MAINE

HILARY NANGLE

Contents

1922
Maine Woods
1934
Bangor &
AROOSTOOK

Stratton
Sugarloaf Mtn
Bingham
Kingfield
Rangeley
Mooselook-meguntic Lake
Skowhegan
Farmington
Belgrade Lakes
Waterville
Bangor
Orono
Amherst
Wesley
Eastport
Campobello Island
Lubec
Machias
Grand Manan
Bucksport
Ellsworth
Milbridge
Jonesport
Beals
Great Wass Island
Searsport
Belfast
Blue Hill
Bar Harbor
Winter Harbor
Cadillac Mtn
Acadia National Park
Sedgwick
Mount Desert Island
Bethel
AUGUSTA
Lincolnville
Islesboro Island
Camden
Penobscot Bay
Rockport
Deer Isle
Swans Island
White Mountain National Forest
Oxford
Lewiston
Auburn
Waldoboro
Rockland
Thomaston
Isle au Haut
Newcastle
Cushing
St. George
Vinalhaven Island
Damariscotta
Wiscasset
Fryeburg
Long Lake
Brunswick
Bath
Sebago
Freeport
Boothbay Harbor
Yarmouth
Monhegan Island
Cornish
PORTLAND
Casco Bay
Old Orchard Beach
Saco
Alfred
Biddeford
Kennebunk
Wells
Berwick
Ogunquit
Dover
Eliot
York
Kittery
NEW HAMPSHIRE
ATLANTIC OCEAN
0 25 mi
0 25 km
© MOON.COM

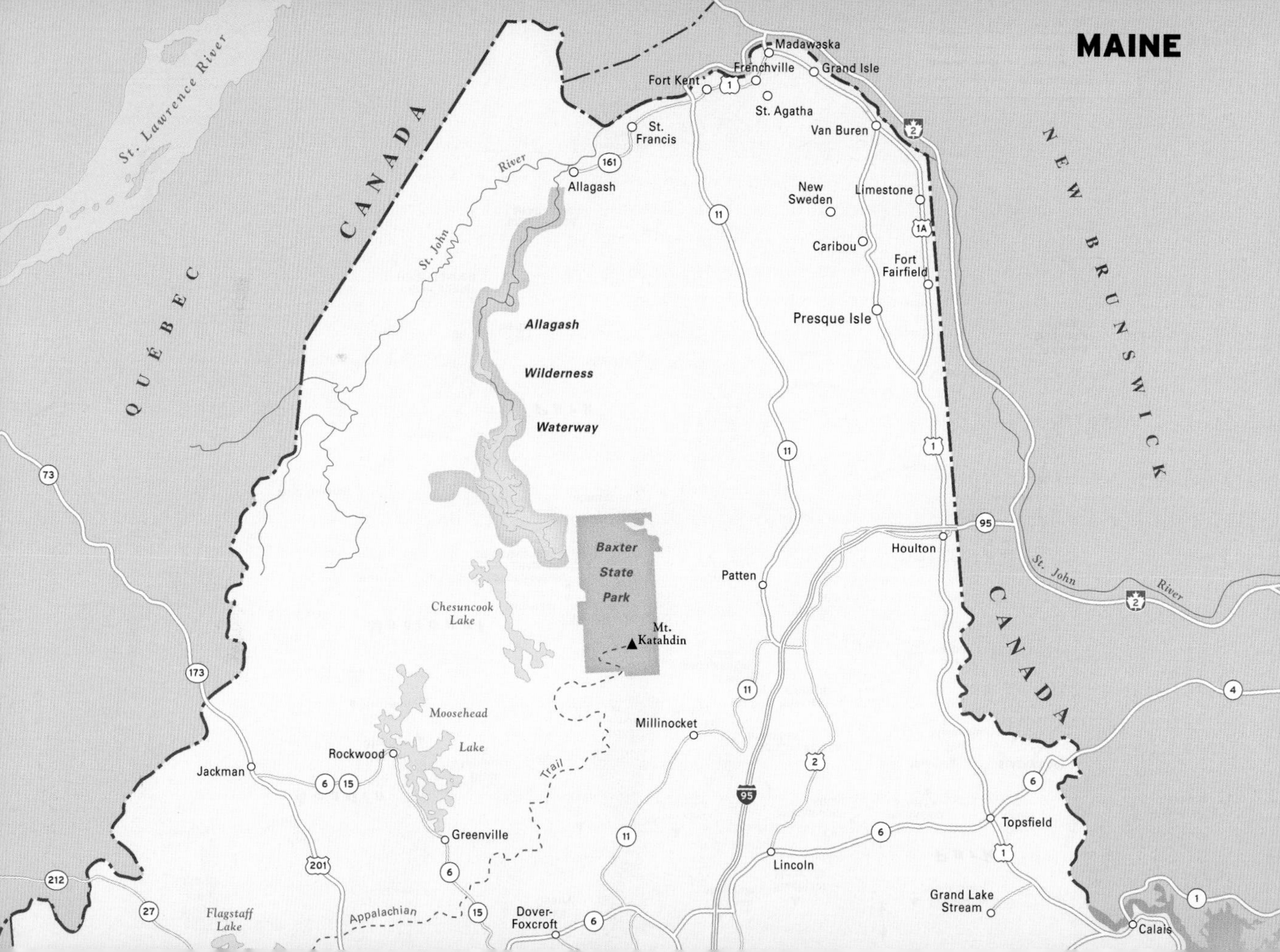

MAINE
QUÉBEC
CANADA
NEW BRUNSWICK
St. Lawrence River
St. John River
Madawaska
Frenchville
Grand Isle
Fort Kent
St. Agatha
Van Buren
St. Francis
Allagash
New Sweden
Limestone
Caribou
Fort Fairfield
Presque Isle
Allagash Wilderness Waterway
Baxter State Park
Mt. Katahdin
Houlton
Patten
Chesuncook Lake
Moosehead Lake
Millinocket
Rockwood
Jackman
Greenville
Trail
Appalachian
Flagstaff Lake
Dover-Foxcroft
Lincoln
Topsfield
Grand Lake Stream
Calais
1
1A
2
4
6
11
15
27
73
95
161
173
201
212

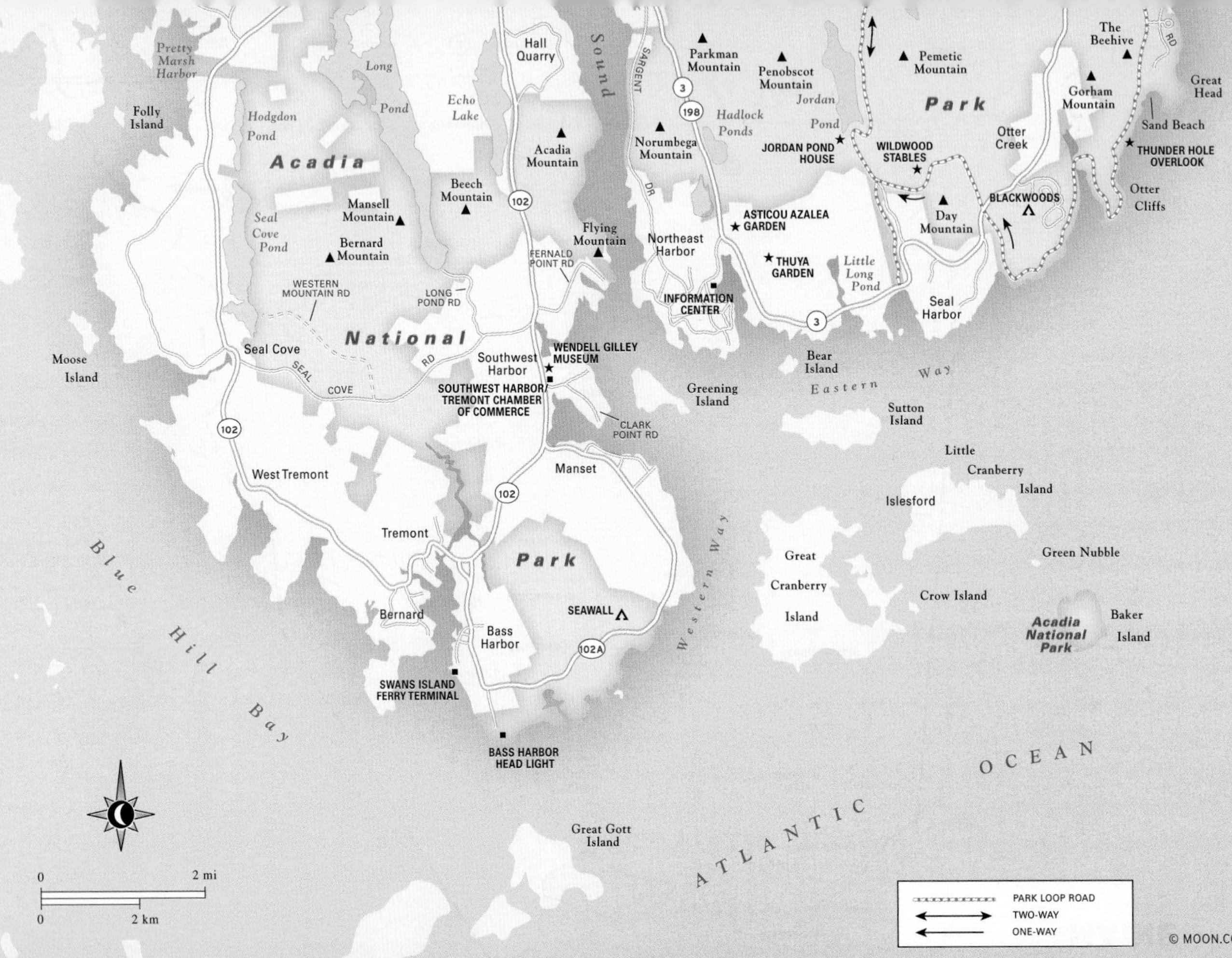
Acadia
National
Park
Park
Pretty Marsh Harbor
Folly Island
Moose Island
Hodgdon Pond
Long Pond
Echo Lake
Seal Cove Pond
Hall Quarry
Sound
Mansell Mountain
Bernard Mountain
Beech Mountain
Acadia Mountain
Flying Mountain
WESTERN MOUNTAIN RD
LONG POND RD
FERNALD POINT RD
SEAL COVE RD
Seal Cove
Southwest Harbor
WENDELL GILLEY MUSEUM
SOUTHWEST HARBOR/ TREMONT CHAMBER OF COMMERCE
CLARK POINT RD
Manset
West Tremont
Tremont
Bernard
Bass Harbor
SWANS ISLAND FERRY TERMINAL
BASS HARBOR HEAD LIGHT
SEAWALL
102
102A
3
198
SARGENT DR
Parkman Mountain
Penobscot Mountain
Pemetic Mountain
Norumbega Mountain
Hadlock Ponds
Jordan Pond
JORDAN POND HOUSE
WILDWOOD STABLES
Northeast Harbor
ASTICOU AZALEA GARDEN
THUYA GARDEN
INFORMATION CENTER
Little Long Pond
Day Mountain
Seal Harbor
Otter Creek
BLACKWOODS
The Beehive
Gorham Mountain
Great Head
Sand Beach
THUNDER HOLE OVERLOOK
Otter Cliffs
RD
Bear Island
Greening Island
Eastern Way
Sutton Island
Little Cranberry Island
Islesford
Western Way
Great Cranberry Island
Green Nubble
Crow Island
Baker Island
Acadia National Park
Great Gott Island
Blue Hill Bay
ATLANTIC OCEAN
0 2 mi
0 2 km
PARK LOOP ROAD
TWO-WAY
ONE-WAY
© MOON.COM

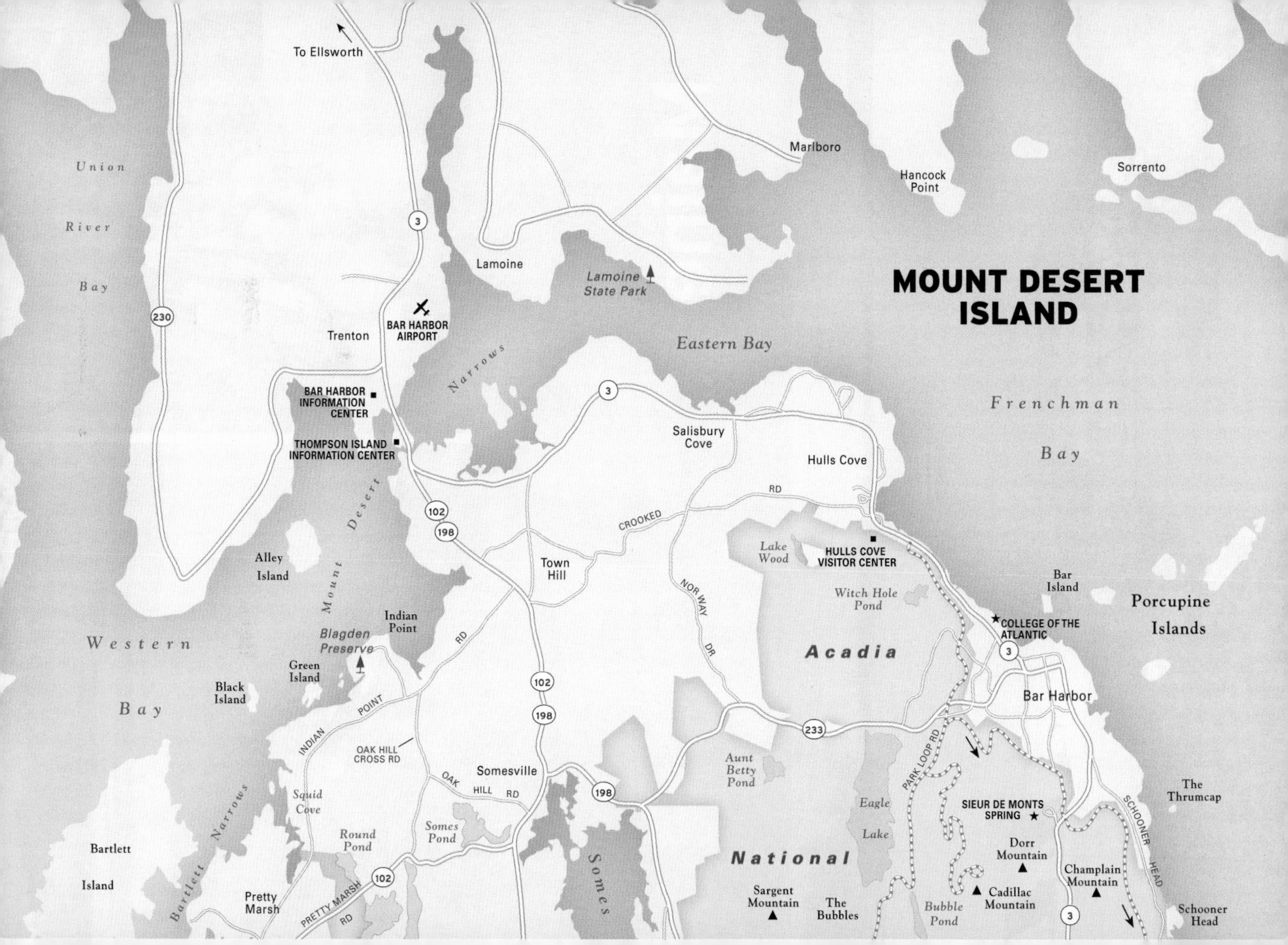

MOUNT DESERT ISLAND
To Ellsworth
Union River Bay
Marlboro
Hancock Point
Sorrento
Lamoine
Lamoine State Park
Trenton
BAR HARBOR AIRPORT
Eastern Bay
Narrows
BAR HARBOR INFORMATION CENTER
THOMPSON ISLAND INFORMATION CENTER
Frenchman Bay
Salisbury Cove
Hulls Cove
Mount Desert
CROOKED RD
Alley Island
Town Hill
Lake Wood
HULLS COVE VISITOR CENTER
NORWAY DR
Bar Island
Witch Hole Pond
Porcupine Islands
Indian Point
COLLEGE OF THE ATLANTIC
Blagden Preserve
Western Bay
Green Island
Acadia
Black Island
INDIAN POINT RD
Bar Harbor
OAK HILL CROSS RD
OAK HILL RD
Somesville
Aunt Betty Pond
PARK LOOP RD
Squid Cove
Eagle Lake
SIEUR DE MONTS SPRING
The Thrumcap
SCHOONER HEAD RD
Bartlett Narrows
Round Pond
Somes Pond
Somes
National
Dorr Mountain
Champlain Mountain
Bartlett Island
Pretty Marsh
PRETTY MARSH RD
Sargent Mountain
The Bubbles
Cadillac Mountain
Bubble Pond
Schooner Head
230
3
102
198
233

DISCOVER

Maine

Tipping the northeastern corner of the United States and comprising 33,215 square miles, Maine boldly promotes itself as "The Way Life Should Be." Not to say that everything's perfect, mind you, but Maine is an extraordinarily special place, where the air is clear, the water is pure, and the traditional traits of honesty, thrift, and ruggedness remain refreshingly appealing.

From the glacier-scoured beaches of the Southern Coast, around spruce-studded islands and Acadia's granite shores, to the craggy cliffs Down East, Maine's coastline follows a zigzagging route that would measure about 3,500 miles if you stretched it taut. Eons ago, glaciers came crushing down from the north, squeezing Maine's coastline into a wrinkled landscape with countless bony fingers reaching toward the sea. Each peninsula has its own character, as does each island, each city, and each village.

Maine's inland is just as exciting, with 6,000 lakes and ponds, 32,000 miles of rivers, and 17 million acres of timberlands for hiking and mountain biking, skiing and snowmobiling, paddling and fishing. This is where intrepid Appalachian Trail hikers finish at the summit of Katahdin, Maine's tallest peak, and determined

Clockwise from top left: colorful buoys; fishing boat; local color on the Schoodic Peninsula; a lighthouse on Isle au Haut; the *WoodenBoat* school in Brooklin; 5 Lakes Lodge in Millinocket.

canoeists can spend a week on the Allagash, a watery lifeline through the wilderness.

Pair natural highs with human pleasures: fine and quirky museums, theatrical and musical performances, artisan studios and art galleries, designer boutiques and specialty shops.

And then there's the food. Lobster, of course, is king, but don't overlook luscious wild blueberries, sweet Maine maple syrup, delicious farmstead cheeses, and the homemade pies and preserves sold at roadside stands and farmers markets. Access to this bounty is why talented chefs are drawn here. But balance a fancy meal with a beanhole or *chowdah suppah,* where you can share a table with locals, the umpteenth-generation Mainers who add character to this special place: the fishermen who make their living from the bone-chilling waters, the lumbermen who know every nook and cranny of the forested wilderness, the farmers who tame the rocky fields. If you're lucky, you might hear a genuine Maine accent (hint: *Ayuh* isn't so much a word as a sharp two-part intake of breath).

A student of Maine-born author Mary Ellen Chase once mused, "Maine is different from all other states, isn't it? I suppose that's because God never quite finished it." Maine may be a work in progress, but it's certainly a masterpiece.

Clockwise from top left: Campobello Island fishing fleet; Thuya Garden in Northeast Harbor; autumn foliage in Acadia National Park; Maine oysters on the half shell.

12 TOP EXPERIENCES

1 **Venture into Acadia National Park:** The East's first national park offers dramatic surf and turf vistas. There's also hiking for all abilities, mountain biking, climbing, fresh- and saltwater paddling . . . name your adventure, you'll find it here (page 306).

2 Feast on Lobster: You'll find lobster in some form at almost every restaurant in Maine, but for the real-deal, head to a traditional, wharf-side shack and feast alfresco on crustaceans plucked fresh from the ocean (page 29).

3 **Paddle a Sea Kayak:** Get up close and personal with Maine's serpentine coastline along the Maine Island Trail (page 278) or on a day trip in the waters of Boothbay Harbor (page 164), Castine (page 271), Deer Isle (page 284), or Mount Desert Island (page 322).

4 Savor Portland Cuisine: Feast on fare from James Beard Award winners (page 105), and other nationally lauded or locally beloved restaurants, breweries, wineries, and distilleries on guided food and beverage tours (page 96).

5 Hike Katahdin: Plan in advance to hike Maine's highest peak, the crown of Baxter State Park and the grand finale of the Appalachian Trail. Or opt for an easier trail and admire this rugged mountain with its Knife Edge trail connecting two peaks from afar (page 457).

6 **Take a Moose Safari:** Increase your odds of seeing these ungainly creatures in the wild on a guided safari in Katahdin Woods and Waters (page 447), Greenville (page 467), or Rangeley Lakes (page 552).

7 Go Island Hopping: Visit the islands of Casco Bay (page 116), Monhegan (page 194), the Fox Islands (page 211), Isle au Haut (page 289), or the Cranberry Isles (page 350).

8 Raft a White-Water River: Dam-controlled releases guarantee white-water thrills from spring into fall on the Kennebec River (page 524) and the Dead and Penobscot Rivers (page 448).

9 Sail Aboard a Windjammer: Plan a multiday excursion sailing the waters of Penobscot Bay from Camden or Rockland (page 206).

10 Flower Power: Garden lovers shouldn't miss the Coastal Maine Botanical Gardens in Boothbay (page 159) or the Garden Preserve's Asticou, Thuya, and Rockefeller Gardens on Mount Desert Island (page 333).

11 **Light Up Your Life:** More than 64 beacons salt Maine's coastline from Kittery to Calais, and most can be viewed on the mainland or on a themed excursion cruise (page 28).

12 **Bike Through the Wilderness:** Mountain biking is increasingly popular in Maine, with the best trail networks in Carrabassett Valley (page 546) and Bethel (page 569).

Planning Your Trip

Where to Go

Southern Coast

Sandy beaches, occasionally punctuated by rocky headlands, are the jewels of the Southern Coast, but this region also oozes history. **Colonial roots** are preserved in historical buildings while the **arts legacy** is honored in museums and galleries. Route 1's endless **shopping** opportunities provide plenty of distraction.

Greater Portland

Brine-scented air, cackling gulls, lobster boats, and fishing trawlers give notice that this is a seafaring town, but it's also **Maine's cultural center,** rich in museums and performing-arts centers, and earns national kudos as a **culinary destination.**

Mid-Coast Region

No region of Maine has more **lobster shacks** or as deep a **maritime history** as this peninsula-rich stretch of coastline, dotted with traditional fishing villages and once-thriving ports and shipbuilding centers. The **Maine Maritime Museum** preserves that heritage; **Bath Iron Works** continues it; and the brick townscapes, renovated mills, and plentiful shops brimming with maritime treasure keep it alive.

Penobscot Bay

Island-studded Penobscot Bay is the **Maine coast in microcosm.** Boat-filled harbors, sandy pocket beaches, soaring spruce trees, and vivid beach roses pepper the shoreline. Gentrifying fishing villages neighbor cosmopolitan towns. **Windjammers** sail by **lighthouses. Antiques shops, art galleries,** and **museums** are as plentiful as lobster boats.

Blue Hill Peninsula and Deer Isle

Water, water everywhere. Around nearly every bend is a river or stream, a cove, a boat-filled harbor, or a serene pond. This inspired and

fishing harbors near Rockland in Penobscot Bay

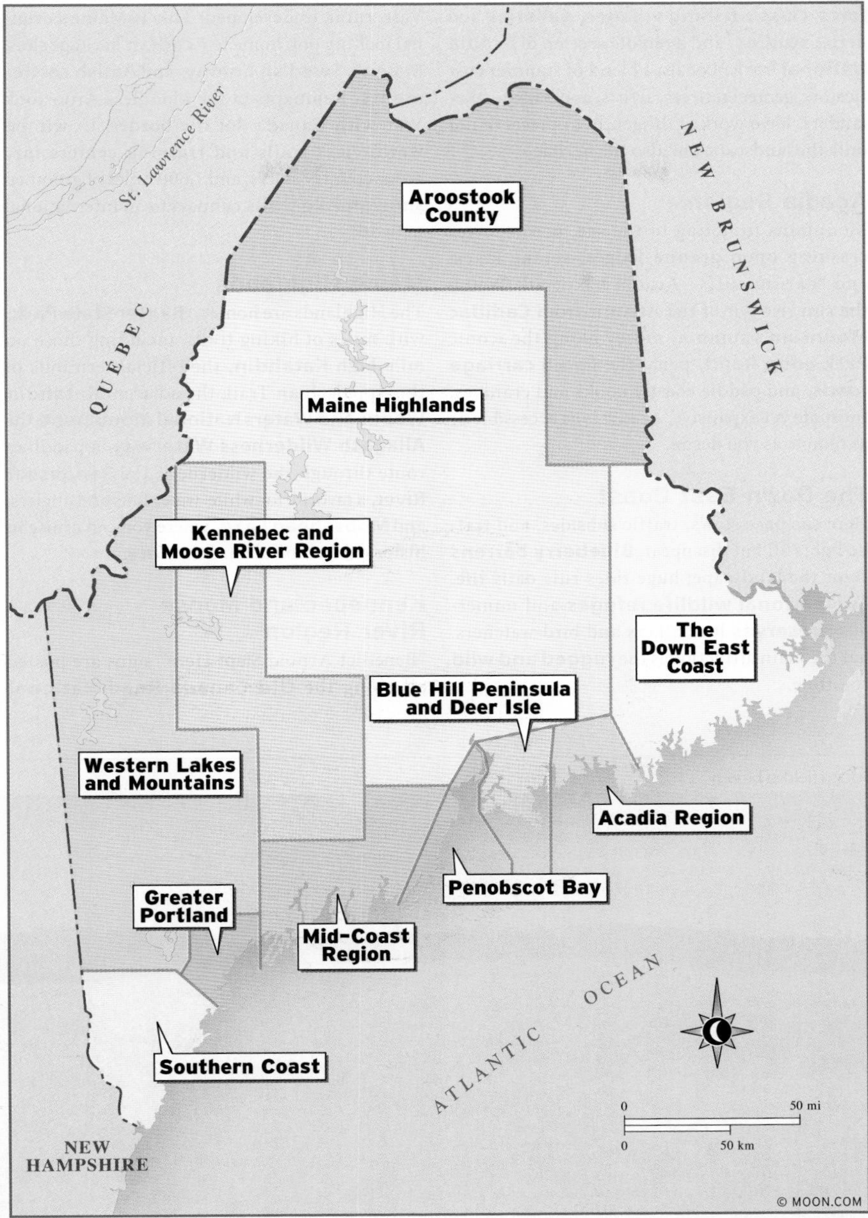
St. Lawrence River
NEW BRUNSWICK
QUÉBEC
Aroostook County
Maine Highlands
Kennebec and Moose River Region
The Down East Coast
Blue Hill Peninsula and Deer Isle
Western Lakes and Mountains
Acadia Region
Penobscot Bay
Greater Portland
Mid-Coast Region
ATLANTIC OCEAN
Southern Coast
0
50 mi
0
50 km
NEW HAMPSHIRE
© MOON.COM

inspiring landscape hosts **historic homes and forts, classic fishing villages, galleries** and **artist studios,** and a remote section of **Acadia National Park.** Locals, a blend of summer rusticators, genteel retirees, artists, and back-to-the-landers, have worked diligently to preserve not only the landscape but also the heritage.

Acadia Region

Mountains tumbling to the sea, ocean waves crashing upon granite ledges, serene lakes, and soaring cliffs—Acadia has it all. Watch the sun rise out of the Atlantic from **Cadillac Mountain**'s summit, mosey along the iconic **Park Loop Road,** pedal the famed **carriage roads,** and paddle coastal nooks and crannies. Intimate yet expansive, Acadia is as accessible or as remote as you desire.

The Down East Coast

Here the pace slows, traffic subsides, and traffic lights all but disappear. **Blueberry barrens** color the landscape; huge tides rule daily life. Two **national wildlife refuges** and numerous **preserves** lure hikers and bird-watchers, but the main attraction is the **rugged and wild** coastline.

Aroostook County

Vast, rural, undeveloped: This is Maine's original melting pot, home to **Acadian** heritage sites, **Maine's Swedish Colony,** and **Amish settlements.** Remnants of the bloodless Aroostook War with Canada dot the border. In winter, world-class trails and training centers lure cross-country skiers, and 1,600 miles of groomed **snowmobile trails** connect to an international network.

Maine Highlands

The Highlands are home to **Baxter State Park,** with miles of hiking trails, including those on mile-high **Katahdin,** the official terminus of the Appalachian Trail; the adjacent **Katahdin Woods and Waters National Monument;** the **Allagash Wilderness Waterway,** a paddling route through the wilderness; the **Penobscot River,** a favorite for white-water fans and anglers; and **Moosehead Lake,** where you can cruise in historical fashion aboard the ***Kate.***

Kennebec and Moose River Region

"Benedict Arnold Slept Here" signs are posted all along the **Old Canada Road National**

potato field in bloom

Scenic Byway, which follows his famous march on Québec. In **Augusta,** the **Maine State Museum** is an excellent introduction to the state, and **Old Fort Western** is the nation's oldest stockade fort. Of course, a **white-water rafting** trip down the Kennebec is a must.

Western Lakes and Mountains

Generations of campers have favored the lakes pocketed in the mountains of western Maine. Cruise Long Lake on the ***Songo River Queen II,*** cast a line in the **Rangeley Lakes,** hike through **Grafton Notch State Park,** or spend a leisurely afternoon splashing in **Sebago** and you'll understand why. In winter, major **alpine resorts** keep things hopping.

Before You Go

High and Low Seasons

Late May to mid-October is prime season, with **July** and **August,** the warmest months, being the busiest. Expect peak-season rates, congested roads, and difficulty getting reservations. Late June and late August tend to be a bit quieter.

September-mid-October is arguably the best time to travel in Maine. Days are warm and mostly dry, nights are cool, fog is rare, the bugs are gone, and the crowds are few. Foliage is turning by early October, usually reaching its peak by mid-month.

In **winter,** especially inland, skiing, snowshoeing, and ice-skating replace hiking, biking, and boating. On the coast, choices in lodging, dining, and activities are fewer, but rates are generally far lower.

Prices and **hours of operation** throughout this book are for **peak season.** In the **off-season,** prices can drop dramatically and operating hours are much more limited. It's not uncommon for a restaurant to close early on a quiet night. In general, days and hours of operation are **subject to change,** so it's a good idea to call ahead or make a **reservation.**

What to Pack

Weather can be unpredictable in Maine, with fog, rain, and temperatures ranging from the low 30s on a cold spring day to the 90s on a hot summer one. But even summer sees days when a **fleece pullover** and a **lightweight, weatherproof jacket** are welcome. A hat and mittens are a plus when venturing far offshore on a boat or climbing inland peaks in spring or fall. Other handy items are **binoculars,** a small **backpack** for day trips or light hiking, and a small or collapsible **cooler** for picnics or storing food.

Unless you're dining at the White Barn Inn, you won't need fancy clothing. Resort casual is the **dress code** in most good restaurants and in downtown Portland, with nice T-shirts and shorts being acceptable almost everywhere in beach communities.

In **winter and spring,** add warm waterproof boots, gloves, a hat, and winter-weight clothing to your list.

The Best of Maine

This itinerary loops though coastal and inland Maine, taking in many of the state's iconic sights. The downside: You'll be doing a fair bit of driving, primarily on two-lane roads where speeds are often 25 mph or lower, and during the season when road construction is a fact of life. While this itinerary is planned as 11 days, you'll be rewarded if you spend more time lingering.

Book your first two nights' lodging in Portland, then book nights 3 and 4 in Rockland or its vicinity; 5 and 6 on Mount Desert Island; 7 and 8 in the Moosehead region; 9 in Rangeley; and 10 in Bethel.

Portland and Vicinity

Day 1: Kennebunkport

Stretch your legs after your journey to Maine with a walk on Kennebunkport's **Goose Rocks Beach,** one of Maine's prettiest. Afterward, mosey along the waterfront to **Dock Square,** where former fishing shacks are now boutiques and galleries, and perhaps indulge in a lobster roll at the **Clam Shack.**

Day 2: Portland

30 MILES; 45 MINUTES

Begin the day with a visit to **Portland Head Light,** a Cape Elizabeth landmark and Maine's oldest lighthouse (1791), perched on the cliffs of 94-acre Fort Williams Park. Spend a few hours in the **Portland Museum of Art,** Maine's premier art museum, and then prowl through the **Old Port and the Waterfront.** End the day with a **sunset cruise on Casco Bay.**

Day 3: Freeport and Bath

35 MILES; 1 HOUR

Make a pilgrimage to giant sports retailer and outfitter **L. L. Bean,** hub of the hubbub in Freeport's outlet bonanza. Spend a few hours shopping or taking a class at the **L. L. Bean Outdoor Discover School.** In the afternoon, visit the **Maine Maritime Museum** in Bath, comprising 10 acres of indoor and outdoor exhibits celebrating the state's nautical heritage.

Rockland and Vicinity

Day 4: Greater Rockland

45 MILES; 1 HOUR

Explore Greater Rockland's many **museums** and **lighthouses.** Or take a day trip to **Monhegan Island** from Port Clyde. This car-free, carefree gem, about a dozen miles off the coast, is laced with hiking trails and has earned renown as the Artists' Island. End the day at the classic **McLoon's Lobster Shack.**

Day 5: Camden and Acadia

85 MILES; 2.25 HOURS

Drive or hike to the top of **Mount Battie** in **Camden Hills State Park,** on the northern fringe of Camden. You'll get a magnificent view of Penobscot Bay. Then continue up the coast to **Mount Desert Island** and begin your explorations of **Acadia National Park.**

Acadia National Park

Day 6: Mount Desert Island

Welcome the day by watching the sunrise from the summit of **Cadillac Mountain.** Afterward, before the crowds arrive, drive the **Park Loop Road,** which covers many of Acadia's highlights. Immerse yourself in the park by going hiking, bicycling, or sea kayaking, or take a carriage ride.

Maine Highlands

Days 7-8: Greenville and Moosehead Lake

130 MILES; 2.75 HOURS

Depart Mount Desert Island and head inland to **Greenville** and **Moosehead Lake.** If time permits, continue to Rockwood and take the shuttle to **Kineo** for a hike.

Book a sunrise or sunset **moose safari.** In the afternoon, enjoy a cruise on the ***Kate*** and

Off the Beaten Path

AROOSTOOK LOOP

It's a pity that few visitors make it to **Aroostook County,** because it is a rural gem with great outdoor resources, including **Aroostook State Park** and rich **Acadian** and **Swedish** heritage sites, not to mention interplanetary travel along the **Maine Solar System Model.** Because of the sheer immensity of the county, you'll want to plan at least four days to a full week.

Be sure to explore the back roads for big views and surprises. Along Route 2 between Sherman Mills and Houlton is **Golden Ridge,** with its panoramic views, as well as a railroad museum and an Amish colony. Route 164 loops out to the **Salmon Brook Historical Society** and **Woodland Bog Preserve.** Tucked just off Route 161 is **Maine's Swedish Colony.**

WAY DOWN EAST

Few folks travel northeast of the Acadia region, but those who do are rewarded with early sunrises, seemingly endless **blueberry barrens,** and big tides. From **Milbridge** through **Calais,** the Maine coast has a much different feel from points south. **Fishing villages** have yet to be gussied up or gentrified, and harbors are filled with working boats, not yachts. Museums, such as the **Burnham Tavern** in Machias, the **Ruggles House** in Columbia Falls, and the **Tides Institute and Museum of Art** in Eastport, are small in size but deep in local—and sometimes national—heritage. Accommodations in Lubec include a former cannery and a former life-saving station. Bring a passport, and **Roosevelt Campobello International Park** is yours to explore.

Spectacular **coastal trails** attract hikers, birders flock to **wildlife preserves,** and sightings of **whales,** seals, and eagles are common. If you continue inland to **Grand Lake Stream,** you'll stumble upon an angler's paradise.

Rangeley Lake

SPORTING CAMP ADVENTURE

Immerse yourself in Maine's forested wilderness at a traditional **sporting camp.** Created more than a century ago to cater to the needs of hunters and anglers, today most are wonderful **family destinations** during the summer. You can **hike, fish, paddle, swim,** search for moose or other wildlife, or simply relax and enjoy the away-from-it-all experience.

Sporting camps dot Maine's North Country, with concentrations around the **Rangeley Lakes** and along the waterways surrounding **Baxter State Park** and **Moosehead Lake.** Many are off the grid, with woodstoves for warmth on chilly evenings and gas lanterns for light, and most include all meals and offer the option to hire a Maine guide for an unforgettable day of activities and explorations.

prowl around the area. End the day with dinner at one of the area's road-accessible sporting camps.

The Forks to Rangeley

Day 9: The Forks and Rangeley

165 MILES; 3.5 HOURS

Depart Greenville and drive to **The Forks** via the **Moosehead Scenic Byway** and **Old Canada Road National Scenic Byway,** perhaps taking a break to stretch your legs on the easy hike into **Moxie Falls.** (Add a day here if you want to go **white-water rafting** on the Kennebec River.) Continue the scenic drive to **Rangeley,** arriving in time to learn about the region's history at the **Rangeley Outdoor Sporting Heritage Museum.**

Day 10: Rangeley

60 MILES; 1.25 HOURS

After a morning hiking, paddling, or fishing, head south on Route 17 over Height of Land, perhaps stopping in **Coos Canyon** to try your hand at panning for gold. Detour off the main road in **Newry** to see the **Artist's Covered Bridge.**

Day 11: Gems of Route 26

75 MILES; 1.75 HOURS

Snake southward through the White Mountain foothills, perhaps exploring **Paris Hill** or **Norway;** the **Shaker Museum,** the world's last inhabited Shaker colony; or **Poland Spring** (there's more here than bottled water). Make the one-hour drive back to Portland.

Lighthouses, Lobster, and L. L. Bean

Maine's biggest draws are the three Ls: lighthouses, lobster, and L. L. Bean. This six-day tour highlights all three and concentrates on the Greater Portland, Mid-Coast, and Penobscot Bay regions. Book your first two nights in Portland, the second two in the Damariscotta area, and the final two in Rockland. If you're arriving by air, use Portland International Jetport.

Day 1

Try to arrive in **Portland** in time to enjoy an afternoon cruise with **Lucky Catch Lobster Tours;** perhaps you'll catch your dinner. If not, you can still enjoy a lobster on the waterfront.

Day 2

Loop out to South Portland and Cape Elizabeth to visit **Spring Point Ledge Light** and **Portland Head Light,** a Maine icon. You won't find a better setting for lunch than the **Lobster Shack,** with views of crashing surf and **Cape Elizabeth Light.** In the afternoon, book a sail or cruise to view the lighthouses salting **Casco Bay.**

Day 3

50 MILES; 1 HOUR

Visit the **Maine Maritime Museum** in **Bath,** and take a **lighthouse cruise** on the **Kennebec River** followed by a mosey down to **Georgetown** for lobster on the wharf at **Five Islands Lobster Company.**

Day 4

35 MILES; 50 MINUTES

Step back in time visiting with lightkeeper Joseph Muise and his family on a **Burnt Island Tour** departing from **Boothbay Harbor.**

Day 5

40 MILES; 1.25 HOURS

Book a daylong excursion to **Monhegan Island** aboard the Hardy Boat out of **New Harbor.** Be sure to visit the museum in the lighthouse keeper's house. Lunch? Lobster at **Fish House Fish,** of course. When you return to the mainland, loop down to Pemaquid Point to view **Pemaquid**

Lobster in the Rough

No Maine visit is complete without a "lobsta dinnah" at a lobster wharf, a rough-and-tumble operation within sight and scent of the ocean. If you spot a place with "Restaurant" in its name, keep going. You want to eat outside, at a picnic table, with a knockout view of boats, islands, and the sea. "Dinners" are served from noonish until around sunset.

Dress casually so you can tackle the lobster without messing up your clothes. If you want beer or wine, call ahead and ask if the place serves it; you may need to bring your own. Lobster devotees cart picnic baskets with hors d'oeuvres, salads, and baguettes—even candles and champagne. Save room for dessert: Many lobster shacks are just as renowned for their pies. Here are my favorite lobster shacks:

- **Chauncey Creek Lobster Pier, Kittery Point** (page 39): The Spinney family has operated this popular spot with views toward Pepperrell Cove since the 1930s.
- **The Lobster Shack, Cape Elizabeth** (page 111): Ocean views, crashing surf, and a lighthouse have enticed lobster lovers to this location since the 1920s.
- **Harraseeket Lunch and Lobster Company, South Freeport** (page 124): Take a break from L. L. Bean and head to this unfussy spot on the working harbor.
- **Erica's Seafood, South Harpswell** (page 137): Enjoy expansive views over Casco Bay from this family-owned shack.
- **Five Islands Lobster Company, Georgetown** (page 152): Watch sailboats playing hide-and-seek amid the spruce-topped islands in the harbor.
- **Round Pond Lobster Co-Op and Muscongus Bay Lobster, Round Pond** (page 179): These two overlook dreamy Round Pond Harbor. The co-op keeps it simple, with lobsters only. Muscongus Bay earns kid-friendly points for its touch tank filled with sea critters.
- **McLoon's Lobster Shack, Spruce Head** (page 192): Pair mighty fine lobster with spruce-fringed island views.
- **Fish House Fish, Monhegan Island** (page 199): It doesn't get much more in the rough than this shack overlooking Monhegan's harbor.

The Lobster Shack

- **Young's Lobster Pound, Belfast** (page 238): Watch boats go to and fro across Belfast's harbor from this shack with seating both inside and on a huge deck.
- **Perry's Lobster Shack, Surry** (page 257): It's worth the drive down Surry Neck to find this tucked-away gem with views to Mount Desert Island.
- **Thurston's Lobster Pound, Bernard** (page 344): The two-story dining area tops a wharf above Bass Harbor.
- **Lunt's Dockside Deli, Frenchboro** (page 352): It's hard to beat this spot, which overlooks a working harbor on Long Island, eight miles off Mount Desert Island.
- **Wharf Gallery & Grill, Corea** (page 364): This shack, with dreamy views over Corea's lobster boat-filled harbor is owned by a sixth-generation lobsterman descended from Corea's first settlers.
- **Quoddy Bay Lobster, Eastport** (page 410): Watch the tide change and boats unload their catches on Passamaquoddy Bay.

Recreation Hotspots

Maine is a vast outdoor playground, with opportunities for both thrill-seeking adrenaline junkies as well as families who prefer an easygoing adventure.

HIKING

- Mile-high **Katahdin** is the terminus of the **Appalachian Trail.** Katahdin tops out on Baxter Peak, which connects to Pamola Peak via the infamous **Knife Edge.**

- For a family-friendly hike with dramatic Katahdin views, walk the easy 0.75-mile **Roaring Brook Nature Trail** in the southeastern corner of Baxter State Park.

MOUNTAIN BIKING

- Pedal between **Carrabassett Valley** and **The Forks** via the **Maine Huts and Trails** system, a corridor through the wilderness with four full-service huts spaced roughly 12 miles apart.

RAFTING

- Paddle Maine's three white-water roller coasters: the **Kennebec River,** the **Penobscot River,** and the **Dead River.**

CANOEING

- The **Allagash Wilderness Waterway** stretches 92 miles from Telos Lake to East Twin Brook through pristine lakes, rapids, and a portage around **Allagash Falls.**

- An easy excursion is a half- to three-day leisurely paddle down the gentle **Saco River.**

SEA KAYAKING

- Paddle along the coast from Kittery to Machias Bay on the **Maine Island Trail,** a 375-mile-long waterway with more than 180 backcountry campsites.

- For first-timers, take an introductory two-hour **harbor paddle,** offered from many coastal communities.

SAILING

- No exercise or experience is required to sail aboard a **Maine windjammer.** All-inclusive sails range from two days to a week.

view from the Appalachian Trail

- Get a sampling with a two-hour **scenic cruise** out of Boothbay Harbor, Rockland, Rockport, Camden, or Bar Harbor.

DOGSLEDDING

- Mush a team of huskies across the frozen **Umbagog Lake** wilderness north of Bethel on a day trip or multiday trek.

ALPINE SKIING AND SNOWBOARDING

- Crowning the summit of **Sugarloaf** is the only lift-serviced skiing in the East above the tree line. Here you'll find runs suitable for both beginners and experts.

- Book a snowcat ride or work up a sweat getting from the lift to **Burnt Mountain,** adjacent to Sugarloaf.

CROSS-COUNTRY SKIING

- Ski groomed trails through Saddleback Mountain at the **Rangeley Lakes Trails Center.**

- Cruise your way along the **Bethel Village Trails,** right in downtown Bethel.

Point Lighthouse, before enjoying **lobster in the rough** in **Round Pond.**

Day 6

50 MILES; 1.5 HOURS

Greet the day with a walk out on the breakwater to **Rockland Breakwater Light.** Afterward, tour the **Maine Lighthouse Museum.** In the afternoon, take a **lighthouse-themed cruise** or **sea kayak tour** out of Rockport or Rockland. En route to yet another lobster dining experience at **McLoon's Lobster Shack** in **Spruce Head,** take the short side jaunt out to **Owls Head Light** in Owls Head.

Farm Fresh

Farm-to-table is so yesterday; in Maine, you don't even have to leave the farm. Many chefs own farms, and at the following restaurants and cafés, ingredients are sourced on-site.

The Well at Jordan's Farm, Cape Elizabeth

Culinary Institute of America-trained chef Jason Williams presides over the **Well** (page 111), a mobile kitchen set amid the fields, greenhouses, and gardens of **Jordan's Farm,** a 122-acre third-generation family farm. Dining is mostly alfresco, with seats at picnic tables, in gazebos, or at the kitchen counter. Visit the farm store before dinner, pick some fresh flowers for the table, and savor a scratch-made farm-fresh meal.

Primo, Rockland

While most places on this list were farms first, **Primo** (page 208), owned by two-time James Beard award-winning chef Melissa Kelly and her partner, Price Kushner, was first a restaurant. Over the years, Kelly and Kushner have cultivated the property, sowing crops and adding gardens, beehives, and livestock. Arrive early to tour the produce and tea gardens, view the hives, and visit with the pigs, chickens, and guinea pigs in the pastures.

Seal Cove Farm, Lamoine

Watch Nubian goats romp in the field and play king of the rock while you wait for your personal pizza to be made and cooked in the outdoor oven at **Seal Cove Farm** (page 305). Pizza menus vary to reflect what's currently fresh from the farm, but each is topped with Seal Cove's various goat cheeses and, if you want, goataroni. Go on a fine day, as there's no indoor seating.

Misty Meadows Organic Farm, Grand Isle

The **Misty Meadows Organic Farm** (page 435), filled with fresh produce, preserves, salted herbs, pickled veggies, baked goods, and even crafts, doubles as a country café featuring Maine spuds with all manner of toppings, as well as typical luncheon fare. There are sweets (oh my, the pies!), a barbecue pit (Thursdays), and hearty daily specials too. There's seating both indoors and outside. Say hello to Princess the pig, if she's hanging around outside.

Stutzman's, Sangerville

Stutzman's (page 480), another third-generation family farm, has a store stocked with farm-fresh produce and a bakery producing scratch-made breads, pies, pastries, and more. You can enjoy lunch or brunch in a café serving soups, salads, desserts, daily specials, and wood-fired pizzas drawing from the farm's bounty.

Riverside Farm Market, Oakland

Enjoy lunch, dinner, or Sunday brunch at **Riverside Farm Market** (page 516), located on the Tyler family's 25-acre working vineyard edging Messalonskee Stream. Everything is made from scratch, there's often live music, and you can dine indoors or on the deck.

Stutzman's in Sangerville

Nezinscot Farm Store and Café in Turner

Apple Acres Farm, Hiram

The best time to visit **Apple Acres Farm** (page 582) is in autumn, when the apple orchard is heavy with fruit and the hills surrounding it are ablaze with color, but stop in anytime for apple-cider doughnuts, ice cream, and oh yes, doughnut ice cream sandwiches, as well as sandwiches, pies, and even a decent lobster roll.

Nezinscot Farm Store and Café, Turner

Come for breakfast, lunch, brunch, or sweets at **Nezinscot Farm Store and Café** (page 607), Maine's first organic dairy farm. Pretty much everything comes from or is made on the farm: veggies from the gardens, meats from the animals, baked goods from the bakery, cheese from the fromagerie, and even house-made charcuterie.

Pietree Orchard, New Sweden

Tabitha King, wife of horror maven Stephen, owns **Pietree Orchard** (page 597), a hilltop orchard with eye-candy mountain views that are gorgeous anytime but glorious in autumn. The farm store carries produce and house-made baked goods and sweets, including cider doughnuts, but plan your visit around the baked-to-order pizzas cooked in the wood-fired oven. You can even go home with a tasty souvenir: Depending on the season, fruit-picking opportunities range from strawberries to pumpkins.

Shhh! Don't tell too many people, but Maine gets fewer leaf peepers than other New England states, so roads are less congested and lodging and dining reservations are easier to score. But do plan in advance. For help in planning, consult www.mainefoliage.com.

MOOSEHEAD AND THE KENNEBEC RIVER

Leaf peepers who make it as far north as **Greenville** are amply rewarded. Plan a minimum of **two nights,** ideally three or more, and spend one full day driving one of the state's most spectacular foliage routes.

- **The Route:** Loop from Greenville over to the Kennebec River and back on Routes 5 to Jackman, 201 south to Bingham, and 16 east to Abbott, and then Route 5 north to return to Greenville. You'll parallel the shorelines of **Moosehead Lake** and the **Moose River** on the Moosehead Lake Scenic Byway before arriving in Rockwood. As you head south, the views along the Old Canada Road Scenic Byway are spectacular. Dip into the **Attean View** rest area for vistas extending toward Canada. Need to stretch your legs? Consider the relatively easy hike to **Moxie Falls.** From here to Bingham, Route 201 can be truly spectacular as it snakes along the Kennebec River.
- **Diversions:** Cruise **Moosehead Lake** aboard the *Kate,* take a **flightseeing tour** or a **moose safari,** or drive to a remote **sporting camp** for lunch.

BETHEL AND RANGELEY

Combine New England's trees with lakes and mountains and you have the best of nature's palette. Divide your lodging between **Bethel** and **Rangeley.**

- **The Route:** From Bethel, take Route 26 north to Errol, New Hampshire, then Route 16 north to Rangeley. Return via Route 17 south to Route 2 west. Heading north, you'll cut through **Grafton Notch State Park** on the Grafton Notch Scenic Byway; the rest of the drive is speckled with mountains, lakes, and streams. Returning south from Rangeley, the Rangeley Lakes National Scenic Byway passes over **Height of Land,** providing dazzling views. The entire route is through prime **moose country,** so keep alert.

blueberry barren, Down East

- **Diversions:** Hike in Grafton Notch or Rangeley, paddle the **Rangeley Lakes,** or pan for gold in **Coos Canyon.**

ACADIA AND DOWN EAST

To the magic foliage mix, add the ocean and top it off with wild blueberry barrens, which turn crimson in foliage season. Book lodging in the **Schoodic region.**

- **The Route:** From Hancock, mosey inland on Route 182 along the Blackwoods Scenic Byway to Cherryfield. Then head south on Route 1A to Milbridge, continuing south on Route 1. In Steuben, dip down Pigeon Hill Road to the Petit Manan section of the **Maine Coastal Islands National Wildlife Refuge** before continuing south on Route 1 to Route 186, which loops around the Schoodic Peninsula via the Schoodic Scenic Byway.
- **Diversions:** Hike **Black** or **Schoodic Mountains,** detour north from Cherryfield to Deblois to see the **blueberry barrens,** bike the Schoodic Loop, head to the carriage roads in **Acadia National Park,** or browse **art galleries.**

Southern Coast

Drive over the I-95 bridge from New Hampshire into Maine's Southern Coast region on a bright summer day and you'll swear the air is cleaner, the sky is bluer, the trees are greener, and the roadside signs are more upbeat. "Welcome to Maine: The Way Life Should Be." (Or is it the way life *used* to be?)

Most visitors come to this region for the spectacular attractions of the justly world-famous Maine coast—the inlets, villages, and especially the beaches—but it's also rich in history. Southernmost York County, part of the original Province of Maine, was incorporated in 1636, only 16 years after the *Mayflower* pilgrims reached Plymouth, Massachusetts. Accordingly, it reeks of history: Ancient cemeteries, musty archives, and architecturally stunning homes and public

Highlights

Look for ★ to find recommended sights, activities, dining, and lodging.

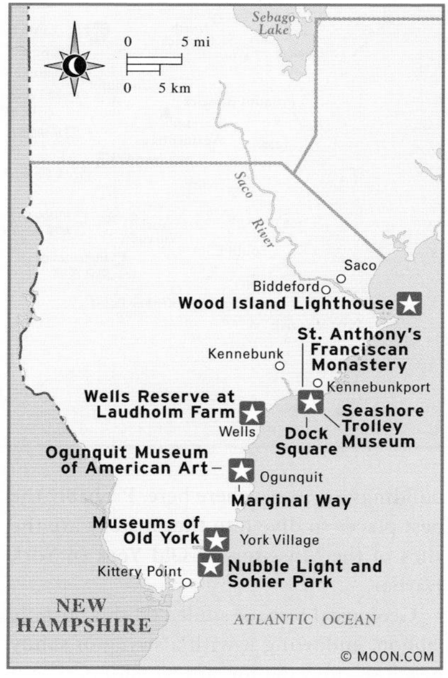

★ **Museums of Old York:** On this campus of historic buildings, you can peek into early life in York, which dates from the 1640s (page 44).

★ **Nubble Light and Sohier Park:** You'll likely recognize this often-photographed Maine coast icon, which is the easiest lighthouse to see in the region (page 44).

★ **Ogunquit Museum of American Art:** It's hard to say which is more jaw-dropping, the art or the view (page 52).

★ **Marginal Way:** Escape the hustle and bustle of Ogunquit with a stroll on this paved shorefront path (page 52).

★ **Wells Reserve at Laudholm Farm:** Orient yourself at the visitors center, where you can learn about the history, flora, and fauna of the area, and then take a leisurely walk to the seashore, passing through a variety of habitats (page 52).

★ **Seashore Trolley Museum:** *Ding-ding-ding* goes the bell, and *zing-zing-zing* go your heartstrings, especially if you're a trolley fan (page 63).

★ **Dock Square:** Brave the shopping crowds and browse the dozens of fishing shacks-turned-boutiques in the heart of Kennebunkport (page 65).

★ **St. Anthony's Franciscan Monastery:** It's hard to believe this oasis of calm is just a short stroll from busy Dock Square (page 66).

★ **Wood Island Lighthouse:** Tour Maine's second-oldest lighthouse and perhaps even climb the tower (page 78).

buildings are everywhere here. Probably the best places to dive into that history are the sites of the Museums of Old York in York Harbor.

Geological fortune smiled on this 50-mile ribbon, endowing it with a string of sandy beaches—nirvana for sun worshippers, but less enchanting to swimmers, who need to steel themselves to be able to spend much time in the ocean, especially in early summer before the water temperature has reached a tolerable level.

Complementing those beaches are amusement parks and arcades, fishing shacks turned chic boutiques, a surprising number of good restaurants given the region's seasonality, and some of the state's prettiest parks and preserves. Spend some time poking around

Previous: Marginal Way; Nubble Light; beach in Ogunquit.

the small villages that give the region so much character; many have been gussied up and gentrified quite a bit, yet retain their seafaring or farming bones.

Some Mainers refer to the Southern Coast as northern Massachusetts. Sometimes it can seem that way, not only for the numbers of Massachusetts plates in evidence but also because many former Massachusetts residents have moved here for the quality of life but continue to commute to jobs in the Boston area. The resulting downside is escalating real estate prices that have forced folks off land that has been in their families for generations and pushed those in traditional seafaring occupations inland. Still, if you nose around and get off the beaten path, you'll find that the real Maine is still here.

PLANNING YOUR TIME

Maine's Southern Coast is a rather compact region, but it's heavily congested, especially in summer. Still, with a minimum of four days, you should be able to take in most of the key sights, including beaches and museums, as long as you don't spend too many hours basking in the sun.

Route 1, the region's primary artery, often has bumper-to-bumper traffic. If you're hopscotching towns, consider using I-95, which has exits for York, Kennebunk, and Saco-Biddeford-Old Orchard Beach. Parking can also be a challenge and expensive, but a trolley system operates in summer and connects most towns, making it easy to avoid the hassles and help the environment.

July and August are the busiest months, with the best beach weather. Spring and fall are lovely, and most attractions are open. In winter, you can walk the beaches without running into another soul, it's easy to get dinner reservations, and lodging prices plummet; the trade-off is that fewer businesses are open.

Kittery

Maine is home to a lot of well-kept secrets, **Kittery** (pop. 9,490) being one of them. Shoppers rarely get beyond the 120-plus outlets along Route 1, but there's equal value in exploring the back roads of Maine's oldest town, settled in 1623 and chartered in 1647. Parks, a small nautical museum, historical architecture, and foodie finds are only a few of the attractions in Kittery and its "suburb," **Kittery Point.** It was also on Kittery's Badger Island that the Continental Navy sloop of war *Ranger,* commanded by John Paul Jones, was launched in 1777. The shipbuilding continues at Portsmouth Naval Shipyard on Kittery's Dennet's Island, the first government shipyard in the United States.

SIGHTS

Avoid the outlet sprawl and see the prettiest part of the area by driving along squiggly Route 103, from the Route 1 traffic circle in Kittery through Kittery Point (administratively part of Kittery) and on to its connection with Route 1A in York. You can even make a day of it, stopping at the sights mentioned here. Watch for cyclists and pedestrians, as there are no shoulders and lots of blind corners and hills.

Kittery Historical and Naval Museum

Maritime history buffs shouldn't miss the small but well-stocked **Kittery Historical and Naval Museum** (200 Rogers Rd. Ext., Rte. 1 just north of the traffic circle, Kittery, 207/439-3080, www.kitterymuseum.com, 10am-4pm Wed. and Sat. mid-Apr.-late May and mid-Oct.-early Nov., 10am-4pm Wed.-Sat. and 1pm-4pm Sun. late May-mid-Oct., $5 adults, $3 ages 7-15, $10 family). A large exhibit hall and a small back room contain ship models, fishing gear, old photos and paintings, and an astonishing collection of scrimshaw (carved whale ivory).

Lady Pepperrell House

The 1760 Georgian **Lady Pepperrell House** (Pepperrell Rd./Rte. 103, just before the Fort McClary turnoff, Kittery Point) is privately owned and not open to the public, but it's worth admiring from afar. Nearby, across from the First Congregational Church, is the area's most visited burying ground. Old-cemetery buffs should bring rubbing gear here for some interesting grave markers. The tomb of Levi Thaxter (husband of poet Celia Thaxter) bears an epitaph written for him by Robert Browning.

Fort McClary State Historic Site

Since the early 18th century, fortifications have stood on this 27-acre headland protecting Portsmouth Harbor from seaborne foes. Contemporary remnants at **Fort McClary** (Rte. 103, Kittery Point, 207/384-5160, daily, $4 nonresident adults, $3 Maine adults, $1 ages 5-11 and nonresident seniors, free resident seniors) include several outbuildings, an 1846 blockhouse, granite walls, and earthworks—all with a view of Portsmouth Harbor. Opposite are the sprawling buildings of the Portsmouth Naval Shipyard. Bring a picnic (covered tables and a lily pond are across the street) and turn the kids loose to run and play. It's officially open May 30-October 1, but the site is accessible in the off-season. The fort is 2.5 miles east of Route 1.

Fort Foster

The only problem with **Fort Foster** (Pocahontas Rd., off Rte. 103, Gerrish Island, Kittery Point, 207/439-3800, 10am-dusk daily late May-early Sept., 10am-8pm Sat.-Sun. Sept.-May, $10 vehicle pass, $5 adult walk-in, $1 child walk-in) is that it's no secret, so parking can be scarce at this 90-acre municipal park at the entrance to Portsmouth Harbor. On a hot day, arrive early. You can swim, hike the nature trails, fish off the pier (state registration required for ages 16 and older), picnic, and investigate the tidepools. Bring a kite; there's almost always a breeze.

ENTERTAINMENT

Kittery Recreation (207/439-3800, www.kitterycommunitycenter.org) presents a **summer concert series** on the common, with the offerings varying from year to year; most of the concerts are free. In addition, live performances, lectures, and movies are held year-round at the center's Star Theatre.

The **Dance Hall** (7 Walker St., 207/703-2083, www.thedancehallkittery.org), sited in a former Grange hall, hosts concerts, dances, and classes.

SHOPPING

You'll find bargains aplenty at Kittery's 120-plus factory outlets (www.thekitteryoutlets.com), a collection of mini-malls clustered along Route 1. Stores include Calvin Klein, Eddie Bauer, J. Crew, Mikasa, Esprit, Lenox, Timberland, Tommy Hilfiger, Gap, Villeroy & Boch, Barbour, Orvis, Le Creuset, and plenty more (all open daily). Anchoring the scene is the **Kittery Trading Post** (301 Rte. 1, Kittery, 207/439-2700 or 888/587-6246, www.kitterytradingpost.com), a humongous sporting goods and clothing emporium.

RECREATION

Brave Boat Harbor

Brave Boat Harbor (207/646-9226), one of the Rachel Carson National Wildlife Refuge's 11 Maine coastal segments, is a beautifully unspoiled 7,500-acre wetlands preserve in Kittery Point. There are hiking trails, but the habitat, home to more than a dozen rare plants and animals, is particularly sensitive here, so be kind to the environment. Take Route 103 to Chauncey Creek Road and continue past the Gerrish Island bridge to Cutts Island Lane. Just beyond it and across a small bridge is a pullout on the left. The 1.8-mile Cutts Island interpretive loop includes a spur ending at a salt marsh. Bring binoculars to spot waterfowl in the marshlands.

FOOD

Seafood and Lobster

If you came to Maine to eat lobster, **Chauncey Creek Lobster Pier** (16 Chauncey Creek Rd., off Rte. 103, Kittery Point, 207/439-1030, www.chaunceycreek.com, 11am-8pm daily mid-May-early Sept., to 7pm Tues.-Sun. early Sept.-Columbus Day) is the real deal. Step up to the window, place your order, take a number, and grab a table (you may need to share) overlooking tidal Chauncey Creek and the woods on the close-in opposite shore. It's a particularly picturesque—and extremely popular—place; parking is a nightmare. BYOB and anything else that's not on the menu.

Quick Bites

Kittery has an abundance of excellent specialty food stores that are perfect for stocking up for a picnic lunch or dinner. Most are along the section of Route 1 between the Portsmouth bridge and the traffic circle, and five are within steps of one another.

At **Beach Pea Baking Co.** (53 Rte. 1, Kittery, 207/439-3555, www.beachpeabaking.com, 7:30am-6pm daily, kitchen open til 5pm), an all-natural bakery and café, you can buy fabulous breads and pastries as well as soups and sandwiches. There's seating indoors and on a patio. Next door is **Golden Harvest** (47 State Rd./Rte. 1, Kittery, 207/439-2113, 9am-7pm Mon.-Sat., 9am-6pm Sun.), where you can load up on luscious produce as well as prepared foods. Across the street is **Terra Cotta Pasta Co.** (52 Rte. 1, Kittery, 207/475-3025, www.terracottapastacompany.com, 9am-7pm Mon.-Sat., 10am-5pm Sun.), where in addition to handmade pastas you'll find salads, soups, sandwiches, prepared foods, and lots of other goodies. Count on **Carl's Meat Market** (25 State. Rd., Kittery, 207/439-1557, 9am-7pm Mon.-Sat., 9am-6pm Sun.), a butcher shop, for awesome burgers and sandwiches. Let your nose guide you into **Byrne & Carlson** (60 Rte. 1, Kittery, 888/559-9778, www.byrneandcarlson.com), which makes elegant and delicious chocolate for connoisseurs.

Lil's (7 Wallingford Sq., Kittery, 207/703-2800, www.lilscafe.com, 6:30am-5pm Mon.-Fri., 7am-5pm Sat., 7am-4pm Sun.) has earned well-deserved fame for its scratch-made fare, especially its crullers. Breakfast and lunch are available. Expect to wait in line; it's worth it.

Mrs. And Me (400 Rte. 1, Kittery, 207/439-1141, www.mrsandme.net, noon-9pm daily) has been dishing out homemade ice cream since 1948.

Want a down-home breakfast or lunch? The **Sunrise Grill** (182 State Rd./Rte. 1, Kittery traffic circle, Kittery, 207/439-5748, www.sunrisegrillinc.com, 7am-2pm Fri.-Tues., $8-13) delivers with waffles, granola, omelets, Diana's Benedict, salads, sandwiches, and burgers.

When Pigs Fly (460 Rte. 1, Kittery, 207/439-4114, www.sendbread.com, 10am-7pm Sun.-Thurs., 10am-8pm Fri.-Sat.) earned renown for its old-world artisanal breads made from organic ingredients. Now it's also home to **When Pigs Fly Wood-Fired Pizzeria** (207/438-7036, www.whenpigsflypizzeria.com, 11:30am-8:30pm Sun.-Thurs., 11:30am-9pm Fri.-Sat., $12-22). Obviously, there's pizza—Neapolitan-style in creative flavor combos—but there are other choices, including house-made charcuterie.

Casual Dining

Ignore the kitschy lighthouse; **Robert's Maine Grill** (326 Rte. 1, Kittery, 207/439-0300, www.robertsmainegrill.com, from 11:30am daily, $13-35) is a fine place to duck out of the shopping madness and enjoy well-prepared seafood and other farm-to-table fare, along with a nice selection of Maine craft beer.

Farm-to-table meets gastropub at the **Black Birch** (2 Government St., Kittery, 207/703-2294, www.theblackbirch.com, from 3:30pm Tues.-Sat., $13-24). Upscale comfort foods—such as Moroccan spiced lamb meatballs, poutine and duck confit, and fish-and-chips—are designed to mix and match and are accompanied by a geek-worthy draft list.

Commitment to using fresh and local foods and a flair for bringing big flavors out of simple ingredients have earned **Anneke Jans** (60 Wallingford Sq., Kittery, 207/439-0001, www.annekejans.net, from 5pm daily, $20-35) kudos far beyond Kittery. This bistro serving creative American fare is a local hot spot with a lively crowd; reservations are recommended. Gluten-free options are available. Complimentary valet parking available on Friday and Saturday evenings.

Bistro 1828 (from 4pm Wed.-Sun., $14-34) at **Frisbee's Wharf** (90 Pepperrell Rd., Kittery Point, 207/703-2028, www.pepperrellcove.com) serves American bistro fare, with dining inside the former store as well as at the rooftop, outdoor **Ski Bar.**

International

Craving Cal-Mex? Some of the recipes in Luis Valdez's **Loco Coco's Tacos** (36 Walker St., Kittery, 207/438-9322, www.locococos.com, 11am-9pm daily, $8-12) have been passed down for generations, and the homemade salsas have flavor and kick. If you're feeling decadent, go for the artery-busting California fries. There are gluten-free and kids' menus too. Choose from self-serve, dining room, or bar seating.

Anju Noodle Bar (7 Wallingford Sq., Kittery, 207/703-4298, www.anjunoodlebar.com, from noon Wed.-Mon., $11-20) gets raves for the okonomiyaki and the pork buns. If you're a hot-sauce fan, pick up a bottle or two of the house-made version to spice up your cooking at home. Pair dinner at the noodle bar with a visit to its sibling, the **Wallingford Dram** (7 Wallingford Sq., Kittery, 207/703-4298, www.thewallingford.com, from 4:30pm Wed.-Sun.), an upscale cocktail bar serving light fare.

Chef Rajesh Mandekar blends techniques drawn from Indian, French, and Italian cuisines to create rave-worthy Indian fare at **Tulsi** (20 Walker St., Kittery, 207/451-9511, www.tulsiindianrestaurant.com, from 4pm Wed.-Fri., from 5pm Tues. and Sat., 11:30am-2:30pm and 5pm-close Sun., $12-24).

For carefully prepared, rustic Italian fare, crafted with an emphasis on locally sourced ingredients, dine at **Festiva Lente** (1 Government Sq., Kittery, 207/703-2287, www.festinalentekittery.com, from 4pm Tues.-Sat., $14-28).

ACCOMMODATIONS

Close to the outlet centers, the **Coachman Inn** (380 Rte. 1, Kittery, 207/439-4434, http://coachmaninn.net, $135-280) is a nicely updated older motel with an outdoor heated pool. Rates include a continental breakfast. Some rooms are pet friendly ($20/pet/day).

Also updated, the pine-shaded **Kittery Inn and Suites** (70 U.S. 1 Bypass, Kittery, 207/439-9324, www.kitteryinnandsuites.com, $140-215) comprises motel rooms, studios with kitchenettes, and two-bedroom cabins. Guests receive a continental breakfast and have use of a saltwater pool and a coin-op laundry.

The **Water Street Inn** (6 Water St., Kittery, 207/994-9735, www.waterstinn.com, $165-250), a handsome brick Victorian, appeals to independent travelers seeking upscale accommodations but not needing an on-site innkeeper. The eight-room inn, renovated in 2018, overlooks the bridge, and has keyless access.

GETTING THERE AND AROUND

Kittery is 60 miles or just over an hour via I-95 from Boston, although it can take longer in summer when traffic backs up at toll booths. It's about eight miles or 15 minutes to York via I-95. Allow about 20 minutes via Route 1, although traffic can be bumper-to-bumper in the stretch by the outlets.

1: Chauncey Creek Lobster Pier 2: Hamilton House
3: Alfred Shaker Museum

1
2
3
118

The Berwicks

Probably the best known of the area's present-day inland communities is the riverside town of South Berwick, thanks to a historical and literary tradition dating to the 17th century, with antique cemeteries to prove it. The 19th- and 20th-century novels of Sarah Orne Jewett and Gladys Hasty Carroll have lured many a contemporary visitor to explore their rural settings, an area aptly described by Carroll as "a small patch of earth continually occupied but never crowded for more than three hundred years."

A ramble through the Berwicks—South Berwick and its siblings—makes a nice diversion from the coast, and because the area is off most visitors' radar screens, it's a good alternative for lodging and dining too.

SIGHTS

Don't blink or you might miss the tiny sign outside the 1774 **Sarah Orne Jewett House Museum and Visitor Center** (5 Portland St./Rte. 4, South Berwick, 207/384-2454, www.historicnewengland.org, 11am-5pm Fri.-Sun. June-Oct. 15, 1st and 3rd Sat. Nov.-May, $8), smack in the center of town. Park on the street and join one of the tours to learn details of the Jewett family and its star, Sarah (1849-1909), author of *The Country of the Pointed Firs,* a New England classic. The adjacent 1854 Greek Revival-style house is now a visitors center with exhibitions and programs. Books by and about Sarah are available in the gift shop. House tours are on the hour until 4pm. The house is one of two local Historic New England properties.

Historic New England's other property, a National Historic Landmark, is the 1785 **Hamilton House** (40 Vaughan's Ln., South Berwick, 207/384-2454, www.historicnewengland.org, 11am-4pm Wed.-Sun. June-Oct. 15, $10). This magnificent Georgian mansion crowns a bluff overlooking the Salmon Falls River and is flanked by handsome colonial gardens. Knowledgeable guides relate the house's fascinating history. (It was the setting for Sarah Orne Jewett's *The Tory Lover.*) Tours begin on the hour, the last at 3pm. In July, the **Sunday in the Garden concert series** ($10, includes house admission) takes place on the lawn; the concert is moved indoors on rainy days. From Route 236 at the southern edge of South Berwick (watch for a signpost), turn left onto Brattle Street and take the second right onto Vaughan's Lane.

Also here is the 150-acre hilltop campus of **Berwick Academy,** Maine's oldest prep school, chartered in 1791 with John Hancock's signature. The coed day school's handsome, gray-stone Romanesque Revival-style William H. Fogg Memorial ("the Fogg") is named for the same family connected with Harvard's Fogg Art Museum. Sarah Orne Jewett helped fund and design the building. Its highlight is an incredible collection of dozens of 19th-century stained glass windows, most designed by Victorian artist Sarah Wyman Whitman, who also designed jackets for Jewett's books. Jewett commissioned the window depicting a dove with a wreath to commemorate the Civil War. A diligent fundraising effort has restored the windows to their former glory.

WORTHWHILE DETOUR

About 25 minutes north of Berwick, via Route 4, is the quiet village of Alfred, home to a Shaker community begun in 1793. In 1931, the Alfred Shakers sold their assets to the Brothers of Christian Instruction and moved in with the Sabbathday Lake Shaker community. The classic Shaker song *Simple Gifts* is attributed to Alfred elder Joseph Brackett. Eight original Shaker buildings and a cemetery remain on Shaker Hill, part of the National Register of Historic Places-listed Alfred Shaker Historic District. The Friends of Alfred Shaker Museum maintain the former carriage house as the **Alfred Shaker**

Museum (118 Shaker Hill Rd., Alfred, www.alfredshakermuseum.com, 1pm-4pm Wed. and Sat. mid-May-early Nov., free). Afterward, treat yourself at **Shaker Pond Ice Cream** (148 Waterboro Rd., Alfred, 207/459-5070, www.shakerpondicecream.com, hours vary seasonally). Take your cone to **Old Sheep Meadows Nursery** (90 Federal St., Alfred, 207/324-5211, www.oldsheepmeadowsnursery.com, hours vary seasonally), where you can explore five acres of display gardens emphasizing hardy root roses, woodland gardens, daylilies, and pre-Civil War apple trees.

RECREATION

When you're ready to stretch your legs, head to **Vaughan Woods State Park** (28 Oldfields Rd., South Berwick, 207/384-5160, 9am-8pm daily late May-early Sept., park trails accessible year-round, $4 nonresident adults, $3 Maine adults, $1 ages 5-11) and wander along the three miles of trails in the 250-acre riverside preserve. It adjoins Hamilton House and is connected via a path, but there's far more parking at the park itself.

ENTERTAINMENT

Another reason to venture inland is to catch a production at the **Hackmatack Playhouse** (538 School St./Rte. 9, Berwick, 207/698-1807, www.hackmatack.org), midway between North Berwick and Berwick. The popular summer theater, performing since 1972, operates from a renovated barn reminiscent of a past era and has 8pm performances Wednesday-Saturday, a 2pm matinee Thursday, and children's shows. Tickets are $25-30.

FOOD

Nature's Way Market (271 Main St., South Berwick, 207/384-3210, 8am-9pm Mon.-Sat., 8am-8pm Sun.) isn't your ordinary health-food store. In addition to healthful fare, it specializes in locally made specialty foods, carries a wide array of wine and beer, and has a butcher shop where you can purchase made-to-order sandwiches.

A local institution since 1960, **Fogarty's** (471 Main St., South Berwick, 207/384-8361, www.fogartysrestaurant.net, 11am-8pm daily, $10-25) has expanded through the years from a simple take-out place to a local favorite for inexpensive American fare and family-friendly dining. Ask for a river-view table in the back room.

At **Thistle Pig** (279 Main St., South Berwick, 207/704-0624, www.thistlepig.com, from 11am Mon. and Thurs.-Sat., from 10am Sun., $17-29), the upscale bistro-fare menu changes frequently to reflect what's fresh and local.

At **Madison's Cafe** (12 Portland St., South Berwick, 207/704-0647, http://madisonscafeofmaine.com, 7am-2pm Tues.-Sat., 8am-2pm Sun., $3-8) is staffed by individuals with intellectual and developmental disabilities.

ACCOMMODATIONS

Innkeepers Ben Gumm and Sally McLaren have turned the 25-room Queen Anne/Eastlake-style Hurd mansion into the **Angel of the Berwicks** (2 Elm St., North Berwick, 207/676-2133, www.angeloftheberwicks.com, $119-179), an elegant antiques-filled inn. The property, listed in the National Register of Historic Places, has 11-foot ceilings, stained glass windows, hand-carved friezes, and ornate mantelpieces. There's even a baby grand piano in the music room. Rates include a full breakfast. It's about a half hour from the coast, and the rates reflect the location, not the grandeur of this special place.

Slip away to **Riverhouse** (72 Vine St., South Berwick, 603/319-1911, http://riverhouse-maine.com, from $195), a handsome and secluded three-room inn overlooking the tidal Salmon Falls River. Two additional guest rooms are in the barn.

GETTING THERE

South Berwick is about 11 miles or 20 minutes from Kittery via Route 236. It's about 10 miles or 20 minutes from South Berwick to York via Routes 236 and 91.

The Yorks

Four villages with distinct personalities—upscale **York Harbor,** historic **York Village,** casual **York Beach,** and semirural **Cape Neddick**—make up the **Town of York** (pop. 12,529). First inhabited by Native Americans, who named it Agamenticus, the area was settled as early as 1624, so history is serious business here. High points were its founding by Sir Ferdinando Gorges and the arrival of well-to-do vacationers in the 19th century. In between were Indian massacres, economic woes, and population shuffles. The town's population explodes in summer, which is pretty obvious in July-August when you're searching for a free patch of York Beach sand or a parking place. York Beach, with its seasonal surf and souvenir shops and amusements, has long been the counterpoint to genteel York Village, but that's changing with the restoration and rebirth of York Beach's downtown buildings and the arrival of tony restaurants, shops, and condos.

History and genealogy buffs can study the headstones in the Old Burying Ground or comb the archives of the Museums of Old York. For lighthouse fans, there are Cape Neddick Light Station ("Nubble Light") and Boon Island, six miles offshore. Rent horses or mountain bikes on Mount Agamenticus, board a deep-sea fishing boat in York Harbor, or spend an hour hiking the Cliff Path in York Harbor. For the kids there's a zoo, a lobster-boat cruise, a taffy maker, and, of course, the beach.

SIGHTS

★ Museums of Old York

Based in York Village, the **Museums of Old York** (207 York St., York Village, 207/363-4974, www.oldyork.org, museum buildings 10am-5pm Tues.-Sat., 1pm-5pm Sun. late May-early Sept., 10am-5pm Thurs.-Sat., 1pm-5pm Sun. early Sept.-mid-Oct., $8-15 adults, $5-10 ages 4-15) are a collection of colonial and postcolonial buildings plus a research library open throughout the summer. Start at the **Jefferds' Tavern Visitor Center** (5 Lindsay Rd., York Village), where you'll need to buy tickets. Don't miss the **Old Burying Ground,** dating from 1735, across the street (rubbings are not allowed). Nearby are the **Old Gaol** and the **School House,** both fun for kids, and the **Emerson-Wilcox House** (guided tours 11:30am, 1:30pm, and 3pm Tues.-Sat., 1:30pm and 3pm Sun.). About 0.5 mile down Lindsay Road on the York River are the **John Hancock Warehouse** and the **George Marshall Store Gallery** (140 Lindsay Rd.), operated in the summer as a respected contemporary art gallery; across the river is the **Elizabeth Perkins House.** Antiques buffs shouldn't miss the Wilcox and Perkins Houses. Both are open by guided tour; other buildings are self-guided. Visit some or all the buildings at your own pace. You can walk to some of the sites from the tavern; to reach others you'll need a car, and parking may be limited.

★ Nubble Light and Sohier Park

The best-known photo op in York is the distinctive 1879 lighthouse known formally as **Cape Neddick Light Station,** familiarly Nubble Light or "the Nubble." Although there's no access to the lighthouse's island, the **Sohier Park Welcome Center** (Nubble Rd., off Rte. 1A, between Long and Short Sands Beaches, York Beach, 207/363-7608, www.nubblelight.org, 9am-7pm daily mid-May-mid-Oct.) provides the perfect viewpoint (and has restrooms). Parking is limited, but the turnover is fairly high. It's not a bad idea, however, to walk from the Long Sands parking area or come by bike (watch for the road's inadequate shoulders). During weekdays this is also a popular spot for scuba divers.

The Yorks

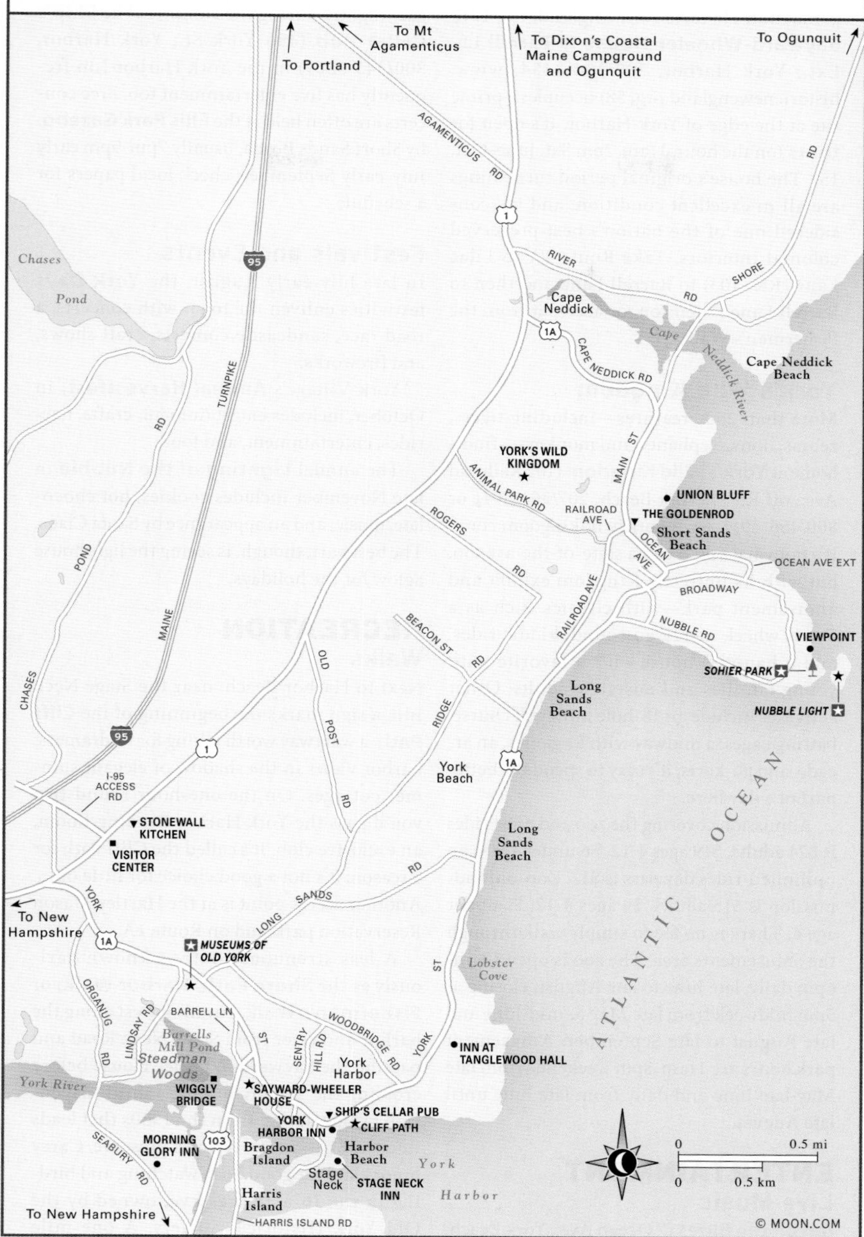
To Mt Agamenticus
To Portland
To Dixon's Coastal Maine Campground and Ogunquit
To Ogunquit
AGAMENTICUS RD
RD
Chases Pond
95
TURNPIKE
RD
MAINE
POND
CHASES
RIVER
SHORE
RD
Cape Neddick
1A
CAPE NEDDICK RD
Cape
Neddick River
Cape Neddick Beach
YORK'S WILD KINGDOM
ANIMAL PARK RD
MAIN ST
UNION BLUFF
THE GOLDENROD
RAILROAD AVE
Short Sands Beach
OCEAN AVE
OCEAN AVE EXT
ROGERS RD
BROADWAY
RAILROAD AVE
NUBBLE RD
VIEWPOINT
SOHIER PARK
NUBBLE LIGHT
BEACON ST
OLD POST RD
RIDGE RD
Long Sands Beach
York Beach
ATLANTIC OCEAN
I-95 ACCESS RD
STONEWALL KITCHEN
VISITOR CENTER
Long Sands Beach
RD
LONG SANDS
YORK
To New Hampshire
MUSEUMS OF OLD YORK
Lobster Cove
ORGANUG RD
LINDSAY RD
BARRELL LN
Barrells Mill Pond
Steedman Woods
ST
SENTRY HILL RD
WOODBRIDGE RD
YORK ST
INN AT TANGLEWOOD HALL
York River
WIGGLY BRIDGE
SAYWARD-WHEELER HOUSE
York Harbor
SHIP'S CELLAR PUB
YORK HARBOR INN
CLIFF PATH
MORNING GLORY INN
103
SEABURY RD
Bragdon Island
Harbor Beach
Stage Neck
STAGE NECK INN
York Harbor
Harris Island
HARRIS ISLAND RD
To New Hampshire
0 0.5 mi
0 0.5 km
© MOON.COM

Sayward-Wheeler House

Owned by the Boston-based nonprofit organization Historic New England, the 1718 **Sayward-Wheeler House** (9 Barrell Ln. Ext., York Harbor, 207/384-2454, www.historicnewengland.org, $8) occupies a prime site at the edge of York Harbor. It's open for **tours** (on the hour, 11am-2pm Sat. June-Oct. 15). The house's original period furnishings are all in excellent condition, and it's considered one of the nation's best-preserved colonial interiors. Take Route 1A to Lilac Lane (Rte. 103) to Barrell Lane and then to Barrell Lane Extension, or access it from the Fisherman's Walk.

York's Wild Kingdom

More than 250 creatures—including tigers, zebras, lions, elephants, and monkeys—find a home at **York's Wild Kingdom** (102 Railroad Ave., off Rte. 1, York Beach, 207/363-4911 or 800/456-4911, www.yorkswildkingdom.com). It's not what you'd call a state-of-the-art zoo, but with its Butterfly Kingdom exhibit and amusement park—with classics such as a Ferris wheel, merry-go-round, kiddie rides, and a haunted house—it's a favorite with young families and nostalgic adults. Other activities include an 18-hole mini golf course, batting cages, a midway with $1 games, an arcade, and go-karts; it's easy to spend the better part of a day here.

Admission covering the zoo and most rides is $24 adults, $19 ages 4-12, $6 under age 4; an unlimited-rides day pass is $12. Zoo-only admission is $15 adults, $9 ages 4-12, $1 under age 4. There is no fee to simply walk through the amusements area. The zoo is open 10am-6pm daily, late June to late August, closing at 5pm midweek from late May to mid-June and late August to late September. Amusement park hours are 11am-8pm weekends from late May-late June and daily from late June until late August.

ENTERTAINMENT

Live Music

Inn on the Blues (7 Ocean Ave., York Beach, 207/351-3221, www.innontheblues.com) has live music or a DJ (acoustic, blues, reggae) nightly during the summer. The **Ship's Cellar Pub** (480 York St., York Harbor, 800/343-3869) in the York Harbor Inn frequently has live entertainment too. Free concerts are often held at the **Ellis Park Gazebo,** by Short Sands Beach, usually 7pm-9pm early July-early September; check local papers for a schedule.

Festivals and Events

In late July-early August, the **York Days** festivities enliven the town with concerts, a road race, sandcastle contests, craft shows, and fireworks.

York Village's **Annual Harvestfest,** in October, includes entertainment, crafts, hayrides, entertainment, and food.

The annual **Lighting of the Nubble** in late November includes cookies, hot chocolate, music, and an appearance by Santa Claus. The best part, though, is seeing the lighthouse aglow for the holidays.

RECREATION

Walks

Next to Harbor Beach, near the Stage Neck Inn, a sign marks the beginning of the **Cliff Path,** a walkway worth taking for its dramatic harbor views in the shadow of elegant summer cottages. On the one-hour round-trip you'll pass the York Harbor Reading Room, an exclusive club. It's called the Cliff Path for a reason; it's not a good choice for little ones. Another access point is at the Hartley Mason Reservation parkland on Route 1A.

A less strenuous route is known variously as the **Shore Path, Harbor Walk,** or **Fisherman's Walk,** running west along the harbor and river from Stage Neck Road and passing the Sayward-Wheeler House before crossing the Wiggly Bridge, a mini suspension bridge dating from the 1930s that leads into the **Steedman Woods** preserve. Carry binoculars for good boat-watching and birding in the 16-acre preserve, owned by the Old York Historical Society. A one-mile double-loop trail takes less than an hour of easy strolling.

Mount Agamenticus

Drive to the summit of **Mount Agamenticus** ("the Big A") and you're at York County's highest point. It's only 692 feet, but on a clear day you'll have panoramic views of ocean, lakes, woods, and sometimes the White Mountains. The 10,000-acre conservation region (www.agamenticus.org), sited within one of the largest remaining expanses of undeveloped forest in coastal New England, is among the most biologically diverse wildernesses in Maine. It includes vernal pools and ponds and is home to rare and endangered species. At the summit are a billboard map of the 40-mile trail network and the **Learning Lodge** (11am-3pm Sat.-Sun. late May-mid-Oct.), with displays, hands-on activities, and a kids' corner. Mountain biking is also hugely popular on Agamenticus. Take a picnic, a kite, and binoculars. In the fall, if the wind is from the northwest, watch for migrating hawks; in winter, bring a sled for the best downhill run in southern Maine. From Route 1 in Cape Neddick, take Mountain Road (also called Agamenticus Road) 4.2 miles west to the access road.

Golf

The **Ledges Golf Club** (1 Ledges Dr., off Rte. 91, York, 207/351-9999, www.ledgesgolf.com) is an 18-hole course with daily public tee times.

Swimming

Sunbathing and swimming are big draws in York, with four beaches of varying sizes and accessibility: **Short Sands Beach, Long Sands Beach, Harbor Beach,** and **Cape Neddick (Passaconaway) Beach.** Bear in mind that traffic can be gridlocked along the beachfront (Route 1A) in midsummer, so it may take longer than you expect to get anywhere. **Lifeguards** are usually on duty 9:30am-4pm mid-June-Labor Day at Short Sands Beach, Long Sands Beach, and Harbor Beach. **Bathhouses** at Long Sands and Short Sands are open 9am-7pm daily in midsummer. The biggest **parking area** (metered) is at Long Sands, but that 1.5-mile beach also draws the most visitors. The scarcest parking is at Harbor Beach near the Stage Neck Inn (two-hour spaces along Route 1A) and at Cape Neddick (Passaconaway) Beach near the Ogunquit town line.

Surfing

Want to catch a wave? For surfing or paddleboard information, lessons, or rentals, call **Liquid Dreams Surf Shop** (171 Long Beach Ave., York, 207/351-2545, www.liquiddreamssurf.com, 8am-8pm daily). It's right across from Long Sands Beach.

Bicycling

Berger's Bike Shop (241 York St., York, 207/363-4070, www.bergersbikeshop.com, 9am-5pm Mon.-Fri., 9am-3pm Sat.) rents hybrid bikes for $40 per full day, $30 per half day; lock and helmet are additional.

Fishing

A local expert on fly fishing, spin fishing, and conventional tackle is **Eldredge Bros. Guide Service** (1480 Rte. 1, Cape Neddick, 207/373-9269, www.eldredgeflyshop.com). Guided fresh- or saltwater fishing trips for one or two anglers begin at $300/four hours.

FOOD

Lobster and Seafood

Locals praise the lobster roll from the **Maine Lobster Outlet** (360 Rte. 1, York, 207/363-9899, http://mainelobsteroutlet.com, 8am-5pm Mon.-Sat., 8am-4pm Sun.) as one of the state's best, and say the clam chowder is excellent. It's takeout only.

Grab an oceanfront seat at **Lobster Cove** (756 York St., York Beach, 207/351-1100, www.lobstercoverestaurant.com, from 8am daily year-round) and watch the waves roll into Long Sands Beach while enjoying lobster or fried seafood.

Quick Bites

Sometimes the line runs right out the door of the low-ceilinged, reddish-brown roadside shack that houses local institution **Flo's Steamed Dogs** (1359 Rte. 1, opposite the Mountain Rd. turnoff, Cape Neddick, no phone, www.floshotdogs.com, 11am-3pm Thurs.-Tues.). There is no menu—just steamed Schultz wieners, buns, chips, beverages, and an attitude. The secret? The spicy, sweet-and-sour sauce, allegedly once sought by the H. J. Heinz corporation. The cognoscenti know to order their dogs only with mayonnaise and the special sauce, not the heretical ketchup or mustard.

See those people with their faces pressed to the glass? They're all watching the taffy makers inside the **Goldenrod** (2 Railroad Ave., York Beach, 207/363-2621, www.thegoldenrod.com, 8am-10pm daily), where machines spew out 180 Goldenrod Kisses a minute, for a total of 65 tons a year, and have been at it since 1896. The Goldenrod is a quaint, seasonal place with a tearoom, a gift shop, an old-fashioned soda fountain with 135 ice cream flavors, and a rustic dining room as well as reasonable prices.

After viewing the Nubble, head across the road to **Dunne's Ice Cream** (214 Nubble Rd., York Beach, 207/363-1277, http://dunnesicecream.com, hours vary seasonally), where unusual flavors complement the standards. Prefer gelato? Look for the **Coppa Magica** (207/703-8227, www.coppamagica.com) gelato van; it makes its own.

Stonewall Kitchen (2 Stonewall Ln., York, 207/351-2712 or 800/207-5267, www.stonewallkitchen.com) concocts imaginative condiments and other food products, many of which have received national awards. You can often watch the jam makers at work. Register in advance for cooking classes. Go there hungry: An espresso bar and an excellent café (8am-4pm Mon.-Sat., 9am-4pm Sun., kitchen closes 3pm, $7-15) are on the premises.

Stop in at the **Gateway Farmers Market** (Greater York Region Chamber of Commerce Visitors Center, Rte. 1, York, 9am-1pm Sat. early-June-early Oct.) and stock up for a picnic. If you still need more, head next door to Stonewall Kitchen.

Family Favorites

The York Harbor Inn's **Ship's Cellar Pub** (Rte. 1A, York Harbor, 11:30am-10pm Mon.-Sat., 4pm-10pm Sun.) attracts even the locals. The menu is the same as in the main dining room (burgers to lobster, $12-42), but the setting is far more casual. The space is designed to resemble the interior of a yacht. There is live music most nights.

Casual Dining

For ocean views paired with a fine-dining atmosphere, book a table at the York Harbor Inn's main dining room, **1637** (Rte. 1A, York Harbor, 207/363-5119, www.yorkharborinn.com, 5:30pm-9pm Mon.-Sat., 10am-2:30pm and 5:30pm-9pm Sun., $12-42). The wide-ranging American menu has something for every taste and budget. An early-bird three-course menu for those seated by 6pm Sunday-Friday is $21.95.

The **Tavern at Chapman Cottage** (370 York St., York Harbor, 207/363-5119, 4pm-9pm Thurs.-Sun., $12-15), owned by the York Harbor Inn, serves an extensive menu of tapas-type fare ($6-16), with a few heftier options ($16-32).

"Food that loves you back" is the slogan for **Frankie and Johnny's Natural Foods** (1594 Rte. 1 N., Cape Neddick, 207/363-1909, www.frankie-johnnys.com, from 5pm Wed.-Sun. summer, reduced hours spring and fall, $30-40). Inside the shingled restaurant, wood floors and pine-colored walls provide the background for the vibrant international fare of chef John Shaw, who trained at the New England Culinary Institute. Vegetarian and vegan choices are always on the menu, along with fish, seafood, and chicken options, and many dishes can be modified for

1: Cape Neddick Light Station, better known as Nubble Light 2: Emerson-Wilcox House in York Village 3: Short Sands Beach 4: Union Bluff hotel in York Beach

1
2
3
4

the gluten-sensitive. Portions are huge, breads and pastas are made in-house, and everything is cooked to order, so plan on a leisurely meal. Bring your own booze, but leave the credit cards behind, since "plastic is not natural."

Chef Justin Walker and his restaurateur wife, Danielle, own ★ **Walkers Maine** (1273 Rte. 1, Cape Neddick, 207/351-1145, from 5pm Wed.-Mon., $15-40), where the New American menu is rooted in fresh and local, including produce from their family farm.

ACCOMMODATIONS

Bed-and-Breakfasts

Built in 1889, the **Inn at Tanglewood Hall** (611 York St., York Harbor, 207/351-1075, www.tanglewoodhall.com, $185-245) was once the summer home of bandleaders Jimmy and Tommy Dorsey. In 2005, it was a York Historical Society decorator show house. It's an elegant, gracious property within walking distance of the beach, yet a world away. Some rooms have gas fireplaces or private porches. Beautiful woodland gardens are another plus. Rates include breakfast.

A boutique bed-and-breakfast catering to romantics, the ★ **Morning Glory Inn** (120 Seabury Rd., York Harbor, 207/363-2062, www.morninggloryinnmaine.com, $215-280) has just five spacious and private guest rooms, each with private patio, balcony, or yard. The living room, in the original section of the house, was a 17th-century cottage barged over from the Isles of Shoals; the newer post-and-beam great room doubles as a dining area where a hot breakfast buffet is served. The property is quiet enough that guests can listen to the birds in the gardens; it's truly a magical setting, far removed yet convenient to everything York offers.

Inns

York Harbor Inn (Rte. 1A, York Harbor, 207/363-5119 or 800/343-3869, www.yorkharborinn.com, $160-499) is an accommodating spot with a country-inn flavor and a wide variety of guest-room and package-plan options throughout the year. The oldest section of the inn is a 17th-century cabin from the Isles of Shoals. Accommodations are spread across the inn, the adjacent Yorkshire House, and four elegantly restored houses, all with resident innkeepers: Harbor Hill and Harbor Cliffs are within steps; the Chapman Cottage and the dog-friendly 1730 Harbor Crest are about a half mile away. Some rooms have four-poster beds, fireplaces, and whirlpools; many have water views. Rates include a generous continental breakfast.

You can't miss the **Stage Neck Inn** (100 Stage Neck Rd., York Harbor, 207/363-3850 or 800/340-9901, www.stageneck.com, year-round, from $400 with breakfast), occupying its own private peninsula overlooking York Harbor. Modern resort-style facilities include indoor and outdoor pools, tennis courts, golf privileges, a spa, a fitness center, varied dining options, and spectacular views from balconies and terraces.

Hotels

Since 1868, the **Union Bluff** (8 Beach St., York Beach, 207/363-1333 or 800/833-0721, www.unionbluff.com, from $260) has stood sentry like a fortress overlooking Short Sands Beach. Guest rooms are split between three buildings, all within spitting distance of the beach. Most have ocean views; some have fireplaces, whirlpool baths, or oceanview decks. Also on the premises: the Beach Street Grill dining room and a pub serving lighter fare. The best deals are the packages, which include breakfast and dinner. The hotel and pub are open year-round; the restaurant is seasonal.

Condominium Suites

Fabulously sited on the oceanfront and overlooking the Nubble, the high-end **ViewPoint** (229 Nubble Rd., York Beach, 207/363-2661, www.viewpointhotel.com, from $425) has nine luxuriously appointed 1-3-bedroom suites with gas fireplaces, fully equipped kitchens, and laundries. On the premises are an outdoor heated pool, a grilling area, gardens, and a playground.

Camping

Dixon's Coastal Maine Campground (1740 Rte. 1, Cape Neddick, 207/363-3626, www.dixonscampground.com, $44-52) has more than 100 well-spaced sites on 26 wooded and open acres. It can accommodate tents and small RVs. Electrical and water hookups are available. For something different, reserve a yurt ($100-135). Facilities include a playground and a good-size outdoor heated pool.

INFORMATION AND SERVICES

The Maine Tourism Association operates a **Maine State Visitor Information Center** (1 Rte. 95, Kittery, 207/439-1319) in Kittery between Route 1 and I-95, with access from either road. It's chock-full of brochures and has restrooms and a picnic area.

For York-area information, head for the Shingle-style palace of the **Greater York Region Chamber of Commerce** (1 Stonewall Ln., off Rte. 1, York, 207/363-4422, www.gatewaytomaine.org), at I-95's York exit. Inside are restrooms. It's open daily in summer.

GETTING THERE AND AROUND

York is about eight miles or 15 minutes via I-95/Maine Turnpike; allow at least 20 minutes via Route 1 from Kittery. It's about seven miles or 15 minutes via Route 1 to Ogunquit, but allow more time in summer.

The Maine Turnpike, a toll road, is generally the fastest route if you're trying to get between two towns. Route 1 parallels the turnpike on the ocean side. It's mostly two lanes and is lined with shops, restaurants, motels, and other visitor-oriented sites, which means stop-and-go traffic that often slows to a crawl. If you're traveling locally, it's best to walk or use the local trolley systems, which have the bonus of saving you the agony of finding a parking spot.

The seasonal **Shoreline Explorer** (207/459-2932, www.shorelineexplorer.com, late June-early Sept.) trolley system makes it possible to travel from York to Kennebunkport without your car. Each town's system is operated separately and has its own fees. **York Trolley 1** (10am-10pm, $2 each way, ages 4 and younger free) operates every 30 minutes between Long and Short Sands Beaches. **Purple 2** ($1 each way, ages 11 and younger ride free, exact change) runs hourly between York's Short Sands Beach and Ogunquit's Perkins Cove.

Ogunquit and Wells

Ogunquit (pop. 892) has been a holiday destination since the indigenous residents named it "beautiful place by the sea." What's the appeal? An unparalleled, unspoiled beach, a shorefront path, a dozen art galleries, and a respected art museum with a view second to none. The town has been home to an art colony attracting the glitterati of the painting world since Charles Woodbury came here in the late 1880s. The summertime crowds continue, multiplying the minuscule year-round population. These days it's an especially gay-friendly community too. Besides the beach, the most powerful magnet is Perkins Cove, a working fishing enclave that looks more like a movie set. The best way to approach the cove is via trolley-bus or on foot, along the shoreline Marginal Way from downtown Ogunquit; midsummer parking in the cove is madness.

Wells (pop. 9,589), once part of Ogunquit and since 1980 its immediate neighbor to the north, was settled in 1640. Nowadays it's best known as a family-oriented community with seven miles of splendid beachfront and lots of antiques and used-book shops strewn along Route 1. It also claims two spectacular nature preserves worth a drive from anywhere. At the southern end of Wells, abutting Ogunquit, is **Moody,** an enclave named after 18th-century settler Samuel Moody.

SIGHTS

★ Ogunquit Museum of American Art

Not many museums can boast a view as stunning as the one at the **Ogunquit Museum of American Art** (543 Shore Rd., Ogunquit, 207/646-4909, www.ogunquitmuseum.org, 10am-5pm daily May 1-Oct. 31, $10 adults, $9 seniors and students, free under age 12), nor can many communities boast such renown as a summer art colony. Overlooking Narrow Cove, 1.4 miles south of downtown Ogunquit, the museum prides itself on its permanent 2,000-piece American art collection. Works by Marsden Hartley, Rockwell Kent, Walt Kuhn, Henry Strater, and Thomas Hart Benton, among others, are displayed in five galleries. Special exhibits are mounted each summer, when there is an extensive series of lectures, concerts, and other programs, including the annual Art by the Sea Gala & Auction, a social-season must. OMAA has a well-stocked gift shop, wheelchair access, and landscaped grounds with sculptures, a pond, and manicured lawns.

★ Marginal Way

No visit to Ogunquit is complete without a leisurely stroll along the **Marginal Way,** the mile-long paved footpath edging the ocean from Shore Road (by the Sparhawk Resort) to Perkins Cove. It has been a must-walk since Josiah Chase gave the right-of-way to the town in the 1920s. The best times to appreciate this shrub-lined shorefront walkway are early morning or when everyone's at the beach. En route are tidepools, intriguing rock formations, crashing surf, pocket beaches, benches for absorbing the views, and a marker listing the day's high and low tides. When the surf's up, keep a close eye on the kids—the sea has no mercy. A midpoint access is at Israel's Head (behind a sewage plant masquerading as a tiny lighthouse), but getting a parking space is pure luck. The only wheels allowed are strollers and wheelchairs.

Perkins Cove

Turn-of-the-20th-century photos show Ogunquit's **Perkins Cove** lined with gray-shingled shacks used by a hardy colony of local fishermen, fellows who headed offshore to make a tough living in little boats. They'd hardly recognize it today. Although the cove remains a working lobster-fishing harbor, several old shacks have been reincarnated as boutiques and restaurants, and photographers go crazy shooting the quaint inlet spanned by a little pedestrian drawbridge. In the cove are galleries, gift shops, restaurants (from fast food to lobster to high-end dining), excursion boats, and public restrooms. I enjoy it best in the early morning, before the crowds arrive. Only a coffee shop at the tip is open then, but you can watch the fishing boats gear up and head out. Parking in the cove is $7 for two hours, but there are some spaces in the back that open up after noon (they are reserved for local fishermen in the morning).

★ Wells Reserve at Laudholm Farm

Known locally as **Laudholm Farm** (the site of the restored 19th-century building that houses the visitors center), **Wells National Estuarine Research Reserve** (342 Laudholm Farm Rd., Wells, 207/646-1555, www.wellsreserve.org) occupies 1,690 acres of woods, beach, and coastal salt marsh on the southern boundary of the Rachel Carson National Wildlife Refuge, just 0.5 mile east of Route 1. Seven miles of trails wind through the property. The best trail is the Salt Marsh Loop, with a boardwalk section leading to an

---

1: sculpture outside the Ogunquit Museum of American Art **2:** snowshoeing at Laudholm Farm **3:** Marginal Way **4:** pedestrian drawbridge over Perkins Cove

1
2
3
4

overlook with panoramic views of the marsh and the Little River inlet. Another winner is the Barrier Beach Walk, a 1.3-mile round-trip that goes through multiple habitats all the way to beautiful Laudholm Beach. Allow 1.5 hours for either; you can combine the two. Some trails are wheelchair-accessible. The informative exhibits in the **visitors center** (10am-4pm daily late May-mid-Oct., 10am-4pm Mon.-Fri. Apr.-late May and mid-Oct.-Nov.) will enhance your enjoyment of the reserve. An extensive schedule includes lectures, nature walks, and children's programs. Reservations are required for some programs. Trails are accessible 7am-dusk. From late May to mid-October, admission ($5 adults, $1 ages 6-16) is charged.

Rachel Carson National Wildlife Refuge

Eleven chunks of coastal Maine real estate between Kittery Point and Cape Elizabeth make up the **Rachel Carson National Wildlife Refuge** (321 Port Rd./Rte. 9, Wells, 207/646-9226, www.fws.gov/refuge/rachel_carson), headquartered at the northern edge of Wells near the Kennebunkport town line. Pick up a *Carson Trail Guide* at the refuge office (parking is limited) and follow the mile-long wheelchair-accessible walkway past tidal creeks, salt pans, and salt marshes. It's a bird-watcher's paradise during migration seasons. Office hours are 8am-4:30pm Monday-Friday year-round; trail access is sunrise-sunset daily year-round. Leashed pets are allowed.

Ogunquit Arts Collaborative Gallery

The **Ogunquit Arts Collaborative Gallery** (Shore Rd. and Bourne Ln., Ogunquit, 207/646-8400, www.barngallery.org, 11am-5pm Mon.-Sat., 1pm-5pm Sun. late May-early Oct., free), also known as the Barn Gallery, features the works of an impressive group of member artists. The OAC is the showcase for the Ogunquit Art Association, established by Charles Woodbury, who was inspired to open an art school in Perkins Cove in the late 19th century. Special programs throughout the season include concerts, workshops, gallery talks, and an art auction.

Ogunquit Heritage Museum

Ogunquit's history is preserved in the **Ogunquit Heritage Museum** (86 Obeds Ln., Dorothea Jacobs Grant Common, Ogunquit, 207/646-0296, www.ogunquitheritagemuseum.com, 1pm-5pm Tues.-Sat. June-Oct., free), which occupies the restored Captain James Winn House, a 1785 Cape house listed in the National Register of Historic Places. Exhibits here and in a new wing focus on Ogunquit's role as an art colony and its maritime heritage, town history, and local architecture.

ENTERTAINMENT

Having showcased top-notch professional theater since the 1930s, the 750-seat **Ogunquit Playhouse** (10 Main St./Rte. 1, Ogunquit, 207/646-5511, www.ogunquitplayhouse.org) knows how to do it right: It presents comedies and musicals late May-mid-November, starring Broadway veterans and a sprinkling of Hollywood stars. The air-conditioned building is wheelchair-accessible. The box office is open daily in season, beginning in early May; tickets range $52-125. The playhouse also presents a children's series. You can take a guided **Backstage Tour** ($5-10, 1-1.5 hours, call for current schedule), viewing the dressing rooms, green room, and backstage while picking up insider info on the stars who have played here over the years. Parking can be a hassle during shows; consider walking the short distance from the Bourne Lane trolley-bus stop.

Live Music

Jonathan's (2 Bourne Ln., Ogunquit, 207/646-4777, http://jonathansogunquit.com) is a twofer find. Downstairs is a casual fine-dining restaurant. Upstairs, national headliners often perform in an intimate venue, where every seat has a great view of the stage. A full bar is available until the show starts. Advance tickets are cheaper than at the door, and dinner guests get preference for seats; all show seats are reserved.

Ogunquit Performing Arts (207/646-6170, www.ogunquitperformingarts.org) presents a full slate of programs, including classical concerts, ballet, and theater, at the **Dunaway Center** (23 School St.). The **Wells Summer Concert Series** runs most Saturday evenings early July-early September at the Hope Hobbs Gazebo in Wells Harbor Park. A wide variety of music is represented, from sing-alongs to swing.

Festivals and Events

Harbor Fest takes place in July in Harbor Park in Wells and includes a concert, crafts fair, parade, and chicken barbecue, along with children's activities.

In August, Ogunquit hosts the annual **Sidewalk Art Show and Sale.**

Capriccio is a performing arts festival in Ogunquit with daytime and evening events held during the first week of September. The second weekend that month, the Wells National Estuarine Research Reserve (Laudholm Farm) hosts the **Laudholm Nature Crafts Festival,** a two-day juried crafts fair with children's activities and guided nature walks.

SHOPPING

Antiques are a Wells specialty. You'll find more than 50 shops with a huge range of prices. The majority are on Route 1. **R. Jorgensen Antiques** (502 Post Rd./Rte. 1, Wells, 207/646-9444) is a phenomenon in itself, filling 11 showrooms in two buildings with European and American 18th- and 19th-century furniture and accessories. **MacDougall-Gionet Antiques and Associates** (2104 Post Rd./Rte. 1, Wells, 207/646-3531) has been in business since 1959, and its reputation is stellar. The 65-dealer shop, in an 18th-century barn, carries American and European country and formal furniture and accessories. The **Farm Antiques** (294 Mildram Rd., Wells, 207/985-2656) specializes in fine English antiques.

If you've been scouring antiquarian bookshops for a long-wanted title, chances are you'll find it at **Douglas N. Harding Rare Books** (2152 Post Rd./Rte. 1, Wells, 207/646-8785 or 800/228-1398). Well-cataloged and organized, the sprawling bookshop stocks upward of 100,000 books, prints, and maps at any given time, plus a hefty selection of Maine and New England histories.

Fans of fine craft, especially contemporary art glass, shouldn't miss **Panache** (307 Main St., Ogunquit, 207/646-4878).

RECREATION

Water Sports

BEACHES

One of Maine's most scenic and unspoiled sandy beachfronts, Ogunquit's 3.5-mile stretch of sand fringed with seagrass is a magnet for hordes of sunbathers, spectators, swimmers, surfers, and sandcastle builders. Getting there means crossing the Ogunquit River via one of three access points. For Ogunquit's **Main Beach**—with a bathhouse and big crowds—take Beach Street. To reach **Footbridge Beach,** which is marginally less crowded, either take Ocean Street and the footbridge or take Bourne Avenue to Ocean Avenue in adjacent Wells and walk back toward Ogunquit. **Moody Beach,** at Wells's southern end, is technically private property, a subject of considerable legal dispute. Lifeguards are on duty all summer at the public beaches, and there are restrooms in all three areas. The beach is free, but parking is $25-30/day and lots fill up early on warm midsummer days. After 3:30pm some parking is free. It's far more sensible to opt for the frequent trolleys.

Wells beaches continue where Ogunquit's leave off. **Crescent Beach** (Webhannet Dr. between Eldredge Rd. and Mile Rd.) is the tiniest, with tidepools, no facilities, and limited parking. **Wells Beach** (Mile Rd. to Atlantic Ave.) is the major (and most crowded) beach, with lifeguards, restrooms, and parking.

Around the other side of Wells Harbor is **Drakes Island Beach** (take Drakes Island Rd. at the blinking light), a less crowded spot with restrooms and lifeguards. Walk northeast from Drakes Island Beach and you'll eventually reach **Laudholm Beach,** with great birding along the way. Summer beach-parking fees (pay-and-display) are $3/hour.

TIDEPOOL EXCURSION

Join marine science educator "Coastal" Carol of **Coast Encounters** (207/831-4436, www.coastencounters.com) on a three-hour, hands-on intertidal excursion ($55 adults, $40 ages 7-18). This is a fabulous way to introduce kids to the beach. Excursions are geared to all family members, from kids to grandparents. Carol even has a special wheelchair available that can travel over the rough terrain.

BOAT EXCURSIONS

Between April and early November, captain Tim Tower runs half-day (departing 4pm, $50 pp) and full-day (departing 7am, $90 pp) **deep-sea fishing trips** aboard the 40-foot ***Bunny Clark*** (207/646-2214, www.bunnyclark.com), moored in Perkins Cove. Reservations are necessary. Tim has a science degree, so he's a wealth of marine biology information. All gear is provided, and the crew will fillet your catch for you; dress warmly and wear sunblock.

Barnacle Billy's Dock at Perkins Cove is home port for the Hubbard family's **Finestkind Cruises** (207/646-5227, www.finestkindcruises.com, no credit cards). Motorboat options consist of 1.5-hour, 14-mile Nubble Light cruises; one-hour cocktail cruises; a 75-minute breakfast cruise complete with coffee, juice, and a muffin; and 50-minute lobster-boat trips. Rates run $22-35 adults, $11-17 children. Also available are 1.75-hour sails ($35 pp) aboard the ***Cricket,*** a locally built wooden sailboat. Reservations are advisable, but usually unnecessary midweek.

OUTFITTERS

At **Wheels and Waves** (365 Post Rd./Rte. 1, Wells, 207/646-5774, www.wheelsnwaves.com), bike or surfboard rentals are $25/day, including delivery to some hotels; a stand-up paddleboard is $50, a single kayak is $55, and a double is $65.

Put in right at the harbor and explore the estuary from **Webhannet River Kayak Rentals** (345 Harbor Rd., Wells, 207/646-9649, www.webhannetriver.com). Rates begin at $25 solo, $50 tandem for two hours.

Paddle the beach-protected Ogunquit River or the Wells estuaries with a kayak from **World Within Sea Kayaking** (17 Post Rd./Rte. 1, Wells, 207/646-0455, www.worldwithin.com). A single kayak is $25/hour or $35/two hours, a double is $35/hour or $50/two hours, and a stand-up paddleboard is $30/hour or $45/two hours. It's based at the Ogunquit River Inn and is only open during the high-tide cycle.

Golf

The 18-hole Donald Ross-designed **Cape Neddick Country Club** (650 Shore Rd., Cape Neddick, 207/361-2011, www.capeneddickgolf.com) is a semiprivate 18-hole course with a restaurant and a driving range.

FOOD

Ogunquit

LOBSTER AND SEAFOOD

Creative marketing, a knockout view, and efficient service help explain why more than 1,000 pounds of lobster bite the dust every summer day at **Barnacle Billy's** (Perkins Cove, 207/646-5575, www.barnbilly.com, 11am-9pm daily seasonally). Billy's has a full liquor license. Try for a spot on the deck, with a front-row seat on Perkins Cove.

Less flashy and less pricey, the **Lobster Shack** (Perkins Cove, 207/646-2941, www.lobster-shack.com, 11am-8pm daily), serves

1: Ogunquit Playhouse 2: a pocket beach off of Marginal Way

OGUNQUIT PLAYHOUSE
1

2

lobsters, meaty lobster rolls, stews, chowders, and some landlubber choices.

QUICK BITES

Eat in or take out from **Village Food Market** (Main St., Ogunquit Center, 207/646-2122, www.villagefoodmarket.com, 6:30am-10pm daily). A basic breakfast sandwich is $3, subs and sandwiches are available in two sizes, and there's a children's menu.

Scrumptious baked goods, tantalizing salads, and vegetarian lunch items are available to go at **Bread and Roses** (246 Main St., 207/646-4227, www.breadandrosesbakery.com, from 7am daily), a small bakery right downtown with a few tables outside.

Harbor Candy Shop (26 Main St., 207/646-8078 or 800/331-5856) is packed with decadent chocolates. Fudge, truffles, and turtles are all made on-site.

The **Egg and I** (501 Main St./Rte. 1, 207/646-8777, www.eggandibreakfast.com, 6am-2pm daily, no credit cards) has more than 200 menu choices and earns high marks for its omelets and waffles. You can't miss it; there's always a crowd. Lunch choices are served after 11am.

Equally popular is **Amore Breakfast** (87 Main St., 207/646-6661, www.amorebreakfast.com, 7:30am-1pm daily). Choose from a dozen omelets and nine versions of eggs Benedict, including lobster and a spirited rancheros version topped with salsa and served with guacamole.

Dine indoors or outside at **Cornerstone Artisanal Pizza & Craft Beer** (221 Main St., 207/646-4118, www.cornerstoneogunquit.com, noon-10pm daily, $11-28), where the menu also includes entrées, salads, small plates, and sandwiches.

INTERNATIONAL

The tapas-heavy menu at **La Orilla** (53 Shore Rd., 207/216-9913, www.laorilladining.com, from 3pm daily, $8-18) specializes in Mediterranean fare with worldly influences. Family-style entrées are available.

At **Caffé Prego** (44 Shore Rd., 207/646-7734, http://cafeprego.com, 7:30am-9pm daily, $12-26), owners Donato Tramuto and Jeffrey Porter have created an authentic taste of Tuscany. They've imported Italian equipment and use traditional ingredients to create coffees, pastries, panini, brick-oven pizzas, pastas, salads, and gelati, served inside or on the terrace.

Chef-owner David Giarusso uses recipes handed down from his great-grandmother, Angelina Peluso, at **Angelina's Ristorante and Wine Bar** (655 Main St./Rte. 1, 207/646-0445, www.angelinasogunquit.com, from 4:30pm daily year-round, $20-35). Dine in the dining room, wine room, lounge, or out on the terrace, choosing from pastas, risottos (the house specialty), and other classics.

Mediterranean fare is finessed with a dollop of creativity and a pinch of Maine flavors at **Five-O** (50 Shore Rd., 207/646-6365, www.five-oshoreroad.com, from 5pm Mon.-Sat., 10am-2pm and 5pm-close Sun., $23-38), one of the region's top restaurants for casual dining. The menu of house-made pastas and entrées changes frequently. Lighter fare ($12-20) is available until 11pm in the lounge, where martinis are a specialty. Valet parking is available.

FAMILY FAVORITES

Boisterous and lively, the **Front Porch** (9 Shore Rd., 207/646-4005, www.thefrontporch.com, from 3pm daily, $12-32) is not for those looking for romantic dining, but it is a good choice for families with divergent tastes. The menu ranges from flatbread pizzas to lobster risotto.

CASUAL DINING

Scratch-made, seasonally inspired, and shareable snacks and small plates make dining at ★ **Northern Union** (261 Shore Rd., 207/216-9639, www.northern-union.me, from 5pm daily, $24-32), an especially enjoyable and fun experience. At this wine-focused restaurant and bar, stick with the small plates ($8-16) and have fun mixing and matching. The servers are especially knowledgeable.

Jonathan's (2 Bourne Ln., 207/646-4777, www.jonathansogunquit.com, from 5pm daily, $25-50) is a lovely oasis, a casual fine-dining venue with clothed tables and big windows overlooking colorful gardens. Much of the fare is sourced from chef Jonathan West's own farm (the Mediterranean pasta, with his farm-raised spicy lamb sausage, is excellent). Kids' and gluten-free menus are available. Upstairs is an intimate space where national acts often perform; check the schedule and consider combining dinner with a show.

There's not much between you and Spain when you snag a window seat at ★ **MC Perkins Cove** (Oarweed Ln., Perkins Cove, 207/646-6263, www.markandclarkrestaurants.com, 11:30am-3:30pm and from 5pm daily late May-mid-Oct., Wed.-Mon. mid-Oct.-Dec. and Feb.-late May, $26-37). Service is attentive, the classic American bistro fare is tops, and in keeping with the style of James Beard Award-winning chefs Mark Gaier and Clark Frasier, it's always fresh. Lighter fare ($12-21) is served in the bar. Off-season events include Sunday jazz brunch ($14-28); Date Night, featuring a three-course prix fixe menu for two (around $50); and Burger Night ($6-10). Reservations are essential for dinner.

Wells

QUICK BITES

For baked goods and made-to-order sandwiches, head to **Borealis Breads** (Rte. 1, no phone, 8:30am-5:30pm Mon.-Sat., 8:30am-3:30pm Sun.), in the Aubuchon Hardware plaza.

Pick up all sorts of fresh goodies at the **Wells Farmers Market** (1:30pm-5pm Wed.) in the Wonder Mountain Fun Park parking lot at 270 Route 1.

In business since 1945, **Congdon's Doughnuts Family Restaurant and Bakery** (1090 Post Rd./Rte. 1, 207/646-4219, www.congdons.com, 6am-2pm daily in summer) serves breakfast and lunch. At 4pm it morphs into **Congdon's After Dark** (http://cadfoodtrucks.com, from 4pm daily), with as many as 10 food trucks on-site, a beer garden, and alcohol served on the covered patio.

For decadent chocolates, cannoli, or hefty sandwiches, pop into the **Bistro at R&R Chocolate** (913 Post Rd./Rte. 1, 207/351-8091, 9am-6pm Mon.-Fri., 9am-4pm Sun.).

For homemade ice cream, dip into **Big Daddy's** (2165 Post Rd./Rte. 1, 207/646-5454, hours vary seasonally).

FAMILY FAVORITES

For fresh lobster, lobster rolls, fish-and-chips, chowders, and homemade desserts, you can't go wrong at the Cardinali family's **Fisherman's Catch** (Harbor Rd./Rte. 1, 207/646-8780, www.fishermanscatchwells.com, 11:30am-9pm daily early May-mid-Oct., $10-26). Big windows in the rustic dining room frame the marsh. There's a kids' menu.

A good steak in the land of lobster? You betcha: The **Steakhouse** (1205 Post Rd./Rte. 1, 207/646-4200, www.the-steakhouse.com, 4pm-9:30pm Tues.-Sun., $16-30) is a great big barn of a place where steaks are hand cut from high-quality corn-fed western beef that has never been frozen. Service is efficient, but the restaurant doesn't take reservations, so be prepared for a long wait.

Tulsi North (231 Post Rd./Rte. 1, 207/360-0443, www.tulsinorth.com, 4pm-9pm Wed.-Sun., $12-24), an Indian restaurant with vegan and gluten-, nut-, and dairy-free options, keeps everyone happy.

FINE DINING

Chef Joshua W. Mather of ★ **Joshua's** (1637 Rte. 1, 207/646-3355, www.joshuas.biz, from 5pm daily, $26-42) grew up on his family's nearby organic farm, and produce from that property highlights the menu. In a true family operation, his parents not only still work the farm, but also work in the restaurant, a converted 1774 home with many of its original architectural elements. Everything is made on the premises, from the fabulous bread to the hand-churned ice cream. The Atlantic haddock, with caramelized onion crust, chive oil, and wild mushroom risotto, is a signature dish, and is alone worth coming for. A vegetarian pasta entrée is offered nightly. Save room for the maple walnut pie with maple ice cream. Reservations are essential for the dining rooms, but the full menu is also served in the bar.

ACCOMMODATIONS

Most properties in this region are open seasonally.

Ogunquit

MOTELS

Request a riverside room at the **Towne Lyne Motel** (747 Main St./Rte. 1, 207/646-2955, www.townelynemotel.com, $115-210), a vintage charmer set back from the highway amid manicured lawns. Some rooms have kitchenettes and/or screened porches.

You're almost within spitting distance of Perkins Cove at the 37-room **Riverside Motel** (159 Shore Rd., 207/646-2741, www.riversidemotel.com, from $265), where you can perch on your balcony and watch the action—or, for that matter, join it. Rates include continental breakfast. The entire 3.5-acre property is smoke-free.

Juniper Hill Inn (336 Main St., 207/646-4501 or 800/646-4544, www.ogunquit.com, year-round, from $224) is a well-run motel-style operation on five acres close to downtown Ogunquit, with a footpath to the beach (15-minute walk). Families especially appreciate the indoor and outdoor pools and coin-operated laundry. Rates include a continental breakfast.

ECLECTIC PROPERTIES

The ★ **Beachmere Inn** (62 Beachmere Pl., 207/646-2021 or 800/336-3983, www.beachmereinn.com, year-round, from $199) occupies an enviable oceanfront location on the Marginal Way, yet is just steps from downtown. The private, family-owned and -operated property comprises an updated Victorian inn, a newer seaside motel, and other buildings. Pocket beaches are just outside the gate. Most rooms have balconies, decks, or terraces; some have fireplaces and/or kitchenettes; almost all have ocean views. There's also a small spa with a hot tub, steam sauna, and fitness room. Breakfast is included, and the inn's Blue Bistro serves lunch and dinner. In season, there's a weekly lobster bake.

It's not easy to land a peak-season cottage at the **Dunes** (518 Main St., 207/646-2612, www.dunesonthewaterfront.com, from $235), but it's worth trying. The meticulously maintained 12-acre property is under its third generation of ownership, and guests practically will their weeks to their descendants. Nineteen tidy, well-equipped one- or two-bedroom housekeeping cottages with screened porches and wood-burning fireplaces, as well as 17 guest rooms, are generously spaced on shady, grassy lawns that roll down to the river, with the dunes just beyond. Facilities include a dock with rowboats, a pool, and lawn games. In peak season, the one- or two-bedroom cottages require a one- or two-week minimum stay; guest rooms require three nights, but last-minute getaway guests can fill in the cracks.

It's not easy to describe the ★ **Sparhawk Oceanfront Resort** (41 Shore Rd., 207/646-5562, www.thesparhawk.com, from $265), a sprawling, one-of-a-kind place popular with honeymooners, families, and seniors. Tradition thrives in this six-acre complex—it's had various incarnations since the turn of the 20th century—and the "Happily Filled" sign regularly hangs out front. Out back is the Atlantic Ocean with forever views, and the Marginal Way starts right here. The property offers a tennis court, gardens, and a heated pool, and breakfast is included in the rates. The 87 guest rooms in four buildings vary from motel-type rooms (best views) to inn-style suites. There's a seven-night minimum July through August, although shorter stays are often possible.

INNS AND BED-AND-BREAKFASTS

The restored **Rockmere Lodge** (40 Stearns Rd., 207/646-2985, www.rockmere.com, year-round, from $198) was built in 1899 for a prominent Maine lumbering family. Near the

Marginal Way on a peaceful street, the handsome home has eight comfortable Victorian guest rooms, most with ocean views. Rates include a generous breakfast. A wraparound veranda, decks, gardens, a gazebo, and a third-floor windowed nook with comfy chairs make it easy to settle in and just watch the passersby.

When you want to be at the center of the action, book a room at **2 Village Square Inn** (14 Village Square Ln., 207/646-5779, www.2vsquare.com, from $199 with breakfast). The walk-to-everything location puts the beach, Marginal Way, shops, restaurants, and more all within footsteps, if you can tear yourself away from the dreamy views, heated outdoor pool, hot tub, and the on-site massage room. Two rooms are dog friendly ($35). Also under the same ownership are the **Nellie Littlefield Inn & Spa** (27 Shore Rd., 207/646-1692, www.nliogunquit.com, from $229), a magnificently restored in-town Victorian; the **Gazebo Inn** (572 Main St., 207/646-3773, www.gazeboinnogt.com, from $249), a carefully renovated 1847 farmhouse and barn within walking distance of Footbridge Beach; and the year-round child- and dog-friendly ($5/night) **Captain's Quarter's** (483 Main St., 207/646-3733, www.captainogt.com, $159-239), a renovated and updated motel.

The plusses of staying at the **Trellis House** (10 Beachmere Pl., 207/646-7909, https://trellishouse.com, from $299), with eight rooms spread out in three buildings, include a convenient in-town location, distant water views, contemporary beachy decor, a full breakfast, and afternoon hors d'oeuvres.

The **Colonial Inn** (145 Shore Rd., 207/646-5191, www.thecolonialinn.com, from $229) is a renovated Victorian-era building with 21st-century comforts. Rooms in the main inn are bright and airy, and some have water views. Family-oriented rooms are in separate buildings, and some have kitchenettes. It's an easy walk to the beach, but if the ocean's too chilly, the hotel has a heated outdoor pool and hot tub. A continental breakfast buffet is provided. The location puts the best of Ogunquit within footsteps.

Fancy an English countryside-style setting with spa amenities? Look no further than the **Beauport Inn** (339 Clary Hill Rd., Cape Neddick, 207/361-2400, www.beauportinn.com, from $269), a stone manor on nine acres with a 40-foot lap pool, outdoor hot tub, sauna, and Turkish steam room, along with four guest rooms and an apartment.

RESORTS

The family-owned ★ **Meadowmere Resort** (74 Main St., 207/646-9661, www.meadowmere.com, from $172) caters to families, with facilities including indoor and outdoor pools, an outdoor hot tub, indoor Roman bath, a spacious, well-equipped health club and spa, barbecue pits, and a restaurant, pub, game room, and guest laundry. The 144 guest rooms, spread across five buildings, include suites designed for families, romantics, and honeymooners as well as standard rooms. The location is excellent: Ogunquit's Main Beach, the Marginal Way, and downtown shops and restaurants are within a 10-15-minute walk (wagons are available for towing gear or kids), and it's on the trolley route. This ultra-green property uses no chemicals in the pools and has an ozone laundry. It's adjacent to Jonathan's, a casual fine-dining restaurant that often features national-caliber shows in an intimate setting. Rates include continental breakfast in season. Open year-round.

The **Cliff House Resort and Spa** (591 Shore Rd., 207/361-1000, www.cliffhousemaine.com, from $500), a self-contained complex, sprawls over 70 acres topping the edge of Bald Head Cliff midway between the centers of York and Ogunquit. Although its roots go back more than a century, it's been rebuilt and in 2016 underwent a complete renovation. The location is spectacular and the facilities and amenities are what you'd expect at a full-service luxury resort.

Wells

Once part of a giant 19th-century dairy farm, the **Beach Farm Inn** (97 Eldredge Rd., 207/646-8493, www.beachfarminn.

com, year-round, $120-169) is a 2.5-acre oasis in a rather congested area 0.2 mile off Route 1. Guests can swim in the pool, relax in the library, or walk 0.7 mile down the road to the beach. Five of the eight guest rooms have private baths (two are detached); 3rd-floor rooms have air-conditioning. Rates include a full breakfast. A cottage rents for $799/week.

Even closer to the beach is **Haven by the Sea** (59 Church St., Wells Beach, 207/646-4194, www.havenbythesea.com, from $229), a heavenly bed-and-breakfast in a former church. Inside are hardwood floors, cathedral ceilings, and stained glass windows. The confessional is now a full bar, and the altar has been converted to a dining area that opens to a marsh-view terrace from which the bird-watching is superb. Guest rooms have sitting areas, and the suite has a whirlpool tub and a fireplace. Guests have plenty of room to relax, including a living area with a fireplace. Rates include a full breakfast and afternoon hors d'oeuvres. Also available is a two-bedroom oceanview apartment.

INFORMATION AND SERVICES

At the southern edge of Ogunquit, right next to the Ogunquit Playhouse, the **Ogunquit Chamber of Commerce's Welcome Center** (Rte. 1, Ogunquit, 207/646-2939, www.ogunquit.org) provides all the usual visitor information and has public restrooms. Ask for the Touring and Trolley Route Map, showing the Marginal Way, beach locations, and public restrooms. The chamber of commerce's annual visitor booklet thoughtfully carries a tide chart for the summer.

Just over the Ogunquit border in Wells (actually in Moody) is the **Wells Information Center** (Rte. 1 at Kimball Rd., 207/646-2451, www.wellschamber.org).

The handsome fieldstone **Ogunquit Memorial Library** (74 Shore Rd., Ogunquit, 207/646-9024) is downtown's only building in the National Register of Historic Places. Or visit the **Wells Public Library** (1434 Post Rd./Rte. 1, Wells, 207/646-8181, www.wells.lib.me.us).

GETTING THERE AND AROUND

Ogunquit is about seven miles or 15 minutes via Route 1 from York. Wells is about six miles or 12 minutes via Route 1 from Ogunquit. From York to Wells, it's about 15.5 miles or 20 minutes on I-95. When traveling in summer, expect heavy traffic and delays on Route 1.

The **Amtrak Downeaster** (800/872-7245, www.amtrakdowneaster.com), which connects Boston's North Station with Portland, Maine, stops in Wells at the **Wells Regional Transportation Center** (696 Sanford Rd.). The Shoreline Explorer trolley connects in season.

C&J (800/258-7111, www.ridecj.com, late May-early Sept.) provides seasonal bus service between New York City and Ogunquit, operating from the visitors center (36 Main St.).

The seasonal **Shoreline Explorer trolley** (207/459-2932, www.shorelineexplorer.com, late June-early Sept.) makes it possible to travel from York to Kennebunkport without your car. Each town's system is operated separately and has its own fees. See the master map and all fee info on the website. Exact change is often required.

Trolley Purple 2 ($1 each way, ages 11 and younger ride free) runs hourly between York's Short Sands Beach and Ogunquit's Perkins Cove. It connects with **Ogunquit Trolley 3** operated by **Ogunquit Trolley** (207/646-1411, $2 one-way, $1.50 ages 10 and younger), which operates along Route 1 to Wells, connecting with **Trolley Blue 4** ($1 one-way, ages 11 and younger free), serving Wells, Wells Beach, and Wells Harbor. **Trolley Blue 4** connects with **Trolley Blue 4b,** and operates between the Wells Regional Transportation Center, where the Amtrak Downeaster train stops, Wells Harbor, and Kennebunkport's Lower Village. **Trolley Orange 5** ($2-4 one-way, $3-6 round-trip, ages 5-11 half fare) connects the Wells Plaza and Wells Regional Transportation Center to Sanford.

The Kennebunks

The world may have first learned of Kennebunkport when George Herbert Walker Bush was president, but Walkers and Bushes have owned their summer estate here for three generations. Visitors continue to come to the Kennebunks (the collective name for **Kennebunk, Kennebunkport, Cape Porpoise,** and **Goose Rocks Beach**) hoping to catch a glimpse of the former first family, but they also come for the terrific ambience, bed-and-breakfasts, boutiques, boats, biking, and beaches.

The Kennebunks' earliest European settlers arrived in the mid-1600s. By the mid-1700s, shipbuilding had become big business in the area. Two ancient local cemeteries—North Street and Evergreen—provide glimpses of the area's heritage. Its historic district reveals Kennebunk's moneyed past and is lined with the homes of the wealthy ship owners and shipbuilders who sent their vessels to the Caribbean and around the globe. Today, unusual shrubs and a dozen varieties of rare maples still line Summer Street—the legacy of ship captains in the global trade. Another legacy is the shiplap construction in many houses, a throwback to a time when labor was cheap and lumber plentiful. Closer to the beach in Lower Village stood the workshops of sailmakers, carpenters, and mast makers whose output drove the booming trade.

Although Kennebunkport (pop. 3,474) draws most of the sightseers and summer traffic, Kennebunk (pop. 10,798) feels more like a year-round community. Its old-fashioned downtown has a mix of shops, restaurants, and attractions. Yes, its beaches are also well known, but many visitors drive right through the middle of Kennebunk without stopping to enjoy its assets.

SIGHTS

★ Seashore Trolley Museum

There's nothing quite like an antique electric trolley to dredge up nostalgia for bygone days. With a collection of more than 250 transit vehicles (and more than two dozen trolleys on display) from around the world, the **Seashore Trolley Museum** (195 Log Cabin Rd., Kennebunkport, 207/967-2800, www.trolleymuseum.org, 10am-5pm daily late May-mid-Oct., 10am-5pm Sat.-Sun. early May and late Oct., $12 ages 16-60, $10 seniors, $9.50 ages 6-15, $5 ages 3-5) verges on trolley mania. Whistles blowing and bells clanging, restored streetcars do frequent trips (last ride at 4:15pm) on a 1.5-mile track into the woods along a rebuilt portion of the Atlantic Shore Line Railway. Ride as often as you wish, and then check out the activity in the streetcar workshop, visit three exhibit carbarns, and go wild in the trolley-oriented gift shop. Bring a picnic lunch and enjoy it here. With a reservation and $100, you can have a "motorman" experience (min. age 18) driving your own trolley (with help, of course) along the line and back. The museum is 1.7 miles southeast of Route 1. It's open during the Christmas Prelude festival. Well-behaved dogs are welcome.

Maine Classic Car Museum

View rare and classic automobiles, including a 1939 Alfa Romeo, one of six left in the world, and a 1948 Tucker, valued at $1.8 million, at the **Maine Classic Car Museum** (2564 Portland Rd./Rt. 1, Arundel, 207/710-6699, 10am-5pm daily, $10 ages 7 and older), based at Motorland Classic Car Showroom & Service Center. The private collection comprises 160 vehicles, of which about 45 are displayed at any time. Also exhibited are related goods and local memorabilia—think advertising, signage, and license plates.

Walker's Point: The Bush Estate

There's no public access to Walker's Point, but

The Kennebunks

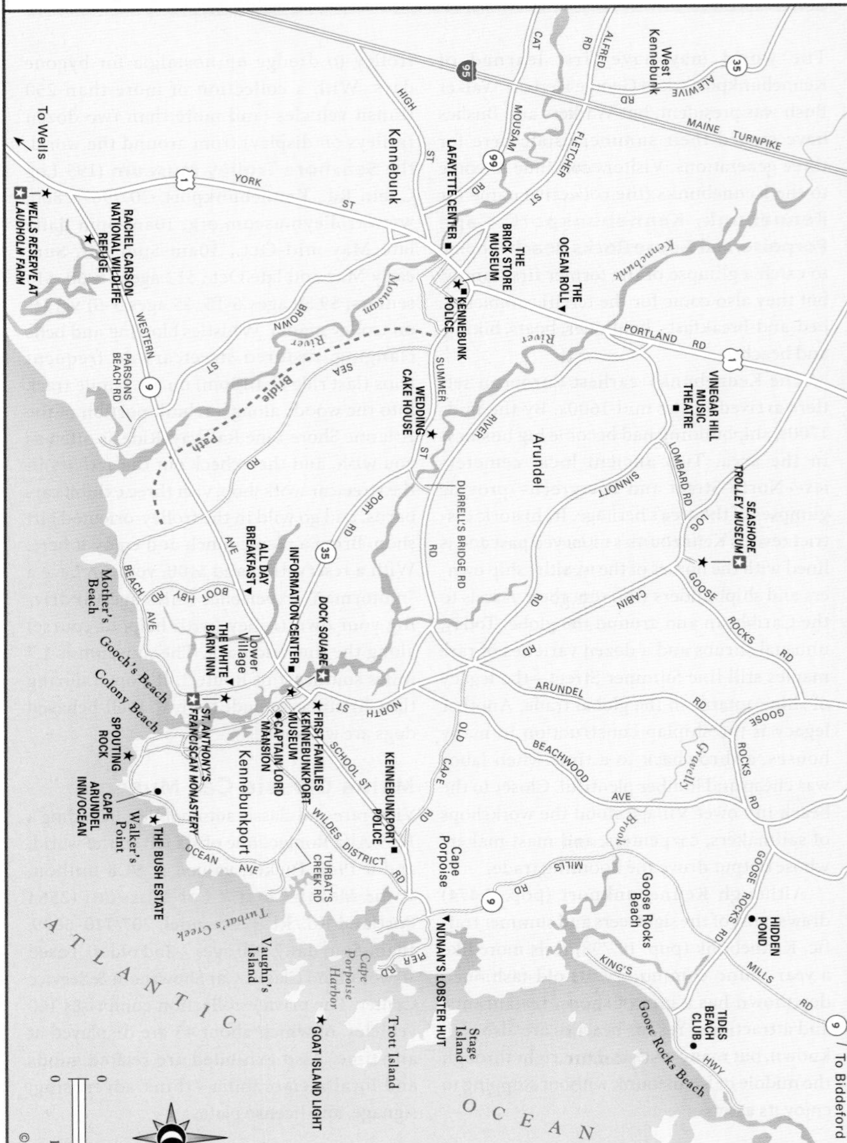

West Kennebunk
Kennebunk
Arundel
Lower Village
Kennebunkport
Cape Porpoise
Goose Rocks Beach
To Wells
To Biddeford
WELLS RESERVE AT LAUDHOLM FARM
RACHEL CARSON NATIONAL WILDLIFE REFUGE
LAFAYETTE CENTER
THE BRICK STORE MUSEUM
THE OCEAN ROLL
KENNEBUNK POLICE
WEDDING CAKE HOUSE
VINEGAR HILL MUSIC THEATRE
SEASHORE TROLLEY MUSEUM
ALL DAY BREAKFAST
INFORMATION CENTER
DOCK SQUARE
THE WHITE BARN INN
FIRST FAMILIES KENNEBUNKPORT MUSEUM
CAPTAIN LORD MANSION
ST. ANTHONY'S FRANCISCAN MONASTERY
SPOUTING ROCK
CAPE ARUNDEL INN/OCEAN
THE BUSH ESTATE
KENNEBUNKPORT POLICE
NUNAN'S LOBSTER HUT
GOAT ISLAND LIGHT
HIDDEN POND
TIDES BEACH CLUB
Mother's Beach
Gooch's Beach
Colony Beach
Walker's Point
Vaughn's Island
Cape Porpoise Harbor
Trott Island
Stage Island
Turbat's Creek
Mousam River
Kennebunk River
Gravelly Brook
Bridle Path
ATLANTIC OCEAN
MAINE TURNPIKE
YORK ST
PORTLAND RD
WESTERN AVE
PARSONS BEACH RD
BROWN ST
SEA RD
SUMMER ST
PORT RD
BEACH AVE
BOOT HBY RD
OCEAN AVE
NORTH ST
SCHOOL ST
WILDES DISTRICT RD
TURBAT'S CREEK RD
RIVER RD
PIER RD
MILLS RD
KING'S HWY
GOOSE ROCKS RD
BEACHWOOD AVE
ARUNDEL RD
CABIN RD
LOG CABIN RD
LOMBARD RD
SINNOTT RD
DURRELL'S BRIDGE RD
OLD CAPE RD
ALEWIVE RD
FLETCHER ST
MOUSAM
ALFRED RD
CAT
HIGH ST
0
1 km
1 mi

you can join the sidewalk gawkers on Ocean Avenue overlooking the late President George H. W. Bush's summer compound. Intown Trolley's regular narrated tours go right past the house, or it's an easy, scenic walk from Kennebunkport's Dock Square. On the way, you'll pass **St. Ann's Church,** whose stones came from the ocean floor, and the paths to **Spouting Rock** and **Blowing Cave,** two natural phenomena that create spectacular water fountains if you manage to be there midway between high and low tides. Right by the compound overlook is **Anchor to Windward,** a 6,000-pound anchor installed by the town in 2009 to honor the former president. Another way to view the residence is from the sea aboard the **schooner *Eleanor*.**

Wedding Cake House

Driving down Summer Street (Rte. 35), midway between the downtowns of Kennebunk and Kennebunkport, it's hard to miss the **Wedding Cake House** (104 Summer St., Kennebunk), a yellow-and-white Federal-style mansion overlaid with gobs of gingerbread and Gothic Revival spires and arches. Bourne, a shipbuilder, built it in 1826, later adding a carriage house. When the carriage house burned, he rebuilt it in this ornate style, and then adorned the house to match it. It's not open to the public.

Cape Porpoise

When your mind's eye conjures an idyllic lobster-fishing village, it probably looks a lot like **Cape Porpoise,** only 2.5 miles from busy Dock Square. Follow Route 9 eastward from Kennebunkport; when Route 9 turns north, continue straight and take Pier Road to its end. From the small parking area, you'll see lobster boats at anchor, a slew of working wharves, and the 19th-century **Goat Island Light,** now automated, directly offshore.

Local History Museums and Tours

Occupying four restored 19th-century buildings in downtown Kennebunk, including the 1825 William Lord store, the **Brick Store Museum** (117 Main St., Kennebunk, 207/985-4802, www.brickstoremuseum.org, 10am-4:30pm Tues.-Fri., 10am-1pm Sat., $7.50 adults, $3 ages 6-16, $6 seniors, $20 family) has garnered a reputation for unusual exhibits, such as a century of wedding dresses, a two-century history of volunteer firefighting, and life in southern Maine during the Civil War. The museum encourages appreciation for the surrounding Kennebunk Historic District with 60-90-minute **architectural walking tours** ($5); they're usually held May-mid-October, but call for a current schedule. If the schedule doesn't suit, the museum sells a walk-it-yourself booklet ($16) and a simple map ($5).

Kennebunk's **Museum in the Streets** (www.themuseuminthestreets.com) comprises 25 sites around town with markers explaining their historical significance.

The **First Families Kennebunkport Museum** (8 Maine St., Kennebunkport, 207/967-2751, www.kporthistory.org, 10am-4pm Mon.-Sat. late May-mid-Oct., $10), also known as the Nott House or White Columns, is owned and maintained by the Kennebunkport Historical Society. The 1853 mansion, considered one of the best examples of Gothic Revival in the country, is filled with original and often rare Victorian furnishings and artifacts and memorabilia covering 200 years of local history. On 45-minute tours, guides relate stories of sea captains, shipbuilders, summer folk, and presidents. A separate gallery is dedicated to the Bush family. Be sure to visit the restored gardens.

★ Dock Square

Even if you're not a shopper, make it a point to meander through **Dock Square,** the heart of Kennebunkport's shopping district, where onetime fishing shacks have been restored and renovated into upscale shops, boutiques, galleries, and dining spots. Some shops, especially those on upper floors, offer fine harbor views. If you're willing to poke around a bit, you'll find some unusual items that make distinctive souvenirs or gifts—pottery, vintage clothing, books, specialty foods, and, yes, T-shirts.

★ St. Anthony's Franciscan Monastery

Long ago, 35,000 Native Americans used this part of town as a summer camp. More recently, so did a group of Lithuanian Franciscan monks who in 1947 fled war-ravaged Europe and acquired the 200-acre **St. Anthony's Franciscan Monastery** (Beach St., Kennebunk, 207/967-2011). They ran a high school here from 1956-1969, and the monks still occupy the handsome Tudor great house, but the well-tended grounds (sprinkled with shrines and a recently restored sculpture created by Vytautas Jonynas for the Vatican Pavilion at the 1964 World's Fair) are open to the public sunrise-sunset daily. A short path leads from the monastery area to a peaceful gazebo overlooking the Kennebunk River. Pets and bikes are not allowed; public restrooms are available.

ENTERTAINMENT

Performing Arts

A renovated 1888 barn is home to the **Vinegar Hill Music Theatre** (53 Old Post Rd., Arundel, 207/985-5552, http://vinegarhillmusictheatre.com), which presents live music drawing from local and national talent.

VentiCordi (207/288-6688, www.venticordi.com, $20 adults, $15 seniors, $5 ages 18 and younger) presents chamber-music concerts at various locations during July and August.

Festivals and Events

Paint the Town Red in February delivers a month of seasonal activities along with food, art, and more. The first two weekends of December mark the festive **Christmas Prelude,** during which spectacular decorations adorn historic homes, candle-toting carolers stroll through the Kennebunks, stores have special sales, and Santa Claus arrives via lobster boat.

The **Art Trail of the Kennebunks** occurs 5pm-7pm on the first Friday of the month.

Kennebunk Parks and Recreation sponsors **Concerts in the Park** (6pm-7:30pm Wed. late June-mid-Aug., free), a weekly series in Lafayette Park.

SHOPPING

Lots of small, attractive boutiques surround **Dock Square,** the hub of Kennebunkport, and flow over the bridge into Kennebunk's Lower Village. Gridlock often develops in midsummer. Avoid driving through here at the height of the season. Take your time and walk, bike, or ride the local trolleys. This is just a sampling of the shopping opportunities.

Antiques and Art

English, European, and American furniture and architectural elements and garden accessories are just a sampling of what you'll find at **Antiques on Nine** (81 Western Ave./Rte. 9, Lower Village, Kennebunk, 207/967-0626). Another good place for browsing high-end antiques as well as home accents is **Hurlbutt Designs** (53 Western Ave./Rte. 9, Lower Village, Kennebunk, 207/967-4110). More than 30 artists are represented at the **Wright Gallery** (5 Pier Rd., Cape Porpoise, 207/967-5053).

Jean Briggs represents nearly 100 artists at her topflight **Mast Cove Galleries** (Maine St. and Mast Cove Ln., Kennebunkport, 207/967-3453, www.mastcove.com) in a handsome Greek Revival house near the Graves Memorial Library. Prices vary widely, so don't be surprised if you spot something affordable. The gallery occasionally sponsors 2.5-hour evening concerts July-August ($25 donation, includes light refreshments). Call for a schedule.

Maine Art Hill (14 Western Ave.,

1: First Families Kennebunkport Museum
2: Seashore Trolley Museum **3:** *Nick's Chance,* a whale-watching boat

1

2

DIXWELL AV
D
P.R. STATION

3

967-5507
FIRST CHANCE
WHALE WATCH
NICK'S CHANCE

Kennebunkport, 207/967-2803, www.maine-art.com) represents more than 40 artists and comprises gallery space, studios, and exhibitions on and around Chase Hill. **Compliments** (Dock Sq., Kennebunkport, 207/967-2269) shows contemporary fine American crafts, with an emphasis on glass and ceramic ware. **Arundel Farm Gallery** (76 Arundel Rd., Arundel, 561/702-6396, www.arundelfarmgallery.com) shows fine art, American craft, and folk art in a carriage house and 1790 farmhouse.

Specialty Shops

Irresistible eye-dazzling costume jewelry, hair ornaments, handbags, scarves, lotions, cards, and other delightful finds fill every possible space at **Dannah** (123 Ocean Ave., Kennebunkport, 207/967-8640).

Scalawags (3 Dock Sq., Kennebunkport, 207/967-2775), a bonanza for pet owners, sells wonderful presents to bring home to furry pals. If traveling with your pooch, ask about local pet-friendly parks, inns, and restaurants, as well as favorite places for walks.

Browse **Daytrip Society** (4 Dock Sq., Kennebunkport, 207/967-4440) and there's a good chance you'll find just the right something from its fun, eclectic selection. Pick up a good read at **Fine Print Booksellers** (28 Dock Sq., Kennebunkport, 207/967-9989).

RECREATION

Parks and Preserves

Thanks to a dedicated coterie of year-round and summer residents, the **Kennebunkport Conservation Trust** (57 Gravelly Brook Rd., Kennebunkport, 207/967-3465, www.kporttrust.org), founded in 1973, has become a nationwide model for land-trust organizations. The trust has managed to preserve from development several hundred acres of land, including 12 harbor islands off Cape Porpoise Harbor. Most of this acreage is accessible to the public, especially via a sea kayak. The trust has even assumed ownership of 7.7-acre Goat Island, with its distinctive lighthouse visible from Cape Porpoise and other coastal vantage points. Check the website for special events and activities.

VAUGHN'S ISLAND PRESERVE

To visit **Vaughn's Island** you'll need to do a little planning, tide-wise: The 96-acre island is about 600 feet offshore. Consult a tide calendar and aim for low tide close to the new moon or full moon, when the most water drains away. Allow yourself an hour or so before and after low tide, but no longer, or you may need a boat rescue. Wear treaded rubber boots, as the crossing is muddy and slippery with rockweed. Keep an eye on your watch and explore the ocean (east) side of the island, along the beach. There's a great view of Goat Island Light off to the east. From downtown Kennebunkport, take Main Street to Wildes District Road. Continue to Shore Road (also called Turbat's Creek Road), go 0.6 mile, jog left 0.2 mile more, and park in the tiny lot at the end.

EMMONS PRESERVE

Also under Kennebunkport Conservation Trust stewardship, the **Emmons Preserve** has five trails meandering through 146 acres of woods and fields on the edge of Batson's River (also called Gravelly Brook). The yellow-blazed trail has the best access to the water. Fall colors here are brilliant, birdlife is abundant, and you can do a loop in half an hour. But why rush? This is a wonderful oasis in the heart of Kennebunkport. From Dock Square, take North Street to Beachwood Avenue (right turn) to Gravelly Brook Road (left turn). The trailhead is on the left.

PICNIC ROCK

About 1.5 miles up the Kennebunk River from the ocean, Picnic Rock is the centerpiece of the **Butler Preserve,** a 14-acre enclave managed by the Kennebunk Land Trust (www.kennebunklandtrust.org). Well named, the rock is a great place for a picnic and a swim, but don't count on being alone. It's an easy 0.75-mile out-and-back. Consider bringing a canoe or kayak (or renting one) and paddling with the tide past beautiful homes and the Cape Arundel Golf Club. From Lower Village Kennebunk, take Route 35 west and hang a right onto Old Port Road. When the road gets close to the Kennebunk River, watch for a sign to the right. Parking is limited.

Water Sports

BEACHES

The Kennebunks are well endowed with sand, but not with parking spaces. Parking permits are required, and you need a separate pass for each town. Many lodgings provide free permits for their guests—ask when making room reservations. Avoid the parking nightmare altogether by hopping aboard the Intown Trolley, which goes right by the major beaches.

The main beaches in **Kennebunk** (east to west, stretching about two miles) are **Gooch's,** which stretches into **Middle Beach,** and **Mother's,** a smallish beach next to Lords Point where there's also a playground. Lifeguards are on duty at Gooch's and Mother's Beaches July to Labor Day. Ask locally about a couple of other beach options. Mid-June to mid-September you'll need to buy a **parking permit** ($25/day, $100/week) at kiosks located along Beach Avenue or online (www.kennebunkmaine.us). Kennebunk also has **beach wheelchairs** ($15/day) available for rental.

Parsons Beach, the least known of the town's beaches, is a lovely swath with limited parking. Ask for directions and pedal to it instead of driving. Dogs are allowed on Kennebunk's beaches before 9am and after 5pm from June 15 to early September, and all day the rest of the year.

Kennebunkport's claim to beach fame is three-mile-long **Goose Rocks Beach,** one of the loveliest in the area. Parking spaces are scarce, and a permit is required late May-early September. **Parking stickers** ($25/day, $100/week) are available from the **Kennebunkport Police Station** (101 Main St., 207/967-4243, 24 hours daily), **Kennebunkport Town Hall** (6 Elm St.), and **Goose Rocks General Store** (3 Dyke Rd., 207/967-4541). To reach the beach, take Route 9 from Dock Square east and north to Dyke Road (Clock Farm Corner). Turn right and continue to the end (King's Hwy.).

No permit is necessary at **Colony Beach** (officially Arundel Beach), across from the Colony resort complex. It's an easy, roughly one-mile walk from Dock Square.

BOAT EXCURSIONS

Join Captain Gary aboard the 87-foot ***Nick's Chance*** (4 Western Ave., Lower Village, Kennebunk, 207/967-5507 or 800/767-2628, www.firstchancewhalewatch.com, $48 adults, $28 ages 3-12, cash only) for the 4.5-hour whale-watching trip to Jeffrey's Ledge, weather permitting. The destination is the summer feeding grounds for finbacks, humpbacks, minkes, the rare blue whale, and the endangered right whale. The boat departs daily late June-early September, weekends only spring and fall, from Performance Marine in Kennebunk's Lower Village. Under the same ownership and departing from the same location is the 65-foot open lobster boat ***Kylie's Chance,*** which departs three times daily in July-August for 1.5-hour scenic lobster cruises ($25 adults, $20 ages 3-12, cash only); the schedule is reduced in spring and fall. A lobstering demonstration is given on most trips, but never on the evening one.

The handsome 55-foot gaff-rigged schooner ***Eleanor*** (Arundel Wharf, 43 Ocean Ave., Kennebunkport, 207/967-8809, www.schoonereleanor.com), built by its captain, Rich "Woody" Woodman, heads out for two-hour sails ($50-60 pp), usually traveling north past Walker's Point to Cape Porpoise and back, weather and tides willing, 1-3 times daily during the summer.

PADDLE SPORTS

You can explore the Kennebunk River by canoe or kayak. **Kennebunkport Marina** (67 Ocean Ave., Kennebunkport, 207/967-3411, www.kennebunkportmarina.com) rents single kayaks ($30 for 2 hours, $50 half day) and double kayaks and canoes ($50 for 2 hours, $70 half day). Check the tide before you depart, and plan your trip to paddle with it rather than against it.

Coastal Maine Kayak & Bike (8 Western Ave., Lower Village, Kennebunk, 207/967-6065, www.coastalmainekayak.com) offers a daylong Cape Porpoise Lighthouse Tour ($85), including guide, instruction, equipment, and snacks; other options are available. Rent single kayaks ($45 for 3 hours, $65 full day) double kayaks ($60 for 3 hours, $80 full day), and stand-up paddleboards ($45 for 3 hours, $65 full day).

SURFING

If you want to catch a wave, stop by **Aquaholics Surf Shop** (166 Port Rd., Kennebunk, 207/967-8650, www.aquaholicsurf.com). The shop has boards, wetsuits, and related gear both for sale and rental, and it offers lessons and surf camps.

Bicycling

Access to the **Eastern Trail** (www.easterntrail.org), the 65-mile section of the East Coast Greenway between Kittery and South Portland, is available at the Kennebunk Elementary School, off Alewive Road, and off Limerick Road in Arundel.

Coastal Maine Kayak & Bike (8 Western Ave., Lower Village, Kennebunk, 207/967-6065, www.coastalmainekayak.com) rents bikes ($10/hour, $35/day), including tandems ($20/hour, $80/day).

Golf

Three 18-hole golf courses make the sport a big deal in the area. **Cape Arundel Golf Club** (19 River Rd., Kennebunkport, 207/967-3494), established in 1897, and **Webhannet Golf Club** (8 Central Ave., Kennebunk, 207/967-2061), established in 1902, are semiprivate and open to nonmembers; call for tee times at least 24 hours ahead. In nearby Arundel, **Dutch Elm Golf Course** (5 Brimstone Rd., Arundel, 207/282-9850) is a public course with rentals, a pro shop, and putting greens.

FOOD

The Kennebunkport Resort Collection operates a dining shuttle between its properties in Kennebunkport and Goose Rocks Beach. It's free for guests at its hotels, but anyone can hop aboard for $5.

Get the lowdown on K-port's food scene on a walking culinary tasting tour with **Maine Foodie Tours** (207/233-7485, www.mainefoodietours.com, $70).

Lobster and Clams

Nunan's Lobster Hut (9 Mills Rd., Cape Porpoise, 207/967-4362, www.nunanslobsterhut.com, from 5pm daily) is an institution. Sure, other places might have better views, but this casual dockside eatery with indoor and outdoor seating has been serving lobsters since 1953.

Adjacent to the bridge connecting Kennebunkport's Dock Square to Kennebunk's Lower Village is another time-tested classic, the **Clam Shack** (Rte. 9, Kennebunkport, 207/967-2560, www.theclamshack.net, 11am-8pm daily). The tiny take-out stand serves some of the state's best lobster rolls, jam-packed with meat and available with either butter or mayo, and delicious fried clams.

Lobster and crab rolls and chowders are the specialties at **Port Lobster** (122 Ocean Ave., Kennebunkport, 207/967-2081, www.portlobster.com, 9am-6pm daily), a fresh-fish store with takeout just northeast of Dock Square.

Pair your lobster with a view of Goat Island Light at **Cape Pier Chowder House** (79 Pier Rd., Cape Porpoise, 207/967-0123, www.capeporpoiselobster.com, from 11am daily).

The **Ocean Roll** (207/450-0332, www.mainelobsterrolls.com, 11am-8pm daily), an extremely popular seasonal food truck selling fresh lobster rolls and fried seafood, parks at the corner of Ross Avenue and Route 1 in Kennebunk.

Quick Bites

All Day Breakfast (55 Western Ave./Rte.

9, Lower Village, Kennebunk, 207/967-5132, 7am-1:30pm daily) delivers on its name.

In addition to the usual general store inventory, **H. B. Provisions** (15 Western Ave., Lower Village, Kennebunk, 207/967-5762, www.hbprovisions.com, 6am-10pm daily) serves breakfast and prepares hot and cold sandwiches, salads, and wraps.

Equal parts fancy food and wine store and gourmet café, **Cape Porpoise Kitchen** (Rte. 9, Cape Porpoise, 207/967-1150, 7am-7pm daily) sells sandwiches, salads, prepared foods, desserts, and everything to go with.

Say *mais oui* to coffee, croissants, savory pies, macarons, and more at **Mornings in Paris** (21 Western Ave., Kennebunk, 207/204-0032, http://morningsinparis.com, from 7am daily).

Enjoy cocktails, small plates, and often live music aboard the **Spirit Restaurant** (4 Western Ave., www.thespiritrestaurant.com, from 11am daily, $10-20), a floating restaurant on a 125-foot schooner anchored on the river by the bridge.

Family Favorites

Extremely popular with locals, **Duffy's Tavern & Grill** (4 Main St., Kennebunk, 207/985-0050, www.duffyskennebunk.com, from 11am daily, $10-23), sited inside a renovated mill in Lafayette Center, is an inviting space with exposed beams, gleaming woodwork, brick walls, and big windows framing the Mousam River. Big-screen high-def TVs make it easy to catch the game while you enjoy American comfort food.

Federal Jack's (8 Western Ave., Lower Village, Kennebunk, 207/967-4322, www.federaljacks.com, 11:30am-10pm daily, $8-26) is the brewpub that gave birth to the Shipyard label. Kids' and gluten-free menus are available. Aim for a seat on the riverfront deck.

It might seem as if chef Richard Lemoine's ★ **Village Tavern** (110 Alfred Rd., West Kennebunk, 207/604-7954, www.villagetavernwestk.com, $13-26, from 4pm daily) is off the beaten path, but don't make the mistake of arriving here without reservations. This justly popular restaurant serves classic as well as updated American fare and also offers child-size portions as well as a separate children's menu. Find it just west of I-95 exit 25.

Casual Dining

Pair a fine wine with light fare at **Old Vines** (141 Port Rd., Lower Village, Kennebunk, 207/967-5766, www.oldvineswinebar.com, from 4pm daily, $14-23), an Old World-meets-New World European-style wine/cocktail bar and tapas restaurant housed in a renovated barn. There's often live music on the patio.

Chef Rebecca Charles of New York's Pearl Oyster Bar opened **Pearl Kennebunk Beach** and **Spat Oyster Cellar** (27 Western Ave., Kennebunk, 207/204-0860, www.pearloysterbar.com, from 5pm Wed.-Sun., $12-25) in 2016. Pearl's seafood-heavy menu ($18-35) celebrates the best of coastal Maine, with options including fried oysters, bouillabaisse, and a lobster roll, along with a few landlubber choices. Spat offers a raw bar and a lighter menu ($10-24).

Musette (2 Pier Rd., Cape Porpoise, 207/204-0707, www.musettebyjc.com, 5:30pm-8:30pm Wed., 7am-1pm and 5:30pm-8:30pm Thurs.-Sat., 7am-1pm Sun., $12-28), owned in part by former White Barn Inn executive chef Jonathan Cartwright, elevates classic Maine comfort foods. A kids' menu is available.

Floor-to-ceiling windows that frame the Kennebunk River breakwater provide perfect views for those indulging at **Stripers Waterside Restaurant** (Breakwater Inn, 133 Ocean Ave., Kennebunkport, 207/967-5333, www.stripersrestaurant.com, 8am-10am, 11am-3pm, and 4pm-9pm daily, $15-28), which serves American regional fare.

Local is the key word at **50 Local** (50 Main St., Kennebunk, 207/985-0850, www.localkennebunk.com, 5pm-9pm Mon.-Sat., $17-32), a downtown Kennebunk bistro specializing in local and organic fare. The menu changes daily, but it's easy to cobble together a meal here that fits your appetite and budget.

The farm-to-fork cuisine at **Earth** (at Hidden Pond resort, 354 Goose Rocks Rd., Kennebunkport, 207/967-6550, www.earthathiddenpond.com, 5pm-10pm daily, $18-55) includes handmade pastas, house-made charcuteries, wood-oven pizzas, and entrées including seafood and meat. The dining room is rustic and the garden views sublime.

The views complement the food at **Hurricane Restaurant** (29 Dock Sq., Kennebunkport, 207/967-9111, www.hurricanerestaurant.com, from 11:30am daily, $24-38). Thanks to a Dock Square location, a menu emphasizing (but not exclusive to) seafood, and a dining room that literally hangs over the river, it reels in the crowds for both lunch and dinner.

The views over the ocean and Walker Point from **Ocean** (208 Ocean Ave., Kennebunkport, 855/346-5700, www.capearundelinn.com, 5pm-9pm daily, $35-50) at the Cape Arundel Inn compete for raves for the continental cuisine. The bar offers a tapas menu.

Fine Dining

European country cuisine reigns at **On the Marsh Bistro** (46 Western Ave./Rte. 9, Lower Village, Kennebunk, 207/967-2299, www.onthemarsh.com, 11:30am-4pm Tues.-Sat., 11:30am-9pm Sun., $28-43), a restored barn overlooking marshlands leading to Kennebunk Beach. The space is infused with arts and antiques and European touches courtesy of owner Denise Rubin, an interior designer with a passion for the Continent. Service is attentive, but the pace is leisurely. Reservations are essential in midsummer. Lighter fare is served in the bar.

One of Maine's biggest splurges is the **White Barn Inn** (37 Beach Ave., Kennebunkport, 207/967-2321, www.whitebarninn.com, from 6pm Mon.-Thurs., from 5:30pm Fri.-Sun.), with haute cuisine and haute prices in a haute-rustic barn. The menu features upscale American cuisine with an emphasis on fresh local ingredients and New England and coastal Maine flavors. Soft piano music accompanies impeccable service. The four-course fixed-price menu is about $125 per person. Also offered is a lobster menu (about $195). Dress nicely—no jeans, shorts, or T-shirts. For more casual dining, opt for the **Bistro** (11:30am-2pm and from 6pm daily, $25-50).

ACCOMMODATIONS

Most Kennebunk-area accommodations stay open through the Christmas Prelude festival, with many B&Bs remaining open year-round. This is not an especially budget-friendly area.

Inns and Hotels

Graciously dominating its 11-acre spread at the mouth of the Kennebunk River, the family-owned **Colony Hotel** (140 Ocean Ave. at King's Hwy., Kennebunkport, 207/967-3331 or 800/552-2363, www.colonymaine.com, from $269) springs right out of a bygone era, and its distinctive cupola is an area landmark. It has had a longtime commitment to the environment, with recycling, waste-reduction, and educational programs. There's a special feeling here, with cozy corners for reading, lawns and gardens for strolling, an oceanview heated saltwater pool, room service, an 18-hole putting green, tennis privileges at the exclusive River Club, bike rentals, massage therapy, and lawn games. The price of rooms includes breakfast. Pets are $30/night.

Hay Creek Hotels operates two high-end boutique properties in the area. Rates include a bountiful continental breakfast and use of bikes. The **Beach House Inn** (211 Beach Ave., Kennebunk, 207/967-3850, www.beachhseinn.com, from $235) faces Middle Beach; splurge on a room with a water view. The **Breakwater Inn, Hotel, and Spa** (127 Ocean Ave., Kennebunkport, 207/967-3118, www.thebreakwaterinn.com, from $279), at the mouth of the Kennebunk River, comprises a beautifully renovated historic inn with wraparound porches and an adjacent, more modern building with guest rooms and a full-service spa. The complex is also home to **Stripers Waterside Restaurant**

(8am-10am, 11am-3pm and from 4pm Wed.-Sat., 8am-10am and 11am-3pm Sun., $15-28).

Families favor the sprawling riverfront ★ **Nonantum Resort** (95 Ocean Ave., Kennebunkport, 207/967-4050 or 888/205-1555, www.nonantumresort.com, from $296) complex, which dates from 1884. It includes a bit of everything, from updated rooms and suites in the main building to modern family suites with kitchenettes in the newer Portside building. Recreational amenities include an outdoor heated pool, docking facilities, lobster-boat and sailing tours, fishing charters, and kayak rentals. A slew of activities are offered daily, including a children's program. Rates include a full breakfast. The water-view dining room is open for dinner daily as well as lunch in July-August. Packages, many of which include dinner, are a good choice. Note: This is a popular wedding venue.

The **White Barn Inn** (37 Beach Ave., Kennebunk, 207/967-2321, www.whitebarninn.com, from $425) is an especially exclusive property and is also home to a well-respected restaurant. Many rooms have fireplaces and marble baths with separate steam showers and whirlpool tubs. Service is impeccable, and amenities are abundant. There's an outdoor heated European-style infinity pool as well as a full-service spa.

The **Kennebunkport Resort Collection** (877/455-1501, www.kennebunkportresortcollection.com) comprises nine upscale or luxury accommodations, all with the expected amenities. A seasonal dinner shuttle provides transportation between them. The nautically themed **Boathouse Waterfront Hotel** (21 Ocean Ave., Kennebunkport, 207/967-8233, from $255) in Dock Square hangs over the river and has a restaurant and lounge with deck. Most guest rooms at the **Cape Arundel Inn & Resort** (208 Ocean Ave., Kennebunkport, 207/967-2125, from $271) overlook crashing surf and the Bush estate. The compound comprises the Shingle-style main inn building; the Rockbound motel-style building; the Carriage House Loft, a large suite on the upper floor of the carriage house; and the adjacent, repurposed former stable house of a grand summer resort. Breakfast is included. Every table in the inn's restaurant (entrées $27-40) has an ocean view. The 16 adorable one- and two-bedroom **Cottages at Cabot Cove** (16 S. Main St., Kennebunkport, 207/967-5424, from $322) have full kitchens. The **Lodge on the Cove** (29 South Main St., 800/879-5778, from $240) is geared to families. The **Yachtsman Lodge and Marina** (59 Ocean Ave., Kennebunkport, 207/967-2511, www.yachtsmanlodge.com, from $399) is a repurposed motel with all bungalow-style rooms opening onto private patios facing the river and pool. The renovated Victorian **Tides Beach Club** (254 Kings Hwy., Kennebunkport, 855/632-3324, from $299) is a hip boutique hotel with a restaurant/lounge on Goose Rocks Beach. A tender oversees beach chairs and umbrellas, provides water, and even delivers lunch. It shares amenities with the nearby, family-oriented **Hidden Pond** (354 Goose Rocks Rd., Kennebunkport, 888/967-9050, from $780), which is tucked in the woods about a mile from Goose Rocks Beach and comprises chic Victorian-esque cottages and bungalows, gardens, a spa, a wellness center, outdoor pools, a pool grill, and the fine-dining restaurant Earth.

Bed-and-Breakfasts

Old Parsonage Guest House (15 School St./Rte. 9, Kennebunkport, 207/967-4352, www.oldparsonageguesthouse.com, $160-225) is less fussy and pricey than most B&Bs, and it also welcomes well-behaved children. The two-bedroom suite and two rooms are smallish but comfy. Accommodating innkeepers go out of their way to assist guests and provide a communal hot breakfast.

Slip away from the crowds at the Gott family's antiques-filled ★ **Bufflehead Cove Inn** (B18 Bufflehead Cove Ln., Kennebunkport, 207/967-3879, www.buffleheadcove.com, from $275), a secluded riverfront home in the woods less than a mile from K-port's action. With a location like this and pampering service, you just might not want to stray from the front porch or dock. Rates include a full breakfast and afternoon treats.

Neighboring the Wedding Cake House, the **Waldo Emerson Inn** (108 Summer St./ Rte. 35, Kennebunk, 207/985-4250, www.waldoemersoninn.com, from $239) has a charming colonial feel, as it should, since the original Dutch gambrel was built in 1784. Poet Ralph Waldo Emerson spent many a summer here, at what was his great-uncle's home. Expect delightful historic details as well as complimentary and honor self-serve bars for cocktails, candy, books, and more. Innkeeper Hana Pevny has traveled widely and has worked as a private chef and culinary instructor.

The elegant Federal-style ★ **Captain Jeffords Inn** (5 Pearl St., Kennebunkport, 207/967-2311 or 800/839-6844, www.captainjeffordsinn.com, from $259), in the historic district, has the ambience of a real captain's house. Expect plush linens in each of the 16 guest rooms and suites: 10 in the main house and 6 additional (including 5 dog-friendly ones) with direct entry in the carriage house ($35/day/dog; pet-sitting available). A three-course breakfast and afternoon tea are included.

The **Captain Fairfield Inn** (8 Pleasant St., Kennebunkport, 207/967-4454, www.captainfairfield.com, from $279) is architecturally modest, but it doesn't scrimp on amenities. The lovely grounds are a fine place to retreat for a snooze in the hammock or a game of croquet. Rates include a tapas-style breakfast and afternoon cookies.

Rivaling the White Barn Inn for service, decor, amenities, and overall luxury is the three-story ★ **Captain Lord Mansion** (Pleasant St., Kennebunkport, 207/967-3141 or 800/522-3141, www.captainlord.com, from $279). Innkeepers Rick and Bev Litchfield have been at it since 1978, and they're never content to rest on their laurels. Each year the inn improves upon seeming perfection. If you want to be pampered and stay in a meticulously decorated, frequently updated, historical bed-and-breakfast with luxurious amenities, original artwork, and even a few cedar closets, look no further. A multicourse breakfast is served to shared tables.

Motels

The nonprofit **Franciscan Guest House** (28 Beach Ave., Kennebunk, 207/967-4865, www.franciscanguesthouse.com, $129-215), on the grounds of the monastery, has accommodations spread among two buildings and three other Tudor-style cottages. This isn't a place for fussbudgets: Decor is vintage 1970s, frills are few, and it's in need of updating. On the plus side: There's a saltwater pool (bring your own pool towels); it's within walking distance of the beach and Dock Square; a continental breakfast is included (hot buffet available, $4 surcharge); and a buffet dinner is often available in summer. There is no daily maid service, but fresh linens and towels are provided daily. The one- to three-bedroom suites are $159-279.

The clean and simple **Cape Porpoise Motel** (12 Mills Rd./Rte. 9, Cape Porpoise, 207/967-3370, www.capeporpoisemotel.com), with rooms ($149), efficiencies and studios ($189), and a two-bedroom cottage ($249), is a short walk from the harbor. Rates include a continental breakfast with homemade baked goods, fresh fruit, cereal, and bagels.

Fontenay Terrace (128 Ocean Ave., Kennebunkport, 207/967-3556, www.fontenayterrace.com, $167-205) borders a tidal inlet and has a grassy and shaded private lawn, perfect for retreating from the hubbub of busy Kennebunkport. A few of the eight guest rooms have water views. A small beach is 300 yards away, and it's a pleasant one-mile walk to Dock Square.

Patricia Mason is the ninth-generation innkeeper at the **Seaside Motor Inn** (80 Beach Ave., Kennebunk, 207/967-4461 or 800/967-4461, www.kennebunkbeach.com,

1: the Clam Shack 2: Nonantum Resort in Kennebunkport 3: Cape Arundel Inn & Resort 4: Colony Hotel

Enjoy Coca-Cola
The Clam Shack
Enjoy Coca-Cola
1
2
3
4

from $269), a property that has been in her family since 1667. The 22-room motel fronts on Gooch's Beach. Rooms are spacious and guests have use of an oceanview hot tub and bicycles. A continental breakfast is included, and a lunch-on-the-beach menu is offered in summer. Kids ages 12 and younger stay free.

Campground

Although you can rent a traditional tent or RV site, glamping is the specialty at **Sandy Pines Campground** (277 Mill Rd., Kennebunkport, 207/967-2483, https://sandypinescamping.com, from $50). Amenities include a heated saltwater pool, kids' areas, a laundry, and a lodge with a general store and snack bar.

INFORMATION AND SERVICES

The **Kennebunk-Kennebunkport-Arundel Chamber of Commerce** (16 Water St., Kennebunk, 207/967-0857, www.visitthekennebunks.com) produces an excellent area guide to accommodations and restaurants, with area maps, bike maps, tide calendars, recreation information, and beach parking permits. The group maintains a seasonal kiosk at 1 Chase Hill in Lower Village.

Check out **Louis T. Graves Memorial Public Library** (18 Maine St., Kennebunkport, 207/967-2778, www.graveslibrary.org) or **Kennebunk Free Library** (112 Main St., 207/985-2173, www.kennebunklibrary.org).

Public restrooms are at Gooch's and Mother's Beaches and at St. Anthony's Franciscan Monastery, and in the Dock Square parking area.

GETTING THERE AND AROUND

Kennebunk is about five miles or 10 minutes via Route 1 from Wells. Kennebunkport is about 6.5 miles or 12 minutes via Routes 1 and 9 from Wells. Connecting Kennebunk and Kennebunkport are four miles of Route 9. From Kennebunk to Biddeford, it's about nine miles or 17 minutes via Route 1. Allow longer for summer congestion in each town.

The **Amtrak Downeaster** (800/872-7245, www.amtrakdowneaster.com) connects Boston's North Station with Portland, Maine, with stops in Wells, Saco, Old Orchard Beach (seasonal), Freeport, and Brunswick. It connects with the seasonal **Shoreline Explorer** (207/324-5762, www.shorelineexplorer.com) trolley system, which operates between York and Kennebunkport. Each town's system is operated separately and has its own fees. The **Shoreline Trolley Blue Line-4b/Kennebunk Shuttle** ($1 one-way, $3 day pass, $10 12-ride pass, free for children under 18) connects Blue Line-4 (serving the Wells Transportation Facility and the Downeaster) with downtown Kennebunk, Lower Village, and Kennebunk's beaches.

Shoreline Trolley Line 6/Intown Trolley (207/967-3686, www.intowntrolley.com, $18, $8 ages 3-17) operates as a narrated sightseeing tour throughout Kennebunk and Kennebunkport. It originates in Dock Square and makes regular stops at beaches and other attractions. The entire route takes about 45 minutes, with the driver providing a hefty dose of local history and gossip. Seats are park bench-style. You can get on or off at any stop.

Old Orchard Beach Area

Seven continuous miles of white-sand beach have been drawing vacation-oriented folks for generations to the area stretching from Camp Ellis in Saco to Pine Point in Scarborough. Cottage colonies and condo complexes dominate at the extremities, but the center of activity has always been and remains Old Orchard Beach.

In its heyday, the **pier at Old Orchard Beach** reached far out into the sea, huge resort hotels lined the sands, and wealthy Victorian folk (including Rose Fitzgerald and Joe Kennedy, who met on these sands in the days when men strolled around in dress suits and women toted parasols) came each summer to see and be seen.

Storms and fires have taken their toll through the years, and the grand resorts have been replaced by endless motels, many of which display *"Nous parlons français"* signs to welcome the masses of French Canadians who arrive each summer. They're joined by young families who come for the sand and surf, and T-shirted and body-pierced young pleasure seekers who come for the nightlife.

Although some residents are pushing for gentrification and a few projects are moving things in that direction, **Old Orchard Beach** (pop. 8,624) remains somewhat honky-tonk, and most of its visitors would have it no other way. French fries, cotton candy, and beach-accessories shops line the downtown, and as you get closer to the pier, you pass arcades and amusement parks. There's not a kid on earth who wouldn't have fun in Old Orchard—even if some parents might find it all a bit much.

Much more sedate are the villages on the fringes. The **Ocean Park** section of Old Orchard, at the southwestern end of town, was established in 1881 as a religious summer-cottage community. It still offers interdenominational services, but it also has an active cultural association that sponsors concerts, Chautauqua-type lectures, films, and other events throughout the summer. All are open to the public.

South of that is **Camp Ellis.** Begun as a small fishing village named after early settler Thomas Ellis, it is crowded with longtime summer homes that are in constant battle with the sea. A nearly mile-long granite jetty—designed to keep silt from clogging the Saco River—has taken the blame for massive beach erosion since it was constructed. But the jetty is a favorite spot for wetting a line and for panoramic views off toward Wood Island Light (built in 1808) and Biddeford Pool. Camp Ellis Beach is open to the public, with lifeguards on duty in midsummer.

Most folks get to Old Orchard by passing through **Saco** (pop. 18,482) and **Biddeford** (pop. 21,277), which have long been upstairs-downstairs sister cities, with wealthy mill owners living in Saco and their workers and workplaces in Biddeford. But even those personalities have always been split—congested commercial Route 1 is part of Saco, and the exclusive enclave of Biddeford Pool is, of course, in below-stairs Biddeford.

Saco still has an attractive downtown, with boutiques and stunning homes on Main Street and beyond. Once blue-collar Biddeford, home to the Biddeford City Theater and the University of New England, now also draws young chefs and entrepreneurs. Still, Biddeford retains its Franco American heritage thanks to the French-speaking workers who sustained the textile and shoemaking industries in the 19th century. The mills on Factory Island between the two cities are being rehabbed to house restaurants, shops, offices, and condos, while honoring their past with a museum.

SIGHTS

Saco Museum

Founded in 1866, the **Saco Museum** (371 Main St., Saco, 207/283-3861, www.

dyerlibrarysacomuseum.org, noon-4pm Tues.-Thurs. and Sun., noon-8pm Fri., 10am-4pm Sat., $5 adults, $3 seniors, $2 ages 7-18) rotates selections from its outstanding collection, including 18th- and 19th-century paintings, furniture, and other household treasures. Lectures, workshops, and concerts are also part of the annual schedule. Admission is free after 4pm Fridays.

★ Wood Island Lighthouse

The all-volunteer **Friends of Wood Island Light** (207/200-4552, www.woodislandlighthouse.org) is restoring Maine's second-oldest lighthouse, which was commissioned by President Thomas Jefferson, built in 1808 (reconstructed in 1858) on 35-acre Wood Island, and abandoned in 1986. In July-August, the organization offers 1.5-hour guided tours ($20 adults, $10 children, recommended donation) of the two-story keeper's house and 42-foot-tall stone tower, relating tales of former keepers and their families. Those age 10 and older can even climb the 60 stairs to the tower's lantern room for splendid views. The tour departs from Vine's Landing in Biddeford Pool. Once on the island, it's about a half-mile walk to the site. Make reservations online; see the website or call for a current schedule.

Harmon Museum

Dip into Old Orchard Beach's history at the Old Orchard Beach Historical Society's **Harmon Museum** (4 Portland Ave., Old Orchard Beach, 207/934-9319, www.harmonmuseum.org, 10am-4pm Mon.-Fri. late June-late Aug., free). Religious groups, the famed pier, destructive fires, Ocean Park, transportation, and celebrities are the subjects of the displays, artifacts, and memorabilia. Interesting anytime, but a great rainy-day activity.

Biddeford Mills Museum

Very much a work in progress, the **Biddeford Mills Museum** (2 Main St., Biddeford, 207/229-6387, www.biddefordmillsmuseum.org) offers tours of the former textile mills, including their underground canals. The two-hour tours ($15) are guided by former mill workers who share their stories along with the history of the mills; call 207/284-8520 or check the website for the current schedule and reservations.

Way Way Store

Dating from the late 1920s, and listed in the National Register of Historic Places, the **Way Way Store** (93 Buxton Rd./Rte. 112, Saco, 207/286-6990, www.waywaystore.com, 10am-9pm daily late May-early Sept., 10am-6pm daily spring and fall) appeals equally to kids and nostalgic adults. Inside this classic general store, constructed from alternating red-and-white concrete blocks and stone pillars, you'll find ice cream, penny candy, produce, and other goodies. It's all rung up on the original register.

ENTERTAINMENT

At 6pm every Thursday late June-Labor Day, **free concerts** are staged in Old Orchard's Memorial Park, followed by **fireworks** at 9:45pm.

Family concerts and other performances are staged at the outdoor **Seaside Pavilion** (8 6th St., Old Orchard Beach, 207/934-2024, www.seasidepavilion.org).

The **Ballpark** (E. Emerson Cummings Blvd., Old Orchard Beach, 207/205-6160, www.oobballpark.com) hosts concerts, shows, baseball games, and other events.

The **Temple** (Temple Ave., Ocean Park, www.oceanpark.org), a 19th-century octagon that seats more than 800, is the venue for concerts and many other programs throughout the summer.

Designed by noted architect John Calvin Stevens in 1896, the 500-seat **City Theater** (205 Main St., Biddeford, 207/282-0849, www.citytheater.org), in the National Register of Historic Places, has been superbly restored, and the acoustics are excellent even when Eva Gray, the resident ghost, mixes it up backstage.

A rainy-day godsend, the **IMAX Theater** (779 Portland Rd./Rte. 1, Saco, 207/282-6234, www.cinemagicmovies.com) has digital sound, stadium seating, a restaurant, and online ticketing.

Festivals and Events

La Kermesse (www.lakermessefestival.com), meaning "the fair" or "the festival," is Biddeford's summer highlight, when nearly 50,000 visitors pour into town in late June to celebrate Biddeford's Franco American heritage. Local volunteers go all out to plan block parties, a parade, games, a carnival, live entertainment, and traditional dancing. Then there's *la cuisine franco-américaine;* you can fill up on boudin, *creton,* poutine, *tourtière, tarte au saumon,* and crepes (although your arteries may rebel).

Check to see the current schedule for the monthly **Biddeford+Saco Art Walk** (www.biddefordsacoartwalk.com).

In July, the parishioners of St. Demetrios Greek Orthodox Church (186 Bradley St., Saco, 207/284-5651) mount the annual **Greek Heritage Festival,** a three-day extravaganza of homemade Greek food, traditional Greek music and dancing, and a crafts fair. Be sure to tour the impressive domed church building.

The beaches come to life in July with the annual **Parade and Sandcastle Contest** in Ocean Park.

Taking place over one weekend in mid-August, Old Orchard Beach's **Beach Olympics** is a family festival of games, exhibitions, and music benefiting Maine's Special Olympics program.

RECREATION

Parks and Preserves

Saco Bay Trails (www.sacobaytrails.org), a local land trust, has produced a helpful trail guide ($12) that includes the Saco Heath, the East Point Sanctuary, and nearly two dozen other local trails. The Cascade Falls Trail, for example, is a half-mile stroll ending at a waterfall. Copies of the guide are available at a number of Biddeford and Saco locations, including the Dyer Library, or from Saco Bay Trails.

EAST POINT SANCTUARY

Owned by Maine Audubon (207/781-2330, www.maineaudubon.org), the 30-acre **East Point Sanctuary** is a splendid preserve at the eastern end of Biddeford Pool. Crashing surf, beach roses, bayberry bushes, and offshore Wood Island Light are all features of the two-part perimeter trail, which skirts the exclusive Abenakee Club's golf course. Allow at least an hour; even in fog, the setting is dramatic. During spring and fall migrations it's one of southern Maine's prime birding locales, so you'll have plenty of company at those times, and the usual street-side parking may be scarce. It's poorly signposted (perhaps deliberately), so you'll want to follow the directions: From Route 9 (Main Street) in downtown Biddeford, take Route 9/208 (Pool Road) southeast about five miles to the Route 208 turnoff to Biddeford Pool. Go 0.6 mile on Route 208 (Bridge Road) and then turn left onto Mile Stretch Road. Continue to Lester B. Orcutt Boulevard, turn left, and go to the end. Be careful: There's poison ivy on the point.

SACO HEATH PRESERVE

Owned by the Nature Conservancy, 1,218-acre **Saco Heath Preserve** is the nation's southernmost "raised coalesced bog," where peat accumulated through eons into two above-water dome shapes that eventually merged into a single natural feature. Pick up a map at the parking area and follow the mile-long, self-guided trail through the woods and then into the heath via a boardwalk. The best time to visit is early-mid-October, when the heath and woodland colors are positively brilliant and insects are on the wane. You're likely to see deer and perhaps even spot a moose, and this is the home of the rare Hessel's hairstreak butterfly. The preserve entrance is on Route 112 (Buxton Road), two miles west of I-95. Pets are not allowed in the preserve.

Amusement Parks

If you have kids, or just love amusement parks, you'll find Maine's best in the Old Orchard area, where sand and sun just seem to complement arcades and rides perfectly. All these parks are seasonal, so call or check websites for current schedules.

The biggie is **Funtown/Splashtown USA** (774 Portland Rd./Rte. 1, Saco, 207/284-5139 or 800/878-2900, www.funtownsplashtownusa.com). Here you can ride Maine's only wooden roller coaster; fly down New England's longest and tallest log flume ride; free-fall 200 feet on Dragon's Descent; or get wet and go wild splashing in the pool or riding speed slides, tunnel slides, raft slides, and river slides. Add a huge kiddie-ride section as well as games, food, and other activities for a full day of family fun. Ticketing options vary by the activities included and height, ranging $31-39 for "Big" (48 inches and taller), $26-30 for "Little" (38-48 inches tall), "Senior" (over age 60), and free for kids under 38 inches tall.

Three miles north of Funtown/Splashtown USA, **Aquaboggan Water Park** (980 Portland Rd./Rte. 1, Saco, 207/282-3112, www.aquabogganwaterpark.com, 10am-6pm daily late June-Labor Day) is wet and wild, with such stomach turners as the Yankee Ripper, the Suislide, and the Stealth, with an almost-vertical drop of 45 feet—enough to accelerate to 30 miles per hour on the descent. Wear a bathing suit that won't abandon you in the rough-and-tumble. Also, if you wear glasses, safety straps and plastic lenses are required. Besides all the water stuff, there is mini golf, an arcade, go-karts, and bumper boats. A day pass for all pools, slides, and mini golf is $24 (48 inches and taller), $19 (under 48 inches tall), and $6 (under 38 inches tall). Monday is $14 general admission. A $34 pass also includes two go-kart rides and unlimited pools, slides, and bumper-boat rides.

The biggest beachfront amusement park, **Palace Playland** (1 Old Orchard St., Old Orchard, 207/934-2001, www.palaceplayland.com) has more than 25 rides and attractions packed into four acres, including a giant waterslide, a fun house, bumper cars, a Ferris wheel, roller coasters, and a

FERRY BEACH STATE PARK

When the weather's hot, arrive early at **Ferry Beach State Park** (95 Bay View Rd., off Rte. 9, Saco, 207/283-0067, www.parksandlands.com, $7 nonresident adults, $5 Maine resident adults, $2 nonresident seniors, $1 ages 5-11), a pristine beach backed by dune grass on Saco Bay. In the 117-acre park are changing rooms, restrooms, a nature center, a lifeguard stand, picnic tables, and a 1.7-mile trail network winding through woodlands, marshlands, and dunes. The 0.4-mile Tupelo Trail passes through a pocket swamp and stand of tupelo trees, both rare at this latitude. Later in the day it's wise to keep the insect repellent handy. It's open daily late May-late September but accessible year-round; trail markers are removed in winter.

Boat Excursions

Join **Nonesuch Oyster Tours** (207/749-5585, www.nonesuchoysters.com, $65 pp) aboard the *Oys-Tour* for a cruise of Nonesuch Oyster Farm, sited in a tidal estuary nature preserve frequented by eagles, sturgeon, and seals. Tours include tasting six freshly harvested oysters. Call for the current schedule.

Golf

Tee off at the **Biddeford-Saco Country Club** (101 Old Orchard Rd., Saco, 207/282-5883) or the challenging 18-hole par-71 **Dunegrass Golf Club** (200 Wild Dunes Way, Old Orchard Beach, 207/934-4513 or 800/521-1029).

Baseball

Baseball fans can head inland to watch the **Sanford Mainers** (Roberts St., Sanford, 207/324-0010, www.sanfordmainers.com), which play in the New England Collegiate Baseball League. The team's stadium, built in 1915 and rebuilt in 1997 after a fire, is famed as the site where, on October 1, 1919, Babe

Old Orchard Beach pier

24,000-square-foot arcade with more than 200 games. An unlimited pass is $38/day; a kiddie pass good for all rides with height limitations is $32; two-day, season, and single tickets are available.

The **Old Orchard Beach pier,** jutting 475 feet into the ocean from downtown, is a mini-mall of shops, arcades, and fast-food outlets. Far longer when it was built in 1898, it has been gradually lopped off by fires and storms. The current incarnation has been here since the late 1970s.

Ruth hit his last homer as a member of the Red Sox. Tickets are $5 adults, $3 students/seniors.

FOOD

Old Orchard Beach

Dining is not Old Orchard's strong point, but the town is a bonanza for cheap eats. Stroll Main Street and out to the pier for hot dogs, fries, pizza, and ice cream.

All-day breakfast and a menu that, except for pizza, tops out at $10 makes convenience store/counter-service restaurant **Tami Lyn's Place** (126 W. Grand Ave., 207/934-4292, www.tamilynsplace.com, 6am-9pm daily) popular for inexpensive family meals.

Dolce Crema Café (1 E. Grand Ave., 207/934-2331, 7:30am-11pm) an order-at-the-counter joint, has options under $10 for all meals and also dishes out gelato.

For casual dining, **Joseph's by the Sea** (55 W. Grand Ave., 207/934-5044, www.josephsbythesea.com, noon-9pm daily, entrées $24-35) is a quiet shorefront restaurant amid all the hoopla. Request a table on the screened patio. The menu is heavy on seafood, but there are choices for steak lovers as well as vegan and gluten-free options. Reservations are advisable in midsummer. **The Roof** (12:30pm-9pm daily, $10-20) serves lighter fare on the restaurant's oceanside deck.

Saco

Craving fast-ish food? The Camire family operates Maine's best homegrown option, **Rapid Ray's** (189 Main St., 207/283-4222, www.rapidrays.biz, 11am-10pm Sun.-Thurs., 11am-11:30pm Fri.-Sat.), a downtown institution since 1953. Burgers, steamed dogs, lobster rolls, and clam cakes are served at the standing room-only joint.

Located on Saco Island in a renovated factory building, the **Run of the Mill Public House & Brewery** (100 Main St., 207/571-9648, www.therunofthemill.net,

11:30am-10pm daily, $10-20) is a 14-barrel brewpub with seasonal outdoor deck seating overlooking the river. Expect pub-fare classics with a few surprises. During summer, when the weather cooperates, an outside grill menu is available.

At **Huot's Seafood Restaurant** (Camp Ellis Beach, 207/282-1642, www.huotsseafoodrestaurant.com, 11:30am-9pm Tues.-Sun., $8-32), under third-generation management, the menu is huge, portions are large, and prices are reasonable. It's a good value for fresh seafood; a children's menu is available and there's a take-out window.

The **New Moon Restaurant** (17 Pepperell Sq., 207/282-2241, http://newmoonafterdark.com, 7:30am-2pm Sun.-Thurs., 7:30am-2pm and 5pm-9pm Fri.-Sat., $16-25) serves rave-worthy breakfasts and lunches in a cheerful yellow house. On Friday and Saturday nights, it offers dinner entrées such as chicken marsala and baked haddock.

Biddeford and Biddeford Pool

For a town grounded in Franco American culture, Biddeford is getting increasingly hip with expanding and interesting choices that are gaining national attention. Ask locally about what's new and popular.

Sweetcream Dairy (40 Main St. building 13, 207/520-2386, from noon daily) makes its own cow-to-cone ice cream.

Take your lobster or fried seafood dinner to an oceanfront picnic table on the grassy lawn behind **F. O. Goldthwaite's** (3 Lester B. Orcott Blvd., Biddeford Pool, 207/284-8872, 7am-7:30pm daily, $4-market rates), an old-fashioned general store. Salads, fried seafood, sandwiches, and kid-friendly fare round out the menu.

Love biscuits? You'll love **Biscuits & Company** (25 Alfred St., 207/710-2333, www.biscuitsandcompany.com, 7:30am-2pm Wed.-Sat., 8:30am-1pm Sun.), an especially popular spot for breakfast and lunch.

If Biddeford has a living room, it's **Elements** (265 Main St., 207/710-2011, www.elementsbookscoffeebeer.com, 7am-10pm Mon.-Thurs., 7am-11pm Fri.-Sat., 8am-6pm Sun.), a combination bookstore, coffee shop, craft-beer bar, and café serving light fare ($6-13) and offering weekend entertainment.

Maine's oldest diner is the **Palace Diner** (18 Franklin St., 207/284-0015, www.palacedinerme.com, 8am-2pm daily, $8-16), a 1926 Pollard that was towed to Maine from Lowell, Massachusetts, by horses in the same year that Lindbergh flew over the Atlantic. It's tucked off Main Street next to city hall.

James Beard Best New Chef and six-time Best Chef Southwest finalist Bowman Brown relocated to New England and opened ★ **Elda** (140 Main St., Biddeford, 207/494-8365, www.eldamaine.com, 5:30pm-9pm Tues.-Sun., $25-29). The small, focused menu emphasizes New England regional fare, with entrées. Your best bet is the four-course prix fixe menu ($58).

ACCOMMODATIONS

The area has hundreds of beds, mostly in motel-style lodgings. The chamber of commerce is the best resource for motels, cottages, and the area's more than 3,000 campsites.

The **Atlantic Birches Inn** (20 Portland Ave./Rte. 98, Old Orchard Beach, 207/934-5295 or 888/934-5295, www.atlanticbirches.com, $150-210) has 10 guest rooms split between a 1902 Victorian designed by John Calvin Stevens and a 1920s bungalow. Breakfast is continental, and there's a swimming pool. The beach is an easy walk. It's open all year, but call ahead in the off-season.

The beachfront **Crest Motel** (35 E. Grand Ave., 207/934-4060, http://crestmotel.com, from $242) is especially popular with families thanks to a playground and a heated indoor pool with retractable roof.

Two family-owned beachfront motels, both with pools, have been recently renovated: the **Edgewater Motor Inn** (57 W. Grand Ave., Old Orchard Beach, 800/203-2034, www.theedgewatermotorinn.com, from $235) and the **Beachwood Motel** (29 W. Grand Ave., Old Orchard Beach, 207/934-2291, www.beachwood-motel.com, from $272).

INFORMATION AND SERVICES

Sources of visitor information are the **Biddeford-Saco Chamber of Commerce and Industry** (207/282-1567, www.biddefordsacochamber.org), **Old Orchard Beach Chamber of Commerce** (207/934-2500 or 800/365-9386, www.oldorchardbeachmaine.com), and **Ocean Park Association** (207/934-9068, www.oceanpark.org).

The **Dyer Library** (371 Main St., Saco, 207/282-3031, www.sacomuseum.org), next door to the Saco Museum, attracts scads of genealogists to its vast Maine history collection. Also check out **Libby Memorial Library** (27 Staples St., Old Orchard Beach, 207/934-4351, www.ooblibrary.org).

GETTING THERE AND AROUND

Biddeford is about five miles or 10 minutes via Route 1 from Kennebunk. From Biddeford to Portland, it's about 18 miles or 25 minutes via I-95 and I-295; allow at least a half hour via Route 1. Downtown Biddeford is about a mile via Route 9 from downtown Saco. From Saco to Old Orchard Beach is about four miles or at least 10 minutes via Route 9, the Old Orchard Beach Road, and Route 5, but it can take twice that in summer traffic.

The **Amtrak Downeaster** (800/872-7245, www.amtrakdowneaster.com) connects Boston's North Station with Brunswick, Maine, with stops in Wells, Saco, Old Orchard Beach (seasonal), Portland, and Freeport. If you're thinking about a day trip, take the train and avoid the traffic and parking hassles.

The **Biddeford-Saco-Old Orchard Beach Transit Committee** (207/282-5408, www.shuttlebus-zoom.com) operates three systems that make getting around simple. The **Old Orchard Beach Trolley** and **Camp Ellis Trolley** (10am-midnight daily late June-Labor Day, $1 one-way, $2 after 6pm, free ages 4 and younger, exact fare required) operate four routes on a regular schedule and connect the towns with Route 1 in Saco. You can flag them down anywhere en route. **ShuttleBus Local Service** provides daily service (except on national holidays) between Biddeford, Saco, and Old Orchard Beach, and connects with the Amtrak stations. One-way fare is $1.50 ages five and older; exact change is required. **ShuttleBus InterCity Service** connects Biddeford, Saco, and Old Orchard with Portland, South Portland, and Scarborough. Fares vary by zones, topping out at $5 for anyone over age five.

Greater Portland

When national magazines highlight the 10 best places to live, eat, work, or play, Greater Portland usually makes the list. The very things that make the area so popular with residents make it equally attractive to visitors. Small in size but big in heart, Greater Portland entices visitors with the staples—lighthouses, lobster, and L. L. Bean—but wows them with everything else it offers. It is the state's cultural hub, with performing arts centers, numerous festivals, and varied museums; it's also a culinary destination, with nationally recognized chefs as well as an amazing assortment and variety of everyday restaurants; and finally, despite its urban environment, it has a mind-boggling number of recreational opportunities. No wonder the National Heritage Trust named it a Distinctive Destination.

Highlights

Look for ★ to find recommended sights, activities, dining, and lodging.

★ **The Old Port and the Waterfront:** Plan to spend at least a couple of hours browsing the shops, dining, and enjoying the energy of this restored historic district (page 88).

★ **Portland Museum of Art:** This museum houses works by masters such as Winslow Homer, John Marin, Andrew Wyeth, Edward Hopper, and Marsden Hartley as well as Monet, Picasso, and Renoir (page 90).

★ **Victoria Mansion:** This house is considered one of the most richly decorated dwellings of its period remaining in the country (page 91).

★ **Portland Observatory:** Climb the 103 steps to the orb deck of the only remaining maritime signal tower on the Eastern Seaboard. You'll be rewarded with views from the White Mountains to Casco Bay's islands (page 92).

★ **Portland Head Light:** This lighthouse, commissioned by President George Washington, sits on the rocky ledges of Cape Elizabeth (page 94).

★ **Lobstering Cruise:** Go out on a working lobster boat in Portland Harbor, see the sights, and perhaps return with a lobster for dinner (page 104).

★ **Casco Bay Tour:** Take a three-hour tour on the mail boat, which stops briefly at five islands en route (page 116).

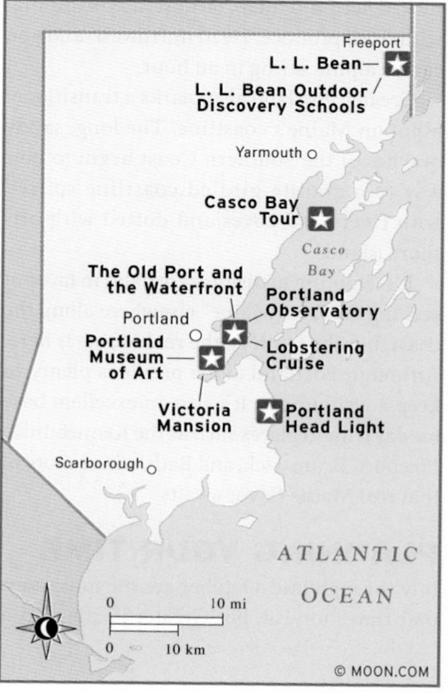

★ **L. L. Bean:** The empire's flagship store is in Freeport. No trip to this shopping mecca is complete without a visit (page 121).

★ **L. L. Bean Outdoor Discovery Schools:** Don't miss the opportunity for an inexpensive introduction to a new sport (page 123).

Portland's population hovers around 66,000, but when the suburbs are included, it climbs to nearly 250,000, making it Maine's largest city by far. Take a swing through the bedroom communities of Scarborough (pop. 18,919), Cape Elizabeth (pop. 9,015), and South Portland (pop. 25,002), and you'll better understand the area's popularity: easily accessible parks, beaches, rocky ledges, and lighthouses are all minutes from downtown, along with a slew of ferry-connected islands dotting Casco Bay. Head north through suburban Falmouth (pop. 11,185) and Yarmouth (pop. 8,349) and you'll arrive in Freeport (pop. 7,879), home of mega-retailer L. L. Bean. En route, you'll still see the vestiges of the region's heritage: sailboats and lobster boats, traps and buoys piled on lawns or along driveways, and, tucked here and there, farm stands brimming with fresh produce. Head northwest, and you can be alpine skiing in an hour.

Greater Portland also marks a transitional point on Maine's coastline. The long, sandy beaches of the Southern Coast begin to give way to a granite-girdled coastline spliced with rivers and coves and dotted with offshore islands.

It's tempting to dismiss Portland in favor of seeking the "real Maine" elsewhere along the coast, but the truth is, the real Maine is here. Although Portland alone provides plenty to keep a visitor busy, it's also an excellent base for day trips to places such as the Kennebunks, Freeport, Brunswick, and Bath, where more of that real Maine flavor awaits.

PLANNING YOUR TIME

July through mid-October are the most popular times to visit, but Greater Portland is a year-round destination, and thanks to it being named *Bon Appetit*'s Restaurant City of the Year in 2018, it's increasingly popular in the quieter months, when it's easier to get reservations at the top restaurants. Spring truly arrives by mid-May, when most summer outfitters begin operations at least on weekends. Salty sea breezes cool summer days and make winter ones seem even chillier. Snow frequently blankets Portland December through March. September is perhaps the loveliest month of the year weather-wise, and by mid-October those fabled New England maples are turning crimson.

To do the region justice, you'll want to spend at least three or four days, more if your plans call for using Greater Portland as a base for day trips to more distant points. You can easily kill two days in downtown Portland alone, what with all the shops, museums, historical sites, waterfront, and neighborhoods to explore. If you're staying in town and are an avid walker, you won't need a car to get to the must-see sights on the peninsula.

Although both Amtrak's Downeaster and the Metro buses reach beyond Portland, to really explore the region, it's best to have a car. Allow a full day for a leisurely tour through South Portland and Cape Elizabeth and on to Prouts Neck in Scarborough.

Rabid shoppers should either stay in Freeport or allow at least a day for L. L. Bean and the 100 or so outlets in its shadow. If you're traveling with a supershopper, don't despair. Freeport has parks and preserves that are light-years removed from the frenzy of its downtown, and the fishing village of South Freeport offers seaside pleasures.

Previous: Portland's harbor; Portland Observatory; Casco Bay ferry.

Greater Portland

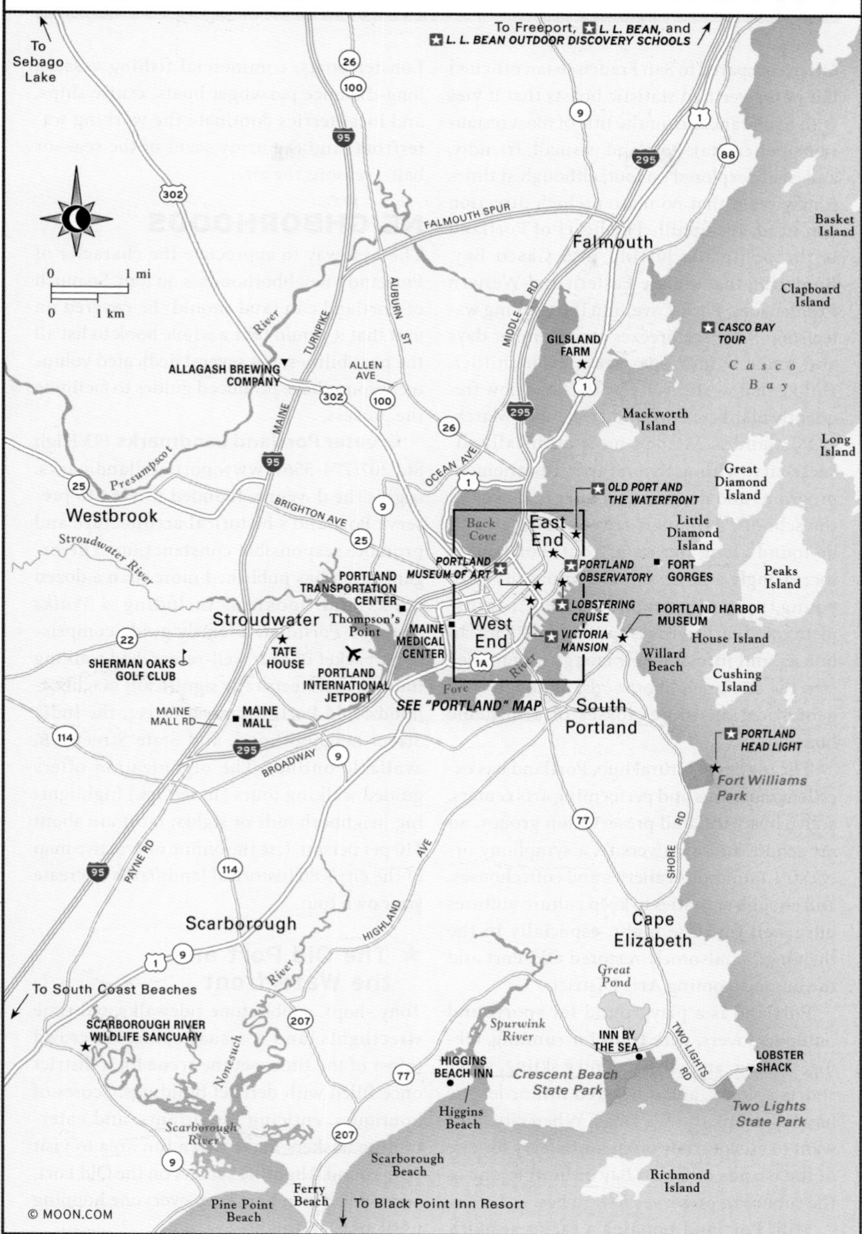

Portland

Often compared to San Francisco (an oft-cited but never-verified statistic boasts that it vies with San Francisco for the title of most restaurants per capita), Portland is small, friendly, and easily explored on foot, although at times it may seem that no matter which direction you head, it's uphill. The heart of Portland is the peninsula jutting into Casco Bay. Bordering that are the Eastern and Western Promenades, Back Cove, and the working waterfront. Salty sea breezes cool summer days and make winter ones seem even chillier. Unlike that western city by the bay, snow frequently blankets Portland December-March.

Portland is Maine's most ethnically diverse city, with active refugee resettlement programs and dozens of languages spoken in the schools. Although salty sailors can still be found along the waterfront, Portland is increasingly a professional community with young, upwardly mobile residents, transplants, and early retirees spiffing up Victorian houses and infusing new energy and money into the city's neighborhoods, although with gentrification comes losses of affordable housing.

The region's cultural hub, Portland has excellent museums and performing arts centers, active historical and preservation groups, an art school and a university, a symphony orchestra, numerous galleries and coffeehouses, and enough activities to keep culture vultures busy well into the night, especially in the thriving, handsomely restored Old Port and the up-and-coming Arts District.

Portland is a playground for sports and outdoors lovers, with trails for running, biking, skating, and cross-country skiing, water sports aplenty, and a beloved minor-league baseball team, the Sea Dogs. When city folks want to escape, they often hop a ferry for one of the islands of Casco Bay or head to one of the suburban preserves or beaches.

Still, Portland remains a major seaport. Lobster boats, commercial fishing vessels, long-distance passenger boats, cruise ships, and local ferries dominate the working waterfront, and the briny scent of the sea—or bait—seasons the air.

NEIGHBORHOODS

The best way to appreciate the character of Portland's neighborhoods is on foot. So much of Portland can (and should) be covered on foot that it would take a whole book to list all the possibilities, but several dedicated volunteer groups have produced guides to facilitate the process.

Greater Portland Landmarks (93 High St., 207/774-5561, www.portlandlandmarks.org) is the doyenne, founded in 1964 to preserve Portland's historical architecture and promote responsible construction. The organization has published more than a dozen books and booklets, including *4 Walks Through Portland,* a family guide comprising a packet of four well-researched walking tours to architecturally significant neighborhoods: Old Port, Congress Street, the India Street neighborhood, and State Street ($8, available online). The organization offers guided walking tours (June-Oct.) highlighting neighborhoods or sights; most are about $10 per person. Use the online interactive map of the city's 80 historical landmarks to create your own tour.

★ The Old Port and the Waterfront

Tony shops, cobblestone sidewalks, old-time streetlights, and a casual upmarket crowd (most of the time) set the scene for a district once filled with derelict buildings. Scores of boutiques, enticing restaurants, and entertaining buskers make this a fun area to visit year-round. Nightlife centers on the Old Port, and a few dozen bars keep everyone hopping until after midnight.

Portland

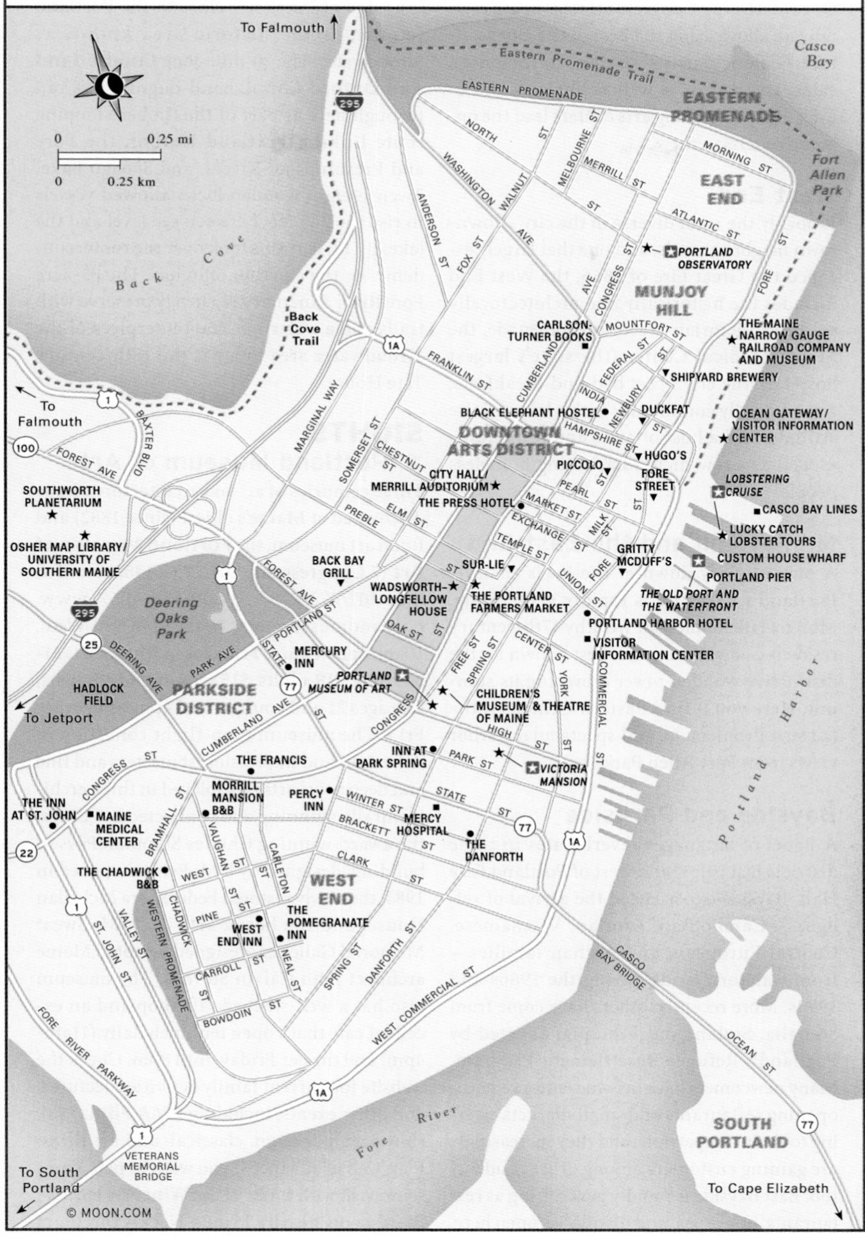
To Falmouth
Eastern Promenade Trail
Casco Bay
EASTERN PROMENADE
NORTH
WASHINGTON AVE
WALNUT ST
MELBOURNE ST
MERRILL ST
MORNING ST
EAST END
Fort Allen Park
ATLANTIC ST
ANDERSON ST
FOX ST
CONGRESS ST
FORE ST
PORTLAND OBSERVATORY
MUNJOY HILL
Back Cove
Back Cove Trail
CARLSON-TURNER BOOKS
MOUNTFORT ST
THE MAINE NARROW GAUGE RAILROAD COMPANY AND MUSEUM
CUMBERLAND AVE
FEDERAL ST
SHIPYARD BREWERY
FRANKLIN ST
MARGINAL WAY
INDIA ST
NEWBURY ST
To Falmouth
BAXTER BLVD
BLACK ELEPHANT HOSTEL
DUCKFAT
OCEAN GATEWAY/ VISITOR INFORMATION CENTER
DOWNTOWN ARTS DISTRICT
HAMPSHIRE ST
FOREST AVE
SOMERSET ST
CHESTNUT ST
HUGO'S
PICCOLO
FORE STREET
LOBSTERING CRUISE
SOUTHWORTH PLANETARIUM
CITY HALL/ MERRILL AUDITORIUM
PEARL ST
THE PRESS HOTEL
MARKET ST
CASCO BAY LINES
PREBLE
ELM ST
EXCHANGE ST
MILK ST
LUCKY CATCH LOBSTER TOURS
OSHER MAP LIBRARY/ UNIVERSITY OF SOUTHERN MAINE
TEMPLE ST
GRITTY MCDUFF'S
CUSTOM HOUSE WHARF
BACK BAY GRILL
SUR-LIE
UNION ST
PORTLAND PIER
Deering Oaks Park
FOREST AVE
WADSWORTH-LONGFELLOW HOUSE
THE PORTLAND FARMERS MARKET
THE OLD PORT AND THE WATERFRONT
PORTLAND ST
OAK ST
PORTLAND HARBOR HOTEL
DEERING AVE
STATE ST
MERCURY INN
FREE ST
SPRING ST
CENTER ST
VISITOR INFORMATION CENTER
PARK AVE
HADLOCK FIELD
PARKSIDE DISTRICT
PORTLAND MUSEUM OF ART
CHILDREN'S MUSEUM & THEATRE OF MAINE
YORK ST
COMMERCIAL ST
To Jetport
CUMBERLAND AVE
CONGRESS ST
HIGH ST
Portland Harbor
INN AT PARK SPRING
PARK ST
VICTORIA MANSION
CONGRESS ST
THE FRANCIS
MORRILL MANSION B&B
PERCY INN
STATE ST
THE INN AT ST. JOHN
MAINE MEDICAL CENTER
BRAMHALL ST
WINTER ST
BRACKETT ST
MERCY HOSPITAL
THE DANFORTH
VAUGHAN ST
CARLETON ST
CLARK ST
THE CHADWICK B&B
WEST ST
WEST END
CHADWICK ST
PINE ST
THE POMEGRANATE INN
WEST END INN
VALLEY ST
ST. JOHN ST
WESTERN PROMENADE
CARROLL ST
NEAL ST
SPRING ST
DANFORTH ST
CASCO BAY BRIDGE
WEST COMMERCIAL ST
BOWDOIN ST
FORE RIVER PARKWAY
OCEAN ST
Fore River
SOUTH PORTLAND
VETERANS MEMORIAL BRIDGE
To South Portland
To Cape Elizabeth
0 0.25 mi
0 0.25 km
© MOON.COM

Congress Street and the Downtown Arts District

Once-declining Congress Street is being revitalized, showcasing the best of the city's culture. Galleries, artists' studios, coffeehouses, cafés, and bistros as well as libraries, museums, and performing arts centers lead the ongoing renaissance.

West End

Probably the most diverse of the city's downtown neighborhoods, and one that largely escaped the Great Fire of 1866, the West End includes the historically and architecturally splendid Victorian Western Promenade, the Maine Medical Center (the state's largest hospital), the city's best bed-and-breakfasts, a gay-friendly community with a laissez-faire attitude, and a host of cafés and restaurants as well as a few niches harboring homeless people.

Munjoy Hill and the East End

A once slightly down-at-the-heels enclave, Portland's East End is rapidly gentrifying. Munjoy Hill, named for wealthy 17th-century resident George Munjoy, is best known for the distinctive wooden tower crowning its summit. Here you'll find Eastern Cemetery, the Eastern Promenade, and spectacular harbor views from Fort Allen Park.

Bayside and Parkside

A Babel of languages reverberates in these districts just below and west of Portland City Hall. Bayside experienced the arrival of refugees—Cambodian, Laotian, Vietnamese, Central European, and Afghan families—from war-torn lands during the 1980s and 1990s. More recently, others have come from Somalia, Sudan, and Ethiopia, assisted by Portland's Refugee Resettlement Program. Many newcomers have become entrepreneurs, opening restaurants and small markets catering to their compatriots, and they increasingly are gaining customers among other residents too. East Bayside is rapidly gentrifying as restaurants, breweries, and distilleries open here.

Stroudwater

Off the downtown peninsula at the western edge of Portland, close to the Portland Jetport, is the historic area known as Stroudwater. The 20-mile-long **Cumberland and Oxford Canal,** hand-dug in 1828, ran through here as part of the timber-shipping route linking Portland Harbor, the Fore and Presumpscot Rivers, and Sebago Lake. Twenty-eight wooden locks allowed vessels to rise the 265 feet between sea level and the lake. By 1870, trains took over the route, condemning the canal to oblivion. The 85-acre Fore River Sanctuary is a lovely preserve with trails and a waterfall. The centerpiece of the Stroudwater area today is the 18th-century Tate House.

SIGHTS

★ Portland Museum of Art

Three centuries of art and architecture can be discovered at Maine's oldest (since 1882) and finest art museum, the **Portland Museum of Art** (7 Congress Sq., 207/775-6148, recorded info 207/773-2787 or 800/639-4067, www.portlandmuseum.org, 10am-6pm Sat.-Wed., 10am-8pm Thurs.-Fri., closed Mon. Oct. 31-late May, $18 adults, $15 seniors and students, free ages 21 and younger and 4pm-8pm every Fri.). The museum's top-flight collection of American and impressionist masters and fine and decorative arts is displayed in three architecturally stunning and connected buildings: the award-winning Charles Shipman Payson building, designed by I. M. Pei and opened in 1983; the newly restored Federal-era McLellan House; and the beaux arts L. D. M. Sweat Memorial Galleries, designed by noted Maine architect John Calvin Stevens. The museum also has a well-stocked gift shop and an excellent café that's open for lunch daily (11am-4pm) and dinner Friday until 8pm. Check the website for current family activities, lectures, and other events, including **PMA Films** ($8), showcasing foreign, classical, and art films. Plan well in advance if you want to pair a museum visit with a tour of the **Winslow Homer Studio** on nearby Prouts Neck—the tours

Winslow Homer

Winslow Homer Studio

Discovering Maine in his early 40s, Winslow Homer (1836-1910) was smitten enough to spend the last 27 years of his life on Prouts Neck, a granite-tipped thumb of land edged with beaches reaching into the Atlantic in Scarborough, just south of Portland. Homer painted some of his greatest works—masterpieces such as *Weatherbeaten, The Fog Warning,* and *The Gulf Stream*—at this oceanfront studio, taking inspiration from the crashing surf, craggy shores, stormy seas, and dense fog. Today, you can stand in the studio and survey the scene for yourself.

Originally the carriage house for the adjacent house owned by Homer's brother Charles, the studio was moved 100 feet and converted to living quarters in 1883 by Portland architect John Calvin Stevens, one of the founders of the Shingle style. The piazza, pergola, and later the painting room were added.

The simplicity of the studio, with its beadboard walls and ceiling, tongue-and-groove floor, and brick fireplace, is pure Maine cottage. Some original furnishings and artifacts add context to understanding Homer. These include the *Snakes! Snakes! Mice!* sign he painted to scare off ladies who might be inclined to visit; the window in which he etched his name; the writings on the wall, such as *"Oh what a friend chance can be when it chooses"*; and a book of family photographs. Copies of his artwork, displays, and a slide show of images are exhibited in the painting room, or "the factory," as he called it. Especially intriguing are the Civil War sketches he made for *Harper's Weekly* while embedded with the Army of the Potomac.

The views from the second-floor piazza are the same as when Homer lived here. Gazing at the open Atlantic, listening to waves crash, gulls cry, and the wind rustling the trees, and maybe wrapped in the damp hush of fog, is perhaps the best place to begin to truly understand Homer's inspiration. After absorbing the view and walking to the oceanfront, you'll see the Homer works at the museum with a far deeper understanding of what made this genius tick.

Homer's ties with the Portland Museum of Art date back to his 1893 exhibition, which included *Signal of Distress.* On the centennial of Homer's death, the museum opened its Charles Shipman Payson wing, honoring the man who funded it and donated 17 paintings by the artist. In 2006, the museum acquired the **Winslow Homer Studio,** a National Historic Landmark, opening it to the public after a six-year project to restore it to its 1910 appearance. The **2.5-hour tours** ($55-65 adults, $25 students) are limited to 10 participants. They depart from the museum. Call or visit the website for the current schedule (207/775-6148, www.portlandmuseum.org). It's wise to make reservations well in advance.

depart from the museum and are limited to 10 participants.

★ Victoria Mansion

The jaws of first-time visitors drop when they enter the Italianate **Victoria Mansion** (109 Danforth St., 207/772-4841, http://victoriamansion.org, 10am-3:45pm daily May-Oct.), also called the Morse-Libby Mansion. It's widely considered the most magnificently ornamented dwelling of its period remaining in the country. The National Historic Landmark is rife with Victoriana: carved marble fireplaces, elaborate porcelain and paneling, a freestanding mahogany staircase, gilded glass chandeliers, and a restored 6- by 25-foot stained glass skylight. It retains more than 90 percent of its original interior, including almost all of Giuseppe Guidicini's unbelievable trompe l'oeil wall paintings. The museum offers two experiences, guided tours or your on own, with docents in various rooms. The schedule varies, so check online or call. It's even more spectacular during the holidays (late Nov.-early Jan., $16 adults, $14 seniors, $5 ages 6-17, $35 family), with yards of roping, festooned trees, and carolers; this is the best time to bring kids, as the house itself may not particularly intrigue them. Ruggles Sylvester Morse, a Maine-born entrepreneur, built the mansion in the late 1850s. He hired 93 craftspeople to complete it. The Gustave Herter-designed interior retains virtually all the original furnishings. Guided 45-minute tours begin every half hour on the quarter hour in season; tours are self-guided during the holidays.

★ Portland Observatory

Providing a head-swiveling view of Portland (and the White Mountains on a clear day), the octagonal red-painted **Portland Observatory** (138 Congress St., 207/774-5561, www.portlandlandmarks.org, 10am-4:30pm daily late May-mid-Oct., last tour at 4:30pm, $10 adults, $8 seniors, $5 ages 6-16, family $30) is the only remaining marine signal tower on the Eastern Seaboard. Built in 1807 at a cost of $5,000 by Captain Lemuel Moody to keep track of the port's shipping activity, the tower has 122 tons of rock ballast in its base. Admission in those days (when only men were allowed to climb the 103 interior steps) was 12.5 cents. Today, admission includes the small museum at the tower's base and a guided tour to the top. Ask about sunset tours.

Wadsworth-Longfellow House

A few blocks down Congress Street from the Portland Museum of Art, you can step back in time to the era of Portland-born poet Henry Wadsworth Longfellow, who lived in the carefully restored **Wadsworth-Longfellow House** (485 Congress St., 207/774-1822, www.mainehistory.org, 10am-5pm Mon.-Sat., noon-5pm Sun. June-Oct., noon-5pm daily May, $15 adults, $13 seniors and students, $4 ages 6-17, $35 family, rates include the museum). Longfellow was here as a child in the early 1800s, long before the brick mansion was dwarfed by surrounding high-rises. Wadsworth and Longfellow family furnishings fill the three-story house, which is owned by the Maine Historical Society. On 45-minute tours (call for times), savvy guides provide insight into Portland's 19th-century life. Don't miss the wonderfully peaceful garden behind the house, which is free to the public.

At the adjacent **Maine Historical Society Museum** ($8 adults, $7 seniors, $2 ages 6-17), you can take in exhibits chronicling five centuries of life in Maine and find an extensive collection of Maine history books in the gift shop. The center also offers 75-minute **historical walking tours** ($15 pp, call for schedule).

Maine Narrow Gauge Railroad Company and Museum

A three-mile ride along Portland's waterfront is the highlight of a visit to the **Maine Narrow Gauge Railroad Company and Museum** (58 Fore St., 207/828-0814, www.mngrr.org, 9:30am-4pm daily mid Apr.-late Oct., $5 adults, $4 seniors, $3 ages 3-12). The museum owns more than three dozen train cars and has others on long-term loan, most from Maine's five historic narrow-gauge railroads, the last of which closed in 1943. You can board a number of the cars and see others undergoing restoration. Train rides (10am-3pm daily, $10 adults, $9 seniors, $6 ages 3-12, includes museum admission) operate on the hour. The track edges Casco Bay along the Eastern Promenade, and the 35-minute ride is a real kid-pleaser. The museum also operates special excursions including ice cream trains, "rails and ales," and Polar Express trains.

1: Victoria Mansion **2:** statue of poet Henry Wadsworth Longfellow in Portland **3:** Portland Head Light

1
2
LONGFELLOW
3

Children's Museum & Theatre of Maine

Here's the answer to parents' prayers: an entire museum in downtown Portland catering to kids. The **Children's Museum & Theatre of Maine** (142 Free St., 207/828-1234, www.kitetails.com, 10am-5pm daily and 5pm-8pm 1st Fri. of month, closed Mon. during school year, $12.50, free for children under 18 months, $2 admission 5pm-8pm 1st Fri., $4 for Camera Obscura only) has lots of hands-on exhibits that encourage interaction and guarantee involvement for a couple of hours. The Camera Obscura, which provides panoramic views over Portland from a room with no windows, is a fun diversion for all ages. Note that the museum plans to move to a new home on Thomas Point as soon as construction is completed.

International Cryptozoology Museum

An eight-foot-tall likeness of a bigfoot greets visitors at former university professor and author Loren Coleman's **International Cryptozoology Museum** (4 Thompson's Point Rd., 207/518-9496, www.cryptozoologymuseum.com, 11am-6pm daily late May-early Sept., 11am-4pm Mon., Wed., and Sun., 11am-6pm Thurs.-Sat. early Sept.-late May., $10 adults, $8 seniors, $5 ages 12 and younger). Coleman is a renowned expert in cryptozoology, the story of hidden animals such as bigfoot, the Loch Ness monster, and the abominable snowman. He has amassed a collection of artifacts such as skulls and footprint castings that lend credence to the existence of these rumored beasts, as well as kitsch that includes movie props and souvenir memorabilia. This is always a big hit with kids.

Southworth Planetarium

Under a 30-foot dome with comfy theater seats and a state-of-the-art laser system, the **Southworth Planetarium** (Science Building, University of Southern Maine, 70 Falmouth St., 207/780-4249, www.usm.maine.edu/planet) presents astronomy shows, with ticket prices around $6. Take Exit 6B off I-295 and go west on Forest Avenue to Falmouth Street (a left turn). The Science Building is on the left past the parking lot.

Osher Map Library

The University of South Maine's **Osher Map Library** (314 Forest Ave., 207/780-4850, www.oshermaps.org, 10am-4pm Tues.-Wed. and Fri., 10am-8pm Thurs., 10am-2pm Sat., free) houses more than 300,000 maps, including works on cosmography, astronomy, navigation, geography, and history, as well as globes, atlases, books, and scientific instruments dating from the late 15th century. Exhibitions feature rare and historic works drawn from the collection. Bring a sweater; the air-conditioning is set for preservation standards. It's attached to the Albert Brenner Glickman Family Library.

Tate House

Just down the street from the Portland International Jetport, in the Stroudwater district, is the 1755 **Tate House** (1270 Westbrook St., 207/774-6177, www.tatehouse.org, 10am-4pm Wed.-Sat., 1pm-4pm Sun., last tour 3pm, June-Oct., $15 adults, $12 seniors, $7 ages 6-12), a National Historic Landmark owned by the Colonial Dames of America. Built by Captain George Tate, who was prominent in shipbuilding, the house overlooks the Stroudwater River and has superb period furnishings and a lovely 18th-century herb garden with more than 70 species. Tours, offered on the hour, last 40 minutes. Cellar-to-attic architecture tours ($18 adults, $10 children) are offered, and garden tours ($15 adults, $7 children) are available by advance reservation.

★ Portland Head Light

Just four miles from downtown Portland in Cape Elizabeth, Fort Williams feels a world away. This oceanfront town park, a former military base, is home to **Portland Head Light** (1000 Shore Rd., Cape Elizabeth,

Lighthouses Tour

Whether in a car or on a bike, it's easy to loop through South Portland and Cape Elizabeth on a lighthouse tour.

Begin just over the Casco Bay Bridge from downtown Portland on Route 77, take Broadway, and continue to Spring Point Marina, turning left at the stop sign and then right onto Madison Street to nine-acre Bug Light Park. A paved walkway leads to **Portland Breakwater Lighthouse,** also known as **Bug Light,** built in 1875. Also here is a memorial commemorating the Liberty ships built on this site during World War II. There's a plan to build an outdoor performing arts center adjacent to the park.

Retrace your route to Broadway and cross it, turning left on Fort Street until it ends at **Southern Maine Community College (SMCC),** overlooking the bay. The best time to come here is evenings and weekends, when there's ample parking. Unless it's foggy (when the signal is deafening) or thundering (when you'll expose yourself to lightning), walk out along the 9,000-foot granite breakwater to the **Spring Point Ledge Light** (207/699-2676, www.springpointlight.org), with fabulous views in every direction. Volunteers typically open it 11am-3pm Saturday and usually Sunday, mid-June-early September ($5; children must be at least 51 inches tall to enter the light). Also here are picnic benches, the remains of Fort Preble, and the **Spring Point Shoreway,** a scenic three-mile path with views to House, Peaks, and Cushings Islands. At the end of the path you'll reach crescent-shaped **Willard Beach,** a neighborhood spot with restrooms, a snack bar, and those same marvelous views.

From the SMCC campus, return on Broadway to the major intersection with Cottage Road and bear left. Cottage Road becomes Shore Road at the Cape Elizabeth town line. Loop into Fort Williams Park and make a pilgrimage to **Portland Head Light,** with **Ram Island Ledge Light** in the distance, before continuing on Shore Road to its intersection with Route 77. Bear left, following Route 77 to Two Lights Road, and follow the signs to 40-acre **Two Lights State Park.** Almost a pocket park, it has picnicking and restroom facilities, but its biggest asset is the panoramic ocean view from atop a onetime gun battery. Summer admission is $7 nonresident adults, $5 Maine resident adults, $2 nonresident seniors, $1 ages 5-11.

Before or after visiting the park, continue on Two Lights Road to the parking lot at the end, where you'll see the signal towers for which Two Lights is named. There's no access to either, and only one still works. If you haven't brought a picnic for the state park, there are few places finer to enjoy the view and a lobster than at the **Lobster Shack.**

207/799-2661, www.portlandheadlight.com, dawn-dusk daily). Commissioned by President George Washington and first lit in 1791, it has been immortalized in poetry, photography, and philately. The surf here is awesome—perhaps too awesome, as the *Annie C. Maguire* was shipwrecked below the lighthouse on Christmas Eve 1886. There's no access to the 58-foot automated light tower, but the restored keeper's house has become the **Museum at Portland Head Light** (10am-4pm daily late May-Oct., 10am-4pm Sat.-Sun. late spring and late fall, $2 adults, $1 ages 6-18). It's filled with local history and lighthouse memorabilia.

TOURS

Self-Guided Walking Tours

Pick up a copy of the free **Portland Freedom Trail map and brochure** (www.mainehistory.org) detailing 13 marked sights related to Portland's role in the Underground Railroad. Among the highlights are the Abyssinian Meeting House, the third-oldest African American meetinghouse still standing in the United States; the First Parish Unitarian Universalist Church, where abolitionist William Lloyd Garrison spoke in 1832; and Mariners' Church, the location of an antislavery bookstore and print shop that printed the first Afrocentric history of the world.

The **Portland Women's History Trail** (http://usm.maine.edu) details seven walks. Among the stops is the site of a long-gone chewing-gum factory where teenage girls worked 10-hour shifts. The trail intersects with two other detailed walking trails, both available online: the **Maine Irish Heritage Trail** (www.maineirishheritagetrail.org) and the **Portland Chinese-American Walking Tour** (http://cafammaine.org/portland-walking-tour).

TOP EXPERIENCE

Food and Beverage Tours

Want the story behind Maine's sustainably and responsibly sourced local fare? Join **Maine Food for Thought** (207/405-0482, www.mainefoodforthought.com) on its three-hour Land, Sea to Fork Tour ($79). You'll visit six noted in-town restaurants for a tasting course along with the story behind the ingredients. Tours meet at the first restaurant, cover about a mile of easy walking, and are limited to a maximum of 14 participants. The mid-afternoon A Toast to Maine Tour ($69-79) lasts 2.5 hours and visits five Old Port locations pairing local fare with land-to-bottle beverages.

Just as the name promises, **Maine Foodie Tours** (10 Moulton St., 207/233-7485, www.mainefoodietours.com, $50-145) delivers a taste of Maine with various two- to three-hour culinary- and beverage-focused walking tours, progressive dinners, and cruises.

Greater Portland has more than two dozen craft **breweries** (http://mainebrewersguild.org), **distilleries** (http://mainedistillersguild.org), **wineries** (www.mainewineryguild.com), and even a mead maker, **Maine Mead Works** (51 Washington Ave., 207/773-6323, www.mainemeadworks.com). Check the websites for current tour and tasting opportunities.

For a more thorough immersion into the local brew scene, book a tour with the **Maine Brew Bus** (207/200-9111, www.mainebrewbus.com, from $65). Minimum age is 21 (ID required).

You'd rather sip wine? Step out on a guided two-hour educational wine walk (from $65) or cruise (from $85) with sommelier Erica Archer of **Wine Wise** (207/619-4630, www.winewiseevents.com).

Nonesuch (www.nonesuchoysters.com, $65) offers two-hour oyster tasting tours aboard the *Oys-Tour*. Participants depart from Pine Point, Scarborough, to visit the oyster nursery and the grow-out site, harvesting and shucking a half dozen to enjoy.

Land-and-Sea Tours

Various commercial operators offer area land-and-sea tours, but frankly, none is first-rate. Guides on each often present incorrect information. Still, such tours are a good way to get the city's general layout. The best of the lot is the 1.75-hour narrated Portland City and Lighthouse Tour in a trolley-bus operated by **Portland Discovery Land and Sea Tours** (Long Wharf, 207/774-0808, www.portlanddiscovery.com, $30 adults, $20 children).

ENTERTAINMENT

The best places to find out what's playing at area theaters, cinemas, concert halls, and nightclubs are the *Portland Phoenix* (www.portlandphoenix.me) and the *Go* supplement in the Thursday edition of the *Portland Press Herald* (www.mainetoday.com). Both have online listings; hard copies are available at bookstores and supermarkets. The *Phoenix* is free.

Nightlife

BREWPUBS AND BARS

Portland is a beer town, with an ever-increasing number of microbreweries and brewpubs, many of which also offer food and/or entertainment. Ask locally for the current hot spots. It's also vigilant about enforcing alcohol laws, so bring valid identification. Bars close at 1am.

Not only is **Gritty's** (396 Fore St., Old

Port, 207/772-2739, www.grittys.com) one of Maine's most popular breweries, but its brewpub was the state's first, having opened in 1988. It serves classic pub fare, and often has live entertainment. Gritty's also has a branch in Freeport.

Far newer on the scene is **Little Tap House** (106 High St., 207/747-4089, www.littletaphouse.com), a gastropub with 14 rotating, Maine-centric taps and a farm-to-table menu.

Beer geeks, here's your happy place: Family-friendly **Novare Res Bier Café** (4 Canal Plaza, 207/761-2437, www.novareresbiercafe.com) carries more than 400 bottled beers from around the world and has more than 33 rotating taps. Pair them with selections from the meat-and-cheese bar, sandwiches, or small plates.

Especially popular in the late afternoon and early evening is **J's Oyster** (5 Portland Pier, 207/772-4828, http://jsoysterportland.com), a longtime fixture (some might call it a dive) on the waterfront known for its raw bar and for pouring a good drink.

Of all Portland's neighborhood hangouts, **Ruski's** (212 Danforth St., 207/774-7604), dating from 1892, is the most authentic—a small, usually crowded onetime speakeasy that rates just as highly for breakfast as for nighttime schmoozing. Expect basic homemade fare for under $10, plus darts and a big-screen TV. Dress down or you'll feel out of place.

Other dress-down neighborhood bars are **Rosie's** (330 Fore St., 207/772-5656, www.rosies-oldport.com) and **Blackstones** (6 Pine St., 207/775-2885, www.blackstones.com), Portland's oldest neighborhood gay bar.

West of I-295, the **Great Lost Bear** (540 Forest Ave., 207/772-0300, www.greatlostbear.com) has 78 brews on tap, representing more than 45 Maine microbreweries plus others from the Northeast. The bear motif and the punny menus are a bit much, but the scratch-made pub fare is very good. It's a kid-pleaser.

WINE AND COCKTAILS

For upscale tippling, where bartenders are elevated to mixologists noted for creative concoctions, head for **Hunt & Alpine** (75 Market St., 207/747-4754, www.huntandalpineclub.com), the **Bearded Lady's Jewel Box** (644 Congress St., 207/747-5384), **Blythe & Barrows** (26 Exchange St., 207/613-9070, www.blythandburrows.com), or the **Top of the East** (157 High St., 207/775-5411), a glass-walled lounge with divine sunset views topping the Westin Hotel.

The **Bramhall** (769 Congress St., 207/805-1978, www.bramhallme.com) and the **Independent Ice Co.** (52 Wharf St., 207/956-7150, https://independentice.com) are especially good choices for whiskey connoisseurs.

Vena's Fizz House (345 Fore St., 207/591-4901, https://venasfizzhouse.com) is equal parts mixology shop—specializing in all-natural fizz sodas—and bar serving cocktails and mocktails made with bitters, shrubs, and switchels. If you like what you drink, you can get the ingredients and the recipe.

Gamers, **Arcadia National Bar** (24 Preble St., 207/747-4958) is your happy place, with pinball and arcade along with craft beer and cocktails and contemporary comfort foods.

It takes persistence to find **Lincolns** (36 Market St., no phone, cash only), a speakeasy on Market Street.

Distillery, brewery, restaurant, bar: **Liquid Riot** (250 Commercial St., 207/221-8889, http://liquidriot.com) offers it all.

Order at the bar at **Maine Craft Distilling** (123 Washington Ave., 207/699-4447, https://mainecraftdistilling.com), which offers cocktails made with its spirits, local craft beers, and small plates.

Lio (3 Spring St., 207/808-7133, www.lio-maine.com) offers 32 wines by the half or full glass, as well as cocktails and a nice menu, allowing you to experiment to find the perfect pairing.

MJ's Wine Bar (1 City Center, 207/772-1400, www.onecitywines.com) often has live music.

The **Drifters Wife** (59 Washington Ave., 207/805-1336, www.drifterswife.com) sells and serves all-natural wines.

Wine? Martini? Dessert? Find it all at **Bar of Chocolate** (38 Wharf St., 207/773-6667). To all that, add cheese and charcuterie at **Gross Confection Bar** (172 Middle St., 207/956-7208, http://grossconfections.com).

LIVE MUSIC AND CLUBS

Scope out the scene when you arrive; the *Portland Phoenix* has the best listings. Most clubs have cover charges. The coolest venue with the hottest acts is **Port City Music Hall** (504 Congress St., 207/899-4990, www.portcitymusichall.com), a three-floor entertainment emporium. **Geno's Rock Club** (625 Congress St., 207/221-2382) has been at it for years, with an emphasis on local bands. **Blue** (650 Congress St., 207/774-4111, www.portcityblue.com) presents local artists and musicians in an intimate, cozy space; traditional Irish music is always featured on Wednesday evening, and jazz on Saturday. Enjoy traditional pub food at **Andy's Old Port Pub** (94 Commercial St., 207/874-2639, http://andysoldportpub.com) while enjoying live acoustic music every night.

Check to see who's playing at **Portland House of Music** (25 Temple St., 207/805-0134, www.portlandhouseofmusic.com), **Empire Live Music & Events** (575 Congress St., 2nd fl., 207/558-2279, http://venue.portlandempire.com), which also hosts an open mic on Mondays, or **Aura** (121 Center St., 207/772-8274, http://aura-maine.com).

Dance club, dive bar, antiques museum? **Bubba's Sulky Lounge** (92 Portland St., 207/828-0549, www.bubbassulkylounge.com) is all that and more. Don your jumpsuit for '80s night on Fridays, when disco pulses on the lighted dance floor, or for the Everything Dance Party on Saturdays, with a DJ, but don't miss checking out all the retro kitsch.

Performing Arts

CONCERT SERIES

The Portland Conservatory of Music presents free weekly **Noonday Concerts** (207/773-5747, www.portlandconservatory.org) at 12:15pm on first Thursdays (First Parish Church, 425 Congress St.) and third Thursdays (Portland Public library, 5 Monument Sq.) October-early April. The music varies widely—perhaps jazz, classical, or choral.

Waterfront Concerts (207/358-9327, www.waterfrontconcerts.com) presents outdoor concerts and events at various Greater Portland venues.

Portland Parks and Recreation sponsors **Summer in the Parks** (207/756-8275, July-Aug., free), an evening concert series and a midday kids' performance series in downtown parks.

Take the ferry to Peaks Island for **Reggae Sundays** (late May to early Sept.) on the deck at Jones Landing (at the ferry landing, Peaks Island, 207/766-4400).

MERRILL AUDITORIUM

The magnificently restored **Merrill Auditorium** (20 Myrtle St., box office 207/874-8200, www.porttix.com) is a 1,900-seat theater inside Portland City Hall on Congress Street, with two balconies and one of the country's only municipally owned pipe organs, the recently restored **Kotzschmar Organ** (207/553-4363, www.foko.org); guided organ tours are offered during the concert season.

Special events and concerts are common at Merrill, and the auditorium is also home to a number of the city's arts organizations. The **Portland Symphony Orchestra** (207/842-0800, www.portlandsymphony.org) and presenting organization **Portland Ovations** (207/773-3150, www.portlandovations.org) have extensive, well-patronized fall and winter schedules; the PSO presents three summer Independence Pops concerts as well. **Opera Maine** (207/879-7678, https://

operamaine.com) performs a major opera each summer.

Tickets for these organizations are available through **PortTix** (207/942-0800, www.porttix.com).

ONE LONGFELLOW SQUARE

Diverse programming is the hallmark of **One Longfellow Square** (207/761-1757, www.onelongfellowsquare.com), an intimate venue for performances and lectures at the corner of Congress and State Streets.

STATE THEATRE

The **State Theatre** (609 Congress St., 207/956-6000, www.statetheatreportland.com), built in 1929 with art deco, Spanish, and Italian decor elements, hosts national touring artists as well as up-and-comers. The State also presents concerts at **Thompson's Point** (www.thompsonspointmaine.com), an outdoor venue edging the Fore River.

PORTLAND STAGE COMPANY

Innovative staging and controversial contemporary dramas are typical of the **Portland Stage Company** (Portland Performing Arts Center, 25A Forest Ave., 207/774-0465, www.portlandstage.org), established in 1974 and going strong ever since. Equity pros present half a dozen plays each winter season in a 290-seat performance space.

Festivals and Events

Summer brings plentiful events, including the **Old Port Festival,** one of the city's largest festivals, usually the first weekend of June. It has entertainment, food and crafts booths, and impromptu fun in Portland's Old Port. The **Greek Heritage Festival,** usually the last weekend of June, features Greek food, dancing, and crafts at Holy Trinity Church (133 Pleasant St.).

Some of the world's top runners join upward of 500 racers in the **Beach to Beacon Race,** held in late July-early August. The 10K course goes from Crescent Beach State Park to Portland Head Light in Cape Elizabeth.

In mid-August the **Italian Street Festival** showcases music, Italian food, and games at St. Peter's Catholic Church (72 Federal St.). Artists from all over the country set up in 350 booths along Congress Street for the annual **Sidewalk Arts Festival** in late August.

The big October wingding is the **Harvest on the Harbor,** a celebration of all things food- and wine-related with tastings, dinners, exhibits, and special events.

The **Maine Brewers' Festival** in November highlights Maine microbreweries. From Thanksgiving weekend to Christmas Eve, **Victorian Holiday** in downtown Portland harks back with caroling, special sales, concerts, a tree lighting, horse-drawn wagons, and Victoria Mansion tours and festivities.

SHOPPING

The Portland peninsula is thick with non-cookie-cutter shops and galleries. The Old Port/Waterfront and Arts District have the highest concentrations, but more and more shops are opening on the East End.

Bookstores

Longfellow Books (1 Monument Way, 207/772-4045) sells new and used books and hosts readings. **Carlson-Turner Books** (241 Congress St., 207/773-4200 or 800/540-7323) and **YES Books** (589 Congress St., 207/775-3233) sell used and rare books. **Print: A Bookstore** (273 Congress St., 207/536-4778, www.printbookstore.com) opened in 2016, proving print is not dead. Pick up a good used read at the **Green Hand** (661 Congress St., 207/253-6808).

Art Galleries

A great way to discover Portland's visual art scene is on the **First Friday Artwalk** (www.creativemaine.com), when in-town galleries host exhibition openings, open houses, meet-the-artist gatherings, and related activities.

Casco Bay Artisans (68 Commercial St., 207/536-1577, http://cascobayartisans.com) represents more than 70 artists from around the world with a focus on Maine. **Greenhut Galleries** (146 Middle St., 207/772-2693, www.greenhutgalleries.com) specializes in contemporary Maine art and sculpture. More than 15 Maine potters—with a wide variety of styles and items—market their wares at the **Maine Potters Market** (376 Fore St., 207/774-1633, www.mainepottersmarket.com).

Specialty Shops

Check out the latest home accessories from Maine-based designer **Angela Adams** (71 Cove St., 800/255-9454).

SOST Linen (5 South St., 774/234-7678) is a must for locally designed and made linen clothing and home wares.

Sea Bags (25 Custom House Wharf, 207/780-0744, http://seabags.com) turns high-performance sails into fashionable bags and totes.

Portland Trading Co. (83 Market St., 207/899-0228, www.portlandtradingco.com) calls itself a general store for modern times, and it's hard to disagree. It's got a bit of this, a little of that, all of it enticing.

For exquisite leather bags crafted in Maine, don't miss **Rough and Tumble** (127 Middle St., 207/808-5042, https://roughandtumbledesign.com). Maine designer **Jill McGowan** (167 Exchange St., 207/772-2199, www.jillmcgowan.com) gained national recognition with her great white shirt; find that and other women's fashions here. Part store, part workroom, **Ferdinand** (243 Congress St., 207/761-2151, http://ferdinandhomestore.com) is chock-full of eclectic finds, including screen prints, jewelry, vintage clothing, and cards created on the owner's letterpress.

The company store for **Planet Dog** (211 Marginal Way, 207/347-8606, www.planetdog.com) is a howling good time for dogs and their owners. You'll find all sorts of wonderful products, and Planet Dog, whose motto is to "think globally and act doggedly," has established a foundation to promote and serve causes such as training dogs for therapy, service, search and rescue, bomb sniffing, and police duty.

RECREATION

Parks, Preserves, and Beaches

Greater Portland is blessed with green space, thanks largely to the efforts of 19th-century mayor James Phinney Baxter, who had the foresight to hire the famed Olmsted brothers to develop an ambitious plan to ring the city with public parks and promenades. Not all the elements fell into place, but the result contributes to what makes Portland such a livable city.

TRAIL NETWORK

Portland Trails (305 Commercial St., 207/775-2411, www.trails.org), a nonprofit land trust, is dedicated to maintaining a 70-mile network of hiking and biking trails in Greater Portland. It has mapped more than 35, including the 2.1-mile Eastern Promenade Trail, a landscaped bayfront dual pathway circling the base of Munjoy Hill and linking East End Beach to the Old Port. A continuing trail connects the Eastern Prom with the 3.5-mile Back Cove Trail, on the other side of I-295. Trail maps are available on the website. Better still, join Portland Trails ($35/year) and support its ambitious efforts.

DOWNTOWN PENINSULA

Probably the most visible of the city's parks, 51-acre **Deering Oaks** (Park Ave. between Forest Ave. and Deering Ave.) is best known for the quaint little duck condo in the middle of the pond. Other facilities and highlights here are tennis courts, a playground, horseshoes, rental paddleboats, a snack bar, the award-winning Rose Circle, a farmers market (7am-noon Sat.), and, in winter, ice-skating. After dark, steer clear of the park.

At one end of the Eastern Promenade, where it meets Fore Street, **Fort Allen Park** overlooks offshore Fort Gorges (coin-operated telescopes bring it closer). A central gazebo is flanked by an assortment of military souvenirs dating as far back as the War of 1812. All along the Eastern Prom are walking paths, benches, play areas, and even an ill-maintained fitness trail—all with that terrific view. Down by the water is **East End Beach,** with parking, some token sand, and the area's best launching ramp for sea kayaks or powerboats. Friends of the Eastern Promenade (www.easternpromenade.org) helps restore and preserve the landscape and sponsors a **free summer concert series** on Thursday evenings as well as the annual **Hidden Gardens of Munjoy Hill** tour in July.

WEST OF THE DOWNTOWN PENINSULA

Looping around tidal **Back Cove** is a 3.5-mile trail for walking, jogging, cycling, or just watching the sailboards and the skyline. Along the way, you can cross Baxter Boulevard and spend time picnicking, playing tennis, or flying a kite in 48-acre **Payson Park,** where parking is available.

The 85-acre **Fore River Sanctuary** (sunrise-sunset daily), managed by Portland Trails, has two miles of blue-blazed trails that wind through a salt marsh, link with the historic Cumberland and Oxford Canal towpath, and pass near **Jewell Falls,** Portland's only waterfall. From downtown Portland, take Congress Street West (Rte. 22) past I-295 to the Maine Orthopedic Center parking lot at the corner of Frost; park in the far corner.

Listed in the National Register of Historic Places, 239-acre **Evergreen Cemetery** (672 Stevens Ave., 207/797-4597, www.friendsofevergreen.org) is Portland's largest urban space. Begun in the mid-1850s and modeled after Mount Auburn Cemetery in Cambridge, Massachusetts, it's an excellent example of the garden cemetery favored by 19th-century romantics. You'll find tree-lined paths, hiking trails, ponds, vistas, and plenty of history. Docents offer **historical walking tours** (call for current schedule, free), or you can download a map and explore on your own. In May, bird-watchers flock here to see warblers, thrushes, and other migratory birds. During peak periods it's possible to see as many as 20 warbler species in a morning, including the Cape May, bay-breasted, mourning, and Tennessee. Naturalists from Maine Audubon often are on-site to help with identification.

CAPE ELIZABETH

Fort Williams (www.fortwilliamspark.com), a 90-acre, town-owned oceanfront park on the site of a former military base, offers much more to explore beyond Portland Head Light. Walk the trails, explore the ruins of the Goddard Mansion, prowl through fortifications, meander through the young arboretum, play tennis, or dip your toes into the surf at the rocky beach. Warning: There's a strong undertow here. The grassy headlands are great places to watch the boat traffic going in and out of Portland Harbor. Bring a picnic lunch or purchase food from one of the food trucks—and don't forget a kite. Admission is free, but pay-and-display metered parking (8am-5pm May-Nov. 1, $2/hour, $10 full day, $15 season) is charged at the most popular areas.

Crescent Beach State Park (Rte. 77, www.parksandlands.com, $8 nonresident adults, $6.50 Maine resident adults, $1 ages 5-11), a 243-acre park with a mile-long beach, changing rooms, a lifeguard, restrooms, picnic tables, and a snack bar, is a favorite with families.

SCARBOROUGH

Scarborough Beach Park (Black Point Rd./Rte. 207, 207/883-2416, www.scarboroughbeachstatepark.com, $6-8 adults, $4-5 children), a long stretch of sand, is the best beach for big waves. Between the parking area and the lovely beach, you'll pass Massacre Pond, named for a 1703 skirmish between resident Native Americans and would-be settlers. The park is open all year for swimming, surfing (permit required), beachcombing, and ice-skating, but on weekends in summer the parking lot fills early. Lifeguards are on duty on sunny days from mid-June to early

September. Rental chairs, umbrellas, and boogie boards as well as surfboards, SUPs, and kayaks are available.

At 3,100 acres, **Scarborough Marsh** (92 Pine Point Rd./Rte. 9, 207/883-5100, www.maineaudubon.org, 9:30am-5pm daily mid-June-early Sept., 9:30am-5:30pm Sat.-Sun. late May and Sept.), Maine's largest salt marsh, is prime territory for bird-watching and canoeing. Rent a canoe (from $20 for 1 hour) at the small nature center operated by Maine Audubon and explore on your own. Other special programs, some geared toward children, include guided bird-watching and wildflower walks and art classes; all require reservations and have reasonable fees. Also here is a walking-tour trail of less than one mile. Pick up a map at the center.

Overlooking the marsh is 52-acre **Scarborough River Wildlife Sanctuary** (Pine Point Rd./Rte. 9), with 1.5 miles of walking trails that loop to the Scarborough River and past two ponds.

FALMOUTH

A 65-acre wildlife sanctuary and environmental center on the banks of the Presumpscot River, **Gilsland Farm** (20 Gilsland Farm Rd., 207/781-2330, www.maineaudubon.org, dawn-dusk daily) is the state headquarters for Maine Audubon. More than two miles of easy, well-marked trails wind through the grounds, taking in salt marshes, rolling meadows, woodlands, and views of the estuary. Observation blinds allow inconspicuous spying during bird-migration season. In the **education center** (9am-4pm Mon.-Fri., 10am-4pm Sat., noon-4pm Sun.) are hands-on exhibits, a nature store, and classrooms and offices. Fees are charged for special events, but otherwise it's all free. The center is 0.25 mile off Route 1.

Once the summer compound of the prominent Baxter family, Falmouth's 100-acre **Mackworth Island** (sunrise-sunset daily year-round, $4 adults, $1 ages 3-11), reached via a causeway, is now the site of the Governor Baxter School for the Deaf. Limited parking is just beyond the security booth on the island. On the 1.25-mile vehicle-free perimeter path, which has great Portland Harbor views, you'll meet bikers, hikers, and dog walkers. Just off the trail on the north side of the island is the late governor Percival Baxter's stone-circled pet cemetery, maintained by the state at the behest of Baxter, who donated this island (as well as Baxter State Park) to the people of Maine. From downtown Portland, take Route 1 across the Presumpscot River to Falmouth Foreside. Andrews Avenue (the third street on the right) leads to the island.

Bicycling

The **Bicycle Coalition of Maine** (207/623-4511, www.bikemaine.org) has an excellent website with info on trails, events, organized rides, bike shops, and more. Another good resource is **Casco Bay Bicycle Club** (www.cascobaybicycleclub.org), a recreational cycling club with rides several times weekly. Check the website for details.

For rentals (from $30/day hybrid, $75/day e-bike) and repairs, visit **Cycle Mania** (65 Cove St., 207/774-2933, www.cyclemania1.com).

View five lighthouses and enjoy a fancy lunch on a half-day tour with **Summer Feet Cycling Adventure** (866/857-9544, www.summerfeet.net, $99). Summer Feet offers plenty of other options, from full-day to week-long trips, including self-guided bicycling tours for which it makes all arrangements and moves luggage. Sister company the **Portland EnCYCLEpedia** (www.portlandmainebike-rental.com) rents bicycles, from $20 half day, and you don't need to book a trip to rent one.

The best locales for island bicycling—fun for families and beginners but not especially challenging for diehards—are Peaks and Great Chebeague Islands, but do remember to follow the rules of the road.

1: Spring Point Ledge Light **2:** shops along the Old Port and Waterfront **3:** Standard Baking Company **4:** State Theatre

1

LeRoux
Kitchen
KITCHENWARE
WINE
2

3
THE STANDARD BAKING CO.
75

4
STATE

Golf

Public courses are plentiful in Greater Portland, but you'll need an "in" to play the private ones. Free advice on helping you choose a course is offered by **Golf Maine** (www.golfme.com).

Sable Oaks Golf Club (505 Country Club Dr., South Portland, 207/775-6257, www.sableoaks.com) is considered one of the toughest and best of Maine's public courses. Since 1998, **Nonesuch River Golf Club** (304 Gorham Rd./Rte. 114, Scarborough, 207/883-0007 or 888/256-2717, www.nonesuchgolf.com) has been drawing raves for the challenges of its par-70 championship course and praise from environmentalists for preserving wildlife habitat; there's also a full-size practice range and green. The City of Portland's **Riverside Municipal Golf Course** (1158 Riverside St., 207/797-3524) has an 18-hole par-72 course (Riverside North) and a 9-hole par-35 course (Riverside South). Opt for the 18-hole course.

Sea Kayaking

With all the islands scattered through Casco Bay, Greater Portland is a sea-kayaking hotbed. The best place to start is out on Peaks Island, 15 minutes offshore via the Casco Bay Lines ferry. **Maine Island Kayak Company** (MIKCO, 70 Luther St., Peaks Island, 207/766-2373, www.maineislandkayak.com) organizes half-day, all-day, and multiday local kayaking trips as well as national and international adventures. An introductory half-day tour in Casco Bay is $70 pp; a full day is $115 pp and includes lunch; sunset trips are $70 pp. Reservations are essential. MIKCO also does private lessons and group courses and clinics (some require previous experience).

TOP EXPERIENCE

★ Lobstering Cruise

Learn all kinds of lobster lore and maybe even catch your own dinner with **Lucky Catch Lobster Tours** (170 Commercial St., 207/233-2026 or 888/624-6321, www.luckycatch.com, $35 adults, $33 seniors, $30 ages 13-18, $20 ages 2-12). Captain Tom Martin offers five different 80-90-minute cruises on his 37-foot lobster boat. On each cruise (except late Sat. and all day Sun.), usually 10 traps are hauled and then processed, and gear is explained. You can even help if you want. Any lobsters caught are available for purchase after the cruise for wholesale boat price (and you can have them cooked nearby for a reasonable rate). Wouldn't that make a nice story to tell the folks back home?

Boat Excursions and Water Taxis

The Old Port wharves are home to several excursion-boat businesses. Each has carved out a niche, so choose according to your interest and schedule. Dress warmly and wear rubber-soled shoes. Remember that all cruises are weather-dependent.

Portland Discover—Land & Sea Tours (Long Wharf, 170 Commercial St., 207/774-0808, www.portlanddiscovery.com) offers a Harbor Lights and Sights Cruise, a Lighthouse Lovers Cruise, and a Sunset Lighthouse Cruise ($19-29 adults, $14-20 ages 3-12).

For a more intimate experience, book a cruise aboard the ***Casco Bay Explorer*** (Long Wharf, 170 Commercial St., 207/775-0727, http://explorecascobay.com), an open boat that holds a maximum of 20 passengers. Options include a 75-minute trip to explore Fort Gorges ($32), a 45-minute seal-watching excursion ($22), and a 50-minute tour of forts and lighthouses ($24).

Cruise up to 20 miles offshore seeking whales with **Odyssey Whale Watch** (Long Wharf, 170 Commercial St., 207/775-0727, www.odysseywhalewatch.com, $49 adults, $39 children 12 and under, $19 infants). Four- to five-hour whale watches aboard the *Odyssey* depart daily from May to early October as well as on spring and fall weekends. (Go easy on breakfast that day, and take preventive measures if you're motion-sensitive.)

Sail quietly across the waters of Casco Bay aboard a windjammer with **Portland**

Schooner Company (Maine State Pier, 56 Commercial St., 207/766-2500, www.portlandschooner.com, late May-Oct., $46 adults, $30 age 12 and under). Two-hour sails are offered daily on three schooners: the 72-foot *Bagheera,* the 88-foot *Wendameen,* and the *Timberwind,* all built in Maine and listed in the National Register of Historic Places.

Create your own itinerary or cruise to a restaurant or other destination aboard a water taxi; prices vary by distance and time. Two offering taxi and charter are **Fogg's Boatworks** (207/232-9609, www.foggsboatwork.com) and **Portland Harbor Water Tours** (207/200-8691, www.portlandharborwatertours.com).

Spectator Sports

A pseudo-fierce mascot named Slugger stirs up the crowds at baseball games played by the **Portland Sea Dogs** (Hadlock Field, 271 Park Ave., 207/879-9500 or 800/936-3647, www.portlandseadogs.com, $9-15), a Class AA affiliate of the Boston Red Sox. The season schedule (early Apr.-Aug.) is available after January 1.

The home court for the **Maine Red Claws** (207/210-6655, www.maineredclaws.com, $8-32), an NBA G League development team for the Boston Celtics, is the **Portland Expo** (239 Park Ave.).

The **Maine Mariners** (207/775-3458, http://marinersofmaine.com, $18-28), an ECHL league hockey team, plays at the **Cross Insurance Arena** (1 Civic Center Sq.).

TOP EXPERIENCE

FOOD

In 2018, *Bon Appétit* named Portland "Restaurant City of the Year." Nine years earlier, the magazine had named Portland "America's Foodiest Small Town." To call Portland a foodie town is an understatement; it's a culinary destination. The downtown alone has more than 100 restaurants, so it's impossible to list even all the great ones—and there are many, with new ones popping up frequently. The city's proximity to fresh foods from both farms and the sea makes it popular with chefs, and its growing immigrant population means it's a good choice for ethnic dining too. If you're especially into the food scene, check www.portlandfoodmap.com, which tracks openings and closures and links to reviews. It also lists the city's food trucks and carts, numbering more than three dozen at last check.

You can also check the "Community News" listings in each Wednesday's *Portland Press Herald.* Under "Potluck," you'll find listings of **public meals,** usually benefiting nonprofit organizations. Prices are always quite low (under $10 for adults, $2-4 for children), mealtimes quite early (5pm or 6pm), and the flavor local.

When you need a java fix, **Coffee by Design** (620 Congress St. and 67 India St., 207/879-2233) is the popular local choice, not only for its fine brews but also for its support of local artists and community causes.

The **Portland Farmers Market** sets up on Wednesdays on Monument Square and on Saturdays in Deering Oaks Park.

Here is a choice selection of restaurants, by neighborhood, with open days and hours provided for peak season. Some don't list a closing time—that's because they shut the doors when the crowd thins.

The Old Port and the Waterfront

If there is a cruise ship in port, avoid restaurants clustered in the heart of the waterfront during lunch. These venues are west of Franklin Street between Congress and Commercial Streets.

SEAFOOD AND LOBSTER

Sam Hayward put Portland on the foodie map by winning Maine's first James Beard Award in 2004. His newest endeavor is **Scales** (68 Commercial St./Maine Wharf, 207/805-0444, www.scalesrestaurant.com, from 5pm daily, $16-40), a harbor-front seafood emporium. The emphasis is on traditional New England favorites, such as steamed or roasted lobster, fresh Gulf of Maine fish, a raw bar, and fried oysters and clams, as well as killer chowders and lobster rolls, all prepared with skilled precision and beautifully presented.

Fresh, beautifully prepared fish, often with a Mediterranean flair, is what you get at **Street and Company** (33 Wharf St., 207/775-0887, www.streetandcompany.net, from 5:30pm daily, $24-40). Tables are tight, and it's often noisy in the informal brick-walled rooms. A third of the tables are held for walk-in diners.

For lobster in the rough, head to **Portland Lobster Company** (180 Commercial St., 207/775-2112, www.portlandlobstercompany.com, 11am-10pm daily). There's a small inside seating area, but it's much more pleasant to sit out on the wharf and watch the excursion boats come and go. Expect to pay in the low $20 range for a one-pound lobster with fries and slaw. Other choices (from $8) and a kids' menu are available.

QUICK BITES

Chocoholics take note: When a craving strikes, head to **Dean's Sweets** (475 Fore St. and 55 Cove St., 207/899-3664) for refined dark-chocolate truffles made without nuts.

Best known for serving the earliest and most filling breakfast around, **Becky's Diner** (390 Commercial St., 207/773-7070, www.beckysdiner.com, 4am-9pm daily) also serves lunch and dinner, all at downright cheap prices.

For gourmet goodies, don't miss **Browne Trading Market** (262 Commercial St., 207/775-7560, 10am-6pm Mon.-Fri., 10am-5pm Sat.). Fresh fish and shellfish fill the cases next to the caviar and cheeses. The mezzanine is literally wall-to-wall wine, specializing in French varietals.

When you're craving carbs, want pastries for breakfast, or need to boost your energy with a sweet, follow your nose to **Standard Baking Company** (75 Commercial St., 207/773-2112, 7am-6pm Mon.-Fri., 7am-5pm Sat.-Sun.), deservedly famous for its handcrafted breads and pastries.

Maple bacon, dark chocolate sea salt, pomegranate, and Allen's Coffee Brandy are just a few of the Maine potato doughnut flavors available at the **Holy Donut** (77 Exchange St., 207/775-7776, https://theholydonut.com, 7am-4pm Mon.-Thurs., 7am-8pm Fri.-Sat., 7am-5pm Sun.).

FAMILY FAVORITES

Enjoy all-natural wood-oven pizza with a harbor view at **Flatbread Company** (72 Commercial St., 207/772-8777, www.flatbreadcompany.com, 11am-9pm Sun.-Thurs., 11am-10pm Fri.-Sat.), part of a small New England chain. Vegan options are available.

Dine aboard a former ferry at **DiMillo's** (25 Long Wharf, 207/772-2216, www.dimillos.com, from 11am daily, $23-33), which has been in biz in one form or another since the late Tony DiMillo opened it in 1954. Still run by his family, this floating restaurant pleases guests with a well-executed, seafood-heavy American menu, great views of the city's working waterfront, and free on-site parking while dining.

CASUAL DINING

Central Provisions (414 Fore St., 207/805-1085, www.central-provisions.com, 11am-10pm daily, $8-24) has earned national kudos for its creative and fresh approach to small-plate dining. Upstairs is an open kitchen with counter seating as well as tables; downstairs is a bar serving Prohibition-era cocktails. The mix-and-match menu offers raw, cold, hot, and sweet preparations.

Plan well in advance to land a reservation at ★ **Fore Street** (288 Fore St., 207/775-2717, www.forestreet.biz, 5:30pm-10pm Sun.-Thurs., 5:30pm-10:30pm Fri.-Sat., entrées from $20). Chef Sam Hayward, renowned for his passionate and creative use of Maine-sourced ingredients, won the James Beard Award for Best Chef in the Northeast in 2004 and has been featured in many foodie publications. Hayward excels at elevating simple foods to rave-worthy dishes. The renovated former warehouse has copper-topped tables, an open kitchen, and industrial-chic decor—but quiet it's not. Those without reservations can show up early to try to land one of the few unreserved tables.

Executive chef Josh Berry presides over the open kitchen at **Union Restaurant** (119 Exchange St., 207/808-8700, www.unionportland.com, 7am-10pm daily, $20-34), sited in the Press Hotel. The menu gives local fare a contemporary spin. Both kids and vegetarian menus are available.

Chef-entrepreneur Harding Lee Smith's the **Grill Room** (84 Exchange St., 207/774-2333, www.thegrillroomandbar.com, 11:30am-2:30pm Mon.-Sat. and from 5pm daily, $21-45) turns out excellent wood-grilled meats and seafood.

INTERNATIONAL

Tiqa (327 Commercial St., 207/808-8840, http://tiqa.net, from 11am Mon.-Sat., 10am-3pm and 5-9pm Sun., $18-34), a light and bright contemporary restaurant, serves farm-fresh pan-Mediterranean fare. Think pasta and kebabs in addition to dishes from southern Europe and the Middle East.

Pasta doesn't get much more authentic than that served at **Paciarino** (470 Fore St., 207/774-3500, www.paciarino.com, 11:30am-2:30pm Mon.-Fri. and 6pm-8:30pm daily, $15-22). Owners Fabiana De Savino and Enrico Barbiero moved here from Milan in 2008, and they make their pastas and sauces fresh daily using recipes from De Savino's *nonna*.

Paolo Laboa, chef-owner of **Solo Italiano** (100 Commercial St., 207/780-0227, www.soloitalianorestaurant.com, from 5pm daily, $25-40) and winner of the 2008 Pesto World Championship, learned Genoese cooking from his mother. His handkerchief pasta with pesto is sublime.

Petite Jacqueline (46 Market St., 207/553-7044, www.bistropj.com, 11am-3pm Mon.-Fri., 10am-3pm Sat.-Sun., from 5pm nightly, $19-26) has earned national accolades for its authentic French bistro cuisine.

Chef Damian Sansonetti arrived in Portland with a distinguished pedigree, and he's living up to expectations with his rustic, authentic central and southern Italian fare at ★ **Piccolo** (111 Middle St., 207/747-5307, www.piccolomaine.com, 5pm-10pm Wed.-Sun., $19-28). Expect a fabulous, leisurely meal professionally served. The restaurant only seats 20, so reservations are a must. On Sundays it also serves a six-course tasting menu ($75) at 6:30pm, limited to six guests. Sansonetti's wife, Ilma Lopez, has earned a Beard nomination for her pastries, so don't skip dessert.

Sushi approaches an art form at **Miyake** (468 Fore St., 207/871-9170, www.miyakerestaurants.com, 11:30am-2pm Mon.-Sat. and 5:30pm-9pm daily). Trained in both French and classical Japanese techniques, chef Masa Miyake has developed a following far beyond Maine for his innovative sushi crafted from primarily local ingredients, including vegetables, fowl, and pork raised on his farm. A four-course tasting menu is $62, the omakase chef's tasting menu is $78, a three-course vegetarian omakase is $35, and à la carte options are $14-19.

East End

These dining spots are all east of Franklin Street, with many on or around Washington Avenue.

QUICK BITES

You can feel good about **Homegrown Herb & Tea** (195 Congress St., 207/774-3484, www.homegrownherbandtea.com, noon-5pm Tues.-Fri., 9am-3pm Sat.), an Ayurvedic shop that blends black, green, and herbal teas and serves light fare, including a delightful lavender shortbread.

Ever had a mashed potato pizza? It's just one of the intriguing choices at **Otto Pizza** (225 Congress St., 207/358-7551, www.ottoportland.com, from 11am daily). Otto's has another location at 576 Congress Street, in the downtown Arts District.

The croissants, pastries, and Roman-style pizzas at **Belleville** (1 North St., 207/536-7463, https://blvl.me, 7am-3pm Tues.-Fri., 8am-3pm Sat.-Sun.) are divine. Find it across from the Portland Observatory.

Just try *not* to walk out with something from **Two Fat Cats Bakery** (47 India St., 207/347-5144, from 8am Tues.-Sun.)—oh, the cookies! The breads! The pies!

Micucci's Grocery Store (45 India St., 207/775-1854, 8am-5:30pm Mon.-Fri., 8am-5pm Sat.) has been serving Portland's Italian community since 1949. It's a great stop for picnic fixings, take-out pizza slabs and sandwiches, and a nice selection of inexpensive wines.

Mainers love their Italian sandwiches, and **Amato's** (71 India St., 207/773-1682, www.amatos.com, 7am-10pm daily) is credited with creating a drool-worthy sub, usually made with ham, cheese, tomatoes, green peppers, black olives, and onions wrapped in a doughy roll and drizzled with oil. Also available is other Italian-inspired fare. Amato's has outlets throughout southern Maine; this one has outdoor patio seating.

The most incredible fries come from **Duckfat** (43 Middle St., 207/774-8080, www.duckfat.com, 11am-10pm daily, $8-14), a casual joint owned by James Beard Award-winning chef Rob Evans. Fries—fried in duck fat, of course—are served in a paper cone and accompanied by your choice of five sauces; the truffle ketchup is heavenly. Want to really harden those arteries? Order the poutine—Belgian fries topped with Maine cheese curds and homemade duck gravy. In addition, Duckfat serves panini, soups, salads, craft sodas, and really good milk shakes; wine and beer are available. Another option is Duckfat's little sibling **Frites Shack** (43 Washington Ave., from noon daily), a walk-up window offering the coveted fries, craft sodas, milk shakes, and shared snack platters.

CASUAL DINING

A trio of restaurants from James Beard Best Chef award-winning chef-owners Andrew Taylor and Mike Wiley line the seaward side of Middle Street. First was ★ **Hugo's** (88 Middle St. at Franklin St., 207/774-8538, www.hugos.net, from 5:30pm Tues.-Sat.), where the blind tasting menu ($90) showcases fresh and local fare from the sea, forest, and field; à la carte entrées range $23-30. Next came **Eventide Oyster Co.** (86 Middle St., 207/774-8538, www.eventideoysterco.com, 11am-midnight daily), a fave of food guru Andrew Zimmern that has also won national accolades. The menu includes nearly two dozen oysters and other shellfish paired with sauces, as well as other seafood (market rates). In 2015, they added the **Honey Paw** (78 Middle St., 207/774-8538, www.thehoneypaw.com, 11am-10pm Wed.-Sat. and Mon., 11am-4pm Sun., $17-28), a "non-denominational noodle bar." Each restaurant is fabulous, but if you're looking for a special night, make reservations and splurge on the tasting menu at Hugo's.

The daily-changing menu at **Drifters Wife** (59 Washington Ave., 207/805-1336, www.drifterswife.com, from 5pm Tues.-Sat., $27-32) is small and appears simple, but the dishes are sophisticated and delicious. The restaurant, which has won national recognition as one of America's best wine restaurants and best new restaurants, evolved out of Maine & Loire, a natural wines shop.

INTERNATIONAL

Traditional Salvadoran foods (think Mexican with attitude) have turned hole-in-the-wall **Tu Casa** (70 Washington Ave., 207/828-4971, www.tucasaportland.com, from 11am Sun.-Fri.) into a must-visit for in-the-know foodies. It's also a budget find, with almost everything on the menu going for less than $10.

Sure, you can cobble together your own heavenly meal from the small plates at **Izakaya Minato** (554 Washington Ave., 207/613-9939, www.izakayaminato.com, from

5pm Mon.-Sat., $10-30), a Japanese gastropub, but why not let chef-owner Thomas Takashi Cooke do it for you by ordering the chef's choice *omakase* menu ($30)?

Barbecue meets southwestern, Caribbean, and Mexican fare at **Terlingua** (40 Washington Ave., 207/808-8502, www.terlingua.me, from 7am-10pm Mon.-Fri., 9am-10pm Sat., 10am-9pm Sun., $9-20).

Cong Tu Bot (57 Washington Ave., 207/221-8022, http://congtubot.com, 5pm-10pm daily, $12-18), a Vietnamese noodle restaurant, offers a menu short on choices but big on flavor.

Middle Eastern fare is the specialty at **Baharat** (91 Anderson St., 207/619-9849, www.baharatmaine.com, from 3pm Tues.-Sun., $12-18), which evolved from a very popular food truck. The sharing plates are a good choice for two ($45) or four ($90), but require up to 45 minutes for preparation.

Arts District and Downtown

These restaurants are clustered downtown, east of High Street.

QUICK BITES

Multiple vendors sell reasonably priced breads, sandwiches, pizzas, crepes, pho, salad, coffees, soups, and more at **Public Market House** (28 Monument Sq., 207/228-2056, www.publicmarkethouse.com, 8am-6pm Mon.-Sat., 10am-5pm Sun.).

Well off most visitors' radar screens is **Artemisia Café** (61 Pleasant St., 207/761-0135, 9am-2pm Wed.-Sun., $10-13), a cheery neighborhood café with a creative American menu.

Nosh Kitchen Bar (551 Congress St., 207/553-2227, www.noshkitchenbar.com, 11:30am-1am Mon.-Sat., 4pm-1am Sun.) serves inspired sandwiches and humongous burgers and, well, noshing fare ($12-21).

CASUAL DINING

For creative Mediterranean-influenced small plates designed to be shared tapas-style, head to ★ **Sur-Lie** (11 Free St., 207/956-7350, www.sur-lie.com, from 4pm Tues.-Sun., $7-20). Can't make up your mind? Chef's choice four- and five-course tasting menus are available for $45-55.

Pursue the perfect pairing at nationally lauded restaurateur and chef Cara Stadler's newest venue, **Lio** (3 Spring St., 207/808-7133, www.lio-maine.com, from 5pm Wed.-Sun., $8-24). The small-plates menu offers contemporary European fare, and about three dozen wines are available by the full or half glass.

For innovative, 100 percent hyperlocal, organic, and gluten-free food, make reservations at **Vinland** (593 Congress St., 207/653-8617, http://vinland.me, from 5pm Wed.-Mon., $13-38). Chef David Levy's menu supports the restaurant's 19-point mission; in short, it's real, healthful, nourishing, delightful, and delicious. A five-course menu is $79; the 19-item tasting menu ($155) requires 24 hours' notice.

A longtimer in the Portland dining scene, **David's** (22 Monument Sq., 207/773-4340, www.davidsrestaurant.com, from 11:30am Mon.-Fri., from 5pm Sat.-Sun, $15-34) serves contemporary American fare as well as pizza; vegetarian, vegan, and gluten-free options are available. Never one to rest on his laurels, chef-owner David Turin opened **David's Opus 10** (Wed.-Sat. mid-June-mid-Sept., $70), an 18-seat fixed-price restaurant within the same space.

Nationally lauded chef Steve Corry blends fresh, local, and seasonal in creative ways on his ever-changing menu at **Five Fifty-Five** (555 Congress St., 207/761-0555, www.fivefifty-five.com, 5pm-9:30pm daily, $22-42). Also available is a five-course chef's menu ($70).

INTERNATIONAL

Cantonese soul food with Maine influence flavors the menu at **Empire Chinese Kitchen** (575 Congress St., 207/747-5063, http://portlandempire.com/kitchen, from 11:30am Wed.-Mon., $6-18), specializing in dim sum and small plates.

Nationally lauded chef Cara Stadler's **Bao Bao Dumpling House** (133 Spring St.,

207/772-8400, www.baobaodumplinghouse.com, from 11:30am Wed.-Sun.) offers traditional and inspired dumplings and small plates. A serving of six dumplings ranges $6-10; other dishes top out around $14.

Masa Miyake's **Pai Men Miyake** (188 State St., 207/541-9204, www.miyakerestaurants.com, 11:30am-11pm Mon.-Thurs., 11:30am-midnight Fri.-Sun., $9-16) is a traditional Japanese noodle bar serving ramen, sushi, and small plates; don't miss the pork buns.

Vegan and vegetarian cuisine comes with an Asian accent at **Green Elephant** (608 Congress St., 207/347-3111, www.greenelephantmaine.com, 11:30am-2:30pm Mon.-Sat. and 5:30pm-9:30pm daily, $12-16).

Duck into chef-owner Asmeret Teklu's **Asmara** (51 Oak St., 207/253-5122, www.asmaramaine.com, 11:30am-10:30pm Tues.-Sat., 3pm-9pm Sun., $13-18) to be transported to East Africa. Traditional Eritrean and Ethiopian dishes, a mix of mild to spicy curried stews, and vegetarian plates are served on *injera,* spongy flatbread made from teff flour that doubles as an eating utensil (silverware is available, if you ask). Entrées are generous and come with a salad and choice of vegetable. Service is leisurely; this is a one-woman show.

Ever-popular **Local 188** (685 Congress St., 207/761-7909, www.local188.com, from 5:30pm daily and 9am-2pm Sat.-Sun.) serves fabulous Mediterranean-inspired food with a tapas-heavy menu. It doubles as an art gallery with rotating exhibits. Most tapas selections are less than $10; heartier choices and entrées begin at $25. There is free parking behind the building.

Authentic Thai street food is served in a cool-yet-sophisticated space at **Boda** (671 Congress St., 207/347-7557, www.bodamaine.com, 5pm-12:45am Sun.-Wed., 5pm-12:45am Thurs.-Sat., $16-20). The dinner menu is served until 9 or 10pm; after that, there's a lighter late-night menu. Vegetarian and gluten-free dishes are available.

Slip into sleek **Emilitsa** (547 Congress St., 207/221-0245, www.emilitsa.com, from 5pm Tues.-Sat., $22-35) for finely crafted authentic Greek dishes paired with Greek wines.

West End

Superb thin-crust pizzas made from all-natural ingredients in usual and unusual flavor combos emerge from the wood-fired oven at **Bonobo** (46 Pine St., 207/347-8267, www.bonobopizza.com, 11:30am-2:30pm Thurs.-Fri. and from 4pm daily, $14-20).

Make reservations in advance to land a much-coveted table at **Chaval** (58 Pine St., 207/772-1110, www.chavalmaine.com, from 5pm daily and 9am-2pm Sun., $17-27), a neighborhood brasserie where chef-owners Damian Samsonetti and Ilma Lopez prepare sophisticated yet approachable Spanish- and French-inspired fare. Do save room for dessert.

Bayside

Breakfast is served all day at the **Miss Portland Diner** (140 Marginal Way, 207/210-6673, www.missportlanddiner.com, 7am-3pm Sun.-Wed., 7am-9pm Thurs.-Sat., $6-18), a 1949 Worcester Diner (car number 818) that was rescued, restored, and reopened in 2007. Snag a counter stool or a booth in the original dining car, or opt for the addition, and then treat yourself to breakfast for dinner.

Full food service is offered on the lanes of **Bayside Bowl** (58 Alder St., 207/791-2695, www.baysidebowl.com, 4pm-11pm Mon.-Thurs., noon-midnight Fri., from 11am Sat.-Sun., $7-13), or you can opt for one of the seating areas. A different menu—think tacos and Mexican bowls—is served on the **Rooftop** (4pm-10pm Mon.-Thurs, from noon Fri.-Sun., $4-5).

Portlanders have long favored **Bayside American Café** (98 Portland St., 207/774-0005, www.baysideamericancafe.com, 7am-2pm daily) for its breakfasts and brunches ($8-17). It doesn't take reservations on weekends, so expect to wait in line.

For a lovely meal in a fine-dining setting, reserve a table at the **Back Bay Grill**

(65 Portland St., near the main post office, 207/772-8833, www.backbaygrill.com, from 5pm Tues.-Sat., $26-38). A colorful mural accents the serene dining room; arts-and-crafts wall sconces cast a soft glow on the white linen-draped tables. The menu, which highlights fresh, seasonal ingredients, isn't innovative but is well prepared, and the wine list is long and well chosen.

The Burbs

Pair a visit to Portland Head Light and Fort Williams with a lobster roll from **Bite Into Maine** (Fort Williams, Cape Elizabeth, 207/420-0294, www.biteintomaine.com, 11am-sold out daily), a mobile food truck also serving vegetarian sandwiches, ice cream, and desserts.

Great sunset views over Portland's skyline, a casual atmosphere, and decent American fare have earned **Saltwater Grille** (231 Front St., South Portland, 207/799-5400, www.saltwatergrille.com, from 11:30am daily, $15-40) an excellent reputation. Dine inside or on the waterfront deck. It's also accessible by water taxi.

If you're venturing out to Cape Elizabeth, detour to the **Good Table** (527 Ocean House Rd./Rte. 77, Cape Elizabeth, 207/799-4663, www.thegoodtablerestaurant.net, 11am-9pm Tues.-Fri., 8am-9pm Sat., 8am-3pm Sun., $10-22), serving home-style favorites as well as Greek specialties.

Make reservations to dine alfresco at the **Well at Jordan's Farm** (21 Wells Rd., Cape Elizabeth, 207/831-9350, www.thewellatjordansfarm.com, 5pm-9pm Tues.-Sat., $28-32), where Jason Williams, a Culinary Institute of America grad, creates dinners from the working farm's bounty and other ingredients sourced locally. Everything is made from scratch. Seating is on picnic tables, in gazebos, or at the four-stool kitchen bar. A three-course, family-style menu, for parties of six or more, is $75 pp.

Sea Glass (40 Bowery Beach Rd./Rte. 77, Cape Elizabeth, 207/299-3134, 7am-9pm daily, $20-46), at the Inn by the Sea, pairs well-prepared American fare with divine ocean views. Dine indoors or on the deck, enjoying seasonally inspired, local, and sustainable entrées such as miso-glazed pollack, butter-poached lobster, or a burger.

Every Mainer has a favorite lobster eatery (besides home), but the **Lobster Shack** (222 Two Lights Rd., Cape Elizabeth, 207/799-1677, www.lobstershacktwolights.com, 11am-8:30pm daily late Mar.-late Oct.), with seating inside and outdoors, tops an awful lot of lists. Seniority helps—it's been here since the 1920s—as does the panoramic vista in the shadow of Cape Elizabeth Light. The menu offers seafood galore, along with salads, burgers, and hot dogs (from $3). Opt for a sunny day; the lighthouse's foghorn can kill your conversation on misty ones.

ACCOMMODATIONS

Downtown Portland

HOSTEL

The family-owned and operated **Black Elephant Hostel** (33 Hampshire St., 207/712-7062, www.blackelephanthostel.com) is sited in a great walk-to-everything location. It has coed and single-sex dorm-style rooms with bunk beds for $40-50 pp; private rooms are $90-140. Linens, a duvet, and a pillow are provided, as are keyed lockers. Decor is wildly colorful, from the outdoor building murals to the indoor ceilings. Communal space includes a comfy lobby lounge and a shared kitchen.

INNS AND BED-AND-BREAKFASTS

All these properties are in older buildings without elevators; stairs may be steep. All include a full breakfast, unless noted otherwise.

Railroad tycoon John Deering built the **Inn at St. John** (939 Congress St., 207/773-6481 or 800/636-9127, www.innatstjohn.com, $129-335) in 1897. The comfortable (if somewhat tired) and moderately priced 39-room hostelry is a good choice for value-savvy travelers who aren't seeking fancy accommodations. The inn welcomes children and pets and even has bicycle storage. Free parking and a meager continental breakfast are provided. Reimbursement for taxi fare from the airport or transportation center is available at a fixed price. Most guest rooms have private baths (some are detached). The downside is the lackluster neighborhood—in the evening you'll want to drive or take a taxi when going out. It's about a 45-minute walk up and over the hill to the Old Port, or around $10 via taxi. Pet-friendly rooms are available ($10/night).

Travel writer Dale Northrup put his experience to work in opening the **Percy Inn** (15 Pine St., 207/871-7638, www.percyinn.com, $159-229) in a handsome brick town house conveniently located just off Longfellow Square. It's best suited for independent-minded travelers who don't desire much contact with the host, who, although always accessible, is rarely on-site. Breakfast is a continental buffet, and you can raid the 24-hour pantry. If you're noise-sensitive, avoid accommodations that open directly into the pantry, kitchen, or breakfast room. Perks include garage storage for bicycles, kayaks, and other equipment.

Sustainability is the goal at **Mercury** (273 State St., 207/420-2420, www.mercuryinn.com, $165-195), a hip bed-and-breakfast sited in an updated Victorian in the city's Parkside neighborhood. Guest rooms are smartly decorated in cream and gray, with blue or yellow accents.

Take a carefully renovated 1830s town house, add contemporary amenities and a service-oriented innkeeper, and the result is the **Morrill Mansion Bed and Breakfast** (249 Vaughan St., 207/774-6900, www.morrillmansion.com, $179-259), on the West End. Six guest rooms and one suite are spread out on the 2nd and 3rd floors. There are no frilly Victorian accents here—the decor is understated yet tasteful, taking advantage of hardwood floors and high ceilings

The Georgian-style **West End Inn** (146 Pine St., 207/772-1377, www.westendbb.com, from $219), built in 1877, has six updated rooms with contemporary amenities. One room has a detached bath, another a private deck. The decor blends traditional furnishings with fun and contemporary accents.

The **Inn at Park Spring** (135 Spring St., 207/774-1059, www.innatparkspring.com, from $230) is housed in an 1835 brick town house, just steps from most Arts District attractions. Choose from handsome guest rooms and a bilevel suite with a kitchenette, living room, and private patio and entrance.

Staying at the **Pomegranate Inn** (49 Neal St. at Carroll St., 207/772-1006, www.pomegranateinn.com, from $269) is an adventure, with faux paintings, classical statuary, contemporary art, antiques, and whimsical touches everywhere—you'll either love it or find it a bit much. The elegant 1884 Italianate mansion has seven guest rooms and a suite.

In the same neighborhood is the intimate **Chadwick Bed & Breakfast** (140 Chadwick St., 207/774-5141, www.thechadwick.com, from $259), with four handsome guest rooms.

Chic and stylish, the **Danforth** (163 Danforth St., 207/879-8755, www.danforthinn.com, from $200), a Lark Hotel, honors its location in a handsome 18th-century brick mansion but updates it with contemporary verve.

FULL-SERVICE HOTELS

You might have trouble finding the **Portland Regency** (20 Milk St., 207/774-4200 or 800/727-3436, www.theregency.com, from $239): This hotel, registered with the National Trust for Historic Preservation as a historic property, is secreted in a renovated armory in the heart of the Old Port. The nicest rooms are the renovated ones, especially those on the 4th floor with decks. Perks include free shuttles to all major Portland transportation facilities. Be forewarned: Room configurations vary widely—some provide little natural light or are strangely shaped. A restaurant, spa, and fitness center are on-site.

One of the city's oldest hotels, the former Eastland, reopened as the **Westin Portland Harborview** (157 High St., 207/775-5411, www.westinportlandharborview.com, from $284) after a complete renovation. It's in the heart of the Arts District, across from the Portland Museum of Art. Rooms have all the bells and whistles you'd expect from a Westin, and amenities include a fitness studio, a spa, a business center, a restaurant, and a great rooftop lounge with panoramic views that on a clear evening extend from the Atlantic to Mount Washington.

The **Francis** (747 Congress St., 207/772-7485, https://thefrancismaine.com, from $335), sited in a historical 1881 brick home designed by architect Francis Fassett, opened as a 15-room boutique hotel in 2017 after a two-year renovation that preserved period architectural details while adding contemporary accents and amenities, with an emphasis on local artwork and products, including in the minibar. Pluses include a 24-hour front desk, a lounge and restaurant, spa services, and comfortable common rooms and nooks.

The ★ **Portland Harbor Hotel** (468 Fore St., 207/775-9090 or 888/798-9090, www.portlandharborhotel.com, from $335), an upscale boutique hotel in the Old Port, is built around a garden courtyard. Rooms, updated in 2018, are plush with a sharp nautical decor accented with local artwork. Complimentary bike rentals are available, and the hotel offers a free local car service. There's a cozy lounge, and the restaurant has 24-hour room service. Ice Bar, an ice sculpture event where you can order your favorite libation from bars made of ice, is held the last weekend of January in the hotel's courtyard and draws a crowd. Some rooms are pet friendly ($25/night).

The ★ **Press Hotel** (19 Exchange St., 207/808-8800, www.thepresshotel.com, from $380) occupies a downtown building that previously housed the state's largest newspaper. The 110-room boutique hotel, a Marriott Autograph Collection property, honors the building's journalistic heritage with a contemporary decor accented with art installations, vintage newsroom-inspired furnishings, wallpapers printed with quirky newspaper headlines, and carpets patterned with jumbled type. It's sited at the head of the Old Port where it intersects with the downtown. Other pluses include an excellent restaurant, a lobby lounge, fitness room, and bicycles. Complimentary transportation is provided to the airport and Portland Transportation Center.

The Burbs

Only a narrow byway separates the **Breakers Inn** (2 Bay View Ave., Higgins Beach, Scarborough, 207/883-4820, www.thebreakersinn.com, from $225 daily, from $1,395 weekly) from the sands of Higgins Beach. This is an old-timey bed-and-breakfast in a turreted, porch-wrapped three-story Victorian built in 1900, converted to an inn in 1932, and operated by the Laughton family since 1956. Every room has an ocean view, including two in the basement. Fancy or frilly, this isn't: You're paying for location, not amenities or the pine-paneled decor. Breakfast is included, picnic lunches are available, and there's a coin-op laundry. Transportation is available from Portland's transportation hubs. No credit cards.

The **Higgins Beach Inn** (34 Ocean Ave., Scarborough, 207/288-6684, www.higginsbeachinn.com, from $249 with breakfast), a classic 1922 summer hotel, reopened in 2017 after a major renovation and updating. Rooms blend coastal ease with contemporary amenities and rusticator beach style. The inn's restaurant, **Shade,** is open for breakfast and dinner ($14-30) and keeps to the beach-casual theme, specializing in locally sourced fare, especially seafood.

The **Black Point Inn Resort** (510 Black Point Rd., Prouts Neck, Scarborough, 207/883-2500 or 800/258-0003, www.blackpointinn.com, from $450 with breakfast) is a classic, unpretentious seaside hotel with a genteel vibe. The historic Shingle-style hotel opened in 1878 at the tip of Prouts Neck, bookended by two beaches and overlooking Casco Bay from one side and south toward Old Orchard from the other. The inn caters to wealthy rusticators who appreciate the gentle updates that preserved the style but added contemporary comforts. Guests have access to

1

2

a private, oceanfront 18-hole golf course, tennis courts, a beach club, the Cliff Walk around the point (passing Winslow Homer's studio), and a lovely, trail-laced woodland bird sanctuary that has ties to Homer's family. The **Point Restaurant** (6pm-8pm daily, $28-38), a fine-dining venue, is open to nonguests by reservation; the less-fussy **Chart Room** (8am-10am and 11:30am-9pm daily, $16-26) serves lighter fare. Don't miss cocktails on the porch at sunset, with views over sand and water to distant Mount Washington. B&B rates are available in spring and fall.

Especially splurge-worthy and well suited for families is the ultra-green, oceanfront ★ **Inn by the Sea** (40 Bowery Beach Rd./Rte. 77, Cape Elizabeth, 207/799-3134 or 800/888-4287, www.innbythesea.com, from around $579), just seven miles south of downtown Portland. Guests stay in handsome rooms, suites, and one- or two-bedroom cottages, most with kitchens or expanded wet bars, comfy living rooms, and big views. This contemporary luxury property offers a cozy lounge, a full-service spa, and a small cardio room. Big windows frame ocean views at **Sea Glass** (207/299-3134, $20-50), serving all meals daily inside or on the deck. Other facilities include an outdoor pool, a *boules* court, wildlife habitats, and a private boardwalk winding through a salt marsh to Crescent Beach State Park. By reservation, dogs are honored guests; they're welcomed with bowls and a bed, receive turndown treats, and have their own room-service and spa menus. Even better, the hotel has a successful foster dog program, so you might end up heading home with a furry friend.

INFORMATION AND SERVICES

The **Visitor Information Center of the Convention and Visitors Bureau of Greater Portland** (14 Ocean Gateway Pier, 207/772-5800, www.visitportland.com) has info and public restrooms. The **Portland Downtown District** (207/772-6828, www.portlandmaine.com) and **LiveWork Portland** (www.liveworkportland.org) have helpful sites.

In the Old Port area, you'll find **public restrooms** at the Visitor Information Center (14 Ocean Gateway Pier), Spring Street parking garage (45 Spring St.), Fore Street Parking Garage (419 Fore St.), and Casco Bay Lines ferry terminal (Commercial St. and Franklin St.). On Congress Street, find restrooms at Portland City Hall (389 Congress St.) and the Portland Public Library (5 Monument Sq.). In Midtown, head for the Cumberland County Civic Center (1 Civic Center Sq.). In the West End, use Maine Medical Center (22 Bramhall St.).

GETTING THERE AND AROUND

Portland is about 100 miles or two hours via I-95 from Boston, although during peak travel periods it can take longer because of congestion and toll lines. It's about 26 miles or 45 minutes via Route 1 from Kennebunk. It's about 17 miles or 20 minutes via Route 295 to Freeport.

The clean and comfortable **Portland Transportation Center** (100 Thompson Point Rd., 207/828-3939) is the base for **Concord Coachlines** (800/639-3317, www.concordcoachlines.com) and the **Amtrak Downeaster** (800/872-7245, www.amtrakdowneaster.com). Parking is $4/day.

The **Metro** (207/774-0351, https://gpmetro.org, $1.50 adults, $1 ages 6-18, $5 day pass, exact change required) bus service makes it easy to get around Portland, South Portland, Westbrook, and Falmouth. Route 1 stops at the Portland Transportation Center and **Greyhound Bus** (950 Congress St., www.greyhound.com), and along Congress Street and the East End. Route 8 services the West End, Old Port, and Waterfront, including **Casco Bay Lines ferry service** (56 Commercial St., www.cascobaylines.com), as well as Bayside. Route 5 services **Portland International Jetport** (207/774-7301, www.

1: Black Point Inn Resort **2:** Inn by the Sea

portlandjetport.org). The **Metro Breez** ($4 adults, $2 ages 6-18) provides express service connecting the Portland Transportation Center, downtown Portland, Yarmouth, Freeport, and Brunswick.

Taxis charge $1.90 for the first 0.1 mile plus $0.30 for each additional 0.1 mile; minimum fare is $5, and airport fares add a $1.50 surcharge.

It's getting easier to get around Portland via bicycle thanks to bike lanes on some roads. See **Portland Trails** (207/775-2411, www.trails.org) for mapped routes.

Parking

Street parking (meters or pay stations) is $1.75/hour, 9am-6pm Mon.-Sat. Parking garages and lots ($2-6/hour, $12-50/day) are strategically situated all over downtown Portland, particularly in the Old Port and near the civic center. Find locations and rates at www.portlandmaine.gov. For winter parking-ban information, call 207/879-0300.

Casco Bay Islands

TOP EXPERIENCE

Casco Bay is dotted with so many islands that an early explorer thought there must be at least one for every day of the year and so dubbed them the Calendar Islands. Truthfully, there aren't quite that many, even if you count all the ledges that appear at low tide. No matter; the islands are as much a part of Portland life as the Old Port.

★ CASCO BAY TOUR

Casco Bay Lines (Commercial St. and Franklin St., Old Port, 207/774-7871, www.cascobaylines.com), the nation's oldest continuously operating ferry system (since the 1920s), is the lifeline between Portland and six inhabited Casco Bay islands. What better way to sample the islands than to take the three-hour ride along with mail, groceries, and island residents? The Casco Bay Lines Mailboat Run stops—briefly—at **Long, Chebeague, Cliff,** and **Little Diamond** and **Great Diamond Islands.** Departures are 10am and 2:15pm daily mid-June-early September, 10am and 2:45pm in other months. Fares are $17 adults, $15 seniors, and $9 ages 5-9.

The longest cruise on the Casco Bay Lines schedule is the nearly six-hour narrated summertime trip (late June-early Sept., $26 adults, $22.50 seniors, $12 ages 5-9) with a two-hour stopover on **Bailey Island,** departing from Portland at 10am daily. Bicycles ($7) and dogs ($4.10) on leashes need separate tickets.

For a shorter island hop, choose any of the island ferry runs and simply stay aboard for the round-trip.

PEAKS ISLAND

Peaks Island is a mere 20-minute ferry ride from downtown Portland, so it's no surprise that it has the largest year-round population. Historically a popular vacation spot—two lodges here were built for Civil War veterans—it was known as Maine's Coney Island at the turn of the 20th century.

Although you can walk the island's perimeter in 3-4 hours, the best way to see it is via bike (extra ferry cost $6.50 adults, $3.25 children), pedaling around clockwise. It can take less than an hour to do the five-mile island circuit, but plan to relax on the beach, savor the views, and visit the museums. Rental bikes are available on the island from Brad Burkholder at **Brad and Wyatt's Bike Shop** (115 Island Ave., Peaks Island, 207/766-5631, 10am-6pm daily, $10/hour, $20/tandem).

Other ways to see the island are on a 75-minute golf-cart tour or two-hour walking tour with **Peaks Island Tours** (207/766-5514, www.peaksislandtours.com, $20 adults, $10 ages 5-12); in a **taxi** (207/518-000, https://

peaksislandtaxi.org, rates vary with distance); or in a golf cart rented through **Mike's Carts** (207/239-1777, www.mikescarts.com, from $70/two hours). Advance reservations are advised for all.

Civil War buffs have two museums worth visiting. The **Fifth Maine Regiment Center** (45 Seashore Ave., Peaks Island, 207/766-3330, www.fifthmainemuseum.org, 11am-4pm daily July-Aug., 11am-4pm Sat.-Sun. late May and Sept.-mid-Oct., $5 pp or $20/family) is a Queen Anne-style cottage built by Civil War veterans in 1888 that now houses exhibits on the war and island history.

Tours at the nearby **Eighth Maine Regimental Memorial** (13 Eighth Maine Ave., Peaks Island, 207/329-3530, https://8thmaineregimentpeaksisland.com, 11am-4pm daily, $5 requested donation) detail the building's fascinating history and its artifacts pertaining to the Eighth Maine as well as material on the island, World War II, and more.

Another museum worthy of a visit just for its quirkiness is the **Umbrella Cover Museum** (207/939-0301, www.umbrellacovermuseum.org, call for current hours, donation), where owner Nancy 3. Hoffman (yes, 3) displays her Guinness World Record collection. Tours end with Hoffman singing "Let a Smile be Your Umbrella" while playing her accordion.

Bring a flashlight and waterproof footwear if you want to prowl around the World War II-era **Battery Steele.** It's located on the ocean side of the island and is well camouflaged with greenery, but it's easy to find with a map. Free maps are available near the ferry dock; detailed color maps are also available for $6 in island stores, but I found the $1 color map available at Brad and Wyatt's Bike Shop handy for a day trip. Or, download a map from https://peaksislandmaine.net.

Food

Both the **Cockeyed Gull** (78 Island Ave., 207/766-2880, www.cockeyedgull.com, 11:30am-8:30pm daily, $10-27) and the **Inn on Peaks Island** (33 Island Ave., 207/766-5100, www.innonpeaks.com, 11am-9pm daily, $10-30) have inside dining as well as outdoor tables with water views.

Accommodations

The spacious cottage-style suites at the **Inn on Peaks Island** (33 Island Ave., 207/766-5100, www.innonpeaks.com, from $289) overlook the ferry dock and have jaw-dropping sunset views over the Portland skyline.

On the other end of the Peaks Island luxury scale is the extremely informal and communal **Eighth Maine Living Museum and Lodge** (13 Eighth Maine Ave., 207/491-1705, www.8thmainepeaksisland.com, $119-139), a rustic shorefront living-history hostel-style lodge overlooking White Head Passage. Its 14 bedrooms, sharing 3 baths and a huge kitchen, allow you to rusticate in much the same manner as the Civil War vets who built this place in 1891 with a gift from a veteran who had won the Louisiana Lottery.

GREAT CHEBEAGUE

Everyone calls Great Chebeague just "Chebeague" (shuh-BIG). Yes, there's a Little Chebeague, but it's a state-owned park and no one lives there. Chebeague is the largest of the bay's islands—4.5 miles long by 1.5 miles wide—and the relatively level terrain makes it easy to get around. Don't bring a car; it's too complicated to arrange. You can bike the leisurely 10-mile circuit of the island in a couple of hours, but unless you're in a hurry, allow time to relax and enjoy your visit.

Stop by the **Museum of Chebeague History** (137 South Rd., 207/846-5237, www.chebeaguehistory.com, 11am-4pm Tues.- Sat., 1pm-4pm Sun.) for an intro to the island's history.

If the tide is right, cross the sand spit from the Hook and explore **Little Chebeague.** Start out about two hours before low tide (preferably around new moon or full moon, when the most water drains away) and plan to be back on Chebeague no later than two hours after low tide.

Back on Great Chebeague, when you're

ready for a swim, head for **Hamilton Beach,** a beautiful small stretch of sand lined with dune grass and not far from the Chebeague Island Inn. Also on this part of the island is **East End Point,** with a spectacular panoramic view of Halfway Rock and the bay.

Food and Accommodations

Get that old-timey island experience at the **Chebeague Island Inn** (61 South Rd., 207/846-5155, www.chebeagueislandinn.com, $189-349), an unfussy historical inn that's been updated. Rooms are small and some share baths. The restaurant serves all meals (breakfast is included), but it's hit or miss.

The **Niblic** (207/846-4146, www.chebeagueislandboatyard.com), at the Chebeague Island Boat Yard, has sandwiches, soups, chowders, and baked goods as well as a nice selection of Maine-made gifts. The **Slow Bell Café** (2 Walker Rd., 207/846-3078), the island's bar, offers pub fare and dinner specials, along with live entertainment on weekends.

GREAT DIAMOND

A century ago, nearly 1,000 personnel were stationed here at Fort McKinley, the largest of five military complexes in Portland Harbor. Now most of the car-free island is a self-contained private community listed in the National Register of Historic Places. The barracks and officers' quarters are now private homes; the quartermaster's storehouse is the Diamond's Edge Restaurant; the quartermaster's office houses an art gallery and museum; and the blacksmith shop houses a restaurant and a general store. Overnight guests have access to the island's amenities, which include walking trails, pebble beaches, and bicycle rentals ($10/day) from the store. Day-trippers can enjoy the restaurant and store, a historical trail, and the volunteer-operated **Fort McKinley Museum** (http://fortmckinleymuseum.weebly.com, check site for current hours, tours $15 adults, $10 children over age 10). Tours of the private community (email tours@diamondcove.com) can also be arranged.

Food

Diamond's Edge Restaurant (Diamond Cove, 207/766-5850, www.diamondsedgerestaurantandmarina.com, 11:30am-2:30pm and 5pm-9pm daily, $22-44), within steps of the Diamond Cove ferry dock, has tables inside, on the porch, and on the lawn. If you need to catch a specific return ferry, make sure to let your server know in advance.

A giant neon pink flamingo sets the island-escape vibe at **Crown Jewel** (255 Diamond Ave., 207/766-3000, www.crownjewelportland.com, 11:30am-10pm Wed.-Mon., $12-20), which delivers on its name. The contemporary American, seafood-heavy menu offers small and large plates.

Accommodations

Step inside the **Inn at Diamond Cove** (22 McKinley Ct., 207/805-9836, www.innatdiamondcove.com, from $309), and it's hard to believe that soldiers once occupied the tony, contemporary accommodations. Most rooms have balconies, though none has a water view. The inn has its own restaurant serving all meals (open to nonguests by reservation) as well as a heated pool.

EAGLE ISLAND

Seventeen-acre **Eagle Island** (207/624-6080, www.pearyeagleisland.org, 10am-5pm mid-June-early Sept., $4-6 adults, $1 ages 5-11), a National Historic Landmark, juts out of Casco Bay, rising to a rocky promontory 40 feet above the crashing surf. On the bluff's crest, Robert Edwin Peary, the first man to lead a party to the North Pole without the use of mechanical or electrical devices, built his dream home. It's now a state historic site that's accessible via an excursion boat from Freeport. The half-day trip usually includes a narrated cruise to the island and time to tour the house, which is filled with Peary family artifacts, and wander the nature trails. Trails

1: Casco Bay ferries **2:** Portland's skyline from Peaks Island

BAY MIST
COCISCO III
1
2

are usually closed until approximately mid-July to protect nesting eider ducks. Peary envisioned the island's rocky bluff as a ship's prow and built his house to resemble a pilothouse. Wherever possible, he used indigenous materials from the island in the construction, including timber drift, fallen trees, beach rocks, and cement mixed with screened beach sand and small pebbles. From the library, Peary corresponded with world leaders, adventurers, and explorers such as Teddy Roosevelt, the Wright brothers, Roald Amundsen, and Ernest Shackleton, and planned his expeditions. Peary reached the North Pole on April 6, 1909, and his wife, Josephine, was on Eagle Island when she received word via telegraph of her husband's accomplishment. After Peary's death in 1920, the family continued to spend summers on Eagle until Josephine's death in 1955. The family then donated the island to the state of Maine. A free self-guided audio tour is available at the welcome center, where you can view a 10-minute video about Peary and the island.

GETTING THERE

Ferries provide regularly scheduled transportation to most islands. Water taxis also service the islands.

Casco Bay Lines (207/774-7871, www.cascobaylines.com) has service to **Peaks, Little Diamond, Great Diamond, Diamond Cove, Long, Chebeague,** and **Cliff Islands.** Round-trip tickets for each island range $8-12 for adults and $4-6 for children/seniors. It's $6.50 for an adult bike and $3.25 for a child bike; animals are $4.10.

Chebeague Transportation Company (207/846-3700, www.chebeaguetrans.com) ferries between causeway-connected Cousins Island, Yarmouth, and Chebeague Island. Round-trip fares are $16 adults, $3 ages 6-11, $6 bicycle. Parking in CTC's lots is $15-20, which includes shuttle to the ferry dock.

Seacoast Tours (207/798-2001, https://seacoasttoursme.com), offers 3.5-hour **Eagle Island** tours departing at 9:30am ($40 adults, $28 children). Trips depart from Freeport.

Freeport

Freeport has a special claim to historical fame—it's the place where Maine parted company from Massachusetts in 1820. The documents were signed on March 15, making Maine its own state.

The region once hosted a booming maritime trade. At the height of the local mackerel-packing industry, countless tons of the bony fish were shipped out of South Freeport, often in ships built on the shores of the Harraseeket River. Splendid relics of the shipbuilders' era still line the streets of South Freeport, and no architecture buff should miss a walk, cycle, or drive through the village. Even downtown Freeport still reflects the shipbuilders' craft, with contemporary shops tucked in and around handsome historic houses. Some have been converted to bed-and-breakfasts, others are boutiques, and one even disguises the local McDonald's franchise.

Today, Freeport is best known as the mecca for the shop-till-you-drop set. The hub, of course, is sporting giant L. L. Bean, which has been here since 1912, when founder Leon Leonwood Bean began making his trademark hunting boots (and unselfishly handed out hot tips on where the fish were biting). More than 120 retail operations now fan out from that epicenter, including many shops carrying Maine-made products.

The town offers plenty for nonshoppers too. You can always find quiet refuge in the town's preserves and parks, along with plenty of local color at the Town Wharf in the still honest-to-goodness fishing village of South Freeport.

An orientation note: Don't be surprised

to receive directions (particularly for South Freeport) relative to "the Big Indian"—a 40-foot-tall landmark at the junction of Route 1 and South Freeport Road. If you stop at the Maine Visitor Information Center in Yarmouth and continue on Route 1 toward Freeport, you can't miss it.

SHOPPING

In Freeport, shopping is the biggest game in town. Anyone who visits is likely to darken the door of at least one shop.

★ L. L. Bean

If you visit only one store in Freeport, it's likely to be "Bean's." The whole world beats a path to **L. L. Bean** (95 Main St./Rte. 1, 207/865-4761 or 800/341-4341, www.llbean.com)—or so it seems in July-August and December. Established as a hunting and fishing supply shop, this giant sports outfitter now sells everything from kids' clothing to cookware on its ever-expanding downtown campus, with separate Hunting & Fishing (flagship); Bike, Boat & Ski; and Home stores. There's also the outlet store—a great source for deals on equipment and clothing—in the Village Square Shops across Main Street.

Until the 1970s, Bean's remained a rustic store with a creaky staircase and a closet-size women's department. Then a few other merchants began arriving, Bean's expanded, and a feeding frenzy followed. The Bean reputation rests on a savvy staff, high quality, an admirable environmental consciousness, and a liberal return policy. Bring the kids—for the indoor trout pond and the aquarium-viewing bulb, the clean restrooms, and the "real deal" outlet store. The main store's open-round-the-clock policy has become its signature; if you show up at 2am, you'll have much of the store to yourself, and you may even spy vacationing celebrities or the rock stars who often visit after Portland shows.

Outlets and Specialty Stores

After Bean's, it's up to your whims and your wallet. The stores stretch for several miles up and down Main Street and along many side streets. Pick up a copy of the *Official Map and Visitor Guide* at any of the shops or restaurants, at one of the visitor kiosks, or at the **Hose Tower Information Center** (23 Depot St., two blocks east of L. L. Bean). All the big names are here, as are plenty of little ones—don't overlook the small shops tucked on the side streets.

SIGHTS

Desert of Maine

So maybe it's a bit hokey, but talk about sands of time: More than 10,000 years ago, glaciers covered the region surrounding the **Desert of Maine** (95 Desert Rd., 207/865-6962, www.desertofmaine.com, early May-mid-Oct., $10). When receding, they scoured the landscape, pulverizing rocks and leaving behind a sandy residue that was covered by a thin layer of topsoil. Jump ahead to 1797, when William Tuttle bought 300 acres and moved his family here along with his house and barn and cleared the land. Now leap to the present and tour where a once-promising farmland has become a desert wasteland. Pick up a map for a self-guided tour or opt for a 35-minute guided one. Kids can hunt for "gems" in the sand. Decide for yourself: Is the desert a natural phenomenon? A human-made disaster? Or does the truth lie somewhere in between?

Chocolate Factory Tour

Pretend you're Willy Wonka on a 30- to 45-minute guided tour of **Wilbur's of Maine Chocolate Confections** (174 Lower Main St., 207/865-4071, http://wilburs.com, $4.50), complete with samples. Call for the current schedule.

Harrington House and Pettengill Farm

A block south of L. L. Bean is the **Harrington House** (45 Main St./Rte. 1, 207/865-3170, www.freeporthistoricalsociety.org, 10am-5pm Tues.-Fri. late May-mid-Oct., free), home of the Freeport Historical Society. Pick up walking maps detailing Freeport's architecture for a small fee. Displays pertaining to Freeport's history and occasional exhibits by local artists are presented in two rooms in the restored 1830 Enoch Harrington House, a property in the National Register of Historic Places.

Also listed in the register is the society's **Pettengill Farm,** a 140-acre 19th-century saltwater farm comprising a circa-1810 saltbox-style house, woods, orchards, a salt marsh, and lovely perennial gardens. The farmhouse is open only during the annual Pettengill Farm Days in the fall, or by appointment, but the grounds are open at all times. From Main Street, take Bow Street 1.5 miles and turn right onto Pettengill Road. Park at the gate, and then walk along the dirt road for about 15 minutes to the farmhouse.

The Big Indian

This 60-foot-tall landmark statute, created by Rodman Shutt in 1968, has welcomed visitors to Freeport since 1969. Originally commissioned by the Casco Bay Trading Post, it was restored in 2005.

ENTERTAINMENT

Shopping seems to be more than enough entertainment for most of Freeport's visitors, but don't miss the **L. L. Bean Summer Concert Series**. At 7:30pm most Saturdays early July-Labor Day weekend, Bean's hosts free big-name family-oriented events in Discovery Park (95 Main St./Rte. 1). Arrive early—these concerts are *very* popular—and bring a blanket or a folding chair.

RECREATION

Parks, Preserves, and Other Attractions

MAST LANDING AUDUBON SANCTUARY

Just one mile from downtown Freeport, **Mast Landing Audubon Sanctuary** (Upper Mast Landing Rd., 207/781-2330, www.maineaudubon.org, free) is a reprieve from the crowds. Situated at the head of the tide on the Harraseeket River estuary, the 101-acre preserve has a little over three miles of signed trails weaving through an apple orchard, across fields, and through pines and hemlocks. The name? Back in the early 1700s, this land was the source of masts for the Royal Navy. To find it, take Bow Street (across from L. L. Bean) one mile to Upper Mast Landing Road and turn left. The sanctuary is 0.25 mile ahead on the left.

Mast Landing Audubon Sanctuary

WOLFE'S NECK WOODS STATE PARK

Five miles of easy to moderate trails meander through 233-acre **Wolfe's Neck Woods State Park** (Wolfe's Neck Rd., 207/865-4465, www.parksandlands.com, $6 nonresident adults, $4 Maine resident adults, $1 ages 5-11), just a few minutes' cycle or drive from downtown Freeport. You'll need a trail map, available near the parking area. The easiest route (and partly wheelchair-accessible) is the Shoreline Walk, about 0.75 mile, starting near the salt marsh and skirting Casco Bay. Sprinkled along the trails are helpful interpretive panels explaining various points of natural history—bog life, osprey nesting, glaciation, erosion, tree decay, and so forth. Guided tours are offered at 2pm daily mid-July-late August, weather permitting. Leashed pets are allowed. Adjacent **Googins Island,** an osprey sanctuary, is off-limits, but you can spy the nesting birds from the mainland (binoculars help). From downtown Freeport, follow Bow Street (across from L. L. Bean) for 2.25 miles; turn right onto Wolfe's Neck Road (also called Wolf Neck Rd.) and go another 2.25 miles.

WOLFE'S NECK CENTER FOR AGRICULTURE & THE ENVIRONMENT

Kids love **Wolfe's Neck Center** (184 Burnett Rd., 207/865-4469, www.wolfesneck.org), a 626-acre saltwater farm dedicated to sustainable agriculture and environmental education. Visit with farm animals and enjoy the property's trails and varied habitats—fields, forests, seashore, and gardens—at no charge. Bicycle ($10-25) and two-hour kayak and canoe ($25-45/tidal cycle) rentals are available. Check to see what programs are being offered—these might include hayrides, farm and garden harvesting and fare, bird-watching, hiking with goats, and more; most range $5-7 pp.

WINSLOW MEMORIAL PARK

Bring a kite. Bring a beach blanket. Bring a picnic. Bring a boat. Bring binoculars. Heck, bring a tent. Freeport's 90-acre oceanfront municipal playground, **Winslow Memorial Park** (207/865-4198, www.freeportmaine.com, $3), has a spectacular setting on a peninsula extending into island-studded Casco Bay. Facilities include a boat launch ($3-5), a campground ($25-35, no hookups), a fishing pier, a volleyball court, scenic trails, a playground, restrooms, picnic facilities, and a sandy beach (the best swimming is at high tide; no lifeguard). On Thursday evenings in July-August, local bands play. The park is 5.5 miles from downtown. Head south on Route 1 to the Big Indian; go left on South Freeport Road and follow it one mile to Staples Point Road. Take a right onto Staples Point Road and follow it to its end.

BRADBURY MOUNTAIN STATE PARK

Six miles from the hubbub of Freeport is tranquil, wooded 590-acre **Bradbury Mountain State Park** (Rte. 9, Pownal, 207/688-4712, www.parksandlands.com, $6 nonresident adults, $4 Maine resident adults, $1 ages 5-11), with facilities for picnicking, hiking, mountain biking, and rustic camping. Pick up a trail map at the gate and take the easy 0.4-mile round-trip Mountain Trail to the 485-foot summit, with superb views east to the ocean and southeast to Portland. It's gorgeous in fall. Or take the Tote Road Trail, on the western side of the park, where the ghost of Samuel Bradbury himself allegedly brings a chill to hikers in a hemlock grove. A playground keeps the littlest tykes happy. The camping fee is $25/site for nonresidents, $15 for residents. The park season is May 15-October 15, but there's winter access for cross-country skiing. A hawk watch takes place mid-March-mid-May. From Route 1, cross over I-95 at Exit 20 and continue west on Pownal Road to Route 9 and head south.

★ L. L. Bean Outdoor Discovery Schools

Since the early 1980s, the sports outfitter's **Outdoor Discovery Schools** (888/552-3261, www.llbean.com) have helped thousands of outdoors enthusiasts improve their skills in fly-fishing, archery, hiking, canoeing, sea kayaking, winter camping, cross-country skiing, orienteering, and even outdoor photography. **Discovery Series Courses** ($25, includes equipment) provide 1.5-2.5-hour lessons in sports such as kayak touring, fly casting, archery, clay shooting, and snowshoeing. Longer fee-based programs, plus canoeing and camping trips, require preregistration well in advance. Some of the lectures, seminars, and demonstrations held in Freeport are free, and a regular catalog lists the schedule. Bean's waterfront **Flying Point Paddling Center** hosts many of the kayaking, saltwater fly-fishing, and guiding programs and is home to the annual **PaddleSports Festival** in June, with free demonstrations, seminars, vendors, lessons, and more.

L. L. Bean Kids' Camp

There's no need to drag your little ones through the outlets or find a sitter when you want to enjoy an adult-oriented experience. Enroll your child, ages 7-12, for a day or a week in Bean's summer **Kids' Camp** (888/552-3261, www.llbean.com). They'll have a blast exploring Maine's great outdoors with skilled instructors and counselors. Activities include canoeing, kayaking, stand-up paddleboarding, archery, fishing, crafts, nature walks, and more. All equipment is provided; you'll need to provide lunch and snacks. You can even arrange for early or late pickup for an additional fee. Rates vary with the schedule.

Boat Excursions

Captain Peter Milholland's **Seacoast Tours** (207/798-2001, https://seacoasttoursme.com) offers a 3.5-hour **Eagle Island** tour ($40 adults, $28 kids) and a 2-hour **Lobstering Demo & Wildlife Cruise** ($35 adults, $20 ages 2-12) aboard the *Pamela B*. He provides a free shuttle from downtown Freeport to the harbor, which saves the excruciating hunt for a parking space.

Kayak, Canoe, and Bike Rentals

Ring's Marine Service (Smelt Brook Rd., South Freeport, 207/865-6143, www.ringsmarineservice.com) rents single kayaks for $35, tandems for $50, and canoes for $30 (all prices per day), with longer-term rentals and delivery available. Bikes are $18 for a half day.

At **Wolfe's Neck Center** (184 Burnett Rd., 207/865-4469, ww.wolfesneck.org) bicycle rentals are $10-25. Kayak and canoe rentals are $30 per tidal cycle.

FOOD

Freeport has an ever-increasing number of places to eat, but there are nowhere near enough restaurants to satisfy hungry crowds at peak dining hours on busy days. Go early or late for lunch, and make reservations for dinner.

Seafood and Lobster

Order lobster in the rough at **Harraseeket Lunch and Lobster Company** (36 Main St., Town Wharf, South Freeport, lunch counter 207/865-4888, lobster pound 207/865-3535, www.harraseeketlunchandlobster.com, 11am-8:45pm daily summer, 11am-7:45pm daily spring and fall, no credit cards). Be prepared for crowds and a wait in midsummer. Fried clams are particularly good here, and they're prepared either breaded or battered. BYOB.

Far more peaceful is **Day's Seafood Takeout** (1269 Rte. 1, Yarmouth, 207/836-3436, www.dayscrabmeatandlobster.com, 11am-dusk Tues.-Sun.), with picnic tables out back overlooking a tidal estuary.

Quick Bites

South of downtown, **Royal River Natural Foods** (443 Rte. 1, 207/865-0046) has a small selection of prepared foods, including soups, salads, and sandwiches, and there is a seating area.

Can't decide what to eat? **Freeport Public Market** (20 Bow St., 207/865-9478, www.freeportmarket.com) is the answer. Under

Shop Local in Freeport

Unlike many outlet centers across the country, Freeport has an excellent mix of local Maine stores in addition to the big-name national company stores. L.L. Bean is the biggie, but you'll find close to three dozen stores with Maine roots. Here's a sampling:

- **Brahms Mount** (115 Main St., 207/869-4026): blankets, linens, and throws woven on antique shuttle looms
- **Brown Goldsmiths & Co.** (11 Mechanic St., 207/865-4126): handcrafted jewelry
- **Cuddledown** (554 Rte. 1, 207/865-1713): bedding, sleepwear, and linens
- **Georgetown Pottery** (148 Main St., 207/865-0060): hand-painted porcelain pottery
- **Island Treasure Toys** (20 Bow St., 207/865-7007): heirloom-quality children's toys
- **Mexicali Blues** (10 Bow St., 207/865-3303): imported clothing and more
- **Maine Woolens** (124 Main St., 207/865-0755): wool and cotton blankets
- **R. D. Allen Freeport Jewelers** (13 Middle St., 207/865-1818): Maine tourmaline jewelry
- **Sea Bags** (6 Bow St., 207/939-3679): nautically inspired totes made from recycled sails
- **Thos. Moser** (149 Main St., 207/865-4519): home furnishings
- **When Pigs Fly** (21 Main St., 207/865-6006): old-world artisan breads
- **Wicked Whoopies** (32 Main St., 207/865-3100): Maine's official snack
- **Wilbur's of Maine Chocolate Confections** (11-13 Bow St., 207/865-4071): house-made chocolates and confections

one roof are order-at-the-counter shops serving crepes, soups, pizza, and more.

Casual Dining

The Harraseeket Inn (162 Main St., 207/865-9377 or 800/342-6423) has two restaurants. The woodsy ★ **Broad Arrow Tavern** (11:30am-10:30pm daily, $10-30), just two blocks north of L. L. Bean but seemingly a world away, is a perfect place to escape shopping crowds and madness. Everything is made from organic and naturally raised foods. Can't decide? There's also an extensive all-you-can-eat lunch buffet (11:30am-2pm Mon.-Sat., $20), offering a bit of everything. The inn's **Maine Harvest** restaurant showcases themed farm-to-table fare, such as beer or wine dinners, and the Lobster Sunday Brunch (11:45am-2pm Sun., $50), a seemingly endless buffet, with chilled Maine lobster among the highlights.

Breakfast is served all day at the **Freeport Cafe** (29 Rte. 1, 207/869-5113, www.thefreeportcafe.com, 6am-2pm Mon.-Thurs., 6am-8pm Fri.-Sat., 6am-4pm Sun., $6-24), but sandwiches, soups, salads, and heftier American and comfort food options also are available. Beer and wine only.

International

At the southern end of downtown and sited in a house just off Main Street is **Li's Place** (51 West St., 207/865-9299, 11am-8:30pm Tues.-Sun., $8-18), a find for Chinese food. The tiny, unadorned year-round restaurant grew out of a seasonal food cart.

Maine meets Italy at **Tuscan Brick Oven Bistro** (140 Main St., 207/869-7200, www.tuscanbrickovenbistro.com, from 11am Mon.-Sat., from 10am Sun., $11-35), where the menu ranges from pizza to ricotta-and-lobster gnocchi to braised local rabbit to wood-grilled Black Angus steak.

Dine indoors or out on the tree-shaded patio at **Azure Italian Café** (123 Main St., 207/865-1237, www.azurecafe.com, from 11:30am Thurs.-Sun., 5pm-9pm Mon. and Thurs., $15-36). Go light, mixing selections from small plates and appetizers, or savor the heartier entrées. The service is pleasant, and the indoor dining areas are accented by well-chosen contemporary Maine artwork. Live jazz is a highlight some evenings.

ACCOMMODATIONS

Downtown

One of Freeport's pioneering bed-and-breakfasts is on the main drag, but away from much of the traffic, in a restored house where Arctic explorer Donald MacMillan once lived. The 19th-century **White Cedar Inn** (178 Main St., 207/865-9099 or 800/853-1269, www.whitecedarinn.com, $149-219) has seven attractive guest rooms and a two-bedroom suite. The full breakfast will power you through a day of shopping, and it's an easy walk back to drop bags as they accumulate.

About a five-minute walk from downtown shops, the **Brewster Inn** (180 Main St., 207/865-4121, https://brewsterhouse.com, from $199) offers five spacious guest rooms and two suites. A multicourse breakfast is included, and guests have access to honor bar wines by the bottle and the Big Brewstah five-tap kegerator, with Maine craft beers.

Two blocks north of L. L. Bean, the ★ **Harraseeket Inn** (162 Main St., 207/865-9377 or 800/342-6423, www.harraseeketinn.com, from $250) is a splendid 84-room country inn with an indoor pool. One room is decorated with contemporary Thomas Moser furnishings; otherwise, decor is colonial reproduction in the two updated historical buildings and a modern addition. Also available is a three-bedroom, two-bath house adjacent to the inn (from $400, includes use of inn facilities, breakfast, and afternoon tea). The inn is especially accessible, so it's a prime choice for anyone with mobility issues. Rates include a hot-and-cold buffet breakfast and afternoon tea with finger sandwiches and sweets—a refreshing break. Pets are permitted in some Carriage House guest rooms for $25, which includes a dog bed, a small can of food, a treat, and dishes. Ask about packages, which offer great value. Children 12 and younger stay free. The inn has long been a leader in the farm-to-table movement. Free transportation is provided to and from Freeport's Amtrak station.

Beyond Downtown

Three miles north of downtown is the **Maine Idyll** (1411 Rte. 1, 207/865-4201, www.maineidyll.com, $84-141), a tidy cottage colony that has been operated by the Marstaller family for three generations. It is a retro throwback and a find for budget travelers. Twenty pine-paneled cottages (from studios to three bedrooms) are tucked under the trees. The Ritz this is not, but some units have kitchenettes and most have fireplaces. A light breakfast is included. Well-behaved pets are welcome for $5.

The family-run, 45-room ★ **Casco Bay Inn** (107 Rte. 1, 207/865-4925 or 800/570-4970, www.cascobayinn.com, $159) is a bit fancier than most motels. It has a pine-paneled lounge with a fieldstone fireplace. The spacious guest rooms have double sinks in the bath area. A continental breakfast with a newspaper is included.

Camping

For anyone seeking peace, quiet, and low-tech camping in a spectacular setting, ★ **Wolfe's Neck Oceanfront Camping** (134 Burnett Rd., 207/865-9307, www.freeportcamping.com, $32-67) is it. Part of the nonprofit Wolfe's Neck Center, the eco-sensitive campground's sites include quiet, car-free, waterfront walk-ins, regular camping, and glamping, as well as a few hookups. Many sites edge the farm's three-mile-long tidal estuary shorefront. Kayak, canoe, and bicycle rentals are available; swimming depends on the tides. Facilities include a playground and snack bar;

bicycle, kayak and canoe rentals are available. Take Bow Street (across from L. L. Bean) to Wolfe's Neck Road, turn right, go 1.6 miles, and then turn left on Burnett Road. Three pet-friendly oceanfront camping cabins are $225-250, plus $10/pet.

The **Desert of Maine** (95 Desert Rd., 207/865-6962, www.desertofmaine.com, $30-45) offers 23 wooded campsites, 18 with water and electricity, for tent and RVs less than 20 feet.

INFORMATION AND SERVICES

Freeport Merchants Association (Hose Tower, 23 Depot St., 207/865-1212 or 800/865-1994, www.visitfreeport.com) produces an invaluable foldout map-guide showing locations of all the shops, plus sites of lodgings, restaurants, visitor kiosks, restrooms, and car and bike parking.

Just south of Freeport is the **Maine Visitor Information Center** (Rte. 1 at I-95 Exit 17, Yarmouth, 207/846-0833), part of the statewide tourism information network. Also here are restrooms, phones, picnic tables, vending machines, and a dog-walking area.

GETTING THERE AND AROUND

Freeport is about 18 miles or 20 minutes via Route 295 from Portland. It's about 10 miles or 15 minutes via Route 295 to Brunswick. You'll need a car to explore beyond the downtown area.

Some **Amtrak Downeaster** (800/872-7245, www.amtrakdowneaster.com) trains stop in Freeport. The station is downtown, eliminating the need for a car unless you want to explore beyond the shops and in-town activities.

The **Metro Breeze** ($4 adults, $2 ages 6-18) provides express service connecting the Portland Transportation Center, downtown Portland, Yarmouth, Freeport, and Brunswick.

Mid-Coast Region

In contrast to the Southern Coast's gorgeous sandy beaches, the Mid-Coast region is characterized by a deeply indented shoreline with snug harbors and long, gnarled fingers of land. This is where you'll find storybook Maine in a panorama format. Lighthouses, fishing villages, country inns, and lobster wharves pepper the peninsulas. The Mid-Coast, as defined in this chapter, stretches from Brunswick to Waldoboro.

The Bath-Brunswick area is one of the least touristy areas of the coast. Not that visitors don't come, but this area has a strong and varied economic base aside from tourism, which means that no matter when you visit, you'll find shops, museums, restaurants, and lodgings open and activities scheduled. Bowdoin College and Bath Iron Works also

Highlights

Look for ★ to find recommended sights, activities, dining, and lodging.

★ **Bowdoin College:** This beautiful, shady campus is home to the Bowdoin College Museum of Art, the Peary-MacMillan Arctic Museum, and the Maine State Music Theater (page 131).

★ **Maine Maritime Museum:** It's easy to while away a half day enjoying this museum's exhibits and riverfront setting (page 144).

★ **Coastal Maine Botanical Gardens:** This seaside garden comprises 250 acres of well-planned exhibits, trails, and art (page 159).

★ **Burnt Island Tour:** Step back in history and visit with a lighthouse keeper's family circa 1950 (page 160).

★ **Pemaquid Point Lighthouse:** It's hard to say which is Maine's prettiest lighthouse—but Pemaquid's is right up there. It's also depicted on the Maine state quarter (page 171).

★ **Colonial Pemaquid and Fort William Henry:** A beautiful setting overlooking John's Bay, a partially reconstructed fort, and remnants from one of the first British settlements in America make this site well worth a visit (page 172).

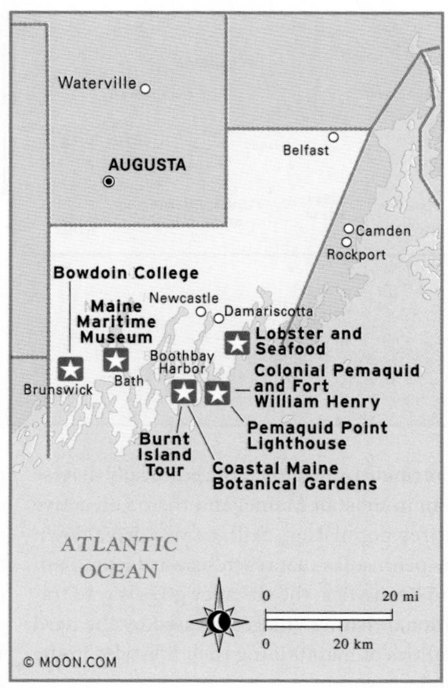

★ **Lobster and Seafood:** Lobster wharves abound in Maine, but the Pemaquid Peninsula has a concentration of scenic spots for lobster lovers (page 179).

Mid-Coast Region

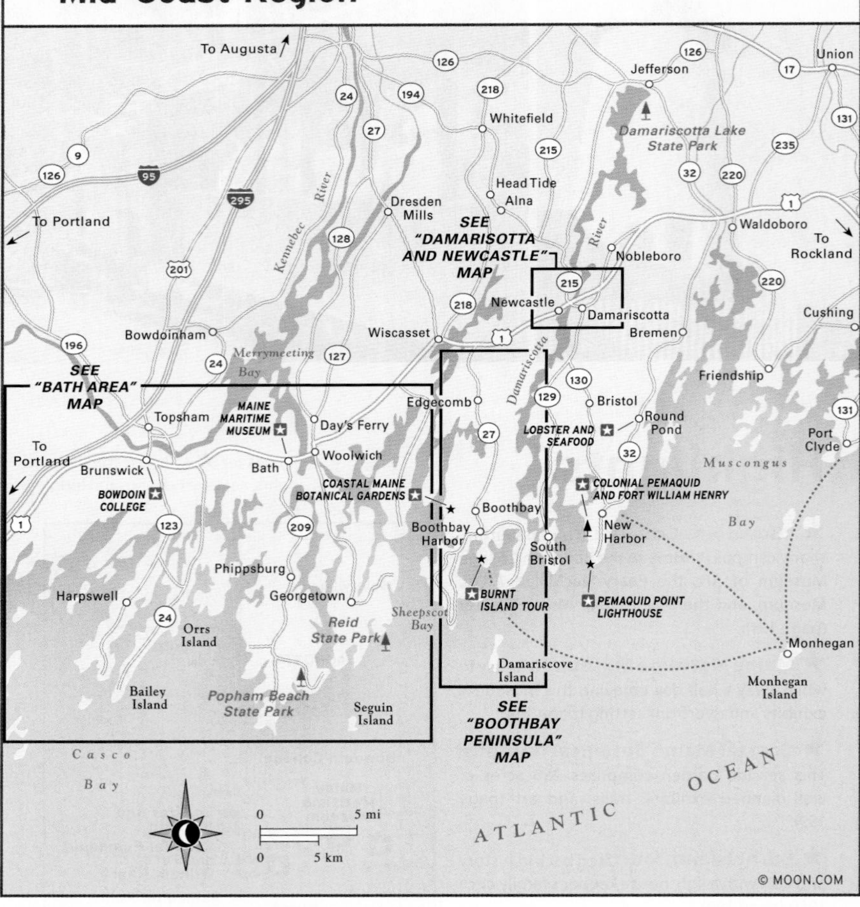

contribute to a region more ethnically diverse than in most of Maine, and there's an active retiree population. Still, as you drive down the peninsulas that reach seaward from Bath and Brunswick, the vibrancy gives way to traditional fishing villages pressed by the hard realities of maintaining such lifestyles in the modern world.

Wiscasset still clings to the nickname of prettiest village in Maine, but for many travelers heading through on Route 1, Wiscasset is nothing but a headache. Traffic often backs up for miles, inching forward through the bottleneck village. Although many are just glad to get through it, those who take time to explore Wiscasset are rewarded with inviting antiques shops and lovely architecture.

The tempo changes northeast of Wiscasset.

Previous: fishing shack in the Harpswells; Pemaquid Point Lighthouse; Boothbay Railway Village.

Traffic eases, and there's less roadside development. Detour down the Boothbay and Pemaquid Peninsulas, and you'll be rewarded with the Maine of postcards. These two peninsulas appear unchallenged as home to more lobster-in-the-rough spots than elsewhere on the coast, and Maine's creative economy is blossoming here, as evidenced by the abundant artists' and artisans' studios.

PLANNING YOUR TIME

Route 1 is the primary artery connecting all the points in the Mid-Coast region, and Wiscasset, a major bottleneck, is smack-dab in the middle. For this reason, it's best to split your lodging and explorations into two parts: south of Wiscasset and north of Wiscasset. Even then, driving down the long fingers of land requires patience. The towns south of Wiscasset are less touristy than those on the Boothbay or Pemaquid Peninsulas, with Orr's and Bailey Islands and the Phippsburg Peninsula being the best places to experience old-time summer flavor.

To cover the region, you'll need 4-5 days. Antiques mavens should concentrate their efforts in Bath, Wiscasset, and Damariscotta. Allow at least two days to appreciate the fine museums in Brunswick and Bath, and another day to tour Wiscasset's historical house museums and nearby fort. If you're an avid or even aspiring kayaker, you'll want time to poke through the nooks and crannies of the coastline in a boat, and if you value parks and preserves, this region offers plenty worth your time.

Brunswick Area

Brunswick, straddling Route 1, was incorporated in 1738 and is steeped in history. It's home to prestigious Bowdoin College, classic homes and churches, several respected museums, and year-round cultural attractions.

Brunswick (pop. 20,278) and **Topsham** (pop. 8,784) face each other across roiling waterfalls on the Androscoggin River. The falls, which Native Americans knew by the tongue-twisting name of Ahmelahcogneturcook ("place abundant with fish, birds, and other animals"), were a source of hydropower for 18th-century sawmills and 19th-20th-century textile mills. Franco Americans arrived in droves to beef up the textile industry in the late 19th century, but eventually lost their jobs in the Great Depression. Those once-derelict mills now house shops, restaurants, and offices.

Brunswick is also the gateway to the **Harpswells** (pop. 4,740), a peninsula-archipelago complex linked by causeways, several bridges, and a unique granite cribstone bridge. Scenic back roads on Harpswell Neck inspire detours to the fishing hamlets of **Cundy's Harbor, Orr's Island,** and **Bailey Island,** and once you're here, it's easy to want to linger.

SIGHTS

★ Bowdoin College

Bowdoin College (Brunswick, 207/725-3000, www.bowdoin.edu) was founded in 1794 as a men's college with a handful of students; coed since 1969, it now has 1,750 students. The college has turned out such noted graduates as authors Nathaniel Hawthorne and Henry Wadsworth Longfellow, sex-research pioneer Alfred Kinsey, U.S. president Franklin Pierce, Arctic explorers Robert Peary and Donald MacMillan, U.S. senators George Mitchell and William Cohen, and a dozen Maine governors. Massachusetts Hall, the oldest building on the 110-acre campus, dates from 1802. The stately Bowdoin pines, on the northeast boundary, are even older. The striking **David Saul Smith Union,** occupying 40,000 square feet in a former athletic building on the east side of the campus, has a café, pub, lounge, and bookstore open to the public. Call for information on admissions and **campus tours** (207/725-3100) and on **concerts, lectures,** and **performances** open to the public (207/725-3375).

Photos and artifacts bring arctic expeditions to life at the small but fascinating **Peary-MacMillan Arctic Museum** (Hubbard Hall, 207/725-3416, www.bowdoin.edu/arctic-museum, 10am-5pm Tues.-Sat., 2pm-5pm Sun., free). Among the specimens are animal mounts, fur clothing, snow goggles, and Inuit carvings—most collected by Arctic pioneers Robert E. Peary and Donald B. MacMillan, both Bowdoin grads. Permanent exhibits highlight the natural and cultural diversity of the arctic. The small gift shop specializes in Inuit books and artifacts.

An astonishing array of Greek and Roman artifacts is only one of the high points at the **Bowdoin College Museum of Art** (Walker Art Building, 207/725-3275, www.bowdoin.edu/art-museum, 10am-5pm Tues.-Sat., 10am-8:30pm Thurs., 2pm-5pm Sun., free). Designed in the 1890s by Charles McKim of the famed McKim, Mead, and White firm, it's a stunning neoclassical edifice with an interior rotunda and stone lions flanking the entry. In 2007, the museum was expanded and modernized, adding a striking bronze-and-glass entry pavilion to preserve the facade while also achieving accessibility. The college's prized Assyrian reliefs, previously in the magnificent rotunda, were moved to a glass-walled addition facing Brunswick's Park Row. The renovated museum is a fitting setting for the impressive permanent collection of 19th- and 20th-century American art and other works.

Pejepscot Historical Society Museums

Side by side in an unusual cupola-topped duplex facing Brunswick's Mall (village green) are two museums operated by the **Pejepscot Historical Society** (207/729-6606, www.pejepscothistorical.org): the **Pejepscot Museum & Research Center** (159 Park Row, Brunswick, 10am-noon and 1pm-4pm Tues.-Sat., free) and the **Skolfield-Whittier House** (161 Park Row, Brunswick, tours at 10am, 11am, 1pm, 2pm, and 3pm Wed.-Sat. late May-mid-Oct., $12 adults, $6 ages 6-16, $30 family). Focusing on local history, the museum has a permanent collection of more than 50,000 artifacts and mounts and hosts an always-interesting special exhibit each year. The 17-room Skolfield-Whittier House, on the right side of the building, looks as though the owners just stepped out for the afternoon. Unoccupied from 1925 to 1982, the onetime sea captain's house has elegant Victorian furnishings and lots of exotic artifacts collected on global seafaring stints.

The Pejepscot Historical Society also operates the **Joshua L. Chamberlain Museum** (226 Maine St., Brunswick, 207/729-6606, tours on the hour 10am-3pm Tues.-Sat., 1pm-3pm Sun. late May-mid-Oct., 10am-3pm Fri.-Sat., 1pm-3pm Sun. mid-Oct.-mid-Nov., $12 adults, $6 ages 6-16, $30 family). Across from First Parish Church, it commemorates the Union army hero of the Civil War's Battle of Gettysburg, who in recent decades has gained long-overdue respect. The partly restored house where Chamberlain lived in the late 19th century (and where Henry Wadsworth Longfellow had lived 30 years earlier) is a peculiar architectural hodgepodge with six rooms of exhibits of Chamberlain memorabilia, much of it Civil War-related. A gift shop stocks lots of Civil War publications, especially ones covering the Twentieth Maine Volunteers. A combination ticket for both historical houses is $16 adults, $10 children, $55 family.

Also under the museum's umbrella is the **Brunswick Women's History Trail.** With more than 20 points of interest, the trail covers such national notables as authors Harriet Beecher Stowe and Kate Douglas Wiggin along with lesser-known lights, including naturalist Kate Furbish, pioneering Maine pediatrician Dr. Alice Whittier, and the

1: Bowdoin College Museum of Art **2:** the cribstone bridge connecting Orr's and Bailey Islands

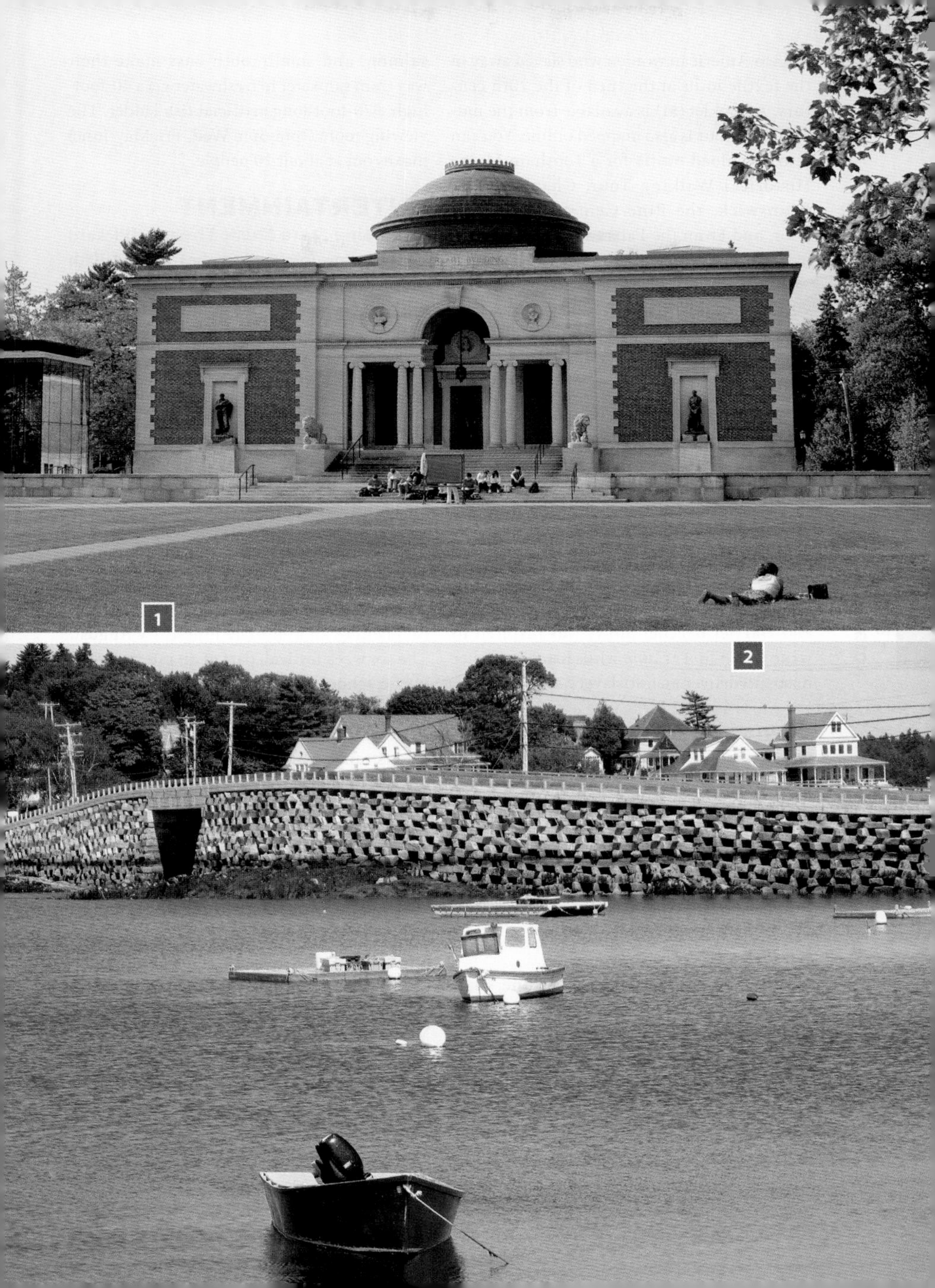
1
2

Franco American women who slaved away in the textile mills at the turn of the 20th century. A booklet ($1) is available from the museum; the tour is also mapped online. You can also download **maps** for a Topsham Maine Historical Walking Tour, Chamberlain's Brunswick, the Pine Cemetery Walking Tour, and From the Falls to the Bay: A Tour of Historic Brunswick, Maine.

The museum also offers guided, 60- to 90-minute **Summer Walking Tours** ($10 adults, $5 children). Each week is a different topic of regional interest, but all depart from the museum. Preregistration is required.

Uncle Tom's Church

Across the street from the Chamberlain museum is the historic 1846 **First Parish Church** (9 Cleveland St. at Bath Rd., Brunswick, 207/729-7331), a Gothic Revival (or carpenter Gothic) board-and-batten structure crowning the rise at the head of Maine Street. Scores of celebrity preachers have ascended this pulpit, and Harriet Beecher Stowe was inspired to write *Uncle Tom's Cabin* while listening to her husband deliver an antislavery sermon here.

Brunswick Literary Art Walk

Cast your eyes downward while walking along Maine Street. Four bronze plaques recognize Brunswick's most famous writers: Henry Wadsworth Longfellow, Nathaniel Hawthorne, Harriet Beecher Stowe, and Robert P. T. Coffin. Each plaque bears a quote from the author commemorated.

Brunswick Fish Ladder

If you're in town mid-May-late June, plan to visit **Brookfield Power's Brunswick Hydro** generating station, also known as **Brunswick Fishway,** straddling the falls on the Androscoggin River and the Brunswick-Topsham town line (Lower Maine St., next to Fort Andross). A glass-walled viewing room lets you play voyeur during the annual ritual of anadromous fish heading upstream to spawn. Amazingly undaunted by the obstacles, such species as alewives (herring), salmon, and smallmouth bass make their way from saltwater to freshwater via a 40-foot-high, 570-foot-long artificial fish ladder. The viewing room (1pm-5pm Wed.-Fri. May-June) maxes out at about 20 people.

ENTERTAINMENT

The **Maine State Music Theatre** (Pickard Theater, Bowdoin College; box office 1 Bath Rd., Brunswick, 207/725-8769, www.msmt.org) has been a summer tradition since 1959. The state-of-the-art, air-conditioned theater brings real pros to its stage for four summer musicals. Performances are at 8pm Tuesday-Saturday; matinees are staged at 2pm on an alternating schedule—each week has matinees on different days. No children under age four are admitted, but special family shows are performed during the season.

The **Bowdoin International Music Festival** (box office 181 Park Row, Brunswick, 207/373-1400, www.bowdoinfestival.org) is a showcase for an international array of classical talent of all kinds late June-early August. The six-week festival, part of an international music school, presents a variety of concert opportunities—enough that there's music almost every night of the week. Venues vary and tickets range from free to $45. Call or check the website for the current schedule.

Second Friday Art Walks (207/725-4366) take place in downtown Brunswick 5pm-8pm on the second Friday of the month May-September. Gallery openings, wine tastings, light refreshments, and other activities are usually part of the mix.

Music on the Mall presents family band concerts at 6pm-8pm Wednesday (Thursday if it rains) in July-August on the Brunswick Mall, the lovely park in the center of town.

Festivals and Events

The first full week of August, the **Topsham Fair** is a weeklong agricultural festival with exhibits, demonstrations, live music, oxen pulls, contests, harness racing, and fireworks at the Topsham Fairgrounds.

The third Saturday of August, the **Maine**

Joshua Chamberlain, Civil War Hero

statue of Joshua Chamberlain

When the American Civil War began in 1861, Joshua Chamberlain was a 33-year-old logic instructor at Bowdoin College in Brunswick; by the time it ended, in 1865, Chamberlain had earned the Medal of Honor for his "daring heroism and great tenacity in holding his position on the Little Round Top" at the Battle of Gettysburg. He was designated by Ulysses S. Grant to formally accept the official surrender of Confederate general John Gordon (both men represented the infantry). He later became governor of Maine (1867-1871) and president of Bowdoin College, but Chamberlain's greatest renown, ironically, came more than a century later—when 1990s PBS filmmakers focused on the Civil War and highlighted his strategic military role.

Joshua Lawrence Chamberlain was born in 1828 in Brewer, Maine, the son and grandson of soldiers. After graduating from Bowdoin in 1852, he studied for the ministry at Bangor Theological Seminary and then returned to his alma mater as an instructor.

With the nation in turmoil in the early 1860s, Chamberlain signed on to help, receiving a commission as a lieutenant colonel in the Twentieth Maine Volunteers in 1862. After surviving 24 encounters and six battle wounds and having been promoted to general (brigadier, then major), Chamberlain was elected Republican governor of Maine in 1866—by the largest margin in the state's history—only to suffer through four one-year terms of partisan politics. In 1871, Chamberlain became president of Bowdoin College, where he remained until 1883. He then dove into speechmaking and writing, his best-known work being *The Passing of the Armies,* a memoir of the Civil War's final campaigns. From 1900 to 1914, Chamberlain was surveyor of the Port of Portland, a presidential appointment that ended only when complications from a wartime abdominal wound finally did him in. He died at the grand old age of 86.

Brunswick's Joshua L. Chamberlain Museum, in his onetime home at 226 Maine Street, commemorates this illustrious Mainer, and thousands of Civil War buffs annually stream through the door in search of Chamberlain "stuff." To make it easier, the Pejepscot Historical Society has produced a helpful map titled "Joshua Chamberlain's Brunswick," highlighting town and college ties to the man—his dorm rooms, his presidential office, his portraits, even his church pew (number 64 at First Parish Church). Chamberlain's gravesite, marked by a reddish granite stone, is in Brunswick's Pine Grove Cemetery, just east of the Bowdoin campus.

Biennially, the museum celebrates **Chamberlain Days** with a symposium that concentrates on his roles in the war and in Maine. Typically, events include lectures by authors and scholars; field trips to places of interest connected with Chamberlain's life; tours of his home, concentrating on the most recent restoration work; musical or dramatic performances; and group discussions.

Highland Games, sponsored by the St. Andrew's Society of Maine, mark the annual wearing of the plaids—but you needn't be Scottish to join in the games, watch the Highland dancing, or browse the arts and crafts booths. (Only a Scot, however, can appreciate that unique concoction called haggis.)

SHOPPING

Downtown Brunswick invites leisurely browsing, with most of the shops concentrated on Maine Street. Take special care when crossing the four-lane-wide street, and do so only at marked crosswalks.

The **Bayview Gallery** (58 Maine St., Brunswick, 800/244-3007) specializes in contemporary New England artists. Nearly two dozen local artists exhibit their works in varied media at **Sebascodegan Artists Gallery** (929 Rte. 123, Harpswell, 207/833-5717).

More than 140 dealers show and sell their wares at **Cabot Mill Antiques** (14 Maine St., 207/725-2855), in the renovated Fort Andross mill complex next to the Androscoggin River.

Part gallery, part resource center, **Maine Fiberarts** (13 Maine St., Topsham, 207/721-0678, www.mainefiberarts.org) is a must-stop for anyone interested in fiber-related artwork: knitting, quilting, spinning, and basketry. If you're interested in finding artists and resources statewide, check out the group's online offerings.

With an eclectic new-book inventory that includes lots of esoterica, **Gulf of Maine Books** (134 Maine St., Brunswick, 207/729-5083) has held the competition at bay since the early 1980s. The fiction selection is particularly good, as are the religion, health, and poetry sections. Poet, publisher, and Renaissance man Gary Lawless oversees everything.

RECREATION

Parks and Preserves

In the village of **Bailey Island,** a well-maintained path edges the cliffs and passes the **Giant Stairs,** a waterfront stone stairway of mammoth proportions. To get there, take Route 24 from Cooks Corner toward Bailey Island and Land's End, keeping an eye out for Washington Avenue, on the left about 1.5 miles after the cribstone bridge. (Or drive to **Land's End,** park the car with the rest of the crowds, survey the panorama, and walk 0.8 mile back along Route 24 to Washington Avenue from there.) Turn onto Washington Avenue, go 0.1 mile, and park at the Episcopal church (corner of Ocean St.). Walk along Ocean Street to the shorefront path. Watch for a tiny sign just before Spindrift Lane. Don't let small kids get close to the slippery rocks on the surf-tossed shoreline. The same advice holds for Land's End, where the rocks can be treacherous.

Thank the **Brunswick-Topsham Land Trust** (108 Maine St., Brunswick, 207/729-7694, www.btlt.org), founded in 1985, for access to the 11-acre shorefront **Alfred Skolfield Preserve,** historically a portage site for Native Americans and later home to a shipyard. One of the two blue-blazed nature-trail loops skirts a salt marsh, where you're apt to see egrets, herons, and ospreys in summer. Take Route 123 (Harpswell Rd.) south from Brunswick about three miles; when you reach the Middle Bay Road intersection (on the right), continue on Route 123 for 1.1 miles. Watch for a small sign and a small parking area on the right.

Tucked behind the Harpswell town office, off Mountain Road linking Route 123 with Route 24, the **Cliff Trail** is a 1.5-mile loop that follows the shoreline along Strawberry Creek, passes through forests with fairy houses, and rises to 150-foot cliffs with dreamy views over Long Reach.

Nearly four miles of trails wind through fields and forests and edge cliffs on the 118-acre **Bowdoin College Coastal Studies Center,** a spectacular chunk of oceanfront tipping an Orr's Island peninsula. To find it, take Route 24 south and then turn right on Bayview Road (just under two miles beyond the bridge). Keep right at the fork. When the road turns to gravel, continue to a parking area with an info kiosk where you can pick up a trail map. The lot only holds six cars.

Swimming

Thomas Point Beach (29 Meadow Rd., Brunswick, 207/725-6009 or 877/872-4321, www.thomaspointbeach.com, 9am-sunset daily mid-May-Sept., $4 adults, $2.50 ages 3-12) is 85 acres of privately owned parkland with facilities for swimming (lifeguard on duty, bathhouses), fishing, field sports, picnicking (500 tables), and camping (75 tent and RV sites for $30-35; no water or sewer hookups, but electricity and a dump station are available). No pets, skateboards, or motorcycles are allowed. The sandy beach is tidal, so the swimming "window" is about two hours before high tide until two hours afterward; otherwise, you're wallowing in mudflats. The same timing applies to kayakers and canoeists. Toddlers head for the big playground; teenagers gravitate to the arcade and the ice cream parlor. From Cooks Corner, take Route 24 south 1.5 miles, turn left, and follow signs for less than two miles to the park.

A popular, family-oriented spot for freshwater swimming is **White's Beach** (Durham Rd., Brunswick, 207/729-0415, www.whitesbeachandcampground.com, $3.50 adults, $2.50 seniors and under age 13). The sandy-bottomed pond maxes out at nine feet. Park facilities include a snack bar, playground, hot showers, and campsites ($25-36). From Route 1 just south of the I-95 exit into Brunswick, take Durham Road 2.2 miles northwest.

Boat Excursions

Departing at noon from the Cook's Lobster House wharf (Cook's Landing) in Bailey Island (off Rte. 24), a large, sturdy **Casco Bay Lines ferry** (207/774-7871, www.cascobaylines.com, $17 adults, $8 ages 5-9) does a 1.75-hour narrated circuit of nearby islands, including Eagle Island, the onetime home of Admiral Robert Peary (there are no stopovers on these circuits). Reservations aren't needed.

Sea Escape Charters (Bailey Island, 207/833-5531, www.seaescapecottages.com) operates two- to six-hour sails aboard the schooner *Alert* ($40-100 adults, $32-80 ages 3-10), a 70-foot Maine-built windjammer. Trips operate out of Sea Escape Cottages, a collection of well-equipped one- or two-bedroom cottages with full kitchens and oceanside decks, along with two suites ($170-205/night, $1,035-1,250/week). Pet-friendly units (extra $25/day) are available.

Captain Len Duda's **Casco Bay Sights-N-Lights** (207/837-1788, www.cascobaysightseeing.com) offers three boating excursions, including two- and three-hour tours of Orr's and Bailey Islands ($135-185 covers two people, plus $25-35 for each additional up to six) and one to Eagle Island, allowing two hours to explore the museum and trails ($40 pp, $18 under age 12). The boat departs from Morse's Cribstone Grill (1945 Harpswell Islands Rd./Rte. 24, Bailey Island).

Paddle Sports

H2Outfitters (Orr's Island, 207/833-5257 or 800/205-2925, www.h2outfitters.com) has been thriving since 1978. Based in a wooden building on the Orr's Island side of the famed cribstone bridge, this experienced company organizes guided sea-kayaking trips, including island camping; all gear is included. A three-hour tour is $75 pp for two; full-day, sunset, and full-moon tours also available. H2O also offers coastal camping trips.

Seaspray Kayaking (207/443-3646 or 888/349-7772, www.seaspraykayaking.com) has bases on the New Meadows River in Brunswick and Sebasco Harbor Resort in Phippsburg as well as rental centers in Georgetown and at Hermit Island Campground, Small Point for kayaks, paddleboards, and canoes. Rentals range $20-35 half day, $25-35 full day. Equipment options include solo and tandem kayaks, recreational kayaks, surf kayaks, paddleboards, SUPs, and canoes. Tours, led by Registered Maine Guides, vary from sunset paddles to three-day expeditions and include moonlight paddles, island-to-island tours, and inn-to-inn tours. Rates begin at $40 per adult. A striper-fishing kayak tour, including tackle and instruction, is $85. Lessons also are available.

If you're an experienced sea kayaker, consider exploring Harpswell Sound from the boat launch on the west side of the cribstone bridge; kayaks can also be put in at Mackerel Cove, near Cook's Lobster House. A launch with plentiful parking is at Sawyer Park on the New Meadows River, on Route 1 just before you cross the river heading north.

FOOD

Lobster and Seafood

You want fresh? You want simple? **Erica's Seafood** (6 Malcolm Dr., South Harpswell,

207/833-7354, www.ericasseafood.com, 11am-7pm daily), a family-owned seasonal takeout on a working wharf overlooking Casco Bay, delivers on both counts. The menu includes lobster and crabmeat rolls, fried seafood, chowders, and burgers. Most seating is outdoors at picnic tables; a few tables are sheltered. Cash only.

The nonprofit Holbrook Community Foundation owns the historical Holbrook's complex, which comprises a Holbrook's General Store (ice cream and penny candy), Hawk's Lobster (selling lobster by the pound and fun items), and **Holbrook's Lobster Grill** (984 Cundy's Harbor Rd., Harpswell, 207/729-9050, www.holbrookwharf.com, 11am-8:30pm daily, $10-20), an order-at-the-counter spot with sheltered and open seating on the wharf.

Other good bets for lobster, along with chowders and fried seafood, are **Gurnet Trading Co.** (602 Gurnet Rd./Rte. 24, Brunswick, 207/729-7300, www.gurnettrading.com, 10am-6pm Mon.-Sat., 10am-4pm Sun., $7-20), serving lunch and dinner daily overlooking Buttermilk Cove; **Giant Stairs Seafood Grille Restaurant** (2118 Harpswell Islands Rd./Rte. 24, 207/833-5000, 7am-8:30pm Thurs.-Sun., $8-25); and **Morse's Cribstone Grill** (1945 Harpswell Islands Rd., Bailey Island, 207/833-7775, 11:30am-8pm Sun.-Thurs., 11:30am-9pm Fri.-Sat., $9-32), perched on the shorefront adjacent to the cribstone bridge.

Arguments rage endlessly about who makes the best chowder in Maine, but the ★ **Dolphin Marina and Chowder House** (Dolphin Marina, 515 Basin Point Rd., South Harpswell, 207/833-6000, www.dolphinmarinaandrestaurant.com, 11:30am-8pm daily May-Oct., $18-36) tops lots of lists for its fish chowder, accompanied by a blueberry muffin. Equally famed is its lobster stew; plus, you can't beat the scenic 13-mile drive south from Brunswick or the spectacular sea and island views through the rounded row of windows of its waterfront building.

Quick Bites

The cafeteria-style ★ **Wild Oats Bakery and Café** (149 Maine St., Tontine Mall, Brunswick, 207/725-6287, www.wildoatsbakery.com, 7am-5pm Mon.-Sat., 8am-5pm Sun.) turns out terrific made-from-scratch breads and pastries, as well as sandwiches, wraps, salads, and soups. It has inside and outside tables, moderate prices, good-for-you salads, and great sandwiches.

H2Outfitters offers guided sea-kayaking trips from its Orr's Island location.

Note: Wild Oats plans to move to Brunswick Landing (off Bath Road near Cooks Corner) in late 2020.

For food on the run—no-frills hot dogs straight from the cart—head for Brunswick's Mall, the village green where **Danny's on the Mall** (no phone) has been cooking dirt-cheap tube steaks since the early 1980s.

Fat Boy Drive-In (Bath Rd./Old Rte. 1, Brunswick, 207/729-9431, http://fatboy-drivein.com, 11am-8pm Thurs.-Tues., $3-16, no credit cards) is a genuine throwback—a landmark since 1955, it boasts carhops, window trays, and a menu guaranteed to clog your arteries. Onion rings, frappés, and BLTs are specialties. Aim for the second Saturday in August, when the annual Sock Hop takes place.

Choose from about 30 flavors of gelato and sorbet at the **Gelato Fiasco** (74 Maine St., Brunswick, 207/607-4002, 11am-11pm daily). You can find these to-die-for gelati statewide, but this is ground zero.

A favorite for *chowdah* is **Salt Cod Cafe** (1894 Harpswell Islands Rd., Orr's Island, 207/833-6210, www.saltcodcafe.com, 7:30am-4pm daily), with a primo location overlooking the cribstone bridge. Sandwiches, wraps, rolls, and baked goods are also available.

The chocolates, truffles, and bark made by Melinda Richter at **Island Candy Company** (Harpswell Islands Rd., Orr's Island, 207/833-6639, 11am-8pm daily in season) are divine, and there are baked goods, ice cream, ice cream sandwiches made with cookies, and a lovely garden too.

The **Brunswick Farmers Market** sets up rain or shine on the Mall (village green) 8am-2pm Tuesdays and Fridays May-November; Friday is the bigger day. The **Brunswick-Topsham Land Trust Farmers' Market** takes place 8:30am-12:30pm Saturdays May-November at Crystal Spring Farm (277 Pleasant Hill Rd.). You'll find produce, cheeses, crafts, condiments, live lobsters, and serendipitous surprises, depending on the season.

Family Favorites

Just over the bridge from Brunswick, in the renovated Bowdoin Mill complex overlooking the Androscoggin River, the **Sea Dog Brewery** (1 Main St., Topsham, 207/725-0162, www.seadogbrewing.com, 11am-1am daily, $12-32) has seating inside and on a deck overhanging the river. The menu ranges from burgers and sandwiches to full-plate entrées. The brewery offers frequent acoustic entertainment, and there are games for kids, a video arcade, and pool tables.

International

Pho fans will find it and other Vietnamese fare at **Lemongrass** (212 Maine St., Brunswick, 207/725-9008, www.lemongrassme.com, 11am-2pm and 4:30pm-9pm daily, $9-19).

You'll find decent sushi and Japanese specialties at **Little Tokyo** (72 Maine St., Brunswick, 207/798-6888, www.littletokyomaine.com, 11:30am-9:30pm daily, $10-25).

Eclectic doesn't begin to describe **Frontier Cafe** (Mill 3, Fort Andross, 14 Maine St. at Rte. 1 overpass, Brunswick, 207/725-5222, www.explorefrontier.com, 11am-9pm Sun. and Tues.-Thurs., 11am-10pm Fri.-Sat., kitchen closes one hour earlier, $13-26), a combination café, gallery, and cinema inspired by founder Michael Gilroy's world travels. The menu includes wonderful market plates emphasizing the cuisine of a country or region—Spain, France, the Middle East, Italy, or global—as well as other worldly flavors, burgers, and vegetarian and vegan options. A café-coffee bar with grab-and-go fare opens 8am Tuesday-Friday, 9am Saturday-Sunday.

Antipasti and Greek platters, *ribollita*, and *arancini* are just a few of the Greek and Italian choices that might appear on the seasonally changing menu at **Enoteca Athena** (97 Maine St., Brunswick, 207/721-0100, www.enotecaathena.com, from 5pm Mon., from 3:30pm Tues.-Sat., $17-22), a casual wine bar with a menu focused on rustic Greek and Italian fare.

Generous portions, moderate prices, efficient service, and narrow aisles are the story at the **Great Impasta** (42 Maine St., Brunswick, 207/729-5858, https://thegreatimpasta.net, 11am-9pm Mon.-Thurs., 11am-10pm Fri.-Sat., $17-28), a cheerful, informal eatery where the garlic meets you at the door. There are gluten-free choices and a "bambino menu" for the kids.

Opa! Pair authentic Greek fare with a Greek wine at **Taverna Khione** (25 Mill St., Brunswick, 207/406-2847, www.tavernakhione.com, 5pm-8pm Tues.-Sun., $20-28). On Sundays, the only option is a three-course menu ($35).

★ **Tao Yuan** (22 Pleasant St., Brunswick, 207/725-9002, www.tao-yuan.me, from 5pm Tues.-Sat., $16-30) wows guests with fresh and innovative Asian cuisine expertly prepared by chef-owner Cara Stadler, who trained with master chefs in France and China and has been nominated for a Beard Award. A blind-tasting menu is $68; a pre-theater version, offered from 5pm-6pm, is $48.

ACCOMMODATIONS

Motels and Inns

Looking rather like the film set of an old-fashioned tearjerker, the family-run **Driftwood Inn** (81 Washington Ave., Bailey Island, 207/833-5461, www.thedriftwoodinnmaine.com, no credit cards, $105-140) has 25 rustic pine-paneled guest rooms in four buildings (some with a private toilet and sink; all with shared showers), six housekeeping cottages ($800-950 per week), a saltwater pool, a stunning view, a dining room, and a take-us-as-we-are ambience. There are no frills, period, but there are oceanfront porches, games, and rare old-fashioned simplicity. You'll fall asleep listening to the waves crash on the rocky shore. It's all on three oceanfront acres near the Giant Stairs. The dining room, open to nonguests by reservation, serves solid Maine fare with an emphasis on seafood late June-early September for $18-24; breakfast is $8. Meals aren't offered during spring and fall. Dogs are allowed in the cottages.

Walk to a beach, the Giant Stairs, and local restaurants from **Cooks Island View Motel** (2041 Harpswell Islands Rd./Rte. 24, Bailey Island, 207/233-7030, http://cooksislandmotel.com, $110-120), a nicely updated motel with 18 rooms and an outdoor pool.

Drive down Route 24, cross the cribstone bridge, and you'll see the **Bailey Island Motel** (1954 Harpswell Islands Rd./Rte. 24, Bailey Island, 207/833-2886, www.baileyislandmotel.com, $159), a congenial, clean, few-frills waterfront spot with 11 guest rooms and wowser views. Kids under 9 stay for free; older children are $15 extra per night. Continental breakfast is included; guests have use of kayaks. A wharf and moorings are available.

The **Brunswick Hotel and Tavern** (4 Noble St., Brunswick, 207/837-6565, www.thebrunswickhotelandtavern.com, from $229) is adjacent to the station where the Concord Coach Lines bus and Amtrak's Downeaster train stop; it's also across from the town green and within steps of Bowdoin College. Historical photographs and nods to Bowdoin's polar bear mascot offset the contemporary decor. Amenities include a restaurant with an outdoor patio and a fitness room. Dog-friendly rooms are available ($50 fee).

Bed-and-Breakfasts

Within walking distance of downtown Brunswick, but across the bridge spanning the Androscoggin River, is the **Black Lantern B&B** (57 Elm St., Topsham, 207/725-4165 or 888/306-4165, www.blacklanternbandb.com, $125-140), Tom and Judy Connelie's lovely 1860s riverfront home. All guest rooms are decorated with an emphasis on comfort, and two have water views. Judy's quilts will warm you on a cool night.

On the outskirts of town, in a rural location smack-dab on Middle Bay, is **Middle Bay Farm Bed and Breakfast** (287 Pennellville Rd., Brunswick, 207/373-1375, www.middlebayfarm.com, year-round,

$170-190), lovingly and beautifully restored by Phyllis Truesdell. Once the site of the Pennell Brothers Shipyard, the farmhouse and sail loft now house guests seeking an away-from-it-all yet convenient location. Four water-view guest rooms in the 1834 farmhouse are decorated with antiques. Two suites in the sail loft each have a living room with a kitchenette and two tiny bedrooms; they share an open porch. All guests receive a full breakfast in the water-view dining room. Bring a sea kayak to launch from the dock if you'd like.

The 1761 **Harpswell Inn** (108 Lookout Point Rd., South Harpswell, 207/833-5509 or 800/843-5509, www.harpswellinn.com, year-round, $180-200) is a comfortable, welcoming, antiques-filled oasis on 2.5 secluded water-view acres. It's tough to break away from the glass-walled great room, but Middle Bay sunsets from the porch can do it. In fall, the foliage on two little islets in the cove turns brilliant red. The bed-and-breakfast has eight guest rooms and two suites ($275).

Thirteen miles south of Cooks Corner, the **Log Cabin** (Rte. 24, Bailey Island, 207/833-5546, www.logcabin-maine.com, from $229) has nine nicely decorated guest rooms with private decks facing the bay, and, weather permitting, splendid sunset views to the White Mountains. Four guest rooms have kitchen facilities; some have gas fireplaces or jetted tubs. There's also an outdoor heated pool. Full breakfast is included; dinner ($19-36) is available.

Right downtown, facing the tree-shaded Mall, is the ★ **Brunswick Inn** (165 Park Row, Brunswick, 207/729-4914 or 800/299-4914, www.brunswickbnb.com, year-round, from $229), a stately 30-room Federal mansion built in 1848. Fine art from a local gallery hangs throughout the inn, complementing the handsome decor. Fifteen comfortable guest rooms are split between the main house and the renovated Carriage House (with two fully accessible guest rooms). There's also a small cottage with a kitchen. Inside the main inn is a laid-back lounge with occasional entertainment. Even if you don't stay here, make reservations for the inn's three-course fixed-price dinners, offered on Tuesday nights ($45).

INFORMATION AND SERVICES

Area information is provided by the **Southern Midcoast Chamber of Commerce** (877/725-8797, www.midcoastmaine.com) and the **Harpswell Business Association** (www.harpswellmaine.org).

GETTING THERE AND AROUND

Brunswick is about 10 miles or 15 minutes via Route 295 from Freeport. It's about nine miles or 15 minutes via Route 1 to Bath.

The **Amtrak Downeaster** (800/872-7245, www.amtrakdowneaster.com) makes daily trips between Boston and Brunswick, with Maine stops in Saco, Wells, Old Orchard (seasonal), Portland, and Freeport.

Bath Area

One of the smallest in area among Maine's cities, **Bath** (pop. 8,514) packs a wallop in only nine square miles. Like Brunswick, it straddles Route 1 and edges a river, but Bath's centuries of historical and architectural tradition and well-preserved Victorian downtown have earned it a prized designation: The National Trust for Historic Preservation named it a Distinctive Destination.

Giant cranes dominate the riverfront cityscape at the huge Bath Iron Works complex, the source of state-of-the-art warships. Less evident (but not far away) is the link to the past: Just south of Bath, in Popham on the Phippsburg Peninsula, is the poorly

Bath Area

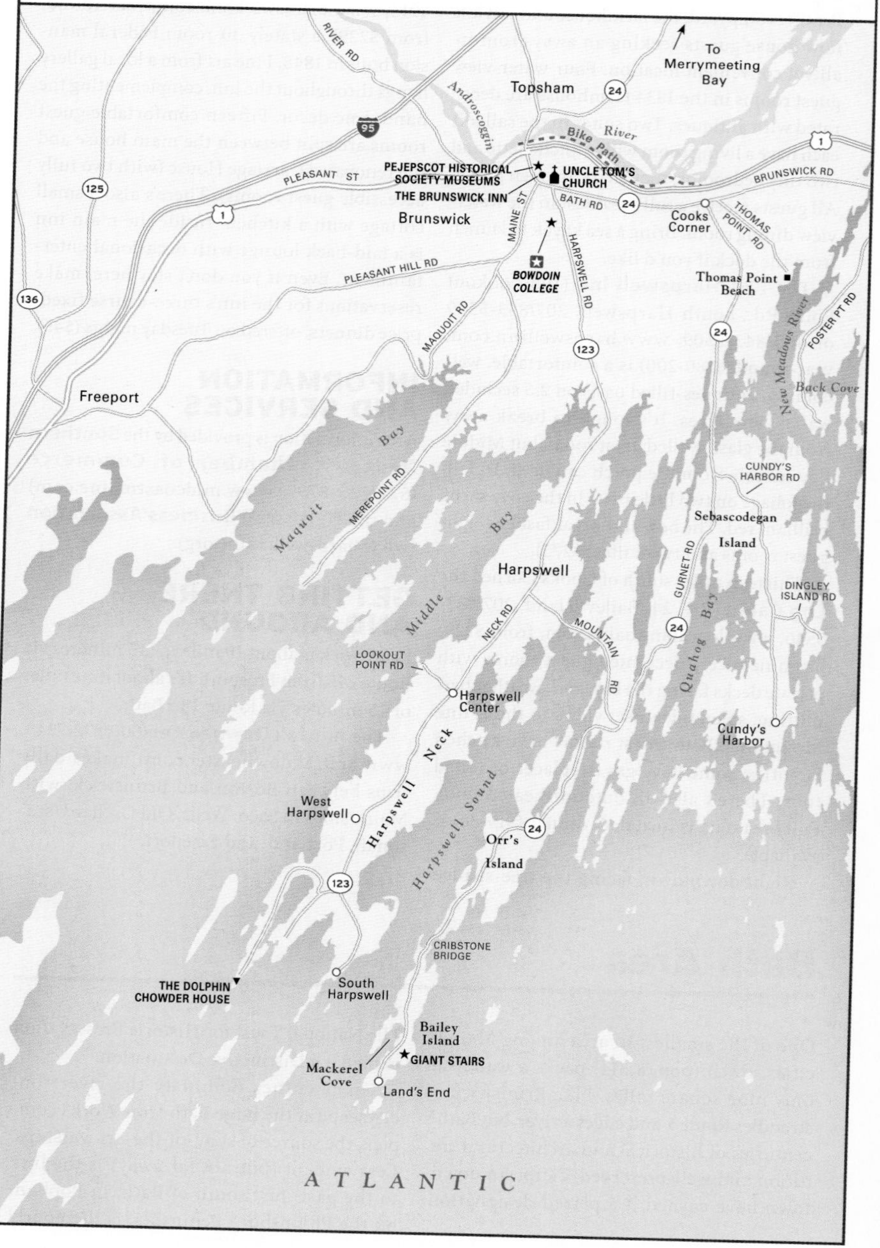

To
Merrymeeting
Bay
Topsham
24
RIVER RD
Androscoggin
River
Bike Path
95
1
125
PLEASANT ST
PEJEPSCOT HISTORICAL
SOCIETY MUSEUMS
UNCLE TOM'S
CHURCH
THE BRUNSWICK INN
BRUNSWICK RD
BATH RD
24
Cooks
Corner
THOMAS
POINT RD
1
Brunswick
MAINE ST
HARPSWELL RD
BOWDOIN
COLLEGE
PLEASANT HILL RD
Thomas Point
Beach
136
MAQUOIT RD
123
24
FOSTER PT RD
New Meadows River
Back Cove
Freeport
Bay
Maquoit
MEREPOINT RD
Bay
Middle
CUNDY'S
HARBOR RD
Sebascodegan
Island
Harpswell
GURNET RD
DINGLEY
ISLAND RD
NECK RD
MOUNTAIN
RD
24
Quahog Bay
LOOKOUT
POINT RD
Harpswell
Center
Cundy's
Harbor
Harpswell Neck
Harpswell Sound
West
Harpswell
24
Orr's
Island
123
CRIBSTONE
BRIDGE
THE DOLPHIN
CHOWDER HOUSE
South
Harpswell
Bailey
Island
GIANT STAIRS
Mackerel
Cove
Land's End
ATLANTIC

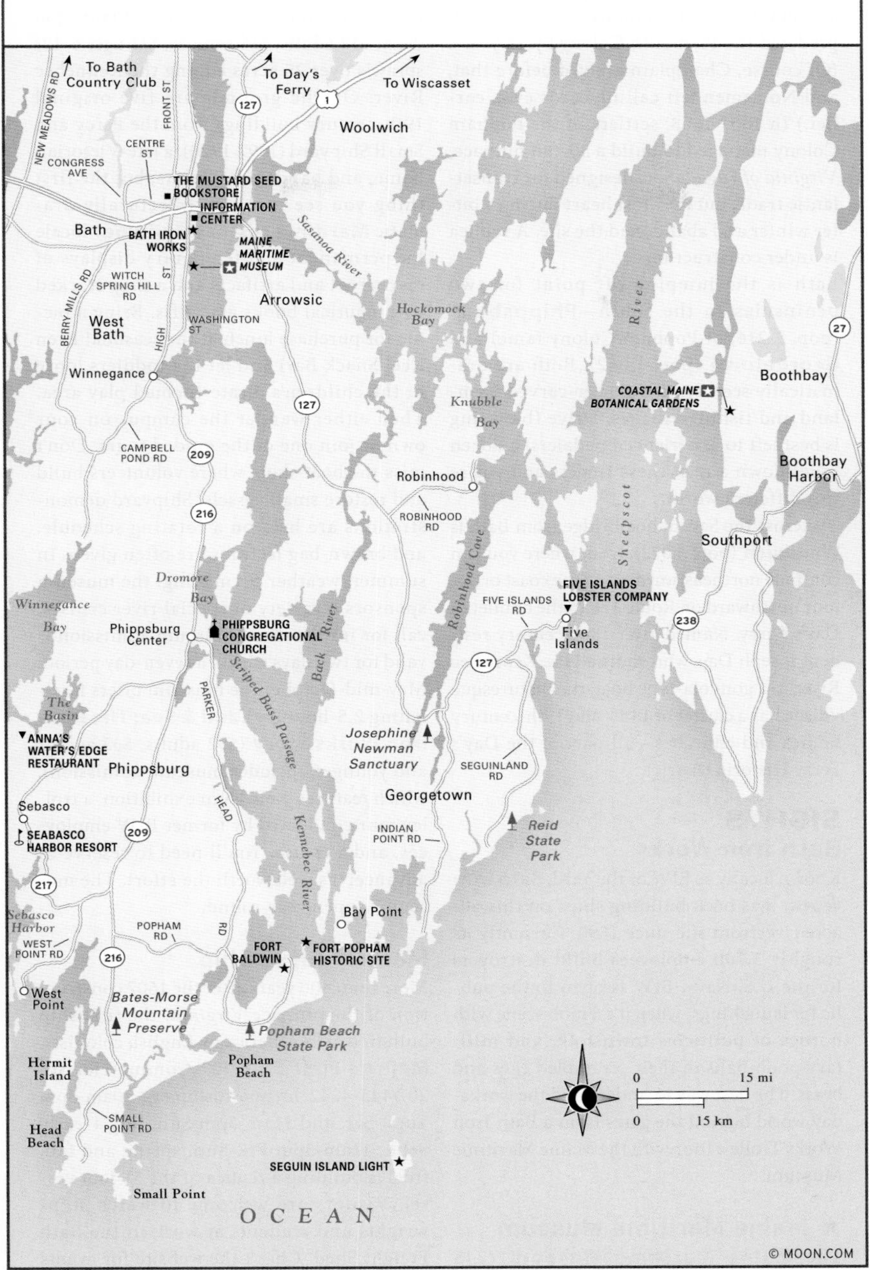
To Bath Country Club
To Day's Ferry
To Wiscasset
NEW MEADOWS RD
FRONT ST
127
1
Woolwich
CENTRE ST
CONGRESS AVE
THE MUSTARD SEED BOOKSTORE
INFORMATION CENTER
Bath
BATH IRON WORKS
Sasanoa River
MAINE MARITIME MUSEUM
WITCH SPRING HILL RD
BERRY MILLS RD
ST
Arrowsic
West Bath
WASHINGTON ST
HIGH
Hockomock Bay
River
27
Winnegance
Boothbay
127
Knubble Bay
COASTAL MAINE BOTANICAL GARDENS
CAMPBELL POND RD
209
Boothbay Harbor
Robinhood
216
ROBINHOOD RD
Sheepscot
Southport
Dromore Bay
Robinhood Cove
FIVE ISLANDS LOBSTER COMPANY
Winnegance Bay
FIVE ISLANDS RD
Phippsburg Center
PHIPPSBURG CONGREGATIONAL CHURCH
Back River
Five Islands
238
127
PARKER
Striped Bass Passage
The Basin
ANNA'S WATER'S EDGE RESTAURANT
Josephine Newman Sanctuary
Phippsburg
SEGUINLAND RD
HEAD
Georgetown
Sebasco
Kennebec River
SEABASCO HARBOR RESORT
209
INDIAN POINT RD
Reid State Park
217
Sebasco Harbor
Bay Point
POPHAM RD
RD
WEST POINT RD
FORT BALDWIN
FORT POPHAM HISTORIC SITE
216
West Point
Bates-Morse Mountain Preserve
Popham Beach State Park
Hermit Island
Popham Beach
0
15 mi
0
15 km
SMALL POINT RD
Head Beach
SEGUIN ISLAND LIGHT
Small Point
OCEAN
© MOON.COM

marked site where a trouble-plagued English settlement, a sister colony to Jamestown, predated the Plymouth Colony by 13 years. (Of course, Champlain arrived before that, and Norsemen left calling cards even earlier.) In 1607-1608, settlers in the Popham Colony managed to build a 30-ton pinnace, *Virginia of Sagadahoc,* designed for transatlantic trade, but they lost heart during a bitter winter and abandoned the site. A replica is under construction.

Bath is the jumping-off point for two peninsulas to the south—**Phippsburg** (pop. 2,216, of Popham Colony fame) and **Georgetown** (pop. 1,042). Both are dramatically scenic, with glacier-carved farmland and fishing villages. Drive (bicycling is best left to experienced pedalers) a dozen miles down any of these fingers and you're in a different world.

Across the Sagadahoc Bridge from Bath is **Woolwich** (pop. 3,072), from where you can continue northeastward along the coast or detour northward on Route 128 to the hamlet of Day's Ferry. Named after 18th-century resident Joseph Day, who shuttled the Kennebec River in a gondola-type boat, the picturesque village has a cluster of 18th- and 19th-century homes and churches—all part of the Day's Ferry Historic District.

SIGHTS

Bath Iron Works

Known locally as BIW or the Yard, **Bath Iron Works** has been building ships on this 50-acre riverfront site since 1890. Currently its roughly 5,700 employees build destroyers for the U.S. Navy. BIW is open to the public for launchings, when it's a mob scene with hordes of politicos, townsfolk, and military pooh-bahs in their scrambled eggs and brass. The best way to understand the workaday world behind the gates is on a Bath Iron Works Trolley Tour with the Maine Maritime Museum.

★ Maine Maritime Museum

The **Maine Maritime Museum** (243 Washington St., Bath, 207/443-1316, www.mainemaritimemuseum.org, 9:30am-5pm daily, $18 adults, $16 seniors, $11 ages 6-12) sprawls over 25 acres edging the Kennebec River. On the grounds are five original 19th-century buildings from the Percy and Small Shipyard (1897-1920), a late-Victorian home, and hands-on exhibits, but the first thing you see is the architecturally dramatic **Maritime History Building,** locale for permanent and temporary displays of marine art and artifacts and a shop stocked with nautical books and gifts. Bring a picnic (or purchase lunch at the seasonal Even Keel Snack Bar) and let the toddlers loose in the children's pirate-themed play area. Then either wander the campus on your own or join one of the guided tours. Don't miss the boat shop, where volunteers build and restore small vessels. Shipyard demonstrations are held on a rotating schedule, and brown-bag lectures are often given. In summer, weather permitting, the museum sponsors a variety of special river cruises; call for information. Museum admission is valid for two days within a seven-day period. May-mid-October the museum offers fascinating 2.5-hour **By Land & Sea: The Bath Iron Works Story** ($52 adults, $33 age 12 and younger, includes museum admission), which features a museum exhibition, a trolley tour conducted by former BIW employees, and a cruise. You'll need to reserve in advance; it's well worth the effort. The museum is open year-round.

Maine's First Ship

More than 400 years after the 1607 construction of the pinnace *Virginia,* the first ship built in North America by English colonists, **Maine's First Ship** (27 Commercial St., 207/443-4242, https://mfship.org, 10am-3pm Tues.-Sat. and 11am-3pm Sun. July 4-early Sept., 11am-3pm Fri.-Sun. spring and fall, free) is building a replica of the 51-foot vessel. Visitors are welcome to watch shipwrights and students at work in the Bath Freight Shed. Check the website for events including lectures, workshops, and guided tours.

Bath Walking Tours

Sagadahoc Preservation (www.sagadahocpreservation.org), founded in 1971 to rescue the city's architectural heritage, details self-guided walking and driving architectural tours on its website. Sagadahoc Preservation also offers an annual house tour, usually in June; check the website for details.

ENTERTAINMENT

Bath's most diversified entertainment setting is the **Center for the Arts at the Chocolate Church** (804 Washington St., Bath, 207/442-8455, www.chocolatechurch.com), a chocolate-brown board-and-batten structure built in 1846 as the Central Congregational Church. Year-round activities at the arts center include music and dance concerts, dramas, exhibits, and children's programs.

At 7pm every Tuesday and Friday mid-June-August, the **Gazebo Concert Series** brings live entertainment to Bath's Library Park. **Summer Saturdays** concerts take place on the Waterfront Park dock.

The **Third Friday Art Walk** takes place 4pm-7pm on the third Friday of the month June to September. From November to April, 50 dealers show their wares at the monthly **Bath Antiques Shows** (www.bathantiquesshows.com, $4) at Bath Middle School.

Throughout the summer, the **Maine Maritime Museum** (207/443-1316) schedules special events, often in concert with visits by tall ships and other vessels. Some of the visiting boats are open to the public for a fee.

The **Drummore Bay Concert Hall** (526 Main Rd./Rte. 209, Phippsburg, 207/446-7199, http://drummorebayconcerthall.com), a renovated Grange hall, is the site of a summer concert series.

SHOPPING

Front and Center Streets are lined with fun independent shops. Bath is home to the **Mustard Seed Bookstore** (74 Front St., Bath, 207/389-4084), a wonderful independent bookstore and tea shop. For cheap beach reads and eclectic finds, visit the **Library Bookstore** (194 Front St., Bath, 207/443-1161).

Smack downtown is **Renys** (86 Front St., 207/443-6251), an only-in-Maine department store that's always worth a looksee. **Markings Gallery** (50 Front St., Bath, 207/443-1499) has three rooms filled with fine Maine craftwork.

Right in the shadow of the Route 1 overpass is an incredible resource for knitters and weavers: **Halcyon Yarn** (12 School St., Bath, 207/442-7909 or 800/341-0282), a huge warehouse of a place that carries domestic and imported yarns, looms, spinning wheels, how-to videos, kits, and pattern books.

About nine miles down Route 127, you'll come to **Georgetown Pottery** (755 Rte. 127, Georgetown, 207/371-2801), a top-quality ceramics studio and shop. A second shop is on Route 1 in Woolwich.

Anyone who appreciates fine woodworking tools *must* visit the Shelter Institute's **Woodbutcher Tools** (873 Rte. 1, Woolwich, 207/442-7938), a retail shop and bookstore five miles north of Bath.

Flea Market

One of Maine's biggest and most enduring flea markets is right on Route 1 north of Bath, often creating near-accidents as rubbernecking motorists slam to a halt. **Montsweag Flea Market** (Rte. 1 at Mountain Rd., Woolwich, 207/443-2809) is a genuine treasure trove about seven miles northeast of Bath's Sagadahoc bridge. It's open from 6:30am weekends May-mid-October, plus on Wednesdays in summer (antiques and collectibles only from 5:30am).

RECREATION

Golf

The 18-hole **Bath Country Club** (Whiskeag Rd., Bath, 207/442-8411) has moderate greens

Looping Around the Phippsburg Peninsula

Thanks to a map and brochures produced by the Phippsburg Business Association and Phippsburg Land Trust (www.phippsburglandtrust.org) and an online guide from the Phippsburg Historical Society (www.phippsburghistorical.com), it's easy to spend the better part of a day or longer exploring the peninsula that extends south from Bath.

About two miles south of Bath is a causeway known as **Winnegance,** a Wabanaki name usually translated as "short carry" or "little portage." Native Americans crossed here from the Kennebec River to the New Meadows River.

It's another 1.3 miles to the **Dromore Burying Ground** (on the right), with headstones dating from 1743. The next mile opens up with terrific easterly views of Dromore Bay. Right in the line of sight is state-owned, 117-acre Lee Island, which is off-limits May-mid-July to protect nesting eagles and waterfowl.

Next you're in **Phippsburg Center,** a shipbuilding depot from colonial days until the early 20th century. Hang a left onto Parker Head Road. After the **Phippsburg Historical Museum** (2pm-4pm Mon.-Fri. summer), in an 1859 schoolhouse, and the Alfred Totman Library, turn left onto Church Lane to see the "Constitution Tree," a huge English linden planted in 1774, in front of the 1802 **Phippsburg Congregational Church.**

Parker Head Road continues southward (watch out for speed bumps) and meets Route 209, which leads to **Popham Beach State Park.** Continue to the end of Route 209 for the **Fort Popham Historic Site,** where parking is woefully inadequate in summer. Youngsters love this place—they can fish from the rocks, explore the 1865 stone fortress, picnic on the seven-acre grounds, and create sandcastles on the tiny beach next to the fort. Resist the urge to swim, though; the current is dangerous, and there's no lifeguard. Across the river is Bay Point, a lobstering village at the tip of the Georgetown Peninsula. **Percy's Store** (207/389-2010), with a handful of tables, is a good bet for pizza, picnic fare, fried dough, and fishing tackle.

Across the cove from the fort is Fort Baldwin Road, a winding one-lane road leading to the shorefront site of the 1607 Popham Colony. Climb the path up Sabino Hill to what's left of World War I-era **Fort Baldwin.** Bring a flashlight if you want to explore the three sections of ruins.

Backtrack about four miles on Route 209, turn left onto Route 216, and head toward **Small Point.** Go about 0.9 mile to Morse Mountain Road, on the left, which leads to the parking area

fees, a pro shop, and a restaurant serving lunch and dinner.

The **Sebasco Harbor Resort** has a nine-hole course, open to nonguests on a space-available basis; call the resort's pro shop (207/389-9060) to inquire. Watch out for the infamous second hole, which gives new meaning to the term *water hole,* and say good morning to Sarah on the sixth tee: If you look nearby, you'll find a gravestone inscribed "Sarah Wallace—1862." A local rhyme goes like this:

Show respect to Sarah
You golfers passing by;
She's the only person on this course
Who can't improve her lie.

Parks and Preserves

The **Kennebec Estuary Land Trust** (KELT, 207/442-8400, www.kennebecestuary.org) maintains three preserves worth a visit; maps of each can be downloaded. Bath's **Thorn Head Preserve,** at the end of High Street, is located on the point where Whiskeag Creek meets the Kennebec River. Allow a half hour for the easy walk to the headland and its stone "picnic" table with views toward Merrymeeting Bay. Allow longer if you want to explore any of the side trails. The **Whiskeag Trail,** a five-mile nonmotorized multiuse urban path, connects the preserve to the Bath YMCA. For terrific views of this section of coast, hike the loop trail to the bedrock summit of Georgetown's **Higgins**

Fort Popham Historic Site

and trailhead for the **Bates-Morse Mountain Preserve.** Farther south are Head Beach and Hermit Island.

Returning northward on Route 216, you'll hook up with Route 209 and then see a left turn (Rte. 217) to Sebasco Harbor Resort. Take the time to go beyond the resort area. When the paved road goes left (to the Water's Edge Restaurant), turn right at a tiny cemetery and continue northward on the Old Meadowbrook Road, which meanders for about four miles along the west side of the peninsula. About midway along is the **Basin,** regarded by sailors as one of the Maine Coast's best "hurricane holes" (refuges in high winds). As you skirt the Basin and come to a fork, bear right to return to Route 209; then turn left on Route 209 and return northward to Bath.

Mountain. The Route 127 trailhead is on the right, 7.6 miles south of Route 1.

REID STATE PARK

If I had to pick my favorite coastal state park, it would be **Reid** (Seguinland Rd., Georgetown, 207/371-2303, www.parksandlands.com, $6-8 adults, $2 seniors, $1 ages 5-11). Surf crashes on One Mile and Half Mile beaches, eagles and osprey soar overhead, kids splash in the lagoon or hunt for seaborne treasures in pools left by the receding tide, and birds nest in the sand dunes and marshlands. Trails lace the 765 acres, but for the biggest reward for the smallest effort, ascend Griffith Head and take in the sweeping seascape views. Facilities include changing rooms with showers, picnic tables, restrooms, and snack bars. The park—14 miles south of Route 1 in Woolwich and two miles off Route 127—is open daily year-round. In winter, bring cross-country skis and glide along the shoreline. Plan to arrive early on summer weekends, when parking is woefully inadequate.

Just 0.5 mile beyond the road to Reid State Park is **Charles Pond,** where the setting is unsurpassed for freshwater swimming in the long, skinny pond. You'll wish this were a secret too, but it isn't. There are no facilities.

BATES-MORSE MOUNTAIN CONSERVATION AREA

Consider visiting Phippsburg's lovely 600-acre **Bates-Morse Mountain Conservation**

Area only if you are willing to be conscientious about the strict rules for this private preserve. A relatively easy four-mile round-trip hike takes you through marshland (you'll need insect repellent) and to the top of 210-foot Morse Mountain, which has panoramic views, and then down to privately owned Seawall Beach. On a clear day you can see New Hampshire's Mount Washington from the summit. No pets or vehicles are allowed, and there are no facilities; stay on the preserve road and the beach path at all times, as the side roads are private. Least terns and piping plovers—both endangered species—nest in the dunes, so avoid this area, especially mid-May-mid-August. Morse Mountain is a great locale for spotting hawks during their annual September migration southward. Pick up a map (and the rules) from the box in the parking area on Morse Mountain Road (marked private), off Route 216 just under a mile south of the intersection with Route 209.

PHIPPSBURG HIKING TRAILS

The **Phippsburg Land Trust** (207/443-5993, www.phippsburglandtrust.org) has prepared a handy free brochure with a map detailing more than a dozen preserves, most with trails. Four—Center Pond, Ridgewell, Spirit Pond, and Sprague Pond—have trail guides available at trailhead boxes.

JOSEPHINE NEWMAN SANCTUARY

A must-see for any nature lover, the 119-acre **Josephine Newman Sanctuary** (Rte. 127, Georgetown), has 2.5 miles of blazed loop trails winding through 119 wooded acres and along Robinhood Cove's tidal shoreline. Josephine Oliver Newman (1878-1968), a respected naturalist, bequeathed her family's splendid property to Maine Audubon (207/781-2330, www.maineaudubon.org), which maintains it today. The 0.6-mile self-guided trail is moderately difficult, but the rewards are 20 informative markers highlighting special features: glacial erratics, reversing falls, mosses, and marshes. The easiest route is the 0.75-mile Horseshoe Trail, which you can extend for another mile or so by linking into the Rocky End Trail. No pets or bikes are allowed. To find this hidden gem, take Route 127 from Route 1 in Woolwich (the road to Reid State Park) for 9.1 miles. Turn right at the sanctuary sign and continue up the narrow, rutted dirt road (ideally no one will be coming the other way) to the small parking lot. A map of the trail system is posted at the marsh's edge and available in the box.

ROBERT P. TRISTRAM COFFIN WILDFLOWER SANCTUARY

The Native Plant Trust (www.nativeplanttrust.org) owns the 177-acre trail-laced **Robert P. Tristram Coffin Wildflower Sanctuary** bordering Merrymeeting Bay in Woolwich. It is home to more than 100 species of wildflowers. To find it, take Route 127 north for 2.2 miles, then Route 128 for 4.5 miles, and look for a small parking area on the left.

Swimming

POPHAM BEACH

On hot July and August weekends, the parking lot at **Popham Beach State Park** (Rte. 209, Phippsburg, 207/389-1335, www.parksandlands.com, $6-8 adults, $2 seniors, $1 ages 5-11), 14 miles south of Bath, fills up by 10am, so plan to arrive early at this huge crescent of sand backed by sea grass, beach roses, and dunes. Facilities include changing rooms, outside showers, restrooms, and seasonal lifeguards. It's officially open April 15-October 30, but the beach is accessible all year.

HEAD BEACH

Just off Route 216, about two miles south of the Route 209 turnoff to Popham Beach, is **Head Beach,** a sandy crescent that's open daily until 10pm. A day-use parking fee ($10) is payable at the small gatehouse; there's a restroom on the path to the beach and a store within walking distance. No pets.

Boat Excursions

The 50-foot ***Yankee*** operates out of Small

Point's Hermit Island Campground Monday-Saturday throughout the summer. You can go on nature cruises, enjoy the sunset, or visit Eagle Island; the schedule is different each day, and rates vary widely by trip. Call for information and reservations (207/389-1788).

The **MV *Ruth,*** a 38-foot excursion boat, runs cruises out of Sebasco Harbor Resort late June-Labor Day. You don't need to be a Sebasco guest to take the trips, but reservations are essential. The schedule changes weekly, but possible options are a Cundy's Harbor lunch cruise, a sunset cruise, and a pirates excursion, with trips ranging 1-2 hours. Call the resort (207/389-1161) for the current week's schedule and rates.

The easiest access to **Seguin Island** (www.seguinisland.org) is via the 30-minute, narrated **Seguin Island Ferry** (207/841-7977, www.fishntripsmaine.com, $35 adults, $25 age 12 and younger), which departs from the harbor near Fort Popham; call for the current schedule. Seguin, 2.5 miles out to sea at the mouth of the Kennebec River, is the site of Maine's second-oldest **lighthouse,** commissioned by George Washington in 1795. The current light, with a first order Fresnel lens, was erected in 1857. Visitors have about two hours to tour the tower and museum, view historical buildings, picnic, and hike five trails. En route, you'll pass Pond Island Lighthouse and likely spot seabirds and perhaps seals and porpoises. Bring your own food and water. Join the **Friends of Seguin Island Light Station** ($30 adults, $75 family) to stay in the two-bedroom **keeper's house** ($250/night) or **camp** ($10/pp).

If you prefer a custom tour, call **River Run Tours** (207/504-2628, www.riverruntours.com). Whether you want to view lighthouses or wildlife or cruise upriver to Swans Island, Captain Ed Rice has a cruise for you. Boat rate is $120/hour while cruising, $50/hour for standby. His comfortable pontoon boat accommodates six; plan on at least two hours.

Paddle Sports

Close to civilization yet amazingly undeveloped **Nequasset Lake** is a great place to canoe. You'll see a few anglers, a handful of houses, and near-wilderness along the shoreline. Personal watercraft and motors over 10 hp are banned. Take Route 1 from Bath across the bridge to Woolwich. Continue to the flashing caution light at Nequasset Road; turn right and go 0.1 mile. Turn left, and left again, into the parking area for the Nequasset Stream Waterfront Park, a popular swimming hole. Launch your canoe and head upstream, under Route 1, to the lake.

Seaspray Kayaking (888/349-7774, www.seaspraykayaking.com) operates from bases at the New Meadows Kayaking Center in West Bath, Hermit Island in Phippsburg, and Sebasco Harbor Resort in Sebasco Estates. Half-day canoe, paddleboard, kayak, and paddle-kayak rentals begin at $15-25 ($10 for each additional hour, up to $25-50 daily), with longer-term rates and delivery available. A variety of guided tours are also offered, with half-day sea kayaking options for $50 adults, $25 children, and specialty paddles, such as sunset or moonlight.

Fishing Charter

Cast a line for stripers, bluefish, mackerel, and more with **Fish'n'Trips Charters** (207/841-7977, www.fishntripsmaine.com). Captain Ethan Derby, a Master Maine Guide, offers half-day cruises beginning at $350, including bait and tackle. The boat departs from the pier adjacent to Fort Popham.

FOOD

Bath

In Waterfront Park on Commercial Street, the **Bath Farmers Market** operates 9am-noon every Saturday May-October.

For breakfast, lunch, or sweets, drop into the **Starlight Café** (15 Lambard St., 207/443-3005, 7am-2pm Mon.-Fri., 8am-2pm Sat., $4-10, cash only), a too-cute and too-tiny basement space across a side street from the Customs House. It's bright and cheerful, and the food is hearty and creative.

Some argue that the state's best thin-crust

pizza (and praiseworthy garlic knots) comes from the ovens at the **Cabin** (552 Washington St., 207/443-6224, www.cabinpizza.com, 10am-10pm Sun.-Thurs., 10am-11pm Fri.-Sat., $5-12, no credit cards), a somewhat rough-and-tumble working-class joint that's been a local fave since 1973. It's across from Bath Iron Works. Avoid it during BIW shift changes (3pm-5pm Mon.-Fri.).

Tuck into **Winnegance Restaurant and Bakery** (36 High St., 207/443-3300, 6am-4pm daily, $6-15), snugged on a corner with views over the Kennebec River and Winnegance Lake, for scratch-made breakfast, lunch, or treats.

Kate and Andy Winglass operate **Mae's Café and Bakery** (160 Centre St. at High St., 207/442-8577, www.maescafeandbakery.com, 8am-2pm daily), a longtime local favorite bakery and café with seating indoors and on a front deck. It's *the* place to go for brunch (reservations are essential on weekends). Most choices are in the $10-15 range. Rotating art shows enliven the open and airy dining rooms.

Finger-licking Memphis-style barbecue, along with other southern specialties, is served in big quantities at **Beale Street Barbeque and Grill** (215 Water St., 207/442-9514, www.mainebbq.com, 11am-9pm Wed.-Sun., $11-30). Everything's made on the premises. Find it next to the municipal parking lot.

Sited in a former metal workshop, **Salt Pine Social** (244 Front St., 207/442-8345, www.saltpinesocial.com, from 5pm Mon. and Wed.-Thurs., and noon-9pm Sat.-Sun., $18-30) is an American bistro with international accents. The atmosphere is casual, the food beautifully presented, and the small plates invite sharing.

Bath Brewing Co. (141 Front St., 207/560-3389, https://bathbrewing.com, from 11:30am daily, $10-18) serves American and pub fare on two floors of its nicely renovated and updated downtown space.

Phippsburg Peninsula

A few notches above a seafood shack, **Anna's Water's Edge Restaurant** (75 Black's Landing Rd., Sebasco Estates, 207/389-1803, www.thewatersedgerestaurant.com, 11am-9pm Wed.-Mon., $5-35) pairs American fare with serene views over island-salted Casco Bay. Eat inside or on shoreline picnic tables.

Even if you're not staying at **Sebasco Harbor Resort** (Rte. 217, Sebasco Estates, 207/389-1161 or 800/225-3819, www.sebasco.com), you can dine in either of its two waterfront restaurants, both with gasp-evoking sunset views and both with children's menus. The **Pilot House** (5:30pm-8:30pm Mon.-Sat., $14-30), the more formal of the two, serves American fare. Below it, the casual **Ledges** (11:30am-10pm daily, $11-22), with indoor and outdoor seating, offers sandwiches, pizzas, lobster, and comfort-food favorites as well as a kids' menu.

Georgetown Peninsula

On the Georgetown Peninsula, **Five Islands Farm** (1375 Rte. 127, Five Islands, 207/371-9383, www.fiveislandsfarm.com, 10:30am-6pm daily) is a fine stop for picnic fixings, with an excellent assortment of Maine cheeses along with breads, meats, chips, salsa, and even wine.

The **Georgetown Country Store** (Five Islands Rd., 207/371-2106, 7am-6pm daily) earns kudos for its lobster rolls as well as other fare, which can range from clam fritters to house-made chili. It's easy to get out of here for $5-10.

Big windows frame sigh-worthy views at **Blue** (96 Seguinland Rd., Georgetown, 207/371-2616 or 855/473-9428, www.greyhavens.com, 5:30pm-9pm Tues.-Sun., $18-34), the restaurant at the Grey Havens Inn. White-draped tables are comfortably spaced in the wood-floored and beadboard-walled and -ceilinged dining room. Chef Esau Crosby's menu emphasizes locally sourced

1: Reid State Park **2:** Five Islands Lobster Company in Georgetown **3:** Sebasco Harbor Resort **4:** Grey Havens Inn

fare and may include choices such as "lazy lobster" or tournedos of beef.

Just over a mile beyond the turnoff to Reid State Park, you'll reach the end of Route 127 at Five Islands. Here you'll find ★ **Five Islands Lobster Company** (1447 Five Islands Rd., Five Islands, Georgetown, 207/371-2990, www.fiveislandslobster.com, 11:30am-8pm daily July-Aug, 11:30am-8pm Sat.-Sun. spring and fall), a classic Maine lobster shack with some of the prettiest views anywhere. Here you can pig out on lobster rolls, better-than-usual onion rings, crab cakes, and, if you must, burgers and hot dogs. Dress down, BYOB, and enjoy the end-of-the-road ambience of this idyllic spot.

ACCOMMODATIONS

Bath

Five generations of the Packard family called the Italianate-style **Benjamin F. Packard House** (45 Pearl St., 207/443-6004, https://benjaminfpackardhouse.com, $159-199) home before it found new life as a bed-and-breakfast. The inn, dating from the 1790s, is in Bath's historic district, an easy walk from the riverfront and downtown shops.

Find elegance and comfort at the **Inn at Bath** (969 Washington St., 207/443-4294 or 800/423-0964, www.innatbath.com, $170-245). Guest rooms in the 1810 Greek Revival-style inn are decorated with antiques. Two have wood-burning fireplaces, and two have two-person jetted tubs. Dogs are a possibility. One room is wheelchair-accessible.

After exploring the region, return to the **Kennebec Inn** (696 High St., 207/443-5324, www.kennebecinn.com, from $195), a mid-19th-century sea captain's home, with four guest rooms spread out in the main house and masterfully restored carriage house. Guests have use of an in-ground pool and a fire pit. A three-course breakfast is served at 8am.

Phippsburg Peninsula

The trouble with staying at the ★ **Sebasco Harbor Resort** (29 Kenyon Rd., Sebasco Estates, 207/613-2147, www.sebasco.com, from $199), a self-contained resort on 550 waterfront acres, is that between the beautiful setting and the bountiful offerings you might not set foot off the premises during your entire vacation. Situated at the mouth of the saltwater New Meadows River, 12 miles south of Bath, Sebasco attracts families who have returned year after year since its 1930 opening. Current owner Bob Smith has brought the resort up to 21st-century standards while keeping its old-style rusticity. You'll have to look far and wide to find a better family resort. Scattered around the well-tended property are the main lodge and a variety of cottages (1-10 bedrooms; the 2-bedroom units with a shared living room are a great choice for families); a four-story cupola-topped lighthouse building edging the harbor; and two suites buildings, Harbor Village and the waterfront Fairwinds Spa, with more contemporary amenities. Kids under age 12 are free; pets are $25/night. Rates that include breakfast and dinner are an additional $50 pp (no charge for 12 and younger when dining with an adult and from the kids' menu). Weekly summer events include a Sunday-evening reception and grand buffet, lobster bakes, bingo, live entertainment, and the twice-weekly Camp Merrit children's program ($25/day, includes lunch). Recreational facilities include two all-weather tennis courts, a nine-hole championship golf course and a three-hole regulation course for beginners and families, the state's largest outdoor saltwater pool, boat tours aboard the *Ruth (from $20/adult, $12/child),* sailing trips, sea-kayak excursions ($50/adult, $25/child), mountain bike tours, candlepin bowling, horseshoes, a playground, a well-equipped fitness center, bike rentals ($10/five hours or $18/day), and as much or as little organized activity as you want.

Step back in history at the ★ **1774 Inn** (44 Parker Head Rd., Phippsburg Center, 207/389-1774, www.1774inn.com, $195-325), a magnificently restored four-square Georgian colonial property, listed in the National Register of Historic Places, with an 1870 ell and barn. Many colonial details have been preserved, including shutters with peepholes and strong bars to defend against attack, paneled wainscoting, ceiling moldings, fluted columns, and wide-plank pine floors. Most of the eight guest rooms (all but two with private baths) have views of the Kennebec River. All are spacious and furnished with antiques. Outside, the inn's four acres roll down to the river. Rates include a full breakfast and evening snacks.

You can walk to beaches or forts from **Stonehouse Manor** (907 Popham Rd., Phippsburg, 877/389-1141, www.stonehousemanor.com, $285-355), a lakeside bed-and-breakfast with distant ocean views, lovely gardens, and an enviable location on Silver Lake. The graceful 1896 mansion-style cottage's architectural features include leaded stained glass windows and oak pocket doors. Rooms are spacious, and the feeling is like being on a private estate. Some bathrooms are detached.

Georgetown Peninsula

It's hard to tear yourself away from the scenery and sanctuary at the **Mooring Bed and Breakfast** (132 Seguinland Rd., Georgetown, 207/371-2790 or 866/828-7348, www.themooringb-b.com, $165-210), the original home of Walter Reid, who donated Reid State Park to the state. His great-granddaughter Penny Barabe and her husband, Paul, have beautifully restored the house, situated on lovely oceanfront grounds with island views. Each guest room has a water view and air-conditioning. There's plenty of room to spread out, including the appropriately named Spanish Room. A full breakfast, afternoon wine and cheese, and freshly baked sweets are included.

Even more secluded is **Coveside Bed & Breakfast** (6 Gotts Cove Ln., Georgetown, 207/371-2807 or 800/232-5490, www.covesidebandb.com, $185-255), occupying an enviable spot on five oceanfront acres near Five Islands. The four guest rooms in the main house and three in the adjacent cottage all have water views; some rooms have fireplaces; one has a jetted tub. A separate building has a TV and exercise room. Guests have access to gardens and the dock on Gotts Cove. Kayak rental can be arranged.

Imagine the perfect Maine seaside inn, and likely it resembles **Grey Havens Inn** (96 Seguinland Rd., Georgetown, 207/371-2616, www.greyhavens.com, from $215). This thoroughly renovated and updated 1904 Shingle-style classic has two turrets, a front porch, and dreamy views over lobster boats, spruce-fringed islands, and the rockbound coast. Public rooms flow, with a massive stone hearth dominating the living room. Guest rooms are comfy and simply decorated in coastal cottage style. Rates include a continental breakfast. The inn's restaurant, Blue, serves dinner ($20-35) Tuesday-Sunday (although it closes for functions).

Camping and Glamping

Plan to book in January if you want a waterfront campsite in midsummer at the Phippsburg Peninsula's **Hermit Island Campground** (6 Hermit Island Rd., Phippsburg, 207/443-2101, www.hermitisland.com, no credit cards). With 270 campsites (no vehicles larger than pickup campers; no hookups) spread over a 255-acre causeway-linked island, this is oceanfront camping at its best. The well-managed operation has a store, a snack bar, a seasonal post office, boat rentals, boat excursions, trails, and seven private beaches. The hub of activity (and registration) is the Kelp Shed, next to the campsite entrance. Open and wooded sites run $45-75 mid-June-Labor Day, $45 early and late in the season. Three small cabins rent for $525-1,400 per week in season. Reservations for a week's stay or longer and for Memorial Day and Labor Day weekends can be made by mail beginning in early January and by phone in early February (call for the exact date). Reservations for stays of less than one week are accepted after March 1. It's open mid-May-Columbus Day, but full operation is really June-Labor Day. The campground is at the tip of the Phippsburg Peninsula. Pets are not allowed.

Channel your inner Tarzan or Jane with a stay at **Seguin Tree Dwellings** (off Rte. 127, Georgetown, 207/751-52241, www.seguinmaine.com, $189-299). Each of the three elevated tree houses has a bathroom, kitchen, electric heaters, views over the Back River, and use of canoes and kayaks. One has a cedar hot tub on an elevated private deck.

INFORMATION AND SERVICES

Visitor Information

A visitors center is located in Bath's renovated train station (restrooms available), adjacent to the Bath Iron Works main yard. It's open year-round with brochure racks and staffed by volunteers May-October. Request copies of the *City of Bath Downtown Map and Guide* and the *Guide to Southern Midcoast Maine.*

Online information is available from **Main Street Bath** (www.visitbath.com), the city's website (www.cityofbath.com), and the **Southern Midcoast Chamber of Commerce** (877/725-8797, www.midcoastmaine.com).

Find **public restrooms** at Bath City Hall (55 Front St.), Patten Free Library (33 Summer St.), Sagadahoc County Courthouse (752 High St.), the visitors center, and in summer at Waterfront Park (Commercial St.).

GETTING THERE AND AROUND

Bath is about 10 miles or 15 minutes via Route 1 from Brunswick. It's about 12 miles or 20 minutes via Route 1 to Wiscasset, but allow up to double that in summer for congestion in Wiscasset.

The **Bath Trolley** (www.cityofbath.com) circulates through the area, with each one-way trip costing $1.

Wiscasset Area

Billing itself as "the Prettiest Village in Maine," **Wiscasset** (pop. 3,732) works hard to live up to its slogan, with quaint street signs, well-maintained homes, and an air of attentive elegance.

Wiscasset ("meeting place of three rivers"), incorporated as part of Pownalborough in 1760, has had its current name since 1802. In the late 18th century it became the shire town of Lincoln County and the largest seaport north of Boston. Countless tall ships sailed the 12 miles up the Sheepscot River to tie up here, and shipyards flourished, turning out vessels for domestic and foreign trade. The 1807 Embargo Act and the War of 1812 delivered a one-two punch that shut down trade and temporarily squelched the town's aspirations, but Wiscasset yards soon were back at it, producing vessels for the pre-Civil War clipper-ship era—only to face a more lasting decline with the arrival of the railroads and the onset of the Industrial Revolution.

In 1973, a large chunk of downtown Wiscasset was added to the National Register of Historic Places. Handsome homes spanning three centuries, many now housing antiques shops, recall the town's glory days.

SIGHTS

A walking tour is the best way to appreciate the Federal, Classical Revival, and even pre-revolutionary homes and commercial buildings in Wiscasset's historic district. If you do nothing else, swing by the homes on High Street.

Historic Houses

Historic New England (207/882-7169, www.historicnewengland.org) owns two Wiscasset properties within easy walking distance of each other. Both are open for tours, offered on the half hour ($8 each).

Once known as the Lee-Tucker House, **Castle Tucker** (2 Lee St., 11am-4pm

Wed.-Sun. June-mid-Oct.) was built in 1807 by Judge Silas Lee and bought by sea captain Richard Tucker in 1858. The imposing mansion has Victorian wallpaper and furnishings, Palladian windows, an amazing elliptical staircase, and a dramatic view over the Sheepscot River. In 1997, Jane Tucker, Richard's granddaughter, deeded the house to Historic New England.

The three-story **Nickels-Sortwell House** (121 Main St./Rte. 1, 11am-4pm Fri.-Sun. June-mid-Oct.) is so close to the road that many motorists miss it. Sea captain William Nickels commissioned the mansion in 1807 but died soon after its completion. For 70 or so years it was the Belle Haven Hotel before Alvin and Frances Sortwell's meticulous Colonial Revival restoration in the early 20th century.

Lincoln County Old Jail

Wiscasset's **Old Jail** (133 Federal St., 207/882-6817, www.lincolncountyhistory.org, noon-4pm Sat.-Sun. June-mid-Oct., $5 adults, free under age 16), completed in 1811, was the first prison in the District of Maine (then part of Massachusetts). Amazingly, it remained a jail—mostly for short-timers—until 1953. Two years after that, the Lincoln County Historical Association took over, and in summer you can check out the 40-inch-thick granite walls, floors, and ceilings; the 12 tiny cells; and historical graffiti penned by the prisoners. Attached to the prison is the 1837 jailer's house, now the **Lincoln County Museum,** containing antique tools, the original kitchen, and various temporary exhibits. A Victorian gazebo overlooking the Sheepscot River is a great spot for a picnic. From Main Street (Rte. 1) in downtown Wiscasset, take Federal Street (Rte. 218) 1.2 miles.

Fort Edgecomb

Built in 1808 to protect the Sheepscot River port of Wiscasset, the **Fort Edgecomb State Historic Site** (Eddy Rd., Edgecomb, 207/882-7777, 9am-5pm daily late May-early Sept., $3-4 adults, $1 ages 5-11) occupies a splendid riverfront spread ideal for picnicking and fishing (no swimming). Many summer weekends feature encampments on the grounds of the octagonal blockhouse that make history come alive with Revolutionary reenactments, period dress, craft demonstrations, and garrison drills. It's off Route 1; take Eddy Road just north of Wiscasset Bridge and go 0.5 mile to Fort Road.

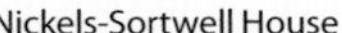
Nickels-Sortwell House

Wiscasset, Waterville, and Farmington Railway

Also historic, but a bit livelier and more fun for kids, is the **Wiscasset, Waterville, and Farmington Railway** (97 Cross Rd., Sheepscot, 207/882-4193, http://wwfry.org, 9am-4pm Sat. year-round and Sun. late May-Oct.), commemorating a narrow-gauge railroad that operated in the early part of the 20th century, from Wiscasset in the south to Albion and Winslow in the north. On the grounds are a museum in the old station (free admission) and train rides along the main-line track running north from Cross Road, on the original roadbed ($10 adults, $5 ages 4-12). Trains depart Sheepscot regularly on weekends; the schedule is a bit complicated, so check the website for operation. From Route 1 in Wiscasset, take Route 218 north 4.7 miles to a four-way intersection and turn left on Cross Road to the museum.

Head Tide Village

Head Tide Village, an eminently picturesque hamlet at the farthest reach of the Sheepscot River tides, is worth a detour, especially in autumn. From Wiscasset, follow Route 218 north for about eight miles and then turn right on Route 194 to find this idyllic pocket, listed in the National Register of Historic Places. From the late 18th century to the early 20th, Head Tide (now part of the town of Alna) was a thriving mill town, a source of hydropower for the textile and lumber industries. All that's long gone, but hints of that era come from the handful of well-maintained 18th- and 19th-century homes in the village center.

Up the hill, the stunning 1838 **Head Tide Church,** another fine example of local prosperity, is usually open 2pm-4pm Saturdays July-August. Volunteer tour guides point out the original pulpit, a trompe l'oeil window, the recently restored 1894 Estey organ, a kerosene chandelier, and walls lined with historical Alna photographs.

Head Tide's most famous citizen was the poet **Edwin Arlington Robinson,** born here in 1869. His family home, at the bend in Route 194, is not open to the public.

Just upriver from the bend in the road is a favorite swimming hole, a millpond where you can join the locals on a hot summer day. Not much else goes on here, and there are no restaurants or lodgings, so Head Tide can't be termed a destination, but it's a village frozen in time—and an unbeatable opportunity for history buffs and shutterbugs, especially in autumn.

FESTIVALS AND EVENTS

Wiscasset's daylong **Annual Strawberry Festival and Country Fair** (St. Philip's Episcopal Church, Hodge St., 207/882-7184) celebrates with tons of strawberries, along with crafts and an auction on the last Saturday in June. The **Alive on the Common** concert series takes place 6pm Thursdays in July and August.

A summer highlight at **Watershed Center for the Ceramic Arts** (207/882-6075, www.watershedceramics.org) is its annual **Salad Days,** a fund-raising event held on the second Saturday in July. For a $40 donation, you choose a handmade pottery plate, fill it from a piled-high buffet of fruit and veggie salads, and take part in an old-fashioned picnic social—and you even get to keep the plate. Afterward, there's plenty of time to explore the center's campus and visit the gallery.

SHOPPING

It's certainly fitting that a town filled end-to-end with antique homes should have more than two dozen individual and collective antiques shops and a few art galleries.

Seventeen exhibitors show their wares in room settings inside the 1799 **Blythe House Antiques** (161 Main St., Wiscasset, 207/882-1280, www.blythehousewiscasset.com).

European and American 19th- and 20th-century painters are the broad focus at **Wiscasset Bay Gallery** (67 Main St./Rte. 1, Wiscasset, 207/882-7682 or 888/622-9445, www.wiscassetbaygallery.com), which schedules high-quality rotating shows throughout the season.

In the handsome open spaces of an early 19th-century brick schoolhouse, the **Maine Art Gallery** (15 Warren St., Wiscasset, 207/882-7511, www.maine-art.com) was founded in 1954 as a nonprofit organization to showcase contemporary Maine artists.

Two miles south of town is **Wiscasset Village Antiques** (563 Rte. 1, Wiscasset, 207/882-40299, http://wiscassetvillageantiques.com), a huge red barn of a place filled with more than 100 dealers showing on three floors.

FOOD

Lobster and Seafood

Red's Eats (Main St. and Water St., Wiscasset, 207/882-6128, 11:30am-5pm Mon.-Thurs., 11:30am-8pm Fri-Sun. early May-mid-Oct., no credit cards), a simple take-out stand, has garnered national attention through the decades for its lobster rolls stuffed with the meat from a whole lobster. It's easy to spot because of the line. Expect to wait, perhaps for an hour or more. Is it worth it? I don't think so, but others rave about the cold lobster rolls, the fried fish, the hot dogs, and the wraps. If you're planning on one of Red's lobster rolls, ask someone who has just bought one the price before you get in line, and make sure you have enough cash. Of course, you can skip the wait with a quick walk across Main Street to the Town Wharf, where **Sprague Lobster** (22 Main St., Wiscasset, 207/882-1236) has a competing stand that many locals prefer. Lines are rare, and the lobster rolls also contain the meat from an entire crustacean.

Quick Bites

Treat's (80 Main St., Wiscasset, 207/882-6192, 7:30am-5:30pm Mon.-Sat., 10am-4pm Sun.) is a superb source for gourmet picnic fixings: sandwiches, soups, wine, cheese, condiments, and artisanal breads and other baked goodies. Take your purchases to the lovely **Sunken Garden,** an almost-unnoticed pocket park created around the cellar hole of a long-gone inn. It's a fine place for a picnic.

Family Favorites

Two miles southwest of downtown Wiscasset, the **Sea Basket Restaurant** (303 Rte. 1, Wiscasset, 207/882-6581, www.seabasket.com, 11am-8pm Wed.-Sun. Mar.-Dec., $4-22) has been serving hearty bowls of lobster stew and good-size baskets of eminently fresh seafood since 1981. It's not a place to seek out, but it is decent on-the-road food.

In a high-visibility location across Route 1 from Red's Eats, **Sarah's Cafe** (Main St./Rte. 1 and Water St., Wiscasset, 207/882-7504, www.sarahscafe.com, 11am-8pm daily, $10-25) is an especially family-friendly spot serving easy-on-the-wallet comfort foods. Food is reliably mundane and the service can be sluggish and indifferent, but crayons keep kids busy. The deck overlooks the Sheepscot River.

Casual Dining

Definitely make reservations if you hope to score seats at **Little Village Bistro** (65 Gardiner Rd./Rte. 27, Wiscasset, 207/687-8232, http://littlevillagebistro.com, 4:30pm-9pm Wed.-Sat., $23-30), a cozy Italian-accented restaurant that turns out excellent fare.

Montsweag Farm Restaurant & Pub (942 Rte. 1, Woolwich, 207/443-6563, https://montsweagfarm.com, from 11am daily, $12-20) comprises a ground-floor pub and a second-floor dining room. The wide-ranging, mostly American menu has a few international surprises as well as vegan, vegetarian, and gluten-free items. Enjoy live music Tuesday through Saturday.

ACCOMMODATIONS

Bed-and-Breakfasts

Named after a famous Maine clipper ship, Paul and Melanie Harris's **Snow Squall Inn** (5 Bradford Rd. at Rte. 1, Wiscasset, 207/882-6892 or 800/775-7245, www.snowsquallinn.com, $120-170) is a renovated mid-19th-century house on the edge of downtown.

Inside are four lovely guest rooms and three family suites. Melanie is a licensed massage therapist and a vinyasa yoga instructor; Paul is a professionally trained chef. It's open all year by reservation.

The **Squire Tarbox Inn** (1181 Main Rd./Rte. 144, Westport Island, 207/882-7693 or 800/818-0626, www.squiretarboxinn.com, mid-Apr.-Dec., $225-290) comprises a late 18th-century main house and an early 19th-century carriage house on a working farm. In 2018, new owners updated the 12 guest rooms without losing their historical charm. Rates include breakfast. Pizza from the inn's woodburning oven is usually offered one night weekly during summer. From downtown Wiscasset, head southwest four miles on Route 1 to Route 144. Turn left and go about 8.5 scenic miles to the inn.

Motels

Fairly close to Route 1 but buffered a bit by century-old hemlocks, the well-maintained **Wiscasset Woods Lodge** (Rte. 1, Wiscasset, 207/882-7137 or 800/732-8168, http://wiscassetwoods.com, $140-190) has been updated over the years with pine and red oak harvested and milled on the eight-acre property. A generous hot breakfast buffet is included. Seven rooms are pet friendly ($10/pet/night). Ask for a room in the back building if you're noise-sensitive.

Camping

Chewonki Campground (235 Chewonki Neck Rd., Wiscasset, 207/882-7426, https://chewonkicampground.com, $55-90), with 47 sites on 50 tidal waterfront acres, also offers a saltwater pool, one-hole golf course, canoe and kayak rentals, and a clay tennis court, as well as the usual campground amenities

INFORMATION AND SERVICES

The **Wiscasset Area Chamber of Commerce** (207/882-9600, www.wiscassetchamber.com) has info on members. Find **public restrooms** on the Town Wharf, on Water Street, and at the Lincoln County Court House.

GETTING THERE AND AROUND

Wiscasset is about 12 miles or 20 minutes via Route 1 from Bath, but allow up to twice that in summer. It's about 13 miles or 20 minutes via Routes 1 and 27 to Boothbay Harbor. It's about 8 miles or 15 minutes via Route 1 to Damariscotta.

Boothbay Peninsula

East of Wiscasset, en route to Damariscotta, only a flurry of signs along Route 1 in Edgecomb hints at what's down the peninsula bisected by Route 27 and framed by the Sheepscot and Damariscotta Rivers. Drive southward down the Boothbay Peninsula Memorial Day-Labor Day, and you'll find yourself in one of Maine's longest-running summer playgrounds.

The three peninsula towns of **Boothbay** (pop. 3,120), **Boothbay Harbor** (pop. 2,165), and, connected by a bridge, **Southport Island** (pop. 606) comprise a maze of islands and peninsulas. When Route 27 arrives at the water, having passed through Boothbay, you're at Boothbay Harbor ("the Harbor"), scene of most of the action. The harbor itself is a boat fan's dream, loaded with working craft and pleasure yachts. Ashore are shops and galleries, restaurants and inns, and one-way streets, traffic congestion, and pedestrians everywhere. But don't despair; it's easy to escape the peak-season crowds in one of the numerous parks and preserves, fine places for a hike or a picnic. Hop on an excursion

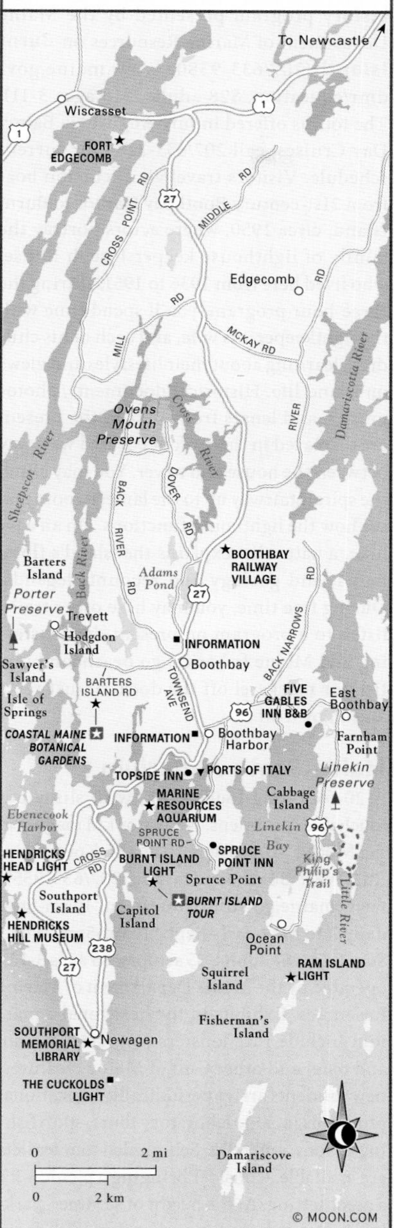

boat to an offshore island, for a whale watch, or for an evening sail around the bay.

Try to save time for quieter spots: East Boothbay, Ocean Point, Southport Island, the Coastal Maine Botanical Gardens, or even the area just over the 1,000-foot-long footbridge stretching across one corner of the harbor. Cross the bridge and walk down Atlantic Avenue to the Fishermen's Memorial, a bronze fishing dory commemorating the loss of hardy souls who've earned a rugged living here by their wits and the sea. Across the street is Our Lady Queen of Peace Catholic Church, with shipwright-quality woodwork.

SIGHTS

TOP EXPERIENCE

★ Coastal Maine Botanical Gardens

The tidal shorefront **Coastal Maine Botanical Gardens** (Barters Island Rd., Boothbay, 207/633-4333, www.mainegardens.org, 9am-6pm daily July-Aug., 9am-5pm daily mid-Apr.-June and Sept.-Oct., $18 adults, $16 seniors, $9 ages 3-17) are masterful, yet still in their youth. The nonprofit project, designed to preserve more than 125 acres of woodlands with a trail network and landscaped pocket "theme" gardens, has grown to encompass 295 acres, with formal gardens, paths, herb and kitchen gardens, woods walks, a fairy village, a five-senses garden, and nearly a mile of waterfront. Artwork is placed throughout. A magical children's garden encourages imagination, play, and discovery in a setting drawing from Maine-related children's literature such as *Blueberries for Sal* and *Miss Rumphius*. Free **Highlight Tours** are offered daily May-October. **Accessible Cart Tours,** offered twice daily, are $10 per person except on Wednesday, when they're free; book at least one week ahead. **Mobility scooter** rentals are available, first come, first served, $8. Operating from the garden's landing is **Sheepscot River Cruises** (207/633-8000), which offers guided cruises aboard the *Beagle,* an electric vessel; call for current offerings. When visiting, allow at least two hours, although you could easily spend a full day here. Feast on fresh produce from the garden at the **Kitchen Garden Café** (11am-3pm daily). Other garden activities include lectures, the Maine Fairy House Festival, a Kitchen Garden Dinner series, and **Gardens Aglow** (4pm-9pm Thurs.-Sun. mid-Nov.-Dec., $16 adults, $14 seniors, $9 children, $41 family), when colorful lights turn the gardens into a winter wonderland. Entrance to the preserve is on Barters Island Road, about 1.3 miles west of Boothbay Center.

Boothbay Railway Village

When George McEvoy's mother ordered him to find a new home for his growing collection of historical memorabilia, including automobiles and defunct narrow-gauge and downsized Maine Central Railroad artifacts, McEvoy purchased 15 acres in Boothbay, constructed a three-quarter-mile-long narrow-gauge track, and in May 1965 opened the **Boothbay Railway Village** (Rte. 27, Boothbay, 207/633-4727, www.railwayvillage.org, 10am-5pm daily late May-mid-Oct., $14 adults, $12 seniors, $7 ages 3-18). Fifty-plus years later, meticulously restored coal-fired steam trains loop through an ever-expanding village comprising 24 buildings, including a functioning steam-boiler workshop, on the now-30-acre campus that feels like a life-size train set. Historical buildings saved and relocated here include Maine Central and Belfast & Moosehead stations, the Boothbay Town Hall, and the Spruce Point Chapel. Exhibits, which range from the significant (60-plus antique vehicles) to the mundane (600 salt-and-pepper sets), help visitors make the connection between industry, everyday life, and the railway. Tickets include riding the steam or diesel trains, Model T rides, demonstrations, and specialty tours; call for current schedule.

★ Burnt Island Tour

Visit with a lighthouse keeper's family, climb the tower into the lantern room, and explore an island during a living- and natural-history program presented by the Maine Department of Marine Resources on **Burnt Island** (207/633-9580, www.maine.gov/dmr/education, $28 adults, $18 ages 3-11). The tour is offered in July-August via Balmy Day Cruises; call 207/633-2284 for current schedule. Visitors travel via excursion boat from 21st-century Boothbay Harbor to Burnt Island, circa 1950, where actors portray the family of lighthouse keeper Joseph Muise, who lived here from 1936 to 1951. During the three-hour program, you'll spend time with the lightkeeper, his wife, and each of his children, learning about their lifestyles and views on island life. Historical documents, photographs, and lenses from 1821 to the present are displayed in the 45-foot covered walkway between the house and tower. You may climb the spiral stairway up to the lantern room and see how the lighthouse functions. On an easy hike, a naturalist explains the island's flora, fauna, and geology and recounts legends. During free time, you may hike other trails, listen to a program on present-day lobstering and Maine fisheries, go beachcombing, fish for mackerel off the dock, or just relax and enjoy it all.

Maine State Aquarium

A 20-foot-long touch tank, with slimy but touchable specimens, is a major kid magnet at the **Maine State Aquarium** (McKown Point Rd., West Boothbay Harbor, 207/633-9559, www.maine.gov/dmr/education, 10am-5pm daily late May-early Sept., 10am-5pm Wed.-Sun. Sept., $7 adults, $5 seniors, $3 ages 3-12), operated by the Maine Department of Marine Resources. Exhibits in the hexagonal aquarium include rare lobsters (oversize, albino, and blue) and other Gulf of Maine creatures; new residents arrive periodically. Educational programs include laboratory tours, sportfishing lessons, and talks. Self-guided tour leaflets are available. Consider bringing a picnic—it's a great setting. At the height of summer, parking is limited, and it's a longish walk from downtown around the west side of the harbor; plan to take the free local trolley-bus.

Southport Island

The nautical shortcut of Townsend Gut separates Boothbay Harbor from **Southport Island.** The island is ideal for a drive-about (or a pedal-about, for experienced cyclists), following Route 27 south to the island's tip and returning north on Route 238. En route are plentiful glimpses of island-salted ocean waters, especially if you explore some of the side roads.

A historic 1810 Cape-style building, carefully restored, is the home of the **Hendricks Hill Museum** (Rte. 27, West Southport, 207/633-1102, www.southportmainehistory.com, 11am-3pm Tues., Thurs., and Sat. July-Aug., free), a community attic filled with all kinds of workaday tools and utensils and fascinating maritime memorabilia. The 11-room museum is about two miles south of the Southport Island bridge, on the right, in the center of West Southport.

From the Southport Village General Store, where you can pick up sandwiches for a picnic, decent lobster rolls, and baked goodies, it's just a hop down Beach Road to **Hendricks Head,** with a nice sandy beach and lighthouse views.

At the island's tip is the **Southport Memorial Library** (207/633-2741). Displayed inside is a collection of mounted tropical butterflies along with 10 signed and numbered Roger Tory Peterson prints.

ENTERTAINMENT

The renovated 1894 **Opera House** (86 Townsend Ave., Boothbay Harbor, 207/633-5159, www.boothbayoperahouse.com) hosts concerts, lectures, dramas, and special events. In July and August, free **band concerts** are held at 7:30pm Thursdays, and free outdoor family movies are shown at 8pm Fridays on the Memorial Library lawn (4 Oak St.). Bring a blanket or folding chair.

There's live entertainment on mid-June to mid-October weekends at **McSeagulls** (14 Wharf St., Boothbay Harbor, 207/633-5900, www.mcseagullsonline.com), which also serves decent food 11:30am-9pm daily. **Mine Oyster** (16 Wharf St., 207/633-6616, www.mineoyster.net) has live entertainment, with an emphasis on dance bands.

Festivals and Events

The **Fishermen's Festival** is a colorful early-season celebration, held the third weekend of April, and includes the Miss Shrimp Princess pageant, a lobster-crate race, plentiful seafood and chowder, contests such as trap hauling, scallop and clam shucking, fish filleting, and net mending, and the blessing of the fleet. There's also a real steal—a lobster-eating contest you can enter for about $5.

June is the month for **Windjammer Days,** two days of festivities centering on traditional windjammer schooners. Highlights are the Windjammer Parade, harbor-front concerts, plenty of food, and a fireworks extravaganza. In early August, the **Boat Builders Festival** features shipyard and boat tours, food, and kids' activities.

From late November through December, the Boothbays dazzle with holiday cheer thanks to **Gardens Aglow** and the **Boothbay Festival of Lights.**

RECREATION

Parks and Preserves

BOOTHBAY REGION LAND TRUST

The **Boothbay Region Land Trust** (137 Townsend Ave., Boothbay Harbor, 207/633-4818, www.bbrlt.org) has preserved more than 1,700 acres, including six islands, with more than 30 miles of trails available. Individual preserve maps as well as a general brochure-map with driving directions are available at the information centers, the trust office, and at trailhead kiosks. The trust also offers a free series of summertime guided walks and paddles in the various preserves, along with talks. A free guide, available at local businesses and info centers, provides details and access points. Here's just a sampling of the possibilities.

Most popular is the **Porter Preserve,** a 19-acre property bordering the Sheepscot

1

2

River. Follow the moderately easy 0.86-mile loop trail and be rewarded with spectacular views, especially at sunset. You might even spy some seals lolling in the ledges at low tide. To get there, take Route 27 south to the monument in Boothbay Center. Bear right on Cory Lane and go 0.3 mile, bearing right again on Barters Island Road for 12.2 miles (perhaps stopping at the Trevett Country Store for lobster rolls or subs to go). Turn left on Kimballtown Road, go 0.5 mile, and then go left at the fork onto Porter Point Road. Park in the small lot just beyond the cemetery.

The 146-acre **Ovens Mouth Preserve** has almost five miles of trails on two peninsulas linked by a 93-foot bridge. The 1.6-mile trail on the east peninsula is much easier than the 3.7 miles of trails on the west peninsula. To get there, from the monument in Boothbay Center, travel 1.7 miles north and then go left on Adams Pond Road. Bear right at the fork and continue 2.2 miles. To get to the east peninsula, bear right at the junction onto the Dover Road Extension. Proceed to the end of the tarred road to the parking lot on the left. To get to the west peninsula, bear left at the junction and continue 0.15 mile to the parking area on the right.

In East Boothbay, on the way to Ocean Point, is the **Linekin Preserve,** stretching from Route 96 to the Damariscotta River. The 2.3-mile white-blazed River Loop (best done clockwise) takes in an old sawmill site, a beaver dam, and great riverfront views. You'll meet a couple of moderately steep sections on the eastern side, near the river, but otherwise it's relatively easy. To get there, take Route 96 for 3.8 miles and look for the parking area and trailhead on the left.

KNICKERCANE ISLAND

This gem is ideal for a picnic, perhaps with a lobster roll from the Trevett Country Store. The island is connected via a bridge, making it a pleasant place to stroll or, if you're brave, swim. Also here is an honest-to-God lobster pound (no, not the kind that serves the tasty crustaceans, but rather the impoundment area for them). The island is off the Barters Island Road causeway. To find it, from Boothbay Center follow signs for the Coastal Maine Botanical Center, then continue until you come to open water on both sides of the road; the parking area is on the left.

1: Coastal Maine Botanical Gardens **2:** lobster shack on the Boothbay Peninsula

BARRETT PARK

On the east side of the harbor, Barrett Park is an oceanfront park on Linekin Bay, with shade trees, picnic tables, swimming, and restrooms. To find it, take Atlantic Avenue and turn left on Lobster Cove Road (at the Catholic church).

Boat Excursions

Two major fleet operators provide practically every type of sea adventure imaginable. Boothbay Harbor's veteran excursion fleet is **Cap'n Fish's Cruises** (Pier 1, Wharf St., Boothbay Harbor, 207/633-3244 or 800/636-3244, www.boothbayboattrips.com, $19-37 adults, $10-20 children). Cap'n Fish's 150-passenger boats do nine varied, mostly 2-3-hour cruises. There's bound to be a tour length and itinerary (seal-watching, lobster-trap hauling, lighthouses, Damariscove Harbor, puffin cruises, and more) that piques your interest. Pick up a schedule at one of the information centers and call for reservations. Cap'n Fish's is the best choice for **whale-watching,** offering 3-4-hour trips departing daily mid-June-mid-October. Tours cost $59 adults, $32 ages 6-14, $19 age 5 and younger, with a rain check if the whales don't show up. Reservations are advisable, especially early and late in the season and on summer weekends. No matter what the weather on shore, dress warmly and carry more clothing than you think you'll need. Motion-sensitive children and adults should plan ahead with appropriate medication. Cap'n Fish's also runs 2.5-hour **puffin-sighting tours** to **Eastern Egg Rock,** circling the island once or twice for the best views. Cruises are offered once

Damariscove Island

Summering Wabanakis knew it as Aquahega, but Damerill's Cove was the first European name attributed to the secure, fjord-like harbor at the southern tip of 210-acre Damariscove Island in 1614, when Captain John Smith of the Jamestown Colony explored the neighborhood. By 1622, Damerill's Cove fishermen were sharing their considerable codfish catch with starving Plimoth Plantation colonists desperate for food. Fishing and farming sustained resident Damariscovers during their up-and-down history, and archaeologists have found rich deposits tracing the story of this early island settlement about seven miles south of Boothbay Harbor.

Rumors persist that the ghost of Captain Richard Pattishall, decapitated and tossed overboard by Indians in 1689, still roams the island, accompanied by the specter of his dog. The fog that often overhangs the bleak, almost-treeless low-slung island makes it easy to fall for the many ghost stories about Pattishall and other one-time residents. In summer, the island is awash with wildflowers, bayberries, raspberries, blackberries, and rugosa roses.

Damariscove Island became a National Historic Landmark in 1978. Since 2005, most of 1.7-mile-long Damariscove has been owned by the **Boothbay Region Land Trust** (1 Oak St., 2nd Fl., Boothbay Harbor, 207/633-44818, www.bbrlt.org). Day-use visitors are welcome on the island anytime, but the northern section (called Wood End) protects the state's largest nesting colony of eiders—nearly 700 nests. Dogs are not allowed.

Access to the island is most convenient if you have your own boat. Enter the narrow cove at the southern end of the island. You can disembark at the dock on the west side of the harbor, but don't tie up here or at the adjacent stone pier. Two guest moorings and two courtesy dinghies are available. The Boothbay Region Land Trust sometimes offers special trips. Summertime caretakers live in the small cabin above the dock, where a trail map is available. Stay on the trail (watch out for poison ivy) or on the shore and away from any abandoned structures; the former Coast Guard station is privately owned.

weekly in June, then three times weekly in July-late August ($39 adults, $17 children).

The harbor's other big fleet is **Balmy Days Cruises** (Pier 8, Commercial St., Boothbay Harbor, 207/633-2284 or 800/298-2284, www.balmydayscruises.com), operating three vessels on a variety of excursions. The *Novelty* does daily one-hour harbor tours ($20 adults, $10 under age 12). Reservations usually are not necessary. The 31-foot Friendship sloop *Bay Lady* offers 90-minute sailing trips ($32 adults, $20 children) daily in summer. Reservations are wise for the *Bay Lady* as well as for the fleet's most popular cruise, a daylong trip to Monhegan Island ($42 adults, $21 ages 3-11) on the *Balmy Days II,* departing at 9:30am and returning at 4:15pm daily early June-late September, plus extended weekends in late May and early October. The three-hour round-trip allows about 3.5 hours ashore on idyllic Monhegan Island.

A far smaller and more personal experience is offered by **Schooner Eastwind Cruises** (20 Commercial St., Boothbay Harbor, 207/633-6598, www.schoonereastwind.com, $44 adults, $25 age 12 and under). A trip aboard *Schooner Eastwind,* a 65-foot traditional wooden schooner built in 2004, is more than a day sail—it's an adventure. Herb and Doris Smith not only built this schooner, but also sailed around the world in their previous boats through the years, providing fodder for many tales. They take passengers on two-hour cruises to the outer islands and Seal Rocks up to four times daily. The boat departs from Fisherman's Wharf.

TOP EXPERIENCE

Paddling

From Memorial Day weekend through September, **Tidal Transit** (18 Granary Way, Chowder House Bldg., Boothbay Harbor,

207/633-7140, www.kayakboothbay.com), near the footbridge, will get you afloat with 3-4-hour guided harbor, wildlife, or sunset sea kayaking tours for around $70.

For do-it-yourselfers, Tidal Transit rents single kayaks ($30/1 hour, $60/day), tandem kayaks ($40/1 hour, $80/day), and stand-up paddleboards ($15/half hour, $45/half day).

FOOD

Boothbay Harbor is not a culinary destination, although it is improving. Go for the views and enjoy the region, but don't expect to be wowed by the food.

Lobster and Seafood

Shannon's Unshelled (11 Granary Way, Boothbay Harbor, www.shannonsunshelled.biz, from 10:30am-sold out daily, cash only), a takeout with a handful of tables, serves lobster rolls made with the meat of a whole lobster on a buttered bun with a side of sea-salted butter, as well as lobster stew, clam chowder, hot dogs, and grilled cheese.

Sit inside or on the deck at **Kaler's Restaurant** (48 Commercial St., Boothbay Harbor, 207/633-5839, www.kalerslobster.com, 11:30am-8pm daily, $9-25), which has a touch tank on the deck to amuse kids. Sure, you can get a lobster, but the menu includes sandwiches, fried and baked seafood, and landlubber choices.

Cozy's Dockside (36 Cozy Harbor Rd., Southport, 207/350-6190, www.oliversrestaurant.com, 11:30am-8pm daily, $8-24) has a stunning location overlooking the harbor and serves family-friendly fare, from hot dogs and burgers to lobster rolls and fried seafood.

On Tuesdays at 5:45pm, the oceanfront **Newagen Seaside Inn** (60 Newagen Colony Rd., Southport, 207/633-5242) offers a lobster bake on the lawn for $45; reservations required.

Well worth the splurge is **Cabbage Island Clambakes** (Pier 6, Fisherman's Wharf, Boothbay Harbor, 207/633-7200, www.cabbageislandclambakes.com, $70, no credit cards). Touristy, sure, but it's a delicious adventure. Board the excursion boat *Bennie Alice* at Pier 6 in Boothbay Harbor, cruise for about an hour past islands, boats, and lighthouses, and disembark at Cabbage Island. Watch the clambake in progress, explore the island, or play volleyball. When the feast is ready, pick up your platter, find a picnic table, and dig in. A cash bar is available in the lodge, as are restrooms. When the weather's iffy, the lodge and covered patio have seats for 100 people. You'll get two lobsters (or half a chicken), chowder, clams, corn, an egg, onions, potatoes, blueberry cake, a beverage, and the boat ride. Clambake season is mid-June-mid-September. The 3.5-hour trips depart at 12:30pm Monday-Friday, 12:30pm and 5pm Saturday, and 11am and 1:30pm Sunday.

Quick Bites

Three general stores deliver local flavors with some fancy touches. It's worth the drive over to Trevett to indulge in a lobster roll or fried clams from the **Trevett Country Store** (207/633-1140), just before the bridge connecting Hodgdon and Barters Islands. Stop into the **Southport General Store** (443 Hendricks Hill Rd., 207/633-6666), serving Southport Island since 1882, for breakfast, pizzas, sandwiches, burgers, lobster rolls, baked goods, and a decent wine selection. On the east side, the **East Boothbay General Store** (255 Ocean Point Rd./Rte. 96, East Boothbay, 207/633-4503) has been serving locals since 1893. These days it sells wine and specialty foods in addition to pizzas (including an awesome breakfast version), excellent sandwiches, salads, and baked goods.

"Free beer tomorrow" proclaims the sign in front of **Bet's Famous Fish Fry** (Village Common, Rte. 27, Boothbay, hours vary seasonally), a take-out stand that's renowned for its generous portions of fresh haddock fish-and-chips perfectly prepared. (Unless you're starving, often a half order will feed two.) There's a nice seating area with picnic tables and a garden.

You can pick up beer, wine, picnic fixings,

and other goodies at **Pinkham's Gourmet Market** (295 Townsend Ave., Boothbay Harbor, 207/633-6236, www.pinkhamseafood.com, 9am-6pm daily), which also offers made-to-order sandwiches and has outdoor seating.

Blue Moon (54 Commercial St., Boothbay Harbor, 207/633-2220, 7:30am-2:30pm daily) is a tiny spot worth seeking out for breakfast and lunch fare. Try to snag one of the porch tables hanging over the harbor.

The seasonal **Boothbay Area Farmers Market** sets up on the Town Commons in Boothbay 9am-noon Thursdays.

Casual Dining

The tapas menu complements the views from the 3rd-floor deck at **Boat House Bistro** (12 The By-Way, Boothbay Harbor, 207/633-0400, www.theboathousebistro.com, 11:30am-9pm daily, $8-39). There are plenty of other options, but the tapas, soups, and salads are the way to go. Vegan and vegetarian choices are available.

For spectacular sunset views, take a spin out to the **Ocean Point Inn** (Shore Rd., East Boothbay, 207/633-4200 or 800/552-5554, www.oceanpointinn.com, 7:30am-10am and 5pm-9pm daily, $12-34). The lobster stew is rave-worthy, there's a nightly vegetarian special, and a children's menu is available.

Dine in either the pub or restaurant at the **Thistle Inn** (55 Oak St., Boothbay Harbor, 207/633-3541, www.thethistleinn.com, 4pm-10pm daily, $12-16 pub, $24-42 restaurant), a cozy spot with intimate dining rooms.

Reopened in 2016 by a local chef with an impressive culinary background, the **Carriage House Restaurant** (388 Ocean Point East Rd., East Boothbay, 207/633-6025, www.eatcarriagehouse.com, 5pm-9pm Tues.-Sat., $14-32) quickly gained a following for its seasonal American fare ranging from sandwiches to heartier dishes.

Real Northern Italian fare prepared by a real Italian chef is the lure for ★ **Ports of Italy** (47 Commercial St., Boothbay Harbor, 207/633-1011, www.portsofitaly.com, from 4:30pm daily, $20-34). Owner Sante Calandri hails from Perugia, but more recently spent 23 years in New York City. This isn't a red-sauce place; expect well-prepared and innovative fare, with delicious homemade pastas and especially good seafood.

Smack-dab in the center of town, adjacent to the footbridge, is **Harborside Tavern** (12 Bridge St., Boothbay Harbor, 207/633-4074, www.harborsidetavern.com, 7:30am-9pm daily, $14-30), a long-standing favorite reinvented under new ownership and serving updated American fare.

ACCOMMODATIONS

If you want to concentrate your time in downtown Boothbay Harbor, shopping or taking boat excursions, stay in town and avoid the parking hassles. Although the town practically rolls up the sidewalks after Gardens Aglow, a few businesses do stay open year-round.

Classic Inns

Over in East Boothbay, the **Ocean Point Inn** (Shore Rd., East Boothbay, 207/633-4200 or 800/552-5554, www.oceanpointinn.com, $125-400) wows with spectacular sunset views and an easygoing ambience that keeps guests returning generation after generation. Lodgings on the sprawling complex include an inn, a lodge, a motel, apartments, and cottages. Most guest rooms have ocean views; some have kitchenettes. The rates, which include a hot buffet breakfast, reflect that this is an older property, and some accommodations are tired; updating is in progress. Also on the premises are a restaurant and tavern with fabulous ocean views, a pier, an outdoor heated pool, a hot tub, and Adirondack chairs set just so on the water's edge. The best deals are the packages.

For those who pine for vacation ease, the ★ **Spruce Point Inn and Spa** (Atlantic

1: Newagen Seaside Inn on Southport Island
2: Blue Heron Seaside Inn 3: a half order of the fish-and-chips at Bet's Famous Fish Fry

1
2
3

Ave., Boothbay Harbor, 207/633-4152 or 800/553-0289, www.sprucepointinn.com, from $255) is the answer. Choose from traditional inn rooms, suites, cottages, and town houses. Decor and prices vary widely. Amenities at the 57-acre resort include a full-service spa and fitness center, freshwater and saltwater pools, tennis courts, a game room, rocky shorefront, and shuttle bus and boat service to downtown (about 1.5 miles, although it seems farther). Rates include use of bicycles, kayaks, paddleboards, shuttles, and a children's program. Dining choices range from poolside to pub-style to fine dining, with prices to match each setting. Pet-friendly accommodations are available for $35/pet/day. The inn holds weddings on many weekends, so aim for midweek.

Get away from it all at the **Newagen Seaside Inn** (60 Newagen Colony Rd., Southport, 207/633-5242 or 800/654-5242, www.newagenseasideinn.com, mid-May-Sept., from $239), an unstuffy, updated, full-service inn with casual dining and views that go on forever. Renovated guest rooms are split among the Main Inn; the Little Inn, where rooms have private decks; and seven cottages. There's a long, rocky shore, a nature trail, and a spa, plus tennis courts, a pool and hot tub, cruiser bikes, guest rowboats, a game room, candlepin bowling, and porches just for relaxing. Rates include a generous buffet breakfast. The Pub (11:30am-2:30pm and 5pm-9pm daily Sun.-Fri., $10-32) is open to nonguests. The inn is six miles south of downtown Boothbay Harbor.

Linekin Bay Resort (92 Wall Point Rd., Boothbay Harbor, 207/633-2494 or 866/847-2103, www.linekinbayresort.com, from $380), a classic old-timey summer sporting camp on 20 wooded oceanfront acres, was reborn under new owners in 2016. The four lodges, 20 cabins, and facilities were updated and brightened, but the all-inclusive summer program remains, comprising lodging, all meals, kids' camps (ages 4-10), sailing instruction, activities, and housekeeping as well as use of the tennis courts, heated saltwater pool, sailboats, canoes, and kayaks. Pet-friendly accommodations are available ($25/day). Room-only rates are available in spring and fall from $140.

Bed-and-Breakfasts

Escape the hustle and bustle at the **Five Gables Inn B&B** (107 Murray Hill Rd., East Boothbay, 207/633-4551, www.fivegablesinn.com, $175-295), which began life as a no-frills summer hotel in the late 19th century. It's gone steadily upmarket since then. Unique touches include wonderful murals throughout and window seats in the gable rooms. All but one of the 16 light and airy guest rooms have Linekin Bay views. The living room is congenial, the gardens are gorgeous, and the porch goes on forever. Rates include a multicourse breakfast and afternoon tea. The inn, on a side road off Route 96 in the traditional boatbuilding hamlet of East Boothbay, is 3.5 miles from downtown Boothbay Harbor.

The charming in-town **Thistle Inn** (55 Oak St., Boothbay Harbor, 207/633-3541, www.thethistleinn.com, $169), an 1861 sea captain's home, has six handsome guest rooms, each named after Maine windjammers with a local connection. A full breakfast is included late May-mid-October, and the inn and its excellent pub and restaurant are open year-round.

The **Harbor House** (80 McKown St., Boothbay Harbor, 800/856-1164, www.harborhouse-me.com, $199-255) is an in-town, mansard-roofed house with eight rooms (some with water views) and a great wraparound porch. A full breakfast is included.

In town and on the water, the **Blue Heron Seaside Inn** (65 Townsend Ave., Boothbay Harbor, 207/633-7020 or 866/216-2300, www.blueheronseasideinn.com, from $285) has an uncluttered, bright interior that belies the building's Victorian vintage. Each room has a waterfront deck; some also have a fireplace and a whirlpool tub. A dock with kayaks and a paddleboat is available. A full breakfast is elegantly served on Wedgwood china.

Topping an in-town hill with sigh-producing views over the inner and outer harbors, and yet just a two-minute walk to shops and restaurants, is ★ **Topside Inn** (60 McKown St., Boothbay Harbor, 207/633-5404 or 888/633-5404, www.topsideinn.com, from $290), a solid 19th-century sea captain's home with two annexes. Innkeepers Buzz Makarewicz and Mark Osborn keep updating the property, opting for a handsome decor with a touch of seaside whimsy. Guest rooms in the three-story main inn are mostly spacious, with nice views. Good books are plentiful, and the rockers on the wraparound porch and Adirondack chairs on the lawn are perfect places to read or relax. Rooms in the annexes have decks and most have at least glimpses of the ocean. Rates in all buildings include breakfast, a self-serve cold buffet with a hot entrée that's served to the table. Hot beverages are available all day; beer, wine, and cocktails are available, as are cheese and charcuterie plates; and on most afternoons, home-baked cookies magically appear in the guest pantry.

Motels and Hotels

Every room at the **Beach Cove Waterfront Inn** (38 Lakeview Rd., Boothbay Harbor, 207/633-0353 or 866/851-0450, www.beachcovehotel.com, $99-220) has a water view, a balcony or deck, a mini-fridge, and a microwave. The renovated property, about one mile from downtown, is extremely popular with families who appreciate its beach, dock, heated saltwater pool, canoes, and rowboats. A light continental breakfast is included.

Since 1955, the Lewis family has owned and operated the **Mid-Town Motel** (96 McKown St., Boothbay Harbor, 207/633-2751, www.midtownmaine.com, $108), a spotless, no-frills vintage motel that's within steps of everything. It's a classic: clean, convenient, and cheap, and the owners couldn't be nicer folks.

Camping

With 150 well-maintained wooded and open sites on 45 acres, **Shore Hills Campground** (553 Rte. 27, Boothbay, 207/633-4782, www.shorehills.com, $32-70) is a popular big-rig destination where reservations are essential in midsummer. Tenting sites are on a separate loop. Also available are two cute cabins, each with bathroom linens provided, $129/night. Leashed pets are allowed, and there's a shuttle service to Boothbay Harbor.

Much smaller, and smack on the ocean, is **Gray Homestead Oceanfront Camping** (21 Homestead Rd., Southport, 207/633-4612, www.graysoceancamping.com, $52-65), a family-run campground with 40 full hookup sites as well as cottages and condos that rent by the week ($700-1,300). A stone beach, a pier, laundry facilities, kayak rentals, and lobsters—live or cooked—are available. There's even a small sandy beach.

INFORMATION AND SERVICES

Providing info about their members are the **Boothbay Harbor Region Chamber of Commerce** (207/633-2353, www.boothbayharbor.com) and the **Boothbay Chamber of Commerce** (207/633-4743, www.boothbay.org).

Find **public restrooms** at the municipal parking lot on Commercial Street (next to Pier 1), the municipal lot at the end of Granary Way, Saint Andrews Hospital, the town offices, the library, and the Maine State Aquarium.

GETTING THERE AND AROUND

Boothbay Harbor is about 13 miles or 20 minutes via Routes 1 and 27 from Wiscasset. It's about 15 miles or 35 minutes to Damariscotta via Routes 27 and 1.

Pemaquid Region

The riverfront towns of **Damariscotta** (pop. 2,218) and **Newcastle** (pop. 1,752) anchor the southwestern end of the Pemaquid Peninsula, while **Waldoboro** (pop. 5,075) anchors the northeastern end. Along the peninsula are **New Harbor** (one of Maine's most photographed fishing villages), **Pemaquid Point** (site of one of Maine's most photographed lighthouses), and ports reputedly used by Captain John Smith, Captain Kidd, and many others. Here too are a restored fortress, Native American historic sites, antiques and crafts shops galore, boat excursions to offshore Monhegan Island, and one of the best pocket beaches in Mid-Coast Maine.

On Christmas Day 1614, famed explorer Captain John Smith anchored on Rutherford Island, at the tip of the peninsula, and promptly named the spot Christmas Cove. Today it is one of three villages that make up the town of South Bristol, the southwestern finger of the Pemaquid Peninsula. **Bristol** (pop. 2,755) and **South Bristol** (pop. 892), covering eight villages on the bottom half of the peninsula, were named after the British port city.

As early as 1625, settler John Brown received title to some of this territory from the Wabanaki sachem (chief) Samoset, an agreeable fellow who learned snippets of English from English cod fishermen. *Damariscotta* (dam-uh-riss-COT-ta), in fact, is a Wabanaki word for "plenty of alewives [herring]." The settlement here was named Walpole but was incorporated in 1847 under its current name.

Newcastle, incorporated in 1763, earned fame and fortune from shipbuilding and brickmaking—which explains the extraordinary number of brick buildings throughout the town. In the 19th century, Newcastle's shipyards sent clippers, Down Easters, and full-rigged ships down the ways and around the world.

Route 1 cuts a commercial swath through Waldoboro without revealing the attractive downtown—or the lovely Friendship Peninsula, south of the highway. Duck into Waldoboro and then follow Route 220 south 10 miles to Friendship for an off-the-beaten-track drive.

Waldoboro's heritage is something of an anomaly in Maine. It's predominantly German, thanks to 18th-century Teutons who swallowed the blandishments of General Samuel Waldo, holder of a million-acre "patent" stretching as far as the Penobscot River. The settlers had a rough life but succeeded in clearing lands and erecting mills. Their descendants went into shipbuilding in a big way, establishing six shipyards and producing more than 300 wooden vessels, including the first five-masted schooner, the 265-foot *Governor Ames*, launched in 1888. Although the *Ames*'s ill-supported masts collapsed on her maiden voyage, repairs allowed her to serve as a coal hauler for more than 20 years, and many more five-masters followed in her wake. It's hard to believe today, but Waldoboro once was the sixth-busiest port in the United States. At the Town Landing, alongside the Medomak River, signage describes the town's shipyards and shipbuilding heritage.

SIGHTS

Chapman-Hall House

Damariscotta's oldest surviving building is the Cape-style **Chapman-Hall House** (270 Main St., Damariscotta, noon-4pm Sat.-Sun. early June-mid-Oct., $5). It was built in 1754 by Nathaniel Chapman, whose family tree includes the legendary John Chapman, better known as Johnny Appleseed. Highlights are the original kitchen and displays of local shipbuilding memorabilia. The house, listed in the National Register of Historic Places, was meticulously restored in the styles of three different eras. Don't miss the antique roses in the back garden. The property is cared for by

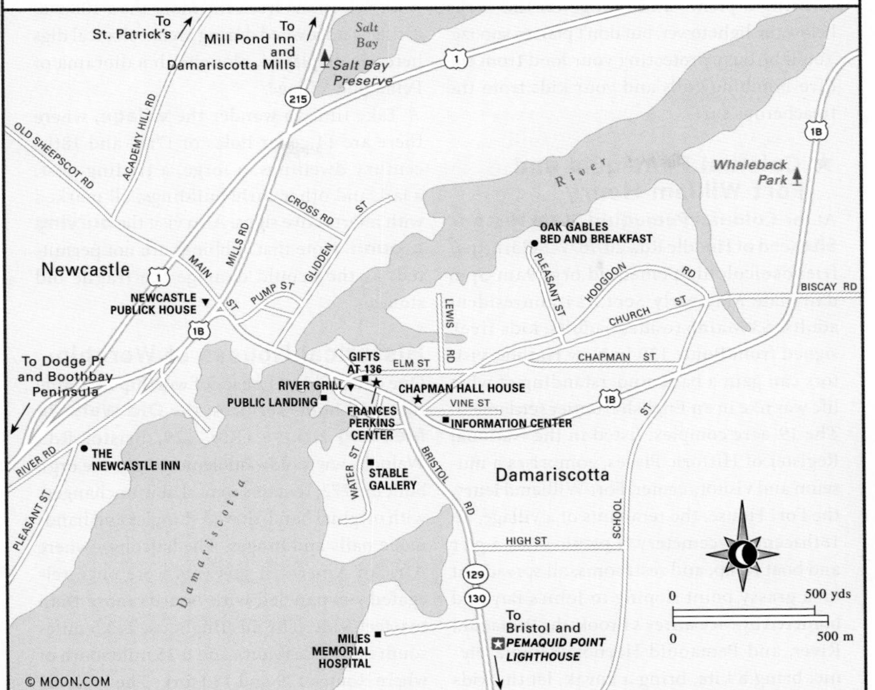

the Lincoln County Historical Society (www.lincolncountyhistory.org), which organizes docent-led tours.

★ Pemaquid Point Lighthouse

One of the icons of the Maine Coast, Pemaquid Point's lighthouse has been captured for posterity by gazillions of photographers and is depicted on a Maine state quarter. The lighthouse, its adjacent keeper's house, and picnic grounds are a town park. Also on the premises is an art gallery. Admission to the grounds, payable at the gatehouse, is $2 (age 12 and older). The lighthouse grounds are accessible all year, even after the museum closes for the season, when admission is free. The point is 15 miles south of Route 1 via winding two-lane Route 130.

Commissioned in 1827, **Pemaquid Point Lighthouse** (www.lighthousefoundation.org) stands sentinel over some of Maine's nastiest shoreline—rocks and surf that can reduce any wooden boat to kindling. Now automated, the light tower is licensed to the American Lighthouse Foundation and is managed by the Friends of Pemaquid Point Lighthouse. Volunteers *aim* to open the tower 10:30am-5pm daily late May-mid-October, weather permitting. There is no charge, but donations are appreciated.

The **Fisherman's Museum** (207/677-2494, 9am-5pm daily mid-May-mid-Oct., donation), in the former lightkeeper's house, points out the pleasures and perils of the lobstering industry and also has displays about shipwrecks and lighthouse memorabilia.

While here, visit the **Pemaquid Art Gallery** (207/677-2752), displaying juried works by the Pemaquid Group of Artists since 1928.

Bring a picnic and lounge on the rocks below the light tower, but don't plan to snooze. You'll be busy protecting your food from the dive-bombing gulls and your kids from the treacherous surf.

★ Colonial Pemaquid and Fort William Henry

At the **Colonial Pemaquid State Historic Site** (end of Huddle Rd., 207/677-2423, http://friendsofcolonialpemaquid.org, 9am-5pm daily late May-early Sept., $4 nonresident adults, $3 Maine resident adults, kids free), signed from Route 130 in New Harbor, visitors can gain a basic understanding of what life was like in an English frontier settlement. The 19-acre complex, listed in the National Register of Historic Places, comprises a museum and visitors center, Fort William Henry, the Fort House, the remnants of a village, an 18th-century cemetery, a picnic area, a pier and boat ramp, and restrooms, all spread out on a grassy point sloping to John's Bay and bordered by McCaffrey's Brook, the Pemaquid River, and Pemaquid Harbor. Bring a picnic, bring a kite, bring a kayak, let the kids run—but do take time to visit the historical sites (a kids' activity book is available for $1). Demonstrations, tours, lectures, and reenactments are part of the site's summer schedule.

Three national flags fly over the ramparts of **Fort William Henry,** a reconstruction of a fort dating from 1692, the second of three that stood here between 1677 and the late 18th century. The forts were built to defend the English settlement of Pemaquid, settled between 1625 and 1628, from the French. From the rebuilt western tower, you'll have fantastic views of John's Bay and John's Island, named for none other than Captain John Smith; inside are artifacts retrieved from archaeological excavations of the 17th-century trading outpost.

The square white **Fort House,** which dates to the late 1700s, houses a research library and archaeology lab as well as a gift shop.

Exhibits at the **museum and visitors center** focus on regional history, from early Native American life through the colonial period. Selections from the more than 100,000 artifacts uncovered during archaeological digs here are displayed, along with a diorama of Pemaquid Village.

Take time to wander the **village,** where there are 14 cellar holes of 17th- and 18th-century dwellings, a forge, a trading post, a jail, and other early buildings, all marked with interpretive signs. Also visit the **burying ground.** Note that rubbings are not permitted, as they could damage the fragile old stones.

Historical Houses of Worship

One of the oldest houses of worship in Maine that still holds services, the **Old Walpole Meeting House** (Rte. 129, Bristol Rd., Walpole, www.oldwalpolemeetinghouse.org), built in 1772, remains remarkably unchanged, with original hand-shaved shingles and handmade nails and hinges. The balcony—where African American servants were once relegated—is paneled with boards more than two feet wide. The meetinghouse is 3.5 miles south of Damariscotta and 0.25 mile south of where Routes 129 and 130 fork. The Walpole Barn, across the main road, has keys if you want to peek inside.

The beautifully restored **Harrington Meeting House** (Old Harrington Rd., off Rte. 130, 2pm-4:30pm Mon., Wed., Fri. July-Aug., donation), begun in 1772 and completed in 1775, now serves as Bristol's local-history museum—town-owned and run by the Pemaquid Historical Association. Behind it is an old cemetery that's fascinating to explore.

A remnant of Waldoboro's German connection is the **Old German Church** (Rte. 32, Waldoboro, 207/832-7742, www.oldgermanmeetinghouse.com, 1pm-4pm daily July-Aug.) and its cemetery. The Reformed Lutheran church, built in 1772 on the opposite side of the Medomak River, was moved across the ice in the winter of 1794. Inside are box pews and a huge hanging pulpit. One of the three oldest churches in Maine, it lost its flock in the mid-19th century when new generations no longer spoke German. A German-language afternoon service is held on the first Sunday of August.

Built in 1808, **St. Patrick's Catholic Church** (Academy Hill Rd., Damariscotta Mills, Newcastle, 207/563-3240, 9am-sunset daily), a solid brick structure with 1.5-foot-thick walls, a rare crypt-form altar, and a Paul Revere bell, is New England's oldest Catholic church in continual use. Academy Hill Road starts at Newcastle Square in downtown Newcastle; the church is 2.25 miles from the square and 1 mile beyond Lincoln Academy.

St. Andrew's Episcopal Church (Glidden St., Newcastle, 207/563-3533), built in 1883, is nothing short of exquisite, with carved-oak beams, a stenciled ceiling, and, for the cognoscenti, a spectacular Hutchings organ.

Frances Perkins Center

For insight into the life of the first female cabinet member in U.S. history, visit the **Frances Perkins Center** (170A Main St., Damariscotta, 207/563-3374, www.francesperkinscenter.org, 10am-2pm Tues.-Sat.). In addition to the small museum honoring Perkins, the secretary of labor from 1933 to 1945, the center often organizes guided tours ($22) of the nearby Perkins Homestead, a National Historic Landmark comprising a 57-acre working farm and brickyard. Dates are limited and preregistration is required.

Old Rock Schoolhouse

Docents garbed in period costumes welcome visitors to Bristol's town-owned one-room **Old Rock Schoolhouse** (158 Rock Schoolhouse Rd., Bristol, 1pm-3pm Wed. and Sun., free), a stone structure dating from 1837 that's one of Maine's oldest schoolhouses.

The Thompson Ice House

On a Sunday morning in February (weather and ice permitting), several hundred helpers and onlookers gather at Thompson Pond, next to the **Thompson Ice House** (1264 Rte. 129, South Bristol, www.thompsonicehouse.com), for the annual ice harvest. Festivity prevails as a crew of robust fellows marks out a grid and saws out 12-inch-thick ice cakes, which are pushed up a ramp to the ice-storage house. More than 60 tons of ice is harvested each year. Sawdust-insulated 10-inch-thick walls keep the ice from melting in this building first used in 1826 and now listed in the National Register of Historic Places. In 1990, the house became part of a working museum (1pm-4pm Wed. and Fri.-Sat. July-Aug., donation), with ice tools and a window view of the stored ice cakes. The grounds, including a photographic display board depicting a 1964 harvest, are accessible for free year-round. The site is 12 miles south of Damariscotta on Route 129.

Glidden Point Oyster Farms

The Damariscotta River produces some of the country's best oysters. Get the scoop on why with a half-hour farm tour of **Glidden Point Oyster Farms** (637 River Rd., Edgecomb, 207/315-7066, www.gliddenpoint.com, $10).

ENTERTAINMENT

Lincoln County Community Theater (2 Theater St., Damariscotta, 207/563-3424, www.lcct.org) owns and operates the historic Lincoln Theater, dating from 1867, where it presents musicals and dramas, concerts, films, and more.

In mid-August, **Olde Bristol Days** features a crafts show, a parade, road and boat races, live entertainment, and fireworks. Damariscotta's people-pleasers are the **Pemaquid Oyster Festival** in September and **Pumpkinfest,** a family event with food, entertainment, and competitions, in October.

SHOPPING

Downtown Damariscotta has a nice selection of independent shops, galleries, and boutiques. Parking in summer is a headache; the municipal lot behind the storefronts has a three-hour limit, and it's often full. You can usually find spots on some of the side streets.

Return of the Alewives

If you're in the Damariscotta area in May and early June, don't miss a chance to go to Damariscotta Mills to see the annual **Alewife Run.** During this time, more than 250,000 alewives (*Alosa pseudoharengus*, a kind of herring) make their way from Great Salt Bay to their spawning grounds in freshwater Damariscotta Lake, 42 feet higher. Waiting eagerly at the top are ospreys, gulls, cormorants, and sometimes eagles, ready to feast on the weary fish. Connecting the bay and the lake is an artificial stone-and-masonry fish ladder (www.damariscottamills.org), a zig-zagging channel where you can watch the foot-long fish wriggle their way onward and upward. The ladder was built in 1807; restoration is ongoing. A walkway runs alongside the route, and informative display panels explain the event. It's a fascinating historical ecology lesson. To reach the fishway, take Route 215 for 1.6 miles west of Route 1. When you reach a small bridge, cross it and take a sharp left down a slight incline to a small parking area. Walk behind the fish house to follow the path to the fish ladder. Try to go on a sunny day—the fish are more active, and their silvery sides glisten as they go.

Antiques

Antiques shops are numerous along Bristol Road (Rte. 130), where many barns have been turned into shops selling everything from fine antiques to less-pedigreed "old stuff." Serious antiques aficionados will find plenty to browse and buy along this stretch of road.

The **Art of Antiquing** (4 Back Shore Rd., Round Pond, 207/529-5300, www.theartofantiquing.com) specializes in antiques and art sourced in Europe and the United Kingdom.

Art Galleries

Worth a visit for the building alone, the **Stable Gallery** (26 Water St., Damariscotta, 207/563-1991, www.stablegallerymaine.com), just off Main Street, was built in the 19th-century clipper-ship era and still has original black-walnut stalls—providing a great foil for the work of dozens of Maine craftspeople. Lining the walls are paintings and prints from the gallery's large stable of artists.

You'll find a carefully curated selection of Maine-made fine and folk arts and crafts as well as artisan chocolates at **Gifts at 136** (136 Main St., Damariscotta, 207/563-1011), an especially fine shop with works in all price ranges.

Betcha can't leave without buying something from **Pemaquid Craft Co-op** (Rte. 130, New Harbor, 207/677-2077), with 15 rooms filled with high-quality works by 50 Maine artisans.

A delightful little off-the-beaten-path find is **Tidemark Gallery** (902 Main St., Waldoboro, 207/832-5109), showing fine arts and crafts from local artists.

The **Philippe Guillerm Gallery** (882 Main St., Waldoboro, 207/701-9085) showcases the works of Guillerm, who travels the world via boat in winter collecting driftwood, which he fashions into amazing works of art.

Specialty and Eclectic Shops

The Pemaquid Peninsula is fertile ground for crafts and gifts, and many of the shop locations provide opportunities for exploring off the beaten path. Artists' studios, galleries, and antiques shops are plentiful. The inventory at **Sherman's Maine Coast Book Shop and Café** (158 Main St., Damariscotta, 207/563-3207) always seems to anticipate customers' wishes, so you're unlikely to walk out empty-handed.

Weatherbird (Main St. and 72 Courtyard St., Damariscotta, 207/563-8993) is a double find. The Main Street shop specializes in women's clothing, and off the alley behind it is the original store, stocked with housewares, wines, toys, cards, and gourmet specialties.

All sorts of fabulous finds, including

specialty foods, wine, books, and Swan Island blankets, fill the **Walpole Barn** (135 Rte. 129, Walpole, 207/563-7050, www.thewalpolebarn.com). Browse home and garden products, whimsies, gourmet foods, and even wines. Another delightful shop in a barn, the **Good Supply** (2016 Bristol Rd., Pemaquid, 207/607-3121) specializes in goods crafted by Maine artists and artisans.

The **Granite Hall Store** (9 Backshore Rd., off Rte. 32, Round Pond, 207/529-5864) is an old-fashioned country store with merchandise ranging from toys to Irish imports. The penny candy, fudge, ice cream, and the old-fashioned peanut-roasting machine captivate the kids.

Bells reminiscent of lighthouses, buoys, and even wilderness sounds are crafted by **North Country Wind Bells** (544 Rte. 32, Round Pond, 877/930-5435, www.northcountrybells.com). Factory seconds are a bargain. In addition to selling heirloom-quality tools, **Lie-Nielsen Toolworks** (264 Stirling Rd./Rte. 1, Warren, 800/327-2520, www.lie-nielsen.com) offers workshops.

Renys

Whatever you do, don't leave downtown Damariscotta without visiting **Renys** (207/563-5757 or 207/563-3011), with stores on each side of Main Street: one sells clothing, the other everything else (although that mix might change). If you can recognize the edges of cut-out labels, you'll find clothes from major retailers at discounted prices. Stock up on housewares, munchies, puzzles, toiletries, shoes, and whatever else floats your boat; the prices can't be beat. This Renys earns bonus points for its classic, old-fashioned soda fountain; go for breakfast, lunch, or ice cream treats.

RECREATION

Parks and Preserves

Coastal Rivers Land Trust (3 Round Top Ln., Damariscotta, 207/563-1388, www.coastalrivers.org) manages more than 33 miles of trails as well as dozens of properties and even some islands. For good descriptions of trails throughout Lincoln County, purchase Paula Roberts's *On the Trail in Lincoln County* ($15.75), which describes and provides directions to more than 60 area walking trails.

GREAT SALT BAY FARM & HERITAGE CENTER

Find a nature center, community gardens, varied habitats with observation platform, and a trail network at this late 18th-century farmstead comprising 115 acres fronting on Great Salt Bay. More than two miles of trails lacing the fields, salt marsh, and shore frontage are open to the public sunrise-sunset daily year-round. To reach the farm from downtown Newcastle, take Mills Road (Rte. 215) to Route 1. Turn right (north) and go 1.4 miles to the blinking light (Belvedere Rd.). Turn left and go 0.4 mile.

SALT BAY PRESERVE HERITAGE TRAIL

The **Salt Bay Preserve Heritage Trail,** a relatively easy three-mile loop around Newcastle's Glidden Point, touches on a variety of habitats and also includes remnants of oyster-shell middens (heaps) going back about 2,500 years. This part of the trail is protected by the federal government; do not disturb or remove anything. To reach the preserve from Newcastle Square, take Mills Road (Rte. 215) about two miles to the offices of the *Lincoln County News* (just after the post office). The newspaper allows parking in the northern end of its lot, but stay to the right, as far away from the buildings as possible, and be sure not to block any vehicles or access ways. Walk across Route 215 to the trailhead and pick up a brochure-map.

WHALEBACK PARK

How often do you get to see ancient shell heaps? **Whaleback Park** is an eight-acre public preserve designed to highlight what remains of the Glidden Midden, ancient oyster-shell heaps across the river from the park viewpoint. (The midden is also visible, but not as easily, from the Salt Bay Preserve Heritage

Trail.) Informational signs explain the history of the midden, allegedly the largest such human artifact north of Florida. The "mini mountain" of castoffs was even vaster until the 1880s, when a factory harvested much of it to make lime. The trailhead and parking is on Business Route 1 opposite and between the Great Salt Bay School and the Central Lincoln County YMCA.

DODGE POINT PRESERVE

In 1989, the state of Maine acquired the now 521-acre **Dodge Point Preserve**—one of the stars in its crown—as part of a $35 million bond issue. To sample what the Dodge Point Preserve has to offer, pick up a map at the entrance and follow the Old Farm Road loop trail, and then connect to the Shore Trail (Discovery Trail), heading clockwise, with several dozen highlighted sites. Consider stopping for a riverside picnic and swim at Sand Beach before continuing back to the parking lot. Hunting is permitted in the preserve, so November isn't the best time for hiking. The Dodge Point parking area is on River Road, 2.6 miles southwest of Route 1 and 3.5 miles southwest of downtown Newcastle.

TRACY SHORE PRESERVE

Walk through a woodland wonderland that extends to rock-ledge shorefront along Jones Cove in South Bristol. Old cellars, moss-covered trails, lichen-covered rocks, a vernal pool, old pasture grounds, and spectacular views highlight this little-known gem, owned by the Damariscotta River Association. It has cliffs and lots of slippery rocks, so be mindful of children. You can connect to another preserve, Library Park, on a link crossing busy Route 129. The trailhead and parking are at the intersection of Route 129 and the S Road, 8.7 miles south of the split from Route 130.

LA VERNA PRESERVE

Roughly 3.5 miles south of the Round Pond post office on Route 130, you'll find this splendid 120-acre **shorefront preserve**, with 2.7 miles of hiking trails passing through woodlands, overgrown farmland, and forested wetlands to 3,600 feet of spectacular ocean frontage. Download a map from the Pemaquid Watershed Association (www.pemaquidwatershed.org).

RACHEL CARSON SALT POND

If you've never spent time studying the variety of sea life in a tidal pool, the **Rachel Carson Salt Pond** is a great place to start. Named after the famed author of *Silent Spring* and *The Edge of the Sea*, who summered in this part of Maine, the salt pond was one of her favorite haunts. The whole point of visiting a tidepool is to see what the tide leaves behind, so check the tide calendar (in local newspapers, or ask at your lodging) and head out a few hours after high tide. Wear rubber boots and beware of slippery rocks and rockweed. Among the many creatures you'll see in this 0.25-acre pond are mussels, green crabs, periwinkles, and starfish. Owned by the Nature Conservancy, the salt pond is on Route 32 in the village of Chamberlain, about a mile north of New Harbor. Parking is limited. Across the road is a trail into a 78-acre inland section of the preserve, most of it wooded. Brochures are available in the registration box.

Golf

The nine-hole **Wawenock Country Club** (Rte. 129, Walpole, 207/563-3938), established in the 1920s, is a challenging and popular public course.

Swimming

The best bet (but also the most crowded) on the peninsula for saltwater swimming is town-owned **Pemaquid Beach Park** (www.bristolparks.org), a lovely tree-lined sandy crescent. There is no lifeguard, but there are cold-water showers and bathrooms and a nature center with exhibits, and the snack bar serves decent food. Admission is $4 for anyone age 12 and older. The beach is just off Snowball Hill Road, west of Route 130.

1: Glidden Point Oyster Farm **2:** sea kayaks

1
2
KAYAKING • ACTIVITIES
RUSH
Schooner Landing

A much smaller beach is the pocket-size sandy area in **Christmas Cove** on Rutherford Island. Take Route 129 around the cove and turn to the right, and then right again down the hill.

One of the area's most popular freshwater swimming holes is **Biscay Pond,** a long, skinny body of water in the peninsula's center. From Business Route 1 at the northern edge of Damariscotta, take Biscay Road (turn at McDonald's) three miles to the pond (on the right, heading east). On hot days, this area sees plenty of cars; pull off the road as far as possible.

Farther down the peninsula, on Route 130, is the **Bristol Mills Swimming Hole at Bristol Dam,** wedged between the road, a dam, and a bridge. Swim at your own risk; no dogs, tobacco, or fireworks permitted.

Boat Excursions

At 9am each day mid-May-early October, the 60-foot powerboat *Hardy III* departs New Harbor for the one-hour trip to **Monhegan,** a Brigadoon-like island a dozen miles offshore where passengers can spend the day hiking the woods, picnicking on the rocks, bird-watching, visiting the museum and galleries, and inhaling the salt air. The return boat leaves for New Harbor at 3:15pm. The cost is $38 adults, $20 ages 2-11, $5 dogs, and reservations are required. Trips operate rain or shine, but strong seas can affect the schedule. From early June to late September there's also a second Monhegan trip—used primarily for overnighters—departing New Harbor at 2pm daily. Early and late in the season, Monhegan trips operate only Wednesday, Saturday, Sunday, and holidays. The *Hardy III* also operates daily 1.5-hour **puffin-watching tours** (5:30pm mid-May-late Aug., $35 adults, $15 ages 2-11) and one-hour **seal-watching tours** (noon daily mid-June-early Sept. and Sept. weekends, $16 adults, $12 children). **Hardy Boat Cruises** (Rte. 32, New Harbor, 207/677-2026, www.hardyboat.com) is 19 miles south of Route 1, based at Shaw's Fish and Lobster Wharf. Parking is $4/day, cash only, at a nearby baseball field.

Damariscotta River Cruises (Schooner Landing, 888/635-4309, www.damariscottarivercruises.com, $31 adults, $16 kids) offers two-hour cruises on the Damariscotta River, with options including oyster farms and seal-watching and happy hour and sunset. It also offers specialty tasting cruises ($70). There's a full bar as well as snacks available for purchase.

Paddle Sports

Midcoast Kayak (47 Main St., Damariscotta, 207/563-5732, www.midcoastkayak.com) has rentals and offers guided tours and lessons on Muscongus Bay and the Damariscotta River. Tours, 2.5-8 hours, range $55-115 and include all sorts of options. If you would rather do it yourself, recreational kayaks, sea kayaks, and SUPs are available at rates beginning at $28 for two hours. Instruction and delivery are also available.

Maine Kayak (20 Colonial Pemaquid Dr., New Harbor, 866/624-6351, www.mainekayak.com) operates from a base near Colonial Pemaquid. Guided options include two-hour wildlife or sunset tours, half- and full-day tours, and multi-day overnights. Rates begin at $50 for the shorter trips. Kayak rentals begin at $30 for two hours.

If you have your own boat or just want to paddle the three-mile length of **Biscay Pond,** you can park at the beach area and put in. Another good launching site is a state ramp off Route 1 in **Nobleboro,** at the head of eight-mile-long **Lake Pemaquid.**

Two preserves are accessible if you have your own boat. Owned by the Damariscotta River Association, 30-acre **Menigawum Preserve (Stratton Island)** is also known locally as Hodgdon's Island. It's at the entrance to Seal Cove on the west side of the South Bristol peninsula. The closest public boat launch is at the Gut, about four miles downriver—a trip better done *with* (in the same direction as) the tide. The best place to land is Boat House Beach, in the northeast corner, which is also a great spot for shelling. Pick up a map from the small box at the north end of the island and follow the perimeter trail clockwise. At the northern end, you'll see osprey nests; at the southern tip are Native American shell middens (do not disturb or remove anything). You can picnic in the pasture but camping and fires are not allowed. Stay clear of the abandoned homesite on the island's west side. The preserve is accessible sunrise-sunset.

Named for a 19th-century local woman dubbed "the Witch of Wall Street" for her financial wizardry, **Witch Island Preserve** is owned by Maine Audubon. The wooded 19-acre island has two beaches, a perimeter trail, and the ruins of the "witch's" house. A quarter mile offshore, it's accessible by canoe or kayak from the South Bristol town landing, just to the right after the bridge over the Gut. Put in, paddle under the bridge, and go north to the island.

FOOD

TOP EXPERIENCE

★ Lobster and Seafood

The Pemaquid Peninsula must have more eat-on-the-dock places per capita than any place in Maine. Some are basic no-frills operations; others are big-time commercial concerns. Each has a loyal following.

Facing each other across the dock in the hamlet of Round Pond are two of my all-time favorite lobster shacks, **Round Pond Lobster Co-Op** (207/529-5725) and **Muscongus Bay Lobster** (207/529-5528). Muscongus has enlarged in recent years, so it has a bigger menu and covered seating, but tiny Round Pond Lobster keeps it simple and oh-so-fresh. Both usually open around 10am daily for lunch and dinner and close around sunset. At either, bring the go-withs, from wine and cheese to bread and chocolates.

Other seasonal lobster wharves salting the peninsula are **Pemaquid Seafood** (32 Co-Op Rd., Pemaquid Harbor, 207/677-2642), with seating inside and out; the no-frills, lobster-only **South Bristol Fishermen's Co-op** (35 Thompson Inn Rd., South Bristol, 207/644-8224); and **Broad Cove Marine Services** (374 Medomak Rd., Bremen, 207/529-5186), a low-key sleeper with nice views.

The biggest and best-known lobster wharf is **Shaw's Fish and Lobster Wharf** (Rte. 32, New Harbor, 207/677-2200 or 800/772-2209, 11am-8pm daily), which has both a raw bar and full bar. Fried seafood dinners run $8-20.

Tucked on a road downtown, the **Lobster Haul** (115 Elm St., 207/682-0110, 11am-7pm daily) is worth finding for lobster, lobster and crab rolls, and lobster tacos as well as Friday night prime rib.

Oysters are the specialty at **Shuck Station** (68 Main St., Newcastle, 207/682-0129, noon-8pm daily, $7-16), but the menu also includes sandwiches, fried seafood, and lobster rolls.

Quick Bites

DAMARISCOTTA

Check out the Moxie memorabilia while enjoying all-day breakfast, lunch, sweets, and coffee at **S. Fernald's Country Store** (50 Main St., Damariscotta, 207/563-8484, www.sfernalds.com, 8am-5pm Mon.-Sat., 9am-5pm Sun.). The candy by the pound is a real kid-pleaser. Sandwiches are available in half and whole sizes.

The burgers, lobster rolls, salads, and fries earn raves at **Larson's Lunch Box** (430 Main St., 207/563-5755, https://larsonslunch.com, 11am-5:30pm Tues.-Sat.), a no-frills take-out stand with a few picnic tables.

Another takeout, the **Village Grill** (28 Biscay Rd., 207/563-2278, 11am-8pm Tues.-Sat.), has earned a solid rep for its barbecue, but it also offers burgers, fried seafood, and specials such as Korean tacos.

In a barn-style building at the northern edge of Damariscotta, **Round Top Ice Cream** (Business Rte. 1, 207/563-5307) has been dishing out homemade ice cream since 1924.

Rising Tide Natural Foods Market (323

Main St., 207/563-5556, www.risingtide.coop, 8am-8pm daily), a thriving co-op organization since 1978, has all the natural and organic usuals, plus a self-service deli section with soups, sandwiches, salads, and entrées; indoor and outdoor seating are available.

The **Damariscotta Area Farmers Market** sets up 9am-noon Fridays mid-May-October at Round Top Farm (Business Route 1) and 3pm-6pm Mondays at Rising Tide Market (323 Main St.).

DOWN THE PENINSULA

You won't find a cozier, less expensive, or more welcoming home-based bakeshop than **Dot's Bakery** (1233 Rte. 32, Round Pond, 207/529-2514, 8am-6pm Wed.-Sun.). Muffins, pies, doughnuts, soups, breads, and even buttermilk pancakes, soups, sandwiches, and pizza are on the menu. Dine in on the central table or take it to go. Call ahead to order pie.

Abundant Bakery (11 Leeman Hill Rd., New Harbor, 207/677-2235, 8am-4:30pm Tues.-Sat.), located across from the public landing, bakes breads, cookies, scones, muffins, pies, and bars, including to-die-for lemon squares.

Big portions of house-made comfort foods have given tiny **Deb's Bristol Diner** (1267 Bristol Rd./Rte. 130, Bristol, 207/563-8005, 6am-2pm Thurs.-Tues.) a great rep.

Just around the corner from Colonial Pemaquid, the **Cupboard Café** (137 Huddle Rd., New Harbor, 207/677-3911, www.thecupboardcafe.com, 8am-3pm Tues.-Sat., 9am-2pm Sun.) is a homey cabin serving fresh-baked goods, breakfasts, and a nice choice of fresh salads, burgers, sandwiches, and specials. Almost everything is made on the premises; the cinnamon and sticky buns are so popular that they've spurred a mail-order business.

WALDOBORO

At the corner of Routes 1 and 220, opposite Moody's Diner, is the warehouse-like building that turns out **Borealis Breads** (1860 Atlantic Hwy./Rte. 1, 207/832-0655, 8am-5pm Mon.-Sat., 9am-4pm Sun.), which started Maine's bread revolution. Using sourdough starters (and no oils, sweeteners, eggs, or dairy products), owner Jim Amaral and his crew produce baguettes, olive bread, lemon fig bread, rosemary focaccia, and about a dozen other flavors; each day has its specialties. Great soups, salads, and excellent sandwiches are available to go.

Virgil Morse opened **Morse's Sauerkraut** (3856 Washington Rd./Rte. 220, 207/832-5569 or 800/486-1605, www.morsessauerkraut.com, 9am-6pm Thurs.-Tues.) farm store in 1918. A century later, fresh sauerkraut is still being produced here, but the rural store has expanded to carry a mind-boggling selection of northern European specialty foods, including cheeses and charcuterie. Also here is a small restaurant (10:30am-4pm) serving traditional German fare ($9-20). Big serve-yourself jars of Morse's pickles are on the tables. Find it eight miles north of Route 1.

Truck drivers, tourists, locals, and notables have been flocking to **Moody's Diner** (Rte. 1 and Rte. 220, 207/832-7785, www.moodysdiner.com, 5am-9pm Mon.-Sat., 6am-9pm Sun., $5-18) since the early 1930s, when the Moody family established this classic eatery on a Waldoboro hilltop. The antique neon sign has long been a Route 1 beacon, especially on a foggy night, and the crowds continue. Expect hearty, no-frills fare and such calorific desserts as peanut butter or walnut pie. After eating, you can buy the cookbook.

Casual Dining

DAMARISCOTTA

Dine upstairs or down at the **Damariscotta River Grill** (155 Main St., 207/563-2992, www.damariscottarivergrill.com, from 11am Mon.-Sat., from 10am Sun., $12-32), where the wide-ranging menu emphasizes fresh seafood. Add $12 to the price of any entrée to include a salad or soup and a dessert.

Locally sourced fare and a craft beer menu make **Newcastle Publick House** (52 Main St., Newcastle, 207/563-3434, www.newcastlepublickhouse.com, 11:30am-10pm daily, $13-24) an ever-popular choice, with seating on two levels and outside.

King Eider's Pub (2 Elm St., Damariscotta, 207/563-6008, www.kingeiderspub.com, 11:30am-9pm daily, $13-38) earns kudos for oysters, crab cakes, single-malt scotches, and good times. A kids' menu is available.

DOWN THE PENINSULA

Pair exploring Fort William Henry with lunch or dinner at the **Contented Sole** (at Fort William Henry, 207/677-3000, www.thecontentedsole.com, 11:30am-9pm daily, $10-20), a rustic waterfront seafood shack with a menu ranging from seafood to pizza. Dine indoors or outside on the dog-friendly dock. There's live music Thursday and Friday nights. Also here is the **Fin Bar** (5pm-9pm Thurs.-Sun.), a 12-seat dining room with a menu emphasizing shared plates ($10-15); reservations required.

Coveside Restaurant (105 Coveside Rd., Christmas Cove, South Bristol, 207/644-8282, www.covesiderestaurant.com, 11:30am-8:30pm daily, $10-28), based at a marina on Rutherford Island, just off the end of the South Bristol peninsula, is open for lunch and dinner as well as light meals. Grab a seat on the deck and watch a steady stream of boaters and summer vacationers during the cruising season. The food quality and service efficiency varies because it's a leased operation, but when it's on, it's hard to beat. There's often live music.

Location, location, location: Right next to Pemaquid Light is the **Sea Gull Shop** (3119 Bristol Rd., Pemaquid Point, 207/677-2374, www.seagullshop.com, 7:30am-3pm Tues.-Thurs., 7:30am-8pm Fri.-Mon., $18-33), a seasonal gift shop, restaurant, and ice cream spot with big views and decent food—pancakes and muffins, for instance, overflowing with blueberries. BYOB.

ACCOMMODATIONS

Inns

Almost on top of Pemaquid Light is the rambling and delightfully old-fashioned **Hotel Pemaquid** (3098 Bristol Rd./Rte. 130, New Harbor, 207/677-2312, www.hotelpemaquid.com, $99-295). Seventeen miles south of Route 1 but just 450 feet from the lighthouse (only one room has a view), the hotel has been welcoming guests since 1900. Hang out in the large, comfortable parlor or on the wraparound veranda. The owners have renovated the property, updating and improving everything without losing the Victorian charm or quirks of an old seaside hotel. Don't expect fancy or fussy. The original inn building has six guest rooms, some with shared baths, as well as five suites. Nine other buildings offer motel-style units, apartments, and cottages. For the Victorian flavor of the place, request an inn room or a suite. There is no restaurant, but the Bradley Inn and the Sea Gull Shop are nearby.

Within easy walking distance of Pemaquid Light and 16 miles south of Route 1, the **Bradley Inn** (3063 Bristol Rd./Rte. 130, New Harbor, 207/677-2105 or 800/942-5560, www.bradleyinn.com, from $165) is a restored late 19th-century three-story inn with restaurant, carriage house, and a cottage amid lovely gardens. Some accommodations have a water view; one has a full kitchen. Room rates include full breakfast and afternoon tea. Dinner is served Wednesday-Saturday.

Innkeeper Julie Bolthuis has breathed new life into the ★ **Newcastle Inn** (60 River Rd., Newcastle, 207/563-5685 or 800/832-8669, www.newcastleinn.com, from $180), an 1860s sea captain's home with 14 guest rooms and suites spread out between the main inn and a carriage house. The lovely grounds descend to the Damariscotta River. Julie serves a full breakfast (on the patio when the weather cooperates), stocks a pantry that includes a bottomless cookie jar, and offers a pub just for guests. One room is dog friendly ($35/day).

Bed-and-Breakfasts

Cozy, comfy, and cluttered with good reads and beloved treasures, **La Vatout** (218 Kaler's Corner, Waldoboro, 207/832-5150, www.

levatout.com, $110-150) is a find for those who want a taste of down-home Maine. Innkeeper Dominika Spetsmann and resident artist Linda Mahoney provide a warm welcome to their in-town, 1830s farmhouse with four guest rooms (two sharing a bath) surrounded by organic gardens and home to a resident cat and dog. The only indoor public area is the dining room, where hearty breakfasts are crafted from local eggs, meats, fish, and grains, along with garden produce. For a real treat, consider the art workshops or nature and food packages, including one that allows you to forage for wild mushrooms with Maine mushroom guru David Spahr, and then return to the inn to prepare a meal.

Martha Scudder provides a warm welcome at **Oak Gables Bed and Breakfast** (36 Pleasant St., Damariscotta, 207/563-1476 or 800/335-7748, www.oakgablesbb.com, year-round, $120-175), a 13-acre hilltop estate overlooking the Damariscotta River. Despite the rather imposing setting, everything's homey, informal, and hospitable. Four spacious second-floor rooms, which can be joined in pairs, share a bath; a guest wing has a full kitchen, a private bath, and a separate entrance. The heated swimming pool is a huge plus, as is the boathouse deck on the river. Guests can harvest blackberries from scads of bushes. Also on the grounds are a three-bedroom cottage ($1,400/week), a riverview one-bedroom apartment ($185/night, $1,100/week), and a studio apartment ($175/night, $975/week), which is usually booked up well ahead.

Wake up with a dip after a restful sleep at the ★ **Mill Pond Inn** (50 Main St./Rte. 215, Damariscotta Mills, Nobleboro, 207/563-8014, www.millpondinn.com, $150-160, no credit cards). The 1780 colonial was restored and converted into an inn in 1986 by delightful owners Bobby and Sherry Whear. The five guest rooms have water views; two have detached bathrooms. After a full breakfast, snooze in a hammock, watch for eagles and great blue herons, pedal a bicycle into nearby Damariscotta, or canoe the pond, which connects to 14-mile-long Damariscotta Lake. Bobby, a Registered Maine Guide, offers fishing trips and scenic tours of the lake in his restored antique Lyman lapstrake (clinker-built) boat. Use of bicycles and a canoe is free for guests. The inn is just a five-minute drive from downtown Damariscotta, but a world away.

The mansard-roofed **Inn at Round Pond** (1442 Rte. 32, Round Pond, 207/809-7386, www.theinnatroundpond.com, year-round, $175-185) commands a sea captain's view of the harbor as it presides over the pretty village of Round Pond. It's an easy walk to a waterfront restaurant, two dueling lobster pounds, an old-timey country store, and a few galleries and shops. Each of the four good-size, air-conditioned rooms has harbor views and sitting areas. There are no TVs and no locks, but there's no reason for either. A full breakfast is included.

Motels and Cottage Colonies

Now here's a bargain. Up a long, winding driveway behind Moody's Diner is **Moody's Motel** (Rte. 1, Waldoboro, 207/832-5362, www.moodysdiner.com, $75-95), in business since 1927; it's likely that little has changed in the meantime. Expect nothing more than a clean and well-run property, and you'll be content. The retro motel and tourist cabins all have screened porches; one has a kitchen. Pets are $10.

Dan Thompson is the third-generation innkeeper at the **Thompson House and Cottages** (95 South Side Rd., New Harbor, 207/677-2317, www.thompsoncottages.net, $500-2,000/week), a low-key, step-back-in-time complex of mostly waterfront rooms, apartments, and cottages split between two mini peninsulas. Apartments are also available by the night ($85-150). Rowboats are available, and there's a library with games, books, and puzzles.

Camping

A favorite with kayakers is **Sherwood Forest Camping** (Pemaquid Trail, New Harbor,

800/274-1593, www.sherwoodforestcampsite.com, $37-45). Facilities include a small camp store, rec room, and a laundry. The campground is just 800 feet from Pemaquid Beach. Two-bedroom rental cabins are $900/week, $149/night when available.

GETTING THERE AND AROUND

Damariscotta is about eight miles or 15 minutes via Route 1 from Wiscasset. It's about 10 miles or 15 minutes via Route 1 to Waldoboro, and about 15 miles or 30 minutes via Route 130 to Pemaquid Point. From Pemaquid Point, it's about 23 miles or 40 minutes via Route 32 to Waldoboro. From Waldoboro, it's about 12 miles or 20 minutes via Route 1 to Thomaston or about 20 miles via Routes 1 and 90 to Camden.

Penobscot Bay

The rugged and jagged shoreline edging island-studded Penobscot Bay is the image that has lured many a visitor to Maine. The coastline here ebbs and flows, rising to rocky headlands, dropping to protected harbors, and linking quiet fishing villages with comparatively cosmopolitan towns. Although the state considers this to be part of the Mid-Coast, this region has a different feel and view, one framed by coastal mountains in Camden and Lincolnville and accented by an abundance of islands.

From Thomaston through Prospect, no two towns are alike except that all are changing, as traditional industries give way to arts- and tourism-related businesses. Thomaston's Museum in the Streets, Rockland's art galleries, Camden's picturesque mountainside harbor,

Highlights

Look for ★ to find recommended sights, activities, dining, and lodging.

★ **Monhegan Historical and Cultural Museum:** View an impressive collection of masters at this museum adjacent to the Monhegan Lighthouse (page 196).

★ **Farnsworth Art Museum and the Wyeth Center:** Three generations of Wyeths are represented in this museum, which also boasts an excellent collection of works by Maine and American masters (page 201).

★ **Owls Head Transportation Museum:** View a fabulous collection of vintage airplanes, automobiles, and even bicycles, many of which are flown, driven, or ridden during weekend special events (page 201).

★ **Rockland Breakwater:** Take a walk on this nearly mile-long breakwater to the lighthouse at the end (open on weekends). It's an especially fine place to watch the windjammers sail in or out of Rockland Harbor (page 202).

★ **Owls Head Light State Park:** The views of Penobscot Bay are spectacular, and it's a great place for a picnic lunch (page 205).

★ **Camden Hills State Park:** If you have time, hike the moderate trail to the summit for a gull's-eye view over Camden Harbor and Penobscot Bay. If not, take the easy route and drive (page 225).

★ **Penobscot Marine Museum:** Learn what life was *really* like during the Great Age of Sail in a town renowned for the number and quality of its sea captains (page 242).

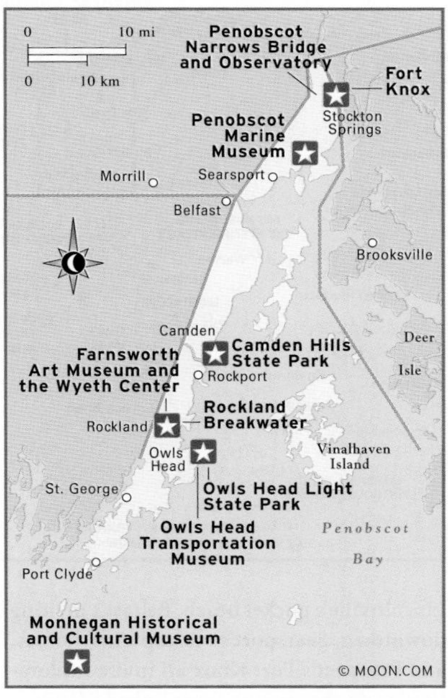

★ **Fort Knox:** A good restoration, frequent events, and secret passages to explore make this late-19th-century fort one of Maine's best (page 245).

★ **Penobscot Narrows Bridge and Observatory:** On a clear day, the views from the 420-foot-high tower, one of only three in the world, extend from Mount Katahdin to Cadillac Mountain (page 245).

Penobscot Bay

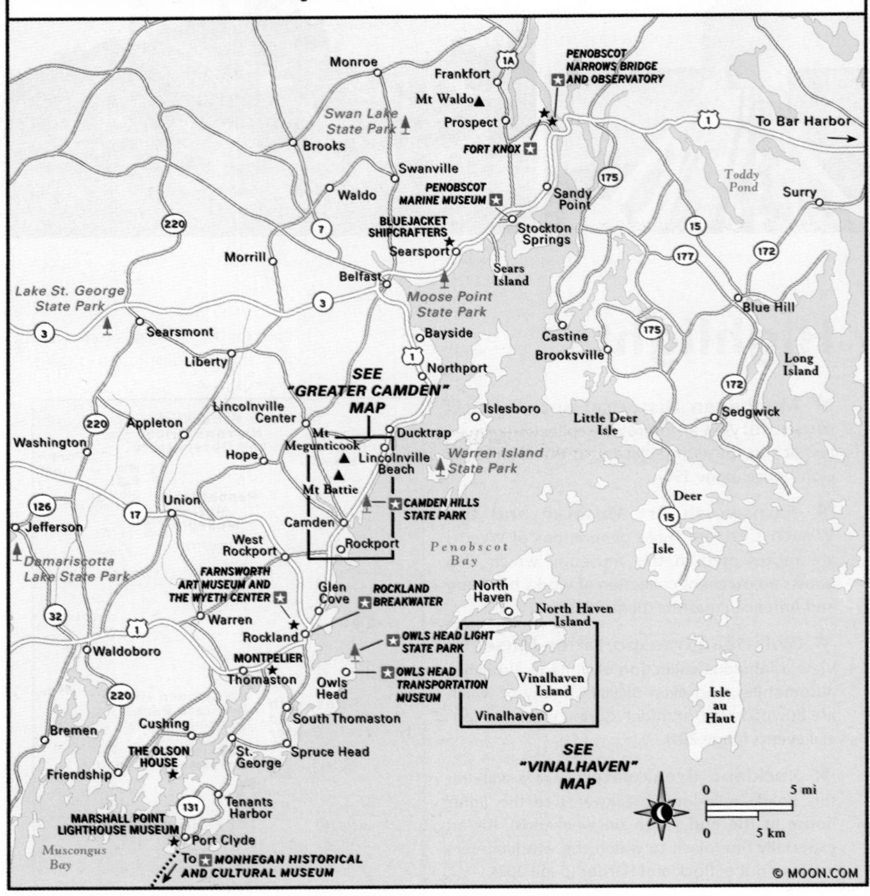

Lincolnville's pocket beach, Belfast's inviting downtown, Searsport's sea captains' homes, and Prospect's Fort Knox all invite exploration, as do the region's ferry-linked islands.

From salty Port Clyde, take the mail boat to Monhegan, an offshore idyll known as the Artists' Island. From Rockland and Lincolnville Beach, car and passenger ferries depart to Vinalhaven, North Haven, Matinicus, and Islesboro. All are occupied year-round by hardy souls, and joined in summer by less-hardy ones. Except for Matinicus, they're great day-trip destinations.

If what appeals to you about a ferry trip is traveling on the water, get a taste of the Great Age of Sail by booking a multiday cruise aboard one of the classic windjammer schooners berthed in Rockland, Rockport, and

Previous: windjammer sailing across Penobscot Bay; Marshall Point Lighthouse; Owls Head Light

Camden. Or simply book a day sail or sea kayak excursion.

Although it's easy to focus on the water, this region is rich in museums and art galleries, antiques and specialty shops, some of the state's nicest inns, and many of its better restaurants.

Most folks arrive in July-August, but autumn—when turning leaves color the hills and are reflected in the sea, the days remain warm, and nights are cool—is an ideal season to visit, especially for leaf peepers who want to get off the beaten track. And in winter, when snow blankets the Camden Hills, you can ski while gazing out over Camden Harbor.

PLANNING YOUR TIME

To hit just the highlights, you'll need at least three days. If you want to relax a bit and enjoy the area, plan on 4-5 days. Make it a full week if you plan on overnighting on any of the offshore islands. In general, lodging is less expensive in Rockland, Belfast, and Searsport than it is in Camden. In any case, head for Monhegan or Vinalhaven on a fine day and save the museums for inclement ones.

Two-lane Route 1 is the region's central artery, with veins running down the peninsula limbs. Yes, traffic backs up, especially in Camden (and in Thomaston on the Fourth of July, when it's closed for a parade), but it rarely stops moving. If your destination is Rockland, take I-95 to Augusta and then Route 17 East; if it's Belfast or north, take I-95 to Augusta and then Route 3 East. Route 90 is a nifty bypass around Thomaston and Rockland, connecting Route 1 from Warren to Rockport. For a less direct route, the **Georges River Scenic Byway** is a 50-mile rural inland route, mostly along Route 131, between Port Clyde and Liberty. It parallels the coast, but it meanders through farmlands and tiny villages and by lakes and rivers, with antiques shops and farm stands along the way. It's simply gorgeous in autumn.

Thomaston Area

Thomaston (pop. 1,558), a little gem of a town, is the gateway to two lovely fingers of land bordering the St. George River and jutting into the Gulf of Maine—the Cushing and St. George Peninsulas.

In 1605, British adventurer Captain George Waymouth sailed up the river now named after him (the St. George River was originally called the Georges River). A way station for Plymouth traders as early as 1630, Thomaston was incorporated in 1777 and officially named after General John Thomas, a Revolutionary War hero.

Industry began with the production of lime, which was used for plaster. A growing demand for plaster, and the frequency with which the wooden boats were destroyed by fire while carrying loads of extremely flammable lime, spurred the growth of shipbuilding and its related infrastructure. Thomaston's slogan became "the town that went to sea."

Seeing the sleepy waterfront today, it's hard to visualize the booming era when dozens of tall ships slid down the ways. But the town's architecture is a testament and tribute to the prosperous past. All those splendid homes on Main and Knox Streets were funded by wealthy ship owners and shipmasters who understood how to occupy the idle hands of off-duty carpenters.

SIGHTS

Knox Museum

As you head north out of Thomaston on Route 1, you'll come face-to-face with an imposing colonial hilltop mansion at the junction with Route 131 South. Dedicated to the memory of General Henry Knox, President George Washington's secretary of war, **Montpelier**

(30 High St., Thomaston, 207/354-8062, http://knoxmuseum.org, 10am-4pm Tues.-Fri., 10am-1pm Sat. late May-early Sept., 10am-4pm Fri., 10am-1pm Sat. early Sept.-mid-Oct., last tour one hour before closing, $10 adults, $8 seniors, $4 ages 5-13, $20 family), home to the **Knox Museum,** is a 1930s replica of Knox's original Thomaston home. The mansion contains Knox family furnishings and other period antiques, all described with great enthusiasm during the 45- to 60-minute tours. Concerts, lectures, and special events occur here periodically throughout the summer; General Knox's birthday is celebrated with considerable fanfare in July. Call for the current schedule.

Museum in the Streets

Montpelier is the starting point for a three-mile walking, cycling, or, if you must, driving tour of nearly 70 sites in Thomaston's **National Historic Landmark District.** Pick up a copy of the tour brochure at one of the local businesses. Included are lots of stories behind the facades of the handsome 19th-century homes that line Main and Knox Streets; the architecture here is nothing short of spectacular. Much of this history is also recounted in the Museum in the Streets, a walking tour taking in 25 informative plaques illustrated with old photos.

Finnish Heritage House

If you're of Finnish descent, pop into the **Finnish Heritage House** (172 St. George Rd./Rt. 131, South Thomaston, www.finnheritage.org, 9am-noon Wed. and Sat. late June-mid-Oct., free), where you can delve into genealogy, purchase Finnish goods and food, and view exhibits. One highlight of the Saturday morning bake and tag sale is *nissa/pulla* (Finnish coffee bread).

EVENTS

Thomaston's **Fourth of July,** an old-fashioned hometown celebration reminiscent of a Norman Rockwell painting, draws huge crowds. A spiffy parade—with bands, veterans, kids, and pets—starts off the morning at 11am, followed by races, crafts and food booths, and lots more. If you need to get *through* Thomaston on the Fourth of July, do it well before the parade or well after noon; the marchers go right down Main Street (Rte. 1), and gridlock forces a detour.

SHOPPING

Thomaston has a block-long shopping street (on Rte. 1), with ample free parking out back behind the stores.

The **Maine State Prison Showroom Outlet** (Main St./Rte. 1 at Wadsworth St., Thomaston, 207/354-9237) markets the handiwork of inmate craftsmen. Some of the souvenirs verge on kitsch; the bargains are wooden barstools, toys (including dollhouses), and chopping boards. You'll need to carry your purchases with you; prison-made goods cannot be shipped.

At the southern end of Thomaston, in a renovated chicken barn, is **Thomaston Place Auction Gallery** (51 Atlantic Hwy./Rte. 1, Thomaston, 207/354-8141, www.thomastonauction.com), the home of Kaja Veilleux, a longtime dealer, appraiser, and auctioneer. Auctions occur frequently, with previews beforehand.

Just south of Thomaston is **Lie-Nielsen Toolworks** (Rte. 1, Warren, 800/327-2520, www.lie-nielsen.com), crafting heirloom-quality hand tools for connoisseurs. Ask about workshops.

FOOD

The bistro menu at the casual **Thomaston Café** (154 Main St./Rte. 1, Thomaston, 207/354-8589, 11am-2pm and 5pm-8pm daily, $18-28) emphasizes seafood.

CAMPING

Located on the Thomaston-Cushing town line, 35-acre **Saltwater Farm Campground** (47 Kalloch Ln., Thomaston, 207/354-6735, www.saltwaterfarmcampground.com) offers open and wooded tent and RV sites overlooking the St. George River. Sites are $325-375/

week; rustic cabins go for $475/week; RV trailers are $850/week. Facilities include a bathhouse, heated pool, hot tub, laundry, store, and play area. The river is tidal, so swimming is best near high tide; otherwise, you're dealing with mudflats.

INFORMATION AND SERVICES

The **Penobscot Bay Region Chamber of Commerce** (800/223-5459, www.mainedreamvacation.com) is the area's best resource.

GETTING THERE AND AROUND

Thomaston is 12 miles or 18 minutes via Route 1 from Waldoboro. It's about 15 miles or 25 minutes via Route 131 to Port Clyde, and about 5 miles or 10 minutes via Route 1 to Rockland.

Cushing Peninsula

Cushing's recorded history goes back at least as far as 1605, when someone named "Abr [maybe Abraham] King"—presumably a member of explorer George Waymouth's crew—inscribed his name here on a ledge (now private property). Since 1789, settlers' saltwater farms have sustained many generations, and the active Cushing Historical Society keeps the memories and memorabilia from fading away. But the outside world knows little of this. **Cushing** (pop. 1,534) is better known as "Wyeth country," the terrain depicted by the famous artistic dynasty of N. C., Andrew, and Jamie Wyeth and assorted other talented relatives.

If you're an Andrew Wyeth fan, visiting Cushing will give you the feeling of walking through his paintings. The flavor of his Maine work is here—rolling fields, wildflower meadows, rocky tidal coves, broad vistas, character-filled farmhouses, and some well-hidden summer enclaves.

SIGHTS

Broad Cove Church

Andrew Wyeth aficionados will recognize the **Broad Cove Church** as one of his subjects. Set alongside Cushing Road en route to the Olson House, it's open most days, so step inside and admire the classic New England architecture. The church is also well known as the site of one of the region's best beanhole bean suppers, usually held on a Saturday in mid-July and attracting several hundred appreciative diners. From Route 1 in Thomaston, at the Maine State Prison Showroom Outlet, turn onto Wadsworth Street and go six miles, then bear left at the fork; the church is 0.4 mile farther, on the right.

The Olson House

Many an art lover makes the pilgrimage to the **Olson House** (noon-5pm Wed.-Sun., last tour 4pm, late May-early Oct., $12, $22 with Farnsworth admission), an iconic site near the end of Hathorne Point Road. The early 19th-century farmhouse appears in Andrew Wyeth's 1948 painting *Christina's World* (which hangs in New York's Museum of Modern Art), his best-known image of the disabled Christina Olson, who died in 1968. In 1991, two philanthropists donated the Olson House to the Farnsworth Art Museum in Rockland, which has retained the house's sparse, lonely, and almost mystical ambience. The clapboards outside remain unpainted, the interior walls bear only a few Wyeth prints (hung close to the settings they depict), and it is easy to sense Wyeth's inspiration for chronicling this place. To find it, from the Broad Cove Church, continue just over one mile, then turn left onto Hathorne Point Road. Go another 1.9 miles to the house. Tours are offered on the hour.

Beanhole Beans

"To be happy in New England," wrote one Joseph P. MacCarthy at the turn of the 20th century, "you must select the Puritans for your ancestors...[and] eat beans on Saturday night." There is no better way to confirm the latter requirement than to attend a beanhole bean supper—a real live legacy of colonial times, with dinner baked in a hole in the ground.

Generally scheduled, appropriately, for a Saturday night (check local newspapers), a beanhole bean supper demands plenty of preparation from its hosts—and a secret ingredient or two. (Don't even think about trying to pry the recipe out of the cooks.) The supper always includes hot dogs, coleslaw, relishes, home-baked breads, and homemade desserts, but the beans are the star attraction. Typically, the suppers are also alcohol-free. They are not only feasts, but also bargains, never setting you back more than about $10.

The beans at the Broad Cove Church's **beanhole bean supper,** served family-style at long picnic tables, are legendary—attracting nearly 200 eager diners. Minus the secrets, here's what happens:

Early Friday morning: Church volunteers load 10 pounds of dry pea and soldier (yellow eye) beans into each of four large kettles and add water to cover. The beans are left to soak and soften for 6-7 hours. Two or three volunteers uncover the churchyard's four rock-lined beanholes (each about three feet deep), fill the holes with hardwood kindling, ignite the wood, and keep the fires burning until late afternoon, when the wood has reduced to red-hot coals.

Early Friday afternoon: The veteran chefs parboil the beans and stir in the seasonings. Typical additions are brown sugar, molasses, mustard, salt, pepper, and salt pork (much of the secret is in the exact proportions). When the beans are precooked to the cooks' satisfaction, the kettle lids are secured with wire and the pots are lugged outdoors.

Friday midafternoon: With the beans ready to go underground, some of the hot coals are quickly shoveled out of the pits. The kettles are lowered into the pits and the coals replaced around the sides of the kettles and atop their lids. The pits are covered with heavy sheet metal and topped with a thick layer of sand and a tarpaulin. The round-the-clock baking begins, and no one peeks before it's finished.

Saturday midafternoon: Even the veterans start getting nervous just before the pits are uncovered. Was the seasoning right? Did too much water cook away? Did the beans dry out? Not to worry, though—failures just don't happen here.

Saturday night: When a pot is excavated for the first of three seatings (about 5pm), the line is already long. The chefs check their handiwork and the supper begins. No one seems to mind waiting for the second and third seatings—while others eat, a sing-along gets underway in the church, keeping everyone entertained.

The Bernard Langlais Sculpture Preserve

En route to or from the Olson House, don't miss the 90-acre **Langlais Sculpture Preserve** (576 River Rd., Cushing, dawn-dusk daily, free), a major stop on the **Langlais Art Trail** (http://langlaisarttrail.org/langlais-preserve). Maine sculptor Bernard "Blackie" Langlais (1921-1977) created more than 3,000 sculptures during his life, and 12 of them, beautifully restored, can be viewed from the quarter-mile ADA-accessible path that winds through the preserve.

St. George Peninsula

The St. George Peninsula is actually better known by some of the villages scattered along its length—**Tenants Harbor, Port Clyde, Wiley's Corner, Spruce Head**—plus the smaller neighborhoods of Martinsville, Smalleytown, Glenmere, Long Cove, Hart's Neck, and Clark Island. Each has a distinct personality, determined partly by the different ethnic groups—primarily Brits, Swedes, and Finns—who arrived to work the granite quarries in the 19th century. Wander through the Seaview Cemetery in Tenants Harbor and you'll see the story: row after row of gravestones with names from across the sea.

A more famous former visitor was 19th-century novelist Sarah Orne Jewett, who holed up in an old schoolhouse in Martinsville, paid a weekly rental of $0.50, and wrote *The Country of the Pointed Firs,* a tale about "Dunnet's Landing" (Tenants Harbor).

Today the picturesque peninsula has salt-water farms, tidy hamlets, a striking lighthouse, spruce-edged tidal coves, an active yachting harbor, and, at the tip, the tiny fishing village of Port Clyde, which serves as a springboard to offshore Monhegan Island.

Port Clyde is likely the best-known community here. (Fortunately, it's no longer called by its unappealing 18th-century name: Herring Gut.) George Waymouth explored Port Clyde's nearby islands in 1605, but you'd never suspect its long tradition. It's a sleepy place, with a general store, low-key inns, a few galleries, and pricey parking.

SIGHTS

Marshall Point Lighthouse and Museum

Not many settings can compare with the spectacular locale of the **Marshall Point Lighthouse Museum** (Marshall Point Rd., Port Clyde, 207/372-6450, www.marshallpoint.org, noon-4pm Sun.-Mon., 10am-4pm Tues.-Sat. late May-mid-Oct., free), a distinctive 1857 lighthouse and park overlooking Port Clyde, the harbor islands, and the passing lobster boat fleet. Bring a picnic and let the kids run on the lawn (but keep them well back from the shoreline). The museum, in the 1895 keeper's house, displays lighthouse and local memorabilia. The grounds are accessible year-round. Take Route 131 to Port Clyde and watch for signs to the museum.

SHOPPING

Art

The St. George Peninsula has been attracting artists for decades, and galleries are abundant. Some have been here for years, and others started up yesterday; most are worth a stop, so keep an eye out for their signs. In early August, a number of renowned artists usually coordinate an open-studio weekend. Well worth a visit is **Mars Hall Gallery** (621 Port Clyde Rd., Tenants Harbor, 207/362-9996), which carries and displays an especially fine selection of Maine art and antiques inside and outside.

Tiny **Lobster Lane Book Shop** (Island Rd., Spruce Head, 207/594-7520) has 50,000 or so treasures for used-book fans. For a few dollars, you can stock up on a summer's worth of reading. The shop, open noon-5pm Saturday-Sunday, is just under a mile east of Route 73, with eye-catching vistas in several directions (except, of course, when Spruce Head's infamous fog sets in).

Despite periodic ownership changes, **Port Clyde General Store** (4 Cold Storage Rd., Port Clyde, 207/372-6543) remains a characterful destination, a two-century-old country store with upscale touches. Stock up on groceries, pick up a newspaper, or buy a sweatshirt. The current owner has gussied it up even more and added a shop and an upstairs gallery featuring Wyeth works.

RECREATION

Swimming and Beachcombing

Drift Inn Beach, named for an early 20th-century summer hotel, is the best public beach on the peninsula. The parking lot, accessible from both Drift Inn Beach Road and Route 131, is about 3.5 miles after the Routes 131 and 73 junction.

Paddle Sports

The St. George Peninsula is especially popular for sea kayaking, with plenty of islands to add interest and shelter. **Port Clyde Kayaks** (Rte. 131, Port Clyde, 207/372-8128, www.portclydekayaks.com) offers half-day, starlight, and full-moon ($60) guided kayaking tours around the tip of the peninsula, taking in Marshall Point lighthouse and the islands. Rental kayaks begin at $200 for five days. Paddleboard rentals are $50 for one day, $200 for five days. Reservations are wise.

If you have kayaking experience, you can launch from the ramp just before the causeway that links the mainland with Spruce Head Island, in Spruce Head (Island Rd., off Rte. 73). Parking is limited. A great paddle goes clockwise around Spruce Head Island and nearby Whitehead (there's a lighthouse on its southeastern shore) and Norton Islands. Duck in for lunch at Waterman's Beach Lobster. At times of new moon and full moon, plan your schedule to avoid low tide near the Spruce Head causeway, or you may become mired in mudflats.

Boat Excursions

The best boating experience on this peninsula is a passenger-ferry trip from Port Clyde to offshore **Monhegan Island**—for a day, overnight, or longer. The trip isn't cheap, and parking adds to the cost, but it's a "must" excursion, so try to factor it into the budget. Port Clyde is the nearest mainland harbor to Monhegan; this service operates all year. **Monhegan-Thomaston Boat Line** (Port Clyde, 207/372-8848, www.monheganboat.com) uses two boats, the ***Laura B.*** (70 minutes each way) and the newer ***Elizabeth Ann*** (50 minutes). Round-trip tickets are $38 adults, $25 ages 2-12, $5 per pet. Leave your bicycle in Port Clyde; you won't need it on the island. Reservations are essential in summer, especially for the 10:30am boat. With advance payment, tickets are held until 30 minutes before departure; there's a $5 fee for cancellations, with no refunds within 24 hours. Parking in Port Clyde is $7/day. If a summer day trip is all you can manage, aim for the first or second boat and return on the last one; don't go just for the boat ride.

During the summer, the Monhegan-Thomaston Boat Line also offers 2.5-hour sightseeing cruises, on a varied schedule, including a **Puffin and Nature Cruise** and a **Lighthouse Cruise**. Each costs $30 adults, $10 children.

Wyeths by Water lobster boat tours (207/372-6600, www.lindabeansperfectmaine.com, $42) depart from the Port Clyde General Store for a 2.5-hour excursion highlighting locations featured in works by N. C. and Andrew Wyeth. The trip includes a lobstering demonstration.

FOOD

Lobster and Seafood

The dreamy island views alone are worth the trip to one of my favorite places, ★ **McLoon's Lobster Shack** (327 Island Rd., Spruce Head, 207/593-1382, www.mcloonslobster.com, 11am-7pm daily). This off-the-beaten-path shack dishes out mighty fine lobster, lobster rolls, lobster stew, crab cakes, and house-made desserts such as strawberry shortcake and blueberry pie. It also grills a good burger. Truly, this place does everything right. While most tables are outside, a few are sheltered by a tent. BYOB.

Quick Bites

Don't be surprised to see the handful of tables occupied at the **'Keag Store** (Rte. 73, Village Center, South Thomaston, 207/596-6810, 5am-9pm Mon.-Sat., 6am-8pm Sun.), one of the most popular lunch stops in the area. (Keag is pronounced "gig"—short for

Wessaweskeag.) Roast-turkey sandwiches with stuffing are a big draw, as is the pizza, which verges on the greasy but compensates with its flavor—no designer toppings, just good pizza. Order it all to go and head across the street to the public wharf, where you can hang out and observe all the comings and goings.

Eat in or just pick up pastries, sandwiches, and even fried foods to go at the **Schoolhouse Bakery** (Rte. 73, Tenants Harbor, 207/372-9608, 7am-2pm Tues.-Sat.).

Casual Dining

White tablecloth dining, harbor views, and good food are the draws at the **Wan-e-set Restaurant** (21 Mechanic St., Tenants Harbor, 207/372-6366, www.eastwindinn.com, 7:30am-9:30am Mon. and Wed., 7:30am-9:30am and 4pm-9pm Tues. and Thurs.-Fri., 7:30am-10:30am and 4pm-9pm Sat.-Sun., $32), located in the Eastwind Inn. Dinner might include sea scallops or filet mignon. For a more casual meal, opt for the inn's **Quarry Tavern** (from 4pm Thurs.-Tues., $12-18), which offers choices such as burgers, fish-and-chips, or lobster tacos.

For a relaxing American dinner, mosey over to the **Craignair Inn Restaurant** (Clark Island Rd., off Rte. 71, Spruce Head, 800/320-9997, www.craignair.com, 5:30pm-8:30pm Wed.-Mon. in season, $17-30), where big windows frame Clark Island and the ocean beyond.

ACCOMMODATIONS

No accommodations on the peninsula are contemporary or modern; for upscale lodgings, stay in Rockland or Camden.

Inns and Bed-and-Breakfasts

The **East Wind Inn** (21 Mechanic St., Tenants Harbor, 207/372-6366, www.eastwindinn.com, $165-250) overlooks an island-dotted harbor. Built in 1860 and originally used as a sail loft, it has a huge veranda, a cozy parlor, harbor-view rooms, and a quiet dining room. Guest rooms, suites, and an apartment are divided between the main inn and the spiffed-up 19th-century former sea captain's home. Rates include a full breakfast.

The decidedly old-fashioned **Craignair Inn** (5 3rd St./Clark Island Rd., off Rte. 71, Spruce Head, 800/320-9997, www.craignair.com, $130-265), built in 1928 to house granite workers, is an unfussy, unpretentious spot with a quiet oceanfront location overlooking the causeway connecting Spruce Head to Clark Island and beyond to open seas. Guest rooms are split between the main inn and the meetinghouse annex; some share baths. Rates include breakfast. Pets are allowed in some rooms for $25/night. The inn has an excellent water-view dining room ($17-30).

Two sister properties, the dog-friendly, circa 1820s **Ocean House** (870 Rte. 131, Port Clyde, 207/372-6691, $145-225) and the **Seaside Inn & Barn Café** (5 Cold Storage Rd., Port Clyde, 207/372-0700), an 1850s sea captain's home, are part of Linda Bean's Perfect Maine empire (www.lindabeansperfectmaine.com). Guest rooms in both are unpretentious; some share baths and some have harbor views. The Seaside's barn houses a seasonal café (4pm-9pm Thurs.-Sat.) serving tapas. From either, you're within steps of the Monhegan boat.

The ocean laps at the front—or is it the back—yard of **Erika's B&B By the Sea** (4 Water St., Spruce Head, 207/691-7124, www.erikasbnb.com, $139-169), a seaside cottage with two private rooms with separate entrances and serene views, one with a queen bed on the second floor and one with twin beds on the first floor. A full breakfast is included, and a one-hour private powerboat cruise is available for $75.

Camping

The third generation now operates **Lobster Buoy Campsites** (280 Waterman's Beach Rd., South Thomaston, 207/594-7546, $28-60), a no-frills oceanfront campground with about 40 sites—28 with water and electric, all with fire ring and picnic table. Bathhouses are adequate but basic, with coin-op showers. You can launch a canoe or kayak from the small, rocky beach. Most sites are open, and Lookout Beach is reserved for tenting. For privacy, opt for sites 24-27, which edge the campground and have shrubbery between them. No credit cards.

GETTING THERE AND AROUND

Port Clyde is about 15 miles or 25 minutes via Route 131 from Thomaston.

Monhegan Island

TOP EXPERIENCE

Eleven or so miles from the mainland lies a unique island community with gritty lobstermen, close-knit families, a longstanding summertime artists' colony, no cars, astonishingly beautiful scenery, and some of the best birdwatching on the Eastern Seaboard. Until the 1980s, the island had only radiophones and generator power; with the arrival of electricity and real phones, the pace has quickened a bit—but not much. Welcome to **Monhegan Island.**

But first a cautionary note: Monhegan has remained idyllic largely because generations of residents, part-timers, and visitors have been sensitive to its fragility. When you buy your ferry ticket, you'll receive a copy of the regulations, all very reasonable, and the captain of your ferry will repeat them. *Heed them, or don't go.*

Many of the regulations have been developed by the Monhegan Associates, an island land trust founded in the 1960s by Theodore Edison, son of inventor Thomas Edison. Firmly committed to preservation of the island in as natural a state as possible, the group maintains and marks the trails, sponsors natural history talks, and insists that no construction be allowed beyond the village limits.

The origin of the name *Monhegan* remains subject to debate; it's either a Maliseet or Micmac name meaning "out-to-sea island" or an adaptation of the name of a French explorer's daughter. In any case, Monhegan caught the attention of Europeans after English explorer John Smith stopped by in 1614, but the island had already been noticed by earlier adventurers, including John Cabot, Giovanni da Verrazzano, and George Waymouth. Legend even has it that Monhegan fishermen sent dried fish to Plimoth Plantation during the Pilgrims' first winter on Cape Cod. Captain Smith returned home and carried on about Monhegan, catching the attention of intrepid souls who established a fishing and trading outpost here in 1625. Monhegan has been settled continuously since 1674, with fishing as the economic base.

In the 1880s, lured by the spectacular setting and artist Robert Henri's enthusiastic reports, gangs of artists began arriving, lugging their easels here and there to capture the surf, the light, the tidy cottages, the magnificent headlands, fishing boats, and even the islanders' craggy features. American, German, French, and British artists have long come here, and they still do; well-known painters associated with Monhegan include Rockwell Kent, George Bellows, Edward Hopper, James Fitzgerald, Andrew Winter, Alice Kent Stoddard, Reuben Tam, William Kienbusch, and Jamie Wyeth.

Officially called Monhegan Plantation, the island has about 60 year-rounders. Several hundred others summer here. A handful of students attend the tiny school through eighth grade; high-schoolers have to pack up and move "inshore" to the mainland during the school year.

Almost within spitting distance of Monhegan's dock (but you'll still need a boat) is whale-shaped **Manana Island,** once the home of a former New Yorker named Ray Phillips. Known as the Hermit of Manana,

Rules for Monhegan Visitors

- Smoking is banned everywhere except in the village.
- Rock climbing is not allowed on the wild headlands on the back side of the island.
- Preserve the island's wild state—do not remove flowers or lichens.
- Bicycles and strollers are not allowed on island trails.
- Camping and campfires are forbidden island-wide.
- Swim only at Swim Beach, just south of the ferry landing—if your innards can stand the shock. Wait for the incoming tide, when the water is warmest (and this warmth is relative). It's wise not to swim alone.
- Dogs must be leashed; carry bags to remove their waste.
- Be respectful of private property; stay on the trails. (As the island visitors guide puts it, "Monhegan is a village, not a theme park.")
- If you're staying overnight, bring a flashlight; the village paths are very dark.
- Carry the island trail map when you go exploring; you'll need it.
- Carry a trash bag, use it, and take it off the island when you leave.

Phillips lived a solitary sheepherding existence on this barren island for more than half a century until his death in 1975. His story had spread so far afield that even the *New York Times* ran a front-page obituary when he died. (Photos and clippings are displayed in the Monhegan Museum.) In summer, youngsters with skiffs often hang around the harbor, particularly Fish Beach and Swim Beach, and you can usually talk one of them into taking you over for a fee. (Don't try to talk them down too much or they may not return to pick you up.) Some curious inscriptions on Manana (marked with a yellow *X* near the boat landing) have led archaeologists to claim that Vikings even made it here, but cooler heads attribute the markings to Mother Nature.

One last note: Monhegan isn't for the mobility-impaired. There's no public transportation, and roads are rough and hilly.

When to Go

If a day trip is all your schedule will allow, visit Monhegan between Memorial Day weekend and mid-October, when ferries from Port Clyde, New Harbor, and Boothbay Harbor operate daily, allowing 5-8 hours on the island—time enough to do an extensive trail loop, visit the museum and handful of shops, and picnic on the rocks. Other months, there's only one ferry per day from Port Clyde, and only three per week November-April, so you'll need to spend the night—not a hardship, but it definitely requires planning.

Almost any time of year, but especially in spring, fog can blanket the island, curtailing photography and swimming (although usually not the ferries). A spectacular sunny day can't be beat, but don't be deterred by fog, which lends an air of mystery you won't forget. Rain, of course, is another matter; some island trails can be perilous even in a misty drizzle.

Practicalities

Monhegan has no bank, but there are a couple of ATMs. Credit cards are not accepted everywhere. Personal checks or cash will do.

The only public restroom is on Horn Hill, just behind the Monhegan House. A donation of $0.50 is requested; don't complain, just drop what you can into the slot to help defray maintenance costs. It's a mere pittance to help keep the island clean.

Electricity is *very* expensive on the island (about $0.70/kilowatt hour, compared with a national average of $0.09). Ask before plugging in a charger for your phone at any restaurant, shop, or other private business, and don't be surprised if you're turned down.

SIGHTS

Monhegan is a getaway destination, a relaxing place for self-starters, so don't anticipate organized entertainment beyond the occasional lecture or narrated nature tour. Bring sturdy shoes (maybe even an extra pair in case trails are wet), a windbreaker, binoculars, a camera, and perhaps a sketchpad or a journal. If you're staying overnight, bring a flashlight for negotiating the unlighted island walkways, even in the village. For rainy days, bring a book. (If you forget, there's a lovely library.) In winter, bring ice skates for use on the Ice Pond.

★ Monhegan Historical and Cultural Museum

The **Monhegan Lighthouse**—activated in July 1824, automated in 1959, and now listed in the National Register of Historic Places—stands at the island's highest point, **Lighthouse Hill,** an exposed summit that's also home to the **Monhegan Historical and Cultural Museum** (207/596-7003, www.monheganmuseum.org, 11:30am-3:30pm daily July-Aug., hours vary June and Sept., $10 adult, $2 ages 10-18, $20 family) in the former keeper's house and adjacent buildings. Overseen by the Monhegan Historical and Cultural Museum Association, the museum has been updated in recent years and is well worth visiting. Exhibits displayed throughout the keeper's house blend artwork by American icons such as Rockwell Kent and James Fitzgerald with historical photos and artifacts downstairs and an emphasis on flora, fauna, and the environment upstairs. The lighthouse tower is open once or twice weekly; call or check the website for the current schedule. Outbuildings have tools and gear connected with fishing and ice cutting, traditional island industries. The replica assistant lightkeeper's house provides a climate-controlled environment for an annual exhibition drawing from works in the museum's impressive collection as well as outside sources. A volunteer is usually on hand to answer questions. Interesting note: Only works by deceased artists are shown, since there are so many talented artists on the island. The museum also owns two buildings designed and built by Rockwell Kent and later owned by James Fitzgerald (www.jamesfitzgerald.org). The house is maintained as a historic house museum, and Fitzgerald's works are displayed in the studio. It's open twice weekly ($5); call for the current schedule.

Monhegan Walking Tour

Plan in advance to arrange for a walking tour of Monhegan focused on its art heritage. Guide **Leith MacDonald** (http://macdonald-artservices.com) shares many of the venues painted by artists. Rates vary with duration.

Artists' Studios

Nearly 20 artists' studios are open to the public during the summer (usually July-August), but not all at once. At least five are open most days—most in the afternoon (Monday has the fewest choices). Sometimes it's tight timewise for day-trippers who also want to hike the trails, but most of the studios are relatively close to the ferry landing. An annually updated map-schedule details locations, days, and times. It's posted on bulletin boards in the village and is available at lodgings and shops.

Winter Works is a crafts co-op and **Lupine Gallery** (207/594-8131) showcases works by Monhegan artists. When you get off the ferry, walk up the hill; one's on the left, and the other is dead ahead. You can't miss them—and shouldn't.

1: Monhegan Historical and Cultural Museum **2:** Monhegan Brewing Company **3:** view of Monhegan Island from Lighthouse Hill

1

2

3

Monhegan Brewing Company

Lobsterman Matt Weber, son of a brewer, and his wife, Mary, a teacher, operate **Monhegan Brewing Company** (Lobster Cove Rd., 207/975-3958, www.monheganbrewing.com). Opened in 2013, they began with Lobster Cove APA and Shipwreck IPA as well as two nonalcoholic sodas. The Webers are working with the Monhegan Island Farm Project, which composts the waste barley. Stop by the tasting room (11am-6pm daily July-Aug., reduced hours spring and fall) to see what's brewing and enjoy a pint in the Trap Room, the trap-enclosed outdoor seating area.

RECREATION

Hiking and Walking

Despite being just over half a mile wide and 1.7 miles long, barely a square mile in area, Monhegan has 18 numbered hiking trails, most of them easy to moderate, covering about 12 miles. All are described in the *Monhegan Associates Trail Map* (www.monheganassociates.org), available at mainland ferry offices and island shops and lodgings or on the website. (The map is not to scale, so the hikes can take longer than may be apparent.)

The footing is uneven everywhere, so Monhegan can present major obstacles to those with disabilities, even on the well-worn but unpaved village roads. Maintain an especially healthy respect for the ocean here, and don't venture too close; through the years, rogue waves on the island's back side have claimed victims young and old.

A relatively easy **day-tripper loop,** with a couple of moderate sections along the back side of the island, takes in several of Monhegan's finest features starting at the southern end of the village, opposite the church. To appreciate it, allow at least two hours. From Main Road, go up Horn Hill, following signs for the **Burnthead Trail** (no. 4). Cross the island to the **Cliff Trail** (no. 1). Turn north on the Cliff Trail, following the dramatic headlands on the island's back side. There are lots of great picnic rocks in this area. Continue to Squeaker Cove, where the surf is the wildest, but be cautious. Then watch for signs to the **Cathedral Woods Trail** (no. 11), carpeted with pine needles and leading back to the village.

When you get back to Main Road, detour up the **Whitehead Trail** (no. 7) to the museum. If you're spending the night and feel energetic, consider circumnavigating the island via the **Cliff Trail** (nos. 1 and 1-A). Allow at least 5-6 hours for this route; don't rush it.

An excellent companion for hiking is the **Monhegan Island Nature Guide,** available widely on the island for $20.

Bird-Watching

One of the East Coast's best bird-watching sites during spring and fall migrations, Monhegan is a migrant trap for exhausted creatures winging their way north or south. Avid bird-watchers come here to add rare and unusual species to their life lists, and some devotees return year after year. No bird-watcher should arrive, however, without a copy of the superb *Birder's Guide to Maine.*

Predicting exact bird-migration dates can be dicey, since wind and weather aberrations can skew the schedule. Generally, the best times are mid-late May and most of September into early October. If you plan to spend a night (or more) on the island during migration seasons, don't try to wing it—reserve a room well in advance.

Around-the-Island Tour

On most days, the **Balmy Days excursion boat** makes a half-hour circuit around the island 2pm-2:30pm for a nominal fee. Ask at the ferry dock.

FOOD

Everything is quite casual on the island, and food is hearty and ample, albeit pricey. None of the full-service restaurants have liquor licenses, so buy beer or wine at one of the stores or bring it from the mainland. In most cases, hours change frequently, so call first. Do look for island-made La Nef Chocolate and Monhegan Coffee Roasters java.

Prepared foods, varying from pastries to sandwiches and salads, are available from **Barnacle Café** (207/596-0371), under the same ownership as the nearby Island Inn; the **Novelty** (207/594-4926), behind and operated by the Monhegan House, which also makes decent New York-style pizza, available by the slice or pie; **Black Duck Emporium** (207/596-7672); and the grocery **L. Brackett & Son** (207/594-2222).

Islanders and visitors flock to the **Monhegan House Restaurant** ($25-35) for breakfast and dinner. The restaurant at the **Island Inn** ($28-39) also welcomes nonguests for breakfast, lunch, and dinner daily. The American dinner menu emphasizes seafood.

You can't get much rougher for lobster in the rough than **Fish House Fish** (Fish Beach, 11:30am-7pm daily). Lobster and crabmeat rolls, locally smoked fish, and homemade stews and chowders are on the menu, as well as fresh lobster. I've found the lobster rolls to be on the meager side; opt instead for the whole crustacean. Take it to the picnic tables on the beach and enjoy.

ACCOMMODATIONS

Island lodgings vary from rustic to comfortable, but none are luxurious. Pickup trucks of dubious vintage meet all the ferries and transport luggage to the lodgings. For cottage renters, Monhegan Trucking charges a small fee for each piece of luggage.

Shining Sails (207/596-0041, www.shiningsails.com, $155-240) lacks the quaintness of the other inns, but the two guest rooms and five efficiencies are comfortable, convenient to the dock, and have private baths. Breakfast (included only in season) is meager continental. "Well-supervised" children are welcome. An additional four apartments ($170-240) are in a separate building. Shining Sails also manages more than two dozen weekly-rental cottages and apartments, with rates beginning around $1,000/week in season.

In the heart of the village, **Monhegan House** (207/594-7983 or 800/599-7983, www.monheganhouse.com, late May-mid-Oct., $190-230, $29 ages 4-12), built in 1870, is a large four-story building with 28 guest rooms. All but two suites ($260) have shared baths; most are on the second floor, with a few powder rooms on the third floor.

The funkiest lodging, and not for everyone, is the **Trailing Yew** (207/596-0440, www.trailingyew.com, $180-195, $50 ages 2-12, no credit cards), which has long been a favorite of artists; check out the annual exhibit in the main building. Spread among six rustic buildings are about 30 guest rooms, most with shared baths (averaging five rooms per bath and not always in the same building), some lighted with kerosene. Rates include breakfast. Breakfast and dinner are served family-style in the old-fashioned dining rooms; both are open to nonguests by reservation. Bring a sleeping bag in spring or fall, as rooms are unheated.

The finest lodging is the **Island Inn** (207/596-0371, www.islandinnmonhegan.com, $195-445), an imposing three-story hotel dating from 1816 that commands a prime chunk of real estate overlooking the harbor. Additional rooms are in the adjacent Pierce Cottage. Most guest rooms have been updated, but retain the simplicity of another era, with painted floors, antique oak furnishings, and comfy beds covered with white down duvets. Just try to resist the siren song of the Adirondack chairs on the expansive veranda and lawn overlooking the ferry landing. Rates for the 32 harbor- and meadow-view guest rooms and suites (some with shared baths) include full breakfast. Add $5 pp daily gratuity and $10/room for a one-night stay.

INFORMATION AND SERVICES

Several free brochures and flyers, revised annually, will answer most questions about planning a day trip or overnight visit to Monhegan. Ferries supply visitors with the *Visitor's Guide to Monhegan Island* and sell the *Monhegan Associates Trail Map* ($1). Both are also available at island shops, galleries, and lodgings. In addition, info is available at www.monheganwelcome.com.

Also check the Rope Shed, the community bulletin board next to the meadow, right in the village. Monhegan's version of a bush telegraph, it's where everyone posts flyers and notices about nature walks, lectures, excursions, and other special events.

GETTING THERE AND AROUND

Ferries travel year-round to Monhegan from Port Clyde at the end of the St. George Peninsula. Seasonal service to the island is provided from New Harbor by **Hardy Boat Cruises** and from Boothbay Harbor by **Balmy Days Cruises.**

Part of the daily routine for many islanders and summer folk is a stroll to the harbor when the ferry arrives, so don't be surprised to see a good-size welcoming party when you arrive. You're the live entertainment.

Monhegan's only vehicles are a handful of pickup trucks owned by local lobstermen, some accommodations, and **Monhegan Trucking.** If you're staying a night or longer and your luggage is too heavy to carry, they'll be waiting when you arrive at the island wharf.

Rockland

A "Share the Pride" campaign—kicked off in the 1980s to boost sagging civic self-esteem and the local economy—was the first step in the transformation of **Rockland** (pop. 7,297). Once a run-down county seat best known for the aroma of its fish-packing plants, the city has undergone a sea change, and in 2010 was named a Distinctive Destination by the National Trust for Historic Preservation. The expansion of the Farnsworth Museum of American Art and the addition of its Wyeth Center was a catalyst. Benches and plants line Main Street (Rte. 1), while independent stores offer appealing wares and coffeehouses and more than a dozen art galleries, along with the Maine Center for Contemporary Art, attracting a diverse clientele. Rockland Harbor is now home to more windjammer cruise schooners than neighboring Camden (which had long claimed the title "Windjammer Capital"). If you haven't been to Rockland in the last decade, prepare to be wowed.

Foresighted entrepreneurs had seen the potential of the bayside location in the late 1700s and established a tiny settlement here called "Shore Village" (or "the Shore"). Today's commercial fishing fleet is one of the few reminders of Rockland's past, when schooners lined the wharves—some to load volatile cargoes of lime destined to become building material for cities all along the Eastern Seaboard, others to head northeast toward the storm-racked Grand Banks and the lucrative cod fishery there. Such hazardous pursuits meant an early demise for many a local seafarer, but Rockland's 5,000 or so residents were enjoying their prosperity in the late 1840s. The settlement was home to more than two dozen shipyards and dozens of limekilns, was enjoying a construction boom, and boasted a newspaper and regular steamship service. By 1854, Rockland had become a city.

The small city remains a commercial hub, with a fishing fleet that heads far offshore and ferries that connect nearby islands. Rockland also claims the title of "Lobster Capital of the World" thanks to Knox County's shipment nationally and internationally of 10 million pounds of lobster each year. The weathervane atop the police and fire department building is a giant copper lobster.

Rockland is more year-round community than tourist town, which adds to its appeal. But visitors pour in during two big summer festivals: the North Atlantic Blues Festival in mid-July and the Maine Lobster Festival in early August. A highlight of the Lobster Festival is King Neptune's coronation of the Maine Sea Goddess—carefully selected from a bevy of local young women—who then sails off with him to his watery domain.

SIGHTS

★ Farnsworth Art Museum and Wyeth Center

Anchoring downtown Rockland is the nationally respected **Farnsworth Art Museum** (16 Museum St., 207/596-6457, www.farnsworthmuseum.org, 10am-5pm Thurs.-Tues., 10am-8pm Wed. summer, 10am-5pm Tues.-Sun. spring and fall, 10am-4pm Wed.-Sun. winter, $15 adults, $13 seniors, $10 students, free under age 17), established in 1948 through a trust fund set up by Rocklander Lucy Farnsworth. With an ample checkbook, the first curator, Robert Bellows, toured the country, accumulating a splendid collection of 19th- and 20th-century Maine-related American art, the basis for the permanent *Maine in America* exhibition.

The 15,000-piece collection today includes works by Fitz Henry Lane, Gilbert Stuart, Eastman Johnson, Childe Hassam, John Marin, Maurice Prendergast, Rockwell Kent, George Bellows, and Marsden Hartley. Best known are the paintings by three generations of the Wyeth family (local summer residents) and sculptures by Louise Nevelson, who grew up in Rockland. (The only larger Nevelson collection is in New York's Whitney Museum of American Art.) The **Wyeth Center,** across Union Street in a former church, contains the work of Andrew, N. C., and Jamie Wyeth. The 6,000-square-foot Jamien Morehouse Wing hosts rotating exhibits.

In the Farnsworth's library—a grand, high-ceilinged oasis akin to an English gentleman's reading room—browsers and researchers can explore an extensive collection of art books and magazines. The museum's education department annually sponsors hundreds of lectures, concerts, art classes for all ages, poetry readings, and field trips. Most are open to nonmembers; some require a fee.

Next door to the museum is the mid-19th-century Greek Revival **Farnsworth Homestead** ($12 adults or $22 with museum), with original high-Victorian furnishings. Looking as though William Farnsworth's family just took off for the day, the house has been preserved rather than restored. Guided tours are offered at 11am, noon, and 1pm Thursday-Sunday late May to mid-October.

The Farnsworth also owns the Olson House, 14 miles away in nearby Cushing, where the whole landscape looks like a Wyeth diorama. Pick up a map at the museum to help you find the house; it's definitely worth the side trip.

Center for Maine Contemporary Art

In 2016, the **Center for Maine Contemporary Art** (21 Winter St., 207/236-2875, www.cmcanow.org, 10am-5pm Mon.-Sat., noon-5pm Sun., $8 adults, $6 seniors and students, free under age 18) moved into a 12,143-square-foot building purpose-designed by Toshiko Mori, who made *Architectural Digest*'s 2014 list of the world's preeminent architects. The striking building provides 4,600 square feet in three galleries to display works by some of Maine's best contemporary artists. Neither museum nor gallery, the nonprofit doesn't have a permanent collection or represent individual artists. It mounts temporary exhibitions, drawing from traditional and nontraditional artistic expressions from both established and emerging artists. It also offers educational programs, workshops, and special events. Admission is free during First Friday Art Walks (5pm-8pm, May-October).

★ Owls Head Transportation Museum

Don't miss this place, even if you're not an old-vehicle buff. A generous endowment has made the **Owls Head Transportation Museum** (Rte. 73, Owls Head, 207/594-4418, www.ohtm.org, 10am-5pm daily, $14 adults, $10 seniors, free under age 18; special events are $18-25 adults) a premier facility for celebrating wings and wheels. Scads of eager volunteers help restore the vehicles and keep them running. On weekends May-October, the museum sponsors air shows (often including aerobatic displays) and car and truck meets for hundreds of enthusiasts. The season highlight is the annual rally and aerobatic show (early Aug.), when more than 300 vehicles gather for two days of festivities. Want your own vintage vehicle? Attend the antique, classic, and special-interest auto auction (third Sun. in Aug.). The gift shop carries transportation-related items. If the kids get bored (unlikely), there's a play area outside with picnic tables. In winter, groomed cross-country skiing trails wind through the museum's 60-acre site; ask for a map at the information desk.

Maine Lighthouse Museum

The headliner at the **Maine Discovery Center** (1 Park Dr.) is the **Maine Lighthouse Museum** (207/594-3301, www.mainelighthousemuseum.org, 10am-5pm Mon.-Fri., 10am-4pm Sat.-Sun. summer, by appt. in winter, $8 adults, $6 seniors, free under age 12), home to the nation's largest collection of Fresnel lenses, along with boatloads of artifacts related to lighthouses, the Coast Guard, and the sea. On view are foghorns, ships' bells, nautical books and photographs, marine instruments, ship models, scrimshaw, and much more.

Project Puffin Visitor Center

If you can't manage a trip to see the puffins, Audubon's **Project Puffin Visitor Center** (311 Main St., 207/596-5566 or 877/478-3346, www.projectpuffin.org, 10am-5pm Thurs.-Tues., 10am-7pm Wed. June-Oct., call for off-season hours) will bring them to you. Live videos of nesting puffins are just one of the features of the center, which also includes interactive exhibits, a gallery, and films, all highlighting successful efforts to restore and protect these clowns of the sea. Ask about children's programs and lectures.

★ Rockland Breakwater

Protecting the harbor from wind-driven waves, the 4,346-foot-long **Rockland Breakwater** took 18 years to build with 697,000 tons of locally quarried granite. In the late 19th century, it was piled up, chunk by chunk, from a base 175 feet wide on the harbor floor (60 feet below the surface) to the 43-foot-wide cap. The **Rockland Breakwater Light**—now automated—was built in 1902 and added to the National Register of Historic Places in 1981. The city of Rockland owns the keeper's house, but the Friends of the Rockland Harbor Lights (www.rocklandharborlights.org) maintains it. Volunteers usually open the lighthouse to the public 10am-5pm Saturday-Sunday late May-mid-October and for special events. The breakwater provides unique vantage points for photographers as well as a place to picnic or catch sea breezes or fish on a hot day, but it is extremely dangerous during storms. Anyone on the breakwater risks being washed into the sea or struck by lightning (ask the local hospital staff; it has happened). Do not take chances when the weather is iffy.

To reach the breakwater, take Route 1 North to Waldo Avenue and turn right. Take the next right onto Samoset Road and drive to the end to **Marie Reed Memorial Park** (with a tiny beach, benches, and limited parking). Or go to the Samoset Resort and walk the path to the breakwater from there.

Sail, Power & Steam Museum

Built on the grounds of the former Snow Shipyard, the **Sail, Power & Steam Museum** (Sharp's Point South, 75 Mechanic St., 207/701-7626, www.sailpowersteammuseum.org, 10am-3:30pm Wed.-Sat., 1pm-4pm Sun., $5 donation requested) is captain Jim Sharp's labor of love. A true character, old salt, and great storyteller, Sharp loves bringing the maritime-related exhibits to life. Concerts are

1: Farnsworth Art Museum **2:** Rockland Breakwater Light **3:** windjammer passing Rockland Breakwater Light under full sail **4:** Owls Head Light

EAT
FARNSWORTH ART MUSEUM
Elm St
ONE WAY
1
2
3
4

frequently held on the site. Free musical jams take place 1:30pm-4pm Sunday. Rockland Folk Arts often presents concerts here; check calendar for dates.

Coastal Children's Museum

If you're traveling with wee ones, the **Coastal Children's Museum** (Sharp's Point South, 75 Mechanic St., 207/596-0300, www.coastalchildrensmuseum.org, 10am-4pm Wed.-Sat., 1pm-4pm Sun., $6 pp or $22 family of four) is just the ticket, with hands-on and educational play exhibits including a touch tank. It's located underneath the Sail, Power & Steam Museum.

Maine Coastal Islands National Wildlife Refuge Visitor Center

Seabird restoration is the focus of the **Maine Coastal Islands National Wildlife Refuge Visitor Center** (91 Water St., 207/594-0600, www.fws.gov/refuge/maine_coastal_islands, 8:30am-4pm Mon.-Fri.), where Friends of Maine's Seabird Islands (www.maineseabirds.org) maintains a handful of exhibits, a theater screening a film about the refuge's work, and an art gallery. They also run special events. Stop in, if only to view the map of the Maine coast in the lobby.

Main Street Historic District

Rocklanders are justly proud of their **Main Street Historic District,** lined with 19th- and early 20th-century Greek and Colonial Revival structures as well as examples of mansard and Italianate architecture. Most now house retail shops on the ground floor; upper floors have offices, artists' studios, and apartments. The chamber of commerce has a map and details.

ENTERTAINMENT

The historic **Strand Theater** (339 Main St., 207/594-7266, www.rocklandstrand.com), opened in 1923, underwent an extensive restoration in the 21st century. Films as well as live entertainment are scheduled. It's also the venue for many **Bay Chamber Concerts** (207/236-2823 or 888/707-2770, www.baychamberconcerts.org) events.

The Historic Inns of Rockland coordinate the annual **January Pies on Parade,** when the inns and dozens of downtown businesses serve a variety of sweet and savory pies as a fund-raiser for the local food pantry. It's always a sellout.

In mid-July, the **North Atlantic Blues Festival** means a weekend of festivities featuring big names in blues. Thousands of fans jam Harbor Park for the nonstop music.

August's **Maine Lobster Festival** is a five-day lobster extravaganza with live entertainment, the Maine Sea Goddess pageant, a lobster-crate race, crafts booths, boat rides, a parade, lobster dinners, and massive crowds. Hotels are full for miles in either direction.

SHOPPING

Galleries

Piggybacking on the fame of the Farnsworth Museum, or at least working symbiotically, art galleries line Rockland's main street and many side streets. Ask around and look around. During the summer, about two dozen of them coordinate monthly openings to coincide with **First Friday Art Walks** (5pm-8pm May-Oct., www.artsinrockland.org), so you can meander, munch, and sip from one gallery to another.

Across from the Farnsworth's side entrance, the **Caldbeck Gallery** (12 Elm St., 207/594-5935, www.caldbeck.com) has gained a top-notch reputation as a must-see (and must-be-seen) space. Featuring the work of contemporary Maine artists, the gallery mounts more than half a dozen solo and group shows May-September each year.

Archipelago (386 Main St., 207/596-0701), on the ground floor of the nonprofit Island Institute, is an attractive retail outlet for talented craftspeople, most from 14 Maine islands and coastal communities.

Other eminently browsable downtown Rockland galleries are **Harbor Square Gallery** (374 Main St., 207/594-8700 or

877/594-8700, www.harborsquaregallery.com), **Dowling Walsh Gallery** (365 Main St., 207/596-0084, www.dowlingwalsh.com), and **Landing Gallery** (409 Main St., 207/239-1223, www.landingart.com).

RECREATION

Parks

★ OWLS HEAD LIGHT STATE PARK

Owls Head Light occupies a dramatic promontory with panoramic views over Rockland Harbor and Penobscot Bay. The 1854 **Keeper's House Interpretive Center & Gift Shop** (10am-4pm daily late May-mid-Oct.) doubles as headquarters for the American Lighthouse Foundation (www.lighthousefoundation.org). The light tower is usually open 1pm-4pm Monday and Wednesday and 10am-4pm Saturday-Sunday (free). The park surrounding the tower has easy walking paths, picnic tables, and a pebbly beach where you can sunbathe or check out Rockland Harbor's boating traffic. If it's foggy or rainy, don't climb the steps toward the light tower: The view evaporates in the fog, the access ramp can be slippery, and the foghorn is dangerously deafening.

Follow signs to reach the park. From North Shore Road, turn left onto Main Street, then left onto Lighthouse Road, and continue along Owls Head Harbor to the parking area. This is also a particularly pleasant bike route—about 10 miles round-trip from downtown Rockland—although the roadside shoulders are poor along the Owls Head stretch.

Swimming

Lucia Beach is the local name for **Birch Point Beach State Park** (www.parksandlands.com, $3-4), one of the best-kept secrets in the area. In Owls Head, just south of Rockland—and not far from Owls Head Light—the spruce-lined sand crescent (free) has rocks, shells, tidepools, and very chilly water. There are outhouses but no other facilities. From downtown Rockland, take Route 73 one mile to North Shore Drive (on your left). Take the next right, Ash Point Drive, and continue past Knox County Regional Airport to Dublin Road. Turn right, go 0.8 mile, and then turn left onto Ballyhac Road (opposite the airport landing lights). Go another 0.8 mile, fork left, and continue 0.4 mile to the parking area.

If frigid ocean water doesn't appeal, head for **Johnson Memorial Park**, a pocket-size sand patch on freshwater **Chickawaukee Lake.** A lifeguard stands watch, and there are restrooms, picnic tables, a snack bar, and a boat launch. In winter, iceboats, snowmobiles, and ice-fishing shacks take over the lake. It's on Route 17, two miles inland from downtown Rockland, an easy pedal on the signposted bicycle path from town.

Golf

The semiprivate **Rockland Golf Club** (606 Old County Rd., 207/594-9322, www.rocklandgolf.com, Apr.-Oct.) is an 18-hole course 0.2 mile northeast of Route 17. For an 18-hole course in an unsurpassed waterfront setting (but with steep rental and greens fees), tee off at the **Samoset Resort** (220 Warrenton St., Rockport, 207/594-2511 or 800/341-1650).

Sea Kayaking

Veteran Maine Guide and naturalist Mark DiGirolamo is the spark plug behind **Breakwater Kayak** (Snow Marine Park, 69 Mechanic St., 207/542-3631, www.breakwaterkayak.com), which has a full range of tours, even multiday ones. A two-hour Rockland Harbor tour is $50, and the all-day Owls Head Lighthouse tour is $115, including lunch. Reservations are advisable. This outfit is particularly eco-sensitive—Mark has a degree in environmental science—and is definitely worth supporting. Maine Audubon often taps Mark to lead natural-history field trips. Dress warmly and bring a filled water bottle.

Boat Excursions

Marine biologist captain Bob Pratt skippers ***A Morning in Maine*** (207/691-7245, www.amorninginmaine.com), a classic 55-foot

TOP EXPERIENCE

Windjamming

In 1936, Camden became the home of the "cruise schooner" (sometimes called "dude schooner") trade when captain Frank Swift restored a creaky wooden vessel and offered sailing vacations to paying passengers. He kept at it for 25 years, gradually adding other boats to the fleet. Now, more than a dozen sail Penobscot Bay's waters. Rockland wrested the Windjammer Capital title from Camden in the mid-1990s and has since held onto it.

Named for their ability to "jam" into the wind when they carried freight up and down the New England coast, windjammers trigger images of the Great Age of Sail. Most member vessels of the Maine Windjammer Association are rigged as schooners, with two or three soaring wooden masts; their lengths range 64-132 feet. Seven are National Historic Landmarks.

These windjammers head out for 3-11 days late May-mid-October, tucking into coves and harbors around Penobscot Bay and its islands. They set their itineraries by the wind, propelled by stiff breezes to Buck's Harbor, North Haven, and Deer Isle. Everything's totally informal and geared for relaxing.

You're aboard for the experience, not for luxury, so expect basic accommodations with few frills, although newer vessels were built with passenger trade in mind and tend to be a bit comfier. Below deck, cabins typically are small and basic, with paper-thin walls—sort of a campground afloat (earplugs are often available for light sleepers). It may not sound romantic, but be aware that the captains keep track of post-cruise marriages. Most boats have shared showers and toilets. If you're type A or given to pacing, don't inflict yourself on the cruising crowd; if you're flexible and ready for whatever, go ahead and sign on. You can help with the sails, eat, curl up with a book, inhale salt air, snap photos, sunbathe, bird-watch, chat up fellow passengers, sleep, or just settle back and enjoy spectacular sailing you'll never forget.

When you book a cruise, you'll receive all the details and directions, but for a typical trip, you arrive at the boat by 7pm for the captain's call to meet your fellow passengers. You sleep aboard at the dock that night and then depart midmorning and spend the next nights and days cruising Penobscot Bay, following the wind, the weather, and the whims of the captain. (Many of the wind-

ketch designed by noted naval architect R. D. (Pete) Culler and built by Concordia Yachts. June-October, *Morning* departs from the middle pier at the Rockland Public Landing three times daily for two-hour sails ($45), with plenty of knowledgeable commentary from Captain Pratt. A 6pm sunset sail is available in July-August.

Maine State Ferry Service

Car and passenger ferries service the islands of Vinalhaven, North Haven, and Matinicus. The Vinalhaven and North Haven routes make fantastic day trips (especially with a bike), or you can spend the night; the Matinicus ferry is much less predictable, and island services are few.

Bicycling

Rentals (from $25), sales, and repair are provided by **Sidecountry Sports** (481 Main St., 207/701-5100, www.sidecountrysports.com).

FOOD

Rockland is gaining a reputation as a foodie destination, with new options opening regularly.

Lobster and Seafood

Claws (543 Main St., 207/596-5600, http://clawsrocklandmaine.com, 11am-9pm daily), a roadside seafood shack, earns raves for its food, views over Penobscot Bay, and seating on the deck or on an enclosed, heated patio. There are a few choices for folks who aren't seafood lovers.

jammers have no engines, only a motorized yawl boat used as a pusher and a water taxi.) You might anchor in a deserted cove and explore the shore, or you might pull into a harbor and hike, shop, and barhop. Then it's back to the boat for chow—windjammer cooks are legendary for creating three hearty all-you-can-eat meals daily, including at least one lobster feast. When the cruise ends, most passengers find it hard to leave.

On the summer cruising schedule, several weeks coincide with special windjammer events, so you'll need to book a berth far in advance for these: mid-June (Schooner Gam, Boothbay Harbor's Windjammer Days), Fourth of July week (Great Schooner Race), Labor Day weekend (Camden's Windjammer Weekend), and the second week in September (Wooden Boat Sail-In). Themed cruises usually include knitting, chocolate- and/or wine-tasting, photography, and family.

Windjammers are a special way to experience Penobscot Bay.

Known for its onboard cuisine is the **Schooner *J. & E. Riggin*** (207/594-1875, www.mainewindjammer.com), captained by the husband-and-wife team of Annie Mahle, author of three cookbooks, and Jon Finger. The **Schooner *Boyd N. Sheppard*** (877/238-1325, www.boydnsheppard.com) offers shorter and food- and wine-themed sails. Many windjammers offering sails out of Camden, Rockland, and Rockport are members of the **Maine Windjammer Association** (800/807-9463, www.sailmainecoast.com), a one-stop resource for vessel and schedule information.

At the **Lobster Shack** (346 Main St., 207/390-0102, 11am-4pm daily), a take-out with outdoor seating sited next to the Farnsworth Museum downtown, lobster rolls, crab rolls, and chowders are the stars, but other homemade soups and specials are equally good. Cash only.

North Beacon Oyster (421 Main St., 207/466-9120, www.northbeaconoyster.com, 4:30pm-9pm Tues.-Sat., $14-28) is a delicious spot for oysters, as well as other fresh seafood options served as small or large plates.

Quick Bites

Grab breakfast before catching a ferry at ★ **Home Kitchen Cafe** (650 Main St., 207/596-2449, www.homekitchencafe.com, 7am-3pm Mon. and Wed.-Sat., 8am-3pm Sun., $8-14), where the huevos rancheros and lobster tacos earn raves. The menu is extensive and creative. Breakfast and lunch are served all day.

Anchoring the other end of Main Street is the **Brass Compass Café** (305 Main St., 207/596-5960, http://thebrasscompasscafe.com, 6am-2pm daily, $10-22), where the portions are big, the prices are small, and most of the ingredients are locally sourced. Sit indoors or on the dog-friendly patio. If you go for breakfast, the fish cakes are a real taste of Maine.

Lots of Rockland-watchers credit the new American cuisine at **Rock City Cafe** (252 Main St., 207/594-4123, www.rockcitycoffee.com, 6am-5pm Sun.-Wed., 6am-6pm Thurs.-Sat., $7-10) with sparking the food renaissance in town. Go for breakfast, lunch, or an afternoon snack, and don't miss the bookstore in back.

Scratch-made bread, pastries, and grab-and-go sandwiches have made **Atlantic Baking Co.** (351 Main St., 207/596-0505, www.atlanticbakingco.com, 7am-6pm Mon.-Sat., 8am-4pm Sun.) a popular spot for a quick informal lunch. There are plenty of tables to enjoy your treats, or take them to the waterfront park.

Main Street Markets (435 Main St., 207/594-8515, www.mainstreetmarkets.com, 9am-6pm Mon.-Sat., 10am-5pm Sun.), a specialty food market and deli, offers breakfast and lunch fare as well as prepared foods to go. It's a great spot to pick up picnic fixings.

Viewing windows let you see into the production area of Maine's first bean-to-bar chocolate company, **Bixby & Co.** (1 Sea St. Pl., 207/691-1778, https://bixbyco.com, 10am-5:30pm Mon.-Sat., 11am-5:30pm Sun.).

The **Rockland Farmers Market** sets up 9am-1pm every Thursday June-September at Harbor Park on Rockland's Public Landing.

Casual Dining

Big flavors come out of the tiny kitchen at **Café Miranda** (15 Oak St., 207/594-2034, www.cafemiranda.com, 11:30am-2pm and 5pm-9pm Mon.-Sat., 10:30am-2pm and 5pm-9pm Sun., $18-27), a perennial local favorite. Chef-owner Kerry Altiero's menu is overwhelming in size and in its flavor contrasts. Many of the appetizers ($6.50-12.50) are enough for a meal. The fresh brick-oven focaccia comes with everything. If you sit at the counter, you can watch the chefs at work. The bar serves beer and wine only. Reservations are essential throughout the summer and on weekends in the off-season; there is patio dining in season.

Live music is often on tap at **Fog Bar & Café** (328 Main St., 207/593-9371, 4:30pm-10pm Thurs.-Mon., $12-25), a gastropub with an eclectic, cross-cultural, frequently changing menu. Monday night features an open mic.

Creative American comfort food is served at **Sammy's Deluxe** (488 Main St., 207/466-9059, www.sammysdeluxe.com, from 5pm Tues.-Sat., $18-26). After a day of exploring, relax at **In Good Company** (415 Main St., 207/593-9110, www.ingoodcompanymaine.com, 4:30pm-9pm daily, $22-28), a casual wine and tapas bar. Sit at the bar and watch chef-owner Melody Wolfertz, a Culinary Institute of America grad, concoct creative small and large plates.

Many places claim to be farm-to-table; two-time James Beard Award-winning chef Melissa Kelly's ★ **Primo** (2 S. Main St./Rte. 73, 207/596-0770, from 5pm Wed.-Mon. July-Aug., shorter hours rest of year, www.primorestaurant.com, $30-38) is the real deal. In the backyard are acres of organic gardens, two greenhouses, beehives, and pastures for the chickens and pigs. Primo is really two experiences under one roof: the intimate and elegant parlor dining rooms downstairs, with their own menu; and the upstairs lounge, with a menu highlighting pizza, cheese and charcuterie, and small plates, making it possible to mix and match a meal of tapas-size portions and stay within a budget. Reservations are essential for the dining rooms, usually at least a week ahead for midsummer weekends—and you still may have to wait when you get there. No reservations are taken for the upstairs lounge. The Sunday $1 oysters always draw a crowd.

International

Ask local pooh-bah chefs where they go on their night off, and the answer often is Keiko Suzuki Steinberger's **Suzuki's Sushi Bar** (419 Main St., 207/596-7447, www.suzukisushi.com, from 5pm Tues.-Sat., $14-28). The food matches the decor: simple yet sophisticated. Sashimi, *nigiri, maki,* and *temaki* choices range $6-13. Reservations are essential.

Authentic Italian cuisine draws repeat customers to **Rustica** (315 Main St., 207/594-0015, www.rusticamaine.com, 5pm-9pm Tues.-Sat., $14-24). The two dining areas are

---

1: Samoset Resort **2:** McLoon's Lobster Shack in Spruce Head **3:** fishing boats near Rockland

1

2

3

comfortable yet refined, with candles on the tables. The fare is fresh and plentiful.

It's hard to say which is better, the views or the fare at the Samoset Resort's **La Bella Vita & The Enoteca Lounge** (220 Warrenton St., 207/594-2511, www.labellavitaristorante.com, 7am-9pm daily, $15-34). Ocean Properties operates other locations of this restaurant, but this one really shines. The flavor is Italian, with pastas, pizzas from the wood-fired oven, and other specialties. Views from the restaurant and deck over the golf course to the ocean are terrific. Sunday brunch is served noon-2:30pm.

ACCOMMODATIONS

If you're planning an overnight stay in the Rockland area the first weekend in August, during the Maine Lobster Festival, make reservations well in advance. Festival attendance runs close to 100,000, so "No Vacancy" signs extend from Waldoboro to Belfast.

Resort

The 221-acre **Samoset Resort** (220 Warrenton St., Rockport, 207/594-2511 or 800/341-1650, www.samosetresort.com, from $325 plus resort fee) commands a spectacular oceanfront site straddling the boundary between Rockland and Rockport, the next town to the north. Built on the ashes of a classic 19th-century summer hotel, the Samoset is a full-service, modern, family-oriented resort. Most of its 178 guest rooms and suites and four cottages have knockout ocean views and all the expected bells and whistles. Facilities include a fitness center with an indoor heated pool, an outdoor zero-entry heated pool with a bar and food service, lighted tennis courts, a children's day camp (ages 5-12, morning and evening sessions), daily planned activities, access to the adjacent Rockland Breakwater, a fabulous 18-hole waterfront golf course, a full-service spa, and an excellent casual, Mediterranean restaurant and lounge with outdoor terrace seating. For a real treat, book the Flume cottage.

Inns and Bed-and-Breakfasts

These bed-and-breakfasts are in Rockland's historic district, within easy walking distance of downtown attractions and restaurants; the first three are members of the **Historic Inns of Rockland Maine** (www.historicinnsofrockland.com), which coordinates the January Pies on Parade event—a blast.

Traveling with Fido and the kiddos? Check into the kid- and pet-friendly **Granite Inn** (546 Main St., 800/386-9036, www.oldgraniteinn.com, $95-215), where you can practically roll out of bed and onto an island ferry. Unlike most historical inns, the decor leans to contemporary and a bit artsy, blending mid-century modern with original artwork as well as antiques. Breakfast is full and satisfying, and might even include a seafood quiche. Front rooms have water views.

The **Limerock Inn** (96 Limerock St., 207/594-2257 or 800/546-3762, www.limerockinn.com, from $170) is a lovely painted lady. The 1890s Queen Anne mansion, with wraparound porch and turret, is listed in the National Register of Historic Places. Each of the eight guest rooms has its own distinct flavor; the Island Cottage Room opens to a private deck overlooking the back gardens. All are elegantly furnished with an emphasis on guest comfort. The inviting decor blends family antiques with mid-century modern furnishings and original art.

Located on a quiet side street a few blocks from downtown, ★ **Berry Manor Inn** (81 Talbot Ave., 207/596-7696 or 800/774-5692, www.berrymanorinn.com, from $229) occupies a meticulously restored manse built in 1898 by wealthy Rocklander Charles Berry as a wedding gift for his wife (thoughtful fellow). High ceilings and wonderful Victorian architectural touches are everywhere, especially in the enormous front hall and two parlors. Guest rooms and suites are spread between the main house and adjacent carriage house. Most have gas fireplaces and whirlpool tubs. A guest pantry is stocked with free soft drinks and juices and sweets—not that you'll be hungry after the extravagant breakfast.

Next door is the Berry Manor Inn's sister property, **Rockland Talbot House** (73 Talbot Ave., 207/593-7393, http://rocklandtalbothouse.com, from $219), which blends B&B with vacation rental. Guests enjoy breakfast but also have use of a refrigerator and microwave.

Hotels

A masterful renovation turned a lackluster downtown property with a primo location facing the ferry terminal into the handsome **Rockland Harbor Hotel** (520 Main St., 800/545-8026, www.rocklandharborhotel.com, from $199). Amenities include a fitness center and a lobby lounge where a complimentary hot breakfast is provided.

The **Lindsey Hotel** (5 Lindsey St., 207/596-7950, https://lindseyhotelmaine.com, from $215) is more like a boutique hotel than a bed-and-breakfast. The 1835 brick Federal has been restored and updated with a nautical motif, contemporary conveniences, and antiques as accent pieces. Don't miss the hidden-from-the-street garden patio. It's smack downtown; a few rooms have glimpses of the water. Rates include a full breakfast.

Industrial-chic decor warmed with reclaimed wood and interior details custom crafted by Lyman Morse Boatbuilding distinguish ★ **250 Main** (250 Main St., 207/594-5994, www.250mainhotel.com, from $319), a 26-room boutique hotel overlooking Harbor Park, designed to highlight a curated collection of contemporary Maine art. Most rooms have water views; some have balconies. Continental breakfast and daily wine socials are offered in the spacious lobby lounge, but you can always take it to the rooftop deck, which has panoramic views over Rockland and the harbor. Some rooms are pet friendly ($50/night).

INFORMATION AND SERVICES

For information, visit the **Penobscot Bay Regional Chamber of Commerce** (Gateway Center, 207/596-0376 or 800/223-5459, www.mainedreamvacation.com).

Find **public restrooms** at the Gateway Center; the Knox County Courthouse (Union St. and Masonic St.); the Rockland Recreation Center (Union St. and Limerock St.), across from the courthouse and next to the playground; the Rockland Public Library; off Tillson Avenue near the municipal parking lots; and the Maine State Ferry Service terminal.

GETTING THERE AND AROUND

Rockland is about five miles or 10 minutes via Route 1 from Thomaston. It's about eight miles or 15 minutes via Route 1 to Camden.

The Fox Islands

TOP EXPERIENCE

Vinalhaven (pop. 1,165) and neighboring **North Haven** (pop. 355) have been known as the Fox Islands since 1603, when English explorer Martin Pring sailed these waters and allegedly spotted gray foxes in his search for sustenance. Nowadays, you'll find reference to that name only on nautical charts, identifying the passage between the two islands as the Fox Islands Thorofare—and there's nary a fox in sight. Each island has its own distinct personality. Vinalhaven is bustling, whereas North Haven is sedate and exclusive.

VINALHAVEN

Vinalhaven, 5 miles wide, 7.5 miles long, and covering 10,000 acres, is 13 miles off the coast of Rockland—a 75-minute ferry trip. The shoreline has so many zigs and zags that no place on the island is more than a mile from the water.

Vinalhaven

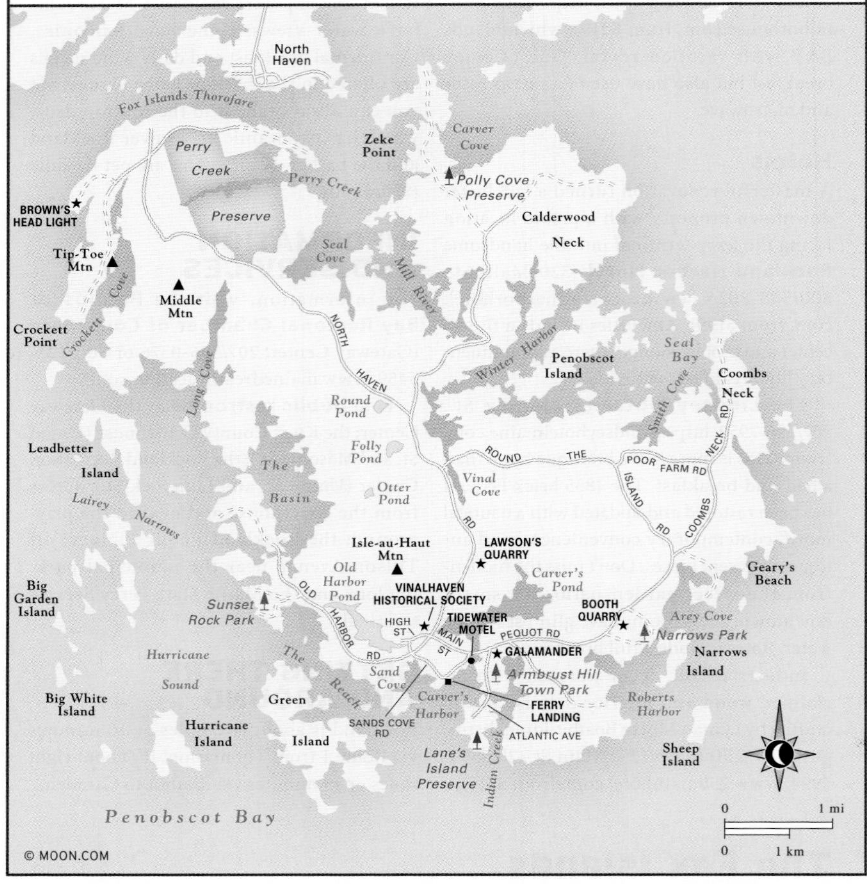

The island is famed for its granite. The first blocks headed for Boston around 1826, and within a few decades, quarrymen arrived from as far away as Britain and Finland to wrestle out and shape the incredibly resistant stone. Schooners, barges, and "stone sloops" left **Carver's Harbor** carrying mighty cargoes of granite destined for government and commercial buildings in Boston, New York, and Washington DC. In the 1880s, nearly 4,000 people lived on Vinalhaven, North Haven, and Hurricane Island. After World War I, demand declined, granite gave way to concrete and steel, and the industry petered out and died. But Vinalhaven has left its mark in the ornate columns, paving blocks, and curbstones of communities as far west as Kansas City.

Vinalhaven is a serious working community, not primarily a playground. Lobstering and fishing are the island's chief industries. Shopkeepers cater to locals as well as visitors, and increasing numbers of artists and artisans work away in their studios. For day-trippers, there's plenty to do—shopping, picnicking, hiking, biking, swimming—but an overnight stay provides a chance to sense the unique rhythm of life on a year-round island.

One Main Street landmark that's hard to miss is the three-story, cupola-topped **Odd Fellows Hall,** a Victorian behemoth built in 1885 for the Independent Order of Odd Fellows Star of Hope Lodge. Artist Robert Indiana, who first arrived as a visitor in 1969, lived here until his 2018 death, decorating the structure with American flag motifs on the lower windows and assorted gewgaws in the upper ones. Plans call for an eventual museum.

At the top of the hill just beyond Main Street (School St. and E. Main St.) is a greenish-blue replica **galamander,** a massive reminder of Vinalhaven's late 19th-century granite-quarrying era. Galamanders, hitched to oxen or horses, carried the stone from island quarries to the finishing shops. Next to the galamander is a colorful wooden bandstand, site of very popular evening band concerts held sporadically during the summer.

The **Vinalhaven Historical Society** (207/863-4410, www.vinalhavenhistoricalsociety.org, 11am-4pm Mon.-Sat. July-Aug. or by appointment, donation) operates a delightful museum in the onetime town hall on High Street, just east of Carver's Cemetery. The building itself has a tale, having been floated across the bay from Rockland, where it served as a Universalist church. The museum's documents and artifacts on the granite industry are particularly intriguing, and special summer exhibits add to the interest. At the museum, request a copy of *A Self-guided Walking Tour of the Town of Vinalhaven and Its Granite-Quarrying History,* a handy little brochure that details 17 in-town locations related to the industry.

For another dose of history, stop by the 1888 **Old Engine House** (Main St., 10am-2pm Mon. and Wed., 1pm-3pm Sat.) to see old firefighting equipment.

First built in 1832 and reconstructed in 1857, **Brown's Head Light** guards the southern entrance to the Fox Islands Thorofare. In 2015, the town turned ownership over to the American Lighthouse Foundation (www.lighthousefoundation.org), which is stabilizing it. Overnight accommodations are planned. To reach the grounds, take North Haven Road about six miles, at which point you'll see a left-side view of the Camden Hills. Continue about another mile to the second road on the left, Crockett River Road. Turn and take the second road on the right, continuing past the Brown's Head Cemetery to the hill overlooking the lighthouse. Check with the foundation for its current status.

Shopping

Most of Vinalhaven's shops are clustered downtown, a short walk from the ferry terminal. **Wind Horse Arts** (50 Main St., 207/863-2262) is filled with artist-owner Alison Thibault's jewelry creations and other finds. **New Era Gallery** (60 Main St., 207/863-9351) sells a well-chosen selection of art in varied media, representing primarily island artisans; don't miss the sculpture garden or barn. **Second Hand Prose** (Main St., 207/863-2258), a used-book store, is run by the Friends of the Vinalhaven Public Library. **Vinalhaven Candy Co.** (35 W. Main St., 207/863-2041) is a kid magnet, but it pleases adults, too, with hand-dipped and soft-serve ice cream and candy galore. **SOST Linen** (56 Main St., 207/863-2361) makes and sells wonderful linen clothing. Pop into **Go Fish** (56 Main St., 207/863-4193) for candy, arts, crafts, clothing, and more. **Zach's Shack** (12 Harbor Rd., 207/313-0042) is one of the few shops not downtown. This small shop filled with Maine-made and artisan-crafted goods is about a 15-minute walk from the ferry terminal (turn left when exiting the ferry terminal lot).

The Saturday-morning anything-goes **flea markets** are an island must, as much for the browsing and buying as for the gossip.

Recreation

PARKS AND PRESERVES

Vinalhaven is loaded with wonderful hikes and walks, some deliberately unpublicized. Since the mid-1980s, the **Vinalhaven Land Trust** (207/863-2543, www.vinalhavenlandtrust.org) has expanded the opportunities. When you reach the island, pick up maps at the land trust's kiosk at **Skoog Memorial Park** (12 Skoog Park Rd., off Sands Cove Rd., west of the ferry terminal) or inquire at the town office or the Paper Store. The trust also offers a seasonal series of educational walks and talks.

Some hiking options are the Perry Creek Preserve, which has a terrific loop trail; Middle Mountain Park; Tip-Toe Mountain; Isle au Haut Mountain; Huber Preserve; and Eleanor L. Campbell Preserve.

No, you're not on the moors of Yorkshire, but you could be fooled in the **Lane's Island Preserve.** Masses of low-lying ferns, rugosa roses, and berry bushes cover the granite outcrops of this sanctuary—and a foggy day makes it even more moorlike and mystical, like a setting for a Brontë novel. The best (albeit busiest) time to come is early August, when you can compete with the birds for blackberries, raspberries, and blueberries. Easy trails wind past old stone walls, an aged cemetery, and along the surf-pounded shore. The preserve is a 20-minute walk (or 5-minute bike ride) from Vinalhaven's ferry landing. Set off to the right on Main Street, through the village. Turn right onto Water Street and then right on Atlantic Avenue. Continue across the causeway on Lane's Island Road and left over a salt marsh to the preserve.

Next to the ferry landing in Carver's Harbor is **Grimes Park,** a wooded pocket retreat with a splendid view of the harbor. Owned by the American Legion, the park is perfect for picnics or for hanging out between boats, especially in good weather.

Just behind the Island Community Medical Center, close to downtown, is **Armbrust Hill Town Park,** once the site of granite-quarrying operations. Still pockmarked with quarry pits, the park has beautifully landscaped walking paths and native flowers, shrubs, and trees—much of it thanks to late island resident Betty Roberts, who made this a lifelong endeavor. From the back of the medical center, follow the trail to the summit for a southerly view of Matinicus and other offshore islands. If you're with children, be especially careful about straying onto side paths, which go perilously close to old quarry holes.

Vinalhaven's harbor

Before the walk, lower the children's energy level at the large playground off to the left of the trail.

BICYCLING

Even though Vinalhaven's 40 or so miles of public roads are narrow, winding, and poorly shouldered, they're relatively level, so a bicycle is a fine way to tour the island.

A 10-mile, 2.5-hour bicycle route begins on Main Street and goes clockwise out on North Haven Road (rough pavement), past Lawson's Quarry, to Round the Island Road (some sections are dirt), and then Poor Farm Road to Geary's Beach and back to Main Street via Pequot Road and School Street. Carry a picnic and enjoy it on Lane's Island, stop for a swim in one of the quarries, or detour down to Brown's Head Light. If you're here for the day, keep track of the time so you don't miss the ferry.

Far more rewarding view-wise, and far shorter, is the out-and-back pedal along **Old Harbor Road to the Basin,** which is rich in wildlife and serves as a seal nursery.

SWIMMING

Two town-owned quarries are easy to reach from the ferry landing. **Lawson's Quarry** is 1 mile from downtown on North Haven Road; **Booth Quarry** is 1.6 miles from downtown via East Main Street. Both are signposted. You'll see plenty of sunbathers on the rocks and swimmers on a hot day, but there are no lifeguards, so swimming is at your own risk. There are no restrooms or changing rooms. Note that pets and soap are not allowed in the water; camping, fires, and alcohol are not allowed in the quarry areas.

Down the side road beyond Booth Quarry is **Narrows Park,** a town-owned space looking out toward Narrows Island, Isle au Haut, and, on a clear day, Mount Desert Island.

For saltwater swimming, take East Main Street 2.4 miles from downtown to a crossroads, where you'll see a whimsical bit of local folk art: the Coke lady sculpture. Turn right (east) and go 0.5 mile to **Geary's Beach** (also called **State Beach**), where you can picnic and scour the shoreline for shells and sea glass.

BOAT EXCURSIONS

See **Vinalhaven by Boat** (207/248-1775, www.vinalhavenbyboat) with captain Mark Jackson aboard the *Ruth,* a small open wooden boat built for pleasure, not speed. The rate ($90/hour) covers up to six people.

Sail through the Fox Islands with **Blue Yonder Sail Charters** (207/491-8551, www.blueyondersailcharters.com), which offers private charters aboard a six-passenger, 40-foot wooden sailboat (from $250 for 2 hours).

PADDLE SPORTS

Sea kayak, canoe, and paddleboard rentals are available at the Tidewater Motel for $40-60 per day, including delivery. A guide can be arranged, but it's not necessary to have one to poke around the harbor or, even better, paddle through the Basin, which is especially popular with birders and wildlife-watchers.

BIRDING AND WILDLIFE-WATCHING

Join ornithologist **John Drury** (207/596-1841, www.maineseabirdtours.com, $90/hour) aboard his 36-foot lobster boat on a birding and wildlife-watching cruise through the islands of Penobscot Bay. Sightings have included Arctic terns, guillemots, shearwaters, petrel, puffins, and eagles, along with seals, dolphins, minke whales, and perhaps even an albatross.

The **Vinalhaven Land Trust** (207/863-2543, www.vinalhavenlandtrust.org) offers weekly **bird walks** from mid-June to mid-September.

Food

Island restaurants change hours frequently; call for current schedules.

QUICK BITES

Baked bean suppers are regularly held at a couple of island locations. Check the local newsletter the *Wind* for details.

If the weather's fine, look for **Greet's Eats** (207/863-2057, 11am-2pm Wed.-Sun.), a take-out wagon on the wharf by the co-op. The lobster rolls earn raves, but there are other options too.

Pick up the fixings for a fancy picnic at **Island Spirits** (32 Main St., 207/863-2192, 10am-6pm Tues.-Sat.), a small gourmet-foods store stocked with wines, beers, cheeses, breads, and other goodies.

For premade or made-to-order sandwiches, stop into **Carver's Harbor Market** (36 Main St., 207/863-4319, 8am-7pm Mon.-Fri., 8am-6pm Sat., 9am-3pm Sun.).

FAMILY FAVORITES

The **Pizza Pitt** (Harbor Wharf, Main St., 207/863-4311, 4pm-8:30pm Wed.-Sun.) is an easy-on-the-budget choice. Another good bet for an American breakfast or lunch is **Homeport Family Restaurant** (82 W. Main St., 207/863-2318, 6am-2pm Fri.-Tues.). For an easy on the budget contemporary tavern menu, pop into the **Sand Bar** (63 Main St., 207/863-4500, from 11am Tues.-Sun., $7-18).

CASUAL DINING

The **Nightingale** (26 Main St., 207/863-5021, noon-2:30pm and 5:30pm-8:30pm Wed.-Mon., $12-26) serves contemporary American fare, with an emphasis on scratch-made from local ingredients.

For contemporary American fare, with a Mediterranean accent, make reservations at **Dot & Millie's** (49 Main St., 207/863-4969, from 6pm Tues.-Sun., $18-28).

Accommodations

If you're planning on staying overnight, don't even consider arriving in summer without reservations. If you're coming for the day, pay attention to the ferry schedule and allow enough time to get back to the boat. The island has no campsites. Rates listed are for peak season.

Convenient to downtown, the **Libby House** (8 Water St., 207/863-4696, www.libbyhouse1869.com, $110-150, no breakfast) is an 1869 Victorian with a two-bedroom apartment and four guest rooms, some sharing a bath.

Your feet practically touch the water when you spend the night at the **Tidewater Motel and Gathering Space** (12 Main St., Carver's Harbor, 207/863-4618, www.tidewatermotel.com, from $190), in two buildings cantilevered over the harbor. The 19-room motel, now operated by the third generation of the Crossman family, is the perfect place to sit on the deck and watch the lobster boats do their thing. Be aware, though, that commercial fishers are early risers, and lobster boat engines can rev up as early as 4:30am on a summer morning—all part of the island pace. Continental breakfast and island shuttle service are included in the rates; sea kayak rentals are available. Kids 10 and under are free. Seven units are efficiencies.

Information and Services

Vinalhaven Chamber of Commerce (www.vinalhaven.org) produces the Visitors Guide ($1). On the island, pick up a copy of Vinalhaven's weekly newsletter, the *Wind,* named after the island's original newspaper, first published in 1884. It's loaded with island flavor: news items, public-supper announcements, editorials, and ads. Copies are available at most downtown locales.

Public restrooms are at the ferry landing and in town at the chamber of commerce office in the big red fire barn.

Getting Around

Don't bring a car unless it is absolutely necessary. If you're day-tripping, you can get to parks and quarries, shops, restaurants, and the historical society museum on foot. If you want to explore farther afield, a bicycle is an excellent option, or you can rent a car from **Vinalhaven Island Car Rental** (207/994-9143, http://vinalhavencarrental.com).

1: Tidewater Motel **2:** ferry connecting Rockland to Vinalhaven and North Haven

1

2

Vinalhaven Taxi (207/720-0056) also provides transportation.

NORTH HAVEN

North Haven (pop. 355), 8 miles long by 3 miles wide, is 12 miles off the coast of Rockland—70 minutes by ferry. The island has sedate summer homes, open fields where hundreds of sheep once grazed, an organic farm, about 350 year-round residents, and a yacht club called the Casino.

Originally called North Island, North Haven had much the same settlement history as Vinalhaven, but being smaller and more fertile, it has developed—or not developed—differently. In 1846, North Haven was incorporated and severed politically from Vinalhaven, and by the late 1800s, the Boston summer crowd began buying traditional island homes, building tastefully unpretentious new ones, and settling in for a whole season of sailing and socializing. Several generations later, summer folk now come for weeks rather than months, often rotating the schedules among slews of siblings. Informality remains the key, though—now more than ever.

The island has two distinct hamlets: North Haven Village, on the Fox Islands Thorofare, where the state ferry arrives; and Pulpit Harbor, particularly popular with the yachting set. The village is easily explored on foot in a morning.

North Haven doesn't offer a lot for the day visitor, and islanders tend not to welcome them with open arms.

Entertainment

Waterman's Community Center (Main St., 207/867-2100, www.watermans.org) provides a place for island residents and visitors to gather for entertainment, events, and even coffee and gossip. It's home to North Haven Arts & Enrichment. Check the schedule on the website to see what's planned.

Shopping

Fanning out from the ferry landing is a delightful cluster of substantial year-round clapboard homes—a marked contrast to the weathered-shingle cottages typical of so many island communities. It won't take long to stroll and visit the handful of shops and galleries, which include **Hopkins Wharf Gallery** on the waterfront and **North Haven Gift Shop** on Main Street.

Recreation

North Haven has about 25 miles of paved roads that are conducive to **bicycling**, but, just as on most other islands, they are narrow, winding, and nearly shoulderless. Starting near the ferry landing in North Haven Village, take South Shore Road eastward, perhaps stopping en route for a picnic at town-owned Mullin's Head Park (also spelled Mullen Head) on the southeast corner of the island. Then follow the road around, counterclockwise, to North Shore Road and Pulpit Harbor. Make advance reservations for a rental bicycle from **North Haven Rentals** (11 Iron Point Rd., 207/867-2282, www.northhavenboatrentals.com, $25/day plus $5/helmet).

Food and Accommodations

Pizza dominates the menu at **Calderwood Hall** (2 Iron Point Rd., 207/867-4700, www.calderwoodhall.com, 5pm-9pm Wed.-Sun., from $14). A market and bakery with prepared foods, baked goods, sandwiches, and more operates here 7am-3pm Wednesday-Saturday. **North Haven Brewing Company** (www.northhavenbrewing.com) operates on the lower level.

If you have wheels, head over to **Turner Farm** (73 Turner Farm Rd., 207/867-4962, www.turner-farm.com), an organic farm dating back 200 years. The location is spectacular, with fields rolling down to the Fox Island Thorofare, and the farm stand (check for seasonal hours) is a great place to pick up fresh meats, produce, and goat cheese. The farm is also the site of frequent family-style

1: Hopkins Wharf Gallery **2:** Turner Farm on North Haven

1

2

barn suppers (five courses, includes beer or wine, $110).

Within walking distance of the ferry is **Nebo Lodge** (11 Mullins Ln., 207/867-2007, www.nebolodge.com, $160-350). Nine rooms, some with shared baths, are decorated with island art, and many have rugs by Angela Adams. Rates include a continental breakfast. Dinner ($24-38) is available from 5pm Tuesday-Saturday July-August, and Friday-Saturday May-June and September-October. Nebo also runs a lobster boat dinner shuttle ($30) from Rockland on select evenings; call for the schedule.

Information

The best source of information about North Haven is the **North Haven Town Office** (Upper Main St., 207/867-4433, www.northhavenmaine.org).

GETTING THERE

The **Maine State Ferry Service** (207/596-2202, www.exploremaine.org) operates six round-trips daily between Rockland and Vinalhaven (75-minute crossing) in summer and three round-trips between Rockland and North Haven (70-minute crossing). From June through September, round-trip tickets are $17.50 adults and $6.25 ages 6-17. Both ferries take cars ($38.50 round-trip, plus $12 reservation fee), but a bicycle ($22.50 round-trip adult bike, $16.25 child bike) will do fine unless you have the time or inclination to see every corner of the islands.

Getting car space on the ferry during midsummer can be a frustrating—and complicated—experience, so *avoid taking a car to the islands*. If you do take a vehicle, give yourself time to find a parking space and perhaps to walk from it to the ferry terminal. If you leave a car at the Rockland lot (space is limited and availability varies), it's $10/24 hours or $50/week. You can also park for free on some of Rockland's side streets and walk, or, for a day trip, park in the city lot between Main Street and the water or Harbor Park.

No official ferry service travels between Vinalhaven and North Haven, even though the two islands are almost within spitting distance of each other. Fortunately, **Brown's Boatyard** (www.brownsboatyard.com) on North Haven provides shuttles on the hour 7am-5pm daily. Call the boat shop (207/867-4621) to arrange a pickup on the Vinalhaven side. The fee is $5 one way, $7 round-trip, $2/bike.

Penobscot Island Air (207/596-7500, www.penobscotislandair.net) flies twice daily to Vinalhaven and North Haven, weather permitting, from Knox County Regional Airport in Owls Head, just south of Rockland. Seat availability is dependent on mail volume. Non-mail flights may be available.

Greater Camden

Camden (pop. 4,850), flanked by **Rockport** (pop. 3,330) to the south and **Lincolnville** (pop. 2,164) to the north, is one of the Mid-Coast's—even Maine's—prime destinations.

Camden is the best known of the three and typifies Maine nationwide, even worldwide, on calendars, postcards, and photo books. Much of its appeal is its drop-dead-gorgeous setting—a deeply indented harbor with parks, a waterfall, and a dramatic mountain backdrop. That harbor is a summerlong madhouse, jammed with dinghies, kayaks, windjammers, mega-yachts, minor yachts, and a handful of fishing craft.

Driven apart by a local squabble in 1891, Camden and Rockport have been separate towns for more than a century, but they're inextricably linked. They share school and sewer systems and an often-hyphenated partnership. On Union Street, just off Route 1, a white wooden arch reads *Camden* on one side and *Rockport* on the other. Rockport has

Greater Camden

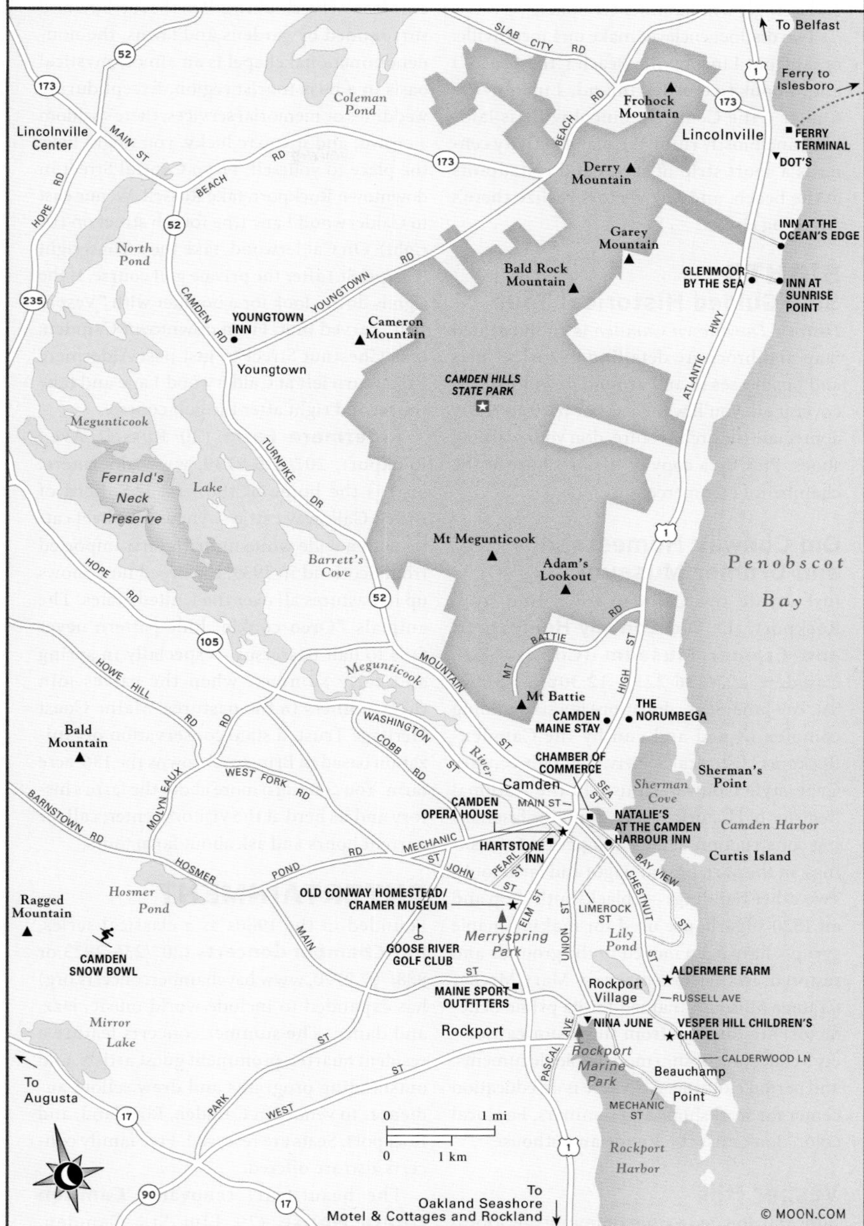

a much lower profile, and its harbor is relatively peaceful—with yachts, lobster boats, and a single windjammer schooner.

Two distinct enclaves make up Lincolnville: oceanfront Lincolnville Beach ("the Beach") and, about five miles inland, Lincolnville Center ("the Center"). Lincolnville is laid-back and mostly rural; the major activity center is a short strip of shops and restaurants at the beach, and few visitors realize there's anything else.

SIGHTS

Self-Guided Historical Tour

Historic Downtown Camden is an illustrated map and brochure detailing historical sites and businesses in and around downtown. To cover it all, you'll want a car or bike; to really appreciate the architecture, don your walking shoes. Pick up a copy of the brochure at the chamber of commerce.

Old Conway Homestead and Cramer Museum

Just inside the Camden town line from Rockport, the **Old Conway Homestead and Cramer Museum** (Conway Rd., Camden, 207/236-2257, 12:30pm-3:30pm Sat. late June-Sept., donation) is a six-building complex owned and run by the Camden-Rockport Historical Society. The 18th-century Cape-style Conway House, in the National Register of Historic Places, contains fascinating construction details and period furnishings; in the barn are carriages and farm tools. Two other buildings—a blacksmith shop and an 1820 sugarhouse used for making maple syrup—have been moved to the grounds and restored. In the contemporary Mary Meeker Cramer Museum (named for its prime benefactor) are displays from the historical society's collection of ship models, old documents, and period clothing. Also here is an education center for workshops and seminars. For local color, don't miss the Victorian outhouse.

Vesper Hill

Built and donated to the community by a local benefactor, the rustic open-air **Vesper Hill Children's Chapel** is dedicated to the world's children. Overlooking Penobscot Bay and surrounded by gardens and lawns, the nondenominational chapel is an almost mystical oasis in a busy tourist region. Except during weddings or memorial services, there's seldom a crowd, and if you're lucky, you might have the place to yourself. From Central Street in downtown Rockport, take Russell Avenue east to Calderwood Lane (the fourth street on the right). On Calderwood, take the second right (Chapel St.) after the private golf course. If the sign is down, look for a boulder with "Vesper Hill" carved in it. From downtown Camden, take Chestnut Street to just past Aldermere Farm; turn left at Calderwood Lane and take the second right after the golf course.

Aldermere Farm (20 Russell Ave., Rockport, 207/236-2739, www.aldermere.org) is the home of the first U.S. herd of Belted Galloway cattle—Angus-like beef cattle with a wide white midriff. First imported from Scotland in 1953, the breed now shows up in pastures all over the United States. The animals' "Oreo-cookie" hide pattern never fails to halt passersby—especially in spring and early summer, when the calves join their mothers in the pastures. Maine Coast Heritage Trust, a state conservation organization based in Brunswick, owns the 136-acre farm. You can learn more about the farm's history and its herd at the visitors center; call for current hours and ask about farm tours.

ENTERTAINMENT

Founded in the 1960s as a classical series, **Bay Chamber Concerts** (207/236-2823 or 888/707-2770, www.baychamberconcerts.org) has expanded to include world music, jazz, and dance. The summer concerts feature a resident quartet, prominent guest artists, and outstanding programs and draw sellout audiences to venues in Camden, Rockland, and Rockport. Seats are reserved. Free family concerts also are offered.

The beautifully renovated **Camden Opera House** (29 Elm St., Camden,

Wine-Tasting

The number of wineries is increasing throughout Maine, and they're especially concentrated in this region. Tour on your own, armed with maps and a passport from the **Maine Winery Guild** (www.mainewinetrail.com).

Draft horses power Brian Smith's **Oyster River Winegrowers** (929 Oyster River Rd., Warren, 207/542-0079, www.oysterriverwine.com, call for hours), a small farm with a vineyard and tasting room. Visit on pizza nights, held 5pm-8pm on Wednesdays during the summer.

More than 3,000 vines are growing on 32 acres at **Breakwater Vineyards** (35 Ash Point Dr., Owls Head, 207/594-1721, www.breakwatervineyard.com), where the tasting room is open noon-5pm Monday-Saturday during summer.

Head inland on Route 17 and then noodle off on the back roads to discover a pair of wineries. At **Sweetgrass Farm Winery and Distillery** (347 Carroll Rd., Union, 207/785-3024, www.sweetgrasswinery.com, 11am-5pm daily May 1-Dec. 31), owner Keith Bodine uses Maine-grown fruits to produce both wines and spirits. Bring a picnic to enjoy while hiking the winery's trails. Carroll Road is between Shepard Hill Road and North Union Road, both north of Route 17, west of Route 131.

Nearby is **Savage Oakes** (174 Barrett Hill Rd., Union, 207/785-5261, www.savageoakes.com, 11am-5pm daily May 1-Oct. 31, Fri.-Sun. Nov. 1-Dec. 25.), where Elmer and Holly Savage and their sons have added winemaking to their second-generation Belted Galloway cattle farm. They grow nine varieties of grapes, both red and white, and produce more than half a dozen wines. Barrett Hill Road is off Route 17 directly opposite Route 131 South.

Gaze out the back door of the **Cellardoor Vineyard** (367 Youngtown Rd., Lincolnville, 207/763-44778, www.mainewine.com, 11am-6pm Mon.-Sat., noon-6pm Sun. early May-mid-Oct., call for off-season hours) and it's possible to think you're in Sonoma Valley. Tucked in the folds of the rolling hills just inland of Lincolnville Beach, Cellardoor occupies a 200-year-old farmhouse and barn overlooking six acres of grapes. During the summer, free wine tours are offered at 2pm daily, and the retail shop offers free wine-tastings daily and food and wine pairings noon-3pm Sundays. You can pick up cheeses and other munchies for an impromptu picnic on the deck.

207/236-7963, box office 207/236-4884, www.camdenoperahouse.com) is the site of many performances by renowned entertainers.

The **Lincolnville Band**, one of the oldest town bands in the country, occasionally plays in the park's Bicentennial Bandstand, built to commemorate the town's 200th birthday.

Festivals and Events

One weekend in February is given over to the **Camden Conference**, an annual three-day foreign-affairs conference with nationally and internationally known speakers. Also in February, the **National Toboggan Championships** features two days of races and fun at the nation's only wooden toboggan chute at the Camden Snow Bowl.

The third Thursday of July is **House and Garden Day**, when you can take a self-guided tour (10am-4:30pm) of significant homes and gardens in Camden and Rockport. Proceeds benefit the Camden Garden Club. **HarborArts**, on the third weekend in July, draws dozens of artists and craftspeople displaying and selling their wares at the Camden Amphitheatre in Harbor Park.

Labor Day weekend is also known as **Windjammer Weekend**, with cruises, windjammer open houses, fireworks, and all kinds of live entertainment in and around Camden Harbor. In September, **Camden International Film Festival** takes place with venues in Camden, Rockland, and Rockport.

Dozens of artists and craftspeople display and sell their wares at the **Fall Festival and Arts and Crafts Show**, the first weekend in October at the Camden Amphitheatre in Harbor Park.

A who's who of entrepreneurs shows up

for the annual **PopTech** conference in late October.

Christmas by the Sea is a family-oriented early-December weekend featuring open houses, special sales, concerts, and a visit from Santa Claus.

SHOPPING

Books

The **Owl and Turtle Bookshop** (33 Bayview St., Camden, 207/230-7335) is a delightful independent bookstore. **Sherman's** (14 Main St., Camden, 207/236-2223), part of a small Maine chain, is an excellent source for books and a whole lot more.

If you want a good read at a great price, **Stone Soup Books** (33 Main St., Camden, no phone), a tiny second-floor shop across from the Lord Camden Inn, is Camden's best source for contemporary used fiction.

Art, Crafts, and Gifts

You'll need to wander the streets to take in all the gift and crafts shops, particularly in Camden. Some are obvious; others are tucked away on side streets and back alleys, so explore.

A downtown Camden landmark since 1940, the **Smiling Cow** (41 Main St., Camden, 207/236-3351) is as good a place as any to pick up Maine souvenirs—a few slightly kitschy, but most reasonably tasteful. Before or after shopping here, head for the rear balcony for coffee and a knockout view of the harbor and the Megunticook River waterfall.

The **Messler Gallery** (25 Mill St., Rockport, 207/594-5611), just off Route 90 and on the campus of the Center for Furniture Craftsmanship, presents rotating shows that focus on woodworking.

Professional boatbuilder Walt Simmons has branched out into decoys and wildlife carvings, and they're just as outstanding as his boats. Walt and his wife, Karen, run **Duck Trap Decoys** (Duck Trap Rd., Lincolnville, 207/789-5363), a gallery-shop that features the work of more than 60 other woodcarvers.

It's a lot easier to get soft, wonderful handwoven and hand-dyed **Swans Island Blankets** (2 Bayview St., Camden, 207/706-7926, and 231 Rte. 1, Northport, 207/338-9691) since the company moved its sales operation off the island near Mount Desert to the mainland, just 2.7 miles north of Lincolnville Beach.

RECREATION

Parks and Preserves

COASTAL MOUNTAINS LAND TRUST

Founded in 1986, the **Coastal Mountains Land Trust** (CMLT, 101 Mt. Battie St., Camden, 207/236-7091, www.coastalmountains.org) has preserved more than 10,000 acres. Maps and information about trails open to the public as well as information about guided hikes and other events are available on the website.

CMLT preserves more than 600 acres on 1,280-foot-high **Bald Mountain,** the fifth-highest peak on the Eastern Seaboard. The somewhat strenuous two-mile round-trip hike accesses the open summit ledges, with grand views over Penobscot Bay. Bald Mountain is home to rare subalpine plants and is a great spot to view migrating hawks in fall. From Route 1 at the southern end of town, take John Street for 0.8 mile. Turn left and go 0.2 mile to a fork. Continue on the left fork (Hosmer Pond Rd.) for two miles. Bear left onto Barnestown Road (passing the Camden Snow Bowl) and go 1.4 miles to the trailhead on the right, signposted Georges Highland Path Barnestown Access. The parking lot holds half a dozen cars. Maps are available in the box. The blue-blazed trail here is relatively easy, requiring just over an hour round-trip, and the summit views are spectacular, especially in fall. Carry a picnic and enjoy it at the top. Avoid this trail in late May-early June, when the blackflies take command, and dress appropriately during hunting season.

The views are almost as fine from the **Beech Hill Preserve**'s open summit, crowned with the Beech Nut, a stone hut dating from 1914, in Rockport. Choose from two trails: The trailhead for the 1.2-mile round-trip Woods Loop Trail is on the Beech Hill Road about a mile off Route 1 (turn across from Hoboken Gardens); the 1.5-mile out-and-back departs from a trailhead on Rockville Street, off Route 1 south of downtown Camden.

FERNALD'S NECK PRESERVE

Three miles of Megunticook Lake shoreline, groves of conifers, and a large swamp ("the Great Bog") are features of **Fernald's Neck Preserve,** on the Camden-Lincolnville line (and the Knox-Waldo County line). Shoreline and mountain views are stupendous, even more so during fall foliage season. The easiest trail is the 1.5-mile Blue Loop at the northern end of the preserve; from it, you can access the 1-mile Orange Loop. From the Blue Loop, take the 0.2-mile Yellow Trail offshoot to Balance Rock for a great view of the lake and hills. Some sections can be wet; wear boots or rubberized shoes, and use insect repellent. From Route 1 in Camden, take Route 52 (Mountain St.) 5.8 miles, bearing left on Fernald's Neck Road. Pick up a map-brochure at the trailhead register. A map is also available at the chamber of commerce office. Dogs are not allowed, and the preserve closes and the gate is locked at 7:30pm.

THE GEORGES RIVER LAND TRUST

A Rockland-based group, the **Georges River Land Trust** (207/594-5166, www.georgesriver.org), whose territory covers the Georges (St. George) River watershed, is the steward for the **Georges Highland Path,** a 50-mile low-impact footpath, with three non-contiguous sections and 11 trailheads. The trail stretches from St. George to Montville (west of Belfast), accessing Rockport and Camden from the back side of the surrounding hills.

★ CAMDEN HILLS STATE PARK

A five-minute drive and a small fee gets you to the top of Mount Battie, centerpiece of 5,650-acre **Camden Hills State Park** (Belfast Rd./Rte. 1, 207/236-3109, www.parksandlands.com, $4-6 adults, $1.50 seniors, $1 children 5-11) and the best place to understand why Camden is "where the mountains meet the sea." The summit panorama is breathtaking and reputedly the inspiration for Edna St. Vincent Millay's poem "Renascence" (a bronze plaque marks the spot); information boards identify the offshore islands. Climb the summit's stone tower for an even better view. The 20 miles of hiking trails (some for every ability) include two popular routes up Mount Battie—an easy hour-long hike from the base parking lot (Nature Trail) and a more strenuous 45-minute hike from the top of Mount Battie Street in Camden (Mount Battie Trail). Or drive up the paved Mount Battie Auto Road. The park has plenty of space for picnics. In winter, ice climbers use a rock wall near the Maiden's Cliff Trail, reached via Route 52 (Mountain St.). The park entrance is two miles north of downtown Camden. Request a free trail map. The park is open mid-May-mid-October, but hiking trails are accessible all year, weather permitting.

MERRYSPRING PARK

Straddling the Camden-Rockport boundary, **Merryspring Park** (31 Conway Rd., Camden, 207/236-2239, www.merryspring.org) is a magnet for nature lovers. More than a dozen well-marked trails wind through woodlands, berry thickets, and wildflowers; near the preserve's parking area are lily, rose, and herb gardens. Admission is free, but donations are welcome. Also free are family programs. Special programs (fee charged) include lectures, workshops, and demonstrations. The entrance is on Conway Road, 0.3 mile off Route 1, at the southern end of Camden. Trails are open dawn-dusk daily.

IN-TOWN PARKS

Just behind the Camden Public Library is the **Camden Amphitheatre** (also called the Bok Amphitheatre, after a local benefactor), a sylvan spot resembling a set for *A Midsummer Night's Dream* (which has been performed here). Concerts, weddings, and all kinds of

Islesboro Excursion

Lying three miles offshore from Lincolnville Beach, 20 minutes via car ferry, is 14-mile-long Islesboro, a year-round community with a population of about 600 that's beefed up annually by a sedate summer colony. Car ferries are frequent enough to make Islesboro an ideal day-trip destination, which is the choice of most visitors partly because food options are few and overnight lodging isn't available. The only camping is on nearby Warren Island State Park—and you have to have your own boat to get there.

The best way to get an island overview is to do an end-to-end auto or bike tour. Pick up an island map at the ferry terminal and explore, heading down to Dark Harbor and Town Beach at the island's bottom, then up to Pripet and Turtle Head at its top. You won't see all the huge "cottages" tucked down long driveways, and you won't absorb island life and its rhythms, but you'll scratch the surface of what Islesboro is about.

En route, you'll pass exclusive summer estates, workaday homes, spectacular seaside vistas, a smattering of shops, and the **Historical Society Museum** (388 Main St., 207/734-6733, www.islesborohistorical.org, call for hours). On the up-island circuit, watch for a tiny marker on the west side of the road (0.8 mile north of the Islesboro Historical Society building). It commemorates the 1780 total eclipse witnessed here—the first recorded in North America. At the time, British loyalists still held Islesboro, but they temporarily suspended hostilities, allowing Harvard astronomers to lug their instruments to the island and document the eclipse.

For nibbles and sips, duck into the **Dark Harbor Shop** (515 Pendleton Point Rd., 207/734-8857), the **Island Market** (113 Main Rd., 207/734-6672), **Durkee's General Store** (867 Main Rd., 207/734-2201) or **Bluewater Bakery** (103 Pendleton Point Rd., 207/734-6608) at the Islesboro Community Center, which is also home to **Art of the Isle Gift Shop** and the Wednesday-morning **Isleboro Farmers' Market**. For a good read, visit **Artisan Books & Bindery** (111 Derby Rd., 207/734-6852).

Allow time before the return ferry to visit the **Grindle Point Sailors' Memorial Museum** (www.townofislesboro.com), a town-owned museum filled with seafaring memorabilia and allegedly home to a benevolent ghost or two. It's in the keeper's house adjacent to **Grindle Point Light** (207/734-2253, www.lighthouse.cc/grindle), which was built in 1850, rebuilt in 1875, and is now automated.

The car ferry ***Margaret Chase Smith*** (207/789-5611, www.exploremaine.org) departs Lincolnville Beach almost every hour on the hour, 8am or 9am-5pm, and departs Islesboro on the half hour, 7:30am-4:30pm. Round-trip fares are $29.50 for a car with driver, $13 adults, $9 ages 6-17, $18 adult bicycles, and $14 kids' bikes. Reservations are $15 extra. A slightly reduced schedule prevails late October-early May. The 20-minute trip crosses a stunning three-mile stretch of Penobscot Bay, with views of islands and the Camden Hills. In summer, avoid the biggest bottlenecks: Friday afternoon (to Islesboro) and Sunday afternoon and Monday holiday afternoons (from Islesboro). The *Smith* remains on Islesboro overnight, so don't miss the last run to Lincolnville Beach. Also providing scheduled and charter transportation is **Quicksilver Water Shuttle** (207/557-0197, http://quicksilvermaine.com, from $10 pp).

other events take place in the park. Across Atlantic Avenue, sloping to the harbor, is **Camden Harbor Park,** with benches, a couple of monuments, and some of the best waterfront views in town. The noted landscape firm of Frederick Law Olmsted designed the park in 1931, and it is listed in the National Register of Historic Places.

Rockport's in-town parks include **Marine Park,** off Pascal Avenue, at the head of the harbor; **Walker Park,** on Sea Street, on the west side of the harbor; **Mary-Lea Park,** overlooking the harbor next to the Rockport Opera House; and **Cramer Park,** alongside the Goose River just west of Pascal Avenue. At Marine Park are the remnants of 19th-century limekilns, an antique steam engine, picnic tables, a boat launch, and a polished granite sculpture of André, a harbor seal adopted by a local family in the early 1960s. André had been honorary harbormaster, ring bearer at weddings, and the subject of several books and a film—and even did the honors at the unveiling of his statue—before he was fatally wounded in a mating skirmish in 1986 at the age of 25.

CURTIS ISLAND

Marking the entrance to Camden Harbor is town-owned **Curtis Island,** with a 26-foot automated light tower and adjoining keeper's house facing into the bay. Once known as Negro Island, it's a sight made for photo ops; the views are stunning in every direction. A kayak or dinghy will get you out to the island, where you can picnic (take water; there are no facilities), wander around, gather berries, or just watch the passing fleet. Land on the Camden (west) end of the island, allowing for the tide change when you beach your boat. Respect the privacy of the keeper's house in summer; it's occupied by volunteer caretakers.

AVENA BOTANICALS MEDICINAL HERB GARDEN

Visitors are welcome at Deb Soule's **Avena Botanicals Medicinal Herb Garden** (219 Mill St., Rockport, 207/594-0694, www.avenabotanicals.com, noon-5pm Mon.-Fri., free), part of an herbal and healing-arts teaching center. More than 150 different medicinal herbs and plants are grown on three organic, biodynamic acres. Pick up a garden map and guide at the entrance, then stroll the paths, meditate on benches, and simply relax. Mill Street is just shy of a mile south of the intersection of Routes 17 and 90 in West Rockport. Check the schedule for guided garden walks ($7) led by Deb Soule. These usually occur twice weekly.

Camden Snow Bowl

More than an alpine ski area, town-owned **Camden Snow Bowl** (20 Barnestown Rd., 207/236-3438, www.camdensnowbowl.com) is a four-season recreation area with tennis courts, public swimming and paddling in Hosmer Pond, and biking and hiking trails, as well as alpine trails for day and night skiing and riding, and Maine's only toboggan chute. The hill is small, but you get glimpses of island-studded Penobscot Bay when descending the trails.

Outfitters

Maine Sport Outfitters (115 Rte. 1, Rockport, and 24 Main St., Camden, 207/236-7120, www.mainesport.com) is a destination for anyone interested in outdoor recreation. The knowledgeable staff can lend a hand and steer you in almost any direction for almost any summer or winter sport. The store sells and rents canoes, kayaks, bikes, SUPs, skis, and tents, plus all the relevant clothing and accessories.

Maine Sport Outdoor School (207/236-8797), a division of Maine Sport, has a full schedule of canoeing, kayaking, hiking, and camping trips. A two-hour guided Camden Harbor tour costs $45 adults, $40 ages 10-15. A four-hour guided harbor-to-harbor tour (Rockport to Camden) is $95 adults, $85 children, including a picnic lunch. Multiday instructional programs and tours are available. The store is 0.5 mile north of the junction of Routes 1 and 90. Bicycle rentals begin at $25/day, calm-water canoes and kayaks are $30-40/day, sea kayaks are $45/day single, $55/day tandem, and SUPs are $55/day.

Orvis-endorsed Maine Master Guide Don Kleiner's **Maine Outdoors** (207/785-4496, www.maineoutdoors.biz, from $375/half day) knows not only the outdoors, but also where to find the fish. He offers fully outfitted bass-fishing trips for serious anglers as well as introductory options for families. Don also offers guided nature exploration expeditions delving into wildlife, geography, history, and the environment at the same rate. Options include canoe exploration, coastal Maine boat trips, eagle watching, and custom adventures.

Paddle Sports

Ducktrap Kayak (2175 Rte. 1, Lincolnville

1

2

Beach, 207/236-8608, www.ducktrapkayak.com) rents sea kayaks ($35-65) and SUPs ($40-80), with rates depending on the type and size; delivery can be arranged.

If you have your own boat, good saltwater launch sites include Eaton Point, at the end of Sea Street in Camden, and Marine Park in Rockport. For freshwater paddling, put in at Megunticook Lake, both its west and east sides; Bog Bridge on Route 105, about 3.5 miles from downtown Camden; Barrett's Cove on Route 52, also about 3.5 miles from Camden; or in Lincolnville's Norton Pond. You can even paddle all the way from the head of Norton Pond to the foot of Megunticook Lake, but use care navigating the drainage culvert between the two.

Swimming

FRESHWATER

The Camden area is blessed with several locales for freshwater swimming—a real boon, since Penobscot Bay can be mighty chilly, even at summer's peak. **Shirttail Point,** with limited parking, is a small sandy area on the Megunticook River. It's shallow enough for young kids and has picnic tables and a play area. From Route 1 in Camden, take Route 105 (Washington Street) 1.4 miles; watch for a small sign on the right. **Barrett's Cove,** on Megunticook Lake, has more parking spaces, though usually more swimmers, and restrooms, picnic tables, and grills as well as a play area. Diagonally opposite the Camden Public Library, take Route 52 (Mountain St.) about three miles; watch for the sign on the left. To cope with the parking crunch on hot summer days, bike to the beaches. You'll be ready for a swim after the uphill stretches, and it's all downhill on the way back.

Lincolnville has several ponds (some would call them lakes). On Route 52 in Lincolnville Center is Breezemere Park, a small town-owned swimming and picnic area on **Norton Pond.** Other Lincolnville options are **Coleman Pond, Pitcher Pond,** and **Knight's Pond.**

SALTWATER

The region's best ocean swimming is at **Lincolnville Beach,** where Penobscot Bay flirts with Route 1 on a sandy stretch of shorefront in the congested hamlet of Lincolnville Beach. On a hot day, the sand is wall-to-wall people; during one of the coast's legendary nor'easters, it's quite a wild place.

Another place for an ocean dip is **Laite Beach Park,** on Bay View Street about 1.5 miles from downtown Camden. It edges Camden Harbor and has a strip of sand, picnic tables, a playground, a float, and a children's amphitheater.

In Rockport, dip your toes into the ocean at **Walker Park,** tucked away on the west side of the harbor. From Pascal Avenue, take Elm Street, which becomes Sea Street. Walker Park is on the left, with picnic tables, a play area, and a small pebbly beach.

Golf

On a back road straddling the Camden-Rockport line, the nine-hole **Goose River Golf Club** (50 Park St., Rockport, 207/236-8488) competes with the best for outstanding scenery.

Day Sails and Excursions

Most day sails and excursion boats operate late May-October, with fewer trips in the spring and fall than in July-August. You can't compare a two-hour day sail to a weeklong cruise on a Maine windjammer, but at least you get a hint of what could be—and it's a far better choice for kids, who aren't allowed on most windjammer cruises.

The classic wooden schooner ***Olad*** (207/236-2323, www.maineschooners.com, $45 adults, $35 under age 13) makes several two-hour sails daily from Camden's Public Landing, weather permitting, late May-mid-October. Captain Aaron Lincoln is a Rockland native, so he's got the local scoop on all the sights.

1: Camden's harbor **2:** Camden Snow Bowl

The 49-passenger ***Appledore*** (207/994-8402, www.appledore2.com), built in 1978 for round-the-world cruising, sails from Bay View Landing beginning around 10am three or four times daily June-October. Most cruises last two hours and cost $40 adults, $25 children. Cocktails, wine, and soft drinks are available.

Over in Rockport, the schooner ***Heron*** (207/236-8605 or 800/599-8605, www.woodenboatco.com) is a 65-foot John Alden-designed wooden yacht launched in 2003. Sailing options include educational eco-tours and sunset happy hour sails ($50 adults, $28 under age 13).

If time is short, Camden Harbor Cruises (207/236-6672, www.camdenharborcruises.com, $30-50 adults, $20-26 ages 2-12) offers a variety of cruises, ranging from one hour to three hours aboard the classic motor launch ***Lively Lady,*** operating from the Public Landing.

Climbing

Scale the cliffs rising above Camden with **Atlantic Climbing School** (207/288-2521, www.climbacadia.com), with half- and full-day options for all ability levels. Rates begin at $80 per half day for a family of four.

FOOD

Quick Bites

ROCKPORT

For health foods, homeopathic remedies, and fresh seasonal produce, pop into **Fresh Off the Farm** (495 Commercial St./Rte. 1, 207/236-3260, 8am-7pm Mon.-Sat., 9am-5:30pm Sun.), an inconspicuous red-painted roadside place that looks like an overgrown farm stand (which it is). Watch for one of those permanent-temporary signs highlighting the latest arrivals, which might include native blueberries or local corn. The shop is 1.3 miles south of the junction of Routes 1 and 90.

At the southern Rockport town line, a sprawling red building is the home of the **Rockport Marketplace and the State of Maine Cheese Company** (461 Commercial St./Rte. 1, 207/236-8895, 9am-6pm Mon.-Sat.). Inside are locally made varieties of cows' milk hard cheeses, all named after Maine locations, as well as hundreds of Maine-made products, from food to crafts.

CAMDEN

The **Camden Farmers Market** (3:30pm-6pm Wed. June-late Sept. and 9am-noon Sat. early May-late Oct.) holds forth at 116 Washington Street.

Made-to-order sandwiches and wraps, homemade soups, veggie burgers, and baked goods are the draws at the **Camden Deli** (37 Main St., 207/236-8343, www.camdendeli.com, 7am-9pm daily), in the heart of downtown, but its biggest asset is the windowed seating overlooking the Megunticook River waterfall. The view doesn't get much better than this (go upstairs for the best angle).

Since the early 1970s, **Scott's Place** (85 Elm St./Rte. 1, 207/236-8751, 10:30am-4pm Mon.-Fri., 10:30am-3pm Sat.), a roadside lunch stand near Renys at the Camden Marketplace, has been dishing up inexpensive burgers and dogs, nowadays adding veggie burgers and salads.

Peek behind the old-fashioned facade at **Boynton-McKay Food Company** (30 Main St., 207/236-2465, http://boynton-mckay.com, 7am-2pm Tues.-Sat., 8am-1pm Sun.) and you'll see an old-fashioned soda fountain, early-20th-century tables, antique pharmacy accessories, and a thoroughly modern café menu. Restored and rehabbed in 1997, Boynton-McKay had been *the* local drugstore for more than a century. The new incarnation features great breakfasts, creative salads and sandwiches, homemade soups, and an espresso bar.

Facing downtown Camden's five-way intersection, **French and Brawn** (1 Elm St., 207/236-3361, 6am-8pm Mon.-Sat., 8am-8pm Sun.) is an independent market that earns the description *super.* Ready-made sandwiches, soups, and other goodies complement the oven-ready take-out meals, high-calorie frozen desserts, esoteric meats, and staff with a can-do attitude.

Before or after hiking in Camden Hills State Park, pop over to **Mount Battie Take Out** (247 Rte. 1, 207/236-6122, 11:30am-7pm Wed.-Mon.) for decent seafood, sandwiches, and ice cream at a fair price.

LINCOLNVILLE

Need a sandwich before heading for the hills or beach? **Dot's** (2457 Rte. 1, 207/706-7922, 7am-5:30pm Mon.-Sat., 8am-3pm Sun.) is the place. It also bakes breakfast goods and treats, makes salads and prepared meals, and sells cheeses and wines. There's seating inside.

Local chef Annemarie Ahearn's oceanfront **Salt Water Farm** (25 Woodward Hill Rd., 207/230-0966, www.saltwaterfarm.com) is a haven for serious foodies. Hands-on cooking classes (around $185 for a four-hour class) and multiday workshops are offered.

The pastries, tarts, pies, strudels, cakes, and breads from the **Red Barn Baking Co.** (2060 Atlantic Hwy./Rte. 1, 207/2301272, 8am-4pm Wed.-Sun.) are alone worth the stop, but the location doubles as the site of a multi-vendor antiques marketplace.

The restored **Lincolnville General Store** (209 Main St., Lincolnville, 207/763-4411, www.lincolnvillegeneral.com, 7am-7pm daily), owned by Phish drummer Jon Fishman and his wife, Briar, offers delicious wood-oven pizzas, hot entrée and salad bars, baked goods, sandwiches, and more.

Casual Dining

ROCKPORT

Dine inside or on the harbor-view patio at **18 Central Oyster Bar & Grill** (28 Central St., 207/466-9055, www.18central.com, from 5pm Thurs.-Tues., $16-34). The well-prepared American menu always includes a vegetarian choice.

Cookbook author and chef Sara Jenkins made a name for herself in Manhattan before returning to Maine in 2016 to open ★ **Nina June** (24 Central St., 207/236-8880, www.ninajunerestaurant.com, 5:30pm-9pm Mon.-Sat., $22-30), a casual Mediterranean trattoria serving rave-worthy fare at reasonable prices. Aim for a seat on the back deck, with views over the harbor, or snag one at the counter to watch the chefs at work in the open kitchen. The menu changes frequently to reflect what's fresh and local.

CAMDEN

The word is out about **Long Grain** (20 Washington St., 207/236-9001, www.longgraincamden.com, 11:30am-2:45pm and 4:30pm-9pm Tues.-Sat., $14-18), a tiny restaurant that's earned kudos and Beard nominations for its outstanding and authentic Pan-Asian cuisine. Flavors are fresh, complex, and layered, and presentation is gorgeous. Make reservations.

Go for the happy hour specials (4pm-6pm daily) at **40 Paper Italian Bistro & Bar** (40 Washington St., 207/230-0111, www.40paper.com, from 4pm Mon.-Sat., $15-30), located in the renovated Knox Mill. Then maybe stick around for the handmade pastas, flatbread pizzas, and other Italian fare.

The **Waterfront Restaurant** (Bay View St., 207/236-3747, www.waterfrontcamden.com, 11:30am-9pm daily, $18-30) has a huge waterside dining deck in town, but you'll need to arrive early to snag one of the tables. Lunches are the most fun, overlooking lots of harbor action; at high tide, you're eye-to-eye with the boats. Most folks rave about the place, but I've found it inconsistent.

For globally inspired, innovative fare, dine at **Fresh & Co.** (1 Bay View Landing, 207/236-7005, www.freshcamden.com, from 5pm Thurs.-Tues, $14-31), which offers small and large plates as well as indoor and outdoor seating.

Fine Dining

CAMDEN

Reservations are a must for the intimate restaurant at the ★ **Hartstone Inn** (41 Elm St., 207/236-4259 or 800/788-4823, www.hartstoneinn.com, 5:30pm-8:30pm daily, $23-30). Michael Salmon, named Caribbean chef of the year when he lived in Aruba, has cooked at the Beard House by invitation. Even Julia Child dined here. The menu changes weekly to use the freshest ingredients. The nightly chef's tasting menu is $55.

Since opening in 2007 to rave reviews, ★ **Natalie's at Camden Harbour Inn** (83 Bayview St., 207/236-7008, www.nataliesrestaurant.com, 5pm-9:30pm daily in season, call off-season, $21-33) has become one of the state's top tables. The dining room was designed to be reminiscent of the Left Bank in Paris a century ago; instead of looking out at the Seine, you're gazing over Camden Harbor. The ambience is fancy here, but resort-casual attire is fine. Fare is modern New England fine dining; options include a four-course fixed price menu ($94, wine pairings available) and an à la carte menu.

LINCOLNVILLE

For a romantic, classic French experience, head a few miles inland to **Youngtown Inn and Restaurant** (581 Youngtown Rd., 207/763-4290 or 800/291-8438, www.youngtowninn.com, from 5:30pm daily, closed Mon. in Aug., $27-34), where chef-owner Manuel Mercier draws on his Parisian heritage and European training. The best deal is the four-course chef's menu ($50). Upstairs are six guest rooms ($200-225, includes breakfast).

ACCOMMODATIONS

Many of Camden's most attractive accommodations (especially bed-and-breakfasts) are on Route 1 (variously disguised as Elm Street, Main Street, and High Street), which is heavily trafficked in summer. If you're sensitive to noise, request a room facing away from the street.

Camden

INNS AND BED-AND-BREAKFASTS

A dozen of Camden's finest bed-and-breakfasts have banded together in the **Camden Bed and Breakfast Association** (www.camdeninns.com), with an attractive brochure and website. Some of them are described here.

The ★ **Hartstone Inn** (41 Elm St., Rte. 1, 207/236-4259 or 800/788-4823, www.hartstoneinn.com, $144-304) is Michael and Mary Jo Salmon's imposing mansard-roofed Victorian close to the heart of downtown. Once inside, you're away from it all. Even more removed are guest rooms in two other buildings under the Hartstone's umbrella. Suites in the Manor House, tucked behind the main inn, have contemporary decor. Guest rooms and suites in the Hideaway, in a residential neighborhood about a block away, have country-French flair. All are elegant; some have fireplaces and whirlpools. And then there's the incredible breakfast. If you get hooked, the Salmons organize culinary classes during the winter, and you can even arrange for a one-on-one cooking experience with Michael. The couple also own Icelandic horses, stabled in South Thomaston, and offer an introductory riding experience.

Opened to guests in 1901, the **Whitehall Inn** (52 High St./Rte. 1, 207/236-3391 or 800/789-6565, www.whitehallmaine.com, from $199) received a head-to-toe renovation and updating when it debuted as a member of the Lark Hotels group in 2015. Lovely gardens, rockers on the veranda, a tennis court, and attentive service all add to the appeal of this historic country inn, famed for its connection to local poet Edna St. Vincent Millay, who first recited her poem "Renascence" to Whitehall guests in 1912. The 36 guest rooms are decorated in neutrals with eye-popping color accents; a few share baths.

Janis and Peter Kesser are the fifth innkeepers at the **Camden Maine Stay** (22 High St./Rte. 1, 207/236-9636, www.mainestay.com, from $200). Like their predecessors, they do everything right, from the comfortable yet elegant decor to the delicious breakfasts and afternoon snacks to the welcoming window candles and garden retreats. The handsome residence, built in 1802, faces busy Route 1 and is just a bit uphill from downtown, but inside and out back, behind the carriage house and barn, you'll feel worlds away.

Three downtown boutique hotels are under the same ownership, and each welcomes dogs in some rooms for $35/night, including a bed, biscuits, bowls, and local dog info. In the heart of downtown Camden, the 36-room **Lord Camden Inn** (24 Main St./Rte. 1, 207/236-4325 or 800/336-4325, www.lordcamdeninn.com, from $215) occupies a historic four-story building (with an elevator). Top-floor rooms have harbor-view balconies. Rates include a breakfast buffet. The luxurious, 10-room Shingle-style **Grand Harbor Inn** (14 Bay View Landing, 877/553-6997, www.grandharborinn.com, from $335) provides a front-row seat on Camden's busy harbor. Perks include 24-hour concierge, evening turndown, and a room-service deluxe continental breakfast. Sited in a renovated 100-year-old industrial building, the 21-room **16 Bay View Hotel** (16 Bay View St., 844/213-7990, http://16bayview.com, from $280) also courts luxury-seeking guests. Some rooms and suites on the upper floor have views over Camden Harbor. A buffet breakfast is included. Vintage, the in-house lounge, offers cocktails and small plates. In summer, the rooftop lounge, the View, delivers on its name.

After years of neglect, Camden's castle, the **Norumbega** (63 High St., 207/236-4646, www.norumbegainn.com, from $319) has been returned to its former opulence by owners Sue Walser and Phil Crispo, but this time, they promise, there's no pretentiousness. Eleven spacious, air-conditioned guest rooms and two suites, some with balconies and terraces, many with panoramic ocean views, are on three floors of this turreted stone mansion by the sea. Phil, a former chef instructor at the Culinary Institute of America and winner on *Chopped,* makes the three-course breakfasts. Multicourse tasting dinners ($95) are available; call for details.

A Relais & Châteaux member, the 1874 **Camden Harbour Inn** (83 Bayview St., 207/236-4200 or 800/236-4200, www.camdenharbourinn.com, from $645) is a boutique bed-and-breakfast complete with 21st-century amenities. It retains the bones of a 19th-century summer hotel, but the decor is contemporary European, with worldly accent pieces and velour furnishings in purples, reds, and silvers. Guest rooms, some with fireplaces, patios, decks, or balconies, have at least a glimpse of Camden's harbor or Penobscot Bay. Service is five-star, right down to chocolates and slippers at turndown. At breakfast, which is included, the menu includes choices such as lobster Benedict as well as a buffet with fresh-baked items, smoked salmon, and other goodies. Snacks are always available. The restaurant, Natalie's, is top-notch. The Dutch owners also speak German, some French, and rudimentary Indonesian and Thai.

MOTELS

The easy-on-the-budget, two-story **Towne Motel** (68 Elm St., Rte. 1, 207/236-3377, www.camdenmotel.com, $124-154) is an easy walk to downtown shops and restaurants. A homemade continental breakfast is provided. One studio is pet friendly.

It's a short stroll into Merryspring Gardens from the 37-room, pet-friendly **Cedar Crest Motel** (115 Elm St./Rte. 1, 207/236-4839, www.cedarcrestinnmaine.com, $150-170), a nicely maintained older property on 3.5 wooded and landscaped acres on the southern edge of downtown Camden. On the premises are an outdoor heated pool, playground, and laundry. A deluxe continental breakfast is included in season. Pet-friendly rooms are $20/night.

CAMPING

Camden Hills State Park (Belfast Rd./Rte. 1, 207/236-3109, $35-45 nonresidents, $25-35 Maine residents) has 112 sites, some with water and electricity, and is wheelchair-accessible. Pets are allowed, showers are free, and the sites are large.

Rockport

MOTELS AND COTTAGE COLONIES

Clean rooms, a convenient location, lovely ocean views from most rooms, and reasonable prices have made the Beale family's **Ledges by the Bay** (930 Rte. 1, Glen Cove, 207/594-8944, www.ledgesbythebay.com, $135-190) motel a favorite among budget-conscious travelers. Most guest rooms have private balconies. Other pluses include a private shorefront, small heated pool, and continental breakfast. Kids 13 and younger stay free in their parents' room.

The all-suites **Country Inn** (8 Country Inn Way/Rte. 1, 207/236-2725 or 888/707-3945, www.countryinnmaine.com, $189-250) is an especially good choice for families thanks to an indoor pool, play areas, a guest laundry, and a small fitness room. Rooms are divided between a main inn and cottage suites. A breakfast buffet and afternoon sweets are included. Pet-friendly rooms are available, $15/night.

Lincolnville

INNS

Private, secluded, and surrounded by 22 acres of woods and gardens, the oceanfront, Shingle-style ★ **Inn at the Ocean's Edge** (Rte. 1, Lincolnville Beach, 207/236-0945, www.innatoceansedge.com, from $339) invites splurging. Most of the spacious rooms have superb ocean views. The grounds are lovely, with lounge chairs placed just so to take in the views and a path to the pebbly shorefront. Amenities include an outdoor, heated, disappearing-edge pool that makes it seem as if you're almost in the ocean, a hot tub, massage service, a sauna, and a fitness room. Rates include a full breakfast and afternoon snacks.

Even more private and secluded is the **Inn at Sunrise Point** (55 Sunrise Point Rd., Lincolnville, 207/236-7716 or 800/435-6278, www.sunrisepoint.com, from $495), an elegant oceanfront retreat with all the bells and whistles you'd expect at these rates. The three handsome rooms in the main house, five separate cottages, and four rooms in the Garden House are all named after Maine authors or artists. Breakfast in the conservatory is divine.

MOTEL AND COTTAGES

A family-run gem, the **Ducktrap Motel** (12 Whitney Rd., Lincolnville, 207/789-5400, www.ducktrapmotel.com, $120-160) is set back from Route 1 and screened by trees. Both the grounds and the rooms are meticulously maintained. Also available are a one-bedroom and a two-bedroom cottage ($150-210). Evenings around the fire pit with music and marshmallows are a highlight.

On 12 hillside acres rolling down to the oceanfront, **Glenmoor by the Sea** (2143 Atlantic Hwy./Rte. 1, 207/236-7905, www.glenmoorbythesea.com, $170-299) is a destination in itself, with 19 cottages and 14 rooms, all recently renovated, two heated outdoor pools, and a nice lawn for activities. Other pluses include an oceanfront deck, tennis court, exercise room, fire pit, and a guest laundry. The motel rooms are close to Route 1, and noise may be a problem; opt for a cottage near the water if you can. A continental breakfast is included. Dogs are allowed in some rooms for $25 per pet/night.

The family-run **Mount Battie Motel** (2158 Atlantic Hwy./Rte. 1, Lincolnville, 207/236-3870 or 800/224-3870, www.mountbattie.com, $170-250) is an environmentally sensitive property with 22 charming motel-style guest rooms, some with water views. The continental breakfast includes home-baked treats.

INFORMATION AND SERVICES

For planning, contact the **Penobscot Bay Regional Chamber of Commerce** (207/236-4404 or 800/223-5459, www.mainedreamvacation.com). Also handy is a map and guide published by the **Lincolnville Business Group** (www.visitlincolnville.com).

Find **public restrooms** in Camden at the Public Landing, near the chamber of commerce, and at the Camden Public Library; in Rockport at Marine Park; and in Lincolnville at the ferry terminal.

GETTING THERE AND AROUND

Camden is about eight miles or 15 minutes via Route 1 from Rockland. It's about 6 miles or 10 minutes via Route 1 from Lincolnville or about 20 miles or 30 minutes via Route 1 from Belfast.

Belfast

Belfast (pop. 6,668) is one of those off-the-beaten-track destinations popular with tuned-in travelers. Chalk that up to its status as a magnet for leftover back-to-the-landers and enough artistic types to earn the city a nod for cultural cool. Belfast has a curling club, a food co-op, a green store, meditation centers, an increasing number of art galleries and boutiques, dance and theater companies, the oldest shoe store in the country, and half a dozen different 12-step, self-help groups. There's a festival nearly every weekend during the summer. It even has a poet laureate.

This eclectic city is a work in progress, a study in Maine-style diversity. It's also a gold mine of Federal, Greek Revival, Italianate, and Victorian architecture. Take the time to stroll the well-planned back streets, explore the shops, and hang out at the gussied-up waterfront.

Separating Belfast from East Belfast, the Passagassawakeag River (puh-sag-gus-uh-WAH-keg) fortunately is known more familiarly as "the Passy." The Indian name has been translated as both "place of many ghosts" and the rather different "place for spearing sturgeon by torchlight." You choose. No matter, you can cross it via a pedestrian bridge.

Many travelers make Belfast a day stop on their way from Camden to Bar Harbor. Truly, Belfast is worth more time than that. Spend a full day or two here and it's likely you'll be charmed, like many of the other urban refugees, into resettling here.

SIGHTS

Historic Walking Tours

No question, the best way to appreciate Belfast's fantastic architecture is to tour by ankle express. At the Belfast Area Chamber of Commerce, pick up the well-researched *Belfast Historic Walking Tour* map-brochure. Among more than 40 highlights on the mile-long self-guided route are the 1818 Federal-style **First Church,** handsome residences on **High Street** and **Church Street,** and the 1840 **James P. White House** (Church St. and Northport Ave.), now an elegant bed-and-breakfast and New England's finest Greek Revival residence. Amazingly for a community of this size, the city has three distinct districts listed in the National Register of Historic Places: Belfast Commercial Historic District (47 downtown buildings), Church Street Historic District (residential), and Primrose Hill Historic District (also residential). Another walking tour is presented by the Belfast Historical Society's **Museum in the Streets,** comprising two large panels and 30 smaller ones highlighting historical buildings and people. Signs are in English and French.

Bayside

Continuing the focus on architecture, just south of Belfast in Northport is the Victorian enclave of Bayside, a neighborhood-y sort of place with small, well-kept gingerbread-trimmed cottages cheek-by-jowl on pint-size lots. Formerly known as the Northport Wesleyan Grove Campground, the village took shape in the mid-1800s as a summer retreat for Methodists. In the 1930s, the retreat was disbanded and the main meeting hall was razed, creating the waterfront park at the heart of the village. Today, many of the colorfully painted homes are rented by the week, month, or summer season, and their tenants are more likely to indulge in athletic rather than religious pursuits. The camaraderie remains, though, and a stroll (or cycle or drive) through Bayside is like a visit to another era. Bayside is four miles south of Belfast, just east of Route 1. If you want to join the fun, try **Bayside Cottage Rentals** (539 Bluff Rd., Northport, 207/338-5355, www.baysidecottagerentals.com).

Temple Heights

Continue south on Shore Road from Bayside to **Temple Heights Spiritualist Camp** (Shore Rd., Northport, 207/338-3029, www.templeheightscamp.org), yet another religious enclave—this one still going. Founded in 1882, Temple Heights has become a shadow of its former self, reduced primarily to the funky 12-room Nikawa Lodge on Shore Road ($50, shared bath, some with ocean views), but the summer program continues thanks to prominent mediums from all over the country. Camp programs mid-June-early September are open to the public; a schedule is published each spring. Spiritualist church services and group healing circles are by donation; Saturday-morning workshops are $30. Better yet, sign up for a 1.5-hour or longer **group message circle** ($20), when you'll sit with a medium and a dozen or so others and receive insights—often uncannily on target—from departed relatives or friends; reservations are requested, and you should plan to arrive a half hour early. Private half-hour readings can be arranged for $50.

Belfast & Moosehead Railroad

The nonprofit Brooks Preservation Society operates the **Belfast & Moosehead Railroad** (207/722-3899, www.brookspreservation.org), which rolls through the inland countryside west of Belfast. The one-hour trips ($16 adults, $6 ages 3-12) aboard vintage trains depart from the **City Point Station** (13 Oak Hill Rd., Belfast); call for the current schedule, which may include options such as pizza or cider-and-doughnuts trains. Also offered are **RailCycle** tours, during which you'll pedal a tandem single-speed bike built specifically for the rails; enclosed footwear is required. Each railcycle holds two people; $30 per cycle or $15 shared with guide.

ENTERTAINMENT

It's relatively easy to find nightlife in Belfast—not only are there theaters and a cinema, but there are usually a couple of bars open at least until midnight and sometimes later. Some spots also feature live music, particularly on weekends. A good source for listings is Belfast Creative Coalition (www.belfastcreativecoalition.org).

If you don't feel like searching out a newspaper to check the entertainment listings, just go to the **Belfast Co-op Store** (123 High St., 207/338-2532) and study the bulletin board. You'll find notices for more activities than you could ever squeeze into your schedule.

Open-mic nights, jazz jams, classes, and lectures pepper the calendar for **Waterfall Arts** (265 High St., 207/338-2222, www.waterfallarts.org).

Two local theater groups stage productions in various venues: the **Belfast Maskers** (207/338-9668, www.belfastmaskers.com) and **Cold Comfort Theater** (207/930-7244, www.coldcomforttheater.com).

The Belfast Garden Club sponsors **Open Garden Days** (www.belfastgardenclub.org) once a week throughout the summer at the homes of club members and friends in and around Belfast. Gardens are usually open 10am-3pm rain or shine; a $5 pp donation is requested to benefit local beautification projects. Check local newspapers or ask at the chamber of commerce for the schedule.

Catch a flick at the restored 1930 art deco **Colonial Theater** (163 High St., 207/338-1930, http://colonialtheater.com).

Festivals and Events

Belfast is a hotbed of events, with a festival scheduled nearly every weekend during the summer.

In early July, soon after the Fourth of July, the **Arts in the Park** festival gets underway at Heritage Park, on the Belfast waterfront. It's a weekend event with two days of music, juried arts and crafts, children's activities, and lots of food booths.

Cheese-rolling, Highland games, and music are just a few of the activities at the midsummer **Maine Celtic Celebration.** In October, the **Belfast Poetry Festival** pairs poets with artists for workshops and readings.

SHOPPING

It's easy and fun to shop in downtown Belfast, which has so far managed to keep the big boxes away. Downtown shops reflect the city's population, with galleries and boutiques, thrift and used-goods stores, and eclectic shops, including a number specializing in books: new, used, and antiquarian. During **Fourth Friday Art Walks** (www.belfastcreativecoalition.org), 5:30pm-8pm May-September, more than a dozen galleries along with street performers and more welcome shoppers.

Specialty Shops

Even if shoes aren't on your shopping list, stop in at "the oldest shoe store in America." Founded in the 1830s, **Colburn Shoe Store** (81 Main St., 207/338-1934 or 877/338-1934) may be old, but it isn't old-fashioned, and it has a bargain basement.

Brambles (2 Cross St., 207/338-3448) is a gardener's delight, with fun, whimsical, and practical garden-themed merchandise.

Left Bank Books (109 Church St., 207/338-9009) is one of those wonderful bookstores that not only has a well-curated selection, but also presents readings and signings.

Seeking an out-of-print treasure or a focused tome? **Old Professor's Bookshop** (99 Main St., 207/338-2006) specializes in new, used, and rare books that answer the big questions: What is? And what matters?

Calling itself a "general store for the 21st century," the **Green Store** (71 Main St., 207/338-4045) carries a huge selection of environmentally friendly products. Whether you're thinking of going off the grid, need a composting toilet, or just want natural-fiber clothing or other natural-living products, this is the place. A very knowledgeable staff can answer nearly any question on environmentally sustainable lifestyles.

About two miles east of Belfast's bridge is the small roadside shop and gorgeous backyard garden of **Mainely Pottery** (181 Searsport Ave./Rte. 1, 207/338-1108). Since 1988, Jeannette Faunce and Jamie Oates have been marketing the work of more than two dozen Maine potters, each with different techniques, glazes, and styles. It's the perfect place to select from a wide range of reasonably priced work.

RECREATION

Parks

Belfast is rich in parks and picnic spots. One of the state's best municipal parks is just on the outskirts of downtown. Established in 1904, **Belfast City Park** (87 Northport Ave., 207/338-1661, free) has lighted tennis courts, an outdoor pool, a pebbly beach, plenty of picnic tables, an unusually creative playground, lots of green space for the kids, and fantastic views of Islesboro, Blue Hill, and Penobscot Bay. For more action right in the heart of Belfast, head for **Heritage Park,** at the bottom of Main Street, with front-row seats on waterfront happenings. Bring a picnic, grab a table, and watch the yachts, tugs, and lobster boats. Every street between the two parks that ends at the ocean is a public right-of-way.

Hiking

The former Belfast & Moosehead Lake Railroad corridor is now the **Belfast Rail Trail on the Passagassawakeag,** a 2.3-mile nonmotorized trail paralleling the Passagassawakeag River that connects the downtown Harbor Walk to City Point.

The **Harbor Walk** follows the downtown

shoreline from Steamboat Landing to the Armistice Bridge, a footbridge crossing the Passy.

Biking

CG Bikes (21 Cross St., 207/218-1206), in the lower level of the United Farmers Market building, rents bicycles for $25 per 24 hours.

Boat Excursions

Take a quick cruise across Belfast Bay from the City Harbor Dock to Young's Lobster Pound and back aboard the ***Back and Forth*** (207/323-5952, www.thebackandforth.com, $18 round-trip), a traditional wooden lobster boat. Special excursions are available, ask for details.

Kayaking

If you don't have your own kayak, **Water Walker Custom Kayak Tours** (152 Lincolnville Ave., 207/338-6424, www.kayak-tour-maine.com) has a full range of options. Owner Ray Wirth, a Registered Maine Guide and American Canoe Association-certified open-water instructor, will arrange customized trips from a few hours to multiple days, as well as provide instruction. Rates vary with length and number of people, but a half-day tour for two is around $160.00.

Curling

The Scottish national sport of curling has dozens of enthusiastic supporters at Maine's only curling rink, the **Belfast Curling Club** (211 Belmont Ave./Rte. 3, 207/338-9851, www.belfastcurlingclub.org), an institution here since the late 1950s. Leagues play regularly on weeknights, and the club holds bonspiels (tournaments) and Learn to Curl sessions several times during the season, which runs late October-early April.

FOOD

Lobster and Seafood

The BYOB **Young's Lobster Pound** (4 Mitchell St., 207/338-1160, 7:30am-8pm daily), a barn of a place just off Route 1 on the east side of the harbor, is the place to go for no-frills, fresh-from-the-sea lobster.

Quick Bites

Wraps are fast food at **Bay Wrap** (20 Beaver St., 207/338-9757, www.thebaywrap.com, 7am-5pm Mon.-Fri., 8am-4pm Sat.). There's no limit to what the staff can stuff into various flavors of tortillas. Eat here or get them to go.

Delicious soups, stews, salads, and sandwiches come out of **Daily Soup** (118 High St., 207/930-0304, 11:30am-3pm Tues.-Fri.), a vest pocket restaurant with only a few seats.

Eat More Cheese (94 Main St., 207/358-9701) carries cheeses from around the world, along with charcuterie, chocolate, and specialty foods.

For homemade ice cream, pop into **Wild Cow Creamery** (31B Front Street, along the Harbor Walk, 207/200-7074, http://thewildcows.com).

The **Belfast Co-op** (123 High St., 207/338-2532, www.belfast.coop, 7:30am-7pm daily) is an experience in itself. You'll have a good impression of Belfast after one glance at the clientele and the bulletin board. Open to members and nonmembers alike, the co-op is a full-service organic and natural foods grocery, with a deli-café serving breakfast, lunch, and take-out fare. There's inside and outdoor seating.

The **Chocolate Drop Candy Shop** (35 Main St., 207/338-0566) is a kid-pleasing, retro-themed ice cream parlor and candy shop.

Scrumptious scratch-made croissants, bagels, and pastries emerge from the ovens at **Moonbat City Baking Co.** (137 Main St., 207/218-1039, 7am-1pm Thurs.-Mon.).

The **Belfast Farmers Market** (Waterfall Arts, 256 High St., 9am-1pm Fri.) provides the perfect opportunity for stocking up for a picnic.

Just try to get out of the **United Farmers Market of Maine** (18 Spring St., 207/218-7005, www.belfastmarket.com, 9am-2pm Sat.) without buying something. This year-round indoor market features more than 50 food and

Visiting Liberty

Seventeen miles west of Belfast, off Route 3, is **Liberty** (www.historicliberty.com), a tiny town with a funky tool store, a quirky museum, a bargain T-shirt shop, and a great state park. Everything is seasonal, running about mid-May-mid-October. Call before visiting if you want to be sure everything's open.

It's a store! It's a museum! It's amazing! More than 10,000 "useful" tools—plus used books and prints and other choice items—fill the three-story **Liberty Tool Company** (57 Main St., 207/589-4771). Drawn by nostalgia and a compulsion for handmade adzes and chisels, thousands of vintage-tool buffs, everyday home hobbyists, and antiques-seekers arrive at this eclectic emporium each year. The collection is beyond amazing, especially in its organization. Owner Skip Brack brings back vanloads of finds almost every week, and after sorting and cleaning, many wind up in this store.

Davistown Museum

The best pieces make it into Brack's **Davistown Museum and Maine Artists Guild** (58 Main St., 207/589-4900, www.davistownmuseum.org, 11am-5pm Thurs.-Sun.), on the 3rd floor of the building housing Liberty Graphics, across the street from Liberty Tool Company. The museum houses not only a history of Maine and New England hand tools but also local, regional, Native American, and environmental artifacts and an amazing collection of contemporary art, highlighted by works by artists such as Louise Nevelson (who used to buy tools across the street), Melitta Westerlund, and Phil Barter.

Downstairs is **Liberty Graphics Outlet Store** (58 Main St., 207/589-4035, www.lgtees.com), selling the eco-sensitive company's overstocks, seconds, and discontinued-design T-shirts. Outstanding silk-screened designs are done with water-based inks, and many of the shirts are organic cotton; prices begin at $7.

Just down Main Street is the old **Liberty Post Office,** a unique octagonal structure that looks like an oversize box. It was built in 1867 as a harness-maker's shop and later used as the town's post office.

A few miles south of downtown, off Route 220, is **Liberty Craft Brewing** (7 Coon Mountain Ln., 207/322-7663, www.libertycraftbrewing.com, 11:30am-8pm Thurs.-Sun.), a family-owned microbrewery serving pub fare such as burgers, bratwurst, and sandwiches.

Two miles west of downtown, **Lake St. George State Park** (Rte. 3, 207/589-4255, $5-7 adults, $1 ages 5-11) is a refreshing find. This 360-acre park has wooded picnic sites with grills along the lake, a beach, rental boats, a playground, volleyball and basketball courts, and five miles of hiking trails. Also available are campsites ($15-25). Afterward, head to **John's Ice Cream** (510 Belfast Ave./Rte. 3, 207/589-3700) for amazing flavors handcrafted on the premises, or good country cooking at the **Olde Mill Diner** (143 Belfast Ave./Rte. 3, Searsmont, 207/342-2999).

If you're up for more inland exploring, weave your way along the **Georges River Scenic Byway,** a 50-mile auto route along the St. George River (aka the Georges River) from its inland headwaters to the sea in Port Clyde. It's lovely anytime, but is especially pretty during foliage season. The official start is at the junction of Routes 3 and 220 in Liberty, but you can follow the trail in either direction or pick it up anywhere along the way. Road signs are posted, but it's far better to obtain a map-brochure at a chamber of commerce or other information locale. Or contact the architects of the route, the **Georges River Land Trust** (207/594-5166, www.georgesriver.org).

craft vendors, with many offering prepared food. Get it to go or settle into the dining area, with big windows overlooking the harbor. Also here is a demonstration kitchen where special dinners, classes, and other events are scheduled.

Family Favorites

A longtime standby for world cuisine, including vegetarian and gluten-free items, **Darby's Restaurant and Pub** (155 High St., 207/338-2339, www.darbysrestaurant.com, from 11:30am daily, $10-25) served tofu before tofu was cool. This place has been providing food and drink since just after the Civil War; the tin ceilings and antique bar are reminders of that. Expect regional American and international comfort foods. It also offers a children's menu.

Casual Dining

You'll have to plan well in advance and win a lottery to dine at chef Erin French's aptly named the **Lost Kitchen** (22 Mill St., Freedom, 207/382-3333, www.findthelostkitchen.com, 5pm-9pm Wed.-Sat., from $135 pp). It's housed in the renovated Mill at Freedom Falls, located about a half hour northwest of Belfast. French's bright takes on comfort foods have garnered her national kudos. Expect a leisurely meal—allow at least three hours to enjoy the fixed-price set menu. See the website for reservation details.

International and Vegetarian

Authentic Neapolitan pizza made by a certified Neapolitan Master Pizza Chef has earned **Meanwhile in Belfast** (2 Cross St., 207/218-1288, www.meanwhile-in-belfast.com, 5pm-8:30pm Wed.-Fri., 11:30am-2:30pm and 5pm-8:30pm Sat.-Sun., $10-22) a solid following for its scratch-made, wood-fired fare.

Delvino's Grill and Pasta House (32 Main St., 207/338-4565, www.delvinos.com, from 11am daily, $10-35) satiates cravings for Italian fare with a menu that includes lasagna, mussels marinara, pizza, and even lobster.

Laan Xang Cafe (18 Main St., 207/338-6338, www.laanxangcafe.com, 11:30am-3pm and 5pm-7pm Mon.-Sat., $11-14), specializing in Thai, Laotian, and Vietnamese fare, is a tiny, mostly take-out spot with a handful of tables on a deck.

Fresh food prepared in creative ways has earned **Chase's Daily** (96 Main St., 207/338-0555, 7am-5pm Tues.-Thurs. and Sat., 7am-8:30pm Fri., 8am-2pm Sun., $18-24) a devoted local following. The emphasis is on vegetarian fare, and most of the produce comes from the Chase family farm in nearby Freedom. The restaurant also serves as an art gallery, farmers market, and bakery. It's not the place for a quiet dinner, as the space is large and tends to be noisy. Dinner and brunch are table service; breakfast and lunch are counter service.

Neighborhood (132 High St., 207/505-0425, 4pm-9pm Tues.-Sat., $16-20) serves an internationally inspired menu with entrées such as tacos, curry, and shrimp and grits, as well as plentiful vegetarian, vegan, and gluten-free options.

ACCOMMODATIONS

Inns and Bed-and-Breakfasts

On a quiet side street, the **Jeweled Turret** (40 Pearl St., 207/338-2304 or 800/696-2304, www.jeweledturret.com, $149-189) is one of Belfast's pioneer bed-and-breakfasts. The 1898 inn is loaded with handsome woodwork and Victorian antiques—plus an astonishing stone fireplace, one of four in the house. The wraparound porches are a fine place to view the gardens while enjoying afternoon tea.

It's an easy walk to downtown from the historic district's **Alden House Inn** (63 Church St., 207/338-2151, www.thealdenhouse.com, $150-220). The 1840 house has distinct architectural features, including a gazebo porch, spiral stairway, two parlors, and a library. Some rooms have detached or shared baths. Breakfast is a highlight, and afternoon tea with freshly baked goods is included.

Motels

The fully renovated **Yankee Clipper Motel** (50 Searsport Ave./Rte. 1, 207/338-2353, www.

yankeeclippermotelbelfast.com, $99-149), a vintage 1950s strip motel on Route 1, has a boutique vibe. All rooms have laminated wood floors, contemporary decor, and neutral colors, along with a microwave and minifridge. There's a guest laundry too.

The clean and affordable **Merrybell Motel** (562 Atlantic Hwy., Northport, 207/338-3018, www.merrybellmotel.com, $99), a nicely renovated vintage mom-and-pop property, hugs Route 1, but has a nice backyard with lawn games, a grill, and picnic tables. A cottage with kitchenette is $149. Pets are negotiable ($20/night).

The nicely updated guest rooms at the oceanfront **Belfast Harbor Inn** (91 Searsport Ave., 207/338-2740, www.belfastharborinn.com, $150-249) are complemented by both indoor and outdoor heated pools—a real plus for families. Rates include a continental breakfast. If you can swing it, request an oceanview room. Five rooms are pet friendly ($20/pet/night).

INFORMATION AND SERVICES

The **Belfast Area Chamber of Commerce** (16 Main St., 207/338-5900, www.belfastmaine.org) produces a regional guide.

Find **public restrooms** at the waterfront Public Landing, in the railroad station, at the Waldo County Courthouse, and at the Waldo County General Hospital.

GETTING THERE AND AROUND

Belfast is about 20 miles or 30 minutes via Route 1 from Camden and about 45 miles or one hour from Augusta and I-95 via Route 3. It's about 6.5 miles or 10 minutes via Route 1 to Searsport.

Searsport Area

Searsport (pop. 2,615) is synonymous with the sea, thanks to an enduring oceangoing tradition that's appropriately commemorated here in the state's oldest maritime museum. The seafaring heyday occurred in the mid-19th century, but settlers from the Massachusetts Colony had already made inroads here 200 years earlier. In the 1750s, Fort Pownall, in nearby **Stockton Springs** (pop. 1,592), was a strategic site during the French and Indian War (the North American phase of Europe's Seven Years' War).

Shipbuilding was underway by 1791, reaching a crescendo 1845-1866, with six year-round shipyards and nearly a dozen more seasonal ones. Ten percent of *all* full-rigged American-flagged ships on the high seas were under the command of Searsport and Stockton Springs captains by 1885—a significant number of them bearing the names Pendleton, Nichols, or Carver. Many of these ships were involved in the perilous China trade, rounding notorious Cape Horn with great regularity.

All this global contact shaped Searsport's culture, adding a veneer of cosmopolitan sophistication. Imposing mansions of seafaring families were filled with fabulous Oriental treasures, many of which eventually made their way to today's Penobscot Marine Museum. Brick-lined Main Street is more evidence of the mid-19th-century wealth, and local churches reaped the benefits of residents' generosity. The Second Congregational Church, known as the Safe Harbor Church and patronized by captains and shipbuilders (most ordinary seamen attended the Methodist church), is ornamented with recently restored Tiffany-style windows and a Christopher Wren steeple.

Another inkling of this area's oceangoing superiority comes from visits to local burial grounds: Check out the headstones at Gordon,

Bowditch, and Sandy Point cemeteries. Many have fascinating tales to tell.

Today the Searsport area's major draws are the Penobscot Marine Museum, the still-handsome brick Historic District, a couple of special state parks, and plentiful antiques shops and flea markets.

The Maine Historic Preservation Commission considers the buildings in Searsport's Main Street Historic District the best examples of their type outside Portland—a frozen-in-time mid-19th-century cluster of brick-and-granite structures. The ground floors often house shops or restaurants; make time to stop in and admire their interiors.

SIGHTS

★ Penobscot Marine Museum

Exquisite marine paintings, historical photographs, ship models, boats, and unusual China-trade objets d'art are just a few of the 10,000 treasures at the **Penobscot Marine Museum** (5 Church St. at Rte. 1, Searsport, 207/548-2529, www.penobscotmarinemuseum.org, 10am-5pm Mon.-Sat., noon-5pm Sun. late May-mid-Oct., $15 adults, $12 seniors, $10 ages 8-16, $40 family), founded in 1936. Allow several hours to explore the exhibits, housed in five separate buildings on the museum's downtown campus. For a start, you'll see one of the nation's largest collections of paintings by marine artists James and Thomas Buttersworth. And the 1830s Fowler-True-Ross House is filled with exotic artifacts from foreign lands. Call or check the website for the schedule of lectures, concerts, and temporary exhibits. This isn't a sophisticated museum, but it is a treasure.

Museum in the Streets

Walk through Searsport's history by visiting a dozen placards detailing historic sites with text in both French and English. Pick up a brochure at the downtown info booth, the Penobscot Maritime Museum, or other local businesses.

BlueJacket Shipcrafters

Complementing the collections at the museum are the classic and contemporary models built by **BlueJacket Shipcrafters** (160 E. Main St./Rte. 1, Searsport, 800/448-5567, www.bluejacketinc.com). Even if you're not a hobbyist, stop in to see the incredibly detailed models on display. BlueJacket is renowned for building one-of-a-kind museum-quality custom models—it's the official model-maker for the U.S. Navy—but don't despair: There are kits here for all abilities and budgets. It's easy to find: Just look for the inland lighthouse on Route 1.

SHOPPING

Shopping in Searsport usually applies to antiques—from 25-cent flea-market collectibles to well-used tools to high-end china, furniture, quilts, and glassware. Strewn along Route 1 are a couple of flea markets.

More than two dozen dealers supply the juried inventory for the **Pumpkin Patch** (15 W. Main St./Rte. 1, Searsport, 207/548-6047), with a heavy emphasis on Maine antiques. Specialties include quilts (at least 80 are always on hand), silver, paint-decorated furniture, Victoriana, and nautical and Native American items.

In excess of 70 dealers sell their antiques and collectibles at the **Searsport Antique Mall** (149 E. Main St./Rte. 1, Searsport, 207/548-2640), making it another worthwhile stop for those seeking oldies but goodies.

RECREATION

Parks

MOOSE POINT STATE PARK

Here's a smallish park with a biggish view—183 acres wedged between Route 1 and a dramatic Penobscot Bay panorama. **Moose Point State Park** (Rte. 1, Searsport, 207/548-2882, $3-4 adults, $1 ages 5-11) is 1.5 miles south of downtown Searsport. Bring a picnic, let the kids hang out and play (there's no swimming, but there's good tidepooling at low tide), or walk through the woods or along the meadow trail.

SEARS ISLAND

After almost two decades of heavy-duty squabbling over a proposed cargo port on Searsport's **Sears Island** (http://friendsofsearsisland.org), the state bought the island for $4 million in 1997. In 2009, a conservation easement was created, forever protecting one of the largest uninhabited islands on the East Coast. The car-free island is a fine place for bird-watching, picnicking, walking, fishing, and cross-country skiing; pick up a brochure at the kiosk. It's linked to the mainland by a causeway and signposted off Route 1. An easy 1.5-mile walk will take you to the island's other side. Bring a picnic and binoculars—and a swimsuit if you're hardy enough to brave the water.

FORT POINT STATE PARK

Within **Fort Point State Park** (Fort Point Rd., Stockton Springs, 207/567-3356, $3-4 adults, $1 ages 5-11) on Cape Jellison's eastern tip are the earthworks of 18th-century **Fort Pownall,** a British fortress built during the French and Indian War; **Fort Point Light,** a square, 26-foot-tall, 19th-century tower guarding the mouth of the Penobscot River, with an adjacent bell tower; shoreline trails; and a 200-foot pier where you can fish or watch birds or boats. Bird-watchers can spot waterfowl—especially ruddy ducks, but also eagles and ospreys. Bring picnic fixings, but stay clear of the keeper's house, which is private property. At the Route 1 fork for Stockton Springs, bear right onto Main Street and continue to Mill Road, in the village center. Turn right and then left onto East Cape Road, and then take another left onto Fort Point Road, which leads to the parking area.

SANDY POINT BEACH

There's a nice sand swath on **Sandy Point Beach,** a town-managed preserve at the mouth of the Penobscot River with walking trails, osprey nests, and a beaver pond. It's at the end of Steamboat Wharf Road (off Route 1) in Stockton Springs.

Bicycling

An especially good ride in this area is the **Cape Jellison** loop in Stockton Springs. Park at Stockton Springs Elementary School and begin the loop from there. Including a detour to Fort Point, the ride totals less than 10 miles from downtown Stockton Springs.

FOOD

Good home cooking with an emphasis on fried food has made **Just Barb's** (24 Main St./Rte. 1, Stockton Springs, 207/567-3886, 6am-8pm Mon.-Sat., 7am-7pm Sun., $11-25) a dandy place for an unfussy meal at a low price. Fried clams and scallop stew are both winners; finish up with a slab of pie or shortcake.

Anglers Restaurant (215 E. Main St./Rte. 1, Searsport, 207/548-2405, www.anglersrestaurant.net, 11am-8pm daily, $7-25) is probably the least-assuming and yet one of the most popular restaurants around. Expect hearty New England cooking, hefty portions, local color, no frills, and a bill that won't dent your wallet. Big favorites are the chowders, stews, and lobster rolls. Desserts are a specialty: The gingerbread with whipped cream is divine, and kids love the "bucket o' worms."

The menu at the **Hichborn** (10 Church St., Stockton Springs, 207/322-8307, www.thehichborn.com, 5pm-9pm Thurs.-Sun., $24-32) emphasizes locally sourced ingredients. Choose from about four entrées served in a lovely dining room in a nicely appointed historical home. Reservations are required.

For a taste of West Africa, dine at **Me Lon Togo** (375 E. Main St./Rte. 1, Searsport, 207/872-9146, www.melontogo.com, 5pm-11pm Sun., $40), which serves a four-course fixed-price menu comprising appetizer, salad, choice of entrée, and dessert.

ACCOMMODATIONS

Inns

The **Homeport Inn** (121 E. Main St., Searsport, 207/548-2259, www.homeporthistoricinn.com, $140-265), a commanding 1861 sea captain's home now listed in the National Register of Historic Places, features seemingly endless antiques-furnished public rooms and guest rooms; some rooms share baths. Shore access is only 100 yards down the road.

The **Captain A. V. Nickels Inn** (127 E. Main St./Rte. 1, Searsport, 207/548-1104, www.captainnickelsinn.com, $135-290) is an oceanside stunner. The cupola-topped mansion, built by the good captain in 1874 as a gift to his bride, is elegantly furnished with European and American antiques. Public rooms range from cozy to expansive. Guest rooms, some with detached baths, are named after ports of call; two suites have decks overlooking the oceans. Rates include an extravagant breakfast.

Motel

The **Yardarm** (172 E. Main St./Rte. 1, Searsport, 207/548-2404, www.searsportmaine.com, $99-140), a well-maintained family-owned small motel with 18 pine-paneled units, is set back from the road and next to BlueJacket Shipcrafters. A continental breakfast is served in a cheery breakfast room in the adjacent farmhouse. Two rooms are pet friendly.

Camping

How can you beat 1,100 feet of tidal oceanfront and unobstructed views of Islesboro, Castine, and Penobscot Bay? **Searsport Shores Camping Resort** (216 W. Main St./Rte. 1, Searsport, 207/548-6059, www.campocean.com) gets high marks for its fabulous setting. About 100 good-size sites (including walk-in oceanfront tenting sites) go for $46-96. Facilities include a private beach, a small store, free showers, a laundry, play areas, a recreation hall, nature trails, kayak rentals, and a volleyball court. Request a site away from organized-activity areas. Bring a sea kayak and launch it here. In early September, the campground hosts Fiber Arts College, a weekend of classes, demonstrations, and camaraderie for spinners, hookers, weavers, and the like.

INFORMATION AND SERVICES

The **Searsport Business and Visitors Guide** publishes a visitors guide and maintains a small self-serve info center in a shed-like building on Route 1 (at Norris St.), across from the Pumpkin Patch antiques shop.

GETTING HERE AND AROUND

Searsport is about six miles or 10 minutes via Route 1 from Belfast. It's about 13 miles or 18 minutes to Bucksport.

Bucksport Area

The new Penobscot Narrows Bridge provides an elegant entry to Bucksport, a longtime rough-and-ready river port and former papermaking town that's slowly gentrifying. Bucksport is no upstart. Native Americans gravitated to these Penobscot River shores in summer, finding a rich source of salmon for food and grasses for basket making. In 1763, the area was officially settled by Colonel Jonathan Buck, a Massachusetts Bay Colony surveyor who modestly named it "Buckstown" and organized a booming shipping business here. His remains are interred in a local cemetery, where his tombstone bears the distinct outline of a woman's leg; this is allegedly the result of a curse by a witch Buck ordered executed, but in fact it's probably a flaw in the granite. The monument is across Route 1 from the Hannaford supermarket, on the corner of Hinks Street.

Just south of town, at the bend in the Penobscot River, **Verona Island** (pop. 544) is best known as the mile-long link between Prospect and Bucksport. **Prospect** is home to the Penobscot Narrows Bridge and Observatory and Fort Knox, guarding the mouth of the Penobscot River. Just before you cross the bridge from Verona to Bucksport, hang a left, then a quick right to a small municipal park with a boat launch and broad views of Bucksport Harbor (and the old paper mill). Admiral Robert Peary's arctic exploration vessel, the *Roosevelt,* was built on this site in 1905 and used in his final 1908 expedition to the North Pole. A scale model can be viewed in the Buck Memorial Library.

Route 1 east of Bucksport leads to **Orland** (pop. 2,225), whose idyllic setting on the banks of the Narramissic River makes it a magnet for shutterbugs. It's also the site of a unique service organization called H.O.M.E. (Homeworkers Organized for More Employment). **East Orland** (officially part of Orland) claims the Craig Brook National Fish Hatchery and Great Pond Mountain (you can't miss it, jutting from the landscape on the left as you drive east on Route 1).

SIGHTS

★ Fort Knox

Looming over Bucksport Harbor, the *other* **Fort Knox** (Rte. 174, Prospect, 207/469-6553, www.maine.gov, 9am-sunset May-Oct., $4-5.50 adults, $2 ages 5-11) is a state historic site just off Route 1. Named for Major General Henry Knox, George Washington's first secretary of war, the sprawling granite fort was begun in 1844. Built to protect the upper Penobscot River from attack, it was never finished and never saw battle. Still, it was, as guide Kathy Williamson says, "very well thought out and planned, and that may have been its best defense." Begin your visit at the Visitor and Education Center, operated by the Friends of Fort Knox, a nonprofit group that has partnered with the state to preserve and interpret the fort. Guided tours are sometimes available. The fort's distinguishing features include two complete Rodman cannons. Wear rubberized shoes and bring a flashlight to explore the underground passages; you can set the kids loose. The fort hosts Civil War reenactments several times each summer as well as a Medieval Tournament, a paranormal-psychic fair, and other events (check the website). The Halloween Fright at the Fort is a ghoulish event for the brave. The grounds are accessible all year. Bring a picnic; views over the river to Bucksport are fabulous.

★ Penobscot Narrows Bridge and Observatory

On a clear day, do not miss the **Penobscot Narrows Bridge and Observatory** (9am-6pm daily July-Aug., 9am-5pm daily May-June and Sept.-Oct., $6-8 adults, $4 ages 5-11, includes fort admission), accessible via Fort Knox. The three-deck observatory caps the bridge's 447-foot-high west tower, with the observatory's top floor sited at 420 feet above the Penobscot River. It's one of only three such structures in the world, and the only one in the United States. You'll zip up in an elevator, and when the doors open, you're facing a wall of glass—it's a bit of a shocker, and downright terrifying for anyone with a serious fear of heights. Ascend two more flights (an elevator is available) and you're in the glass-walled observatory; the views on a clear day extend from Katahdin to Mount Desert Island. Even when it's hazy, it's still a neat experience.

Alamo Theatre

The 1916 **Alamo Theatre** (85 Main St., Bucksport, 207/469-0924 or 800/639-1636, event line 207/469-6910, www.oldfilm.org, 9am-4pm Mon.-Fri. year-round) shows not only contemporary films but also indie and local ones. Before each feature, it screens archival shorts about New England produced or revived by the unique **Northeast Historic Film,** which is headquartered here. NHF has more than 10 million feet of film in its archives, including rarities. Celebrities ranging from Ken Burns to Oprah Winfrey have requested footage for projects. Stop in, survey the restoration, visit the displays (donation requested), and browse the Alamo Theatre Store for antique postcards, T-shirts, toys, and reasonably priced videos on ice harvesting, lumberjacks, maple sugaring, and other traditional New England topics.

H.O.M.E.

Adjacent to the flashing light on Route 1 in Orland, **H.O.M.E.** (Homeworkers Organized for More Employment, 207/469-7961) is tough to categorize. Linked with the international Emmaus Movement founded by a French priest, H.O.M.E. was started in 1970 by Lucy Poulin and two nuns at a nearby convent. The quasi-religious organization shelters refugees and the homeless, operates a soup kitchen and a car-repair service, runs a day-care center, and teaches work skills in a variety of hands-on cooperative programs. Seventy percent of its income comes from sales of crafts, produce, and services. At the Route 1 **store** (Rte. 1 and Upper Falls Rd., 9am-4:30pm daily), you can buy handmade quilts, organic produce, maple syrup, and jams—and support a worthwhile effort. You can also tour the craft workshops on the property.

Bucksport Waterfront Walkway

Stroll the one-mile paved walkway from the Bucksport-Verona Bridge to Webber Docks. Along the way are historical markers, picnic tables, a gazebo, restrooms, and expansive views of the harbor and Fort Knox.

SHOPPING

Locals come just as much for the coffee and conversation as the selection of new and used reads at **BookStacks** (71 Main St., Bucksport, 207/469-8992). You'll find a smattering of antiques and curiosity shops dotting Route 1.

Stubborn Cow Glass (55 Main St., Bucksport, 207/433-7505), a working stained glass studio and gallery, sells gorgeous works in all sizes.

It's difficult to decide where to look first in the **Lighthouse Arts Center** (86 Main St., Bucksport, 207/702-9135, www.lighthouseartscenter.com). Fine art and crafts by more than 60 artisans fills the spacious gallery, which has big windows overlooking Bucksport Harbor.

Just south of Route 1 is **Wild Blueberry Patch Gift Shop** (Allen's Wild Maine Blueberries, Rte. 15, Orland, 207/469-7060), a tiny blue cottage next to the Allen family's blueberry processing building. Stop in for fresh, canned, frozen, or dried wild Maine blueberries and all manner of blueberry merchandise, from baking mixes to T-shirts.

RECREATION

Craig Brook National Fish Hatchery

For a day of hiking, picnicking, swimming, canoeing, and a bit of natural history, pack a lunch and head for 135-acre **Craig Brook National Fish Hatchery** (306 Hatchery Rd., East Orland, 207/469-6701, www.fws.gov/northeast/craigbrook), on Alamoosook Lake. Turn off Route 1 6 miles east of Bucksport and continue 1.4 miles north to the parking area. The **visitors center** (8am-4pm Mon.-Sat. summer, free) offers interactive displays on Atlantic salmon (don't miss the downstairs viewing area), displays of fly-fishing artifacts and memorabilia, maps, and a restroom. The grounds are accessible 6am-sunset daily year-round. Established in 1889, the U.S. Fish and Wildlife Service hatchery raises sea-run Atlantic salmon for stocking seven Maine rivers. The birch-lined shorefront has picnic tables, a boat launch, an Atlantic salmon display pool, additional parking, and a spectacular cross-lake view. Watch for eagles, ospreys, and loons.

Great Pond Mountain Wildlands

Encompassing two parcels of land and roughly 4,300 acres, the Great Pond Mountain Wildlands is a jewel. Acquired by the **Great Pond Mountain Conservation Trust** (207/469-7190, www.greatpondtrust.org) in 2005 after a decade of negotiation, the Wildlands comprises two sections. The larger 3,420-acre parcel surrounds Hothole Valley, including Hothole Brook, prized for its trout, and shoreline on Hothole Pond. The smaller 875-acre tract includes two miles of frontage on the Dead River (not to be confused with the Dead River of rafting fame in northwestern Maine) and reaches up Great Pond Mountain and down to the ominously named Hellbottom Swamp. The land is rich with wildlife: black bears, moose, bobcats, and deer, to name just a few species; plus, with the pond, swamp, and river, it's ideal for birdwatching. The 14 miles of woods roads lacing the land are open for walking, mountain biking, and snowshoeing, and the waterways invite fishing and paddling. Avoid the area during hunting season. Snowmobiling is permitted; ATVs are banned. Access to the Dead River tract is from the Craig Brook National Fish Hatchery; follow Don Fish Road to the Dead River Gate and Dead River Trail. The South Gate to Hothole Pond Tract is on Route 1 just southwest of Route 176. There's a parking lot at the gate, or, when it's open, you can drive in along Valley Road about 2.5 miles to another parking area.

The biggest rewards for the 1.8-mile easy-to-moderate hike up 1,038-foot **Great Pond Mountain** are 360-degree views. On a clear day, Baxter State Park's Katahdin is visible from the peak's north side. In fall, watch for migrating hawks. Access is via gated private property beginning about a mile north of Craig Brook National Fish Hatchery on Dog Fish Road in East Orland. Roadside parking is available near the trailhead, but during fall foliage season you may need to park at the hatchery. Pick up a brochure at the trailhead, stay on the trail, and respect the surrounding private property. For a longer hike, access the Great Pond Mountain Trail via the Dead River Trail and Connector, a moderately difficult multiuse gravel trail, for a total distance of seven miles.

FOOD

Carrier's Mainely Lobster (corner of Rtes. 1 and 46, 207/469-1011, www.carriersmainelylobster.com, 11am-8pm daily) doesn't look like much, but it's owned by a fishing family and is the best local spot for lobster or fried seafood. The large lobster roll is filled with meat from about two of the tasty crustaceans. There's an indoor dining room out back as well as picnic tables.

Roughly 100 yards up the road is another local fave that's stood the test of time. **Crosby's Drive-In and Dairy Bar** (30 Rte. 46, Bucksport, 207/469-3640, 10:30am-7:30pm daily) has been dishing out burgers, dogs, fried seafood, and ice cream since 1938.

Now here's something different: **Friars' Brewhouse Tap Room** (84 Main St., Bucksport, 207/702-9156, 11:30am-7pm Tues.-Sat., $8-16) is run by two Franciscan friars who brew Belgian-style craft beer, bake bread and treats, and serve a light menu (sandwiches, cheese/charcuterie plates, lobster rolls, etc.) in a diner-esque space with religious accents.

Walk down the alley next to the Dairy Port to find **Verona Wine and Design** (77 Main St., Bucksport, 207/745-0731, www.veronawineanddesign.com, 4pm-9pm Mon. and Wed.-Fri., noon-9pm Sat.-Sun., $5-19), a wine and tapas restaurant with seating indoors as well as on a private patio out back. Make a meal from shareables, sandwiches, appetizers, and desserts.

MacLeod's (63 Main St., Bucksport, 207/469-3963, http://macleodsrestaurant.com, from 4pm Sun.-Thurs., from noon Fri.-Sat., $10-25) is Bucksport's most popular and enduring restaurant. Some tables in the pleasant dining room have glimpses of the river and Fort Knox. The wide-ranging American menu has choices for all tastes and budgets. Reservations are wise for Saturday nights.

ACCOMMODATIONS

Inn

If only the six simple guest rooms at the old-timey **Alamoosook Lakeside Inn** (off Route 1, Orland, 207/469-6393 or 866/459-6393, www.alamoosooklakesideinn.com, year-round, $165) actually overlooked the lake, it would be the perfect rustic lakeside lodge. The property is gorgeous, and the location is well suited for exploring the area. All guest rooms, decorated in country style, have windows and doors opening onto a long, enclosed sunporch overlooking the lake (so if the curtains are open, other guests passing by can see into the room). The lodge has 1,300 feet of lakefront and is great for wildlife-watching and fishing (especially for bass, trout, salmon, and pickerel), and guests may use the inn's canoes and kayaks. Paddle across the lake to the fish hatchery for a hike up Great Pond Mountain. If the weather doesn't cooperate, retreat to the basement rec room, with games, a fireplace, a library, and even a kitchenette. A full breakfast is served. Two rooms are pet friendly ($15/night). Note: The inn often hosts events.

In downtown Bucksport, the 40-room **Fort Knox Park Inn** (64 Main St., Bucksport, 207/469-3113, www.fortknoxparkinn.com, $120-150) is a four-story motel right at the harbor's edge. A light continental breakfast is included. Be sure to request a water view, preferably on an upper floor, or you'll be facing a parking lot.

Motel

On the edge of downtown and set back from Route 1, the **Bucksport Motor Inn** (70 Rte. 1, Bucksport, 207/469-3111 or 800/626-9734, www.bucksportmotorinn.com, $119) is a family-owned, vintage 1956 motel that's being updated; be sure to ask for one of the renovated rooms. Perks include refrigerators and microwaves. Some rooms are dog friendly ($15).

Camping

The rivers, lakes, and ponds between Bucksport and Ellsworth make the area especially appealing for camping, and sites tend to be cheaper than in the Bar Harbor area. Six miles east of Bucksport, on the shores of 10-mile-long Toddy Pond, which reaches 100 feet in depth in some places, is **Balsam Cove Campground** (286 Back Ridge Rd., East Orland, 207/469-7771, www.balsamcove.com, late May-late Sept., $30-70), which leans toward bigger RVs. Facilities on the 50 acres include 60 wooded waterfront or water-view tent and RV sites, rental cabins ($76-84), on-site rental trailers ($100-105), a dump station, a store, laundry, free showers and Wi-Fi, boat rentals, and freshwater swimming. Dogs are welcome on camping sites for $2 per night. During July and August, especially on weekends, reservations are wise.

INFORMATION AND SERVICES

The best source for local info is the **Bucksport Bay Area Chamber of Commerce** (207/469-6818, www.bucksportbaychamber.com).

In Bucksport, **public restrooms** next to the town dock (behind the Bucksport Historical Society) are open spring-fall. Restrooms are open year-round in the Gateway gas station (at the Route 1 traffic light next to the Bucksport bridge) and in the Bucksport Municipal Office (Main St., Mon.-Fri.).

GETTING THERE AND AROUND

Bucksport is about 20 miles or 35 minutes via Route 15 from Bangor. It's about 17 miles or 25 minutes via Routes 1 and 15 to Blue Hill, about 22 miles or 30 minutes via Route 1 to Ellsworth, and about 18 miles or 30 minutes via Routes 175 and 166 to Castine.

Blue Hill Peninsula and Deer Isle

The Blue Hill Peninsula, once dubbed "the Fertile Crescent," is unique. Few other locales harbor such a high concentration of artisans, musicians, and on-their-feet retirees juxtaposed with topflight wooden-boat builders, lobstermen, and umpteenth-generation Mainers. Perhaps surprisingly, the mix seems to work.

Anchored by the towns of Bucksport to the east and Ellsworth to the west, the peninsula comprises several enclaves with markedly distinct personalities. Blue Hill, Brooklin, Brooksville, Sedgwick, Castine, Deer Isle, and Stonington are stitched together by a network of narrow, winding country roads. Thanks to the mapmaker-challenging coastline and a handful of freshwater ponds and rivers, there's a view of water around nearly every bend.

Highlights

Look for ★ to find recommended sights, activities, dining, and lodging.

★ **Parson Fisher House:** More than just another historic house, the Parson Fisher House is a remarkable testimony to one man's ingenuity (page 253).

★ **Flash! In the Pans Community Steelband:** Close your eyes when you hear this phenomenal steel-pan band and you might think you're on a Caribbean island rather than in Maine (page 253).

★ **Blue Hill Mountain:** It's a relatively easy hike for fabulous 360-degree views from the summit of Blue Hill Mountain (page 256).

★ **Holbrook Island Sanctuary State Park:** Varied hiking trails and great birding are the rewards for finding this off-the-beaten-path preserve (page 261).

★ **Castine Historical Tour:** A turbulent history detailed on signs throughout town makes Castine an irresistible place to tour on foot or by bike (page 269).

★ **Sea Kayaking:** Hook up with "Kayak Karen" in Castine for a tour (page 271).

★ **Haystack Mountain School of Crafts:** Don't miss an opportunity to visit this internationally renowned crafts school, which has an award-winning architectural design in a stunning setting (page 276).

★ **Nervous Nellie's:** Sculptor Peter Beerits's ever-expanding whimsical world captivates all ages—and it's free (page 278).

★ **Arts and Crafts Galleries:** Given the presence of the Haystack Mountain School of Crafts, it's no surprise to find dozens of fabulously talented artisans on Deer Isle (page 280).

★ **Acadia National Park:** Isle au Haut's limited access makes this remote section of the park truly special. It's unlikely you'll have to share the trails—or the views—with more than a few other people (page 290).

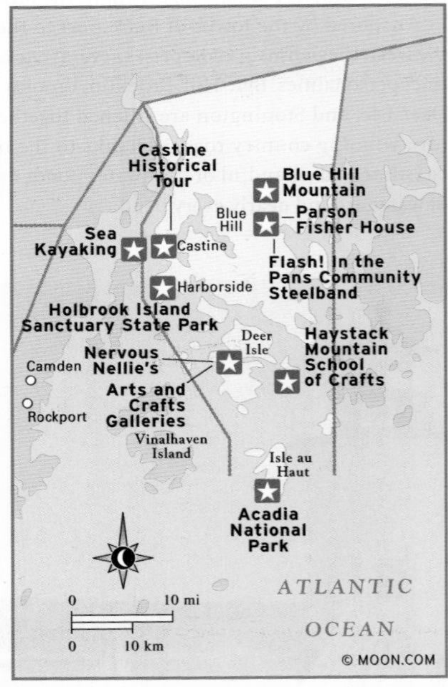

You can watch the sun set from atop Blue Hill Mountain; tour the home of the fascinating Jonathan Fisher; stroll through the village of Castine (charming verging on precious), whose streets are lined with regal homes; visit *WoodenBoat* magazine's world headquarters in tiny Brooklin; and browse top-notch studios and galleries throughout the peninsula. Venture a bit inland of Route 1, and you find lovely lakes for paddling and swimming and another hill to hike.

After weaving your way down the Blue Hill Peninsula and crossing the soaring pray-as-you-go bridge to Little Deer Isle, you've entered the realm of island living. Sure, bridges and causeways connect the points, but the farther down you drive, the more removed from civilization you'll feel. The pace slows; the population dwindles. Fishing and lobstering are the mainstays; lobster boats rest near many homes, and trap fences edge properties. If your ultimate destination is the section of Acadia National Park on Isle au Haut, the drive down Deer Isle to Stonington helps to disconnect you from the mainland. To reach the park's acreage on Isle au Haut, you'll board the Isle au Haut ferryboat for the trip down Merchant Row to the island.

PLANNING YOUR TIME

To truly enjoy this region, you'll want to spend at least 3-4 days here, perhaps splitting your lodging between two or three locations. The area demands leisurely exploring; you won't be able to zip from one location to another. Traveling along the winding roads, discovering galleries and country stores, and lodging at traditional inns are all part of the experience.

Arts fans will want to concentrate their efforts in Blue Hill, Deer Isle, and Stonington. Outdoor-oriented folks should consider Deer Isle, Stonington, or Castine as a base for sea kayaking or exploring the area preserves. For architecture and history buffs, Castine is a must.

No visit to this region is complete without at least a cruise by, if not a visit to, Isle au Haut, an offshore island that's home to a remote section of Acadia National Park. Allow at least a few hours for a ride on the mail boat, but if you can afford the time, spend a full day hiking the park's trails. Don't forget to pack food and water.

Blue Hill

Twelve miles south of Route 1 is the hub of the peninsula, **Blue Hill** (pop. 2,686), exuding charm from its handsome old homes to its waterfront setting to the shops, restaurants, and galleries that boost its appeal.

Eons back, Native American summer folk gave the name Awanadjo (small, hazy mountain) to the mini-mountain that looms over the town and draws the eye for miles around. The first permanent settlers arrived in the late 18th century, after the French and Indian War, and established mills and shipyards. More than 100 ships were built here between Blue Hill's incorporation in 1789 and 1882, bringing prosperity to the entire peninsula. Throughout the 19th century and into the 20th, Blue Hill's granite industry boomed, reaching its peak in the 1880s. Scratch the Brooklyn Bridge and the New York Stock Exchange and you'll find granite from Blue Hill's quarries.

Critical to the town's early expansion was its first clergyman, Jonathan Fisher, a remarkable fellow who has been likened to Leonardo

Previous: a lighthouse on Isle au Haut; lobster boats in Stonington; Haystack Mountain School of Crafts.

Blue Hill Peninsula and Deer Isle

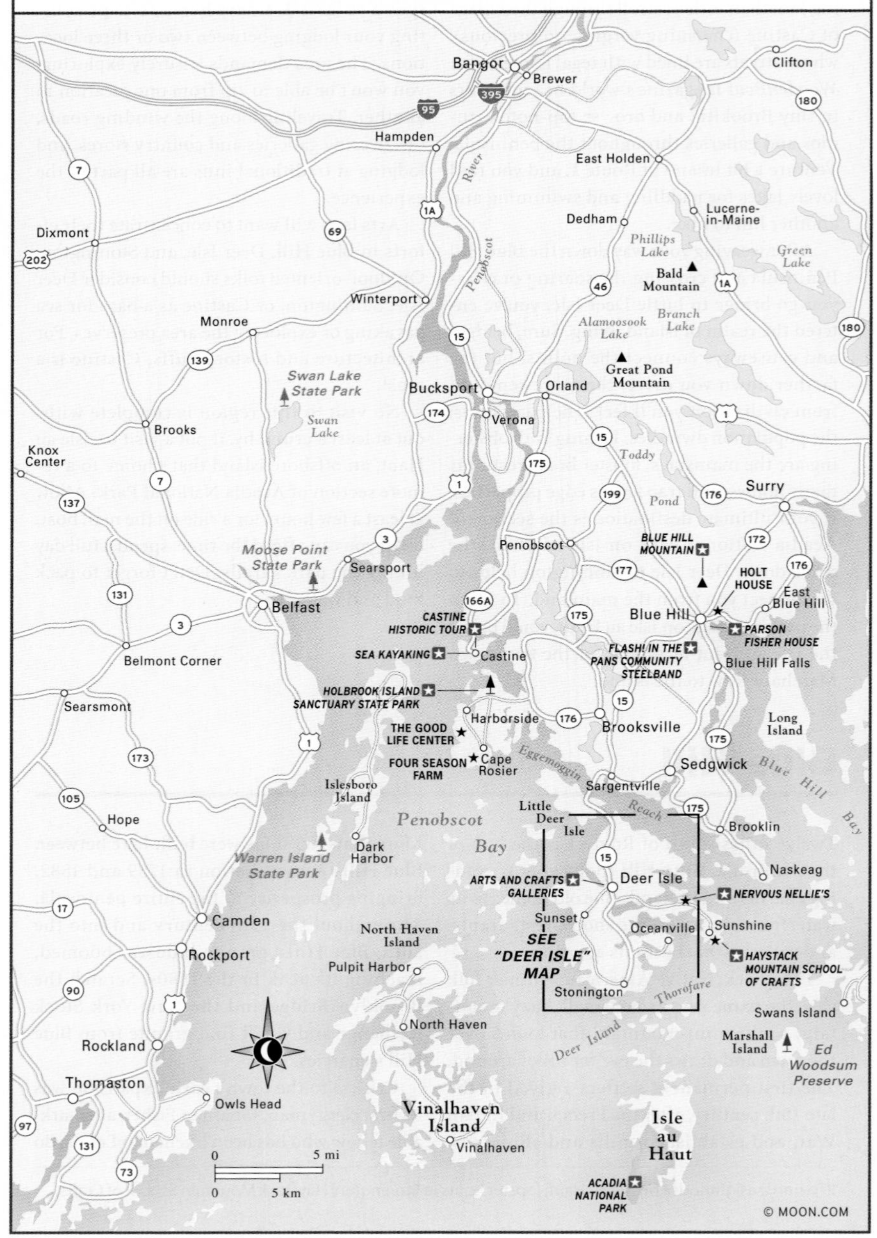

da Vinci. In 1803, Fisher founded Blue Hill Academy (predecessor of today's George Stevens Academy), then built his home (now a museum), and eventually left an immense legacy of inventions, paintings, engravings, and poetry.

At the height of industrial prosperity, tourism took hold, attracting steamboat-borne summer boarders. Many succumbed to the scenery, bought land, and built waterfront summer homes. Thank these summer folk and their offspring for the fact that music has long been a big deal in Blue Hill. The Kneisel Hall Chamber Music School, established in the late 19th century, continues to rank high among the nation's summer music colonies.

Scoot over to neighboring **Surry** (pop. 1,466) for an oceanfront lobster shack with views over Mount Desert Island followed by to-die-for ice cream or for a boating excursion with a famous captain.

SIGHTS

★ Parson Fisher House

Named for a brilliant Renaissance man who arrived in Blue Hill in 1794, the **Parson Fisher House** (44 Mines Rd./Rte. 15/176, 207/374-2459, www.jonathanfisherhouse.org, 1pm-4pm Thurs.-Sat. early July-early Sept., 1pm-4pm Fri.-Sat. early Sept.-mid-Oct., $5) immerses visitors in period furnishings, inventions, and Jonathan Fisher lore. And Fisher's feats are breathtaking: He was a Harvard-educated preacher who also managed to be an accomplished painter, poet, mathematician, naturalist, linguist, inventor, cabinetmaker, farmer, architect, and printmaker. In his spare time, he fathered nine children and founded a school. Fisher also pitched in to help build the yellow house on Tenney Hill, which served as the Congregational church parsonage. Now it contains intriguing items created by Fisher that volunteer tour guides delight in explaining, including a camera obscura. Don't miss it.

Historic Sights

In downtown Blue Hill, a few steps off Main Street, stands the **Holt House** (3 Water St., www.bluehillhistory.org, 1pm-4pm Tues. and Fri., 11am-2pm Sat. July-mid-Sept., $3 adults, free under age 13), home of the Blue Hill Historical Society. Built in 1815 by Jeremiah Holt, the Federal-style building contains restored stenciling, period decor, and masses of memorabilia contributed by local residents. In the carriage house are even more goodies, including old tools, a sleigh, carriages, and more.

Walk or drive up Union Street (Rte. 177), past George Stevens Academy, and wander the **Old Cemetery,** established in 1794. If gnarled trees and ancient headstones intrigue you, there aren't many good-size Maine cemeteries older than this one.

Bagaduce Music Lending Library

One of Maine's more unusual institutions is the **Bagaduce Music Lending Library** (49 South St., 207/374-5454, www.bagaducemusic.org, 10am-4pm Mon.-Fri. or by appointment), where you can borrow from a collection of more than 250,000 titles. The library also has a performance hall and offers a concert series ($20) featuring musicians performing selections from its collection. Annual membership is $25 ($15 for students 18 and younger); fees range $1-4 per piece.

Scenic Route

Parker Point Road (turn off Rte. 15 at the Blue Hill Public Library) takes you from Blue Hill to Blue Hill Falls the back way, with vistas en route toward Acadia National Park. For more serene views, drive the length of **Newbury Neck**, off Route 172 in Surry; you might even bookend the drive with a lobster dinner at the tip, followed by an ice cream back in downtown Surry.

ENTERTAINMENT

★ Flash! In the Pans Community Steelband

If you're a fan of steel-band music, the **Flash! In the Pans Community Steelband**

(207/374-2172, www.flashinthepans.org) usually performs somewhere on the peninsula 7:30pm-9pm Mondays mid-June to early September. Local papers carry the summer schedule for the nearly three-dozen-member band, which deserves its devoted following. Admission is usually a small donation to benefit a local cause.

Other Live Music

Since 1922, chamber-music students have been spending summers perfecting their skills and demonstrating their prowess at the **Kneisel Hall Chamber Music School** (Pleasant St./Rte. 15, 207/374-2811, www.kneisel.org). Festival concerts by faculty and guest artists run Friday evenings and Sunday afternoons late June-late August. The concert schedule is published in the spring, and reserved-seating tickets ($35 inside, $25 on the porch outside, nonrefundable) can be ordered online or by phone. Other opportunities to hear the students and faculty include young-artist concerts, children's concerts, open rehearsals, and more. Kneisel Hall is about 0.5 mile from the center of town.

Chamber music continues in winter thanks to the volunteer **Blue Hill Concert Association** (207/326-4666, www.bluehillconcertassociation.org), which presents concerts January-March at the Congregational church. Recommended donation is $30.

Blue Hill Bach (207/590-2677, www.bluehillbach.org), formed in 2011 to present Baroque music, presents a summer Bach Festival. **Surry Arts: At The Barn** (8 Cross Rd., Surry, 207/669-9216, http://surryartsandevents.com) presents a wide range of performances, from flamenco guitar to jazz to classical to blues. **Bagaduce Music Lending Library** (49 South St., Blue Hill, 207/374-5454, www.bagaducemusic.org) presents concerts in its performance hall.

Theater

The **New Surry Theatre** (18 Union St., 207/200-4720, www.newsurrytheatre.org) stages musicals and classics from November through August. **Bagaduce Theatre** (176 Mills Point Rd., Brooksville, 207/801-1536, www.bagaducetheatre.com) presents plays starring Equity actors from May into September.

Lectures

The **Shaw Institute** (55 Main St., 207/374-2135, www.shawinstitute.org), a nonprofit scientific research organization focused on chemical exposure and climate change, sponsors an evening lecture series.

Festivals and Events

WERU's annual **Full Circle Fair** is usually held in mid-August at the Blue Hill Fairgrounds (Rte. 172, north of downtown Blue Hill). Expect world music, good food, crafts, and socially and environmentally progressive talks. On Labor Day weekend, the **Blue Hill Fair** (Blue Hill Fairgrounds, Rte. 172, 207/374-9976) is one of the state's best agricultural fairs. Both the **Foliage, Food & Wine Festival** and **Word. Blue Hill Literary Arts Festival** take place in October.

SHOPPING

Perhaps it's Blue Hill's location near the renowned Haystack Mountain School of Crafts. Perhaps it's the way the light plays off the rolling countryside and onto the twisting coastline. Perhaps it's the inspirational landscape. Whatever the reason, numerous artists and artisans call Blue Hill home, and top-notch galleries are abundant.

The **Liros Gallery** (14 Parker Point Rd., 207/374-5370 or 800/287-5370, www.lirosgallery.com) has been dealing in Russian icons since the mid-1960s. Prices are high, but the icons are fascinating. The gallery also carries Currier & Ives prints, antique maps, and 19th-century British and American paintings. Just up the street is the **Cynthia Winings Gallery** (24 Parker Point Rd., 917/204-4001, www.cynthiawiningsgallery.com), which

1: Parson Fisher House 2: Blue Hill

1

2

shows contemporary works by local artists. From here it's a short walk to **Blue Hill Bay Gallery** (Main St., 207/374-5773, www.bluehillbaygallery.com), which represents contemporary artists in various media.

Don't miss **Jud Hartmann** (79 Main St., at Rte. 15, 207/374-9917, www.judhartmanngallery.com). The spacious, well-lighted, in-town gallery carries Hartmann's limited-edition bronze sculptures of the woodland Native Americans of the Northeast. Hartmann often can be seen working on his next model in the gallery—a real treat. He's a wealth of information about his subjects, and he loves sharing the mesmerizing stories he's uncovered during his meticulous research.

Handworks Gallery (48 Main St., 207/374-5613, www.handworksgallery.org) sells a range of fun, funky, utilitarian, and fine-art crafts, including jewelry, furniture, rugs, wall hangings, and clothing, by more than 50 Maine artists and craftspeople.

Rackliffe Pottery (130 Ellsworth Rd./Rte. 172, 207/374-2297 or 888/631-3321, www.rackliffepottery.com), noted for its vivid blue wares, also makes its own glazes and has been producing lead-free pottery since 1969. **Mark Bell Pottery** (Rte. 15, 207/374-5881), in a tiny building signaled only by a small roadside sign, is the home of exquisite, award-winning porcelain by the eponymous potter. It's easy to understand why his wares have been displayed at the Smithsonian Institution's Craft Show as well as at other juried shows across the country. The delicacy of each vase, bowl, or piece is astonishing, and the glazes are gorgeous. Twice each summer he has kiln openings—must-go events for collectors and fans.

Blue Hill Books (26 Pleasant St./Rte. 15, 207/374-5632, www.bluehillbooks.com) is a wonderful independent bookstore that organizes an "authors series" during the summer.

RECREATION

Parks and Preserves

Blue Hill Heritage Trust (157 Hinckley Ridge Rd., Blue Hill, 207/374-5118, www.bluehillheritagetrust.org, 8:30am-5pm Mon.-Fri.) works hard at preserving the region's landscape. Trail maps for all sites can be downloaded from the website. It also presents a Walks and Talks series, with offerings such as a mushroom walk and talk, a full-moon hike up Blue Hill Mountain, and farm tours. Many include talks by knowledgeable folks on complementary topics. The trust publishes *Hiking Trails & Public Access Points of the Greater Blue Hill Peninsula,* a 60-page booklet with details about trails, boat launches, swimming spots, and preserves.

★ BLUE HILL MOUNTAIN

Mountain seems a fancy label for a 943-footer, yet Blue Hill Mountain stands alone, visible from Camden and even beyond. On a clear day, head for the summit and take in the wraparound view encompassing Penobscot Bay, the hills of Mount Desert, and the Camden Hills. In mid-June the lupines along the way are breathtaking; in fall the colors are spectacular, with reddened blueberry barrens added to the variegated foliage. Go early in the day, as this is a popular, easy-to-moderate hike. Allow about 1.5 hours for the Osgood Trail, a two-mile out-and-back from the Mountain Road trailhead. For more challenge, connect with the moderate-to-challenging Hayes Trail, about one mile each way.

Take Route 15 (Pleasant St.) to Mountain Road and follow it 0.8 mile to the trailhead (on the left) and the small parking area (on the right). You can also walk (uphill) on the one-mile Post Office Trail.

The easy-to-moderate Becton Trail departs from the Turkey Farm Road trailhead (0.6 mi. off Rte. 172) and continues approximately two miles to the summit.

BLUE HILL TOWN PARK

At the end of Water Street is a small park with a terrific view, along with a small pebble beach, picnic tables, a portable toilet, and a playground.

Outfitters

The **Activity Shop** (139 Mines Rd.,

Forever Farms

Family farms are experiencing a resurgence in Maine. According to the **Maine Farmland Trust** (207/338-6575, www.mainefarmlandtrust.org), since 2002, Maine has gained more than 1,000 farms and it leads the nation in attracting young farmers. It leads the New England states in agricultural production, contributing $2 billion to the state's economy each year.

Maine is the world's largest producer of brown eggs and wild blueberries; it ranks eighth in the country in production of potatoes and second in production of maple syrup, and it ranks second in New England for both milk and livestock production. But much of the recent growth has been in smaller farms that grow vegetables and/or raise small livestock for local sale. Farm stands and farmers markets, community-supported agriculture programs, demand for fresh local fare in local restaurants, and growing public awareness of the importance of knowing where food originates all contribute to the strength of Maine's farms. Impressive statistics, yes, but there's a cloud on the horizon. The rising cost of land combined with the aging of the farmers who own much of the state's agricultural land threatens Maine's farming future.

Maine Farmland Trust is working to bridge that gap. The nonprofit organization's mission is to protect Maine's farmland and to support farmers and the future of farming in Maine. It does this in two primary ways: Protecting farmland with conservation easements that ensure that the land will always be available for farming, and increasing farm viability by giving farmers support with business planning and market development to help them prosper. The seedbed of farmland preservation in Maine is the Blue Hill Peninsula, where the **Blue Hill Heritage Trust** (BHHT, 207/374-5118, www.bluehillheritagetrust.org) has preserved more than 2,000 acres of farmland since 1989. One of the driving forces behind the BHHT's efforts is local farmer Paul Birdsall, who helped found the organization in 1985 and then went on to help found Maine Farmland Trust in 1999. Birdsall's 360-acre Horsepower Farm is one of 13 permanently preserved agricultural properties on the peninsula. Birdsall is the elder of four generations on the family farm in Penobscot. Back in the 1980s, when he recognized that development was pushing the cost of land higher than farmers could afford, he began to purchase available farmland, preserve it with easements, and then resell it to farmers, such as Philip and Heather Retberg of Quills End Farm, a 105-acre property in Penobscot.

The battle to preserve Maine's farmland is at a crucial stage. Over the next 10 years, ownership of as much as 400,000 acres of farmland is expected to change as aging farmers retire. Since its founding, Maine Farmland Trust has supported more than 500 farm families and protected more than 55,000 acres of farmland. It is working to support 1,000 families and to protect 100,000 acres. Doing so is expected to cost $50 million, but it will help ensure Maine's food security, and the economic impact of that investment is projected to be more than $50 million annually.

207/374-3600, www.theactivityshop.com) rents bicycles for $115/week and canoes, kayaks, and paddleboards for $125-245/week, including delivery on the peninsula.

Boat Excursions

Join captain Linda Greenlaw, of *Perfect Storm* fame, for the **Perfect Tour** (207/479-3000, https://theperfecttour.com) aboard the *Earnest*. Operating from Perry's Lobster Shack in Surry, Greenlaw offers two- to eight-hour custom charters beginning at $600 for two hours. Options include Catch Your Dinner: Lobster Fishing 101, Cocktail Cruise, Sunset Cruise, and Floating Picnic, in addition to fishing, bird-watching, and wildlife-watching.

FOOD

Lobster and Seafood

For lobster, fried fish, and a decent lobster roll, head to the **Fish Net** (163 Main St., 207/374-5240, 11am-8pm daily), an inexpensive, mostly take-out joint on the eastern end of town.

It's not easy to find ★ **Perry's Lobster Shack** (1076 Newbury Neck Rd., Surry, 207/667-1955, www.perryslobstershack.com, noon-9pm daily, no credit cards), but those seeking a classic lobster-shack experience should make the effort. This traditional Maine lobster shack is about five miles down Newbury Neck, just after the Causeway Place beach. Expect lobster, lobster and crab rolls, corn, chips, mussels, and clams. From the pier-top picnic tables, you're overlooking the water with Mount Desert Island as a backdrop. Unlike most lobster shacks, this one has wait service.

Quick Bites

With a full bar, indoor and outdoor seating, and a boatyard location on Webber's Cove, the **Boatyard Grill** (13 E. Blue Hill Rd., 207/374-3533, noon-9pm Thurs.-Mon., from $10) attracts the sailing and drinking crowd, who appreciate its laid-back, Caribbean-esque style. The menu ranges from burgers to lobster. There's often live music on Saturdays.

Picnic fare and pizza are available at **Merrill & Hinckley** (11 Union St., 207/374-2821, 6am-9pm Mon.-Fri., 7am-9pm Sat., 8am-8pm Sun.), a quirky, 150-year-old family-owned grocery and general store.

The **Blue Hill Wine Shop** (138 Main St., 207/374-2161, 10am-5:30pm Mon.-Sat.), tucked into a converted horse barn, carries more than 1,000 wines, plus teas, coffees, breads, and cheeses.

The **Blue Hill Co-Op and Café** (70 South St., 207/374-2165, http://bluehill.coop, 7am-8pm daily) sells organic and natural foods. Breakfast items, sandwiches, salads, and soups are available in the café.

For premium ice cream and gelato in creative and classic flavors, dip into **Pugnuts Ice Cream Shop** (1276 Surry Rd., Surry, 7am-9pm Mon.-Fri., 8am-9pm Sat.-Sun.).

Peninsula Provisions (5 Maine St., Blue Hill, 207/619-4986, 8am-5pm Mon-Fri., 8am-3pm Sat.) shares its space with a florist and sells coffee, ice cream, baked goods, and chocolates.

Blue Hill's first solar-powered nanobrewery, **DeepWater Brewing Co.** (33 Tenney Hill Rd., 207/374-2441, 4:30pm-9pm Tues.-Sun., $14-20) serves pub-style fare. Ask about tours of the brewery, located in a beautifully renovated historic barn behind the pub.

A good choice or breakfast or lunch, the **Harbor House of Blue Hill Café** (27 Water St., Blue Hill, 207/374-7027, 7am-2pm Tues.-Sat.) has indoor and outdoor seating.

Local gardeners, farmers, and craftspeople peddle their wares at the **Blue Hill Farmers Market** (9am-11am Sat. late May-mid-Oct.). Demonstrations by area chefs and artists are often on the agenda. From late May to late August and from mid-September to early October, the Saturday market is at the Blue Hill Fairgrounds; late August through mid-September, it moves to the Blue Hill Congregational Church.

Family Favorites

Marlintini's Grill (83 Mines St./Rte. 15, 207/374-2500, www.marlintinisgrill.com, from 11am daily, $10-20) is half sports bar, half restaurant. You can sit in either, but the best spot is on the screened-in porch. The menu includes soups, salads, burgers, fried seafood, rib eye, and nightly home-style specials; there's a kids' menu too. The portions are big, the service is good, and the food is decent.

Just south of town is **Barncastle** (125 South St., 207/374-2300, www.barn-castle.com, noon-8pm Tues.-Sat., $10-20), serving a creative selection of wood-fired pizzas in three sizes as well as sandwiches, subs, panini, calzones, salads, and comfort foods in a lovely Shingle-style cottage. There are vegetarian options. Expect to wait for a table; this is one popular spot.

Casual Dining

For breakfast, lunch, or dinner, tuck into **Sandy's Blue Hill Café** (40 Main St., 207/374-5550, http://sandysbluehillcafe.com, 7am-2pm Mon., 7am-2pm and 5pm-8pm Thurs.-Sun., $14-24), which also roasts its own coffee. The eclectic dinner menu ranges from

1: Thurston Co. 2: Blue Hill Inn 3: Perry's Lobster Shack

THE THURSTON CO.
STAURANT&BAR
1

BLUE HILL
INN
EST. 1840
2

turkey burgers and curry to espresso-dusted filet mignon and crispy duck.

The **Thurston Co.** (66 Main St., 207/374-7166, http://thethurstonco.com, 5pm-9pm Wed.-Mon., $16-32) occupies a historic forge building hanging over Mill Stream in downtown Blue Hill. The contemporary American menu reflects chef Matt Thurston's Louisiana childhood, culinary training in Colorado, and his more recent positions at Maine restaurants.

Fine Dining

For a lovely dinner by candlelight, make reservations at ★ **Arborvine** (33 Upper Tenney Hill/Main St., 207/374-2119, www.arborvine.com, 5:30pm-9pm Tues.-Sun., $28-36), a conscientiously renovated, two-century-old Cape-style house with four dining areas, each with a different feel and understated decor. Chef-owner John Hikade and his wife, Beth, prepare classic entrées such as crispy roasted duckling and roasted rack of lamb. Their mantra has been fresh and local for more than 30 years.

ACCOMMODATIONS

What's old is new at **Barncastle** (125 South St., 207/374-2330, www.barn-castle.com, $125-195), a late 19th-century Shingle-style Victorian that's listed in the National Register of Historic Places. It opens to a two-story foyer with a split stairway and balcony. Rooms and suites open off the balcony. All are spacious, minimally decorated, and offer contemporary accents. Rates include a continental breakfast. The downstairs tavern serves pizza, salads, and sandwiches; noise can be a factor.

The **Farmhouse Inn** (578 Pleasant St., Blue Hill, 207/374-5286, www.thefarmhouseinnmaine.com, $150-250) comprises a beautifully renovated 1870s farmhouse and connected barn, sited on 48 acres at the base of Blue Hill Mountain and about three miles from downtown Blue Hill. Guest rooms in the barn are small; those in the farmhouse offer more space. All guests have use of the public rooms, including one with table tennis, and a backyard fire pit.

Imagine a classic country inn, and the ★ **Blue Hill Inn** (Union St./Rte. 177, 207/374-2844 or 800/826-7415, www.bluehillinn.com, from $200) would be it. Built as a private residence in 1830 and converted to an inn in 1841, the antiques-filled inn is just steps from Main Street's shops and restaurants. Ten guest rooms and a suite have real chandeliers, four-poster beds, down comforters, fancy linens, and braided and Oriental rugs. Rear rooms overlook the extensive cutting garden, with chairs and a hammock. A three-course breakfast is served in the elegant dining room. Afternoon refreshments with sweets appear in the living room daily, and superb hors d'oeuvres are served 6pm-7pm in two elegant parlors or the garden. Also available are two year-round, pet-friendly suites with cooking facilities in the contemporary Cape House.

The ★ **Wave Walker Bed and Breakfast** (28 Wavewalker Ln., Surry, 207/667-5767, www.wavewalkerbedandbreakfast.com, from $265) has a jaw-dropping location near the tip of Newbury Neck. It sits on 20 private acres with 1,000 feet of shorefront as well as woods and blueberry fields. The newly built inn is smack on the oceanfront, with views across the water to Mount Desert Island. Four spacious guest rooms have wowser views. Guests also have use of a living room, sunroom, and oceanfront deck. A full hot breakfast is served. Kayaks are available. A separate two-bedroom-plus-loft cottage rents for $1,800 per week.

INFORMATION AND SERVICES

The **Blue Hill Peninsula Chamber of Commerce** (207/374-3242, www.bluehillpeninsula.org) is the best source for information on Blue Hill and the surrounding area.

Public restrooms are in the Blue Hill Town Hall (Main St.), Blue Hill Public Library (Main St.), and Blue Hill Memorial Hospital (Water St.).

GETTING THERE AND AROUND

Blue Hill is about 17 miles or 25 minutes via Routes 1 and 15 from Bucksport. It's about 14 miles or 20 minutes via Route 172 to Ellsworth, about 8 miles or 15 minutes via Route 15 to Brooksville, and about 20 miles or 35 minutes via Routes 15, 175, 199, and 166 to Castine.

Brooksville, Sedgwick, and Brooklin

I'm going to let you in on a secret, a part of Maine that seems right out of a time warp—a place with general stores and family farms, where family roots go back generations and summer rusticators have returned for decades. Nestled near the bottom of the Blue Hill Peninsula and surrounded by Castine, Blue Hill, and Deer Isle, this often-missed area—home to the towns of **Brooksville, Sedgwick,** and **Brooklin**—offers superb hiking, kayaking, and sailing, plus historic homes, unique shops, and artist studios.

BROOKSVILLE

Brooksville (pop. 934) drew the late Helen and Scott Nearing to Harborside on Cape Rosier. Their book *Living the Good Life* made them role models for back-to-the-landers, who still come today. **Buck's Harbor** (a harbor in Brooksville and the general locale for what passes as the center of town) is the setting for *One Morning in Maine,* one of Robert McCloskey's beloved children's books.

Sights

THE GOOD LIFE CENTER

Forest Farm, home of the late Helen and Scott Nearing, is now the site of the **Good Life Center** (372 Harborside Rd., Harborside, 207/326-8211, www.goodlife.org). Advocates of simple living and authors of 10 books on the subject, the Nearings created a trust to perpetuate their farm and philosophy. Resident stewards lead **tours** (usually 1pm-5pm Thurs.-Mon. mid-June-early Sept., Sat.-Sun. early Sept.-mid-Oct., $10 donation). Ask about the schedule for the traditional Monday-night meetings (7pm), featuring free programs by gardeners, philosophers, musicians, and other guest speakers. Occasional work parties, workshops, and conferences are also on the docket. From Route 176 in Brooksville, take Cape Rosier Road and go 8 miles, passing Holbrook Island Sanctuary. At the Grange Hall, turn right and follow the road 1.9 miles to the end. Turn left onto Harborside Road and continue 1.8 miles to Forest Farm, across from Orrs Cove.

FOUR SEASON FARM

About a mile beyond the Nearings' place is **Four Season Farm** (609 Weir Cove Rd., Harborside, 207/326-4455, http://fourseasonfarm.com), the lush organic farm owned and operated by internationally renowned gardeners Eliot Coleman and Barbara Damrosch. Both have written numerous books and articles and starred in TV gardening shows. The experimental market garden, a model for small-scale sustainable agriculture, operates year-round. Visitors are welcome to drive in and around the farm; a farm stand operates 10am-2pm Saturdays.

Recreation

★ HOLBROOK ISLAND SANCTUARY STATE PARK

In the early 1970s, foresighted benefactor Anita Harris donated to the state 1,230 acres in Brooksville that would become the **Holbrook Island Sanctuary** (207/326-4012, www.parksandlands.com, free). From Route 176, between West Brooksville and South Brooksville, head west on Cape Rosier Road, following brown-and-white signs for the sanctuary. Trail maps and bird checklists

Scenic Routes

Cape Rosier

Get way, way off the beaten path with a loop around **Cape Rosier,** the westernmost arm of the town of Brooksville. The Cape Rosier loop takes in Holbrook Island Sanctuary, Goose Falls, the hamlet of Harborside, and plenty of water and island views. Note that some roads are unpaved, but they usually are well maintained.

No one seems to know how **Caterpillar Hill** got its name, but its reputation comes from a panoramic vista of water, hills, and blueberry barrens—with a couple of convenient picnic tables where you can stop for lunch, photos, or a ringside view of the sunset and fall foliage. From the 350-foot elevation, the views take in Walker Pond, Eggemoggin Reach, Deer Isle, Swans Island, and even the Camden Hills. The signposted rest area is on Route 175/15; watch out for the blind curve when you pull off the road.

Between Sargentville and Sedgwick, Route 175 offers elevated views of Eggemoggin Reach, with shore access to the Benjamin River just before you reach Sedgwick village.

Naskeag Point Road begins off Route 175 in "downtown" Brooklin, heads down the peninsula for 3.7 miles, passing the entrance to *WoodenBoat* Publications, and ends at a small shingle beach (limited parking) on Eggemoggin Reach. You'll find picnic tables, a boat launch, a seasonal toilet, and a marker commemorating the 1778 Battle of Naskeag, when British sailors came ashore from the sloop *Gage,* burned several buildings, and were run off by a ragtag band of local settlers.

are available in boxes at trailheads or at park headquarters. The easy Backshore Trail (about 30 minutes) starts here, or go back a mile and climb the steepish trail to **Backwoods Mountain** for the best vistas. Other attractions include shorefront picnic tables and grills, four old cemeteries, super birdwatching during spring and fall migrations, a pebble beach, and a stone beach. Leashed pets are permitted, but no bikes are allowed on the trails, and camping is not permitted. The park is officially open May 15 to October 15, but the access road and parking areas are plowed in winter for cross-country skiers.

Theater

Bagaduce Theatre (176 Mills Point Rd., Brooksville, 207/801-1536, www.bagaducetheatre.com) presents plays starring Equity actors at the Fowler Farm from May into September.

Shopping

When you need a slate sink, a claw-foot tub, brass fixtures, or a Palladian window, **Architectural Antiquities** (52 Indian Point Ln., Harborside, 207/326-4938, www.archantiquities.com), on Cape Rosier, is just the ticket—a restorer's delight. It's open all year by appointment; ask for directions when you call.

Makers' Market (30 Bagaduce Rd., Brooksville, 207/812-3703) is a double hit: Not only is it a shop carrying locally produced crafts and treasures, it's home to the **Ecouture Textile Studio,** where Amelia Poole handcrafts one-of-a-kind scarves, clothing, and art from all-natural and sustainable textiles—including cotton, silk, and linen—dyed with plant-sourced colors.

Food

QUICK BITES

In North Brooksville, where Route 175/176 crosses the Bagaduce River, stands **Bagaduce Lunch** (145 Franks Flat, Penobscot, 11am-7pm Thurs.-Tues., 11am-3pm Wed.), a take-out shack named an "American Classic" by the James Beard Foundation in 2008. Owners Judy and Mike Astbury buy local fish and clams. Check the tide calendar and go when the tide is changing; order fried clams, settle in at a picnic table, and watch the reversing falls. If you're lucky, you might sight an eagle, osprey, or seal.

Lunch is the specialty at **Buck's Harbor Market** (6 Cornfield Hill Rd., South Brooksville, 207/326-8683, www.bucksharbormarket.com, 8am-6pm daily), a low-key, marginally gentrified general store popular with yachties in summer. Pick up sandwiches, cheeses, prepared foods, breads, and treats for a Holbrook Island adventure.

You often can find **Tinder Hearth**'s (1452 Coastal Rd., Brooksville, 207/326-8381, http://tinderhearth.com) organic, wood-fired, European-style breads and pastries in local shops and at farmers markets, but you can buy them right at the bakery on Tuesdays and Fridays. On some evenings, Tinder Hearth bakes thin-crust pizzas. Reservations are required; call for the current schedule and menu. The bakery is on the west side of Route 176 north of the Cape Rosier Road.

Family-run **Strong Brewing Company** (7 Rope Ferry Rd., Sedgwick, 207/359-8722, http://strongbrewing.com, noon-8pm daily) is open for tastings and often has live music. Find it at the intersection of Routes 15 and 176.

Three varieties of English-style hard cider are specialties at the **Sow's Ear Winery** (Rte. 176 at Herrick Rd., Brooksville, 207/326-4649, no credit cards), a minuscule operation in a funky two-story shingled shack. Winemaker Tom Hoey also produces sulfite-free blueberry, chokecherry, and rhubarb wines; he'll let you sample it all. Ask to see his cellar, where everything happens. Lining the walls in the tiny tasting room/shop are books, also for sale, that concentrate on architecture and history, with specialty areas highlighting Gothic arches and Russian history, but including plenty of other esoteric topics.

CASUAL DINING

Behind the Buck's Harbor Market is ★ **Buck's Restaurant** (6 Cornfield Hill Rd., Brooksville, 207/326-8688, www.bucksrestaurant.weebly.com, 5:30pm-8:30pm Mon.-Sat., $21-33), where guests dine at white-clothed tables inside or on a screened porch. The American menu reflects what's locally available, has a few international accents, and changes frequently.

The **Oakland House Dining Room** (435 Herrick Rd., Brooksville, 207/359-8521, www.oaklandhouse.com), 7:30am-10am and from 5:30pm Tues.-Sat., 7:30am-10am, 11am-2pm, and from 5:30pm Sun., $12-38), serves a farm-to-table, American breakfasts, dinners, and Sunday brunch in a lovely porch-style room.

Accommodations

COTTAGE COLONIES

The two operations in this category feel much like informal family compounds—places where you quickly become an adoptee. These are extremely popular spots where successive generations of hosts have catered to successive generations of visitors, and reservations are usually essential for July-August. Many guests book for the following year before they leave. We're not talking fancy: The cottages are old-shoe rustic, of varying sizes and decor. Most have cooking facilities; one colony includes breakfast and dinner in July-August. Both have hiking trails, playgrounds, rowboats, and East Penobscot Bay on the doorstep.

The fourth generation manages the **Hiram Blake Camp** (220 Weir Cove Rd., Harborside, 207/326-4951, www.hiramblake.com, Memorial Day-late Sept., no credit cards), but other generations pitch in and help with gardening, lobstering, maintenance, and kibitzing. Fifteen one- to six-bedroom cottages line the shore of this 100-acre property, which has been in family hands since before the Revolutionary War. The camp itself dates from 1916. Don't bother bringing reading material: The dining room has ingenious ceiling niches lined with countless books. Guests also have the use of rowboats, and kayak rentals are available. Home-cooked breakfasts and dinners are served family-style; lobster is always available at an additional charge. Much of the fare is grown in the expansive gardens. Other facilities include a dock, a recreation room, a pebble beach, and an outdoor chapel. There's a one-week minimum (beginning Sat. or Sun.) from late June through August, when cottages go for $1,200-3,700 per week (including breakfast, dinner, and linens). Off-season rates (no meals or linens, but cottages have cooking facilities) are $785-2,750 per week. Pets are welcome.

The ninth generation took over **Oakland House Cottages by the Side of the Sea** (435 Herrick Rd., Brooksville, 207/359-8521, www.oaklandhouse.com, from $225) in 2018. Much of this rolling, wooded land fronting on Eggemoggin Reach was part of the original king's grant way back in 1765. Eight nicely furnished and well-equipped one- and two-bedroom cottages are tucked along the shoreline or in the trees, and two newly renovated rooms and two-bedroom suites are in the main inn. Other pluses are trails threading through the woods and providing access to viewpoints and a pocket beach. An on-site restaurant offers breakfast and dinner. Rental canoes, kayaks, paddleboards, bikes, and fishing gear are available; sailboat and powerboat excursions are offered; and horseback riding and tennis can be arranged. Two cottages are dog friendly ($25/night).

GUEST HOUSE

Sited on the lovely Oakland House Seaside Resort grounds is **Acorn Guesthouse** (435 Herrick Rd., Brooksville, 207/359-8521, www.mainehostel.com), offering a mix of dorm-style, private, and semiprivate rooms, with rates ranging $60-99/room. Living spaces, bathrooms, and the kitchen are shared. Linens and towels are provided.

Getting There and Around

Buck's Harbor, Brooksville, is about eight miles or 15 minutes from Blue Hill via Routes 15, 175, and 176. From Buck's Harbor, it's about eight miles or 15 minutes to Harborside on Cape Rosier via Route 176 to the Cape Rosier Road or about nine miles or 15 minutes to Sedgwick.

SEDGWICK

Incorporated in 1789, **Sedgwick** (pop. 1,196) once included all of Brooklin and part of Brooksville. Now wedged between the two, it includes the hamlet of **Sargentville,** the **Caterpillar Hill** scenic overlook, and a well-preserved complex of historic buildings.

Sights

HISTORICAL SIGHTS

Now used as the museum and headquarters of the Sedgwick-Brooklin Historical Society, the 1795 **Reverend Daniel Merrill House** (Rte. 172, Sedgwick, 2pm-4pm Sun. July-Aug., donation) was the parsonage for Sedgwick's first

1: El El Frijoles in Sedgwick 2: Oakland House Cottages by the Side of the Sea

1
2

permanent minister. Inside the house are period furnishings, old photos, toys, and tools; a few steps away are a restored 1874 schoolhouse, an 1821 cattle pound (for corralling wandering bovines), and a hearse barn. Pick up a brochure during open hours and guide yourself around the buildings and grounds. The **Sedgwick Historic District,** crowning Town House Hill, comprises the Merrill House and its outbuildings, plus the imposing 1794 Town House and the 23-acre Rural Cemetery (the oldest headstone dates from 1798) across Route 172.

Recreation

PARKS AND PRESERVES

Just south and below the Caterpillar Hill scenic overlook, take the Cooper Farm Road to find two preserves, one for an easy-to-moderate hike and the other for a swim or paddle.

The Blue Hill Heritage Trust's **Cooper Farm at Caterpillar Hill** offers a three-loop trail network winding through blueberry barrens and woods. If you follow the entire outer loop, it's 1.5 miles round-trip, but you can shorten or lengthen that via the cross trails. In late July and August, help yourself to the blueberries.

Afterward, continue a bit farther along Cooper Farm Road to Landing Road, which leads to the **Sedgwick/Brooksville Town Landing** on Walker Pond. You'll find docks and floats, picnic tables, and a small sand beach with shallow water. It's a fine place to picnic, swim, paddle, or launch a small boat.

Shopping

Most local businesses are small, owner-operated shops, which means they're often catch-as-catch-can.

Don't miss the "world's smallest bookstore," Bill Henderson's **Pushcart Press Bookstore** (380 Christy Hill, Sedgwick, 207/266-2531). It's a trove of literary fiction both used and new, including editions of the *Pushcart Prize: Best of the Small Presses* annual series. Sales help support Pushcart fellowships.

Mermaid Woolens (34 Reach Rd., Sedgwick, 207/359-2747, www.mermaidwoolens.com), source of Elizabeth Coakley's wildly colorful hand-knit vests, socks, and sweaters. They're pricey but worth every nickel. Call first.

Food

★ **El El Frijoles** (41 Caterpillar Rd./Rte. 15, Sargentville, 207/359-2486, www.elelfrijoles.com, 11am-8pm Wed.-Sat., $6-16)—that's *L. L. Beans* to you gringos—gets raves for its made-from-scratch California-style empanadas, burritos, and tacos, many of which have a Maine accent. Try the spicy lobster burritos or a daily special, such as ranchero shrimp tacos. Dine in the screen house or on picnic tables on the lawn; there's a play area for children.

Getting There and Around

Sedgwick is about eight miles or 15 minutes via Route 175 from Brooksville. It's about 5 miles (10 minutes) to Brooklin via Route 175 or 10 miles (15 minutes) to Blue Hill via Route 172.

BROOKLIN

Brooklin (pop. 824) is known by many travelers, thanks to two magazines: the *New Yorker* and *WoodenBoat.* Wordsmiths extraordinaire E. B. and Katharine White "dropped out" to Brooklin in the 1930s and forever afterward dispatched their splendid material for the *New Yorker* from here. In 1977, *WoodenBoat* magazine moved its headquarters to Brooklin, where its 60-acre shore-side estate attracts builders and dreamers from all over the globe.

Sights

WOODENBOAT PUBLICATIONS

On Naskeag Point Road, 1.2 miles from Route 175 in downtown Brooklin, a small sign marks the turn to the world headquarters of ***WoodenBoat*** (Naskeag Point Rd., Brooklin, 207/359-4651, www.woodenboat.com, 7:30am-6pm Mon.-Fri., 9am-5pm Sat.).

E. B. White: Some Writer

Every child since the mid-1940s has heard of E. B. White—author of the memorable *Stuart Little, Charlotte's Web,* and *Trumpet of the Swan*—and every college kid for decades has been reminded to consult *The Elements of Style.* But how many realize that White and his wife, Katharine, were living not in the big city but in the hamlet of North Brooklin, Maine? It was Brooklin that inspired Charlotte and Wilbur and Stuart, and it was Brooklin where the Whites lived very full, creative lives.

Abandoning their desks at the *New Yorker* in 1938, Elwyn Brooks White and Katharine S. White bought an idyllic saltwater farm on the Blue Hill Peninsula and moved here with their young son, Joel. Andy (as E. B. had been dubbed since his college days at Cornell) produced 20 books, countless essays and letters to editors, and hundreds (maybe thousands?) of "newsbreaks"—those wry clipping-and-commentary items sprinkled through each issue of the *New Yorker.* Katharine continued wielding her pencil as the magazine's standout children's-book editor, donating many of her review copies to Brooklin's Friends Memorial Library. (The library also has two original Garth Williams drawings from *Stuart Little,* courtesy of E. B., and a lovely garden dedicated to the Whites.) Katharine's book, *Onward and Upward in the Garden,* a collection of her *New Yorker* gardening pieces, was published in 1979.

E. B. White died on October 1, 1985, at the age of 86. He and Katharine and Joel left large footprints on this earth, but perhaps nowhere more so than in Brooklin.

Buy magazines, books, clothing, and all manner of nautical merchandise at the handsome store, stroll the grounds, or sign up for one of the dozens of one- and two-week spring, summer, and fall courses in seamanship, navigation, boatbuilding, sail making, marine carving, and more; tuition varies by course and duration. Special courses are geared to kids, women, pros, and all-thumbs neophytes; the camaraderie is legendary, and so is the cuisine. School visiting hours are 8am-5pm Monday-Saturday June-October.

Shopping

Virginia G. Sarsfield handcrafts paper products, including custom lampshades, calligraphy papers, books, and lamps, at **Handmade Papers** (113 Reach Rd., Brooklin, 207/359-8345, www.handmadepapersonline.com).

It's worth the mosey out Flye Point to find **Flye Point Sculpture Garden & Art Gallery** (436 Flye Point Rd., Brooklin, 207/610-0350), where Peter Stremlau displays fine works in varied media by Maine-based and Maine-inspired artists. Wander through gardens and woodlands accented with sculptures. More sculptures, as well as paintings and accordion books, are inside the gallery. The waterfront location is spectacular.

Leaf and Anna (12 Reach Rd., 207/359-5030), in Brooklin village, is a browser's delight, filled with garden and kitchen must-haves, items for boats, and books.

Food

QUICK BITES

The **Brooklin General Store** (4 Reach Rd., junction of Rte. 175 and Naskeag Point Rd., Brooklin, 207/359-8359, http://brooklingeneralstore.com, 6am-8pm Mon.-Fri., 6am-7pm Sat.-Sun.), dating from 1866 but completely rebuilt in 2017, carries groceries, beer and wine, newspapers, and local chatter as well as sandwiches, breakfast treats, baked goods, and pizza.

CASUAL DINING

Fresh farm-to-table fare is served at the **Brooklin Inn Restaurant** (Rte. 175, Brooklin, 207/359-2777, www.thebrooklininn.com, 8:30am-1:30pm daily café, 5:30pm-8:30pm Tues.-Sat. restaurant, $16-33). Also here is the **Pub** (5pm-10pm Tues.-Sun.), with a food cart on Sunday evenings.

Accommodations

It's an easy walk to the village center from the **Maine Hideaway Guest House** (19 Naskeag Point Rd., Brooklin, 207/610-2244, www.themainehideaway.com, $115-135), a nicely renovated and updated 1874 Victorian with contemporary decor. Rates include breakfast. Some rooms share baths. Also available are an apartment and a two-story suite ($165).

New owners in 2019 have updated and renovated the **Brooklin Inn** (Rte. 175, Brooklin, 207/359-2777, www.thebrooklininn.com, $145-175), which offers four handsome guestrooms.

CAMPING

With 730 feet of waterfront on Eggemoggin Reach and 16 wooded acres, **Oceanfront Camping @ Reach Knolls** (666 Reach Rd., Brooklin, 207/359-5555, www.reachknolls.com, $29 tent, $39 RV, no credit cards) is a no-frills campground with 32 wooded sites, some with water views. The camp office has free showers and potable water; there is no water at the sites. The campground can accommodate RVs up to 35 feet in length, and electricity is available. There are privies and a dump station. A path leads to the pebbly beach where you can launch a kayak.

Getting There and Around

Brooklin is about five miles or 10 minutes via Route 175 from Sedgwick. It's about 12 miles or 20 minutes to Blue Hill via Route 175 or about 18 miles or 30 minutes to Deer Isle Village via Routes 175 and 15.

INFORMATION AND SERVICES

The best source of information about the region is the **Blue Hill Peninsula Chamber of Commerce** (207/374-2281, www.bluehillpeninsula.org).

Local **Penobscot Bay Press** (www.penobscotbaypress.com), which publishes a collection of local newspapers, also maintains an excellent website, with listings for area businesses as well as articles highlighting area happenings.

Castine

Castine (pop. 1,366) is a gem—a serene New England village with a tumultuous past. It tips a cape, surrounded by water on three sides, including the entrance to the Penobscot River, which made it a strategic defense point. Once beset by geopolitical squabbles, saluting the flags of three different nations (France, Britain, and the Netherlands), its only crises now are local political skirmishes. This is an unusual community, a National Register of Historic Places enclave that many people never find. The town celebrated its bicentennial in 1996. Today a major presence is the Maine Maritime Academy, yet Castine remains the quietest college town imaginable.

What visitors discover is a year-round community with a busy waterfront, an easy-to-conquer layout, a handful of traditional inns, wooded trails on the outskirts of town, an astonishing collection of splendid Georgian and Federalist architecture, and water views nearly every which way you turn.

HISTORY

Originally known as Fort Pentagouet, Castine received its current name courtesy of Jean-Vincent d'Abbadie, Baron de Saint-Castin. A young French nobleman manqué who married a Wabanaki princess named Pidiwamiska, d'Abbadie ran the town in the second half of the 17th century and eventually returned to France.

A century later, in 1779, occupying British troops and their reinforcements scared off potential American seaborne attackers (including Col. Paul Revere), who turned tail up the Penobscot River and ended up scuttling their more than 40-vessel fleet—a humiliation known as the Penobscot Expedition and still regarded as one of the worst naval defeats for the United States.

When the boundaries for Maine were finally set in 1820, with the St. Croix River marking the east rather than the Penobscot River, the last British Loyalists departed, some floating their homes north to St. Andrews in New Brunswick, Canada, where they can still be seen today. For a while, peace and prosperity became the bywords for Castine—with lively commerce in fish and salt—but it all collapsed during the California gold rush and the Civil War trade embargo, leaving the town down on its luck.

Of the many historical landmarks scattered around town, one of the most intriguing must be the sign on "Wind Mill Hill," at the junction of Route 166 and State Street:

> On Hatch's Hill there stands a mill. Old Higgins he doth tend it. And every time he grinds a grist, he has to stop and mend it.

In smaller print, just below the rhyme, comes the drama:

> Here two British soldiers were shot for desertion.

Castine has quite a history indeed.

SIGHTS

★ Castine Historical Tour

To appreciate Castine fully, you need to arm yourself with the Castine Merchants Association's visitors brochure-map (all businesses and lodgings in town have copies) and follow the numbers on bike or on foot. With no stops, walking the route takes less than an hour, but you'll want to read dozens of historical plaques, peek into public buildings, shoot some photos, and perhaps even do some shopping.

The **Wilson Museum** (107 Perkins St., 207/326-8545, www.wilsonmuseum.org, 10am-5pm Mon.-Fri., 2pm-5pm Sat.-Sun. late May-late Sept., free), a cabinet of curiosities founded in 1921, contains an intriguingly eclectic but well-presented two-story collection of prehistoric artifacts, ship models, dioramas, baskets, tools, and minerals assembled over a lifetime by John Howard Wilson, a geologist-anthropologist who first visited Castine in 1891 (and died in 1936). Among the exhibits are Balinese masks, ancient oil lamps, cuneiform tablets, Zulu artifacts, pre-Inca pottery, and assorted local findings. It's well worth visiting.

Next door is the late 18th-century **John Perkins House,** moved to Perkins Street from Court Street in 1969 and restored with period furnishings. It's open in July and August for guided tours (on the hour, 2pm-5pm Sun. and Wed., $5).

Across the street and open the same days and hours as the Perkins House are the **Village Blacksmith** and the **Woodshop,** both with free demonstrations.

At the end of Battle Avenue stands the 19th-century **Dyce Head Lighthouse,** no longer operating; the keeper's house is owned by the town. Alongside is a public path (signposted Enter at Your Own Risk) leading via a wooden staircase to a tiny patch of rocky shoreline and the beacon that has replaced the lighthouse.

The highest point in town is **Fort George,** site of a 1779 British fortification. Nowadays, little remains except grassy earthworks, but there are interpretive displays and picnic tables.

Main Street, descending toward the water, is a feast for historic architecture fans. Artist Fitz Hugh Lane and author Mary McCarthy once lived in elegant houses along the elm-lined street (neither building is open to the public). On Court Street between Main and Green Streets stands turn-of-the-20th-century **Emerson Hall,** site of Castine's municipal offices.

Across Court Street, **Witherle Memorial Library,** a handsome early 19th-century building on the site of the 18th-century town jail, looks out on the Town Common. Also facing the Common are the Adams and Abbott Schools, the former still an elementary school. The **Abbott School** (10am-4pm

Maine Maritime Academy

the *State of Maine,* Maine Maritime Academy's training ship

The state's only merchant-marine college—one of only seven in the nation—occupies 35 acres in the middle of Castine. Founded in 1941, the academy awards undergraduate and graduate degrees in such areas as marine engineering, ocean studies, and marina management, preparing a student body of about 950 men and women for careers as ship captains, naval architects, and marine engineers.

The academy owns a fleet of 60 vessels, including the historic gaff-rigged research schooner *Bowdoin,* flagship of arctic explorer Admiral Donald MacMillan, and the 500-foot training vessel *State of Maine,* berthed down the hill at the waterfront. The *Bowdoin*, the Official Vessel of the State of Maine, is a National Historic Landmark. In 1996-1997, the *State of Maine,* formerly the U.S. Navy oceanographic research vessel *Tanner,* underwent a $12 million conversion for use by the academy. It is still subject to deployment, and in 2005, the school quickly had to find alternate beds for students using the ship as a dormitory when it was called into service in support of rescue and rebuilding efforts after Hurricane Katrina in New Orleans.

Weekday **tours of the campus** can be arranged through the admissions office (207/326-2206 or 800/227-8465 outside Maine, www.mainemaritime.edu). Campus highlights include the three-story Nutting Memorial Library, in Platz Hall; the Henry A. Scheel Room, a cozy oasis in Leavitt Hall containing memorabilia from late naval architect Henry Scheel and his wife, Jeanne; and the well-stocked bookstore (Curtis Hall, 207/326-9333).

Mon.-Sat., 1pm-4pm Sun. July-early Sept., reduced schedule spring and fall, donation), built in 1859, has been carefully restored for use as a museum and headquarters for the **Castine Historical Society** (207/326-4118, www.castinehistoricalsociety.org). A big draw at the volunteer-run museum is the 24-foot-long Bicentennial Quilt, assembled for Castine's 200th anniversary in 1996. The historical society, founded in 1966, organizes lectures, exhibits, and special events (some free) in various places around town.

On the outskirts of town, across the narrow neck between Wadsworth Cove and Hatch's Cove, stretches a rather overgrown canal (signposted British Canal) scooped out by the occupying British during the War of 1812. Effectively severing land access to the town of Castine, the Brits thus raised havoc, collected local revenues for eight months, and then departed for Halifax with enough funds to establish Dalhousie College, now Dalhousie University. Wear waterproof boots to walk the canal route; the best time to go is at low tide.

If a waterfront picnic sounds appealing, settle in on the grassy earthworks along the harbor-front at **Fort Madison,** site of an 1808 garrison (then Fort Porter) near the corner of Perkins and Madockawando Streets. The views from here are fabulous, and it's accessible all year. A set of stairs leads down to the rocky waterfront.

Tours

The **Castine Historical Society** (17 School St., 207/326-4118, www.castinehistoricalsociety.org) offers free, guided walking tours at 10am Saturdays in July and August. Private tours may be available on other days; call for details.

Or, opt for a one-hour tour aboard *Scarlet,* a five-passenger, street-legal golf cart operated by the nonprofit **Castine Touring Company** (207/326-5088, $10pp). It operates 10am-5pm daily during the summer season, departing from the Town Dock.

ENTERTAINMENT

See what's on the calendar for the Castine Arts Association (www.castinearts.org). Possibilities for live music include **Danny Murphy's Pub** (on the wharf, tucked underneath the bank and facing the parking area and harbor) and Jazz Tuesdays at the **Pentagoet Inn.**

The **Wilson Museum** (107 Perkins St., 207/326-8545, www.wilsonmuseum.org) frequently schedules concerts, lectures, and demonstrations. The **Trinitarian Church** often brings in high-caliber musical entertainment.

Bastille Day in July is celebrated with food, tours, open studios, music, the Picnic en Blanc (you must wear white), and more.

Castine sponsors the intellectual side of the early August Wooden Boat Regatta. The **Castine Yacht Club** brings in a who's who of big-name sail-related designers and racers for this annual lecture series. Other events include on-the-dock boat tours and limited sailing opportunities.

SHOPPING

Gallery B (5 Main St., 213/839-0851, www.gallerybgallery.com) shows fine art and sculpture. The **Compass Rose Bookstore** (3 Main St., 207/326-5034) specializes in maritime history, coastal Maine-based authors, and environmental history, and doubles as a coffee bar. Oil paintings by local artists Joshua and Susan Adam are on view at **Adam Gallery** (140 Battle Ave., 207/326-8272).

RECREATION

Witherle Woods

The 185-acre **Witherle Woods,** owned by Maine Coast Heritage Trust (www.mcht.org), is a popular walking area with a 4.2-mile maze of trails and old woods roads leading to the water. Many Revolutionary War-era relics have been found here; if you see any, do not remove them. Access to the preserve is via a dirt road off Battle Avenue, between the water district property (at the end of the wire fence) and the Manor's exit driveway, and diagonally across from La Tour Street. You can download a map from the website.

TOP EXPERIENCE

★ Sea Kayaking

Castine Kayak Adventures (17 Sea St., 207/866-3506, www.castinekayak.com) is spearheaded by Maine Guide Karen Francoeur, or "Kayak Karen," as she's known locally. All skill levels are accommodated, but Karen is particularly adept with beginners, delivering wise advice from beginning to end. Three-hour half-day trips are $55; six-hour full-day tours are around $110 and include lunch. Sunset tours, 2.5 hours, are $55; the sunrise tour includes a light breakfast for $55. Bioluminescent Night Paddle tours, under the stars (weather permitting), run about 2.5-3 hours and are $65 per person. If you have your own boat, call Karen; she knows these waters. She offers instruction for all levels as well as

2

Here CAPTAIN JURRIAEN AERNOUTS of the DUTCH FRIGATE FLYING HORSE

1674

Having captured FORT PENTAGOET August 1674, took formal possession of ACADIA, in the name of his SOVEREIGN, WILLIAM, PRINCE of ORANGE, by burying a glass bottle containing a copy of his commission and a declaration of his official act, naming the conquered territory

NOVA HOLLANDIA

a Maine Sea Kayak Guide course. Karen also rents kayaks (from $45/day single, $60 double) and **bicycles** ($20/day).

Swimming

Backshore Beach, a crescent of sand and gravel on Wadsworth Cove Road (turn off Battle Ave. at the Castine Golf Club), is a favorite saltwater swimming spot, with views across the bay to Stockton Springs. Be forewarned, though, that ocean swimming in this part of Maine is not for the timid. The best time to try it is on the incoming tide, after the sun has had time to heat up the mud. At mid- to high tide, it's also the best place to put in a sea kayak.

Golf

The nine-hole **Castine Golf Club** (200 Battle Ave., 207/326-8844, www.castinegolfclub.com) dates to 1897, when the first tee required a drive from a 30-step-high mound. Willie Park Jr. redesigned it in 1921.

Boat Excursions

Guildive Cruises (207/701-1421, www.castinecruises.com) offers two different ways to enjoy Castine from the water. The ***Guildive***, constructed in 1934 and captained by Kate Kana and Zander Parker, offers two-hour sails, departing up to three times daily from the Wharf at 15 Sea Street, for $50; sunset sails, which include a light appetizer, are $55. ***Lil' Toot*** offers two excursions by reservation: one to Holbrook Island that allows about 3.5 hours to enjoy the parklands and the other a 1.5-hour harbor tour ($42.50pp).

FOOD

Quick Bites

The **Castine Farmers Market** takes place on the Town Common 9am-11:30am Thursdays.

Luscious baked goods fill the counter of **Castine Variety** (5 Main St., 207/326-9920, 7am-8pm Mon.-Fri., 7am-7pm Sat.-Sun., $6-22), a restored former general store. The menu blends classic American fare with Hawaiian and Southeast Asian flavors, a nod to the owner's background. BYOB.

MarKels (26 Water St., 207/326-9510, www.markelsbakehouse.com, 7am-2pm daily), a higgledy-piggledy eatery of three rooms and a deck at the end of an alleyway tucked between Main and Water Streets, is a delicious find for breakfast, lunch, or sweets. Stop here for coffee, juices, pastries, interesting snacks and salads, homemade soups, specials, and delicious sandwiches.

The **Captain's Catch** (Town Dock, 207/460-4212, 11am-7pm daily), a waterfront take-out stand, is an excellent bet for summer classics such as lobster and crab rolls, burgers, and haddock sandwiches. You can't beat the location or the view, and much of the menu is locally sourced and made from scratch.

Your best bet for late-night eats is **Danny Murphy's Pub** (5 Sea St., on the wharf, tucked underneath the bank facing the parking area and harbor, 207/326-1004, 4pm-10pm daily), a sports bar with video games, a pool table, and frequent live entertainment. The pizza gets high marks.

Family Favorites

On a warm summer day, it's hard to find a better place to while away a few hours than **15 Sea Street Bar & Grill** (15 Sea St., 207/326-9045, noon-9pm Thurs.-Sun., $17-30). Next to the Town Dock, it's a barn of a place, with an outside deck and front-row windjammer-watching seats in summer. The American menu emphasizes seafood.

Casual Dining

Jazz music plays softly and dinner is by candlelight at the ★ **Pentagöet** (26 Main St., 207/326-8616 or 800/845-1701, www.pentagoet.com, from 6pm Tues.-Sat., $18-34). In fine weather, you can dine on the porch. Choices vary from roasted *loup de mer* to slow-cooked lamb shank, or simply make a meal of small plates and starters, such as crab cakes and a salad. Don't miss the

1: Castine waterfront 2: an interpretive sign in Castine

1

2

lobster bouillabaisse or the chocolate *budino*, a scrumptious warm Italian pudding that melts in your mouth (a must for chocoholics). Enjoy live jazz on the porch 5pm-8pm Tuesdays in July and August.

ACCOMMODATIONS

Inns

Castine is not the place to come if you require in-room phones, air-conditioning, or fancy bathrooms. The pace is relaxed and the accommodations reflect the easy elegance of a bygone era.

The three-story Queen Anne-style ★ **Pentagöet Inn** (26 Main St., 207/326-8616 or 800/845-1701, www.pentagoet.com, May-late Oct., $135-295) is the perfect Maine summer inn, right down to the lace curtains billowing in the breeze, the soft floral wallpapers, and the intriguing curiosities that accent but don't clutter the guest rooms. Innkeepers Jack Burke, previously with the U.S. Foreign Service, and Julie Van de Graaf, a pastry chef, took over the century-old inn in 2000 and have given it new life, upgrading rooms and furnishing them with Victorian antiques, adding handsome gardens, and carving out a niche as a dining destination. The inn's 16 guest rooms are spread between the main house and the adjoining, pet-friendly, renovated 1791 Federal-style Perkins House. A hot buffet breakfast, afternoon refreshments, and evening hors d'oeuvres are provided. Jack holds court in the pub (chock-full of vintage photos and prints as well as exotic antiques), advising guests on activities and opportunities. Borrow one of the inn's bikes and explore town or simply walk—the Main Street location is convenient to everything Castine offers.

The venerable **Castine Inn** (41 Main St., 207/326-4365, www.castineinn.com, $150-235) has 19 second- and third-floor guest rooms and suites; some have water views; a few are air-conditioned. Public space includes a formal living room as well as a wraparound porch overlooking the gardens. Breakfast ($9 guests, $10 public) is served in the dining room, which features a wraparound mural of Castine.

Rental Properties

For summer cottage rentals, contact **Saltmeadow Properties** (7 Main St., 207/326-9116, www.saltmeadowproperties.com).

INFORMATION AND SERVICES

Castine has no local information office, but all businesses and lodgings in town have copies of the Castine Merchants Association's visitor's brochure-map. For additional information, go to the **Castine Town Office** (Emerson Hall, 67 Court St., 207/326-4502, www.castine.me.us, 8am-3:30pm Mon.-Fri.). Find **public restrooms** by the dock, at the foot of Main Street.

GETTING THERE AND AROUND

Castine is about 16 miles or 25 minutes via Routes 1, 175, and 166 from Bucksport. It's about 20 miles or 35 minutes via Routes 166, 199, and 175 from Blue Hill.

1: John Perkins House 2: Pentagöet Inn

Deer Isle

"Deer Isle is like Avalon," wrote John Steinbeck in *Travels with Charley*—"it must disappear when you are not there." **Deer Isle,** the name of both the island and its midpoint town, has been romancing authors and artisans for decades, but it is unmistakably real to the quarry workers and fishermen who've been here for centuries. These longtimers are a sturdy lot, as Steinbeck recognized: "I would hate to try to force them to do anything they didn't want to do."

Measuring about nine miles north to south (plus another three miles for Little Deer Isle), the island of Deer Isle today has a handful of hamlets (including **Sunshine, Sunset, Mountainville,** and **Oceanville**) and two towns—**Stonington** (pop. 1,043) and **Deer Isle** (pop. 1,975). A suspension bridge over Eggemoggin Reach links the Blue Hill Peninsula with Little Deer Isle; from there, a sinuous 0.4-mile causeway connects to the northern tip of Deer Isle.

Deer Isle remains an artisans' enclave, anchored by the Haystack Mountain School of Crafts. Studios and galleries are plentiful, although many require tooling along back roads to find them. Stonington, a rough-and-tumble fishing port with an idyllic setting, is slowly being gentrified. Locals are holding their collective breath, hoping that any improvements don't change the town too much. Already, real estate prices and accompanying taxes have escalated way past the point where many a local fisherman can hope to buy, and in some cases maintain, a home.

HISTORY

Early 18th-century maps show no name for Deer Isle, but by the late 1800s, nearly 100 families lived here, supporting themselves first by farming, then by fishing. In 1789, when Deer Isle was incorporated, 80 local sailing vessels were scouring the Gulf of Maine in pursuit of mackerel and cod, and Deer Isle men were circling the globe as yachting skippers and merchant seamen. At the same time, in the once-quiet village of Green's Landing (now called Stonington), the shipbuilding and granite industries boomed, spurring development, prosperity, and the kinds of rough high jinks typical of commercial ports the world over.

Green's Landing became the "big city" for an international crowd of quarrymen carving out the terrain on Deer Isle and nearby Crotch Island, source of high-quality granite for Boston's Museum of Fine Arts, the Smithsonian Institution, a humongous fountain for John D. Rockefeller's New York estate, and less showy projects all along the Eastern Seaboard. The heyday is long past, but the industry did extend into the 20th century (including a contract for the pink granite at President John F. Kennedy's Arlington National Cemetery gravesite). Today, Crotch Island is the site of Maine's only operating island granite quarry. For the best views, take one of the excursion boats or ferries headed to Isle au Haut.

SIGHTS

Sightseeing on Deer Isle means exploring back roads, browsing the galleries, walking the trails, hanging out on the docks, and soaking in the ambience.

★ Haystack Mountain School of Crafts

The renowned **Haystack Mountain School of Crafts** (Sunshine Rd., Deer Isle, 207/348-2306, www.haystack-mtn.org) in Sunshine is open to the public on a limited basis, but if it fits into your schedule, go. Anyone can visit the school store or walk down the central stairs to the water; to see more of the campus, take a tour (1pm Wed., $5), which includes a video, viewing works on display, and the opportunity to visit some studios. Beyond that,

Deer Isle

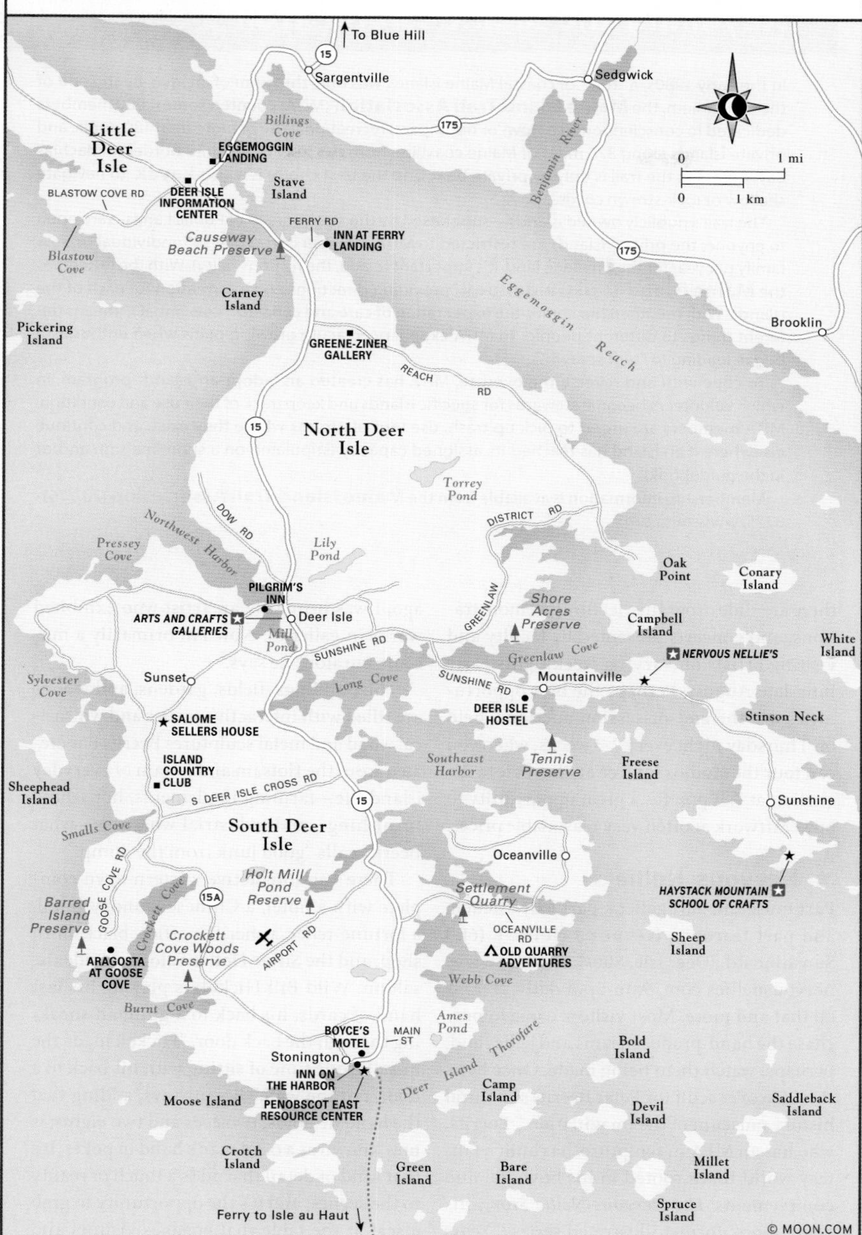
To Blue Hill
15
Sargentville
Sedgwick
175
Little Deer Isle
Billings Cove
EGGEMOGGIN LANDING
Benjamin River
0
1 mi
1 km
BLASTOW COVE RD
DEER ISLE INFORMATION CENTER
Stave Island
FERRY RD
INN AT FERRY LANDING
Causeway Beach Preserve
Blastow Cove
Carney Island
Eggemoggin Reach
Brooklin
Pickering Island
GREENE-ZINER GALLERY
REACH RD
North Deer Isle
Torrey Pond
DOW RD
Northwest Harbor
DISTRICT RD
Pressey Cove
Lily Pond
Oak Point
Conary Island
PILGRIM'S INN
ARTS AND CRAFTS GALLERIES
Deer Isle
GREENLAW
Shore Acres Preserve
Campbell Island
Mill Pond
SUNSHINE RD
Greenlaw Cove
White Island
NERVOUS NELLIE'S
Sylvester Cove
Sunset
Long Cove
Mountainville
SALOME SELLERS HOUSE
DEER ISLE HOSTEL
Stinson Neck
ISLAND COUNTRY CLUB
Southeast Harbor
Tennis Preserve
Freese Island
Sheephead Island
S DEER ISLE CROSS RD
Sunshine
Smalls Cove
South Deer Isle
GOOSE COVE RD
Oceanville
Holt Mill Pond Reserve
Crockett Cove
15A
Settlement Quarry
HAYSTACK MOUNTAIN SCHOOL OF CRAFTS
Barred Island Preserve
AIRPORT RD
OCEANVILLE RD
Sheep Island
Crockett Cove Woods Preserve
OLD QUARRY ADVENTURES
ARAGOSTA AT GOOSE COVE
Webb Cove
Burnt Cove
Ames Pond
BOYCE'S MOTEL
MAIN ST
Bold Island
Stonington
Deer Island Thorofare
INN ON THE HARBOR
Camp Island
Moose Island
PENOBSCOT EAST RESOURCE CENTER
Devil Island
Saddleback Island
Crotch Island
Green Island
Bare Island
Millet Island
Spruce Island
Ferry to Isle au Haut
© MOON.COM

TOP EXPERIENCE

Kayaking the Maine Island Trail

In the early 1980s, a "trail" of coastal Maine islands was only the germ of an idea. By the end of the millennium, the **Maine Island Trail Association** (MITA) counted some 4,000 members dedicated to conscientious (i.e., low- or no-impact) recreational use of more than 180 public and private islands along 375 miles of Maine coastline from the New Hampshire border to Machias Bay. Access to the trail is only by private boat, and the best choice is a **sea kayak**, to navigate shallow or rock-strewn coves.

The trail's publicly owned islands—supervised by the state Bureau of Public Lands—are open to anyone; the private islands are restricted to MITA members, who pay $45/individual or $65/family per year for the privilege (and, it's important to add, the responsibility). With the fee comes the **Maine Island Trail Guidebook,** providing directions and information for each of the islands. With membership comes the expectation of care and concern. "Low impact" means different things to different people, so MITA experienced acute growing pains when enthusiasm began leading to "tent sprawl."

To cope with and reverse the overuse, MITA has created an "adopt-an-island" program, in which volunteers become stewards for specific islands and keep track of their use and condition. MITA members are urged to pick up trash, use tent platforms where they exist, and continue elsewhere if an island has reached its assigned capacity (stipulated on a shoreline sign and/or in the guidebook).

Membership information is available from the **Maine Island Trail Association** (207/761-8225, www.mita.org).

there are slide programs, lectures, demonstrations, and concerts presented by faculty and visiting artists on varying weeknights early June-late August. Perhaps the best opportunities are the end-of-session auctions, held on Thursday night every 2-3 weeks, when you can tour the studios for free at 7pm before the auction at 7:30pm. It's a great opportunity to buy craftwork at often very reasonable prices.

★ Nervous Nellie's

Part museum, part gallery, part jelly kitchen, and part tearoom, **Nervous Nellie's** (600 Sunshine Rd., Deer Isle, 800/777-6845, www.nervousnellies.com, 9am-5pm daily, free) is all that and more. Most visitors come to purchase the hand-produced jams and jellies and, perhaps, watch them being made. Once here, they discover sculptor Peter Beerits's "natural history museum of the imagination." Beerits, who has an MFA in sculpture, has built a fantasy world that's rooted in his boyhood and complements *The Nervous Nellie Story,* his comic-book-format illustrated series. "Years ago, I was primarily an artist who exhibited works in galleries. Now I'm primarily a museum curator," he says.

The buildings, fields, gardens, and woods are filled with interactive scenes and whimsical wood and metal sculptures Beerits has created from the flotsam and jetsam of everyday island life—farming implements, household furnishings, and industrial whatnots—what Beerits calls "good junk from the dump."

There's an interactive western town complete with a hotel, a Chinese laundry, a jail, a fortune-teller, a sheriff's office, blacksmith shop, and the Silver Dollar Saloon. Inside the saloon, Wild Bill Hickok is playing his last hand of cards, his back to a gunman sneaking through the back door. "Hickok made the mistake one time of sitting with his back to a door, not the wall," Beerits says, adding that the hand he holds, two aces and two eights, is now known as a dead man's hand in poker. It's that kind of detail that adds a touch of reality to the scenes, and it's the opportunity to grab a seat at the table that engages visitors and keeps the cameras clicking. The West fades into the Mississippi Delta, where blues music draws visitors into Red's Lounge, where a pianist and guitarist crank out the blues, while a couple flirts in a corner booth.

Beerits moved the original Hardy's Store here. Like a living-history museum, it provides a glimpse into island life decades ago. No detail is overlooked, from the red hot dogs and buns in the steamer to the pickled eggs on the counter, from Neville Hardy at the register to the women seated out front eyeing the gas pump. As in every exhibit, fans have left notes, often illustrated, sharing their thoughts and impressions.

Many visitors take in these sights and then settle into the café for a snack, not realizing that there's more to see. In the woods behind, King Arthur's knights in shining armor, some larger than life, guard and inhabit the Grail Castle. Continue down the path, and you'll arrive at a woodlands church, another of Beerits's projects.

You can easily spend an hour here, and there's no admission; wander freely. Beerits will gladly explain his creations, if he's free. He offers free insider tours at 1pm on select Sundays. The property is also home to **Nervous Nellie's Jams and Jellies,** known for outstanding, creative condiments. You can peek into the kitchen to see the jams being made. The self-serve **Mountainville Café,** open May-early October, offers tea, coffee, and scones—with, of course, delicious Nervous Nellie's products; sampling is encouraged. Stock up, because they're sold in only a few shops. Also sold is a small, well-chosen selection of Maine products. Really, trust me, you must visit this place.

Historic Houses and Museums

There's more to the 1830 **Salome Sellers House** (416 Sunset Rd./Rte. 15A, Sunset Village, 207/348-6400, www.dishistoricalsociety.org, 1pm-4pm Wed.-Fri. mid-June-mid-Sept., donation) than first meets the eye. A repository of local memorabilia, archives, and intriguing artifacts, it's also the headquarters of the **Deer Isle-Stonington Historical Society.** Sellers, matriarch of an island family, was a direct descendant of *Mayflower* settlers. She lived to be 108, a lifetime spanning 1800-1908, earning the record for oldest recorded Maine resident. The house contains Sellers's furnishings, and in a small exhibit space in the rear is a fine exhibit of baskets made by Maine Native Americans. Behind the house are the archives, heritage gardens, and an exhibit hall filled with nautical artifacts. Enthusiastic volunteer guides, many of them island natives, bring all this to life. They love to provide tidbits about various items; seafarers' logs and ship models are particularly intriguing, and don't miss the 1920s peapod, the original lobster boat on the island. The house is just north of the Island Country Club and across from Eaton's Plumbing.

Close to the Stonington waterfront, the **Deer Isle Granite Museum** (51 Main St., Stonington, 207/367-6331, www.deerislegranitemuseum.org, noon-5pm Tues., Thurs., and Sat.-Sun. July-Aug.) was established to commemorate the centennial of the quarrying business hereabouts. The best feature of the small museum is a 15-foot-long working model of Crotch Island, center of the industry, as it appeared at the turn of the 20th century. Flatcars roll, boats glide, and derricks move—it all looks very real. Donations are welcome.

Another downtown Stonington attraction is a Lilliputian complex known as the **Miniature Village.** Beginning in 1947, the late Everett Knowlton created a series of replicas of local buildings and displayed them on granite blocks in his yard. Since his death, they've been restored and put on display each summer in town—along with a donation box to support the upkeep. The village is set up on East Main Street (Rte. 15), below Hoy Gallery.

Pumpkin Island Light

A fine view of Pumpkin Island Light can be had from the cul-de-sac at the end of the Eggemoggin Road on Little Deer Isle. If heading south on Route 15, bear right at the information booth after crossing the bridge and continue to the end.

Maine Center for Coastal Fisheries

The purpose of the **Maine Center for Coastal Fisheries** (13 Atlantic Ave., Stonington, 207/367-2708, www.penobscoteast.org) is "to energize and facilitate responsible community-based fishery management, collaborative marine science, and sustainable economic development to benefit the fishermen and the communities of Penobscot Bay and the Eastern Gulf of Maine." Bravo to that! At its **Discovery Wharf** (10am-4pm Sun.-Fri., free) are educational displays and interactive exhibits, including virtual reality experiences, a touch wall, and a touch tank highlighting Maine fisheries and the Gulf of Maine ecosystem. One of the driving forces behind the venture is Ted Ames, who won a $500,000 MacArthur Fellowship "genius grant" in 2005.

ENTERTAINMENT

Stonington's 1912 **Opera House** (207/367-2788, www.operahousearts.org) is home to Opera House Arts, which hosts films, plays, lectures, concerts, family programs, and workshops year-round.

Bird-watchers flock to Deer Isle in mid-May for the annual **Wings, Waves & Woods Weekend** (www.deerisle.com).

Mid-July brings the **Stonington Lobsterboat Races** (207/348-2804), very popular competitions held in the harbor, with lots of possible vantage points. Stonington is one of the major locales in the lobster boat-racing circuit.

The **Peninsula Potters Studio Tour and Sale** (www.peninsulapotters.com) is held in October, when more than a dozen potters from Blue Hill to Stonington welcome visitors.

Want to meet locals and learn more about the area? **Island Heritage Trust** (www.islandheritagetrust.org) sponsors a series of walks, talks, and tours late May to mid-September. For information and reservations, call 207/348-2455.

SHOPPING

The greatest concentration of shops is in Stonington, where galleries, clothing boutiques, and eclectic shops line Main Street.

In "downtown" Deer Isle Village, Candy and Jim Eaton now operate the **Periwinkle** (8 Main St., Deer Isle, 207/348-2256), stocking it with a fun mix of books, handicrafts, and niceties.

Just beyond the Opera House, **Dockside Books & Gifts** (62 W. Main St., Stonington, 207/367-2652) carries just what its name promises, with a specialty in marine and Maine books. The rustic two-room shop has spectacular harbor views.

The **Dry Dock** (24 Main St., Stonington, 207/367-5528) carries women's clothing, unique jewelry, and intriguing housewares.

Outfitter **Old Quarry Ocean Adventures** operates an in-town Stonington camp store at 9 Thurlow Hill Road, where you can sign up for trips as well as purchase gear.

★ Arts and Crafts Galleries

Thanks to the presence and influence of Haystack Mountain School of Crafts, supertalented artists and artisans lurk in every corner of the island. Most galleries are tucked away on back roads, so watch for roadside signs. Many have studios open to the public where you can watch the artists at work.

LITTLE DEER ISLE

Alfred's Roost (360 Eggemoggin Rd., 207/348-6699) is a fun gallery and working glass studio in an old schoolhouse. Ask Dusty Eagen to share mascot Alfred Peabody's life story.

DEER ISLE

The **Greene-Ziner Gallery** (73 Reach Rd., 207/348-2601, www.melissagreene.com) is

1: monument at Stonington's harbor 2: Haystack Mountain School of Crafts 3: Nervous Nellie's

1

2

3

a double treat. Melissa Greene turns out incredible painted and incised pottery—she's represented in the Smithsonian's Renwick Gallery—and Eric Ziner works magic in metal sculpture and furnishings. Your budget may not allow for one of Melissa's pots (in the four-digit range), but I guarantee you'll covet them. The gallery also displays the work of several other local artists. Also here is a farm stand with baked goods, produce, and more.

The **Frederica Marshall Gallery** (81 N. Deer Isle Rd., 207/348-2782, www.fredericamarshall.com) is a multifaceted find. Marshall is a master brush painter who delights in explaining Japanese sumi-e work and demonstrating the brushes that vary from a cat's whisker to four horsetails in size. She also has a classroom and offers workshops ranging from two hours to four days in length. Her husband, Herman Kidder, operates **Kidder Forge** on the same property. His knives forged from old tools are available in the gallery.

One of the island's premier galleries is Elena Kubler's **Turtle Gallery** (61 N. Deer Isle Rd./Rte. 15, 207/348-9977, www.turtlegallery.com), in a handsome space formerly known as the Old Centennial House Barn (owned by the late Haystack director Francis Merritt) and the adjacent farmhouse. Group and solo shows of contemporary paintings, prints, and crafts are hung upstairs and down in the barn; works by gallery artists are in the farmhouse; and there's usually sculpture in the gardens both in front and in back. It's just north of Deer Isle Village, across from the Shakespeare School.

In the village, **Deer Isle Artists Association** (55 Main St., 207/348-2330, www.deerisleartists.com) features two-week exhibits of paintings, prints, drawings, and photos by member artists. The **Devta Doolan Studio** (3 Main St., 207/348-3134) shows Doolan's fine gold jewelry. **Summerall/Mozelle Gallery** (13 Main St., 207/460-2329) shows fine jewelry as well as fine craftwork by about a dozen artists

STONINGTON

Cabinetmaker Geoffrey Warner features his work at **Geoffrey Warner Studio** (431 N. Main St., 207/367-6555, www.geoffreywarnerstudio.com). Warner mixes classic techniques with contemporary styles and Eastern, nature-based arts and crafts accents to create some unusual and rather striking pieces. He also crafts the budget-friendly ergonomic Owl stool as well as offers kits and workshops. Ask about studio tours.

The **gWatson Gallery** (68 Main St., 207/367-2900, www.gwatsongallery.com) is a fine-art gallery representing a number of top-notch painters and printmakers. Occasionally it hosts live music. More paintings, many in bold, bright colors, can be found at Jill Hoy's **Hoy Gallery** (80 Main St., 207/367-2368, www.jillhoy.com). On the other end of Main Street, **Marlinespike Chandlery** (58 W. Main St., 207/348-2521, www.marlinespike.com) specializes in ropework, both practical and fancy.

RECREATION

Parks and Preserves

Foresighted benefactors have managed to set aside precious acreage for respectful public use on Deer Isle. The **Nature Conservancy** (207/729-5181, www.nature.org) owns two properties: **Crockett Cove Woods Preserve** and **Barred Island Preserve.** The conscientious steward of other local properties is the **Island Heritage Trust** (420 Sunset Rd., Sunset, 207/348-2455, www.islandheritagetrust.org, 8am-4pm Mon.-Fri.). At the trust's office you can pick up notecards, photos, T-shirts, and helpful maps and information on hiking trails and nature preserves. Proceeds benefit the Island Heritage Trust's efforts; donations are appreciated.

SETTLEMENT QUARRY

One of the easiest, shortest walks in the area leads to an impressive vista. From the parking lot on Oceanville Road (just under one mile off Rte. 15), marked by a carved granite sign, it's about five minutes to the top of the old **Settlement Quarry,** where the viewing platform (aka the "throne room") takes in the panorama—all the way to the Camden Hills on a good day. In early August, wild raspberries are an additional enticement. Three short loop trails lead into the surrounding woods. A map is available in the trailhead box.

EDGAR TENNIS PRESERVE

The **Edgar Tennis Preserve** (sunrise-sunset daily), off Sunshine Road, has very limited parking, so don't try to squeeze in if there isn't room; schedule your visit for another hour or day. But do go, and bring at least a snack, if not a full picnic, to enjoy on one of the convenient rocky outcroppings. Allow at least 90 minutes to enjoy the walking trails, one of which skirts Pickering Cove, providing sigh-producing views. Another trail leads to an old cemetery. Parts of the trails can be wet, so wear appropriate footwear. Bring binoculars for bird-watching. To find the preserve, take Sunshine Road 2.5 miles to Tennis Road and follow it to the preserve.

SHORE ACRES PRESERVE

The **Shore Acres Preserve,** a gift in 2000 from Judy Hill to the Island Heritage Trust, comprises old farmland, woodlands, clam flats, a salt marsh, and granite shorefront. Three walking trails connect in a 1.5-mile loop, with the Shore Trail section edging Greenlaw Cove. As you walk along the waterfront, look for the islands of Mount Desert rising in the distance and seals basking on offshore ledges. Do not walk across the salt marsh, and try to avoid stepping on beach plants. To find the preserve, take Sunshine Road 1.2 miles and then bear left at the fork onto Greenlaw District Road. The preserve's parking area is just shy of one mile down the road. Park only in the parking area, not on the paved road.

CROCKETT COVE WOODS PRESERVE

Donated to the Nature Conservancy by eco-conscious local artist Emily Muir, **Crockett Cove Woods Preserve** is Deer Isle's natural gem—a coastal fog forest laden with lichens and mosses. Four interlinked walking trails cover the whole preserve, starting with a short nature trail. Pick up the helpful map-brochure at the registration box. Wear rubberized shoes or boots, and respect adjacent private property. From Deer Isle Village, take Route 15A to Sunset Village. Go 2.5 miles to Whitman Road and then to Fire Lane 88.

BARRED ISLAND PRESERVE

Owned by the Nature Conservancy but managed by the Island Heritage Trust, **Barred Island Preserve** was donated by Carolyn Olmsted, grandniece of noted landscape architect Frederick Law Olmsted, who summered nearby. A former owner of adjacent Goose Cove Lodge donated an additional 48 acres of maritime boreal fog forest. A single walking trail, one mile long, leads from the parking lot to the point. At low tide, and when eagles aren't nesting, you can continue out to Barred Island. Another trail skirts the shoreline of **Goose Cove,** before retreating inland and rejoining the main trail. From a high point on the main trail, you can see more than a dozen islands, many of which are protected from development, as well as **Saddleback Ledge Light,** 14 miles distant. To get to the preserve, follow Route 15A to Goose Cove Road and then continue to the parking area on the right. If it's full, return another day.

HOLT MILL POND PRESERVE

The Stonington Conservation Commission administers the town-owned **Holt Mill Pond Preserve,** where more than 47 bird species have been identified (bring binoculars). It comprises four habitats: upland spruce forest, lowland spruce-mixed forest, freshwater marsh, and saltwater marsh. A self-guiding nature trail is accessible off Airport Road. Look for the Nature Trail sign just beyond the medical center. The detailed, self-guiding trail brochure, available at the trailhead kiosk, is accented with drawings by noted artist Siri Beckman.

AMES POND

Ames Pond is neither park nor preserve, but it might as well be. On a back road close to Stonington, it's a mandatory stop in July-August, when the pond wears a blanket of pink and white water lilies. From downtown Stonington, take Indian Point Road just under a mile east to the pond.

CAUSEWAY BEACH AND SCOTT'S LANDING

If you're itching to dip your toes into the water, stop by **Causeway Beach** along the causeway linking Little Deer Isle to Deer Isle. It's popular for swimming and is also a significant habitat for birds and other wildlife. On the other side of Route 15 is **Scott's Landing,** with more than 20 acres of fields, trails, and shorefront.

ED WOODSUM PRESERVE AT MARSHALL ISLAND

The Maine Coast Heritage Trust (www.mcht.org) owns **Marshall Island,** the largest undeveloped island on the Eastern Seaboard. Since acquiring it in 2003, the trust has added 10 miles of hiking trails on three inter-connected loops. After exploring, picnic on Sand Cove beach on the southeastern shore. For transportation, check with **Old Quarry Ocean Adventures** (130 Settlement Rd., Stonington, 207/367-8977, www.oldquarry.com) or ***Bert & I*** (207/460-8679). Primitive camping is available by **reservation** (207/729-7366) at designated sites; fires require a **permit** (207/827-1800).

Sporting Outfitters and Guided Trips

The biggest operation is **Old Quarry Ocean Adventures** (130 Settlement Rd., Stonington, 207/367-8977, www.oldquarry.com), with a broad range of outdoor adventure choices. Bill Baker's ever-expanding enterprise rents canoes, kayaks, sailboats, bikes, moorings, platform tent sites, and cabins. Bicycle rentals are $22 per day or $110 per week. Sea kayak rentals are $70 per day for a single, $85 for a tandem. Two-hour, half-day, and weekly rentals are available. Other options include canoes, SUPs, rowboats, and sailboats; check the website for details. For all boat rentals, you must demonstrate competency in the vessel. They'll deliver and pick up anywhere on the island for a fee of $30 each way; it's $50 for off-island deliveries. All-day guided sea kayaking tours are $130 pp; half-day tours are $65 pp. Plenty of other options are available, including sunset tours and family trips.

A Registered Maine Guide leads overnight kayaking-camping trips on nearby islands. Rates, for kayak rental and guide, begin around $300 per adult for one night, with a three-person minimum; add meals for $12 per person. If you're bringing your own kayak, you can park your car ($8/night up to two nights, $7/night for three or more nights) and launch from here ($6/boat for launching); they'll take your trash and any trash you find. Old Quarry is off the Oceanville Road, less than a mile from Route 15, just before you reach the Settlement Quarry preserve. It's well signposted.

Guided Walks

The **Island Heritage Trust** (402 Sunset Rd., Sunset, 207/348-2455, www.islandheritagetrust.org), along with the Stonington and Deer Isle Conservation Commissions, sponsors a Walks and Talks series. See the website or call for information and reservations.

TOP EXPERIENCE

Sea Kayaking

The waters around Deer Isle, with lots of islets and protected coves, are extremely popular for sea kayaking, especially off Stonington. The six-mile paddle from Stonington to Isle au Haut is best left to experienced paddlers, especially since fishing folks refer to kayakers as "speed bumps."

Driftwood Kayak (17 Hardy's Hill Rd., Deer Isle, 617-957-8802, www.driftwood-kayak.com) offers fully outfitted guided one- to three-day trips in the waters off Deer Isle from $190 pp.

Swimming

The island's only major freshwater swimming hole is the **Lily Pond,** northeast of Deer Isle Village. Just north of the Shakespeare School, take the Quaco Road about a half mile. Park and take the path to the pond, which has a shallow area for small children (and a toilet).

Boat Excursions

The **Isle au Haut Boat Company** (27 Seabreeze Ave., Stonington, 207/367-5193 or 207/367-6516, www.isleauhaut.com) offers a number of scenic cruises. A narrated 1.25-hour Scenic Harbor Cruise, during which the crew hauls a string of lobster traps, departs Stonington at 2pm Monday-Saturday ($24 adults, $12 under age 12). Special puffin trips and lighthouse tours are available on a limited basis ($75 adults, $45 under age 12, call for schedule). A Crotch Island Quarry trip includes a guided walking tour (limited schedule, $50 adults, $25 kids). Another option is to cruise over and back to Isle au Haut without stepping foot off the boat ($24 adults). Dockside parking is around $12, or find a spot in town and save the surcharge.

Yet another aspect of the **Old Quarry Ocean Adventures** (Stonington, 207/367-8977, www.oldquarry.com) empire are sightseeing cruises. The schedule and options change year to year, but usually include a three-hour Sightseeing and Natural History Eco Cruise ($45 adults, $35 under age 16). Also available is a 1.5-hour sunset cruise, departing one hour before sunset for $175/four. And if that's not enough, Old Quarry also offers five-hour puffin and pelagic tours ($75 adults, $50 kids), half-day lighthouse trips ($55 adults, $40 kids), and hourly island shuttles ($30 pp). Or, if none of this floats your boat, you can also arrange for a custom charter for $175 per hour. Old Quarry also offers special trips in conjunction with the Island Heritage Trust. For information or reservations, call 207/348-2455.

Cruise through East Penobscot Bay aboard the mail boat ***Katherine*** (207/701-9316, $24 adults, $12 under age 12), which departs from the Deer Isle Yacht Club at 9:30am Monday-Saturday for a two-hour excursion taking in Eagle, Butter, Barred, and Great Spruce Head Islands. Call for reservations, parking details, and to confirm the time.

Former Stonington harbormaster Steve Johnson enjoys sharing Stonington Harbor's highlights aboard the ***Bert & I*** (207/460-8679 or 207/367-2991, http://deerislecabinwithboattours.com, $140/hour for 4-6 passengers). Options include Stonington Harbor, lighthouse, island, seal-watching, and sunset tours ranging 1-2 hours. Ask about his drop-off service to Green Island, where you can spend a few hours exploring, picnicking, and swimming in a freshwater quarry (from about $25 pp).

FOOD

Options for dining are few, and restaurants suffer from a lack of consistency. Patience is more than a virtue here; it's a necessity.

Lobster and Seafood

LDI Lobster (202 Little Deer Isle Rd., Little Deer Isle, 207/348-2843, 11am-7pm daily), a sister property of the Boatyard Grill in Blue Hill, serves fresh lobster and seafood, along with options for landlubbers and vegetarians.

Quick Bites

Coffee zealots praise **44 North Coffee** (70 Main St., Stonington, 207/348-3043, https://44northcoffee.com, 6:30am-5pm Mon.-Tues. and Sat, 6:30am-8:30pm Wed.-Fri., 8am-2pm Sun.), a spacious café serving coffee and pastries. On Wednesday through Friday evenings, it also serves beer and wine. 44 North also operates a tiny shop out of its roastery (7 Main St., Deer Isle, 207/348-5208, 8am-4pm Mon.-Fri., 8am-2pm Sat.), where you can grab a cuppa and a baked treat.

Burnt Cove Market (Rte. 15, Stonington,

207/367-2681, 6am-9pm daily) sells pizza, fried chicken, and sandwiches, plus beer and wine.

The **Fairway Café** (442 Sunset Rd., Deer Isle, 207/348-2379, www.islandcountryclub.net, 11am-2pm daily), located at the Island Country Club, is a good bet for a reasonably priced lunch.

The Island Community Center (6 Memorial Ln., just off School St., Stonington) is the locale for the lively **Island Farmers Market** (10am-noon Fri. late May-late Sept.), with more than 50 vendors selling smoked and organic meats, fresh herbs and flowers, produce, gelato and yogurt, maple syrup, jams and jellies, fabulous breads and baked goods, chocolates, ethnic foods, crafts, and so much more. Go early; items sell out quickly.

If you're based at Old Quarry, the **Old Quarry Take Out** (7am-8pm daily) offers breakfast, lunch, and dinner, as well as ice cream and lobster.

The **Deer Isle Night Market** takes place 4pm-6pm Tuesdays late May through November, when food vendors set up at 11 Main Street.

Family Favorites

Fried seafood, lobsters, burgers, ice cream, and other usuals are available at **There's a Treat Takeout** (495 N. Deer Isle Rd./Rte. 15, 207/348-9444, 11am-7pm daily), a popular and inexpensive family spot with picnic tables and a playground. Simple sandwiches, burgers, and dogs start at $3, while fried seafood baskets begin around $12.

Harbor Cafe (36 Main St., Stonington, 207/367-5099, 6am-8:30pm daily, $7-25) is *the* place to go for breakfast (you can eavesdrop on the local fisherfolk if you're early enough), but it's also open for lunch and dinner. Food varies, as does the service; the best advice is to stick to the basics or go for the fish fry with free seconds on Friday nights.

The views are top-notch from the dining area at the harbor-side **Stonecutters Kitchen** (5 Atlantic Ave., Stonington, 207/367-2442, www.stonecutterskitchenme.com, 11am-8pm daily, $10-25), an order-at-the-counter deli offering sandwiches, fried fare, lobster, and good pizza. The entrance is through the Harbor View Store (207/367-2530, 4am-8pm Mon.-Fri., 6am-8pm Sun.), where you can pick up breakfast sandwiches in the wee hours.

Casual Dining

Gaze over lobster boats to-ing and fro-ing around spruce-and-granite-fringed islands from **Acadia House Provisions** (27 Main St., Stonington, 207/367-2555, http://acadiahouseprovisions.com, 4:30pm-8:30pm Tues., 11:30am-1:30pm and 4:30pm-8:30pm Wed.-Sat., $12-28), a culinary bright spot fronting on the harbor in downtown Stonington. Chef Ryan McCaskey of Chicago's Acadia Restaurant (recipient of two Michelin stars) opened here in 2019, serving an American farm-to-table menu.

At ★ **Aragosta at Goose Cove** (300 Goose Cove Rd., Deer Isle, 207/348-6900, www.aragostamaine.com, 5pm-9pm Mon. and Thurs.-Fri., 10am-2pm and 5pm-9pm Sat.-Sun., $25-40), every table in the bi-level dining room and outdoor porch has a dreamy water view. The emphasis is on seafood, but chef Devin Finigan's oft-changing New American menu draws from what's currently available from local farms, foragers, and fishers. She also makes her own charcuterie, salts, and ice cream.

Seafood and house-made pastas are the specialties at **Fin & Fern** (25 Seabreeze Ave., Stonington, 207/348-3111, http://finandfernme.com, 11am-8:30pm Wed.-Sun., $15-35), which overlooks the ferry terminal. Chef-owner Andrew Chappel traveled the world as a private chef aboard private yachts before landing here. Parking can be a challenge.

ACCOMMODATIONS

Inns and Bed-and-Breakfasts

Eggemoggin Reach is almost on the doorstep at the **Inn at Ferry Landing** (77 Old Ferry Rd.,

1: Deer Isle's coastline 2: Stonington's Opera House 3: LDI Lobster 4: Aragosta at Goose Cove

1
2
OPERA HOUSE.
LDI LOBSTER
3
4

Deer Isle, 207/348-7760, www.ferrylanding.com, $130-185), overlooking the abandoned Sargentville-Deer Isle ferry wharf. The view is wide open from the inn's great room, where guests gather to read, play games, talk, and watch passing windjammers. Professional musician Gerald Wheeler has installed two grand pianos in the room; it's a treat when he plays. His wife, Jean, is the hospitable innkeeper, managing three water-view guest rooms and a suite. The Mooring, an annex that sleeps five, is rented by the week ($1,500 without breakfast). The inn is open year-round except Thanksgiving and Christmas.

The ★ **Inn on the Harbor** (45 Main St., Stonington, 207/367-2420 or 800/942-2420, www.innontheharbor.com, from $170) is exactly as its name proclaims—its expansive deck hangs right over the harbor. Although recently updated, the 1880s complex still has an air of unpretentiousness. Most of the 14 guest rooms and suites, each named after a windjammer, have fantastic harbor views and private or shared decks where you can keep an eye on lobster boats, small ferries, windjammers, and pleasure craft; binoculars are provided. Street-side rooms can be noisy at night. Rates include a continental buffet.

Pilgrim's Inn (20 Main St., Deer Isle, 207/348-6615, www.pilgrimsinn.com, early May-mid-Oct., from $199) comprises a beautifully restored colonial building with 12 rooms and three newer cottages overlooking the peaceful Mill Pond. The inn, listed in the National Register of Historic Places, began life in 1793 as a boardinghouse named the Ark. Rates include a full breakfast. Dinner (5pm-7pm Sun.-Thurs., $14-37) is available for guests.

★ **Aragosta at Goose Cove** (300 Goose Cove Rd., Deer Isle, 207/348-6900, www.aragostamaine.com, from $280) is a spectacular 21.9-acre oceanfront property with comfy suites and cottages sprinkling the woodlands and ledges. Rates include access to the private beach as well as a full breakfast in the main lodge. The restaurant also serves dinner and brunch on weekends. It's adjacent to Barred Island Preserve.

Motels

Right in downtown Stonington, just across the street from the harbor, is **Boyce's Motel** (44 Main St., Stonington, 207/367-2421 or 800/224-2421, www.boycesmotel.com, year-round, $89-175). The 11 units have refrigerators; some have kitchens and living rooms, and one has two bedrooms. Across the street, Boyce's has a private harbor-front deck for its guests. Ask for rooms well back from Main Street to lessen street noise. Some rooms are pet friendly ($15/stay); restrictions apply.

Hostel and Bunkhouse

The rustic-bordering-on-primitive **Deer Isle Hostel** (65 Tennis Rd., Deer Isle, 207/348-2308, www.deerislehostel.com, $30-70, no credit cards), set near the Tennis Preserve, is overseen by owner Dennis Carter, a Surry native and local stoneworker and carpenter. The three-story, timber-frame building is completely off the grid, with a pump in the kitchen for water, an outhouse, outdoor hot water-can shower, and solar-powered lighting. Carter hand-cut the granite for the basement, and the timbers in the nail-free frame are hand-hewn from local blown-down spruce. He expects guests to work in the extensive organic gardens, using produce for shared meals prepared on a woodstove, the sole source of heat. The goal is sustainability, not profit. Communal dinners are available nightly—guests either help with preparation or make a $7-10 contribution. Accommodations include private and dorm rooms and huts. Kids 11-14 are $20; kids 10 and younger are $15. Bedding is provided; sleeping bags are not permitted.

Old Quarry Ocean Adventures Bunkhouse (130 Settlement Rd., Stonington, 207/367-8977, www.oldquarry.com, $70-90 d) sleeps up to eight in three private rooms; weekly rates as well as whole-building rates are available. Guests use the campground bathhouse facilities. Bring your own sleeping bag or linens, or rent them for $4.

Rustic Cottages

When you truly want to escape the trappings

of civilization, make reservations for one of four rental cottages on **Eagle Island** (207/701-9316, www.eagleislandrentals.com, from $750 per week) located in East Penobscot Bay, about 2.5 miles off Deer Isle. The private island is off the grid, and not all cottages have indoor plumbing, but it is a very special experience for those who don't mind roughing it with basic comforts. Rates range $750/week for a cozy camp with outhouse and solar shower to $2,250/week for a six-bedroom former boarding home with indoor plumbing.

Camping

Plan ahead if you want to camp at **Old Quarry Ocean Adventures Campground** (130 Settlement Rd., Stonington, 207/367-8977, www.oldquarry.com, $45-75 d), with both oceanfront and secluded platform sites for tents and just three RV sites. Each additional adult is $15. Kids under age 16 are $8. Leashed pets are permitted ($2/stay); Wi-Fi is $3 per stay. Parking is designed so that vehicles are kept away from most campsites, but you can use a garden cart to transport your equipment between your car and your site. The campground is adjacent to the Settlement Quarry preserve.

INFORMATION AND SERVICES

The **Deer Isle-Stonington Chamber of Commerce** (207/348-6124, www.deerislemaine.com) has a summer information booth on a grassy triangle on Route 15 in Little Deer Isle, 0.25 mile after crossing the bridge from Sargentville (Sedgwick).

Find **public restrooms** at the Atlantic Avenue Hardware pier and the Stonington Town Hall on Main Street, Chase Emerson Library in Deer Isle Village, and behind the information booth on Little Deer Isle.

GETTING THERE AND AROUND

Deer Isle Village is about 12 miles or 25 minutes via Route 15 from Brooksville. Stonington is about six miles or 15 minutes via Route 15 from Deer Isle Village.

Isle au Haut

TOP EXPERIENCE

Eight miles off Stonington lies 4,700-acre **Isle au Haut,** roughly half of which belongs to Acadia National Park. Pronounced variously as "I'll-a-HO" or "I'LL-a-ho," the island has nearly 20 miles of hiking trails, excellent birding, and a tiny village.

Around 40-50 souls call Isle au Haut home year-round, and most of them eke out a living from the sea. Each summer, the population temporarily swells with day-trippers, campers, and cottagers—then settles back in fall to the measured pace of island life.

Samuel de Champlain, threading his way through this archipelago in 1605 and noting the island's prominent central ridge, named it Isle au Haut (High Island). Appropriately, the tallest peak (543 feet) is now named Mount Champlain.

Peletiah Barter, the island's first European settler, arrived in 1792 and his descendants still live and work here. Incorporated in 1874, Isle au Haut earned a world record during World War I, when all residents were members of the Red Cross. Electricity came in 1970, and phone service in 1988.

More recent fame has come to the island thanks to island-based authors Linda Greenlaw, of *Perfect Storm* fame, who wrote *The Lobster Chronicles,* as well as several cookbooks and mysteries. Although her books piqued interest in the island, Isle au Haut remains uncrowded and well off the beaten tourist track.

Most of the southern half of the

six-mile-long island belongs to Acadia National Park, thanks to the wealthy summer visitors who began arriving in the 1880s. It was their heirs who, in the 1940s, donated valuable acreage to the federal government. Today, this backcountry division of the national park has a well-managed 19-mile network of trails, a few lean-tos, several miles of unpaved road, a lighthouse inn, and summertime passenger-ferry service to the park entrance. The National Park Service has a no-promote policy regarding Isle au Haut; unless you ask about it, you won't be told about it.

In the island's northern half are the private residences of fishing families and summer folk, a minuscule village (including a market, gift shop, and post office), and a five-mile stretch of paved road. All vehicles on the island are owned by residents.

Folk singer Gordon Bok penned the lyrics to *The Hills of Isle au Haut:*

The winters drive you crazy
And the fishin's hard and slow
You're a damn fool if you stay
But there's no better place to go

TOP EXPERIENCE

★ ACADIA NATIONAL PARK

Mention **Acadia National Park** and most people think of Bar Harbor and Mount Desert Island, where more than three million visitors arrive each year. The Isle au Haut section of the park sees maybe 5,000-7,500 visitors annually, with a daily cap of 128. The limited boat service, the remoteness of the island, and the scarcity of campsites contribute to the low count, leaving the trails and views for only a few hardy souls.

About a third of a mile from the town landing, where the year-round mail boat and another boat dock, is the **Park Ranger Station** (207/335-5551), where you can pick up trail maps and park information—and use the island's only public facilities. Do yourself a favor, though: Plan ahead by downloading Isle au Haut maps and information from the Acadia National Park website, www.nps.gov/acad, and instead opt for the boat to the park's dock.

RECREATION

Hiking

Hiking on Acadia National Park trails is the major recreation on Isle au Haut, and even in the densest fog you'll see valiant hikers going for it. A loop road circles the whole island; an unpaved section goes through the park, connecting with the mostly paved nonpark section. Walking on that is easy. Beyond the road, none of the park's 19 miles of trails could be labeled "easy"; the footing is rocky, rooted, and often squishy. But the park trails are well marked, and the views—of islets, distant hills, and the ocean—make the effort worthwhile. Go prepared with proper footwear. If you're day-tripping, consult with the ranger who meets the park boat about the best options for your ability, as most first-time visitors overestimate the amount of terrain they can cover.

The most-used park trail is the 7.6-mile round-trip **Duck Harbor Trail,** connecting the town landing with Duck Harbor. You can either use this trail or follow the island road—mostly unpaved in this stretch—to get to the campground when the summer ferry ends its Duck Harbor runs.

Even though the summit is only 314 feet, **Duck Harbor Mountain** is the island's toughest trail. Still, it's worth the 2.4-mile round-trip effort for the stunning 360-degree views from the summit. Option: Rather than return via the trail's steep, boulder-strewn sections, cut off at the Goat Trail and return to the trailhead that way.

For terrific shoreline scenery, take **Western Head Trail** and **Cliff Trail** at the island's southwestern corner. They form a nice four-mile loop around Western Head. The route follows the coastline, ascending ridges and cliffs and descending to rocky beaches, with some forested sections. Options: Close

1: trailhead at Acadia National Park on Isle au Haut
2: a lighthouse on Isle au Haut

NATIONAL PARK SERVICE
Department of the Interior
Duck Harbor
Isle au Haut
Acadia National Park
1
2

the loop by returning via the Western Head Road. If the tide is out (and *only* if it's out), you can walk across the tidal flats to the quaintly named Western Ear for views back toward the island. Western Ear is privately owned, so don't linger. The **Goat Trail** adds another four miles (round-trip) of moderate coastline hiking east of the Cliff Trail; views are fabulous and bird-watching is good, but if you're here only for a day, you'll need to decide whether there's time to do this and still catch the return mail boat. If you do have the time and the energy, you can connect from the Goat Trail to the **Duck Harbor Mountain Trail.**

Rangers recommend **Eben's Head** for those visiting with young children. This short, easy loop skirts the coastline and takes in two cobble beaches that are ideal for beachcombing and splashing. An offshoot climbs a rocky knob guarding the entrance to Duck Harbor; it's a fine place for a picnic, but keep youngsters away from the edges.

Bird-Watching

Isle au Haut's offshore location makes it a popular stopover for migrating bats; shorebirds, including purple sandpipers; songbirds; and raptors, including bald eagles. It's also renowned as a wintering haven for harlequin ducks.

Swimming

For freshwater swimming, head for **Long Pond,** a skinny, 1.5-mile-long swimming hole running north-south on the east side of the island, abutting national park land. There's a minuscule beach-like area on the southern end with a picnic table and a float. If you're here only for the day, though, there's not enough time to do this *and* get in a long hike. Opt for the hiking—or do a short hike and then go for a swim (the shallowest part is at the southern tip).

FOOD AND ACCOMMODATIONS

Options for food are extremely limited on Isle au Haut, so if you're coming for a day trip, bring sufficient food and water. If you want to camp overnight, plan well in advance. The island's only inn converted to a vacation rental in 2019.

Food

Isle au Haut is pretty much a BYO place—and for the most part, that means BYO food.

Thanks to the **Isle au Haut General Store** (207/335-5211, www.theislandstore.net), less than a five-minute walk from the town landing, you won't starve. The summer inventory includes all the makings for a great picnic.

And then there's the **Maine Lobster Lady** (207/669-2751, 11am-6pm Tues.-Sun.), Diana Santospago's seasonal takeout serving lobster in many forms, chowders, and fried seafood and whoopie pies as well as breakfast sandwiches, pies, milk shakes, ice cream, and iced coffee. Find her parked at the General Store. There are picnic tables with umbrellas on the thoroughfare's edge.

Camping

Online reservations open April 1 at 10am for the five six-person lean-tos at **Duck Harbor Campground** (207/335-5551, www.recreation.gov). The season runs May 15 to October 15; the fee is $20/night. The maximum stay is three nights and you can only stay once during each calendar year.

Unless you don't mind backpacking nearly five miles to reach the campground, try to plan your visit between mid-June and late September, when the mail boat makes a stop in Duck Harbor. It's wise to check with the **Isle au Haut Boat Company** (207/367-5193, www.isleauhaut.com) for the current ferry schedule before choosing dates for a lean-to reservation.

1: Isle au Haut General Store 2: Isle au Haut Boat Company 3: Duck Harbor

THE ISLAND STORE
1

MISS LIZZIE
2

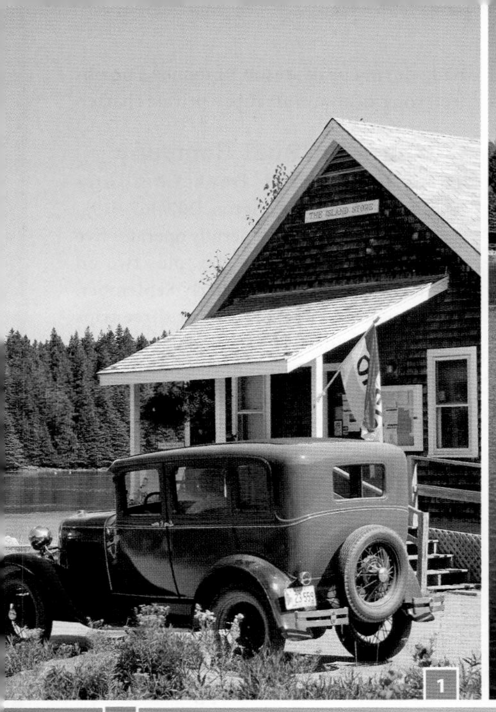

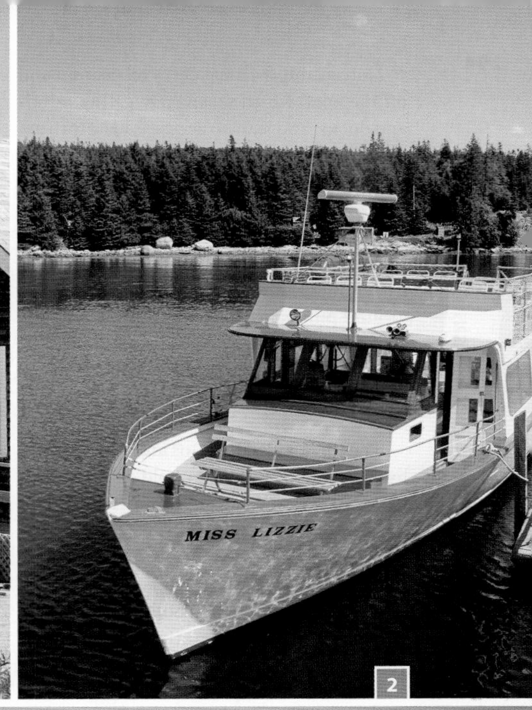

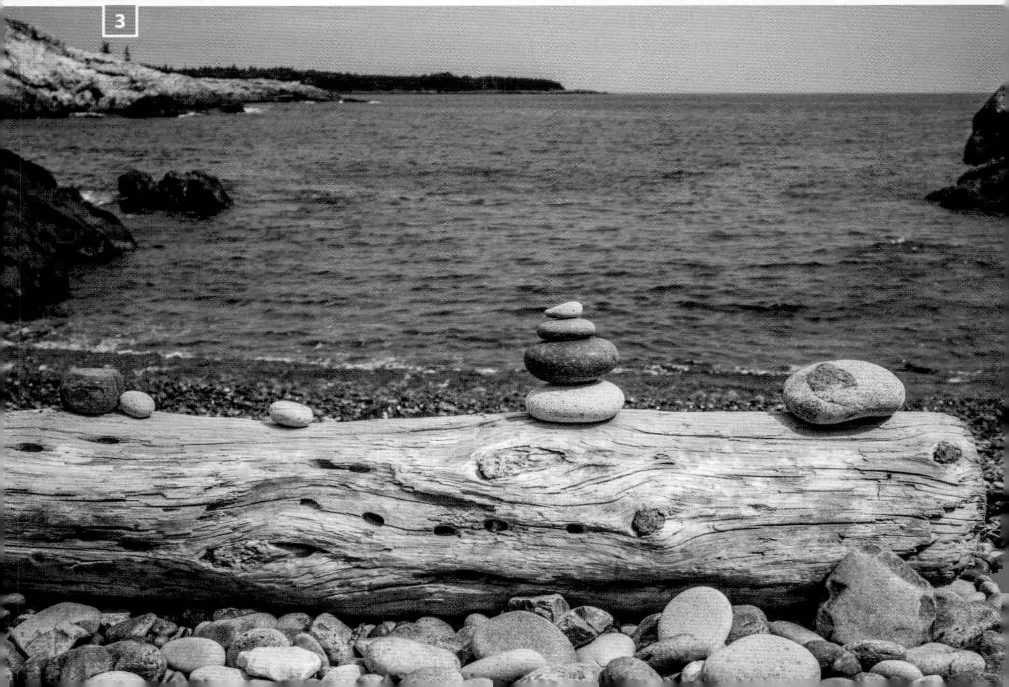
3

Note: Campers must carry all gear on and off the boat, which means navigating ramps and docks, and lean-to access is via a trail ascending rocky and rooted terrain. The distance from boat to campground is roughly 0.25 mile.

Trash policy is carry-in/carry-out, so pack a trash bag or two with your gear. Also bring a container for carting water from the campground pump, because it's 0.3 mile from the lean-tos. It's a long walk to the general store for food—when you could be off hiking the island's trails—so bring enough to cover your stay.

The three-sided lean-tos are big enough (8 by 12 feet, 8 feet high) to hold a small (two-person) tent, so bring one along if you prefer being fully enclosed. A tarp will also do the trick. (Also bring mosquito repellent—some years, the critters show up here en masse.) No camping is permitted outside of the lean-tos, and nothing can be attached to trees. If you're even tempted by the idea of trying to sneak off and backpack into the park for an overnight, forget it: The island is small and rangers, boat captains, and locals keep track of the comings and goings. Don't risk federal fines.

INFORMATION AND SERVICES

Information about the section of Acadia National Park on Isle au Haut is available both online (www.nps.gov/acad) and at the ranger station (207/335-5551), about 0.3 mile from the town landing boat dock. General information on the island is available online from **Isle au Haut Community Development Corporation** (http://isleauhaut.org) and **Isle au Haut Boat Company** (www.isleauhaut.com).

GETTING THERE

Two companies offer transportation to Isle au Haut's town landing. Use Isle au Haut Boat Company if your destination is the park, as it lands right at Duck Harbor twice daily during peak season. If money's no object, you can always arrange a private charter.

Isle au Haut Boat Company

The **Isle au Haut Boat Company** (Seabreeze Ave., Stonington, 207/367-5193, www.isleauhaut.com) generally operates five daily trips Monday-Saturday, plus two on Sunday from mid-June to early September. Other months, there are two or three trips Monday-Saturday. The best advice is to request a copy of the current schedule, covering dates, variables, fares, and extras.

Round-trips April-mid-October are $40 adults, $20 kids under age 12 (two bags per adult, one bag per child). Round-trip surcharges include bikes ($22) and kayaks/canoes ($46 minimum). Weather seldom affects the schedule, but be aware that heavy seas could cancel a trip.

There is twice-daily ferry service, early June-mid-September, from Stonington to Duck Harbor, at the edge of Isle au Haut's Acadia National Park campground. For a day trip, the schedule allows you 4.5 hours on the island Monday-Saturday and 5 hours on Sunday. No boats or bikes are allowed on this route, and no dogs are allowed in the campground. A ranger meets the boat in Duck Harbor and provides an orientation and campsite check-in. Before mid-June and after Labor Day, you'll be off-loaded at the Isle au Haut town landing, about 4.5 miles from Duck Harbor. The six-mile passage from Stonington to the Isle au Haut town landing takes 45 minutes; the trip to Duck Harbor is 1.25 hours.

Ferries depart from the Isle au Haut Boat Company dock (Seabreeze Ave., off E. Main St. in downtown Stonington). Parking ($12) usually is available next to the ferry landing. Arrive at least an hour early to get all this settled so you don't miss the boat.

Old Quarry Ocean Adventures

Also offering seasonal service to Isle au Haut is **Old Quarry Ocean Adventures** (Stonington, 207/367-8977, www.oldquarry.

com), which transports passengers on the *Nigh Duck*. The boat usually leaves Old Quarry at 9am and arrives at the island's town landing at 9:45am, returning from the same point at 5pm. The fee is $40 round-trip for adults, $30 for children under age 16. Bring your own bike for free or rent one from Old Quarry for $22/day. The boat can carry kayaks for $10. Old Quarry also offers a taxi service to Isle au Haut for $175 each way. Note: Old Quarry only services the town dock, not the park dock.

Acadia Region

Summer folk have been visiting Mount Desert Island (MDI) for millennia. The earliest Native Americans discovered fabulous fishing and clamming, good hunting and camping, and invigorating salt air. Today's arrivals find variations on the same theme: thousands of lodgings and campsites, hundreds of restaurant seats, dozens of shops, plus 40,000 acres of Acadia National Park.

It's no coincidence that artists were a large part of the 19th-century vanguard here: The dramatic landscape, with both bare and wooded mountains descending to the sea, still inspires all who see it. Once the word got out, painterly images began confirming the reports, and the surge began. Even today, no saltwater locale on the Eastern Seaboard can compete with the variety of scenery on Mount Desert Island.

Highlights

Look for ★ to find recommended sights, activities, dining, and lodging.

★ **Park Loop Road:** If you do nothing else on Mount Desert, drive this magnificent road that takes in many of Acadia National Park's highlights (page 308).

★ **The Carriage Roads:** Whether you walk, bike, or ride in a horse-drawn carriage, make a point of seeing Mr. Rockefeller's roads and bridges (page 308).

★ **Hiking:** Hiking is one of the best ways to experience Acadia, and trails range from easy rambles over flat terrain to near-vertical climbs on ladder trails (page 310).

★ **Abbe Museum:** The downtown Abbe Museum and its seasonal museum at Sieur de Monts Spring are fascinating places to learn about Maine's Native American heritage (page 316).

★ **Dive-In Theater Boat Cruise:** Got kids? Don't miss this tour, where Diver Ed brings the undersea world aboard (page 323).

★ **Northeast Harbor's Gardens:** "Magical and enchanting" best describes Asticou, Thuya, and Rockefeller Gardens. Zen-like Asticou is best seen in spring; Thuya delivers color through summer; Rockefeller peaks in early August (page 333).

★ **Wendell Gilley Museum:** Gilley's intricately carved birds, from miniature shorebirds to life-size birds of prey, are a marvel to behold (page 339).

★ **Seal Cove Auto Museum:** A must for fans of antique automobiles, the museum hosts one of the largest collections of Brass Era vehicles in the country, including a few extremely rare models (page 340).

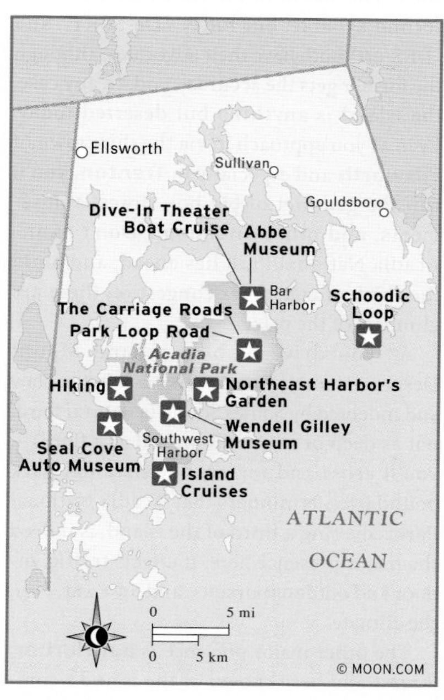

★ **Island Cruises:** Kim Strauss shares his deep knowledge of island ways and waters on the lunchtime cruise that allows time to explore Frenchboro (page 343).

★ **Schoodic Loop:** A scenic six-mile road edges the pink-granite shores of Acadia National Park's only mainland section and accesses hiking trails and picnic spots (page 355).

Those pioneering artists brilliantly portrayed this area, adding romantic touches to landscapes that really need no enhancement. From the 1,530-foot summit of Cadillac Mountain, you'll sense the grandeur of it all—the slopes careening toward the bay and the handful of islands below looking like the last footholds between Bar Harbor and Bordeaux.

For nearly four centuries, controversy has raged about the pronunciation of the island's name, and we won't resolve it here. French explorer Samuel de Champlain apparently gets credit for naming it *l'Ile des Monts Deserts* (island of bare mountains) when he sailed by in 1604. The accent in French would be on the second syllable, but today "De-SERT" and "DES-ert" both have their advocates, although the former gets the accuracy nod. In any case, the island is anything but deserted today. Even as you approach it, via the shire town of **Ellsworth** and especially in **Trenton,** you'll run the gauntlet of big-box stores, amusements, and other diversions. Don't panic: Acadia National Park lies ahead, and amid the thick of consumer congestion there are glimpses of the prize.

As you drive or bike around Mount Desert—vaguely shaped like a lobster claw and indented by Somes Sound (a natural fjard, not as deep or as steeply walled as a fjord)—you'll cross and recross the national park boundaries, reminders that Acadia National Park, covering a third of the island, is indeed the major presence here. It affects traffic, indoor and outdoor pursuits, and, in a way, even the climate.

The other major presence is **Bar Harbor,** largest and best known of the island's communities. It's the source of just about anything you could want, from T-shirts to tacos, books to bike rentals. The contrast with Acadia is astonishing, and the park struggles to maintain its image and character. And yet, even in Bar Harbor, the park's presence is felt.

Bar Harbor shares the island with **Southwest Harbor, Tremont,** and a number of small villages: **Bass Harbor, Bernard, Northeast Harbor, Seal Harbor, Otter Creek, Somesville,** and **Hall Quarry.** From Bass, Northeast, and Southwest Harbors, private and state ferries shuttle bike and foot traffic to offshore **Swans Island, Frenchboro** (Long Island), and the **Cranberry Isles** (and cars to Swans Island).

Stay on Route 1 instead of taking Route 3 to the island, and the congestion disappears. The towns lining the eastern shore of Frenchman Bay—**Hancock, Sullivan, Winter Harbor,** and **Gouldsboro**—have some of the best views of all: front-row seats facing the peaks of Mount Desert Island. It's no wonder many artists and artisans make their homes here. And at the tip of the **Schoodic Peninsula,** a stunning pocket of Acadia National Park sees only a fraction of the visitors who descend on the main part of the park.

PLANNING YOUR TIME

So much to do, so little time—that's the lament of most visitors. You can circumnavigate Mount Desert Island in a day, hitting the highlights along the Park Loop with just enough time to *ooh* and *aah* at each, but to appreciate Acadia, you need time to hike the trails, ride the carriage roads, get afloat on a whale-watching cruise or a sea kayak, visit museums, and explore an offshore island or two. A week or longer is best, but you can get a taste of Acadia in 3-4 days. Do note: a new congestion plan will require advance reservations for some of the park's highlight.

The region is very seasonal, with most restaurants, accommodations, and shops open mid-May-mid-October. May and June bring the new greens of spring and blooming rhododendrons and azaleas in Northeast Harbor's Asticou Garden, but mosquitoes and blackflies are at their worst and weather is temperamental—perhaps sunny and hot one day, damp and cold the next, making for a

Previous: view over Jordan Pond; beaver lodge in Corea Heath; Schoodic Peninsula beach.

Acadia Region

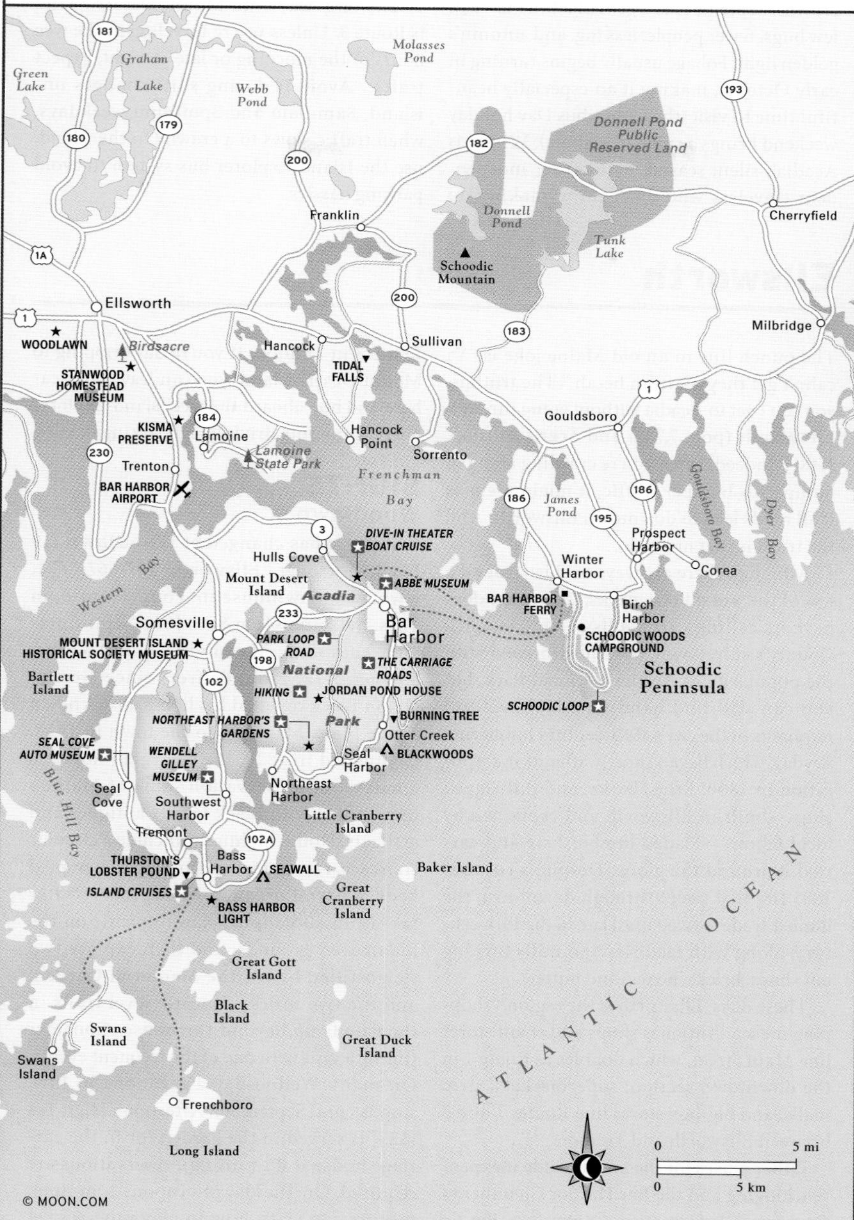

packing nightmare. July and August bring summer at its best, along with the biggest crowds. September is a gem of a time to visit: few bugs, fewer people, less fog, and autumn's golden light. Foliage usually begins turning in early October, making it an especially beautiful time to visit (the Columbus Day holiday weekend brings a spike in visitors). Winter is Acadia's silent season, best left for independent travelers who don't mind making do or perhaps making a meal of peanut butter crackers if an open restaurant can't be found.

The only way onto Mount Desert Island is Route 3. Unless you're traveling in the wee hours of the morning or late at night, expect traffic. Avoid it during shift changes on-island, 8am-9am and 3pm-4pm weekdays, when traffic slows to a crawl. On the island, use the Island Explorer bus system to avoid parking hassles.

Ellsworth

The punch line to an old Maine joke is "Ya cahn't get they-ah from he-ah." The truth is, you can't get to Acadia without going through **Ellsworth** (pop. 7,741) and **Trenton** (pop. 1,481). Indeed, when you're crawling along in bumper-to-bumper traffic, it might seem as if all roads lead to downtown Ellsworth. And the truth is that many do.

Although there are ways to skirt around a few of the worst bottlenecks, the region does have its calling cards. Ellsworth, Hancock County's shire town, has mushroomed with the popularity of Acadia National Park, but you can still find handsome architectural remnants of the city's 19th-century lumbering heyday, which began shortly after its incorporation in 1800. Brigs, barks, and full-rigged ships—built in Ellsworth and captained by local fellows—loaded lumber here and carried it around the globe. Despite a ruinous 1855 fire that swept through downtown, the lumber trade thrived until late in the 19th century, along with factories and mills turning out shoes, bricks, boxes, and butter.

These days, Ellsworth is the region's shopping mecca. Antiques shops and small stores line Main Street, which doubles as Route 1 in the downtown section; supermarkets, strip malls, and big-box stores line Routes 1 and 3 between Ellsworth and Trenton.

Other pluses for the area include inexpensive lodging and the Bar Harbor Chamber of Commerce Information Center location on Route 3 in Trenton. If you're day-tripping to Mount Desert Island, you can leave your car here and hop aboard the free Island Explorer bus, eliminating driving and parking hassles.

SIGHTS

Woodlawn

Very little has changed at **Woodlawn** (19 Black Horse Dr., Ellsworth, 207/667-8671, www.woodlawnmuseum.com, 10am-5pm Tues.-Sat., 1pm-4pm Sun. June-Sept., 1pm-4pm Tues.-Sun. May and Oct., $12 adults, $5 ages 5-12, grounds free) since George Nixon Black donated his home, also known as the Black Mansion, to the town in 1928. Completed in 1828, the Georgian house is a marvel of preservation—one of Maine's best—filled with Black family antiques and artifacts. House highlights include a circular staircase, rare books and artifacts, canopied beds, a barrel organ, and lots more. After taking an audio tour, plan to picnic on the manicured grounds, and then explore two sleigh-filled barns, the Memorial Garden, and the two miles of mostly level trails in the woods up beyond the house. Consider timing a visit with one of the frequent events: On many Wednesday afternoons in July, August, and September, Afternoon High Tea ($25) is served in the garden (or in the carriage house if it's raining); reservations are required. On Tuesday afternoons 2pm-4pm, visitors can learn how to play nine-wicket golf croquet on the tournament-sized court ($10, includes equipment). On Route 172, watch for the small sign 0.25 mile southwest of U.S. 1, and turn into the winding uphill driveway.

Birdsacre

En route to Bar Harbor, watch carefully on the right for the sign that marks **Birdsacre** (289 High St./Rte. 3, Ellsworth, 207/667-8460, www.birdsacre.com, sunrise-sunset daily, donation), a 200-acre urban sanctuary. Wander the trails in this peaceful preserve, spotting wildflowers, birds, and well-labeled shrubs and trees, and you'll have trouble believing you're in prime tourist territory. One trail, a boardwalk loop through woods behind the nature center, is accessible for wheelchairs and strollers.

Noted ornithologist Cordelia Stanwood once lived in the 1850 **Stanwood Homestead Museum** (10am-4pm daily June-September) at the sanctuary entrance. Birdsacre is also a wildlife rehabilitation center, so expect to see all kinds of winged creatures, especially hawks and owls, in various stages of recuperation. Some will be returned to the wild, and others remain here for educational purposes. Stop by the **nature center** (10am-4pm daily June-Sept., volunteer dependent) for even more exhibits.

Kisma Preserve

I can't stress this enough: **Kisma Preserve** (446 Bar Harbor Rd./Rte. 3, 207/667-3244, Trenton, www.kismapreserve.org, 10am-6pm daily mid-May-late fall) is not a zoo; it's a nonprofit educational facility, and everything revolves around preserving and protecting the animals, most of which are either rescues or retirees. Rules are strictly enforced—no running, loud voices, or disruptive behavior is permitted. The easiest way to view the animals is on a one-hour guided tour (about $20). Guides educate visitors about the biology of the animals, how they came to be here, and whether they'll be returned to the wild. For serious animal lovers, the preserve offers behind-the-scenes tours and close-ups; there are even options for camping in the preserve. It truly is a special place, home to more than 100 exotic and not-so-exotic creatures, with an emphasis on wolves and bears. Donations are essential to Kisma's survival, and yes, it's pricey, but so is feeding and caring for these animals.

Downeast Scenic Railroad

The all-volunteer **Downeast Rail Heritage Preservation Trust** (Railroad Siding Rd., Washington Junction, Hancock, 866/449-7245, www.downeastscenicrail.org) has restored a 1948 diesel engine and rehabilitated portions of the Calais Branch Line. Saturday-Sunday (late May-mid-Oct.) you can board the two vintage coaches, an open flatcar, or the caboose for a roughly 11-mile, 90-minute scenic excursion ($17 adults, $9 ages 3-12) to Ellsworth Falls and back. Work continues on the track to Green Lake, which will allow a 24-mile round-trip. If you're a train buff, ask about volunteer opportunities. From downtown Ellsworth, take Main Street northeast for 2.3 miles to Railroad Siding Road.

Telephone Museum

Discover life before cell phones at the **Telephone Museum** (166 Winkumpaugh Rd., Ellsworth 207/667-9491, www.thetelephonemuseum.org, 1pm-4pm Sat. July 1-Sept. 30 or by chance, $10 adults, $5 children), a hands-on museum with the East's largest collection of old-fashioned switching systems. Find it 10 miles north of Ellsworth, 1 mile off Route 1A toward Bangor.

Flightseeing

Get an eagle's-eye view of the area from either of these two businesses.

Scenic Flights of Acadia (1044 Bar Harbor Rd./Rte. 3, Trenton, 207/667-6527, www.scenicflightsofacadia.com) offers low-level flightseeing services in the Mount Desert Island region. Flights range 15-75 minutes, with prices beginning around $50 per person with a two-passenger minimum.

Scenic Biplane and Glider Rides (968 Bar Harbor Rd./Rte. 3, Trenton, 207/667-7627, www.acadiaairtours.com) lets you soar in silence with daily glider flights. The one- or two-passenger gliders are towed to an altitude of at least 2,500 feet and then released. An FAA-certified pilot guides the glider. Rates begin at $220 for a 25-minute flight for one or two. Other options include rides in an open-cockpit biplane (from $150 for two) and helicopter rides (from $75 pp). All flights are subject to an airport fee.

ENTERTAINMENT

Ellsworth has three free summer series (http://myellsworth.com). The **Ellsworth Concert Band** performs Wednesday evenings at the Harbor Park Gazebo. **Outdoor family movies** are shown at sunset Thursdays at the Knowlton Playground on State Street (donations appreciated). **Concerts** are staged at Waterfront Park at 6pm on Fridays.

Ace lumberjack "Timber" Tina Scheer has been competing around the world since she was seven, and she shows her prowess at the **Great Maine Lumberjack Show** (127 Bar Harbor Rd./Rte. 3, Trenton, 207/667-0067, www.mainelumberjack.com, 7pm daily mid-June-early Sept., 4pm Sat. and 2pm Sun. early Sept.-mid-Oct., $13 adults, $12 over age 62, $9 ages 4-11). During the 75-minute "Olympics of the Forest," you'll watch two teams compete in 12 events, including ax throwing, crosscut sawing, logrolling, speed climbing, and more. Some events are open to participation. If you want to learn skills, one-hour lessons for up to six participants are $60-75. Performances are held rain or shine. Seating is under a roof, but dress for the weather if it's inclement. The ticket office opens at 6pm. The venue is dog friendly.

The carefully restored art deco **Grand Auditorium of Hancock County** (100 Main St., Ellsworth, 207/667-9500, www.grandonline.org) is the year-round site of films, concerts, plays, and art exhibits.

SHOPPING

Specialty Shops

You're unlikely to meet a single person who has left **Big Chicken Barn Books and Antiques** (1768 Bucksport Rd./Rte. 1, Ellsworth, 207/667-7308, www.bigchickenbarn.com) without buying something. You'll find every kind of collectible on the vast first floor, courtesy of more than four dozen dealers. Climb the stairs for books, magazines, old music, and more. With free coffee, restrooms, and 21,000 square feet of floor space, this place is addictive. The Big Chicken is 11 miles east of Bucksport, 8.5 miles west of Ellsworth.

Just south of downtown, in the historic 1838 courthouse at the corner of Court Street and Route 1, is **Courthouse Gallery Fine Art** (6 Court St., Ellsworth, 207/667-6611, www.courthousegallery.com), showcasing works by some of Maine's top contemporary artists.

The 40-plus-dealer **Old Creamery Antique Mall** (13 Hancock St., Ellsworth, 207/667-0522) fills 6,000 square feet on two jam-packed floors. Around the corner is **Atlantic Art Glass** (25 Pine St., Ellsworth, 207/664-0222, www.atlanticartglass.com), where you can watch Linda and Ken Perrin demonstrate glassblowing and buy their contemporary creations.

Don't miss **Rooster Brother** (29 Main St./Rte. 1, Ellsworth, 800/866-0054, www.roosterbrother.com) for gourmet foods and its kitchen emporium. You can easily pick up all the fixings for a fancy picnic here.

John Edwards Market (158 Main St., Ellsworth, 207/667-9377) is a twofold find: Upstairs is a natural-foods store; downstairs is the Wine Cellar Gallery, showcasing Maine artists throughout the year.

Union River Book & Toy Co. (100 Main St., Ellsworth, 207/667-6604, www.unionrivertoys.com) is filled with books, toys, games, puzzles, dolls, stuffed animals,

---

1: Birdsacre wildlife rehabilitation center **2:** Seal Cove Farm **3:** Woodlawn

1
2
3

puppets, and more to keep the kiddos happy should the weather turn gloomy. Out back is a café.

Stock up on Maine-made jams, syrups, honeys, and other specialty foods at **Maine's Own Treats** (68 Rte. 3/Bar Harbor Rd., Trenton, 207/667-8888).

Discount Shopping

The **L. L. Bean Factory Store** (150 High St./Rte. 1, Ellsworth, 207/667-7753) carries everything from clothing to sporting equipment, but don't expect a full range of sizes or designs—that said, I've never left empty-handed.

Across the road is **Renys Department Store** (Ellsworth Shopping Center, 175 High St./Rte. 1, Ellsworth, 207/667-5166, www.renys.com), a Maine-based discount operation with a "you never know what you'll find" philosophy. Trust me, though, you'll find something here.

Marden's (461 High St./Rte. 3, Ellsworth, 207/669-6035, www.mardenssurplus.com) is another Maine "bit of this, bit of that" enterprise with the catchy slogan "I shoulda bought it when I saw it." Good advice.

FOOD

Lobster and Seafood

It's hard to say which is better—the serene views or the tasty lobster—at **Union River Lobster Pot** (8 South St., 207/667-5077, www.lobsterpot.com, 4pm-9pm daily June-early Sept., 5pm-8:30pm early Sept.-mid-Oct., $15-24). It's tucked behind Rooster Brother, right on the banks of the Union River. The menu includes far more than lobster, with chicken, fish, meat, and pasta dishes, and a kids' menu is available. Remember to save room for the pie, especially the blueberry.

Far more touristy is **Trenton Bridge Lobster Pound** (Bar Harbor Rd./Rte. 3, 207/667-2977, www.trentonbridgelobster.com, 11am-7:30pm Mon.-Sat. late May-mid-Oct.), on the right next to the bridge leading to Mount Desert Island. Watch for the "smoke signals"—steam billowing from the huge vats.

Jordan's Snack Bar (200 Down East Hwy./Rte. 1, 207/667-2174, www.jordanssnackbar.com, 11am-7pm Wed.-Mon.) has an almost cult following for its crabmeat rolls and fried clams. Wednesday cruise-ins (6pm-9pm) usually feature live entertainment and draw up to 50 vintage cars. Kids will love the game room and playground.

Quick Bites

Order breakfast anytime at the **Riverside Café** (151 Main St., Ellsworth, 207/667-7220, 7am-2pm daily, $4-12). As for the name? It used to be down the street, overlooking the Union River.

Less creative but no less delicious are the home-style breakfasts at **Martha's Diner** (Renys Plaza, 151 High St., Ellsworth, 207/664-2495, www.marthasdiner.com, 6am-2pm Tues.-Sun.), where lunch is also served 11am-2pm Tuesday-Saturday. Booths are red leatherette and Formica, and the waitresses may call you "doll."

Big flavors come out of tiny **86 This** (125 Main St., Ellsworth, 207/610-1777, www.86thismaine.com, 11am-8pm Mon.-Fri., 11am-4pm Sat.), a wrap-and-burrito joint. The flavors are rich, the portions are generous, and wraps are named after the owners' favorite indie bands.

On the upper end of Main Street, **Flexit Café and Bakery** (192 Main St., Ellsworth, 207/412-0484, http://flexitcafe.com, 6:30am-5pm Mon.-Sat., 7:30am-3pm Sun.) serves breakfast and lunch daily, with vegan and gluten-free options available.

Serendib (2 State St., Ellsworth, 207/664-1030, www.serendibellsworth.com, 10:30am-7:30pm Tues.-Sat., $12-16) serves authentic Indian-Sri Lankan cuisine prepared by owner Sanjeeva Abeyasekera, a native of Sri Lanka.

Morton's Moo (9 School St., Ellsworth, 207/266-9671, hours vary seasonally) deserves its giant reputation for homemade Italian gelato, *sorbetto,* and ice cream in creative flavors. It's half a block off Main Street behind Flexit.

New York-style thin-crust pizza, by the slice or the pie, is served at **Finelli Pizzeria** (12 Rte. 1, Ellsworth, 207/664-0230, www.finellipizzeria.com, 11am-8pm Sun.-Thurs., 11am-9pm Fri.-Sat., $11-14), where the pizza dough and focaccia are made fresh daily. Other options include calzones, pastas, subs, and salads.

Mosey through Lamoine to **Seal Cove Farm** (202 Partridge Cove Rd./Rte. 204, Lamoine, 207/667-7127, www.mainegoatcheese.com, noon-7pm Fri.-Sat., noon-5pm Sun., $12), a working goat farm best known for its handcrafted artisan cheeses. Adjacent to the small farm stand is an outdoor wood-burning oven. Ten-inch handcrafted pizzas are made not only with Seal Cove's fresh goat and mixed-milk cheeses, but also with seasonal, farm-fresh produce. There's a small picnic pavilion. Human kids will get a kick out of watching the goat kids romp in the pasture.

Casual Dining

Provender Kitchen & Bar (112 Main St., Ellsworth, 207/610-1480, www.eatprovender.com, 5pm-9pm Tues.-Sat., 9am-2pm Sun., $16-36) serves contemporary American fare in a historical setting complete with polished wood booths and soft lighting.

ACCOMMODATIONS

The Kelley family's **Isleview Motel** (1169 Bar Harbor Rd./Rte. 3, Trenton, 207/667-5661 or 866/475-3843, www.isleviewmotelandcottages.com, $65-99) comprises a motel, one- and two-bedroom cottages, and a few "sleep-and-go" rooms above the office, all decorated in country style. Rates include a light continental breakfast.

The family-owned **Open Hearth Inn** (Bar Harbor Rd./Rte. 3, Trenton, 207/667-2930 or 800/655-0234, www.openhearthinn.com, $90-160) is clean, convenient, and replete with retro charm. Choose an inn room, a 1950s tourist court-style cottage, a motel room, or an apartment. Free pickup at Bar Harbor Airport is offered during business hours. On most mornings, homemade muffins are available in the office, along with tea and coffee. It's less than 0.25 mile from the bridge connecting Trenton to Mount Desert Island and within walking distance of four lobster restaurants.

The **Acadia Sunrise Motel** (952 Bar Harbor Rd./Rte. 3, Trenton, 207/667-8452, www.acadiasunrisemotel.com, $90-150) has undergone a sea change since its 1985 origin as a strip mall. Perks include an outdoor heated pool, playground, and a guest laundry. Ask for a room at the back, away from the street noise and overlooking the airport, with the ocean and Acadia's mountains in the distance. Pets are welcome ($15-25).

If all you want is a good bed in a clean room, the rainbow-colored **Twin Hills Cottages of Acadia** (210 Twin Hill Rd., Ellsworth, 207/667-8390, www.twinhillscottages.com, $99-129), a nicely updated vintage 1948 motor court facing Route 1 south of town, fits the bill with comfortably renovated one- and two-bedroom cabins.

Tucked away in Lamoine, the **Chocolate Chip Bed & Breakfast** (720 Lamoine Beach Rd., Lamoine, 207/610-1691, www.chocolatechipbb.com, $135-160) treats guests to all kinds of chocolate treats, from muffins in the morning to cookies at night. Eric and Sue Hahn's lovingly rebuilt early 19th-century pond-side farmhouse has four comfy guest rooms decorated in country style, all with hardwood floors and handmade quilts.

Camping

The 55-acre oceanfront **Lamoine State Park** (23 State Park Rd./Rte. 184, Lamoine, 207/667-4778, www.parksandlands.com, mid-May-mid-Oct., $30, reservations $5/night) is equally convenient to the Schoodic region and Mount Desert Island. Facilities include a picnic area with a spectacular view, a boat launch, a children's play area, a tree house, and a dump station. Camping is available at 62 mostly wooded sites; several are oceanfront. No hookups are available (except for one site designated for the disabled). The campground has a modern bathhouse with free hot showers. Reserve online with a credit card, or call 207/624-9950 or 800/332-1501 on weekdays. Leashed pets are allowed; cleanup is required.

INFORMATION AND SERVICES

The **Ellsworth Area Chamber of Commerce** (207/667-5584, www.ellsworthchamber.org) also covers Trenton.

The **Thompson Island Visitors Center** (Rte. 3, Thompson Island, 207/288-3411) represents the Mount Desert Island Regional Chambers of Commerce, which includes the Trenton Chamber of Commerce. An Acadia National Park ranger is usually stationed here, and park passes are available.

Find **public restrooms** in City Hall (City Hall Ave.) in downtown Ellsworth, open 24 hours daily; the library (46 State St.); the chamber of commerce; and the picnic area and boat launch (Water St.).

GETTING THERE AND AROUND

Ellsworth is about 14 miles via Route 172 from Blue Hill. It's about 20 miles or 30-45 minutes, depending on traffic, to Bar Harbor.

Route 1 of the **Island Explorer** (www.exploreacadia.com) bus system, which primarily serves Mount Desert Island with its fleet of propane-fueled fare-free vehicles, connects the Hancock County/Bar Harbor Airport in Trenton with downtown Bar Harbor. Operated by Downeast Transportation, the Island Explorer runs late June-mid-October.

Before or after visiting Mount Desert Island, if you're headed farther Down East—to Lamoine, the eastern side of Hancock County, and beyond—there's a good shortcut from Trenton. About five miles south of Ellsworth on Route 3, just north of the Kisma Preserve, turn east onto Route 204, bear left at the T intersection, and then take your first right, following Route 204/Pinkhams Flats Road. Turn right onto Mud Creek Road, which wiggles through a salt marsh and eventually spits out on Route 1 just west of Franklin.

Acadia National Park on Mount Desert Island

TOP EXPERIENCE

Rather like an octopus, or perhaps an amoeba, **Acadia National Park** extends its reach here and there on Mount Desert Island. The first national park east of the Mississippi River and the only national park in the northeastern United States, it was created from donated parcels—a big chunk here, a tiny plot there—and slowly but surely fused into its present-day size of more than 46,000 acres. Within the boundaries of this splendid space are mountains, lakes, ponds, trails, fabulous vistas, and several campgrounds. Each year more than two million visitors bike, hike, and drive into and through the park. Yet even at the height of summer, when the whole world seems to have arrived, it's possible to find peaceful niches and less-trodden paths.

Acadia's history is unique among national parks and is indeed fascinating. Several books have been written about some of the high-minded (in the positive sense) and high-profile personalities who provided the impetus and wherewithal for the park's inception and never flagged in their interest and support. Just to spotlight a few, we can thank George B. Dorr, Charles W. Eliot, and John D. Rockefeller Jr. for the park we have today.

The most comprehensive guide to the park and its surrounding area is *Moon Acadia National Park.*

NATIONAL PARK INFORMATION

Entrance fees for Acadia are charged May-October. Seven-day passes are $30 for private motorized vehicles carrying 15 passengers or fewer; $25 for motorcycles; and $15 for pedestrians, hikers, and bikers. An annual pass to Acadia is $55. An interagency annual pass covering all federal recreation sites is $80. Seniors (age 62 and older) can purchase an annual interagency pass for $20 or a lifetime pass for $80. An interagency annual military pass is free for active-duty U.S. military personnel and their dependents. A lifetime access pass for citizens or permanent residents with disabilities is free. To see if your family qualifies for the annual Every Kid in a Park 4th grade pass (covering the passholder and everyone else in your vehicle), visit www.everykidinapark.gov. Passes are available at the visitors centers, park campgrounds, the Sand Beach entrance station, and online. Avoid lines by purchasing online, but be sure your dates are firm and don't forget to print out the pass.

Congestion Management

Acadia might seem as if it's bursting at the seams during peak season and holidays, especially for the top sights. The park sees 3.5 million visitors annually (ranking in the top 10 of all national parks), with most of those concentrated between 8am and 5pm in July and August.

The park expects to begin implementing a new transportation plan beginning in 2021. Elements of this plan call for reservations for private vehicles through timed entry at peak times for Cadillac Mountain, Ocean Drive, and Jordan Pond, meaning you'll have to make a reservation and pay a fee to visit these sites in a vehicle. For updated details, visit www.nps.gov/acad.

Hulls Cove Visitor Center

The modern **Hulls Cove Visitors Center** (Rte. 3, Hulls Cove, 207/288-3338, 8:30am-4:30pm daily Apr. 15-June 30 and Sept. 1-Oct. 31, 8am-6pm daily July-Aug.) is eight miles southeast of the head of Mount Desert Island and is well signposted. Here you can buy your park pass; rendezvous with pals; make reservations for ranger-guided natural and cultural history programs; watch a 15-minute film about Acadia; buy books, park souvenirs, and audio guides; and use the restrooms. Pick up a copy of the **park's event calendar,** which lists activities along with tide calendars, and the schedule for the excellent **Island Explorer** shuttle bus system, which operates late June-Columbus Day. The Island Explorer is supported by park entrance fees as well as by Friends of Acadia and L. L. Bean. If you have children, enroll them in the park's free **Junior Ranger program.** To earn a Junior Ranger patch, they must complete the activities in an age-appropriate workbook, attend ranger-led programs, and promise to take care of Acadia. Once they've completed the book, stop by the **Junior Ranger Table** (8:30am-10:30am and 2pm-4pm daily) to be sworn in by a ranger.

Thompson Island Visitor Center

As you cross the bridge from Trenton toward Mount Desert Island, you might not even notice that you arrive first on tiny **Thompson Island,** site of a visitors center (8am-6pm daily mid-May-mid-Oct.) established jointly by the chambers of commerce of Mount Desert Island's towns and Acadia National Park. In season, a park ranger is usually posted here to answer questions and provide basic advice on hiking trails and other park activities, but consider this a stopgap—be sure to continue to the park's main visitors center.

Bar Harbor Village Green

The park maintains a small **information center** (8am-5pm late June-mid-Oct.) in downtown Bar Harbor on the Village Green, adjacent to the Island Explorer bus stop on Firefly Lane. Park and bus information, as well as visitor passes, are available here.

SIGHTS

★ Park Loop Road

The 27-mile **Park Loop Road** takes in most of the park's big-ticket sites. It begins at the visitors center, winds past several of the park's scenic highlights (with parking areas), ascends to the summit of **Cadillac Mountain,** and provides overlooks to magnificent vistas. Along the route are trailheads and overlooks as well as **Sieur de Monts Spring** (Acadia Nature Center, Wild Gardens of Acadia, Abbe Museum summer site, and the convergence of several spectacular trails), **Sand Beach, Thunder Hole, Otter Cliffs, Fabbri picnic area** (where there's one wheelchair-accessible picnic table), **Jordan Pond House, Bubble Pond,** and **Eagle Lake.** Just before you get to Sand Beach, you'll see the Park Entrance Station, where you'll need to buy a pass if you haven't already done so.

Start at the parking lot below the Hulls Cove Visitor Center and follow the signs; part of the loop is one-way, so you'll be doing the loop clockwise. Traffic gets heavy at midday in midsummer, so aim for early morning or late afternoon, if you can. Maximum speed is 35 mph, but be alert for gawkers and photographers stopping without warning, and pedestrians dashing across the road from stopped cars or tour buses.

Allow a couple of hours so you can stop along the way. You can rent an audio tour on cassette or CD for $13 (including directions, an instruction sheet, and a map) at the Hulls Cove Visitor Center. Another option is to pick up the drive-it-yourself tour booklet ***Motorist Guide: Park Loop Road*** ($4.50), available at the Thompson Island and Hulls Cove Visitor Centers.

★ The Carriage Roads

In 1913, John D. Rockefeller Jr. began laying out what eventually became a 57-mile carriage road system, and he oversaw the project through the 1940s. Motorized vehicles have never been allowed on these lovely graded byways, making them real escapes from the auto world. Devoted now to multiple uses, the "Rockefeller roads" see hikers, bikers, baby strollers, wheelchairs, and even horse-drawn carriages.

Pick up a free copy of the carriage road map at any of the centers selling park passes. The busiest times are 10am-2pm.

The most crowded carriage roads are those closest to the Hulls Cove Visitor Center—the Witch Hole Pond Loop, Duck Brook, and Eagle Lake. Avoid these, opting instead for roads west of Jordan Pond, or go early in the morning or late in the day. Better still, go off-season, when you can enjoy the fall foliage (late Sept.-mid-Oct.) or winter's cross-country skiing.

You can rent bicycles in Bar Harbor, Northeast Harbor, or Southwest Harbor. Note: Only Class 1 e-bikes (up to 20mph but only when pedaling) are allowed on the carriage roads.

In 2015, David Rockefeller gave approximately 1,000 acres surrounding Little Long Pond to the Land & Garden Preserve (www.gardenpreserve.org), which also manages Asticou and Thuya Gardens in Northeast Harbor. Be forewarned that hikers are allowed on the carriage roads here, but bicyclists are not. The no-biking areas are signaled with Green Rock Company markers. The carriage-road map clearly indicates the biking and no-biking areas. Bicyclists must be especially speed-sensitive on the carriage roads, keeping an eye out for hikers, horseback riders, small children, and the hearing impaired.

1: Bass Harbor Head Light **2:** Sand Beach **3:** Ship Harbor Nature Trail

1
2
3

HORSE-DRAWN CARRIAGE RIDES

To recapture the early carriage roads era, take one of the horse-drawn open-carriage tours run by **Carriages of Acadia** (Wildwood Stables, 21 Dane Farm Rd., Seal Harbor, 877/276-3622, www.acadiahorses.com), one mile south of the Jordan Pond House. One- and two-hour trips start at 9am daily mid-June to mid-October. Reservations are not required, but they're encouraged, especially in midsummer. The two-hour tours ($40 adults, $16 ages 6-12, $11 ages 2-5) are better. Choose from the two-hour **Day Mountain Summit** ride at 4pm or the **Mr. Rockefeller Bridge Tour**, taking in three bridges, at 9:45am or 1:45pm. If you can't spare two hours, the one-hour loop around Day Mountain is $24 for adults, $14 for children, and $9 ages 2-5. Two carriages are wheelchair-accessible, carrying up to two wheelchairs and four additional passengers; call in advance to reserve space on these. Private trips are available; call for current pricing.

Bass Harbor Head Light

At the southern end of Mount Desert's western "claw," follow Route 102A to the turnoff toward **Bass Harbor Head Light.** Drive or bike to the end of Lighthouse Road, walk down a steep wooden stairway, and look up and to the right. Voilà! Bass Harbor Head Light, its red glow automated since 1974, stands sentinel at the eastern entrance to Blue Hill Bay. The Coast Guard is conveying ownership of the 2.5-acre property housing the 1858 lighthouse and 1876 tower and fog bell to the park.

Baker Island

The best way to get to—and to appreciate—history-rich Baker Island is on the ranger-narrated Baker Island cruise booked through **Bar Harbor Whale Watch Company** (1 West St., Bar Harbor, 207/288-2386 or 888/942-5374, www.barharborwhales.com, mid-June-mid-Sept., $49 adults, $27 ages 6-14, $9 under age 6). The five-hour tours include access via motorized skiff to the 130-acre island, which has a farmstead, a lighthouse, and intriguing rock formations. The return trip provides a view of Otter Cliffs from the water (bring binoculars and look for climbers), Thunder Hole, Sand Beach, and Great Head. Call or check the website for departure times.

RECREATION

★ Hiking

If you're spending more than a day on Mount Desert Island, plan to buy a copy of *A Walk in the Park: Acadia's Hiking Guide,* by Tom St. Germain, which details more than 60 hikes, including some outside the park. Remember that pets are allowed on park trails, but only on leashes no longer than six feet. Four of the Island Explorer bus routes are particularly useful for hikers, alleviating the problems of backtracking and car-jammed parking lots. Here's a handful of favorite Acadia hikes, from easy to rugged.

Three easy trails are ideal for young families. **Jordan Pond Nature Trail** starts at the Jordan Pond parking area. This is an easy, wheelchair-accessible, one-mile wooded loop trail; pick up a brochure at the beginning of the trail. **Ship Harbor Nature Trail** starts at the Ship Harbor parking area, on Route 102A between Bass Harbor and Seawall Campground, in the southwestern corner of the island. The easy 1.3-mile loop trail leads to the shore; pick up a brochure at the trailhead. Ship Harbor is particularly popular among bird-watchers seeking warblers, and you just might spot an eagle while you picnic on the rocks. An even easier trail, with its parking area just east of the Ship Harbor parking area, **Wonderland** is 1.4 miles round-trip—a great hike that delivers a microcosm of the island's ecosystems.

A moderate 1.4-mile loop, the **Great Head Trail** starts at the eastern end of Sand Beach, off the Park Loop Road. Park in the Sand Beach parking area and cross the beach to the trailhead. Or take Schooner Head Road from downtown Bar Harbor and park in the small area where the road dead-ends. There

With a Little Help from Our Friends

As we watch federal funding for national parks lose headway year after year, every park in the United States needs a safety net like **Friends of Acadia** (FOA, 207/288-3340 or 800/625-0321, www.friendsofacadia.org), a dynamic organization headquartered in Bar Harbor. Propane-powered shuttle-bus service needs expanding? FOA finds a multimillion-dollar donor. Well-used trails need maintenance? FOA organizes volunteer work parties. New connector trails needed? FOA gets them done. No need seems to go unfilled.

FOA—one of Acadia National Park's greatest assets—is both reactive and proactive. It's an amazingly symbiotic relationship. When informed of a need, the Friends stand ready to help; when they themselves perceive a need, they propose solutions to park management and jointly figure out ways to make them happen. It's hard to avoid sounding like a media flack when describing this organization.

Friends of Acadia was founded in 1986 to preserve and protect the park for resource-sensitive tourism and myriad recreational uses. Since then, FOA has contributed more than $27 million to the park and surrounding communities for trail upkeep, carriage road maintenance, seasonal park staff funding, and conservation projects. FOA also cofounded the Island Explorer bus system and instigated the Acadia Trails Forever program, a joint park-FOA partnership for trail rehabilitation. More than 40 trails have been rehabilitated or built through the program.

As part of its efforts to reduce traffic congestion on Mount Desert Island, FOA purchased land in Trenton for an off-island transit and welcome center and sold approximately 150 acres to the Maine Department of Transportation for the facility. The organization constructed a community trail on the remaining land. The Acadia Land Legacy Partnership between FOA, Acadia National Park, Maine Coast Heritage Trust, and conservation donors purchases or protects privately held lands in or adjacent to Acadia's borders; recent achievements include the purchase of 62 acres on Seal Cove Pond and the permanent protection of 1,400 acres of intact woods and wetlands bordering Acadia's Schoodic District. FOA also helps fund more than 150 seasonal positions serving the park.

You can join FOA and its roughly 5,000 members and support this worthy cause; memberships start at $40/year. You can also lend a hand while you're here: FOA and the park organize **weekly volunteer work parties** (8:20am-12:30pm Tues., Thurs., and Sat. June-mid-Oct.) for Acadia trail, carriage road, and other outdoor maintenance. Call the recorded information line (207/288-3934) for the work locations, or call the FOA office for answers to questions. The meeting point is park headquarters (Eagle Lake Rd./Rte. 233, Bar Harbor), about three miles west of town. Take your own water, lunch, and bug repellent. Dress in layers and wear closed-toe shoes. More than 12,000 volunteer hours go toward this effort each year.

Each summer, Friends of Acadia also sponsors a cadre of **Ridge Runners** and **Summit Stewards,** who work under park supervision and spend their days on the summit of Cadillac Mountain and out and about on trails repairing cairns, watching for lost hikers, and handing out Leave No Trace information. FOA also hires more than a dozen area teens each summer for the Acadia Youth Conservation Corps, which does trail and carriage road work, and Cadillac Summit Stewards, who work atop Acadia's highest mountain to protect the fragile alpine environment and the visitor experience there. And, FOA's seasonal Acadia Digital Media Team captures still photographs and videos to help share the story of the park, the organization, and their programs.

If you happen to be in the region on the first Saturday in November, call the FOA office to register for the **annual carriage road cleanup,** which usually draws up to 500 volunteers. Bring water and gloves; there's a free hot lunch at midday for everyone who participates. It's dubbed Take Pride in Acadia Day—indeed an apt label.

are actually two trail loops here, both of which have enough elevation to provide terrific views.

Another moderate hike with great views is the 1.8-mile round-trip **Gorham Mountain Trail.** It's a great family hike, as kids especially love the Cadillac Cliffs section. Access is off the Park Loop Road, just beyond Thunder Hole.

The moderate hike to **Beech Mountain**'s summit has a fire tower, from which you can look out toward Long Pond and the Blue Hill Peninsula. A knob near the top is a prime viewing site for the migration of hawks and other raptors in September. Round-trip on the wooded route is 1.1 miles, although a couple of side trails can extend it. You'll have less competition here in this quieter part of the park. Take Route 102 south from Somesville, heading toward Pretty Marsh. Turn left onto Beech Hill Road and follow it to the parking area at the end.

Beehive Trail and **Precipice Trail** are the park's toughest routes, with sheer faces and iron ladders; Precipice is often closed (usually mid-Apr.-late July) to protect nesting peregrine falcons. If challenges are your thing and these trails are open (check beforehand at the visitors center), go ahead. But a fine alternative in the difficult category is the **Beachcroft Trail** on Huguenot Head. Also called the Beachcroft Path, the trail is best known for its 1,500 beautifully engineered granite steps. Round-trip is 2.4 miles, or you can continue a loop at the top, taking in the **Bear Brook Trail** on Champlain Mountain, for about 4.4 miles. The parking area is just north of Route 3, near Sieur de Monts Spring.

Rock Climbing

Acadia has a number of splendid sites prized by climbers: the sea cliffs at Otter Cliffs and Great Head; South Bubble Mountain; Canada Cliff (on the island's western side); and the South Wall and the Central Slabs on Champlain Mountain. If you haven't tried climbing, never do it yourself without instruction. **Acadia Mountain Guides Climbing School** (228 Main St., Bar Harbor, 207/288-8186 or 888/232-9559, www.acadiamountainguides.com) and **Atlantic Climbing School** (67 Main St., 2nd fl., Bar Harbor, 207/288-2521, www.acadiaclimbing.com) both provide instruction and guided climbs. Costs vary depending on the site, experience level, session length, and number of climbers.

Swimming

Slightly below the Park Loop Road (take Island Explorer Route No. 3—Sand Beach), **Sand Beach** is the park's and the island's biggest sandy beach. Lifeguards are on duty during the summer, and even then, the biggest threat can be hypothermia. The saltwater is terminally glacial—in mid-July it still might not reach 60°F. The best solution is to walk to the far end of the beach, where a warmer shallow stream meets the ocean. Avoid the parking lot scramble by taking the Explorer bus.

The park's most popular freshwater swimming site, staffed with a lifeguard and inevitably crowded on hot days, is **Echo Lake,** south of Somesville on Route 102 and well signposted (take Island Explorer Route No. 7—Southwest Harbor).

If you have a canoe, kayak, or rowboat, you can reach swimming holes in **Seal Cove Pond** and **Round Pond,** both on the western side of Mount Desert. The eastern shore of **Hodgdon Pond** (also on the western side of the island) is accessible by car via Hodgdon Road and Long Pond Fire Road. **Lake Wood,** at the northern end of Mount Desert, has a tiny beach, restrooms, and auto access. To get to Lake Wood from Route 3, head west on Crooked Road to unpaved Park Road. Turn left and continue to the parking area, which will be crowded on a hot day, so arrive early.

Park Ranger Programs

Pick up a copy of ***Acadia Weekly,*** which details the ranger programs available (or download it ahead of time at www.nps.gov/acad). Don't miss these possibilities for learning more about the park's natural and cultural history.

The park ranger programs, lasting 1-3 hours, are great—and most are free. During July-August there are dozens of weekly programs. Included are birding, dusk, sunset, photo, and geology walks; mountain hikes; carriage road explorations by foot or bike; stargazing programs; touch tank talks; and activities geared to young families. Some programs require reservations, others do not; reservations can be made up to three days in advance (207/288-8832).

Park rangers also give evening lectures during the summer in the amphitheaters at Blackwoods and Seawall Campgrounds.

FOOD

Jordan Pond House

The only restaurant within the park is the **Jordan Pond House** (Park Loop Rd., 207/276-3316, www.acadiajordanpondhouse.com, 11am-9pm daily), a modern facility in a spectacular waterside setting. Jordan Pond House began life as a rustic 19th-century teahouse; wonderful old photos line the walls of the current incarnation, which went up after a disastrous fire in 1979. Afternoon tea is still a tradition, with tea, popovers, and strawberry jam served on the lawn until 5pm daily in summer, weather permitting, but it's no secret, especially with bus tours and cruisers, so it's likely you'll wait for a table. The locally based Acadia Corporation managed Jordan Pond House for 80 years, but in a controversial 2014 decision, the park service awarded the contract to an out-of-state concessionaire. Unfortunately, the overall experience has declined, while the prices have risen.

CAMPING

Mount Desert Island has at least a dozen commercial campgrounds, but there are only two—Blackwoods and Seawall—within park boundaries on the island; neither has hookups. Both have seasonal restrooms (no showers), dump stations, and seasonal amphitheaters where rangers present evening programs. Reservations for both are handled by Recreation.gov (877/444-6777, www.recreation.gov, credit card required).

Blackwoods Campground

Year-round **Blackwoods,** just off Route 3, five miles south of Bar Harbor, has 306 sites. Because of its location on the east side of the island, it's also the more popular of the two campgrounds. Reservations are suggested May 1-October 31, when the fee is $30/site/night. Reservations can be made up to six months ahead. In April and November, camping is $15; in December-March it's free with a permit. A trail connects the campground to the Ocean Drive trail system.

Seawall Campground

Reservations are accepted for half of the 214 sites at **Seawall Campground,** on Route 102A in the Seawall district, four miles south of Southwest Harbor; the rest are first come, first served. In midsummer, you'll need to arrive as early as 8:30am (when the ranger station opens) to secure an unreserved site. Seawall is open late May-September. The cost is $30/night for drive-up sites and $22/night for walk-in tent sites.

RV length at Seawall is limited to 35 feet, with the width limited to an awning extended no more than 12 feet. Generators are not allowed in the campground.

Mount Desert Island with Kids

Acadia National Park is a great place to introduce kids to the great outdoors. Between park visits, you'll find plenty of other activities with real kid appeal. Here are a few sure bets.

IN THE PARK

Before arriving, register either by phone or online for **Acadia Quest,** an experiential scavenger hunt in the park. At park headquarters, sign kids up as **Junior Rangers.** Then pick and choose from the **ranger-led activities** that appeal to your family's interests and abilities. Good choices for **easy family hikes** include the Ocean Path, Jordan Pond Nature Trail, Ship Harbor Nature Trail, and Wonderland. If you're into **geocaching,** ask about the park's EarthCache Program (www.nps.gov/acad/earthcache.htm).

SLIMY SEA CREATURES

You can't beat the wow appeal of **Diver Ed's Dive-in Theater Boat Cruise** (207/288-3483 or 800/979-3370, www.divered.com). Ed dives to the depths with an underwater camera while you wait on board and watch the action. When he resurfaces, he brings along with him a variety of creatures from the depths for passengers to see, feel, and learn about.

LOBSTER LORE

Even if the kids won't eat lobster, they'll be fascinated by the info presented on the two-hour cruises aboard the ***Lulu*** (56 West St., Bar Harbor, 207/963-2341 or 866/235-2341, www.lululobsterboat.com).

HANDS-ON NATURE

"Please touch" is the philosophy at the **George B. Dorr Museum of Natural History** (105 Eden St./Rte. 3, Bar Harbor, 207/288-5015, www.coa.edu, 10am-5pm Tues.-Sat., donation), a small museum on the College of the Atlantic campus in Bar Harbor. Kids have the opportunity to touch fur, skulls, and even whale baleen.

FERRY HOPPING

Spend the better part of a day on the **Cranberry Isles,** visiting both Big and Little Cranberry and either walking or biking around, or take the passenger ferry to **Winter Harbor** and hop on the Island Explorer bus to visit the Schoodic section of Acadia National Park. En route, watch for seals, seabirds, and lobster boats hauling traps.

NATIVE AMERICAN CULTURE

Check with the **Abbe Museum** (26 Mt. Desert St., Bar Harbor, 207/288-3519, www.abbemuseum.

Bar Harbor and Vicinity

In the late 19th century and well into the 20th, **Bar Harbor** (pop. 5,235), founded in 1796 as the town of Eden, grew to become one of the East Coast's fanciest summer watering holes. In those days, ferries and steam yachts arrived from points south, large and small resort hotels sprang up, and exclusive mansions (quaintly dubbed "cottages") were the venues of parties thrown by summer-resident Drexels, DuPonts, Vanderbilts, and prominent academics, journalists, and lawyers. The "rusticators" came for the season with huge entourages of servants, children, pets, and horses. The area's renown was such that by the 1890s, even the staffs of the British, Austrian,

org, 10am-5pm daily late May-early Nov.) about scheduled special programs for kids, and time your visit to take advantage of them. There's a resource room for children downstairs and a few other kid-friendly exhibits at this Native American history museum, but the events bring it all to life.

NATURALIST'S NOTEBOOK

Bookstore? Museum? Arts space? Exploratorium? The **Naturalist's Notebook** (16 Main St., Seal Harbor, 207/801-2777, www.thenaturalistsnotebook.com) is all that and more, with three floors of engaging, kid-friendly exhibits, books, and treasures.

LAUGH FEST

Improv Acadia (15 Cottage St., Bar Harbor, 207/288-2503, www.improvacadia.com) stages a family-friendly show every evening.

I SCREAM, YOU SCREAM

The ultimate kid-in-a-candy-store experience is at **Ben & Bill's** (66 Main St., Bar Harbor, 207/288-3281 or 800/806-3281), where you can buy not only chocolates made on-site but also to-die-for ice cream in both adult- and kid-pleasing flavors.

OLYMPICS OF THE FOREST

Expert lumberjack Tina Scheer and her crew exhibit the most amazing skills at the **Great Maine Lumberjack Show** (Rte. 3, Trenton, 207/667-0067, www.mainelumberjack.com, 7pm daily mid-June-early Sept., 4pm Sat. and 2pm Sun. early Sept.-mid-Oct.). During the 75-minute performance, two teams compete in 12 events, including ax throwing and logrolling. You can participate in some and even arrange for your youngster to learn how to logroll. Talk about a great story for that "what I did on my summer vacation" assignment.

FAMILY NATURE CAMP

Explore tidepools, learn about animal tracks, discover the diversity of bats, go whale-watching, and take a hike and learn about the natural world in the process at the College of the Atlantic's **Family Nature Camp** (800/597-9500, www.coa.edu/summerprograms). This **hands-on, participatory, naturalist-led program** provides plenty of fodder summer vacation stories. The minimum age is five; extended family is welcome. Camp includes campus lodging, meals, field trips, and some boat tours.

and Ottoman embassies retreated here for the summer from Washington DC.

The establishment of the national park in 1919 and the arrival of the automobile changed the character of Bar Harbor and Mount Desert Island; the creation of the income tax, two World Wars, and the Great Depression took an additional toll in myriad ways, but the coup de grâce for Bar Harbor's era of elegance came with the Great Fire of 1947, a wind-whipped conflagration that devastated more than 17,000 acres on the eastern half of the island and leveled gorgeous mansions, humble homes, and more trees than anyone could ever count. Only three people died, but property damage was estimated at more than $23 million. Whole books have been written about the October inferno; fascinating scrapbooks in Bar Harbor's Jesup Memorial Library dramatically relate the gripping details of the story. Even though some of the elegant

Bar Harbor

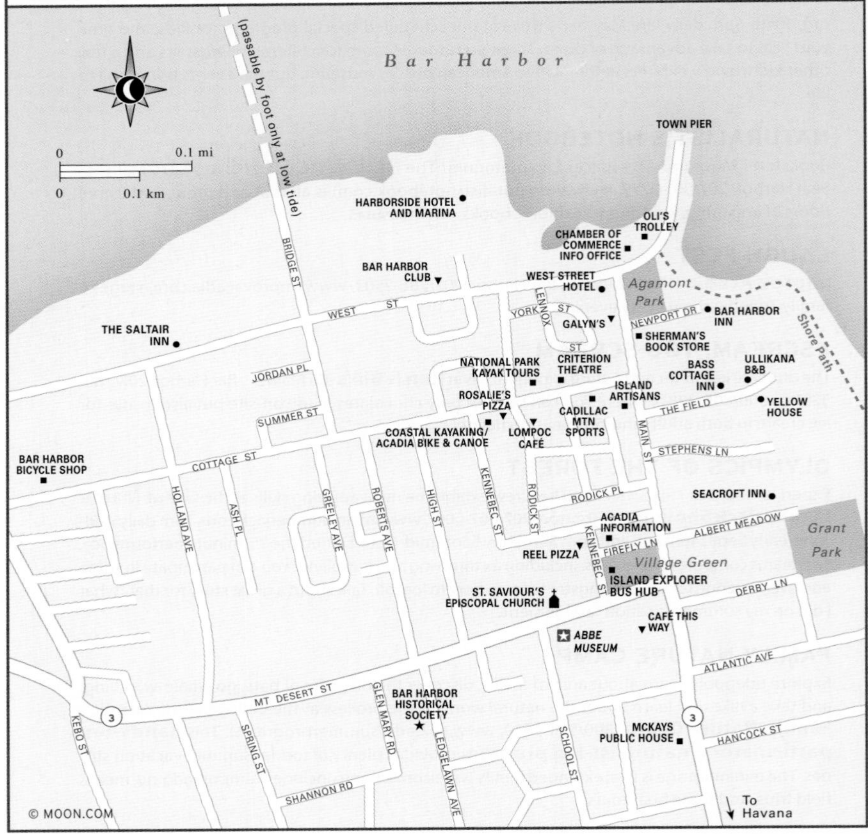

cottages have survived, the fire altered life here forever.

Bar Harbor often gets a bad rap for crowds. It's the island's largest town and the shopping hub; it's also where tour buses and cruise ships dock. That said, it's not hard to slip away to enjoy the town's sights and charms, of which there are many.

SIGHTS

★ Abbe Museum

The fabulous Abbe Museum, Maine's only Smithsonian affiliate, is a superb introduction to prehistoric, historic, and contemporary Native American tools, crafts, and other cultural artifacts, with an emphasis on Maine's Micmac, Maliseet, Passamaquoddy, and Penobscot people. Everything about this privately funded museum, established in 1927, is tasteful. It has two campuses: The **main campus** (26 Mount Desert St., Bar Harbor, 207/288-3519, www.abbemuseum.org, 10am-5pm daily May-Oct., 10am-4pm Thurs.-Sat. Nov.-Dec. and Feb.-Apr., $8 adults, $4 ages 11-17) is home to a collection spanning nearly 12,000 years. In creating the core exhibit, *People of the First Light*, museum staff worked with 23 Wabanaki curatorial consultants and four Native artists, among others. Museum-sponsored events include crafts workshops, hands-on children's programs, archaeological field schools, and the **Native American Festival** (usually the first Sat. after July 4).

Admission to the in-town Abbe also includes admission to the **museum's original site** (10am-5pm daily late May-mid-Oct.), in the park about 2.5 miles south of Bar Harbor at Sieur de Monts Spring, where Route 3 meets the Park Loop Road. Inside a small but handsome building listed in the National Register of Historic Places are displays from a 50,000-item collection. Admission to only the Sieur de Monts Spring Abbe is $3 adults, $1 ages 11-17, and admission paid here can be credited to admission to the main museum.

While you're at the original Abbe Museum site, take the time to wander the paths in the adjacent **Wild Gardens of Acadia,** a collection of more than 400 plant species native to Mount Desert Island. Twelve separate display areas, carefully maintained and labeled by the Bar Harbor Garden Club, represent native plant habitats; pick up the map-brochure that explains each.

St. Saviour's Episcopal Church

St. Saviour's (41 Mt. Desert St., Bar Harbor, 207/288-4215), completed in 1878 in downtown Bar Harbor, contains Maine's largest collection of Tiffany stained glass windows. Ten originals are here; an 11th was stolen in 1988 and replaced by a locally made window. Of the 32 non-Tiffany windows, the most intriguing is a memorial to Clarence Little, founder of the Jackson Laboratory and a descendant of Paul Revere. Images in the window include the laboratory, DNA, and mice. In July-August, the church is open for self-guided tours 9am-5pm daily; you can pick up a brochure in the back. It's also open for tours on Sundays following the 10am service. In the off-season, call for the schedule or make an appointment. If old cemeteries intrigue you, spend time wandering the 18th-century town graveyard next to the church.

Bar Harbor Historical Society

The **Bar Harbor Historical Society** is housed in the **La Rochelle Mansion and History Museum** (127 West St., Bar Harbor, 207/288-0000, www.barharborhistorical.org, 10am-4pm Mon.-Sat. mid-May-mid-Oct., free), a Georgian waterfront mansion that survived the Great Fire of 1947. Exhibits and collections let visitors understand life in the famed summer colony before that devastating event. Exhibitions also highlight renowned landscape designer Beatrix Farrand, architect Frank L. Savage, and the grand hotels.

For a sample of Bar Harbor before the great fire, wander over to upper West Street, which is listed in the National Register of Historic Places thanks to the remaining grand cottages that line it.

College of the Atlantic

A museum, a gallery, gardens, and a pleasant campus for walking are reasons to visit the **College of the Atlantic** (COA, 105 Eden St./Rte. 3, Bar Harbor, 207/288-5015, www.coa.edu), which specializes in human ecology, or humans' interrelationship with the environment.

In a handsome renovated building that originally served as the first Acadia National Park headquarters, the **George B. Dorr Museum of Natural History** (10am-5pm Tues.-Sat., donation) showcases regional birds and mammals in realistic dioramas made by COA students. The biggest attraction for children is the please-touch philosophy, allowing them to reach into a touch tank to feel fur, skulls, and even whale baleen. The museum gift shop has a particularly good collection of books and gifts for budding naturalists.

Across the way is the **Ethel H. Blum Gallery** (207/288-5015, ext. 254, 11am-4pm Mon.-Sat. summer, Mon.-Fri. during the academic year), a small space that hosts some intriguing exhibits.

The campus is home to a number of gardens (www.coa.edu/gardens). Find the **Beatrix Farrand Garden,** created by the renowned garden designer in 1928, behind

Kaelber Hall. It contains more than 50 varieties of roses and was the prototype for the rose garden at Dumbarton Oaks in Washington DC. Both are known for Farrand's use of garden rooms, such as the walled terraces in this garden.

The **Turrets Seaside Garden,** fronting on the ocean, was restored by a student in 2005. The central fountain, created by alumnus Dan Farrenkopf of Lunaform Pottery, was installed in 2009. Adjacent to the Turrets is a **sunken garden,** created in a foundation. It's been restored a couple of times, and in 2015, the COA Gardening Club started maintaining it, eventually turning it into a sustainable, low-maintenance, edible garden. The 1st floor of the **Turrets,** a magnificent 1895 seaside cottage that's now an administration building, can be explored.

The college also offers excellent and very popular weeklong sessions of **Family Nature Camp** (800/597-9500, www.coa.edu/summer, July-early Aug., $950-1,100 adults, $500 ages 15 and younger). It's essential to register well in advance; ask about early-season discounts. Families are housed and fed on the campus and explore Acadia National Park with expert naturalist guides.

Check the college's calendar of events for lectures, conversations, and other activities. The campus is 0.5 mile northwest of downtown Bar Harbor on Island Explorer Route 2/ Eden Street.

Garland Farm

Fans of landscape architect Beatrix Farrand should visit **Garland Farm** (475 Bayview Dr., Bar Harbor, 207/288-0237, www.beatrixfarrandsociety.org), the ancestral home of Lewis Garland, who managed Farrand's Reef Point property. When Farrand dismantled that property in 1955, she moved here with the Garlands, engaging an architect to build an addition to the original farmhouse and barn using architectural elements from Reef Point. The property was sold a few times, and greatly reduced in size, until the Beatrix Farrand Society purchased it in 2004. The society aims to restore Garland Farm to its Farrand-era design and condition and to create a center for the study of design and horticulture. The property, now listed in the National Register of Historic Places, hosts special events and programs. Garland Farm is open for visits one or two days per week for guided or self-guided tours ($5 suggestion donation) or by appointment; call or check the website for the current schedule. Horticulture-related programs ($20) fill the summer calendar.

JAX

World renowned in genetic research, scientists at the **Jackson Laboratory for Mammalian Research** (600 Main St./Rte. 3, Bar Harbor, 207/288-1429, www.jax.org) study cancer, diabetes, muscular dystrophy, heart disease, and Alzheimer's disease, among others—with considerable success. The nonprofit research institution, locally called JAX or just "the lab," is also renowned for its genetics databases and for producing genetically defined laboratory mice, which are shipped to research labs worldwide. The lab offers free one-hour public researcher-led tours (limited to 15 people; min. age 12; preregistration required) one day per week from mid-June to early October. If this is on your must-do list, plan ahead: The tours often sell out well in advance. The visitor program changes every summer, so call for current details.

Bar Harbor and Park Tours

The veteran of the Bar Harbor-based bus tours is **Acadia National Park Tours** (ticket office in Testa's Restaurant, Bayside Landing, 53 Main St., Bar Harbor, 207/288-0300, www.acadiatours.com, May-Oct., $32.50 adults, $20 under age 13). A 2.5-3-hour naturalist-led tour of Bar Harbor and Acadia departs at 10am and 2pm daily from Testa's Restaurant, across from Agamont Park near the Bar Harbor Inn, in downtown Bar Harbor. Reservations are advised in midsummer and during fall foliage season (late Sept.-early Oct.); pick up reserved tickets 30 minutes before departure.

If you're under a time crunch, take the one-hour trolley-bus tour operated by **Oli's Trolley** (ticket office 1 West St., Bar Harbor, 207/288-5443 or 866/987-6553, http://olistrolley.com, $25 adults, $15 age 11 and younger), which includes Bar Harbor mansion drive-bys and the Cadillac Mountain summit. The ticket office is downtown at Harbor Place, next to the town pier on the waterfront. Dress warmly if the air is at all cool; it's an open-air trolley. Reservations are advised. The trolley also does 2.5-hour park tours 2-5 times daily late April-October ($40 adults, $25 age 11 and younger); 4-hour park tours ($65 adults, $40 age 11 and younger); and 1.5-hour sunset Cadillac Mountain tours ($25 adults, $15 age 11 and younger). Restroom stops are offered. Tours depart from the boardwalk at the Harborside Hotel, 55 West Street.

MDI Tours (207/808-0413, www.mditours.com, $100/hour) offers small, mixed-group (max. 5 guests), and private 3-5-hour park and island tours in Chevy Suburban SUVs. Local islanders guide the tours.

Although the Island Explorer buses do reach a number of key park sights, they are not tour buses. There is no narration, the bus cuts off the Park Loop at Otter Cliffs, and it excludes the summit of Cadillac Mountain.

Bird-Watching and Nature Tours

For private tours of the park and other parts of the island, contact Michael Good at **Down East Nature Tours** (150 Knox Rd., Bar Harbor, 207/288-8128, www.downeastnaturetours.com). A biologist and Maine Guide, Good is simply batty about birds. He has spent more than 25 years studying the birds of North America, and he has even turned his home property on Mount Desert Island into a bird sanctuary. Good specializes in avian ecology in the Gulf of Maine, giving special attention to native and migrating birds. Whether you're a first-timer wanting to spot eagles, peregrine falcons, shorebirds, and warblers, or a serious bird-watcher seeking to add to your life list, perhaps with a Nelson's sparrow, Good's your man. Prices begin at $135 pp for four hours and include transportation from your lodging; kids are half price. Bring your own binoculars; Good supplies a spotting scope.

ENTERTAINMENT

The **Bar Harbor Town Band** performs for free at 8pm Monday and Thursday evenings July-mid-August in the bandstand on the Village Green (Main St. and Mt. Desert St., Bar Harbor).

You never know quite what's going to happen at **Improv Acadia** (15 Cottage St., Bar Harbor, 207/288-2503, www.improvacadia.com, late May-mid-Oct., $20 adults, $15 age 12 and younger). Every show is different, as actors use audience suggestions to create comedy sketches. Shows are staged once or twice nightly. Dessert, snacks, and drinks are available. The 8pm show in July and August is family friendly.

The **Bar Harbor Music Festival** (207/288-5744 July-Aug., 212/222-1026 off-season, www.barharbormusicfestival.org), a summer tradition since 1967, emphasizes up-and-coming musical talent in a series of classical, jazz, and pop concerts, and even an opera in early July-early August, at various island locations including an annual outdoor concert in Acadia National Park. Tickets are $30-45 adults, $15 students, and can be purchased online or at the festival office building (59 Cottage St., Bar Harbor). Reservations are advised.

Every evening from 7pm to 11pm, **pianist Bill Trowell** plays in the Great Room Piano Lounge at the Bluenose Hotel (90 Eden St., Bar Harbor, 207/288-3348, www.barharborhotel.com).

Built in 1932 and listed in the National Register of Historic Places, the **Criterion Theatre** (35 Cottage St., Bar Harbor, 207/288-0829, www.criteriontheatre.org) is a beautifully restored, 877-seat art deco classic, with an elegant floating balcony. It now hosts performances, movies, and special events.

Festivals and Events

Bar Harbor is home to numerous special events; here's just a sampling. For more, call 800/345-4617 or visit www.barharbormaine.com.

In early June, the annual **Acadia Birding Festival** (www.acadiabirdingfestival.com) attracts bird-watchers with guided walks, boating excursions, tours, talks, and meals.

The **Abbe Museum Indian Market** brings together Native American artists in mid-May. In late June, **Legacy of the Arts** is a weeklong celebration of music, art, theater, dance, and history, with tours, exhibits, workshops, concerts, lectures, demonstrations, and more.

The **Fourth of July** is always a big deal in Bar Harbor, celebrated with a 6am blueberry pancake breakfast, a 10am parade, an 11am seafood festival, a band concert, and fireworks. A highlight is the Lobster Race, a crustacean competition drawing contestants such as Lobzilla and Larry the Lobster in a four-lane saltwater tank on the Village Green. Independence Day celebrations in the island's smaller villages always evoke a bygone era.

The Abbe Museum, the College of the Atlantic, and the Maine Indian Basketmakers Alliance sponsor the annual **Native American Festival** (10am-4pm first Sat. after July 4, free), featuring baskets, beadwork, and other handicrafts for sale as well as Indian drumming and dancing.

In even-numbered years, the **Mount Desert Garden Club Tour** (www.gcmdgardenday.com) presents a rare chance to visit some of Maine's most spectacular private gardens on a Saturday in late July.

The September **Acadia Night Sky Festival** (www.acadianightskyfestival.com) celebrates Acadia's stellar stargazing with arts and science events, presentations, and activities.

SHOPPING

Bar Harbor's boutiques—running the gamut from attractive to kitschy—are indisputably visitor-oriented; most shut down for the winter.

More than 100 Maine artisans are represented at **Island Artisans** (99 Main St., Bar Harbor, 207/288-4214, www.islandartisans.com), and the quality is outstanding. You'll find basketwork, handmade paper, wood carvings, blown glass, jewelry, weaving, metalwork, ceramics, and more.

Gallery? Funky gift store? Museum? It's hard to categorize the **Rock & Art Shop** (13 Cottage St., Bar Harbor, 207/288-4800). Fossils, gems, minerals, bug-filled marbles, and preserved sea horses are part of the intriguing mix, most of which carries educational signs.

Bark Harbor (150 Main St., Bar Harbor, 207/288-0404) is the place to pick up the perfect souvenir for your cat or dog.

Toys, cards, and newspapers blend in with the new-book inventory at **Sherman's Book Store** (56 Main St., Bar Harbor, 207/288-3161). It's just the place to pick up maps and trail guides for fine days and puzzles for foggy days.

RECREATION

Walks

A real treat is a stroll along downtown Bar Harbor's **Shore Path** (6:30am-dusk daily), a well-trodden granite-edged byway built around 1880. Along the craggy shoreline are granite-and-wood benches, town-owned **Grant Park** (great for picnics), birch trees, and several handsome mansions that escaped the 1947 fire. Offshore are the four Porcupine Islands. Leashed pets are allowed. Plan 30-45 minutes for the mile loop, beginning next to the town pier and the Bar Harbor Inn and returning via Wayman Lane and Main Street.

Check local newspapers or the Bar Harbor Chamber of Commerce visitor booklet for the times of low tide, then walk across the gravel bar to wooded **Bar Island** (formerly Rodick's Island) from the foot of Bridge

1: Dive-In Theater Boat Cruise **2:** Shore Path **3:** Bar Harbor's waterfront **4:** low tide in Bar Harbor

1
STARFISH ENTERPRISE
OSPREY
2
LIGHTHOUSE TOURS 288-2386
3
4

Street in downtown Bar Harbor. Shell heaps recorded on the eastern end of the island indicate that Native Americans enjoyed this turf in the distant past. You'll have the most time to explore the island during new-moon or full-moon low tides, but that's still no more than 4 hours—about 1.5 hours before and after low tide. Be sure to watch the time so you don't get trapped (for up to 10 hours). The foot of Bridge Street is also an excellent kayak-launching site.

About a mile from downtown along Main Street (Rte. 3) is **Compass Harbor,** a section of the park where you can stroll through woods to the water's edge and explore the overgrown ruins of Acadia National Park cofounder George Dorr's home.

Five trails wind through the Nature Conservancy's forested 110-acre **Indian Point-Blagden Preserve**, a rectangular parcel with island, hill, and bay vistas. Seal-watching and bird-watching are popular, and there are harbor seals on offshore rocks as well as woodpeckers and 130 other species in blowdown areas. To spot the seals, plan your hike around low tide, when they'll be sprawled on the rocks close to shore. Wear rubberized shoes. Bring binoculars or use the telescope installed here. To keep from disturbing the seals, watch quietly and avoid jerky movements. Park near the preserve entrance and follow the Big Woods Trail, which runs the length of the preserve. A second parking area is farther in, but then you'll miss much of the preserve. When you reach the second parking area, just past an old field, bear left along the Shore Trail to see the seals. Register at the caretaker's house (just beyond the first parking lot, where you can pick up bird and flora checklists), and respect private property on either side of the preserve. It's open dawn-6pm daily year-round. From the junction of Routes 3 and 102/198, continue 1.8 miles to Indian Point Road and turn right. Go 1.7 miles to a fork and turn right. Watch for the preserve entrance on the right, marked by a Nature Conservancy oak leaf.

Bicycling

With all the great biking options, including 33 miles of carriage roads open to bicycles and some of the best roadside bike routes in Maine, you'll want to bring a bike or rent one here.

The Minutolo family's **Bar Harbor Bicycle Shop** (141 Cottage St., Bar Harbor, 207/288-3886, www.barharborbike.com), on the corner of Route 3, has been in business since 1977. If you have your own bike, stop here for advice on routes—the Minutolos have cycled everywhere on the island and can suggest the perfect mountain-bike or road-bike loop based on your ability and schedule. The shop has rentals varying from standard mountain bikes to full-suspension models and even tandems, as well as all the accessories and gear you might need; rates begin at about $30/day. Hours in summer are 8am-6pm daily, 9am-5pm spring and fall.

If hills are your biking nemesis, consider renting an electric bicycle from **Pedego Electric Bikes Acadia** (55 West St., Bar Harbor, 207/664-9181). These battery-assist bikes let you get as much of a workout as you desire, with six settings ranging from no assist to high assist, as well as a throttle, for an extra push when necessary. Do ask for where these are permitted, as not all are allowed in all parts of the park. Rates begin at $55/four hours or $100/day; reservations are wise.

TOP EXPERIENCE

Sea Kayaking

National Park Kayak Tours (39 Cottage St., Bar Harbor, 207/288-0342 or 800/347-0940, www.acadiakayak.com) limits its Registered Maine Guide-led tours to a maximum of six tandem kayaks per trip. Four-hour morning, midday, afternoon, or sunset paddles are offered, including shuttle service, a paddle and safety lesson, and a brief stop, for $55 pp in July-August, $50 off-season. Trips cover about six miles on the western side of the island and include transportation. Multiday camping trips also are offered. Try to make reservations at least one day in advance.

Half-day, full-day, and multiday sea kayak tours are on the schedule organized by **Coastal Kayaking Tours** (48 Cottage St., Bar Harbor, 207/288-9605 or 800/526-8615, www.acadiafun.com). The best option for beginners is the 2.5-hour harbor tour ($48 pp). A half-day family tour, departing at 1pm, can handle kids age eight and over ($58 pp). A 2.5-hour sunset cruise ($48 pp) begins around 5pm, depending on season. All trips are weather-dependent, and reservations are essential.

Golf

Duffers first teed off at **Kebo Valley Golf Club** (100 Eagle Lake Rd./Rte. 233, Bar Harbor, 207/288-5000, www.kebovalleyclub.com, May-Oct.) in 1888, making this Maine's oldest club and the eighth oldest in the nation. The 17th hole became legendary when it took President William Howard Taft 27 strokes to sink a ball in 1911. Kebo is very popular, with a gorgeous setting, an attractive clubhouse, and decent food service, so booking tee times is essential; you can reserve up to six days in advance.

Boat Excursions

★ DIVE-IN THEATER BOAT CRUISE

You don't have to go diving in these frigid waters; others will do it for you. When the kids are clamoring to touch slimy sea cucumbers and starfish at various touch tanks in the area, they're likely to be primed for Diver Ed's **Dive-In Theater Boat Cruise** (207/288-3483 or 800/979-3370, www.divered.com), departing from the College of the Atlantic pier (105 Eden St., Bar Harbor). Ed Monat, former Bar Harbor harbormaster and College of the Atlantic grad, heads the crew aboard the 46-passenger *Starfish Enterprise*. The boat goes a mile or two offshore, where Ed, a professional diver, goes overboard with a video camera and a mini-Ed who helps put things in proportion. You and the kids stay on deck, all warm and dry, along with Captain Evil, who explains the action on a TV screen. There's communication back and forth, so the kids can ask questions as the divers pick up urchins, starfish, crabs, lobsters, and other sea life. When Ed resurfaces, he brings a bag of touchable specimens—another chance to pet some slimy creatures (which go back into the water after show-and-tell). It's a great concept. Watch the kids' expressions—this is a big hit. The two-hour trips depart three times daily Monday-Saturday and once on Sunday early July-early September; fewer trips are made in spring and fall. The cost is $42 adults, $37 seniors, $32 ages 5-11, $16 under age 5. Advance reservations are required.

WHALE-WATCHING AND PUFFIN-WATCHING

Whale-watching boats go as far as 20 miles offshore, so no matter what the weather in Bar Harbor, dress warmly and bring more clothing than you think you'll need—even gloves, if you're especially sensitive to cold. I've been out on days when it's close to 90°F on the island but feels more like 30°F in a moving boat on the open ocean. Motion-sensitive children and adults should plan in advance for appropriate medication, such as seasickness pills or patches. Adults are required to show a photo ID when boarding the boat.

Whale-watching, puffin-watching, and combo excursions are offered by **Bar Harbor Whale Watch Company** (1 West St., Bar Harbor, 207/288-2386 or 800/942-5374, www.barharborwhales.com), sailing from the town pier (1 West St.) in downtown Bar Harbor. The company operates under various names, including Acadian Whale Watcher, and has a number of boats. Most trips are accompanied by a naturalist (often from Allied Whale at the College of the Atlantic), who regales passengers with all sorts of interesting trivia about the whales, porpoises, seabirds, and other marinelife spotted along the way. In season, some trips go out as far as the puffin colony on Petit Manan Light. Trips depart daily late May-late October, but with so many options it's impossible to list the schedule; call for the

Adopt-a-Whale

Here's a trump card: When everyone else is flashing photos of kids or grandkids, you can whip out images of your very own adopted whale. And for that, you can thank Allied Whale's **Adopt-a-Whale** program at the College of the Atlantic (COA) in Bar Harbor.

In 1972, COA established Allied Whale, a marine-mammal laboratory designed to collect, interpret, and apply research on the world's largest mammal. Although Allied Whale's primary focus is the Gulf of Maine, its projects span the globe and involve international scientific collaboration. Since 1981, part of the research has involved assembling an enormous photo collection (more than 25,000 images) for identification of specific humpback and finback whales (with names such as Quartz and Elvis) and tracking of their migration routes. The photo catalog of finbacks already numbers more than 1,000.

And here's where the adoption program comes in—it's a way to support the important research being done by Allied Whale and its colleagues. If you sign up as an adoptive "parent" for a year, you'll receive a Certificate of Adoption, a large color photo and a biography of your whale, its sighting history, an informational booklet, and an Adopt-a-Whale/Allied Whale bumper sticker. It's a superb gift for budding scientists. The adoption fee is $30 for a single whale or $40 for a mother and calf.

For further information, contact **Allied Whale** (207/288-5644, www.barharborwhalemuseum.org/adopt2.php).

latest details. Tickets are around $65 adults, $35 ages 6-14, $14 under age 6. A portion of the ticket price benefits Allied Whale, which researches and protects marine animals in the Gulf of Maine. Trips may extend longer than the time advertised, so don't plan anything else too tightly around the trip.

Sailing **Scenic Nature Cruises** (1.5-2 hours) and kid-friendly **Lobster/Seal Watch Cruises** (1.5 hours) are also offered. Rates for these are around $34 adults, $20 ages 6-14, and $14 for kids under 6.

Captain Steve Pagels, under the umbrella of **Downeast Windjammer Cruises** (207/288-4585 or 207/288-2373, www.downeastwindjammer.com), offers 1.5-2-hour day sails on the 151-foot steel-hulled *Margaret Todd*, a gorgeous four-masted schooner with tanbark sails that he designed and launched in 1998, or the *Bailey Louise Todd*. Trips depart at 10am, 2pm, and around sunset daily mid-May-mid-October (weather permitting) from the Bar Harbor Inn pier, just east of the town pier in downtown Bar Harbor. You'll get the best wildlife sightings on the morning trip, but better sailing on the afternoon trip; there's live music on the sunset one. A park ranger narrates some sails, which adds to the experience. Buy tickets at the pier, at the office (27 Main St.), or online with a credit card; arrive at least half an hour before departure. The cost is $42-48 adults, $39-44 seniors, $32-46 ages 6-11, $7-12 ages 2-5. Dogs are welcome on all sails.

SEA VENTURE

Captain Winston Shaw's custom boat tour by **Sea Venture** (207/288-3355, www.svboattours.com) lets you design the perfect trip aboard *Reflection*, a 20-foot motor launch. Captain Shaw, a Registered Maine Guide and committed environmentalist, specializes in nature-oriented tours. He's the founder and director of the Coastal Maine Bald Eagle Project, and he was involved in the inaugural Earth Day celebration in 1970. He's been studying coastal birds for more than 30 years. You can pick from 10 recommended cruises lasting 1-8 hours, or design your own. In any case, the boat is yours. The boat charter rate is $130/hour for up to two people, $150 for three or four, and $200 for five or six. Captain Shaw can also arrange for picnic lunches. On longer trips, restroom stops are available. The boat departs from the Atlantic Oceanside Hotel pier, 119 Eden Street/Route 3 in Bar Harbor.

LOBSTER CRUISE

When you're ready to learn *the truth* about lobsters, sign up for a two-hour cruise aboard the ***Lulu*** (55 West St., Bar Harbor, 207/288-3136, www.lululobsterboat.com), a traditional Maine lobster boat that departs up to four times daily from the Harborside Hotel and Marina. The captain and crew provide an entertaining commentary on anything and everything, but especially about lobsters and lobstering. They'll haul a lobster trap and explain intimate details about the hapless critters. This is a real kid-pleaser, but adults are equally entertained. Reservations are required. Cost is $35 adults, $32 seniors and active U.S. military, $20 ages 2-12.

FOOD

You won't go hungry in Bar Harbor. For sit-down restaurants, make reservations as far in advance as possible. Expect reduced operations during spring and fall; few places are open in winter.

Mount Desert Island is a seasonal community, and restaurant days and hours change frequently, so always call ahead. Also note that staffing is always a challenge in the region, and many businesses import workers from overseas. By the time waiters and waitresses have been fully trained, the season is almost over.

Lobster and Seafood

Nearly every restaurant in town serves some form of lobster (my top choice for a lobster roll is the Side Street Café).

Dine inside or on the dock at **Stewman's Lobster Pound** (35 West St., 207/288-0346, www.stewmanslobsterpound.com, 11am-10pm daily), where the menu ranges from burgers to lobster.

Although it lacks the oceanfront location, **West Street Café** (76 West St., Bar Harbor, 207/288-5242, www.weststreetcafe.com, 11am-9pm daily) is a fine spot for a lobster dinner at a fair price. There are other items on the menu, but the reason to go here is for the lobster (market price). A kids' menu is available. Go before 6pm for early-bird specials.

Quick Bites

Tastings ($6) are offered daily at **Bar Harbor Cellars** (854 Rte. 3, Bar Harbor, 207/288-3907, www.barharborcellars.com). The winery, located at Sweet Pea Farm, is in the early stages of using organic techniques to grow hybrid grapes. In the meantime, it's making wines from European and California grapes. Also here is a Maine chocolate room and a small selection of complementary foods, such as olives, cheese, and crackers.

Only a masochist could bypass **Ben & Bill's Chocolate Emporium** (66 Main St., Bar Harbor, 207/288-3281 or 800/806-3281, www.benandbills.com, from 10am daily), which makes homemade candies and more than 50 ice cream flavors (including a dubious lobster flavor); the whole place smells like the inside of a chocolate truffle. Closing hours depend on the season and crowds, but it's usually open until late in the evening.

That said, the most creative flavors come from **Mt. Desert Island Ice Cream** (7 Firefly Ln., Bar Harbor, 207/288-0999, and 325 Main St., Bar Harbor, 207/288-5664, www.mdiic.com). It's made in small batches, just five gallons at a time, using the finest ingredients. We're talking creamy, rich, and delicious ice cream in wild flavors.

Inexpensive, but with a healthful menu, is the **Take-A-Break Café** (105 Eden St., Bar Harbor, 207/288-5015, www.coa.edu, 7:30am-9:30am, 11:30am-1pm, and 5:30pm-6:30pm Mon.-Fri. during the academic year) in Blair Dining Hall, at the College of the Atlantic. If you find yourself on the college campus, perhaps for a boat tour or museum visit, consider eating here. The prices are especially inexpensive, there are always vegetarian, vegan, gluten-free, and meat choices, and the selection is organic and local whenever possible.

After 30 years as a specialty beer pub, the

Lompoc Café & Bookstore (36 Rodick St., Bar Harbor, 207/288-9392, www.lompoccafe.com, hours vary, $12-16) has matured into a casual café and book shop. Go for pizzas, salads, and sandwiches, along with bocce in the beer garden. They also serve light breakfast fare.

Another good spot for healthful and vegetarian fare is **Thrive Juice Bar & Kitchen** (51 Rodick St., Bar Harbor, 207/801-9340, http://thrivebarharbor.com, 8am-4pm daily), which specializes in smoothies, but also has salads, bowls, and wraps.

When it comes to American pub-grub favorites, such as burgers and fish sandwiches, the **Thirsty Whale Tavern** (40 Cottage St., Bar Harbor, 207/288-9335, www.thirstywhaletavern.com, 11am-9pm daily, $8-20) does it right.

For breakfast or brunch, you can't beat **2 Cats** (130 Cottage St., Bar Harbor, 207/288-2808 or 800/355-2828, http://twocatsbarharbor.com, 7am-1pm daily, $8-15). Fun, funky, and fresh best describe both the restaurant and the food. Dine inside or on the patio.

Choco-Latte (240 Main St., Bar Harbor, 207/801-9179, www.choco-lattecafe.com, 7am-8pm daily) aims to make all of its chocolates in house from organic Criollo cacao sourced from women-owned co-ops in Chiapas and Veracruz, Mexico. Pair them with an organic coffee or a hot chocolate or even a house-made bagel.

Between Mother's Day and late October, the **Eden Farmers Market** operates out of the YMCA parking lot off Lower Main Street in Bar Harbor, 9am-noon Sundays. You'll find fresh meats and produce, local cheeses and maple syrup, yogurt and ice cream, bread, honey, preserves, and even prepared Asian foods.

Picnic Fare and Prepared Foods

Although a few of these places have some seating, most are for the grab-and-go crowd.

A good choice for take-out fare is **Downeast Deli** (65 Main St., Bar Harbor, 207/288-1001, 8am-9pm daily). You can get both hot and cold fresh lobster rolls as well as other sandwiches, soups, and salads.

At **Adelmann's Deli & Grill** (224 Main St., Bar Harbor, 207/288-0455, 11am-7pm daily), build-your-own lunch sandwiches are $11. Choose from a variety of breads, Boar's Head-brand meats and cheeses, veggies, condiments, and more.

Peekytoe Provisions (244 Main St., Bar Harbor, 207/801-9161, http://peekytoeprovisions.com, 11am-7pm Wed.-Mon., $4-16) is a great spot to pick up prepared as well as made-to-order soups, salads, sandwiches, and specials, most made from local and sustainable ingredients.

Brewpubs and Microbreweries

The Lompoc Café's signature Bar Harbor Real Ale and five or six others are brewed by the **Atlantic Brewing Company** (15 Knox Rd., Town Hill, in the upper section of the island, 207/288-2337, www.atlanticbrewing.com). Free brewery tours, including guided tastings, are given daily at 2pm, 3pm, and 4pm late May-mid-October; arrive one hour before tour time to secure tickets. Also operating here in summer is **Mainely-Meat Bar-B-Q** (207/288-9200, 11:30am-8pm daily, $8-20), offering pulled pork, chicken, ribs, and similar fare for lunch and dinner.

Atlantic also operates **Atlantic Brewing Midtown** (52 Cottage St., Bar Harbor, 207/801-9700, 11am-9pm daily), where it brews small-batch beers seven barrels at a time. Those as well as other Atlantic beers are offered in the tasting room. There's often live music in the evenings.

Family Favorites

An unscientific but reliable local survey gives the best-pizza ribbon to **Rosalie's Pizza & Italian Restaurant** (46 Cottage St., Bar Harbor, 207/288-5666, www.rosaliespizza.com, 4pm-10pm daily, $7-20), where the Wurlitzer jukebox churns out tunes from the 1950s. Rosalie's earns high marks for consistency with its homemade pizza (gluten-free crust available), in four sizes or by the slice, along with calzones and subs; there are lots of vegetarian options. The Italian dinners—spaghetti, eggplant parmigiana, and others—are all less than $10, including a garlic roll. Beer and wine are available. Avoid the downstairs lines by heading upstairs and ordering at that counter, or call in your order.

Route 66 Restaurant (21 Cottage St., Bar Harbor, 207/288-3708, www.barharborroute66.com, from 11am daily, $12-25), filled with 1950s memorabilia and metal toys, is a fun restaurant that's a real hit with children (check out the Lionel train running around just below the ceiling). The standard American menu includes kids' choices. No raves here, just okay food in a fun atmosphere.

Efficient, friendly cafeteria-style service makes **EPI's Pizza** (8 Cottage St., Bar Harbor, 207/288-5853, 7am-9pm daily July-Aug., 7am-3pm daily Sept.-June) an excellent choice for budget Italian fare.

On a clear day, you can't beat the panoramic views over Bar Harbor, Frenchman Bay, and the Porcupine Islands from the **Looking Glass Restaurant** (Wonder View Inn, 50 Eden St., Bar Harbor, 207/288-5663, www.wonderviewinn.com, 7am-10:30am and 5:30pm-9pm daily, $14-38). It's quite casual, with choices ranging from sandwiches to rack of lamb. The deck is dog friendly. Go for breakfast after watching sunrise from Cadillac.

Most folks come to **Sweet Pea's Café** (854 Rte. 3, Bar Harbor, 207/801-9078, www.sweetpeascafemaine.com, 11am-9pm Wed.-Sun., $15-25) for the wood-oven sourdough pizzas, topped with fresh-from-the-farm greens, veggies, and local seafood, but the mussels and the oyster starters earn raves. It's located on a working farm, with dining inside or outside looking over pasturelands where horses graze.

Casual Dining

Chef Karl Yarborough draws inspiration for his ever-changing, creative menu at **Ciao** (135 Cottage St., Bar Harbor, 207/801-9110, www.ciaobarharbor.com, $10-20) from family travels during the winter and pairs it with fresh and local ingredients, resulting in intriguing combos such as lobster and chorizo or pear bruschetta.

When you're craving fresh and delicious fare but not a heavy meal, the ★ **Side Street Café** (49 Rodick St., Bar Harbor, 207/801-2591, www.sidestreetbarharbor.com, 11am-10pm daily, $11-26) delivers with an upscale tavern-fare menu complete with burgers, mac-and-cheese, salads, ribs, Tex-Mex, and even full lobster dinners. The venue tends to be noisy, but you also can sit on the streetside deck. It's open year-round. In 2019, the restaurant opened the **Annex** (51 Rodick St., 4pm-10pm daily), serving craft cocktails and sharable small plates, with live music nightly.

Cocktails, small plates, and crepes are the specialties at **Project Social** (16 Mount Desert St., Bar Harbor, 207/801-9293, www.socialbarharbor.com, 11am-10pm daily, $12-34), a trendy spot facing the Village Green. There's often live music.

Set back from the road behind a garden is the very popular **McKays Public House** (231 Main St., Bar Harbor, 207/288-2002, www.mckayspublichouse.com, 5pm-9pm daily, $12-32), a comfortable pub with seating indoors in small dining rooms or at the bar, or outdoors in the garden. The best bet is the classic pub fare, although fancier entrées are available.

Once a Victorian boardinghouse and later a 1920s speakeasy, **Galyn's Galley** (17 Main St., Bar Harbor, 207/288-9706, www.galynsbarharbor.com, 11am-10pm daily Mar.-Nov., $16-44) has been a downtown dining mainstay since 1986. Lots of plants, modern decor, reliable service, and several indoor and outdoor dining areas contribute to the loyalty of the clientele. Reservations are advisable in midsummer. Be seated before 6pm to enjoy the early-bird lobster special.

Casual, friendly, creative, and reliable defines **Cafe This Way** (14 Mt. Desert St., Bar Harbor, 207/288-4483, www.cafethisway.com, 7am-11:30am and 5:30pm-9:30pm Mon.-Sat.,

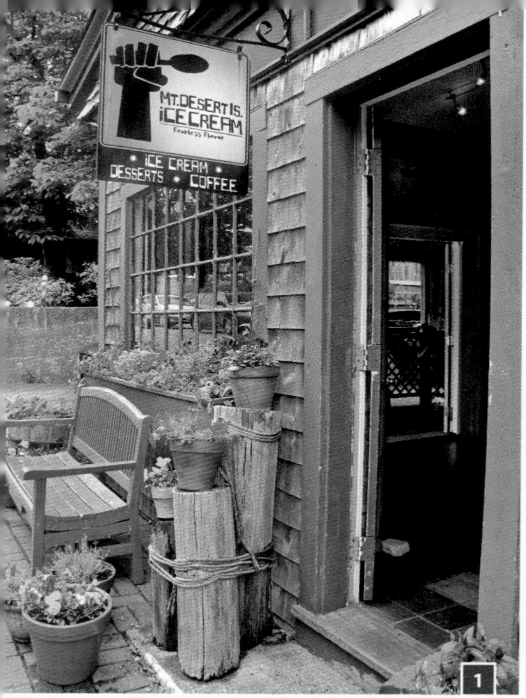

1

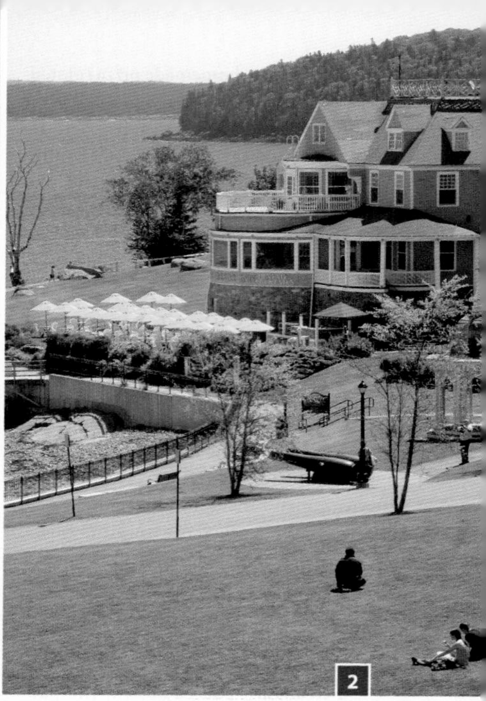

2

3

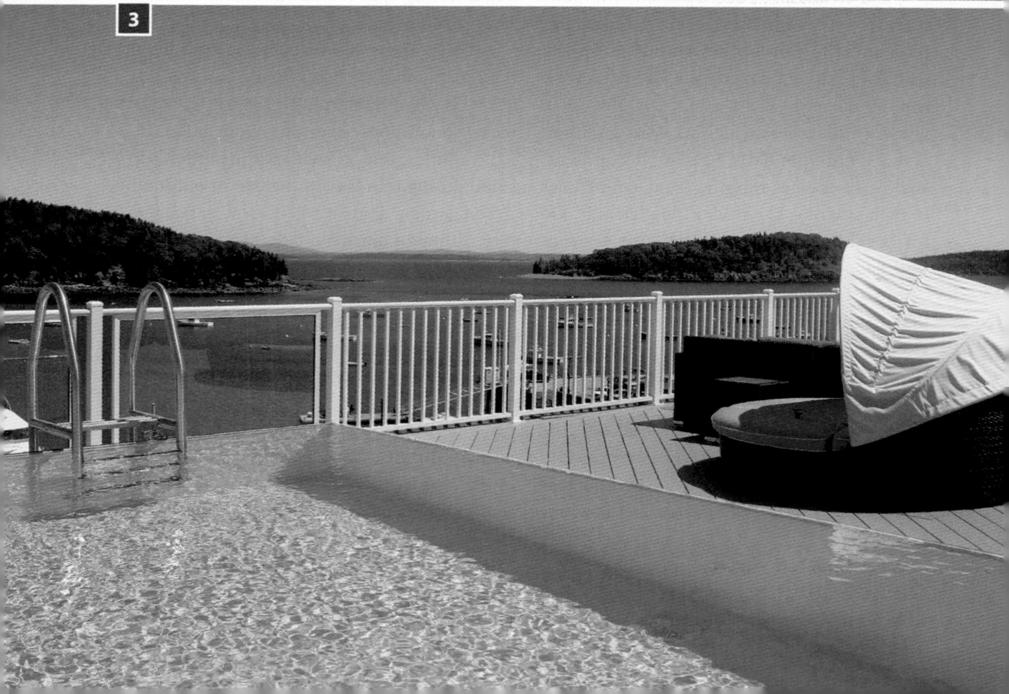

8am-1pm and 5:30pm-9:30pm Sun., $22-30), where it's easy to make a meal out of the small plates ($10-15). Vegetarians will be happy here. The breakfast menu is a genuine wake-up call ($6-12).

Dine inside or on the porch of chef-co-owner Bobby Will's seasonally inspired, New American, farm-to-table restaurant **Salt & Steel** (321 Main St., Bar Harbor, 207/288-0447, www.machebistro.com, 5pm-10pm Tues.-Sun., $28-35). Can't decide? A four-course tasting menu is available.

International

La Bella Vita Ristorante (55 West St., Bar Harbor, 207/288-5033, www.labellavitaristorante.com, 7am-10pm daily, $12-35), at the Harborside Hotel, does an excellent job with Italian fare, including antipasti, pizzas, pastas, and classics such as veal scaloppini or chicken piccata. Dine inside or out.

For "American fine dining with Latin flair," head to ★ **Havana** (318 Main St., Bar Harbor, 207/288-2822, www.havanamaine.com, 5pm-10pm daily May-Nov. and 9:30am-2pm Sun. late May-late Aug., call for off-season hours, $20-42), where the innovative menu changes frequently to take advantage of what's locally available. Inside, bright orange walls and white tablecloths set a tone that's equally festive and accomplished. There's also garden seating. For a lighter meal, consider **Parrilla** (from 4pm daily, $8-26), Havana's street-side outdoor bar with an Argentinian-style wood-fired grill. It serves a selection of small and large plates.

Fine Dining

Five miles south of Bar Harbor, in the village of Otter Creek, which itself is in the town of Mount Desert, is the inauspicious-looking **Burning Tree** (Rte. 3, Otter Creek, 207/288-9331, 5pm-10pm Wed.-Mon. late June-early Oct., closed Mon. after Labor Day, $26-34), which is anything but nondescript inside. Chef-owners Allison Martin and Elmer Beal Jr. have created one of Mount Desert Island's better restaurants, but it can get quite noisy when busy—which it usually is. The specialties are imaginative seafood entrées and vegetarian dishes. At the height of summer, service can be a bit rushed, and the kitchen runs out of popular entrées. Do make reservations.

1: Mt. Desert Island Ice Cream **2:** Bar Harbor Inn **3:** the rooftop pool at the West Street Hotel

ACCOMMODATIONS

Unless otherwise noted, these properties operate seasonally; most are open May-October. Rates listed are for peak season.

Hotels and Motels

If all you want is an air-conditioned room with a bed, **Robbins Motel** (396 Rte. 3, Bar Harbor, 207/288-4659, www.robbinsmotel.com, $69), an older property, has 30 small and unadorned (some might call them dismal) pine-paneled guest rooms with queen beds. There is no charm and it's not quiet, but it's cheap and clean. Off-season rates are as low as $40. Also available is a one-bedroom apartment with a full kitchen for $79.

The **Belle Isle Motel** (910 Rte. 3, Bar Harbor, 207/288-5726, www.belleislemotel.net, $99-109), a vintage mom-and-pop roadside motel, delivers clean and affordable lodgings. On the premises are a heated pool, playground, picnic area, and guest laundry. Dogs are welcome for $15/night.

Also on the lower end of the budgetary scale, the **Edenbrook Motel** (96 Eden St./Rte. 3, Bar Harbor, 207/288-4975 or 800/323-7819, www.edenbrookmotelbh.com, $129-179) comprises four vintage motel buildings tiered up a hillside. Some rooms on the upper levels have panoramic views of Frenchman Bay. New owners in 2018 began updating the rooms, so rates are creeping upward. It's across from the College of the Atlantic, about 1.5 miles from Acadia's main entrance, and 1 mile from downtown.

On the edge of downtown, across from the College of the Atlantic, are two adjacent sister properties tiered up a hillside: **Wonder**

View Inn & Suites (50 Eden St., Bar Harbor, 207/288-3358, www.wonderviewinn.com, $140-315) and the **Bluenose Hotel** (90 Eden St., Bar Harbor, 207/288-3348 or 800/445-4077, www.barharborhotel.com, from $240). The pet-friendly ($20/pet/night) Wonder View comprises four older motels on 14 acres of estate-like grounds with grassy lawns and mature shade trees, an outdoor pool, and a restaurant. The estate was the home of famed mystery writer Mary Roberts Rinehart, who coined the phrase "The butler did it." Guest rooms vary widely, and rates reflect both style of accommodation and views. The Bluenose comprises two buildings. Almost all of Mizzentop's rooms and suites are spacious and have fabulous views and balconies; some also have fireplaces. Stenna Nordica guest rooms, accessed from outdoor corridors, are more modest. Also here are a spa, fitness center, indoor and outdoor pools, and a lounge with live music every evening. All properties need updating, but they're clean and fine, if you're not persnickety.

The family-owned **Highbrook Motel** (94 Eden St./Rte. 3, Bar Harbor, 207/288-3591 or 800/338-9688, www.highbrookmotel.com, $175-215) comprises two buildings across from the College of the Atlantic. Rooms have in-room mini-fridges. The upper building is pricier, but offers more privacy. Rates include a grab-and-go continental breakfast.

On the edge of town, the **Cromwell Harbor Motel** (359 Main St., Bar Harbor, 207/288-3201 or 800/544-3201, www.cromwellharbor.com, $180) comprises four buildings set back from the road on nicely landscaped grounds with a heated outdoor pool.

One of the town's best-known, most visible, and best-situated hotels is the **Bar Harbor Inn** (1 Newport Dr., Bar Harbor, 207/288-3351 or 800/248-3351, www.barharborinn.com, from $300), a sprawling complex on eight acres overlooking the harbor and islands. The 153 rooms and suites vary considerably in style, from traditional inn to motel, and are in three different buildings. Continental breakfast is included, and special packages, with meals and activities, are available—an advantage if you have children. The kids will appreciate the heated outdoor pool; adults might enjoy the full-service spa. Also under the same management and ownership (www.bar-harbor-hotels.com) is the family-oriented **Acadia Inn** (98 Eden St., Bar Harbor, 207/288-3500, www.acadiainn.com, from $229), located between the park entrance and downtown Bar Harbor. A hot-and-cold breakfast buffet is included.

The appropriately named **Harborside Hotel & Marina** (55 West St., Bar Harbor, 207/288-5033 or 800/238-5033, www.theharborsidehotel.com, from $599) fronts on the water in downtown Bar Harbor. Most of the guest rooms, studios, and suites, all updated in 2019, have a water view and a semi-private balcony. Some have large outdoor hot tubs. The resort fee allows access to the beautifully restored Bar Harbor Club, with a full-service spa, fitness center, tennis courts, and oceanfront heated pool. Also on the premises are a second outdoor pool, a good casual Italian restaurant, a pier, and a marina. Sharing use of those facilities is a sister property, the **West Street Hotel** (50 West St., 877/905-4498, www.theweststreethotel.com, from $599), a tony spot with a rooftop pool (ages 18 and older only) overlooking downtown, the harbor, islands, and the ocean. Rooms have a nautical vibe, and those on the West Street side have harbor-view balconies.

Inns and Bed-and-Breakfasts

An in-town find for families, the **Seacroft Inn** (18 Albert Meadow, Bar Harbor, 207/288-4669 or 800/824-9694, www.seacroftinn.com, $120-160) is well situated just off Main Street and near the Shore Path. All rooms in Bunny and Dave Brown's white gabled cottage have refrigerators and microwaves; a continental breakfast is available for $5 per person. Housekeeping is available for $10 per day. Some rooms can be joined as family suites.

Outside of town, in a serene location with fabulous views of Frenchman Bay, is the **Inn at Bay Ledge** (150 Sand Point Rd.,

Bar Harbor, summer 207/288-4204, www.innatbayledge.com, $175-395), an elegant, casual retreat tucked under towering pines atop an 80-foot cliff. Terraced decks descend to a pool and onto the lawn, which stretches to the cliff's edge. Stairs descend to a private stone beach below. Almost all guest rooms have water views; some have private decks. A sauna and a steam shower are available. In the woods across the street are cottages, which lack the view but have use of the inn's facilities. Also on the premises is the Summer House ($495), a shingled cottage with a deck 25 feet from the edge of Frenchman Bay.

Built in 1880, and operated as a B&B by the same family for more than 30 years, the **Shore Path Cottage** (24 Atlantic Ave., Bar Harbor, www.shorepathcottage.com, $215-305) offers an enviable location with sigh-worthy sea views and private access to Bar Harbor's Shore Path. It's secreted away and yet just a few minutes' walk to all downtown attractions. Comfy and spacious rooms, full breakfasts, afternoon snacks, and on-site bicycle rental are just a few of the plusses of this special spot.

Situated on one oceanfront acre in the West Street Historical District, the ★ **Saltair Inn** (121 West St., Bar Harbor, 207/288-2882, www.saltairinn.com, from $239) was originally built in 1887 as a guesthouse. Innkeepers Kristi and Matt Losquadro and their family now welcome visitors in eight updated guest rooms, most of which are quite spacious, and five of which face Frenchman Bay. Frills vary by room but might include whirlpool tubs, fireplaces, and balconies. A full breakfast is served either in the dining room or on the water-view deck. It's steps from downtown, but really, with a location like this, why leave?

Alpheus Hardy, Bar Harbor's first cottager, built the Tudor-style **Ullikana** (16 The Field, Bar Harbor, 207/288-9552, https://ullikana.com, from $280) in 1885. It's tucked in a quiet downtown location close to the Shore Path and neighboring **Bass Cottage** (14 The Field, Bar Harbor, 207/288-1234, www.basscottage.com, from $280), a grand 1885 building. Experienced innkeepers Eddie and Judy Hemmingsen own both. Each has a boutique hotel vibe and a guest pantry stocked with snacks. Some rooms have working fireplaces, whirlpool tubs, and/or private terraces with water views. Guests at both inns take breakfast at the Bass Cottage and afternoon refreshments at the Ullikana.

Completing the trio of inns sited in the Field is the **Yellow House Bed & Breakfast** (15 The Field, 207/288-5100, www.yellowhousemaine.com, from $325), a lovely 1872 summer cottage. The seven-room inn, moved to its current location in 1885, blends gentle ease with contemporary comforts. Innkeepers Pat and Chris Coston welcome guests warmly and provide expert guidance. Enjoy breakfast on the inviting wraparound porch overlooking a sculpture garden or in the parlor.

Camping

Mount Desert Island's private campgrounds are located at the northern end of the island, down the center, and in the southwest corner. Most are also on the routes of the free Island Explorer bus service, making it easy and economical—and preferable—to leave your car or RV at your campsite and avoid the parking problems between late June and Columbus Day.

Family owned and operated, **Bar Harbor Campground** (409 Rte. 3, Bar Harbor, 207/288-5185, www.thebarharborcampground.com, $30-45) caters to families and offers a heated pool, a recreation hall, and a play area. It doesn't accept advance reservations, nor does it take credit cards. Many of the 300 sites have ocean views. Hookups are available.

The Baker family has operated **Hadley's Point Campground** (33 Hadley Point Rd., Bar Harbor, 207/288-4808, www.hadleyspoint.com, May 15-mid-Oct., $32-50) since 1969. Tent sites are nicely spaced in the woods and have a sense of privacy; big-rig sites, located in fields, are tight. Camping cabins ($90) are furnished with one queen and two twin beds and a bathroom with metered shower; pets are permitted for $10 per night. Facilities include a laundry, a heated pool, shuffleboard courts, horseshoes, and a playground. A public saltwater beach with a boat launch is within walking distance. The campground is eight miles from Bar Harbor.

INFORMATION AND SERVICES

The **Bar Harbor Chamber of Commerce** (1201 Bar Harbor Rd./Rte. 3, Trenton, 207/288-5103, www.barharbormaine.com) is open daily in summer. The chamber's **downtown branch** (2 Cottage St., Bar Harbor, 8am-4pm daily), which it shares with Acadia National Park in winter, is open year-round.

If you're traveling with kids, have them check out the ***Kids' Guide to MDI*** (https://cfournier1.wixsite.com/mysite) written by third-graders at Conners Emerson School in 2015-16.

Find **public restrooms** at the park visitors centers and in downtown Bar Harbor in Agamont Park, Harbor Place at the town pier, adjacent to the Village Green, and on the School Street side of the athletic field.

GETTING THERE AND AROUND

Bar Harbor is about 20 miles or 30-45 minutes, depending on traffic, via Route 3 from Ellsworth; about 45 miles or 75 minutes via Routes 1A and 3 from Bangor; and about 275 miles or five hours via Routes 195 and 3 from Boston. It's about 12 miles or 20 minutes via Routes 233 and 198 or 20 miles or 35 minutes via Route 3 to Northeast Harbor.

Make it easy on yourself and help improve the air quality by leaving your car at your lodging (or if day-tripping, at the Bar Harbor Chamber of Commerce on Route 3 in Trenton) and taking the Island Explorer bus. Route 8/Trenton connects the airport with the downtown

Bar Harbor has metered parking, with payment either at individual meter or kiosk. Rates for street and lot parking vary from $1.50-2/hour (quarters, credit card, or Park Mobile app), depending upon location.

Schoodic Passenger Ferry

Although Winter Harbor is roughly 43 miles or 1.15 hours from Bar Harbor by car, it's only about 7 miles by water.

The summer schedule for the **Bar Harbor Ferry** (207/288-2984, www.barharborferry.com, round-trip $28 adults, $20 children) is coordinated with the Island Explorer bus's summertime Schoodic route, so you can board the ferry in Bar Harbor, pick up the bus at the dock in Winter Harbor, and be shuttled along the Schoodic Loop. Stop where you like for a picnic or a hike, and then board a later bus. Take the last bus back to the ferry and return to Bar Harbor. It makes for a super car-free excursion. It operates at least four times daily mid-June-mid-Oct.

Northeast Harbor

Ever since the late 19th century, the upper crust from Philadelphia has been summering in and around Northeast Harbor. Sure, they also show up in other parts of Maine, but it's hard not to notice the preponderance of Pennsylvania license plates surrounding Northeast Harbor's elegant "cottages" mid-July-mid-August.

Actually, even though Northeast Harbor is a well-known name with special cachet, it isn't even an official township: It's a zip-coded village within the town of **Mount Desert** (pop. 2,053), which collects the breathtaking property taxes and doles out the municipal services.

The attractive boutiques and restaurants

in Northeast Harbor's small downtown area cater to a casually posh clientele, and the well-protected harbor attracts a tony crowd of yachties. For their convenience, a palm-sized annual directory, *The Redbook,* discreetly lists owners' summer residences and winter addresses—but no phone numbers.

Except for three spectacular public gardens and two specialized museums, not much here is geared to budget-sensitive visitors—but there's no charge for admiring the scenery.

Although all of Mount Desert Island is seasonal, Northeast Harbor is especially so. Many businesses don't open until early July and close in early September.

SIGHTS

Somes Sound

As you head toward Northeast Harbor on Route 198 from the northern end of Mount Desert Island, you'll begin seeing cliff-lined Somes Sound, on your right. The glacier-sculpted fjard (not as deep or as steeply walled as a fjord) juts five miles into the interior of Mount Desert Island from its mouth between Northeast Harbor and Southwest Harbor. Watch for the right-hand turn for Sargent Drive (no RVs allowed) and follow the lovely, granite-lined route along the east side of the sound. Halfway along, a marker explains the geology of this spectacular natural inlet. There aren't many pullouts en route, and traffic can be fairly thick in midsummer, but don't miss it. **Suminsby Park,** located off Sargent Drive, 400 feet from Route 3, is a fine place for a picnic. The park has rocky shore access, a hand-carry boat launch, picnic tables, grills, and a pit toilet. An ideal way to appreciate Somes Sound is from the water—sign up for an excursion out of Northeast Harbor or Southwest Harbor.

TOP EXPERIENCE

★ Gardens

If you have the slightest interest in gardens, allow time for Northeast Harbor's two marvelous public gardens, both operated by the nonprofit **Mount Desert Land and Garden Preserve** (207/276-3727, www.gardenpreserve.org).

ASTICOU AZALEA GARDEN AND THUYA GARDEN

One of Maine's best spring showcases is the **Asticou Azalea Garden,** a 2.3-acre pocket where about 70 varieties of azaleas, rhododendrons, and laurels—many from the classic Reef Point garden of famed landscape designer Beatrix Farrand—burst into bloom. When Charles K. Savage, beloved former innkeeper of the Asticou Inn, learned the Reef Point garden was being undone in 1956, he went into high gear to find funding and managed to rescue the azaleas and provide them with the gorgeous setting they have today, across the road and around the corner from the inn. Serenity is the key—with a Japanese sand garden that's mesmerizing in any season, stone lanterns, granite outcrops, pink-gravel paths, and a tranquil pond. Try to visit early in the season and early in the morning to savor the effect. Blossoming occurs May-August, but the prime time for azaleas is roughly mid-May-mid-June.

The garden is on Route 198, at the northern edge of Northeast Harbor, immediately north of the junction with Peabody Drive (Rte. 3). Watch for a tiny sign on the left (if you're coming from the north), marking access to the parking area. A small box suggests a $5 donation, and another box contains a garden guide ($2). Pets are not allowed in the garden. Take Island Explorer Route 5 (Jordan Pond) or Route 6 (Brown Mountain) and request a stop. Note: The Asticou Stream Trail, a lovely meander through fields and woods and down to the shoreline, connects the garden to the town. Look for a small signpost across from the Route 3 entrance to the garden.

Behind a carved wooden gate on a forested hillside not far from Asticou lies an enchanted garden also designed by Charles K. Savage as a semiformal English herbaceous garden, inspired by Beatrix Farrand

and interpreted for coastal Maine. Special features of **Thuya Garden** are perennial borders and sculpted shrubbery. On a misty summer day, when few visitors appear, the colors are brilliant. Adjacent to the garden is **Thuya Lodge** (207/276-5130), former summer cottage of Joseph Curtis, donor of this awesome park. The lodge, with an extensive botanical and horticultural library and quiet rooms for reading, is open 10am-4:30pm daily late June-Labor Day. The garden is open 7am-7pm daily. A collection box next to the front gate requests a $5 donation per adult. To reach Thuya, continue on Route 3 beyond Asticou Azalea Garden and watch for the Asticou Terraces parking area (no RVs; two-hour limit) on the right. Cross the road and climb the Asticou Terraces Trail (0.4 mile) to the garden. Allow time to hang out at the three lookouts en route. Alternatively, drive 0.2 mile beyond the Route 3 parking area, watching for a minuscule Thuya Garden sign on the left. Go 0.5 mile up the steep, narrow, and curving driveway to the parking area (but walking up reaps higher rewards). Or take Island Explorer Route 5 (Jordan Pond) and request a stop.

Note: It's possible to connect Asticou and Thuya Gardens by walking the Asticou Hill Trail, which follows an old road, or hiking the moderately difficult (lots of exposed roots) Eliot Mountain Trail. The Asticou Hill Trail road across from the Asticou Inn provides access to both; it's a private road, but foot traffic has a right-of-way.

ABBY ALDRICH ROCKEFELLER GARDEN

The **Abby Aldrich Rockefeller Garden** (207/276-3330 in season, www.gardenpreserve.org, $15), located in Seal Harbor, was created between 1926 and 1935, when the Rockefellers turned to renowned designer Beatrix Farrand to create a garden using treasures they'd brought back from Asia. The enclosed garden is a knockout, accented with English floral beds, Korean tombstone figures, a moon gate, woodland and water gardens, and even yellow roof tiles from Beijing. You can also stroll to the terrace of what was the Eyrie, the former Rockefeller summer home, removed in 1963. The garden is only open from mid-July to early September, and admission is limited and reservations are required; check the website for current details, and make plans well in advance. A garden guide with map is provided, but you're free to explore at your own pace. Although gorgeous anytime, the garden comes into peak bloom

Asticou Azalea Garden

during the first two weeks of August. Hint: Most visitors arrive right at the session's start. Avoid the crowds by showing up a little later.

Petite Plaisance

On Northeast Harbor's quiet South Shore Road, **Petite Plaisance** (35 South Shore Rd., Northeast Harbor, 207/276-3940, www.petiteplaisanceconservationfund.org, Tues.-Sat. June 15-Aug. 31, donation) is a special-interest museum commemorating noted Belgian-born author and college professor Marguerite Yourcenar (pen name of Marguerite de Crayencour), the first woman elected to the prestigious Académie Française. From 1950 to 1987, Petite Plaisance was her home, and it's hard to believe she's no longer here; her intriguing possessions and presence fill the two-story house, of particular interest to Yourcenar devotees. In 2014, the French Ministry of Culture added Petite Plaisance to its registry of illustrious houses. Free hour-long tours of the 1st floor are given, by advance appointment only. Tours are offered in French or English, depending on visitors' preferences; French-speaking visitors often make pilgrimages here. No children under age 12 are allowed. Call at least a day ahead, between 9am and 4pm, to schedule an appointment. Yourcenar admirers should request directions to Brookside Cemetery in Somesville, seven miles away, where she is buried.

Great Harbor Maritime Museum

Annual exhibits focusing on the maritime heritage of the Mount Desert Island area are held in the small, eclectic **Great Harbor Maritime Museum** (124 Main St., Northeast Harbor, 207/276-5262, 10am-5pm Tues.-Sat. late June-Labor Day, donation), housed in the old village fire station and municipal building. ("Great Harbor" refers to the Somes Sound area—Northeast, Southwest, and Seal Harbors, as well as the Cranberry Isles.) Yachting, coastal trade, and fishing receive special emphasis. Look for the canvas rowing canoe, built in Veazie, Maine, between 1917 and 1920; it's the only one of its kind known to exist today.

ENTERTAINMENT

Since 1964, the **Mount Desert Festival of Chamber Music** (207/266-2550, www.mtdesertfestival.org) has presented concerts in the century-old Neighborhood House on Main Street at 8:15pm Tuesdays mid-July-mid-August. Tickets ($30 general admission) are available at the Neighborhood House box office Monday-Tuesday during the concert season, online, or by phone reservation.

SHOPPING

Upscale shops, galleries, and boutiques with clothing, artwork, housewares, and antiques line Main Street, making for intriguing browsing and expensive buying (check the sale rooms of the clothing shops for bona fide bargains). The season is short, though, with some shops open only in July-August.

One must-visit is **Shaw Contemporary Jewelry** (100 Main St., 207/276-5000 or 877/276-5001, www.shawjewelry.com, year-round). Besides the spectacular silver and gold beachstone jewelry created by Rhode Island School of Design alumnus Sam Shaw, the work of more than 100 other jewelers is displayed exquisitely. Plus there are sculptures, Asian art, and rotating art exhibits. It all leads back toward a lovely light-filled garden. Prices are in the stratosphere, but appropriately so. As one well-dressed customer was overheard sighing to her companion: "If I had only one jewelry store to go to in my entire life, this would be it."

If you're traveling with children or if you have any interest in art, science, or nature, don't miss the **Naturalist's Notebook** (16 Main St., Seal Harbor, 207/801-2777, www.thenaturalistsnotebook.com), a shop and exploratorium. Owned by artist-photographer Pamelia Markwood and her *Sports Illustrated* writer-editor husband, Craig Neff, the shop has three stories full of engaging exhibits, books, and treasures.

The Maine Sea Coast Mission

the Maine Sea Coast Mission's *Sunbeam V*

Remote islands and other isolated communities along Maine's rugged coastline may still have a church, but few have a full-time minister; fewer yet have a health care provider. Yet these communities aren't entirely shut off from either preaching or medical assistance.

Since 1905, the **Maine Sea Coast Mission** (207/288-5097, www.seacoastmission.org), a nondenominational, nonprofit organization rooted in a Christian ministry, has offered a lifeline to these communities. The mission serves nearly 2,800 people on eight different islands, including Frenchboro, the Cranberries, Swans, and Isle au Haut, as well as others living in remote coastal locations on the mainland. Its numerous, much-needed services include a Christmas program; in-school, after-school, and summer school programs; emergency financial assistance; food assistance; a thrift shop; ministers for island and coastal communities; scholarships; and health services.

Many of these services are delivered via the mission's ***Sunbeam V,*** a 75-foot diesel boat that has no limitations on when, and few on where, it can travel. In winter, it even serves as an icebreaker, clearing harbors and protecting boats from ice damage. During your travels in the Acadia region, you might see the *Sunbeam V* homeported in Northeast Harbor or on its rounds.

A nurse and a minister usually travel on the ship. The minister may conduct services on the island or on the boat, which also functions as a gathering place for fellowship, meals, and meetings. The minister also reaches out to those in need, the marginalized, or the ill, and often helps with island funerals. Onboard telemedicine equipment enables the nurse to provide much-needed health care, including screening clinics for diabetes, cholesterol, and prostate and skin cancer; flu and pneumonia vaccines; and tetanus shots.

The mission welcomes donations and volunteers. You can make a difference.

RECREATION

Boat Excursions

Northeast Harbor is the starting point for a couple of boat services headed for the **Cranberry Isles.** The vessels leave from the commercial floats at the end of the concrete municipal pier on Sea Street.

The 75-foot ***Sea Princess*** (207/276-5352, https://barharborcruises.com) carries visitors as well as an Acadia National

Park naturalist on a 2.75-hour morning trip around the mouth of Somes Sound and out to Little Cranberry Island (Islesford) for a 50-minute stopover. The boat leaves Northeast Harbor at 10am daily mid-May-mid-October. A narrated afternoon trip departs at 1pm on the same route. Other trips operate, but not daily. These include 1.5-hour scenic and sunset Somes Sound cruises. Fees range $26-32 adults, $16-19 ages 6-12, $7 up to age 5. Reservations are advisable for all trips, although even that provides no guarantee, since the cruises require a 15-passenger minimum.

Downeast Friendship Sloop Charters (Northeast Harbor Municipal Marina, 41 Harbor Dr., 207/266-5210, www.downeastfriendshipsloop.com) operates two traditional Friendship sloops, the *Helen Brooks* and the *Linda*. Private charters range $275-425, covering up to six passengers; shared trips are $85 per person for about three hours. A sunset sail is a lovely way to end a day.

FOOD

Quick Bites

In the **Pine Tree Market** (121 Main St., Northeast Harbor, 207/276-3335, 8am-6pm Mon.-Sat., 9am-5pm Sun.), you'll find gourmet goodies, a huge wine selection, a resident butcher, fresh fish, a deli, homemade breads, pastries, sandwiches, and salads. The market offers free delivery to homes and boats.

Pop into **Milk & Honey** (3 Old Firehouse Ln., Northeast Harbor, 207/276-4003, http://milkandhoneykitchen.com, 8am-4pm daily, $7-10) for especially good made-to-order sandwiches (10am-2pm), along with soups, salads, and sweets. Find it tucked behind Shaw Contemporary Jewelry.

Breakfast pastries, prepared sandwiches, soups and salads, and dinners-to-go are all available at **123 Main** (123 Main St., Northeast Harbor, 207/276-4166, www.123neh.com, 8:30am-4:30pm daily).

From June well into October, the **Northeast Harbor Farmers Market** sets up each Thursday, 9am-noon, across from the Kimball Terrace Inn on Huntington Road.

Family Favorites

The homemade doughnuts are reason enough to visit the **Colonel's Restaurant and Bakery** (143 Main St., Northeast Harbor, 207/288-4775, www.colonelsrestaurant.com, 8am-9pm daily), but tucked behind the bakery is a full-service restaurant, serving everything from burgers to prime rib, as well as the usual seafood musts ($10-25). Its kids' menu and casual atmosphere draws families, and it can be quite boisterous inside. There's also a deck out back and a separate bar area, which often is the quietest spot with the fastest service.

ACCOMMODATIONS

Inns

For more than 100 years, the genteel **Asticou Inn** (Rte. 3, Northeast Harbor, 207/276-3344 or 800/258-3373, www.asticou.com, from $250) has catered to the whims and weddings of Northeast Harbor's well-heeled summer rusticators. Hardwood floors are topped with elaborate rugs, rooms are papered with floral or plaid wallpapers, and gauzy ruffled curtains blow in the breeze. It's all delightfully old-fashioned, but also tired, lacking contemporary amenities, and in need of updating, yet most guests would have it no other way. The inn tops a lawn that slopes down to the yacht-filled harbor, and cocktails and lunch are served daily on the porch overlooking the heated pool, clay tennis court, and water. Accommodations are spread out between the main inn, three cottages, and four funky Topsiders, which seem inspired by the old *Jetsons* TV show. The nicest rooms and suites face the harbor. The inn's restaurant serves breakfast, lunch, and dinner daily. Try to plan a late-May or early-June visit; you're practically on top of the Asticou Azalea Garden, Thuya Garden is a short walk away (or hike via the Eliot Mountain Trail), and the rates are lowest. Asticou is a popular wedding venue, so if you're looking for a quiet weekend, check the inn's event schedule before booking a room.

Three miles from Northeast Harbor, in equally tony Seal Harbor, is a true bargain, the **Lighthouse Inn and Restaurant** (12 Main St./Rte. 3, Seal Harbor, 207/276-3958, www.lighthouseinnandrestaurant.com, $85-105). Sure, the three guest rooms (one small, one very large with a kitchenette) are dated and dowdy, but at these prices, who cares? Downstairs is a restaurant (11am-8pm daily) with equally reasonable prices. It's a short walk to Seal Harbor.

Bed-and-Breakfasts

The **Colonel's Suites** (143 Main St., Northeast Harbor, 207/288-4775, www.colonelssuites.com, from $199), above the bakery/restaurant of the same name, provide comfortable accommodations with modern amenities. Rates include a full breakfast in the restaurant.

In 1888, architect Fred Savage designed the two Shingle-style buildings that make up the three-story **Harbourside Inn** (Main St., Northeast Harbor, 207/276-3272, www.harboursideinn.com, mid-June-mid-Sept., $210-350). The owners preserved the old-fashioned feel by decorating the 11 spacious guest rooms and three suites with antiques, yet modern amenities include some kitchenettes. Most rooms have working fireplaces. A light continental breakfast is served. Trails to Norumbega Mountain and Upper Hadlock Pond leave from the back of the property.

Motels

Although it's overdue for an overhaul, you can't beat the location of the **Kimball Terrace Inn** (10 Huntington Rd., Northeast Harbor, 207/276-3383 or 800/454-6225, www.kimballterraceinn.com, $170-255). The three-story motel faces the harbor, and every guest room has a patio or private balcony (ask for a harbor-facing room). Bring binoculars for yacht-spotting. The motel has an outdoor pool and a restaurant. It's a short walk from Northeast Harbor's downtown. Like the Asticou, it's a popular wedding venue. Some rooms are pet friendly ($25/day).

INFORMATION AND SERVICES

The harbor-front information bureau of the **Mount Desert Chamber of Commerce** (18 Harbor Rd., Northeast Harbor, 207/276-5040, www.mountdesertchamber.org) covers the villages of Somesville, Northeast Harbor, Seal Harbor, Otter Creek, Pretty Marsh, Hall Quarry, and Beech Hill.

Find **public restrooms** at the end of the building housing the Great Harbor Maritime Museum, in the town office on Sea Street, and at the harbor.

GETTING THERE AND AROUND

Northeast Harbor is about 12 miles or 20 minutes via Routes 233 and 198 or 20 miles/35 minutes via Route 3 from Bar Harbor. It's about 13 miles or 25 minutes to Southwest Harbor.

Northeast Harbor is served by Route 5 (Jordan Pond) and Route 6 (Brown Mountain) of the Island Explorer bus system.

Southwest Harbor and Vicinity

Southwest Harbor (pop. 1,764) is the hub of Mount Desert Island's "quiet side." In summer, its tiny downtown district is probably the busiest spot on the whole western side of the island (west of Somes Sound), but that's not saying a great deal. "Southwest" has the feel of a settled community, a year-round flavor that Bar Harbor sometimes lacks. And it competes with the best in the scenery department. The Southwest Harbor area serves as a very convenient base for exploring Acadia National Park, as well as the island's less-crowded villages and offshore Swans Island, Frenchboro, and the Cranberry Isles.

The quirky nature of the island's four town boundaries creates complications in trying to categorize various island segments. Officially, the town of Southwest Harbor includes only the villages of **Manset** and **Seawall,** but nearby is the precious hamlet of **Somesville.** The Somesville National Historic District, with its distinctive arched white footbridge, is especially appealing, but traffic gets congested here along Route 102, so rather than just rubbernecking, plan to stop and walk around.

The "quiet side" of the island becomes even quieter as you round the southwestern edge into **Tremont** (pop. 1,563), which includes the villages of **Bernard; Bass Harbor,** home of Bass Harbor Head Light and ferry services to offshore islands; and **Seal Cove.** Tremont occupies the southwestern corner of Mount Desert Island. It's about as far as you can get from Bar Harbor, but Island Explorer Route No. 7/Southwest Harbor comes through regularly.

Be sure to visit these small villages. Views are fabulous, the pace is slow, and you'll feel as if you've stumbled upon "the real Maine."

SIGHTS

★ Wendell Gilley Museum

In the center of Southwest Harbor, the **Wendell Gilley Museum** (Herrick Rd. and Rte. 102, Southwest Harbor, 207/244-7555, www.wendellgilleymuseum.org, 10am-5pm Tues.-Sat. July-Aug., 10am-4pm Tues.-Sat. June and Sept.-Oct., $5 adults, $2 ages 5-12) was established in 1981 to display the lifework of local woodcarver Wendell Gilley (1904-1983), a onetime plumber who had gained a national reputation for his carvings by the time of his death. The museum houses more than 200 of his realistic bird specimens carved over more than 50 years. Summer exhibits also feature other wildlife artists. Many days, a local artist gives woodcarving demonstrations, and members of the local carving club often can be seen whittling away. The gift shop carries an ornithological potpourri, including books, binoculars, and carving tools. Kids over age eight appreciate this more than younger ones. Carving workshops range from 90-minute introductory lessons for adults and children ($25, includes kit and admission), offered most weekdays during the summer, to multiday classes on specific birds.

Somesville Historical Museum and Gardens

The tiny **Somesville Historical Museum and Gardens** (Rte. 102, Somesville, 207/276-9323, www.mdihistory.org, 10am-4pm daily late June-late Aug., 10am-4pm Sat.-Sun. Sept.-mid-Oct., donation) is adjacent to the gently curving white bridge in Somesville, so there's a good chance you're going to stop nearby, if just for a photo. In season, the heirloom garden, filled with flowering plants and herbs of the 19th and early 20th centuries, is beautiful. The one-room museum has local artifacts and memorabilia displayed in a themed exhibit that changes annually. You can purchase a walking-tour guide to Somesville in the museum. If you're especially interested in history, ask about the museum's programs, which include speakers, demonstrations, and workshops.

Charlotte Rhoades Park and Butterfly Garden

It's easy to miss the **Charlotte Rhoades Park and Butterfly Garden** (Rte. 102, Southwest Harbor, 207/244-5405, www.rhoadesbutterflygarden.org, donation appreciated), but that would be a mistake. This tiny seaside park was donated to the town in 1973, and the butterfly garden was established in 1998 to promote conservation education. A kiosk is stocked with butterfly observation sheets, and there's often a volunteer docent on duty on Thursday mornings. Check the website for info about garden tours. Time a visit with the annual butterfly release in July (reservations required). The park is on the water side of Route 102 between the Causeway Golf Club and the Seal Cove Road.

Country Store Museum

Stepping inside the former general store that's now headquarters for the **Tremont Historical Society** (Shore Rd., Bass Harbor, 207/244-9753, www.tremontmainehistory.us, 1pm-4pm Mon., Wed., and Fri. July-mid-Oct.) is like stepping into the 1800s. Displays highlight the local heritage. If you're lucky, seventh-generation islander Muriel Davisson might be on duty and regale you with stories about her aunt, author Ruth Moore. You can buy copies of Moore's books here—good reads all. The museum is across from the Seafood Ketch.

★ Seal Cove Auto Museum

The late Richard C. Paine Jr.'s Brass Era (1895-1917) car collection, one of the largest in the country, is nicely displayed and identified in the **Seal Cove Auto Museum** (1414 Tremont Rd./Rte. 102, Seal Cove, 207/244-9242, www.sealcoveautomuseum.org, 10am-5pm daily May-Oct., $6 adults, $5 seniors, $4 ages 13-17, $2 ages 5-12). All vehicles are in as-found condition; this ranges from fresh-from-the-barn to meticulously restored. It's easy for kids of any age to spend an hour here, reminiscing or fantasizing. Among the highlights are a 1913 Peugeot with mahogany skiff body; a 1915 F.R.P., the only one in existence; an original 1903 Ford Model A, the first car commercially produced by the Ford Motor Co.; and a 1909 Ford Model T "Tin Lizzie," from the first year of production. The oldest car in the collection is an 1899 DeDion-Bouton, one of the earliest cars produced in the world. The museum is about six miles southwest of Somesville. Or, if you're coming from Southwest Harbor, take Route 102 north to Seal Cove Road (partly unpaved) west to the other side of Route 102 (it makes a giant loop) and go north about 1.5 miles. This is not on the Island Explorer route.

The Maine Granite Industry Historical Society Museum

Delve into the history of Maine granite at the **Maine Granite Industry Historical Society Museum** (62 Beech Hill Cross Rd., Mount Desert, 207/244-7299, www.mainegraniteindustry.org, 10am-4pm Tues.-Sun. Apr. 1-Nov. 30, winter by appt., donation). Founder and curator Steven Haynes oversees a collection comprising hundreds of tools, photographs, ledgers, books, and other artifacts related to quarry workers, blacksmiths, stonecutters, and stone carvers. Immigrants from countries including Italy, Finland, Sweden, Norway, and Portugal worked quarries in nine Maine counties, and the granite can still be seen in public buildings, including churches, courthouses, and libraries, as well as bridges throughout the country. Displays show the difference between granite from different quarries. Haynes is a wealth of information, and he loves to share his passion. He's often carving and polishing at the site.

Harding Wharf

Drive to the end of the Bernard village road, and you can't miss the faux lighthouse on Harding Wharf. The attached fishing shack was built in 1891 by the Murphy family, who lived in Centennial House across the road. They sold it to Charles Harding in 1927, and it remained in the family until Charles's brother Clarence sold it to Nancy and Irving

Silverman in 1981. Later that year, the Silvermans attached their colorful collection of 29 historical wooden lobster buoys to the seaward side of the shack.

ENTERTAINMENT

Acadia Repertory Theatre

Somesville is home to the **Acadia Repertory Theatre** (Rte. 102, Somesville, 207/244-7260, www.acadiarep.com, $26 adults, $22 seniors, students, and military, $13 under age 16), which has been providing first-rate professional summer stock on the stage of Somesville's antique Masonic Hall since 1973. Classic plays by Oscar Wilde, Neil Simon, and even Molière have been staples, as has the annual Agatha Christie mystery. Performances in the 148-seat hall run at 8:15pm Tuesday-Sunday late June-late August, with 2pm matinees on the last Sunday of each play's run. Special children's plays are performed at 10:30am Wednesdays and Saturdays in July-August. Tickets for children's theater programs are $9 adults, $6 children.

Lecture and Concert Series

During July-August, the Claremont Hotel (22 Claremont Rd., Southwest Harbor, 207/244-5036 or 800/244-5036, www.theclaremonthotel.com) sponsors a **free weekly lecture series**, with noted experts, at 8:15pm on Thursday evenings. Past topics have ranged from the Art of the Maine Coast to Cameo Fever: From Catherine the Great to Scarlett O'Hara. It also offers a **Saturday evening concert series** ($15), with music ranging from jazz to classical.

Festivals and Events

During July-August, the Wednesday **Pie Sale** at the Somesville Union Meeting House is always a sellout.

In early August, the annual **Claremont Croquet Classic,** held on the grounds of the classic Claremont Hotel, is open to all ages.

In October, Smuggler's Den Campground, on Route 102 in Southwest Harbor, is home to **Acadia's Oktoberfest** (207/244-9264, www.acadiachamber.com), a weekend celebration with wine, beer, food, and music.

The **Acadia Night Sky Festival** (www.acadianightskyfestival.com), in September, includes lectures, movies, sky-viewing opportunities, and other activities.

SHOPPING

Southwest Harbor

Intriguing galleries and independent shops fill downtown Southwest Harbor.

Fine art of the 19th and early 20th centuries, most depicting Maine and Mountain Desert Island, is the specialty at **Clark Point Gallery** (46 Clark Point Rd., Southwest Harbor, 207/244-0920). **Cornerstone Gallery** (322 Main St., Southwest Harbor, 207/244-5918) carries original works by local artists and artisans. **Southwest Harbor Artisans** (360 Main St., Southwest Harbor, no phone) is a cooperative effort operated by Maine artisans.

You can stop in at the **Hinckley Ship'Store** (130 Shore Rd., Southwest Harbor, 207/244-7100 or 800/446-2553, www.hinckleyshipstore.com) and pick up books, charts, and all sorts of Hinckley-logo gear. The Hinckley Company, a name of stellar repute since the 1930s, is one of the nation's premier boatbuilders. There are no tours of the Hinckley complex, but most yachters can't resist the urge to look in at the yard.

Bernard and Seal Cove

Linda Fernandez Handknits (Bernard Rd., Bernard, 207/244-7224) sells beautiful hand-knit sweaters, mittens, hats, socks, Christmas stockings, and embroidered pillowcases, all handcrafted by the talented and extended Fernandez family. The kids' lobster sweaters are especially cute.

Potters Lisbeth Faulkner and Edwin Davis can often be seen working in their studio at **Seal Cove Pottery & Gallery** (Kelleytown Rd., Seal Cove, 207/244-3602). In addition to their functional hand-thrown or hand-built pottery, they exhibit Davis's paintings as well as crafts by other island artisans.

RECREATION

Hiking

At the Southwest Harbor/Tremont Chamber of Commerce office, or at any of the area's stores, lodgings, and restaurants, pick up a free copy of the *Trail Map/Hiking Guide,* a very handy foldout map showing more than 20 hikes on the west side of Mount Desert Island. Trail descriptions include distances, time required, and skill levels (easy to strenuous).

Bicycle Rentals

Southwest Cycle (370 Main St., Southwest Harbor, 207/244-5856, www.southwestcycle.com) will fix you up with maps and lots of good advice for three loops (10-30 miles) on the western side of Mount Desert. Rentals begin around $25 for a full day, with multi-day discounts available. The shop also rents every imaginable accessory, from baby seats to tag-a-longs.

Golf

The ocean-hugging nine-hole **Causeway Club** (Fernald Point Rd., 207/244-3780) is more challenging than it looks.

Boat Excursions

★ ISLAND CRUISES

High praise goes to **Island Cruises** (Little Island Marine, Shore Rd., Bass Harbor, 207/244-5785, www.bassharborcruises.com), operated by captain Eli Strauss, for its narrated 3.5-hour lunch cruise to Frenchboro. The 49-passenger *R. L. Gott,* which Eli's dad, Kim, built, departs at 11am daily during the summer. Eli was born navigating these waters, and his experience shows not only in his boat handling but also in his narration. Expect to pick up lots of local heritage and lore about once-thriving and now abandoned granite-quarrying and fishing communities, the sardine industry, and lobstering, and to see seals, cormorants, guillemots, and often eagles. The trip allows enough time on Frenchboro for lunch. You could bring a picnic, but it's a treat to have lunch at Lunt's, where the menu ranges from hot dogs to lobster. Afterward, stroll through the village and visit the small museum before returning through the sprinkling of islands along the 8.3-mile route. Eli also hauls a trap or two and explains lobstering. He earns major points for maneuvering the boat so that passengers on both sides get an up-close view of key sights. It's an excellent, enthralling tour for all ages. Round-trip cost is $40 adults, $20 ages 3-11.

Island Cruises also does a two-hour **afternoon nature cruise** among the islands that covers the same topics but spends a bit more time at seal ledges and other spots ($35 adults, $20 ages 3-11). On either trip, don't forget to bring binoculars. Island Cruises also offers private charters: from $270 for two hours aboard a six-passenger sailboat; from $310 for two hours aboard a six-passenger powerboat. You'll find the Island Cruises dock by following signs to the Swans Island ferry and turning right at the sign shortly before the state ferry dock.

1: footbridge in Somesville 2: Long Pond

SAIL ACADIA

Sail Acadia (207/266-5210, www.downeastfriendshipsloop.com) offers two ways to cruise. Sail aboard the 1899 *Alice E*, the oldest Friendship sloop sailing today. Shared trips are $85 pp; private charters start at $275, covering up to six passengers. Or learn about lobster fishing on a two-hour tour aboard the *Elizabeth T* ($40), a wooden lobster boat built on Mount Desert Island. During the cruise, you'll haul a few traps as well as view a seal colony, a century-old osprey nest, and Bear Island Lighthouse.

DEEP-SEA FISHING

Go fishing with **Acadia Deep Sea Fishing Tours** (Beal's Wharf, Clark Point Rd., Southwest Harbor, 207/244-5385, www.acadiafishingtours.com, half day $69 adults, $49 ages 5-12) aboard the 43-foot *Vagabond,* and you might return with a lobster. The boat goes 8-20 miles offshore for mackerel, bluefish, codfish, and more. All equipment is included; dress warmly and come prepared with seasickness medications. Non-fishing passengers pay $10 less.

BOAT RENTALS AND LESSONS

Mansell Boat Rental Co. (135 Shore Rd., Manset, 207/244-5625, www.mansellboatrentals.com), next to Hinckley, rents sailboats and powerboats by the day or week, including a keel day-sailor for $195 per day and a 17-foot Boston Whaler for $295 per day. Also available are private sailing lessons: $295 for a two- to three-hour sail lesson cruise for one or two, which includes rigging and unrigging the boat.

Paddling

SEA KAYAKING AND STAND-UP PADDLEBOARDING

On the outskirts of Southwest Harbor's downtown is **Maine State Kayak** (254 Main St., Southwest Harbor, 207/244-9500, www.mainestatekayak.com). Staffed with experienced, environmentally sensitive kayakers (all are Registered Maine Guides), the company offers three- to four-hour guided trips ($55-75 pp). Most popular is the four-hour Wildlife Excursion. Maine State Kayak also offers stand-up paddleboarding with its partner **Acadia SUP.** Options include a two-hour lake session or ocean trip, each is $50 including instructor and gear, and a 75-minute yoga class ($25).

CALM-WATER PADDLING

Just west of Somesville (take Pretty Marsh Rd.) and across the road from Long Pond, **National Park Canoe & Kayak Rental** (145 Pretty Marsh Rd./Rte. 102, Mount Desert, 207/244-5854, www.nationalparkcanoerental.com, mid-May-mid-Oct.) makes canoeing and kayaking a snap. Just rent the boat, carry it across the road to Pond's End, and launch it. Be sure to pack a picnic. Rates range $32-42 for a three-hour canoe, kayak, or paddleboard rental. A do-it-yourself sunset canoe or kayak tour (5pm-sunset) is $22 per person. The late fee is $10 per half hour. Reservations are essential in July-August.

If you've brought your own canoe or kayak, launch it at Pond's End. It's four miles to the south end of the lake. If the wind kicks up, skirt the shore; if it really kicks up from the north, don't paddle too far down the lake, because you'll have a difficult time getting back.

Another option is to launch your canoe on the quieter, cliff-lined southern end of the lake, much of which is in the national park. To find the put-in, take the Seal Cove Road (on the east end of downtown Southwest Harbor). Go right on Long Cove Road to the small parking area at the end near the pumping station. You can also put in from the Long Pond Fire Road, off Route 102 in Pretty Marsh.

Almost the entire west side of **Long Pond** is Acadia National Park property, so plan to picnic and swim along here; tuck into the sheltered area west of Southern Neck, a crooked finger of land that points northward from the western shore. Stay clear of private property on the east side of the lake.

FOOD

Lobster and Seafood

Few restaurants have as idyllic a setting as ★ **Thurston's Lobster Pound** (9 Thurston Rd., Bernard, 207/244-7600, www.thurstonforlobster.com, 11am-8pm daily, market rates), which overlooks lobster boat-filled Bass Harbor. The screened dining room practically sits in the water. Also on the menu: chowders, sandwiches, and terrific desserts. Read the directions at the entrance and order before you find a table on one of two levels. Thurston's also has a full bar, with a huge stone hearth, deck, and roll-up walls that allow as much or as little of the weather in as necessary. It's an extremely popular place to relax with a drink overlooking the sighworthy harbor.

Eat, drink, and be messy is the slogan at **Beal's Lobster Pier** (182 Clark Point Rd., Southwest Harbor, 207/244-3202, www.bealslobster.com, 11am-9pm daily). Go for the lobster, but if you're traveling with landlubbers, there are burgers, fried fish, salads, sandwiches, and even veggie burgers on the menu. There's also a kids' menu. Both sheltered and outdoor seating is available on the wharf.

Vintage burger-joint-style takeout meets lobster shack at **Charlotte's Legendary Lobster Pound** (465 Seawall Rd./Rte. 102A, Southwest Harbor, 207/244-8021, www.charlotteslegendarylobsters.com, 11am-8:30pm daily), an order-at-the-window, eat-on-picnic-tables spot that earns raves for its lobster and lobster rolls. And the entertainment: 1950s music, Wiffle ball, deer that regularly roam in the fields, and Nigerian dwarf goats.

Quick Bites

Pick up picnic fare at **Sawyer's Market** (344 Main St., Southwest Harbor, 207/244-3315, 5:30am-8pm daily in summer). For wine, cheese, and gourmet goodies, head across the street to **Sawyer's Specialties** (353 Main St., Southwest Harbor, 207/244-3317, 9am-6pm Mon.-Sat.). For reasonably priced all-hours takeout fare including pizzas, prepared dinners, sandwiches, and more, head into **Gott's Store** (111 Bass Harbor Rd., Southwest Harbor, 207/244-3431, 3:30am-10pm daily).

Here's a breakfast you can feel good about: **Common Good Café** (19 Clark Point Rd., Southwest Harbor, 207/244-3007, www.commongoodsoupkitchen.org, 7:30am-11:30am Tues.-Sun., donation) offers a self-serve buffet comprising hot popovers, slow-simmered steel-cut oatmeal, tea, and coffee, along with accompaniments including maple syrup and plain and flavored butters. Most seating is outdoors. The volunteer-run program raises funds for the Common Good Soup Kitchen Community, which distributes free soup to shut-ins, offers a winter community meal, and oversees a winter clothing program, among other things. Be as generous as you can in your donation; remember just one popover with tea is about $12 at the Jordan Pond House, while here you can eat as many as you like. That said, no one monitors it, and if you're on a tight budget, just give what you can. Every penny is appreciated. You might also consider picking up a package of the popover mix.

Island Bound Treats (302 Main St., Southwest Harbor, 207/266-3253, 9:30am-2pm Mon.-Sat.) makes scrumptious tripleberry, strawberry rhubarb, and blueberry pies.

Some of the island's most creative sandwiches and pizza toppings emerge from **Little Notch Cafe** (340 Main St., Southwest Harbor, 207/244-3357, 8am-9pm daily, $9-20), next to the library in Southwest Harbor's downtown. Also available are Little Notch Bakery's famed breads, a couple of pasta choices, and homemade soups, stews, and chowders.

College of the Atlantic students run **Beech Hill Farm** (171 Beech Hill Rd., Mount Desert, 207/244-5204, 9am-4pm Tues.-Sat.), a 73-acre property with Maine Organic Farmers and Gardeners Association-certified organic gardens. Also here are acres of heirloom apple trees as well as forestland. Visit the farm stand for fresh produce as well as other organic or natural foods including cheeses and baked goods.

Family Favorites

Good chowders, sandwiches, fried clams, lobster rolls, and even pizza are served at the cozy **Quietside Cafe** (360 Main St., Southwest Harbor, 207/244-9444, 11am-10pm Mon.-Sat., 11am-8pm Sun., $6-18), with seating indoors or on picnic tables outside. Do save room for Frances's sky-high homemade blueberry and key lime pies.

Café Dry Dock (357 Main St., Southwest Harbor, 207/244-5842, www.cafedrydockinn.com, 11am-9:30pm daily, $10-25) earns kudos for longevity—it's been here for more than 30 years—as well as its reliably good food and service. Just skip the fries, which are baked. Dine inside or on the deck. There's usually live music on Wednesday evenings.

Casual Dining

Good food, good coffee, and good wine complement the Mediterranean-influenced menu at **Sips** (4 Clark Point Rd., Southwest Harbor,

207/244-4550, www.sipsmdi.com, 7am-9pm Mon.-Sat., 7am-noon Sun.), a congenial place. Small- and large-plate and tapas-style choices range $8-28; the risottos are especially good. A children's menu is available.

New American is the specialty at **Coda** (18 Village Green Way, Southwest Harbor, 207/244-8133, www.codasouthwestharbor.com, from 5pm Mon.-Sat., $14-35), where everything is made from scratch. There's often live entertainment.

Sure, there's seating inside the harbor-hugging **Seafood Ketch Restaurant** (47 Shore Rd., Bass Harbor, 207/244-7463, www.seafoodketch.com, 11am-10pm daily), but aim for a table on the patio so you can watch the lobster boats go to and fro. There are a few "landlubber delights," but the menu favors fresh seafood dishes—including the baked lobster-seafood casserole, a recipe requested by *Gourmet* magazine. Most entrées run $20-28, but sandwiches and lighter fare are available. This is a prime family spot, with a kids' menu and also a gluten-free menu. In early summer, be sure to bring bug dope if sitting outside. Follow signs for the Swans Island ferry terminal.

Fine Dining

Red sky at night, diners delight: Gold walls, artwork, wood floors, and a giant hearth set a chic tone for **Red Sky** (14 Clark Point Rd., 207/244-0476, www.redskyrestaurant.com, 5:30pm-9pm Wed.-Mon., entrées $24-35), one of the island's tonier restaurants. The creative fare emphasizes fresh seafood, hand-cut meats, and local organic produce; there's always a vegetarian choice.

ACCOMMODATIONS

Inns

If you're pining for the "old Maine," stay at the **Claremont Hotel** (22 Claremont Rd., Southwest Harbor, 207/244-5036 or 800/244-5036, www.theclaremonthotel.com), an elegant, oceanfront grande dame dressed in mustard-yellow clapboard with a spectacular six-acre hilltop setting overlooking Somes Sound. Dating from 1884, the main building has 24 guest rooms, most of them refurbished yet pleasantly old-fashioned and neither fussy nor fancy; if you want techie frills, go elsewhere. Additional guest rooms are in the Phillips House, Rowse House, and Cole Cottage. Rates for guest rooms begin around $135 in spring and fall and rise as high as $315 in August and include a buffet breakfast. Also on the premises are 14 cottages ($325-645). Guests have access to croquet courts, a clay tennis court, one-speed cruiser bikes, rowboats, and a library. The most popular time here is the first week in August, during the annual Claremont Croquet Classic. Children are welcome.

Bed-and-Breakfasts

Most of Southwest Harbor's bed-and-breakfasts are clustered downtown, along Main Street and the Clark Point Road.

Built in 1884, the mansard-roofed Victorian **Inn at Southwest** (371 Main St./Rte. 102, Southwest Harbor, 207/244-3835, www.innatsouthwest.com, $160-235) has 13 dormers and a wraparound wicker-furnished veranda. Seven 2nd- and 3rd-floor guest rooms—named for Maine lighthouses and full of character—are decorated with a mix of contemporary and antique furnishings. Breakfast and afternoon sweets are included.

Comfortable, spacious rooms, many with water views, welcome guests to the **Clark Point Inn** (109 Clark Point Rd., Southwest Harbor, 207/2440-9828, www.clarkpointinn.com, $169-249). The location is steps from the ferry dock and an easy walk to downtown. A multicourse breakfast and evening sweets are provided. It's open year-round.

The elegant Queen Anne **Kingsleigh Inn 1904** (373 Main St., Southwest Harbor, 207/244-5302, www.kingsleighinn.com, $195-325) has eight rooms, some with private harbor-facing decks, on three floors. The best splurge is the Turret Suite, with a fireplace,

1: Thurston's Lobster Pound **2:** Birches Bed and Breakfast

1
2

private deck, and a telescope trained on the harbor. Breakfast and afternoon refreshments are included, and homemade chocolates and port wine are replenished daily in guest rooms.

The linden-blossom fragrance can be intoxicating in summer at the **Lindenwood Inn** (118 Clark Point Rd., Southwest Harbor, 207/244-5335 or 800/307-5335, www.lindenwoodinn.com, $189-349). The inn's 15 guest rooms, split between two buildings, and poolside bungalow are decorated in a sophisticated yet comfortable style. After you hike Acadia's trails, the heated pool and hot tub are especially welcome, and after that, perhaps enjoy a drink while shooting pool or playing darts. Some guest rooms have harbor views.

Even glimpsed through the trees from the road, the ★ **Birches Bed and Breakfast** (46 Fernald Point Rd., Southwest Harbor, 207/244-5182, www.thebirchesbnb.com, from $269) is appealing. A wooded drive winds down to the large home facing the ocean, near the mouth of Somes Sound. It's just 350 yards to the Causeway Golf Club and a short walk to the Flying Mountain trailhead and Valley Cove fire road with access to the Acadia and St. Sauveur trails. Built as a summer cottage in 1916, the Birches retains that casual summer ease, right down to the stone fireplace in the living room and the croquet court on the lawn. Guest rooms are especially large and comfortably decorated; most have water views, and one has a sleeping porch. Innkeeper Susi Homer, whose grandfather built this magical retreat, treats guests like family. Her breakfasts and itinerary planning are legendary. A five-bedroom, pet-friendly cottage also is available. Open year-round; advance reservations required off-season.

Set on a corner, well back from Clark Point Road, is ★ **Harbour Cottage Inn** (9 Dirigo Rd., Southwest Harbor, 207/244-5738 or 888/843-3022, www.harbourcottageinn.com, from $269). Built in 1870 as the annex for the island's first hotel, it's now a lovely bed-and-breakfast with eight guest rooms and three suites decorated in a colorful and fun cottage style. Some guest rooms have jetted baths and/or fireplaces. Rates include a multicourse breakfast. Also part of Harbour Cottage is **Pier One,** which offers five truly waterfront updated suites (from $1,605/week), including a studio cottage; shorter stays are often available. Guests of Pier One have private use of a 150-foot pier, and they can dock or launch canoes, kayaks, or other small boats from right outside their doors; dockage is available for larger boats. It's all within walking distance of downtown.

Each of the four spacious oceanview guest rooms at **Ann's Point Inn** (79 Ann's Point Rd., Bass Harbor, 207/244-9595, www.annspointinn.com, from $355) has a king bed covered in luxurious linens, a gas fireplace, and all the amenities you might expect, including robes and slippers. The inn, sited on a private waterfront lot at the tip of Ann's Point, pampers guests with a hot tub and a sauna, plus afternoon hors d'oeuvres and evening sweets. Even better, the inn's green and sustainable practices include solar-powered electricity and hot water and garden-fresh fare at breakfast. All this is on two acres with 690 feet of shorefront, from which you can watch eagles soar and lobster boats at work.

Motels and Cottages

Smack on the harbor and just a two-minute walk from downtown is the appropriately named **Harbor View Motel & Cottages** (11 Ocean Way, Southwest Harbor, 207/244-5031, www.harborviewmotelandcottages.com). The family-owned complex comprises motel rooms ($100-250/night or $610-950/week) spread out in two older, somewhat dowdy one-story buildings and a newer three-story structure fronting the harbor. A meager continental breakfast is served to motel guests July to early September. Also on the premises are housekeeping cottages and an apartment ($150-210/night or $850-1380/week), ranging from studios to two-bedrooms. Pets are welcome in some units ($10/day or $60/week).

Directly across from the famed seawall and adjacent to the park, the **Seawall Motel**

(566 Seawall Rd./Rte. 102A, Southwest Harbor, 207/244-9250 or 800/248-9250, www.seawallmotel.com, $140) is a no-surprises two-story motel (upstairs guest rooms have the best views). Kids 12 and younger stay free, and there's a laundry. The location is primo for bird-watchers. A hearty continental breakfast buffet is included.

Bass Harbor Cottages and Country Inn (95 Harbor Dr./Rte. 102A, Bass Harbor, 207/244-3460, www.bassharborcottages.com) fronts on Bass Harbor. Accommodations are basic but clean; there's no maid service. The sturdy white home has three guest rooms ($159-279). Also on the premises are a number of rustic cottages and suites (from $159 daily, $1,600 weekly).

Cottage Rentals

L. S. Robinson Co. (337 Main St., Southwest Harbor, 207/244-5563, www.lsrobinson.com) has an extensive list of cottage rentals in the area. The Southwest Harbor/Tremont Chamber of Commerce (329 Main St., Southwest Harbor, 207/244-9264 or 800/423-9264, www.acadiachamber.com) also keeps a helpful listing of privately owned homes and cottages available for rent.

Camping

Acadia National Park's Seawall Campground is on this side of the island.

Built on the site of an old quarry, on a hillside descending to rocky frontage on Somes Sound, **Somes Sound View Campground** (86 Hall Quarry Rd., Mount Desert, 207/244-3890, off-season 207/244-7452, www.ssvc.info, late May-mid-Oct., $30-70) is among the smallest campgrounds on the island, with about 60 sites, most geared to tents and vans. Rustic camping cabins and glamping tents are $70-90 per night. Facilities include hot showers (if you're camping on the lowest levels it's a good hike up to the bathhouse), a heated pool, a boat launch, kayak, canoe, and paddleboat rentals, and a fishing dock. You can swim in the sound from a rocky beach. Leashed pets are allowed. It's two miles south and east of Somesville and a mile east of Route 102.

The **Smuggler's Den Campground** (Rte. 102, Southwest Harbor, 207/244-3944, www.smugglersdencampground.com, $40-75) is a midsized, pet-friendly campground between Echo Lake and downtown Southwest Harbor. Trails access back roads to Echo Lake (1.25 miles) and Long Pond (1 mile) as well as 25 miles of Acadia National Park trails. Big-rig sites are grouped in the top third, pop-ups and small campers are in the middle third, and tenting sites are in the lower third and in the woods rimming the large recreation field. Also available are cabins ($625 camping, $1,375 with kitchen and bath, per week). Facilities include a laundry, free hot showers, Wi-Fi, a heated pool and kiddie pool, and a four-acre recreation field with horseshoe pits, half-court basketball, and lawn games.

On the eastern edge of Somesville, just off Route 198 at the head of Somes Sound, the ★ **Mount Desert Campground** (516 Somes Sound Dr./Rte. 198, Somesville, 207/244-3710, www.mountdesertcampground.com, $39-70) is centrally located for visiting Bar Harbor, Acadia, and the whole western side of Mount Desert Island. The campground has 152 wooded tent sites, about 45 on the water, spread out on 58 acres. Reservations are essential in midsummer—one-week minimum for waterfront sites, three days for off-water sites in July-August. (Campers book a year ahead for waterfront sites here.) This popular and low-key campground gets high marks for maintenance, noise control, and convenient tent platforms. Another plus is the Gathering Place, where campers can relax, play games, use free Wi-Fi, and purchase coffee and fresh-baked treats or ice cream. No pets are allowed July-early September, and no trailers over 20 feet are permitted. Kayak, canoe, and stand-up paddleboard rentals are available.

INFORMATION AND SERVICES

The **Southwest Harbor/Tremont Chamber of Commerce** (329 Main St.,

Southwest Harbor, 207/244-9264 or 800/423-9264, www.acadiachamber.com) stocks brochures, maps, menus, and other local info.

In downtown Southwest Harbor, **public restrooms** are at the southern end of the parking lot behind the Main Street park and near the fire station. There are portable toilets at the town docks and at the Swans Island ferry terminal in Bass Harbor.

GETTING THERE AND AROUND

Southwest Harbor is about 13 miles or 25 minutes via Routes 198 and 102 from Northeast Harbor. It's about 14 miles or 25 minutes to Bar Harbor.

Southwest Harbor, Tremont, and Bass Harbor are serviced by Route No. 7 (Southwest Harbor) of the Island Explorer bus system.

Islands Near Mount Desert

TOP EXPERIENCE

Sure, Mount Desert is an island, but for a sampling of real island life, you'll want to make a day trip to one of the offshore islands. Most popular are the **Cranberry Isles** and **Swans Island,** but don't overlook **Frenchboro,** an off-the-radar gem.

CRANBERRY ISLES

The **Cranberry Isles** (pop. 141), south of Northeast and Seal Harbors, comprise Great Cranberry, Little Cranberry (called Islesford), Sutton, Baker, and Bear Islands. Islesford and Baker include property belonging to Acadia National Park. Bring a bike to explore the narrow, mostly level roads on the two largest islands, Great Cranberry and Islesford, but remember to respect private property. Unless you've asked permission, do not cut across private land to reach the shore.

The Cranberry name has been attributed to 18th-century loyalist governor Francis Bernard, who received these islands along with all of Mount Desert as a king's grant in 1762. Cranberry bogs (now long gone) on the two largest islands evidently caught his attention. Permanent European settlers arrived in the 1760s, and there was even steamboat service by the 1820s.

Lobstering and other fishing industries are the commercial mainstays, boosted in summer by the various visitor-related pursuits. Artists and writers come for a week, a month, or longer; day-trippers spend time on Great Cranberry and Islesford. There are no inns on either.

Largest of the islands is **Great Cranberry,** with a general store, a small historical museum with a café, and a gift shop, but not much else except pretty views. Public restrooms are located near the dock and at the museum.

The second-largest island is **Little Cranberry,** locally known as Islesford. It's easy to spend the better part of a day here exploring. Begin at the **Islesford Historical Museum** (207/288-3338, www.nps.gov/acad, free), operated by the National Park Service. The exhibits focus on local history, much of it maritime, so displays include ship models, household goods, fishing gear, and other memorabilia. Also on Islesford are a handful of galleries and a general store. Public restrooms are near the museum.

For lunch, bring a picnic or head to the **Islesford Dock** (207/244-7494, http://islesforddock.com, 11am-3pm and 5pm-9pm Tues.-Fri., 10am-3pm and 5pm-9pm Sat.-Sun. July-Aug., $13-32), where views across to Acadia's mountains are incredible, especially at sunset. A kids' menu is available.

1: passenger ferry bound for the Cranberry Isles **2:** Isleford Dock restaurant **3:** Islesford Historical Museum

1
2
3
National Park Service
U.S. Department of the Interior
Islesford
Historical Museum
Acadia National Park

Day Trip to Frenchboro, Long Island

Since Maine has more Long Islands than anyone cares to count, most of them have other labels for easy identification. Here's a case in point—a Long Island known universally as Frenchboro, the name of the village that wraps around Lunts Harbor. With a year-round population hovering around 60, Frenchboro has had ferry service only since 1960. Since then, the island has acquired phone service, electricity, and satellite TV, but don't expect to notice much of that when you get here. One of only 15 Maine coastal islands that still supports a year-round population, Frenchboro is an especially quiet place, where islanders live as islanders always have—making a living from the sea and being proud of it. Frenchboro is the subject of *Hauling by Hand,* a fascinating, well-researched "biography" published in 1999 by eighth-generation islander Dean Lunt.

In 1999, when roughly half of the island (914 acres, including 5.5 miles of shorefront) went up for sale by a private owner, an incredible fund-raising effort collected nearly $3 million, allowing purchase of the land in 2000 by the Maine Coast Heritage Trust. Some of the funding helped restore the village's church and one-room schoolhouse. Since then, thanks to a gift from David Rockefeller, it's expanded to include Rich's Head, adding 192 acres and three miles of shoreline. Visitors now have access to more than 10 miles of hiking trails, though take heed: most are rustic and unmarked. Today the preserve comprises 1,159 acres—more than 80 percent of the island, including about eight miles of shoreline. You can download an island map from Maine Coast Heritage Trust (www.mcht.org), which owns the preserve, or pick up one at the museum. No camping or fires are permitted.

Frenchboro is a delightful day trip. A good way to get a sense of the place is to take the 3.5-hour lunch cruise run by captain Ian Strauss of **Island Cruises** (Little Island Marine, Shore Rd., Bass Harbor, 207/244-5785, www.bassharborcruises.com). For an even longer day trip to Frenchboro, plan to take the passenger ferry *R. L. Gott* during her weekly run for the Maine State Ferry Service. Each Friday early April-late October, the *R. L. Gott* departs Bass Harbor at 8am, arriving in Frenchboro at 9am. The return trip to Bass Harbor is at 6pm, allowing nine hours on the island. The **Maine State Ferry Service** (207/244-3254, daily recorded info 800/491-4883, http://maine.gov/mdot/ferry/frenchboro) uses the ferry *Captain Henry Lee,* the same vessel used on the Swans Island route, for service to Frenchboro on Wednesday, Thursday, and Sunday, but none of these trips allows any time on the island.

When you go, take a picnic with you, or stop at **Lunt's Dockside Deli** (207/334-2902, http://luntsdeli.com, 11am-3pm), open only in July-August. It's a very casual establishment—order at the window, grab a picnic table, and wait for your name to be called. Lobster rolls and fish chowder are the specialties, but there are plenty of other choices, including sandwiches, hot dogs, and even vegetable wraps. Of course, you can get lobster too. Prices are low, the view is wonderful, and you might even get to watch lobsters being unloaded from a boat.

The **Frenchboro Historical Society Museum** (207/334-2924, www.frenchboro.lib.me.us, free), just up from the dock, has interesting old tools, other local artifacts, and a small gift shop with mostly island-made goods. It's usually open afternoons Memorial Day-Labor Day. The island has a network of easy and not-so-easy maintained trails through the woods and along the shore; some can be squishy, and some are along boulder-strewn beachfront. The trails are rustic, and most are unmarked, so proceed carefully. In the center of the island is a beaver pond. There's a restroom above the Dockside Deli and two others near the museum.

Every year since 1961, on the second Saturday of August, Frenchboro hosts its annual **Lobster Festival** (www.frenchboro-dinner.org), a midday meal comprising lobster, chicken salad, hot dogs, coleslaw, homemade pies, and more, served rain or shine, with proceeds benefiting a local cause. Islanders and hundreds of visitors gather in the village for the occasion, which also includes live music, the All the Road We Got footrace (almost 5K), children's games, a raffle, silent auction, and more. The Maine State Ferry makes a special run that day.

Getting There

Do call to confirm current ferry schedules, as online versions aren't always accurate.

Beal and Bunker (207/244-3575) provides year-round mail and passenger boat service to the Cranberries from Northeast Harbor. The schedule makes it possible to do both islands in one day. The summer season, with more frequent trips, runs late June-Labor Day. The boats make a variety of stops on the three-island route (including Sutton in summer), so be patient as they make the circuit. It's a people-watching treat. If you just did a round-trip and stayed aboard, the loop would take about 1.5 hours. Round-trip tickets (covering the whole loop, including intra-island trips if you want to visit both Great Cranberry and Islesford) are $32 adults, $16 ages 3-11, free under age 3. Bicycles are $8 round-trip. The off-season schedule operates early May-mid-June and early September-mid-October; the winter schedule runs mid-October-April. In winter, the boat company advises phoning ahead on what Mainers quaintly call "weather days."

The **Cranberry Cove Ferry** (upper town dock, Clark Point Rd., Southwest Harbor, 207/244-5882, cell 207/460-1981, www.downeastwindjammer.com) operates a summertime service to the Cranberries mid-May-mid-October. The ferry route begins at the upper town dock (Clark Point Rd.) in Southwest Harbor and makes stops in Manset and Great Cranberry before reaching Islesford an hour later and reversing the itinerary; it's two hours total if you stay on the boat. (Stops at Sutton can be arranged.) In summer (July-Aug.) there are six daily round-trips, with fewer trips in June and September. Round-trip fares are $32 adults, $22 children, $8 bicycles.

SWANS ISLAND

Six miles off Mount Desert Island lies scenic, roughly 7,000-acre **Swans Island** (pop. 332; www.swansisland.org), named after Col. James Swan, who bought it and two dozen other islands as an investment in 1786. As with the Cranberries, fishing is the year-round way of life here, with lobstering being the primary occupation. In summer the population practically triples with the arrival of artists, writers, and other seasonal visitors. The island has no campsites, few public restrooms, and only a handful of guest rooms. Visitors who want to spend more than a day tend to rent cottages by the week.

You'll need either a bicycle or a car to get around on the island, as the ferry comes in on one side and the village center is on the other. Should you choose to bring a car, it's wise to make reservations for the ferry, especially for the return trip. Bicycling is a good way to get around, but be forewarned that the roads are narrow, lack shoulders, and are hilly in spots.

Sights include the **Swans Island Lobster & Marine Museum** (Ferry Rd., 207/244-3254, http://swansislandlobsterandmarinemuseum.org, 11am-3pm Mon.-Fri. June-late Sept., donation) and **Lighthouse Park/Hockamock Head Light** (207/526-4025, www.burntcoatharborlight.com), where you'll find hiking trails. A one-bedroom apartment in the keeper's house is available for weekly rental (www.swansislandvacations.com/Lighthouse.html, $1,000).

A Swans Island summer highlight is the **Sweet Chariot Music Festival,** a three-night midweek extravaganza in early August geared to boaters.

Overnight accommodations are available at the **Harbor Watch Inn** (111 Minturn Rd., 207/526-4563 or 800/532-7928, www.swansisland.com, $115-195) and the **Carter House** (207/266-0958 or 207/526-4198, $95). For sustenance, try **TIMS, The Island Market & Supply** (40 North Rd., 207/526-4043, www.tims-swans-island.com).

Getting There and Around

Swans Island is a six-mile, 40-minute trip on the state-operated car ferry *Captain Henry Lee,* operated by the **Maine State Ferry Service** (207/244-3254, daily recorded info 800/491-4883, http://maine.gov/mdot/ferry/swansisland). The ferry makes up to six round-trips a day, the first from Bass

Harbor at 7:30am Monday-Saturday and at 9am Sunday, and the last from Swans Island at 4:30pm. From June through September, round-trip tickets are $17.50 adults and $6.25 ages 6-17; bikes are $22.50 round-trip adult bike, $16.25 child bike; cars are $38.50 plus $12 reservation fee. Only four reservations are accepted for vehicles; be in line at least 15 minutes before departure or you risk forfeiting your space.

To reach the Bass Harbor ferry terminal on Mount Desert Island, follow the distinctive blue signs, marked Swans Island Ferry, along Routes 102 and 102A.

Southwest Cycle (Main St., Southwest Harbor, 207/244-5856 or 800/649-5856) rents bikes by the day and week and is open year-round. It also has ferry schedules and Swans Island maps. For the early-morning ferry, you'll need to pick up bikes the day before; be sure to reserve them if you're doing this in July-August.

Schoodic Peninsula

Slightly more than 2,366 of Acadia National Park's acres are on the mainland Schoodic Peninsula; the rest are all on islands, including Mount Desert. World-class scenery and the relative lack of congestion, even at the height of summer, are just two reasons to sneak around to the eastern side of Frenchman Bay. Other reasons are abundant opportunities for outdoor recreation, two scenic byways, and dozens of artists' and artisans' studios tucked throughout this region.

Still, the biggest attractions in this area are the spectacular vignettes and vistas—of offshore lighthouses, distant mountains, and close-in islands—and the unchanged villages. **Winter Harbor** (pop. 516), known best as the gateway to Schoodic, shares the area with an old-money, low-profile, Philadelphia-linked summer colony on exclusive Grindstone Neck.

Gouldsboro (pop. 1,737), including the not-to-be-missed villages of **Birch Harbor, Corea,** and **Prospect Harbor,** earned its own minor fame from Louise Dickinson Rich's 1958 book *The Peninsula,* a tribute to her summers on Corea's Cranberry Point, "a place that has stood still in time." Since 1958, change has crept into Corea, but not so as you'd notice. It's still the same quintessential lobster-fishing community, perfect for photo ops. A new section of the Maine Coastal Islands National Wildlife Reserve, the 431-acre **Corea Heath Unit,** has taken over former navy lands along Route 195 in Corea. In another initiative, the Frenchman Bay Conservancy acquired the 600-acre Northern Corea Heath, across the highway from the Corea Heath Unit and home to Grand Marsh and Grand Marsh Bay.

Between Ellsworth and Gouldsboro are **Hancock** (pop. 2,394), **Sullivan** (pop. 1,236), and **Sorrento** (pop. 274). Venture down the oceanside back roads and you'll discover an old-timey summer colony at Hancock Point.

Meander inland to find the **Donnell Pond Public Reserved Land,** a spectacular chunk of mostly undeveloped lakes for boating and fishing, peaks for hiking, and even a beach for camping.

TOP EXPERIENCE

SCHOODIC SECTION OF ACADIA NATIONAL PARK

The smaller and less touristed Schoodic section of Acadia isn't as overpowering as that on Mount Desert, but it's no less powerful. Even though it's on the mainland, it feels more remote, and the landscape has a raw edge, with too-frequent fog shrouding the stunted and scraggly spruce clinging to its pink granite shores.

As with so much of Acadia's acreage on

Scenic Byways

The Schoodic region boasts not one but two designated scenic byways: the **Schoodic National Scenic Byway,** which wraps around the peninsula, and the **Blackwoods Scenic Byway,** an inland blue highway cutting through the Donnell Pond Public Reserved Land. If time permits, drive at least one of these routes. Ideally, you'd do both, because the scenery differs greatly. The best option is to connect the two via Route 1, creating a loop that includes lakes and forests, mountains and fields, ocean and rocky coast. If you have only one day to explore this region, this route takes in the best of it. In early to mid-October, when the fall foliage is at its peak, the vistas are especially stunning.

The 29-mile Schoodic National Scenic Byway stretches from Hancock on Route 1 to Gouldsboro and then south on Route 186 and around the Schoodic Peninsula, ending in Prospect Harbor. A detailed guide is available at www.schoodicbyway.org. Along the route are seven outdoor **Kids Quest** sites designed to engage families in the region's history, culture, and ecology. A detailed guide is available at www.schoodicbyway.org.

The 12.5-mile Blackwoods Scenic Byway moseys along Route 182 inland of Route 1, from Franklin to Cherryfield. It slices through the Donnell Pond Public Reserved Land, edges lakes and mountains, and passes through small villages. You'll find access to trailheads and boat launches at Donnell Pond and Tunk Lake. Blueberry barrens, which turn crimson in autumn, can be seen on the rolling hills around Franklin and Cherryfield. Although Cherryfield is beyond the Schoodic region, it's a beautiful town to visit, filled with stately Victorian homes. It's also the self-proclaimed wild blueberry capital of the world. Maps and information are available at www.blackwoodsbyway.org.

Mount Desert Island, the Schoodic section became part of the park largely because of the deft diplomacy and perseverance of George B. Dorr. In 1928, when local landowners objected to donating their acreage to a national park tagged with the Lafayette name (geopolitics being involved at the time), Dorr managed to obtain congressional approval for the 1929 name change to Acadia National Park, with Schoodic among the lands included.

To reach the park boundary from Route 1 in Gouldsboro, take Route 186 south to Winter Harbor. Continue through town, heading east, and then turn right and continue to the park entrance sign, just before the bridge over Mosquito Harbor.

You can also tour the park using the free Island Explorer bus, which circulates through Winter Harbor, around the Schoodic Loop, and on to Prospect Harbor, with stops along the way.

★ Schoodic Loop

The major sights of Acadia's Schoodic section lie along the six-mile one-way road that meanders counterclockwise around the tip of the Schoodic Peninsula. You'll discover official and unofficial picnic areas, hiking trailheads, offshore lighthouses, a welcome center with exhibits, and turnouts with scenic vistas. Also named the Park Loop Road, it's best referred to as the Schoodic Loop, to distinguish it from the one on Mount Desert Island. Begin at the **Schoodic Woods Campground Welcome Center,** where you can pick up information and, should you choose, leave your car to explore via bicycle or the Island Explorer bus.

While a car may seem the most convenient way to see the sights, you'll actually be better served looping via bicycle (rentals available at the ferry dock or near the park entry road) or by riding the bus. This section of the park is gaining in popularity, and the increase in cars is straining the designated parking areas along the loop. Once you're on the one-way section, parking is allowed only in designated pull-offs and parking lots, and these often are filled. With a bike, you can stop where and when you want. The bus picks up at non-designated stops, if you flag it down. If driving, be especially vigilant around bicyclists; many families include young or novice cyclers, and if you see a viewpoint you like with room to pull off, stop; it's a long way around to return. Note: Neither RVs nor trailers are allowed on the loop beyond the campground.

The first landmark is **Frazer Point Picnic Area,** with lovely vistas, picnic tables, and wheelchair-accessible restrooms. Other spots are fine for picnics, but this is the only official one. The area takes its name from Thomas Frazer, a free African American and the first recorded nonnative resident of Winter Harbor. He operated a saltworks here and was listed in the 1790 census. From here, the road becomes one-way. No parking is allowed in the right lane.

From this side of Frenchman Bay, the views of Mount Desert Island's summits are gorgeous, rising beyond islands sprinkled here and there.

Drive 1.5 miles from the picnic area to **Raven's Head,** an unmarked, Thunder Hole-type cliff with sheer drops to the churning surf below and fabulous views. There are no fences, and the cliffs are eroded, so it's not a good place for little ones. The trail is unsigned, but there's a small pullout on the left side of the road opposite it. Be extremely careful here, stay on the path (the environment is very fragile and erosion is a major problem), and stay well away from the cliff's edge.

At 2.2 miles past the picnic area, watch for a narrow, unpaved road on the left, across from an open beach vista. It winds for one mile (keep left at the fork) up to a tiny parking circle, from which you can follow the trail (signposted Schoodic Trails) to the open ledges on 440-foot **Schoodic Head.** From the circle, there's already a glimpse of the view, but it gets much better. If you bear right at the fork, you'll come to a grassy parking area with access to the Alder Trail (over to the Blueberry Hill parking lot) and the Schoodic Head Trail.

Continue on the Schoodic Loop Road and hang a right onto a short, two-way spur to **Schoodic Point.** On your right is the **Schoodic Institute** campus (207/288-1310, www.sercinstitute.org), on the site of a former top-secret U.S. Navy base that became part of the park in 2002. At the entrance is a small info center (with ADA-accessible restroom), staffed by volunteers and park rangers. Continue up the road to the restored **Rockefeller Welcome Center** (10am-4pm daily late May-mid-Oct., 10am-4pm Mon.-Fri. mid-Oct.-late May). Inside are exhibits highlighting Schoodic's ecology and history, the former navy base's radio and cryptologic operations, and current research programs. The Schoodic Institute also offers ranger-led activities, lectures by researchers or nationally known experts addressing environmental topics related to the park and its surroundings, and other programs and events. Check the online calendar for current opportunities.

Continue out to **Schoodic Point,** the highlight of the drive, with surf crashing onto big slabs of pink granite. Be extremely cautious here; chances of rescue are slim if a rogue wave sweeps someone offshore. In peak season, you may have to make a loop or two of the parking lot to score a space. Alternatively, park at the Schoodic Institute and walk 0.4 mile to the point.

From Schoodic Point, return to the Loop Road. Look to the right and you'll see Little Moose Island, which can be accessed at low tide. Be careful, though, not to get stranded here—ask at the info center for safe crossing times. Continue about one mile past the Schoodic Point/Loop Road intersection to the **Blueberry Hill** parking area, a moorlike setting where the low growth allows almost 180-degree views of the bay and islands. There are a few trails in this area—all eventually converging on **Schoodic Head,** the highest point on the peninsula. (Don't confuse this with Schoodic Mountain, which is well north of here.) Across and up the road a bit is the trailhead for the 180-foot-high **Anvil**

Educating for the Future

The Schoodic section of Acadia National Park is well on the way to becoming a world-class center for the study of science and nature, thanks to a history of benefactors dating back to the early 19th century. Maine native and Wall Street tycoon John G. Moore once owned most of Schoodic Point. In 1927, George Dorr persuaded Moore's heirs to donate the land to the Hancock County Trustees of Public Reservations, with the stipulation that the land be used as a public park and for the "promotion of biological and other scientific research." Seven years later, more than 2,000 acres of the peninsula were donated to Acadia National Park.

The timing was perfect. John D. Rockefeller Jr. was working with the National Park Service to construct the Park Loop Road on Mount Desert Island. The U.S. Naval Radio Station on Otter Point was in the way, so Rockefeller, working with Dorr, helped the National Park Service collaborate with the U.S. Navy to relocate the station to Schoodic Point. Six buildings were constructed. Most noteworthy is Rockefeller Hall, a French Norman Revival-style mansion designed by New York architect Grosvenor Atterbury, who used a similar design for the park's carriage road gatehouses on Mount Desert Island.

In 1935, the U.S. Naval Radio Station at Schoodic Point was commissioned, and by the late 20th century, the 100-acre campus comprised more than 35 buildings and was home to 350 employees. When the station closed in 2002, the land was returned to the park for use as a research and education center.

It took 10 years and millions of dollars to transform the former navy base. The campus now offers housing and dining facilities for individual researchers, groups, and conferences; classrooms; laboratories; and a modern 124-seat auditorium, all in the inspirational setting of Schoodic Point. A renovated Rockefeller Hall, listed in the National Register of Historic Places, now serves as Schoodic's welcome center, with exhibits highlighting Schoodic's ecology and history, the former navy base's radio and cryptologic operations, and current research programs. Credit for the renovations goes to local benefactor Edith Robb Dixon, who donated $1 million in the name of her late husband, Fitz Eugene Dixon Jr.

Schoodic Institute at Acadia National Park (207/288-1310, www.schoodicinstitute.org) is the nonprofit that partners with Acadia to manage the campus and advance science and education throughout the park and the region. Schoodic Institute connects education with research, while managers at Acadia National Park rely on the research to restore Acadia's ecosystems and improve their resiliency in the face of rapid environmental changes.

The Schoodic Institute offers education and research programs aimed not only at scientists and researchers but also at students and teachers. The institute also hosts Acadia National Park's artist-in-residence program and works with the park to present programs, lectures, special events, and ranger-led activities; check the online calendar for current offerings. Among these are "bio blitzes," in which teams of specialists and volunteers research the park's flora and fauna in minute detail. In 2013-2014, a two-year blitz focused on beetles found more than 100 species never previously identified in the park.

headland; a pullout on the right side holds about three cars.

As you continue along this stretch of road, keep your eyes peeled for eagles, which frequently soar here. There's a nest on the northern end of Rolling Island; you can see it with binoculars from some of the roadside pullouts.

From Blueberry Hill, continue 1.2 miles to a pullout for the East Trail, the shortest and most direct route to Schoodic Head. From here, it's about another mile to the park exit, in Wonsqueak Harbor. It's another two miles to the intersection with Route 186 in Birch Harbor.

ENTERTAINMENT

Winter Harbor's biggest wingding is the annual **Lobster Festival** (www.acadia-schoodic.org), held the second Saturday in

Gallery Hopping in Hancock and Sullivan

From Route 1 take Eastside Road, just before the Hancock-Sullivan Bridge, and drive 1.6 miles south to the Wray family's **Gull Rock Pottery** (103 Gull Rock Rd., Hancock, 207/422-3990, www.gullrockpottery.com). Torj and Kurt Wray created this gallery, which daughter-in-law Akemi Wray now runs. She's continued crafting their wheel-thrown, hand-painted, dishwasher-safe pottery decorated with cobalt-blue-and-white Japanese-style motifs, but has added some of her own designs. Complementing the indoor gallery is an outdoor oceanfront sculpture gallery with views to Mount Desert Island.

Cross the Hancock-Sullivan Bridge and then take your first left off Route 1 onto Taunton Drive to find the next four galleries, beginning with Dan Farrenkopf's and Phid Lawless's **Lunaform** (66 Cedar Ln., Sullivan, 207/422-0923, www.lunaform.com), set amid beautifully landscaped grounds surrounding an old quarry. At first glance, it appears that many of the wonderfully aesthetic garden ornaments created here are hand-turned pottery, when in fact they're hand-turned steel-reinforced concrete. Take the first right off Taunton Drive onto Track Road, proceed 0.5 mile, then turn left onto Cedar Lane.

Return to Taunton Drive and take the next right onto Quarry Road, then a left on Whales Back Drive, a rough dirt lane, to find granite sculptor Obadiah Bourne Buell's **Stone Designs Studio and Granite Garden Gallery** (124 Whales Back Rd., Sullivan, 207/422-3111, www.stonedesignsmaine.com). Bourne displays his home accents and garden features in a self-serve gallery adjacent to a quarry and in the surrounding gardens. This really is a magical spot, and if you time it right, you might be able to see the sculptor at work.

Continue north on Taunton Road as it changes its name to South Bay Road. Bet you can't keep from smiling at the whimsical animal sculptures and fun furniture of talented sculptor-painter

August. The daylong gala includes a parade, live entertainment, lobster-boat races (a serious competition in these parts), crafts fair, games, and more crustaceans than you could ever consume.

Concerts, art classes, coffeehouses, workshops, and related activities are presented year-round by **Schoodic Arts for All** (207/963-2569, www.schoodicarts.org). Many are held at historic Hammond Hall in downtown Winter Harbor. A summer series presents monthly concerts on Friday evenings May-October. In early August, the two-week **Schoodic Arts Festival** is jam-packed with daily workshops and nightly performances for all ages.

The **Pierre Monteux School for Conductors and Orchestra Musicians** (Rte. 1, Hancock, 207/422-3280, www.monteuxschool.org), a prestigious summer program founded in 1943, has achieved international renown for training dozens of national and international classical musicians. It presents two well-attended concert series late June-July. The Wednesday series (7:30pm, $15 adults) features chamber music; the Sunday concerts (5pm, $25 adults, $5 students) feature symphonies. An annual free family concert usually is held in early to mid-July. All concerts are held in the school's Forest Studio; payment is accepted via cash or check only. At both series, kids younger than 18 admitted free with an adult.

Seeking to add more vibrancy and diversity to the peninsula's entertainment offerings and to indulge their own interests in music and the sciences, the owners of Oceanside Meadows Inn created the **Institute for the Arts and Sciences** (207/963-5557), which presents a series of Thursday-night events late June-late September, with a break during the Schoodic Arts Festival. The wide-ranging calendar includes lectures and concerts as well as art shows. Some are free; others are $10-12 in advance or $12-15 at the door.

On Monday evenings in July-August, weather permitting, the **Frenchman Bay Conservancy** (207/422-2328, www.

Philip Barter. His work is the cornerstone of the eclectic **Philip Barter Studio Gallery** (318 South Bay Rd., Sullivan, 207/422-3190, www.bartergallery.com). The gallery, open by chance or appointment, is 2.5 miles off Route 1.

Continue on South Bay Road (note that it becomes dirt for a roughly 0.5-mile section) and turn left, heading north, when it meets Route 200/Hog Bay Road. Almost immediately on your left is Charles and Susanne Grosjean's **Hog Bay Pottery** (245 Hog Bay Rd./Rte. 200, Franklin, 207/565-2282, www.hogbay.com), in operation since 1974. Inside the casual, laid-back showroom are Charles's functional, nature-themed pottery and Susanne's stunning handwoven wool rugs. Pottery seconds are often available.

Next, head south on Route 200/Bert Gray Road. Handwoven textiles are the specialty at **Moosetrack Studio** (388 Bert Gray Rd./Rte. 200, Sullivan, 207/422-9017, www.moosetrackweaving.com), where the selections range from handwoven area rugs to shawls of merino wool and silk. Camilla Stege has been weaving since 1969, and her exquisite work reflects her experience and expertise. The gallery is 1.8 miles north of Route 1.

Continue south. Just before the intersection with U.S. 1 is a double hit. Artist Paul Breeden, best known for the remarkable illustrations, calligraphy, and maps he's done for *National Geographic*, Time-Life Books, and other national and international publications, displays and sells his paintings at the **Spring Woods Gallery and Willowbrook Garden** (19 Willowbrook Ln., Sullivan, 207/422-3007, www.springwoodsgallery.com or www.willowbrookgarden.com). Also filling the handsome modern gallery space are paintings by Ann Breeden. Be sure to allow time to meander through the shady sculpture garden, where there's even a playhouse for kids.

frenchmanbay.org) presents a concert series at its Tidal Falls Preserve. Pack a picnic supper or purchase fare from a food truck. Music might include jazz, steel pan drums, ukuleles, or an orchestra.

SHOPPING

You can find just about anything at the **Winter Harbor 5 and 10** (Main St., Winter Harbor, 207/963-7927). It's the genuine article, an old-fashioned five-and-dime that's somehow still surviving in the age of Walmart.

Prospect Harbor Soap Co. (4 Duck Pond Rd. at Rte. 186, Winter Harbor, 207/963-7598, www.prospectharborsoapco.com) maintains an outlet where you can purchase lotions, handmade soaps, and other skin-care products.

Galleries

From Route 1, loop down to Winter Harbor and back up on Route 186 through Prospect Harbor to find these galleries.

An old post office houses **Lee Art Glass** (679 S. Gouldsboro Rd./Rte. 186, Gouldsboro, 207/963-7280). The fused-glass tableware is created by taking two pieces of window glass and firing them on terra-cotta or bisque molds at 1,500°F. What makes the result so appealing are the colors and the patterns—crocheted doilies or stencils—impressed into the glass. The almost magical results are beautiful and delicate-looking, yet functional.

In the village center is **Artisans & Antiques** (357 Main St., Winter Harbor, 207/963-2400), a 15-member group shop with a nice mix of craftwork and treasures.

Winter Harbor Antiques and Works of Hand (424-426 Main St., Winter Harbor, 207/963-2547) is a double treat: Antiques fill one building, and a well-chosen selection of distinctive works by local craftspeople and artists fills the other. It's across from Hammond Hall and set behind colorful, well-tended gardens.

Works by contemporary Maine artists, including noted painters and sculptors associated with the Schoodic International Sculpture Symposium, are shown in rotating shows at **Littlefield Gallery** (145 Main St., Winter Harbor, 207/963-6005, www.littlefieldgallery.com).

The folk-art funk begins on the exterior of the **Salty Dog Gallery/Hurdy Gurdy Man Antiques** (173 Main St., Prospect Harbor, 207/963-7575), a twofold find. The lower level is filled with fun folk-art vintage goods. Upstairs, owner Dean Kotula displays his fine art, documentary-style photographic prints.

Visiting the **U.S. Bells Foundry and Watering Cove Pottery** (56 W. Bay Rd./Rte. 186, Prospect Harbor, 207/963-7184, www.usbells.com) is a treat for the ears, as browsers try out the many varieties of cast-bronze bells made in the adjacent foundry by Richard Fisher. If you're lucky, he may have time to explain the process—particularly intriguing for children and a distraction from their instinctive urge to test every bell in the shop. The store also carries quilts by Richard's wife, Cindy, and wood-fired stoneware and porcelain by their daughter-in-law Liza Fisher. U.S. Bells is 0.25 mile up the hill from Prospect Harbor's post office.

Here's a nifty place: **Chapter Two** (611 Corea Rd., Corea, 207/963-7269, www.chaptertwocorea.com) is home to Spurling House Gallery, Corea Rug Hooking Company, and Accumulated Books Gallery. Spread out in three buildings is a nice selection of used and antiquarian books, fine crafts, and hand-hooked rugs. Yarn, rug-hooking supplies, and lessons are available.

Continue on the same road to **Bartlett House Quilts** (667 Corea Rd. Corea, 207/963-2659), where Carmen Jensen Weeks creates gorgeous and colorful quilts designed by Kaffe Fassett and Liza Prior Luch.

Down the first dirt lane after the Corea Post Office is the **Corea Wharf Gallery** (13 Gibbs Ln., 207/963-2633, www.coreawharfgallery.com). Inside a humble wharf-top fishing shack are historical photographs of Corea, taken in the 1940s-1960s by Louise Z. Young, born in Corea in 1919. She was a friend of painter Marsden Hartley, and took many candid photographs of him around the area. Young also worked with noted photographer Berenice Abbott. Also here are artifacts from Corea's history, especially ones connected to fishing. The gallery doubles as a lobster shack selling lobster, lobster rolls, hot dogs, and more.

RECREATION

Preserves

The very active **Frenchman Bay Conservancy** (FBC, 207/422-2328, www.frenchmanbay.org) manages a number of small preserves dotting the region, and most have at least one trail providing access; you can download maps from the site. The conservancy publishes a free *Short Hikes* map, available locally, that provides directions to several of these.

TIDAL FALLS PRESERVE

FBC's 8-acre **Tidal Falls Preserve** (off Eastside Rd., Hancock) is sited on the shores of the Taunton River, at Frenchman Bay's only reversing falls (roiling water when the tide turns). It's an idyllic spot, with a visitor center, kayak launch, pavilion with rooftop observatory, and picnic tables overlooking the falls and ledges, where seals often slumber at low tide. The Monday Music program, 6pm-7:30pm July-August, features live music and food trucks. Dogs are not permitted.

COREA HEATH

The 600-acre **Northern Corea Heath** is spectacular property, with divergent ecosystems including bogs, ledges, and mixed-wood forest. *Heath* is a local word for peatland or bog, and this one is a rare coastal plateau bog, distinguished because it rises above the surrounding landscape. Natural features include pitcher plants, sphagnum mosses, rare vascular plants, and jack pines. It's a fabulous place for bird-watching too, and the preserve borders a section of the Maine Coastal Islands National Wildlife Refuge. A one-mile trail loops through the preserve. Trail access is signed on Corea Road, 1.9 miles from the Route 195 intersection.

DONNELL POND PUBLIC RESERVED LAND

More than 15,000 acres of remote forests, ponds, lakes, and mountains have been preserved for public access in **Donnell Pond Public Reserved Land** (Maine Bureau of Parks and Lands, 207/827-1818, www.parksandlands.com), north and east of Sullivan. The reserve includes five peaks taller than 900 feet, a 1,940-acre wetland, and 35 miles of freshwater shoreline, making it especially rich in bird sightings. Hikers can climb Schoodic, Black, Caribou, and Tunk Mountains for expansive views taking in Frenchman Bay and Mount Desert Island; paddlers and anglers have Donnell Pond, Tunk Lake, Spring River Lake, Long Pond, Round Pond, and Little Pond, among others. Route 182, an official Scenic Highway, snakes through the Donnell Pond preserve. Hunting is permitted, so take special care during hunting season.

The hiking isn't easy here, but it isn't technical, and the options are many. The interconnecting trail system takes in Schoodic Mountain, Black Mountain, and Caribou Mountain. Follow the Schoodic Mountain Loop clockwise, heading westward first. To make a day of it, pack a picnic and take a swimsuit (and don't forget a camera and binoculars for the summit views). On a brilliantly clear day, you'll see Baxter State Park's Katahdin, the peaks of Acadia National Park, and the ocean beyond. In late July-early August blueberries are abundant on the summit. For such rewards, this is a popular hike, so don't expect to be alone, especially on fall weekends when the foliage is spectacular.

The Black Mountain ascent begins easily enough and then climbs steadily through the woods, easing off a bit before reaching bald ledges. Continue to the true summit by taking the trail past Wizard Pond. Views take in the forested lands, nearby lakes and peaks, and Acadia's more distant peaks. You can piggyback it with Schoodic Mountain, using that trailhead as a base for both climbs. Another possibility is to add Caribou Mountain. That loop exceeds seven miles, making for a full day of hiking.

Trailheads are accessible by either boat or vehicle. To reach the vehicle-access trailhead for Schoodic Mountain from Route 1 in East Sullivan, drive just over four miles northeast on Route 183 (Tunk Lake Rd.). Cross the Maine Central Railroad tracks and turn left at the Donnell Pond sign onto an unpaved road (marked as a jeep track on the USGS map). Go about 0.25 mile and then turn left for the parking area and trailhead for Schoodic Mountain, Black Mountain, Caribou Mountain, and a trail to Schoodic Beach. If you continue straight, you'll come to another trailhead for Black and Caribou Mountains. Water-access trailheads are at Schoodic Beach and Redman's Beach.

Tours and Workshops

Check with the **Schoodic Insitute** (207/288-1310, www.schoodicinstitute.org), which offers multi-day birding tours, photographic workshops, and other activities including lodging and meals.

Down East Sunrise Trail

The multi-use, gravel-surface **Down East Sunrise Trail** (www.sunrisetrail.org), a joint effort by the Maine Department of Transportation and Maine Department of Conservation, stretches 85 miles along a rehabilitated discontinued railroad bed between Washington Junction, in Hancock, and Ayers Junction, south of Calais. Maps, available to download from the website, show trailheads, highlights, and parking lots along the route. The 30-mile section between Washington Junction and Cherryfield roughly follows the Down East coastline of the Schoodic region. Additional access points include Franklin and Sullivan; see the map for details and directions.

1
2
3
4

The seven-mile Franklin Crossing-to-Tunk Lake Road section edges Schoodic Bog and the southwest corner of the Donnell Pond Public Reserved Land and offers fine views of Schoodic Mountain. There's limited parking on both ends: the Franklin Crossing intersection with Route 182 and the Tunk Lake Road intersection on Route 183.

Bicycling

The Maine Department of Transportation has mapped and provides info on area bicycle routes. These include the Schoodic Peninsula, with 10-, 12-, and 24-mile loops, and the Downeast Route/East Coast Greenway Trail, a 140-mile trail stretching from Ellsworth to Calais. PDF maps with tour details are available at www.exploremaine.org, or you can pick up a copy of *Explore Maine by Bike: 33 Loop Bicycle Tours* at any of the Maine Visitor Centers. Do be extremely careful pedaling in this region, because, as in much of Maine, shoulders are few and traffic moves swiftly.

The best choices for cycling are the **Schoodic Loop,** the **carriage roads** in the park, and the quiet roads of **Grindstone Neck** and **Corea.**

Sea Schoodic Kayak and Bike (8 Duck Pond Rd., Winter Harbor, 833/724-6634) rents bicycles for $25/day. It's wise to make advance reservations.

Canoeing and Kayaking

Experienced sea kayakers can explore the coastline throughout this region. Canoeists can paddle the placid waters of Jones Pond on the Schoodic Peninsula. In Donnell Pond Public Reserved Land, the major water bodies are **Donnell Pond** (big enough by most gauges to be called a lake) along with **Tunk Lake, Spring River Lake,** and **Long Pond;** all are accessible for boats (even, alas, powerboats). In early August, Round Mountain, rising a few hundred feet from Long Pond's eastern shore, is a great spot for gathering blueberries and huckleberries.

To reach the boat-launching area for Donnell Pond from Route 1 in Sullivan, take Route 200 north to Route 182. Turn right and go about 1.5 miles to a right turn just before Swan Brook. Turn and go not quite two miles to the put-in; the road is poor in spots but adequate for a regular vehicle. The Narrows, where you'll put in, is lined with summer cottages ("camps" in the Maine vernacular); keep paddling east to the more open part of the lake. Continue on Route 182 to find the boat launches for Tunk Lake and Spring River Lake (hand-carry only). Canoeists and kayakers can access Tunk Stream from Spring River Lake.

Also accessed from Route 182 is **Flanders Pond,** 2.9 miles off Route 1 on the Flanders Pond Road. It's a beautiful pond, with islands and mountain views. The public park has a parking area and an offshore float, as the pond is also a local swimming spot.

RENTALS

Sea Schoodic Kayak and Bike (8 Duck Pond Rd., Winter Harbor, 833/724-6634,) has rental kayaks stashed on Jones Pond ($45 double, $35 single). Visit the shop for directions, keys, PFDs, and paddles.

GUIDED TOURS

Antonio Blasi is a Master Maine Sea Kayak and Recreational Guide whose **Hancock Point Kayak Tours** (58 Point Rd., Hancock, 207/266-4449, http://schoodicmaineguide.com) offers guided paddles on Frenchman Bay or on an area lake. A three-hour bay paddle, including all equipment, safety and paddling demonstrations, and usually an island break, is $45/seat double kayak, $55 single kayak. A 1.5-hour lake tour is $55 pp single or double or $75 for two adults and one small child. Overnight kayak camping trips are $150 pp.

1: Schoodic Peninsula **2:** bikes on the Schoodic Loop **3:** Wharf Gallery & Grill **4:** cottages on the Schoodic Peninsula

Aquaterra Adventures (2695 Rte. 1, Sullivan, 207/422-0303, www.aquaterra-adventures.com, $65) offers four-hour guided sea-kayaking tours in protected Flanders Bay, open to ages 8 and older.

Boat Excursions

Cruise aboard the 40-foot *Tricia Clark* to Petit Manan Island, home to Petit Manan Light, and view puffins, seals, and other seabirds with **Acadia Puffin Cruise** (88 Sargent St., Winter Harbor, 207/598-7900, https://acadiapuffincruise.com). The 2.5-hour cruise costs $75 adults, $45 ages 6-12, $20 ages 5 and younger. Complimentary snacks, waters, and binoculars are available on board.

Swimming

The best freshwater swimming in the area is at **Jones Beach** (sunrise-sunset daily), a community-owned recreation area on Jones Pond in West Gouldsboro. Here you'll find restrooms, a nice playground, picnic facilities, a boat launch, a swim area with a float, and a small beach. The beach is located at the end of Recreation Road, off Route 195, which is 0.3 mile south of Route 1. Leashed pets are permitted.

Two beach areas on Donnell Pond are also popular for swimming: **Schoodic Beach** and **Redman's Beach** both have picnic tables, fire rings, and pit toilets. It's a 0.5-mile hike to Schoodic Beach from the parking lot. Redman's Beach is only accessible by boat. Other pocket beaches are also accessible by boat or via roadside pullouts.

A sand beach on a remote freshwater pond is the reward for a 0.25-mile hike into the Frenchman Bay Conservancy's **Little Tunk Pond Preserve.** From Route 1 in Sullivan, take Route 183 about five miles, then look for the parking area on the left. Just east of that is the **Spring River Lake Beach Day Use Area,** with parking and toilets.

Golf

Play the nine-hole **Grindstone Neck Golf Course** (Grindstone Ave., Winter Harbor, 207/963-7760, www.grindstonegolf.com) just for the dynamite scenery and for a glimpse of this exclusive late 19th-century summer enclave.

FOOD

Lobster and Seafood

The **Lobstore** (258 Newman St./Rte. 186, Winter Harbor, 207/963-8600, www.thelobstore.net, 11am-7pm daily) is more than a seafood market. Pick up fresh fish for your campsite or kitchen, or opt for chowder, lobster cooked to order, and even sushi.

You'd be hard-pressed to find a better place to enjoy a lobster than the ★ **Wharf Gallery & Grill** (13 Gibbs Ln., Corea, 207/963-8888, www.corealunch.com, 11am-4pm daily), an eat-on-the-wharf lobster shack overlooking dreamy, lobster boat-filled Corea Harbor. The menu includes lobster rolls, lobster grilled cheese (trust me, try it), crab claws, oysters, hot dogs, sausages, and ice cream. Owner Joe Young is a sixth-generation lobsterman and a descendant of Corea's original settlers. Images taken by his aunt, photographer Louise Z. Young, are displayed in the shed gallery. Ask Joe to share a few stories about his aunt and the family's relationship with painter Marsden Hartley; he's a great storyteller.

Tracey's Seafood (2719 Rte. 1, Sullivan, 207/422-9072, $5-20, 11am-8pm daily) doesn't look like much from the road, but don't be fooled. The Tracey family harvests the clams and catches the lobsters, shucks and picks, and dishes out ultra-fresh lobster, chowders, and fried seafood. There's a take-out window and picnic tables on the lawn as well as a dining room with wait service. Portions are big, prices are low—$5 burgers, two-fer lobster rolls (usually around $12-18, but I've seen them as low as $10), and a Friday fish fry with free seconds. Don't miss the homemade pies.

The **Fisherman's Galley** (7 Newman St./Rte. 186, Winter Harbor, 207/963-5585, www.fishermansgalleymaine.com, 4pm-9pm Mon.-Sat. late June-early Sept., $3-16) is a cool, rustic, earth-friendly lobster and seafood spot, with options for landlubbers and a full bar with Maine craft beers on tap. Guests order at the counter, and the food is delivered to their tables. The menu makes it easy to cobble together a meal that fits your appetite and budget. Dine inside, outside under a tent, or get a lobster boil in a bucket to go.

Quick Bites

There's no food in the park's Schoodic section, nor are there a lot of food options on the Schoodic Peninsula itself. You won't go hungry, but a little advance planning can go a long way.

Make a point to attend one of the many **public suppers** held throughout the summer in this area and in so many other rural corners of Maine. Typically benefiting a worthy cause, these usually feature beans or spaghetti or the serendipity of potluck. Everyone saves room for the homemade pies. Notices of such suppers are usually posted on public bulletin boards in country stores and in libraries, on signs in front of churches, and at other places that people gather. Local newspapers also often detail such events.

Pick up groceries or premade or made-to-order fare at the **Dunbar Store** (1983 Rte. 1, Sullivan, 207/422-0280, 7am-7pm Mon.-Sat., 8am-4pm Sun.).

J. M. Gerrish (352 Main St., Winter Harbor, 207/963-7000, 8am-3pm Wed.-Sun.) has had its ups and downs, but locals are confident that the century-old store is now back in local, reliable hands. Open for breakfast and lunch, it also has a classic ice cream counter along with a small penny candy section.

Pick up veggies, meats, eggs, cheeses, and handcrafted fiber products as well as jams, preserves, and baked goods at the **Winter Harbor Farmers Market** (Newman St., Winter Harbor, 9am-noon Tues. late June-early Sept.).

Stock up on gourmet goodies at **Grindstone Neck of Maine** (311 Newman St./Rte. 186, Winter Harbor, 207/963-7347 or 866/831-8734, www.grindstoneneck.com), just north of downtown Winter Harbor, which earns high marks for its smoked salmon, spreads and pâtés, and smoked cheeses, all made without preservatives or artificial ingredients.

Defying its name, **Sullivan Harbor Smokehouse** (Rte. 1, Hancock, 207/422-3735 or 800/422-4014, www.sullivanharborfarm.com) is in spacious modern digs in Hancock. Big interior windows allow visitors to see into the production facility from the retail shop/tasting room.

Take Route 182 to Route 200 (Eastbrook Rd.) and go 1.6 miles to family-operated **Shalom Orchard Organic Winery** (158 Eastbrook Rd., Franklin, 207/565-2312, www.shalomorchard.com). The certified-organic farm is well off the beaten path but worth a visit for its organic fruit and wines as well as for its yarns, pelts, fleece, and especially the views of Frenchman Bay from the hilltop.

German and Italian presses, Portuguese corks, and Maine fruit all contribute to the creation of Bob and Kathe Bartlett's award-winning dinner and dessert wines at **Bartlett Maine Estate Winery** (175 Chicken Mill Pond Rd., Gouldsboro, 207/546-2408, www.bartlettwinery.com, 10am-5pm Mon.-Sat. June-Oct., or by appointment), just north of the Schoodic Peninsula. Founded in 1982, the winery produces more than 20,000 gallons annually in a handsome wood-and-stone building designed by the Bartletts. Not ones to rest on their many laurels, in 2008, the Bartletts introduced grape wines, and more recently, the **Spirits of Maine Distillery** (do try the Rusticator Rum). There are no tours, but you're welcome to sample for a small tasting fee. Reserve wines—the dry blueberry is excellent—and others of limited vintage are sold only on-site. A sculpture garden patio makes a nice spot to relax. Bartlett's is 0.5 mile south of Route 1 in Gouldsboro.

International

Downeast Mexican Takeout (22 Old Rte. 1, Gouldsboro, 207/963-4043, 11am-7pm Tues.-Sun., $3-9) doesn't look like much, but it turns out excellent, made-to-order homemade

Michoacán Mexican fare. Patience is key here, as it takes a while to prepare, especially if there are other orders in the queue. Seating is outdoors on picnic tables.

Have a hankering for Korean? Sonye Carroll and family serve bibimbap, *boul-koh-kee,* barbecued ribs, and kimchee, along with top-notch crabmeat rolls, as well as burgers and dogs, homemade doughnuts, and Gifford's ice cream, at the seasonal **YU Takeout** (674 Rte. 1, Hancock, 207/412-0944, 11am-8pm daily, $8-20).

Family Favorites

Good food served by friendly folks is what pulls the locals into **Chester Pike's Galley** (2336 U.S. 1, Sullivan, 207/422-8200, 7am-2pm daily, $5-15). The prices are low and the portions are big. If you're on a diet, don't even *look* at the glass case filled with fresh-baked pies, cakes, and cookies. Go early if you want to snag one of the homemade doughnuts (and order dessert first).

The best place for grub and gossip in Winter Harbor is **Chase's Restaurant** (193 Main St., Winter Harbor, 207/963-7171, 7am-8pm Tues.-Sun., $8-28), a seasoned but updated, no-frills booth-and-counter operation turning out straightforward American fare and decent seafood.

Shoot pool, play darts or horseshoes, watch the game on TV, sip a cold drink, and savor a burger or fried seafood at the family-friendly the **Pickled Wrinkle** (9 E. Schoodic Dr., at the intersection with Rte. 186, Birch Harbor, 207/963-7916, www.thepickledwrinkle.com, 11am-9pm daily, $9-23). Don't be fooled by the humble appearance; the owners know their way around the kitchen and opt for local and organic whenever possible. That said, the overall atmosphere is more tavern than restaurant. There's often live music; Thursday jazz nights always draw a crowd. The Friday-night all-you-can-eat haddock fry is a deal.

Don't be put off by "Wilbur," the lobster sculpture outside **Ruth & Wimpy's Kitchen** (792 Rte. 1, Hancock, 207/422-3723, www.ruthandwimpys.com, 2pm-9pm Mon.-Sat., $10-28). You'll probably see a crowd as well. This family-fare standby serves hefty sandwiches, lobster, pizza, pasta, and steak. Antique license plates and collections of miniature cars and trucks accent the interior.

Casual Dining

The gastropub menu at **Ironbound** (1513 U.S. 1, Hancock, 207/422-3395, www.ironboundinn.com, from 5pm Tues.-Sun. mid-June-mid-Oct., $12-37) ranges from burgers and salads to halibut and rib eye, making it easy to please everyone. The atmosphere is casual, with wood floors and undressed tables. The fare complements the setting, with ingredients sourced locally whenever possible. Play bocce on the lawn while enjoying the outside bar, the Bounder.

Aim for a table either outdoors on the terrace or by the window at **Bunker's Wharf** (260 E. Schoodic Dr., Birch Harbor, 207/963-9111, 11am-9pm daily, $15-35), which overlooks postcard-perfect Wonsqueak Harbor. The New American menu emphasizes seafood—the crab cakes and the lobster stew earn raves—and of course there's lobster, but there are choices for landlubbers, and vegetarians can mix and match a meal from starters, salads, and pasta. Or go for lunch and opt for a burger, crab cake BLT, or portobello burger.

Chef Mike Poirier and baker Alice Letcher's the ★ **Salt Box** (10 Newman St., Winter Harbor, 207/422-9900, http://saltboxmaine.com, 5pm-9pm Wed.-Sun. late May-early Oct. and noon-3pm Fri.-Sun. July-Aug., $23-36), in a contemporary building overlooking the harbor, has earned a following. The decor is open and upscale, the creative New American fare is sophisticated yet approachable and focused on fresh seasonal ingredients, and the service is excellent. It's easy to make a meal from small plates and salads, or opt for entrées such as farm gnocchi, lobster mac, or cioppino.

Fine Dining

The unpretentious dining rooms at the ★ **Crocker House Country Inn** (967 Point Rd., Hancock Point, 207/422-6806, www.crockerhouse.com, 5:30pm-9pm daily May-Oct., 5:30pm-8:30pm Fri.-Sun. Apr. and Nov.-Dec., entrées $29-38) provide a setting for well-prepared Continental fare crafted from fresh and local ingredients; reservations are essential, as this is one of the area's most consistent and popular dining spots.

Another dependable dining experience is **Chipper's** (1239 U.S. 1, Hancock, 207/422-8238, www.chippersrestaurant.com, from 5pm Wed.-Sat.). Owner Chipper Butterwick opened his popular restaurant in 1995 and expanded the simple Cape-style building in 2010, adding a pub. The restaurant's wide-ranging menu includes rack of lamb and chateaubriand, but the emphasis is on seafood; the crab cakes earn rave reviews. Entrées include a sampling of tasty haddock chowder and a salad, but save room for the homemade ice cream for dessert. Entrées are in the $25-35 range, but some appetizer-salad combos provide budget options, and lighter fare ($6-16) is available in the pub.

ACCOMMODATIONS

Inns and Bed-and-Breakfasts

Sited on a bluff with sweeping views over Frenchman Bay, the **Bluff House Inn** (57 Bluff House Rd., Gouldsboro, 207/963-7805, www.bluffinn.com, year-round, $95-185) offers guest rooms in a 1980s post-and-beam lodge, a two-bedroom apartment, and one-room cabins. Verandas wrap around the 1st and 2nd floors of the lodge, so bring binoculars for sighting ospreys and bald eagles. Settle by one of two stone fireplaces or grab a seat by the window. Lodge rooms are a bit dated, but new owners in 2019 plan updates. Breakfast is expanded continental. Pet-friendly rooms are available for $15/stay.

Taunton River Bed & Breakfast (19 Taunton Dr., Sullivan, 207/422-2070, www.tauntonriverbandb.com, $115-125), sited in a 19th-century farmhouse with river views, is warm and inviting, formal without being stuffy. Two of the three guest rooms share a bath. It would be easy to spend the day just sitting on the porch swing, but it's an easy pedal or drive to local art galleries. The inn is just a stone's throw off Route 1, so traffic din might bother the noise-sensitive.

Sustainable living is the focus of Karen and Ed Curtis's peaceful **Three Pines Bed and Breakfast** (274 East Side Rd., Hancock, 207/460-7595, www.threepinesbandb.com, year-round, $125), fronting on Sullivan Harbor just below the Reversing Falls. Their quiet, off-the-grid 40-acre oceanfront organic farm is home to a llama, rare-breed chickens and sheep, ducks, and bees as well as a large organic garden, berry bushes, an orchard, and greenhouses. Photovoltaic cells provide electricity, and appliances are primarily propane powered; satellite technology operates the phone, TV, and Wi-Fi systems. Two inviting guest rooms have private entrances and water views. A full vegetarian breakfast (with fresh eggs from the farm) is served. Bicycles and a canoe are available. You can walk or pedal along an abandoned railway line down to the point, and you can launch a canoe or kayak from the yard. Children are welcome; pets are a possibility.

Follow Hancock Point Road 4.8 miles south of Route 1 to the three-story, gray-blue **Crocker House Country Inn** (967 Point Rd., Hancock, 207/422-6806, www.crockerhouse.com, $125-180), Rich and Liz Malaby's antidote to Bar Harbor's summer traffic. Built as a summer hotel in 1884, the inn underwent rehabbing a century later, but it retains a delightfully old-fashioned air despite now offering contemporary conveniences. Breakfast is included. A few bicycles are available, and clay tennis courts are nearby. If you're arriving by boat, request a mooring. The inn's dining room, open nightly for dinner in season, is a draw in itself. Some rooms are pet friendly.

Watch lobster boats unload their catch at the dock opposite **Elsa's Inn on the Harbor** (179 Main St., Prospect Harbor, 207/963-7571, www.elsasinn.com, $140-175), with views overlooking the harbor and beyond to a lighthouse. Every room has an ocean view, and a few have separate entrances. Innkeepers Scott and Cherrie Markwood pamper their guests with nice linens, down duvets, and afternoon refreshments. A hearty hot breakfast is served either indoors in the dining room or outside on the porch or patio After a day of exploring, settle into a rocker on the veranda and gaze over the boat-filled harbor out to Prospect Harbor Light.

Although **Ironbound** (1513 U.S. 1, Hancock, 207/422-3395 www.ironboundinn.com, $175-195), a four-room inn located above the restaurant of the same name, is right on Route 1, when you're on the garden-view balconies, or on the lawn out back, you're oblivious to any traffic. Rooms are bright and airy (some allow pets, $15), and guests have use of a comfy sitting area downstairs, adjacent to the restaurant. Rates include continental breakfast. Guests can arrange for a private lobster boat tour. The inn adjoins Crabtree Neck Conservation Trust lands, laced with trails and a pond.

Just off Route 1, the balcony-wrapped, oceanfront **Acadia Bay Inn Bed and Breakfast** (12 Miramar Ave., Sullivan Harbor, 207/422-0127, https://www.acadiabayinn.com, $199-289) offers serene views across Frenchman Bay to the peaks of Mount Desert and stairs down to the shore. Dinner and picnic lunches are available with advance reservation. Rates include a full breakfast.

Overlooking the Gouldsboro Peninsula's only sandy saltwater beach, **Oceanside Meadows Inn** (Rte. 195, Corea Rd., Prospect Harbor, 207/963-5557, www.oceaninn.com, May-mid-Oct.) is an eco-conscious retreat on 200 acres with organic gardens, wildlife habitat, and walking trails. Fourteen guest rooms are split between the nine-bedroom 1860s captain's house and the seven-bedroom, 1820 Shaw farmhouse next door. Rooms have a comfy, old-fashioned shabby-chic decor. Note that there are no TVs or air-conditioning, and many of the bathrooms are tiny. In 2019, for family reasons, the owners switched from bed-and-breakfast operation ($178-219) to weekly vacation rentals ($7,665-9,065/house), but they're considering returning to B&B operation.

Cottages

Roger and Pearl Barto, whose family roots in this region go back five generations, have four rental accommodations on their Henry Cove oceanfront property, **Main Stay Cottages** (66 Sargent St., Winter Harbor, 207/963-2601, www.mainstaycottages-rvpark.com, $99-135). Most unusual is the small, one-bedroom Boat House, which has stood since the 1880s. It hangs over the harbor, with views to **Mark Island Light,** and you can hear the water gurgling below at high tide (but it is cramped, be forewarned). Other options include a very comfortable efficiency cottage, a one-bedroom cottage, a 2nd-floor suite with a private entrance, and a four-bedroom house ($150-250/night). All have big decks and fabulous views over the lobster boat-filled harbor; watch for the eagles that frequently soar overhead. Main Stay is on the Island Explorer bus route and a short walk from where the Bar Harbor Ferry docks.

The views to Mount Desert are dreamy from **Edgewater Cabins** (25 Benvenuto Ave., Sullivan, 207/422-6414 May 15-Oct. 15, 603/472-8644 rest of year, www.edgewatercabins.com, $595-995/week), a colony of seven housekeeping cottages on a spit of land jutting into Frenchman Bay. The well-tended four-acre property has both sunrise and sunset water views, big trees for shade, and lawns rolling to the shorefront. Stays of at least three nights ($95-175/night) are possible, when there's availability. Also offered are boat tours of Frenchman Bay aboard the *Edgewater II* (from $45pp for two hours).

Camping

None of the area campgrounds offer showers, but showers ($4 for six minutes), as well as a laundry ($3/wash or dry), are available at the **Schoodic Marine Center** (88 Sargent

St., Winter Harbor, 207/963-7449, www.schoodicinstitute.org, 6am-9pm).

A handful of authorized primitive campsites can be found on **Tunk Lake** (southwestern corner) and **Donnell Pond** (at Schoodic Beach and Redman's Beach), all accessible on foot or by boat. Each has a table, a fire ring, and a nearby pit toilet. Many of the sites are on the lakefront. All are first come, first served with no fees or permits required; they are snapped up quickly on midsummer weekends. You can camp elsewhere within this public land, except in day-use areas, but fires are not permitted at unofficial sites.

Acadia National Park's 90-site **Schoodic Woods Campground** (Park Loop Rd., Schoodic Peninsula, 877/444-6777 or 518/885-3639 international, www.recreation.gov, credit or debit card required, $22-60) is sited on an approximately 1,400-acre property over which Acadia National Park holds a conservation easement. It's located about a mile south of Route 186, north of the Frazer Point Picnic Area. Sites include remote walk-in tenting, drive-in tenting, and RV sites with water and electricity. There is also a welcome center and an amphitheater with National Park Service programming. Hiking trails connect it to Schoodic Head, and nonmotorized paths link the east and west sides of the peninsula.

The primitive, commercial, self-serve, backcountry-style **Acadia East Campground** (547 Rte. 1, Gouldsboro, 833/246-2267, www.acadiaeastcampground.com, $32) opened in 2018 with 6 tent sites on 8.8 wooded acres and plans to expand to 30 sites over the next few years. You must bring your own water and take out all trash. There's a vault toilet. Each site has a fire ring and picnic table. It's dog friendly.

The Bartos, owners of **Main Stay Cottages and RV Park** (66 Sargent St., Winter Harbor, 207/963-2601, www.mainstaycottages-rvpark.com, $48), have a 10-site campground overlooking Henry Cove. It's designed for self-contained RVs, as there are no restrooms or showers on-site; sewer, water, electric, and Wi-Fi are available.

INFORMATION

For advance information about eastern Hancock County, contact the **Schoodic Peninsula Chamber of Commerce** (207/963-7658, www.acadia-schoodic.org). Another source for advance information is **Downeast & Acadia Regional Tourism** (207/546-3600 or 888/665-3278, www.downeastacadia.com). Also covering the area is the **Ellsworth Area Chamber of Commerce** (207/667-5584, www.ellsworthchamber.org).

To plan ahead, see the **Acadia National Park** website (www.nps.gov/acad), where you can download a Schoodic map.

For information on the **National and Maine Scenic Byways** in this region, visit www.byways.org or www.exploremaine.org/byways.

GETTING THERE AND AROUND

Winter Harbor is about 25 miles via Routes 1 and 186 from Ellsworth. It's about 20 miles or 30 minutes to Milbridge, on the Down East coast. Although Winter Harbor is roughly 43 miles or 1.15 hours from Bar Harbor by car, it's only about 7 miles by water. You can get here by seasonal passenger ferry from Bar Harbor or bus from Ellsworth, but you'll need a vehicle or bicycle to explore beyond the part of the Schoodic Peninsula that's served by the Island Explorer bus.

The **Bar Harbor Ferry** (207/288-2984, www.barharborferry.com, round-trip $28 adults, $20 children) operates at least four times daily mid-June-mid-Oct. between downtown Bar Harbor and the Schoodic Marine Center in Winter Harbor, and coordinates with the free **Island Explorer** (www.exploreacadia.com) bus's summertime Schoodic route, Route 8. Pets and bicycles are free.

The Down East Coast

The term *Down East* is rooted in the direction the wind blows; the prevailing southwest wind powered 19th-century sailing vessels along this rugged coastline. But to be truly Down East, in the minds of most Mainers, you have to be physically here in Washington County—a stunning landscape of waterways, forests, blueberry barrens, rocky shoreline dotted with islands and lighthouses, and independent pocket-size communities, many still dependent upon fishing or lobstering for their economies.

At one time, most of the Maine coast was as underdeveloped as this part of it. You can set your clock back a generation or two while you're here; you'll find no giant malls, only a couple of fast-food joints, and two—count 'em—traffic lights. For the most part, your choices

Highlights

Look for ★ to find recommended sights, activities, dining, and lodging.

★ **Maine Coastal Islands National Wildlife Refuge:** More than 300 bird species have been sighted at Petit Manan Point. Even if you're not a bird-watcher, come for the hiking and, in August, the blueberries (page 376).

★ **Great Wass Island Preserve:** The finest natural treasure in this part of Maine is the Great Wass Archipelago, partly owned by the Nature Conservancy, with opportunities for hiking and bird-watching (page 381).

★ **Cutler Coast Public Reserve:** If you're an avid hiker, don't miss this spectacular preserve with nearly a dozen miles of beautifully engineered trails (page 386).

★ **Machias Seal Island Puffin Tour:** An excursion boat departs from Cutler for Machias Seal Island, home to Atlantic puffins, as well as razorbill auks, Arctic terns, and common murres (page 387).

★ **Quoddy Head State Park:** This park features the iconic candy-striped West Quoddy Head Light, as well as recreational opportunities like cliff-side hiking trails, beachcombing, and bird-watching (page 391).

★ **Roosevelt Campobello International Park:** Make it an international vacation by venturing over to this New Brunswick park, home to the Roosevelt Cottage and miles of hiking trails (page 399).

★ **Whale-Watching:** Sail into Passamaquoddy Bay with Island Cruises, pass the Old Sow whirlpool, and ogle seabirds and whales (page 402).

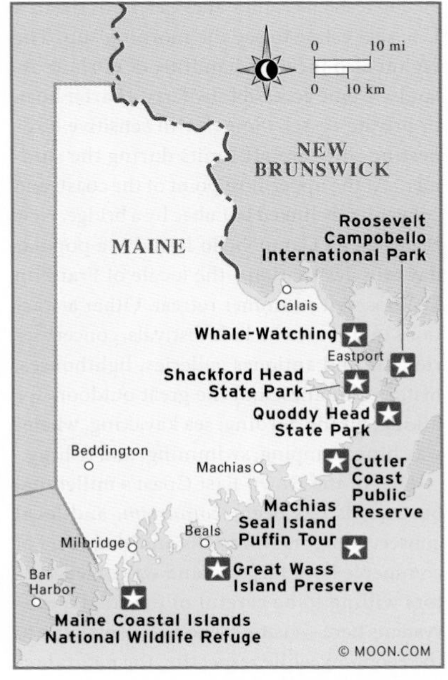

★ **Shackford Head State Park:** The rewards for this easy hike are panoramic views over Cobscook Bay from Eastport to Campobello (page 406).

are limited to family-style restaurants specializing in home cooking with an emphasis on fresh (usually fried) seafood and lobster rolls. Nor will you find grand resorts or even not-so-grand hotels. Motels, tourist cabins, and small inns and bed-and-breakfasts dot the region. The upside is that prices too are a generation removed. If you're searching for the Maine of your memories or your imagination, this is it.

When eastern Hancock County flows into western Washington County, you're on the Down East Coast (sometimes called the Sunrise Coast). Stretching from Steuben eastward to Jonesport, Machias, and Lubec—then "around the corner" to Eastport and Calais—Washington County is twice the size of Rhode Island, covers 2,528 square miles, has about 30,000 residents, and stakes a claim as the first U.S. real estate to see the morning sun. The region also includes handfuls of offshore islands—some accessible by ferry, charter boat, or private vessel. (Some, with sensitive bird-nesting sites, are off-limits during the summer.) At the uppermost point of the coast, and conveniently linked to Lubec by a bridge, New Brunswick's Campobello Island is a popular day-trip destination—the locale of Franklin D. Roosevelt's summer retreat. Other attractions in this area include festivals, concert series, art and antiques galleries, lighthouses, historical homes, and the great outdoors for hiking, biking, birding, sea kayaking, whale-watching, camping, swimming, and fishing.

One of the Down East Coast's millennial buzzwords has been *ecotourism,* and local conservation organizations and chambers of commerce have targeted and welcomed visitors willing to be careful of the fragile ecosystems here—visitors who will contribute to the economy while respecting the natural resources and leaving them untrammeled, who don't cross the fine line between light use and overuse. Low-impact tourism is essential for this area. However, outfitters are few and far between.

One natural phenomenon no visitor can affect is the tide—the inexorable ebb and flow, predictably in and predictably out. If you're not used to it, even the 6-10-foot tidal ranges of southern Maine may surprise you. But along this coastline, the tides are astonishing—as much as 28 feet difference in water level within six hours. Old-timers tell stories of big money lost betting on horses racing the fast-moving tides.

Another surprise to visitors may be how early the sun rises—and sets—on the Sunrise Coast. Keep in mind that if you cross into Canada from either Lubec or Calais, you enter the Atlantic time zone, and you'll need to set your clock ahead one hour.

Yet another distinctive natural feature of Washington County is its blueberry barrens (fields). Depending on the time of year, the fields will be black (torched by growers to jump-start the crop), blue (ready for harvest), or crimson (fall foliage, fabulous for photography). In early summer, a million rented bees set to work pollinating the blossoms. By August, when a blue haze forms over the knee-high shrubs, bent-over bodies use old-fashioned wooden rakes to harvest the ripe berries. It's backbreaking work, but the employment lines usually form quickly when newspaper ads announce the start of the annual harvest.

Warm clothing is essential in this corner of Maine. It may be nicknamed the Sunrise Coast, but it also gets plenty of fog, rain, and cool temperatures. Temperatures tend to be warmer, and the fog diminishes, as you head a bit inland, but you can never count on that. Mother Nature is an accomplished curveball pitcher, and El Niño and La Niña periodically provide an assist.

Previous: Lubec waterfront; sculptures at the St. Croix Island International Historic Site; Roosevelt Campobello International Park.

The Down East Coast

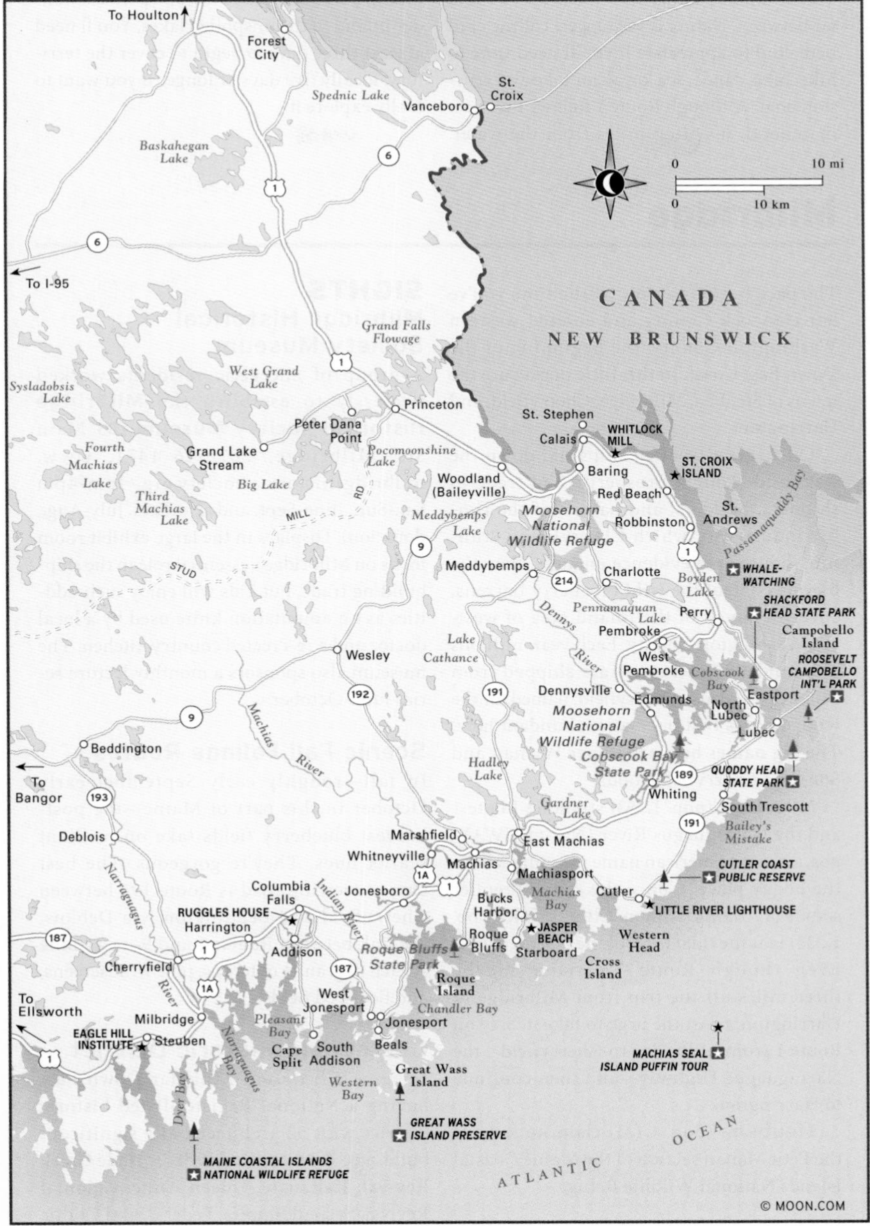

PLANNING YOUR TIME

Down East Maine is not for those in a hurry. Traffic ambles along, and towns are few and far between. Nature is the biggest calling card here, and to appreciate it you'll need time to hike, bike, canoe, sea kayak, or take an excursion boat. Although Route 1 follows the coast in general, it's often miles from the water. You'll want to ramble down the peninsulas to explore the seaside villages, see lighthouses, or hike in parks and preserves, and perhaps wander inland to the unspoiled lakes. You'll need at least three days to begin to cover the territory, ideally five days or longer if you want to really explore it.

Milbridge

The pace begins to slow by the time you've left Hancock County and entered western Washington County, the beginning of the Down East Coast. In this little pocket are the towns of Steuben, Milbridge, Cherryfield, and Harrington.

Once, great wooden ships slid down the ways and brought prosperity and trade to shippers, builders, and barons of the timber industry, of which Cherryfield's stunning houses are evidence enough. Now the barons control the wild blueberry barrens, covering much of the inland area of western Washington County. Each year, millions of pounds of blueberries are shipped from Milbridge and also Cherryfield, named for the wild cherries that once were abundant here. The big names here are Jasper Wyman and Sons and Cherryfield Foods.

Milbridge (pop. 1,353) straddles Route 1 and the Narraguagus River (Nar-ra-GWAY-gus, a Native American name meaning "above the boggy place"), once the state's premier source of Atlantic salmon. **Cherryfield** (pop. 1,232) is at the tidal limit of the Narraguagus. Even though Route 1A trims maybe three miles off the trip from Milbridge to Harrington, resist the urge to take it. Stay on Route 1 from Milbridge to Cherryfield—the Narraguagus Highway—and then continue to Harrington.

Steuben's (pop. 1,131) claim to fame is the Petit Manan section of the Maine Coastal Islands National Wildlife Refuge.

SIGHTS

Milbridge Historical Society Museum

A group of energetic residents worked tirelessly to establish the **Milbridge Historical Society Museum** (83 Main St., Milbridge, 207/546-4471, www.milbridgehistoricalsociety.org, 1pm-4pm Sat.-Sun. June-Sept. and also Tues. July-Aug., donation). Displays in the large exhibit room focus on Milbridge's essential role in the shipbuilding trade, but kids will enjoy such oddities as an amputation knife used by a local doctor and a re-created country kitchen. The museum also sponsors a monthly lecture series June-October.

Scenic Fall Foliage Routes

In fall—roughly early September-early October in this part of Maine—the post-harvest blueberry fields take on brilliant scarlet hues. They're gorgeous. The best barren-viewing road is Route 193 between Cherryfield and Beddington, via Deblois, the link between Routes 1 and 9—a 21-mile stretch of granite outcrops, pine windscreens, and fiery-red fields.

Cherryfield Historic District

Imagine a little town this far Down East having a National Register-listed historic district with 52 architecturally significant buildings. Architectural styles include Greek Revival, Italianate, Queen Anne, Colonial Revival, Second Empire, Federal, and Gothic

Maine Fisheries Trail

According to the National Marine Fisheries Service, the proportion of Maine workers employed in commercial fishing is more than 10 times the percentage nationwide. Maine's **Downeast Fisheries Trail** (www.downeastfisheriestrail.org) stretches along Route 1 from Penobscot Bay to Cobscook Bay, but here in Washington County, where the percentage of fishing folks is even higher, you're in the thick of it.

Of the hundreds of sardine canneries that peppered coastal Maine's waterfront, none remain. Once, groundfish such as cod were a major fishery for boats heading to sea from ports such as Jonesport, Lubec, and Eastport, but now they're all but gone. These days, commercial fishermen harvest clams, elvers, crabs, alewives, scallops, urchins, shrimp, marine worms, and even seaweed, in addition to fish and lobster; hatcheries seek to replenish species such as sea-run salmon; and farms raise Atlantic salmon, oysters, and mussels.

The mapped trail comprises 45 sites celebrating Maine's maritime heritage and marine resources, from the Penobscot Marine Museum in Searsport to the Cobscook Bay Resource Center in Eastport. Marked sites allow you to delve into Maine's fishing and maritime heritage by visiting fish hatcheries, aquaculture facilities, active fishing harbors, processing plants, working wharves and piers, and related historical sites. You can request a printed copy of the map by calling 207/581-1435.

Revival—dating 1803-1940, with most from the late 19th century. Especially impressive for such a small town are the Second Empire-style homes. The **Cherryfield-Narraguagus Historical Society** (88 River Rd., Cherryfield, 207/546-2076, 1pm-4pm Sat. summer) created a free brochure-map, *Walking Tour of the Cherryfield Historic District*. It's available for download from the Downeast & Acadia Regional Tourism (http://downeastacadia.com/story/cherryfield).

ENTERTAINMENT

The biggest event in this end of Washington County is **Milbridge Days,** in late July, drawing hundreds of visitors. The Saturday-afternoon highlight is the codfish relay race—hilarious enough to have been featured in *Sports Illustrated* magazine and on national television. The four-member teams, clad in slickers and hip boots, really do hand off a greased cod instead of the usual baton. Also on the schedule are a blueberry pie-eating contest, parade, kids' games, an auction, cribbage tournament, crafts booths, and more. The relay race has been going since the mid-1980s; the festival has been going for a century and a half.

The **Eagle Hill Institute** (59 Eagle Hill Rd., Steuben, 207/546-2821, www.eaglehill.us) presents advanced natural history seminars and scientific illustration workshops as well as public lectures by recognized experts. Past topics have included Of Bugs and Birds, A Relationship in Peril; Wild Mushrooms; A Date with Mount Everest; Lizzie van Lew: The North's Most Successful Spy During the Civil War; and The Maine Bumble Bee Atlas. The institute also sponsors various opportunities to meet and mingle with scientists and others. If you're especially interested in natural history and the arts, the institute offers longer programs as well.

SHOPPING

Arthur Smith (Rogers Point Rd., Steuben, 207/546-3462) is the real thing when it comes to chain-saw carvings. He's an extremely talented folk artist who looks at a piece of wood and sees an animal in it. His carvings of great blue herons, eagles, wolves, porcupines, flamingoes, and other creatures are incredibly detailed, and his wife, Marie, paints them in lifelike colors. Don't expect a fancy studio; much of the work can be viewed roadside.

Also in Steuben, but on the other end of

the spectrum, is **Ray Carbone** (460 Pigeon Hill Rd., Steuben, 207/546-2170, www.raycarbonesculptor.com), whose masterful wood, stone, and bronze sculptures and fine furniture are definitely worth stopping to see or buy. Don't miss the granite sculptures and birdbaths in the garden.

Contemporary Maine art by local artists and artisans is shown in rotating shows at **Schooner Gallery** (59 Main St., Milbridge, 207/546-3179, www.schoonergallery.com), where you can also preorder a handsome wreath for the holidays.

RECREATION

★ Maine Coastal Islands National Wildlife Refuge

Restoring and managing colonies of nesting seabirds is the focus of the **Maine Coastal Islands National Wildlife Refuge,** which spans 250 coastal miles and comprises more than 60 offshore islands and four mainland parcels totaling more than 8,200 acres spread out in five sections. Occupying a peninsula in Steuben with 10 miles of rocky shoreline and three offshore islands is the refuge's outstandingly scenic **Petit Manan Division** (Pigeon Hill Rd., Steuben, 207/546-2124, www.fws.gov/refuge/maine_coastal_islands, sunrise-sunset daily year-round). The remote location means it sees only about 15,000 visitors per year, and most of those are likely birders, as more than 300 different bird species have been sighted here. Among the other natural highlights are stands of jack pine, coastal raised peatlands, blueberry barrens, freshwater and saltwater marshes, granite shores, and cobble beaches. Note: There is no visitors center.

The moderately easy, 4-mile round-trip Birch Point Trail and the slightly more difficult, 1.8-mile round-trip Hollingsworth Trail loop provide splendid views and opportunities to spot wildlife along the shore and in the fields, forests, and marshlands. The Hollingsworth Trail, looping to the shoreline, is the best of the preserve's paths. This is foggy territory, but on clear days you can see the 123-foot lighthouse on Petit Manan Island, 2.5 miles offshore (for a closer look at the puffin colony there, book a trip on an excursion boat from Milbridge). The Birch Point Trail passes through blueberry fields to the shoreline of Dyer Bay. Family-friendly interpretive signage explains flora and fauna along the route.

From Route 1, on the east side of Steuben, take Pigeon Hill Road. Six miles down is the first parking lot, for the Birch Point Trail; another 0.5 mile takes you to the parking area for the Hollingsworth Trail, where space is limited. If you arrive in August, help yourself to blueberries. Cross-country skiing is permitted in winter.

Pigeon Hill

It doesn't require too much effort to hike Pigeon Hill and reap views taking in Cadillac Mountain, Petit Manan Light, and the island-studded Bold Coast from its 317-foot summit, the highest point on Washington County's coastline. Since acquiring this 170-acre preserve, **Downeast Coastal Conservancy** (207/255-4500, www.downeastcoastalconservancy.org) has enhanced the original trail and added new ones. The preserve now has 1.6 miles of linked trails to the summit ledges; the shortest route, 0.8 mile round-trip, ascends steeply but swiftly. For the best views on the descent, take the Summit Loop and Silver Mine Trails; the latter passes an abandoned silver mine (not much to see but a pile of rocks). The trailhead is on the western side of Pigeon Hill Road, 4.5 miles south of Route 1. If you continue on the road, you'll end up at the Petit Manan Point Division of the Maine Coastal Islands National Wildlife Refuge.

McClellan Park

You can picnic, hike, and camp at this oceanfront park in Milbridge. Go tidepooling, clamber over rocks, or just admire the views

1: Cherryfield Historic District **2:** Vazquez Mexican Takeout

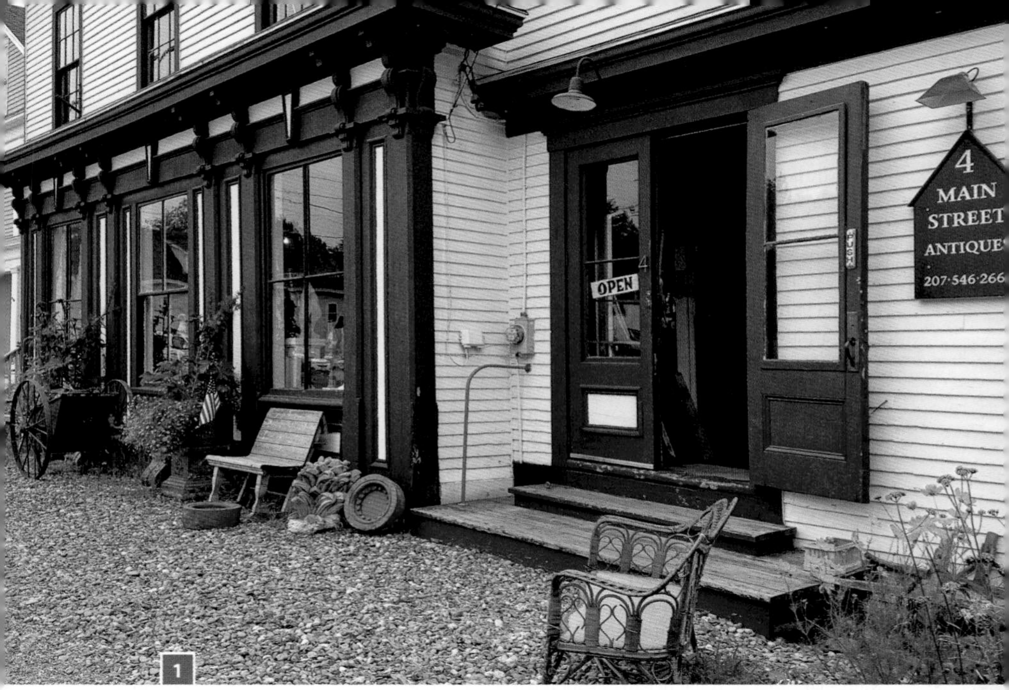

1

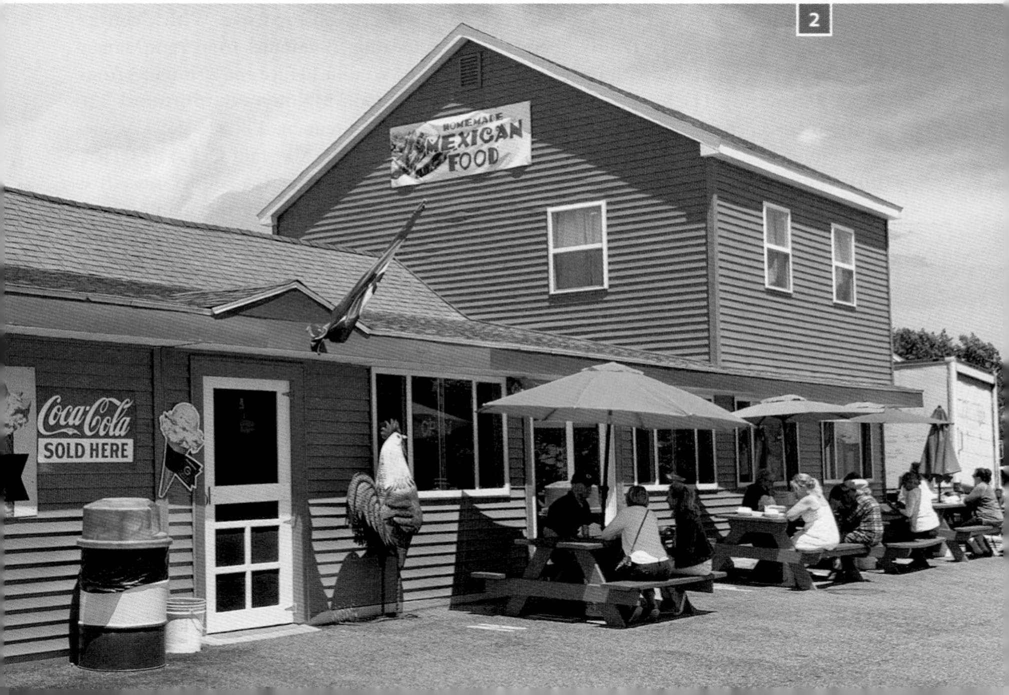

2

over the rugged islands offshore. From Route 1, take Wyman Road approximately 4.5 miles.

Boat Excursions

Captain Jamie Robertson's **Robertson Sea Tours and Adventures** (Milbridge Marina, Fickett's Point Rd., 207/483-6110 or 207/461-7439, www.robertsonseatours.com, May 15-Oct. 1) offers cruises from the Milbridge Marina aboard the *Kandi Leigh* or the *Susan Jane*, a pair of classic Maine lobster boats. Options include puffins and seabirds, whale-watching, lighthouses, lobstering, and a full-day combo. Prices range $60-350 adults, $45-185 children for the 2-6-hour cruises. Boat minimums may apply.

FOOD

Quick Bites

Thank the migrant community who arrive here in summer to pick blueberries for ★ **Vazquez Mexican Takeout** (38 Main St., Milbridge, 207/598-8141, 10am-7pm Mon.-Sat., $3-12). What began as a food truck serving authentic Mexican fare to blueberry pickers has evolved into a family-operated permanent take-out spot, with picnic tables inside and outside. The food is excellent, the portions are generous, and the Mexican fare is delicious and authentic, with house-made tortillas and salsas. In July and August, it opens at 6am for breakfast.

Fire & Dough Wood Fired Pizza (164 Main St., Milbridge, 207/546-8116, www.fireanddoughdowneast.com, 11:30am-7pm Wed.-Sun., $7-10), a mobile kitchen, offers 10-inch pizzas; outdoor seating only.

Family Favorites

Home cooking, from shepherd's pie to fried fish, comes out of the kitchen at **Scovils Millside Dining** (1276 Main St./Rte. 1, Harrington, 207/483-6544, 7am-7pm Tues.-Sun., $5-18), a family-run restaurant near the intersections of Routes 1 and 1A. The Friday all-you-can-eat fish fry is $10.

Milbridge House (20 Main St., 207/544-4454, www.milbridgehouse.com, 6am-2pm Tues.-Sun., $6-20) serves home-style comfort food for breakfast and lunch.

Expect big portions of home-cooked fare at **44 Degrees North** (17 Main St., Milbridge, 207/546-4440, www.44-degrees-north.com, 11am-8pm Mon.-Sat., $10-30). The front room is family oriented, with booths, tables, and cheerful decor. The back room doubles as a sports bar. As is usually the case in this part of Maine, there's a case full of mouthwatering desserts.

CAMPING

Town-owned **McClellan Park** (Wayman Rd., Milbridge, 207/542-2422, $10/site), a gift to the town in 1925 from George B. McClellan, son of a Civil War general, has 14 primitive wooded campsites, each with picnic table and fire ring. The 10-acre oceanfront park, sited on Tom Leighton Point at the mouth of Narraguagus Bay, has a picnic area and excellent views of undeveloped islands.

Since 1958, the Ayr family has welcomed campers at its quiet, well-off-the-beaten-path property on Joy Cove. With a convenient location 15 minutes from Petit Manan National Wildlife Refuge and 20 minutes from Schoodic Point, **Mainayr Campground** (321 Village Rd., Steuben, 207/546-2690, www.mainayr.com, late May-mid-Oct., $30-33) has 32 mostly wooded tenting and RV sites (five with full hookups). Also on the premises are a playground, a laundry, a beach for tidal swimming, clamming flats, a grassy launch area for kayaks and canoes, a camp store, berries for picking, and fresh lobsters.

INFORMATION

Info on the area is available from the **Milbridge Area Merchants Association** (www.milbridge.org).

GETTING THERE AND AROUND

Milbridge is about 20 miles or 25 minutes via Routes 186 and 1 from Winter Harbor. It's about 25 miles or 30 minutes via Routes 1 and 187 to Jonesport.

Jonesport and Beals Area

Between western Washington County and the Machias Bay area is the molar-shaped Jonesport Peninsula, reached from the west via the attractive little town of **Columbia Falls,** bordering Route 1. First settled around 1762, Columbia Falls still has a handful of houses dating from the late 18th century, but its best-known structure is the early-19th-century Ruggles House.

On the banks of the Pleasant River, just south of Columbia Falls, **Addison** (pop. 1,266) once had four huge shipyards cranking out wooden cargo vessels that circled the world. Today, the town may be best known as the haunt of painter John Marin, who first came to Maine in 1914.

Jonesport (pop. 1,370) and **Beals Island** (pop. 508) remain traditional hardworking fishing communities. Beals, connected to Jonesport via an arched bridge over Moosabec Reach, is named for Manwarren Beal Jr. and his wife, Lydia, who arrived around 1773 and quickly threw themselves into the Revolutionary War effort. But that's not all they did—the current phone book covering Jonesport and Beals Island lists dozens of Beal descendants (as well as dozens of Alleys and Carvers, other early names). Even more memorable than Manwarren was his six-foot, seven-inch descendant Barnabas, dubbed "Tall Barney." The larger-than-life fellow became the stuff of legend all along the Maine Coast.

Also legendary here is the lobsterboat design known as the Jonesport hull. Souped-up versions of the design are consistent winners in the summertime lobsterboat race series.

There's little here in terms of attractions, never mind lodging or dining, but self-sufficient, outdoor-oriented visitors and history buffs should enjoy the area's simple pleasures and raw beauty.

SIGHTS

Ruggles House

Behind a picket fence on a quiet street in Columbia Falls stands the remarkable **Ruggles House** (146 Main St., Columbia Falls, 207/483-4637, www.ruggleshouse.org, 10am-4pm Mon.-Sat., noon-4pm Sun. mid-June-mid-Oct., $5 adults, $2 ages 6-12). Built in 1818 for Judge Thomas Ruggles—lumber baron, militia captain, even postmaster—the tiny house on a grand scale boasts a famous flying (unsupported) staircase, intricately carved moldings, a Palladian window, and unusual period furnishings. Rescued in the mid-20th century and maintained by the Ruggles House Society, this gem has become a magnet for savvy preservationists. A quarter mile east of Route 1, it's open for hour-long guided tours.

Wreaths Across America Museum

Wreaths Across America has earned international fame for its annual wreath-laying at Arlington National Cemetery. This **museum** (4 Point St., Columbia Falls, 877/385-9504, www.wreathsacrossamerica.org, 9am-4pm Mon.-Fri., free), located at its headquarters, shows films and showcases items donated to the company over the years by veterans and their families. You can tour this heart-tugging memorial to American soldiers on your own or with a guide.

Wild Salmon Resource Center

Established in 1922, the **Wild Salmon Resource Center** (107 Main St., Columbia Falls, 207/483-4336, www.mainesalmonrivers.org, 9am-4pm Mon.-Fri., free), on the Pleasant River, has educational displays and a library. The basement-level, volunteer-run fish hatchery raises 50,000 Atlantic salmon fry annually. Staff welcome visitors and explain the efforts to save Maine's endangered salmon.

1

2

Downeast Institute for Applied Marine Research and Education

University of Maine at Machias professor Brian Beal founded the Beals Island Regional Shellfish Hatchery, now the **Downeast Institute** (Black Duck Cove, Great Wass Island, 207/497-5769, www.downeastinstitute.org), a marine field station for the University of Maine at Machias. Free tours are available; call ahead. Children's summer marine science camps are offered, usually lasting three days.

ENTERTAINMENT

For a taste of real Maine, don't miss the Downeast Salmon Federation's April **Smelt Fry** (207/483-4336), held under a riverside tent in Columbia Falls.

The biggest annual wingding hereabouts is Jonesport's **Fourth of July** celebration, with several days of special activities, including barbecues, a beauty pageant, kids' games, fireworks, and the famed **Jonesport Lobster Boat Races** in Moosabec Reach.

SHOPPING

You can't miss the humongous blueberry housing **Wild Blueberry Land and Heritage Center** (1067 Rte. 1, Columbia Falls, 207/483-2583, www.wildblueberrylandmaine.com). Step inside to find blueberry everything, from baked goods—including pies—to blueberry-themed merchandise ranging from scented candles to condiments. Displays chronicle the region's wild blueberry heritage.

Nelson Decoys/The Puffin Gift Shop/Downeast Art Gallery (13 Cranberry Ln., Jonesport, 207/497-3488) is equal parts shop, gallery, and museum. Inside are not only hand-carved decoys and birds, but also creations by other area artists and artisans. It's in an old schoolhouse, just off Main Street downtown.

1: fishing shack in Jonesport 2: Ruggles House

RECREATION

★ Great Wass Island Preserve

Allow a whole day to explore 1,576-acre Great Wass Island, an extraordinary preserve, even when it's drenched in fog—a not-infrequent event. Owned by the **Nature Conservancy** (207/729-5181, www.nature.org), the preserve is at the tip of Jonesport's peninsula. The best hiking routes are the wooded 2.2-mile Little Cape Point and 2.3-mile Mud Hole Trails, retracing your path for each or looping them via the shoreline for a 4.5-mile loop (allow about five hours). Note that neither is flat, the terrain is often uneven, and the exposed bedrock can be slippery. Expect to see beachhead irises (like a blue flag) and orchids, jack pines, a rare coastal peat bog, seals, pink granite, pitcher plants, lots of warblers, and maybe some grouse. Carry water and a picnic; wear bug repellent. No camping, fires, or pets are allowed, and there are no toilet facilities; access is during daytime only. To reach the preserve from Route 1, take Route 187 to Jonesport (12 miles) and then cross the arched bridge to Beals Island. Continue across Beals to the Great Wass causeway (locally called "the Flying Place") and then go three miles on Black Duck Cove Road to the parking area (on the left). Watch for the Nature Conservancy oak-leaf symbol. At the parking area, pick up a trail map and a bird checklist.

Boat Excursions

Operating as **Coastal Cruises** (Kelley Point Rd., Jonesport, 207/598-7473, www.cruisedowneast.com), captain Laura Fish and her brother Harry Fish offer three-hour Moosabec Reach cruises in the *Overtime,* a working lobster boat, or *Dorothy Helen,* a flat-bottom outboard skiff. Among the sights are Moose Peak Light and the islands of Moosabec Reach. Rates are $200 for the skiff, which takes up to three passengers, and $375 for the lobster boat, which holds up to six passengers. Reservations are required. Trips depart from Jonesport and operate May-mid-October.

FOOD

Pop into **Columbia Falls General** (150 Main St., Columbia Falls, 207/483-8092, 9am-5pm Wed.-Thurs., 9am-7pm Fri., 10am-7pm Sat., 10am-4pm Sun.) for local products, baked goods, penny candy, ice cream, and more.

Jonesport Pizza Shop (187 Main St., Jonesport, 207/497-2187, 4am-8pm Mon.-Sat.), locally known as Nellie's, does decent pizza and subs. Across the bridge, **Bayview Takeout** (42 Bayview Dr., Beals, 207/497-3301, 11am-8pm daily) delivers on its slogan, "Wicked Good Food." Burgers and subs run $4-10, with seafood at market rates.

ACCOMMODATIONS

How about staying in a beautiful modern farmhouse overlooking the water—with llamas lolling outside? At **Pleasant Bay Bed and Breakfast** (386 West Side Rd., Addison, 207/483-4490, www.pleasantbay.com, year-round, $60-170), a 110-acre working farm, Joan Yeaton and Jerry Metz manage to pamper llamas as well as their two-legged guests. Three miles of trails wind through the 110 acres, and a canoe is available for guests. Three lovely guest rooms (private and shared baths) and one suite all have water views. Rates include breakfast. The farm borders Pleasant Bay, 3.9 miles southwest of Route 1.

Proprietor Dorothy Higgins's **Cranberry Cove Cottage Studio** (56 Kelley Point Rd., Jonesport, 207/598-6138, cranberry-cove@hotmail.com, $125) occupies the loft of a restored carriage house. Kayaks are provided. Pets are welcome. Rates decrease with the length of stay.

Camping

The town of Jonesport operates the low-key, no-frills **Henry Point Campground** (Henry Point, Kelley Point Rd., Jonesport, 207/598-2274, early May-Labor Day, $25) on two acres with fabulous views over Sawyer Cove and Moosabec Reach. Showers and washing machines are available across the cove at Jonesport Shipyard (207/497-2701). The campground is exposed to wind off the water, so expect nights to be cool. Sites are allocated on a first-come, first-served basis. From Route 187 at the northeastern edge of Jonesport, turn right onto Kelley Point Road and then right again to Henry Point.

INFORMATION

The town maintains a website (www.townofjonesport.com) with listings of area businesses.

GETTING THERE AND AROUND

Jonesport is about 25 miles or 30 minutes via Routes 1 and 187 from Milbridge. It's about 22 miles or 30 minutes via Routes 187 and 1 to Machias.

Machias Bay Area

The only negative thing about **Machias** (muh-CHAI-us, pop. 1,221) is its Micmac Indian name, meaning "bad little falls" (even though it's accurate—the midtown waterfall here is treacherous). A contagious local esprit pervades this shire town of Washington County thanks to antique homes, a splendid river-valley setting, Revolutionary War monuments, and a small university campus.

An ideal time to land here is during the renowned annual Machias Wild Blueberry Festival, the third weekend in August, when harvesting is underway in Washington County's blueberry fields and you can stuff your face with blueberry everything—muffins, jam, pancakes, ice cream, and pies. You can also collect blueberry-logo napkins, T-shirts, magnets, pottery, and jewelry. The biggest highlights: the summer musical parody and the pie-eating contest. Unless you're attending it, avoid the area that weekend.

Among the other summer draws are a chamber-music series, hiking, biking, and sea kayaking.

Also included within the Machias sphere are the towns of **Roque Bluffs, Jonesboro, Whitneyville, Marshfield, East Machias,** and **Machiasport.** Just to the east, between Machias and Lubec, are the towns of **Whiting** and **Cutler.**

HISTORICAL SIGHTS

History is a big deal in this area, and since Machias was the first settled Maine town east of the Penobscot River, lots of enthusiastic amateur historians have helped rescue homes and sites dating from as far back as the Revolutionary War.

English settlers, uprooted from communities farther west on the Maine Coast, put down permanent roots here in 1763, harvesting timber to ensure their survival. Stirrings of revolutionary discontent surfaced even at this remote outpost, and when British loyalists in Boston began usurping some of the valuable harvest, Machias patriots plotted revenge. By 1775, when the armed British schooner *Margaretta* arrived as a cargo escort, local residents aboard the sloop *Unity,* in a real David-and-Goliath episode, chased and captured the *Margaretta.* On June 12, 1775, two months after the famed Battles of Lexington and Concord (and five days before the Battle of Bunker Hill), Machias Bay was the site of what author James Fenimore Cooper called "the Lexington of the Sea"—the first naval battle of the American Revolution. The name of patriot leader Jeremiah O'Brien today appears throughout the Machias area—on a school, a street, a cemetery, and a state park. In 1784, Machias was incorporated; it became the shire town in 1790.

Museums

One of 21 homes in the entire country designated as most significant to the American Revolution, the 1770 **Burnham Tavern** (14 Colonial Way, Machias, 207/733-4577, www.burnhamtavern.com, 10am-3pm Mon.-Fri. July-Aug. or by appointment, $5 adults, $1-2 kids) comes to life on one-hour guided tours. Upstart local patriots met here in 1775 to plot revolution against the British. Job and Mary Burnham's tavern-home next served as an infirmary for casualties from the Revolution's first naval battle, just offshore. Lots of fascinating history lies in this National Historic Site, maintained by the Daughters of the American Revolution. Hanging outside is a sign reading "Drink for the thirsty, food for the hungry, lodging for the weary, and good keeping for horses, by Job Burnham."

Headquarters for the Machiasport Historical Society and one of the area's three oldest residences, the 1810 **Gates House** (344 Port Rd., Machiasport, 207/255-8461, 12:30pm-4:30pm Tues.-Fri. July-Aug., or by appointment, free) was snatched from ruin and restored in 1966. The building, listed in the National Register of Historic Places, overlooks Machias Bay and contains fascinating period furnishings and artifacts, many related to the lumbering and shipbuilding era. The museum, four miles southeast of Route 1, has limited parking on a hazardous curve.

O'Brien Cemetery

Old-cemetery buffs will want to stop at **O'Brien Cemetery,** resting place of the town's earliest settlers. It's next to Bad Little Falls Park, close to downtown, off Route 92 toward Machiasport. A big plus here is the view, especially in autumn, of blueberry barrens, the waterfall, and the bay.

Fort O'Brien State Historic Site

The American Revolution's first naval battle was fought just offshore from **Fort O'Brien** (207/726-4412, www.parksandlands.com, free) in June 1775. Now a State Historic Site, the fort was originally built to guard Machias during the Revolutionary War and was later rebuilt several times. Only Civil War-era

Two Scenic Routes

The drives described below can also be bike routes (easy to moderately difficult) but be forewarned that the roads are narrow and shoulderless, so caution is essential. Heed biking etiquette.

ROUTE 191, THE CUTLER ROAD

Never mind that Route 191, between East Machias and West Lubec, is one of Maine's most stunning coastal drives—you can still follow the entire 27-mile stretch and meet only a handful of cars. **East Machias** even has its own historic district, with architectural gems dating from the late 18th century along High and Water Streets. Farther along Route 191, you'll find fishing wharves, low moorlands, a hamlet or two, and islands popping over the horizon. The only peculiarly jarring note is the 26-tower forest of North Cutler's Naval Computer and Telecommunications Station, nearly 1,000 feet high—monitoring global communications—but you'll see this only briefly. (At night, the skyscraping red lights are really eerie, especially if you're offshore aboard a boat.) Off Route 191 are minor roads and hiking trails worth exploring, especially the coastal trails lacing Cutler Coast Public Preserve. About three miles south of the Route 191 terminus is **Bailey's Mistake,** a hamlet with a black-sand (volcanic) beach. The name? Allegedly it stems from one Captain Bailey who, misplotting his course and thinking he was in Lubec, drove his vessel ashore here one night in the late 19th century. Unwilling to face the consequences of his lapse, he and his crew off-loaded their cargo of lumber and built themselves dwellings. Whether true or not, it makes a great saga. Even though it's in the town of **Trescott,** and the hamlet is really South Trescott, everyone knows this section as Bailey's Mistake.

ROUTE 92, STARBOARD PENINSULA

Pack a picnic and set out on Route 92 (beginning at Elm Street in downtown Machias) down the 10-mile length of the Starboard Peninsula to a stunning spot known as the Point of Maine. Along the way are the villages of Larrabee, Bucks Harbor, and Starboard, all part of the town of Machiasport. In Bucks Harbor is the turnoff (a short detour to the right) to **Yoho Head,** a controversial upscale development overlooking Little Kennebec Bay.

South of the Yoho Head turnoff is the sign for **Jasper Beach.** From the Jasper Beach sign, continue 1.4 miles to two red buildings (the old Starboard School House and the volunteer fire department). Turn left onto a dirt road and continue to a sign reading Driveway. Go around the right side of a shed and park on the beach. (Keep track of the tide level, though.) You're at **Point of Maine,** a quintessential Down East panorama of sea and islands. On a clear day, you can see the offshore **Libby Island Light,** the focus of Philmore Wass's entertaining narrative *Lighthouse in My Life: The Story of a Maine Lightkeeper's Family.*

earthworks remain. Officially the park is open Memorial Day weekend-Labor Day, but it's accessible all year. Take Route 92 from Machias about five miles toward Machiasport; the parking area is on the left.

OTHER SIGHTS

Maine Sea Salt Company

Season your visit with a tour of the **Maine Sea Salt Company** (11 Church Ln., Marshfield, 207/255-3310, www.maineseasalt.com), which produces sea salt in its solar greenhouses and shallow pools using evaporation and reduction of seawater. Free tours (available 9am-5pm most days May-late Oct., call first) explain the process and include tastings of natural, seasoned, and smoked salts.

Little River Lighthouse

Friends of the **Little River Lighthouse** (207/259-3833, www.littleriverlight.org) usually open the restored lighthouse and tower for tours once or twice each summer. Transportation is provided to the island from Cutler Harbor. Donations benefit care and maintenance of the 1876 beacon.

ENTERTAINMENT

The **University of Maine at Machias** (207/255-1384, www.machias.edu) is the cultural focus in this area, particularly during the school year.

If the **Machias Ukulele Club** is performing anywhere, don't miss them. **Machias Bay Chamber Concerts** (207/255-3849, www.machiasbaychamberconcerts.com, $15 suggested donation per adult, free for students 18 and younger) are held at 7pm on Tuesday evenings in July at the Centre Street Congregational Church. Art exhibits accompany concerts.

The **Machias Wild Blueberry Festival** (www.machiasblueberry.com) is the summer highlight, running Friday-Saturday the third weekend in August and featuring a pancake breakfast, road races, concerts, crafts booths, a baked-bean supper, a homegrown musical, and more. The blueberry motif is everywhere. It's organized by Centre Street Congregational Church, United Church of Christ, in downtown Machias.

SHOPPING

Influenced by traditional Japanese designs, Connie Harter-Bagley markets her dramatic raku ceramics at **Connie's Clay of Fundy** (335 Main St./Rte. 1, East Machias, 207/255-4574, www.clayoffundy.com), on the East Machias River, four miles east of Machias. If she's at the wheel, you can also watch her work.

Flower-design majolica pottery and whimsical terra-cotta items are April Adams's specialties at **Columbia Falls Pottery** (4 Main St., Machias, 207/483-4075, www.columbiafallspottery.com), an appealing shop in a rehabbed country store next to the Ruggles House.

RECREATION

Parks, Preserves, and Beaches

BAD LITTLE FALLS PARK

At Bad Little Falls Park, alongside the Machias River, stop to catch the view from the footbridge overlooking the roiling falls (especially in spring). Bring a picnic and enjoy this midtown oasis tucked between Routes 1 and 92.

JASPER BEACH

Thanks to a handful of foresighted year-round and summer residents, spectacular crescent-shaped **Jasper Beach**—piled high with ocean-polished stones—has been preserved by the town of Machiasport. There is no sand here, just seemingly endless smooth rocks in intriguing shapes and colors. According to the Maine Geological Survey, although the beach is named for jasper, a form of iron-enriched silica, the disc-shaped red volcanic stone here is rhyolite; the rounder ones are granites and quartzites. Resist the urge to fill your pockets with souvenirs. From Route 1 in downtown Machias, take Route 92 (Elm Street) 9.5 miles southeast, past the village of Bucks Harbor. Watch for a large sign on your left. The beach is on Howard's Cove, 0.2 mile off the road and accessible year-round. There are no facilities.

ROQUE BLUFFS STATE PARK

Southwest of Machias, six miles south of Route 1, is **Roque Bluffs State Park** (Roque Bluffs Rd., Roque Bluffs, 207/255-3475, www.parksandlands.com). Saltwater swimming this far north is for the young and brave, but this 274-acre park on Schoppee Point also comprises 60-acre Simpson Pond, with freshwater warm and shallow enough for toddlers and the old and timid. Facilities include primitive changing rooms, outhouses, hiking trails, a play area, and picnic tables; there is no food and there are no lifeguards. Views go on forever from the wide-open, half-mile-long sweep of sand-and-pebble beach. Keep an eye out for eagles and sea ducks. Admission is $6 nonresident adults, $4 Maine resident adults, $1 ages 5-11 (the fee box relies on the honor system). The park is open daily May 15-September 15, but the beach is accessible year-round.

★ CUTLER COAST PUBLIC RESERVE

On the seaward side of Route 191, about 4.5 miles northeast of Cutler's center, watch for the parking area for the **Cutler Coast Public Reserve,** a spectacular preserve with nearly a dozen miles of beautifully engineered hiking trails. Originally about 2,100 acres, this preserve expanded fivefold in 1997 when several donors, primarily the Richard King Mellon Foundation, deeded to the state 10,055 acres of fields and forests across Route 191 from the trail area, creating a phenomenal tract that now runs from the ocean all the way back to Route 1. It is Maine's second-largest public-land gift after Baxter State Park. Today the park is popular with wildlife-watchers: Birding is great, and you might spot whales (humpback, finback, northern right, and minke), seals, and porpoises. If you're here in August, you can stock up on blueberries and even some wild raspberries.

The easiest trail is the 2.8-mile round-trip Coastal Trail through a cedar swamp and spruce-fir forest to an ocean promontory and back. For a longer hike, take the 5.5-mile round-trip Black Point Brook Loop, which progresses along a stretch of moderately rugged hiking southward along dramatic tree-fringed shoreline cliffs. Allow 5-6 hours for the hike and bring binoculars and a camera; the views from this wild coastline are fabulous, and the granite ledges overlooking the surf are great places for a picnic. Precipitous cliffs and narrow stretches can make the shoreline section of this trail perilous for small children or insecure adults, so use extreme caution and common sense. Insect repellent is helpful for the inland boggy stretches. Another option, the 9.2-mile Fairy Head Loop, starts the same way as the Black Point Brook Loop but continues southward along the coast, leading to three primitive campsites (stoves only, no fires) available on a first-come, first-served basis. Unless you have gazelle genes, this longer loop almost demands an overnight trip.

There are no facilities in the preserve. Information on the preserve, including a helpful map, is available from the **Maine Bureau of Parks and Lands** (207/287-3821, www.parksandlands.com).

BOG BROOK COVE PRESERVE

Adjacent to the Cutler Coast Public Preserve, on Route 191, is Maine Coast Heritage Trust's

Wild Blueberry Land and Heritage Center

(www.mcht.org) **Bog Brook Cove Preserve.** Between the two preserves, this is the largest contiguous area of conservation land in the state outside of Acadia National Park. Bog Brook Cove's lands flow from Cutler into neighboring Trescott and include nearly three miles of ocean frontage with headlands, smashing views of Grand Manan Island, gravel beaches, coastal peatlands, and 10-acre Norse Pond. The moderate, three-mile Norse Pond Trail takes in the pond and rises to a headland, with views over the Grand Manan Channel, before descending to Bog Brook Cove and a rocky beach. The northern access, via Moose River Road, begins with a 0.2-mile wheelchair/stroller-accessible trail to an overlook, before continuing as a footpath to Moose Cove. The challenging, 2.3-mile Ridge Trail comprises two loops.

Water Sports

If you've brought your own sea kayak, there are public launch ramps in Bucks Harbor (east of Rte. 92, the main Machiasport road) and at Roque Bluffs State Park. You can also put in at Sanborn Cove, beyond the O'Brien School on Route 92, about five miles south of Machias, where there's a small parking area. Before setting out, check the tide calendar and plan your strategy so you don't have to slog through acres of muck when you return.

Sunrise Canoe and Kayak (188 Main St., Machias, 207/255-3375, www.sunrisecanoeandkayak.com) rents canoes and kayaks for $25-45/day and offers sea kayak excursions ($65 half day, $110 full day) on Machias Bay, including one to a petroglyph site. It also offers guided day trips and fully outfitted multiday canoeing and kayaking excursions on the Machias and St. Croix Rivers and along the Bold Coast. Owner Rob Scribner is a third-generation Maine Guide.

The **Machias River,** one of Maine's most technically demanding canoeing rivers, is a dynamite trip mid-May-mid-June, but no beginner should attempt it. The best advice is to sign on with an outfitter or guide. The run lasts from four days up to six days if you start from Fifth Machias Lake. Expect to see wildlife such as ospreys, eagles, ducks, loons, moose, deer, beavers, and snapping turtles. Be aware, though, that the Machias is probably the buggiest river in the state, and blackflies will form a welcoming party. In addition to Sunrise Canoe and Kayak, Bangor-based **Sunrise Expeditions** (207/942-9300, www.sunrise-exp.com) also offers fully outfitted trips.

Boat Excursions

★ MACHIAS SEAL ISLAND PUFFIN TOUR

Andy Patterson, skipper of the 40-foot *Barbara Frost,* operates the **Bold Coast Charter Company** (207/259-4484, www.boldcoast.com), homeported in Cutler Harbor. Andy provides knowledgeable narration, answers questions in depth, and shares his considerable enthusiasm for this pristine corner of Maine. He is best known for his five-hour puffin-sighting trips to Machias Seal Island (departing between 7am and 8am daily mid-May-Aug., $150, no credit cards); the trip is unsuitable for small children or adults who are susceptible to seasickness. Daily access to the island is restricted and swells can roll in, so passengers occasionally cannot disembark, but the curious puffins often surround the boat, providing plenty of photo opportunities. No matter what the air temperature on the mainland, dress warmly and wear sturdy shoes. The *Barbara Frost*'s wharf is on Cutler Harbor, just off Route 191. Look for the Little River Lobster Company sign; you'll depart from the boat launch. All trips are dependent on weather and tide conditions, and reservations are required. Note: Reserve early, because trips can sell out months in advance.

FOOD

Watch the local papers for listings of **public suppers, spaghetti suppers,** or **baked-bean suppers,** a terrific way to sample the culinary talents of local cooks. Most begin at 5pm, and it's wise to arrive early to get near

Puffins

The chickadee is the Maine state bird, and the bald eagle is our national emblem, but probably the best-loved bird along the Maine Coast is the Atlantic puffin, a member of the auk family. Photographs show an imposing-looking creature with a quizzical mien; amazingly, this larger-than-life seabird is only about 12 inches long. Black-backed and white-chested, the puffin has bright orange legs, "clown makeup" eyes, and a distinctive, rather outlandish red-and-yellow beak. Its diet is fish and shellfish.

Almost nonexistent in this part of the world as recently as the 1970s, the puffin (or "sea parrot") has recovered dramatically thanks to the unstinting efforts of Cornell University ornithologist Stephen Kress and his **Project Puffin** (www.projectpuffin.org). Starting with an orphan colony of two on remote Matinicus Rock, Kress painstakingly transferred nearly a thousand puffin chicks (also known fondly as "pufflings") from Newfoundland and used artificial nests and decoys to entice the birds to adapt to and reproduce on Eastern Egg Rock in Muscongus Bay.

In 1981, thanks to the assistance and persistence of hundreds of interns and volunteers, and despite the predations of great black-backed gulls, puffins finally were fledged on Eastern Egg, and the rest, as they say, is history. Within 20 years, more than three dozen puffin couples were nesting on Eastern Egg Rock, and still more had established nests on other islands in the area. Kress's methods have received international attention, and his proven techniques have been used to reintroduce bird populations in remote parts of the globe. In 2001, *Down East* magazine singled out Kress to receive its prestigious annual Environmental Award.

HOW AND WHERE TO SEE PUFFINS

Puffin-watching, like whale-watching, involves heading offshore, so be prepared with warm clothing, rubber-soled shoes, a hat, sunscreen, binoculars, and, if you're motion-sensitive, appropriate medication.

Eastern Egg Rock colony: Maine Audubon naturalists accompany tours aboard **Hardy Boat Cruises** (Rte. 32, New Harbor, 207/677-2026, www.hardyboat.com, 1.5 hours, mid-May-late Aug., $35 adults, $15 ages 2-11), out of **New Harbor,** and **Cap'n Fish's Cruises** (Pier 1, Wharf St., Boothbay Harbor, 207/633-3244 or 800/636-3244, www.boothbayboattrips.com, 2.5 hours, June-late Aug., $39 adults, $17 children), out of **Boothbay Harbor.**

Petit Manan colony: Excursion boats operated by **Bar Harbor Whale Watch Company** (1 West St., Bar Harbor, 207/288-2386 or 800/942-5374, www.barharborwhales.com, 3.5-4 hours, daily late May-mid-Aug., around $65 adults, $35 ages 6-14, $14 under age 6) depart from **Bar Harbor**, and those operated by **Robertson Sea Tours and Adventures** (Milbridge Marina, Fickett's Point Rd., 207/483-6110 or 207/461-7439, www.robertsonseatours.com, 3 hours, mid-May-mid-Aug., $75 adults, $55 children) depart from **Milbridge.**

Machias Seal Island colony: The best daily up-close-and-personal opportunities for puffin-watching along the Down East Coast—specifically on Machias Seal Island—are with **Bold Coast Charters** (207/259-4484, www.boldcoast.com, 5 hours, daily mid-May-Aug., about $150 pp), which departs from **Cutler.** Weather permitting, you'll be allowed to disembark on the 20-acre island.

If you can't get afloat to see puffins, the next best thing is a visit to the **Project Puffin Visitor Center** (311 Main St., Rockland, 877/478-3346), where you can view exhibits, a film, and live video feeds of nesting puffins.

ADOPT-A-PUFFIN PROGRAM

Stephen Kress's Project Puffin has devised a clever way to enlist supporters via the Adopt-a-Puffin program (www.projectpuffin.org). For a $100 donation, you'll receive a certificate of adoption, biography, and book.

the head of the line. The suppers often benefit needy individuals or struggling nonprofits, and where else can you eat nonstop for less than $10?

Quick Bites

Craving something healthful? The **Whole Life Natural Market** (4 Colonial Way, Machias, 207/255-8855, www.wholelifemarket.com, 9am-5pm Mon.-Sat.) houses the **Saltwater Café** (9am-2pm Mon.-Sat.), serving salads, soups, sandwiches, and baked goods made from organic fruits, vegetables, and grains as well as hormone-free dairy products. When the café isn't open, grab-and-go foods are usually available in the store. The **French Cellar** (4 Colonial Way, Machias, 207/255-4977), which carries fine wines, craft beers, and a nice selection of cheeses, shares the building.

Another source for fresh, healthful foods is the **Machias Valley Farmers Market** (9am-1pm Fri.-Sat. May-Oct.). It's held on "the dike," a low causeway next to the Machias River. It's usually a good source for blueberries in late July-August.

Riverside Take-Out (Rte. 1, Machias, 207/263-7676, 11am-7pm Thurs.-Sun.), a trailer-esque shack in a dirt lot wedged between road and river, doesn't look like much, but road-food cognoscenti heap praise on the monster haddock burger, house-made onion rings, and sweet potato fries as reasons alone to stop.

For authentic German take-out fare, stop by **Jo's World Famous Schnitzel Wagon** (54 Water St., Machias, 207/200-3001, 11am-7pm Mon.-Sat.), a food truck that moves around town.

Family Favorites

★ **Helen's** (111 Main St./Rte. 1, Machias, 207/255-8423, www.helensrestaurantmachias.com, 6am-8pm Mon.-Sat., 7am-2pm Sun., $6-30), an institution in these parts since 1950, is on the banks of the Machias River, with great views, especially from the deck, where cocktails and apps are served. Save room for the legendary wild blueberry pie.

Family-owned and very popular all day long is the **Blue Bird Ranch Family Restaurant** (78 Main St./Rte. 1, Machias, 207/255-3351, www.bluebirdranchrestaurant.com, 6am-8:30pm daily, $6-25), named for the Prout family's other enterprise, the Blue Bird Ranch Trucking Company. Service is efficient, the food is hearty, the desserts are homemade, and the portions are ample in the three dining rooms.

ACCOMMODATIONS

Inns and Cabins

After a meticulous restoration, Michael and Liz Henry opened the **Talbot House Inn** (509 Main St., E. Machias, 207/259-1103, www.thetalbothouseinn.com, $115) in a Mansard-roofed mansion that served as a stop on the Underground Railroad. The house is rife with architectural riches, but the bathrooms (some shared) are modern.

The **Chandler River Inn** (654 Rte. 1, Jonesboro, 207/434-2540, www.chandlerriverinn.com, $135-165) reopened in 2019 after new owners made much-needed updates to this lovely, late 18th-century, five-room bed-and-breakfast on 20 riverside acres. Kayaks are available for use on the river, when launching from the inn. Dinner may be available.

The second generation now operates **Micmac Farm Guesthouses** (47 Micmac Ln., Machiasport, 207/255-3008, www.micmacfarm.com, $105/night, $650/week). Stay in one of Anthony and Bonnie Dunn's three rustic but comfortable and well-equipped cottages with kitchenette and dining area, and you'll find yourself on the deck over the tidal Machias River and watching for seabirds, seals, and eagles. (Note: Mosquitoes can be pesky.) Pets and children are welcome. There's also a river-view room in the restored 18th-century Gardner House, with a private bath with whirlpool tub ($125, includes a light breakfast). All guests have use of the farmhouse, including a library.

Motels

For inexpensive digs, you can't beat the **Blueberry Patch** (550 Rte. 1, Jonesboro, 207/434-5411, www.blueberrypatchmotel.com, $80-100), a clean and bright motel and tourist cabins, with three efficiency units. Robert and Tammie Alley provide homespun hospitality with a few extras. There's a pool and a small playground. If you're taller than six feet, choose a motel room rather than a cabin; the cabin bathrooms are tiny. Morning muffins—blueberry, of course—and coffee are included. Some rooms are pet friendly.

Don't judge the **Margaretta Inn** (330 Main St., Machias, 207/255-6671, www.margarettainn.com, $110-125) by its exterior. Completely renovated in 2014, this vintage 1960s motel offers a lot of bang for your buck. The 12 air-conditioned rooms have mini-fridges, microwaves, and duvet-topped beds dressed in white.

Most of the 28 guest rooms and six efficiencies at the two-story **Machias River Inn** (109 Main St./Rte. 1, Machias, 207/255-4861, www.machiasriverinn.com, year-round, $124-175) overlook the tidal Machias River. Next door is Helen's Restaurant—famed for seasonal fruit pies and an all-you-can-eat weekend breakfast buffet. Well-behaved dogs ($10/dog/night) are welcome. The motel is within easy walking distance of downtown, which makes it perfect if you're here for the Blueberry Festival.

Lighthouse

Yes, you can spend a night or more at **Little River Lighthouse** (Cutler, 877/276-4682, www.littleriverlight.org, $150-225), thanks to the Friends of Little River Lighthouse. Three guest rooms sharing two baths are available, but you have to bring food, bottled water, towels, bed linens or sleeping bags, and all personal items (soap, shampoo) and clean up after yourself. Guests have use of a kitchen. Transportation to the lighthouse is provided, but you have to coordinate your arrival with the tide. No children younger than 12.

INFORMATION AND SERVICES

The **Machias Bay Area Chamber of Commerce** (85 E. Main St., Machias, 207/255-4402, www.machiaschamber.org) stocks brochures, maps, and information on area hiking trails.

GETTING THERE AND AROUND

Machias is about 22 miles or 30 minutes via Routes 1 and 187 from Jonesport. It's about 28 miles or 40 minutes via Routes 1 and 189 to Lubec.

Lubec

As the nation's easternmost point, **Lubec** (pop. 1,359) is literally the beginning of the United States. Settled in 1780 as part of Eastport, it split off in 1811 and was named for the German port of Lübeck. The town's most famous resident was Hopley Yeaton, first captain in the U.S. Revenue-Marine (now the U.S. Coast Guard), who retired here in 1809.

With appealing homes and more than 90 miles of meandering waterfront, Lubec conveys the aura of realness. (Lubec residents love to point out that the closest traffic light is 50 miles away.) Along the main drag, Water Street, a number of shuttered buildings, many undergoing restoration, reflect the town's roller-coaster history. Once the world's sardine capital, Lubec no longer has a packing plant, but new businesses are slowly arriving, and each year the town looks a bit spiffier. These days, the summer residents far outnumber year-rounders. Arrive here on a fine summer day and it's easy to understand why so many visitors are smitten and, seduced by the views and the real estate prices, purchase a piece of a dream.

Be sure to bring appropriate identification if planning on crossing the International Bridge to Campobello Island, New Brunswick, home to Roosevelt Campobello International Park and a few other noteworthy sites.

SIGHTS

★ Quoddy Head State Park

Beachcombing, bird-watching, hiking, picnicking, and an up-close look at Maine's only red-and-white-striped lighthouse are the big draws at 541-acre **Quoddy Head State Park** (973 S. Lubec Rd., Lubec, 207/733-0911, www.parksandlands.com, 9am-sunset May 15-Oct. 15, $3-4 adults, $1 children), the easternmost point of the United States. Begin with a stop at the **visitors center** (207/733-2180, www.westquoddy.com, 10am-4pm daily late May-early July and early Sept.-mid-Oct., 10am-4:30pm Mon.-Sat., 10am-4pm Sun. July-Aug., free), located in the 1858 keeper's house and operated by the enthusiastic all-volunteer West Quoddy Head Light Keepers Association. Inside are exhibits on lighthouse memorabilia, local flora and fauna, and area heritage; a gallery displaying local works; and a staffed information desk.

The current **West Quoddy Head Light,** towering 83 feet above mean high water, was built in 1857. (Its counterpart, Head Harbour Lightstation, aka East Quoddy Head Light, is on New Brunswick's Campobello Island.) Views from the lighthouse grounds are fabulous, and whale sightings are common in summer. The lighthouse tower is open the Saturday after July 4; during Maine Open Lighthouse Day, usually held in September; and other times when Coast Guard personnel are on-site and available. Check the visitors center website for dates.

The cliffs of Canada's Grand Manan Island are visible from the park's grounds. The four-mile round-trip, moderately difficult **Coastal Trail** follows the 90-foot cliffs to Carrying Place Cove. The easy, mile-long **Bog Trail** loops via boardwalk through a unique moss and heath bog; a second bog is designated as a National Natural Landmark. The one-mile **Coast Guard Trail** loops out to an observation point; the western half is accessible to motorized wheelchairs and non-motorized with assistance. Be forewarned that the park gate is locked at sunset. In winter the park is accessible for snowshoeing. From Route 189 on the outskirts of Lubec, take South Lubec Road (well signposted) to West Quoddy Head Road. Turn left and continue to the parking area.

Mulholland Market and McCurdy's Herring Smokehouse

Lubec Landmarks (207/733-2197, www.lubeclandmarks.org) is working to preserve these local landmarks. The **smokehouse complex** (10am-4pm Wed.-Sun., $3 donation), one of the last herring-smoking operations in the country (closed in 1991 and now a National Historic Landmark), can be seen on the water side of Water Street. In 2007, after years of effort, it reopened to the public. You can tour it on your own, or volunteer guides will explain the exhibits, which include hands-on ones for kids. Next door, **Mulholland Market Gallery** (50 Water St., 10am-4pm daily), the organization's headquarters, doubles as a community center. Inside are displays about the smokehouses, exhibits of local art, and a small gift shop. It is volunteer-operated, so hours aren't set in stone.

Robert S. Peacock Fire Museum

Worth a look-see for fans of old fire equipment, the small **museum at the fire station** (40 School St., Lubec, 207/733-2341) is open by request at the adjacent town office.

Lubec Breakwater

The region's humongous tides and dramatic sunsets over Johnson Bay can be appreciated from the town's breakwater. **Lost Fishermen's Memorial Park,** honoring

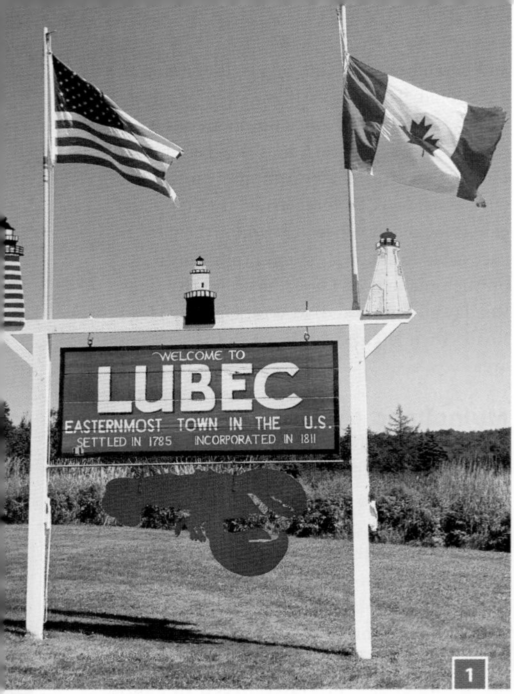

WELCOME TO
LUBEC
EASTERNMOST TOWN IN THE U.S.
SETTLED IN 1785 INCORPORATED IN 1811

1

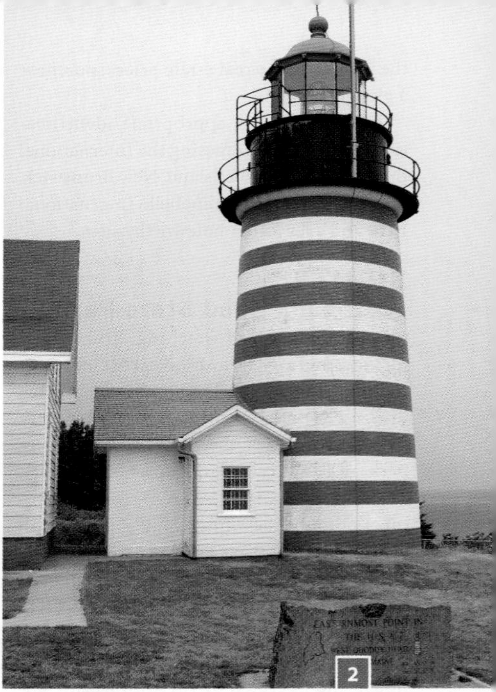

2

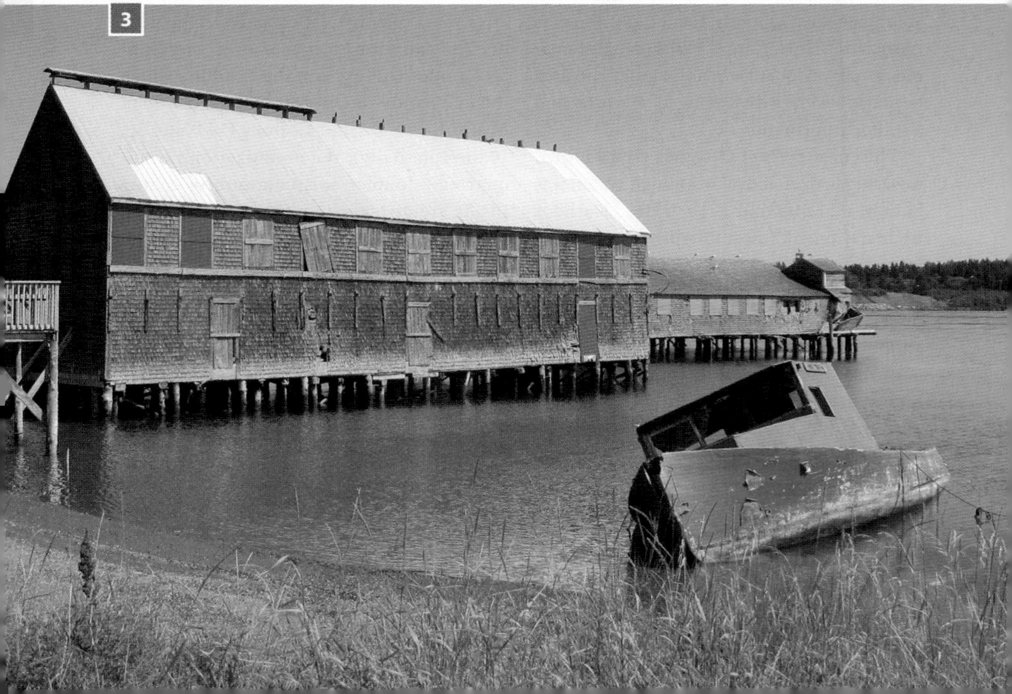

3

regional fishermen lost at sea, provides views across the channel to Campobello Island and red-capped **Mulholland Point Lighthouse,** an abandoned beacon built in 1885 that's now part of Roosevelt Campobello International Park. As the tide goes out—18 or so feet—you'll see hungry harbor seals dunking for dinner. And if you're lucky, you might spot the eagles that nest nearby (bring binoculars).

ENTERTAINMENT

Classical music is the focus (for the most part) at **SummerKeys** (207/733-2316 or 973/316-6220 off-season, www.summerkeys.com), a music camp for adults, no prior experience required, with weeklong programs in piano, voice, oboe, flute, clarinet, guitar, violin, and cello. Recently it expanded its offerings to writing and photography. Free concerts by visiting artists, faculty, and students are held at 7:30pm Wednesday evenings late June-early September in the Congregational Christian Church on Church Street.

Live music is often on tap at Cohill's Inn and Lubec Brewing Co., both on Water Street, and live jazz often enlivens Crow Tree Gallery, usually on Sundays. The **Lubec Area Musicians' Philanthropic Society** (www.lampsdowneast.org) offers a free summer concert series.

The **Masons' Music and Barbecue,** held most Thursday evenings from late June to late August at the town bandstand on Main Street, includes an all-you-can-eat cookout ($10 adults, $4 children) and a free concert.

Timber-frame buildings built by the **Cobscook Community Learning Center** (Timber Cove Rd., Trescott, 207/733-2233, www.thecclc.org) house an open pottery studio, a fiber-arts studio, and multipurpose classrooms. The year-round programs offered include open-jam music nights, workshops, talks, adult education, indigenous education, sustainable and value-added eco-ventures, youth programs, and more.

Birders flock to the Cobscook Bay area for the **Down East Spring Birding Festival** (207/733-2233, www.downeastbirdfest.org), held annually in late May. Guided and self-guided explorations, presentations, and tours fill the schedule, and participation is limited, so register early.

The **Bay of Fundy International Marathon,** a Boston Marathon qualifier, is a big draw in June.

SHOPPING

In downtown Lubec, **Wags and Wool** (24 Water St., Lubec, 207/733-4714) caters to knitters and dog lovers, with natural fibers, local yarns, handknit sweaters, socks, and gloves, and dog toys and accessories; **Seventh Stream Gift Shop** (38 Water St., Lubec, 207/263-5903) carries bath and body products and a nice selection of New England made crafts and products; and **Shop by the Sea** (69 Johnson St., Lubec, 207/733-4400) at the Inn on the Wharf, offers a wide selection of treasures, from postcards to original paintings, clothing to stuffed animals.

Monica's Chocolates (100 County Rd./Rte. 189, Lubec, 866/952-4500, www.monicaschocolates.com, 8am-8pm daily) gives meaning to the term *sinfully delicious.* Monica Elliott creates sumptuous handmade gourmet chocolates using family recipes from her native Peru. Her hot chocolate, not always available, is swoon-worthy. Monica also sells jewelry and sweaters and other items from Peru.

Lighthouse buffs must stop at **West Quoddy Gifts** (Quoddy Head Rd., one mile before the lighthouse, 207/733-2457). It's stocked with souvenirs and gift items, most with a lighthouse theme.

Fred and Patty Hartman's **DownEast Drawings and Wildlife Art Gallery** (Rte. 189, Whiting, 207/733-0988) is filled with award-winning artwork featuring the flora and fauna of the region. Shanna Wheelock displays her gorgeous pottery as well as fine

1: Lubec, the easternmost point in the country
2: West Quoddy Head Light **3:** former smokehouse on Lubec's waterfront

Tides

Nowhere in Maine is the adage "Time and tide wait for no man" truer than along the Washington County coastline. The nation's most extreme tidal ranges occur in this area, so the hundreds of miles of tidal shore frontage between Steuben and Calais provide countless opportunities for observing tidal phenomena. Every six hours or so, the tide begins either ebbing or flowing. The farther Down East you go, the higher (and lower) the tides. Although tides in Canada's Bay of Fundy are far higher, the highest tides in New England occur along the St. Croix River at Calais.

Tides govern coastal life—particularly Down East, where average tidal ranges may be 10-20 feet and extremes approach 28 feet. Everyone is a slave to the tide calendar, which coastal-community newspapers diligently publish. Boats tie up with extralong lines, clammers and worm diggers schedule their days by the tides, hikers must plan for shoreline exploring, and kayakers need to plan their routes to avoid getting stuck in the muck.

Tides, as we learned in school, are lunar phenomena, created by the moon's gravitational pull; the tidal range depends on the lunar phase. Tides are most extreme at new and full moons—when the sun, moon, and Earth are aligned. These are spring tides, supposedly because the water springs upward (the term has nothing to do with the season). And tides are smallest during the moon's first and third quarters—when the sun, Earth, and moon have a right-angle configuration. These are neap tides (*neap* comes from an Old English word meaning "scanty"). Other lunar and solar phenomena, such as the equinoxes and solstices, can also affect tidal ranges.

The best time for shoreline exploration is on a new-moon or full-moon day, when low tide exposes mussels, sea urchins, sea cucumbers, starfish, periwinkles, hermit crabs, rockweed, and assorted nonbiodegradable trash. Rubber boots or waterproof, treaded shoes are essential on the wet, slippery terrain.

Caution is also essential in tidal areas. Unless you've carefully plotted tide times and heights, don't park a car, bike, or boat trailer on a beach. Make sure your sea kayak is lashed securely to a tree or bollard, don't take a long nap on shoreline granite, and don't cross a low-tide land spit without an eye on your watch.

A perhaps apocryphal but almost believable story goes that one flatlander stormed up to a ranger at Cobscook Bay State Park one bright summer morning and demanded indignantly to know why they had had the nerve to drain the water from her shorefront campsite during the night. When it comes to tides...you have to go with the flow.

craft by other Maine artists at **Crow Town Gallery** (406 South Lubec Rd., Lubec, 207/904-9169).

RECREATION

Boat Excursions

Explore Cobscook, Fundy, and Passamaquoddy Bays on a 2.5-hour tour with **Downeast Charter Boat Tours** (31 Johnson St., Lubec, 207/733-2009, www.downeastcharterboattours.com, $69 adults, $49 age 12 and younger) aboard the 25-foot lobster boat *Lorna Doone*. Options include whale-watching, lighthouses, history and folklore, marinelife, and the Old Sow whirlpool.

Jet-boat whale-watching tours are offered aboard the *Tarquin* from the **Inn on the Wharf** (60 Johnson St., Lubec, 207/733-4400, www.theinnonthewharf.com). The 2.5-3-hour tours are $50 adults, $25 kids under age 12.

Hiking and Walking

Two preserves run by the Maine Coast Heritage Trust (www.mcht.org) are fine places for a walk. The **Hamilton Cove Preserve**'s 1.5 miles of ocean frontage are highlighted by cobble beaches, rocky cliffs, and jaw-dropping views (on a clear day) of Grand Manan. To find it, take Route 189 to South Lubec Road toward Quoddy Head, but bear right at the fork on Boot Cove Road and continue 2.4 miles to a small parking lot on the left. There's a kiosk with maps about 100 feet down the trail. It's 0.8 mile to an observation platform and another 0.5 mile to the bench at the trail's end. For more expansive views, hike 1.2 miles to the summit of Benny's Mountain.

Continue on Boot Cove Road another 1.5 miles to find **Boot Head Preserve,** with dramatic cliffs and ravines that epitomize the region's Bold Coast reputation. The trail passes through a rare coastal raised peatland before continuing to a viewing platform on the coast. From the parking lot to Boot Cove via the Coastal Trail is 1.25 miles; return via the Interior Trail for another 0.75 mile.

For information on other hikes in the area, pick up a copy of *Cobscook Trail Guide,* with maps and trail details. It's available for about $7 at local stores or from the Quoddy Regional Land Trust Office on Route 1 in Whiting. Another resource available locally is *Self-Guided Birding Explorations, Washington County, Maine,* published in conjunction with the Down East Spring Birding Festival. It lists and maps walks and hikes, and notes habitats and bird species.

A 20-mile network of trails and gravel roads winds through the Edmunds Unit of the **Moosehorn National Wildlife Refuge** (207/454-7161, www.fws.gov/refuge/moosehorn, sunrise-sunset daily, free), which straddles Route 1 between Whiting and Dennysville and also fronts on Cobscook Bay adjacent to the state park. The refuge, the northernmost in the United States along the Atlantic Flyway for migratory birds, is a favorite among birders.

In 2010, *Travel + Leisure* magazine named Lubec one of the best beach towns in the country. Where's the beach, you ask? **Mowry Beach,** owned by the Downeast Coastal Conservancy (www.downeastcoastalconservancy.org), is at the end of Pleasant Street; continue past the wastewater treatment plant to a parking lot. Follow the path over the dunes to the beach. When the tide rolls out, remnants of a drowned ice age forest are revealed. Also here is a wheelchair-accessible 0.4-mile boardwalk designed for sighting nesting, migrating, and wintering birds, including warblers, finches, waxwings, hawks, and northern shrikes.

Biking and Kayaking

The **Wharf** (60 Johnson St., Lubec, 207/733-4400) rents bikes for $18/day as well as kayaks for $25-35.

FOOD

Lobster and Seafood

Fisherman's Wharf (69 Johnson St., Lubec, 207/733-4400, www.theinnonthewharf.com, 7am-8pm daily, $12-28), at the Inn on the Wharf, is in a renovated oceanfront sardine factory. There's seating inside and on a small deck, with panoramic views over Cobscook Bay to Eastport's Shackford Head. Seafood is the specialty, but there are landlubber choices and a full bar too.

Quick Bites

Fresh seafood takeout is available at **Becky's Seafood** (145 Main St., Lubec, 207/733-2228, 11am-6pm Mon.-Sat., 11am-2pm Sun., $5-32); it's nothing fancy, nothing fussy, but it is cheap and good.

Breakfast and lunch are served at **Sally Ann's Café & Market** (52 Water St., Lubec, 207/733-2879, 8am-5pm Wed.-Sat, no credit cards). There are a handful of tables inside, and one on the waterside deck.

Up for an adventure? Check out the **Most Absurd Bar in the World: A Sculpture** (45 Main St., Dennysville, 207/726-4466, $10-14) at the Hansom House. Melinda and Jonathan Jaques spent six years restoring and, *ahem,* decorating the wood shed and great room. A 25-foot stained glass ceiling sculpture as well as the flotsam and jetsam of everyday life fills every available ceiling and wall space and much of that in between. It's occasionally open (usually Friday and Saturday evenings) for light fare, such as chowders, chili, and crab cakes, along with beer and wine; call for the current schedule.

Casual Dining

Lubec Brewing Company (41 Water St., Lubec, 207/733-4555, 11am-8:30pm Thurs.-Sun., $13-25) serves craft beer and organic food, and **Juji's at the Lubec Brewing Co.** serves weekly changing menus of scratch-made fare crafted primarily from locally sourced ingredients for lunch and dinner. It doubles as a live music venue.

Craving Italian? Dine inside or on the waterside deck at **Frank's Dockside Restaurant** (20 Water St., Lubec, 207/733-4484, 11am-7pm Thurs.-Tues., $12-25). If the weather's nice, aim for a back-deck seat at the **Water Street Tavern & Inn** (12 Water St., Lubec, 207/733-2477, from 5pm daily, $12-28). Seafood is the specialty.

Good burgers, chowders, pastas, and other choices as well as Guinness, Smithwick's, and microbrews have earned **Cohill's Inn** (7 Water St., Lubec, 207/733-4300, www.cohillsinn.com, noon-3pm and 5pm-8:45pm Wed.-Mon., $12-29) an enthusiastic two thumbs up from locals and visitors alike. The dining room has excellent water views, and there's often entertainment on Saturday afternoon. The deck is dog friendly.

ACCOMMODATIONS

Many visitors use Lubec as a base for day trips to Campobello Island (passport or passport card necessary), so it's essential to make reservations at the height of summer. Several lodgings are also available on Campobello.

Inns and Bed-and-Breakfasts

Built in 1860 by a British sea captain, ★ **Peacock House Bed and Breakfast** (27 Summer St., Lubec, 207/733-2403 or 888/305-0036, www.peacockhouse.com, $125-175) has long been one of Lubec's most prestigious residences. Among the notables who have stayed here are Donald MacMillan, the famous Arctic explorer, as well as U.S. senators Margaret Chase Smith and Edmund Muskie. Now innkeeper Mary Beth Hoffman welcomes guests to the inn's three rooms and four suites; some have water views, and one is wheelchair-accessible. The spacious public rooms include a library, parlor with baby grand, and gathering room that flows to a deck and lovely gardens.

Unusual antiques fill the guest rooms and sitting room of the 19th-century **Home Port Inn** (45 Main St., Lubec, 207/733-2077, www.homeportinn.com, $110-145), ensconced on a Lubec hilltop. Each of the seven guest rooms has a private bath, although some are detached; some rooms have water views. Rates include a full breakfast.

Ellen and Jack Gearrin extend a warm Irish welcome to guests at **Cohill's Inn** (7 Water St., Lubec, 207/733-4300, www.cohillsinn.com, $105-150), which overlooks the Bay of Fundy on one side and the Narrows on the other. There are no frills or fuss in the simply but nicely furnished guest rooms. A continental breakfast is included in the rates. Downstairs is a popular and reliable pub, but service ends at 9pm, so it's quiet at night. The inn is dog friendly.

The waterfront **Water Street Tavern & Inn** (12 Water St., Lubec, 207/733-2477, www.watersttavernandinn.com, $95-250) has three nicely appointed rooms and two suites. All guests have access to a gathering room with comfy seating, big views, and a kitchenette. Also available is a two-bedroom water-view cottage for $1,050 per week.

Motels

The pleasantly updated **Eastland Motel** (385 County Rd./Rte. 189, Lubec, 207/733-5501, www.eastlandmotel.com, $90) has 20 guest rooms. A homemade continental breakfast is included in the rates. A few dog-friendly rooms are available ($10 per dog).

Apartments, Suites, and Houses

Renovations to the former Lubec Sardine Company's Factory B created the ★ **Inn**

1: Wags and Wool in downtown Lubec **2:** Mowry Beach **3:** Frank's Dockside Restaurant **4:** Water Street Tavern & Inn

WAGS
WOOL
83
Wags & Wool
Yarn
Needles & Notions
Patterns & Books
Beautiful One-of-a-kind
Handknit Sweaters
Organic Catnip
Frank's Dockside Restaurant
TAVERN & INN
WELCOME
LUBEC
12
1
2
3
4

on the Wharf (60 Johnson St., Lubec, 207/733-4400, www.theinnonthewharf.com, $115-190), comprising rooms, suites, and a restaurant, while preserving the working waterfront. Guest rooms have use of a common kitchen and dining area and a laundry. Two-bedroom, two-bathroom apartments have full kitchens and laundry facilities. All have incredible views. Also on the premises are a yoga studio and bike and kayak rentals. A whale-watching boat departs from the wharf. That's all great, but what really distinguishes this property is that hidden on the basement level are huge tanks holding lobsters, crabs, and eels; an area for processing the periwinkle harvest; and other intriguing spots where you might catch local fishing folks bringing in their catches. Also available are three rental houses with varying configurations; call for details.

Bill Clark rescued the former Coast Guard station at West Quoddy Head and restored, renovated, and reopened it as ★ **West Quoddy Station** (S. Lubec Rd., Lubec, 207/733-4452 or 877/535-4714, www.quoddyvacation.com, $120-330). The bluff-top complex comprises well-equipped self-catering studios and one- to five-bedroom cottages, all done in 1950s style but with contemporary amenities. Views are stupendous, and you can walk to West Quoddy Head. Weekly rentals run $800-2,200. It's dog friendly.

Camping

A 3.5-mile network of nature trails, picnic spots, great bird-watching and berry picking, hot showers, a boat launch, and wooded shorefront campsites make ★ **Cobscook Bay State Park** (Rte. 1, Edmunds Township, 207/726-4412, www.parksandlands.com, $20-30/site/night, $5 reservation fee, 2-night minimum) on the 888-acre Moosehorn Reserve, one of Maine's most spectacular state parks. It's even entertaining just to watch the 24-foot tides surging in and out of this area at five or so feet per hour; there's no swimming because of the undertow. Reserve well ahead to get a place on the shore. There are no hookups, but there's a dump station for RVs. To guarantee a site in July-August, call 207/624-9950 (800/332-1501 in Maine) or visit www.campwithme.com. The park is open daily mid-May-mid-October; trails are groomed in winter for cross-country skiing, and one section goes right along the shore.

INFORMATION AND SERVICES

The **Association to Promote and Protect the Lubec Environment** (888/347-9302, www.visitlubecmaine.com) is the best source for local information. The **Lubec Historical Society & Museum** (135 Main St., Lubec, 207/733-2994, www.lubechistoricalsociety.com, 10am-3pm, Mon., Wed., and Fri., free) also offers local info.

Find public restrooms at the Lubec Marina and the public library.

GETTING THERE AND AROUND

Island Discovery Tours (506/752-1901, http://campobellosightseeing.blogspot.com) offers three-hour van tours of Campobello Island for CAD$40, with pickup available in Lubec. Walking tours are CAD$35/hour.

The **Franklin D. Roosevelt Memorial Bridge** connects Lubec to Campobello Island (passport, passport card, or enhanced driver's license required for return).

The **Eastport-Lubec ferry** (207/546-2927, http://downeastwindjammer.com, $25 adults, $14 ages 2-11, bikes $6) makes four round-trips Tuesday-Sunday mid-June to mid-September.

Lubec is approximately 28 miles or 40 minutes via Routes 1 and 189 from Machias. It's about 40 miles or one hour via Routes 189, 1, and 190 to Eastport.

Campobello Island

Just over the Franklin D. Roosevelt Memorial Bridge from Lubec lies nine-mile-long, unspoiled **Campobello Island** (pop. 1,000), in Canada's New Brunswick province. Most visitors come to see the place where President Franklin D. Roosevelt, along with other wealthy Americans, summered, but few take the time to explore the charms of Roosevelt's "beloved island." Those who do find a striking lighthouse that's open for tours, hiking trails, carriage roads for biking, whale-watching excursions, and spectacular vistas.

It's interesting to note that before becoming a summer retreat for wealthy Americans, Campobello was the feudal fiefdom of a Welsh family. King George III awarded the grant to Captain William Owen in 1767, and he arrived in 1770. When Benedict Arnold fled the United States as a traitor, he settled here and in St. John, New Brunswick, overseeing a lucrative business smuggling goods between New Brunswick and the states, before moving to England in 1792.

SIGHTS

★ Roosevelt Campobello International Park

Since 1964, **Roosevelt Campobello International Park** has been under joint U.S. and Canadian jurisdiction, commemorating U.S. president Franklin D. Roosevelt. FDR summered here as a youth, and it was here that he came down with infantile paralysis (polio) in 1921. The park, covering most of the island's southern end, has well-maintained trails and carriage roads, picnic sites, and dramatic vistas, but its centerpiece is the imposing Roosevelt Cottage, one mile northeast of the bridge.

Stop first at the park's **visitors center** (459 Rte. 774, Welshpool, 506/752-2922 in season, www.fdr.net), where you can pick up brochures (including a trail map, bird-watching guide, and bog guide), sign up for Tea with Eleanor and/or a Fun Tour, peruse displays about the Roosevelts and their relationship with the island, and see a short video setting the stage for the cottage visit. Ask about other guided hikes and tours, which may include beach, bog, and grounds.

ROOSEVELT COTTAGE

It's a short walk from the visitors center to the **Roosevelt Cottage** (10am-6pm Atlantic time, 9am-5pm Eastern time, mid-May-mid-Oct., free). Little seems to have changed in the 34-room red-shingled "cottage" overlooking Passamaquoddy Bay since President Roosevelt last visited in 1939. Free 30-minute guided tours of the house depart every 15 minutes from 10am to 5:45pm. Each guide gives the tour a different spin, and all are engaging and fun. The Roosevelt Cottage grounds are beautifully landscaped, and the many family mementos—especially those in the late president's den—bring history alive. It all feels very personal and far less stuffy than most presidential memorials.

TEA WITH ELEANOR

Don't miss the engaging one-hour **Tea with Eleanor** program, during which park interpreters tell stories about the remarkable Eleanor Roosevelt, highlighting the first lady's history and her many feats, while guests enjoy tea and cookies at the Wells-Shober Cottage. Two programs are available. The 11am free tea is first come, first served, with tickets available each day from the visitors center. Because it fills so quickly, the park has added a Reserved Tea (3pm daily, $14 pp, age 12 and younger free). The reserved tea also includes a booklet of cookie recipes compiled by Eleanor's granddaughter.

FUN TOUR

On the one-hour **Fun Tour,** guides take guests behind the scenes, sharing stories and

1
2
Lubec, Maine
3
4

secrets about the park and the people who called it home. The free tour, limited to 15 participants, is offered twice daily on a first-come, first-served basis. Get tickets at the visitors center.

AN EVENING AT THE COTTAGE

Twice a month, the park's An Evening at the Cottage presents **Roosevelt Park Radio Hour** at the Adams Estate overlooking Friar's Bay. The program includes dinner and a re-creation of FDR's Fireside Chats.

THE PARK BY BICYCLE OR CAR

Carriage roads lace the park, and although you can drive them, a bike, if you have one, is far more fun. Options include **Cranberry Point Drive,** 5.4 miles round-trip from the visitors center; **Liberty Point Drive,** 12.4 miles round-trip, via Glensevern Road, from the visitors center; and **Fox Hill Drive,** a 2.2-mile link between the other two main routes. En route, you'll have access to beaches, picnic sites, spruce and fir forests, and great views of lighthouses, islands, and the Bay of Fundy.

Just west of the main access road from the bridge is the **Mulholland Point picnic area,** where you can spread out your lunch next to the distinctive red-capped lighthouse overlooking Lubec Narrows. A marine biology exhibit in the red shed adjacent to it highlights seals, whale rescue, tides, and other related topics.

HIKING AND PICNICKING

Within the international park are 8.5 miles of walking-hiking trails, varying from dead easy to moderately difficult. Easiest is the 1.2-mile (round-trip) walk from the visitors center to **Friar's Head picnic area,** named for its distinctive promontory jutting into the bay. For the best angle, climb up to the observation deck on the headland. Grills and tables are here for picnickers. Pick up a brochure at the visitors center detailing natural sights along the route.

1: Roosevelt Cottage 2: Head Harbour Lightstation
3: view from Mulholland Point Light
4: Campobello's active fishing fleet

The most difficult—and most dramatic—trail is a 2.4-mile stretch from **Liberty Point to Raccoon Beach,** along the southeastern shore of the island. Precipitous cliffs can make parts of this trail risky for small children or insecure adults, so use caution. Liberty Point is incredibly rugged, but observation platforms make it easy to see the tortured rocks and wide-open Bay of Fundy. Along the way is the SunSweep Sculpture, an international art project by David Barr. At broad Raccoon Beach, you can walk the sands, have a picnic, or watch for whales, porpoises, and ospreys. To avoid returning via the same route, park at Liberty Point and walk back along Liberty Point Drive from Raccoon Beach. If you're traveling with nonhikers, arrange for them to meet you with a vehicle at Con Robinson's Point.

You can also walk the park's perimeter, including just more than six miles of shoreline, but only if you're in good shape, have waterproof hiking boots, and can spend an entire day on the trails. Before attempting this, however, inquire at the visitors center about trail conditions and tide levels.

Herring Cove Provincial Park

Far too few people visit 1,049-acre **Herring Cove Provincial Park** (506/752-7010 or 800/561-0123), with picnic areas, 95 campsites, a four-mile trail system, a mile-long sandy beach, freshwater Glensevern Lake, a restaurant with fabulous views, and the nine-hole championship-level **Herring Cove Golf Course** (506/752-2467). The park is open early June-September. Admission is free.

Head Harbour Lightstation

Consult the tide calendar before planning your assault on **Head Harbour Lightstation,** also called **East Quoddy Head Light,** at Campobello's northernmost tip. The 51-foot-tall light, built in 1829, is on an islet accessible only at low tide. The distinctive white light tower bears a huge red cross. (You're likely to pass near it on whale-watching trips out of Eastport or Lubec.) From the Roosevelt

Cottage, follow Route 774 through the village of Wilson's Beach and continue to the parking area. A stern Canadian Coast Guard warning sign tells the story: "Extreme Hazard. Beach exposed only at low tide. Incoming tide rises 5 feet per hour and may leave you stranded for 8 hours. Wading or swimming are extremely dangerous due to swift currents and cold water. Proceed at your own risk."

It's worth the effort for the bay and island views from the lighthouse grounds, often including whales and eagles. Getting there requires navigating ladders and slippery rocks. You can make the trip during a four-hour window around dead low tide (be sure your clock coincides with the Atlantic-time tide calendar).

The **Friends of the Head Harbour Lightstation** (916 Rte. 774, Welshpool, www.campobello.com/lighthouse), a local nonprofit, have restored the lighthouse and adjacent keeper's house. The group continues to maintain the property, and access fees support the effort. You can see the light from the nearby grounds at no charge, but if you want to hike out to the island or visit the light, the suggested donation is $5. Add a lighthouse tour, including climbing the tower, for $10; the family maximum for the walk or the tour is $25 (cash only). You can support the efforts with a membership, available for $15 individual or $25 family.

TOURS

Island Discovery Tours (506/752-1901, http://campobellosightseeing.blogspot.com) offers 2.5-hour van tours of Campobello Island for $25, with pick up available on the island or in Lubec. Walking tours are $20/hour.

RECREATION

★ Whale-Watching

Island Cruises (506/752-1107 or 888/249-4400, www.bayoffundywhales.com, $58 adults, $48 age 11 and younger, $53 age 65 and older) depart three times daily from Head Harbour Wharf for scenic, 2.5-hour whale-watching cruises aboard the *Mister Matthew,* a 37-foot traditional Bay of Fundy fishing boat that carries 20 passengers. Captain Mackie Greene is a member of the Fundy Whale Rescue Team, so he has great insights and stories to share. Sightings might include minke, finback, humpback, and perhaps even northern right whales.

FOOD

Don't expect culinary creativity on Campobello, but you won't starve, either—at least during the summer season.

The ★ **Pier** (6 Pollock Cove Rd., Wilson's Beach, 506/752-2200, 11:30am-8pm daily, CAD$11-18), new in 2018, should have been called the View. Sit indoors or on the deck and watch for whales while enjoying soups, salads, sandwiches, burgers, or a few heftier choices. The specialty is seafood, fried or baked. There's often live music on Sunday nights.

Expect generous portions, friendly service, super-fresh fish, and decadent desserts at **Family Fisheries** (1979 Rte. 774, Wilson's Beach, 506/752-2470, www.familyfisheries.com, 11:30am-9pm daily, CAD$6-28), a seafood restaurant and fish market toward the island's northern end.

Roosevelt Campobello International Park operates the **Prince Café** (506/752-6055, 10am-4pm daily) in the restored 1920s-era Prince Cottage, next to the Roosevelt Cottage. Light breakfasts and lunch are served cafeteria-style.

Herring Cove Restaurant (136 Herring Cove Rd., Welshpool, 506/752-1092, 8am-8pm daily, CAD$5-30), at the golf course with a water-view deck, has a full bar and offers a full menu. It serves the island's best breakfast. A kids' menu is available.

ACCOMMODATIONS

In midsummer, if you'd like to overnight on the island, reserve lodgings well in advance; Campobello is a popular destination. The nearest backup beds are in Lubec, and those fill too.

Check into the **Pollock Cove Inn & Cottages** (2455 Rte. 774, Wilson's Beach, 506/752-2300, CAD$75-175), spread out on a grassy oceanfront bluff, and watch for whales and porpoises from the point. Options at the recently renovated property range from small rooms best for a quick overnight stay to two-bedroom cottages with full kitchens. The adjacent Pier restaurant serves lunch and dinner.

The **Owen House** (11 Welshpool St., Welshpool, 506/752-2977, www.owenhouse.ca, late May-mid-Oct., CAD$104-210) is an old-shoe comfortable (think quirky and a bit tired), early 19th-century B&B on 10 acres on Deer Point overlooking Passamaquoddy Bay and Eastport in the distance. Nine guest rooms (two with shared baths) on three floors are decorated with antiques and family treasures along with owner Joyce Morrel's paintings (Joyce grew up in this house) and assorted handmade quilts. Don't expect fancy or techy amenities. Joyce and innkeeper Jan Meiners are very active in the lighthouse preservation efforts.

Equally enticing are the views from **An Island Chalet** (115 Narrows Rd., Welshpool, 506/752-2971, www.anislandchalet.com, CAD$125-180), a colony of waterfront housekeeping cabins overlooking the Lubec Narrows. Each cabin has a loft suite with queen bed, twins downstairs, a full kitchen, and a front porch.

The 95-site campground at **Herring Cove Provincial Park** (506/752-7010, http://parcsnbparks.ca, CAD$28-31) is a gem. It's underused, so crowds are rare. Sites (from tents to RVs) are tucked in the woods near Herring Cove Beach. Also available are rustic shelters ($43). On the premises are a restaurant, nine-hole golf course, picnic grounds, and hiking trails that connect with adjacent Campobello International Park.

INFORMATION AND SERVICES

Be aware that there's a one-hour time difference between Lubec and Campobello. Lubec, like the rest of Maine, is on Eastern time; Campobello, like the rest of New Brunswick, is on Atlantic time, an hour ahead. As soon as you reach the island, set your clock ahead an hour.

There is no need to convert U.S. currency to Canadian money for use on Campobello; U.S. dollars are accepted everywhere on the island, but prices tend to be quoted in Canadian dollars.

Off the bridge, stop at the **Adventure Centre** (44 Rte. 774, Welshpool, 506/752-7043, May-Oct.) on your right for island and park maps, tide info for lighthouse visits, and New Brunswick visitor information.

For information about the island, visit **Campobello Tourism Association** (www.visitcampobello.com).

Public restrooms are at the Adventure Centre and the Roosevelt Campobello International Park visitors center.

GETTING THERE AND AROUND

Campobello is connected by bridge to Lubec. From Campobello you can also continue by ferry to New Brunswick's Deer Island and on to Eastport or make the Quoddy Loop and continue to Letete, New Brunswick, and visit St. Andrews before crossing the border at Calais and returning south to Eastport.

To visit the island, you'll have to pass immigration checkpoints on the U.S. and Canadian ends of the **Franklin D. Roosevelt Memorial Bridge** (U.S. Customs, Lubec, 207/733-4331; Canada Border Services, Campobello, 506/752-1130). Be sure to have the required identification: a passport or a passport card.

The funky two-stage boat-and-barge **East Coast Ferries** (877/747-2159, www.eastcoastferriesltd.com, no credit cards, passport or passport card required) departs Campobello for Deer Island on the hour 9am-7pm Atlantic time late June-early September; the fare is $18/car and driver plus $5/passenger over age 12, $30 maximum per car, $10/motorcycle, $6 bicycle and passenger. All fares are subject to a fuel surcharge. A separate free ferry connects Deer Isle to Letete, near St. Andrews. It departs Deer Isle on the hour 6am-10pm Atlantic time, and on the half-hour 7:30am-6:30pm.

Eastport and Vicinity

When you leave Whiting, the gateway to Lubec and Campobello, and continue north on Route 1 around Cobscook Bay, it's hard to believe that life could slow down any more than it already has, but it does. The landscape's raw beauty is occasionally punctuated by farmhouses or a convenience store, but little else.

Edmunds Township's (pop. 342) claims to fame are its splendid public lands—Cobscook Bay State Park and a unit of Moosehorn National Wildlife Refuge. Just past the state park, loop along the scenic shoreline before returning to Route 1.

Pembroke (pop. 840), once part of adjoining **Dennysville** (pop. 342), is home to Reversing Falls Park, where you can watch and hear ebbing and flowing tides draining and filling Cobscook Bay. **Perry** (pop. 889) is best known for the Sipayik Indian Reservation at Pleasant Point, a Passamaquoddy settlement two miles east of Route 1 that has been here since 1822. Route 191 cuts through the heart of the reservation.

From Sipayik, on the mainland, you hopscotch from one dollop of land to another and finally reach the city (yes, it's officially a city) of **Eastport** (pop. 1,331), on Moose Island. The sardine industry was introduced in the late 19th century, and five canneries once operated here, employing hundreds of local residents, who snipped the heads off herring and stuffed them into cans.

Settled in 1772 and home to the deepest natural seaport in the continental United States, Eastport has had its ups and downs, mostly mirroring the fishing industry. It's on a two-steps-forward-one-step-back upswing as people "from away" have arrived to soak up the vibe of a small town with a heavy Down East accent. Artists, artisans, and antiques shops are leading the town's rejuvenation as a tourist destination, with the Tides Institute at the forefront. When the Fox Network reality-TV series *Murder in Small Town X* was filmed here, the city morphed into the village of Sunrise, Maine, and local residents happily filled in as extras. The huge waterfront statue of a fisherman is a remnant of the filming.

Until 1811 the town also included Lubec, which is about 2.5 miles across the water via boat but more than 40 miles in a car. A passenger ferry connects the two.

SIGHTS

Historical Walking Tour

The best way to appreciate Eastport's history is to pick up and follow the route in *A Walking Guide to Eastport,* available locally for $2.75. The handy map-brochure spotlights the city's 18th-, 19th-, and early 20th-century homes, businesses, and monuments, many now in the National Register of Historic Places. Among the highlights are historic homes converted to bed-and-breakfasts, two museums, and a large chunk of downtown Water Street, with many handsome brick buildings erected after a disastrous fire swept through in 1886. Also look for interpretive signage downtown, especially along the Breakwater Walkway.

Raye's Mustard Mill Museum

How often do you have a chance to watch mustard being made in a turn-of-the-20th-century mustard mill? Drive by **J. W. Raye and Co.** (83 Washington St./Rte. 190, Eastport, 207/853-4451 or 800/853-1903, www.rayesmustard.com, 8:30am-4pm Mon.-Fri., 10am-5pm Sat.-Sun.) at the edge of Eastport and stop in for a free 15-minute tour (offered as schedules permit; call first) of North America's last traditional stone-ground mustard mill. You'll get to see the granite millstones, the mustard seeds being winnowed, and enormous vats of future mustard. Raye's sells mustard under its own label and

1: Herring Cove Golf Course **2:** Owen House B&B

produces it for major customers under their labels. The shop stocks all of Raye's mustard varieties (samples available), other Maine-made food, and gift items, and it also has a small café where you can buy coffee, tea, and light fare. Both Martha Stewart and Rachael Ray have discovered Raye's, which has won both gold and bronze medals at the World-Wide Mustard Competition. Note: While the mill is undergoing restoration, the store has moved to 54 Water Street in downtown Eastport.

The Tides Institute and Museum of Art

One of downtown Eastport's most promising additions is the **Tides Institute and Museum of Art** (43 Water St., 207/853-4047, www.tidesinstitute.org, 10am-4pm Tues.-Sun., donation appreciated), which is actively building significant cultural collections focused on the U.S.-Canada northeast coast but with an eye to the broader world. It's also producing new works employing printmaking, letterpress, photography, bookbinding, oral history, and other media. Among the significant items in its collection are works by Martin Johnson Heade and Paul Caponigro, a fine selection of baskets by Native Americans, and two organs made by the local Pembroke organ company in the 1880s. Rotating summer shows highlight both the permanent collections and loaned works. The institute also offers programs, demonstrations, and workshops by visiting and resident artists at **StudioWorks** (48 Water St.) and cultural programming, such as concerts, readings, and art installations, in the acoustically divine **Free Will North Church Project Space** (82 High St.), with a beautiful Baroque-style organ. It also coordinates the annual New Year's Eve cross-border celebration, ringing in the new year twice with sardine and maple leaf drops.

Pleasant Point Reservation

To get to Eastport, you pass through the Passamaquoddy's Sipayik or **Pleasant Point Reservation** (www.wabanaki.com). Ask locally or check the website to find basket makers and other traditional artists who might sell from their homes. The decorative baskets are treasures that escalate in price as makers gain recognition and win awards. It's a real treat to be able to buy one from the maker.

Scenic Detour

If time allows a short scenic detour, especially in fall, turn left (northwest) off Route 1 on Route 214 and drive 10 miles to quaintly named **Meddybemps** (pop. 157), allegedly a Passamaquoddy word meaning "plenty of alewives [herring]." Views over Meddybemps Lake, on the north side of the road, are spectacular, and you can launch a canoe or kayak into the lake here, less than a mile beyond the junction with Route 191 (take the dead-end unpaved road toward the water).

★ Shackford Head State Park

Shackford Head (off Deep Cove Rd., Eastport, www.parksandlands.com, sunrise-sunset daily, free), crowning a peninsula that juts into Cobscook Bay, has 3.2 miles of wooded trails. Easiest is the 1.2-mile round-trip to Shackford Head Overlook and its continuation onto the steeper Ship Point Trail, which adds another 0.4 mile. The trail rises gently to a 175-foot-high headland with wide-open views of Eastport and, depending on weather, Campobello Island, Lubec, Pembroke, and even Grand Manan. This state preserve is a particularly good family hike. Also here is a memorial with plaques detailing the history of five Civil War ships that were decommissioned and burned on Cony Beach by the U.S. government between 1901 and 1920. Eastport's huge tides allowed the ships to be brought in and beached and then taken apart as the tide receded. Fourteen Eastport men served on four of the ships. The trailhead and parking area are just east of the Boat School.

Reversing Falls Park

There's plenty of room for adults to relax and kids to play at **Reversing Falls Park** in West

Pembroke—plus shorefront ledges and a front-row seat overlooking a fascinating tidal phenomenon. The park is connected via hiking trails to the Downeast Coastal Conservancy's **Reversing Falls Conservation Area** (www.downeastcoastalconservancy.org), a nearly 200-acre property with 1.5 miles of shorefront and 70 acres of coastal wetlands. Pack a picnic and then check newspapers or information offices for the tide times so that you can watch the saltwater surging through a 300-yard-wide passage at about 25 knots, creating a whirlpool and churning "falls." The park is at Mahar Point in West Pembroke, 7.2 miles south of Route 1. Coming from the south (Dennysville), bear right off Route 1 onto Old County Road in West Pembroke and continue to Leighton Point Road. Turn right on Young's Cove Road and continue to the park.

Gleason Cove

This quiet park and boat launch is a delightful place to walk along the shorefront or to grab a table and spread out a picnic while drinking in the dreamy views over fishing weirs and islands in Passamaquoddy Bay. To get here, take Shore Road (opposite the New Friendly Restaurant) and then take a right on Gleason Cove Road.

ENTERTAINMENT

The **Eastport Arts Center** (36 Washington St., Eastport, 207/853-4650, www.eastportartscenter.com) is an umbrella organization for local arts groups, with headquarters and performance space in a former church. You can pick up a brochure with a complete schedule, which usually includes concerts, workshops, films, puppet shows, productions by local theater group **Stage East,** and other cultural events. Also based here is the **Passamaquoddy Bay Symphony Orchestra,** formed in 2007 by conductor Trond Saeverud, who doubles as concertmaster of the Bangor Symphony Orchestra.

Concerts and other programs are sometimes held in the waterfront amphitheater between Water Street and the waterfront walkway. It's marked by *Nature's Grace,* a granite sculpture carved by New Brunswick artist Jim Boyd.

Festivals and Events

For a small community, Eastport manages to pull together and put on plenty of successful events during the year.

Eastport's annual four-day **Fourth of July—Old Home Week** extravaganza includes a parade, pancake breakfasts, barbecues, a flea market, an auction, races, live entertainment, and fireworks. This is one of Maine's best Fourth of July celebrations and attracts a crowd of more than 10,000. Lodgings are booked months in advance, so plan ahead.

Indian Ceremonial Days, a three-day Native American celebration, includes children's games, canoe races, craft demos, talking circles, fireworks, and traditional food and dancing at Sipayik, the Pleasant Point Reservation in Perry, the second weekend in August.

The **Eastport Salmon & Seafood Festival** (www.eastportsalmonfest.org) in early September usually includes craft demonstrations, arts and crafts vendors, educational exhibits, boat trips to view salmon farms, music, and other activities.

The three-day **Eastport Pirate Festival** (www.eastportpiratefestival.com) in September features live music, parades, children's activities, reenactments, and races.

A great resource for area happenings is **CulturePass** (www.culturepass.net), which covers the entire Passamaquoddy Bay region. Pair it with the **Artsipelago: Two Countries One Bay Passport** (www.artsipelago.net), a cultural guide to the international Passamaquoddy Bay region.

SHOPPING

Eastport has long been a magnet for artists and craftspeople yearning to work in a supportive environment, but the influx has increased in recent years.

Especially worth seeking out are the **Commons** (51 Water St., Eastport, 207/853-4123), displaying works by artisans from the region and farther afield, and woodworker Roland LaVallee's **Crow Tracks** (11 Water St., Eastport, 207/853-2336), filled with intricate carvings of birds and local fauna; the tiny garden entryway doubles the pleasure of a visit.

The **Eastport Gallery** (109 Water St., Eastport, 207/853-4166) is a cooperative with works in varied media. The gallery also sponsors the annual **Paint Eastport Day,** usually held the second Saturday in September, when anyone is invited to paint a local scene; a reception and "wet paint" auction follow.

More than 20 artists from the region are represented at **Eastport Breakwater Gallery** (93 Water St., Eastport, 207/853-4773).

Indulge your sweet tooth at **Sweeties Downeast** (80 Water St., Eastport, 207/853-3120), where candy, nuts, fancy popcorn, and homemade fudge are sold by the pound.

Stop in, if only for a few minutes, at **S. L. Wadsworth and Son** (42 Water St., Eastport, 207/853-4343), the oldest ship chandlery in the country and the oldest retail business in Maine. In addition to hardware and marine gear, you'll find nautical gifts, souvenirs, and copies of Eastport-set mysteries penned by local author Sarah Graves. **Ellerson Guitars** (20 Key St., Eastport, 207/853-4692) is the home studio of guitarist and luthier John Squib.

You never know what you'll find at the **Eastport Flea for All,** which sets up on the sea walk downtown on Saturday mornings from late May through September.

A number of very talented artists and artisans are tucked along the back roads of the area. You might get lucky and find them open, but it's wise to call before making a special trip. These include **Wrenovations** (6 Steam Mill Rd., Robbinston, 207/454-2382), with stained glass art creations by Mark Wren and braided rugs by his wife, Arlene; **Susan Designs** (behind Loring's Body Shop, 416 Gin Cove Rd., Perry, 207/853-4315), where gifted fiber artist Susan Plachy sells her quilts, dolls, and rustic furniture; and **Done Roving Yarns** (20 Charlotte Rd., Charlotte, 207/454-8184, http://doneroving.com), for gorgeous yarns and fiber-art classes.

RECREATION

Boat Excursions

Eastport Windjammers (207/853-2500 or 207/853-4303, www.eastportwindjammers.com) offers a 2.5-3-hour whale-watching and lobster cruise ($50 adults, $35 ages 5-12, $20 under age 5) departing at 1:30pm daily and heading out into the prime whale-feeding grounds of Passamaquoddy Bay—passing the Old Sow whirlpool (the largest tidal whirlpool in the Northern Hemisphere), salmon aquaculture pens, and Campobello Island. En route you'll see bald eagles, porpoises, possibly puffins and ospreys, and a lighthouse. En route back, lobster traps are hauled, with specimens placed in a touch tank. The best months for viewing whales are July and August, but Butch is a skilled spotter, so if they're there, he'll find them. A two-hour sunset cruise ($40 adults, $30 children) departs the Eastport Pier (call for times). Ignore the name; trips are aboard a 49-passenger lobster boat. Also available are three-hour fishing trips aboard the *Lady H* ($55 adults, $34 under age 12).

Fish for shark, tuna, cod, pollock, and haddock aboard the *Vonnie and Val,* a 33-foot sportfishing boat, with **Fundy Breeze Charters** (109 Water St., Eastport, 207/853-4660, www.fundybreeze.com). A full day is $125 pp with a $600 boat minimum; a half day is $65 pp with a $300 minimum. Also offered are lighthouse ($55), puffin ($100), and whale-watching ($55-110) tours; boat minimums apply for all. Tours depart from the Eastport Chowder House dock.

FOOD

Lobster and Seafood

When the weather's clear, there's

1: Eastport's pier **2:** Kilby House Inn B&B **3:** Quoddy Bay Lobster

1
2
3
Classic
Classic
SOLO

nothing better than lobster at ★ **Quoddy Bay Lobster** (7 Sea St., Eastport, 207/853-6640, 10am-6pm Tues.-Sat., noon-4pm Sun.). Lobster is the headliner—you can watch boats unload their catch, it's that fresh. Other options include wraps, salads, and chowders. There's even a kids' menu. Eat indoors or on picnic tables (some sheltered) hugging the harbor.

Seafood, natch, is the specialty at the bilevel **Eastport Chowder House** (167 Water St., Eastport, 207/853-4700, 11am-9pm daily, $13-25). There's a bar downstairs and a harborfront deck too.

Quick Bites

Dastardly Dick's Wicked Good Coffee (68 Water St., Eastport, 207/853-2090, 7am-2pm Tues.-Fri., 7am-noon Sat.) serves light breakfasts and lunches. On most Saturdays, the **Eastport Farmers Market** runs 11am-1pm at 5 Washington Street.

Of course **Pie Ladies' Bakery** (423 Rte. 1, Triangle Plaza, Pembroke, 207/217-9660, www.pieladiesbakery.com, 8am-2pm Wed.-Sat.) serves pie. It's also a handy stop for breakfast, lunch, homemade treats, or coffee.

It's worth the slight detour off Route 1 to purchase hot- and cold-smoked salmon as well as smoked salmon sticks and smoked haddock at **Maine-ly Smoked Salmon** (555 South Meadow Rd., Perry, 207/853-4794, www.mainelysmokedsalmon.com, 9am-5pm daily).

Look for the **ShoFar Farms** (www.shofarfarms.com, from $8) mobile brick oven around the area, or check the schedule on its website.

Family Favorites

The aptly named **New Friendly Restaurant** (1014 Rte. 1, Perry, 207/853-6610, 11am-8pm daily, $5-20) lays on home-cooked offerings for "dinnah" (a Maine-ism meaning "lunch").

A downtown Eastport institution since 1924, the **WaCo Diner** (Bank Square, Eastport, 207/853-9226, 6am-2pm daily, $8-20), pronounced WHACK-o, could refer to Washington County or to Nelson Watts and Ralph Colwell, who started it as a lunch cart. Expect diner fare with an emphasis on seafood. It's a good choice for breakfast. If the weather's fine, aim for a seat on the waterside deck.

Old Sow Grill (31 Water St., Eastport, 207/853-2823, 4pm-10pm Sun.-Tues., noon-10pm Wed.-Sat., $14-28), serves American fare in two dining rooms and a water-view deck. There's often live music on weekends.

ACCOMMODATIONS

Although musician and retired teacher Greg Noyes, innkeeper at the ★ **Kilby House Inn B&B** (122 Water St., Eastport, 800/853-4557, www.kilbyhouseinn.com, $100-125), grew up closer to Ellsworth, his great-great-grandfather was born in Eastport. Greg bought the Kilby House in 1992 and has masterfully updated and renovated the 1887 Victorian into a lovely four-bedroom inn filled with antiques (some original to the house), clocks, a grand piano, and an organ. Some bathrooms are small, but the hospitality and location, just one block off the ocean and two blocks from downtown, make up for that. Breakfast is served at 8am in the formal dining room. In the carriage house behind the inn is an adorable self-catered studio apartment with a private deck, full kitchen, and laundry ($150/day, $850/week).

On the second floor of the **Commons** (51 Water St., Eastport, 207/853-4123, www.thecommonseastport.com), a renovated downtown building on the waterfront, are two nicely appointed two-bedroom apartments with full kitchens, decks, and spectacular harbor views. Tide Watcher has two baths and rents for $1,365/week; Water's Edge has one bath and rents for $1,050/week. Shorter stays may be possible.

INFORMATION AND SERVICES

One of the best resources is the free ***Artsipelago: Two Countries One Bay* guidebook and map** (www.artsipelago.net), available locally and online, which details the arts and culture of the Passamaquoddy Bay region on both sides of the border, sorted by town. Listings include artists, cultural institutions, galleries, farmers markets, farms, local foods, ferries, festivals, film, historic sites, lighthouses, music, parks/natural sites, and theater.

Brochures are available at the **Quoddy Maritime Museum and Visitor Center** (70 Water St., Eastport, 10am-6pm daily June-Sept.), where you can see a huge model of the failed 1936 Passamaquoddy Tidal Power Project, an idea whose time hadn't come when it was proposed. Information is also available from the **Eastport Chamber of Commerce** (207/853-4644, www.eastportchamber.net).

Public restrooms are available in the Port Authority building on the waterfront.

GETTING THERE AND AROUND

The **Eastport-Lubec ferry** (207/546-2927, https://downeastwindjammer.com, $25 adults, $14 ages 2011, bikes $6) makes four round-trips Tuesday-Sunday mid-June to mid-September.

Eastport is about 40 miles or one hour via Routes 189, 1, and 190 from Lubec. It's about 28 miles or 40 minutes to Calais via Routes 190 and 1.

Calais and Vicinity

Calais (CAL-us, pop. 3,123) is as far as you'll get on the coast of Maine; from here on, you're headed inland. Europeans showed up in this area as early as 1604, when French adventurers established an ill-fated colony—the root of Acadian/Cajun civilization in the New World—on St. Croix Island in the St. Croix River, 16 whole years before the Pilgrims even thought about Massachusetts. After a winter-long debacle, all became relatively quiet until 1779, when the first permanent settler arrived. Southeast of Calais is tiny **Robbinston** (pop. 574), a booming shipbuilding community in the 19th century but today little more than a blip on the map.

Calais is both a river town and a major border crossing into New Brunswick, Canada, so you'd think it would be a lively spot, but the economy struggles here, with many of the downtown storefronts empty.

SIGHTS

St. Croix Island International Historic Site

Acadian/Cajun civilization in North America has its roots on **St. Croix Island,** an International Historic Site under joint U.S. and Canadian jurisdiction (Rte. 1, Red Beach Cove, eight miles south of Calais, 207/454-3871, www.nps.gov/sacr, free). The island is the site of the earliest European settlement in North America north of Florida, established by French explorers Samuel de Champlain and Pierre du Gua de Monts in 1604. Doomed by disease, mosquitoes, lack of food, and a grueling winter, 35 settlers died; in spring the emaciated survivors abandoned their effort and moved on to Nova Scotia. In 1969, archaeologists found the graves of 23 victims. The only monument on the island is a commemorative plaque dating from 1904.

Unless you have your own boat, you can't get to the island, but you can stop at the mainland **visitors center** (9am-5pm Thurs.-Mon. June and Sept., 9am-5pm daily July-Aug.), partake in interpretative programs, and enjoy the heritage trail, with bronze statues depicting personnel and cultures important to the colony's development. The trail ends on the point with views of the island. Also here are picnic tables, restrooms, a gravel beach, and a boat launch.

Whitlock Mill Lighthouse

From the lovely Pikewoods Rest Area, beside Route 1 about four miles southeast of Calais, there's a prime view of 32-foot-high **Whitlock Mill Lighthouse** on the southern shore of the St. Croix River. Built in 1892, the green flashing light is accessible only over private land, so check it out from this vantage point.

Calais-Robbinston Milestones

A quirky little local feature, the **Calais-Robbinston milestones** are a dozen red-granite chunks marking each of the 12 miles between Robbinston and Calais. Presaging today's highway mile markers, late-19th-century entrepreneur and journalist James S. Pike had the stones installed on the north side of Route 1 to keep track of the distance while training his pacing horses.

Alexander Art Trail

Here's a fun diversion. Take Route 9 inland and follow signs to discover the **Alexander Art Trail** (70 Barros Lake Rd., Alexander, 207/454-3563, www.arttrail.net, 8am-sunset daily, $2 donation) the largest hand-carved outdoor sculpture collection in Maine, comprising more than two dozen hand-carved figures.

RECREATION

Parks and Preserves

DEVIL'S HEAD

About six miles south of Calais, watch for signs on the river side of the road pointing to **Devil's Head.** The site has a mile of frontage on the St. Croix River estuary and views to St. Croix Island. A road with two parking areas descends to the shoreline, and there are pit toilets and a marked hiking trail. Approximately 1.5 miles long, the trail loops from the road, leading to the highest point of coastal land north of Cadillac Mountain. (The headland was originally called d'Orville Head, which morphed into Devil's Head.)

PIKE'S PARK

Calais has a lovely riverfront park at the foot of North Street. Pike's is the perfect place for a picnic. From here you have access to the 1.5-mile **Calais Waterfront Walk.**

FOOD

A bright spot downtown, **Crumbs Café & Bake Shoppe** (257 Main St., 207/454-8995, 7am-3pm Tues.-Fri., 11am-2pm Sat., $5-9) serves breakfast fare, sandwiches, panini, soups, chowders, and sweets.

Fried foods, burgers, pizza, and reasonably priced dinner plates have earned **Yancy's** (332 North St., Calais, 207/454-8200, 11am-8pm Wed.-Sat., $4-14) a solid reputation with families.

The **Nook and Cranny** (575 Airline Rd./Rte. 9, Baileyville, 207/454-3335, www.nookncrannyrestaurant.com, 11am-9pm Tues.-Sun., $10-20) doesn't look like much from the outside, but the interior is cozy, and the wide-ranging menu has a bit of this and some of that. A summer Sunday brunch buffet ($14) is served 11am-2pm.

ACCOMMODATIONS

The same family has operated the **International Motel** (626 Main St., Calais, 207/454-7515 or 800/336-7515, www.theinternationalmotel.com, $75-180) since 1955, and while clean, the rooms are tired. Opt for a room in the newer Riverview building. Pet-friendly rooms are available.

Twelve miles south of Calais, the Gothic-style, gingerbread-trimmed **Redclyffe Shore Motel** (Rte. 1, Robbinston, 207/454-3270, www.redclyffeshoremotorinn.com, $89-130) caps a bluff jutting into the St. Croix River where it widens into Passamaquoddy Bay. The overall property needs updating, but the 16 few-frills motel units have sunset-facing river views; opt for one with a balcony.

INFORMATION AND SERVICES

The **Maine Visitor Information Center** (39 Union St., Calais, 207/454-2211) has free

Wi-Fi, clean restrooms, and scads of brochures, including those produced by the **St. Croix Valley Chamber of Commerce** (207/454-2308 or 888/422-3112, www.visitstcroixvalley.com). The information center is open 8am-6pm daily mid-May-mid-October, 9am-5:30pm daily the rest of the year.

Public restrooms are available at the Maine Visitor Information Center and at the St. Croix International Heritage Site in Red Beach.

Pay attention to your watch—Calais is on Eastern time, whereas St. Stephen and the rest of New Brunswick is on Atlantic time, one hour later.

GETTING THERE AND AROUND

Calais is about 28 miles or 40 minutes from Eastport via Routes 190 and 1. It's about 95 miles or two hours and 15 minutes to Bangor via Routes 1 and 9.

If you plan to cross into Canada, you'll have to pass **immigration checkpoints** on both the U.S. (Calais, 207/454-3621) and Canadian (St. Stephen, 506/466-2363) ends of the bridges. Be sure to have the required identification (passport or passport card) and paperwork.

Grand Lake Stream

For a tiny community of 109 year-rounders, Grand Lake Stream has a well-deserved, larger-than-life reputation. It's the center of a vast area of rivers and lakes, ponds and streams—a recreational paradise, and more than 35,000 acres, including 62 miles of shore frontage, has been preserved by the **Downeast Lakes Land Trust** (www.downeastlakes.org). It's the town at the end of the world, remote in every sense of the word, yet just a half hour or so inland from Calais.

The famous stream is a narrow three-mile neck of prime scenic and sportfishing water connecting West Grand Lake and Big Lake. A dam spans the bottom of West Grand, and just downstream is a state-run salmon hatchery. Since the mid-19th century, the stream and its lakes have been drawing fishing fans to trout and landlocked-salmon spawning grounds, and fourth and fifth generations now return here each year.

Fly-fishing enthusiasts arrive May-June for landlocked salmon and smallmouth bass (the stream itself is fly-fishing only); families show up July-August for canoeing, bird-watching, swimming, fishing, and hiking; hunters arrive in late October for game birds and deer; and snowmobilers, snowshoers, and cross-country skiers descend as the snow piles up.

Canoe building has contributed to the area's mystique. The distinctive Grand Lake canoe (or "Grand Laker"), a lightweight, square-sterned, motorized 20-footer, was developed in the 1920s specifically for sportfishing in these waters. In the off-season, several villagers still hunker down in their workshops and turn out these stable cedar beauties. (Interested? Call Bill Shamel, 207/796-8199.)

RECREATION

The region has the greatest concentration of Registered Maine Guides in the state, which gives you an indication of the fishing, hunting, and canoeing opportunities here. Truly the best way to experience Grand Lake Stream is with a member of the **Grand Lake Stream Guides Association** (www.grandlakestreamguides.com). The website lists members and specialties. You can arrange for one of these skilled guides to lead you on a fishing expedition, wildlife or photographic safari, or canoeing trip for a half day or longer.

Hiking

If you're in Grand Lake Stream only for the day, head for the **public landing** (bear right after the intersection with the Pine Tree Store), where you'll find a parking area, a dock, a portable toilet, and a boat launch. You can also walk the path on the eastern shore of the stream. Or, armed with a map from the Pine Tree Store, hike the 2.6-mile **Little Mayberry Cove Trail** edging the western shoreline of West Grand Lake.

Folk Art Festival

A great time to visit the village is the last full weekend in July for the annual **Grand Lake Stream Folk Art Festival** (207/796-8199, www.grandlakestreamfolkartfestival.com, 10am-5pm Sat.-Sun., $8), held on the town's grassy ball field. Tents shelter approximately 50 top-notch juried artisans. Nonstop bluegrass and folk music is another attraction. An exhibit highlights the region's canoe-building tradition, and another displays antique and contemporary quilts. Leashed pets are welcome on festival grounds.

FOOD

The heart of Grand Lake Stream is the **Pine Tree Store** (3 Water St., Grand Lake Stream, 207/796-5027). People have been getting their gas and groceries here for more than 60 years. It's also a good source of local information (and gossip), and it offers breakfast fare, pizza, sandwiches, and general-store merchandise.

The **Old School Family Restaurant** (46 Main St., Princeton, 207/796-5254, 5am-7pm Mon.-Fri., 6am-7pm Sat., 6am-3pm Sun.) is a find for fans for good home cookin' at reasonable prices. Go for breakfast; the homemade toast is reason enough. Dinner options range from sandwiches to a fried seafood platter ($7-19).

Both Leen's Lodge and Weatherby's open their dining rooms to guests by reservation. Expect to pay $25-40 for a full meal.

ACCOMMODATIONS

Cabin accommodations, with or without meals, are the lodgings of choice in Grand Lake Stream, and there's enough variety for every taste and budget. Few guests stay one night; most stay several days or a week. Rates quoted below are for two; many cabins can sleep more than that, and pp rates may be lower for extra people. Some housekeeping cabins require your own sheets and towels. Most camps have boat rentals for about $25-50/day (a motor brings the total to about $60-95).

Weatherby's (3 Water St., Grand Lake Stream, 877/796-5558, www.weatherbys.com) an Orvis-endorsed fly-fishing lodge with roots in the late 1800s, is an institution in these parts. Guests stay in 15 rustic cottages and cabins, all with fireplace or woodstove, screened porch, and bathroom. Meals are served in the main lodge, a comfy spot with a library of sporting books and magazines, fly-tying bench, and piano. American Plan rates (from $199 pp adults, $85 ages 10-15, $65 ages 4-9) include breakfast, lunch, and dinner; housekeeping rates, no meals, are $70 pp, $29 ages 5-15. Dogs are $15/day.

Leen's Lodge (207/796-2929 or 800/995-3367, www.leenslodge.com, May-Oct., from $185 pp), on a spacious wooded shore and peninsula of West Grand Lake, has 10 small and large rustic cabins with baths. Rates include breakfast, pack lunch, and dinner. Children 6-12 pay $12 multiplied by their age; children 5 and younger are free. Housekeeping rates are also sometimes available. Leashed pets are welcome, and kennels are provided. BYOB. Canoe and motorboat rentals should be arranged in advance.

Grand Lake Lodge (207/796-5584, www.grandlakelodgemaine.com, from $55 pp, no credit cards), on the shore of West Grand Lake and two blocks from the village center and with a safe swimming area, is a particularly good choice for families. Dogs are allowed for $20/each.

The **Lakeside** (14 Rolfe St., Princeton, 888/677-2874, www.thelakeside.org, $70-85) is set well back from Route 1 on Lewy Lake, which flows through Long Lake into Big Lake. The five housekeeping cabins along the lakeshore are geared to sports-oriented folks; they're clean but basic. Guide services and boat rentals are available.

INFORMATION AND SERVICES

The volunteer-run **Grand Lake Stream Chamber of Commerce** (www.grandlakestream.org) produces a brochure listing accommodations, shops, and services.

GETTING THERE

Grand Lake Stream is about 32 miles or 45 minutes from Calais via Route 1 and the Grand Lake Stream Road. It's about 80 miles or 1.75 hours to Houlton via Route 1 or about 115 miles or 2.25 hours to Bangor via Routes 1 and 9.

Aroostook County

Welcome to the Crown of Maine. When Mainers

refer to "The County," they're referring to Aroostook, a Micmac Indian word meaning "bright" or "shining." At 6,453 square miles, Maine's largest county—the largest east of the Mississippi—is bigger than Connecticut and Rhode Island combined, but its population numbers fewer than 68,000 residents (that's roughly 11 per square mile), and fully a quarter of them live in only two smallish cities, Presque Isle and Caribou. People may be scarce, but Aroostook has the largest density of moose and black bear in the Lower 48.

This is Maine's big-sky country, an awesome place to view the northern lights. In places, the landscape seems to go on forever. Neat farmhouses and huge, half-buried potato-storage barns anchor vast

Highlights

Look for ★ to find recommended sights, activities, dining, and lodging.

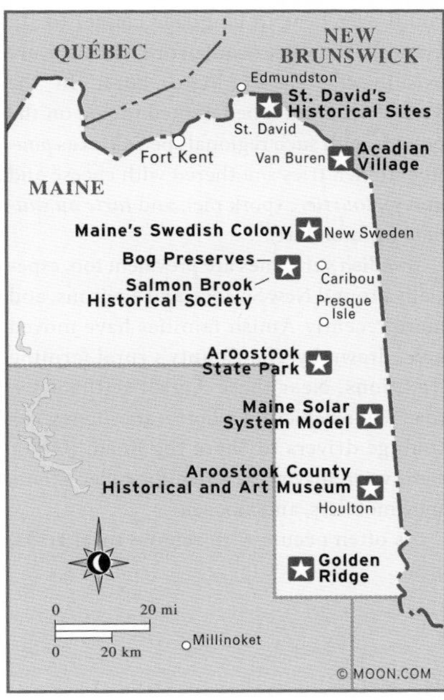

★ **Maine Solar System Model:** Stretching 95 miles along Route 1 between Houlton and Presque Isle is a three-dimensional scale model of the solar system (page 420).

★ **Aroostook County Historical and Art Museum:** There are plenty of treasures here for history buffs, including military artifacts dating from the Civil War (page 421).

★ **Golden Ridge:** Route 2, between Sherman Mills and Houlton, passes along the ridge top, with panoramic views from Katahdin to distant lakes (page 423).

★ **Salmon Brook Historical Society:** Learn about the traditional potato-farm lifestyle at this National Register of Historic Places-listed property and museum (page 425).

★ **Maine's Swedish Colony:** It's an authentic touch of Sweden, and the best time to visit is during the annual June Midsommar Festival (page 426).

★ **Aroostook State Park:** Maine's first state park has opportunities for hiking, swimming, and boating (page 428).

★ **Bog Preserves:** In early summer, schedule a walk at the Woodland Bog Preserve with Nature Conservancy steward Richard Clark to learn about the flora and fauna and see rare orchids (page 428).

★ **Acadian Village:** Delve into Maine's Acadian history and heritage on a guided tour of 16 antique and replica buildings (page 432).

★ **St. David's Historical Sites:** Learn about Acadian heroine Tante Blanche, visit a typical homestead and school, and see where the Acadians first landed (page 433).

undulating patches of potatoes, broccoli, and barley. Potato fields define The County—bright green in spring, varied shades of pink, purple, yellow, and white in mid-July, dirt-brown and gold just before the autumn harvest.

Aroostook is perhaps best known as a winter destination. Legions of snowmobilers (often called "sledders") crisscross The County every winter, exploring hundreds of miles of the incredible Interconnecting Trail System (ITS). It's also earned an international reputation for its Olympic biathlon-training center, which hosts World Cup Nordic events.

The County's agricultural preeminence sets it apart from the rest of Maine, but so do its immigrant cultures. Acadian culture permeates the northernmost St. John Valley, where the French dialect is unlike anything you'll ever hear in language classes (or in France). Islands of Acadian or French culture exist in other parts of Maine, but it's in "the Valley" that you'll be tempted to pile on the pounds with such regional specialties as *poutine* (french fries smothered with cheese and gravy), *tourtière* (pork pie), and *tarte au saumon* (salmon tart).

Swedish surnames are prevalent too, especially around New Sweden and environs, and more recently Amish families have moved here, drawn by The County's rural farming traditions. Near these Amish settlements, road signs depicting a horse-and-buggy encourage drivers to Share the Road. (Other signs warn drivers to watch for roller-skiers, snowmobilers, and moose).

As often occurs with remote rural areas, The County sometimes gets a bum rap (never from the snowmobiling crowd) among downstaters and others who've never been here. But it deserves notice—for the scenery if nothing else. Admittedly, it's a long haul, but you're guaranteed a totally different Maine experience. For many visitors, there's a sensation of traveling back 20 or 30 years to an era when life was simpler, communities were small, and everyone greeted each other by name.

To truly appreciate The County, detour off Route 1 and explore the crossroads and often-gravel byways. Trust me, it's worth it.

PLANNING YOUR TIME

Covering such a large expanse of geography takes time. While you can loop around Aroostook's periphery in one long day, you'll need 3-4 days to explore the region and tease out its charms. Do note that lodging and restaurant options tend to be unfussy and few.

Snowmobilers and cross-country skiers come January-March, when The County measures its snow in feet, not inches.

In June, newly planted potato fields resemble Ireland in their vibrant greens, although the blackflies and mosquitoes can be annoying. Midsommar is the best time to visit the Swedish colony. In mid-July, the potato fields are in bloom. Most museums and historical sites are open during the summer, so that's the best time for history buffs to visit. Days are long and temperatures moderate, also making it ideal for hikers, cyclists, and paddlers.

Autumn comes early, with leaves beginning to turn color in late August in the northern parts of The County.

Previous: St. John River; a sculpture at Acadian Village; part of the Maine Solar System Model.

Aroostook County

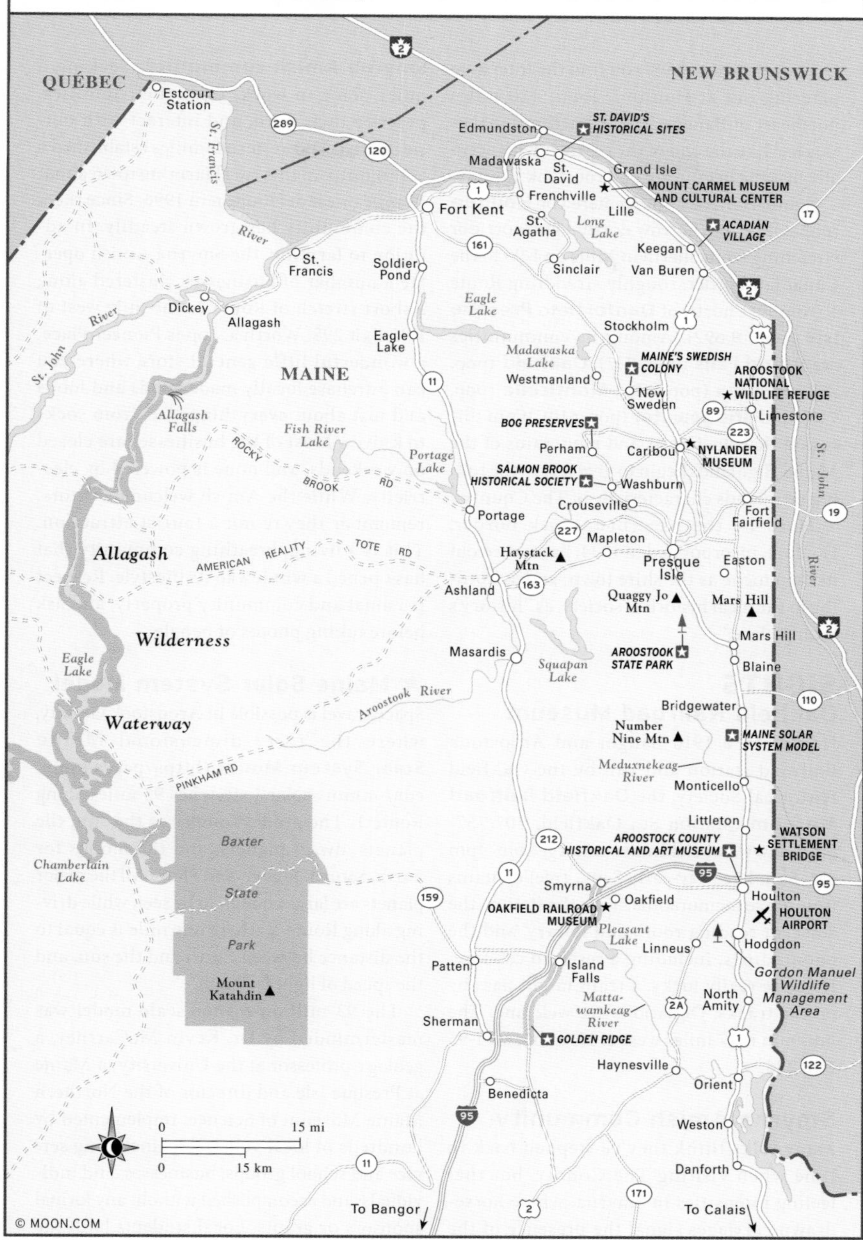

AROOSTOOK COUNTY

Southern Aroostook County

Driving north on I-95, you find the interstate petering out at Houlton, about 120 miles northeast of Bangor. That sometimes makes this feel like the end of the earth, but it's actually just the beginning of Aroostook County.

Southern Aroostook, centered on **Houlton** (pop. 6,123), is a narrow north-south corridor stretching from Sherman Mills on I-95 to the Canadian border, roughly straddling Route 1 from just north of **Danforth** to **Presque Isle** (pop. 9,692). Among its communities are **Island Falls** (pop. 837), **Oakfield** (pop. 737), **Smyrna** (pop. 442), **Monticello** (pop. 790), and **Bridgewater** (pop. 610). It's in this region that the forests and mountains of the Maine Highlands begin to give way to the rolling farmlands characteristic of The County.

Hard by the New Brunswick border, Houlton, incorporated in 1834, has carved out its own niche as the shire town, and, according to the local historical society, as "history's hiding place."

SIGHTS

Oakfield Railroad Museum

Housed in a 1910 Bangor and Aroostook Railroad station and run by the Oakfield Historical Society, the **Oakfield Railroad Museum** (Station St., Oakfield, 207/757-8575, www.oakfieldmuseum.org, 1pm-4pm Sat.-Sun. late May-early Sept., free) contains iron-horse memorabilia. Tour the station, the adjacent reading room and library, and the outbuildings, including a restored caboose. If you're really lucky, a train might pass by on the tracks. Donations are welcome. The museum is 17 miles west of Houlton, off I-95 Exit 286.

Smyrna Amish Community

Many folks think they've stepped back in time when visiting The County, but that feeling intensifies in Smyrna, where horse-drawn carriages signal the presence of the **Smyrna Amish community.** Seeking a quiet place to work, raise their families, practice their faith, and interact with outsiders, five Midwestern families established a community in this rural farming town about 15 miles west of Houlton in 1996. Since then, the community has grown steadily. In addition to farming, the Smyrna Amish operate a number of businesses clustered along a short stretch of Route 2, one mile west of I-95 Exit 295. Worth a stop is Pioneer Place, a wonderful little general store where you can purchase locally made goods and foods and just about everything else, from socks to knives. Most of the businesses are closed on weekends, and none is powered by electricity. While the Amish welcome visitors, remember they're not a tourist attraction. This is a living, breathing community that has opened a window to its lifestyle. Respect personal and community property, and ask before taking photos of people.

★ Maine Solar System Model

Space travel is possible in Aroostook County, where the three-dimensional **Maine Solar System Model** (http://pages.umpi.edu/~nmms/solar/) stretches 95 miles along Route 1. The model comprises the sun, the planets, dwarf planets, and the moons for Earth, Saturn, Jupiter, and Pluto. All the major planets are large enough to be seen while driving along Route 1, where one mile is equal to the distance between Earth and the sun, and the speed of light is 7 mph.

The 93-million-to-one scale model was masterminded by Dr. Kevin McCartney, a geology professor at the University of Maine at Presque Isle and director of the Northern Maine Museum of Science; implemented by hundreds of local volunteers, including service and school groups, businesses, and individuals; and accomplished without any formal sponsors or grants. Local students built the planets. It's really quite a marvel of can-do grassroots community spirit.

Pluto, only 1 inch in diameter, is embedded in a wall in the lobby of the Visitor Information Center in Houlton, just off Route 1, north of the I-95 interchange. Other models are mounted on 10-foot-tall posts and dot parking lots and fields along the route. The project is detailed and mapped both in a brochure, available at the center, and on the Internet. If heading north, begin in Houlton and set your odometer to zero at the info center.

Market Square Historic District

An arced pedestrian bridge across the Meduxnekeag River in Houlton links Gateway Crossing, on Route 1, with Market Square's 28 turn-of-the-20th-century buildings listed in the National Register of Historic Places (the architecture is lovely, but unfortunately more than a few storefronts are empty). Along the bridge and walkway (both wheelchair-accessible) are markers detailing Houlton's downtown history. A walking guide is available at the **Greater Houlton Area Chamber of Commerce** (109 Main St., Houlton), two blocks up Main Street. On the Route 1 side, illustrated plaques detailing more history along with flora and fauna pepper an easy 0.2-mile round-trip riverside trail.

★ Aroostook County Historical and Art Museum

The 1903 White Memorial Building, the Colonial Revival residence that houses the Greater Houlton Area Chamber of Commerce, is also home to the **Aroostook County Historical and Art Museum** (109 Main St., 207/532-6984, http://houltonmuseum.wixsite.com/acham, 1pm-4pm Tues.-Fri., 9am-1pm Sat. June-early Sept., donation) containing a fine collection of photos, books, vintage clothing, antique tools, and housewares. You can wander through on your own, but a guide will bring the collection to life. Of particular interest are military artifacts from the Civil War, Hancock Barracks, and the Camp Houlton POW internment camp.

If you're especially keen on history, ask museum staff to provide information about and direct you to two noteworthy local historical sites, although frankly, there isn't much to see at either.

The U.S. Army established **Hancock Barracks** in 1828 to protect American border settlements and garrisoned 200 troops there during the 1838-1839 Aroostook War. It provided frontier training for West Point graduates, and Gen. Robert E. Lee visited here. To find the overgrown, gated site in Garrison Park, take Route 2 toward the airport and turn left onto Garrison Road, near the top of the hill.

The still functioning **Houlton International Airport** was established in 1941 as Houlton Army Air Base. Neutrality laws prevented U.S.-built planes from flying directly from the United States to Britain, so during the months before the attack on Pearl Harbor, planes were known to land in Houlton and then be towed by tractor across the border to Canada for takeoff on the highway. In 1944, part of the base became Camp Houlton, Maine's largest **German POW camp.** Nearly 4,000 German prisoners lived here in barracks while laboring in lumber camps, canneries, potato farms, and paper mills. The original World War II airport control tower (one of the few surviving in the country), one POW camp building, a few foundations, and a small memorial are all that remain of the era. To find the site, take Route 2 east from downtown. At the T intersection, bear right and then right again on Aviation Road.

Watson Settlement Bridge

About six miles north of Houlton, amid typical Aroostook farmland in Littleton, stands Maine's northernmost (yes, and easternmost) covered bridge, built in 1911 and last used in 1985. The wood-truss bridge, straddling a branch of the Meduxnekeag River, feels quite forlorn, a remnant of the past just sitting here unused (except, unfortunately,

1

2

3

RESTAURANT
GRAMMY'S
COUNTRY
INN
532-7808

4

AROOSTOOK COUNTY
EST. 1937
HISTORICAL & ART
MUSEUM of HOULTON

by graffiti artists). Maine once had 120 or so covered bridges; only nine remain, and this is the only one using the Howe truss system. For the prettiest route to the bridge from Houlton, take Foxcroft Road from Route 2 and continue 6.1 miles; turn left onto Carson Road. From Route 1 in Littleton, go right on Carson Road, which winds its way down to the river (bear left at the fork). The quicker route is to head north on Route 1 4 miles from the I-95 interchange and then go right on Carson Road for 2.9 miles.

Scenic Routes

★ GOLDEN RIDGE

The interstate is the fastest route to Houlton, but Route 2, from Sherman Mills through Oakfield and Smyrna, is the best choice for moseyers, and it really isn't that much longer. The far-less-traveled route passes through gorgeous countryside dotted with farms, lakes, and small villages. The views from Golden Ridge, a section between Island Falls and Oakfield, reach to Katahdin and beyond. Watch for potato barns, unique structures built into the ground for cold potato storage. Most have a gambrel roof topping the landscape.

MILLION-DOLLAR VIEW SCENIC BYWAY

South of Houlton and stretching eight miles along Route 1 between Danforth and Orient is an especially scenic drive that passes over Peekaboo Mountain and offers panoramic views over the Chiputneticook chain of lakes into Canada to the east, and to Katahdin on the west. It's also prime moose-watching country. There are two scenic pullouts, one with views west to Katahdin, the other with views east across the lakes into Canada.

RECREATION

Houlton is at the fringe of prime **snowmobiling** country. The crowds tend to head up the road to Presque Isle, Caribou, and the St. John Valley, but there are plenty of trails here. For information on snowmobiling in the Houlton area, contact the chamber of commerce or the **Maine Snowmobile Association** (207/622-6983, www.mesnow.com), which can put you in touch with local snowmobile clubs. Some snowmobile trails cross into Canada. Carry a passport or passport card when you are near the border. The Houlton border crossing is open 24 hours daily.

1: Watson Settlement Bridge 2: Amish buggy in Aroostook County 3: Grammy's Country Inn 4: Aroostook County Historical and Art Museum

FOOD

Homemade doughnuts, cinnamon buns, and other treats emerge from the kitchen at **Sadie's Bakery** (5 Water St., Houlton, 207/532-6650, 6:30-am-2pm Tues.-Fri., 6:30am-noon Sat.), a hole-in-the-wall that's been in biz since 1948. The **Houlton Farmers Market** sets up on Market Square downtown 9am-1pm Saturdays.

For breakfast, lunch, or a good java, pop into **Wired Houlton** (23 Market Sq., Houlton, 617/388-9619), which doubles as an art gallery.

Maple syrup and honey are produced at **Spring Break** (3315 Rte. 2, Smyrna Mills, 207/757-7373, www.mainemapleandhoney.com), a sugarhouse and Maine-made gift shop near the Amish colony.

Family Favorites

For humongous portions (even by County standards), home cooking, good service, and local color, ★ **Grammy's Country Inn** (1687 Bangor Rd., Linneus, 207/532-7808, 8am-9pm Mon.-Fri., 7am-9pm Sat., 7am-8pm Sun., $9-28) is the choice. It's nothing fancy, mind you, but where else might you find deep-fried lobster on the menu? Order conservatively, and even then, plan on having leftovers. Do save room for dessert, which includes two-fisted whoopie pies. The best part though is that nearly everything on the menu is less than $14.

It's easy to spot the **Blue Moose Lodge** (180 Rte. 1, Monticello, 207/538-0991, www.

thebluemooselodge.com, 11am-8pm Wed.-Sat., 7am-7pm Sun., $7-19): Just look for the blue moose. Rather nondescript on the exterior, inside it's warm, inviting, and lodge-like. The family-operated restaurant serves home-style fare at better-than-reasonable prices.

Casual Dining

Hidden in the back of the small downtown Fishman Mall and displaying the work of local artists, the **Courtyard Café** (61 Main St., Houlton, 207/532-0787, www.thecourtyardcafe.biz, 11am-2pm and 5pm-8pm Tues.-Thurs., 11am-2pm and 5pm-9pm Fri., 5pm-9pm Sat., $12-32) is well worth finding. Dine either in the main restaurant or the more casual bar. The American menu changes frequently, and often includes international accents.

First Settler's Lodge (341 Rte. 1, Weston, 207/448-3000, www.firstsettlerslodge.com, 5pm-8pm Fri.-Sat., $12-25) serves American fare with a view.

ACCOMMODATIONS

On the Million-Dollar View Scenic Byway, about 28 miles south of Houlton, ★ **First Settler's Lodge** (341 Rte. 1, Weston, 207/448-3000, www.firstsettlerslodge.com, $140-150) is a spoiler with spectacular views east to the East Grand Lakes and west to Katahdin. Guests staying in the four very spacious rooms (some ideal for families), group room with multiple beds, or honeymoon suite with private deck have use of an expansive and comfy cathedral-ceilinged great room with deck overlooking Katahdin, back gardens overlooking the lakes, and a well-equipped guest kitchen. Breakfast is included; dinner is available. Pets are welcome for $45/stay. Hiking/snowshoeing trails descend to the lake.

Clean, well-maintained, and regularly updated, **Ivey's Motor Lodge** (Rte. 1, Houlton, 207/532-4206 or 800/244-4206 in Maine, www.iveysmotorlodge.com, $145-175) wins folks over with good-size guest rooms, friendly service, and amenities unexpected in an older motel. Rates include a hot-and-cold continental buffet. On the premises is a pub with a big-screen TV.

The **Shiretown Motor Inn** (282 North Rd./Rte. 1, Houlton, 207/532-9421 or 800/441-9421, www.shiretownmotorinn.com, $120-150) has an indoor pool and a fitness room. Rates include continental breakfast. Some rooms are pet friendly ($10).

INFORMATION AND SERVICES

The **Greater Houlton Chamber of Commerce** (109 Main St., Houlton, 207/532-4216, www.greaterhoulton.com) is in the same 1903 Colonial Revival building as the Aroostook Historical and Art Museum. Request the *Walking Guide to Market Square Historic District*.

The **Maine Visitor Information Center** (28 Ludlow Rd., Houlton, 207/532-6346), with brochures and maps covering the entire state, is open 9am-5pm weekdays year-round, with weekend and extended weekday hours in summer. **Restrooms** are also available. **Aroostook County Tourism** (888/216-2463, www.visitaroostook.com) has information on and links for the entire county.

GETTING THERE

Houlton is about 80 miles or 1.75 hours from Grand Lake Stream via Route 1 or about 120 miles or 1.75 hours from Bangor via I-95. It's about 42 miles or 50 minutes to Presque Isle.

Central Aroostook County

Ahh. Sighs of contentment are common in a region where folks know their neighbors, crime is rare, and the only traffic jams are caused by slowly moving farm equipment. In addition to road signs urging drivers to be wary of moose, there are others encouraging sharing the road with roller-skiers and Amish horse-and-buggies.

Most of the 60,000 acres planted with spuds in Maine are found in the "Potato Triangle," the region framed by **Presque Isle** (pop. 9,692) to the south, **Caribou** (pop. 8,189) to the north, and **Fort Fairfield** (pop. 3,496) on the Canadian border, tied together by the zigzagging course of the Aroostook River. Farmhouses, potato barns, and rolling fields dominate the landscape—and when those fields bloom in mid-July, it's one of the prettiest sights around. Northeast of Caribou is **Limestone** (pop 2,314); south of Presque Isle is **Mars Hill** (pop. 1,493). Each is a day's stage ride from the others, about 13 miles, making it easy to explore the region from one base. South of Fort Fairfield is **Easton,** home to another Amish community.

Outdoor enthusiasts, especially, will find miles of multiuse trails, two small alpine ski areas, and impressive cross-country facilities that have hosted World Cup events. Cross-country skiing was introduced to Maine by settlers of the Swedish Colony, the region northwest of Caribou anchored by **New Sweden** (pop. 602) and **Stockholm** (pop. 253).

SIGHTS

Most historical sites in the area are run by volunteers, so hours change frequently. It's wise to call before making a special trip.

Northern Maine Museum of Science

Science wunderkind Kevin McCartney, a geology professor and the powerhouse behind the Maine Solar System scale model, also gets credit for the **Northern Maine Museum of Science,** located in Folsom Hall at the **University of Maine at Presque Isle** (UMPI, 181 Main St./Rte. 1, Presque Isle, 207/768-9400). Hallways in the three-story science building have been turned into a free teaching museum, where you can take in all manner of scientific and mathematical exhibits, with displays varying from bottle-nosed dolphins to DNA. Also here is the sun, the epicenter of the Route 1 solar system model. Nothing is high-tech, but it's enjoyable and well presented.

★ Salmon Brook Historical Society

Here's a worthwhile two-for-one deal, with lots of charm and character: In tiny downtown Washburn, across from the First Baptist Church, the **Salmon Brook Historical Society** (1267 Main St./Rte. 164, Washburn, 207/455-4339) operates the **Benjamin C. Wilder Homestead,** an 1852 farmhouse in the National Register of Historic Places, and the **Aroostook Agricultural Museum** in the adjacent red barn. The well-restored 10-room house has period furnishings and displays; the barn contains old tools and antique cookware and pottery. The museums, on 2.5 acres, are open July 4-early September, call for current hours, and other times by appointment. Admission is free, but donations are welcome. Washburn is 11 miles northwest of Presque Isle and 10 miles southwest of Caribou.

Nylander Museum

If you were an eccentric self-educated geologist and needed a place to display and store everything you'd accumulated, you'd create a place like the **Nylander Museum** (393 Main St., Caribou, 207/493-4209, cariboumaine.org, donation). Swedish-born Olof Olssen

Nylander traveled the world collecting specimens, settled in Caribou, and bequeathed his work, including 6,000 fossils and 40,000 shells, to the city. Since his 1943 death, the museum has acquired other collections: butterflies, mounted birds, and additional geological specimens. It's all displayed in two small galleries. Call for current hours.

★ Maine's Swedish Colony

Maine's Swedish Colony (www.maineswedishcolony.info) comprises New Sweden, Stockholm, and Woodland, and spills over into neighboring towns, including Westmanland, Connor, Madawaska Lake, and Caribou. The best time to visit is during the **Midsommar Festival,** on the closest weekend to Midsummer Day (June 21), when sites are open for tours and residents don traditional Swedish costumes and celebrate the year's longest day. Activities include decorating a maypole, Swedish dancing, a smorgasbord, concerts, and a prayer service. Non-Scandinavians are welcome to join in.

New Sweden is eight miles northwest of downtown Caribou via Route 161. At the **New Sweden Historical Society Museum** (Capitol Hill Rd. and Station Rd., New Sweden, 207/896-5200, noon-4pm Wed.-Fri., 1pm-4pm Sat.-Sun. early June-mid-Sept., donation), three floors of memorabilia reflect the rugged life in this frontier community. An exact replica of the colony's "Kapitoleum" (capitol), the museum was built in 1971 after fire leveled the original structure. Check out the museum's guestbook: Visitors have come from all over Scandinavia to see this cultural enclave. The museum is open. Next door, in the **Capitol Hill School,** a gift shop carries Swedish items. Out back is a monument with the list of the original settlers.

Continuing east on Station Road, you'll pass **W. W. Thomas Memorial Park** on the left, a great spot for a picnic, with a play area for kids and a dramatic vista over the rolling countryside. Concerts occur periodically in the band shell. About 0.2 mile farther are the circa-1870 **Larsson/Ostlund Log Home,** one of the colony's oldest buildings, and the shingled **Lars Noak Blacksmith and Woodworking Shop,** another remnant of the early settlers, both listed in the National Register of Historic Places.

Back in Caribou, **Monica's Scandinavian Imports** (176 Sweden St., Caribou, 207/493-4600) is chock-full of imported goods, from linens to clothing, cheese, and jewelry.

Scenic Routes

With so much open space in The County, particularly in the Potato Triangle, drivers and bicyclists can enjoy great long vistas. One route is **Route 164** between Caribou and Presque Isle, half of it along the Aroostook River. On the way, you can check out the museums in Washburn or detour on the multiuse trail.

Another scenic drive is **Route 167,** between Presque Isle and Fort Fairfield; the 12-mile stretch is especially dramatic in mid-July when the rolling fields are draped with pink and white potato blossoms and Fort Fairfield puts on its annual Potato Blossom Festival.

If you're even a bit adventurous and have a trustworthy vehicle, explore the back roads in this region. Although many are quite hilly, they're worth the effort for cyclists too. Be forewarned that many have gravel sections, but they're usually well maintained. Don't be surprised to come across roller-skiers or Amish buggies. Expect to find big views from hilltop ridges and honor stands for potatoes and other fresh produce. Good choices are the roads east of Route 1 in the Easton area and the Tangle Ridge Road, in Woodland.

TOURS

The **Presque Isle Historical Society** (207/762-1151, www.pihistory.org) offers a wide range of ways to experience the city, including two-hour guided walking tours, one-hour tours of the 1875 **Vera Estey House Museum,** guided walking tours of the historic Fairmount Cemetery, haunted hearse tours, mystery history tours, and three-hour narrated city tours and foliage tours aboard Molly the Trolley. Fees range from free to $5.

One Potato, Two Potato

Potato stands pepper Aroostook County's highways and byways.

Native to South America, the potato is king in Aroostook County, where 90 percent of Maine's spuds grow on more than 60,000 acres. The output makes Maine the country's fifth- to eighth-largest producer (depending on the harvest).

Aroostook County's potato heritage dates back more than 150 years, says fourth-generation potato farmer Keith LaBrie of LaBrie's Farms in St. Agatha. "It became a staple on family farms generations ago," LaBrie says. "Back 50, 60 years ago, there were thousands of small growers, with 15-20-acre farms. Those have consolidated into 300-500-acre farms, and the harvesting is mechanized now for efficiency."

In the past, he says, Maine predominantly grew the round, white table stock variety. Recently there's been more of a move toward russet types. While most of what Maine grows is used for processed french fries and potato chips, Maine potatoes are now being used to produce Cold River Vodka (www.coldrivervodka.com), made and sold in Freeport.

Potato fields are in full blossom in mid-July. Different varieties produce differently colored blossoms, so there will be white in one field, purple in another. Look for roadside sheds selling new potatoes, usually by the honor system.

Annual festivals in Fort Fairfield and Houlton celebrate the blossoms and the harvest; potatoes appear on every restaurant menu and family table; and countless roadside stands peddle them by the bag. Although high schools still close for 2-3 weeks in September so students (and teachers) can assist with the harvest, most of the work is done mechanically these days.

Now, if you don't get enough of this potato business while you're here in The County, there's always a membership in the **Organic Potato of the Month Sampler Club.** Eight months a year, **Wood Prairie Farm** (49 Kinney Rd., Bridgewater, 800/829-9765, www.woodprairie.com), an organic farm in Bridgewater, sends its members an eight-pound gift box of three different kinds of organic potatoes. The package comes with postcards and recipes, so you're all set. The base price for the eight-month club is $299; one month is $39.95.

Information on the potato industry is available from the **Maine Potato Board** (207/764-4148, www.mainepotatoes.com).

RECREATION

Parks and Preserves

★ AROOSTOOK STATE PARK

Aroostook State Park (State Park Rd., Presque Isle, 207/768-8341, www.parksandlands.com, $3-4 adults, $1 ages 5-11 and seniors) has the distinction of being Maine's first state park, created in 1939, when inspired citizens of Presque Isle donated 100 acres of land to the state. The park has grown significantly since then; it now comprises nearly 1,000 acres, encompassing Quaggy Jo Mountain and Echo Lake and providing plentiful opportunities for hiking, water sports, snow sports, camping, and more. Quaggy Jo comes from the Micmac word *quaquajo,* which translates as "twin-peaked." Allow 2-3 hours for the moderate (with steep sections) three-mile hike (clockwise) via the North Peak, North-South Peak Ridge, and South Peak Trails to take in both summits; the views, especially from North Peak, are superb. After hiking, have a lakeside picnic and then cool off with a swim or fish for brook trout. Public boat access is available and canoe or kayak rentals are $3 per hour. The park is equally inviting in winter, when a selection of trails are open for cross-country skiing. Groomed snowmobile trails also pass through the park.

★ BOG PRESERVES

About six miles west of Caribou, the **Woodland Bog Preserve** is home to several rare orchid species and 80 bird species (nearly 90 have been banded here). Nearby is **Salmon Brook Lake and Perham Wetlands,** a northern white cedar bog that's home to numerous rare plants. Trails and boardwalks ease exploring these areas, but do wear waterproof shoes and use strong insect repellent.

Multiuse Trails

From Washburn, you can access two crushed-stone multiuse trails that are popular with mountain bikers, ATV riders, and snowmobilers: the 75-mile **Aroostook Valley Rail Trail** passes through fields and woods and edges streams and the Aroostook River between Washburn, Stockholm, Van Buren, Mapleton, and Caribou. Access in Washburn is via Station Road off Route 164. Park in downtown Washburn, and carry plenty of water. From Caribou, you can go to Stockholm and on to Van Buren (29 miles one-way). Or begin in Carson (just west of Caribou) and go to New Sweden (9 miles one-way). The 40-mile **Southern Bangor & Aroostook Rail Trail** connects Presque Isle with Houlton.

Golf

Laid out during the era of Prohibition, the border-crossing 18-hole **Aroostook County Country Club** (234 Russell Rd., Fort Fairfield, 800/980-8747, www.avcc.ca) has its parking lot and pro shop in the U.S., but the course and the alcohol-serving clubhouse are in Canada.

Paddling

Perception of Aroostook (9 Caribou Rd./Rte. 1, Presque Isle, 207/764-5506, www.perceptionofaroostook.com) rents canoes and kayaks and will provide shuttles for the easy-going, 10-mile calm-water paddle on the Aroostook River from Washburn to Presque Isle.

Winter Sports

Twenty miles of professionally designed world-class cross-country skiing trails are available free at the **Maine Nordic Heritage Center** (Nordic Heritage Access Rd., off Rte. 167, Presque Isle, 207/492-1444, www.nordicheritagecenter.org), part of the Maine Winter Sports Center. One of the world's best internationally licensed cross-country facilities, the center has hosted international biathlon and cross-country races. The facilities include 20.5 miles of Nordic trails, a 30-point biathlon range, 0.6-mile paved and lighted roller-ski loop, 2.5-mile lighted trail, and visitors center with equipment rentals. Afterward, finish up with a sauna in the lodge. Best of all, the trails are free. The facility also has 20 miles of marked mountain bike trails.

Snowmobile rentals are available at the **Sled Shop** (108 Main St., Presque Isle, 207/764-2900, www.thesledshopinc.com). Rates begin at $250/day. Links to local snowmobile clubs are on its website.

ENTERTAINMENT

Agriculture exhibits, harness racing, live entertainment, and fireworks are all part of Presque Isle's **Northern Maine Fair** (www.northernmainefairgrounds.com), the biggest country fair in this part of Maine, held from late June to early July.

One of The County's biggest wingdings is the **Maine Potato Blossom Festival** held in Fort Fairfield in mid-July. It features pageantry, potatoes, crafts, potatoes, entertainment, potatoes, fireworks, and potatoes.

FOOD

As with other parts of Maine, Aroostook County has frequent **public suppers** throughout the summer. Visitors are welcome, even encouraged (most suppers benefit a good cause), so check the papers, line up early, and enjoy the local food and color.

Quick Bites

Breakfast is served all day along with the usual home-style fare at the **Riverside Inn Restaurant** (399 Main St., Presque Isle, 207/764-1447, 5am-2pm Sat.-Thurs., 5am-8pm Fri., 6am-3pm Sun., $5-12).

Farms Bakery & Coffee Shop (118 Bennett Dr., Caribou, 207/493-4508, 6am-2pm Tues.-Sat.) is the place to go for scratch-made croissants, delicious pastries, and light lunches.

Just try to resist the cookies and pastries at **Café Demoiselles** (483 Main St., Presque Isle, 207/760-7587, http://www.cafedemoiselles.com, 7am-2pm Tues.-Sat., $4-8), which also serves sweet and savory crepes along with smoothies and coffees.

Retro **Burger Boy** (344 Sweden St., Caribou, 207/498-2329, 10:30am-9pm Mon.-Sat., 11am-9pm Sun.) has been serving fresh-ground burgers, house-made fries, and decent shakes since 1968. Burgers start at $2.46.

For farm-fresh ice cream, dip into **Goughan's Farm** (875 Fort Fairfield Rd./Rte. 161, Caribou, 207/498-6565, 8am-5pm Mon.-Sat., noon-5pm Sun. Mar.-mid-Dec.), where you can pair a visit with a round of miniature golf or a stop at the petting barn.

Stock up on picnic goodies at the **Presque Isle Farmers Market** (8:30am-1pm Sat. mid-May-mid-Oct.) in the Riverside Pavilion on Riverside Drive.

Family Favorites

When you're craving Italian fare, **Mascoto's Italian Restaurant** (6 Center St., Caribou, 207/492-2422, 11am-9pm Mon.-Sat., $8-20) does it well, from pastas to pizzas.

Inexpensive home cooking is the draw for **Frederick's Restaurant** (507 Main St., 207/498-3464, 11am-8pm Tues.-Sat., noon-7pm Sun., $8-21).

The **Irish Setter Pub** (710 Main St., Presque Isle, 207/764-5400, from 11am daily, $9-20) specializes in pub fare and Irish comfort food.

Aroostook County's first craft brewery, **Northern Maine Brewing Co.** (22 Main St., Caribou, 207/490-0000, 4pm-9pm Wed.-Thurs., 4pm-10pm Fri.-Sat., $10-25) emphasizes local sourcing for its beers and updated pub fare.

Time a visit to the Swedish Colony to enjoy a meal at **Eureka Hall Restaurant and Tavern** (5 School St., Stockholm, 207/896-5868, 4:30pm-11pm Thurs.-Sat., 3pm-8pm Sun.), serving American fare in a sit-down setting upstairs ($14-25) and tavern-style pizza and subs downstairs ($9-18). There's often live music. Do call, as hours change frequently.

Casual Dining

The frequently changing New American menu at ★ **Café Sorpreso** (415 Main St., Presque Isle, 207/764-1854, http://cafesorpreso.com, 5pm-8pm Mon., 11am-2pm and

AROOSTOOK COUNTY
AGRICULTURAL MUSEUM
1
2
3
4
NEW SWEDEN HISTORICAL MUSEUM

5pm-8pm Tues.-Sat., $18-30), a contemporary downtown restaurant, emphasizes fresh and, when possible, local Maine foods.

Fine Dining

At ★ **Canterbury Royale** (182 Sam Everett Rd., Fort Fairfield, 207/472-4910, www.canterburyroyale.com, Tues.-Sat., $52-80), guests are immersed in an elegant Old World European setting for five-course diners featuring haute French cuisine served in a private dining room. Guests order entrées in advance, and half-sisters and classically trained chefs Barbara Boucher and Renee O'Neill choose the other courses. Tables are set with crystal, silver, elaborate candelabras, and marble accents. Plan far in advance, as only two parties are seated each evening.

ACCOMMODATIONS AND CAMPING

Lodging choices are few in this region, and none are fancy. It's smart to have reservations.

The ★ **Old Iron Inn B&B** (155 High St., Caribou, 207/492-4766, www.oldironinn.com, $99-125) comes by its name honestly. Hundreds of antique irons are displayed through the in-town 1913 arts and crafts-style house, and Dr. Kevin McCartney, a geology professor and 2016 Fulbright scholar, can recount the background of each one. Three guest rooms are comfortably furnished with quilts and oak antiques. Settle into the living room with a choice from the extensive magazine selection or choose a good read—there are plenty of mysteries, along with Lincoln and aviation libraries—from the well-stocked bookcases. Known for her culinary talent, Kate McCartney serves a delicious breakfast in the Victorian dining room. Ask Kevin about the Maine Solar System or the Science Museum at UMPI, both of which he pioneered.

Patronized primarily for its convenient downtown site, the clean but dated **Northeastland Hotel** (436 Main St., Presque Isle, 207/768-5321 or 800/244-5321, www.northeastlandhotel.com, $135-150), built in 1934, has 50 spacious guest rooms. Children age 12 and under stay free.

The 148-room **Presque Isle Inn and Convention Center** (Rte. 1, Presque Isle, 207/764-3321 or 800/533-3971, www.presqueisleinn.com, $120-140) is tired and service is spotty, but it's the area's best full-service lodging. Amenities include a restaurant, health club, indoor pool, and coin laundry. Pets are welcome.

Just south of town, the two-story **Caribou Inn and Convention Center** (Rte. 1, Caribou, 207/498-3733, www.caribouinn.com, $110-155), a sister property of the Presque Isle Inn, has 72 large, comfortable—albeit tired—guest rooms and suites. Facilities include an indoor pool, a health club, a restaurant, and a coin-op laundry. Kids under age 13 stay free. Pet-friendly rooms are available for a small fee.

Fieldstone Cabins & Rainbow Cove RV Park (287 Lake Shore Dr., Stockholm, 207/551-9319 or 207/768-1688), overlooking Madawaska Lake, offers five well-equipped cabins (from $125/night or $600/week to $180/night or $900/week) and 20 RV sites ($30/night or $140/week).

Campsites at **Aroostook State Park** (State Park Rd., Presque Isle, 207/624-9950 or 800/332-1501, parksandlands.com, $15 Maine residents, $25 nonresidents) are wooded and close to Echo Lake.

INFORMATION

Local info is available from the **Central Aroostook Chamber of Commerce** (207/764-6561, www.pichamber.com) and the **Caribou Chamber of Commerce** (207/498-6156 or 800/722-7648, www.cariboumaine.net).

Aroostook County Tourism (888/216-2463, www.visitaroostook.com) and **Aroostook Outdoors** (www.goaroostookoutdoors.com) have information and web links for the entire county.

1: Salmon Brook Historical Society **2:** Saturn, part of the Maine Solar System Model **3:** potato barn **4:** New Sweden Historical Society Museum

GETTING THERE

Presque Isle is about 42 miles or 50 minutes via Route 1 from Houlton. It's about 56 miles or 1.25 hours to Fort Kent via Route 1.

United operates daily nonstop flights to **Northern Maine Regional Airport** in Presque Isle (PQI, 650 Airport Dr., 207/764-2550, www.flypresqueisle.com) from Newark's Liberty International, Boston's Logan Airport, and Portland Jetport. While at the airport, check out the **Presque Isle Air Museum** (207/764-2542), which displays historical photos and memorabilia from Presque Isle's impressive aviation history in two corridors.

The St. John Valley

Settled by Acadians in 1785, the St. John Valley isn't quite sure whether it should be the 51st state or Canada's 11th province. Valley hallmarks are huge Roman Catholic churches, small riverside communities, tidy homes, an eclectic French patois, and a handful of unique culinary specialties—all thanks to a twist of fate.

Henry Wadsworth Longfellow's immortal epic poem *Evangeline* relates a saga of *le grand dérangement,* when more than 10,000 French-speaking Acadians tragically lost their lease on Nova Scotia after the British expelled them for disloyalty in 1755—a date engraved ever since in the minds of their thousands of descendants now living on the American and Canadian sides of the St. John River. (Thousands more of their kin ended up in Louisiana, where Acadian-Cajun traditions also remain strong.) Acadian heritage sites pepper the valley.

In this part of Maine, Smiths and Joneses are few—countless residents bear such names as Cyr, Daigle, Gagnon, Michaud, Ouellette, Pelletier, Sirois, and Thibodeau. In **Van Buren** (pop. 2,171), **Grand Isle** (pop. 467), **Madawaska** (pop. 4,035), **St. Agatha** (pop. 747), and **Frenchville** (pop. 1,087), French is the mother tongue for 97 percent of the residents, who refer to the Upper St. John Valley as *chez nous* ("our place"), their homeland.

Religion is as pervasive an influence as language. When a Madawaska beauty represented Maine in the Miss America contest in 1995, the local *St. John Valley Times* admonished its readers: "Keep your fingers crossed and your rosaries hot."

Between Madawaska and Fort Kent, detour off Route 1, via Route 162, into the lovely lake district, locally known as the "back settlements," through the town of St. Agatha (usually pronounced the French way: "Saint a-GAHT") and the village of Sinclair. T-shaped **Long Lake** is the northernmost of the Fish River Chain of Lakes, extending southwest to Eagle Lake.

West of Fort Kent are the tiny and tinier riverside communities of **St. John** (pop. 267), **St. Francis** (pop. 485), **Allagash** (pop. 239), and **Dickey,** the latter two serving as endpoints for two of Maine's most popular long-distance canoe routes: the St. John River and the Allagash Wilderness Waterway.

The 104-mile **St. John Valley Scenic and Cultural Byway** ties the region together. It stretches from Allagash to Hamlin following the St. John River on Route 1, but also detouring out Route 162 to Cyr Plantation, St. Agatha, and Sinclair. From Fort Kent to Portage, Route 11 south doubles as a **Fish River Maine Scenic Byway.** It's lovely anytime, but especially spectacular during autumn foliage, when brilliant colors roll down hills, dapple open vistas, and reflect in the smattering of lakes and ponds.

SIGHTS

★ Acadian Village

In the hamlet of Keegan, about two miles

The Bloodless Aroostook War

Fort Kent Blockhouse

Aroostook County's major brush with historical notoriety occurred in 1839, with the skirmish known as the Aroostook War. Always described as "bloodless"—since there were no casualties (other than a farmer accidentally downed by friendly fire)—the war was essentially a boundary dispute between Maine and New Brunswick that had simmered since 1784, when New Brunswick was established.

The 1783 Treaty of Paris had set the St. Croix River as the Washington County line, but loopholes left the northernmost border ill-defined. Maine feared losing timber-rich real estate to Canada, and matters heated up when 200 burly militiamen descended on the region in early 1839 to defend the young state's territory. About 3,000 troops ended up supporting the Maine cause, and legendary war hero General Winfield "Old Fuss and Feathers" Scott was sent to Augusta for three weeks in March 1839 to negotiate the successful truce.

After the "war," Aroostook was incorporated as a county, and by 1842 the Webster-Ashburton Treaty (sometimes also called the Treaty of Washington), negotiated by Daniel Webster and Lord Ashburton, brought a long-awaited peace that opened the area for stepped-up settlement.

Among the remnants of the Aroostook War are two wooden blockhouses, one an original and a National Historic Site, on the banks of the St. John River in **Fort Kent** (page 434), the other a replica on the Aroostook River in Fort Fairfield.

northwest of downtown Van Buren, is a prominent reminder of the heritage in this valley. Begun as a small-scale bicentennial project in 1976, the **Acadian Village** (Rte. 1, Van Buren, 207/868-5042, http://acadianvillage.mainerec.com, noon-5pm daily June 15-Sept. 15, $7 adults, $5 children) is a 2.5-acre open-air museum comprising 19 antique and replica buildings.

Mount Carmel Museum and Cultural Center

As with the other religion-dominated communities in the valley, the most prominent landmark in the Lille village of **Grand Isle** (pop. 467) is the decommissioned Catholic church, a Baroque, twin golden-domed building undergoing long-term restoration as a nonprofit bilingual museum and cultural center. Built in 1908-1909, Our Lady of Mount Carmel Church had its first mass on New Year's Day 1910 and its last in 1978. Since historian, preservationist, and renaissance man Don Cyr acquired the wooden church in 1984, he has organized concerts and other events under the aegis of the nonprofit **Association culturelle et historique du Mont-Carmel** (207/895-3339, www.museeculturel.org). He also shares his collection of Acadian antiques and artifacts inside the museum. The church is usually open noon-4pm Sunday-Friday, mid-June-early September.

★ St. David's Historical Sites

As you reach the eastern edge of Madawaska, you can't help but notice the bell tower of the imposing brick **St. David Catholic Church,** established in 1871. The 1911-1913 building draws from Renaissance and Baroque Italian architecture and is listed in the National Register of Historic Places.

Inside, check out the high arched ceiling, domed altar, and stained glass windows.

Just east of St. David's is the one-room **Tante Blanche Museum** (Rte. 1, St. David Parish, Madawaska, 207/728-4518, 11am-3pm Fri.-Sun. summer, free), containing Acadian artifacts. Run by the Madawaska Historical Society (207/728-6412), the log museum commemorates Marguerite Blanche Thibodeau Cyr ("Tante Blanche"), an Acadian heroine during a 1797 famine. On-site volunteers answer questions and provide guidance. The museum's campus also includes the 1870 **School House No. 1** and the circa 1840 **Albert House.**

Continue down the 0.5-mile gravel road to the riverfront, where a 14-foot-high marble **Acadian Cross** marks the reputed 1785 landing spot of Acadians expelled by the British from Nova Scotia and New Brunswick. During the annual Acadian Festival, the landing is reenacted.

Fort Kent Blockhouse

Built in 1839 during the decades-long U.S.-Canada border dispute known as the Aroostook War, the **Fort Kent Blockhouse** (Blockhouse Rd., Fort Kent, 9am-5pm daily late May-early Sept., $2-3 adults), a National Historic Landmark, is the only remnant of a complex that once included barracks, a hospital, and an ammunition hoard. Bring a picnic and commandeer a table in the pretty little riverside park just below the fort.

The First Mile

The bridge to Canada marks the northern end of historic U.S. Route 1, with Key West, Florida, anchoring the southern end. You are 318 miles north of Portland, 368 miles north of the New Hampshire border at Kittery, and 2,209 miles north of Key West.

Madawaska Four Corners Park

Dedicated to long-distance motorcycling, **Madawaska Four Corners Park** (213 W. Main St., 207/436-7451, www.madawaskafourcorners.org, free) represents the Northeast in the nationwide Four Corners Tour. Check in to the Welcome Center, ask about the Maine Four Corners Experience Tour, and snap a few pics. You can download a video tour for the paver stones.

St. Agatha Historical House and Preservation Center

This tiny town (pop. 747) has one heck of a museum: the **St. Agatha Historical House and Preservation Center** (534 Main St., St. Agatha, 207/543-6911, http://ste-agathehistoricalsociety.com, 1pm-4pm Tues.-Sun. mid-June-early Sept., donation). Volunteers assist guests touring both the oldest house in town and the museum, which is chock-full of interesting artifacts and exhibits (carvings, textiles, farm equipment, religious and school goods, and much more). It's easy to while away an hour or so here.

RECREATION

Multiuse Trail

The 17-mile crushed-stone **Saint John Valley Heritage Trail** (www.mainetrailfinder.com), a rail-to-trail project along the former Fish River Railroad bed, parallels the south bank of the St. John River, passing through farmlands and forests between Fort Kent and St. Francis, where the historical turntable has been preserved. The trail connects with area ATV and snowmobile trails and is part of the National Park Service's Acadian interpretation efforts.

Paddling

The **St. John River,** the longest free-flowing river east of the Mississippi, doubles as the international border. Public boat access points are plentiful, but be sure to land only on the U.S. shoreline. A good resource is **Northern Forest Canoe Trail** (www.northernforestcanoetrail.org).

Long Lake has two access points: a **picnic and recreation area** (Rte. 162, St. Agatha) on the western shore with a boat launch, a beach, grills, and restrooms, and **Birch Point Beach** (Chapel Rd., St. David, on the east side of Long Lake; turnoff to the beach at St. Michael's Chapel), with a picnic area.

Nordic Skiing

The **Fort Kent Outdoor Center** (33 Paradise Circle Rd., Fort Kent, 207/834-6203, www.10thmtskiclub.org) has hosted World Cup Biathlon events. This biathlon and cross-country facility has 7.5 miles of biathlon trails, plus an additional 18 miles of cross-country trails, a lighted roller-ski loop, a wax building, a stadium, and a 30-station biathlon range. The Tenth Mountain Lodge, with a sauna and a fireplace, is a comfy place to relax after a day on the trails. The center's access road is 1.6 miles south of downtown Fort Kent off Route 1. A trail pass is $15 adults, $10 ages 7-18; a snowshoe pass is $10/$5. Rental equipment is available. Guided ski or snowshoe safaris are $10.

Snowmobiling

This is prime sledding country. The best resource for trail info is **Fort Kent SnoRiders** (www.fortkentsnoriders.com). At **Top of Maine Rentals** (379 Aroostook Rd./Rte. 11, Fort Kent, 207/834-3095) expect to pay around $200 for a one-day rental.

ENTERTAINMENT

Spectators crowd the snowy streets to watch Fort Kent's five-day **Can Am Crown International Sled Dog Races** (www.can-am-crown.net), held in March. Special locations offer vantage points for watching teams competing in races of 30, 60, and 250 miles. A mushers' award ceremony caps the festivities.

Madawaska hosts the Franco-American **Acadian Festival** (www.acadianfestival.com), with a historical reenactment, tournaments, a fishing derby, Acadian food, music and dancing, a parade, and a featured-family reunion in mid-August.

Catch a flick at the **Skylite Drive-In** (304 11th Ave., Madawaska, 207/728-7538, http://www.skylitedrivein.com), the northernmost drive-in theater east of the Mississippi. If you're lucky, you might catch the insanely popular fried Oreos as the special in the snack bar.

FOOD

Quick Bites

Check local papers and bulletin boards for notices about **public suppers,** an inexpensive way to break bread with the locals.

Misty Meadows Organic Farm (1164 Main St., Grand Isle, 207/895-8015, 8am-3pm daily, $7-15) dishes out farm-fresh organic veggies and comfort foods with an Acadian and Quebequois accent. The very casual restaurant doubles as a shop selling crafts and farm fare. Saturdays feature barbeque.

Purchase *ployes* mix, farm-fresh produce, and local crafts at **Bouchard's Country Store** (Rte. 161, Fort Kent, 207/843-3237, http://ployes.com, 10am-5:30pm Tues.-Fri., 9am-4pm Sat.).

Walk into **Doris's Cafe** (345 Market St./Rte. 161, Fort Kent Mills, 207/834-6262, 5am-2pm Mon.-Sat.), and conversation ceases as every head in the place turns to see the stranger. Not to worry—chatter quickly resumes, and you can catch all the local gossip. Expect American, Acadian, and French-Canadian comfort food. Pretty much everything on the menu is less than $10.

Family Favorites

Ask anyone in the valley: When it comes to *ployes* (buckwheat pancakes), *creton* (a meat spread), and chicken stew, no one does it better than ★ **Dolly's** (Rte. 1, Frenchville, 207/728-7050, 6:30am-9pm Wed.-Mon., $5-18), a valley institution since 1988. Go early for the chicken stew—it always sells out.

Prime rib is the specialty at the **Swamp Buck** (250 W. Main St./Rte. 1, Fort Kent, 207/834-3055, 11am-9pm Mon.-Sat., 9am-9pm Sun., $12-26), but the American menu ranges from decent burgers to blackened haddock. On Sunday mornings there's a buffet breakfast from 9am-1pm.

INN of Acadia
Welcome
Voyageur Lounge
1
2
3
Misty Meadows
THE DIONNES'
Maine
A/C IS running! Please keep door closed
Steak & Eggs Skillet
Fried Greenbeans
Fried Pickles
Salade à la Crème Sure
WELCOME
Don't forget To Sign Our Guest Book!!

Casual Dining

The multicultural menu at the **Voyageur Lounge** (4:30pm-8pm Mon.-Thurs., 4:30pm-9pm Fri.-Sat., $7-30), within the Inn of Acadia, has something for everybody. There's often entertainment Friday and Saturday nights.

For the best panorama in town, dine at the **Lakeview Restaurant** (9 Lakeview Dr., St. Agatha, 207/543-6331, www.lakeviewrestaurant.biz, 11am-9pm daily, $4-30), with sweeping views over Long Lake. The wide-ranging American menu has a choice and price for every taste and budget. An all-you-can-eat breakfast buffet is served on Sunday mornings in winter.

Orchids (121 Fraser Ave., Madawaska, 207/728-9232, www.orchidsfinedining.com, 11am-8pm Wed.-Fri., 4pm-8pm Sat.-Sun., and 9am-1pm Sun., $20-30) serves American fare in the former Fraser Mansion.

Huge steaks and giant lobsters are the specialties at the ★ **Long Lake Sporting Club Resort** (Rte. 162, Sinclair, 207/543-7584 or 800/431-7584, www.longlakesportingclub.com, from 11am daily, $18-32). The deck and dining room have fabulous views over Long Lake.

ACCOMMODATIONS AND CAMPING

The ★ **Inn of Acadia** (384 St. Thomas St., Madawaska, 207/728-3402, www.innofacadia.com, $105-150), a boutique inn, is housed in a former convent. This is The County's finest lodging, with 15 rooms and four suites decorated in a sleek, contemporary style. Also here are a café, lounge, fitness studio, and guest laundry. Rates include continental breakfast. Dinner is offered in the Voyageur Lounge, where there's acoustic music on Friday and Saturday evenings. Airport shuttles are available.

Just across the road from the lake, the **Long Lake Motor Inn** (596 Main St./Rte. 162, St. Agatha, 207/543-5006, www.stagatha.com/longlake, $85-100) has 18 spacious guest rooms, 11 of them with lake views (and great sunrises). There are also two pet-friendly two-bedroom lakefront units with kitchenettes. Continental breakfast is included, and there's a lounge on the premises.

Clean, comfortable, and inexpensive, the downtown **Northern Door Inn** (356 W. Main St., Fort Kent, 207/834-3133, www.northerndoorinn.com, $100) has a nice gathering area in the lobby, where a light continental breakfast is served. Don't look for fancy; this place is old and due for a major updating. Kids age 12 and under stay free; pets are $5 each per night.

The **Lakeview Camping Resort** (9 Lakeview Dr., St. Agatha, 207/543-6331, www.lakeviewrestaurant.biz) has 80 mostly wooded sites, with areas for RVs ($30-38) and tents ($24). Also on-site are a convenience store, a shower house, and a restaurant.

INFORMATION AND SERVICES

For local information, check with the **St. John Valley Chamber of Commerce** (356 Main St./Rte. 1, Madawaska, 207/728-7000, www.stjohnvalleychamber.org) and the **Greater Fort Kent Area Chamber of Commerce** (291 W. Main St./Rte. 1, Fort Kent, 207/834-5354 or 800/733-3563, www.fortkentchamber.com). **Aroostook County Tourism** (888/216-2463, www.visitaroostook.com) has info and links for the entire county.

An excellent companion when touring the St. John Valley is *Voici the Valley Cultureway*, a guidebook and CD highlighting the heritage and sights. Purchase locally ($15) or in advance from the **Musée Culturel** (207/895-3339, http://museeculturel.org/shop). Another resource is

1: Inn of Acadia **2:** sculpture outside the Tante Blanche Museum **3:** Misty Meadows Organic Farm

the National Park Service (www.nps.gov/maac); its 1994 publication *Acadian Culture in Maine* is available online (http://acim.umfk.maine.edu).

GETTING THERE AND AROUND

Fort Kent is about 56 miles or 1.25 hours from Presque Isle via Route 1. It's about 96 miles or 2.25 hours to Patten via Route 11.

If you're planning to pass through the U.S.-Canada border stations in Van Buren (207/868-3391), Madawaska (207/728-4376), or Fort Kent (207/834-5255), have the proper identification and paperwork. For crossings into the United States, see www.cbp.gov. For crossings into Canada, see www.cbsa-asfc.gc.ca. Remember that New Brunswick is on Atlantic time, an hour ahead of Eastern time.

Maine Highlands

Home to the state's highest mountain, largest lake, and a national monument, the Maine Highlands, which cover all of Piscataquis County and the northern two-thirds of Penobscot County, typify the rugged North Woods. Here you'll find the Katahdin Woods and Waters National Monument, 40-mile-long Moosehead Lake, the appealing frontier town of Greenville, the headwaters of the Allagash Wilderness Waterway, and Baxter State Park, home to mile-high Katahdin.

Sport hunters and anglers have always frequented the North Woods, and they still do. But sportsmen and back-to-the-landers are increasingly sharing their untamed turf with a new generation of visitors. Sporting camps originally built for rugged anglers and hunters now

Highlights

Look for ★ to find recommended sights, activities, dining, and lodging.

★ **Patten Lumbermen's Museum:** A visit to this replica of a lumber camp will cure any romantic notions about being a lumberjack (page 445).

★ **Maine Boom Houses:** Paddle or cruise to these artifacts from the log-driving era (page 445).

★ **Hiking in Baxter State Park:** Choose from more than 200 miles of trails crowned by Katahdin, the state's tallest peak (page 455).

★ **Cruise on the *Kate*:** See Moosehead Lake from the water on a historic vessel (page 462).

★ **Kineo:** It's worth the effort to get a close-up view of Kineo's iconic cliffs and take in the view from its summit (page 464).

★ **Moose Safaris:** You can't go home without spotting at least one moose, so go with a guide who knows where they hang out (page 467).

★ **Gulf Hagas Reserve:** Nicknamed the Grand Canyon of the East, the 3.5-mile-long gorge makes a spectacular hike (page 478).

★ **Stephen King-dom:** Learn all about the master of horror on a guided tour to Bangor-area sites (page 485).

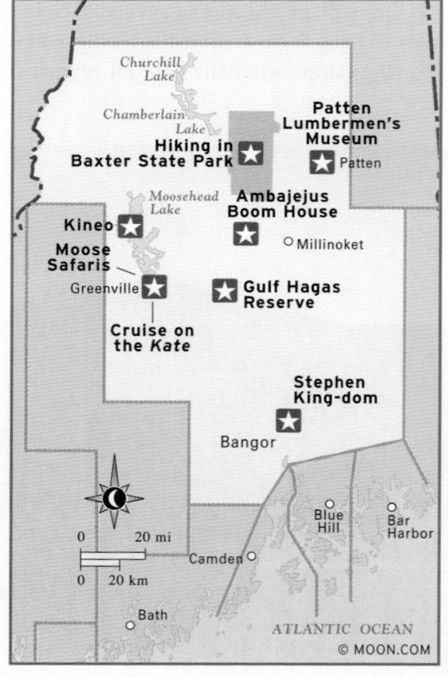

welcome photographers, birders, and families, especially during summer; white-water rafting, canoeing—including two of Maine's best-known classic trips, the Allagash and St. John—kayaking, and snowmobiling are all big business; and hikers have found nirvana in a vast network of trails, particularly the huge, carefully monitored trail system in Baxter State Park.

In the 1970s, environmental concerns forced paper companies to halt the perilous river-run log drives that took their products to market. This cessation not only cleaned up the rivers but also spared the lives of the hardy breed of men who once made a living unjamming the logs in roiling waters. The alternative now is roads, lots of them, mostly unpaved—a huge network that has opened up the area to more and more outdoors enthusiasts. More recently, the region began gaining national attention thanks to Roxanne Quimby, who made her fortune from Burt's Bees. In 2016, she donated land holdings adjacent to and east of Baxter State Park to create the new Katahdin Woods and Waters National Monument.

Stay at one of this region's primitive forest campsites and you'll really sense the wilderness—owls hoot, loons cry, frogs croak—and yes, insects annoy. No matter how much civilization intrudes, it's still remote and wild. As one writer put it, "Trees grow, die, fall, and rot, never having been seen by anyone. They litter the shores of lakes, form temporary islands, block streams, and quickly eradicate paths."

The air gateway to the region is Bangor, Maine's second-largest city and home to horror maven Stephen King. Between Bangor and nearby Orono, a university town, there's enough "cultcha" to balance the wilderness.

PLANNING YOUR TIME

If you merely want a taste of the wilderness, you can swoop from Bangor up to Millinocket on Route 11, segue over to Greenville on the Golden Road, and return to Bangor via Monson, Guilford, and Dover-Foxcroft on Route 15 in two days. But if you really want to experience the North Woods, you'll need time to paddle, hike, and explore—requiring at least three days, ideally a week or longer. Greenville makes a fine base for exploring the region; it's on the edge of the wilderness, within striking distance of Baxter State Park and the Penobscot River, on the shore of Moosehead Lake, and surrounded by endless opportunities for outdoor recreation. Hikers and paddlers will prefer camping in Baxter State Park or the Katahdin Woods and Waters National Monument.

From mid-May to early July, the blackflies are more than annoying. When they begin to wane, the mosquitoes take up the charge. Arm yourself with bug repellent. DEET is the strongest. One Baxter State Park ranger I spoke with swore by Bounce dryer sheets—place one under a cap and the other under your shirt around the waistline to create a "force field" that keeps the bugs from biting.

Most timber-company throughways remain there for all to use, but never forget that the logging trucks *own* them—in more ways than one. As they barrel along, give them room—and some slack as well; you may even be glad they're there, especially if you get lost. *DeLorme's Maine Atlas* is essential for exploring the area, but every time the loggers begin working a new patch, they open new roads, so the cartographers can barely keep up.

Finally, never underestimate the North Woods: Bring versatile clothing (more than you think you'll need), don't strike out alone without telling anyone, stock up on insect repellent and water, use a decent vehicle (4WD if possible), and carry a flashlight, maps, and a compass. Perhaps most important, be a conscientious, eco-sensitive visitor.

Previous: Baxter State Park; the steamboat *Kate;* moose in the Maine Highlands.

Maine Highlands

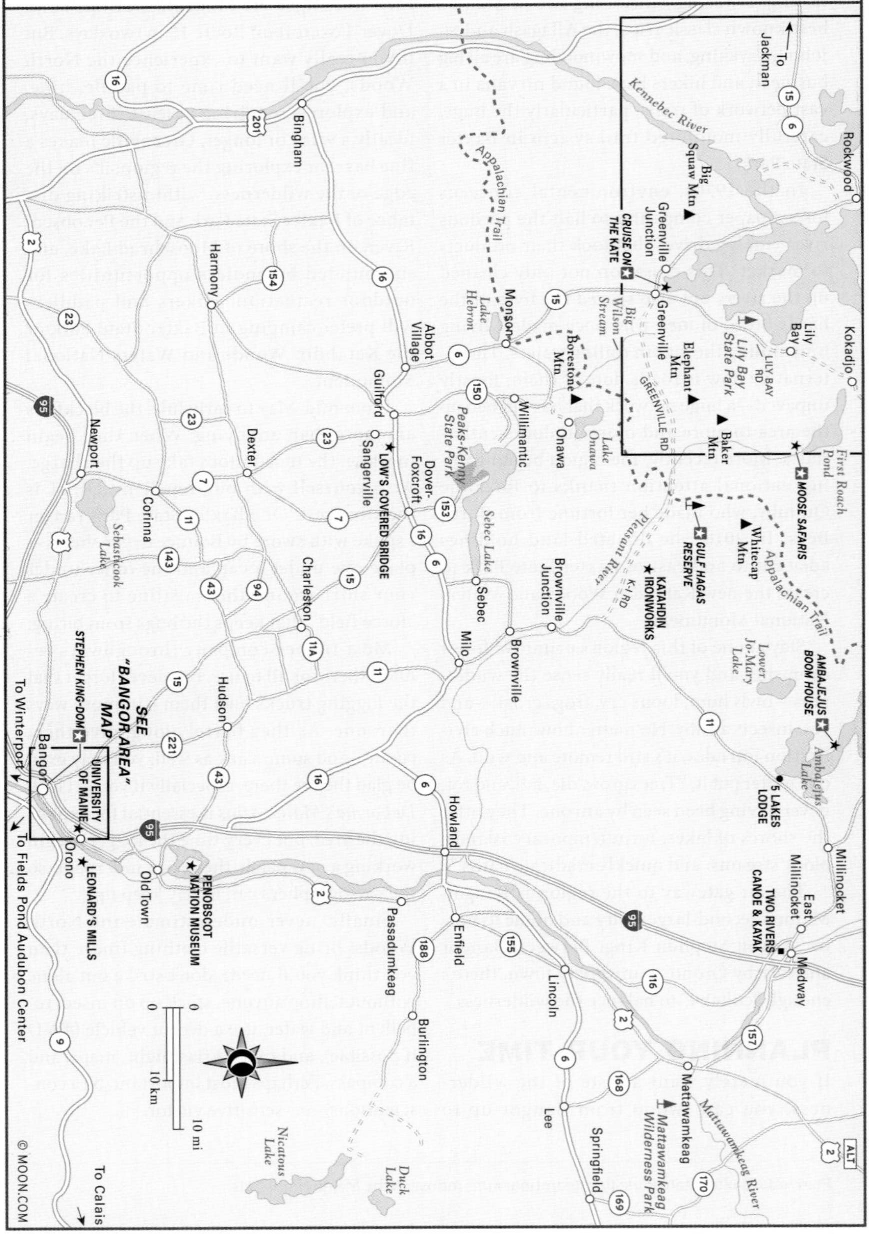

To Jackman
Kennebec River
Rockwood
Big Squaw Mtn
Greenville Junction
CRUISE ON THE KATE
Greenville
Big Wilson Stream
Lily Bay
Lily Bay State Park
LILY BAY RD
Kokadjo
Elephant Mtn
GREENVILLE RD
Baker Mtn
First Roach Pond
MOOSE SAFARIS
Appalachian Trail
Bingham
Monson
Lake Hebron
Borestone Mtn
Willimantic
Onawa
Lake Onawa
Abbot Village
Harmony
Guilford
Peaks-Kenny State Park
Dover-Foxcroft
Sebec Lake
Pleasant River
K-I RD
GULF HAGAS RESERVE
Whitecap Mtn
KATAHDIN IRONWORKS
Brownville Junction
Brownville
Sebec
Milo
Lower Jo-Mary Lake
AMBAJEJUS BOOM HOUSE
Ambajejus Lake
5 LAKES LODGE
Millinocket
East Millinocket
TWO RIVERS CANOE & KAYAK
Medway
Newport
Dexter
Sangerville
LOW'S COVERED BRIDGE
Corinna
Sebasticook Lake
Charleston
Hudson
SEE "BANGOR AREA" MAP
STEPHEN KING-DOM
UNIVERSITY OF MAINE
Bangor
To Winterport
Orono
LEONARD'S MILLS
Old Town
PENOBSCOT NATION MUSEUM
Howland
Passadumkeag
Enfield
Lincoln
Burlington
Mattawamkeag
Mattawamkeag Wilderness Park
Mattawamkeag River
Lee
Springfield
Nicatous Lake
Duck Lake
To Fields Pond Audubon Center
To Calais
0 10 mi
0 10 km

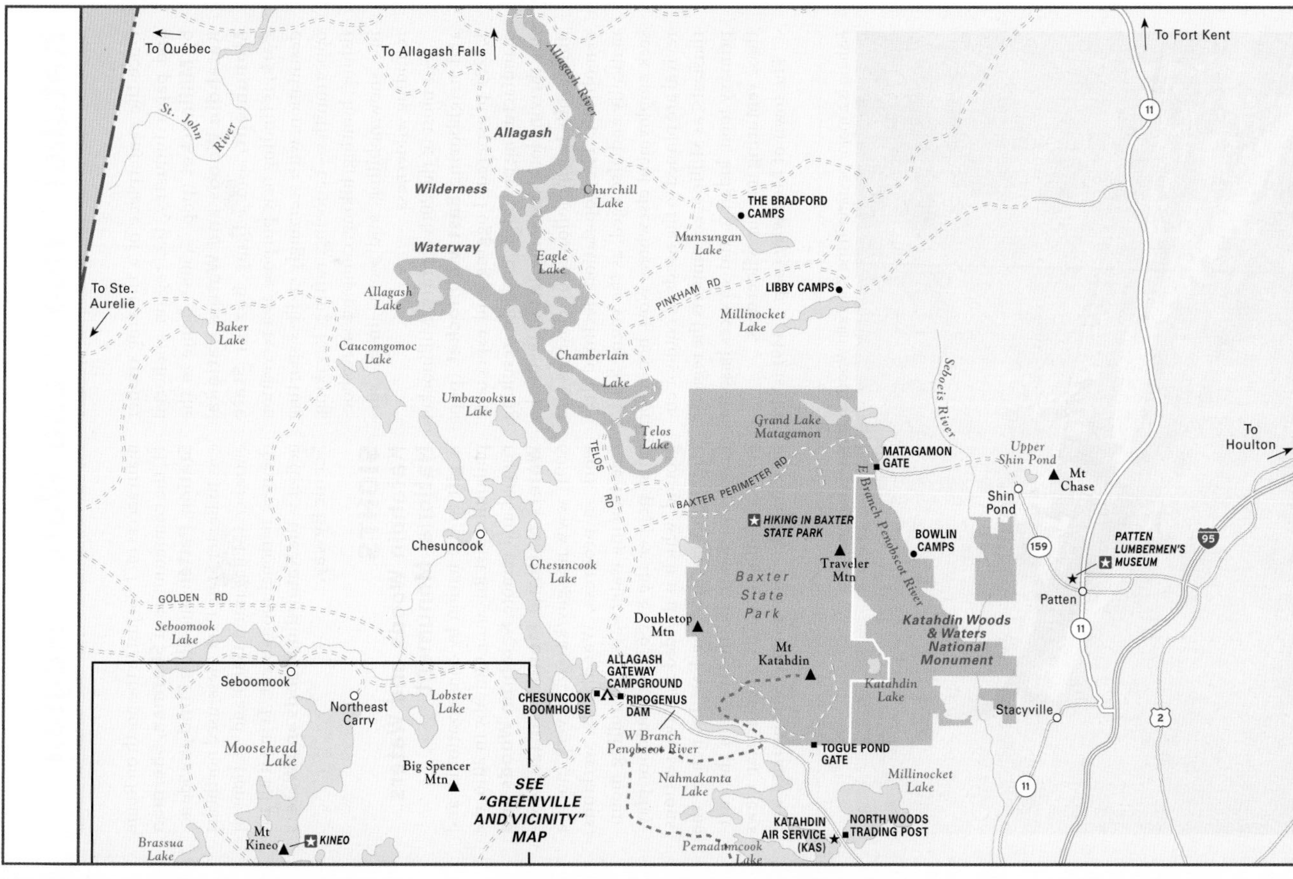
To Québec
To Allagash Falls
To Fort Kent
St. John River
Allagash River
Allagash
Wilderness
Waterway
Churchill Lake
THE BRADFORD CAMPS
Munsungan Lake
Eagle Lake
To Ste. Aurelie
Allagash Lake
PINKHAM RD
LIBBY CAMPS
Millinocket Lake
Baker Lake
Caucomgomoc Lake
Chamberlain Lake
Seboeis River
Umbazooksus Lake
Grand Lake Matagamon
Telos Lake
TELOS RD
To Houlton
MATAGAMON GATE
Upper Shin Pond
Mt Chase
Shin Pond
BAXTER PERIMETER RD
E Branch Penobscot River
HIKING IN BAXTER STATE PARK
BOWLIN CAMPS
159
PATTEN LUMBERMEN'S MUSEUM
95
Chesuncook
Chesuncook Lake
Traveler Mtn
Baxter State Park
Patten
GOLDEN RD
Doubletop Mtn
Katahdin Woods & Waters National Monument
11
Seboomook Lake
Mt Katahdin
ALLAGASH GATEWAY CAMPGROUND
Seboomook
Northeast Carry
Lobster Lake
CHESUNCOOK BOOMHOUSE
RIPOGENUS DAM
Katahdin Lake
Stacyville
2
W Branch Penobscot River
TOGUE POND GATE
Moosehead Lake
Big Spencer Mtn
SEE "GREENVILLE AND VICINITY" MAP
Nahmakanta Lake
Millinocket Lake
KATAHDIN AIR SERVICE (KAS)
NORTH WOODS TRADING POST
Mt Kineo
KINEO
Brassua Lake
Pemadumcook Lake

Katahdin Woods and Waters Region

Once the centerpiece of a thriving timber and paper industry, the region anchored by **Millinocket** (pop. 4,506), home to the **Katahdin Woods and Waters National Monument,** and edging **Baxter State Park,** is finding new purpose as a recreation destination, with seemingly endless sporting opportunities—canoeing, rafting, kayaking, fishing, hunting, hiking, camping, snowshoeing, snowmobiling, and more—in the surrounding wilderness.

For most of the 20th century, Millinocket and neighboring **East Millinocket** (pop. 1,723) prospered. Logging and especially manufacturing provided good jobs, resulting in a thriving local economy. In the 1990s, the mill layoffs began, followed by closures and demolition. The population declined dramatically and also aged, as the young left to seek employment elsewhere. Now, hopes for revival are pinned to the needs of outdoor enthusiasts, as Millinocket remains the region's primary food, lodging, and services base for those venturing into the wilderness.

The town of **Medway** (pop. 1,349) is the main access off I-95; just to the north on Route 11, the communities of **Sherman, Sherman Station, Patten,** and **Shin Pond** provide access to Baxter State Park's less-used northeast entrance (Matagamon Gate) and sections of the new national monument. Tying it all together is the **Katahdin Woods and Waters Scenic Byway.**

SIGHTS

Katahdin Woods and Waters National Monument

A gift to the nation by conservationist and philanthropist Roxanne Quimby in 2016, the rugged and remote **Katahdin Woods and Waters National Monument** (207/456-6001, www.nps.gov/kaww) is very much a work in progress. Woodlands, wetlands, free-flowing waterways, and rolling mountains pepper the 87,563-acre outdoor playground, which is divided into two sections. Highlights include the East Branch of the Penobscot River, hiking trails in the eastern Katahdin foothills, spectacular views of Katahdin, and unique biodiversity and

Fishing is a major pastime in the Katahdin Woods and Waters region.

geology. Culturally, the lands are important to the Penobscot Indian Nation, recall the era of lumbermen and river drivers, and have ties to Henry David Thoreau, John James Audubon, and Theodore Roosevelt. Outdoor enthusiasts can hike, fish, camp (first come, first served), paddle, ski, snowshoe, watch wildlife, and stargaze here, although facilities are primitive at best. Sited west of Route 11 and east of Baxter State Park, in the Unorganized Territories north of Millinocket and south of Patten, the monument is remote and without many services, with access via gravel woods roads that are best suited for vehicles with high ground clearance.

Access the monument's North Matagamon entrance via Route 159 to the Grand Lake Road. To access the southern section, take Route 11 to the gravel Swift Brook Road, which connects with the 14-mile Katahdin Loop Road. Note: Yield to logging equipment and trucks on the Swift Brook Road. Frankly, unless you're planning on camping, hiking, or paddling, there's not much to see. For more information, visit the monuments office in downtown Millinocket.

Katahdin Woods and Waters Scenic Byway

One of the easiest ways to get a sense of the monument, without entering it, is via the 89-mile **Katahdin Woods and Waters Scenic Byway** (www.katahdinwoodsandwaters.com). The route winds between Millinocket and Patten, following the Baxter State Park Road and Routes 11 (also known as the Grindstone Rd.) and 159, offering views of Maine's highest peak and taking in museums and sights en route. A map-brochure, detailing the byway and sights and services along it, can be picked up locally.

Here's my recommended detour from the byway: On a clear day, detour west off Route 11 on the Happy Corner Road, about two miles south of downtown Patten; follow it about two miles to the Frenchville Road, on your right, and take that (gravel in sections) north to a T intersection. At the intersection, bear right on the Waters Road, which will connect with Route 159, and from there turn right to return to Route 11 and Patten. The biggest rewards for this loop are the panoramic views of Katahdin from the Happy Corner Road; the rest is a delightful country byway, with some nice ridge views east from the Frenchville Road. It's simply gorgeous in autumn.

★ Patten Lumbermen's Museum

About 40 miles northeast of Millinocket, 0.5 mile west of downtown Patten and about 25 miles southeast of Baxter State Park's Matagamon Gate, is a family-oriented museum commemorating the lumberman's grueling life. The nine buildings at the open-air **Patten Lumbermen's Museum** (61 Shin Pond Rd./Rt. 159, Patten, 207/528-2650, www.lumbermensmuseum.org, 10am-4pm Tues.-Sun. July-mid-Oct., 10am-4pm Fri.-Sun. spring, $10 adults, $8 seniors, $5 ages 4-12) tell the tale of timber in the 19th and early 20th centuries: cramped quarters, hazardous equipment, rugged terrain, and nasty weather. Lots of working gear and colorful dioramas appeal to children, and there are picnic tables, a snack bar, and room to roam. A summer highlight is the annual **beanhole bean dinner** (beans baked underground overnight), held the second Saturday in August.

★ The Maine Boom Houses

The last log drive on the West Branch of the Penobscot occurred in 1979. For a vision of that era, wander into the post office to view John W. Beauchamp's 1942 oil-on-canvas *Logging in the Maine Woods*, a New Deal mural. Better yet, visit one or both restored boom houses maintained by the **West Branch Historical Preservation Committee** (http://themaineboomhouses.org). Each is filled with incredible lumbering-era artifacts, photos, paintings, and signage that bring the era to life. If you're lucky, former river driver and now curator and caretaker Chuck Harris will be on site to answer

Maine's Big Dig: The Golden Road

The era of nimble lumberjacks driving logs downriver ended in the early 1970s when Maine's paper companies began building roads into the wilderness for access to their timberlands. The most famous of these, the Golden Road, runs from Millinocket around the top of Moosehead Lake to the Québec border. It took nearly 1,000 workers almost five years to build the private, 96-mile, mostly unpaved road. Completed in 1975 and originally called the West Branch Haul Road, Maine's version of the Big Dig reputedly earned its current name from the cost ($3.2 million) of construction.

The Golden Road is the most scenic link between Millinocket and Greenville, comprising a 71-mile trip, two-thirds unpaved, through the wilderness. Red-and-white mile markers tacked to trees tick off the distance—if you can spot them. Driving this route is a true adventure, but it's not for everybody. If you're not used to driving backwoods dirt roads, this might not be the place to start. If you choose to do so, it's vital to ask about the road's condition—if there has been a lot of cutting going on along the route or if it has been a while between gradings, it could be in uncomfortably rough shape. Remember, it's a private road built for trucks and logs, not cars and people.

When driving from Millinocket, you'll exit the Golden Road after about 48 miles. Watch for a fork in the road, with a crude sign denoting Greenville Road; if you make it to the North Woods checkpoint, you've overshot it. The Greenville Road then parallels Moosehead Lake's east shore to Greenville. Keep an eye peeled for moose, deer, and even black bears.

Remember that you are entering true wilderness. There are no gas stations, restaurants, lodgings, or anything but water, trees, and wildlife, and cell phone service is spotty at best. Go prepared with a full tank of gas, bottles of water, energy bars, bug repellent, and a good spare tire. Bicycles, motorcycles, ATVs, and horses are not allowed on the road.

Should you meet a logging truck along the way, pull way, way over and let it pass. If it's loaded, it might be carrying as much as 100,000 pounds of logs.

questions and share stories. Both are open May 15 to September 15; admission is free, but donations are needed and appreciated.

Ambajejus Boom House, on Ambajejus Lake, is listed in the National Register of Historic Places. Erected here in 1906, the structure was used as a rest stop for 65 years by rugged river drivers, lumbermen who "boomed out" (collected with immense chains) and actually rode logs downstream to the sawmills. The only access is via boat: arrange a cruise through the Big Moose Inn (scheduled; for private, provide at least 48 hours' notice), book a canoe rental or guided trip with New England Outdoor Center, or do it yourself. If you go on your own, launch your boat in Spencer Cove, near Katahdin Air Service, on the west side of the Golden Road, and paddle or motor out and around to the right, to the head of the lake. Stay close to shore, as the wind can pick up unexpectedly.

Although called a boom house, the 1916 **Chesuncook Boom House** on Chesuncook Lake actually was a boarding house capable of accommodating 24 men. Like Ambajejus, the house at Dam Point appears as if the crew is out working. In front is the 1971 Woodsmen's Memorial; behind it is a barn, also filled with artifacts. The state maintains a boat launch here. From Millinocket, follow the Baxter State Park Road to the Golden Road, continue on the gravel road to the Chesuncook Lake Road (signed for Allagash Gateway Campsites), between mile markers 32 and 33, turn right, and follow it to the end.

Flightseeing

Based at Ambajejus Lake, about eight miles northwest of Millinocket on the road to Baxter State Park, **Katahdin Air Service** (KAS, Millinocket, 866/359-6246, www.katahdinair.com) provides access to wilderness locations in every direction—but the scenic floatplane flights are outstanding even if you have no particular destination. Fall-foliage trips are beyond fabulous. Rates begin at $105 per person (2-person minimum) for a half-hour mountain flight. You'll fly over Katahdin and the Penobscot River's West Branch, perhaps spotting moose en route. The best flight, though, is an hour-long trip over Baxter State Park to the Allagash Wilderness Waterway and back along the West Branch ($225 pp). Flights operate daily late May to October, weather permitting.

Katahdin Air Service is also a major link in the sporting-camp network, flying guests into and out of the remote camps via floatplane. When you contact a sporting camp for rate information, request the rates for floatplane access. It won't be cheap, but it's safe and fun. For a token sporting-camp experience without an overnight, sign up for one of KAS's "fly 'n' dine" trips. For $225 per person (2-person minimum, covering meals and transport), it'll fly you into a sporting camp for dinner and take you back afterward. It's a delicious adventure.

If you prefer your plane to have wheels, book a sightseeing flight with **West Branch Aviation** (Millinocket Municipal Airport, 164 Medway Rd., Millinocket, 207/723-4375, www.westbranchaviation.com). The rate is $89 per person for a half hour, $149 per person for a full hour, with a two-person minimum on all flights.

SHOPPING

North Light Gallery (256 Penobscot Ave., Millinocket, 207/723-4414 or 800/970-4278, www.artnorthlight.com) is well worth a stop. Owner Marsha Donahue specializes in art from the Katahdin-and-Lakes School, and she shows the works of about a dozen select artists and artisans. You can't miss the building; Donahue has painted murals on the exterior.

If you can't leave without a photograph of a moose, bear, or other wildlife, Mark Picard's **Moose Prints Gallery** (58 Central St., Millinocket, 207/447-6906, www.markpicard.com) is a must-stop.

Stock up on last-minute head-into-the-woods needs at **North Woods Trading Post** (Baxter State Park Rd., Millinocket, 207/723-4326, 7am-9pm daily). Pick up bottled water (there's no place to buy it in the park), fill the gas tank, purchase technical gear and clothing, take advantage of the free Wi-Fi (just ask for the password), find the perfect map or book, have a bite (food's good), and pick Tom's brain for suggestions (he's from these parts and was a ranger at Chimney Pond for years).

SUMMER RECREATION

Mattawamkeag Wilderness Park

Talk about a well-kept secret that shouldn't be: Check out the town-owned **Mattawamkeag Wilderness Park** (Rte. 2, Mattawamkeag, 207/736-4881 or 888/724-2465, www.mw-park.com), about an hour's drive southeast of Baxter State Park's southern gate. The park's well-managed facilities include 15 miles of trails, picnic tables, restrooms, free hot showers, a recreation hall, a playground, a sandy beach (on the Mattawamkeag River), and fishing for bass, salmon, and trout. There's also access to fine canoeing, including flat-water and Class V white water, on one of northern Maine's most underused rivers. And you can stay the night at one of the 50 wooded campsites and 11 lean-tos. The entrance is about eight miles east of Route 2 on an unpaved logging road locally called "the park road"; it's signposted on Route 2. Day use is $3/person or $7/car. Camping fees are $22-35/site/night; seven sites have hookups. The park is open daily late May-October.

TOP EXPERIENCE

Moose-Spotting

New England Outdoor Center (800/766-7238, www.neoc.com) offers three-hour guided moose-spotting tours via vans for $53 adults, $43 ages 5-12; a full-day tour via van and pontoon boat is $149, including a packed lunch.

Boat Excursions

For those who don't want to brave a canoe, kayak, or raft, the **Big Moose Inn** (207/723-8391, www.bigmoosecabins.com) makes it easy to get out on the lakes to see the wildlife and Katahdin or the Ambajejus Boom House. Options include 2-3-hour trips (from $20 pp); boat minimums may apply and you must make reservations at least a day or two in advance.

Mountain Biking

Katahdin Area Trails (http://katahdinareatrails.org) is constructing a network of mountain biking/nordic skiing trails on Hammond Ridge and Black Cat Mountain. The first six miles of single-track trails opened in 2019. Eventually, it will comprise 30-50 miles of biking trails and a gravity park. Current access is from New England Outdoor Center, which rents mountain bikes.

Penobscot River Trails (2540 Grindstone Rd./Rte. 11, Soldiertown TWP, 207/746-5807, http://penobscotrivertrails.org) offers more than 15 miles of carriage road-style trails on 5,000 acres along the East Branch of the Penobscot River. Access is off Route 11, approximately 12 miles north of Route 157 in Medway.

Water Sports

CANOEING AND KAYAKING

This part of Maine is a canoeist's paradise, well known as the springboard for Allagash Wilderness Waterway and St. John River trips.

Close to Millinocket, experienced canoeists and kayakers may want to attempt sections of the **East and West Branches of the Penobscot River,** but no neophyte should try them. We're talking Big Water. Refer to the *AMC River Guide* for details, or contact one of the local outfitters such as New England Outdoor Center or Maine Quest Adventures.

A relatively gentle, early summer canoe trip ideal for less-experienced paddlers is on the **Seboeis River,** between the Shin Pond-Grand Lake Road and Whetstone Falls, about 24 miles. Even easier, and a good family trip, is the flat-water run putting in below Whetstone Falls (west of Stacyville) and taking out before Grindstone Falls.

If you launch your canoe early in the day on **Sawtelle Deadwater,** a reservoir near Shin Pond and west of Patten, you're bound to see moose. From Shin Pond, head northwest, crossing the Seboeis River at about six miles, and then turn right onto the next unpaved road and continue less than two miles to the water. You can also reach the Deadwater off the parallel paved Huber Road. Canoe rentals are available at Shin Pond Village.

TOP EXPERIENCE

WHITE-WATER RAFTING

Maine's biggest white-water rafting region is around the Forks, the area of the Kennebec Valley where the Kennebec and Dead Rivers meet, but the second-largest area is along the West Branch of the Penobscot River near Millinocket. One-day Penobscot River rafting trips pass through Ripogenous Gorge (a rip-roaring chasm of roiling Class IV and V white water), go over nine-foot Nesoudnehunk Falls, and travel through a few other Class IV rapids and a few ponds, all in the shadow of Katahdin. It's a fabulous adventure, and a riverside lunch is included.

The primary rafting outfitter here is the **New England Outdoor Center** (NEOC, Black Cat Rd., off Baxter State Park Rd., Millinocket, 207/723-5438 or 800/766-7238, www.neoc.com), based in an updated and renovated historical sporting camp on Millinocket Lake overlooking Katahdin. NEOC organizes West Branch rafting trips from $74 pp, depending on which part of the river, day, and month. Packages including meals and lodging are available. NEOC is a full-service outdoor adventure resort, with lodging, dining, and guided recreational services.

FISHING

Water, water everywhere. That means primo fishing, including streams, rivers, and walk-in and fly-in ponds for brook trout; ponds and lakes for splake and lake trout; rivers and lakes for landlocked salmon; brooks and streams for wild and native brook trout; lakes for brown trout; and streams and rivers for bass. The Maine Department of Inland Fisheries and Wildlife (www.mefishwildlife.com) produces *Fishing Opportunities in Maine,* which details where to fish for what. Fishing licenses and other info also are available on the website.

For local info and supplies visit **Two Rivers Canoe and Tackle** (2323 Medway Rd./Rte. 157, Medway, 207/746-8181, www.tworiverscanoe.com).

Guided and outfitted fishing trips for one or two anglers with **Maine Quest Adventures** (Rte. 157, Medway, 207/746-9615, www.mainequestadventures.com) are $300 full day with lunch, $200 half day with a snack; multiday trips are also available.

Serious anglers should consider one of the sporting camps listed in *Accommodations*.

WINTER RECREATION

Winter can be magical in the North Country, where snow is usually measured in feet, not inches.

Snowmobiling

More than 350 miles of the Interconnecting Trail System (ITS) crisscross the Millinocket area, including some trails that run right through town. Local snowmobile clubs produce excellent trail maps available from the Katahdin Area Chamber of Commerce. Snowmobile enthusiasts might also want to visit the Northern Timber Cruisers Snowmobile Club's **Antique Snowmobile Museum** (Millinocket Lake Rd., Millinocket, 207/723-6203, www.northerntimbercruisers.com, weekends in winter or by appointment), which contains about three dozen antique machines. The clubhouse also serves food.

Snowmobile rentals ($279), clothing rentals ($10-25), shuttles, and guided trips are available from the **New England Outdoor Center's Twin Pine Snowmobile Rentals** (800/634-7238, www.neoc.com), based at Twin Pine Camps, near ITS 86 in Millinocket. A three-hour guided trip is $169 for a single, $199 for two/sled. Rentals require a $1,000 security deposit on a credit card.

Cross-Country Skiing

The Northern Timber Cruisers also groom and track more than 20 miles of free wilderness cross-country trails. Begin at the clubhouse on Baxter State Park Road 1.6 miles northeast of Millinocket. For trail conditions, call 207/723-4329.

FOOD

While the local options are improving, most of what's available is good home cookin', and you're welcome anywhere in jeans.

Patten

Order pizzas, soups, and sandwiches made with house-made bread at the **Hangar** (at the airport, 53 North Rd., Patten, 207/528-2555, 10am-7pm Tues.-Sat., $6-16), and then settle at a table inside or out.

Debbie's Deli & Pizza (2 Founders St., Patten, 207/528-2012, 4am-9pm Mon.-Sat., 6am-9pm Sun., $5-18) is the downtown choice for hearty home-style cooking and house-made breads, pastries, and pies.

Millinocket

The **Appalachian Trail Café** (210 Main St., Millinocket, 207/723-6720, 5am-8pm daily, $6-12) knows how to feed hungry hikers, rafters, anglers, and other outdoor adventurers. Breakfast is served all day, but burgers, fried foods, and other budget-friendly comfort foods join the menu for lunch.

For pizza, subs, pastas, and calzones, locals recommend **Angelo's Pizza Grille** (118 Penobscot Ave., Millinocket, 207/723-6767, 10:30am-9pm Mon.-Sat., $8-20) downtown.

The downtown **Scootic In Restaurant** (70 Penobscot Ave., Millinocket, 207/723-4566, www.scooticin.com, 11am-10pm Mon.-Sat., 4pm-10pm Sun., $9-30) has a full bar, and kids are welcome. Expect American comfort foods with a few surprises, and seating both indoors and on a patio.

Enjoy contemporary American fare paired with eye-candy views over Millinocket Lake to Katahdin while dining at **River Drivers Restaurant** (off Baxter State Park Rd., 207/723-8475 or 800/766-7238, www.neoc.com, 4pm-9pm daily, $14-32) on New England Outdoor Center's Twin Pine campus. Breakfast and lunch are served in peak seasons.

Dine on one of the antique oak tables in the bright dining room or on the screened-in porch at **Fredericka's** in the Big Moose Inn (Baxter State Park Rd., Millinocket, 207/723-8391, www.bigmoosecabins.com, 5pm-9pm Wed.-Sun. July-Aug., 5pm-9pm Wed.-Sat. Sept.-June, $18-30). The creative American menu emphasizes fresh and local ingredients. Pub fare is served at the inn's **Loose Moose Bar and Grill** (from 5pm daily, $8-22).

ACCOMMODATIONS

Patten

Patten is a good choice if you're accessing Baxter State Park's North Gate or the Katahdin Woods and Waters National Monument's northern parcels.

Choose from cabins ($129-189) or inn rooms with shared baths ($98-150) or a family room with private bathroom ($200) at **Mt. Chase Lodge** (1517 Shin Pond Rd., Mount Chase, 207/528-2183, https://mt-chaselodge.com, $110), which edges Upper Shin Pond. Breakfast is included for inn guests and available for $15 for cabin guests. Dinner, served Wednesday-Sunday, is from $30 per person. A meal plan including breakfast and dinner is from $40 adults, $23 ages 4-12. Owners Mike and Lindsay Downing (she grew up here) can help with planning activities or arrange for guided half-day ($200 for 2 people) or full-day ($350 for 2 people) adventures.

Eight miles off the access road to Baxter's northern gate and edging Katahdin Woods and Waters lands, **Bowlin Camps** (Bowlin Pond Rd. off Rte. 159, Patten, 207/528-2022, www.bowlincamps.com), a traditional fishing and hunting camp on the shore of the Penobscot River's East Branch, welcomes family groups, especially in July-August. Kids love the suspension bridge across the river, and there are trails to ponds and two waterfalls. An easy 16-mile canoe run starts here (rentals are available), and someone will meet you at the other end. Cabins are rustic, heated with woodstoves; all have private baths and gas and electric lights, some have kitchenettes, and one is accessible. Summer rates in cabins begin around $150 pp/night, including family-style meals served in the main lodge. Children ages 5-10 are half price; dogs are $15. Snowmobilers and cross-country skiers frequent the place in winter.

Matagamon Wilderness (Grand Lake Rd., Patten, 207/446-4635, www.matagamonwilderness.com) is just a few miles from Baxter's Matagamon gate. On the premises and bordering the East Branch of the Penobscot River are 36 wilderness campsites that can accommodate up to a 42-foot RV ($32) and six housekeeping cabins ($125-200), a general store with food service, and boat rentals. Pets are allowed in the campground for $10/stay.

Millinocket

Hikers take note: The **Appalachian Trail Lodge** (33 Penobscot Ave., Millinocket, 207/723-4321, www.appalachiantraillodge.com) provides cheap sleeps ($25 bunk, $55 private room with shared bath, $95 suite with kitchen) and caters to you with hiking and Bangor airport shuttles, coin-op laundry, and two kitchenettes.

The 48-room **Baxter Park Inn** (935 Central St./Rte. 157, Millinocket, 207/723-9777, www.baxterparkinn.com, $130-150) is an updated, older motel just east of downtown. Perks include a continental breakfast,

1: Ambajejus Boom House 2: 5 Lakes Lodge 3: North Woods Trading Post 4: Chesuncook Boom House

1
2
NOVELTIES
TEE SHIRTS
COFFEE AND
WINE
SODA
SOUVENIRS
MAPLE SYRUP
ICE CREAM
NORTH WOODS
3
4
WEST BRANCH
WILLIAM HILTON
2

indoor pool and sauna, and guest laundry. It's right on ITS 83. Pets are allowed with a signed waiver for $10.

In downtown Millinocket, knowledgeable innkeepers Micki and Fred Schumacher extend a warm welcome at the **Young House Bed and Breakfast** (193 Central St., Millinocket, 207/723-5452, www.theyounghousebandb.com, $130). The guest rooms aren't big or fancy, but the public rooms include a parlor with a baby grand. A full breakfast is included.

Big Moose Inn (Baxter State Park Rd., Millinocket, 207/723-8391, www.bigmoosecabins.com), sited on Millinocket Lake, midway between Millinocket and Baxter State Park's southern boundary, is especially popular with white-water rafters. It's part inn, part cabin colony, part campground, and steeped in Maine woods traditions. That's especially true in the main lodge, with a mix of smallish shared-bath rooms ($65 pp) and suites with private baths ($160-199). On the grounds are tent sites ($13 pp), RV sites ($17 pp) and lean-tos ($16 pp), plus 14 cabins that sleep 2-16 ($60 pp; minimum varies by cabin; bring your own towels). Canoe or kayak rental is $5/hour or $20/day. The inn has a restaurant and pub, and North Woods Trading Post, with prepared food and supplies, is next door. Some cabins and campsites are pet friendly ($20/pet/day plus $200 security deposit).

Area natives Rick and Debbie LeVasseur built ★ **5 Lakes Lodge** (46 Marina Dr., South Twin Lake, Millinocket, 207/723-5045, www.5lakeslodge.com, $215-295), a handsome two-story log lodge on a spit of land extending into South Twin Lake. Soaring windows and a stone fireplace dominate the two-story living room, with stunning views of Katahdin over the chain of lakes. The LeVasseurs provide canoes and kayaks for their guests on the pebble beach out front; small fishing boats are available for rental at the dock out back, where flightseeing tours will pick up guests. Rates include a full breakfast. It's a fine place for wildlife-watching: eagles and loons nest on the interconnecting lakes, and Rick has a few "guaranteed" moose-spotting sites. Many evenings he takes guests on an eagle-sighting cruise. Also available is a two-bedroom loft apartment ($300).

Ground zero for year-round sporting outfitter **New England Outdoor Center** (off Baxter State Park Rd., Millinocket, 800/766-7238, www.neoc.com, from $260) is its lakefront, Katahdin-view Twin Pine campus, an oasis of civilization in the wilderness just southeast of Baxter State Park. Facilities include a lodge with full-service restaurant and lounge, a recreation hall with a sauna and games, and use of canoes, kayaks, and docking facilities. The lakeside accommodations range from small cabins to green-built guesthouses, all with full kitchens. Pets are accommodated ($20/night, includes bed and bowls).

Wilderness Sporting Camps

The two excellent sporting camps listed here have long-standing reputations. Both require 60-90-minute drives on unpaved roads; it's worth the splurge to arrive by floatplane. Anglers usually frequent the camps in spring, July-August is the best time for families, and hunters come in autumn.

About 150 miles north of Bangor, ★ **Libby Camps** (Millinocket Lake, 207/435-8274, www.libbycamps.com), on the east shore of a different Millinocket Lake than the one near Millinocket, is flanked by Baxter State Park and the Allagash Wilderness Waterway. Matt and Ellen Libby, the third generation to run this 1890 fishing and hunting camp, have ceded daily management to their son Matt-John and his wife, Jess, and their young family; daughter Alison and her husband help out too. If you catch a trophy salmon or brook trout at this Orvis-endorsed fly-fishing lodge, they'll ready it for the taxidermist. Ten comfortable cabins have flush toilets, propane lights, and quilt-topped beds. The basic daily rate, including three meals, a boat, and a cabin, is $225 pp per day. Pets are allowed. Hearty meals are served close to an enormous stone fireplace in the handsome log-beam lodge. Canoes, kayaks, and motorboats are available for guests, and there's a sandy beach. The Libbys also own 10 "outpost cabins" on wildly remote ponds. Both Matts are licensed pilots; they'll fly you in on a seaplane from the Presque Isle Airport or Matagamon Lake near Patten, or you can arrange transport with other flying services.

The only sporting camp on a pristine lake, the ★ **Bradford Camps** (Munsungan Lake, 207/746-7777, winter 207/439-6364, www.bradfordcamps.com) is owned by Igor and Karen Sikorsky. (If the name rings a bell, think helicopters.) The scenery and sunsets are magnificent, the loons are mystical, and moose sightings are frequent. Eight good-size log cabins (with bathrooms and propane lamps), lined up along the lakefront, are $210 pp per day or $1,360/week; the family rate for two adults and two kids under 18 is about $3,550/week. Rates include excellent meals served family-style in the lake-view lodge. Most fascinating is the antique ice house, containing brilliantly clear ice cut arduously from the lake the previous winter. Canoes and kayaks are free for guests, a boat with a motor and gas is $75/day, and hiking trails await. A fly rod and gear is $30/day, waders are $40/day. A guide (from $300/day) is essential for fishing these waters—noted for rare blue-back trout—and helpful for canoeing a nearby stretch of the Allagash. If you're an aviation fan, ask about the Sikorsky Seminar weekend, usually in July. Karen and Igor can arrange flights from Millinocket Lake, or you can drive 60 miles over rough logging roads and pay $40 pp gate fees. No credit cards.

Campgrounds

The Scanlin family owns and manages **Allagash Gateway Camps** (207/723-9215 or 207/692-7317, www.allagashgatewaycamps.com), sited off the Golden Road, about 40 miles northwest of Millinocket (allow 90 minutes as roads are rough with some unpaved sections). The property edges Chesuncook, Maine's third largest lake, and offers cabins and campsites scattered along the shoreline. The five cabins have cooking facilities, but share outhouses and a shower house ($40 pp plus $10 per dog/night). Campsites include shorefront and forested ($15-45/night; dogs $10/stay). Canoe and kayak rentals and shuttles are available.

Probably the closest you can get to Baxter's south gate with an RV is **Chewonki's Big Eddy Campground** (Mile 28.5 on the Golden Rd., 207/882-7323, https://bigeddy.chewonki.org). Many of the 75-acre campground's primitive sites (about $14/pp) edge the Penobscot River at the famed Big Eddy landlocked salmon pools. Only five can accommodate RVs and trailers (up to 28 feet). Also available are rustic and camping cabins ($45-60 pp). Dogs are a possibility in some accommodations ($5/dog/night).

New England Outdoor Center's **Penobscot Outdoor Center Campground** (off Baxter State Park Rd.), the closest private campground to the southern entrance of Baxter, has bunkhouses (from $60), cabin tents (from $46), and tenting sites (around $15 pp). Frills include a hot tub, bar, and some food service in the base lodge. No hookups, no water, no pets.

INFORMATION AND SERVICES

The **Katahdin Area Chamber of Commerce** (1029 Central St./Rte. 157, Millinocket, 207/723-4443, www.katahdinmaine.com) is based in a small prefab building at the eastern edge of Millinocket.

Just east of Northern Plaza in Millinocket, Baxter State Park Headquarters, open weekdays, has **public restrooms,** as does Millinocket's municipal building (197 Penobscot Ave.) and the chamber of commerce.

Pets are not allowed in Baxter State Park. For doggie day or overnight care, try **Katahdin Kritters Pet Resort** (20 Dirigo Dr., East Millinocket, 207/746-8040, http://katahdinkritters.com).

GETTING THERE AND AROUND

Millinocket is about 72 miles or 1.25 hours from Bangor via I-95. It's about 85 miles or two hours to Greenville via Routes 11 and 6 or 70 miles and two hours via the (mostly unpaved) Baxter State Park, Golden, Greenville, and Lily Bay Roads.

Katahdin Air Service (KAS, Millinocket, 866/359-6246, www.katahdinair.com) has an excellent half-century reputation of offering charter floatplane flights to remote campsites and sporting camps May to November.

Baxter State Park

Consider the foresight of Maine governor Percival Proctor Baxter. After years of battling the state legislature to protect the area around Katahdin, Maine's highest mountain, he bade good-bye to state government in 1925 and proceeded to implement his dream. Determined to preserve this chunk of real estate for Maine residents and posterity, he pleaded the cause with landowners and managed to accumulate an initial 5,960-acre parcel—the nucleus of today's 209,644-acre Baxter State Park—and donated it to the state in 1931. From then on, he acquired and donated more and more bits and pieces, adding his last 7,764-acre parcel in 1962, just seven years before his death at the age of 93. The governor's prescience went far beyond mere purchases of land; his gift carried stiff restrictions that have been little altered since then. And thanks to interest accrued on his final bequest, as well as small and large donations from park users and supporters, park authorities have been able to add even more acreage—including a splendid 4,119-acre parcel donated in 2006 and another 143 acres, including 4,000 feet of waterfront on Katahdin Lake, acquired in 2013.

Percival Baxter was by no means the first to discover this wilderness. His best-known predecessor was author Henry David Thoreau, who climbed Katahdin in 1846 from what's now Abol Campground, but who never reached the summit. He didn't even reach Thoreau Spring (4,636 feet), named in his honor, but he did wax eloquent about the experience, claiming, "It was the fresh and natural surface of the planet Earth, as it was made forever and ever."

Today this fantastic recreational wilderness has 51 mountains, 24 higher than 3,000 feet; more than 225 miles of trails; and more than 60 named ponds. One rough unpaved road (limited to 20 mph) circles the park. No gasoline, drinking water, or food is available; camping is carry-in, carry-out.

Camping, in fact, is the only way to sleep in Baxter—at tent sites, lean-tos, bunkhouses, or rustic log cabins. Competition for sleeping space can be fierce on midsummer weekends; it's pure luck to find an opening, so you need to plan well ahead. Guaranteeing a spot, particularly one of the coveted 22 cabins, means reserving well in advance (no refunds). The rewards are rare alpine flowers, unique rock formations, pristine ponds, waterfalls, wildlife sightings (especially moose), dramatic vistas, and in late September, spectacular fall foliage.

The hiking here is incomparable. Peakbaggers accustomed to 8,000-footers (or more) may be unimpressed by the altitudes, but no one should underestimate the ruggedness of Baxter's terrain or the vagaries of the weather in this unique microclimate.

Regulations

The list of rules (www.baxterstateparkauthority.com/rules) is long at Baxter, and park rangers make the rounds to ensure enforcement. In the end, the rules are what make Baxter so splendid. Here are a few choice ones, but read through for any that might pertain to your plans.

No oversized vehicles, motorcycles, motorbikes, or ATVs are allowed in the park; **bicycles** are allowed only on maintained roads and on the Dwelley Pond Trail. The narrow, rough Perimeter Road is not particularly bike-friendly; when weather has been especially dry, bicyclists end up with mouthfuls of dust. **Snowmobiles** are restricted to certain areas; check with park rangers.

The park bans the use of **cell phones, TVs, radios, drones** and **CD or cassette players.** Noise levels in the park are strictly monitored by the rangers. There are no pay phones in the park, but all park rangers have radiophones.

No domestic animals are allowed in the park.

Baxter in Winter

The roads aren't plowed, campgrounds are closed, and the lakes and ponds are frozen solid, but Baxter authorities allow winter use of the park—with a multipage list of rigid restrictions. If this sounds appealing, contact the Baxter State Park Authority (www.baxterstateparkauthority.com/index.htm) for winter information.

DAY USE

Most day-use visitors are here to hike. On summer and fall weekends, you'll need to arrive early—even if you're not climbing Katahdin—because the day-use **parking areas** fill up. (There are only 284 day-use parking spots in the park; reserve in advance for $5.) On weekends, a long line forms before dawn at the Togue Pond Gate. A notice board at each gatehouse specifies which day-use parking areas are closed and which are open; there's almost always some place to park (although never alongside the Perimeter Road or campground access roads), and zillions of trails to hike, even if it may not be what you had in mind. So plan to arrive early (no later than 7am to hike Katahdin) or be prepared to be totally flexible about your hiking choice.

The northern end of the park is much less used than the southern end, so consider entering via the northern **Matagamon Gate** and hiking the wonderful trails in that part of Baxter. Take I-95 Exit 264 (Sherman) and then drive another 33 miles west, via Patten and Shin Pond, to Matagamon Gate.

Picnic areas, some with only a single table, season the park; most of the vehicle-accessible campgrounds also have picnic areas where noncampers are welcome. At the campgrounds, park in the day-use parking area, not the campers' lots.

INTERPRETIVE PROGRAMS AND GUIDES

Park rangers offer a range of family, evening campground, and Walk-with-a-Ranger programs. Call or check online for the current schedule. Also available online are a listing of bird species and a wildflower checklist.

★ HIKING

Baxter's 200 or so miles of trails could occupy hikers for their entire lives. There's no such thing as "best" hikes, but some are indeed better (for various reasons) than others. Below is a range of options; consult the most recent edition of Stephen Clark's *Katahdin: A Guide to Baxter State Park and Katahdin* for details and more suggestions.

Trails originating at campgrounds all have registration clipboards; sign-in is required for Katahdin hikes and encouraged for all other hikes. All trails are blue-blazed, except for white-blazed ones that are part of the Appalachian Trail. Carved brown signs appear at all major trail junctions. All hikers are required to carry a flashlight.

Wear technical or wool clothing, not cotton. Jeans can be a real drag (literally) if you get soaked in a stream, waterfall, or rainstorm. If you're planning to hike Katahdin, bring more layers than you think you'll need. Bring plenty of insect repellent, especially in June, when the blackflies are on the rampage. Wear light-colored long pants and a long-sleeved shirt and sweater with tight-fitting wrists and a snug collar.

Nature Trails and Family Hikes

Baxter has three easy nature trails that make ideal hikes for families with a range of age and skill levels. Nature-trail maps are available at park headquarters, the park entrance gates, and the nearest ranger stations to the trailheads. The 1.8-mile **Daicey Pond Nature Trail,** beginning at Daicey Pond Campground, circumnavigates the pond counterclockwise, taking about an hour. In August, help yourself to the raspberries near the circuit's end. Best of all, you can extend the hike at the end by renting a canoe ($1/hour or $8/day) at the campground's ranger station, in the shadow of Katahdin's west flank. After that, take the easy 1.2-mile round-trip hike from the campground access road to Big Niagara Falls.

The other nature trails are **South Branch Nature Trail,** a 0.7-mile walk starting at South Branch Campground in the northern part of the park, and **Roaring Brook Nature Trail,** a 0.8-mile walk starting near Roaring Brook Campground in the southeastern corner of the park, with dramatic views of Katahdin's east flank.

Other easy-to-moderate good family hikes are Trout Brook Mountain, Burnt Mountain, and Howe Brook Trail—all in the northern section of the park. Burnt Mountain has a fire tower at the top, and you'll need to climb the tower to see the view; the summit itself is quite overgrown. In the southern end of the park, the easy 1.4-mile **Cranberry Pond Trail** leads from Togue Pond Gate to a boggy pond. An easy 5.2-mile round-trip from Daicey Pond Campground goes to **Lily Pad Pond** and then via canoe to **Windy Pitch Ponds.** Plan to picnic en route alongside Big Niagara Falls. (Before departing, stop at the Daicey Pond office and pick up the keys for the canoe locks at Lily Pad Pond.)

Howe Brook Trail, departing from South Branch Campground, requires fording the brook several times in summer, so wear waterproof footgear. The reward, higher up, is a series of waterfalls and little pools where the kids can swim (the water is frigid), and flat boulders where you can picnic and sunbathe. In the fall, the foliage on this hike is especially gorgeous. For this six-mile hike, allow about four hours round-trip for lunch, a swim, and dawdling. Afterward, rent a canoe at the campground ($1/hour or $8/day) and paddle around scenic Lower South Branch Pond, in the shadow of North Traveler Mountain.

In 2006, after a multimillion-dollar fundraising campaign, the Trust for Public Land donated 4,119 acres on the park's eastern flank to the Baxter State Park Authority. Centerpiece of the parcel is spectacular **Katahdin Lake**—long coveted by Percival Baxter for inclusion in the park. The 6.6-mile (round-trip) hike to Katahdin Lake, via the trailhead at Avalanche Field in the southeastern corner of the park, is relatively easy. If you're inclined to linger longer at the lake, year-round accommodations in the form of housekeeping ($45 adults, $30 ages 12-17) and American Plan (with all meals, $148 pp adults, $65 pp ages 6-12) options are available in the eight lakeside log cabins managed by Holly and Bryce Hamilton at **Katahdin Lake Wilderness Camps** (207/837-1599, www.katahdinlakewildernesscamps.com/home.html). Note: The only access is by foot (3.3 miles) or floatplane.

Moderate Hikes

Good hikes generally classified as moderate are Doubletop Mountain, Sentinel Mountain, and the Owl. If you decide to hike **Doubletop Mountain,** start at the Nesowadnehunk (Ne-SOWD-na-hunk) Field trailhead and go south to Kidney Pond Campground, an eight-mile one-way trek, up and over and down. It's much less strenuous this way. Allow about six hours.

Allow about six hours also for the **Sentinel Mountain Trail** from Daicey Pond Campground (6.6 miles round-trip) or Kidney Pond Campground (4 miles round-trip). It's not difficult; the only moderate part involves a boulder field about midway up. Take a picnic and hang out at the top; the view across to Katahdin, the Owl, and Mount

O-J-I is splendid. With binoculars, you'll probably spot moose in the ponds below. If the weather has been rainy, do not hike the Owl. It verges on being strenuous even under normal conditions.

TOP EXPERIENCE

Katahdin

Mile-high **Katahdin,** northern terminus of the Appalachian Trail, is the Holy Grail for most Baxter State Park hikers—and certainly for Appalachian Trail through-hikers, who have walked 2,158 miles from Springer Mountain, Georgia, to get here. Thousands of hikers scale Katahdin annually via several different routes. The climb is strenuous, requires a full day, and is not suitable for small children; kids under age six are banned above the tree line. You'll be a lot happier and a lot less exhausted if you plan to camp in the park before and after the Katahdin hike. Cut-off time for most trails ascending Katahdin is noon.

Katahdin, by the way, is a Native American word meaning "greatest mountain"—hence there's no need to refer to it as "Mount" Katahdin. The Katahdin massif actually comprises a single high point (Baxter Peak, 5,267 feet) and several neighboring peaks (Pamola Peak, 4,902 feet; Hamlin Peak, 4,756 feet; and the three Howe Peaks, 4,612-4,734 feet).

Even though Thoreau never made it to Katahdin's summit (Baxter Peak), countless others have, and the mountain sees a virtual traffic jam in summer and fall, particularly late in the season, when most of the through-hikers are nearing the end of their odyssey. Some hikers make the summit an annual ritual; others consider it a one-time rite of passage and then opt for less-trodden paths and less-strenuous climbs.

Rangers post weather reports at 7am daily at all the campgrounds. Heed them. Katahdin has its own biome, and the weather on the summit can be dramatically different from that down below. At times, especially in high-wind and blowing-snow conditions, park officials close trails to the summit. They don't do it frivolously; Katahdin is literally a killer.

Besides the requisite photo next to the **Baxter Peak summit sign,** Katahdin's other "been there, done that" experience is a traverse of the aptly named **Knife Edge,** a treacherous 1.1-mile-long granite spine (minimum width three feet) between Baxter and Pamola Peaks. If you can stand the experience, hanging on for all you're worth next to a 1,500-foot drop, go for it; the views are incredible. But don't push beyond your personal limits; you're hours from the nearest hospital.

The most-used route to Baxter Peak is the **Hunt Trail,** a 10-mile round-trip that coincides with the Appalachian Trail from Katahdin Stream Campground; allow at least eight hours round-trip. Other routes start from Russell Pond, Chimney Pond, Roaring Brook, and Abol Campgrounds. See Stephen Clark's *Katahdin* guide for specific route information.

CAMPING

Facilities at 11 campgrounds vary from cabins to tent sites, lean-tos, and bunkhouses; there also are several backcountry campsites supervised by the nearest campground rangers.

All the campgrounds close October 15; they open on various dates beginning May 15. One hike-in campground (Chimney Pond) opens June 1. Fees are $32/night for a lean-to or tent site, $21/night for backcountry sites, $12 pp per night in a bunkhouse, and $57/night for a two-person cabin. Reserve online.

The park's only cabins are in the southwest corner—at **Daicey Pond Campground** (10 cabins) and **Kidney Pond Campground** (12 cabins). Daicey Pond has the best views—Katahdin from every cabin, and the sunrises are unmatched. With two exceptions, Kidney Pond cabins overlook the pond and surrounding woods, but not the mountains; Doubletop Mountain is behind the campground. All cabins have woodstoves (for heating only), gas lanterns, outhouses, outside fireplaces, and beds; bring your own linens, water, food, and whatever else you think you might need.

1
2

Chimney Pond and **Russell Pond Campgrounds** are hike-in; the distance from the Roaring Brook parking area to Chimney Pond is 3.3 miles, and to Russell Pond is 7 miles. Chimney Pond has a bunkhouse and nine four-person lean-tos. Russell Pond has a bunkhouse, five lean-tos, and three tent sites—all arranged around the pond, where you can also rent canoes ($1/hour or $8/day).

The campgrounds in the northern part of the park, near the Matagamon Gate, tend to be less busy and far quieter than those closer to the main gate and Katahdin. **South Branch Pond Campground** has an eight-person bunkhouse, 12 lean-tos, and 21 tent sites in an especially idyllic setting; the best sites are the lean-tos and walk-in sites edging the pond. The campground offers great swimming and has canoe and kayak rentals ($1/hour, $8/day). **Trout Brook Campground** has one lean-to, 14 tent sites, and four group sites.

June-August, bring fabric screening if you're staying in a lean-to; a tarp may foil the blackflies, mosquitoes, and no-see-ums, but you don't want to suffocate.

Getting Reservations

Reservations for any campsite within the park for the dates May 15-October 15 operate on a rolling basis and must be made beginning four months in advance by mail, in person at park headquarters, via phone, or online. For instance, to request a site or sites for July 14, you'll need to mail your reservation to arrive no earlier than March 14 (see www.baxterstateparkauthority.com/camping for the reservation schedule). July gets booked up first, then August; weekends are more crowded than weekdays. Maximum length of stay is 7 nights per campground, 14 nights total in the park. If you make a reservation and can't keep it, be considerate and call or email the park headquarters to cancel, even though you won't receive a refund. It will give someone else a chance to enjoy the beauty of Baxter.

1: Katahdin, in Baxter State Park 2: view of Katahdin from Daicey Pond Campground

PARK ACCESS, INFORMATION, AND SERVICES

Unless you're hiking the Appalachian Trail (AT), the only way to enter the park is via one of two gates. **Togue Pond Gate** at the southern end of the park is the choice for visitors from Greenville or Millinocket and is the more used gate. At the northeast corner of the park is **Matagamon Gate,** accessible via I-95, Patten, and Shin Pond Road. Both gates are open 6am-10pm early May-mid-October. After Columbus Day, the gates are open 6am-7pm, weather permitting.

Before you enter the park, check your fuel gauge and fill your tank: there are no fuel stations in the park.

If you have camping reservations, don't arrive at the park with more people than your receipt indicates; the rangers at the gate check this, and the campground rangers even do body counts to be sure you haven't stuffed extra people into cabins or lean-tos.

Maine residents have free daytime use of the park—one of Governor Baxter's stipulations. At the gates, **nonresidents** pay $15/vehicle for a day pass; a nonresident season pass is $39 (a rental car with Maine plates doesn't qualify). Everyone must pay for camping.

A day-use **Katahdin-access parking reservation** is $5. Maine residents can make one at any time beginning April 1 for the summer season; nonresidents can make a reservation beginning two weeks before their intended hike. Reservations are held until 7am on the reservation date. All other parking areas in the park are first come, first served.

There is no public transportation to or within Baxter State Park. RVs are allowed, but the maximum size permitted is 9 feet high, 7 feet wide, and 22 feet long (or 44 feet for a car and trailer). Baxter is not a drive-through park. The park's 43-mile unpaved **Perimeter Road,** connecting the Togue Pond and Matagamon Gates, is narrow and corrugated, evidently deliberately so; it's designed for access, not joyriding.

The Allagash and St. John Rivers

ALLAGASH WILDERNESS WATERWAY

In 1966, Maine established a 92-mile stretch of the Allagash River as the Allagash Wilderness Waterway (AWW), a northward-flowing collection of lakes, ponds, and streams starting at Telos Lake and ending at East Twin Brook, about six miles before the Allagash meets the St. John River. Also recognized as a National Wild and Scenic River, the waterway's habitats shelter rare plants, 30 or so mammal species, and more than 120 bird species. Canoeing season usually runs from late May (after "ice-out") to early October. Water and insect levels are high and water temperature is low in May-June; July-August are the most crowded but have better weather; September can be chilly, but the foliage is fabulous. Allow 7-10 days to paddle the Allagash. Arranging a flexible schedule gives you enough slack to wait out strong winds on the three largest lakes. Such a schedule also allows time for a leisurely pace, side trips, and fishing along the way.

En route, you might detour into **Allagash Lake,** a pristine, motor-free oasis; ponder the two Lombard Hauler **steam engines,** rusted-out relics of the Eagle Lake and Umbazooksus Railroad, abandoned on a narrow spit of land seemingly in the middle of nowhere; **Chase Rapids,** an exhilarating nine-mile stretch of white water just below Churchill Dam; and **Allagash Falls,** a dramatic 40-foot drop 8 miles before the end of the waterway and 13 miles before the river meets the St. John.

There are 80 signposted campsites along the waterway; all are first come, first served. During July-August, when canoe traffic is fairly heavy, canoers shouldn't wait too late in the day to set up camp. Sites are $12 pp per night for nonresidents, $6 pp per night for Maine residents. Children under age 10 are free. Fees are payable in advance at the ranger station where you enter the waterway.

The **Maine Bureau of Parks and Lands** (Northern Region, 106 Hogan Rd., Bangor, 207/941-4014, www.parksandlands.com) manages AWW operations. During the season, rangers are stationed at key sites along the route. Download a brochure from the website. For seasonal water-level information, call the **Forest Service** (207/435-7963, 8am-5pm daily late Apr.-mid-Dec.). Two excellent resources for the paddle are the **Northern Forest Canoe Trail** (802/496-2285, www.northernforestcanoetrail.org) and Allagash: Maine's Wild and Scenic River, a pictorial overview by naturalist Dean Bennett.

The AWW is accessible from Greenville or Millinocket, or from the Aroostook County community of Ashland by private logging roads. You'll need to pay the **North Maine Woods** (207/435-6213, www.northmainewoods.org) gate fees when you cross onto timber-company land ($11/day Maine residents, $16 nonresidents; ages 17 and younger or 70 and older have free day use; cash or check only). Official access points with parking areas are Chamberlain Thoroughfare Bridge, Churchill Dam, Umsaskis Thoroughfare, and Michaud Farm.

THE ST. JOHN RIVER

Like the Allagash, the St. John has long been associated with the timber industry—and the spring log drives when huge loads of giant logs were driven *upstream* and eventually to the mills. The history of the late 19th- and early 20th-century lumbering era is especially colorful, loaded with tales of unbelievably rugged conditions and equally rugged characters. It's only a memory since the log drives ended, but you'll see remnants of the era along the way.

The prime season on the St. John is May-early June. North Maine Woods (NMW) monitors daily water levels on the river; call a day in advance (207/435-6213) to confirm that water flow is adequate, especially after mid-June. NMW suggests 3,000 cfs (cubic feet per second) as a mini-

Allagash River

mum for enjoyable paddling—to avoid grounding out or extensive portaging—but experienced canoeists recommend 2,000 cfs.

Camping is allowed only at designated sites; all are first come, first served. Between Baker Lake and Allagash village, there are 28 signposted riverside camping areas with a total of more than 60 sites. If a site is filled, you'll have to move on, anywhere from two to five more miles. About half of the sites have at least one sheltered picnic table, a real plus that saves rigging tarps for meals in rainy weather. Other facilities are outhouses and fire rings. Sites are $12 pp per night for nonresidents, $10 pp per night for Maine residents. Children under age 15 are free. Even though the St. John has no dams, a heavy rainstorm can cause the river to rise as much as three feet overnight. Secure your canoe for the night as high as possible.

Download a St. John River brochure with maps, campsites, and other pertinent info from **North Maine Woods** (207/435-6213, www.northmainewoods.org), the nonprofit recreational manager for this area. The North Maine Woods gate fee is $11/day Maine residents, $16 nonresidents; ages 17 and under or 70 and older have free day use; cash or check only.

There are five main access points for the St. John River, plus the final takeout point downriver at the top of Maine. From the southernmost point, **5th St. John Pond,** it's 143 miles to the town of Allagash. The easiest way to get here is via floatplane from Greenville. Downstream are **Baker Lake, St. Juste Road Bridge,** and **Moody Bridge,** the latter being best for low-water conditions; drive in via Ashland (about 3.5 hours on American Realty Rd.). By the time you get to **Blanchet/Moody Bridge,** you're more than halfway downriver—almost not worth the trip. Shuttle arrangements can be complicated for St. John trips. Work out all details in advance.

GUIDES

Veteran guide services that offer trips on both the St. John and the Allagash Rivers include the Cochrane family's **Allagash Canoe Trips** (207/237-3077, www.allagashcanoetrips.com) and Blaine Miller's **Allagash Guide Inc.** (207/634-3748, www.allagashguide.com). Costs vary for guided trips, usually including everything except transportation to Maine; figure around $175-200 pp per day.

Information

Books, maps, and information are available at **Baxter State Park Headquarters** (64 Balsam Dr., Millinocket, 207/723-5140, www.baxterstateparkauthority.com, 8am-5pm Mon.-Fri. year-round), at campground ranger stations, and at the Togue Pond Visitor Center. More information is available from **Friends of Baxter State Park** (www.friendsofbaxter.org).

Pick up a *Day Use Hiking Guide* at the visitors center or at park headquarters. The fold-out map, quite sketchy, also has basic info on major park trails.

Greenville and Vicinity

Greenville (pop. 1,646) is the jumping-off point for the North Woods—ground zero for floatplanes and ski-planes maintaining contact with remote hamlets and sporting camps. Although barely larger than a small town, it's the big city for tinier communities in every direction. In truth, it's a bit like a frontier town itself. Greenville edges **Moosehead Lake**—Maine's largest—from its southern end. Moosehead is 40 miles long and covers 117 square miles, but counting all the niches and notches, its shoreline runs to more than 400 miles.

The origin of the lake's name has to be from the large number of antlered critters hereabouts, especially along the shore toward the outposts of **Rockwood** or **Kokadjo.** In addition to moose-watching, outdoor pursuits include swimming, boating, fishing, camping, hiking, white-water rafting, golfing, picnicking, birding, skiing, snowshoeing, and snowmobiling. In spring, summer, and fall, you can also cruise the lake aboard an antique steamer.

Moosehead has been attracting outdoors enthusiasts, primarily hunters and anglers, since the 1880s. The long haul from lower New England, ending with the passenger train from Bangor, apparently was worth it for the clean air, prime angling, and chance to rough it. That era has long passed, and the clientele has changed noticeably, but Greenville's downtown still has a rustic air, the outlying hamlets even more so.

Greenville was incorporated in 1836, just before the timber industry began to take off. Steamboats hauled huge corrals ("booms") of logs down the lake to the East Outlet of the Kennebec River (East and West Outlets are both on the west side of Moosehead Lake), where river drivers took over. All that ended in the 1970s, but a cruise aboard the *Katahdin* recalls that colorful era.

Greenville's lakeshore twin, **Greenville Junction,** once a busy rail crossroads, is now one of those blink-and-you'll-miss-it places, but you can still eat and sleep here. Twenty miles northwest of Greenville on Route 6/15 is the small hamlet of Rockwood, the closest spot to Kineo, a lake icon marked by cliffs. One of the best Kineo views is from the public boat landing, on a loop road just off Route 6/15; the road then continues west, along Brassua Lake and the aptly named Moose River, to **Jackman**—a lovely 30-mile drive popular with moose-watchers.

When you make inquiries about the Moosehead area, you'll hear lots of references to "ice-out." It's almost a season—the time when winter's ice releases its grip on the lake and spring and summer activities can begin. Depending on the severity of the winter, ice-out occurs anywhere in early-late May. Fisherfolk arrive, plumbing begins to work, and a few weeks later the blackfly larvae start to hatch. Spring is underway.

SIGHTS

★ Cruise on the *Kate*

During the logging era, the steamboat *Katahdin*, a 1914 wooden vessel, towed log booms across Moosehead Lake. Now

Greenville and Vicinity

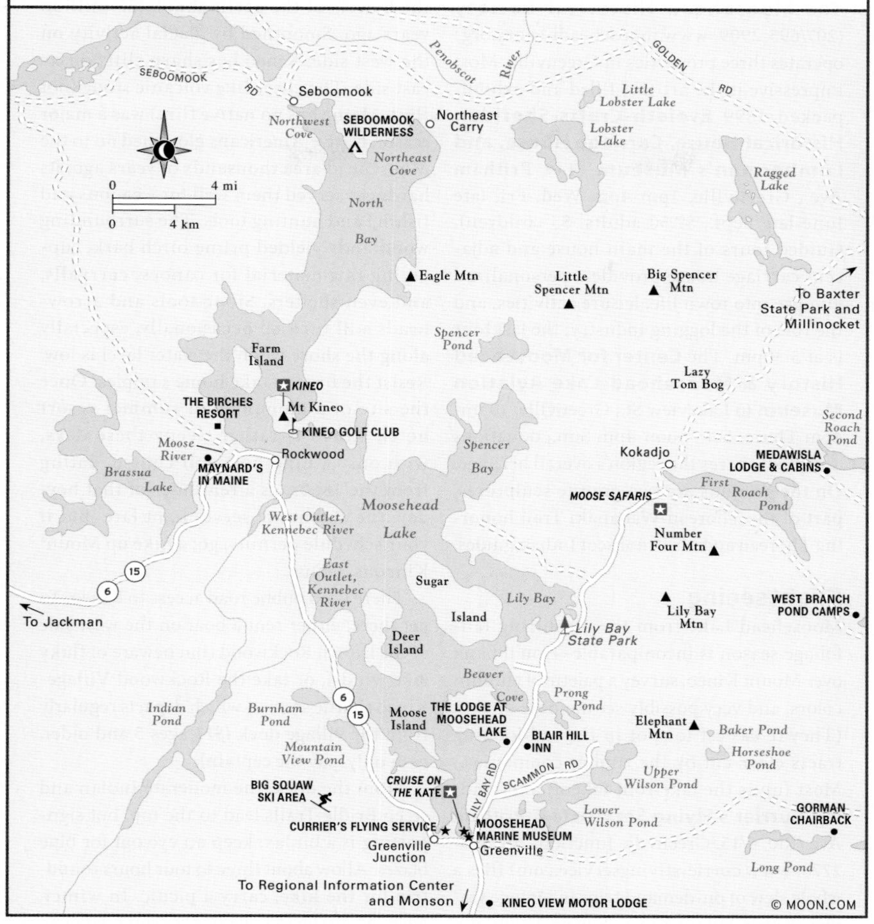

converted to diesel, the *Kate*, as it's known locally, cruises on 40-mile-long Moosehead Lake from its base at the bottom of the lake next to the **Moosehead Marine Museum** (12 Lily Bay Rd., Greenville, 207/695-2716, www.katahdincruises.com). The best trip for children is the regular three-hour Sugar Island Cruise (the schedule changes annually). Tickets are $35 adults, $30 seniors, $18 ages 11-16, $10 ages 3-10. Lunch is available for purchase on the five-hour **Mount Kineo cruise** ($45 adults, $40 seniors, $23 ages 11-16, $15 ages 2-10). An all-day head-of-lake trip (call for rates), including breakfast and dinner, often operates the last Saturday of September, when it's chilly, but the fall foliage is fantastic. There is indoor and outdoor seating, and food is available on board. Smoking and high-heeled shoes are not allowed; the boat is wheelchair-accessible. Be sure to check out the museum exhibits while here.

Moosehead Historical Society Museums

The **Moosehead Historical Society** (207/695-2909, www.mooseheadhistory.org) operates three properties in Greenville. Most impressive is the artifact-filled and exhibit-packed 1899 **Eveleth-Crafts-Sheridan Historical House, Carriage House, and Lumberman's Museum** (444 Pritham Ave., Greenville, 1pm-4pm Wed.-Fri. late June-late Sept., $7.50 adults, $3 children). Guided tours of the main house and adjacent carriage house provide a personalized glimpse into town life, leisure activities, and the role of the logging industry; the last tour is at 3:30pm. The **Center for Moosehead History & Moosehead Lake Aviation Museum** (6 Lakeview St., Greenville, 10am-4pm Thurs.-Sat., noon-4pm Sun., donations accepted) shares the region's overall heritage. On the grounds are two granite sculptures, part of the Thoreau-Wabanaki Trail honoring Thoreau and his Penobscot Indian guides.

Flightseeing

Moosehead Lake from the air during fall-foliage season is incomparable—you'll bank over Mount Kineo, survey a palette of autumn colors, and very possibly see a moose or two. (They're easiest to spot in the sad-looking tracts clear-cut by the timber companies.) Most fun is the lakefront takeoff and landing. **Currier's Flying Service** (447 Pritham Ave./Rte. 6/15, Greenville Junction, 207/695-2778, www.curriersflyingservice.com) flies a whole slew of on-demand trips in vintage seaplanes over Mount Kineo, Squaw Mountain, and Katahdin. Costs range $45-180 pp with a two-passenger minimum. Call to arrange a flight schedule; planes depart from Greenville Junction, where the Currier family also operates a small gift shop, selling Sue Currier's hand-sewn wall hangings.

★ Kineo

Moosehead Lake's most distinctive landmark, at the lake's "waistline," is **Mount Kineo,** a 763-foot-high chunk of green-tinged rhyolite or felsite that erupted from the bowels of the earth about 425 million years ago. Smoothed by glacial activity on the west side, Kineo has sharp cliffs on its east side. The chert-like volcanic stone (not flint; Maine has no native flint) was a major reason Native Americans glommed on to the Moosehead area thousands of years ago; its hardness served them well for weapons and fishing and hunting tools. The surrounding woodlands yielded prime birch bark, supplying raw material for canoes, carryalls, and even shelters. Stone tools and arrowheads still turn up occasionally, especially along the shore when the water level is low. Resist the urge to take home samples. Once the site of a monumental summer resort hotel, Kineo is rather sleepy these days, with only a nine-hole golf course, dating from the 1860s, as a reminder of that heyday; the clubhouse serves light fare. But if your schedule permits, go; a hike up Mount Kineo is a must.

There is no public road access to Kineo. To get there, either rent a boat on the west side of the lake in Rockwood (but beware of fluky lake winds), or take the Rockwood Village-Kineo shuttle service, which departs regularly from the village dock ($13 ages 5 and older, cash only, pay the captain).

From the dock, the moderate Indian and steep Bridle Trails lead to the top, but signposting is a bit lax; keep an eye out for blue blazes. Allow about three to four hours round-trip for the hike; carry a picnic. In winter, when Moosehead Lake freezes solid, you can get to the Kineo peninsula by snowmobile (weather and common sense determine the schedule), but the trails are too full of snow for hiking.

ENTERTAINMENT

Gazebo concerts are offered Thursday evenings during July and August. On Friday

---

1: the steamboat *Kate* 2: flightseeing planes
3: view of Mount Kineo 4: downtown Greenville

KATAHDIN
N91549
SHAW BLOCK
·1893·
MOOSEHEAD
LAKE
SOUVENIRS
INDIANSTORE
KAMP
KAMP
ANTIQUES
1
2
3
4

nights, there's usually **family entertainment** in Thoreau Park.

Moosemainea, an annual month-long moose-oriented festival sponsored by the Moosehead Lake Region Chamber of Commerce, combines canoe, rowboat, and mountain-bike races; a family fun day; moose safaris; and even a "best moose photo" contest. Register your own moose sightings on a huge map at the chamber of commerce. Events take place in Greenville and Rockwood mid-May-mid-June.

The **Thoreau-Wabanaki Trail Festival,** in late July, celebrates Henry David Thoreau's three visits to the region with workshops, activities, and presentations.

In early September, the four-day **International Seaplane Fly-In** draws seaplanes from all over New England for public breakfasts, a two-day crafts fair, flightseeing, and more. Beds are very scarce during the Fly-In, so either book well ahead to be part of it or wait for another time to visit.

In February, the **100-Mile Wilderness Sled Dog Race** attracts dog teams from throughout the Northeast.

SHOPPING

Greenville and the surrounding area are filled with shops selling moose-related and woodsy-themed merchandise.

The lakeside **Artisan Village** downtown is a fun place to shop for handmade works. The **Indian Hill Trading Post** (Rte. 15, Greenville, 207/695-2104 or 800/675-4487, www.indianhill.com) offers one-stop shopping for camping gear, clothing, footwear, fishing and hunting licenses, souvenirs, and groceries. It has an ATM.

At the downtown crossroads, the **Moosehead Lake Indian Store at Kamp Kamp** (Pritham Ave., Greenville, 207/695-0789) is jam-packed with woods-related merchandise, from moose and bear doodads to antiques.

Gabriel's Studio (Rte. 6/15, Greenville, 207/695-3968) carries an excellent selection of inexpensive new and gently used books.

RECREATION

Multisport Outfitters

The biggest and best outfitter in this neck of the woods is **Northwoods Outfitters** (Main St., Greenville, 866/223-1380 or 207/695-3288, www.maineoutfitter.com), in downtown Greenville, right across from the *Katahdin*. Northwoods should be your first stop no matter what your choice of activity. These folks are the region's outdoor pros. Even if you have your own equipment and have no need for a guide, stop in for advice and information, maps, and perhaps a cup of java and some final posting from the civilized world from its **Internet Café.** Northwoods does it all, offering rental equipment, shuttles, and guided trips: moose safaris, lake cruises, mountain biking, hiking, sailing, canoeing, white-water rafting, fishing, dogsledding, snowmobiling, snowshoeing, and so on. Even better, it uses guides who are passionate about their individual sports. It's open 9am-5pm daily, with extended hours during peak seasons.

Guided Excursions

Maine Guide Chris Young provides personalized service on his **Young's Guide Service** (207/695-2661, https://youngsguideservice.com) private trips. Options range from moose safaris, fishing, and cruises through wilderness waterways aboard a motor-driven canoe. Rates begin around $225 for two, for a 3-4-hour trip.

Ed Mathieu is the chief honcho of **Moose Country Eco Tours** (191 N. Dexter Rd., Sangerville, 207/876-4907, http://moosecountryecotours.com), usually operating in the Greenville area. Options include birding, paddling, covered bridges, and waterfalls. A 3-5-hour tour for three or fewer is $90 per person.

Lily Bay State Park

Lining the eastern shore of Moosehead Lake, **Lily Bay State Park** (Lily Bay Rd., Greenville, 207/695-2700, www.parksandlands.com, $4-6 adults, $2 seniors, $1 ages 5-11, free under age 5) is the place to go for moose-watching, fishing, picnicking, hiking, canoeing, swimming, birding, and camping at some of Maine's most desirable waterfront sites. The park is open 7am-11pm daily May 1-October 15, but it's accessible in winter for cross-country skiing and snowmobiling. From Greenville, head north on Lily Bay Road for eight miles; the park is on the left.

★ Moose Safaris

Of course you want to see a moose, and while there's a good chance you'll see one along the road or in a waterway during your travels, taking a moose-sighting tour by land or boat led by a registered Maine Guide increases the chances. **Northwoods Outfitters** offers three-hour moose safaris by land or water (from $50 pp). For an elevated view, **Currier's** does its moose-watching from the air.

If you go on your own, swampy **Lazy Tom Bog** is one of the region's best moose-watching haunts. Plan to go soon after sunrise or just before sunset. From Greenville, take the Lily Bay Road north to Kokadjo, 18 miles. A mile later, when the road forks, take the left fork (signposted Spencer Pond Camps). Continue 0.5 mile to a small bridge. Park on either side of the bridge and have your camera ready, preferably with a long lens. If you want to emerge from your car, or even stick your lens through the open window, you may need to douse yourself with insect repellent. And try to keep the kids quiet.

Hiking

Except for early June, when blackflies torment woodland hikers as well as moose, the Greenville area is sublime for hiking. The chamber of commerce has a list that includes hiking directions for **Number Four Mountain, Big and Little Squaw Mountains, Big and Little Spencer Mountains,** and **Elephant Mountain** (a B-52 crash site). Also ask at the chamber for directions to **Moose Mountain,** off Route 6/16, topped with the first fire tower in the United States. It's a bit rickety, but it's still there. The hike is moderate to difficult and takes about four hours round-trip.

Mountain Biking

Given all the backwoods trails, mountain biking is very popular. You can bring a bike and strike out on your own, rent a bike, or go with a guide or group. Remember, however, that bicycles are *not* allowed on logging roads; the huge lumber trucks are intimidating enough for passenger vehicles, never mind bicycles.

Mountain bike rentals are available from **Northwoods Outfitters** for $25/day. Also available are kids' bikes, child seats, and Trail-a-Bikes.

Twenty miles north of Greenville, the **Birches Resort** (Rockwood, 207/534-7305, www.birches.com) rents mountain bikes ($35/day) and sends you off on its network of trails.

Water Sports

In addition to Lily Bay State Park, there's fine swimming at **Red Cross Beach** in downtown Greenville. The parking area is near the Masonic Temple on Pritham Avenue, and a short path through the woods leads to the beach. You'll find lifeguards, picnic tables, and floats. Another swimming spot is at the boat launch in Greenville Junction.

PADDLE SPORTS

If you're not an experienced paddler, be cautious about canoeing or kayaking on Moosehead Lake. The sheltered bays and coves are usually safe, but you can have serious trouble in the open areas—especially the stretch between Rockwood and Kineo. Do not attempt it; even pros have been swamped by rogue winds on that route. At Lily Bay State Park, you can launch a canoe from the waterfront campsites and easily make it to Sugar Island.

At **Northwoods Outfitters,** canoe rentals are $40, kayak rentals began at $30; weekly rentals and deliveries are available, as is shuttle service.

POWERBOAT RENTALS

If you want to explore Moosehead Lake's numerous nooks and crannies, **Wilson's**

The Ungainly, Beloved Moose

Everyone loves Maine's bulbous-nosed and top-heavy state animal. Maine's Department of Inland Fisheries and Wildlife estimates that the state is home to more than 60,000 moose, most in the North Woods, the highest population in the lower 48 states. It's pretty likely that you'll encounter one if you're driving the roads or hiking the trails in the Maine Highlands region.

MOOSE SAFETY

The moose's long legs put its head and shoulders about windshield level, and a crash can propel the animal headfirst through the glass. Human and animal fatalities are common in moose crashes. Moose pay no heed to those yellow-and-black diamond-shaped moose-crossing signs, but officials post them near typical moose hangouts, so slow down when you see them. At night, be even more careful, as moose don't tend to focus in on headlights (as deer do), and their eyes don't reflect at an angle that drivers can see.

Moose have no history of harming humans, but stay out of their way during "the rut," when they're charging around and out of the woods looking for females in heat. This usually occurs mid-September-mid-October, when the foliage is at its peak, hikers are out and about, and Moose Lottery winners are in hot pursuit.

MOOSE HUNTING

Moose hunting, officially sanctioned, is somewhat controversial, partly because the creatures seem to present little sporting challenge. But they are a challenge, not because of wile or speed but because of heft. Imagine dragging one of these fellows out of the woods to a waiting truck; it's no mean feat. In Maine's annual Moose Lottery—a herd-thinning scheme concocted by the Department of Inland Fisheries and Wildlife—hunters receive permits to shoot moose in specific zones in late September-mid-October. At official state weighing stations, the hapless moose are strung up, weighed, tested for parasites, and often butchered on the spot by freelance meat packagers. Moose meat is actually tasty.

MOOSE SPOTTING

During daylight hours, especially early and late in the day, keep your binoculars and camera handy. In late spring and early summer, pesky flies and midges drive the moose from the deepest woods, so you're more likely to see them close to the roadside.

Moose are vegetarians, preferring new shoots and twigs in aquatic settings, so the best places to see them are wetlands and ponds fringed with grass and shrubs. These spots are likely to be buggy too, so slather yourself with insect repellent.

on Moosehead Lake (66 Wilsons Rd., Greenville Junction, 207/695-2549, www.wilsonsonmooseheadlake.com) rents 14-16-foot fishing skiffs for $110-150/day. Careful: The lake is shallow.

FLY-FISHING

The **Maine Guide Fly Shop and Guide Service** (34 Greenville Rd., Greenville, 207/695-2266, www.maineguideflyshop.com) will set you up with a guide and all the equipment you need to do it right. A guided drift-boat experience, including lunch and gear, is $450 for up to two people.

Golf

The most popular, scenic, and windswept course in the area is the nine-hole **Kineo Golf Club** (207/534-9012, www.mooseheadlakegolf.com), built for the 500 or so guests at the turn-of-the-20th-century Mount Kineo House. At every turn you'll see Mount Kineo, or Moosehead Lake, or both. Access is by boat shuttle.

Moose have extremely acute senses of hearing and smell, but their eyesight is pitiable. If you're utterly quiet and stay downwind of them, they probably won't spot you.

Try one of the following hot spots to catch a glimpse:

- Sandy Stream Pond, Baxter State Park
- Grassy Pond, Baxter State Park
- Russell Pond, Baxter State Park
- Sawtelle Deadwater, off Shin Pond Road, about seven miles northwest of Shin Pond
- Lazy Tom Bog, off Lily Bay Road, about 19 miles north of Greenville
- Route 6/15, between Greenville Junction and Rockwood, on the west side of Moosehead Lake
- The Golden Road, between Ripogenus Dam and Pittston Farm

Winter Sports

SNOWMOBILING

The biggest winter pursuit hereabouts is snowmobiling, thanks to an average 102-inch annual snowfall and 300 miles of Greenville-area trails connecting to the entire state network. It's pretty competitive trying to get a bed in winter if you don't plan well ahead. Incidentally, if you're curious about how people get around northern Maine in winter, check out the parking lot at the Greenville school complex (Pritham Ave.): The vehicle of choice is the snowmobile. The chamber of commerce has snowmobile trail maps and can put you in touch with local snowmobile clubs. Thanks to these energetic clubs, trails are well maintained and signposted.

A particularly popular loop is the 160-mile **Moosehead Trail,** which circumnavigates Moosehead Lake. It travels from Greenville to Rockwood to Pittston Farm, Seboomook, Northeast Carry, and Kokadjo, and then back to Greenville. You can start at any access point along the route and go in either direction.

For snowmobile rentals or guided tours,

contact Northwoods Outfitters. Rates begin around $250/day for a rental sled. A three-hour guided tour is $149 pp.

CROSS-COUNTRY SKIING

The **Birches Resort** (Rockwood, 207/534-7305, www.birches.com) has 40 miles of groomed cross-country ski trails winding through an 11,000-acre nature preserve. A trail pass is $14 full day, $11 half day for adults; kids are $10 or $8. Full-day rates include use of the hot tub and sauna. Equipment rentals are available at the Birches Ski Touring Center.

For a real adventure, ski between the **Appalachian Mountain Club**'s (www.outdoors.org) wilderness lodges—Medawisla, Little Lyford, and Gorman Chairback—and the privately owned West Branch Pond Camps. More than 30 miles of groomed wilderness trails connect the properties, which welcome adventurers with woodstove-heated cabins and hot family-style meals. Both guided and self-guided adventures are available, as is a gear shuttle.

FOOD

The range of dining experiences in and near Greenville is surprisingly broad. While choices are plentiful in summer, they're scanty in the off-season.

Quick Bites

Extremely popular among local residents is **Flatlanders** (36 Pritham Ave., Greenville, 207/695-3373, from 11am daily, $6-19). The best choice is the broasted chicken, which one waitress described as "kinda like fried chicken but cooked in a pressure cooker so it's more healthy." Whatever; everyone agrees it's tasty.

Buy pizza and subs, beer and wine coolers, and worms and crawlers at **Jamo's** (34 Pritham Ave., Greenville, 207/695-2201, 5am-9pm Mon.-Thurs., 5am-10pm Fri.-Sat., 6am-9pm Sun.). OK, skip the latter pairing, but the pizza's decent, and the Dagwood sandwiches, made on fresh-baked pita bread, earn raves.

The **Farm at Moosehead** (300 Moosehead Lake Rd./Rte. 15, 207/695-0182, http://thefarm300.com, 4pm-8pm Thurs.-Sat.) specializes in wood-fired pizza and slow-smoked baby back ribs, but it also offers specials. There's no seating; it's take-out only.

Casual Dining

A dining bright spot in downtown Greenville, **Rod-N-Reel Cafe** (44 Pritham Ave., Greenville, 207/695-0388, 4pm-9pm Wed.-Sun., $12-28) reels them in with reliable home-style food with flair. Fish is the dominant theme, from the name to the decor to the menu, but you can get steaks, chicken, and pasta, as well as lighter fare. Friday and Saturday are prime rib nights. Hours are sporadic.

For upscale pub food, dine at the **Stress-free Moose** (65 Pritham Ave., Greenville, 207/695-3100, from 11am daily, $10-20), with seating indoors and on a big wraparound porch. There's often live music; it can be quite loud inside.

At **Kelly's Landing** (Rte. 6/15, Greenville Junction, 207/695-4438, www.kellysatmoosehead.com, 7am-9pm daily year-round, $11-30), the food is hit or miss, but you can't beat the location and lake views. If the weather's fine, dine on the deck; if not, the dining rooms have big windows facing the water. A kids' menu is available. An all-you-can-eat buffet breakfast is served Sunday 8am-11am. There's always a crowd, and boaters can tie up at the dock.

The **Dockside Inn and Tavern** is slated to open it its downtown location edging the lake for the 2020 summer season.

Sporting Camp Fare

Go to ★ **Maynard's in Maine** (131 Maynards Rd., 207/534-7703 or 888/518-2055, www.maynardsinmaine.com), a classic sporting lodge, for the experience. It's not gourmet fare, just good home cookin'. Maynard's is open to nonguests (breakfast 7am-9am daily, dinner 5:30pm-7:30pm daily, reservations required). There's a full menu for breakfast and a choice of two entrées at dinner ($22-26), which includes soup or salad and rolls. Everything is homemade or baked and served family-style in the pleasant dining room. BYOB.

If you're willing to drive a good 10 miles into the woods to dine, book a table at **West Branch Pond Camps** (Kokadjo, 207/695-2561, www.westbranchpondcamps.com). This is the real deal, a traditional sporting camp amid wilderness, with mountain and water views. A set menu is offered at 6pm Monday-Saturday and at noon Sunday; prices range $25-35, depending on the meal. Dining here is an adventure, and the food never disappoints; everything is made from scratch in a historical kitchen. If you're worried about making the drive at night, make reservations for Sunday's noon turkey dinner. Advance reservations are required.

Fine Dining

The elegant ★ **Blair Hill Inn** (Lily Bay Rd., 207/695-0224) serves a fixed-price six-course menu ($79) 5:30pm-8:30pm Thursday-Saturday evenings in the elegant dining room and adjacent glassed-in porch high on a hill with sweeping sunset views over Moosehead Lake. The inn has an indoor wood-burning grill, so meats and fish are grilled, and much of the produce comes from the inn's greenhouses and gardens. Almost everything is made from scratch; special diets can be accommodated, including vegan with notice. It's open mid-June-mid-October. Arrive early to enjoy a sunset cocktail in the lounge or on the porch.

ACCOMMODATIONS

Lodging in the area varies from just a few grades above camping to exquisite country inns and lodges.

Country Inns

Combine a Victorian hillside manse, eye-popping views of Moosehead Lake, and English manor house decor and ambience, and the result is the ★ **Blair Hill Inn** (Lily Bay Rd., Greenville, 207/695-0224, www.blairhill.com, from $399), where Dan and Ruth McLaughlin (escapees from the software industry) have created a relaxing, elegant retreat. Ten spacious guest rooms in the magnificent 1891 home are furnished with comfy antiques and accented with ornate woodwork, fabulous lighting, and fine paintings. Some have working fireplaces and most have expansive lake views. A truly gourmet breakfast is included, and a five-course dinner ($79 pp) is available Thursday-Saturday. The inn also serves guest-only dinners by reservation on Tuesday, Wednesday, and Sunday; ask for details when you book a room. If you want a different angle on the expansive views, relax in the dining room, living room, or comfy lounge; even better, score a seat on the front porch. The inn also has a well-equipped fitness room and a spa offering facials, scrubs, and massages. The grounds include lovely gardens, greenhouses, a huge barn, and rolling lawns edged with stone walls. Service is top-notch, yet unobtrusive; the innkeepers will arrange activities and make recommendations on request.

Elegance and comfort are also bywords at the **Lodge at Moosehead Lake** (Lily Bay Rd., Greenville, 207/695-4400, www.lodgeatmooseheadlake.com, from $449), although the woodsy decor might be a little much for some guests. Each of the five guest rooms in the main building has a theme—Trout, Loon, Moose, Totem, and Bear—and each has beds and mirrors hand-carved by local woodworking master Joe Bolf, plus lots of accessories to carry out its motif. All but the Trout have dramatic views of Moosehead Lake. Whirlpool tubs and fireplaces are in each room. An adjacent Carriage House has four water-view suites, including a two-bedroom with a kitchen and big deck. Breakfast is included. In-house and safari camp dinners are available to guests; these vary seasonally. Two suites are dog friendly (70 pounds max, $35/night).

Motels

The **Kineo View Motor Lodge** (Rte. 15, Greenville, 207/695-4470 or 800/659-8439,

2
Welcome to
Kokadjo
Population
Not many

3

4
MAYNARDS

www.kineoview.com, $99-119), three miles south of Greenville, sits on a prime hilltop spot with a dead-on view of Mount Kineo and gorgeous sunsets. The chalet-style three-story motel has 12 good-size guest rooms and a suite with a full kitchen and fireplace ($200). Rates include continental breakfast late May-mid-October. This is a great place to bring kids—there's lots of acreage to run around, including nature trails. Outside are picnic tables and a grill. Some rooms accommodate pets ($10 by reservation).

You're practically *in* the lake at **Chalet Moosehead** (12 N. Birch St., Greenville Junction, 207/695-2950 or 800/290-3645, www.mooseheadlodging.com, $135-180). The newer two-story building is where you want to stay; first- and second-floor guest rooms have whirlpool tubs and private balconies with dynamite views. The older two-story section has seven basic, somewhat tired, guest rooms, some with kitchenettes. Kids age five and under stay free; dogs ($20/night) are allowed in the older units. Dock space is free if you bring your own boat, and guests have free use of canoes, paddleboats, gas grills, and a private swimming area.

Sporting Camps and Rental Cabins

If cell service or Internet access is important to you, or if you're uncomfortable driving on dirt roads, be sure to ask before booking any of these.

Ease into sporting camp life at **Maynard's in Maine** (Rockwood, 207/534-7703 or 888/518-2055, www.maynardsinmaine.com). Meals are served in the central lodge; guests stay in cabins, all with full baths and most with views over the Moose River to the Blue Ridge (a blaze of color during foliage season). The food is great—freshly made and home-baked. At first glance it may seem more run-down than rustic, but the cabins are comfy, the mattresses firm, and the plumbing is inside. Rates, including breakfast, dinner, and a packed lunch, are $95 adults, $45 ages 3-12; without meals, it's $55 adults, $25 ages 3-12. Cabins have 1-3 bedrooms. Dogs are allowed for $20/stay. Motorboat rental is $65/day, canoes and kayaks are $20-25.

Eric Stirling is the fourth-generation host at **West Branch Pond Camps** (Kokadjo, 207/695-2561, www.westbranchpondcamps.com). Lining the shore of First West Branch Pond, overlooking White Cap Mountain, are nine classically rustic cabins with indoor plumbing and evening electricity. For wilderness lovers who prefer a tad of comfort, this is the real thing. The camps are set on 30 private acres surrounded by conservation lands. Fly-fishing, hiking, and paddling are the major pursuits. If you're hoping to spot a moose, well, the gangly mammals often stroll right through the property, even peeking in the kitchen window. Speaking of the kitchen: When the bell rings for meals, guests head to the 1890 lakeside lodge and vacuum up the hearty cuisine described in one upscale national magazine as "simple, soulful Yankee cooking." BYOB. Cross-country skiers and snowshoers come in winter, when heat is by woodstove and there are privies as well as two heated bathhouses, each with shower and toilet. The daily rate is $125 pp, $80 ages 12-17, $50 ages 5-11, which includes meals, lodging, firewood, linens, and use of rowboats, kayaks, and canoes. Well-behaved pets are $20/stay.

The **Appalachian Mountain Club** (603/466-2727, www.outdoors.org) operates three trail-connected traditional sporting camps in the 100-Mile Wilderness region. **Little Lyford,** dating from 1874 and sitting near Gulf Hagas and the Appalachian Trail, Little Lyford Pond, and the Pleasant River, is the most primitive. Guests stay in nine cabins or a 12-bed bunkhouse, all sharing a central bathhouse with hot showers, a winter sauna, and composting toilets. It's a full-service lodge with three daily meals provided. Dogs are welcome for $10/night/dog. ★ **Gorman Chairback** on the shores of Long Pond is the newest and provides the most amenities. It

1: view from Blair Hill Inn **2:** Kokadjo landscape **3:** West Branch Pond Camps **4:** Maynard's in Maine

has four cabins with bathrooms, eight renovated cabins, a bunkhouse sleeping 10, and a new environmentally friendly lodge with showers and a winter sauna. A third lodge, **Medawisla,** sited where the Roach River flows into Second Roach Pond, comprises a new lodge, four new waterfront cabins, five deluxe en-suite cabins, two 16-bed bunkhouses, and a wood-fired winter sauna. For all, heat is by woodstove. Canoes, kayaks, and snowshoes are available. Packages that include gear shuttle for lodge-to-lodge skiing are available. Rates vary by season, and you'll get the best price if you join the AMC. Nonmember rates, including meals, begin at $105 pp for bunkhouse lodging and $150 pp for a private cabin.

Forty-three miles northeast of Greenville is **Nahmakanta Lake Camps** (207/731-8888, www.nahmakanta.com), Don and Angel Hibbs's oasis in the wilderness on Nahmakanta Lake. Nine restored cabins right on the lake have screened porches, full kitchens, and woodstoves. There is no electricity. Each cabin has a private but separate bathroom. Choose from the full American Plan, including all meals ($160 pp per day adults, plus $8 multiplied by age for ages 1-17); the Modified American Plan, including supper ($125 pp per day adults, $6 multiplied by age for children); or housekeeping ($90 pp per day adults, $4 multiplied by age for kids). Canoes and kayaks are provided; boats and motors are $60/day; guides are available. Summer access is via 25 miles of gravel roads or floatplane. Dogs ($20/stay) are welcome with advance notice.

Six inviting but primitive (outhouses) housekeeping cabins welcome guests to ultra-quiet **Spencer Pond Camps** (806 Spencer Pond Rd., Beaver Cove, 207/745-1599, http://spencerpond.com, $150), the only accommodations on Spencer Pond. Each cabin is comfy and cozy, with quilts on the bed, kerosene and gas lights, a woodstove for heat, and a working kitchen. Young adults and students traveling with family are $30, ages 12 and younger are free; $25/pet. Rates include linens, firewood, and use of canoes, kayaks, and mountain bikes. Guided explorations with Registered Maine Guides can be arranged.

Camping

The **Maine Forest Service** supervises and maintains free campsites with fireplaces and outhouses, many on the shores of Moosehead Lake. Most are accessible only by boat on a first-come, first-served basis. For information, contact the Maine Forest Service **office** (downtown Greenville, 207/695-3721).

At the northern end of Moosehead Lake, about 5.5 miles south of the Golden Road, **Seboomook Wilderness Campground** (2538 Seboomook Rd., Seboomook, 207/280-0555, www.seboomookwildernesscampground.com, campsites from $20, cabins from $55) has 87 wooded and open tent and RV sites, Adirondack shelters, and housekeeping cabins (no linens), many right on the water. Everything is very rustic, although there is a central bathhouse with flush toilets and free hot showers. Request a site on the eastern side, away from the long-term RV area. Facilities include a small, shallow beach and a grocery store with a lunch counter. History buffs take note: This was the site of a World War II German POW camp. Seboomook's store is open all winter for snowmobilers and cross-country skiers; campsites are open mid-May-November. Canoes, kayaks, and motorboat rentals are available. The campground is about 28 unpaved miles north of Rockwood.

You can't get much closer to the water than some of the primitive sites at **South Inlet Wilderness Campground** (Frenchville Rd., Kokadjo, 207/695-2474 evenings, 207/695-3954 winter, $18-30). Although near a dirt road, many of the sites front on First Roach Pond. Facilities include a beach, a boat launch, privies, fire rings, and picnic tables.

Plan well in advance to snag one of the primo waterfront sites at **Lily Bay State Park** (Lily Bay Rd., Greenville, 207/695-2700); on weekends July-August, campsite reservations are essential, with a two-night minimum (call 207/624-9950 from outside Maine,

800/332-1501 in Maine, or visit www.campwithme.com). Only the lucky will find a last-minute space, even though there are 93 sites in two clusters; none have hookups. Camping fees are $30 nonresidents, $20 Maine residents, plus the reservation fee of $5/site/night.

INFORMATION AND SERVICES

The **Moosehead Lake Region Chamber of Commerce** (888/876-2778, www.mooseheadlake.org) has information about member businesses and area activities.

State agencies with offices in Greenville are the **Maine Warden Service** (MWS, 207/695-3756) and the **Maine Forest Service** (MFS, Lakeview St., Greenville, 207/695-3721), where you can view a Smokey Bear display. The Greenville MWS office, with jurisdiction for all search-and-rescue missions of Maine's acreage, undertakes at least one search-and-rescue mission per week. The MFS, besides fire-spotting duty, is also responsible for a number of public campsites in the region.

In Greenville, the Indian Hill Trading Post has **public restrooms,** as do the chamber of commerce office and the Moosehead Marine Museum, next to the *Katahdin* wharf. In Greenville Junction and Rockwood, there are restrooms at the public boat landings.

GETTING THERE AND AROUND

Greenville is about two hours from Millinocket via Routes 11 and 6/15 or 70 miles and two hours via the (mostly unpaved) Baxter State Park, Golden, Greenville, and Lily Bay Roads. It's about 34 miles or 45 minutes to Dover-Foxcroft via Route 6/15 and about 50 miles or one hour to Jackman via Route 6/15. It's about 72 miles or 1.5 hours from Bangor via Route 15.

Greenville flying services operating small pontoon- or ski-equipped planes act as the lifelines to remote North Woods sporting camps, campsites, rivers, lakes, and ponds inaccessible overland. In some cases, road access exists, but you'll jeopardize your vehicle, your innards, and maybe your life along the way. **Currier's Flying Service** (Pritham Ave./Rte. 6/15, Greenville Junction, 207/695-2778, www.curriersflyingservice.com) and **Jack's Air Service** (Pritham Ave., Greenville, 207/695-3020, www.jacksairservice.com), based in downtown Greenville, provide on-demand charter service to remote locales. Both firms have flat hourly rates if you want to create your own itinerary.

Many of the **roads** in the Greenville area are unpaved; paper-company roads tend to be the best maintained, because access is essential for their huge log trucks and machinery. But others, especially roads leading to sporting camps, can become tank traps in spring (April-May) and after a heavy downpour. Check road conditions before setting out during those times, especially if you don't have a 4WD vehicle. Ask the chamber of commerce, the Maine Forest Service, the county sheriff, or the sporting camp owners.

Dover-Foxcroft Area

At the bottom of Piscataquis (piss-CAT-uh-kwiss) County, **Dover-Foxcroft** (pop. 4,213) is the county seat, hub for the surrounding towns of **Milo** (pop. 1,847), **Brownville Junction** (pop. 1,250), **Sangerville** (pop. 1,343), **Guilford** (pop. 1,521), **Abbot** (pop. 714), and **Monson** (pop. 686). Here's an area that's often overlooked, probably because Greenville, Moosehead Lake, Baxter State Park, and Katahdin Woods and Waters National Monument are just up the road. But it's easy to spend a couple of days exploring here—notably for dramatic Gulf Hagas Reserve and Borestone Mountain Sanctuary, but also for a handful of out-of-the-way towns few visitors get to appreciate.

Incorporated in 1822, Monson, a lakeside blink 20 miles northwest of Dover-Foxcroft and 15 miles south of Greenville, has an old reputation and a new one. The old one comes from its slate quarries, first mined in the 1870s, which shipped slate around the nation for sinks, roof tiles, blackboards, and even urinals. A considerable Finnish community grew up here to work the quarries; their descendants still celebrate traditional Finnish holidays. Although the industry has declined, and only one company still operates, Monson slate monuments adorn the gravesites of John F. Kennedy and Jacqueline Kennedy Onassis.

Monson's current fame comes from Appalachian Trail (AT) through-hikers, whose energetic grapevine carries the word about the town's hospitality to the rugged outdoors folk nearing the end of their arduous trek from Springer Mountain, Georgia. The Monson stopover comes just before the AT leg known as the 100-Mile Wilderness, so it's a place to regroup, clean up, and rev up for the grueling, isolated week-plus ahead. It's also growing as an arts colony.

Sangerville, incorporated in 1813, is the birthplace of the infamous Sir Harry Oakes, a colorful adventurer who acquired a fortune in Canadian gold mining. Murdered in bed in his Nassau, Bahamas, mansion in 1943, gazillionaire Oakes was interred in Dover-Foxcroft. His killer was never found. Also born in Sangerville was Sir Hiram Maxim, inventor of the Maxim gun.

SIGHTS

Low's Covered Bridge

In 1987, the raging Piscataquis River, swollen by spring rains, wiped out 130-foot-long **Low's Covered Bridge,** near Sangerville. Named after settler Robert Low, the original bridge was built in 1830 and replaced in 1843 and 1857. The current incarnation, a well-made replica, reopened in 1990 at a cost of $650,000. It's one of only nine covered bridges in Maine. Close to Route 16/6/15, the bridge is 3.7 miles east of Guilford and 4.5 miles west of Dover-Foxcroft.

Katahdin Iron Works

Only a lonely stone blast furnace and a charcoal kiln remain at **Katahdin Iron Works,** the site of a once-thriving 19th-century community where iron mining produced 2,000 tons of ore a year and steam trains brought tourists to the three-story Silver Lake House to "take the waters" at Katahdin Mineral Springs. Today most visitors drive down the unpaved 6.5 miles from Route 11 and stop just across the road, at the North Maine Woods **KI Checkpoint,** for hiking in Gulf Hagas Reserve. Entrance to the KI site (as it's known locally) is free, but you'll have to pay a fee to proceed on the road.

Lake Onawa

Four-mile-long **Lake Onawa** is the mountain-ringed setting for the charming hamlet of Onawa, once linked to civilization only by train. Then came the road, and passenger service ceased, leaving Onawa as a summer colony with a year-round population of three. A prime attraction is an incredible 126-foot-high wooden railroad trestle (featured in one of Stephen King's films). During World War II, the trestle was protected by African American security guards, among them Edward Brooke, the late U.S. senator from Massachusetts. The 1,400-foot-long trestle, officially the Ship Pond Stream Viaduct, soars over Ship Pond Stream at the southern end of the lake, about 0.5 mile beyond the cluster of cottages. The best way to view it is by boat; put in at the public landing at the end of Boat Landing Road. To reach Onawa, from Route 6/16/15 at the northern edge of Monson, take the Elliotsville Road northeast; turn right at the Big Wilson Stream bridge, and then take the next left onto Onawa Road. Continue about three miles to the settlement.

Harrigan Learning Center and Museum

Worldly travelers and backpackers Tom and Nancy Harrigan established the **Harrigan Learning Center and Museum** (24 Gerrish Rd., Milo, 207/279-1796, www.trcmaine.org/

harrigan, 10am-4pm Wed., Sat., and Sun., $9 adults, $5 ages 4-18) adjacent to the Three Rivers Kiwanis-Milo-Brownville building in order to share their impressive collection of fossils, minerals, and Native American artifacts from around the globe. Exhibits focus on paleontology, archaeology, and gems and minerals, and there's a discovery room showcasing fluorescent minerals under ultraviolet light. It's a superlative collection that's well displayed. Even better, Tom is often there to answer questions or guide you through it all.

Monson

Downtown Monson, which hugs the shore of Hebron Lake, is worth a poke around, not only for the local historical society museum, but also for the increasing number of shops and galleries. If you have a canoe or kayaks, you can put in at the public landing on Hebron Street.

ENTERTAINMENT

Live music, community theater, movies, and other entertainment are regularly scheduled at the **Center Theatre for the Performing Arts** (20 E. Main St., Dover-Foxcroft, 207/564-8943, www.centertheatre.org), sited in a nicely renovated 300-seat movie theater. Ask about the local doctor who was married on stage during a presentation by the Maine Hysterical Society, complete with reception line during intermission.

The one-day **Maine Whoopie Pie Festival** (www.mainewhoopiepiefestival.com) is held the fourth Saturday in June in Dover-Foxcroft, with tastings, tours, crafts, and entertainment.

The **Piscataquis Valley Fair** (www.piscataquisvalleyfair.com) takes place the fourth weekend in August. A family-oriented traditional county fair, it features agricultural exhibits, a pig scramble, a homemade ice cream parlor, fireworks, and a carnival.

Contra and Finn dances often take place on Saturday nights at the **Finnish Farmers Club.** Look for the small sign hanging in front of the white frame building two miles south of Monson village on the west side of Route 6/15. Expect dancing, perhaps traditional costumes, coffee, and pulla bread along with Finnish folk music.

RECREATION

Peaks-Kenny State Park

Get organized to arrive at **Peaks-Kenny State Park** (Sebec Lake Rd., Dover-Foxcroft, 207/564-2003, www.parksandlands.com, $5-7 adults, $2 seniors, $1 ages 5-11, free under age 5) well before 11am on weekends in June-August—after that, you may be turned away or have to wait. This particularly scenic park wrapping around South Cove on 14-mile-long Sebec Lake has 50 picnic sites, a playground, a lifeguard-staffed sandy beach, 10 miles of hiking trails, and 56 campsites. Canoe and kayak rentals are $3/hour.

Hiking

MONSON APPALACHIAN TRAIL VISITOR CENTER

Stop by the **AT Visitor Center** (6 Tenny Hill Rd., Monson, 207/573-016), located in the Monson Historical Society Building, for hiker info, trail maps, and trail conditions as well as for regional activities, such as wildlife viewing, day hikes, white-water rafting, and ATV trails. Ask about guided walks and hikes as well as presentations.

For details on these or other hikes, consult *North Woods Walks* by Christopher Keene (a guide for Northwoods Outfitters) or AMC's *Maine Mountain Guide,* available in local bookstores.

BORESTONE MOUNTAIN SANCTUARY

Owned and maintained by the Maine Audubon Society (www.maineaudubon.org), **Borestone Mountain Sanctuary** (Elliotsville Rd., Elliotsville Plantation, 207/631-4050, 8am-sunset daily May-Oct., $5 adults, $3 ages 6-18 and over age 60) is a 1,600-acre preserve that provides a wonderful hiking experience. The two-mile (each way) moderately difficult trail to the rocky

Conserving for the Future

Anyone who has visited Maine's North Woods knows that this landscape of woods, water, and mountains is a treasure. While the state and federal government had protected bits and pieces, most notably Baxter State Park, Nahmakanta, and Gulf Hagas, it was a hopscotch pattern that left the connecting areas, including those sheltering the famed 100-Mile Wilderness section of the Appalachian Trail, vulnerable.

Enter the **Appalachian Mountain Club (AMC),** which in 2003 launched the Maine Woods Initiative, a strategy for land conservation that combines outdoor recreation, resource protection, sustainable forestry, and community partnerships in the 100-Mile Wilderness region. Through its work on the initiative, AMC is protecting land from development and maintaining public access for recreation in perpetuity.

In 2003, the AMC acquired the Katahdin Iron Works tract, a spectacular 37,000-acre parcel of wilderness that includes the headwaters of the West Branch of the Pleasant River and abuts federally protected Gulf Hagas. That wasn't enough. In 2009, the AMC acquired the Roach Ponds Tract, which abuts not only the Katahdin Iron Works Tract but also the state's Nahmakanta Public Reserved Land. The purchase of the 29,500-acre Roach Ponds tract was a historic transaction that marked the creation of a 63-mile-long corridor of conservation land stretching from the AMC's Katahdin Iron Works property near Greenville north to Baxter State Park. The holdings comprise nearly 650,000 acres of conservation land that's a playground for outdoor enthusiasts.

Within the AMC's 66,500-acre Maine Woods Property alone are more than two dozen ponds, more than 80 miles of managed recreational trails and ski routes, more than 150 miles of dirt roads, and a 21,000-acre ecological reserve to protect the West Branch watershed as well as a few other special zones to protect other vital ecological resources. The remaining acreage is a working forest, maintained with sustainable techniques, and open to hunters, anglers, paddlers, mountain bikers, wildlife-watchers, skiers, snowshoers, and campers.

Even better, it's possible to immerse oneself in this chunk of heaven without sacrificing all creature comforts. Within the Maine Woods Property are three AMC-managed sporting camps: Medawisla Wilderness Lodge and Cabins, Little Lyford Lodge and Cabins, and Gorman Chairback Lodge and Cabins; the privately owned West Branch Pond Camps; and a mix of drive-in, hike-in, and paddle-in campsites.

open summit delivers ample rewards at the top: full-circle views that include Lake Onawa below and the mountains of the 100-Mile Wilderness. Foliage season is especially dramatic here. Allow 4-5 hours for the four-mile round-trip, including a halfway-up stop at the Sunrise Pond Visitor Center, with displays on local flora and fauna; don't miss it. Pets are not allowed. From Route 6/16/15 at the northern edge of Monson, take the partly unpaved Elliotsville Road northeast 8.5 miles to the trailhead.

APPALACHIAN TRAIL

Sample the country's eastern footpath from the trailhead north of Monson on Route 6/15, just south of Spectacle Ponds. Unless you're a serious hiker, you won't want to venture too far, as this is one of the most difficult sections of the trail.

★ GULF HAGAS RESERVE

Hiking in and around **Gulf Hagas Reserve,** a spectacular 400-foot-high, 3.5-mile-long wooded and rocky gorge along the West Branch of the Pleasant River, requires registering first at the **KI Checkpoint** (207/965-8135, www.northmainewoods.org) operated by North Maine Woods, the forest recreation-management association. (KI is short for Katahdin Iron Works.) The checkpoint is one of the entrances into the **KI Jo-Mary Multiple Use Forest,** a 175,000-acre working forest. (Jo-Mary is the name of a legendary Native American chief.) The checkpoint is open 6am-9pm (sometimes later on midsummer weekends) from early May to Columbus Day. The staffers have maps of the reserve ($2) and KI Jo-Mary ($3); do not hike Gulf Hagas without the map. Access is $15 for nonresidents, $10 for Maine residents. No bicycles, motorcycles, or ATVs can go beyond this point. Camping at one of the 60 scenic primitive sites in this area costs an extra $12 nonresident/$10 resident pp per night. It's wise to call the checkpoint ahead of time to reserve one of the sites, which have outhouses, picnic tables, and fire rings. The campground has a carry-in, carry-out policy. There's also a commercial campground here.

It's about seven miles from the checkpoint to one of the two parking areas; remember that logging trucks have the right of way on this road. En route from your vehicle toward the gulf, you'll go through the **Hermitage,** a 35-acre preserve of old-growth pines. Gulf Hagas Reserve, a National Natural Landmark that's part of the Appalachian Trail corridor, is no cakewalk. Almost weekly, rangers have to rescue injured or lost hikers who underestimate the terrain. Ledges are narrow, with 100-foot drop-offs, and rain can make them perilous. Leave rambunctious children at home; the section beyond **Screw Auger Falls** is particularly dangerous for kids under age 12. Wear waterproof hiking boots—you have to cross a stream to gain access to the reserve.

Caveats aside, the hike is fantastic—especially mid-September-early October, when the leaves are gorgeous and the bugs have retreated. Carry a compass and a flashlight and allow 6-8 hours for the 8.3-mile canyon circuit (although there are shortcuts if you tucker out before the end). Most hikers do the loop clockwise. North Maine Woods trails are blue-blazed; a spur of the Appalachian Trail is white-blazed. The trails are open mid-May-late October, but atypical weather can affect the schedule. The checkpoint is 11.5 miles northwest of Brownville Junction (6.5 miles northwest of Rte. 11).

The Appalachian Mountain Club's Little Lyford Camps is a convenient base for hiking Gulf Hagas.

Multiuse Trails

From its Newport base on the north side of Route 7 to its end near Fairview Street in Dover-Foxcroft, the 27-mile **Newport/Dover-Foxcroft Rail Trail** passes through towns and rural countryside, including farms, woods, and wetlands, and edges Sebasticook and Corundel Lakes, the east branch of the Sebasticook River, and the Piscataquis River.

Peaks-Kenny State Park on Sebec Lake

The 10-mile **Guilford Memorial River Walk** edges the Piscataquis River from Guilford to Abbot. The trailheads are off Route 15 in Guilford, east of the athletic fields, and at the Sangerville Station bridge on Route 23.

Water Sports

Lakes and rivers color much of the map blue in this region. If you have your own boat, quiet-water paddling options include the Sebec River above Milo, the Piscataquis River above the dam in Guilford, Lake Hebron in Monson, and Branns Mill Pond in Dover-Foxcroft.

Merrill's Marina (8 Cotton Brook Rd., Dover-Foxcroft, 207/564-2617, www.boat-sebeclake.com) rents Old Town canoes and kayaks for $35/day or $275/week with a $125 security deposit.

FOOD

Dover-Foxcroft

For a light bite, duck into **Center Coffee House** (22 E. Main St., 207/802-8052, www.centercoffeehouse.com, from 6:30am Mon.-Fri., from 8am Sat., from 9am Sun.), a popular spot for coffee. It also offers a handful of breakfast and lunch dishes ($3-6).

Spruce Mill Farm & Kitchen (920 W. Main St., 207/564-0300, 9am-5:30pm Wed.-Fri., 8am-3pm Sat., $5-12) uses fresh, organically grown veggies and other local ingredients in its scratch-made breads, soups, sandwiches, and pastries.

Good home cooking with a few surprises packs the **Nor'easter Restaurant** (44 North St., 207/564-2122, 11am-8pm Tues.-Sun., $6-18), a congenial place with country-style decor and seating both at the counter and tables.

★ **Stutzman's** (891 Doughty Hill Rd., 207/564-8596, 11am-2pm Wed.-Thurs., 11am-7pm Fri.-Sat., 10am-1pm Sun.), on the back road between Sangerville and Dover-Foxcroft, began life as a farm market but has grown to include a justly popular café. Go for the wood-fired pizzas, fresh salads and sandwiches, and soups and specials ($8-15). The pizza buffet, usually available Friday-Saturday and sometimes midweek, includes soups, salad, and dessert ($10); the Sunday brunch ($12) features live music.

Butterfield's Ice Cream (946 W. Main St., 207/564-2513) has been dishing out homemade premium ice cream since 1950.

Monson

The century-old **Monson General Store** (12 Greenville Rd., 207/997-3800, 6:30am-7pm daily, $4-12) underwent a complete renovation, reopening in 2017. It offers fresh local foods, baked goods, soups, sandwiches, and salads.

Spring Creek Bar-B-Q (26 Greenville Rd./Rte. 15, 207/997-7025, www.springcreekbar-b-qmaine.com, 11am-7pm Thurs., 11am-8pm Fri.-Sat., 11am-5pm Sun., $5-12) has been dishing out rave-worthy 'cue for nearly two decades. Prices and portions are geared to Appalachian Trail hikers, so you won't go hungry or poor. About the hours: It stays open until the food's gone and opens other days "on a whim."

Reasonably priced pub fare is served at the **Lakeshore House** (9 Tenney Hill Rd./Rte. 5/15, 207/997-7069, www.thelakeshorehouse.com, from 11:30am Tues.-Sun., $10-21), a casual spot overlooking Lake Hebron with seating indoors and out. Thursday night is open mic 6pm-9pm, and on summer Sundays there's live music 3pm-6pm.

Here's a surprise: Chef Marilou Ranta's multi-course fixed-price menus draw on her Philippine heritage at the **Quarry** (15 Tenney Hill Rd., Monson, 207/997-3486, 6pm-10pm Thurs.-Mon.), a lakeside fine-dining venue with gorgeous sunset views that pair well with the presentation and service. The five-course dinner menu changes regularly and costs around $65. Reservations are required.

Milo

Awesome doughnuts, bismarcks, cinnamon buns, cream horns, and other drool-worthy

1: Stutzman's 2: Monson General Store 3: Low's Covered Bridge

1

MONSON GENERAL STORE

2

3

pastries are reason enough to stop at **Elaine's Cafe & Bakery** (38 Main St./Rte. 11, 207/943-2705, www.elainesbakerycafe.com, 6am-5pm Tues.-Sun.), a cheerful riverside spot on the north side of the bridge. In addition, inexpensive breakfasts are served until 11:30am daily.

ACCOMMODATIONS

Bed-and-Breakfasts

Just beyond the Dover-Foxcroft area, but close enough, the ★ **Brewster Inn** (37 Zion's Hill Rd., Dexter, 207/924-3130, www.brewsterinn.com, $89-159) is an attractive 19-room mansion listed in the National Register of Historic Places. Built for Maine governor and U.S. Senator Ralph Brewster, it was remodeled in 1934 by John Calvin Stevens. The knotty-pine Game Room was the governor's private hideout, and you can probably guess who once slept in the Truman Room. Breakfast is a generous buffet with one hot dish. Innkeepers Mark and Tina Stephens have been remodeling the rooms and restoring the lovely gardens to their mid-20th-century splendor.

The **Mill Inn** (5 E. Main St., Dover-Foxcroft, 207/805-8839, http://dfmill.com, $125-145), located in a masterfully renovated and repurposed downtown mill on the Piscataquis River, opened in 2015 with six handsome, industrial-chic guest rooms.

Neither hostel nor B&B, the **Lakeshore House** (9 Tenney Hill Rd./Rte. 5/15, Monson, 207/997-7069, www.thelakeshorehouse.com) is a continually evolving lakeside business housing hiker-oriented guest rooms, a pub, and canoe and kayak rentals on Lake Hebron. All guests share three baths, a living room, and a kitchenette. A laundry is available, $5 per wash/dry including soap. A bunkroom bed is $25. A semi-private double is $79. A private single room is $50.

Hostels

Headquarters for Appalachian Trail through-hikers, and a home-away-from-home since 1977, is the legendary **Shaw's Boarding Home** (Pleasant St., Monson, 207/997-3597, www.shawshikerhostel.com). To weary hikers, this welcoming no-frills operation feels like the Hyatt Regency. Short-haul hikers are also welcome, as are snowmobilers in winter; couch potatoes will feel totally out of place. The home can accommodate nearly three dozen guests in varied arrangements—private rooms in the main house ($50 s, $60 d), bunkhouse beds ($25 pp), and tent sites ($12). A lumberjack-quality breakfast is $9, and dinner is $12-15. For small fees, shuttle and mail-drop service and laundry facilities are available; parking for short-haulers is $1/day.

Camping

Within the boundaries of the KI Jo-Mary Multiple Use Forest is a single commercial campground, **Jo-Mary Lake Campground** (Upper Jo-Mary Lake, Millinocket, 207/723-8117, www.jmlcampground.com, mid-May-late Sept.), on the southern shore of five-mile-long Upper Jo-Mary Lake. Despite being remote, the campground has 70 sites, flush toilets, hot showers, laundry facilities, a snack bar, plenty of play space for kids, and a sandy beach. Sites are $24/night plus a $10/day gate fee. From Brownville Junction, take Route 11 northwest about 15 miles, turn left onto an unpaved road, stop at the Jo-Mary Checkpoint, and then continue six miles northwest to the campground.

North Maine Woods (92 Main St., Ashland, 207/435-6213, www.northmainewoods.org) manages campsites within KI Jo-Mary. These include authorized campsites with steel fire rings, cedar picnic tables, and privies, and primitive, designated fire permit sites, which require a fire permit. Campsites are $12/night plus user fees: $10/day for Maine residents, $15/day for nonresidents; those younger than age 18 or older than 70 have free day use. No credit cards.

Peaks-Kenny State Park (Sebec Lake Rd., Dover-Foxcroft, 207/564-2003) has 56 campsites. On weekends July-August, reservations are essential (call 207/624-9950 from outside Maine, 800/332-1501 in Maine, or visit www.campwithme.com). Nonresident camping fees are $40/site/night, Maine residents

$30/site/night, plus the reservation fee of $5/site/night; no hookups. Leashed pets are allowed.

INFORMATION

Local information is available from the **Southern Piscataquis County Chamber of Commerce** (100 South St./Rte. 7, Dover-Foxcroft, 207/564-7533, www.spccc.org). For information about Gulf Hagas Reserve and the KI Jo-Mary Multiple Use Forest, contact **North Maine Woods** (207/435-6213, www.northmainewoods.org).

GETTING THERE

Dover-Foxcroft is about 34 miles or 45 minutes from Greenville via Route 6/15. It's about 53 miles or just over an hour from Millinocket via Route 11. It's about 38 miles or 50 minutes to Bangor via Route 15.

Bangor Area

Maine's Queen City is best identified by a trio of kings, but its appeal extends to those on a pauper's budget. Home to king of horror Stephen King, Bangor was folksinger Roger Miller's destination in "King of the Road" and is home to a gigantic statue of king of the woods Paul Bunyan. One would think with so many kingly claims, **Bangor** (BANG-gore) would be nicknamed the King City, but for reasons long forgotten, it's been promoted as the Queen City since the late 19th century.

Bangor incorporated in 1791, but when explorer Samuel de Champlain landed here in 1604 (an event commemorated by a plaque downtown, next to Kenduskeag Stream), the Queen City bore the Native American name of Kenduskeag, meaning "eel-catching place." Now you can stroll alongside Kenduskeag Stream, duck into shops and an increasing number of restaurants, and end the evening with music, a show, or perhaps trying your luck at the state's first slots.

Lumber capital of the world in the 19th century, Bangor highlights fine specimens of Victorian, Italianate, Queen Anne, and Greek Revival architecture—and who knows, you might see legendary author Stephen King in your travels. Part of what King enjoys about Bangor is that locals are used to him and accord him "normal person" treatment.

Orono (pop. 10,362), home of the University of Maine's flagship campus, is part college town, part generic Maine village, and a fine example of the tail wagging the dog. More than 11,000 university students converge on this Bangor suburb every year, fairly overwhelming the year-round population.

Old Town (pop. 7,840) is perhaps best known for the world's oldest continuously operating canoe manufacturer, **Old Town Canoe Company** (125 Gilman Falls Rd./Rte. 43, Old Town, 207/827-1530, http://oldtowncanoefactoryoutlet.com), incorporated in 1904 and turning out as many as 400 boats a month within two years. In 1915, its list of dealers included Harrod's in London and the Hudson's Bay Company in far northern Canada, and Old Town had supplied canoes to expeditions in Egypt and the Arctic.

Under separate tribal administration and linked to Old Town by a bridge built in 1951, **Indian Island Reservation** is home to about 400 Penobscot Indians.

SIGHTS

The Standpipe

A distinctive west-side landmark is the **Thomas Hill Standpipe.** The 1.75-million-gallon riveted-steel water tower and observatory, built in 1897, is a National Historic and American Water Landmark. Some say it's the Queen City's crown, and a case can be made that it resembles one when viewed from afar. The Standpipe is open four days each year for tours, usually once per season. At these times visitors can climb the interior staircase

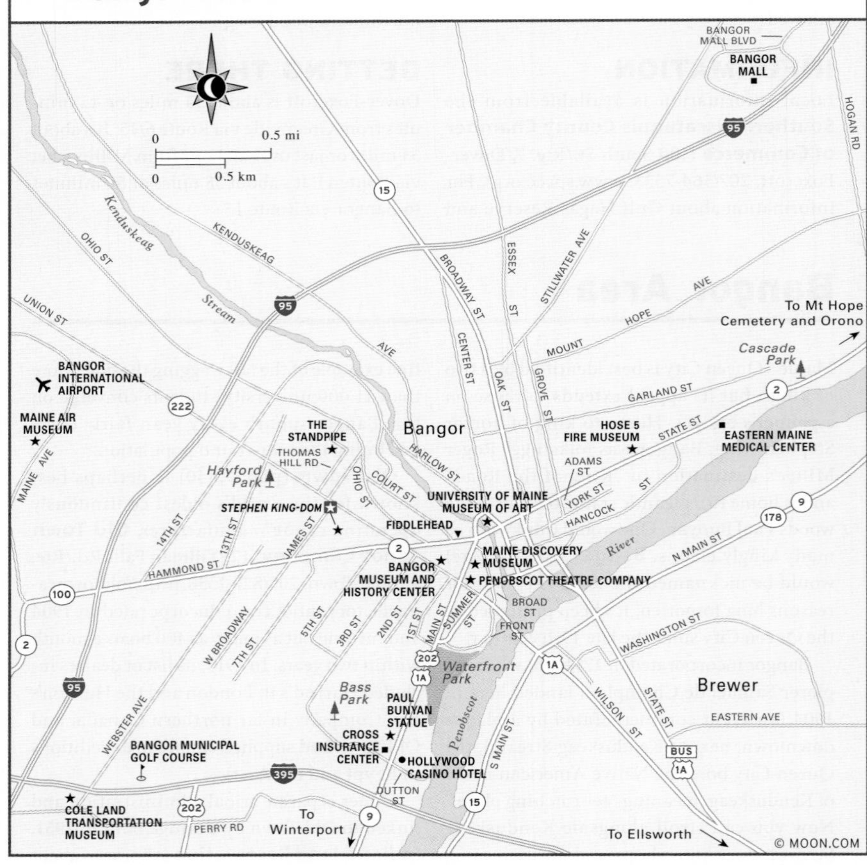

circling to the top and access the great view from the observation platform. For tour information, call the **Bangor Water District** (207/947-4516, www.bangorwater.org).

Paul Bunyan Statue

Bangor's Victorian-era fortunes were built on the millions of trees felled in the North Woods and driven down the Penobscot River to the city's busy port. Super-logger Paul Bunyan is a native son, born in Bangor on February 12, 1834—stop into the city clerk's office to see his birth certificate. This explains the 31-foot-tall statue of him in front of the Cross Center. Weighing 3,200 pounds, the colorful statue was erected in 1959 during the city's 125th anniversary. Inside the base is a time capsule due to be opened in 2084. In Bunyan's hand is a peavey, a genuine Maine-made tool: After observing the difficulties river drivers were having shepherding logs down the Penobscot River with the traditional cant dog, local blacksmith Joseph Peavey invented the tool that bears his name.

★ Stephen King-dom

Maine native and naturalized hometown boy, horror honcho Stephen King is anything but a myth. Born in Portland, he has lived in Bangor since 1980, and you may spot him around town (especially at baseball and basketball games). His turreted mansion on West Broadway looks like a set from one of the movies based on his novels and stories—complete with a wrought-iron front gate and fence festooned with iron bats and cobwebs. Heed the No Trespassing sign; the best-selling author has had his share of odd encounters with off-the-wall devotees.

For an immersion into Stephen King-dom, book a tour with Stuart Tinker's **SK Tours** (25 Thomas Hill Rd., 207/947-7193, www.sk-tours.com). Tinker, a King expert, has been featured on TV and quoted in magazines. A three-hour tour ($45 pp ages 13 and older) visits about 30 sites related to the author, from places where he's lived to locations featured in his books as well as filming locations. Pets are welcome with advance notice.

Bangor Museum and History Center

Built by a wealthy attorney in 1836 and listed in the National Register of Historic Places, the handsome brick Thomas A. Hill House, home of the **Bangor Museum and History Center** (159 Union St., Bangor, 207/942-1900, www.bangorhistoricalsociety.org, 10am-4pm Mon.-Fri., noon-4pm Sat., donation), on the corner of High Street, has been restored to Victorian elegance, with period furnishings, Maine paintings, and special exhibits.

The center offers a good variety of 90-minute guided walking tours ($10 pp) focused on Bangor's history, with options including Historic Homes, the Great Fire of 1911, and the Devil's Half Acre. If you prefer to tour on your own, download an overview of historical landmarks, architectural highlights, and National Register properties from the center's website.

Mount Hope Cemetery

In a state where burial grounds often command views to die for, the standout is **Mount Hope Cemetery** (207/945-6589, www.mthopebgr.com, 7:30am-7:30pm daily Apr.-Oct., 7:30am-4pm daily Nov.-Mar.), established in 1834, consecrated in 1836, and easily the state's loveliest. Here you can hobnob with some of Maine's dearly departed. Among the sights are unusual grave markers, including one elevated sarcophagus, and the

The best way to see Stephen King's Bangor is on a specialty tour.

graves of Hannibal Hamlin, Abe Lincoln's vice president during the Civil War, and gangster Al Brady, listed as public enemy number one and killed in a firestorm of bullets in downtown Bangor in 1937. Also of note is the 20-foot-tall Soldier's Monument, erected in 1864 and among the oldest Civil War monuments in the country. Inspired by the design of Mount Auburn Cemetery in Cambridge, Massachusetts, 264-acre Mount Hope is more park than cemetery—with gardens, ponds, bridges, paved paths, lots of greenery, a few picnic tables, and wandering deer. The entrance to the green-fenced cemetery is at 1048 State Street (Rte. 2), about 0.25 mile east of Hogan Road. The **Bangor Museum and History Society** (207/942-1900, www.bangorhistoricalsociety.org, $10) offers tours; call or check its website for the schedule.

University of Maine Museum of Art

Bangor scored a coup when it lured the **University of Maine Museum of Art** (UMMA, Norumbega Hall, 40 Harlow St., Bangor, 207/561-3350, www.umma.umaine.edu, 10am-5pm Tues.-Sat., free) downtown. The pocket-size museum's primary strengths are photography and contemporary works on paper, and its focus is on modern and contemporary art. Among the significant items in the museum's collection of more than 3,800 original works are pieces by John Marin, Roy Lichtenstein, Willem de Kooning, and Alex Katz. Exhibits are displayed in one permanent and three changing galleries. Entrance is via a bridge from the riverside park between Hammond and Central Streets downtown.

Kenduskeag Stream Trail

Pick up a copy of the Kenduskeag Stream map at the visitors bureau and follow it to 13 marked sites, including where Portuguese navigator Esteban Gómez landed in 1525, followed by French geographer Samuel de Champlain in 1604. Also on the trail is Lovers Leap, a 150-foot-tall cliff where a Native American couple plunged to their deaths after being denied permission to marry.

Maine Discovery Museum

Here's a major kid magnet with a wide range of interactive exhibits that encourage creative play. The **Maine Discovery Museum** (74 Main St., Bangor, 207/262-7200, www.mainediscoverymuseum.org, 10am-5pm Mon.-Sat., 11am-4pm Sun., $7.50) occupies more than 22,000 square feet on three floors. Seven interactive permanent exhibit areas feature nature, geography, art, science, anatomy, Maine children's literature, and music.

Air, Fire, and Transportation Museums

On the grounds of Bangor International Airport, the **Maine Air Museum** (98 Maine Ave., Bangor, 207/941-6757, www.maineairmuseum.com, 10am-4pm Sat., noon-4pm Sun. early June-early Sept., $6 adults, $1 kids, $10 family) is a fledgling museum operated by the Maine Aviation Historical Society and dedicated to the history of Maine aviation.

Kids get a kick out of the firefighting artifacts and fire trucks at the **Hose 5 Fire Museum** (247 State St., Bangor, 207/945-3229, 9am-noon Sat. early May-late Oct., free), in an 1897 fire station.

Children love the **Cole Land Transportation Museum** (405 Perry Rd., Bangor, 207/990-3600, www.colemuseum.org, 9am-5pm daily May-mid-Nov., $7 adults, $5 seniors, free under age 19), a sprawling facility founded by Bangor trucking magnate Galen Cole. More than 200 19th- and 20th-century vehicles—just about anything that has ever rolled across Maine's landscape—fill the museum. Besides vintage cars, there are fire engines, tractors, logging vehicles, baby carriages, even a replica railroad station. And this being Maine, the museum believes it owns the country's largest collection of snow-removal equipment.

Outside are picnic tables and a covered bridge to walk over and under. The museum is near the junction of I-95 and I-395.

University of Maine

Orono's major sights are on the 660-acre campus of the **University of Maine** (UMO, www.umaine.edu), a venerable institution founded in 1868 as the State College of Agriculture and Mechanical Arts. It received its current designation in 1897 and now awards bachelor's, master's, and doctoral degrees. The oldest building on campus is North Hall, an updated version of the original Frost family farmhouse.

Information about the campus, including guided tours, is available from the **visitors center** (Buchanan Alumni House, 160 College Ave., University of Maine, Orono, 207/581-3740, 10am-3pm Mon.-Fri. and noon-3pm Sat. during the academic year). Guided campus tours are offered daily.

One of the newest buildings, built in 1986 and renovated in 2009, is the **Collins Center for the Arts,** scene of year-round activity. Located on the second floor is the expanded **Hudson Museum** (207/581-1901, 9am-4pm Mon.-Fri., 11am-4pm Sat. and before selected performances, free), spotlighting traditional and contemporary world cultures in three contiguous galleries. The World Cultures Gallery comprises eight display areas, organized by theme, including one devoted to the museum's superlative Palmer collection of pre-Columbian artifacts. The Maine Indian Gallery highlights the museum's impressive Maliseet, Micmac, Passamaquoddy, and Penobscot holdings. Temporary exhibitions fill the Merritt Gallery.

The Maine sky takes center stage at the **Emera Astronomy Center and M. F. Jordan Planetarium** (167 Rangeley Rd., 207/581-1341, http://astro.umaine.edu). Multimedia presentations help explain the workings of our universe and bring astronomy to life. Comet collisions and rocketing asteroids keep the kids transfixed. Program scheduling varies; call ahead to reserve space in the 45-seat auditorium. Planetarium programs are $6 adults, $4 kids under age 12.

At the eastern edge of the campus, the seven-acre **Lyle E. Littlefield Ornamental Trial Garden** (Rangeley Rd., 207/594-2948) contains more than 2,500 plant species, many being tested for winter durability. The best time to come is early June, when crabapples and lilacs put on their perennial show. The garden is open daily; bring a picnic. Horticulture fans will also enjoy the 10-acre riverside **Fay Hyland Arboretum,** on the western edge of campus.

In the last agricultural building on campus (the barn predates UMO), the **Page Farm and Home Museum** (207/581-4100, 9am-4pm Tues.-Sat.) houses a collection of farm implements and home items; on-site are a one-room schoolhouse, a blacksmith's shop, heritage gardens, and a general store stocked with goods made by local artisans.

Parking is a major sticking point at UMO, so you'll need a parking permit for most areas except the Maine Center for the Arts and the sports complex when events are taking place. For other times and lots, you can obtain a free one-day permit either from campus security or the parking office. For more information call 207/581-4047.

Penobscot Nation Museum

Don't be put off by the humble exterior of Indian Island's **Penobscot Nation Museum** (12 Down St., Indian Island, 207/827-4153, www.penobscotnation.org, free, donation appreciated); inside it's jam-packed with Native American historical artifacts and artwork, including exhibits of baskets, beadwork, dress, antique tools, and birchbark canoes. Jewelry, dream catchers, and other handcrafted items are for sale in the small store. Call for current hours.

In the island's Protestant cemetery is the grave of **Louis Sockalexis,** the best Native American baseball player at the turn of the 20th century. Allegedly, his acceptance onto Cleveland, Ohio's baseball team spurred management to dub the team the Indians—a name that has stuck.

After visiting the museum, if you continue to the stop sign and bear right, you'll come to a riverside park with interpretive signage and trails accented with sculptures. It's a fine place for a picnic lunch.

Leonard's Mills

Officially known as the **Maine Forest and Logging Museum** (262 Government Rd., Bradley, 207/974-6278, www.leonardsmills.com, $3 donation), **Leonard's Mills** re-creates a 1790s logging village, with a sawmill, a blacksmith shop, a covered bridge, a log cabin, and other buildings. The site is accessible roughly sunrise-sunset year-round, but the best times to visit are during the museum's special-events days (the schedule varies) when dozens of museum volunteers don period dress and bring the village to life. Demonstrations, beanhole bean suppers, hayrides, antique games, and kids' activities are all part of the mix. The season's biggest event is **Living History Days,** a two-day festival held the first weekend in October ($10 adults, $5 children). An ongoing museum project is the restoration to working condition of one of the old Lombard Haulers, an important part of the North Woods story. The museum is on Penobscot Experimental Forest Road in Bradley, 1.3 miles southeast of Route 178. It's directly across the river from Orono, but the only bridges are north (Old Town-Milford) and south (Bangor-Brewer). After visiting, dip into **Spencer's Ice Cream** (77 Main St., Bradley, 207/827-8670), which has been dishing out homemade ice cream since 1930.

ENTERTAINMENT

More than a century ago, when cabin-feverish lumberjacks roared into Bangor for R&R, they were apt to patronize Fan Jones's "establishment" on Harlow Street. Adult entertainment is still available in the city, but so is higher-brow stuff. That said, nights in Bangor are pretty quiet for a city.

Founded in 1896, Maine's **Bangor Symphony Orchestra** (207/942-5555 or 800/639-3221, www.bangorsymphony.com) has an enviable reputation as one of the country's oldest and best community orchestras. During the regular season (September-May), monthly concerts are presented weekends at the Maine Center for the Arts in Orono. The orchestra occasionally performs in summer too.

After visiting the Penobscot Nation Museum on Indian Island, walk the island's interpretative trails.

Bangor's professional theater company, **Penobscot Theatre** (131 Main St., Bangor, 207/942-3333, www.penobscottheatre.org) performs classic and contemporary comedies and dramas September-early June in the 1920 Bangor Opera House.

UMO's **Collins Center for the Arts** (207/581-1755, www.collinscenterforthearts.com) is the year-round site of concerts, dramas, and other events with big-name performers. See what's on the schedule at the **Gracie Theatre** (1 College Circle, Husson College, Bangor, 207/941-7888, www.gracietheatre.com).

During the summer, **Waterfront Concerts** (www.waterfrontconcerts.com) brings big-name entertainment to the open-air Darling's Waterfront Pavilion on the riverfront; most shows require tickets, but some are free. In the winter, the venue shifts to the downtown Cross Center.

On most Tuesday evenings late spring-summer, the **Bangor Band** (www.bangorband.org) performs free outdoor concerts; check the website for schedules and locations. Every Thursday evening in June-July, the **Cool Sounds of Summer** free outdoor concerts are held in West Market Square. Bangor Library also sponsors a summer concert series on its lawn.

Festivals and Events

In April (usually the third Saturday), the **Kenduskeag Stream Canoe Race** is an annual 16.5-mile spring-runoff race sponsored by Bangor Parks and Recreation (207/992-4490, www.kenduskeagstreamcanoerace.com). It draws upward of 700 canoes and thousands of spectators and finishes in downtown Bangor. The best location for taking in the action is Six Mile Falls—take Broadway (Rte. 15) about six miles northwest of downtown.

In late July-early August, the **Bangor State Fair,** held in Bass Park, is a huge 10-day affair with agricultural and crafts exhibits, a carnival, fireworks, sinful food, and big-name live music.

In early December, at the Hudson Museum on the Orono campus of the University of Maine, the **Maine Indian Basketmakers Sale and Demonstration** includes Maine Indian baskets, carvings, jewelry, and traditional arts. Demonstrations, drumming, and singing are all on the agenda.

SHOPPING

In Bangor, browse, eat, sip, and buy at the **Antique Marketplace and Café** (65 Maine St., Bangor, 207/941-2111 or 877/941-2111, www.antiquemarketplacecafe.com). Filling two floors are a wide range of antiques, along with used books and a café (9am-5pm Mon.-Sat., noon-5pm Sun.). The **Rock & Art Shop** (36 Central St., Bangor, 207/947-2205) blends nature, art, and yes, rocks into an unusual shopping experience.

The world's oldest continuously operating canoe manufacturer, **Old Town Canoe Company** (125 Gilman Falls Rd./Rte. 43, Old Town, 207/827-1530, http://oldtowncanoefactoryoutlet.com), incorporated in 1904 and was turning out as many as 400 boats a month within two years. In 1915, its list of dealers included Harrod's in London and the Hudson's Bay Company in far northern Canada, and Old Town had supplied canoes to expeditions in Egypt and the Arctic. Quality is high at Old Town, so its boats are pricey, but you can visit the **Old Town Canoe Factory Outlet Store** and look over the supply of "factory-blemished" canoe and kayak models. You may end up with a real bargain. There's also a full line of paddles, jackets, compasses, and other accessories.

RECREATION

Fields Pond Audubon Center

South of Bangor-Brewer (although it feels as if you're heading east) is the Maine Audubon Society's **Fields Pond Audubon Center** (216 Fields Pond Rd., Holden, 207/989-2591, http://maineaudubon.org). About four miles of footpaths wind through 229 acres of woods, fields, marshes, and lakeshore, all open sunrise-sunset daily year-round. (Wear waterproof shoes or boots; parts of the trail can be wet.) Canoe rentals are available. Pick up brochures and maps at the **L. Robert Rolde Nature Center** (9am-4:30pm Tues.-Fri.). A full schedule of programs occurs here throughout the year, including lectures, nature walks, slide talks, and even a nature-book discussion group. Cost averages $5-10 pp. A nature store carries books, cards, and gifts.

Bangor City Forest and Orono Bog

Here's a double treat that's rich in flora and fauna. About nine miles of trails and more than four miles of roads meander through the 680-acre working **Bangor City Forest** (http://cityforest.bangorinfo.com). Accessible through the Bangor City Forest, the mile-long **Orono Bog Boardwalk** (Tripp Dr., Bangor, 207/581-2850, www.oronobogwalk.org), a National Natural Landmark, is wheelchair-accessible and has a restroom, benches every 200 feet, and interpretative signage. A series of **guided nature walks** (207/866-2578) are offered 9am-10:30am Saturdays early June-late October. Most are free; reservations are recommended. The forest and bog parking area is on Tripp Road, off Stillwater Avenue, about midway between the Bangor Mall and Kelly Road. Leashed pets are allowed in the forest, but not the bog.

FOOD

Quick Bites

A downtown landmark since 1978, **Bagel Central** (33 Central St., Bangor, 207/947-1654, www.bagelcentralbangor.com, 6am-6pm Mon.-Fri., 6am-2pm Sat.-Sun.) is a cheerful spot to meet, greet, and grab some handmade bagels, great deli sandwiches, soups, and more. It's operated under Orthodox rabbinical supervision.

A breakfast and lunch favorite among vegans and vegetarians is **Fork & Spoon** (76 Main St., Bangor, 207/433-7646, www.forkandspoon.me, 7am-6pm Mon.-Fri., 8am-6pm Sat., 10am-3pm Sun.), which offers smoothies, salads, grain bowls, sandwiches on housemade bread, baked goodies, and ice cream.

Harvest Moon Deli (72 Columbia St. and 366 Griffin Rd., Bangor, 258 State St., Brewer, and 18 Mill St., Orono, 207/947-3354, www.harvestmoondeli.com, 10am-4pm daily) is a rock star when it comes to sandwiches, with more than a dozen named for rock icons such as Jimi Hendrix, Jerry Garcia, and Janis Joplin, along with classics, salads, and build-your-own options.

The **Bangor Farmers' Market** sets up in Abbott Square, 11am-2pm Sundays.

Brewpubs and Draft Houses

It's the 14-plus rotating taps of craft brews that bring most folks to **Nocturnem Draft Haus** (56 Main St., Bangor, 207/907-4380, www.nocturnemdrafthaus.com, from 3pm Mon.-Sat.). Pairing well with the world-class brews are cheeses and charcuterie, burgers, sandwiches, and salads served by a knowledgeable staff. There's live music every weekend, and outside seating during the summer.

Across the bridge is **Mason's Brewing Co.** (15 Hardy St., Bangor, 207/989-6300, http://masonsbrewingcompany.com, 10:30am-10:30pm daily, $12-18), a riverside brewpub with seating inside or out.

Family Favorites

Convenient to I-95 Exit 180, **Dysart's** (Coldbrook Rd., Hermon, 207/947-8732, www.dysarts.com, $9-18) is a truckers' destination resort—you can grab some grub, shower, shop, phone home, play video games, fuel up, and even sneak a bit of shut-eye. For real flavor, opt for the truckers' dining room, where the music is country and dozens of bleary-eyed drivers have reached the end of their transcontinental treks. If you're here with a carload, order an 18-Wheeler—18 scoops of ice cream with a collection of toppings. No question, Dysart's is unique, and it's open 24 hours daily year-round.

Beer aficionados love **Geoghan's Pub** (570 Man St., Bangor, 207/945-3730, www.

geaghans.com, $10-12), which serves traditional pub fare with an Irish accent.

A bit more upscale and extremely popular locally, **Blaze** (18 Broad St., Bangor, 207/922-2660, www.blazebangor.com, 11am-9pm Mon.-Sat., 10am-9pm Sun.) is a comfy choice for inspired American fare and brick-oven pizza ($14-30).

Orono's veteran restaurant is **Pat's Pizza** (11 Mill St., Orono, 207/866-2111, http://patspizzaorono.com, 10:30am-midnight daily, $5-12), a statewide family-owned chain founded here in July 1931 by C. D. "Pat" Farnsworth. Subs, calzones, burgers, and "tomato Italian" entrées fill out the menu.

Casual Dining

Seasonally appropriate comfort foods with pizzazz are served at ★ **Fiddlehead** (84 Hammond St., Bangor, 207/942-3336, www.thefiddleheadrestaurant.com, 4pm-9pm Tues.-Fri., 5pm-10pm Sat., 5pm-9pm Sun., $17-34), a downtown restaurant with a cozy neighborhood feel. Owners Laura Albin, who runs the front of the house, and Melissa Chaiken, the chef, are especially accommodating of vegetarians and the glucose intolerant, but the menu, which changes quarterly, ranges from burgers to seafood and draws heavily from the owners' farm.

11 Central (11 Central St., Bangor, 207/922-5115, www.11centralbangor.com, 4pm-9pm daily, $15-30), an American bistro, serves steaks, pastas, seafood, and pizzas in a casual yet stylish downtown spot with a hip vibe and a touch of candlelight elegance.

Every college town needs a **Woodman's** (31 Main St., Orono, 207/866-4040, www.woodmansbarandgrill.com, from 4pm daily, $12-30), a casual restaurant with a menu ranging from burgers to filet mignon. Don't go looking for culinary wonders here, just good food and service.

ACCOMMODATIONS

Bangor has all the major budget and mid-priced chains but few independent B&Bs or inns.

If you're flying in or out of Bangor Airport, you can't beat the convenience of the **Four Points Sheraton Hotel** (307 Godfrey Blvd., Bangor, 207/947-6721 or 800/228-4609, www.fourpointsbangorairport.com, from $155), which is linked to the terminal by a skyway. It has a restaurant, fitness room, and an indoor pool. Pets are permitted for $20/stay.

Hollywood Casino Hotel & Raceway (500 Main St., Bangor, 877/779-7771, www.hollywoodcasinobangor.com, $199-349) is downtown. Facilities include a restaurant, café, lounge, fitness center, and the casino. The best rooms have river views. Airport shuttles are available.

University Inn Academic Suites (5 College Ave., Orono, 207/866-4921 or 800/321-4921, www.universityinnorono.com, $125-160), a renovated and well-maintained motel overlooks the Stillwater River. Rates include a hot breakfast buffet and afternoon libations. Also on-site are an outdoor heated pool with bar service and a family recreation center. There's a dock for boat launching; canoe and kayak rentals are available.

At the three-story **Black Bear Inn** (4 Godfrey Dr., Orono, 207/866-7120 or 800/528-1234, www.blackbearinnorono.com, $140-305), decorated with a black bear theme, the priciest guest rooms are the hot-tub suites. Rates include hot buffet breakfast. Pet-friendly rooms are available.

INFORMATION AND SERVICES

The best source for local information is the **Greater Bangor CVB** (519 Main St., Bangor, 207/947-5205, www.visitbangormaine.com).

Two **Maine Visitor Information Centers** (8am-6pm daily) are just south of Bangor on I-95, one on each side of the highway. The modern gray-clapboard buildings have racks of statewide information, agreeable staffers, clean restrooms, vending machines, and covered picnic tables. Northbound, the center is at mile 175 (207/862-6628); southbound, it's at mile 179 (207/862-6638).

GETTING THERE AND AROUND

Bangor International Airport (BIA, 287 Godfrey Blvd., Bangor, 207/992-4600, www.flybangor.com) is served by major U.S. carriers.

Concord Coachlines (1039 Union St./Rte. 222, Bangor, 207/945-4000 or 800/639-3317, www.concordcoachlines.com) connects Bangor with Augusta, Portland, and points south via direct and coastal routes.

Cyr Bus Line (207/827-2335 or 800/244-2335, www.johntcyrandsons.com) operates one round-trip daily between Aroostook County and Bangor, stopping in Bangor at the Greyhound and Concord bus terminals.

Operating once daily between Bangor and Calais is **West's Coastal Connection** (207/546-2823 or 800/596-2823, www.westbusservice.com), stopping in Bangor at the Concord terminal as well as at the airport.

The **Community Connector** (207/992-4670, www.bangormaine.gov) bus service provides transportation between Bangor, Brewer, Old Town, Veazie, Orono, and Hampden. The fare is $1.50; exact change required.

By car, Bangor is about 72 miles or 1.15 hours from Millinocket via I-95 and about 72 miles or 1.5 hours from Greenville via Route 15. It's about 10 miles or 15 minutes to Orono via I-95, about 130 miles or 2 hours to Portland via I-95, and about 48 miles or 1.25 hours to Bar Harbor via Routes 1A and 3.

Kennebec and Moose River Region

For more than 3,000 years, Maine's Kennebec River and Québec's Chaudière River have been the primary routes for trade and migration between Québec City and the sea. People and goods have moved through history along this corridor: farmers migrating north, hoping to profit from the Québec market; French, Irish, and British families moving south in search of opportunity; escaping slaves following the Underground Railroad north; economic opportunists smuggling alcohol south during Prohibition. The most famous traveler was Benedict Arnold, who followed the route on foot and in bateaux with a band of colonial militia in 1775 in his ill-fated attempt to capture Québec City from the British.

The Kennebec wends its way through Somerset and Kennebec

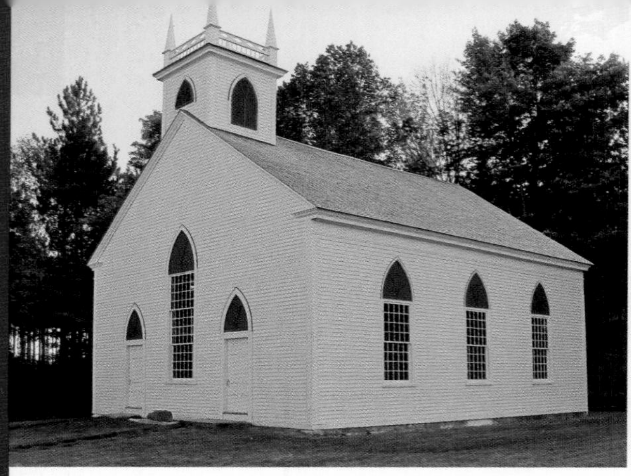

Highlights

Look for ★ to find recommended sights, activities, dining, and lodging.

★ **Maine State Museum:** Spend a few hours immersed in Maine's history and pick up all kinds of "Well, what do you know?" trivia (page 498).

★ **Old Fort Western:** The nation's oldest stockaded fort hosted Benedict Arnold on his march to Québec (page 499).

★ **Pownalborough Court House:** President John Adams once handled a trial in this pre-Revolutionary riverside courthouse (page 499).

★ **Colby College Museum of Art:** American art is on display in this recently expanded campus museum (page 512).

★ **L. C. Bates Museum:** View all sorts of eccentric natural-history relics and then walk the trails in the forest (page 518).

★ **South Solon Meetinghouse:** From the exterior it looks like just another New England meetinghouse—inside, however, wow (page 523)!

★ **Moxie Falls:** It's a short hike to one of New England's tallest waterfalls (page 524).

★ **Old Canada Road National Scenic Byway:** Benedict Arnold marched his troops along a good stretch of this route along the Kennebec River (page 524).

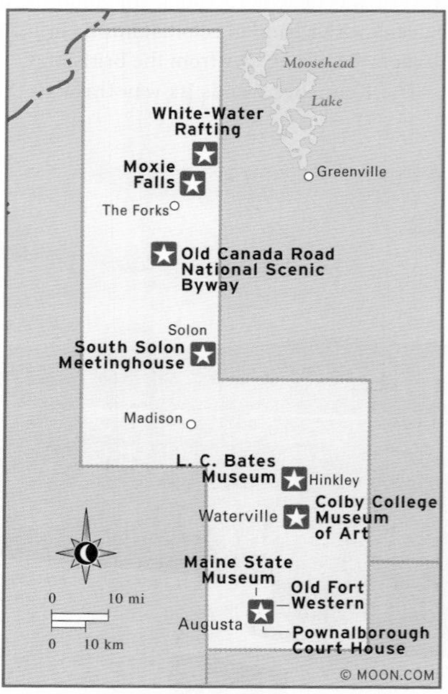

★ **White-Water Rafting:** For thrills, take a wild guided ride down the Kennebec River (page 524).

Counties from Indian Pond through The Forks, Bingham, Skowhegan, Waterville, Augusta, and Richmond, and then on toward the sea at Bath. Augusta, the state's capital, is rich in historical sites that are balanced by the modern shops and restaurants in Hallowell. Waterville is home to Colby College, alone worth a visit for its Museum of Art. The region's lovely lake districts—Belgrade Lakes, China Lakes, and Winthrop Lakes—have been favorite summer destinations for generations upon generations. On the outskirts are rural farming communities such as Unity, home to an Amish colony and an annual organic-foods fair that draws urbanites and back-to-the-landers alike.

In the late 20th century, the textile and paper mills that drove the region's economy began cutting back and closing, and businesses in their communities did the same. Now many of those old mills are being renovated into new housing and business complexes, and ecotourism is booming. From Skowhegan north, the wilderness lakes, rivers, forests, and mountains provide endless opportunities for outdoors-oriented folks. On the culinary front, Skowhegan is now Maine's bread center and Somerset County has the distinction of being the country's top producer of maple syrup.

Traditional outdoor sports such as hunting, fishing, hiking, camping, and boating were joined by white-water rafting in 1976. That's the year timber companies stopped floating logs down the Kennebec to their lumber mills and gutsy outdoorsman Wayne Hockmeyer decided to take a rubber raft through the Kennebec Gorge. He survived, and since then, white-water rafting has mushroomed, focusing long-overdue attention on the beautiful Upper Kennebec Valley and creating a whole new crowd of enthusiasts for this region. Augmenting that is the Maine Huts and Trails system, which connects The Forks to Carrabassett Valley, in the Western Lakes and Mountains.

PLANNING YOUR TIME

Depending on your interests, you can swim, canoe, raft, hike, mountain bike, snowmobile, or cross-country ski; tour museums and historic sites; take walking tours; shop; or blend it all into one rich excursion of history, heritage, culture, and adventure.

Getting around the region is easy: Route 201 parallels the Kennebec River from one end to the other. The downside is that the two-lane highway is also the major artery from Québec to the U.S. coast, and it may seem as if everyone else but you is simply trying to get from point A to point B in record time. Traffic generally isn't heavy, but it can be disconcerting to have a big rig on your bumper on the narrow and winding stretches of the road. Once you're above Skowhegan, moose also become a danger. Be wary, especially around dawn and dusk or in early spring, when moose often lick salt residue on roadsides.

Think of Route 201 as the region's spine, and Routes 2, 3, 16, 17, and 27 as crucial vertebrae linking it to Maine's Western Lakes and Mountains, Highlands, and Mid-Coast regions. There's a good chance you're going to pass through the region if you're gallivanting around the state. From Norridgewock, Route 201A parallels the river on its western banks, passing through Madison and the Ansons and pretty farm country before rejoining Route 201 in Bingham.

Unless you're a snowmobiler, May-October is the best time to appreciate this part of Maine. In May-June, blackflies are notorious and can make outdoor pleasures—with the exception of fishing—true misery. July-September, when both the air and water are warm, is the best time for white-water rafting, for recreation on the lakes, and for hiking. In late September-early October, when

Previous: Attean View Rest Area; South Solon Meetinghouse; Moxie Falls.

Kennebec and Moose River Region

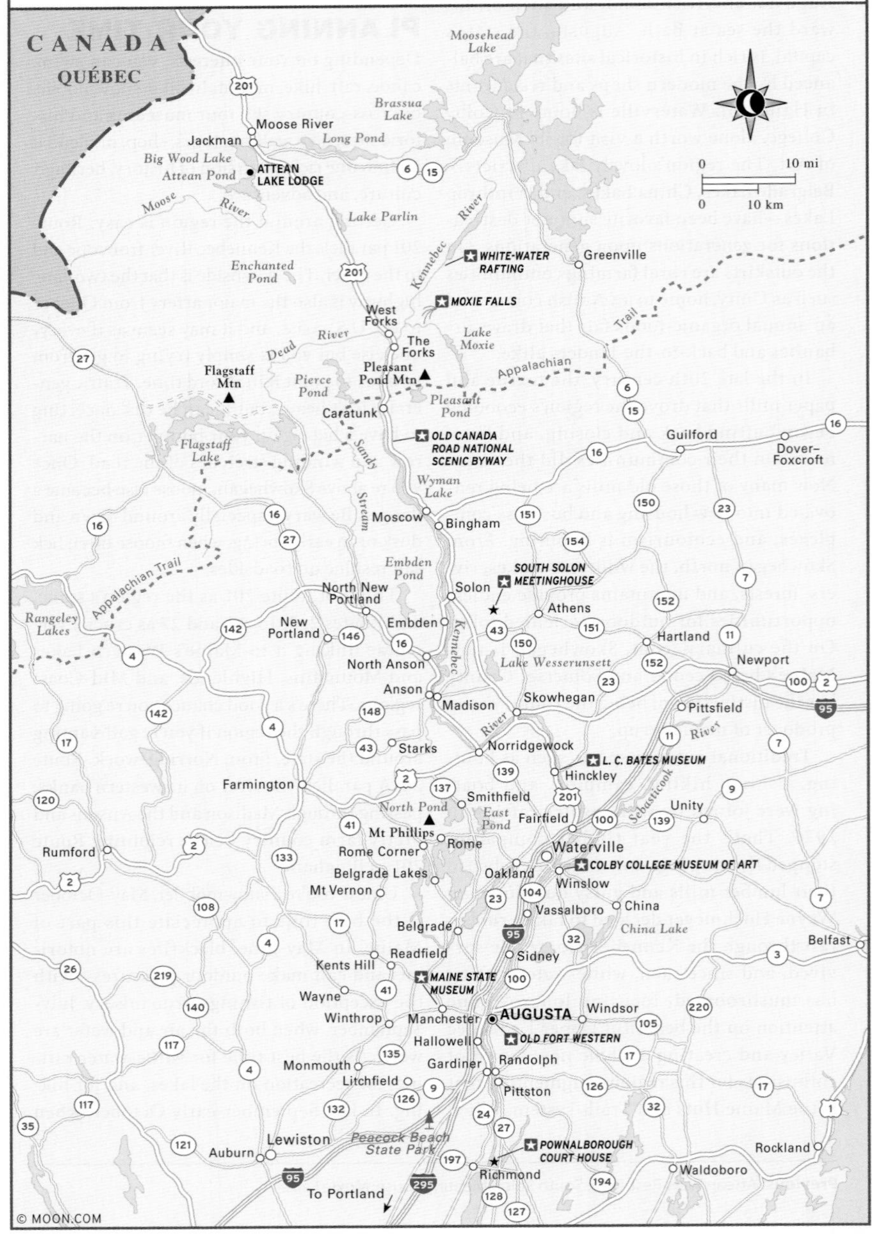

the foliage is at its peak, driving the northern stretch of Route 201, a National Scenic Byway, is glorious.

Outdoor enthusiasts will want to spend at least 2-3 days in and around The Forks or Jackman region, where rafting, canoeing, and hiking opportunities are plentiful. Plan on another 1-2 days to visit the cultural diversions clustered in Augusta and Waterville. Of course, generations of folk spend a week or longer every summer in the lakes regions surrounding Augusta, but you can dip your toes in for a sample in a day or two.

If you're history-minded—or just interested in "heritage touring"—consider following the **Kennebec-Chaudière International Corridor,** a historic route that stretches from Bath, Maine, to Québec City. Native Americans took it on foot and by canoe; Benedict Arnold used it; and enterprising 19th-century traders found it invaluable for moving their wares between the United States and Canada. Along the route are museums, churches, dramatic scenery, and French and American cultural centers. The heritage, people, and landscape are brought to life on a CD, *Deep Woods and River Roads,* narrated by Nick Spitzer, folklorist and host of Public Radio International's *American Routes.* It can be purchased at museums and visitors centers along the route.

Augusta and Vicinity

As the state capital, **Augusta** (pop. 19,136) is where everything is supposed to happen. A lot does happen here, but don't be surprised to find the imposing State House and lovely governor's mansion the centerpieces of a relatively sleepy city. Augusta is the seventh-largest city in Maine and no megalopolis, but it *is* the heart of state government and central Maine.

Pilgrims first settled here on the banks of the Kennebec River in the 17th century, and Boston merchants established Fort Western in the mid-18th century. Augusta was named state capital in 1827.

The three best-known communities south of Augusta—Hallowell, Gardiner, and Richmond—all scale down hillsides to the river, making their settings especially attractive. In **Hallowell** (pop. 2,381), settled in 1762, the main thoroughfare still retains the air of its former days as a prosperous port and source of granite and ice. The entire downtown, with brick sidewalks and attractive shops and restaurants, is a National Historic District.

Six miles south of Augusta, **Gardiner** (pop. 5,800), the "Tilbury Town" of noted author Edwin Arlington Robinson, claims more buildings in the National Register of Historic Places than any of its neighbors. The Gardiner Historic District includes more than 45 downtown buildings. Main Street is a gem, and although still too many storefronts are empty, there's a bit of a buzz here. Besides Robinson, another prominent Gardiner resident was Laura Howe Richards, author of *Captain January* and daughter of Julia Ward Howe, who wrote "The Battle Hymn of the Republic." (The yellow Federal-style home where Richards and her husband raised seven children, at 3 Dennis Street, is not open to the public.) Most outstanding of Gardiner's mansions (also not open to the public) is Oaklands, a Gothic Revival home built in 1836 by the grandson of founding father Dr. Sylvester Gardiner, a wealthy land speculator.

Just over the border in Sagadahoc County, **Richmond** (pop. 3,411), also flush with handsome buildings, was the site of a Russian émigré community in the 1950s. Here's a town that awaits rediscovery. Just over the bridge is a pre-Revolutionary courthouse, and north of that, also on the river, is the starting point of Benedict Arnold's march to Québec.

West of Augusta, amid the Winthrop

Lakes region, the town of **Monmouth** (pop. 4,104) is the site of Cumston Hall, a dramatic turn-of-the-20th-century structure that now houses the Theater at Monmouth as well as the municipal offices and public library.

SIGHTS

Maine State House

From almost every vantage point in Augusta, your eye catches the prominent dome of the **Maine State House,** centerpiece of the government complex on the west side of the Kennebec River. Occupying the corner of State and Capitol Streets, the State House dates from 1832, when it was completed to the design of famed Boston architect Charles Bulfinch, who modeled it on his Massachusetts State House design. Only a dozen years had passed since Maine had separated from Massachusetts; Augusta had become the state capital in 1827. Granite for the building came from quarries in nearby Hallowell; the total construction cost was $145,000. Atop the oxidized copper dome stands a gold-gilded sculpture, *Lady Wisdom.* In the early 20th century, space needs forced a major expansion of the building, leaving only the eight-columned front portico as the Bulfinch legacy.

Visitors are welcome to wander around the State House (after clearing entry screening), but check first to see whether the legislature is in session. If so, parking becomes scarce, the hallways become congested, and access may be restricted. The best place to enter the building is on the west side, facing the more modern state office building; the entrance is marked "Maine State House." Pick up the useful brochure for a self-guided tour, or better still, take a free 45- to 60-minute guided tour, usually available hourly, 9am-noon weekdays. Call ahead (207/287-2301; tours are organized by the Maine State Museum) to arrange it, or ask at the kiosk.

On the Blaine House side of the State House is a replica of the **Liberty Bell,** with the same dimensions, weight, aged-oak yoke, iron straps, hand-forged bolts, and inscription. The bell was crafted in 1950, when the U.S. Department of the Treasury donated one to each state to promote the Savings Bond Independence Drive.

★ Maine State Museum

If the Smithsonian is the nation's attic, welcome to Maine's attic—and a well-organized one at that. At the **Maine State Museum** (State House Complex, Augusta, 207/287-2301, www.mainestatemuseum.org, 9am-5pm Tues.-Fri., 10am-4pm Sat., $3 adults, $2 ages 6-18 and seniors, $10 family, no credit cards), gears and tools spin and whir in the intriguing *Made in Maine* industrial exhibits, focusing on quarrying, ice harvesting, fishing, agriculture, lumbering, and shipbuilding. A spiraled archaeological exhibit covers the past 12 millennia of Maine's history. Some displays are interactive, and all exhibits are wheelchair-accessible. Gallery guides are available in French, German, Spanish, Japanese, and Russian. During the winter, the museum sponsors a free lecture series, and special programs occur throughout the year. A small gift shop stocks historical publications and Maine-related gifts and toys. The museum is part of the state government complex that includes the State House and the Maine State Library. The museum and library share a building, separated by a parking lot from the State House.

The Blaine House

In 1833, a year after the State House was ready for business, retired sea captain James Hall finished his elegant new home across the street. But it was not until 29 years later, when prominent politico James G. Blaine assumed ownership, that the house became the hotbed of state and national political ferment. No underachiever, Blaine was a Maine congressman and senator, Speaker of the U.S. House, U.S. secretary of state under two presidents, and Republican candidate for the presidency. Two decades after his death, Blaine's widow donated the family home to the state of Maine; it has been the governor's mansion ever since.

Free 25-minute guided tours of the ground-floor public areas of the **Blaine House** (State St. and Capitol St., Augusta, www.blainehouse.org) are available through the Maine State Museum; call 207/287-2301 for the current schedule. Reservations are required at least three days in advance for security clearance.

★ Old Fort Western

Built in 1754 for the French and Indian War and restored as recently as 1988, **Old Fort Western** (16 Cony St., Augusta, 207/626-2385, www.oldfortwestern.org, 10am-4pm daily July-Aug., 11am-4pm Fri.-Mon. spring and fall, $10 adults, $6 ages 6-14, $25 family), reputedly North America's oldest remaining wooden garrison, has witnessed British, French, and Native Americans squabbling over this Kennebec riverfront site. Benedict Arnold and his troops camped here during their 1775 march to Québec. Today, costumed interpreters help visitors travel through time to the 18th century; hands-on demonstrations—butter churning, musket drill, barrel building, weaving, even vinegar making—occur daily Fourth of July-Labor Day.

★ Pownalborough Court House

If you're an architecture fan or a history buff, don't miss the 1761 **Pownalborough Court House** (River Rd./Rte. 128, Dresden, 207/882-9628, www.lincolncountyhistory.org, 10am-4pm Tues.-Sat., noon-4pm Sun. July-Aug., 10am-4pm Sat., noon-4pm Sun. June and Sept.-mid-Oct., $5 ages 15 and older), a pre-Revolutionary riverfront courthouse listed in the National Register of Historic Places. President John Adams once handled a trial in this mid-18th-century frontier community (named Pownalborough) established by French and German settlers. During the 30-minute tour of the three-story courthouse, docents delight in pointing out the restored beams, paneling, and fireplaces, as well as the on-site tavern that catered to judges, lawyers, and travelers. Walk a few hundred feet south and you'll find a cemetery with graves of Revolutionary War, War of 1812, and Civil War veterans. Also here are maintained trails along the riverfront and in the woods. From Richmond, take Route 195, crossing the river, and then Route 128 north.

Walking and Driving Tours

Many of Hallowell's distinctive homes have stories to tell. Stop by **Hallowell City Hall** (1 Winthrop St., 207/623-4021) to pick up a copy of the *Museums in the Streets* map or visit www.historichallowell.org.

Fans of poet **Edwin Arlington Robinson** will find a map of Gardiner-area ("Tilbury Town") sites at www.earobinson.com.

ENTERTAINMENT

Six miles south of Augusta, the 1864 **Johnson Hall Performing Arts Center** (280 Water St., Gardiner, 207/582-7144, www.johnsonhall.org) is the year-round site of plays, lectures, art camps, after-school programs, classes, concerts, and more.

Maine's enduring Shakespearean theater is the **Theater at Monmouth** (796 Main St./Rte. 132, Monmouth, box office 207/933-9999 or 800/769-9698 in Maine, www.theateratmonmouth.org, $34), based in Monmouth's architecturally astonishing **Cumston Hall.** Completed in 1900, the Romanesque Victorian structure has columns, cutout shingles, stained glass, and a huge square tower. The interior is equally stunning, with frescoes and a vaulted ceiling. The theater's summer season, performed by professionals in rotating repertory, runs early July-August. Shakespeare usually gets the nod for one or two of the four plays. Tickets for the family show are $15 adults, $10 children.

During the school year, the **University of Maine at Augusta** campus schedules lectures, concerts, and other performances. Check with the school (student activities 207/621-3000, ext. 3442, or information center 877/862-1234, www.uma.edu) for current information.

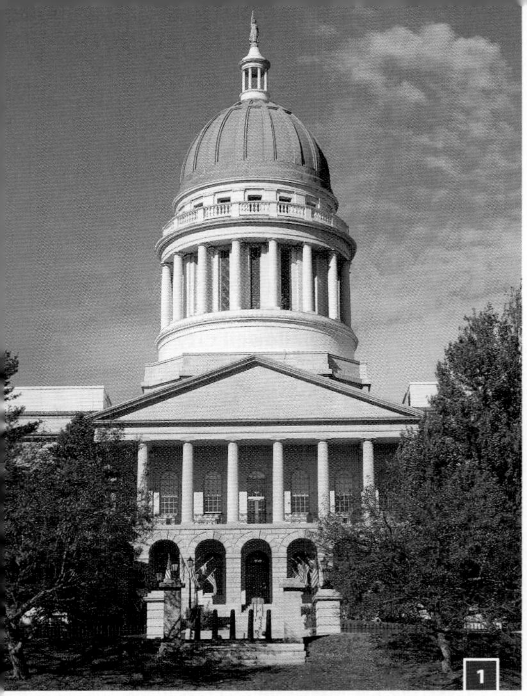
1

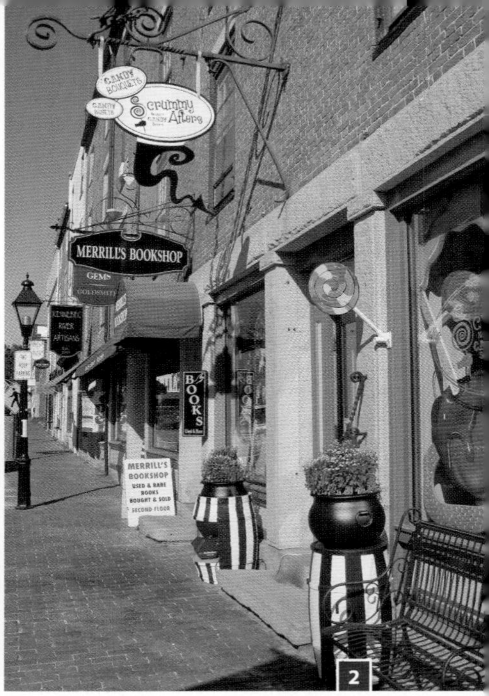
Scrummy Afters
MERRILL'S BOOKSHOP
GEMS
KENNEBEC RIVER ARTISANS
BOOKS
MERRILL'S BOOKSHOP
USED & RARE BOOKS
BOUGHT & SOLD
SECOND FLOOR
2

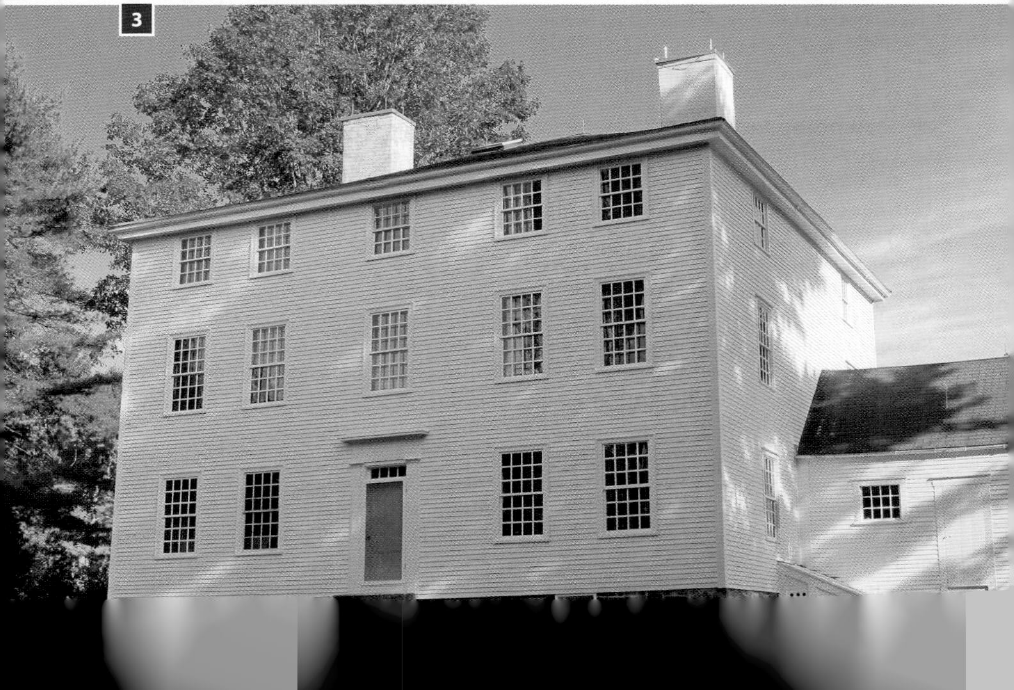
3

The Russians Were Coming

In the 1950s, the sleepy Kennebec River town of Richmond, 12 miles south of Maine's state capital, became the center of a unique and unlikely colony as several hundred Russian-speaking refugee families settled among the area's villages and rolling farmland. The Kennebec Valley, economically depressed and remote from other Russian immigrant centers in the United States, seems an improbable choice for a Slavic enclave. Yet Richmond soon boasted a Russian restaurant, a Russian boot-maker's shop, a balalaika orchestra, and even onion domes—on St. Alexander Nevsky, Maine's first Russian Orthodox church, which celebrated its 50th anniversary in 2003. Russian was heard on Richmond's streets, and Russian-speaking children enrolled in local schools. At the time, Richmond had the distinction of being home to the largest rural Russian-speaking population in the country.

The settlement was the brainchild of Baron Vladimir von Poushental, a swashbuckling veteran of the czar's World War I air force. Fleeing the Bolshevik Revolution, he landed in New York, where his personality and family connections gained him entry to a series of managerial jobs, if not to the wealth he had enjoyed as a Russian noble. In 1947, von Poushental, an expert marksman and dedicated hunter, decided to retire to a modest cabin in the Kennebec Valley, where he had hunted and fished for many years. There he began buying up abandoned farms and promoting the valley's attractions to fellow Russian émigrés. The climate and countryside resembled Russia's, he said, and land was cheap. For a few thousand dollars, a refugee could buy a house and 30 acres. To create a nucleus for the settlers, the baron donated a 400-acre farm to the aging veterans of Russia's White armies, and he helped them establish a retirement home and an Orthodox chapel.

And so they came: Ukrainians, Russians, Belorussians, and Cossacks; professors, farmers, artists, and carpenters. Some came directly from Europe's displaced-persons camps, others from homes and jobs in U.S. cities where they had lived for years. The settlers shared a common language, their Orthodox faith, a zest for life, and a hatred of the Soviet regime. The younger émigrés worked, raised families, and became part of the larger American community around them. Their elderly parents felt more comfortable associating with other Russian-speakers.

Today the boot-maker and restaurant are gone. Most of the elderly—the old émigrés from pre-Communist Russia—are dead, their Cyrillic gravestones dotting the Richmond cemetery. Their grandchildren, Russian Americans, have merged successfully into the mainstream United States. Most have married outside their ethnic group, and many have taken jobs outside the Kennebec Valley, not necessarily by choice. Yet a fair number still live and work in the area. In a way that might have surprised even von Poushental, who died in 1978, the colony he sponsored took root and flourished in a part of the country he loved.

Festivals and Events

In June, the **Maine Fiber Frolic** (www.fiberfrolic.com) celebrates fiber, fiber animals, and fiber arts at the Windsor Fairgrounds. Expect llamas, alpacas, angora rabbits, sheep, goats, and other livestock as well as demonstrations, workshops, and exhibits.

In mid-June and again in mid-to-late August, the annual **Blistered Fingers Family Bluegrass Music Festival** (www.blisteredfingers.com) takes place at the Litchfield Fairgrounds in Litchfield.

The Augusta area seems to claim more country fairs than any other part of the state. Each has a different flavor, but there are always lots of animals, games, and junk food, often a carnival, and sometimes harness racing. Don't miss an opportunity to attend at least one. Good bets are the **Monmouth Fair** in early August; the **Windsor Fair** in late August; and the **Litchfield Fair** during the second weekend in September.

1: Maine State House **2:** Merrill's Bookshop in downtown Hallowell **3:** Pownalborough Court House

SHOPPING

Two towns south of Augusta draw shoppers. Both **Hallowell** and **Gardiner** have boutiques, restaurants, specialty shops, and antiques stores.

The **Harlow Gallery** (100 Water St., Hallowell, 207/622-3813), headquarters for the Kennebec Valley Art Association, serves as a magnet not only for its member artists but also for friends of art.

Fifteen dealers show a broad range of antiques at the **Hallowell Antique Mall** (191 Water St., Hallowell, 207/430-8315), on the southern edge of downtown.

The apt slogan at **Merrill's Bookshop** (134 Water St., 2nd fl., Hallowell, 207/623-2055) is "Good literature from Edward Abbey to Leane Zugsmith." John Merrill has an eye for unusual rare and used books, so you may walk out with a personal treasure.

"Guns. Wedding Gowns. Cold Beer." The sign outside **Hussey's General Store** (510 Ridge Rd./Rte. 32 at Rte. 105, Windsor, 207/445-2511, www.husseysgeneralstore.com) says it all. With merchandise spread out on three floors, there isn't much that Hussey's doesn't have, and that bridal department does a steady business. Its slogan: "If we don't have it, you don't need it." From Augusta, take Route 105 about 11 miles east to Route 32; Hussey's is on the corner. If you're at the Windsor Fairgrounds, the store is only about two miles farther north on Route 32.

RECREATION

Parks and Preserves

On the east side of State Street, between the State House and the river, is **Capitol Park,** a great place for a picnic after visiting the Maine State Museum, the State House, and the Blaine House. In the park is the **Maine Vietnam Veterans Memorial,** a dramatic "you are there" walk-through monument erected in 1985.

VILES ARBORETUM

On the east side of the Kennebec River, the **Viles Arboretum** (153 Hospital St./Rte. 9, Augusta, 207/621-0031, www.vilesarboretum.org, dawn-dusk daily) devotes 224 acres to more than 300 varieties of trees and shrubs, and it's laced with nearly six miles of trails. The Viles Arboretun Art Trail displays the state's largest permanent outdoor art collection, with many pieces for sale. If you're a birder, bring binoculars; more than 150 species have been spotted here. Well-designed planting clusters include hosta and rhododendron collections, a rock garden, an antique

The Theater at Monmouth is an architectural gem.

apple orchard, and the Governors Grove, with a white pine dedicated to each Maine governor. Stop first at the **Viles Visitor Center** (8am-4:30pm Mon.-Fri.) to pick up a trail map. Leashed pets are allowed; smoking is not permitted on the grounds. During the winter, the trails are groomed for cross-country skiing. Admission is free; donations are appreciated. A farmers market sets up here 2pm-5pm Fridays in summer.

Next to the arboretum parking lot is **Cony Cemetery** (also known as Knight Cemetery), one of Augusta's oldest, with gravestones dating from the late 18th century. Old-cemetery buffs will want to check it out, but rubbings are not permitted.

KENNEBEC VALLEY GARDEN CLUB PARK

Escape the shopping hubbub in this pocket of tranquility at the Augusta Civic Center. Designed in 1974 by Lyle Littlefield, a professor of horticulture at the University of Maine, it's now maintained by club members. Within the two-acre park's borders are a water-lily pond rimmed with cattails, two formal gardens, and trails edged by perennials. Nearby are children's butterfly and hummingbird gardens and woodlands with wildflowers.

JAMIES POND WILDLIFE MANAGEMENT AREA

Maine's Department of Inland Fisheries and Wildlife manages this 840-acre preserve. The 107-acre pond, stocked with brook trout and splake, appeals equally to anglers, birders, wildlife-watchers, and paddlers. Mapped trails weave through the surrounding woodlands. Access is from Outlet Road, just west of the Maple Hill Farm Inn in Hallowell.

VAUGHN WOODS & HISTORIC HOMESTEAD

Just steps from downtown Hallowell, paths weave through **Vaughn Woods** (207/622-9831, http://vaughanhomestead.org, donations appreciated), a Hobbit-like landscape with a babbling brook, a pond, stone bridges (undergoing restoration), and a dam. The parking area is on the corner of Middle Street and Litchfield Road. The **Homestead,** home to seven generations of the Vaughn family, is open for scheduled tours (10am Tues. July-Aug., $10 pp, reservations required) and during public events.

Swan Island

The Maine Department of Inland Fisheries and Wildlife (IF&W) manages **Swan Island Wildlife Management Area** (207/547-5322, http://www.maine.gov/swanisland) on **Swan Island** in the middle of the Kennebec River. The four-mile-long island, settled in the early 1700s, once had as many as 95 resident farmers, fishermen, ice cutters, and shipbuilders; five houses still exist. Now it's home to more than 30 species of Maine wildlife unable to live in the wild. Its siting at the head of Merrymeeting Bay makes it ideal not only for wildlife-watchers, but also for birding enthusiasts. Whether you come for the day or to stay in the primitive campground, unless you're arriving by canoe or kayak, you'll need to call or make an online reservation.

Seven miles of well-marked trails lace the island; one trail takes 30 minutes, another takes three hours end to end. No license is needed for fishing, but even private boats need permission to land here (near the campground); small boats are not recommended because of 10-foot tidal variations. Bikes are permitted on the 4.5-mile dirt main road only, and cars and pets are not allowed. Canoe and kayak rentals are available from the campground for $10/hour or $35/day.

Each of the campground's 10 well-spaced lean-tos sleeps six. You'll find picnic tables, fireplaces, and outhouses; firewood and potable water are provided. Cost is $20 pp. There's a two-night maximum. The policy is carry-in, carry-out, so bring trash bags. A tour truck meets campers at the island dock and transports them the 1.5 miles to the campground. The same truck does the island tour.

Getting here requires a five-minute ferry ride from a dock in Richmond, next to the town-owned Waterfront Park on Route 24. The boat operates four times daily May-October; reservations are required. Day-use admission is $8 over age 5. Pack a picnic lunch; fireplaces at the campground are available for day use if no campers are using them, but bring tinfoil for cooking. Alcohol is not allowed on the island.

Bicycling

You can walk, bike, ski, or run the **Kennebec River Rail Trail** (KRRT), keeping an eye peeled for bald eagles, salmon, and just the general flow of the Kennebec. The Friends of KRRT (www.krrt.org) maintains the 6.5-mile riverside trail connecting Augusta's Waterfront Park to Gardiner. About 0.5 mile of the trail is along Route 201/Water Street in Hallowell.

Golf

Ten miles north of Augusta and 12 miles south of Waterville, the **Natanis Golf Club** (Webber Pond Rd., Vassalboro, 207/622-3561, www.natanisgc.com) has been the site of many a Maine golf tournament. Named after a trusted Indian guide, the Natanis club has two separate 18-hole courses.

Fishing

Fish for stripers and bluefish on the Kennebec River with Gardiner-based **Maine Experience Guide Service** (207/215-3828, www.maineexperienceguideservice.com) with Master Maine Guide Jay Farris. Rates begin at $325 for four hours and cover up to two people.

FOOD

Local Flavors

Almost everything on the menu is made in-house at the **Downtown Diner** (204 Water St., Augusta, 207/623-9695, 5am-2pm Mon.-Fri., 6am-2pm Sat., 7am-1pm Sun., $4-14), a reliable spot for inexpensive, good home cookin' in the spot once occupied by Hersey's Shoe Store, which the marquee still advertises.

Great breads, delish cookies, premade quiche, and other treats come from **Slates Bakery** (161 Water St., Hallowell, 207/622-4104, 7am-6pm Mon.-Sat., 7am-4pm Sun.).

Put your lights on for service at **Fast Eddies** (1308 Rte. 202, Winthrop, 207/377-5550, www.fasteddiesdrivein.com, 11am-8pm daily late Apr.-mid-Oct., $2-20), but even if you opt for carhop service, make it a point to visit the dining room, where James Dean, Elvis, Marilyn Monroe, and Betty Boop preside over a cool collection of 1950s memorabilia. Burgers, shakes, fried foods, and homemade ice cream are the draws. Wednesday Cruise Nights, late May-August, feature live entertainment and attract antique-car buffs.

Pastries, hearty breakfasts, and fat sandwiches are the lures to **Annabella's Bakery & Café** (2 Main St., Richmond, 207/737-7165, 6:30am-2pm Wed.-Sat., 6:30am-1pm Sun.). Dine in or take it to go and enjoy your meal in the riverside park across the street.

The yummy aromas of Old World-style baking are reason enough to venture off the beaten path to find **Black Crow Bakery** (232 Plains Rd., Litchfield, 207/268-9927, 7am-7pm Tues.-Sat.), where the specialty, a Tuscan loaf, is as pretty as it is tasty. Almost all the breads baked in the brick oven are sourdough-based, and every day features a different loaf, perhaps Sicilian, olive herb, focaccia, the fantastic apricot-almond, or Greek cheese. A modern mixer is Mark and Tinker Mickalide's only high-tech tool; they operate a very traditional bakery in their 1810 farmhouse's former summer kitchen, even grinding their own grains on Maine granite. The shop, which operates on the honor system, is across from the Legion Hall, between I-495 and the Litchfield Fairgrounds.

Worth the trip for excellent homemade ice cream is **Tubby's** (512 Main St., Wayne, 207/685-8181, www.tubbysicecream.com, 11:30am-8:30pm daily), a seasonal spot with waterfront tables. It also serves sandwiches ($3-10) as well as a decent lobster roll.

For a fresh lobster or crabmeat roll, pop into **Hallowell Seafood and Produce** (197

Water St., Hallowell, 207/621-0500, 9am-6pm daily), on the southern edge of downtown. No seating, but you can take it to the riverside park across the street.

The **Farmers Market at Mill Park** at the old Edwards Mill site on the north end of Water Street operates 2pm-6pm Tuesdays. The **Gardiner Farmers Market** sets up on the Common 3pm-6pm Wednesdays.

Family Favorites

Fill up and feel good about it with big portions of top-notch fried food at the **Red Barn** (455 Riverside Dr., Augusta, 207/623-9485, 9am-8pm Tues.-Sun., $4-20). Locals love this place, and in turn the owner and staff generously support community causes. The $25 fried chicken family meal easily feeds four.

The first-rate ★ **A-1 Diner** (3 Bridge St., Gardiner, 207/582-4804, 7am-8pm Mon.-Sat., 8am-1:30pm Sun., $8-16) is the real thing, a genuine classic diner. The menu, however, goes well beyond diner fare. How about Moroccan roasted veggies and hummus or soba noodles with spicy broth, shrimp, and veggies? There's also a regular diner menu. Sunday brunch draws a crowd.

If you're feeding bottomless-stomached teens, **Lucky Garden** (222 Water St., Hallowell, 207/622-3465, www.luckygardenme.com, from 11am daily, $9-30) is a great choice. The restaurant, with a nice dining room overlooking the river, is locally known for its sesame chicken. The all-you-can-eat buffets, 11am-2:30pm daily ($9), and dinner, 4:30pm-8pm Thurs.-Sun. ($13), are ideal for those with big appetites.

Brewpubs and Tap Rooms

It's the 20-ounce pint glass, not politics, that helped christen the **Liberal Cup** (115 Water St., Hallowell, 207/623-2739, www.theliberalcup.com, 11:30am-10pm daily, $8-14), a brewpub and restaurant where owner Geoffrey Houghton, who studied in Britain, brews great ales. Homemade is true of the contemporary pub fare.

For wood-fired, thin-crust pizza and good brews, snag a table at **Cushnoc Brewing Co.** (243 Water St., Augusta, 207/213-6332, www.cushnocbrewing.com, 11am-10pm daily, $12-18).

In fine weather, aim for a seat on the riverside deck at the **Quarry Tap Room** (122 Water St., Hallowell, 207/213-6173, http://www.quarrytaproom.com, from 11am daily, $10-14), a gastropub with 36 rotating taps featuring microbrews, half of them from Maine. There's often live music.

Casual Dining

Don't let the location inside a hotel deter you from **Cloud 9** (Senator Inn and Spa, 284 Western Ave., Augusta, 207/622-5804, www.senatorinn.com, 6:30am-9pm Mon.-Sat., 6:30am-2pm Sun., $10-30). The chefs are committed to using local ingredients and take great care in preparing the fare. Choices vary from wood-oven pizzas to handmade pastas, burgers and fries to filet mignon.

Ask anyone where to eat in the Augusta area and chances are high that the answer will be ★ **Slates** (163 Water St., Hallowell, 207/622-9575, www.slatesrestaurant.com, 3:30pm-8:30pm Mon., 11:30am-9pm Tues., 8am-9pm Wed-Sat., 10am-2pm Sun.), the Energizer Bunny of local restaurants. Founded in 1979, it just keeps improving. Dinner options range from pizza and crepes to housemade fettuccini and tenderloin au poivre; most are in the $12-30 range. Vegetarian fare is available. There's usually live music on Monday nights.

Dining is by reservation only at the **Sedgley Place** (54 Sedgley Rd., Greene, 207/946-5990 or 800/924-7778, www.sedgleyplace.com, seatings on the hour Wed.-Sun.), in a lovely Federal-style homestead. The five-course American menu ($33-40) changes weekly; request vegetarian and children's portions ahead of time. Book a 5pm table if attending a performance at Theater of Monmouth.

ACCOMMODATIONS

On the western side of the city, close to I-95 but convenient to downtown and the capitol complex, is the **Senator Inn and Spa** (284 Western Ave., Augusta, 207/622-5804 or 877/772-2224, www.senatorinn.com, $120-324), with a decent restaurant, a full-service spa, and indoor and outdoor heated pools. Rooms vary widely; opt for a renovated one, ideally a spa suite. Pets are allowed in certain rooms for $12/night. Rates include an expanded continental breakfast.

Bed-and-Breakfasts

On a back road only 10 minutes from the State House, 130-acre ★ **Maple Hill Farm Bed and Breakfast Inn and Conference Center** (11 Inn Rd., off Outlet Rd., Hallowell, 207/622-2708 or 800/622-2708, www.maplebb.com, $130-220) provides a green, rural respite. Eight guest rooms in the informal renovated 1890s farmhouse overlook woods, fields, gardens, and even the Camden Hills. Some guest rooms have double whirlpool tubs, gas fireplaces, and private decks. Public areas include a living room, a guest kitchenette, a hot tub, and a sauna. Breakfast is a custom-cooked affair from a menu that features the inn's fresh eggs as an option. No pets are permitted because of the delightful farm animals, including llamas, cows, and goats. The eco-aware inn has a wind-generating turbine, extensive solar panels, and other green initiatives. Maple Hill Farm is three miles west of downtown Hallowell, next to an 800-acre wildlife preserve with an extensive trail network and a wonderful pond.

About 10 miles southwest of Augusta but a world removed is **A Rise and Shine B&B** (19 Moose Run Dr./Rte. 135, Monmouth, 207/933-9876, www.riseandshinebb.com, $140-170), the former Woolworth family estate overlooking Lake Cobbosseeconte in Monmouth. Lorette Comeau and Tom Crocker restored the main house; now it's a prize, with Lorette's hand-painted murals in a few of the eight guest rooms. The overall atmosphere is low key yet inviting, with plenty of shared public rooms—a great room, a living room, a dining room, a huge patio, and a TV room—to spread out and relax. Rates include a full breakfast. Two 1st-floor rooms connect through a bath for a family suite. The property previously was a racehorse farm, so horses can be accommodated by arrangement.

Architect, innkeeper, and Maine native Shawn Dolley spent three years meticulously renovating a turreted 1905 Christian Science church in Gardiner into the **Stone Turret** (17C Lincoln Ave., Gardiner, 207/319-4010, www.thestoneturret.com, $130-180), a sophisticated B&B where guests immerse in the history of the building and the city while enjoying contemporary decor and amenities blended with original architectural features, such as tin ceilings and stained glass windows. It's a short walk to downtown shops and restaurants.

INFORMATION

Local information is available from the **Kennebec Valley Chamber of Commerce** (207/623-4559, www.augustamaine.com), the **Hallowell Area Board of Trade** (207/620-7477, www.hallowell.org), and the **Kennebec Valley Tourism Council** (207/623-4884, www.kennebecvalley.org).

GETTING THERE AND AROUND

Cape Air Airlines (866/227-3247, www.capeair.com), a JetBlue affiliate, operates flights year-round between Boston's Logan Airport and the **Augusta State Airport** (AUG, 75 Airport Rd., Augusta, 207/626-2306).

Concord Coachlines (Augusta Transportation Center, 9 Industrial Dr., Augusta, 800/639-3317, www.concordcoachlines.com) operates bus service among Portland, Augusta, and Bangor, connecting with the Maine coast, Boston, and points south.

By car, Augusta is roughly 60 miles or 55 minutes from Portland via I-295 and I-95. It's roughly 34 miles or one hour from Belfast via Route 3, and roughly 75 miles or just over an hour from Bangor via I-95. It's roughly 17 miles or 30 minutes to Belgrade Lakes via Route 27.

Belgrade Lakes Area

The Belgrade Lakes area is one of those Proustian memories-of-childhood places where multigenerational family groups return year after year for idyllic summer visits full of nothing but playing, hiking, swimming, fishing, listening for the loons, watching sunsets, and dreading the return to civilization (as the famous North Pond hermit did, avoiding detection for nearly three decades). It was the inspiration for *On Golden Pond*—playwright Ernest Thompson spent his childhood summers here. Today's parents, recalling carefree days at one of the many Belgrade-area summer camps, now send their own kids to camp here, or they rent lakefront cottages and devote their energies to re-creating those youthful days.

Water, water everywhere: Mosey along the back roads and it seems as if there's yet another body of water around every other bend. Belgrade's chain of lakes includes seven major lakes and ponds: Long Pond, North Pond, Great Pond, East Pond, Salmon Pond, McGrath Pond, and Messalonskee Lake (also known as Snow Pond), as well as numerous smaller ones; as you continue south, so do the lakes and ponds. Camps and cottages are sprinkled around their shores. Roadside put-ins and boat launches, from which you can put in a canoe, kayak, or powerboat, can be found on every lake. This is a great area just to strap a canoe or kayak on the car and wander, stopping wherever seems interesting for a paddle. Incidentally, the village of Belgrade Lakes, heart of the region, has its own post office but is part of the towns of **Belgrade** (pop. 3,189) and **Rome** (pop. 1,010).

Since the Belgrade Lakes area is tucked in between Waterville and Augusta, those cities serve as the easily accessible commercial and cultural hubs for Belgrade visitors.

Directly west of Belgrade Lakes village is the charming, out-of-the-way hamlet of **Mount Vernon** (pop. 1,640), founded in 1792 and worth a visit by car or bike. North of that is **Vienna** (VI-enna, pop. 570); south is lovely **Kents Hill,** home to a prep school and part of the town of **Readfield** (pop. 2,598).

SIGHTS

DEW Haven

Lions and tigers and bears, oh, my! And monkeys, camels, wallabies, ostriches, a binturong, a hyena, and, well, the list goes on. Allow at least an hour to visit **DEW Haven** (918 Pond Rd./Rte. 41, Mount Vernon, 207/293-2837, www.dewhaven.com, 10am-5pm Tues.-Sun. mid-June-late Aug., 10am-5pm Sat.-Sun. early May-mid-June and early Sept.-mid-Oct., $15 ages 13-64, $10 ages 4-12 and seniors). Kids love the hands-on stuff at Julie and Bob Miner's innovative nonprofit zoo, where they raise and rehabilitate exotic and other animals, enhancing rare and endangered breeds, and educate visitors about them. Bob, a disabled Vietnam vet, has rescued animals from zoos and shows and even New York City apartments. Julie and Bob have hand-raised and bottle-fed many of these animals from infancy, and they enter every cage. Bob kisses the bears and the lions, and Julie nuzzles the panther, but visitors watch from behind a double fence; trust me, it's plenty close enough, especially when you learn such facts as that the hyena has the strongest jaw pressure of any land mammal. Join a tour if available during your visit. Find DEW midway between Mount Vernon village and Kents Hill. Note: Whining children are strongly discouraged.

ENTERTAINMENT

Under the auspices of **Snow Pond Center for the Arts** (www.snowpond.org), free concerts by students and faculty are offered late June-mid-August at the **New England Music Camp** (Lake Messalonskee, Sidney, 207/465-3025, www.nemusiccamp.com). Call or check the website for current schedule. Weekend concerts are at the outdoor "Bowl-in-the-Pines" (bring a blanket or folding chair); midweek performances take place in Alumni Hall.

SHOPPING

Mosey and poke around the back roads and you'll be rewarded with a handful of galleries and whatnot shops.

Cars and canoes are about the only things you can't buy at **Day's Store** (Main St./Rte. 27, Belgrade Lakes, 207/495-2205, www.go-2days.com), a legendary institution since 1960. From firewater to fishing tackle, sandwiches (including the Long Pond Grinder) to souvenirs, and more than a dozen kinds of homemade fudge, it's a general store par excellence. Don't expect fancy; the local flavor provides its character. Long Pond is at its back door, providing access by boat or car.

The seasonal branch of Waterville's **Maine Made and More Shop** (129 Main St./Rte. 27, Belgrade Lakes, 207/872-7378), a summer landmark since 1980, is the place to stock up on tasteful gifts and crafts: jams and maple syrup, cards and guidebooks, T-shirts and sweatshirts, stuffed moose, and even shoes.

The talented duo of potter Mark Hutton and weaver Hillary Hutton sell their gorgeous handcrafted works from their home-based **Hutton Studios** (277 Tower Rd., Vienna, 207/293-3686, www.huttonstudios.com), open by chance or by appointment.

RECREATION

Parks and Views

Just north of Day's Store in Belgrade Lakes village is a cute little picnic area on Long Pond, **Belgrade Peninsula Park** (5:30am-10:30pm daily), next to an old dam. Late in the day it's a great spot for sunset-watching and fishing; no camping or fires are permitted. The Belgrade Lakes Conservation Corps restored it in 1996, and there is space for five carefully parked cars.

Another scenic standout, with a super photo op of Long Pond and Belgrade Lakes village, is the state-maintained overlook at **Blueberry Hill** on the west side of Long Pond. From Route 27, just south of Belgrade Lakes village, take Castle Island Road west about three miles to Watson Pond Road. Turn right (north) and continue about 1.5 miles. (Another 2.8 miles north of Blueberry Hill is the trailhead for French's Mountain.)

Golf

Golf has taken center stage here ever since the opening of the splendid **Belgrade Lakes Golf Club** (West Rd., Belgrade Lakes, 207/495-4653, www.belgradelakesgolf.com) in 1998. Designed by noted British expert Clive Clark, the course is an 18-hole standout, and the view from the elegant clubhouse is dazzling.

Hiking

Proactive in protecting much of the region's beautiful land for hiking and responsible enjoyment, the **7 Lakes Alliance** (207/495-6039, www.7lakesalliance.org) has a terrific trail map and hiking guide to the Kennebec Highlands—although it doesn't show every protected acre, since the alliance is managing to protect land faster than it can print maps.

The two good hikes listed here are included on the map, which can also be obtained at local general stores such as Day's. Both hikes are just north of Belgrade Lakes village in the town of Rome. Neither leads to a particularly high elevation, but their summits are isolated enough to provide panoramic vistas.

For lots of gain, little pain, and a good family hike, head for **French Mountain,** on the west side of Long Pond. To reach the trailhead from Route 27, go about 4.2 miles north of Belgrade Lakes village and turn left onto Watson Pond Road, then continue 0.7 mile; the trail (signposted) begins on the left. Allow about 20 minutes to reach the 716-foot summit, with fantastic views of Long Pond, the village, and Great Pond. Take a picnic (and a litter bag) and stretch out on the ledges. It's 0.8-mile round-trip.

A marginally tougher yet still-easy hike is **Mount Phillips,** a 755-footer with summit views of Great Pond. Allow about 30 minutes to reach the top via the 1.4-mile blue-blazed loop trail from the Route 225 trailhead. Take Route 225 from Rome Corner (Logan's Country Antiques is at the fork). Continue 1.5 miles to the trailhead (on the left), across from Starbird Lane.

Water Sports

Good places for swimming are **Long Pond Public Beach** on Lakeshore Drive in Belgrade Lakes village (near Sunset Grille) and at the Belgrade Community Center, on Route 27 just south of the village. In addition to the lakefront, the center also has a pool open to nonresidents for a nominal fee during community swim hours.

FISHING

Fishing is a big deal here, particularly in May-June and September (the season runs Apr. 1-Oct. 1). Among the 20 species in the seven major lakes and ponds are landlocked salmon, brown trout, black bass, pickerel, white perch, and brook trout. You'll have to stick to bag, weight, and length limits. Pick up tackle and nonresident fishing licenses at **Day's Store** (Main St., Belgrade Lakes, 207/495-2205 or 800/993-9500).

Cast a line for northern pike with **Maine Wilderness Tours** (207/557-9933, www.mainewildernesstours.com). Trips include rod, reel, tackle, and bait, with rates beginning at $225 for four hours for up to three anglers.

BOATING

Great Pond Marina (25 Marina Dr., Belgrade Lakes, 207/495-2213, www.greatpondmarina.com) rents runabouts (from $325/two days), pontoon boats (from $477/two days), kayaks ($30/day single, $50/day double), and paddleboards ($45/day). A security deposit is required.

Snow Pond Cruises offers a variety of charter pontoon boat cruises on Snow Pond. Rates begin at $19 for a one-hour tour with a minimum of four people.

Roller-Skating

Here's a throwback: When the windows are open, it feels as if you could dive out into the water at **Sunbeam Roller Rink** (828 Village Rd./Rte. 8, Smithfield, 207/416-2400), an old-fashioned roller-skating rink dating from 1922 and edging North Pond. It's usually open late April through October; call for current hours.

FOOD

Quick Bites

Stop in at **Day's Store** (182 Main St./Rte. 27, Belgrade Lakes, 207/495-2205, www.go2days.com, 7am-9pm daily) for pizza, sandwiches, and baked goodies. It also sponsors afternoon waterfront concerts on many summer Saturdays.

Hello, Good Pie Bakery & Gourmet Kitchen (39B Main St., Belgrade Lakes, 207/485-2323, http://hellogoodpieco.com, 7am-2pm Sun. and Wed., 7am-6pm Thurs.-Sat.) is a delicious stop for baked treats, deli sandwiches, soups, salads, and other sweets.

Detour down by the old millstream to the **Olde Post Office Café** (366 Pond Rd., Village Center, Mount Vernon, 207/293-4978, 7am-2:30pm Sun.-Fri., 7am-2:30pm and 5pm-9pm Sat.). Sandwiches, salads, panini, and wraps fill the menu along with baked goodies. Grab a seat inside or on the screened porch overlooking the stream or lake. Don't miss the old wheel-driven mill across the street. There's live music Saturday evenings.

Casual Dining

For more than 50 years the **Village Inn and Tavern** (157 Main St., Belgrade Lakes, 207/495-3553, www.villageinnandtavern.com, 5pm-9pm daily, $16-33) has been known for its 12-hour roast duck, but the American menu includes other choices from seafood to pasta.

Sadie's Boathouse Restaurant (25 Marine Dr., Great Pond Marina, Belgrade

Johnson
Johnson
Johnson
1

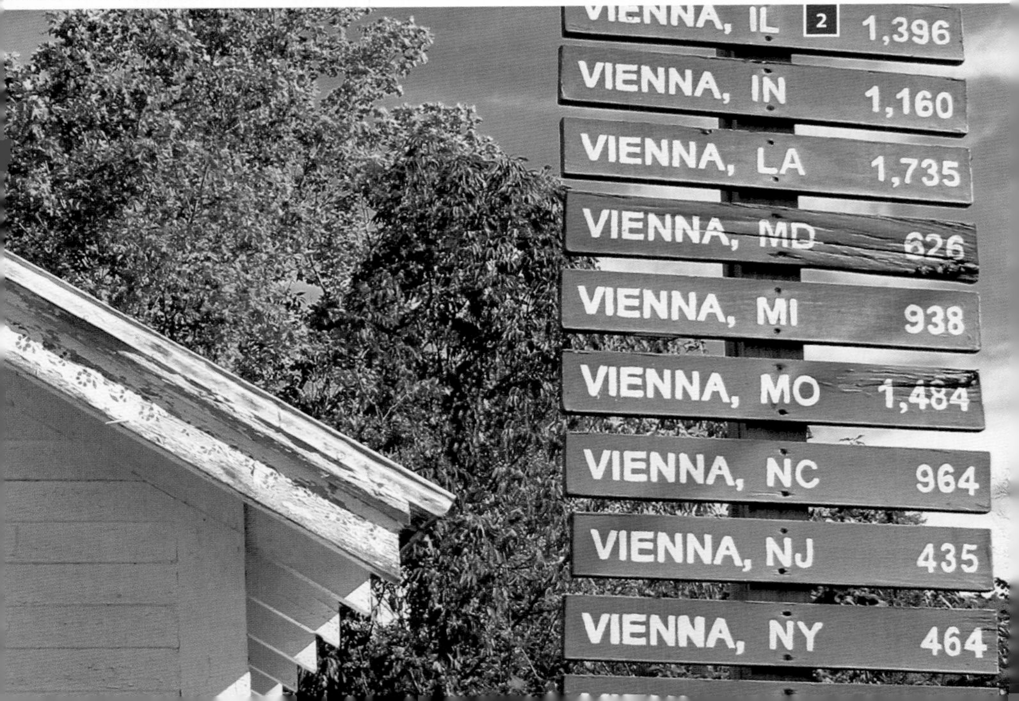

VIENNA, IL 1,396
2
VIENNA, IN 1,160
VIENNA, LA 1,735
VIENNA, MD 626
VIENNA, MI 938
VIENNA, MO 1,484
VIENNA, NC 964
VIENNA, NJ 435
VIENNA, NY 464

Lakes, 207/495-4045, 5pm-9pm Fri.-Sat., $20-33) is a fine place to enjoy lake views along with classic American fare. Opt for the porch; it can be loud by the bar.

ACCOMMODATIONS

Fall asleep to the cries of loons at the **Village Inn and Tavern** (157 Main St., Belgrade Lakes, 207/495-3553, www.villageinnandtavern.com, $165-185 rooms, $225-245 suites), sited smack downtown, but fronting on Great Pond and with views to Long Pond across the street. One canoe and a double kayak are available for guests. Pets welcome in some rooms for $35/night.

The **Pressey House Lakeside Bed and Breakfast** (32 Belgrade Rd., Oakland, 207/465-3500, www.presseyhouse.com, $169-259) occupies a mid-19th-century octagonal house with an ell and a barn at the head of nine-mile-long Messalonskee Lake (also known as Snow Pond). The family-friendly inn has five good-size suites, most with kitchens. Rates include a full breakfast. Relax in the great room, which has a huge brick fireplace dividing it in two, or on the patio. You can borrow the canoe, kayaks, or a paddleboat to explore the lake. Find the Pressey House just west of Waterville on the eastern edge of the Belgrade Lakes region, a five-minute drive from I-95 Exit 127.

You can almost dive into Lake Minnehonk from the back porch of the **Lakeside Loft** (386 Pond Rd./Rte. 41, Mount Vernon, 207/293-4855, www.thelakesideloft.com, $109-219). Three self-catering units with cooking facilities face the lake, and guests have access to the living room as well as a kayak, canoes, backpacks, and in winter, snowshoes. There's also Wi-Fi and a video library.

Sporting Camps

These classic Belgrade-area Maine sporting camps retain the flavor of those much farther north, and they're a heck of a lot easier to reach when driving from the south. These three are American Plan, so meals are included. In general, spring and late-season rates are lower.

Established in 1910 and still operated by the same family, **Bear Spring Camps** (60 Jamaica Point Rd., Rome, 207/397-2341, www.bearspringcamps.com, mid-May-early Oct.) is one of the state's largest sporting camps, with 32 rustic cottages on 400 wooded acres. All overlook the North Bay of nine-mile-long Great Pond. Each cottage has its own dock; rental motorboats, kayaks, canoes, and even a pontoon boat are available. Other facilities include a sandy beach, a tennis court, and hiking trails. Cottages have 1-4 bedrooms with rates from $1,085 per week for two, including all meals, served in the main lodge. In traditional style, lunch (called "dinner") is the main meal of the day. Cabins are available only by the week mid-June to Labor Day. Pets are not allowed.

Founded in 1909, **Alden Camps** (3 Alden Camps Cove, Oakland, 207/465-7703, www.aldencamps.com, mid-May-late Sept.) has an incredibly loyal following that includes multigenerational guests. The 18 rustic cottages face great sunrises across three-mile-long East Pond (a.k.a. East Lake). Meals are hearty and surprisingly creative, with about a dozen or so entrée choices nightly. The Friday night lobster bake or clam bake is a longstanding tradition. BYOB. The 40-acre spread has a clay tennis court, a sandy beach, a waterskiing boat, and a kids' play area. Rates vary with cottage size and occupancy, beginning around $156 pp per night or $933 pp per week for a studio. Children under age 12 are $26-94/day or $155-562/week, depending on age. Pets are grudgingly allowed for $30/day. A 17 percent resort fee is charged. Boat rentals begin at $40/day or $240/week; canoes and kayaks are free. Alden Camps is seven miles off I-95 Exit 127.

Castle Island Camps (Castle Island Rd., Belgrade Lakes, 207/495-3312, www.castleislandcamps.com, May-mid-Sept.) occupies all of tiny Castle Island, a blip on the

1: fishing boats in the Belgrade Lakes region
2: sign in Vienna, Maine

causeway-bridge dividing Long Lake. What a location! The 12 lakefront rustic cabins, each with screened porch, are geared to anglers, but they're popular with families in summer who want a simple old-fashioned lake-based holiday. Rates are $96 s, $175 d per night; $650 s, $1,200 d/week; kids' rates, $40-75, vary with age. Rental boats ($60/day with gas) and kayaks and paddleboards ($25/day) are available.

Seasonal Rentals

For cottage rentals, call **Day's Real Estate** (207/495-2104, www.belgraderental.com).

INFORMATION

Local information is available from the **Belgrade Lakes Region Business Group** (www.belgradelakesmaine.com) and the **Kennebec Valley Tourism Council** (207/623-4884, www.kennebecvalley.org).

Summertime in the Lakes (www.sumbelnews.com), a widely available free tabloid with ads, features, and calendar listings, is an especially helpful local publication that appears weekly during the summer.

GETTING THERE

By car, Belgrade Lakes is roughly 17 miles or 30 minutes from Augusta via Route 27. It's roughly 18 miles or 30 minutes to Waterville via Routes 27 and 11. It's roughly 20 miles or 30 minutes to Farmington.

Waterville and Vicinity

Most visitors are drawn to **Waterville** (pop. 15,722) by Colby College, an elite liberal arts institution whose students and faculty give a college-town flavor to this former mill town, incorporated in 1802. The school's Museum of Art is reason enough to visit this small city. Other draws include a fabulous film festival and the nation's oldest blockhouse, in nearby **Winslow** (pop. 7,794).

As early as 1653, Europeans set up a trading entrepôt here, calling it Teconnet, and commerce with Native Americans thrived until the onset of the Indian Wars two decades later. In the late 19th century, a contingent of Lebanese immigrants arrived, finding employment in the town's mills, and many of their descendants have become prominent community members. Best known of these is favorite son and former U.S. Senate Majority Leader George J. Mitchell, who still returns to spend time with family here.

Venture east to the rolling farmlands of **Unity** (pop. 2,099) to find Maine's organic farming center as well as Unity College and an Amish community.

SIGHTS

Colby College

Crowning Mayflower Hill, two miles from downtown Waterville, is **Colby College** (Mayflower Hill, Waterville, 207/872-3000, www.colby.edu). Colby's 1,800 students attend a huge variety of liberal arts programs on a 714-acre campus noted for its handsome Georgian buildings. Founded by Baptists in 1813 as the all-male Maine Literary and Theological Institution, Colby received its current name in 1867 and went coed in 1871. Campus tours are available through the **admissions office** (207/859-4828 or 800/723-3032, 8am-5pm Mon.-Fri., 8am-noon Sat.).

★ COLBY COLLEGE MUSEUM OF ART

With the 2013 opening of the Alfond-Lunder Family Pavilion, Colby's **Museum of Art**

(207/859-5600, 10am-5pm Tues.-Sat., noon-5pm Sun., free), in the Bixler Art and Music Center, became the state's largest art museum in terms of gallery space. Over the years, it's earned an especially distinguished reputation for its remarkable permanent collection of 18th-20th-century American art, which was cemented with the donation of the Lunder Collection, valued at $100 million and comprising more than 500 objects. These include works by Winslow Homer, Sol LeWitt, John Singer Sargent, and Georgia O'Keeffe, to name just a few, as well as 300 works by James McNeill Whistler.

The new galleries are the latest milestone in the museum's growth. In 1996, it opened its $1.5 million Paul J. Schupf Wing to house 415 paintings and sculptures created by artist Alex Katz over a 50-year period. In July 1999, the architecturally stunning $1.3 million Lunder Wing opened, expanding the museum's exhibit space to 28,000 square feet. Other significant holdings include works by Gilbert Stuart and John Marin, and in 2016, the museum acquired Picasso's *Voillard Suite*, a rare series comprising 100 etchings. In addition to the permanent collections, special solo and group shows are mounted throughout the year. And don't miss the tasteful gift shop. The museum is on the east side of the campus's main quadrangle.

Also on the campus is the **Perkins Arboretum and Bird Sanctuary,** with three nature trails. Bring a picnic and blanket and stretch out next to Johnson Pond. In winter there's ice-skating on the pond.

Fort Halifax

The two-story **Fort Halifax** (Bay St., Winslow) stands sentinel where the Sebasticook River meets the Kennebec River. A National Historic Landmark and the nation's oldest blockhouse, it was built in 1754 of doweled logs during the French and Indian War. In 1987, after rampaging Kennebec floodwaters swept the building away, more than three dozen of the giant timbers were retrieved downstream and the blockhouse was meticulously reassembled on its original site. The surrounding park is a great place for a picnic, with tables dotting shaded grassy lawns rolling to the river's edge.

Two Cent Bridge

Dating from 1903, the 700-foot-long **Two Cent Bridge** (officially the Ticonic Footbridge) spans the Kennebec from Benton Avenue in Winslow to Front Street in Waterville (at the base of Temple St.). Back then, pedestrian commuters working at the paper mill in Winslow paid $0.02 to cross. This suspension footbridge, which operated until 1973, was rehabilitated in 2012. Stroll across the restored bridge and replica tollbooth for good views of Ticonic Falls, the waterfall that likely inspired author Richard Russo's Pulitzer-prize-winning novel *Empire Falls.*

Redington Museum

Home of the Waterville Historical Society, the **Redington Museum and Apothecary** (62 Silver St., Waterville, 207/872-9439, www.redingtonmuseum.org, 10am-3pm Tues.-Sat. Memorial Day weekend-Labor Day, tours 10am, 11am, 1pm, 2pm, $5 adults, kids free with adult) has a particularly intriguing replica of a 19th-century pharmacy filled with authentic pharmaceutical antiquities. Early settler Asa Redington built the Federal-style house in 1814 for his son, William.

Johnny's Selected Seeds

If you're a gardener, farmer, horticulturalist, or just plain curious, take a 15-minute drive east of Waterville to visit the research farm of **Johnny's Selected Seeds** (Foss Hill Rd., Albion, 207/861-3900, www.johnnyseeds.com). Guided tours are offered on select summer dates; call for schedule and reserve in advance. Or visit the store (955 Benton Ave., Winslow, 207/238-5327). The eponymous seed source has a national reputation. More than 2,000 varieties of herbs, veggies, and flowers are grown in the trial gardens, which were

1

2

started in 1973. Known for high-quality seeds and service, the company makes good on anything that doesn't sprout.

ENTERTAINMENT

Once the haunt of vaudevillians, the renovated turn-of-the-20th-century **Waterville Opera House** (93 Main St., 207/873-5381, tickets 207/873-7000, www.operahouse.com), above city hall, is now the site of plays, dance performances, and concerts throughout the year.

About 20 minutes northeast of Waterville in rural Unity is **Unity Centre for the Performing Arts** (42 Depot St., Unity, 207/948-7469, http://uccpa.unity.edu), a 200-seat theater built by Bert and Coral Clifford and donated to Unity College in 2007.

Festivals and Events

One of Maine's premier art-film houses, the two-screen **Railroad Square Cinema** (17 Railroad Sq., Waterville, 207/873-6526, www.railroadsquarecinema.com) is the home of the **Maine International Film Festival** (MIFF, 207/873-7000, www.miff.org), which has brought such luminaries as Glenn Close and Keith Carradine to town to receive Mid-Life Achievement Awards. The 10-day summer festival screens about 100 films representing about 50 filmmakers.

A gathering of New England's best fiddlers, the **East Benton Fiddlers' Convention** (207/453-2017) draws close to 2,000 enthusiasts to open-air performances at the Littlefield farm in East Benton. The convention happens noon-dusk the last Sunday in July.

Downtown Waterville is the site of midsummer **Taste of Waterville.** The food-focused one-day festival is usually held on a Wednesday. There's alfresco dining along with music for kids and adults.

During the third weekend in September, sleepy Unity comes alive with the **Common Ground Fair,** a celebration of organic foods and country life sponsored by the Maine Organic Farmers and Gardeners Association. There are exhibits, demonstrations, livestock, social and political action groups, and more.

During the academic year, and less often in summer, **Colby College** (207/859-4353, www.colby.edu/news) is the venue for exhibits, lectures, concerts, performances, and other events.

1: Two Cent Bridge **2:** Fort Halifax

FOOD

Quick Bites

Jorgensen's Café (103 Main St., Waterville, 207/872-8711, 7am-5pm Mon.-Sat., 7am-3pm Sun.) is a downtown institution. Bagels, muffins, breakfast sandwiches, and an espresso bar attract morning crowds; lunch comprises specialty sandwiches, with every kind of deli meat available, plus quiche, salads, and soups. It's also the local outlet for Kennebec Chocolates.

Nothing's finer on a hot summer day than a banana, black licorice, peanut butter-chocolate chip, or other homemade ice cream from **North Street Dairy Cone** (127 North St., Waterville, 207/873-0977, noon-8pm daily).

An extremely popular hangout, **Big G's Deli** (Benton Ave., Winslow, 207/873-7808, www.big-g-s-deli.com, 6am-7pm daily, $5-12) began as a sandwich shop in 1986 and now seats 200. It's renowned for enormous "name" sandwiches such as the Miles Standwich (nearly a whole turkey dinner), all on thick slices of homemade bread (half sandwiches are available). You can enjoy breakfast until noon. Order at the counter and try for a seat, or get it to go for the mother of all picnics.

The **Grand Central Café** (10 Railroad Sq., 207/872-9135, 5pm-8pm Mon.-Wed., 11am-8pm Thurs., 11am-9pm Fri.-Sat., $9-20) is a local favorite for fancy brick-oven pizza. It also serves vegan and vegetarian fare.

Tea lovers take refuge in **Selah Tea Café** (177 Main St., Waterville, 207/660-9181, www.selahteacafe.com, 7am-7pm Mon.-Fri., 8am-5pm Sat.-Sun.), a cozy spot serving breakfast, sandwiches, soups, and salads in addition to fine teas.

Venture inland to **Unity Charcuterie** (41 Lealynn Dr., Unity, 207/948-1777, 10am-noon and 1pm-5pm Tues.-Wed. and Fri.-Sat.), where Amish butcher Matthew Secich handcrafts sausage and other specialty foods. While here, don't miss the fresh glazed doughnuts, available Wednesdays year-round and Saturdays in summer at the **Amish Community Market** (368 Thorndike Rd., Unity, 207/948-4174, 8am-5pm Mon.-Wed. and Fri.-Sat.).

The **Downtown Waterville Farmers Market** (2pm-6pm Thurs.) sets up at Head of Falls by the Two Cent Bridge.

Casual Dining

Fresh, flavorful American cuisine with varied ethnic inspirations makes dining at the **Last Unicorn** (98 Silver St./Rte. 201, Waterville, 207/873-9363, www.thelastunicornrestaurant.com, 11am-9pm Mon.-Sat., $18-26) a tasty adventure. Creative appetizers and an extensive wine and cocktail list are other pluses of this friendly place, which has patio dining in summer.

The **Riverside Farm Market** (291 Fairfield St., Oakland, 207/465-4439, www.riversidefarmmarket.com, 10am-2:30pm Wed.-Sat.) doubles as a casual restaurant (11am-2pm Wed.-Sat., 5:30pm-8:30pm Thurs.-Sat., 10am-2pm Sun., $15-29) serving fabulous sandwiches, soups, and salads with a Mediterranean bent, along with scrumptious baked goods and designer coffees. You also can pick up baked goods or lunch—soups, salads, quiche, and sandwiches—at the deli and baked-goods counter. Everything on the contemporary American menu is made from scratch.

The emphasis is on seafood at **18 Below Raw Bar** (18 Silver St., Waterville, 855/242-1665, www.18belowrawbar.com, 4pm-10pm Tues.-Sun., $14-28), but landlubbers and vegetarians will find a few options.

International

It doesn't look like much from the outside—or on the inside, for that matter—but the little **Lebanese Cuisine** (34 Temple St., Waterville, 207/873-7813, 9am-4pm Mon.-Fri., 9am-1pm Sat., $4-10) delivers on its name, with authentic dishes, including stuffed grape leaves, spinach and feta pastries, and a divine baklava. No credit cards.

ACCOMMODATIONS

Chains dominate area lodging, but the Pressey House, in the Belgrade Lakes area, is convenient to Waterville.

Guests at **84 The Pleasant Street Inn** (84 Pleasant St., Waterville, 207/680-2515, www.84pleasantstreet.com, $65-99) have access to a full kitchen, a dining area, and a living room, making it easy to feel at home. Five guest rooms have full baths, one has a half bath, and one has a shared bath. It's clean and cozy, and rates include a self-serve continental breakfast.

Colby College's investments in downtown Waterville include the **Lockwood Hotel,** a four-story, 53-room boutique hotel with a full-service restaurant that's expected to open in late 2020.

INFORMATION

The best sources of local information are the **Mid-Maine Chamber of Commerce** (207/873-3315, www.midmainechamber.com) and the **Kennebec Valley Tourism Council** (207/623-4884, www.kennebecvalley.org).

GETTING THERE

By car, Waterville is roughly 23 miles or 28 minutes from Augusta via I-95 and roughly 18 miles or 30 minutes from Belgrade Lakes via Routes 27 and 11. It's roughly 20 miles or 25 minutes to Skowhegan via I-95 and Route 201.

Skowhegan Area

The Wabanaki named **Skowhegan** (skow-HE-gun, pop. 8,589), meaning "the place to watch for fish," because that's just what the early Native Americans did at the Kennebec River's twin waterfalls. Their spears were ready when lunch came leaping up the river. The island between the falls later formed the core for European settlement of Skowhegan, the largest town in and the county seat of Somerset County. These days, plans are in the works to create a Run of River, a downtown white-water park.

Favorite daughter Margaret Chase Smith, one of Maine's preeminent politicians, put Skowhegan on the map, and even since her 1995 death, admirers and historians have made pilgrimages to her former home.

Another local institution is the nationally and internationally renowned Skowhegan School of Painting and Sculpture, founded in 1946 as a summer residency program. One of the few art schools in the United States offering workshops in fresco painting, Skowhegan provides 65 artists with a bucolic 300-acre lakeside setting for honing their skills and interacting with peers and prominent visiting artists. Gaining admission is highly competitive for the nine-week program. Skowhegan's annual summer lecture series, featuring big names in the art world, is open to the public.

These days, Skowhegan is earning fame as the state's bread-making center, thanks to the presence of Maine Grains at the Somerset Grist Mill, which is turning out flours from stone-milled local grains, and the annual Kneading Conference and companion Artisan Bread Fair in late July.

In the early 18th century, the town of **Norridgewock** (NORE-ridge-wok, pop. 3,367) was a French and Indian stronghold against the British. A century earlier, French Jesuit missionaries had moved in among the Norridgewock Indians at their settlement here and converted them to Catholicism. Best known of these was Father Sébastien Râle, beloved of his Indian parishioners. In 1724, taking revenge for Indian forays against them, a British militia detachment marched in and massacred the priest and his followers, a major milestone during what was known as Dummer's War. Today, a granite monument to Father Râle stands at the scene; it's found at Old Point, along the Kennebec River about two miles south of downtown Madison, close to the Madison-Norridgewock town boundary.

Meaning "smooth water between rapids," Norridgewock was the last bit of civilization for Benedict Arnold and his men before they headed into the Upper Kennebec wilderness on their march to Québec in 1775. Stopping for almost a week, they spent most of their time caulking their leaky bateaux. Today the town has a slew of handsome 18th- and 19th-century homes and a downtown that's undergoing a revival.

SIGHTS

Margaret Chase Smith Library

Beautifully sited on Neil Hill, high above the Kennebec River, the **Margaret Chase Smith Library** (56 Norridgewock Ave., Skowhegan, 207/474-7133, www.mcslibrary.org, 10am-4pm Mon.-Fri., donation) bulges with fascinating memorabilia from the life and times of one of Maine's best-known politicians, who spent 32 years in the U.S. House and Senate and died in 1995. Over the entrance door is her signature red rose; inside is a 20-minute video describing her career. In 2000, the library held a special commemoration of the 50th anniversary of Senator Smith's "declaration of conscience" speech, in which she courageously castigated Senator Joseph McCarthy for his "Red Scare" Communist witch-hunting tactics. During her years in the U.S. House and Senate, "The Lady from Maine" would return to her constituents—and she was never too busy to autograph place mats at her favorite local restaurant or to wave from her chair in her house's street-side solarium. Ask if a staff member is available to show you Senator Smith's house, connected to the library on the 15-acre estate. (She was born at 81 North Ave. in Skowhegan.) The library is closed the week between Christmas and New Year's Day. The complex is 0.5 mile west of Route 201 (Madison Ave.).

Skowhegan History House

When you enter the handsome redbrick **Skowhegan History House** (66 Elm St., Skowhegan, 207/474-6632, www.skowheganhistoryhouse.org, $2 adults, $1 children and seniors), with only half a dozen rooms, you'll find it hard to believe that blacksmith Aaron Spear built it in 1839 for his family of 10 children. Skowhegan treasures—antique clocks, china, and other furnishings—now fill the two-story structure, which has a commanding view over the Kennebec River and heirloom gardens. The house, located just west of Route 201 at the junction of Elm and Pleasant Streets, is staffed by volunteers and open from late May to mid-October; call for hours.

Skowhegan Indian Monument

Rising 62 feet above its pedestal and weighing 24,000 pounds, the giant wooden **Skowhegan Indian Monument** (http://langlaisarttrail.org) was carved in 1969 by Maine sculptor Bernard Langlais, a Skowhegan School of Painting alum who died in 1977. Known nationally for his work, Langlais dedicated the monument to the Native Americans who first settled this area. One hand holds a spear, the other holds a stylized fishing weir. Restored in 2014, it's just off Route 201, tucked in the back corner of a parking lot behind a Cumberland Farms at the intersection with High Street. Skowhegan was the recipient of 25 other Langlais pieces, which are being restored and placed around town. Find these and others on the Langlais Art Trail (http://langlaisarttrail.org).

Skowhegan Historic District

Bounded roughly by Water and Russell Streets and Madison Avenue, the **Skowhegan Historic District,** close to the Kennebec River, contains 38 turn-of-the-20th-century buildings from the town's heyday as a commercial center. After the arrival of trains in 1856, the wireless telegraph in 1862, and telephones in 1883, Skowhegan saw incredible prosperity. It's worth a walkabout to admire the architectural details of a bygone era. Many buildings are undergoing restoration and now house independent businesses and shops.

★ L. C. Bates Museum

Offbeat doesn't begin to describe this treasure chest. In a Romanesque building, listed in the National Register of Historic Places, on the Good Will-Hinckley School campus, which was established in 1889 as a school for disadvantaged children, the **L. C. Bates Museum** (Rte. 201, Hinckley, 207/238-4250, www.gwh.org, 10am-4:30pm Wed.-Sat., 1pm-4:30pm Sun. Apr.-mid-Nov., 10am-4:30pm Wed.-Sat. mid-Nov.-Mar. or by appointment, $3 adults, $1 under age 17) is a way-cool, way-retro museum, with a broadly eclectic collection focusing on natural history. Among the treasures in the dozen or so rooms are hundreds of mounted rare birds, priceless Native American artifacts, and a trophy marlin caught by Ernest Hemingway. Dress warmly if you visit in winter; it's not heated.

Behind the museum, visit the arboretum and nature trails, open dawn-dusk. *Forest Walking Trails* maps are available in the museum. Alongside the trails are monuments to prominent conservationists. The turreted brick-and-granite building is five miles north of I-95 Exit 133, between Fairfield and Skowhegan.

Pedestrian Bridges

Two downtown bridges across the Kennebec are worth crossing just for the views. Spanning the river's South Channel, the **Swinging Bridge** connects Skowhegan Island (from Arnold Trail Park, behind the ice cream stand) to Alder Street, off West Front Street. First built in 1883, floods in 1888, 1901, 1936, and 1987 damaged or destroyed the wire footbridge. Its latest incarnation was unveiled in 2006, when the town completely renovated it.

The **Skowhegan Walking Bridge** spans the river about a block below the dam, opposite where Route 201 North and Route 2 split downtown. This one traces its history back to 1856, when it was constructed for the Somerset and Kennebec Railroad. The following year it was carried away by floodwaters. A wooden bridge followed, and then a steel one, also destroyed by floodwaters. The current bridge dates from 1988.

ENTERTAINMENT

Theaters

For a dose of nostalgia, catch a flick at the 350-car **Skowhegan Drive-In** (Waterville Rd./Rte. 201, Skowhegan, 207/474-9277, www.skowhegandrivein.com), a landmark since 1954. Nightly double features start at dusk or whenever the sun disappears. Gates open at 7:30pm.

Built in 1901, the **Lakewood Theater** (Rte. 201, Madison, 207/474-7176, www.lakewoodtheater.org), on the shores of Lake Wesserunsett six miles north of Skowhegan, is a step back in time. Maine's oldest summer theater presents nine musicals, comedies, and light dramas each season. Performances are at 8pm Thursday-Saturday and at 4pm every other Sunday, plus matinees at 2pm every other Wednesday late May-mid-September. On matinee Wednesday, there is also a 7pm evening performance. Tickets are $22-35 adults and about $18 ages 4-17. Consider pairing it with dinner at the restaurant and perhaps an overnight at the inn.

Lectures and Concerts

Performing arts events are sometimes scheduled in Skowhegan's **Opera House** inside the circa 1909 city hall, where Booker T. Washington spoke in 1912.

In mid-June-early August, the evening **Barbara Fish Lee Lecture Series** draws nationally and internationally noted artists to participate in its lecture and presentation series at the Old Dominion Fresco Barn at the Skowhegan School of Painting and Sculpture (207/474-9345, www.skowheganart.org).

A **concert series** is held at **Skowhegan's Coburn Park** at 5pm Sundays during July-August.

Festivals and Events

Mega-size omelets made in the world's largest omelet pan, a parade, a crafts fair, live entertainment, a carnival, and fireworks are among the features of the **Central Maine Egg Festival.** It's held for nearly a week at Manson Park in Pittsfield mid-July. The biggest day is Saturday.

Artisan bread bakers and those interested in learning about growing and milling grains converge in Skowhegan for the annual late July **Kneading Conference** and its companion **Artisan Bread Fair.**

Founded in 1818 and billed as the country's oldest agricultural fair in continual operation, the **Skowhegan State Fair** is a 10-day extravaganza with agricultural exhibits galore, live entertainment, harness racing, food booths, a carnival, and a demolition derby at the Skowhegan Fairgrounds (Rte. 201, Skowhegan) early-mid-August.

The annual **Skowhegan Craft Brew Festival** (www.skowhegancraftbrewfest.com), with live music and farm-to-table fare, occurs on a Saturday in late August.

SHOPPING

Discounts of up to 50 percent are typical for athletic-shoe seconds at the **New Balance Factory Store** (12 Walnut St., Skowhegan, 207/474-6231). The store also carries sportswear, socks, sports bags, and such. The outlet is just off Route 201 (W. Front St.) south of the Kennebec. The turn is next to Skowhegan Savings Bank.

The retail factory outlet for **Dog Not Gone** (40 Dane Ave., Skowhegan, 207/479-5500, www.dognotgone.com) carries the

SCULPTOR
BERNARD LANGLAIS
BORN OLD TOWN MAINE
1921-ALUMNUS OF SKOWHEGAN
SCHOOL OF PAINTING & SCULPTURE
MR LANGLAIS DIED 1977
SKOWHEGAN INDIAN
THIS SCULPTURE IS DEDICATED
TO THE MAINE INDIANS
THE FIRST PEOPLE TO USE
THESE LANDS IN PEACEFUL WAYS
1
2 
3 
MARGARET
CHASE SMITH
LIBRARY

company's Maine-made insect-repelling clothing for people and pets.

The **Fairfield Antiques Mall** (382 Rte. 201, Fairfield, 207/453-4100) boasts that it's the state's largest antiques group shop. Judge for yourself; it's 2.5 miles north of the I-95 interchange. In downtown Skowhegan, **Hilltop Antiques** (48 Water St., 207/474-0055) has 27 rooms brimming with finds on three floors.

About 20 talented area artists show their works at the cooperatively owned **River Roads Artisans Gallery** (75 Water St., Skowhegan).

RECREATION

Parks

Donated to the town by former Governor Abner Coburn, **Coburn Park,** a wonderful riverside oasis, has a lily pond, memorial gardens (including a hospice garden and a Margaret Chase Smith rose garden), a summer concert series at the gazebo, pagodas, and more than 100 species of trees and shrubs. Bring a picnic, grab a table, and enjoy. The park is on Water Street (Rte. 2, 0.6 miles east of Rte. 201).

Lake George Regional Park (off Rte. 2, Skowhegan and Canaan, 207/474-1292, www.lakegeorgepark.org, $6 adults, $2 ages 5-11) has boating, swimming, two sandy beaches, hiking and walking trails, playing fields, and picnicking in two sections framing Lake George.

About three miles north of Solon, close to the Solon-Bingham town line and just north of the area known as Arnold's Landing, is **Arnold's Way Rest Area,** with covered picnic tables, grills, and an outhouse. Interpretive panels here mark the first of two dozen panels along the Old Canada Road Scenic Byway at Moscow, The Forks, Parlin Pond, and Attean, interpreting area history and heritage.

Golf

The 18-hole **Lakewood Golf Course** (Rte. 201, Madison, 207/474-5955, www.lakewoodgolfmaine.com), five miles north of Skowhegan, dates from 1925.

1: Skowhegan Indian Monument **2:** Kennebec River **3:** Margaret Chase Smith Library

FOOD

Quick Bites

Just south of downtown, the **Snack Shack** (100 Waterville Rd./Rte. 201, Skowhegan, 207/474-0550, www.snackshackme.com, 11am-8pm Tues.-Sat., $3-15) never disappoints for fried foods or sandwiches. It has a few tables, but most folks get takeout. Classic, antique, and hot rod vehicles fill the lot for Cruz-in Tuesday 4pm-dusk.

An 1864 bank now houses the **Bankery** (87 Water St., Skowhegan, 207/474-2253, www.thebankery.com, 7:30am-6pm Mon.-Sat., $3-10), a fine source for made-from-scratch baked goods as well as soups, chowders, flatbreads, quiches, and other treats. You can even watch the bakers at work.

More than two dozen fat sandwiches, as well as flatbread pizzas, salads, and a soup of the day, draw locals into **Kel-Matt Café** (147 Madison Ave./Rte. 201, Skowhegan, 207/474-0200, www.kelmatcafe.com, 11am-3pm Mon.-Fri., 11am-2pm Sat., $8-10). Service is friendly and efficient.

I scream, you scream, and in Maine everyone screams for **Gifford's Ice Cream** (307 Madison Ave./Rte. 1, Skowhegan, no phone, www.giffordsicecream.com). At this roadside institution, you can lick whoopie pie, Maine tracks, Denali peanut butter Iditarod, or Maine wild blueberry flavors while playing miniature golf.

The **Skowhegan Farmers Market** sets up at the Somerset Grist Mill, at the corner of Court and High Streets, 9am-1pm Saturdays May to October. While here, visit the mill's **Flour, Feed, and Dry Goods** store to purchase organic, Maine-grown stone-milled grains.

Family Favorite

At **Ken's Family Restaurant** (414 Madison Ave./Rte. 201, Skowhegan, 207/474-3120, www.kensfamilyrestaurant.com, 11am-8pm daily, $5-24), in its second generation of Dionne family ownership, fried food is the specialty, although you'll find plenty more on this American menu.

Casual Dining

Two doors from the Towne Motel, in a renovated 19th-century home, the **Heritage House Restaurant** (182 Madison Ave., Skowhegan, 207/474-5100, www.hhrestaurant.com, lunch buffet 11:30am-2pm Tues.-Fri., dinner 5pm-9pm Mon.-Sat., $20-30) is Skowhegan's favorite special-occasion restaurant. Apricot-mustard chicken breast is a specialty. Reservations are advisable on weekends. The lunch buffet runs $8.50-10.

Pair a show at the Lakewood Theatre with a meal at the lakeside **Lakewood Inn Restaurant** (76 Theatre Rd., Madison, 207/858-4403, www.lakewoodtheater.org, from 5pm Wed.-Sat., 10am-2pm Sun., $21-36), serving a wide-ranging, internationally accented, contemporary American menu that pleases all palates. Hours are extended on show days.

Everything served at the ★ **Miller's Table at Maine Grains** (42 Court St., Skowhegan, 207/612-5322, https://mainegrains.com, 11am-2:30pm Mon.-Tues., 11am-2:30pm and 4pm-9pm Wed.-Fri., 8am-9pm Sat., $10-24) is scratch-made, from breakfast fare to the wood-fired pizzas to dinners. Time a visit to coincide with a gristmill tour; call for current schedule. Indoor seating is limited; reservations are encouraged. There are sheltered outside tables too.

ACCOMMODATIONS

Convenient to downtown, the **Towne Motel** (172 Madison Ave./Rte. 201 N., Skowhegan, 207/474-5151 or 800/843-4405, http://thetownemotel.com, mid-May-mid-Oct., $115-140) has 33 guest rooms; some with kitchenettes. Continental breakfast is included. The large outdoor pool is great for kids.

Sleep where the stars slept at the **Colony House Inn Bed and Breakfast** (79 Beach Rd., Madison, 888/268-2853, www.colonyhouseinn.com, $48 pp), a lovely—although tired—lakefront historical B&B adjacent to the Lakeside Theater. The 1929 John Calvin Stevens-designed Shingle-style inn is wrapped in old-style elegance, with a nice screened porch and a many-windowed dining room where a full breakfast is served. The prices reflect the old-fashioned bathrooms and the need for updating and TLC. One guest room has a private bath, two lake-facing guest rooms are connected by a bath, and two other guest rooms share a bath. Also on the premises are two cottages ($600-700/week or $100/night): one lakefront, one lakeview. Within walking distance are the theater, a restaurant, a golf course, and a spiritualist camp that has been running for more than 125 years. Rent a boat, or simply settle into one of the Adirondack chairs on the lawn and gaze out at Lake Wesserunsett; it's heaven.

INFORMATION AND SERVICES

The **Skowhegan Area Chamber of Commerce** (23 Commercial St., Skowhegan, 207/474-3621 or 888/772-4392, www.skowheganchamber.com) has info, as does **Main Street Skowhegan** (207/612-2571, www.mainstreetskowhegan.org), and the town's website (www.skowhegan.org). More information is available from the **Kennebec Valley Tourism Council** (207/623-4884, www.kennebecvalley.org).

GETTING THERE

By car, Skowhegan is roughly 20 miles or 25 minutes from Waterville via I-95 and Route 201. It's roughly 45 miles or one hour to Bingham via Route 201.

Solon to Jackman

Route 201, from **Solon** (pop. 1,053) north to **Jackman** (pop. 862), is a National Scenic Byway threading through the rural towns of **Bingham** (pop. 922), **Moscow** (pop. 512), and **The Forks** (pop. 37). Until the arrival of white-water rafting in the late 1970s, the Upper Kennebec Valley was best known to anglers, hunters, timber truckers, and families who'd been summering here for generations. Long before that, before dams changed the river's flow patterns, Native Americans used the Kennebec as a convenient chute from the interior's dense forests to coastal summer encampments. In 1775, Col. Benedict Arnold led more than 1,000 men up this river in a futile campaign to storm Québec City's ramparts.

Midway between Skowhegan and The Forks, 23 miles in each direction, Bingham is also right on the 45th parallel and thus equidistant between the North Pole and the equator (3,107 miles in each direction). The town was named for William Bingham, an influential colonial-era banker and land speculator who made a fortune in privateering. Roscoe Vernon "Gadabout" Gaddis, TV's pioneering Flying Fisherman, built Bingham's funky grass airfield, the Gadabout Gaddis Airport.

Just north of Bingham is Moscow, home of the 155-foot-high Wyman Dam, harnessing the Kennebec River for hydroelectric power. Backed up behind the dam is gorgeous Wyman Lake, lined with birches, evergreens, frequent pullouts (great for shutterbugs), and a small lakeside picnic area on the west side of Route 201.

Appropriately named, The Forks stands at the confluence of the Kennebec and Dead Rivers. Although neither looks particularly menacing from the Route 201 bridge, both draw legions of white-water rafters and kayakers for the Class III-IV rapids on the dam-controlled waters.

Surrounded by mountains, Jackman is the valley's frontier town, the last outpost before the Québec border, 16 miles northward. Founded as a railway stop for lumber trains, it's now a linchpin in the international snowmobile trail system. Wander into local businesses and you'll likely hear a French lilt to the conversation.

From Bingham to Jackman, Route 201 is better known as "Moose Alley." Even though state transportation officials have built rumble strips into the road and littered the roadsides with flashing yellow lights and cautionary Moose Crossing signs, drivers still barrel along, and every year fatalities occur. Those who drive carefully, though, have a treat in store: Moose sightings are relatively frequent, especially early and late in the day. If you notice a car or two pulled off the road, it's likely someone has spotted a moose. (Another Moose Alley in this area—a pretty sure bet for spotting one of the behemoths—is Route 6/15 from Jackman east to Rockwood.)

SIGHTS

★ South Solon Meetinghouse

The **South Solon Meetinghouse** (www.southsolonmeetinghouse.org, no official hours, usually left open), a serene white-clapboard 1842 New England meetinghouse now listed in the National Register of Historic Places, sits at a crossroads in the hamlet of South Solon. The classic Gothic Revival exterior provides no clues about the eye candy inside. One of the founders of the Skowhegan School of Painting and Sculpture rescued the church from ruin in the 1930s; in the 1950s, fresco artists selected in a stiff competition were given a free hand to paint the place with only the following guidance: "There shall be no limitation of subject matter; however, bearing in mind the religious character of the building, which has been non-sectarian from its inception, it's suggested that the New and Old Testaments offer rich and suitable subject matter. This material should be interpreted in imaginative terms which allow complete freedom to develop symbols, associations, or legends." The riot of color followed until every square inch of wall and ceiling was frescoed with interdenominational religious scenes. (A fresco program continues at the Skowhegan School.) A binder, available in the entry foyer, is filled with information about the frescoes. The South Solon Historical Society cares for the property. The meetinghouse is on the corner of South Solon Road and Meetinghouse Road, north of Route 43 and east of Route 201.

★ Moxie Falls

Here's a big reward for little effort: One of New England's highest waterfalls, **Moxie Falls,** which drops 92 feet, is one of the easiest to reach. From Route 201, just south of the Kennebec River bridge in The Forks, drive two miles east on Moxie Pond Road to the signposted parking area. From here, via an easy, wide trail with steps and a boardwalk, it's one mile to viewing platforms overlooking the falls. Allow a relaxed hour for the round-trip; if it's hot, cool off in the stepped pools. Avoid the falls in June, when blackflies will have you for lunch.

★ Old Canada Road National Scenic Byway

The **Old Canada Road Scenic Byway** (www.fhwa.dot.gov/byways) on Route 201 between Lakewood and the Canadian border is gorgeous in any season but drop-dead spectacular in autumn, when every curve along the winding two-lane road reveals a red, gold, orange, and green palette.

It's also a historical route. Benedict Arnold marched his troops along the Kennebec River to the north of Moscow before crossing the river and turning inland. Rest stops along the route have interpretative signage and picnic tables. Two of the prettiest are **Wyman Lake Rest Area,** about midway between Bingham and The Forks, and **Attean View Rest Area,** just south of Jackman (climb the Owl's Head Trail for an even more spectacular view). The rest area in The Forks, just before the bridge, is a great place to watch rafts float by at the end of their thrilling white-water trip down the Kennebec River. Detour into the neat little hamlet of **Caratunk,** a smidgen east of Route 201 on the way to Pleasant Pond.

For a glimpse into the region's glorious past, visit the **Old Canada Road Historical Society** (16 Sidney St., Bingham, www.oldcanadaroad.org, 1pm-5pm Fri., 11am-4pm Sat.).

Flightseeing

Get a bird's eye view of the rivers, lakes, and mountains with Pilot Thomas Coleman, owner of **Wings, Woods & Waters** (207/356-8794), with pickup available in Caratun, The Forks, or Jackman. The fee is $75 pp for 20 minutes.

RECREATION

Recreation is the big focus in this part of Maine. Among the opportunities in the Upper Kennebec Valley are hiking, canoeing, kayaking, bicycling, fishing, and snowmobiling—just for a start—but the big business is white-water rafting, based in and around The Forks.

TOP EXPERIENCE

Water Sports

★ WHITE-WATER RAFTING

Carefully regulated by the state, the rafting companies have come a long way since the sport really took off in the early 1980s. Most have sprawling base complexes and have diversified year-round into other adventure sports such as mountain biking, paddlesports, camping, rock climbing, horseback riding, snowmobiling, and cross-country skiing.

The focus of white-water rafting in this region is the **East Branch of the Kennebec River,** a 12-mile run from the Harris Station hydroelectric dam, below Indian Pond, to The Forks. The dam's controlled water releases

1: interpretive sign along the Old Canada Road National Scenic Byway **2:** Attean View Rest Area

1
River Towns / Les villes le long de la rivière
2

produce waves of up to eight feet, and the trip begins with a bang in the Alleyway. The highlight is Magic Falls, a Class IV drop that appears as nothing more than a horizon line when approaching it but that has the punch to flip rafts. The excitement is concentrated in the first half of the trip; by the end of it, you're just floating along, but that provides opportunities for swimming, water fights between rafts, and perhaps kayaking. Some companies also break for a riverside lunch. Kennebec trips operate early May-mid-October.

Most of the rafting companies also organize trips on the oddly named **Dead River,** but serious water releases occur only half a dozen times during the season, mostly on spring weekends. Competition is stiff for space on the exhilarating 16-mile run through Class III-V white water from below Grand Falls to The Forks. The biggest thrill is Poplar Hill Falls. In July-August, the Dead River lives up to its placid name, and outfitters organize moderately priced Sport-Yak and family rafting trips.

The cost of a one-day Kennebec River trip ranges $70-130 pp, depending on whether it's a weekday, weekend, special release, or in midsummer. Prices include a hearty cookout or lunch either along the river or back at base camp. The cost of the one-day Dead River trip ranges $79-140 pp. Scads of economical package rates are available—covering lodging, meals, and other activities—especially early and late in the season. Be forewarned that all outfitters have age minimums, usually 10 on the upper Kennebec and 15 on the Dead. Some also impose a weight minimum.

Trips start early in the morning and you'll be exhilarated but dog-tired at the end of the day, so it's wise to bookend the trip with nearby lodging. Most of the outfitters have accommodations and dining for every budget. The camaraderie is contagious when everyone around you is about to go rafting or has just done it.

About a dozen outfitters operate on the Kennebec and Dead Rivers. The oldest and biggest is **Northern Outdoors** (1771 Rte. 201, The Forks, 800/765-7238, www.northernoutdoors.com), with extensive base facilities including lodging, dining, rentals, and more.

CANOEING AND KAYAKING

If you're a neophyte canoeist, if you have never done a multiday trip, or if you want to go en famille, your baptismal expedition probably ought to be the three-day **Moose River Bow Trip,** an easy 45-mile loop (ergo "bow") with mostly flat water. Of course, you can do this yourself, and you don't even need to arrange a shuttle, but a guided trip has its advantages—not the least of which is that the guides provide the know-how for the beginners, they do the cooking and cleanup, and they're a big help for portaging.

Experienced Maine Guides Andy and Leslie McKendry operate **Cry of the Loon Kayak Adventures** (207/668-7808, www.cryoftheloon.net), which offers a food-, equipment-, instruction-included guided three-day Moose River Bow trip ($425 pp, with only one portage). Maximum group size is eight and minimum four. Andy and Leslie will also do one-day guided trips ($60 pp with lunch). If you want to be on your own, they rent kayaks and canoes for $25/day, paddleboards for $30/day. Avoid June, when the blackflies descend; the water level can be a problem in August for the bow trip. Cry of the Loon's base is 6.5 miles east of Jackman on Route 15.

Maine Huts and Trails

The nonmotorized multiuse **Maine Huts and Trails** (www.mainehuts.org) network, which extends about 50 miles from Carrabassett Valley to The Forks, has a full-service hut sited about two miles below Grand Falls on the Dead River, making it easy to hike or bike the trail or even hike in, and then paddle out. It's also open to skiers and snowshoers.

Hiking

The **Appalachian Trail** (AT), extending 2,158 miles from Springer Mountain, Georgia,

The Benedict Arnold Trail

"A tragic masterpiece of bad timing, bad maps, and bad luck" is author Ogden Tanner's summation of Col. Benedict Arnold's march to Québec. Even though Arnold's expedition has been little more than a footnote to history, it's an incredible story, and one best appreciated during a visit to this region.

Arnold marched his troops up the Kennebec River Valley before crossing it and veering inland and up along the Carrabassett River. From Pittston to the Carrying Place (10 miles north of Bingham) and along Route 27, between Kingfield and the border, Arnold Trail historical markers note the expedition's rest stops and obstacles, and reveal other details.

When you see the terrain, you'll begin to understand some of the rigors endured by Arnold (before his change of heart and alliance) and his men when they chose a route through the Kennebec Valley to attack the British in Québec City in 1775. Although he later betrayed the Revolutionary cause, Arnold was in good graces when he set out that fall with 1,100 adventurers to remove the English from their Québec stronghold.

In Pittston, six miles south of Augusta, the expedition assembled 220 locally made bateaux and then continued up the Kennebec River to Augusta, camping at Old Fort Western, Skowhegan, and Norridgewock—cutting a swath through the Kennebec River Valley before portaging westward at Carrying Place Township to the Western Lakes and Mountains region and on into Canada. Afflicted by disease, hunger, cold, insects, and unforgiving terrain, the group was devastated before dragging into Québec City in December 1775.

If you're interested in Arnold, pick up a copy of *Following Their Footsteps: A Travel Guide and History of the 1775 Secret Expedition to Capture Québec* by Stephen Clark. The book includes history, maps, canoe routes, and an appendix of places to visit along the way.

to the summit of Maine's Katahdin, crosses the Upper Kennebec Valley near Caratunk, just south of The Forks. The *Appalachian Trail Guide to Maine* provides details for reaching several sections of the white-blazed trail accessible to short-haul hikers. Crossing the 70-yard-wide Kennebec at this point would be a major obstacle were it not for the seasonal free ferry service operated for AT hikers by the Maine Appalachian Trail Club (www.matc.org). Check the website for the current schedule. Do not attempt to ford the river.

Other hikes abound, but access is often through a maze of logging roads or through territory where active logging may change landmarks. Ask locally for directions to the trailheads to **Sally Mountain, Number 5** (topped with a fire tower), **Coburn Falls,** and **Kibby Mountain** (with an observation deck).

Mountain Biking

Mountain biking is growing in popularity here, but be forewarned that this is logging country, and on the woods roads, logging trucks and equipment have the right of way; don't mess with them. Your best bet is the **Maine Huts and Trails.**

The **Kennebec Valley Trail,** an easy eight-mile multiuse gravel trail, follows an old narrow-gauge railroad bed between the Williams Dam public landing, alongside the Kennebec River in Solon, and the Gaddis Airport, on the southern outskirts of Bingham. The scenic route roughly shadows the river and is especially gorgeous in autumn. Note: A rugged section of the trail continues to North Anson.

In the Jackman area, an easy-to-moderate 10-mile trip is the **Sandy Bay Loop,** beginning seven miles north of downtown Jackman. The trail follows mostly jeep roads and includes hill climbs along a section on Route 201. Jackman's chamber office has a recreational map detailing this route and others in the area.

Snowmobiling and ATVing

The region is a snowmobiling hotbed, with

hundreds of miles of groomed snowmobile trails that connect east to the Moosehead Lake area, west to the Sugarloaf area, and north into Canada. Most double as ATV trails.

Escape into the wilderness with **Northern Outdoors** (1771 Rte. 201, The Forks, 800/765-7238, www.northernoutdoors.com). If you're comfortable exploring the backwoods on your own, rental snowmobiles begin at $210/half day/single sled; clothing rental is $45. Better yet, go with a guide; half-day tours begin at $175 (not including rental). ATV rentals begin at $165/half day.

FOOD

Fine dining simply doesn't exist in this region, but you'll find good home cooking. It's always wise to ask locally about current reputations, as they do seem to change with the wind as cooks blow in and out of town or head downriver. Most of the rafting companies also operate restaurants.

Thompson's Restaurant (348 Main St./Rte. 201, Bingham, 207/672-3330, 7am-2pm Sun. and Wed., 7am-7pm Thurs.-Sat., $6-14) has been around forever, serving inexpensive, no-nonsense fare. Don't miss the doughnuts.

Gas, food, clothing: You can get it all at **Berry's General Store** (Rte. 201, The Forks, 207/663-4461, 5am-7pm daily), an institution in these parts.

Hawk's Nest Lodge, Restaurant & Pub (2989 Rte. 201, West Forks, 207/663-2020, www.hawksnestlodge.com, 7am-8pm daily, $11-29) serves pizza, sandwiches, salads, and some heftier entrées.

Home cookin' is also the specialty at **Mama Bear's** (420 Main St., Jackman, 207/668-4222, 4am-noon Mon., 4am-8pm Tues.-Fri., 6am-8pm Sat., 6am-noon Sun., $6-15). Slide into a booth and check out the engraved tables and the historical pics lining the walls. This tiny spot was Jackman's original A&P store.

The **Kennebec River Pub and Brewery at Northern Outdoors Restaurant** (Rte. 201, The Forks, 800/765-7238, www.northernoutdoors.com, 7am-9pm daily early May-late Oct. and late Dec.-late Mar., $10-20) caters to the rafting and recreating crowd, but it's one of the best bets around. The pub-style dinner menu ranges from burgers to steak tips.

ACCOMMODATIONS

Most of the white-water rafting companies have lodging, and it's convenient to stay where you play. But if you aren't rafting, staying at these places can be a bit overwhelming, especially with the après-raft party atmosphere. If you're planning to be in this area during snowmobiling season, especially in Jackman, book well in advance; the lodgings get chockablock with sledders.

The custom-designed post-and-beam **Hawk's Nest Lodge, Restaurant & Pub** (2989 Rte. 201, West Forks, 207/663-2020, www.hawksnestlodge.com, $129-250), built in 2004, is especially popular with rafters and sledders. The pine-paneled guest rooms are spacious and have custom furnishings. Most have river views. One especially family-friendly, two-story suite was constructed on the site of a climbing wall, and the handholds remain. Chainsaw carvings by Maine Guide Jeff Samudosky accent the property.

★ **Attean Lake Lodge** (Birch Island, Jackman, 207/668-3792, www.atteanlodge.com, Memorial Day-Sept.), an upscale rustic cottage colony geared to families, is a slice of heaven. Owned by the Holden family since 1900, it's on Birch Island in the center of island- and rock-sprinkled Attean Lake (also called Attean Pond). Fourteen well-maintained log cabins (some old, some new, 2-6 beds) have baths, fireplaces, gas or kerosene lamps, and porches with mesmerizing views of the lake and surrounding mountains. Guests tend to collect in the new main lodge, with its cathedral ceiling, stone fireplaces, and window-walled dining room, where a choice-of-menu breakfast and dinner are served; a box lunch is provided. Kids love the sandy beach. Motorboats are $30/day; canoes, kayaks, paddleboats, and a sailboat are free. July-Labor Day, rates for two adults are $460/day, including three meals (wine and beer are available), but nobody stays just one night. Early and late in the season, rates are $360 d per day; children's rates are much lower. Be sure to paddle across the pond and climb **Sally Mountain** (about 1.5 miles round-trip) for views that stretch as far as Katahdin; in fall, the foliage vistas are fabulous. Access to the island is via the lodge launch, a five-minute run.

★ **Sky Lodge** (748 Main St., Moose River, 207/668-2171, https://skylodge.unity.edu, from $120), owned and operated by Unity College, was built in 1929 as an executive sporting getaway then rechristened Sky Lodge by its next owners, two World War II airmen. In 2018, Unity College acquired through donation this spectacular 150-acre estate overlooking the Moose River Valley. The main log lodge has stone fireplaces anchoring each end of the two-story great room, rimmed with a balcony. Also here is a lounge with full bar and TV, a pool room, a dining room, and a porch. Accommodations include rooms and suites in the main log lodge ($120-225), cabins ($165-365), a motel annex ($95-110), bunkhouses ($55), and a few rental houses ($225-375). Some are pet friendly ($25/night). Guests have use of an outdoor saltwater pool and cross-country and snowshoeing trails. The lodge can arrange trail rides, floatplane rides, golf, and guided fly-fishing excursions. Also on the premises are an antique auto museum and a railroad museum with working models. Dinner is available most weekends and some midweek days, call for details, entrées ($28-35).

The nicest motel in town is **Bishop's Country Inn Motel** (461 Main St., Jackman, 207/668-3231 or 888/991-7669, www.bishopsmotel.com, $95-115/summer, $110-130/winter). A breakfast buffet is included and there's a coin-op laundry. It's directly across Route 201 from Bishop's Store, where you can get everything else you might possibly want or need, and even grab a meal.

Lake Parlin Lodge (6003 Rte. 201, Parlin Pond Township, 207/668-9060, www.lakeparlinlodge.com) has six one- and two-bedroom lakeside cabins, all with full kitchens and propane fireplaces ($175-275). There are also four rooms in the main lodge ($120).

Camping

How often do you find a campground in the National Register of Historic Places? That's the case at the **Evergreens Campground and Restaurant** (Rte. 201A, Solon, 207/643-2324, www.evergreenscampground.com), on a prehistoric site used by Native Americans about 4,000 years ago as well as by Benedict Arnold on his march to Quebec. Many stone tools and weapons excavated here are now in the Maine State Museum in Augusta; a small collection is displayed at the campground. The campground has mostly wooded sites (tent sites $16, RV sites $29, dogs $10), some right on the Kennebec River. Cabins are $33 pp ($132 with kitchen), dogs $10. Rental canoes, kayaks, and tubes are available by the day, and shuttle service is available. There is a small launch fee for people bringing their own boats, and a guest fee. The restaurant, open 5pm-8pm Friday-Saturday for dinner and 8am-11am Saturday-Sunday for breakfast, has a bar and a riverfront deck. Directly across the river (technically in Embden) is a huge outcrop covered with ancient Indian petroglyphs; eagles can often be seen on this shore. The campground, a mile south of the center of Solon, is open all year, except mud season (spring), and caters to snowmobilers in winter.

Indian Pond Campground (1675 Indian Pond Rd., The Forks, 800/371-7774, mid-Apr.-mid-Oct., $14 pp), next to Harris Station on the East Branch of the Kennebec, where Upper Kennebec rafting trips begin, has 27 tent and RV sites that have picnic tables and fire rings but no hookups. There also are 13 water-access primitive sites. Other facilities include showers, restrooms, an RV dump station, laundry machines, and a boat launch. Leashed pets are allowed. You can hike from here to Magic Rock and watch Kennebec River rafters surging through Magic Falls. To reach the campground from Route 201 in The Forks,

1

Mama Bear's Restaurant
BREAKFAST • LUNCH • DINNER
RESTAURANT
RESTAURANT
HOME COOKING
RESTAURANT

2

Sky Lodge

3

OPEN
OPEN
Hawk's Nest
LODGE

take Lake Moxie Road (also called Moxie Pond Rd.) about five miles east; turn left (north) onto Harris Station Road and continue eight miles to the campground gatehouse.

On Heald Stream in Moose River, a mile east of downtown Jackman, the **Moose River Campground and Cabins** (207/668-4400, www.mooserivercampground.org, mid-May-mid-Oct.) has 48 tent and RV sites close to a picturesque old dam site. Now crumbling from disrepair, the dam was once part of a thriving turn-of-the-20th-century lumber mill that employed more than 700 workers to turn out 35 million board feet annually. Open and wooded campsites are $25-40. Housekeeping cabins are $35 pp. Canoe rentals are available. Facilities include a snack bar, a swimming pool, a trout pond, a laundry room, and a children's play area.

INFORMATION

Local information is available from **The Forks Area Chamber of Commerce** (The Forks, 207/663-4430, www.forksarea.com), the **Jackman/Moose River Region Chamber of Commerce** (207/668-4171 or 888/633-5225, www.jackmanmaine.org), and **Kennebec Valley Tourism Council** (207/623-4884, www.kennebecvalley.org).

GETTING THERE

By car, Bingham is roughly 45 miles or one hour from Skowhegan via Route 201. It's roughly 50 miles or one hour from Bingham to Jackman via Route 201. From Jackman, it's roughly 50 miles or 1 hour to Greenville via Route 6/15, and it's 110 miles or 2.25 hours to Québec City via Routes 201, 173, and 73.

1: Mama Bear's in Jackman **2:** Sky Lodge **3:** Hawk's Nest Lodge, Restaurant & Pub

Western Lakes and Mountains

The recreational variety of Maine's Western Lakes and Mountains—about 4,500 outstandingly scenic square miles of Franklin, Oxford, Androscoggin, and Cumberland Counties—is astonishing. In winter, the state's two alpine powerhouses—Sunday River and Sugarloaf—entice skiers and riders from throughout the Northeast and even abroad. Smaller, family-oriented ski areas deliver fewer on-mountain amenities but offer more wallet-friendly prices. Cross-country and snowshoeing trails also lace the region, dogsledding is increasingly popular, and snowmobiling is big business. Now add hut-laced trails for winter hiking and ponds for skating.

Still, winter is the off-season in much of this region. The multitude of lakes, ponds, rivers, and streams satisfy recreational boaters and

Highlights

Look for ★ to find recommended sights, activities, dining, and lodging.

★ **Flagstaff Scenic Boat Tours:** Learn the fascinating history of the flooded village and enjoy wilderness scenery on a guided cruise (page 542).

★ **Sugarloaf:** The summit snowfields are the only lift-accessible skiing and riding above the tree line in the East (page 543).

★ **Maine Huts and Trails:** Hike, bike, paddle, ski, or snowshoe from hut to hut on this spectacular wilderness trail (page 545).

★ **Mountain Biking:** Multi-use and dedicated mountain-biking trails make it easy to explore the region's mountains and visit pristine waterways (pages 546 and 569).

★ **Rangeley Outdoor Sporting Heritage Museum:** Learn about the sporting legends who made Rangeley famous (page 551).

★ **Grafton Notch State Park:** This is a spectacular chunk of real estate, with hiking trails, waterfalls, and picnic areas (page 566).

★ ***Songo River Queen II:*** Take in views to Mount Washington on a cruise across Long Lake (page 584).

★ **Paris Hill:** Take a walk around this hidden hilltop National Historic District (page 592).

★ **Poland Spring:** Tour through the history of famed Poland Spring Water and Hiram Ricker's family empire (page 599).

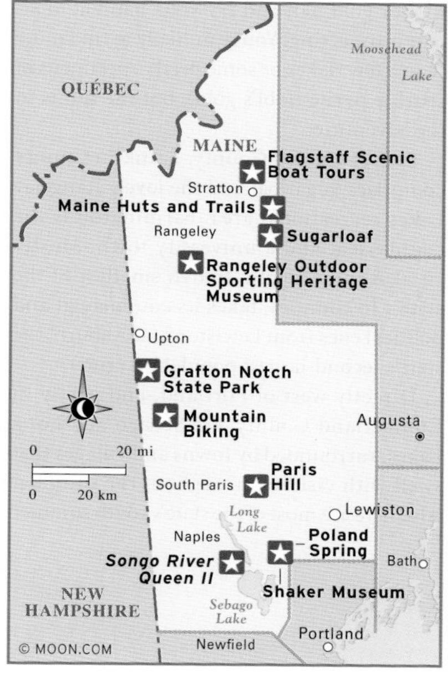

★ **Shaker Museum:** Visit the world's last inhabited Shaker community (page 599).

anglers, while the mountains attract hikers and mountain bikers. One of the most rugged stretches of the 2,158-mile Appalachian Trail, which runs from Georgia to Maine, passes through this area.

Of Maine's nine covered bridges (seven originals and two carefully built replicas), five are in the Western Lakes and Mountains—including the picturesque "Artist's Covered Bridge," near Sunday River, my favorite because you can ski through the forest and suddenly come upon it.

Sprawling, mountainous Oxford County, backed against New Hampshire, has fabulous trails for hiking and rivers for canoeing. There's gold—and all kinds of other minerals—in the Oxford Hills; the official state gemstone, tourmaline, an intriguing stone that turns up in green, blue, or pink, is most prevalent in western Maine. Grab a digging tool or gold pan and try your hand at amateur prospecting. You're unlikely to find more than a few flakes or some pretty specimens of sparkly pyrite (fool's gold), but the fun is in the adventure.

East of Oxford County, Franklin County comprises Sugarloaf and the lovely Rangeley Lakes recreational area. Farmington is the county seat and a university town. Mostly rural Androscoggin, fourth smallest of the state's 16 counties, takes its commercial and political cues from Lewiston and Auburn, the state's second-largest population center.

Directly west of Portland, and partly in Cumberland County, are Sebago and Long Lakes, surrounded by towns and villages that swell with visitors throughout the summer. Also here are most of the state's youth summer camps—some many generations old. During the annual summer-camp parents' weekend in July, Bridgton's tiny besieged downtown feels like Times Square at rush hour.

PLANNING YOUR TIME

If you're coming for warm-weather recreation—boating, swimming, hiking, and simply playing in the great outdoors—you'll find it here in abundance. And in July-August, you won't be alone on the Route 302 corridor stretching from Windham through Bridgton. Skip north to the Oxford Hills, Bethel, and the Kingfield region, and the crowds diminish. Bethel, home to Sunday River, and Kingfield, the nearest big town to Sugarloaf, come to life during the ski season, but otherwise are quiet places to escape, recreate, and especially to enjoy fall's foliage. If winter sports are your priority, late February-mid-March usually brings the best combination of snow and temperatures.

While you can loop through this region in 3-4 days, to get the most out of the summer recreational opportunities, pick one spot and explore from there. Good hubs are Rangeley, Bethel, Bridgton, and Naples.

If you're interested in Franco American culture, plan on spending the better part of a day in the Lewiston-Auburn area. For antiquing, slip over to Cornish. For fishing, make Rangeley your base. No matter where you stay, don't overplan. The region's riches demand that you get off the highways and byways and onto the back roads. Wander around and you'll stumble on spectacular views, great hikes, country stores, and swimming holes.

Previous: Rangeley Lake; ice cream stand; Bigelow Preserve.

Farmington Area

Farmington (pop. 7,760), the county seat and northwestern Maine's commercial hub, has a thriving and easily walkable downtown that's home to a respected University of Maine campus. Also here are a community ski area and an unusual opera museum. What's more, mountain towns and scenery stretch out and beyond in every direction. Less than an hour's drive north of town is the Carrabassett Valley, a recreation stronghold made famous by the year-round Sugarloaf alpine resort. Off to the northwest are the fabled Rangeley Lakes. Nearby towns, including **Wilton** (pop. 4,116), **Weld** (pop. 419), **New Sharon** (pop. 1,407), **Temple** (pop. 528), and **Industry** (pop. 929), offer mountains for hiking, lakes for swimming and paddling, and farm stands.

And, lest we forget, Farmington's leading candidate for favorite son is Chester Greenwood, who, in 1873, rigged beaver fur, velvet, and a bit of wire to create "Champion ear protectors"—called earmuffs these days—when he was only 15. The clever fellow patented his invention and then went on to earn 100 more patents for such things as doughnut hooks and shock absorbers. His early-December birthday inspires the quirky annual Chester Greenwood Day celebration in downtown Farmington.

SIGHTS

Nordica Homestead Museum

Gem-encrusted gowns, opera librettos, lavish gifts from royalty, and family treasures fill the handful of rooms in the **Nordica Homestead Museum** (116 Nordica Ln., Farmington, 207/778-2042, www.lilliannordica.com, tours 1pm-5pm Tues.-Sun. June-Sept. 15, $5 adults, $2 children), birthplace of Lillian Norton (1857-1914), better known as Madame Lillian Nordica, the legendary turn-of-the-20th-century Wagnerian opera diva. Her influence still pervades the house, where scratchy recordings play in the background and newspaper clippings line the walls. No opera buff should miss this. A guide is on hand to answer questions. Take Route 4/27 north from Farmington and turn right (east) onto Holley Road; the farm is 0.5 mile down the road.

RECREATION

Mount Blue State Park

Mount Blue State Park (299 Center Hill Rd., Weld, 207/585-2261, www.parksandlands.com), covering nearly 8,000 acres in two sections, is one of Maine's best-kept secrets. Yes, it's crowded in summer, but mostly with Mainers. It offers multilevel hiking, superb swimming, wooded campsites, mountain scenery, and daily interpretive natural-history programs in summer. There are movies on weekends, guided hikes, weekly guest speakers, even gold-panning expeditions—you'll never be bored. Swimming and camping are on Lake Webb's west side; the Center Hill section, including the trail to Mount Blue itself, is on the lake's east side. The main entrance, with a two-mile access road, is eight miles from Weld, on the lake's west side. Day-use admission is $7 nonresident adults, $5 Maine resident adults, $1 ages 5-11, nonresident seniors $2, resident seniors free. Canoe rentals are $3/hour. Winter brings snowshoeing, snowmobiling, and cross-country skiing on groomed trails.

Hiking

You're getting into western Maine's serious mountains here, so there are plenty of great hiking opportunities, running the gamut from a cakewalk to a workout.

In Weld, a deservedly popular hiking route goes up 3,187-foot **Mount Blue,** in the eastern section of Mount Blue State Park. From Route 142 in Weld village, follow signs and take Maxwell Road and then Center Hill Road about 2.5 miles to the parking area for Center

Western Lakes and Mountains

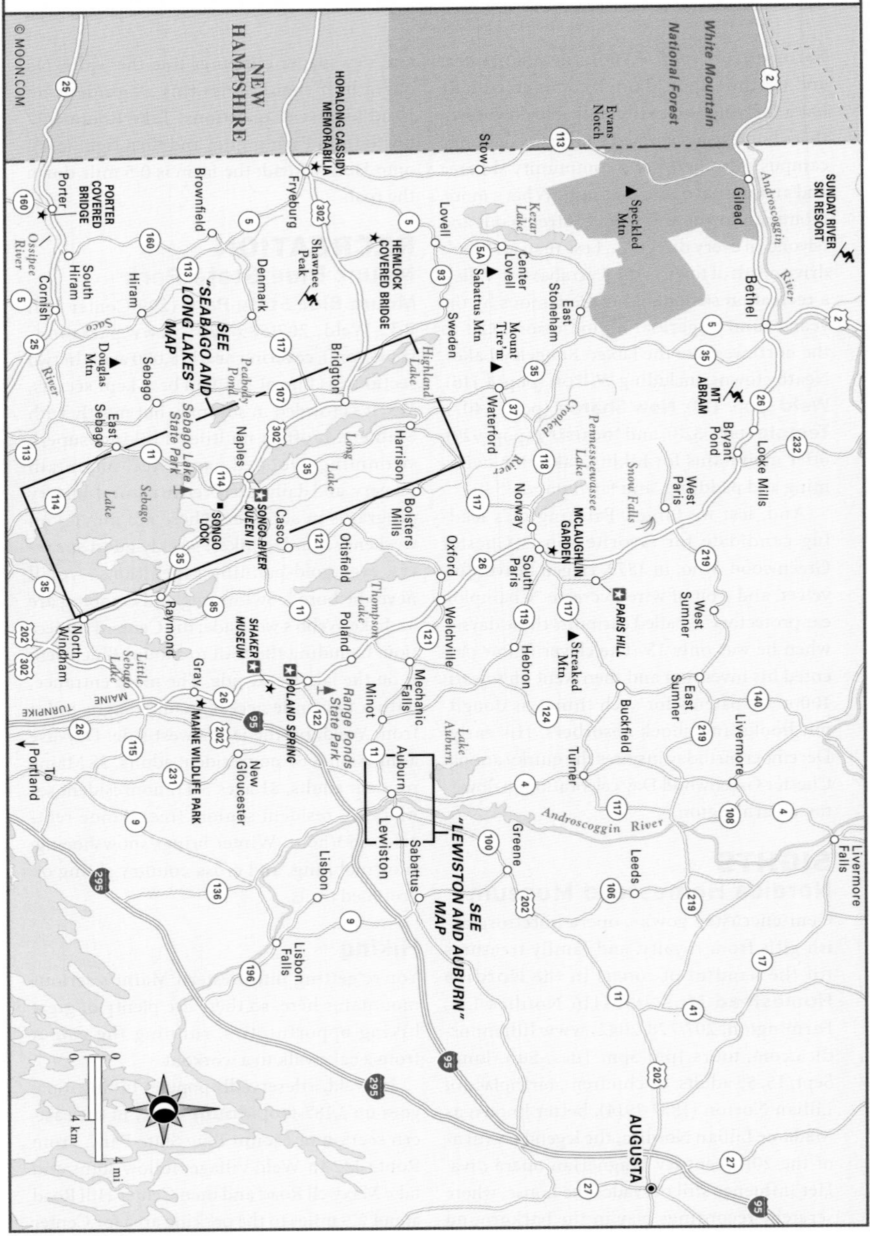

White Mountain National Forest
NEW HAMPSHIRE
Evans Notch
Stow
Gilead
SUNDAY RIVER SKI RESORT
Androscoggin River
Speckled Mtn
Kezar Lake
HOPALONG CASSIDY MEMORABILIA
Fryeburg
Brownfield
Porter
PORTER COVERED BRIDGE
Ossipee River
Lovell
Center Lovell
HEMLOCK COVERED BRIDGE
Shawnee Peak
Sabattus Mtn
East Stoneham
Bethel
MT ABRAM
Bryant Pond
Locke Mills
West Paris
Snow Falls
Pennesseewassee Lake
Crooked River
Mount Tire'm
Waterford
Sweden
Highland Lake
Bridgton
Denmark
Hiram
South Hiram
Cornish
Saco River
Douglas Mtn
Sebago
East Sebago
SEE "SEABAGO AND LONG LAKES" MAP
Peabody Pond
Sebago Lake State Park
Sebago Lake
Naples
Long Lake
Harrison
Bolsters Mills
Norway
MCLAUGHLIN GARDEN
South Paris
PARIS HILL
West Sumner
East Sumner
Streaked Mtn
Hebron
Buckfield
Turner
Livermore
Livermore Falls
Leeds
Oxford
Otisfield
Casco
SONGO RIVER QUEEN II
SONGO LOCK
Thompson Lake
Welchville
Mechanic Falls
Minot
Poland
Range Ponds State Park
POLAND SPRING
SHAKER MUSEUM
Raymond
North Windham
Little Sebago Lake
Gray
MAINE WILDLIFE PARK
MAINE TURNPIKE
New Gloucester
Lake Auburn
Auburn
Lewiston
SEE "LEWISTON AND AUBURN" MAP
Androscoggin River
Greene
Sabattus
Lisbon
Lisbon Falls
To Portland
AUGUSTA
0 4 mi
0 4 km

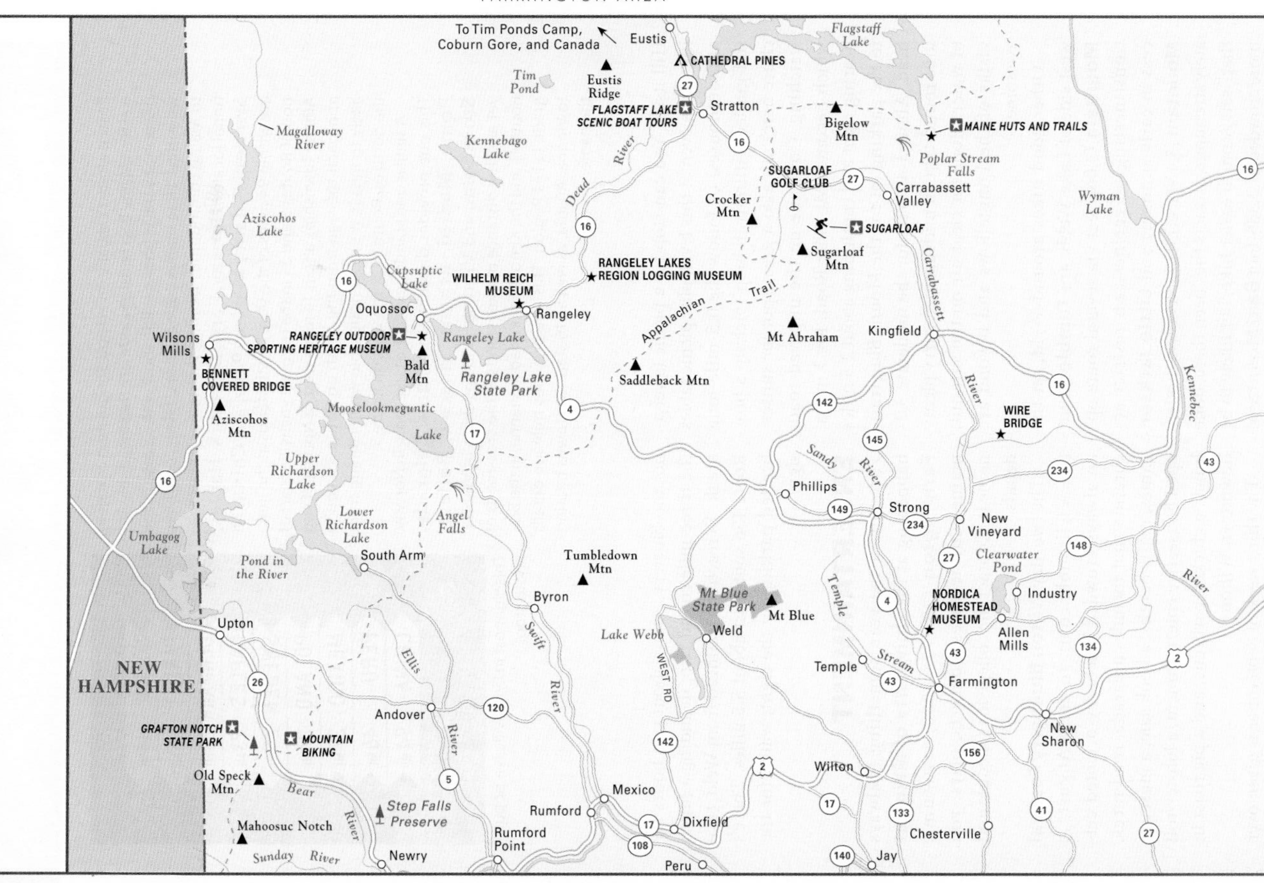
To Tim Ponds Camp, Coburn Gore, and Canada
Eustis
CATHEDRAL PINES
Flagstaff Lake
Tim Pond
Eustis Ridge
FLAGSTAFF LAKE SCENIC BOAT TOURS
Stratton
Bigelow Mtn
MAINE HUTS AND TRAILS
Magalloway River
Kennebago Lake
Dead River
Poplar Stream Falls
SUGARLOAF GOLF CLUB
Carrabassett Valley
Wyman Lake
Aziscohos Lake
Crocker Mtn
SUGARLOAF
Sugarloaf Mtn
RANGELEY LAKES REGION LOGGING MUSEUM
Cupsuptic Lake
WILHELM REICH MUSEUM
Appalachian Trail
Oquossoc
Rangeley
Carrabassett River
Mt Abraham
Kingfield
Kennebec River
Wilsons Mills
RANGELEY OUTDOOR SPORTING HERITAGE MUSEUM
Rangeley Lake
Bald Mtn
Rangeley Lake State Park
BENNETT COVERED BRIDGE
Saddleback Mtn
Aziscohos Mtn
Mooselookmeguntic Lake
WIRE BRIDGE
Upper Richardson Lake
Sandy River
Phillips
Lower Richardson Lake
Angel Falls
Strong
New Vineyard
Umbagog Lake
South Arm
Clearwater Pond
Pond in the River
Tumbledown Mtn
Industry
Temple Stream
Mt Blue State Park
Mt Blue
NORDICA HOMESTEAD MUSEUM
Byron
Upton
Lake Webb
Weld
Allen Mills
Swift River
WEST RD
Temple
NEW HAMPSHIRE
Ellis River
Farmington
Andover
New Sharon
GRAFTON NOTCH STATE PARK
MOUNTAIN BIKING
Wilton
Old Speck Mtn
Bear River
Mexico
Step Falls Preserve
Rumford
Mahoosuc Notch
Dixfield
Rumford Point
Chesterville
Sunday River
Newry
Jay
Peru

International Maine

Posted almost casually on an undistinguished corner in western Maine is a roadside landmark that inevitably appears in any travel book or slide show with a sense of the whimsical. Nine markers direct bikers, hikers, or drivers to Maine communities bearing the names of international locales: **Norway, Paris, Denmark, Naples, Sweden, Poland, Mexico, Peru,** and **China.** All are within 94 miles of the sign, which stands at the junction of Routes 5 and 35 in the burg of Lynchville (part of Albany Township), about 14 miles west of Norway. If you approach the sign from the south on Route 35, you're likely to miss it; it's most noticeable when coming from the north on Route 35 or the west on Route 5.

A similar one stands next to the Lake Store in Norway. This one provides distances to **Lisbon, Belgrade, Rome, Madrid, Athens, Moscow, Belfast, Stockholm,** and **Vienna.** And speaking of Vienna, yet another distance marker stands at the crossroads of Route 41 and the Kimball Falls Road in Vienna, in the Belgrade Lakes Region. This one provides mileage details to Vienna, Austria, as well as 16 stateside towns bearing the name.

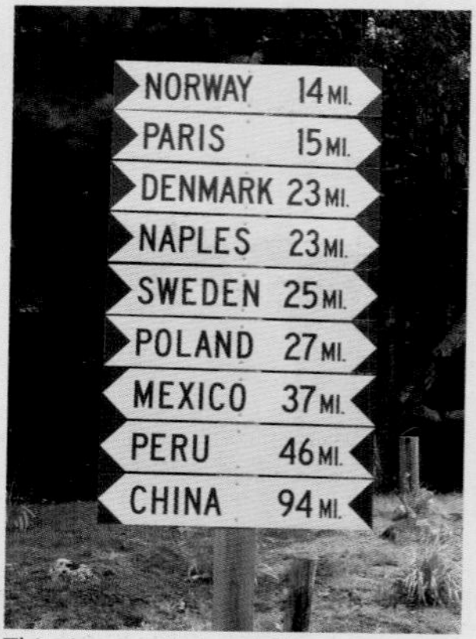

This signpost in Lynchville is a popular photo stop.

Hill itself. You can stop for a picnic (sweeping views even at this level, plus picnic tables and outhouses) or follow the 0.5-mile-long self-guided nature-trail loop (pick up a brochure here). It's also a great spot for sunset-watching. Continue up the unpaved road, which becomes Mt. Blue Road, for 3 miles, bearing right and continuing about 2.5 miles to the parking lot for the Mount Blue trailhead. Allow 3-4 hours for the moderate 3.2-mile round-trip. In midsummer, carry plenty of water. Hope for clear air on the summit; vistas of the Longfellows and beyond are awesome.

Other good hikes around Weld, on the west side of Lake Webb, are **Tumbledown Mountain** (3,068 feet via several route options; nesting peregrines can restrict access in early summer) and **Little Jackson Mountain** (3,434 feet). Tumbledown, moderately strenuous, attracts the "been there, done that" set. A much easier hike, but likely to be more crowded, is 2,386-foot **Bald Mountain,** with a scoured summit fine for picnics if it's not too blustery. Allow about two hours for the three-mile round-trip, including a lunch break. To reach the trailhead from Weld, take Route 156 southeast about 5.5 miles. There's limited parking on the right; watch for the sign.

ENTERTAINMENT

Throughout the year, something is always happening at the **University of Maine at Farmington** (207/778-7000, www.umf.maine.edu): lectures, concerts, plays, you name it. Contact the college for schedule and details.

The two-day **Wilton Blueberry Festival** (www.wiltonbbf.com), in early August, is an always-crowded blueberry-oriented celebration that includes a parade, road races, games, crafts booths, a book sale, a museum open house, live entertainment, a lobster-roll lunch, a chicken barbecue, and a pig roast in downtown Wilton.

The third week of September is given over to the **Farmington Fair,** a weeklong country fair with agricultural exhibits, a parade, harness racing, and live entertainment at the Farmington Fairgrounds.

The first Saturday in December, Farmington honors a native son on **Chester Greenwood Day.** Festivities commemorating the inventor of earmuffs include a road race, an oddball earmuff parade, a polar-bear swim, and other activities.

SHOPPING

Fans of fine craft simply must visit **SugarWood Gallery** (248 Broadway, Farmington, 207/778-9105), which features the work of more than 100 western Maine artisans.

It's hard to resist the cheerful, welcoming ambience at **Devaney Doak and Garrett Booksellers** (193 Broadway, Farmington, 207/778-3454, www.ddgbooks.com), not to mention the children's corner piled high with books, toys, and games. Around the corner, **Twice-Sold Tales** (155 Main St., Farmington, 207/778-4411) has a well-chosen and well-organized selection; Maine titles are a specialty, and prices are reasonable.

I always introduce visiting friends to **Renys** (24 Broadway, Farmington, 207/778-4641), and they always leave with at least a bag or two. From clothing to cleaning supplies to electronics to food, Renys has it all at budget-friendly prices.

Fletchers' Mill (1687 New Vineyard Rd./Rte. 27, New Vineyard, 855/535-3824, https://fletchersmill.com), 10 miles north of Farmington, crafts and sells cooking tools, including salt and pepper mills, rolling pins, and accessories.

FOOD

Quick Bites

If you'll be camping or staying in a condo or cottage with cooking facilities, swing by **Whitewater Farm** (28 Mercer Rd./Rte. 2, Mercer, 207/778-4748) or **Sandy River Farms** (580 Farmington Falls Rd./Rte. 2, Farmington, 207/778-3835) for local naturally raised meats, poultry, dairy products, and produce. Sandy River also sells its fresh, custard-style ice cream here.

There's always a line at **Gifford's Ice Cream** (Rte. 4/27, Farmington, 207/778-3617, 11am-10pm daily summer, 11am-9pm daily spring and fall), a longtime take-out spot.

My favorite Farmington order-at-the-counter is **Soup for You! Cafe** (222 Broadway, Farmington, 207/779-0799, 10:30am-7pm Mon.-Sat.), which oozes college-town funk and concocts sandwiches and tasty soups; usually about six are made daily, with vegan, vegetarian, and gluten-free options. Nothing on the menu is more than $10.

The **Farmington Farmers Market** sets up in the courthouse parking lot (129 Main St., Farmington, 9am-noon Sat. May-Oct.). You'll find herbs, homemade bread, cheeses, and organic meats and produce.

Casual Dining

Breakfast, lunch, dinner, even tapas—the **Homestead Bakery Restaurant** (186 Broadway, Farmington, 207/778-6162, www.homesteadbakery.com, 8am-9pm Mon.-Sat., 8am-2pm Sun., $10-24) serves it all. There's plenty of ethnic variety—Mediterranean, Mexican, Thai—as well as pub-style classics and pizza. A martini and wine bar, with couches by a fireplace, provides cozier seating.

Step back in time and savor the views from the **Kawanhee Inn** (12 Ann's Way/Rte. 142, Weld, 207/585-2000, www.maineinn.net, 5pm-9pm Tues.-Sun., hours vary spring and fall, $18-35). The lakefront setting is spectacular, especially at sunset. Reservations are recommended. Lighter fare ($9-12) is served in the pub.

The former Bass Shoe factory now houses **Calzolaio Pasta Co.** (248 Main St., Wilton, 207/645-9500, www.calzolaiopasta.com, 11am-9pm Mon.-Sat., 9am-9pm Sun., $9-30), which prepares decent Italian fare, from brick-oven pizzas and homemade pastas to specialty entrées such as veal saltimbocca and Sicilian chicken. There are kids', vegetarian, and gluten-free menus too. Opt for an outdoor riverside table if the weather's fine.

Ompah! For Mediterranean street food, head to **White Fox Taverna** (108 Narrow Gauge Sq., 207/778-9369, 4pm-9pm Wed.-Fri., 11am-9pm Sat.-Sun., $10-25). There's often live music on Friday nights.

ACCOMMODATIONS

Just west of Farmington, **Wilson Lake Inn** (183 Lake Rd., Wilton, 207/645-3721 or 800/626-7463, www.wilsonlakeinn.com, $149-269) is a well-maintained family-owned property with rooms, studios, and extended-stay two-bedroom suites with kitchens. The grounds are lovely, with gardens and a lawn leading to the lakefront. Sightseeing flights leave from the inn's dock. Rates include a continental breakfast and use of canoes, kayaks, and rowboat.

Step back in time at **Kawanhee Inn** (12 Ann's Way/Rte. 142, Weld, 207/585-2000, www.maineinn.net, late May-mid-Oct.), a rustic, lakefront lodge-style inn and cabins tucked under the shelter of towering pines. Owners Chris and Jodi Huntington have renovated the cabins and updated the rooms, all while preserving the classic 1920s style (the plumbing has a mind of its own). Sunsets in this mountain-and-lake setting on six-mile-long Lake Webb are lovely; loons' cries add to the magic. Eleven 2nd-floor guest rooms with shared and private baths in the large main lodge are $110-165/day. Cabins ($200-300/night, from $1,200/week) vary in age, size, and facilities; all have lake views, fieldstone fireplaces, and screened-in porches. Pets are welcome for $35/dog/night plus a $200 security deposit (some restrictions, call). Guests receive continental breakfast and have use of canoes and kayaks and a sandy beach.

Camping

Mount Blue State Park (299 Center Hill Rd., Weld, 207/585-2261, www.parksandlands.com) has 136 wooded sites but no hookups. Camping fees are $30/site for nonresidents, $20 for Maine residents. Reservations are handled through the state-park reservation system; from out of state call 207/287-3824 at least two weeks ahead or book reservations online from February 1 at www.campwithme.com. The reservation fee is $5/site/night, with a two-night minimum.

INFORMATION

Downtown Farmington (www.downtownfarmington.com) has local information and listings.

GETTING THERE AND AROUND

Farmington is roughly 40 miles or 50 minutes from Augusta via Route 27. It's about 22 miles or 30 minutes to Kingfield via Route 27. It's about 40 miles or one hour to Rangeley via Route 4.

Sugarloaf Area

The thread tying together the Sugarloaf area is the Carrabassett River, which winds its way through the smashingly scenic **Carrabassett Valley** from the **Sugarloaf** area through **Kingfield** and on to **North Anson,** where it tumbles over treacherous falls and flows into the mighty Kennebec River. On both sides of the valley, the Longfellow and Bigelow Ranges boast six of Maine's ten 4,000-footers—a hiker's paradise.

Flanking the west side of the valley is the huge Sugarloaf resort. In 1951, Kingfield businessman Amos Winter and some of his pals, known locally as the "Bigelow Boys," cut the first ski trail from the snowfields above the tree line atop Sugarloaf Mountain, dubbing it "Winter's Way." A downhill run required skiing three miles to the base of the trail and then strapping on animal skins for the uphill trek. Three runs on wooden skis would be about the daily max in those days. By 1954, the prophetically named Winter and some foresighted investors had established the Sugarloaf Mountain Ski Club; the rest, as they say, is history.

Sugarloaf is the dominant presence the relatively new town of **Carrabassett Valley** (pop. 781). It bills itself as a year-round resort, which is true, but winter is definitely the peak season, when the head count is highest and so are the prices. Everything's open and humming November-late April; spring skiing often extends into May. More recently, the valley has gained status for its well designed, mapped, and maintained mountain-biking trails.

Before Amos Winter brought fame and fortune to his hometown and the valley, **Kingfield** was best known as a timber center and the birthplace of the Stanley twins (designers of the Stanley Steamer). Today it's an appealing slice-of-life rural town, with handsome old homes and off-mountain beds and restaurants and two museums.

In **Stratton,** a village in **Eustis** (pop. 618), old-timers reminisce over the towns of Flagstaff and Dead River—already historic two centuries before they were consigned to the history books in the 1950s. That's when the Long Falls Dam, built on the Dead River, backed up the water behind it, inundated the towns, and created 20,000-acre Flagstaff Lake. The hydroelectric dam now controls the water flow for spring white-water rafting on the Dead River.

Flagstaff owes its name to Col. Benedict Arnold, whose troops en route to Québec in 1775 flew their flag at the site of today's Cathedral Pines Campground. After struggling up the Kennebec River to the spot known as the Carrying Place, the disheartened soldiers turned northwest along the Dead River's North Branch at Flagstaff and then on through the Chain of Ponds to Canada.

Route 27, from Kingfield to the Canadian border at Coburn Gore, is an officially designated Scenic Highway, a 54-mile stretch that's most spectacular in mid-late September-early October. But there's no pot of gold at the end; there's not much to Coburn Gore except a customs outpost, a convenience store (with fuel), and a few dwellings.

SIGHTS

Stanley Museum

Here's a reason to go back to school: The small but captivating **Stanley Museum** (40 School St., Kingfield, 207/265-2729, www.stanleymuseum.org, 11am-4pm Tues.-Sun. June-Oct., 11am-4pm Tues.-Fri. Nov.-Apr., or by appointment, $4 adults, $3 seniors, $2 ages 12-18), located in the town's old schoolhouse, is dedicated to educating visitors about Kingfield's most famous native sons, twin brothers Francis Edgar (F. E.) and Freelan Oscar (F. O.) Stanley. Although best known for the Stanley Steamer, the identical twins' legacy of invention and innovation extends far beyond either the automobile or Kingfield. These versatile overachievers also invented the photographic dry plate, eventually selling out to George Eastman. Freelan Stanley, the first to climb Mount Washington by car, later became a noted violin maker. He was also a talented portrait artist—one of his subjects was poet Henry Wadsworth Longfellow—and he's credited with inventing the airbrush. Also in the museum are hundreds of superb photographs (and glass-plate negatives) by the twins' clever sister, Chansonetta Stanley Emmons, and work by Chansonetta's artist-daughter, Dorothy. The museum gift shop contains auto-related books, pamphlets, and other specialty items.

Ski Museum of Maine

Established in 1995, the **Ski Museum of Maine** (256 Main St., Kingfield, 207/265-2023, www.skimuseumofmaine.org, 9am-5pm daily, free) exhibits artifacts and memorabilia documenting Maine's role in the growth and development of skiing, from immigrant

Swedes to manufacturing to resorts. The museum is sited above the Sugarloaf Outlet Ski Shop, and it's wise to call ahead to verify hours in the off-season and summer.

Nowetah's American Indian Museum

A bold, in-your-face sign announces the driveway to **Nowetah's American Indian Museum** (2 Colegrove Rd., off Rte. 27, New Portland, 207/628-4981, 10am-5pm daily, free), an astonishing repository of hundreds of Maine Indian baskets and bark objects—plus porcupine-quill embroidery, trade beads, musical instruments, soapstone carvings, and other Native American esoterica. Übercollector Nowetah Cyr, a descendent of St. Francis Abenaki and Paugussett Indians, loves explaining unique details about the artifacts she's displayed here since 1969. In the museum's gift shop are many Native American craft pieces as well as books. It's 16 miles north of Farmington.

Wire Bridge

About seven miles south of Kingfield and not far from Nowetah's museum, twenty-five-foot-tall shingled towers announce the entrance to the **Wire Bridge** suspended over the Carrabassett River in New Portland. Built in 1864-1866 at a cost of $2,000, with steel supports imported from England, the bridge is in the National Register of Historic Places. Locals often refer to it as "rustproof" for its stainless-steel construction, or "flood-proof" for its longtime survival despite nasty spring floods. To find the bridge from Route 146 in New Portland, turn north onto Wire Bridge Road and follow signs for less than a mile.

Dead River Historical Society Museum

Unless you're a rabid history fan or have an area connection, many local historical society museums can be a bit of a snore. Not so the **Dead River Historical Society** (Main St., Stratton, 11am-3pm Sat.-Sun. July-Aug., donation), which contains fascinating memorabilia from the two villages submerged when the Dead River was dammed and Flagstaff Lake created.

★ Flagstaff Scenic Boat Tours

Join Master Maine Guide Jeff Hinman and **Flagstaff Scenic Boat Tours** (Eustis, 207/246-2277, www.flagstaffboattours.com) for a pontoon boat tour on Flagstaff Lake. Hinman relates the story of the flooded villages below the surface and points out wildlife en route. This is a fabulous way to experience the region in summer or in fall, when the colors are popping. Options include a 2.5-hour historical tour ($40 pp) and a 4.5-hour luncheon cruise to the Maine Huts and Trails Flagstaff Hut ($50 pp). Boat minimum is four people.

Benedict Arnold Trail

In the fall of 1775, Benedict Arnold led Continental troops north from Augusta with the goal of capturing Québec. He followed the Kennebec River, then portaged to the Dead River, following it to Chain of Ponds near the Québec border. The **Maine High Peaks Scenic Byway** traces Arnold's route north on Route 27 from Kingfield to Coburn Gore, with roadside historical markers along the way. It's a gorgeous drive, especially in autumn, when leaves are turning and snow might fringe the peaks.

PICNIC AND REST AREAS

Several riverside and viewpoint rest areas on or near Route 27 make picnicking almost mandatory, especially in autumn, when the leaf colors are splendid. On Route 27, roughly halfway between Kingfield and the Sugarloaf access road, a picnic area is sandwiched between the highway and the Carrabassett River, just north of Hammond Field Brook.

About 12 miles north of the Sugarloaf access road, turn left (west) onto Eustis Ridge Road and go two miles to the Eustis Ridge picnic area, a tiny park with an expansive view of the Bigelow Range.

Finally, on Route 27, about 23 miles north

of Sugarloaf, there's another scenic picnic area, this one alongside the Dead River on the east side of the highway.

★ Sugarloaf

The king of Maine's alpine resorts, **Sugarloaf** (Carrabassett, 207/237-2000 or 800/843-5623, www.sugarloaf.com) is a four-season destination resort with alpine skiing and snowboarding, snowshoeing, cross-country skiing, and ice-skating in winter; golf, hiking, and mountain biking during warmer months; and ziplining during all seasons. A compact base village has a hotel, an inn, and gazillions of condos as well as restaurants, a chapel, a few shops, and a base lodge housing a snow school and rental operations. The separate Outdoor Center, linked via shuttle and trails, houses cross-country skiing and mountain-biking operations and has an ice-skating rink.

ALPINE SKIING AND RIDING

At 4,237 feet, Sugarloaf is not only Maine's highest skiing mountain, it also has the only lift-serviced above-tree-line terrain in the East. Well over 100 named trails and glades on more than 1,000 acres, served by 15 lifts ranging from a T-bar to detachable high-speed quads, ribbon its 2,820 vertical feet. Even beginners can ski from the summit, a 3.5-mile descent via the longest run. **Snowcat skiing** is offered on adjacent **Burnt Mountain,** the resort's side-country terrain. Although the resort has produced national and international ski and snowboard champions (two-time Olympic snowboard-cross gold medalist Seth Wescott calls it home), Sugarloaf has always been especially family-friendly, with day care and all kinds of children's ski and entertainment programs.

SUGARLOAF OUTDOOR CENTER

On Route 27 about a mile south of the Sugarloaf access road is the entrance to the **Sugarloaf Outdoor Center** (207/237-6830), geared in winter toward cross-country skiing, snowshoeing, and ice-skating. Some sections of the 63-mile cross-country skiing trail network are on Maine Public Reserve Land, and some are on Penobscot Indian Nation land. Also at the Outdoor Center is an Olympic-size outdoor ice-skating rink, lighted on weekend nights and holiday weeks. The glass-walled lodge looking out on Sugarloaf Mountain has ski, snowshoe, and skate rentals, plus a casual café. Cross-country lessons are available. Call for current hours and fees for all programs, and ask about special events such as guided moonlight tours and snowshoe tours. In summer, the center is a mountain biking hub.

GOLF

Designed by Robert Trent Jones Jr., and regularly ranked in national golf magazines as Maine's top course, the 18-hole, par-72 **Sugarloaf Golf Club and Golf School,** a town-owned course managed by Sugarloaf, meanders through woods and alongside the Carrabassett River in the shadow of the Longfellow Range. You get what you pay for; greens fees are steep. Tee times are essential; book a week or two in advance for weekends. Sugarloaf's golf school offers multiday programs all summer, with special weeks designed for Women's Golf School and Junior Golf Camp. Club rentals and private lessons are available; carts are mandatory. A driving range, a pro shop, and a café round out the facilities.

OTHER ACTIVITIES

Summer activities at Sugarloaf include guided hikes, boat trips, moose-spotting tours, mountain biking, fly-fishing, scenic chair rides, and wilderness cookouts. Seventy-five-minute zip-line tours ($45 pp) on seven lines varying from 160 to 260 feet in length are offered year-round. A guided 90-minute off-road Segway tour is $59.

ANTIGRAVITY CENTER

A partnership between Sugarloaf, the town, and CVA (Carrabassett Valley Academy, a ski preparatory school at the mountain's base that has produced many Olympians), the

1
2
3
Hamlin's
4

Antigravity Center (207/237-5566, www.carrabassettvalley.org), locally called the AGC, is the answer to a parent's frustration when the weather doesn't cooperate. It houses a gym, a climbing wall, a skate park, trampolines, a weight room, and more, and fitness classes are offered. Call for current hours and programs.

ENTERTAINMENT

Sugarloaf is entertainment central in these parts. Every night in winter there's live music somewhere here, so you can hopscotch from the Bag to Gepetto's to the Rack (owned by Olympic gold medalist Seth Wescott) and back again.

The last full week in January is **White White World Week,** Sugarloaf's winter carnival, with discount lift tickets, reduced lodging rates, ski races, fireworks, a torchlight parade, and other special events.

Sugarloaf meets the Caribbean during **Reggae Fest** with spring skiing, reggae bands day and night, and lots of boisterous fun over a mid-late-April weekend.

In late June or early July, the annual **Kingfield POPS concert** features the Bangor Symphony Orchestra, an arts and crafts festival, a garden tour, and more.

RECREATION

Multisport Trails

The town-owned **Narrow Gauge Trail** begins at Campbell Field on the east side of Route 27 near the foot of the Sugarloaf access road and continues seven miles, gradually downhill, to the Carrabassett Valley Town Park. The trail follows the abandoned narrow-gauge railway bed along the river. Pack a picnic and wear a bathing suit under your biking duds; you'll be passing swimming holes along the way. In winter, it's groomed weekly for cross-country skiing. From the trail, you can connect to the Maine Huts and Trails network.

1: Wire Bridge 2: Sugarloaf 3: pontoon tour boat on Flagstaff Lake 4: mountain bikers at Sugarloaf

★ Maine Huts and Trails

The **Maine Huts and Trails system** (207/265-2400, www.mainehuts.org), an easygoing 12-foot-wide wilderness highway for hikers, mountain and fat-tire bikers, snowshoers, cross-country skiers (it's groomed in winter), and even paddlers, opened in 2008 in Carrabassett Valley. By 2016, it had expanded to more than 80 trail miles stretching eastward to The Forks.

Four comfy (practically luxe) off-the-grid, full-service lodges are spaced roughly 10-12 miles—or a day's hike—apart. Each provide beds (including a pillow but not bedding) in dorms heated to 60°F in winter (private and family rooms available) and hot meals. The main lodges have composting toilets, hot showers, and gathering rooms with comfy furnishings. Rates begin at $99 pp in a shared room, with breakfast, lunch, and dinner.

Huts are located at **Stratton Brook,** with views of the Bigelow Mountains, Sugarloaf, and the Carrabassett Valley, accessed from a trailhead from a spur trail just north of the Sugarloaf Mountain access road; **Poplar Falls,** in the shadow of Little Bigelow Mountain, accessed from the Carrabassett Valley trailhead off Route 27; on the shores of **Flagstaff Lake,** accessed via a trailhead on the Long Falls Dam Road north of North New Portland or by boat across the lake; and at **Grand Falls** on the Dead River near The Forks, from which you can arrange a white-water paddle or raft trip. This is absolutely gorgeous territory, and the trail's design makes it welcoming to beginning hikers and mountain bikers and especially families. Pricing varies by season and choice of accommodations. Trust me: Even if you only hoof or cruise in for lunch, this is an experience that should be incorporated into every vacation in this region.

Hiking

Just east of Stratton (eight miles northwest of Sugarloaf) is the dedicated hiker's dream: 35,000-acre **Bigelow Preserve** is all public land thanks to conservationists who organized a statewide referendum and yanked it from developers' hands in 1976. Within the preserve are the multiple peaks of the Bigelow Range—the Horns Peaks (3,810 and 3,831 feet), West Peak (4,150 feet), Avery Peak (4,088 feet), and Little Bigelow (3,040 feet), as well as 3,213-foot Cranberry Peak. In the fall when the hardwoods all change colors, the vistas are incomparable. In winter, snowmobilers crisscross the preserve, and cross-country skiers often take advantage of their trails, especially along the East Flagstaff Road, where you might be able to stop for hot chocolate at volunteer-staffed Bigelow Lodge. The trailhead for Cranberry Peak (6.6 miles round-trip, moderate to strenuous) is next to Route 27 at the southern end of Stratton village.

About five miles southeast of Stratton, the **Appalachian Trail** (AT) crosses Route 27 and continues north and then east across the Bigelow Peaks, the spine of the Bigelow Range. You can get to the AT here, or drive back northwest 0.5 mile on Route 27 and go 0.9 mile on rugged unpaved Stratton Brook Road to another AT trailhead. In any case, if you do the whole AT traverse, 16.5 miles from Route 27 to East Flagstaff Road, you'll probably want to arrange a shuttle at East Flagstaff Road (via Long Falls Dam Rd. from North New Portland). The white-blazed AT route is strenuous; four free campsites with lean-tos are sited along the way. (The most-used campsite is Horns Pond, where space can be tight.) You can detour to the Maine Huts' Flagstaff hut too.

Cathedral Pines is a fine spot for an easy family hike, ski, or snowshoe. Maintained paths slice and loop through a majestic red pine stand and out a boardwalk over a bog. Find the trailhead and parking across from Cathedral Pines Campground, at the corner of Route 27 and Eustis Ridge Road, about 3.5 miles north of the intersection with Route 16 in Stratton.

An easy-to-moderate family hike, combining a picnic and swim, goes to the twin cascades of **Poplar Stream Falls.** Off Route 27 in Carrabassett Valley, leave your car at the Maine Huts parking lot and walk northeast 1.5 miles to the falls, veering off the Maine Huts and Trails system. Pack a picnic and let the kids have a swim.

Depending on your enthusiasm, your stamina level, and your time frame (and maybe the weather), there are plentiful options for short hikes along the AT or on a number of side trails. Preserve maps are usually available at the Sugarloaf Area Info Center (on Route 27 in Valley Crossing), but for planning your hikes, request or download a copy of the Bigelow Preserve map-brochure from the **Maine Bureau of Parks and Lands** (22 State House Station, Augusta, 207/287-3821, www.parksandlands.com). Also helpful is the *Appalachian Trail Guide to Maine.*

TOP EXPERIENCE

★ Mountain Biking

Mountain biking is an excellent way to explore the area's mountains, streams, and forests. **Carrabassett Region NEMBA** (http://carrabassett.nemba.org) maintains an ever-increasing network of world-class mountain-biking trails spanning more than 100 miles, with loop options for all abilities. Printed maps are available at most trailheads, or you can download them from the NEMBA website, which also lists special events, rides, and socials, and trail conditions. Both the Narrow Gauge trail and Maine Huts and Trails network permit mountain biking. **Allspeed Cyclery** (207/779-3951, www.allspeed.com), based at the Outdoor Center, rents full-suspension bicycles ($89/day adults, $29-49/day kids). **Carrabassett Valley Bike** (207/935-8863, www.carrabassettvalleybike.com), based at Valley Crossing, rents bicycles for $50/day or $35/four hours.

Water Sports

Along the **Carrabassett River** between Kingfield and the Sugarloaf access road are half a dozen **swimming holes** used by generations of locals. Several spots have natural waterslides and room for shallow dives. Look for roadside pullouts with parked cars.

On mountain-rimmed **Flagstaff Lake** in Eustis, about 11 miles north of Sugarloaf, the town-owned beach next to the Cathedral Pines Campground has a playground and changing rooms. There are no lifeguards, but there's also no admission fee. (Do not use the campground's beach unless you're staying there.)

The **Outpost Adventure Center at Sugarloaf** (207/237-6875) rents single kayaks for $29 half day, $59 full day; double kayaks, canoes, and stand-up paddleboards for $39 half day, $69 full day.

Moose-Spotting

Head up Route 27 to Route 16 and go west. Early or late in the day, perhaps en route to dinner in Rangeley, you're almost guaranteed to see a moose in the boggy areas or near the sand and salt piles stored for winter use. Just remember to drive slowly and watchfully. No one wins when you hit a moose. Sugarloaf resort offers guided moose-spotting tours.

FOOD

Ask locally about two-fer nights, offered midweek at various restaurants. During holidays and winter weekends, make reservations.

Sugarloaf Resort

Boyne, Sugarloaf's corporate parent, owns and operates most of the restaurants on the mountain. These include: **45 North** (Sugarloaf Mountain Hotel, 2092 Access Rd., 207/237-4220, 7am-10am and 4pm-10pm daily, $18-38), a family-friendly restaurant with a rustic barn style and a New American menu; **Bullwinkle's Grill** (207/237-2000, sometimes open for dinner), the only on-mountain venue, located off Tote Road on the mountain's western side, with access via snowcat; and the ski-in/ski-out **Shipyard Brew Haus** (Sugarloaf Inn, Access Rd., 207/237-6834, 7am-10pm daily, $10-25).

In the base village, the independently owned **Bag and Kettle** (207/237-2451, www.thebagandkettle.com, 11am-close daily late Nov.-mid-Apr., $9-30), known locally as the Bag, is famous for its Bag Burgers, soups, and wood-fired pizzas, although the menu is much broader than that; Blues Monday features live music.

Alice and Lulu's (207/235-6111, www.aliceandlulus.com, 10am-6pm Sun.-Mon., 10am-8pm Fri.-Sat.) is a European-style Alpine wine bar with cheeses, charcuterie, tapas, raclette, and a few other entrées ($9-28); it also offers brunch and lunch.

D'Ellies (207/237-2490, 8am-3pm daily), another independent, is one of Sugarloaf Village's most popular eateries for sandwiches, homemade soups, salads, and hearty breakfasts.

Two-time Olympic gold medalist Seth Wescott is one of the partners in the **Rack** (Access Rd., 207/237-2211, http://therackbbq.com, from 4pm daily, $12-32), where you can view his memorabilia and, when he's around, chat with him while enjoying hearty ribs. This is an especially popular après-ski spot, with frequent live music.

Carrabassett Valley

Hug's (3001 Rte. 27, Carrabassett Valley, 207/237-2392, 4:30pm-9:30pm Wed.-Sun., $15-24), a northern Italian restaurant that is open in winter only, is always jam-packed. Be forewarned: Tables are tight and there's little space to wait for one. But the food is good, the atmosphere festive, the pesto breadsticks are addictive, and the family-style salad is delicious. Kids' portions are available.

Tufulio's (Rte. 27, Valley Crossing, Carrabassett Valley, 207/235-2010, 5pm-9pm daily, $10-26), another Italian-accented family favorite, makes the valley's best pizza. The shrimp-and-artichoke pesto pie is tops. In summer you can eat on the deck. It opens at 4pm for a popular happy hour. Two-fer night is Sunday.

At the **SugarBowl** (1242 Rte. 27, Carrabassett Valley, 207/235-3300, www.sugarbowlmaine.com, 4pm-10pm Mon.-Fri., noon-10pm Sat.-Sun., $12-18), you can bowl, watch the game on 17 large-screen TVs, visit the arcade, or try the golf simulator, while enjoying upscale pub fare.

Kingfield

The **Orange Cat Cafe** (329 Main St., Kingfield, 207/265-2860, www.orangecatcafe.com, 7am-3pm Mon.-Sat., 8am-3pm Sun.), in the "brick castle," is a favorite for breakfast sandwiches and pastries, homemade soups, creative sandwiches, salads, and other goodies. There's often live music.

Like burritos? You'll love **Rolling Fatties** (268 Main St., Kingfield, 207/399-9246, http://rollingfatties.com, 3pm-8pm Thurs., noon-8pm Fri.-Sat., noon-6pm Sun.). The casual order-at-the-counter restaurant sited in an in-town farmhouse features burritos and bowls crafted from GMO-free and locally raised foods. In the summer, the truck is often on the road; check the website for details.

An old reliable, **Longfellow's** (Rte. 27, Kingfield, 207/265-2561, www.longfellowsme.com, 11am-9pm daily, $12-24), serves a New American menu. Service is friendly, prices are reasonable, and the best tables have views over the river out back. Two-fer night is Tuesday.

The area's top fine-dining restaurant is **One Stanley Avenue** (1 Stanley Ave., Kingfield, 207/265-5541, www.stanleyavenue.com, 5pm-9:30pm Tues.-Sun. mid-Dec.-mid-Apr., $21-35), a Kingfield magnet since 1972 with a menu that never changes (entrées are noted with the year they were added to the menu). Cocktails in the Victorian lounge precede a dining experience: unobtrusive service, understated decor, and entrées such as roast duck with rhubarb glaze, chicken with fiddleheads, and sage rabbit. Reservations are essential on winter weekends.

Stratton

Decent home cooking at reasonable prices is served at the **Looney Moose Cafe** (9 Main St., 207/246-3000, 7am-2pm Tues.-Sun.).

For well-prepared, seasonally driven upscale American fare, make reservations at the ★ **Coplin Dinner House** (8252 Rte. 27, 207/246-0016, http://coplindinnerhouse.com, from 5pm Wed.-Sun., $24-39), occupying a restored farmhouse on the outskirts of Stratton Village. Wednesday is two-fer night. Lighter fare ($26-24) is served in the Tiger Lily Lounge.

ACCOMMODATIONS

When you've had a long day on the slopes, a bed close by can be mighty tempting—plus you can be upward bound quickly in the morning. But such convenience doesn't come cheaply, so your budget may dictate where you decide to stay. The choices are on the mountain at Sugarloaf, in Carrabassett Valley near the Sugarloaf access road, or farther afield in Kingfield, Stratton, Eustis, and beyond. On weekends and holiday periods, on-mountain beds are scarce to nonexistent, so reservations well in advance are necessary. Keep in mind that winter is peak season; expect lower rates in summer.

Many area accommodations provide discount passes for cross-country skiing at the Sugarloaf Outdoor Center, a nice little perk.

Sugarloaf

Accommodations are available all year at the resort (800/843-5623), and prices vary widely depending on the property and the dates. Possibilities include condominiums and two hotels. The winter-only **Sugarloaf Inn** (207/237-0088), conveniently situated adjacent to the Sawduster double chairlift, has 42 guest rooms (some in need of a facelift). The imposing **Sugarloaf Mountain Hotel** (207/237-2222 or 800/527-9879), with 119 varied guest rooms and suites and two penthouses, is in the village center. All reservations booked by Sugarloaf include use of the **Sugarloaf Sports and Fitness Club** (207/237-6946), in the Sugartree condo complex on Mountainside Road. In winter, packages with lift tickets are your best bet.

Just south of the mountain access road but on the shuttle route is **Hostel of Maine** (3004 Town Line, Carrabassett Valley, 207/237-2077, www.hostelofmaine.com, $185-255), a purpose-built log structure with bunkrooms (from $45), family rooms (from $199), private rooms (from $145), and spacious living rooms, including one with a stone fireplace. Rates include a hearty continental breakfast.

Kingfield

Slumber in history at the 1918 **Herbert Grand Hotel** (246 Main St., Kingfield, 207/265-2000 or 800/843-4372, www.herbertgrandhotel.com, $90-140), an antiques-filled, three-story, 26-room Victorian hotel in downtown Kingfield. Rooms vary widely; some are a bit quirky, but all were updated in 2016. The inn has a pub ($8-12), and a continental breakfast is included.

Next door to One Stanley Avenue restaurant and under the same ownership, **Three Stanley Avenue** (3 Stanley Ave., Kingfield, 207/265-5541, www.stanleyavenue.com, $80-95) has been a B&B since the early 1980s. The antiques-filled yellow Victorian (built by Bayard Stanley, younger brother of the famed Stanley Steamer twins) has three first-floor guest rooms with private baths and three second-floor guest rooms sharing two baths. It's all very welcoming, with comfortable wicker chairs on the front porch and a traditional gazebo, formerly a bandstand, in the backyard. Rates include a full breakfast served at the adjacent restaurant.

The **Inn on Winter's Hill** (33 Winter Hill St., Kingfield, 207/340-1020, https://wintershill.com, $150-250), originally the home of Amos Winter, has had a few lives; now it's a welcoming country inn. Rooms are distributed between the historic main house, with Victorian splendor, and the newer Barn, with a more contemporary feel. The restaurant serves breakfast ($12) and dinner, New American comfort food ($14-36). Pet-friendly rooms are $20/night.

Stratton and Eustis

A wonderful traditional sporting camp, **Tim Pond Camps** (Eustis, 207/243-2947, www.timpond.com) has been operating since 1877, when guests took so long to get here that they stayed the whole summer. Harvey and Betty Calden have owned this idyllic lakeside retreat since 1981. Eleven rustic log cabins dot the woods on either side of a modern-rustic lodge where everyone gathers three times a day for great comfort food; the dinner bell rings promptly at 5:30pm. BYOB. Daily rates are $240 pp, including all meals and use of a classic Rangeley boat with a motor and gas, and a canoe; it's half price for ages 5-12. Pets are $15/visit. Fly-fishing for brook trout is the prime pursuit (every spring a fly-fishing school is offered), but it's a fine place just to relax and listen to the loons. A family discount is available in July-August. Cabins have full baths, electricity until 10pm, daily maid service, and fascinating guest journals. Tim Pond Camps is at the northern end of mile-long Tim Pond, on a dirt road about 10 miles west of Route 27.

The updated **Spillover Motel and Inn** (Rte. 27, Stratton, 207/246-6571, http://spillovermaine.com), seven miles north of Sugarloaf, makes an excellent base for skiing or hiking. Choose from comfy motel rooms (from $99) or opt for the inn ($175), one mile away, where guests have kitchen access and share two bathrooms; robes and slippers are provided. Rates at both include a continental breakfast that can be upgraded to a hot breakfast.

Camping

With 115 wooded sites (most with hookups) on 300 acres, nonprofit **Cathedral Pines Campground** (Rte. 27, Eustis, 207/246-3491, www.gopinescamping.com, $32-40) has one of Maine's most scenic locations. It's set amid gigantic red pines and surrounded by mountains on the shore of Flagstaff Lake. Look for the marker that designates this site as one of Benedict Arnold's stops during his march to Québec City in 1775. Facilities include a recreation hall, a bathhouse, laundry, a swimming beach, basketball, a playground, canoe rentals, and paddleboat rentals. Pets are allowed. The campground is 26 miles south of the Québec border.

Just five miles south of the Quebec border, in the midst of pond-speckled, mountain-cradled wilderness, is **Natanis Point Campground** (19 Natanis Point Rd., Chain of Ponds Township, 207/297-2694, www.natanispointcampground.com, $25), with 61 grassy sites, some waterfront on Natanis or Round Ponds. Amenities include a sandy beach, a boat launch providing access to five miles of interconnecting lakes, and direct access to a 150-mile ATV trail.

INFORMATION

Sugarloaf (5092 Access Rd., Carrabassett Valley, 207/237-2000, www.sugarloaf.com) provides information on anything and everything on the mountain. During the ski season, the free tabloid *Sugarloaf This Week*, published biweekly, carries comprehensive information about on-mountain activities. It's available everywhere on the mountain and throughout the valley and beyond.

If you're staying on the mountain or in the valley and have cable TV, tune to channel 17 (WSKI) for weather, snow, trail, and lift updates, plus an entertainment rundown.

GETTING THERE AND AROUND

Kingfield is roughly 22 miles or 30 minutes from Farmington via Route 27. It's about 15 miles or 25 minutes to Sugarloaf via Route 27. It's about 42 miles or one hour to Rangeley via Routes 27 and 16.

The free **Sugarloaf Explorer** shuttle service (207/237-6853, www.sugarloafexplorer.com) operates 8am-approximately midnight daily during the winter season; it's on an on-call basis midweek and on a set schedule on weekends and during holiday periods. Various routes serve the condos, outdoor center, and valley.

Rangeley Lakes Area

Rangeley (pop. 1,168), incorporated in 1855, is the centerpiece of a vast system of lakes and streams surrounded by forested mountains. Rangeley is a catchall name. First applied to the town (formerly known as the Lake Settlement), it now also refers to the lake and the entire region. "I'm going to Rangeley" could indicate a destination anywhere in the extensive network of interconnecting lakes, rivers, and streams backing up to New Hampshire. The Rangeley Lakes make up the headwaters of the Androscoggin River, which technically begins at Umbagog Lake and flows seaward for 167 miles to meet the Kennebec River in Merrymeeting Bay, near Brunswick and Topsham.

Excavations have revealed evidence of human habitation in this area as long ago as 9000 BC. More than 8,000 stone tools and other artifacts were uncovered at the Vail site, on the edge of Aziscohos Lake. Native Americans certainly left their linguistic mark here, too, with tongue-twisting names applied to the lakes and other natural features. Mooselookmeguntic means "where hunters watch moose at night"; Umbagog means "shallow water"; Mollychunkamunk (a.k.a. Upper Richardson Lake) means "crooked water"; Oquossoc means "landing place"; and Kennebago means "land of sweet water." The town's more prosaic name comes from 19th-century landowner Squire James Rangeley.

The region has been a vacation magnet since the late 1800s, drawing outdoors enthusiasts who came first by stagecoach and later by rail and steamer to breathe in the unspoiled air, paddle and fish the clear waters, hike mountain trails, and hunt in vast wildlands. Folks still come today for many of the same reasons, but to these add golf, tennis, and winter sports that include skiing, snowshoeing, ice fishing, and especially snowmobiling. Recreation is the primary attraction, but there are also cultural events, old-fashioned annual festivals and fairs, a few museums, and shops selling antiques, books, sportswear, and crafts.

Southeast of Rangeley, the town of **Phillips** (pop. 1,028), was the birthplace of fly-fishing legend Cornelia T. "Fly Rod" Crosby (1854-1946), recipient of the first Registered Maine Guide license issued by the state—the imprimatur for outdoors professionals. Crosby, who wrote columns for the local paper later syndicated in Boston, Chicago, and New York, was a fanatic angler and hunter who always kept a china tea set neatly stowed in her gear.

Along Route 17 about 23 miles south of Oquossoc is Coos Canyon, in the town of **Byron** (pop. 145), where gold was found in the early 1800s on the East Branch of the Swift River. Amateur prospectors still flock to the area, but don't get your hopes up—it's more play than profits.

SIGHTS

★ Rangeley Outdoor Sporting Heritage Museum

Don and Stephanie Palmer began collecting artifacts relating to the region's rich sporting heritage back in the mid-1990s, and as the collection grew, they realized they needed a museum to house it. Opened in 2010 after a major fundraising effort and expanded in 2012, the **Rangeley Outdoor Sporting Heritage Museum** (Rte. 17, Oquossoc Village, 207/864-5647, www.rangeleyoutdoormuseum.org, 10am-4pm Wed.-Sun. May-June and Sept.-Oct., daily July-Aug., $5 over age 12) has engaging exhibits that tell the stories of Rangeley's many sporting luminaries, including Fly-Rod Crosby; fly-tier Carrie Stevens; taxidermist, painter, and angler Herb Welch; and boatbuilder Herbie Ellis. You enter through a reconstructed 1890 log cabin, which sets the tone. This museum is a community treasure, and locals and summer residents are helping it grow its collections with finds from their attics. Don't miss it. As a five-year-old remarked when I visited, "This museum is so cool."

Wilhelm Reich Museum

Controversial Austrian-born psychoanalyst and natural scientist Wilhelm Reich (1897-1957), noted expert on sexual energy, chose Rangeley for his residence and research. Hour-long guided tours of the **Wilhelm Reich Museum** (Dodge Pond Rd., Rangeley, 207/864-3443, www.wilhelmreichtrust.org, 1pm-5pm Wed.-Sun. July-Aug., 1pm-5pm Sat. Sept., $8 adults, free under age 13), his handsome fieldstone mansion, include a slide presentation covering Reich's life, eccentric philosophy, experiments, and inventions such as the orgone accumulator and the cloudbuster. Reich is buried on the estate grounds. Views are spectacular from the roof of the museum, also known as Orgonon, so bring binoculars and a camera. A nature-trail system, including a bird blind, winds through the wooded acreage. The museum hosts free outdoor-oriented natural-science programs 2pm-4pm Sundays.

Rangeley Lakes Scenic Byway

While most visitors reach Rangeley via Route 4 from the Farmington area, another popular route is Route 17 from the Rumford-Mexico area. When you reach Byron on the Swift River, you enter the 35-mile **Rangeley Lakes Scenic Byway,** stretching from Byron north to Oquossoc and then southward down Route 4 through Rangeley to Madrid. The label is unquestionably deserved, especially in autumn when the vibrant colors are unforgettable. The two-lane road winds through the rural woods of western Maine, opening up periodically to reveal stunning views of lakes, streams, forested hillsides, and the Swift River. You might even see a moose. Highlights are two signposted viewpoints—**Height of Land** and the **Rangeley Scenic Overlook**—surveying Mooselookmeguntic and Rangeley Lakes, respectively. Height of Land, 11 miles south of Oquossoc, adjoins the Appalachian Trail.

Maine Forestry Museum

Renovated and upgraded in 2015, the three-story **Maine Forestry Museum** (221 Stratton Rd./Rte. 16, Rangeley, 207/864-3939, www.maineforestrymuseum.org, 10am-4pm Wed.-Sun. mid-June-early Sept. or by appointment, donation) is home to an eclectic assortment of lumberjack paraphernalia, artifacts, and samples of traditional artwork created in the camps. Call first; I've found it closed even during posted open hours.

Bennett Covered Bridge

Spanning the Magalloway River beneath Aziscohos Mountain, the 93-foot-long, Paddleford truss-type **Bennett Covered Bridge,** built in 1901 and closed to traffic in 1985, sees far fewer visitors than most of Maine's eight other covered bridges. The setting, in the hamlet of Wilsons Mills, makes for great photos, so it's worth detouring on the unpaved road next to the Aziscohos Valley Camping Area, 0.3 mile west of Route 16 and 28 miles west of Rangeley.

Sandy River and Rangeley Lakes Railroad

The **Sandy River and Rangeley Lakes Railroad** (128 Bridge St., Phillips, 207/788-3621, www.srrl-rr.org) dates to 1879, when the first section was constructed to connect northern Franklin County with Farmington, the terminus of the Maine Central Railroad. Since 1969, volunteers have been working to restore and reopen a section of the original narrow-gauge track. Visit the station, then board a restored 1884 passenger car for the 50-minute round-trip ride to the museum and roundhouse. The train operates June-mid-October on an erratic schedule. Fares are $6 adults, $1 ages 6-12. Call or check the website for current season info and schedule; even then, it's dependent on the availability of equipment and operators. Rail fans might also want to check out the Railroad Room of the nearby **Phillips Historical Society** (Main St., Phillips). It's open 1pm-3pm on the first and third Sunday June-early October.

TOP EXPERIENCE

Moose-Spotting

The likelihood of spotting one of these gangly critters can be quite high, if conditions are ripe. Route 16 between Rangeley and Stratton is well known as "moose alley," especially in the boggy areas close to the road. Sunrise and sunset are the best times for sighting moose. Keep your camera handy, and drive slowly; no one wins in a moose-car collision, and fatal accidents are not uncommon on this unlighted stretch.

Flightseeing

The best way to put the region in perspective is from the air. **Acadian Seaplanes** (2640 Main St., 207/864-5307, www.acadianseaplanes.com) offers tours of the Rangeley region via floatplane (beginning at $65 pp for 15 minutes). Also available are a rafting tour ($199 pp) and Fly & Dine trips ($179 pp including meal) to a remote sporting camp for dinner.

Quill Hill

If you lack the time, will, or ability to hike for views, drive 4.5 miles to the summit of **Quill Hill** (Rte. 27, 7.3 miles north of Rangeley, $10/car). The 2,848-foot summit provides 360-degree views of the surrounding wilderness, especially stunning in foliage season and at sunset. Picnic tables and a wheelchair-accessible path make it a great spot for the whole family.

ENTERTAINMENT

The great outdoors is the Rangeley region's biggest source of entertainment, but there are some options for rainy days and evening fun.

Rangeley Friends of the Arts (RFA, 2493 Main St., 207/864-5000, http://rangeleyarts.org) is a local cultural organization that promotes the arts in the region through concerts, events, scholarships, and school programs. The organization is based at **Lakeside Theater.**

Hungry for a good time? Check out **Moose**

Alley (2809 Main St., Rangeley, 207/864-9955, http://moosealley.me), with a 10-lane bowling alley, an arcade, a billiards room, live music on most Friday and Saturday nights, sporting events on 22 HD screens, and a menu heavy on sandwiches, salads, burgers, and pizza ($9-13).

Festivals and Events

Hardly a day goes by in July and August without something scheduled. At other times, events are less frequent.

Avid snowmobilers shouldn't miss the annual January **Snodeo,** held for one day in Rangeley. Events at the family-oriented festival include competitions, food, games, an auction, raffles, live entertainment, radar runs, children's events, a snowmobile parade, antique snowmobile displays, fireworks, and more.

Expert white-water paddlers arrive in spring for the **Smalls to the Wall Steep Creek Race** down the Sandy River and over the steep steps of Smalls Falls, usually in mid- to late April.

The last weekend in July, **Logging Museum Festival Days** includes a parade, a beanhole bean supper, lumberjack events, and the Little Miss Woodchip contest. It's held on the Maine Forestry Museum grounds on Route 16.

Downtown Rangeley comes alive the third Thursday in August for the **Annual Blueberry Festival,** a daylong celebration of the blueberry harvest, with sales of everything blueberry.

SHOPPING

The new-book selection is distinguished at **Books, Lines & Thinkers** (Main St., Rangeley, 207/864-4355) thanks to owner Wess Connally, a former high school English teacher in Rangeley.

Ecopelagicon: A Nature Store (7 Pond St., Rangeley, 207/864-2771) emphasizes eco-oriented gifts, books, toys, games, and cosmetics. It also arranges guided paddling, snowshoeing, and hiking tours.

RECREATION

Parks

RANGELEY LAKE STATE PARK

With 1.2 miles of lake frontage and panoramic views toward the mountains, **Rangeley Lake State Park** (S. Shore Dr., Rangeley, 207/864-3858, www.parksandlands.com, $4-6 adults, $2 ages 5-11 and seniors) gets high marks for picnicking, swimming, fishing, birding, boating, and camping. The swimming "beach" is a large patch of grass. None of the 50 campsites is at water's edge, but a dozen have easy shore access. (For camping reservations, visit www.campwithme.com; from out of state call 207/287-3824 at least two business days in advance. Maine residents call 800/332-1501.) If you're doing any boating, stay close to shore until you're comfortable with the wind conditions; the wind picks up very quickly on Rangeley Lake, especially in the south and southeast coves near the park. Camping is $30/site nonresidents, $20 for Maine residents, plus $5/site/night for a reservation; there are no hookups, but there are hot showers. The park, four miles off Route 17, is open mid-May-September, but it's accessible in the winter for cross-country skiing and snowmobiling.

LAKESIDE PARK

In downtown Rangeley, overlooking both lake and mountains, lovely, grassy **Lakeside Park** has a tiny beach and a safe swim area, grills and covered picnic tables, tennis courts, a playground with plenty of swings, lots of lawn for running, and a busy boat launch. Restrooms are open when a lifeguard is on duty. Access is from Main Street (Rte. 4) near the Parkside and Main Restaurant and the chamber of commerce office.

SMALLS FALLS

One of Maine's most accessible cascades, **Smalls Falls** is right next to Route 4 at a state rest area 12 miles south of Rangeley. Pull into the parking area and walk a few steps to the overlook for an overview, and ascend the trail for a closer view of the four waterfalls: a 3-foot

Mooselookmeguntic Lake / Le Lac Mooselookmeguntic
The Students Island fish story
Carrie Stevens and the Grey Ghost
1
2
Outdoor Heritage
MUSEUM
Rangeley Lakes Historical Society
GIFT SHOP
WEDS-SUN
3
Oquossoc Lady II
4

fall at the bottom, a 14-foot horsetail, a 25-foot fall in two sections, and a 12-foot horsetail. Keep hiking to see smaller falls. Bring a picnic. Locals love to swim in the pools between the falls. The rest area is officially open mid-May-October, but it's easy to park alongside the highway early and late in the season.

Preserves

Since its founding in 1991, **Rangeley Lakes Heritage Trust** (RLHT, Rte. 4, Oquossoc, 207/864-7311, www.rlht.org) has preserved more than 13,650 acres, including 50 miles of water frontage, 15 islands, and Bald Mountain. Trail maps can be printed from the website.

HUNTER COVE WILDLIFE SANCTUARY

Loons, ducks, and other waterfowl are the principal residents of **Hunter Cove Wildlife Sanctuary.** While walking the three miles of easy blazed trails, best covered in a clockwise direction, keep an eye out for the blue flag iris, which blossoms throughout the summer. You may even spot a moose. If you launch a canoe into Hunter Cove and paddle under the Mingo Loop Road bridge early in the season, you'll come face-to-face with nesting cliff swallows. To reach the sanctuary, take Route 4 west of downtown Rangeley for about 2.5 miles, turning left into the preserve across the road from Dodge Pond. It's signposted. The preserve is open sunrise-sunset daily, and admission is free.

Hiking

Hiking opportunities in this region are plentiful, and indeed there are numerous hiking guidebooks that provide details on more serious endeavors. Here's a sampling of a few hikes that reap big rewards for basic efforts. Wear appropriate footwear and carry water, snacks or lunch, and bug repellent.

1: Height of Land on the Rangeley Lakes Scenic Byway **2:** Rangeley Outdoor Sporting Heritage Museum **3:** Rangeley Region Lake Cruises **4:** canoe on Rangeley Lake

BALD MOUNTAIN

Centerpiece of a 1,953-acre parcel of Maine Public Reserve Land, **Bald Mountain** is a relatively easy two-hour 2.6-mile round-trip hike that ascends less than 1,000 feet, yet the minimal effort leads to stunning views of Rangeley, Cupsuptic, and Mooselookmeguntic Lakes—not to mention the surrounding mountains. Even three-year-olds can tackle this without terrifying their parents. Pack a picnic. The trailhead is on Bald Mountain Road in Oquossoc, about a mile south of Route 4 and roughly across from the entrance to Bald Mountain Camps. Park well off the road.

ANGEL FALLS

Dropping 90 feet straight down, dramatic **Angel Falls** is one of New England's highest cascades. Even in midsummer, you'll be fording running water, so wear rubberized or waterproof shoes or boots. The best time to come is autumn, when most of the rivulets have dried up and the woods are brilliantly colorful. Allow 1-1.5 hours for the easy-to-moderate 1.4-mile round-trip hike. The trail is mostly red-blazed, with the addition of orange strips tied at crucial points. From Oquossoc, take Route 17 south about 18.5 miles to Houghton and turn right on an unpaved road; continue across a bridge and then turn right on Bemis Road for another 3.5 miles. From the parking lot, walk along the road to the trailhead. This is a popular hike, so you should see other cars. The trail leads off to the left.

PIAZZA ROCK AND SADDLEBACK MOUNTAIN

A distinctive landmark on the western slope of Saddleback Mountain, **Piazza Rock** is a giant cantilevered boulder 600 feet off the Appalachian Trail (AT). The hike up is easy to moderate—not a cakewalk, but fine for families—and travels along the white-blazed AT from Route 4. From downtown Rangeley, go seven miles southeast on Route 4 and park in the lot on the south side of the highway. Piazza Rock is 1.2 miles northeast of the highway.

If you continue on the AT from Piazza Rock, it's another four miles to the summit of 4,116-foot **Saddleback Mountain,** but most hikers take the shorter route up the mountain from the ski area's base lodge. To get there from Rangeley, go south on Route 4 to Dallas Hill Road and then go 2.5 miles to Saddleback Mountain Road. From the lodge, follow the orange trail markers. Expect a stiff breeze and 360-degree vistas. A trail map is available at the lodge.

CASCADE STREAM GORGE

A 16-foot cascade, a 2,000-foot gorge, and well-placed picnic tables are the rewards for completing this short but sometimes steep trail. Allow about 30 minutes for the one-mile round-trip white-blazed trail without stops. From downtown Rangeley, head south 3.5 miles on Route 4, turning left on Cascade Road, left on Town Hall Road, and then right up a steep drive, bearing right again into the parking area.

Other excellent hikes west and north of Rangeley are **Aziscohos Mountain** and **West Kennebago Mountain.** Both are easy to moderate, have terrific views from their summits, and require 3-4 hours round-trip from their trailheads. West Kennebago has a fire tower.

FLY ROD CROSBY TRAIL

The first 20 miles of the **Fly Rod Crosby Trail** opened in August 2012. Eventually, the trail, named for Maine's first registered guide, Cornelia "Fly Rod" Crosby, will stretch 45 miles from Strong to Oquossoc. The first section begins in Phillips and continues northwest through Madrid and Sandy River Plantation, first following an abandoned railroad bed and then veering into the backcountry before ending at Saddleback Mountain. The sections from Strong to Phillips and continuing from Saddleback to Oquossoc are under development by the nonprofit High Peaks Alliance (www.highpeaksalliance.org); find a trail map on the website with directions to current trailheads.

Boat Excursions

Cruise the waters of Rangeley Lake aboard the *Oquossoc Lady* or Grey Ghost with **Rangeley Region Lake Cruises** (207/864-2038, www.rangeley-lakes.com). Scenic lake, sunset, and fall foliage cruises last 1.5 hours and cost $35 adults, $10 ages 2-10. Special sunset and full-moon cruises are scheduled when the sunset and full-moon rise occur within the same hour.

Water Sports

FISHING

The Rangeley Lakes area earned its vaunted reputation for world-class fishing. Diehard anglers will always show up in May-early June, lured by landlocked salmon and brook trout. The region boasts of being the birthplace of contemporary fly-fishing, and indeed many famous flies originated here. The best fly-fishing correlates with the waves of fly hatches late May-early July. The Big Three for fly-fishing are the **Kennebago, Magalloway,** and **Rapid Rivers. Upper Dam** on Mooselookmeguntic Lake is another hot spot. If you're serious about fishing, arrange to be flown into a wilderness pond.

The best local source of information on fly-fishing is **Rangeley Region Sport Shop** (2529 Main St., Rangeley, 207/864-5615, www.rangeleysportshop.com), which also sells gear and offers wade-guiding services for $200 half day, $350 full day.

PADDLING

Canoeing and kayaking are splendid throughout this region. Be forewarned, though, that Rangeley and Mooselookmeguntic Lakes are much larger than they look, and they have wide-open expanses where fluky winds can kick up suddenly and mightily and swamp boats.

If you're looking for pristine waters where motorboats are banned, opt for **Saddleback Lake, Loon Lake, Little Kennebago Lake,** or **Quimby Pond,** all fairly close to Rangeley.

Other nearby paddling choices are the **Cupsuptic River,** the lower **Kennebago**

Paddle Across Maine

You can paddle an ancient Native American route through the mountains and wilderness of northern New England and Québec. The 740-mile **Northern Forest Canoe Trail** (802/496-2285, www.northernforestcanoetrail.org) begins in Old Forge, New York, and passes through 35 communities in Vermont, Québec, New Hampshire, and Maine, following lakes, rivers, and streams, both flat water and white water, before finishing in Fort Kent. While some dedicated paddlers have completed the trek from start to finish, most folks dabble in various areas.

More than 350 miles of the waterway are in Maine. The trail enters the state via Umbagog Lake in section 8 and then progresses through the Rangeley Lakes and across Flagstaff Lake to Spencer Stream before crossing into the Kennebec River Valley region, following the Moose River, and finishing section 10 in Moosehead Lake. Sections 11 through 13 pass from the lake to the West Branch of the Penobscot and on to Chesuncook Lake. From here, it follows the Allagash Wilderness Waterway to its confluence with the St. John River at the tip of Maine.

If you get serious about paddling it, the trail is mapped in 13 sections (sections 8-13 are in Maine; maps are $10 each, available online or in local shops; the full set is $60). The maps detail the waterways, portages, dams, communities en route, and natural sights. Also beneficial is the *Northern Forest Canoe Trail Guidebook* ($25). Much information is available online, with even more available to those who join Northern Forest Canoe Trail; membership is $35.

River, and **Mooselookmeguntic Lake.** Slightly farther afield are **Upper and Lower Richardson Lakes,** both wonderfully scenic, as is **Umbagog Lake** (um-BAY-gog), straddling the Maine-New Hampshire border. The **Cupsuptic, Kennebago,** and **Magalloway Rivers** are all easy Class I waters. The Rangeley Lakes Area Chamber of Commerce has produced a suggested canoeing itinerary for the Rangeley Lakes chain, including information about wilderness campsites en route. Some of the campsites require reservations and fire permits.

Rangeley Region Lake Cruises (207/864-2038, www.rangeley-lakes.com) also offers guided Mothership kayak trips from the Grey Ghost pontoon boat. Trips on Rangeley Lake are $65 adults, $40 ages 12-15. Trips on Mooselookmeguntic, Cupsuptic, and Upper Richardson are $75 adults, $50 ages 12-15.

Besides being a place that has fishing, camping, and hunting gear as well as water toys, outdoor clothing, and unique gifts, **River's Edge Sports** (Rte. 4, Oquossoc, 207/864-5582, www.riversedgesports.com) also rents canoes, kayaks, and paddleboards. Rates start at $25/day or $125/week. For $50, including canoe or single kayak rental, River's Edge will shuttle you and the canoe up the Kennebago River to the start of an idyllic 2-3-hour downstream paddle to Route 16 and your car; go at sunrise for the best chance of spotting a moose.

Ecopelagicon (7 Pond St., Rangeley, 207/864-2771, www.ecopelagicon.com) rents kayaks for use on Haley Pond for a short paddle or to take to your camp. Single kayaks rent for $32/day, $25/half day, or $12/hour; doubles are $36, $28, and $15; canoes are $30, $22, $12; SUPs are $45, $30, $15. Long-term rates are available. Delivery and pickup are available for a fee.

MOTORBOATING

The easiest way to explore these massive lakes is by motorboat. Most lakes have public access points, but these may be busy. Put-ins for Rangeley Lake include the state park, Lakeside Park, and off Route 4 in Oquossoc. The best one for Mooselookmeguntic is Haines Landing, at the end of Route 4. There's another ramp off Route 16 west, approximately four miles from the intersection with Route 4. Also off Route 16 is the Mill Brook access for Lake Richardson and the Black Cove Campground access for Aziscohos (be careful, as it's extremely shallow in places). Maine has strict rules about boating. For information, contact the **Maine Department of Inland Fisheries and Wildlife** (www.maine.gov/ifw) or a local outfitter.

Motorboat rentals from **Lakeside Convenience & Marina** (2582 Main St., Rangeley, 207/864-5888, www.lakesideon-rangeley.com) begin at $230/day, $150/half day.

Golf

Noted golfers have been teeing off at **Mingo Springs Golf Course** (Country Club Rd., Rangeley, 207/864-5021) since 1925, when the course started with nine holes. Today's 18-hole, par-70 course boasts panoramic vistas of lakes and mountains—and sometimes an annoying breeze. Golf-and-lodging packages are available at the adjacent Country Club Inn.

Gold Panning

"Gold bought, sold, and lied about here" proclaims the sign outside **Coos Canyon Rock and Gift Shop** (472 Swift River Rd., Byron, 207/364-4900, www.cooscanyonrockandgift.com), a family operation since 1956. Check out the exhibits of some of the nuggets found in the Swift River and then rent equipment and try it yourself. A pan and trowel for use on-site are free, with a $5 deposit. Off-site use is $2.50/day for a pan and screen, $1 for a trowel, or $15-20 for a fancier sluice box ($100 deposit). It's a relatively inexpensive lesson in patience.

Winter Sports

ALPINE SKIING AND SNOWBOARDING

Saddleback (207/864-5671 or 866/918-2225, www.saddlebackmaine.com), a family-oriented area, with a 2,000-foot vertical drop off a 4,116-foot summit, closed in 2015. It's expected to reopen in 2020 after infrastructure improvements.

CROSS-COUNTRY SKIING AND SNOWSHOEING

The volunteer-operated nonprofit **Rangeley Lakes Cross Country Ski Club** (524 Saddleback Mountain Rd., 207/864-4309, www.xcskiresorts.com/rangeley) operates the **Rangeley Lakes Trails Center,** with 55 kilometers of mapped trails lacing through the Saddleback preserve on lower Saddleback Mountain. Maps are available at the center, where a yurt serves as the lodge. Trails are open 9am-4pm daily. Full-day ski passes are $20 adults, $12 ages 7-18; full-day snowshoe passes are $10 adults, $5 kids; and fat-tire bike passes are $15 adults, $12 kids. Equipment rental is available: $20 for skis, boots, and poles; $10 for snowshoes; $55 for fat-tire bikes.

The summer nature trails at the **Wilhelm Reich Museum** are accessible for free cross-country skiing or snowshoeing 9am-4pm weekdays.

ICE-SKATING

A local skating club maintains an ice rink on **Haley Pond.** Free skate rentals are available from **Ecopelagicon** (3 Pond St., Rangeley, 207/864-2771). Haley Pond is also home to a winter pond hockey tournament in February.

SNOWMOBILING

Snowmobiling is big business in Rangeley, and in winter most accommodations and lodgings cater to it. The Rangeley area, linked to the state's **Interconnected Trail System** (ITS) via ITS 84, 89, and 117, has its own well-marked 150-mile groomed network thanks to the diligent efforts of the local Rangeley Lakes Snowmobile Club (www.rangeleys-nowmobile.com). A family club membership is $45; individual membership is $30. Club gatherings and events are a good way to get the local scoop. Popular rides include a 65-mile lake loop; all or part of the 300-mile Black Fly Loop, which circles through Franklin and Somerset Counties; Kennebago Mountain; and even into Canada on the 12,500-mile international circuit. There are no local trail fees, but support at local fund-raisers is appreciated.

Rangeley Power Sports (2770 Main St., Rangeley, 207/305-5233, www.rangeleypowersports.com) rents sleds for $175 half day, $200-300 full day. Snowmobile clothing and gear rentals also are available.

FOOD

Check the local newspaper for announcements of **public suppers,** featuring chicken, beans, spaghetti, or just potluck. Most suppers benefit charitable causes, cost under $10 pp, and provide an ample supply of local color.

Quick Bites

While bagels are the specialty at **Moosely Bagels** (2588 Main St., Rangeley, 207/864-5955), the menu offers a full range of breakfast and lunch options. Eat inside or on the back lake-view deck.

"Meet me at the Frosty" is Rangeley's summertime one-liner, a ritual for locals and visitors alike. **Pine Tree Frosty** (Main St., Rangeley, 207/864-5894), a tiny takeout near Haley Pond and the Rangeley Inn, serves ever-popular Gifford's ice cream in dozens of flavors along with good-size lobster rolls and superb onion rings.

Oquossoc Grocery (Rte. 4, Oquossoc, 207/864-3662) has fresh-baked doughnuts, sandwiches, and pizza.

Family Favorites

Try to snag a table on the deck overlooking the park and lake at **Parkside and Main** (2520 Main St./Rte. 4, Rangeley, 207/864-3774, from 11:30am daily, $8-22). The American menu varies from burgers to steak; stick with the homemade soups and salads or simpler preparations, and don't miss the homemade blue cheese dressing. In summer there's often entertainment on the deck.

Watch the game while sipping cold beer and chowing good burgers, nachos, hand-cut fries, and similar fare at ever-popular **Sarge's Sports Pub and Grub** (Main St., Rangeley, 207/864-5616, http://sargessportspub.com, from 11am daily), which has covered outdoor seating. More substantial entrées ($10-17) are served after 5pm, and there's even a kids' menu. Weekends there's often live entertainment.

The **Red Onion** (Main St./Rte. 4, Rangeley, 207/864-5022, http://therangeleyredonion.com, 11am-9pm daily, $10-20) is a barn of a place serving soups, sandwiches, chili, pizzas made on homemade dough, and comfort fare. Portions are large.

In winter, watch deer feed in the woods and in the summer, dine outside at the **Gingerbread House** (55 Carry Rd., Oquossoc, 207/864-3602, www.gingerbreadhouserestaurant.net, 7:30am-3pm Wed.-Sat., 7am-11:30am Sun., $10-16), serving the usual breakfast fare and pub favors for lunch.

Several sporting camps in the Rangeley area open their dining rooms to nonguests, primarily for dinner, during the summer. Grab the opportunity to sample the sporting-camp ambience and the comfort food that brings guests back from one generation to the next. One of the best is the lakefront restaurant at **Bald Mountain Camps** (Bald Mountain Rd., Oquossoc, 207/864-3671, www.baldmountaincamps.com, $12-35), which offers well-prepared, American fare. Make dinner reservations well in advance, and aim for sunset. Hours vary by season. It also serves lunch in peak seasons.

Casual Dining

Huge windows frame dramatic views of Rangeley Lake from the dining room of the hilltop **Country Club Inn** (56 Country Club Rd., Rangeley, www.countryclubinnrangeley.com, 6pm-8pm Wed.-Sun., $25-32). White tablecloths drape the well-spaced tables, and the Continental fare complements the view. If the weather's fine, begin with cocktails on the deck overlooking the lake.

Cozy and inviting, ★ **Forks in the Air Mountain Bistro** (2485 Main St., Rangeley, 207/864-2883, www.forksintheair.com, 4pm-9pm daily, $16-34) serves seasonal, updated New England cuisine.

The Rangeley Inn's **Tavern** (207/864-3341, 3pm-9pm nightly late June-late Oct., call for off-season hours, $12-34) at the Rangeley Inn, serves a limited comfort food menu.

The sunset view over Rangeley Lake with the White Mountains as a backdrop is reason alone to reserve a table at **Loon Lodge** (16 Pickford Rd., Rangeley, 207/864-5666, www.loonlodgeme.com, 5pm-9pm Tues.-Sat., $21-31), where the menu features updated American fare.

At **45th Parallel Wood Fired Grille** (17 Rumford Rd./Rt. 4, Oquossoc, 207/864-3001, 11am-9pm Wed.-Mon., $10-24), expect not only wood-grilled ribs, brisket, and steak, but also pan-seared and fresh seafood, and burgers and sandwiches, some with an international accent.

Excellent food at affordable prices reel folks into the **Hungry Trout Grille and Bar** (2303 Main St., Rangeley, 207/864-5044, http://rangeleysaddlebackinn.com/restaurant, 4pm-9pm Tues.-Sat., $11-20), where Chef Brian Anderson prepares American comfort food with pizazz. The restaurant is extremely popular, for good reason, but it doesn't take reservations. It's located at the Rangeley Saddleback Inn.

ACCOMMODATIONS

Inns and Motels

The **Country Club Inn** (56 Country Club Rd., Rangeley, 207/864-3831, www.countryclubinnrangeley.com, mid-May-mid-Oct. and late Dec.-Mar.) claims the same fabulous lake-and-mountain panorama as the adjacent Mingo Springs Golf Course. Nineteen 1960s-style lake-view guest rooms are $149-169 with breakfast, $129-139 room only; ask about golf packages. Decor is classic lodge: two huge fireplaces in the living room accented by wildlife trophies, and lots of pine paneling everywhere. The inn is superbly maintained and run, and there's an outdoor pool. Pets are a possibility. The inn is 2.2 miles west of downtown Rangeley.

Since acquiring the venerable **Rangeley Inn** (2443 Main St., Rangeley, 207/864-3341, www.therangeleyinn.com, $125-300) in 2013, owner Travis Ferland has been working to restore the rambling, downtown Victorian-era hotel to its former glory. Rooms in the main inn retain Victorian charm (right down to those squeaky floors), those in the tavern wing have been tastefully renovated, and those in pet-friendly ($15/night) Haley Pond Lodge have water views. Guests have free use of canoes and kayaks on the pond. The main building houses a **tavern** (3pm-9pm daily in season, $13-18) serving contemporary pub fare. Rates include a continental breakfast.

Families love the **Rangeley Saddleback Inn** (2303 Main St./Rt. 4, Rangeley, 207/864-3434, $130-160) as much for the service as for the amenities, which include an indoor saltwater pool, hot tub, on-site restaurant, and grab-and-go breakfast. Four rooms are pet friendly.

The sunset views over Rangeley Lake are sigh-worthy from **Loon Lodge** (16 Pickford Rd., Rangeley, 207/864-5666, www.loonlodgeme.com, $125-185), which also houses a popular restaurant and pub. Beyond the back deck, the lawn rolls down to the lake, so you can wake with a morning swim.

Bed-and-Breakfasts

Rob Welch, a retired principal, and his wife, Jan, a schoolteacher, are the enthusiastic hosts at ★ **Pleasant Street Inn B&B** (104 Pleasant St., Rangeley, 207/864-5916, www.pleasantstreetinnbb.com, $154-184), perched on a quiet hillside less than half a mile from downtown. The Welches have completely renovated and expanded a traditional Maine farmhouse to include five good-size guest rooms. There's plenty of room to spread out in the guest parlor with a TV, spacious living room, and dining area, where a full breakfast is served. Guests also have access to a pantry stocked with afternoon refreshments, as well as a computer. In the winter, you can watch Rob feed the deer in the backyard.

The **Highland Heath House** (100 Kendall Farm Trail, Rangeley, 207/864-2441, www.highlandheathhouse.com, $160-195) is a handsome log home overlooking Rangeley Lake and offering three guest rooms and a suite decorated in upscale cabin style, a great room with a wood-burning fireplace, and a BYOB pub on the lower level.

Sporting Camps and Cabin Colonies

Stephen Philbrick is the third-generation owner of **Bald Mountain Camps** (Bald Mountain Rd., Oquossoc, 207/864-3671, www.baldmountaincamps.com, from $150), a family-oriented traditional sporting camp edging Mooselookmeguntic Lake. Established in 1897, the operation has 14 winterized, rustic waterfront log cabins sleeping 2-8 people. Each has a porch, a fireplace, a living room, individual bedrooms, and efficiency or full kitchen; daily housekeeping is available. The lake-view lodge has a dining room and lounge. Among the activities are swimming at the sandy beach, fishing, tennis, boating, and waterskiing. There's a playground for kids. Pets are $15/night.

Expect to hear lots of loons and see plenty of moose at **Grant's Kennebago Camps** (Kennebago Rd., Rangeley, 207/864-3608 or 800/633-4815, www.grantscamps.com, mid-May-mid-Oct.), a classic sporting camp built in 1905 on remote five-mile-long Kennebago Lake. Seriously dedicated fly-fishers fill up the beds in May and September; families take their places July-August (check the family packages). Daily rates for the 18 rustic cabins, with private baths and hot showers, are $165-195/adult, including three meals daily in the water-view dining room and use of sailboats, paddleboards, and bikes mid-July-mid-September. Children ages 7-12 are $60/night; children under age 6 are free. Pets are $15/night/pet. The main lodge's lake-view dining room is open to nonguests for all meals by reservation, but the hearty cuisine makes it a popular place, so call well ahead; BYOB. Canoe, kayak, and motorboat rentals range $40-65/day. Access to Grant's is via a gated nine-mile road from Route 16, west of Rangeley. The gate is open 7am-6pm only; if you're coming just for dinner, Grant's will arrange for access.

Avid fly-fishers have been heading to **Lakewood Camps** (207/243-2959, www.lakewoodcamps.com, no credit cards) for more than 150 years. The lakefront cabins are by Middle Dam, which separates Lower Richardson Lake from the famed Rapid River. The cold and wild Rapid River, which falls nearly 1,100 feet in fewer than

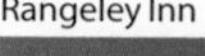
Rangeley Inn

eight miles, is restricted to fly-fishing. Landlocked salmon and brook trout are found in both the lake and river, but the lake is also home to togue (lake trout). Much of this area is protected Maine Public Reserve Land. Walk the Carry Road, which parallels the river, and you'll pass the home where Louise Dickinson Rich lived when she wrote *We Took to the Woods*. The daily rate ($225 pp, $175 ages 12-16, $120 ages 6-11) includes all meals and boat transportation as well as use of canoes and kayaks; rowboats are $25; a motorboat with gas is $95. Guests stay in simple lakeside cabins that have Franklin fireplaces, generator-powered electricity, and full baths. Dogs are $25/night.

On a quiet cove about four miles west of town, **Hunter Cove on Rangeley Lake** (office 334 Mingo Loop Rd., cabins Hunter Cove Rd., Rangeley, 207/864-3383, www.huntercove.com) has eight rustic-modern well-equipped waterfront cabins on six acres. Each has one or two bedrooms, a screened porch, and a woodstove. Rates are $190-250/night or $1,300-1,500/week. Pets are $15/day. It's open year-round, with lower rates off-season and midweek. From here, it's an easy paddle to the western edge of the Hunter Cove Wildlife Sanctuary, and Mingo Springs Golf Course is nearby.

Houseboats

Immerse in Rangeley Lake life with a few nights aboard a houseboat with **Just Add Water Floating Camps** (724 Shore Rd., Oquossoc, 443/852-1125, http://thefloatingnomad.com). Choose from two self-contained houseboats, *Roam* (from $215/night) or the larger Nomad (from $265/night). You'll need to bring food; drinking water is provided. Opt to stay dockside, anchored just off shore, or anchored in a secluded cove. Total bliss! You can even arrange guided cruises, paddles, hikes, or yoga afloat. Owner Rheanna Sinnett is a Registered Maine Guide, licensed boat captain, certified yoga instructor, and former Navy helicopter pilot.

Camping

In addition to the nonprofit and commercial campgrounds described here, the Rangeley Lakes Region Chamber of Commerce maintains a list of no-fee and low-fee **remote wilderness campsites** throughout the Rangeley Lakes.

The **Maine Forest Service** (Rte. 16, Oquossoc, 207/864-5545), responsible for more than a dozen no-fee primitive campsites, will provide a copy of its list on request. The office also issues fire permits.

The **Stephen Phillips Memorial Preserve Trust** (Oquossoc, 207/864-2003, www.stephenphillipswildernesscamping.com) oversees 60 primitive tent sites on both the east and west shores of Mooselookmeguntic Lake and on Students, Toothaker, and other islands, all within a 400-acre preserve that includes more than four miles of lakefront. Mainland sites are large and private; each has a fire ring, picnic table, and water access. Island sites and those on the west shore are accessible only by boat. Canoe rentals are available for $15/day or $25 overnight. Nightly cost is $20/site for two people, ages 6-17 are $5, extra adults are $10, dogs are $5 each.

At the southeast corner of Aziscohos Lake, **Black Brook Cove Campground** (Lincoln Pond Rd., Lincoln Plantation, 207/486-3828, www.blackbrookcove.com, from $26) provides three different kinds of camping experiences: The main campground has 30 tent and RV sites with hookups; the secluded east shore area has 26 wooded waterfront sites for small, self-contained units and tents; and the 20-acre boat-accessible Beaver Island, out in the lake, has nine wilderness sites, with another seven around the lake. The remote sites include outhouses. The main campground facilities include coin-op showers, a private beach, a convenience store, and rental boats and canoes.

The Rangeley Lakes Heritage Trust owns and operates lakefront **Cupsuptic Lake Park & Campground** (Rte. 16, Oquossoc, 207/864-5249, www.cupsupticcampground.

com), with 42 RV sites, 23 tent sites, 4 fully equipped cabin tents, and 6 day-use sites. Options include wilderness, island, and wooded sites, with rates beginning at $27. Rental boats are available, and dogs are permitted ($3/day). Also on-site are a recreation hall, a sandy beach, and rental boat slips.

Seasonal Rentals

The **Morton and Furbish Agency** (207/864-5777 or 888/218-4882, www.rangeleyrentals.com) has a wide selection of daily, weekly, and monthly rental cottages, camps, houses, and condos for winter and summer use. The chamber of commerce can also assist with seasonal rentals.

INFORMATION AND SERVICES

The **Rangeley Lakes Region Chamber of Commerce** (Lakeside Park, Rangeley, 207/864-5364 or 800/685-2537, www.rangeleymaine.com) produces annual guides to lodgings and services; the useful *Maine's Rangeley Lakes Map* costs $4. **Public restrooms** are in a building adjacent to the chamber.

GETTING THERE

Rangeley is about 42 miles or one hour from Kingfield via Routes 27 and 16. It's about 65 miles or 1.5 hours to Bethel via Routes 17 and 2.

Bethel and Vicinity

Bethel (pop. 2,607), a classic New England village tucked in the folds of the White Mountains, showcases white-steepled churches, an ivy-covered brick prep school (Gould Academy), lovely antique homes, a main street dotted with shops and restaurants, a top-notch historical museum, and a sprawling inn on the common—all easily explored on foot. Six miles away, Sunday River, one of New England's largest alpine resorts, draws skiers and snowboarders to its modern slopes and lodges. The Ellis, Bear, and Androscoggin Rivers wind through the region, and in the river valleys are two covered bridges, a handful of ponds, and many working farms. Bookending the region are two spectacular notches: Evans Notch, in the White Mountain National Forest, and Grafton Notch, a state park. East of Bethel along the Androscoggin River are **Rumford** (pop. 5,841), birthplace of former Secretary of State Edmund Muskie, as well as the don't-blink villages of **Rumford Point, Center Rumford,** and **Hanover** (pop. 238). Just south of town is the village of **Bryant Pond,** in Woodstock, pop. 1,277, where a huge telephone sculpture honors Bryant Pond Telephone Company for its heritage as the last crank phone system in the country; the dial tone arrived in 1983.

Thanks to Sunday River, winter is peak season here. In addition to skiing and riding, activities include snowshoeing, snowmobiling, dogsledding, skijoring, ice-skating, ice fishing, even ice climbing. Spring brings canoeists and anglers. Summer is lovely, with hiking for all abilities, biking, boating, fishing, rockhounding in local quarries, and golfing. Autumn is still surprisingly undiscovered. It's perhaps the region's prettiest season, when visitors can take advantage of all the summer activities and do so under a canopy of blazing crimson, gold, and orange backed by deep evergreen.

Bethel's "modern" history dates from 1774, when settlers from Sudbury, Massachusetts, called it Sudbury Canada, a name reflected in the annual Sudbury Canada Days festival. Another present-day festival, Mollyockett Day, commemorates one of the area's most intriguing historical figures, a Pequawket Indian woman named Mollyockett. She practiced herbal medicine among turn-of-the-19th-century settlers, including a baby named Hannibal Hamlin. Her remedies proved effective in snatching Abraham Lincoln's future vice president from death in 1809. (The incident actually occurred in the Hamlin home on Paris Hill, southeast of Bethel.) Mollyockett died August 2, 1816, and is buried in the Woodlawn Cemetery on Route 5 in Andover.

North of Bethel, **Andover** (pop. 821) has become a word-of-mouth favorite among through-hikers and section hikers on the Appalachian Trail (AT), which snakes by about eight miles to the west. It's Maine's southernmost town near the AT, and the hikers pile into Andover for a break in August-September after negotiating the Mahoosuc Range, one of the AT's toughest sections.

East of Bethel is tiny **Locke's Mills** (officially in the town of Greenwood, pop. 830, the birthplace of L. L. Bean of sports-retailing fame).

SIGHTS

Maine Mineral and Gem Museum

Slated to open in time for Maine's 2020 bicentennial, the **Maine Mineral and Gem Museum** (57 Main St. Bethel, 207/824-3036, www.mainemineralgemmuseum.org, 10am-5pm Mon.-Sat.) promises to showcase one of the world's most extensive collections, as well as interactive exhibits and archival documents relating to Maine mining, minerals, and gems. Meteorites, fossils, and other minerals are part of the collection. Tours of area mines will be available. Call or check the website for its current status.

Covered Bridges

Often called the **Artist's Covered Bridge** because so many artists have committed it to canvas, an 1872 wooden structure stands alongside a quiet country road north of the Sunday River Ski Resort. Kids love running back and forth across the disused bridge, and in summer they can swim below it in the Sunday River. The bridge is 5.7 miles northwest of Bethel; take Route 2 toward Newry, turn left at the Sunday River Road, and then bear right at the fork. The bridge is well signposted, just beyond a small cemetery.

About 20 miles north of Bethel in South Andover, the **Lovejoy Bridge,** built in 1867, is one of the lesser-visited of Maine's nine covered bridges. It's also the shortest. Spanning the Ellis River, a tributary of the Androscoggin, the 70-foot-long bridge is 0.25 mile east of Route 5 but not visible from the highway; it's about 7.5 miles north of Rumford Point. In summer, local kids use the swimming hole just below the bridge.

Historical Houses and Tours

The **Bethel Historical Society** (Bethel Common, 14 Broad St., Bethel, 207/824-2908, www.bethelhistorical.org), one of the state's best regional historical societies, maintains two adjacent downtown properties. Listed in the National Register of Historic Places, the 1813 Federal-style **Dr. Moses Mason House** (1pm-4pm Thurs.-Sat. July-Aug. or by appointment, $5 adults, $3 ages 6-12, $10/family, includes guided tour) is a carefully restored eight-room museum. Particularly significant in the museum are the hall murals painted by noted itinerant muralist Rufus Porter or his nephew Jonathan Poor. Dr. Moses Mason, a local physician and true Renaissance man, was elected to Congress a dozen years after Maine achieved statehood and served two terms. The Mason House is adjacent to the 1821 **O'Neil Robinson House** (10am-4pm Tues.-Fri. year-round and 1pm-4pm Sat. July-Aug., donation), which has exhibit galleries and a small museum shop. Ask about the Hidden History Tours of the museum's archival storage barn.

Pick up the society's free *Walking Tour of Bethel Hill Village* brochure, available from the society or chamber of commerce. It provides detailed information on 29 buildings and monuments in the downtown area's Historic District. Officially, more than 60 structures are included in the district. Allow an hour to appreciate the 19th- and 20th-century architecture. Check the museum's website for guided walking tours.

ENTERTAINMENT

At **Sunday River Ski Resort,** there's live entertainment in several locations on weekends and during school vacations. The resort also runs the Black Diamond Family Entertainment Series, with performances such as vaudeville, marionettes, storytelling, and circus acts.

The hot spots for après-ski into the night are the **Foggy Goggle** at Sunday River; the **Matterhorn** (Sunday River Access Rd., 207/824-6836, www.matterhornskibar.com), a classic ski bar accented with cool alpine memorabilia and featuring live weekend entertainment; and year-round **Suds Pub** (207/824-6558, www.thesudburyinn.com) at the Sudbury Inn, where Thursday's Hoot Night has been an open-mic tradition since 1987.

Festivals and Events

In mid-June, the annual three-day **Trek Across Maine: Sunday River to the Sea** draws nearly 2,000 cyclists for the 180-mile bike expedition from Bethel to Rockland, proceeds from which benefit the Maine Lung Association. Registrations are accepted on a first-come, first-served basis, and the trek is usually fully booked by April. Pledges are required, and there's a registration fee. Call 800/458-6472 for details.

The third Saturday in July, on Bethel Common in downtown Bethel, **Mollyockett Day** commemorates a legendary turn-of-the-19th-century Native American healer with a parade, children's activities, a crafts fair, food, and fireworks.

Andover presents a parade, live entertainment, children's games, art and flower shows, antique cars, a barbecue, and a beanhole bean supper the first weekend in August as part of **Andover Old Home Days.** The second weekend that month at the Moses Mason House in Bethel, **Sudbury Canada Days** commemorates Bethel's earliest settlers with traditional crafts, an art show, a parade, croquet, a bean supper, and a contra dance.

The **North American Wife Carrying Championship** takes place at Sunday River in October. During winter, Sunday River's calendar is chock-full of events.

SHOPPING

Check out the strikingly unusual designs and glazes at **Bonnema Potters** (146 Main St., Bethel, 207/824-2821), in a handsomely restored studio across the street from the Sudbury Inn.

The Artist's Covered Bridge crosses the Sunday River in Newry.

Maine Line Products (297 Main St./Rte. 26, Greenwood, 207/875-2522, http://mainelineproducts.com) is a source of whimsical, Maine-made souvenirs for your whimsical friends, as well as serious gifts such as jams, syrup, fudge, and wind chimes.

Shaker-reproduction furniture and a home store filled with decorative items and accessories and wood ware can be found at **S. Timberlake Home Store** (158 Rte. 2, Bethel, 207/824-1149, www.stimberlake.com).

RECREATION

Parks and Preserves

STEP FALLS PRESERVE

Mahoosuc Land Trust (207/824-3806, www.mahoosuc.org) manages **Step Falls Preserve,** which is ideal for family hiking—an easy one-hour round-trip through the woods alongside an impressive series of cascades and pools that invited swimming. Pick up a map at the trailhead. Bring a picnic and have lunch on the rocks along the way. The waterfalls are most dramatic in late spring; the foliage is most spectacular in fall; the footing can be dicey in winter. The trailhead for the preserve is on Route 26, 8 miles northwest of Route 2 and 10 miles southeast of the New Hampshire border. If the lot is full, return another time.

★ GRAFTON NOTCH STATE PARK

Nestled in the mountains of western Maine, **Grafton Notch State Park** (Rte. 26, Grafton Township, 207/824-2912 or 207/624-6080 off-season, www.parksandlands.com, $3-4 adults, $1 ages 5-11 and seniors; payment is on the honor system) boasts splendid hiking trails, spectacular geological formations, and plenty of space for peace and quiet. It's hard to say enough about this lovely park, a must-visit. Bring a picnic. Highlights include **Screw Auger Falls, Mother Walker Falls,** and **Moose Gorge Cave.**

The best (but not easiest) hike is the **Table Rock Loop,** a 2.4-mile moderate-to-strenuous two-hour circuit from the main trailhead (signposted Hiking Trails) at the edge of Route 26. The trailhead parking area is four miles inside the park's southern boundary and 0.8 mile beyond the Moose Cave parking area. Part of the route follows the white-blazed Appalachian Trail; otherwise, the trail is orange- and blue-blazed. Some really steep sections are indeed a challenge, but it's well worth the climb for the dramatic mountain views from aptly named Table Rock.

Another favorite moderate-to-strenuous hike goes up **Old Speck Mountain** (4,180 feet), third highest of Maine's ten 4,000-footers and part of the Mahoosuc Range. The 28-foot-high viewing platform on the restored fire tower gets you above the wooded summit for incredible 360-degree views of the White Mountains, the Mahoosuc Range, and other mountains and lakes. Allow a solid seven hours for the 7.6-mile round-trip from the trailhead on the west side of Route 26 in Grafton Notch. The route follows the white-blazed Appalachian Trail (AT) most of the way; the tower is about 0.25 mile off the AT. Although there's a route map at the trailhead (the same location as the Table Rock hike), the best trail guide for this hike is in John Gibson's *50 Hikes in Southern and Coastal Maine.*

If you're driving along Route 26 early or late in the day, keep a lookout for moose; have your camera ready and exercise extreme caution. You'll usually spot them in boggy areas, munching on aquatic plants, but when they decide to cross a highway, watch out—unlike us, they don't look both ways. And their eyes don't reflect headlights, so be vigilant after dark. Moose-car collisions are too often fatal for both moose and motorists.

THE MAHOOSUC RANGE

South and east of Grafton Notch State Park is a 27,253-acre chunk of **Maine Public Reserve Land** (Bureau of Parks and Lands, 207/778-3821, www.parksandlands.com) known as the Mahoosucs, or the Mahoosuc Range, where the hiking is rugged and strenuous but the scenic rewards are inestimable.

The Appalachian Trail traverses much of the reserve, and its hikers insist that the mile-long Mahoosuc Notch section, between Old Speck and Goose Eye Mountains, is one of their biggest challenges on the 2,158-mile Georgia-to-Maine route, requiring steep ascents and descents with insecure footing, gigantic boulders, and narrow passages. If you're an experienced hiker, go for it, and use reliable guidebooks and maps, preferably USGS maps. You can download a map and guide from the website.

WHITE MOUNTAIN NATIONAL FOREST

About 49,800 acres of the 770,000-acre **White Mountain National Forest** (www.fs.usda.gov/whitemountain) lie on the Maine side of the border with New Hampshire. Route 113, roughly paralleling the border, bisects the **Caribou-Speckled Mountain Wilderness,** the designated name for this part of the national forest. It's all dramatically scenic, with terrific opportunities for hiking, camping, picnicking, swimming, and fishing.

A drive through **Evans Notch** along Route 113, north to south between Gilead and Stow (and continuing to Fryeburg), is worth a detour. It takes about 30 minutes without stops, but bring a picnic and enjoy the mountain views from the tables at the Cold River Overlook, about a mile south of the Evans Notch high point. Route 113 is too narrow for bikes in midsummer, when logging trucks and visitor traffic can be fairly dense. During fall, when the foliage is brilliant, this route is spectacular and off the usual tourist paths. The road is closed in winter. If you plan on stopping or hiking, Evans Notch requires a parking permit ($5 for 7 days). Some locations have an "iron ranger" allowing payment of $3/parking place/day.

An easy family hike is the **Albany Brook Trail,** one mile each way between the Crocker Pond Campground (at the end of Crocker Pond Rd.) and the northern shore of Round Pond.

Outfitters and Guide Services

These companies provide rentals, guide services, and support for many of the sports detailed below. They're also great resources if you've brought your own equipment.

The Maine Guides at **Bethel Outdoor Adventure** (BOA, 121 Mayville Rd./Rte. 2, Bethel, 207/824-4224 or 800/533-3607, www.betheloutdooradventure.com) are pros at canoeing, kayaking, and stand-up paddleboarding. They'll also shuttle you upriver, so you don't have to fight the current. Rates range $50-70 with shuttle, $35-40 without. Also offered are guided canoeing and kayaking trips by advance reservation, beginning at $75 half day, and fishing trips, $300pp half day (minimum 6 people). Customers have access across a 500-foot-long suspension, passenger bridge across the Androscoggin River to a quiet one-mile walking trail on Hastings Island. BOA also operates a riverside campground with sites for tents and RVs ($24-39).

Locke Mountain Guide Service (1 Bear River Rd., Newry, 207/381-7322) offers half-day ($280) and full-day with lunch ($400) float-fishing trips on the Androscoggin River aboard its 2013 Clackacraft drift boat, which comfortably carries two anglers and an oarsman. Other options included guided wade-fishing trips into native brook trout and landlocked salmon waterways and lake and pond trips that are ideal for introducing kids to fishing.

Veteran professional guides Polly Mahoney and Kevin Slater of **Mahoosuc Guide Service** (1513 Bear River Rd., Newry, 207/824-2073, www.mahoosuc.com) lead wilderness canoe trips not only in the Bethel area but also on the Allagash, Penobscot, and St. John Rivers, as well as in Québec. With extensive wilderness backgrounds in such locales as Labrador and the Yukon, management experience with Outward Bound, a flair for camp cooking, and a commitment to Native American traditions, Polly and Kevin are ideal trip leaders.

Hiking and Walking

Much of the hiking in this area is within the various parks and preserves, but a fun family hike not in that category is the easy-to-moderate ascent of **Mount Will** in Newry, on the outskirts of Bethel. The Bethel Conservation Commission has developed a 3.2-mile loop trail that provides mountain and river views and has interpretive signs; allow about 2.5 hours to do the loop. At the chamber of commerce information center, pick up a Mount Will map-brochure, which explains three different hiking options. Find it on the west side of Route 2/26, 1.9 miles north of the Riverside Rest Area—a terrific spot, incidentally, for a post-hike picnic next to the Androscoggin River.

The wheelchair-accessible **Bethel Recreational Path** is about 1.5 miles long and parallels the Androscoggin River. It begins at Davis Park (Rte. 26 and Intervale Rd.), where there's also a skateboard park, picnic tables, a boat launch, and a playground, and ends near Bethel Outdoor Adventure on Route 2. Expect to share it with joggers, in-line skaters, and cyclists. The **Androscoggin River Recreational Walking Trail** covers 1.5 miles, beginning at the Riverside Rest Area on Route 2, just east of the Sunday River access road, and continuing to the River View Resort.

Water Sports

ANDROSCOGGIN RIVER

The rivers in the Bethel area are a paddler's dream, varying from beginner and family stretches to white-water sections for intermediate and advanced canoeists. Fortunately, the major artery, the Androscoggin River, seldom has low-water problems, and you'll see lots of islands as well as eagles, moose, and a beaver dam. West of Bethel there's an old cable from a onetime ferry crossing.

The 42-mile **Androscoggin River Canoe Trail,** created in 2001 by the **Mahoosuc Land Trust** (207/824-3806, www.mahoosuc.org), provides access points to the river spaced about five miles apart, from the Shelburne Dam in New Hampshire to Rumford. An interactive map is available online.

The annual 170-mile **Androscoggin River Source to the Sea** (www.androscogginwatershed.org) has paddling events celebrating the river's revival from years of unbridled pollution.

POND PADDLING

Just east of Locke Mills, before the **Littlefield Beaches Campground** (207/875-3290, www.littlefieldbeaches.com), you can put in at **Round Pond,** on the south side of Route 26, and continue into North and South Ponds. Bring a picnic, and before you head out, enjoy it across the road at the lovely state rest area.

FISHING

The 26-mile stretch of the Upper Androscoggin River between the New Hampshire border and Rumford Point; its tributaries, the Wild, Pleasant, Sunday, and Bear Rivers; and local brooks are popular with anglers seeking rainbows, brookies, browns, and landlocked salmon. Even during the peak of summer, it's possible to catch smallmouth bass on the Andro.

Pick up a copy of *A Guide to Local Fishing* at the Bethel Area Chamber of Commerce.

Biking

The Bethel Area Chamber of Commerce has sheets detailing about a dozen rides in the region, with lengths varying from a five-mile Village Restaurant Ride (don't be deceived; it takes in Paradise Hill, a killer for Sunday cyclists) to the 53-mile covered bridge cruise. For an easy pedal, follow the Sunday River Road as it continues out past Artist's Covered Bridge. It's mostly level and winding, paralleling the river and providing beautiful mountain views.

Bicycle rentals (mountain bikes, road bikes, and fat-tire bikes) are available from **Barker Mountain Bikes** (53 Mayville Rd., Bethel, 207/824-0100, www.barkermountainbikes.com), a full-service shop.

TOP EXPERIENCE

★ MOUNTAIN BIKING

Mahoosuc Pathways (207/200-8240, www.mahoosucpathways.org) oversees hiking, snowshoe, Nordic, and mountain/fat-tire trails throughout the region. These include the Bacon Hill mountain biking trails and the Bethel Village Trails system, with 8km of snowshoe and fat-tire trails.

Mt. Abram (Greenwood) broke ground in 2019 on the first phase of what is expected to become the state's largest mountain bike park. The first phase, three miles of lift-serviced gentle trails for beginners on the resort's west side, are expected to open in 2020. Rental bikes will be available.

Golf

Thanks to its spectacular setting, the 18-hole championship course at the **Bethel Inn and Country Club** (Bethel Common, Bethel, 207/824-2175, www.bethelinn.com) wows every golfer who plays here. Tee times are required, and caddies are available. Also based here is the **Guaranteed Performance School of Golf** (800/654-0125, www.gpgolfschool.com).

The area's newest course is the 18-hole, Robert Trent Jones Jr.-designed course at **Sunday River Ski Resort** (207/824-3000, www.sundayriver.com).

Sunday River Mountain Park

Sunday River (10am-4pm Thurs.-Sun. late June-Aug., 10am-4pm Fri.-Sun. early Sept.-mid-Oct.) offers **scenic lift rides** ($15 ages 13 and older, $10 ages 6-12); **twin ziplines** ($15), **bungee trampoline** ($10), a **climbing wall** ($10), and **disc golf** ($15 for 18 holes with chondola ride, $5 disc rental).

Winter Recreation

SUNDAY RIVER SKI RESORT

Sprawling octopus-like over eight connected mountains, **Sunday River** (Sunday River Rd., Newry, 207/824-3000 or 800/543-2754, snow phone 207/824-6400, www.sundayriver.com) defines the winter sports scene in this area, with downhill skiing and snowboarding, ice-skating, cross-country skiing, phenomenal snowmaking capability, slope-side lodging, and plentiful amenities that include a spa, night skiing, entertainment, restaurants, and lodging. Its 870 acres are laced with 135 designated trails and glades, terrain parks and pipes, a snow-tubing area, serviced by 15 lifts and three base lodges (South Ridge is the main one). Don't even consider leaving the base without a trail map, and make sure everyone in your party knows exactly where to meet for lunch or at day's end.

Sunday River is also home to **Maine Adaptive Skiing** (800/639-7770, www.maineadaptive.org), which provides free lessons and tickets for alpine and cross-country skiing and snowboarding for people with physical disabilities. Reservations are required.

Sunday River has day-care facilities in three locations (reservations are advised), a ski school, rental equipment, a free on-mountain trolley-bus service, and plenty of places to grab a snack or a meal at a wide range of prices. Call or check the website for current ticket prices; one-day tickets purchased at the window are priciest, so be smart and buy online in advance for the best price.

CROSS-COUNTRY SKIING

Right in downtown Bethel, the **Bethel Village Trails** (207/824-6276, www.mahoosucpathways.org, $18 adult day pass, $12 ages 7-17), based at the Bethel Inn Resort, has about 25 trails groomed for classic and skate skiing and five miles of snowshoe and fat-tire biking trails on the inn's scenic golf course. The ski shop has a wax room and a snack bar with seating areas. Ski and snowshoe rentals and half-day tickets are available. Note: Ask about the ski, swim, sauna special that includes a day pass along with use of the pool and sauna at the Bethel Inn Resort.

About 30 miles of trails wind through 1,000 acres along the Androscoggin River at **Carter's Cross-Country Ski Center** (786 Intervale Rd., Bethel, 207/824-3880, www.

cartersxcski.com, $15 adults, $10 ages 6-18), which offers a lodge and ski shop with a snack bar. Rental skis and snowshoes are available. It also rents two off-the-grid trailside lodges (from $99, including trail pass) and offers room in its lodge ($99).

ICE-SKATING

Picture an old-fashioned Currier and Ives winter landscape with skaters skimming a snow-circled pond and you'll come close to the scene on Bethel Common in winter. Bring a camera. The groomed arena, in the downtown historic district, is usually ready for skaters by Christmas vacation. Sunday River Ski Resort also has a rink; skating is free, and rental skates are available.

DOGSLEDDING

When they're not off leading multiday dogsledding trips in the Mahoosucs or on Umbagog Lake (rates begin around $725 pp), or even with the Inuit in Canada's Nunavut Territory ($6,185 pp) or snowshoeing with the Cree in Québec (from $3,025 pp), Kevin Slater and Polly Mahoney of **Mahoosuc Guide Service** (1513 Bear River Rd., Newry, 207/824-2073, www.mahoosuc.com) will bundle you in a deerskin blanket and take you on a one-day dogsled trip on Umbagog Lake, beyond Grafton Notch State Park. Wear goggles or sunglasses; the dogs kick up the snow. Insulted parkas and footwear, a campfire lunch, and warm drinks are included in the $300-325 pp fee. Trips are limited, and they're very popular; book well in advance.

In winter, there is a three-day Learn-to-Mush package at **Telemark Inn Wilderness Lodge** (591 King's Hwy., Mason Township, 207/836-2703, www.newenglanddogsledding.com, $1,075 pp d, $1,475 s, plus 10 percent gratuity) that includes three half-day guided mushing experiences, three nights' lodging, and all meals. Other options are available. The off-the-grid inn, with five guestrooms sharing baths, creates its own electricity via wind and photovoltaics. Meals are family style.

FOOD

Quick Bites

You can feel good when eating at the **Good Food Store** (212 Mayville Rd./Rte. 2, Bethel, 207/824-3754 or 800/879-8926, www.goodfoodbethel.com, 9am-8pm daily, $5-8). The combination store and takeout sells both good food and food that's good for you, and it stocks an array of natural foods. Create an

Join Mahoosuc Guide Service on a dogsledding trip.

instant picnic with sandwiches, salads, and soups, even beer and wine. If you're renting a condo and don't feel like cooking or eating out, you can pick up homemade soups, stews, and casseroles to go.

Sharing the premises is **Smokin' Good BBQ** (212 Mayville Rd./Rte. 2, Bethel, 207/824-4744, www.smokingoodbarbecue.com, 11:30am-7:30pm Fri.-Sun., $8-20), operating from "Graceland," an orange graffiti-covered trailer. A transplanted Texan turned me on to this gem. Choices include pulled pork, beef brisket, ribs, chicken, and sides such as barbecue beans, slaw, and corn bread. Dress for the elements: Outside seating only.

Baked goods made daily from scratch from all-natural ingredients have earned **DiCocoa's Bakery and Marketplace** (119 Main St., Bethel, 207/824-5282, www.cafedicocoa.com, 7am-4pm Thurs.-Mon.) a solid following. Go for the fabulous baked goods, but don't miss the lunch specials. The bakery doubles as a market selling fancy foods and take-home meals. It also makes scrumptious gelato, and I think the chocolate chip cookies are among the best I've ever had. On Saturday nights from January through March, it offers a **Gentle Dining** series ($65, BYOB), with each week's menu focused on a different country.

The **Bethel Farmers Market** sells good-for-you produce and other items 9am-1pm Saturdays late-May-mid-October, on Route 26 (at Parkway) next to Norway Savings Bank at the southern edge of town.

Head to the **Local Hub** (224 Main St., Greenwood, 207/875-0011, http://localhubmaine.com, 7am-8pm Sun.-Wed., 7am-9pm Thurs.-Sat.) for scratch-made breads and baked goods, smoothies, sandwiches, salads, pizzas, and ready-to-eat meals made from local, farm-fresh ingredients whenever possible.

Butcher Burger Bethel (188 Main St., Bethel, 207/824-1171, 11:30am-9pm daily, $10-23) serves burgers, sandwiches, and comfort foods.

Family Favorites

Frequently cited as one of the country's best classic ski bars, the **Matterhorn Ski Bar** (292 Sunday River Rd., Newry, 207/824-6271, www.matterhornskibar.com, from 3pm Mon-Fri., from 11:30am Sat.-Sun., $13-33) is a barn-style restaurant that is *the* après-ski spot in Bethel. Check out the bar, made from 120 skis. The wide-ranging menu includes the region's best pizzas, cooked in a wood-burning oven, along with kids' choices. Most afternoons there's après-ski acoustic entertainment. Live entertainment, usually rock bands, begins at 9:30pm on Friday-Saturday. It's open only in winter.

Suds Pub (151 Main St., Bethel, 207/824-2174 or 800/395-7837, www.thesudburyinn.com, 11:30am-9:30pm daily, $10-16), situated on the lower level of the Sudbury Inn, is a relaxing family-friendly hangout serving classic tavern fare and a few entrées. The full bar has 29 beers on tap.

Decent home-style cooking, a relaxed kid-friendly atmosphere, free popcorn, a children's menu, and options ranging from pizza to steak are the draws at **Rooster's Roadhouse** (159 Mayville Rd./Rte. 2, Bethel, 207/824-0309, www.roostersroadhouse.com, 11:30am-10pm daily, $9-30).

Breakfast is served all day at the **Little Red Hen Diner** (28 S. Main St., Andover, 207/392-2253, www.littleredhendiner.com, 6:30am-2pm Sun. and Tues.-Thurs., 6:30am-8pm Fri.-Sat., $5-11), although midday wraps, sandwiches, burgers, and quesadillas are available. On Thursday nights May-October, a Mexican buffet is served. Year-round, Friday nights feature prime rib, maple-glazed salmon, and parmesan-crusted haddock ($16-20), and Saturday nights is an all-you-can-eat Italian buffet ($12 adults, $7 under age 10). Save room for the homemade ice cream and pies.

The Bethel Inn's **Millbrook Tavern & Grille** (Bethel Common, Bethel, 207/824-2175, www.bethelinn.com, 11:30am-9pm daily mid-May-mid-Oct., 5pm-9pm Sun.-Thurs., noon-9pm and 5pm-9pm Fri.-Sat.

mid-Dec.-early Mar., $12-32) serves pub fare, with seating indoors in a sports-tavern atmosphere or on the terrace. There's often live music on summer weekends.

International

Cho Sun (141 Main St., Bethel, 207/824-7370, www.chosunrestaurant.com, 5pm-9pm Wed.-Sun., $18-27) is in a lovely New England Victorian house decorated with Asian art and antiques. Sushi is a specialty, but owner Pok Sun Lane's Korean fare draws on her heritage.

Classic Italian fare is served at **22 Broad Street** (22 Broad St., Bethel, 207/824-3496, www.22broadstreet.com, 5pm-close daily, $20-38), located in the Greek Revival-style 1848 Gideon Hastings House across from the Bethel Inn. The restaurant's martini bar opens at 4:30pm.

Casual and Fine Dining

Brian's (43 Main St., Bethel, 207/824-1007, http://briansbethel.com, 4pm-9pm Thurs.-Mon., $19-33) is a popular bistro serving comfort food with updated New American and international flavors. Lunch is available 11:30am-3pm Saturdays, July-September.

ACCOMMODATIONS

Conveniently, the **Bethel Area Chamber of Commerce Reservations Service** (800/442-5826, www.bethelmaine.com) provides toll-free lodging assistance for more than 1,000 beds in member B&Bs, motels, condos, and inns. If you're planning a winter visit, however, particularly during Thanksgiving and Christmas holidays, February school vacation, or the month of March, plan ahead to score a bed near the slopes.

Keep in mind that peak season (ergo the highest room rates) in this part of Maine is in winter, not summer. Some lodgings also have higher rates for fall foliage in September-October.

Sunday River Lodging

On-mountain lodging options at **Sunday River** (207/824-3000, reservations 800/543-2754, www.sundayriver.com) include 425 guest rooms and suites in two full-service hotels—the **Grand Summit** and the **Jordan Grand Hotel**—as well as hundreds of slopeside condos and town houses in seven different clusters. Both hotels have restaurants and cafés, indoor and outdoor heated pools, tennis courts, video game rooms, and lots of extra amenities; the Jordan Grand is in an isolated location. Most guest rooms have full kitchen facilities. Except for the dorm rooms, lodging packages include lift tickets. Prices for accommodations and activity packages vary widely.

Country Inn

Bethel's grande dame, the **Bethel Inn and Country Club** (21 Broad St., Bethel, 207/824-2175 or 800/654-0125, www.bethelinn.com) faces the Bethel Common in the historic district; in the backyard is a golf course backed by the White Mountains. Rooms are spread out between the traditional main inn and outbuildings. Also on the premises are 1-3-bedroom condominiums. Guest rooms vary widely in decor and quality; ask for a recently updated one. This is a full-service resort, and amenities include golf, tennis, a health club with a saltwater pool and a sauna, a game room, a lakeside outpost for swimming and boating, and a summer children's program. Inn rates, including breakfast, begin at around $155. Children under age 12 stay free in the same room. Rates with dinner are available. Some accommodations permit dogs for $35/night.

Bed-and-Breakfasts

Innkeepers John and Jeanette Poole pamper guests with upscale linens, afternoon and evening refreshments, and rave-worthy breakfasts at the **Holidae House B&B** (85 Main St., Bethel, 207/824-3400, www.holidaehouse.com, $135-160), a cozy and comfy Victorian in the heart of downtown.

For a quiet stay within walking distance of downtown shops, restaurants, and attractions, opt for the **Bethel Hill Bed and Breakfast** (66 Broad St., Bethel, 207/824-2161, www.

bethelhill.com, $149-189), a handsome inn with three spacious guest rooms tastefully decorated with antiques. A full breakfast is included.

Traveling with your pooch? **Paws Inn** (372 Walkers Mill Rd./Rte. 26, Bethel, 207/824-6678, www.pawsinn.net, $90-115) takes dog-friendly lodging to the extreme. Carolyn Bailey provides two guest rooms, dog beds or crates, fenced-yard and barn play areas, doggie snacks, and plenty of love. Doggie day care is available. You only need bring food for your dog and proof of vaccinations; Carolyn prepares a full breakfast. The property is two miles south of downtown.

Motels

The **Inn at the Rostay** (186 Mayville Rd./Rte. 2, Bethel, 207/824-3111 or 888/754-0072, www.rostay.com, $90-140) is a motel that acts like an inn. Rooms are spread between three buildings. On the five-acre premises are a pool, hot tub, and picnic pavilion. Guests can have a full breakfast ($8), served in a dining room adjacent to a guest parlor. Some rooms are pet friendly ($20).

For clean, cheap, and convenient digs, check into Ruthie's **Bethel Village Motel** (88 Main St., Bethel, 800/882-0293, www.bethelvillagemotel.com, from $85), smack downtown in a walk-to-everything location behind Ruthie's boutique.

Camping

South Arm Campground (62 Kennett Dr., Andover, 207/364-5155, www.southarm.com) has 38 lakeside wilderness sites ($15/family), including island sites accessible only by boat, with transportation available. A bit less remote on a peninsula is the full-service main campground with 65 wooded sites ($24-32), all with water and 30-amp electricity; it has a marina, modern bathhouses, and a bakery and general store. From here, you can fly-fish the Rapid River, canoe the lake, fish, paddle (rentals available), take a sunset moose cruise, walk a section of the Appalachian Trail, bike logging roads, or just relax in this little slice of heaven.

Just south of its namesake, **Grafton Notch Campground** (1471 Bear River Rd./Rte. 26, Newry, 207/824-2292, www.campgrafton.com, $28) is a small, no-frills campground with 15 wooded sites with fire rings and picnic tables, a modern bathhouse, and a dump station ($10), but no hookups. Leashed dogs are permitted. Don't expect real quiet, though; you can hear the trucks on Route 26, but you

Bethel Inn and Country Club

can't beat the location if you want to hike in the state park.

Tucked away on the Ellis River, **Lone Mountain Campground** (424 Main St., Andover, 207/392-0019, https://lonemountaincamping.com, $28-40) offers sites for tents through big rigs, along with hot showers, access to hiking, ATV, and equestrian trails, and a sandy beach.

Thirteen miles west of Bethel is the seven-acre **Hastings Campground** (877/444-6777 for credit card reservations, recreation.com, $20), one of four campgrounds along Route 113 in the White Mountain National Forest. The 24-site campground is primitive, with no hookups or showers, but it does have vault toilets, a hand pump for water, access to fishing and hiking, and it is wheelchair-accessible. Route 113 is especially scenic, so this is a prime location for extensive hiking in the national forest. Trail information and maps are available from the Evans Notch Ranger District office. The campground is in Gilead, three miles south of Route 2.

When you really yearn to escape, try to snag one of the seven first-come, first-served sites at **Crocker Pond Campground** ($18), located in the White Mountain National Forest. No reservations are accepted, so be prepared with a contingency plan. The campground, set amid white pines on the edge of Crocker Pond, has a hand pump for water and a vault toilet. Nonmotorized boats are permitted. To find the campground, from Route 2 in West Bethel, take Flat Road and travel 5.8 miles, and then turn right at the sign and continue another 0.5 mile down a dirt road.

INFORMATION AND SERVICES

The **Bethel Area Chamber of Commerce** (Cross St., Bethel, 207/824-2282 or 800/442-5826, www.bethelmaine.com) has information and public **restrooms.**

GETTING THERE AND AROUND

Bethel is roughly 65 miles or 1.5 hours from Rangeley via Routes 17 and 2. It's about 36 miles or 50 minutes to Fryeburg via Route 5, about 24 miles or 30 minutes to South Paris via Route 26, and about 70 miles or 1.5 hours from Portland via Route 26.

The free **Bethel Explorer** (www.mountainexplorer.org) bus service operates between Bethel and Sunday River. View current schedule online.

At Sunday River, the free **Sunday River Trolley** (207/824-3000) circulates throughout the resort, operating weekends Thanksgiving-Christmas and then daily from mid-December to early April. It runs on a 30-minute cycle, 8am-1am weekdays and 7am-1am weekends and holidays.

Fryeburg Area

Fryeburg (pop. 3,449), a crossroads community on busy Route 302, is best known as the funnel to and from the factory outlets, hiking trails, and ski slopes of New Hampshire's North Conway and the White Mountains. Except during early October's annual extravaganza, the giant Fryeburg Fair, Fryeburg is rarely on anyone's itinerary. That's a shame: The mountain-ringed community has lots of charm, historic homes, the flavor of rural life, and access to miles of Saco River canoeing waters.

Incorporated in 1763, Fryeburg is Oxford County's oldest town; even earlier it was known as Pequawket, an Indian settlement and trading post. Skirmishes with white settlers routed the Native Americans in 1725 during Dummer's War (also known as

Lovewell's War). Casualties were heavy on both sides; Lovewell and the Pequawket chief were among the fatalities.

In 1792, Fryeburg Academy, a private school on Main Street, was chartered; the school's Webster Hall is named after famed statesman Daniel Webster, whose undistinguished teaching career at the school began and ended in 1802. Among the students at the time was Rufus Porter, who later gained renown as a muralist, inventor, and founder of *Scientific American* magazine. Today the school is one of a handful of private academies in Maine that provide public secondary education, a uniquely successful private-public partnership.

Just north of Fryeburg is the town of **Lovell** (pop. 1,140), with three hamlets—known collectively as the Lovells—strung along Route 5, on the east side of gorgeous Kezar Lake. Anyone who has discovered Kezar Lake yearns to keep it a secret, but the word is out. The mountain-rimmed lake is too beautiful.

SIGHTS

Hemlock Covered Bridge

The 116-foot-long **Hemlock Covered Bridge,** built in 1857 over the "Old Saco," or "Old Course," a former channel of the Saco River, is in the hamlet of East Fryeburg, just west of Kezar Pond. It's accessible by car, but if you have a mountain bike, this is a peaceful pedal on a nice dirt road. The best time to visit is July-October; mud or snow can prevent car access in other months, and June is buggy. From the Route 5/302 junction in Fryeburg, take Route 302 east 5.5 miles to Hemlock Bridge Road. Turn left (north) and go about three miles on a paved and then unpaved road to the bridge. Or paddle under the bridge on a detour from the Saco River.

Doll Museum

View 10,000 dolls from around the world at the **Hazel & Owen Currier Doll Museum** (103 Lovell Rd., Fryeburg, www.currierdollmuseum.org, 10am-2pm Wed.-Thurs. July-Aug. or by appointment spring and fall, $5 donation). For 45 years, Hazel Currier collected dolls. In 2015, she donated them, including Barbie, Cabbage Patch, Shirley Temple, American Girl, Dresden, and other collections, to the Fryeburg Historical Society, which now displays it in the 1847 Fryeburg Town House.

Hopalong Cassidy Memorabilia

When he died in 1956, longtime Fryeburg resident Clarence Mulford, author of the Hopalong Cassidy books, left his extensive collection of Western Americana, including models, copies of his books, research materials, and more, along with enough money to display them, to the **Fryeburg Public Library** (515 Main St., Fryeburg, 207/935-2731, www.fryeburgmaine.org/town-departments/library).

ENTERTAINMENT

See what's on tap at the **Leura Hill Eastman Performing Arts Center** (Fryeburg Academy, Fryeburg, 207/935-9232, www.fryeburgacademy.org).

Singer-songwriter Carol Noonan has created a phenomenal 200-seat performing arts center on her hilltop farm. **Stone Mountain Arts Center** (695 Dug Way Rd., Brownfield, 866/227-6523, www.stonemountainartscenter.com) brings in nationally renowned performers such as Roseanne Cash, Shemekia Copeland, Sweet Honey in the Rock, Leo Kottke, and Paula Poundstone, to name a few. All events take place in the barn, and preshow dinners ($20-25) are available by reservation. Credit cards are taken for reservations, but cash or checks are preferred for actual payment. Print out a copy of the directions—this place is in the boonies.

The **Lovell Brick Church for the Performing Arts** (www.lovellbrickchurch.org) is the site of a summer entertainment series, with performances May-September.

In summer, **outdoor concerts** are held Tuesday nights at the gazebo in Bradley Park (or in the fire barn, if it's raining).

Festivals and Events

The big shindig in these parts is the **Fryeburg Fair** (www.fryeburgfair.com), the last country fair of the season. It's held the first week of October, sometimes including a few days in September. It's Maine's largest agricultural fair and an annual event since 1851. A parade, a carnival, craft demonstrations and exhibits, harness racing, pig scrambles, children's activities, ox pulling, and live entertainment are all here, as are plenty of food booths (it's sometimes called the "Friedburg" Fair). More than 300,000 turn out for eight days of festivities, so expect traffic congestion. The fair runs Sunday-Sunday, and the busiest day is Saturday. No dogs are allowed on the 180-acre site. Spectacular fall foliage and mountain scenery just add to the appeal.

SHOPPING

It's hard to believe that the jewelry and crafts inside the **Harvest Gold Gallery** (Rte. 5, Center Lovell, 207/925-6502, www.harvestgoldgallery.com) are more stunning than the setting overlooking Kezar Lake. Magnificent gold jewelry, much of it accented with Maine gemstones, is made on the premises. More than 200 American artisans are also showcased here, and the owners are extremely knowledgeable about whom they represent.

Far less high-end but no lower in quality are the crafts at **Weston's** (48 River St./Rte. 113 N., Fryeburg, 207/935-2567, www.westonsfarm.com). The mostly locally made selection at the seventh-generation family farm includes baskets, bears, pillows, candles, and more.

RECREATION

Hiking

The area's easiest and therefore busiest trail is the 20-minute hike up **Jockey Cap,** named for a cantilevered ledge that has long since disappeared. At the summit, with a 360-degree view of lakes and mountains, is a monument to Admiral Robert Peary, the Arctic explorer who once lived in Fryeburg. The monument's metal edge is a handy cheat sheet, with profiles and names of all the mountains you see—more than four dozen of them. The trail is fine for kids, but keep a close eye on the littlest ones; the drop-off is perilous on the south side. Jockey Cap is also popular with rock climbers and boulder mavens. The trailhead is on Route 302, half a mile east of the Routes 5 and 302 intersection; park on the far left side of the Jockey Cap Country Store lot. And here's a bit of trivia: Jockey Cap was the site of Maine's first ski tow.

Allow about half an hour to reach the summit of **Sabattus Mountain,** in Lovell. This is an especially good family hike, easy and short enough for small children. Carry a picnic and enjoy the views at the top, especially from the ledges of the more open second summit. You'll see the White Mountains, Pleasant Mountain, and skinny Kezar Lake; in fall it's fabulous. To reach the trailhead from Fryeburg, take Route 5 North to Center Lovell. About 0.8 mile after the junction of Routes 5 and 5A, turn right onto Sabattus Road. Go about 1.6 miles, bearing right at the fork onto an unpaved road. Continue another 0.5 mile to a parking area on the left; the trailhead is across the road. The round-trip loop trail is 1.4 miles.

Other good hikes in this area are **Mount Tom** (easy, about 2.5 hours round-trip), just east of Fryeburg; **Burnt Meadow Mountain** (moderately difficult, about four hours round-trip to the north peak, with good views of the Presidential Range), near Brownfield; and **Mount Cutler** (moderately difficult, about two hours round-trip), near Hiram.

Water Sports

Fryeburg has two public beaches that double as canoe put-ins. **Weston's Beach** (River St./

Rte. 5 N., just off Rte. 302) is a swath of sand extending into the Saco River that gets wider as the summer progresses and the river level drops. Another sandy beach is adjacent to **Canal Bridge Campground,** just off Route 5 heading toward Lovell.

CANOEING

The **Saco River,** whose headwaters are in Crawford Notch, New Hampshire, meanders 84 miles from the Maine border at Fryeburg to the ocean at Saco and Biddeford. Its many miles of flat water, with intermittent sandbars and a few portages, make it wonderful for canoeing, camping, and swimming, but there's the rub: The summer weekend scene on the 35-mile western Maine stretch sometimes looks like bumper boats at an amusement park, especially weekends and holidays, and it can be quite raucous—with large parties towing canoes filled with beer. Aim for midweek or late September-early October, when the foliage is spectacular, the current is slower, noise levels are lower, and the crowds are busy elsewhere. Day trips are easy, but for a longer one, figure about 2 mph and you can do the Fryeburg-to-Hiram segment with two overnight stops, including a couple of interesting side-trip paddles to Hemlock Bridge, Pleasant Pond, and Lovewell's Pond. If you put in at Swan's Falls in Fryeburg (www.sacorivercouncil.org, parking $10/day), you won't have to deal with portages between there and Hiram. For multiday trips, you'll need to get a **fire permit** (free; available at some local stores), or stay at one of the commercial campgrounds.

Saco River Canoe and Kayak (Rte. 5, Fryeburg, 207/935-2369, www.sacorivercanoe.com), close to the convenient put-in at Swan's Falls, rents canoes and tandem kayaks ($45/day Fri.-Sun. July-Aug., $33/day midweek and off-season) and provides delivery and pickup service along a 50-mile stretch of the Saco River. Shuttle fees range $7-16 for two canoes.

If the crowds on the Saco become a bit much, head east or north with your canoe or kayak to the area's lakes and ponds, even to **Brownfield Bog,** a favorite with birders. Prime canoeing spots are **Lovewell Pond** and **Kezar Pond** in Fryeburg; **Kezar Lake** in Lovell; and **Virginia Lake** in Stoneham. A north wind kicks up on Kezar Lake, so stay close to shore. The most spectacular is mile-long Virginia Lake, nudged up against White Mountain National Forest. To see a house on the wooded shoreline is a rarity. The rough access road (off Rte. 5 between North Lovell and East Stoneham) is a mechanic's delight, but persevere; tranquility lies ahead.

The easiest way to see beautiful Kezar Lake is by renting a boat from **Kezar Lake Marina** (219 W. Lovell Rd., Lovell, 207/925-3000, www.kezarlake.com). Canoes and kayaks rent for $25/day. A 13-foot Boston Whaler begins at $50 half day, $90 full day.

Winter Sports

SNOWMOBILING

More than 600 miles of groomed trails are accessible from Fryeburg. For information and sled rental, try **Northeast Snowmobile Rentals** (532 Main St./Rte. 302, Fryeburg, 800/458-1838, www.northeastsnowmobile.com). Rates for three hours begin around $110 Sunday-Friday, $170 Saturday/weekend/holiday.

FOOD

Local Flavors

Rosie's Restaurant at the Lovell Village Store (Rte. 5, Lovell, 207/925-1255, 5am-8pm Mon.-Sat., 6am-7pm Sun.) is always packed. Expect good food, friendly service, and a never-too-late-for-breakfast/never-too-early-for-lunch menu. Just up the road, the **Center Lovell Market and Restaurant** (1007 Main St., Center Lovell, 207/925-1051, 7am-2pm Sun.-Mon., 7am-8pm Tues.-Sat.) is a bit more upscale.

Weston's Farm, established by the Weston family in 1799 and now operated by the seventh generation, edges the Saco River and is across from Weston's Beach. Stop at **Weston's Farm Stand** (48 River St./Rte. 113 N., Fryeburg, 207/935-2567, www.

1

2

westonsfarm.com, 9am-6pm daily mid-May-Dec. 24) for all kinds of picnic and cottage fixings, from fresh produce and local meats to cheese and maple syrup.

Casual Dining

Chef-co-owner and Culinary Institute of America grad Jonathan Spak crafts contemporary American fare with international accents at the ★ **Oxford House Inn** (548 Main St., Fryeburg, 207/935-3442, www.oxfordhouseinn.com, 5:30pm-9pm Wed.-Sun., $15-34). The four dining rooms appear formal, but this is a casual place; request a table on the glassed-in back porch to watch the sun set behind the White Mountains. Dinner reservations are wise.

If you have a hankering for barbecue and good times, the **302 West Smokehouse & Tavern** (636 Main St., Fryeburg, 207/935-3021, www.302west.com, 11am-10pm Mon.-Sat., 9am-10pm Sun., $12-26) delivers on both counts. There are big portions of ribs and barbecued entrées; salads, seafood, burgers, and Mex also are available. If there's entertainment, plan on a crowd; this place is crazy popular with locals. If the weather's nice, grab a seat on the back deck.

Beer geeks, here's your happy place. Fronting on the golf course yet hidden on a back road is a local secret with a big reputation—**Ebenezer's Pub** (44 Allen Rd., off W. Lovell Rd., Lovell, 207/925-3200, from noon daily summer, shorter hours off-season). *Beer Advocate* has named it one of the world's best beer bars. Most folks come for the Belgian beer selection—with 35 on tap and more than 700 by the bottle, it's easily the best in New England, some say in the entire country. And if you're not a fan of Belgian brews, there are dozens of other beer choices. Complementing that is good pub fare, burgers, sandwiches, salads, and pizzas ($8-15), as well as heartier entrées ($15-25). Dine on the screened-in porch or inside the tavern and bar. Every August, Ebenezer's puts on an extravagant multi-course Belgian dinner with beer pairings as part of its weeklong Belgian Beer Festival.

ACCOMMODATIONS

If you're planning to be in the area during the Fryeburg Fair, you'll need to reserve beds or campsites months ahead, in some cases a year in advance.

Inns and Bed-and-Breakfasts

The ★ **Oxford House Inn** (548 Main St./Rte. 302, Fryeburg, 207/935-3442 or 800/261-7206, www.oxfordhouseinn.com, $195) is better known for its dining, but upstairs are four spacious and inviting guest rooms. Rear rooms have bucolic views over the Saco River Valley farmlands to the White Mountains. Breakfasts, served in the mountain-view dining room on the inn's porch, are every bit as creative as the inn's dinner menus.

The **Old Saco Inn** (125 Old Saco Ln., Fryeburg, 207/925-3737, www.oldsacoinn.com, $145-220) sits on 65 quiet acres bordering the old course of the Saco River. A huge lawn rolls down to the river's edge; rising beyond are the distant White Mountains. Trails meander through the woods and fields, canoes and kayaks are available, and there's a driving range (10am-6pm Wed.-Sun., $5/40 balls). Centerpiece of the main inn is a two-story dining room centered on a huge hearth. It's home to the **Bistro** (from 5pm Thurs.-Sat., $10-25), serving an American menu with international accents. There's a guest library with cozy nooks in the upstairs mezzanine. Guest rooms are spread out between the inn and the adjacent carriage house. Most have private entrances; some have decks; one has a detached but private bath. A full breakfast is included, served either indoors or on the porch.

If you're traveling with your pooch, you'll adore the **Admiral Peary Inn Bed and Breakfast** (27 Elm St., Fryeburg, 207/935-1269, www.admiralpearyinn.com, $139-189), named for the famed Arctic explorer who briefly resided here. What distinguishes

1: Hemlock Covered Bridge **2:** Admiral Peary Inn Bed and Breakfast this inn are the spacious and plentiful public rooms: the front library, a parlor, dining room, huge kitchen with dining area, great room with fireplace and 50-inch TV, pool table nook, and large three-season porch, not to mention the back deck and yard. Innkeeper Donna Pearce has updated the decor, opting for handsome and comfy over froufrou and frilly. The inn, dating from the 1860s, is in a quiet residential area that's an easy walk to downtown. Dogs stay free as long as they can vouch for the behavior of their people. Rates include a full breakfast.

Cottage Resort

The *New York Times* once headlined a story on **Quisisana** (42 Quisisana Dr., Center Lovell, 207/925-3500, www.quisisanaresort.com, no credit cards) as "Where Mozart Goes on Vacation." By day, the staff at this elegantly rustic 47-acre retreat masquerade as waiters and waitresses, chambermaids, boat crew, and kitchen help; each night, presto—they're the stars of musical performances worthy of Broadway and concert-hall ticket prices. Since 1947 it has been like this at "Quisi," with staff recruited from the nation's best conservatories. Veteran managers attuned to guests' needs keep it all working smoothly.

The frosting on all this culture is the setting—a beautifully landscaped pine grove on the shores of sandy-bottomed Kezar Lake, looking off to the White Mountains and dramatic sunsets. No wonder reservations for the lodge rooms and 38 neat white cottages are hard to come by. The New York-heavy clientele knows to book well ahead, often for the same week, and new generations have followed their parents here. In July-August, a one-week minimum Saturday-Saturday reservation is required. Rates begin at $225 pp, including meals, musical entertainment, tennis, and nonmotorized boats. Beer and wine only are available. Quisisana's season runs mid-June to late August.

Camping

Paddling is the major focus at **Woodland Acres Campground** (Rte. 160, Brownfield, 207/935-2529, www.woodlandacres.com), which offers rental canoes and kayaks ($60/day, includes shuttle service to one location; reduced rates for additional days). The staff makes it all very convenient, even suggesting more than half a dozen daylong and multiday canoe trips for skill levels from beginner to expert. This well-maintained campground on the Saco River has 109 wooded tent and RV sites ($36-48). Leashed pets are allowed ($2.50/day). From Fryeburg, take Route 5/13 southeast to Route 160; turn left (north) and go a mile to the campground.

Also in Brownfield, and also geared toward paddlers, is **River Run** (Rte. 160, Brownfield, 207/452-2500, www.riverruncanoe.com), with 27 large primitive tent sites ($15 pp, no hookups) on 100-plus acres next to the Saco River's Brownfield Bridge. Canoe and kayak rentals ($26-45) and shuttle service ($9-30) are available.

The Saco River Recreational Council maintains rustic **Swans Falls Campground** (198 Swans Falls Rd., Fryeburg, 207/935-3395, www.sacorivercouncil.org, $15 pp, $25 min./night) on the Saco River just north of Fryeburg. The wooded grounds have 18 campsites with picnic tables and fire rings. There's also a visitor center and a store. This is a very busy canoe and kayak access point on the Saco River.

INFORMATION

The **Greater Bridgton Lakes Region Chamber of Commerce** (207/647-3472, www.mainelakeschamber.com) covers Fryeburg.

GETTING THERE AND AROUND

Fryeburg is roughly 36 miles or 50 minutes from Bethel via Route 5. It's about 20 miles or 25 minutes to Cornish via Route 5 and about 15 miles or 20 minutes to Bridgton via Route 302.

Cornish

Folded in the foothills of the White Mountains and well off the radar screen of most tourists, Cornish and neighboring Limerick, which edges Lake Sokokis, are rural charmers filled with architectural gems and dotted with antiques and eclectic shops. Lovely to visit spring through fall, they're especially treasured during foliage season, not only for the leaves but also for the apple harvest. Local historians boast that in the 1850s many of Cornish's splendid homes were moved by oxen from other parts of town to the main drag to be close to the stagecoach route. The Cornish area is convenient to Sebago, Portland, and the Southern Coast.

SIGHTS

Porter Covered Bridge

Just west of Cornish, this lovely bridge linking Oxford and York Counties and the towns of Porter and Parsonsfield spans the Ossipee River. Officially known as the **Parsonsfield-Porter Historical Bridge,** the current 152-foot double-pan, Paddleford construction dates from 1859. The best view is from Route 160, just south of what passes as downtown.

ENTERTAINMENT

The **Ossipee Valley Fair** is an old-fashioned four-day agricultural fair with tractor pulling, animal exhibits, live entertainment, food booths, games, and a carnival. It's in South Hiram the second weekend in July.

The **Ossipee Valley Music Festival** (www.ossipeevalley.com), a long weekend of bluegrass, fiddling, and acoustical music, takes place in mid to late July.

Apple Acres Farm (www.appleacresfarm.com) hosts an autumn **bluegrass festival.**

A great time to visit Cornish is the last Saturday in September, when the annual **Apple Festival** (207/625-7447, www.cornishmaine.org), held in downtown Cornish, celebrates the area's major crop with music, a crafts fair, and even an apple-pie contest. You can overdose all day on apples and stock up for winter, and do it just as fall foliage is starting to appear. For a spectacular panorama of fall colors along the Ossipee and Saco River Valleys, drive up Towles Hill Road (left turn, just west of town).

SHOPPING

Antiques and artisans' shops dominate Cornish's genuinely quaint and walkable downtown. Here's a sampling: **Cornish Trading Company** (19 Main St./Rte. 25, 207/625-8387) is a terrific group antiques shop in the handsome three-story Masonic building. Across the street is **Full Circle Artisan's Gallery & Bead Emporium** (12 Main St., 207/625-7725), carrying fine craft by regional artists. **At Once All Agog** (28 Main St., 207/625-3322) sells puzzles, toys, games, and books. **Village Jewelers** (Main St., 207/625-8958) has a drool-worthy selection of Maine gems. **Evie's Eclectic Collections** (Main St., 207/625-8916) delivers on its name, with merchandise displayed in a beautifully restored mansion.

RECREATION

Back Country Excursions (43 Woodward Rd., Parsonfield, 207/625-8189, www.bikebackcountry.com) has 30 miles of dedicated mountain-biking trails for all abilities as well as a technical terrain park for thrill-seekers on an 8,800-acre private recreational and logging preserve. Instruction and guided rides are available. Reserve ahead; all rides require a guide. Rates are $60 for a full day with lunch, $50 without lunch, or $30 half day, which includes access to showers and maps. Bikes rent for $45; a helmet is $5. You also can rent a canoe for paddling local waterways for $20. Camping and lodging are available.

FOOD

In addition to pick-your-own apples in autumn, **Apple Acres Farm** (363 Durgintown Rd., Hiram, 207/625-4777, http://appleacresfarm.com) operates the Treehouse Tavern, which is justifiably popular for apple-cider doughnuts, luncheon fare, and desserts.

On one of those lazy, hazy days of summer, you'd be hard-pressed to find a better spot to enjoy burgers, fried food, and an ice cream than the humble **Sokokis Seafood Shack** (174 Washington St., Limerick, 207/793-2600, 11:30am-9pm Tues.-Sun., $5-20), a lakeside takeout with picnic tables.

Expect big portions of American homestyle and Italian fare at **Phat Boy's Café** (172 Main St., Cornish, 207/625-7980, 7am-8pm daily, $10-20). All-you-can-eat fried haddock for about $18 is served nightly.

★ **Krista's Restaurant** (2 Main St., Cornish, 207/625-3600, www.kristasrestaurant.com, from 11:30am Mon. and Wed.-Fri., from 8am Sat.-Sun., $11-28) serves fabulous, fresh, New American fare for all meals in huge portions in its cheery rooms and on a screened deck overhanging a gurgling stream.

Fresh seafood is served at **Bay Haven Lobster Pound** (101 Maple St., Cornish, 207/625-7303, 11am-8pm Tues.-Thurs. and Sun., 11am-9pm Fri.-Sat., $10-30), operated by a fishing family. Portions are very generous; prices are reasonable. Dress down, order the humongous fisherman's platter—and plan on sharing.

ACCOMMODATIONS

Smack-dab downtown is the 1824 **Inn at Cornish** (2 High St., Cornish, 207/625-8501, www.cornishinn.com, $150-195), a three-story gently updated classic with a wraparound porch and a dining room, where breakfast is served. The 16 guest rooms are simple yet comfortable.

The barn-red **Midway Country Lodging** (712 S. Hiram Rd., Cornish, 207/625-8835, www.mainemidwaylodging.com, $99-145) is a motel-like inn, or maybe an inn-like motel with mountain views and nice gardens.

The handsome brick Greek Revival-style **Jeremiah Mason Bed & Breakfast** (40 Main St., Limerick, 207/793-4858, www.jeremiahmasonhouse.com, $55-75), built by a wealthy banker in 1859, retains the elegance—and the prices—of a bygone era. Spacious antiques-accented guest rooms have chandeliers, marble fireplaces, and floor-to-ceiling windows. Rates include a full breakfast; less expensive rooms have half-baths; pet-friendly rooms are available.

INFORMATION

Area info is available from the **Cornish Association of Businesses** (207/625-8856, www.cornish-maine.org) and www.limerickmaine.com.

GETTING THERE AND AROUND

Cornish is roughly 20 miles or 25 minutes from Fryeburg via Route 5. It's about 23 miles or 35 minutes to Bridgton via Routes 5 and 117. It's about 35 miles or 50 minutes to Portland via Route 25.

Sebago and Long Lakes

When Greater Portland residents say they're headed *upta camp*, most likely they're headed to a summer cottage here. The area along the shores of Sebago and Long Lakes includes the two major hubs of **Bridgton** (pop. 5,210) and **Naples** (pop. 3,872), as well as the smaller communities of **Sebago** (pop. 1,719) and **Harrison** (pop. 2,730) and the larger communities of **Raymond** (pop. 4,436), **Casco** (pop. 3,742), and **Windham** (pop. 17,001), as well as numerous smaller ponds and lakes.

When the summer-vacation boom began in the mid-19th century and then erupted after the Civil War, visitors flowed into this area via stagecoach, the Cumberland and Oxford Canal, and later the Bridgton and Saco Railroad. The 28-lock canal, opened in 1830 and shut down in 1870, connected Portland's Fore River with Sebago and Long Lakes. Its only working remnant is the Songo Lock in Naples, on the Songo River between Brandy Pond and Sebago Lake.

Sebago is an apt Native American word meaning "large, open water"; it's the state's second-largest lake (after Moosehead), and fluky winds can kick up suddenly and toss around little boats, so be prudent. Now a major water source for Greater Portland, the lake reportedly served as the crossroads for major Native American trading routes, and artifacts still occasionally surface in the Sebago Basin area.

Engage in a heart-to-heart with an adult vacationing in this area and you're likely to find someone trying to recapture the past—the carefree days at summer camp in the Sebago and Long Lakes region. The shores of Sebago, Long, and Highland Lakes shelter dozens of children's camps that have created several generations of Maine enthusiasts—"people from away" who still can't resist an annual visit. Unless your own kids are in camp, however, or you're terminally masochistic, do not appear in Bridgton, Naples, or surrounding communities on the last weekend in July. Parents, grandparents, and surrogate parents all show up then for the midseason summer-camp break, and there isn't a bed or restaurant seat to be had in the entire county and often beyond. Gridlock is the rule.

Aside from that, this mountain-lake setting has incredible locales for canoeing, swimming, hiking, fishing, golfing, camping, biking, ice-skating, snowshoeing, and skiing. Maine's first ski lift opened in 1938 on Pleasant Mountain, now the Shawnee Peak ski area.

These lakes are quite convenient to Portland—Sebago is the large body of water you'll see to the west as you descend into the Portland Jetport.

SIGHTS

Narramissic, the Peabody-Fitch Farm

Built in 1797 and converted to Federal style in 1828, **Narramissic, the Peabody-Fitch Farm** is the crown jewel of the **Bridgton Historical Society** (207/647-3699, www.bridgtonhistory.org). The homestead includes a carriage house, an ell, a barn, a blacksmith shop, and historical gardens. The barn has its own story: It's known as the Temperance Barn because the landowners were avowed teetotalers, so the volunteer barn-raisers earned only water for their efforts. Narramissic is a relatively recent name, given to it by the 20th-century owner who donated it to the historical society in 1986. The name is a Native American word meaning "hard to find," reflecting her lengthy search for a family summer home. But it also suits the circuitous route, fortunately signposted, to the South Bridgton farm from downtown Bridgton: Take Main Street to Route 117 south and turn left on Route 107, then right on Ingalls Road. The

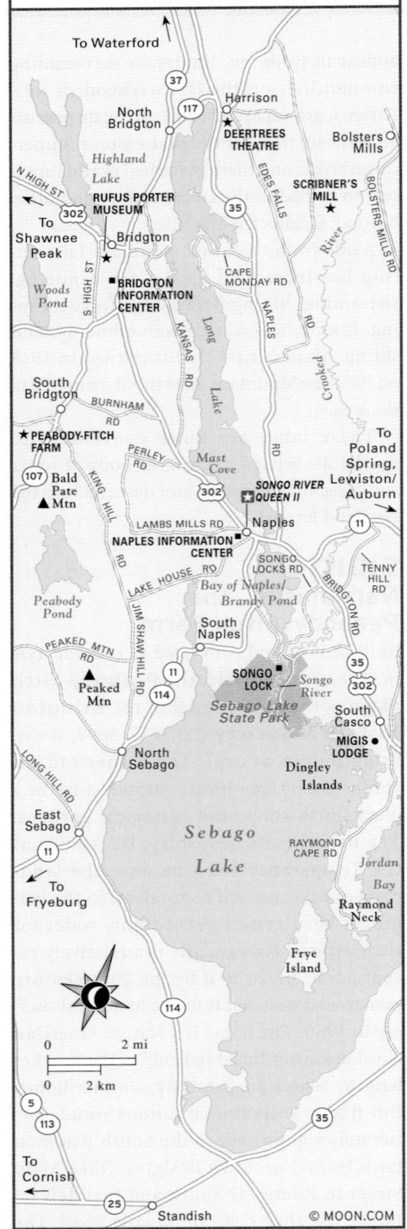

grounds are open during daylight hours for hiking and picnicking; call for open house hours and tours.

★ *Songo River Queen II*

Berthed in downtown Naples is the ***Songo River Queen II*** (Bay of Naples Causeway/Rte. 302, Naples, 207/693-6861, www.songoriver-queen.net, $18-28 adults, $9-14 children), a 93-foot Mississippi stern-wheeler replica that operates one- and two-hour narrated cruises on Long Lake mid-May-mid-October. On board are restrooms and a snack bar.

Presidential Maine

Inspired by a famous western Maine signpost giving directions to nine Maine towns named for foreign cities and countries, Boy Scouts in Casco decided to create some competition—a directional sign for 10 Maine towns named for U.S. presidents. The marker stands next to the village green in **Casco,** at the corner of Route 121 and Leach Hill Road, pointing to towns such as Washington (76 miles), Lincoln (175 miles), Madison (96 miles), and Monroe (114 miles). There's even a Clinton (84 miles).

If you're here in the fall, take time to detour briefly to Casco's "million-dollar view." Continue south from the signpost less than two miles on Route 121 to Route 11 (Pike Corner), then turn right (west) and go about 0.5 mile to Quaker Ridge Road and turn left (south). Views are spectacular along here, especially from the Quaker Hill area.

Rufus Porter Museum

The early-19th-century itinerant artist's murals and paintings are the focus at the **Rufus Porter Museum** (121 Main St., Bridgton, 207/647-2828, www.rufusportermuseum.org, 10am-4pm mid-June-mid-Oct., $8 adults, $4 students), which opened in the restored John and Maria Webb House in 2016. Porter, the founder of *Scientific American* magazine, painted landscapes on the walls of homes throughout New England. Most were unsigned. The museum, which occupies two historic downtown buildings, the Webb House

Family-Size Alpine Areas

Maine's big resorts get most of the attention, but for young families or anyone on a budget, the smaller resorts provide not only a fun experience but also a good value. Perhaps the vertical range isn't as grand, but really, how often do you ski 2,000 feet without stopping? All of these little guys have night skiing, most have tubing parks, and some have cross-country trails too. If you're searching for areas with soul, for friendly faces, and places where kids matter, head to these slopes.

Lost Valley (200 Lost Valley Rd., off Young's Corner Rd., Auburn, 207/784-1561, www.lostvalleyski.com) is a vest-pocket ski area secreted in the barely rolling countryside outside Auburn. Don't be deceived by the hill's diminutive size. Although the vertical drop is only 240 feet, it was enough to produce four Olympians: Karl Anderson and Anna, Julie, and Rob Parisien. This is an especially family-friendly area; the base lodge doubles as the local babysitting service—parents just naturally watch out for one another's kids. According to Olympian Julie Parisien, who has coached local youth, you may be able to make only 10 turns from top to bottom, but that's 10 good turns. And that's what matters.

Maine's oldest ski area is **Shawnee Peak** (Rte. 302, Bridgton, 207/647-8444, www.shawneepeak.com), an increasingly popular destination given its proximity to Portland (45 miles). I have a soft spot for the area where I spent my youth—bring your family, and you'll likely understand why. The setting is rural and undeveloped, and Pleasant Mountain appears to rise out of Moose Pond. The views, which take in Mount Washington and the Presidential Range of the White Mountains, are calming, almost inspirational. It's one of the largest night-skiing facilities, acreage-wise, in New England. Arrive at night, and you'll notice that the trails spell out the word LOV in 1960s-block-style lettering. The mountain skis bigger than its 1,300-foot vertical range indicates, as it has two faces, with open slopes on one and squiggly trails ribboning the other.

For anyone weak in the wallet or overawed by megaresorts, **Mount Abram** (Howe Hill Rd., off Rte. 26, Lockes Mills, 207/875-5002, www.skimtabram.com) is the solution. This longtime family favorite is something of a sleeper. Most folks drive right by on their way to glitzy Sunday River, just up the road. A savvy few turn off Route 26 in Locke Mills, drawn by this resort's commitment to family skiing and a decent 1,150-foot vertical range. The segregated learning area, tubing park, night lights, cross-country loop, low-key atmosphere, and lack of crowds make it a real gem.

A real success story is **Black Mountain of Maine** (39 Glover Rd., Rumford, 207/364-8977, www.skiblackmountain.org), where prices are low and spirit is high. Recent investments in the 1,150-vertical-foot hill include new lifts and new trails, and the owners have added snowmaking and made the property smoke-free. Another plus is the cross-country trail system, designed by two-time Olympian Chummy Broomhall.

The Farmington Ski Club operates **Titcomb Mountain Ski Area** (180 Ski Slope Rd., West Farmington, 207/778-9031, www.titcombmountain.com), an all-volunteer operation with a modest 350-foot vertical drop. It's the hill where two-time Olympic gold medalist Seth Wescott played as a youth. In addition to the alpine terrain, there are nine miles of groomed trails for cross-country skiing and snowboarding (a potential solution for mixed marriages or partnerships). The operating schedule coincides with school hours, so it's open late afternoon and evenings, weekends, and daily during vacation weeks. Yes, it's a club, but nonmembers are welcome.

and the Church House, exhibits Porter's inventions, writings, and murals.

Scribner's Mill

In use by three generations of the Scribner family between 1847 and 1962, **Scribner's Saw Mill and Homestead** (207/585-6455, Scribner's Mill Rd., Harrison, www.scribnersmill.org) is an accurately reconstructed (and working) sash sawmill museum. It's open 1pm-4pm on first and third Saturdays from late May-early September.

ENTERTAINMENT

Tucked away on a back road in Harrison, east of Long Lake, dramatic-looking 278-seat

Deertrees Theatre and Cultural Center (156 Deertrees Rd., Harrison, 207/583-6747, www.deertrees-theatre.org) is a must-see even if you don't attend a performance. The acoustically superior building, constructed of rose hemlock in 1936, is in the National Register of Historic Places and has seen the likes of Rudy Vallée, Ethel Barrymore, Tallulah Bankhead, and Henry Winkler; restoration of the rustic building in the 1990s has given it an exciting new life. During the summer season, there's something going on nearly every night—musicals, plays, comedy, folk, jazz, blues, and weekly children's performances. The theater is signposted off Route 117 in the Harrison woods. Also here is a gallery and café.

From mid-July to mid-August, the **Sebago-Long Lake Chamber Music Festival** (207/583-6747, www.sebagomusicfestival.org, $25 adults, free under age 22) brings Tuesday evening chamber-music concerts to Harrison's Deertrees Theatre. Advance booking is essential for this popular series, founded in 1975.

Sunday evening **band concerts** around the gazebo behind the Naples Information Center are free mid-July-mid-August. Bring a chair or blanket to the Village Green (Rte. 302, Naples).

One of a dying species, **Bridgton Twin Drive-In** (Rte. 302, Bridgton, 207/647-8666, cash only) screens two shows nightly beginning at dusk in July and August.

Festivals and Events

Shawnee Peak ski area (207/647-8444, www.shawneepeak.com) has a full schedule of family-oriented special events, including races, throughout the winter; call or check the website for information.

The **Maine Blues Festival** (www.mainebluesfestival.com), in June, celebrates Maine's blues artists over three days and across multiple venues.

The third Saturday in July, Bridgton is the scene of the **Annual Art in the Park** exhibition and sale, a mad success since its inception.

SHOPPING

Anchored by **Renys** (151 Main St., 207/647-3711), where you can buy just about anything portable at great prices, Bridgton offers the region's best collection of interesting shops, with most housed in historic buildings along the town's main drag. Among these are **Gallery 302** (112 Main St., 207/647-2787), with more than 60 member artists, and **Bridgton Books** (140 Main St., 207/647-2122), an independent bookstore carrying 20,000 titles, including new, selected used, and bargains, along with cards, puzzles, and more.

Hole in the Wall Studioworks (1544 Roosevelt Trail/Rte. 302, Raymond, 207/655-4592, www.holeinthewallstudioworks.com) sells an especially fine selection of American-made art and crafts. Don't miss the sculpture garden.

Maine-made crafts and a luscious selection of yarns are at **Rosemary's Gift & Yarn Shop** (39 Roosevelt Trail/Rte. 302, Windham, 207/894-5770, www.maine-crafts.com).

RECREATION

Sebago Lake State Park

Fourth largest of Maine's state parks, 1,400-acre **Sebago Lake State Park** (11 Park Access Rd., Naples, 207/693-6613 late June-Labor Day, 207/693-6231 off-season, www.parksandlands.com, $6-8 adults, $2 seniors, $1 ages 5-11) is one of the most popular—so don't anticipate peace and quiet here in July-August. Swimming and picnicking are superb, fishing is so-so, and personal watercraft are an increasing hazard. During the summer, park officials organize lectures, hikes, and other activities. The park is open mid-May-October, but there's winter access to 4.5 miles of groomed cross-country skiing trails—mostly beginner terrain.

1: *Songo River Queen II* **2:** Deertrees Theatre and Cultural Center

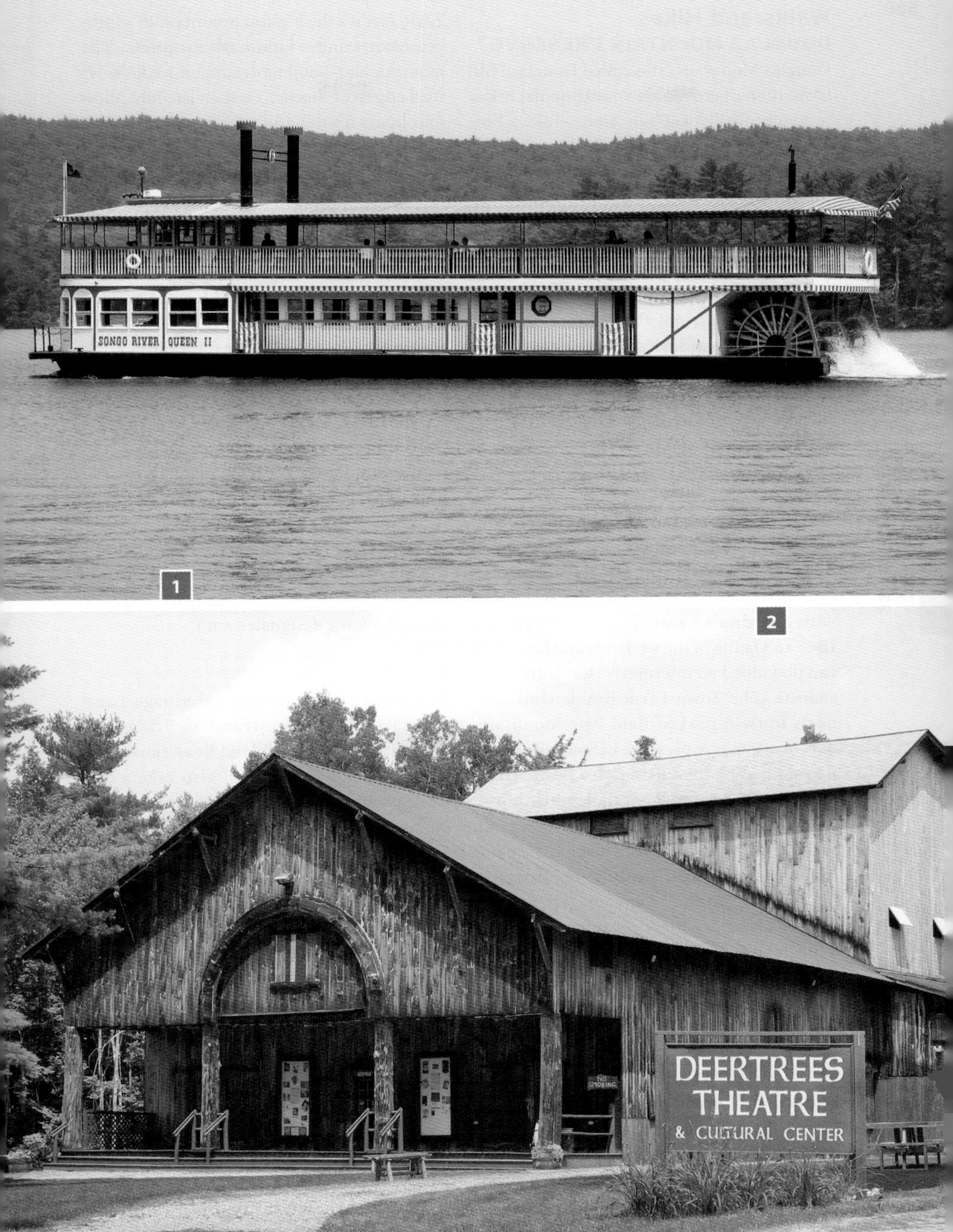
SONGO RIVER QUEEN II
1
2
NO SMOKING
DEERTREES THEATRE
& CULTURAL CENTER

Walks and Hikes

DOUGLAS MOUNTAIN PRESERVE

Douglas Mountain (also called Douglas Hill) is one of southern Maine's most popular hikes, so you probably won't be alone. Take a brochure from the registration box, and follow the moderate Woods Trail to the 1,415-foot summit, a 30-minute walk at most. At the top is a 0.7-mile nature-trail loop, plus a 16-foot stone tower with a head-spinning view. In the fall, the vistas are incomparable. Be eco-sensitive and stick to the trails in this 169-acre preserve. Pets are not allowed. The trails are accessible dawn-dusk. The trailhead is off Route 107 in Sebago: Take Dyke Mountain Road 0.8 mile to Douglas Mountain Road, then follow signs to the parking area ($3).

HOLT POND AND BALD PATE MOUNTAIN

The Holt Pond Preserve comprises 450 mostly wetland acres in Naples and is owned by the **Lakes Environmental Association** (207/647-8580, www.mainelakes.org). A trail with boardwalks makes it easy to spot the flora and fauna in the wetlands and bogs. You can download an interpretive guide from the website. The Town Farm Brook Trail connects to twin-peaked Bald Pate Mountain, part of a 486-acre preserve in South Bridgton maintained by the **Loon Echo Land Trust** (207/647-4352, www.loonecholandtrust.org). Bald Pate's trail network is open year-round, and there's a kiosk with trail maps at the parking lot (signposted off Rte. 107). The first peak has views to Pleasant Mountain, and the summit peak is bald, with panoramic views. Pack a lunch and plan for a full day if you decide to connect the two preserves. If you come in winter, some of Bald Pate's trails are groomed for cross-country skiing.

PLEASANT MOUNTAIN

Loon Echo Land Trust also manages this nearly 2,000-acre preserve on the eastern sides of the Shawnee Peak alpine resort on Pleasant Mountain in Bridgton. Six interconnecting trails provide access to the main summit—at 2,000 feet it's the highest mountain in southern Maine and a landmark for pilots. The most popular—and most suitable for kids—is the Ledges (or Moose) Trail. In late July, allow four hours for the 3.5-mile round-trip so you can pick blueberries on the open ledges midway up. At the top there's plenty of space for spreading out a picnic overlooking panoramic vistas of woods, lakes, and mountains. From Bridgton, drive 5.75 miles west on Route 302 to Mountain Road (just after the causeway over Moose Pond). Turn left (south) at signs for Shawnee Peak ski area and go 3.3 miles to the trailhead for the Ledges (or Moose) Trail; parking is limited.

PONDICHERRY PRESERVE

In downtown Bridgton is this 66-acre preserve with two miles of trails, many with boardwalks, lacing woodlands, fields, and wetlands, including a mile of stream frontage. Easiest access is from the public parking lot behind the Magic Lantern Theater. Pick up a trail map at the trailhead kiosk. Leashed dogs are allowed on one designated trail.

Swimming

Besides two sandy beaches at Sebago Lake State Park, and the strand at Bridgton's Highland Park on Highland Road (just steps from downtown), you can also take a dip while picnicking at an unmarked picnic area on the island midway across Bridgton's Route 302 Moose Pond causeway.

Golf

The 18-hole **Bridgton Highlands Country Club** (Highland Ridge Rd., Bridgton, 207/647-3491, www.bridgtonhighlands.com) course is outstandingly scenic and very popular, especially at the height of summer. Starting times are required.

Less expensive but also scenic is the **Naples Golf and Country Club** (Rte. 114, Naples, 207/693-6424, www.naplesgolfcourse.com), established in 1922. Light meals are available at the clubhouse.

The championship-level **Point Sebago**

Golf Club (Rte. 302, Casco, 207/655-2747, www.pointsebago.com, May-mid-Oct.) is part of the 800-acre family-oriented Club Med-style Point Sebago Resort. Call for starting times at the 18-hole course, which is open to the public. Golf-and-lodging packages are available.

Water Sports

You can rent a pontoon boat, a powerboat, or if you must, a personal watercraft, or PWC, often referred to by the trademarked name Jet Ski.

Both **Naples Marina** (1565 Roosevelt Trail, Raymond, 207/693-6254, www.naplesmarinamaine.com) and **Causeway Marina** (780 Roosevelt Trail, Naples, 207/693-6832, www.causewaymarina.com) rent powerboats, including pontoon boats, runabouts, and fishing boats.

If you've brought a **canoe or kayak,** don't launch it into Sebago Lake; save it for the smaller lakes and ponds, where the winds are more predictable and the boat traffic is less congested.

FOOD

Restaurants in this region tend to get swamped in summer, especially when camper parents are dropping off, picking up, or visiting their kids. Reservations are wise.

Local Flavors

The **Bridgton Farmers Market** is held 8am-1pm Saturdays mid-May to early October behind Renys.

Conveniently situated across from a lakeside picnic area at the intersection of Routes 302 and 85, the **Good Life Market** (1297 Roosevelt Trail, Raymond, 207/655-1196, www.thegoodlifemarket.com, 7am-7pm daily, $7-10) is a great place to pick up sandwiches, salads, fresh-baked treats, wine, and specialty foods.

Breakfast and only breakfast is served at **Chute's Cafe and Bakery** (Rte. 302, South Casco, 207/655-7111, 6am-12:30pm daily, $6-16).

In addition to providing catering and prepared meals-to-go, **Marie's Kitchen** (939 Roosevelt Trail, Naples, 207/693-2021, www.marieskitchennaples.com, 11:30am-2pm Mon.-Wed., 11:30am-6pm Thurs.-Fri., 9am-6pm Sat., 9am-2pm Sun.) serves breakfast and lunch.

Beth's Kitchen Cafe (108 Main St., Bridgton, 207/647-5211, http://bethskitchencafe.com, 7am-3pm daily) is a pleasant spot for breakfast, lunch, and baked goods; beer and wine are available.

Standard Gastropub (233 Main St., Bridgton, 207/647-4100, 11am-10pm daily, $10-20) attracts fans of barbecued and smoked foods along with North American craft brews. The space is small, the flavors big. Snag a table or take it to go.

Casual Dining

For more than 25 years, the **Black Horse Tavern** (26 Rte. 302, Bridgton, 207/647-5300, www.theblackhorsetavern.com, 11am-9pm Mon.-Sat., 10am-9pm Sun., $12-30) has been a reliable choice for good food in a pleasant, tavern-style atmosphere. A kids' menu is available.

For well-prepared classic Italian fare, make reservations at **Vivo's Country Italian Kitchen & Bar** (18 Depot St., Bridgton, 207/647-8488, www.vivoitalian-bridgton.com, from 5pm daily, $19-28), tucked behind Renys.

Craving a bit of Irish craic? The **Black Bear Café** (215 Roosevelt Trail, Naples, 207/693-4770, www.theblackbearcafe.com, from 4pm daily, $15-32) delivers. The pleasant Irish pub is accented with a tin ceiling and local artwork. Dinner choices—burgers, salads, and pub-style classics—as well as a kids' menu make it easy to please everyone. There's live music most evenings in summer.

Nonguests can dine at **Migis Lodge** (Migis Lodge Rd., South Casco, 207/655-4524, www.migis.com) on Sebago Lake by advance reservation. Breakfast is $18, lunch is $22, a five-course dinner served in the dining room Monday-Thursday is $50, the waterside lobster bake on Friday nights and the buffet dinner in

Noble
House
INN
VACANCY
1

2

the dining room on Saturday nights are each $55; all prices plus tax and 18 percent gratuity. Dining room meals require a jacket. No credit cards.

Built on the site of an old mill, the **Old Mill Tavern** (56 Main St., Harrison, 207/583-9077, www.oldemilltavern.com, 11:30am-9pm daily, $11-26) serves a tavern menu emphasizing comfort foods. The vibe is local, with live entertainment on weekends.

ACCOMMODATIONS

Bed-and-Breakfasts

The ★ **Noble House Inn** (81 Highland Rd., Bridgton, 207/647-3733, www.noblehousebb.com, year-round, $165-275) is a grand turn-of-the-20th-century Victorian with nine warmly decorated guest rooms, some with screened porches or jetted tubs. Guests have use of a comfortable sitting room, a living room with a grand piano and an organ, and a great veranda. A short walk brings you to Bridgton's Highland Park on the lake, with swimming, picnicking, and boating access. Rates include a full breakfast and access to a bottomless cookie jar.

The nicely updated, four-story **Lakeview Inn** (15 Lake House Rd., Naples, 207/693-9099, www.lakeviewinnmaine.com, year-round, $189-229) began its life in 1906 as a boardinghouse for young women working the town's lakeside resorts. Now the 16 guest rooms, some with lake views, have an unfussy, welcoming decor. Rates include a multicourse breakfast and snacks.

Resort

Welcome to heaven: At ★ **Migis Lodge** (Migis Lodge Rd., South Casco, 207/655-4524, www.migis.com, no credit cards), on the east side of Sebago Lake, guests often confirm their next year's July or August booking before they depart for home. Don't let that dissuade you; there often are openings. The rustic elegance of 100-acre Migis, along with attentive service and a fabulous lakeside setting, have drawn big-name guests since the resort was established in the early 20th century. Guests stay in spacious cabins within steps of the lake; each has a wood-burning fieldstone fireplace and is decorated in inviting Polo Ralph Lauren-meets-L. L. Bean style. Men wear jackets for dinner, and there is a supervised meal and playtime for children during dinner hours. All this comes at a price, which includes almost everything, from sailboats, canoes, and kayaks to island cookouts, waterskiing, tennis courts, a children's program, and even a weekly lobster bake; exclusions include boats with motors, massages, and alcohol. Summer rates for the 35 lake-view 1-6-bedroom cottages and six lodge rooms begin around $350 pp, varying with the season and the accommodation. This is a fabulous place for an autumn foliage retreat, when rates are far lower.

1: Noble House Inn in Bridgton **2:** Migis Lodge on Sebago Lake

Camping

Plan well ahead to land one of the 250 sites at **Sebago Lake State Park** (11 Park Access Rd., Naples, 207/693-6613 late June-Labor Day, www.parksandlands.com, reservations in Maine 800/332-1501, out of state 207/624-9950 or www.campwithme.com). Despite its popularity, well-spaced sites provide some privacy. Rates are $35 nonresidents, $25 Maine residents with a $5/night reservation fee. Some sites have water and electric hookups ($10 premium/night).

Seasonal Rentals

Krainin Real Estate (800/639-2321, www.krainin.com) handles weekly and monthly rentals for cottages on Sebago and Long Lakes as well as many of the surrounding smaller lakes and ponds. Krainin also arranges rentals on **Frye Island,** a 1,000-acre summer community in the middle of Sebago Lake that's accessible only by car ferry.

INFORMATION

The **Greater Bridgton Lakes Region Chamber of Commerce** (207/647-3472, www.mainelakeschamber.com) has an attractive information center (with public restrooms) 0.5 mile south of downtown Bridgton on Route 302.

The **Sebago Lakes Region Chamber of Commerce** (Windham 207/892-8265, Naples 207/693-3285, www.sebagolakeschamber.com) operates two information centers: one on Route 302 in Windham, and a seasonal one on the Naples village green.

GETTING THERE AND AROUND

Bridgton is roughly 23 miles or 35 minutes from Cornish via Routes 5 and 117. It's about 10 miles or 15 minutes to Waterford via Route 17, about 19 miles or 30 minutes to South Paris via Route 117, and about 23 miles to Poland via Routes 302 and 11. It's 15 miles or 20 minutes to Fryeburg or one hour to Portland, either via Route 302.

Oxford Hills

Sandwiched between the Lewiston-Auburn area and the Bethel area, with Sebago and Long Lakes off to the south, the Oxford Hills region centers on **Norway** (pop. 5,014) and **South Paris** (pop. 2,267).

Oxford County's official seat is Paris. The town of **West Paris** (pop. 1,812) is in fact mostly *north* of Paris and South Paris. Within the boundaries of West Paris is the hamlet of North Paris. Fortunately, there's no East Paris, but there is the tiny enclave of **Paris Hill,** a pocket paradise worthy of a detour.

West Paris gained its own identity when it separated from Paris in 1957, but its traditions go way back. The Pequawket Indian princess Mollyockett, celebrated hereabouts as a healer, supposedly buried a golden treasure under a suspended animal trap, hence the name of Trap Corner for the junction of Routes 26 and 219 in West Paris. No such cache has been uncovered. More recent traditions in West Paris come from Finland, home of many 19th- and early-20th-century immigrants who gravitated to this area.

Norway's name comes not from Europe or Norwegian settlers but rather from a variation on a Native American word for waterfalls—referring to the cascades on the town's Pennesseewassee (PEN-a-see-WAH-see) Lake (called Norway Lake locally), which powered 19th-century mills. European settlement began in 1786. The town was the birthplace of C. A. Stephens (1844-1931), who wrote weekly stories for a 19th-century boys' magazine, *Youth's Companion,* for 55 years. Colorfully reflective of rural Maine life, the entertaining tales were collected in *Stories from the Old Squire's Farm,* published in 1995. Norway was known as the "Snowshoe Capital of the World" during the early 20th century, when snowshoes made locally by Mellie Dunham were used on the 1909 Peary expedition to the North Pole and by World War II troops. The multitalented Dunham also earned fame as one of the nation's top fiddlers.

Waterford (pop. 1,553) is a delight, especially the National Historic District known as Waterford Flat (or Flats), with classic homes and tree-lined streets alongside Keoka Lake in the shadow of Mount Tir'em. It's a 19th-century village frozen in time. Visit during foliage season, and you may never leave.

SIGHTS

★ Paris Hill

On Route 26, just beyond the northern edge of South Paris, a sign marks one end of Paris Hill Road, a four-mile loop that reconnects farther along with Route 26. As you head uphill, past an old cemetery, you'll arrive at a Brigadoon-like enclave of elegant 18th- and 19th-century homes—a National Historic District with dramatic views off to the White Mountains and the lakes below. The centerpiece of the road is **Paris Hill Common,** a pristine park in front of the birthplace of Hannibal Hamlin

1
2
HAMLIN
Memorial Library
& Museum
1822
HAMLIN
MEMORIAL HALL

(1809-1891), vice president during Abraham Lincoln's first term. The house is not open to the public.

South of the green stands the **Hamlin Memorial Library & Museum** (16 Hannibal Hamlin Dr., 207/743-2980, www.hamlin.lib.me.us, 11am-5pm Tues., 1pm-6pm Thurs., 10am-2pm Sat.), the only Paris Hill building open to the public, where you can bone up on the history of this pocket paradise. Visit the library's website to download a copy of the Paris Hill walking tour. Most children (and adults) get a kick out of entering a public library that was once a town jail. This one, built in 1822, held as many as 30 prisoners until 1896. Three prisoners somehow escaped in the 1830s, abandoning one of their pals stuck in the wall opening they had created. In 1902, the jail became the library, retaining the telltale signs of jail-bar hinges in the granite walls. Admission is free to the library's upper-level museum section, but donations are welcome. The library has no heat, so dress warmly.

A great time to visit is on the third Saturday in July, for the annual **Founder's Day Classic Car Exhibit** ($10 adults, $2 ages 12 and younger), when Robert and Sandra Bahre open the garage on the Hamlin estate to share their world-renowned collection. Among the prizes are Packards, Duesenbergs, Stutz Bearcats, a Tucker, a Thomas Flyer, vintage race cars, and other models.

Finnish-American Heritage Center

In the early 20th century, hundreds of Finnish immigrants moved to Maine's Oxford Hills. The **Finnish-American Heritage Center** (8 Maple St., West Paris, www.mainefinns.org) relates their story. The building, which began life as a hotel before being converted to a boardinghouse for immigrant Finnish men, then later an American Legion post, is open to visitors 2pm-4pm Sunday in July-August. Inside are displays, a library, and a gift shop. The center also presents occasional cultural events and meals, which are promoted in local papers.

McLaughlin Garden

For more than 60 years, Bernard McLaughlin had lovingly tended his two-acre perennial garden alongside Route 26, eventually surrounded by commercial development, and he'd always welcomed the public into his floral oasis. In 1995, at the age of 98, McLaughlin died, stipulating in his will that the property be sold. Eager developers eyed it, but loyal flower fans dug in their heels, captured media attention, created a nonprofit foundation, and managed to buy the property—the beginning of the little miracle. The **McLaughlin Garden** (97 Main St., South Paris, 207/743-8820, www.mclaughlingarden.org, dawn-dusk daily early May-late Oct., donation appreciated) lives on, with its 98 varieties of lilacs along with lilies and irises and so much more. The garden's main paths are wheelchair-accessible. Check the website for special events and programs. Also on the premises are a homestead and barn (10am-4pm Tues.-Sun.) with a gift shop and tea room offering light fare. Call in advance to arrange a guided tour ($8 pp) or $50 for five or fewer.

Downtown Norway

After most of **downtown Norway** (www.norwaydowntown.org) burned during the Great Fire of 1894, it was rebuilt in brick and wood, reflecting the Victorian era's considerable embellishments. The Maine Historic Preservation Commission considers the downtown, now a National Historic District, one of the state's best examples of period architecture. It's currently undergoing a renaissance, with artists and entrepreneurs breathing new life into vacant storefronts and empty buildings. A historical walking tour, detailing the history of many buildings, is available online and in the downtown info kiosk.

In 2013, 10 years after the 1894 **Norway Opera House,** a National Historic Register property with a distinctive clock tower, was designated one of Maine's most endangered historical properties, phase one of a massive grassroots preservation effort was completed and street-level shops opened. The next phase will rehab and reopen the 2nd-floor opera hall. Also undergoing restoration is the distinctive **Gingerbread House.**

RECREATION

Parks and Preserves

A 300-foot gorge on the Little Androscoggin River is the eye-catching centerpiece of **Snow Falls** rest area, an easy-off, easy-on roadside park where you can picnic on a table alongside the waterfall. Trucks whiz by on the highway, but the noise of the water usually drowns them out. The rest area is on Route 26, about six miles north of the center of South Paris.

Western Foothills Land Trust (207/739-2124, www.wfltmaine.org) owns **Roberts Farm Preserve** (64 Roberts Rd.). The 165-acre preserve is webbed with over seven miles of trails for hiking, Nordic skiing, snowshoeing, and mountain biking, and it also has a trail for the physically challenged that meets ADA standards. It's a short and easy walk to a lovely vista with views over Lake Pennesseewassee. The preserve is located just off Routes 1887/117, 0.2 mile south of the lake.

Hiking

The most popular Oxford Hills hikes are particularly family-friendly—no killer climbs or even major ascents, no bushwhacking, just good exercise and some worthwhile views. In July-mid-August, don't be surprised to encounter clusters of summer campers, since camp counselors all over this region regularly gather up their kids and take them out on the trails or paddling the ponds. If you're spending more than a day hiking in this area, pick up a copy at bookstores and gift shops of *Hikes in and Around Maine's Lake Region* by Marita Wiser; it's the best available advice on this area.

It's hard to resist a hike up **Mount Tir'em** (1,104 feet)—if only to disprove its name. Actually, it's supposedly a convolution of a Native American name. The only steep section is at the beginning, after the memorial marker dedicated to 19th-century Waterfordite Daniel Brown, for whom the unblazed trail is named. Allow an hour or so for the 1.4-mile round-trip, especially if you're carrying a picnic. Allow time on the summit ledges to take in the views—all the way to Sebago on a clear day. From downtown Waterford (Rte. 35), take Plummer Hill Road about 300 feet beyond the community center. The unmarked trailhead is on the west side of the road where it branches.

Straddling the Paris-Buckfield-Hebron town boundaries, the half-mile **Streaked Mountain** (pronounced STREAK-ed) trail climbs 800 feet, often steeply, to an expansive 1,770-foot summit with communications towers and vistas as far as Mount Washington. Pack a picnic. If you're here in early August, take along a small pail to collect wild blueberries. In late September-early October, it's indescribable, but remember to wear a hunter-orange hat or vest once hunting season has started—or tackle the trail on a Sunday, when there's no hunting. Allow about 1.5 hours for the one-mile round-trip, especially if you're picnicking and blueberry-picking. To reach the trailhead from South Paris, take Route 117 west to Streaked Mountain Road, on the right (south); turn and go about 0.5 mile. Park well off the road. (You can also climb Streaked from the east, but it's a much longer hike that requires waterproof footwear.)

Golf

At nine-hole **Paris Hill Country Club** (355 Paris Hill Rd., Paris, 207/743-2371), founded in 1899, you'll find a low-key atmosphere, reasonable greens fees, cart rentals, and a café. The rectangular course has all straight shots; the challenges come from slopes and unexpected traps.

1: birthplace of Vice President Hannibal Hamlin in Paris Hill **2:** Hamlin Memorial Library & Museum

It's not just golfers who patronize the nine-hole **Norway Country Club** (Lake Rd./Rte. 118, Norway, 207/743-9840); this is a popular spot to have lunch (11am-7pm) or kick back on the club porch and admire the mountain-lake scenery.

Spectator Sports

If you're partial to guerrilla warfare on wheels, the place to be is **Oxford Plains Speedway** (Rte. 26, Oxford, 207/539-8865, www.oxfordplains.com), Maine's center for stock-car racing. From late April-mid-September, souped-up high-performance vehicles careen around the track in pursuit of substantial monetary prizes. Almost all races begin at 6:30pm.

Sleigh Rides

Don your winter warmies and snuggle under a lap blanket on a 40-minute sleigh ride with **High View Farm** (4 Leander Harmon Rd., Harrison, 207/596-1601, www.high-view-farm.com, $70 for four, plus $5 each additional person). Add a stop in the woods for a bonfire with roasted marshmallows and hot chocolate for $35. Rides are offered 11am-7pm, are private, and are by reservation only.

ENTERTAINMENT

Established in 1972 by the late mime master Tony Montanaro, **Celebration Barn Theater** (190 Stock Farm Rd., South Paris, 207/743-8452, www.celebrationbarn.com) specializes in physical theater entertainment, but other performances salt the schedule. Performances are open to the public in the 125-seat barn at 8pm most Saturdays June-August. Reservations are required; most tickets run $10-18. The theater also offers residential workshops for aspiring mimes, storytellers, comedians, and the like.

The **Oxford Casino** (Rte. 26, Oxford, 207/539-6700, www.oxfordcasino.com) has slot machines and table games.

Festivals and Events

More than 100 artists participate in the **Norway Music & Arts Festival** (www.nmaaf.org), the second weekend in July, which also has street entertainment and other activities.

Founders' Day (www.hamlin.lib.me.us) brings craft and antiques exhibits, music, and an antique-car open house to Paris Hill Common in Paris Hill the third Saturday in July. A special highlight is a one-day showing of Robert and Sandra Bahre's world-class collection of more than 60 vehicles, including Packards, Duesenbergs, Stutz Bearcats, and more.

The name of North Waterford's **World's Fair** (www.waterfordworldsfair.org) seems sort of cheeky for this three-day country medley of agricultural events, egg-throwing contests, a talent show, live music, dancing, and more in mid-July.

The family-oriented four-day agricultural **Oxford County Fair** (www.oxfordcounty-fair.com), "The Horse-Powered Fair," held in mid-September, features 4-H exhibits, a beauty pageant, a pig scramble, live entertainment, an apple-pie contest, and plenty of crafts and food booths at the Oxford County Fairgrounds.

SHOPPING

Norway's Main Street has the best selection of independent shops in the area, with many offering works by local artists. These include the **Tribune Books & Gifts** (430 Main St., Norway, 207/739-6200), which often hosts readings and book groups; **Fiber & Vine** (402 Main St., 207/739-2664), a must for knitters and wine lovers; and two Western Maine Art Group facilities, the **Lajos Matolcsy Arts Center** (480 Main St., Norway, 207/739-6161, www.westernmaineartgroup.org) and the **Main Street Gallery** (426 Main St.).

Frost Farm Gallery (27 Pikes Hill, Norway, 207/743-8041, www.frostfarmgallery.com) hosts rotating exhibits.

Peruse more than 13,000 new, used, and out-of-print books as well as artwork at the **Maine Bookhouse** (1545 Main St./Rte. 26, Oxford, 207/743-9300, www.themainebookhouse.com).

It's hard to resist inhaling deeply upon entering **Maine Balsam Fir Products** (16 Morse Hill Rd., West Paris, 800/522-5726, www.mainebalsam.com), filled with balsam pillows, neck rolls, draft stoppers, trivets, and sachets along with oil, soap, clothing, quilts, and more, all jammed in a one-room shop adjacent to where the balsam products are made. Tours are offered when the schedule permits—just ask.

FOOD

Quick Bites

An emphasis on all-natural meats and local ingredients, along with occasional concerts and wine tastings and the area's best coffee, make **Café Nomad** (450 Main St., Norway, 207/739-2249, www.cafenomad.com, 7am-4pm Mon.-Thurs., 7am-9pm Fri., 8am-3pm Sat., $8-14) an especially popular local spot for breakfast, lunch (sandwiches), drinks, or dinner.

Pop into **Taste of Eden Vegan Café** (238 Main St., Norway, 207/739-6090, www.tasteofedencafe.com, 11am-5:30pm Mon.-Thurs., 11am-2:30pm Sun., $6-8) for inexpensive vegan fare, including soups, sandwiches, and daily specials.

A bright spot in the lackluster hubbub on the fast-food strip is **Rising Sun Cafe and Bakery** (130 Main St./Rte. 26, South Paris, 207/743-7046, www.risingsuncafebakery.com, 6am-4pm Tues.-Fri., 7am-2pm Sat., $6-8), a local fave for light fare.

"Everything Shirley makes is good," a regular told me as I debated between the scones, cookies, muffins, soups, pies, beans, and other homemade treats at **Hungry Hollow Country Store** (28 Bethel Rd./Rte. 26, West Paris, 207/674-3012, 7am-5:30pm Mon.-Sat., 10am-5:30pm Sun.). Everything is made from scratch using unbleached flour and natural sea salt, and is prepared without trans fats.

Local produce, honey, organic meat, perennials, preserves, syrup, cheese, and baked goods are all part of the stock at **Norway Farmers Market,** which sets up downtown at Witherell Park on Main St. 2pm-6pm Thursdays late May-October.

In addition to fresh produce, **Smedburg's Farm** (1408 Main St., Oxford, 207/743-6723, 7am-7pm daily) sells fresh bread, pies, prepared foods, condiments, cheeses, and farm-made ice cream. Another farm stand worth a look-see is **Crestholm Farm Stand and Ice Cream** (177 Main St., Oxford, 207/539-8832, http://crestholmfarm.com, 9am-8pm daily), which also sells farm-made ice cream and has a free petting zoo.

Yet another choice for homemade ice cream is the **Inside Scoop** (156 Main St., South Paris, 207/461-2300, http://www.insidescoopmaine.com, 11am-9pm daily), offering both hard and soft serve.

Family Favorites

Norway Brewing Company (237 Main St., Norway, 207/739-2126, www.norwaybrewing.com, 2pm-9pm Mon.-Fri., 11am-3pm and 4pm-9pm Sat.-Sun., $9-16) serves snacks, small plates, sandwiches, and a couple of heartier choices, along with kid-pleasers, in its taproom and garden.

Depending on the season, you can pick fresh strawberries, blueberries, apples, or pumpkins at **Pietree Orchard** (803 Waterford Rd., Sweden, 207/647-9419, www.pietreeorchards.com), owned by author Tabitha King (wife of author Stephen), but the best reasons to go are for the cider doughnuts and the brick-oven pizza (available daily 11:30am-3pm). Enjoy your food on the picnic tables overlooking the orchards with views to distant mountains. The farm store also sells house-made breads, pies, jams, and other goodies.

Craving 'cue? **Smokin' Dave's Backyard BBQ & Grill** (230 Main St., Norway, 207/744-2578, www.smokindavesbackyardbbq.com, from 11am Wed.-Sun., $6-15) delivers, with a family- and budget-pleasing menu.

It doesn't look like much from the exterior, but **Riverside Lodge & Sauna** (20 Paris Hill Rd., Paris, 207/744-2412, www.riversidelodgeandsauna.com, 4pm-9pm Thurs.-Sat., 3pm-8pm Sun., $5-20) dishes out good pizzas, hearty soups, and comfort food specials. Call in advance and book a private wood-fired sauna or a massage.

Wood oven-fired pizza is the specialty of **Oxbow Beer Garden** (420 Rte. 26., Oxford, 207/539-5178, https://oxbowbeer.com, from 4pm Wed.-Sun., $10-18), with inside and outdoor seating.

Casual Dining

Bret and Amy Baker have meticulously renovated an 1896 former judge's mansion into the region's best restaurant at ★ **76 Pleasant St.** (76 Pleasant St., Norway, 207/744-9040, www.76pleasantstreet.com, from 5pm Tues.-Sun. July-Aug, fewer nights off season, $23-28). The two dining rooms and lounge balance comfortable, contemporary furnishings with the building's architectural elegance. Dining is a treat, with seasonal New American choices.

Open since 1976, **Maurice Restaurant** (109 Main St./Rte. 26, South Paris, 207/743-2532, www.mauricerestaurant.com, lunch 11am-1:30pm Tues.-Fri., dinner 4pm-8pm Tues.-Sat., brunch 11am-1:30pm Sun., $12-24) has stood the test of time; the decor reflects its age. Renowned for French cuisine when it opened, it now also offers homestyle classics. It's had its ups and downs over the decades, but it remains one of the region's reliable options.

By reservation, Barbara Vanderzanden will prepare a four-course dinner for inn guests and nonguests at the peaceful **Waterford Inne** (258 Chadbourne Rd., Waterford, 207/583-4037, www.waterfordinne.com, no credit cards). The leisurely meal is $48 pp; spring for it, as she does a wonderful job. BYOB.

ACCOMMODATIONS

Barbara Vanderzanden's traditionally elegant ★ **Waterford Inne** (258 Chadbourne Rd., Waterford, 207/583-4037, www.waterfordinne.com, $135-200), an antiques-filled 19th-century farmhouse on 25 open and wooded acres with a pond, is everything a classic country inn should be. Rooms are bright and airy and one has a woodstove and porch. Public rooms are spacious and inviting, as is the screened-in porch. A full breakfast is included; a scrumptious four-course dinner is available by reservation for $48. Children are welcome, and pets are allowed for $25 per night. The inn is close to East Waterford, 0.5 mile west of Route 37. No credit cards.

The **Bear Mountain Inn** (364 Waterford Rd./Rte. 35, South Waterford, 207/583-4404, www.bearmtninn.com, from $180), a beautifully updated 1820s B&B overlooking Bear Pond (it's really a lake), is one of those places that's hard to leave, especially after you settle in on the pond-view terrace or the beach. On the premises are boats, docks, hammocks, a lake-view hot tub, even trails up Bear and Hawk Mountains. The self-contained sugar maple cottage, with fireplace and kitchenette, is pet friendly ($20).

INFORMATION

The **Oxford Hills Chamber of Commerce** (4 Western Ave., South Paris, 207/743-2281, www.oxfordhillsmaine.com) produces an annual magazine that's an interesting read and is far less promotional than the usual CC material. **Downtown Norway Maine** (www.norwaydowntown.org) covers Norway.

GETTING THERE AND AROUND

South Paris is roughly 19 miles or 30 minutes from Bridgton via Route 117. It's about 14 miles or 22 minutes from Poland via Route 26, about 24 miles or 45 minutes to Lewiston via Routes 26 and 11. Plan on 24 miles or 30 minutes to Bethel via Route 26 and 45 miles or 65 minutes to Portland via Route 26 and I-95.

Poland Spring

The section of Route 26 between the Maine Turnpike (I-95) exit in Gray and **Poland** (pop. 1,795) is rich in historical sites and worthwhile attractions, including a wildlife park, the world's last inhabited Shaker village, the remains of the Poland Spring House, and the source of famed Poland Spring water.

It was the water's fame that helped the Ricker family grow a small hotel into the Poland Spring House, a 300-room hotel that was an architectural and technological marvel. Also on their 5,000-acre property was the world's first resort golf course and one of the first courses designed by Donald Ross. During the resort's heyday in the early 20th century, the richest and most powerful people in the country gathered in Poland Spring to play golf and discuss world policy. Almost every U.S. president from Ulysses S. Grant to Theodore Roosevelt stayed here. Other guests and visitors of note include Babe Ruth, Alexander Graham Bell, Mae West, Betty Grable, and Judy Garland; Charles Lindbergh flew over the hotel on July 25, 1927, but was unable to land because of the crowds.

The Poland Spring House was destroyed by fire in 1975, but the Maine State Building and the All Souls Chapel remain open to visitors, and the original spring that started it all can be viewed.

SIGHTS

★ Poland Spring

It was Poland Spring Water that built Hiram Ricker's family empire, and a visit to Poland Spring should include **Poland Spring Preservation Park** (207/998-7143, www.polandspring.com, 9am-4pm Thurs.-Sat.), home to the Poland Spring Museum and Spring House (both free), to learn about the legendary healing power of the water. The Maine State Building and All Souls Chapel are also both maintained by the **Poland Spring Preservation Society** (207/998-4142, www.polandspringps.org, 9am-4pm Mon. and Thurs.-Sat., 9am-11am Sun. late May-mid-Oct., 9am-4pm Fri.-Sat., 9am-11am Sun. spring and fall, donation requested).

Begin at the **Poland Spring Museum,** where exhibits detail the history of the famed water and explain its origins. The water won the Medal of Excellence at the 1893 Chicago World's Fair, and the Grand Prize at the 1904 St. Louis World's Fair. After touring the exhibits, visit the Spring House. Nature trails lace the grounds and connect to the other sites.

The three-story octagonal **Maine State Building** was built as the state pavilion for the 1893 Chicago World's Fair. Afterward, Ricker bought it for $30,000 and moved it to Maine aboard a special freight train and then via horse-drawn wagon to Ricker Hill, where it was reassembled piece by piece. One year later, it reopened as a library and art museum as part of the Ricker family's centennial celebration of their settlement at Poland Spring. Although it suffered years of neglect in the mid-20th century, it has been restored and is now operated by the Poland Spring Preservation Society as a museum and art gallery. Also displayed here is the Maine Golf Hall of Fame collection.

The Ricker Family built the adjacent **All Souls Chapel** in 1912 with donations from guests and staff of the Poland Spring House. The 1926 Skinner pipe organ and a set of Westminster chimes are still in working order.

★ Shaker Museum

Only a handful of Shakers remain in the world's last inhabited Shaker community, located three miles south of Poland Spring Resort. Nonetheless, the members of the United Society of Shakers, an 18th-century religious sect, keep a relatively high profile with a living-history museum, craft workshops, a store, publications, a mail-order herb and gift business, and even a music CD. (See their website for the wonderful herb and herbal tea catalog.) Each year more than 8,000 visitors arrive at **Sabbathday Lake Shaker Community** (707 Shaker Rd., New Gloucester, 207/926-4597, 10am-4:30pm Mon.-Sat., http://maineshakers.com) to catch a glimpse of an endangered lifestyle. The 75-minute basic guided tours ($10 adults, $2 ages 6-12) begin at 10:30am and are given every hour on the half hour, except for the last tour of the day, given at 3:15pm. Entry to the *Creating Chosen Land: Our Home 1783-1920* exhibit, or a Shaker Herb Garden Tour, is $7 adults, $2 kids; both are included with the guided tours. The Shakers also welcome the public to their 10am Sunday Meeting worship, where men and women enter through separate doors and sit separately. Check the special events calendar for workshops, demonstrations, herb garden tours, and the annual **Maine Festival of American Music** concert weekend. No pets are permitted on the grounds.

Twice each year on Saturdays in late May and mid-October, the Friends of the Shakers at Sabbathday Lake (www.friendsoftheshakers.org), a nonprofit group (annual membership $30 individual, $40 family), organizes **Friends' Work Day,** when 3-4 dozen volunteers show up at 10am to do spring and fall cleanup chores. The all-day work party includes a communal dinner.

Maine Wildlife Park

If you want to see where Maine's wild things are, visit the **Maine Wildlife Park** (56 Game Farm Rd., Gray, 207/657-4977, www.mainewildlifepark.com, 9:30am-6pm daily mid-Apr.-early Nov., gate closes 4:30pm, $7.50 ages 13-59, $5.50 ages 4-12 and 60 plus), located four miles south of the Shaker Village. Today the park is a temporary haven for orphaned and injured wildlife, although those who cannot survive in the wild live here permanently. Approximately 30 native species of wildlife can be seen at this state-operated wildlife refuge, including such ever-popular species as moose, black bears, white-tailed deer, and bald eagles.

In addition to the wildlife, there are numerous interactive exhibits and displays to view, nature trails to explore, the Warden Museum, a fish hatchery, a nature store, a snack shack, trails, and even picnic facilities. Special programs and exhibits are often offered on weekends mid-May-mid-September. The park offers a Photographer's Pass, which

Sabbathday Lake is the last inhabited Shaker community in the world.

provides special access to wildlife enclosures, for $50/hour by advance reservation only. Bring quarters to purchase food to feed the critters. During July-August, wildlife talks and a children's story and craft program are often offered; call for current schedule. At any time, this is a great spot for young families.

The park is 3.5 miles north of the Maine Turnpike (I-95) Exit 63. From the coast, take Route 115 from Main Street in downtown Yarmouth to Gray, and then head north on Route 26 for 3.5 miles.

ENTERTAINMENT

Each summer, **Poland Spring Preservation Society** hosts a series of weekly concerts, held either outdoors, in the Maine Inn, or in the All Souls Chapel. The music varies from acoustic guitar to jazz.

RECREATION

Range Ponds State Park

Brimming with swimmers when the temperature skyrockets, **Range Ponds State Park** (Empire Rd., Poland, 207/998-4104, www.parksandlands.com) has a swimming area that includes a lifeguard and a bathhouse. The park also offers picnicking as well as a playground and two miles of nature trails. (Part of the trail verges on a marsh; be prepared with bug repellent.) The beach, parking, restrooms, and picnic tables are wheelchair-accessible. Most of the park's acreage was once the estate of Hiram Ricker, owner of Poland Spring Water (now owned by Perrier/Nestle). Bring a canoe or kayak and launch it into Lower Range Pond. Admission is $8 nonresident adults, $6 Maine resident adults, $2 nonresident seniors, $1 ages 5-11; the park is open mid-May-mid-October. From Lewiston-Auburn, take Route 202/11/100 South to Route 122. Turn right (east) and continue to Empire Road in Poland Spring; the turnoff to the park is well signposted.

Pineland Farms

Once a home for people with developmental disabilities, the campus of **Pineland Farms** (15 Farm View Dr., New Gloucester, 207/688-4539, www.pinelandfarms.org, $5) was closed in 1996. Now the foundation-owned property comprises 19 buildings and 5,000 acres of working farmland, and much of it is open for recreation. Walk or ski the trails, sight birds in the fields and woods, stroll through the one-acre public garden planted with more than 130 varieties of perennials and 6,000 flowering annuals, fish the pond or skate on it in winter, play tennis or disc golf, go mountain biking or orienteering, or visit the Equestrian Center. It's a vast outdoor playground, but your first stop should be the market and visitors center (8am-7pm daily) to see a list of events (frequent ones include guided farm tours and family experiences), pick up maps, pay any necessary fees, shop for farm-fresh products, or even grab breakfast, lunch, or snacks in the café. Dogs are not allowed on the grounds.

Golf

The 18-hole **Poland Spring Country Club** (41 Ricker Rd., off Rte. 26, Poland Spring, 207/998-6002) was laid out in 1896 on the grounds of the long-gone Poland Spring House, a health spa. In 1915, Donald Ross added the second nine.

FOOD

Pair a paddle with a comfort meal at **Cyndi's Dockside** (Rte. 26 causeway, Poland Spring, 207/998-5008, www.dockside.me, 11:30am-8pm Sun.-Wed., 11:30am-9pm Thurs.-Sat., $9-24), a lakeside restaurant with a boat-rental facility on Middle Range Pond. Burgers, sandwiches, fried seafood, and lobster provide something for everyone, and there's a kids' menu too. Kayak, canoe, and paddleboat rentals are $8/hour.

You can't go wrong at the **New Gloucester Village Store** (405 Intervale Rd., New Gloucester, 207/926-4224, www.ngvillagestore.com, 6am-9pm Mon.-Sat., 7:30am-8pm Sun., $8-20), a bakery/deli with a wood-fired oven. Pizzas, sandwiches on house-made bread, salads, and breakfast fare are available, and there are also prepared foods to go and an extensive selection of wine and beer.

Just a few miles from the Shaker Village is **Bresca and the Honey Bee** (106 Outlet Rd., New Gloucester, 207/926-3388, www.brescaandthehoneybee.com, 11am-3pm Sat.-Sun., ice cream 11am-5pm daily late June-early Sept., $4-10, cash only), a take-out snack shack with a small café on Outlet Beach. What makes this place special is that it's operated by Krista Kearns Desjarlais, a respected chef who earned national kudos for a restaurant she owned in Portland. Salads, burgers, hot dogs, wood-grilled fare, house-made ice cream, and other specials are served during summer. During the rest of the year, she sells pastries, ployes, savory hand pies, and other goodies. If you want access to the beach and lake, admission is $5 adults, $3 ages 3-13.

Prefer frozen custard? **Ruby Rose Frozen Custard** (1184 Maine St., Poland, 207/998-2262, from noon daily) dishes out delicious, homemade frozen custard in regular and creative flavors. Don't miss the chocolate chip cookie custard sandwiches.

ACCOMMODATIONS

On the shores of Tripp Lake, the **Wolf Cove Inn Bed and Breakfast** (5 Jordan Shore Dr., Poland, 207/998-4976, www.wolfcoveinn.com, from $249) is a delightful spot to recoup. A dozen guest rooms and suites, some with fireplaces and/or spa tubs, and one cabin are named after Maine icons. Rates include a three-course breakfast and afternoon refreshments. Paddle around in one of the inn's canoes, kayaks, or rowboats, hang out on the private beach or dock, go for a swim in the lake, or relax in the gazebo. Sunsets are magnificent here. Ask about private lakefront dinners. A few rooms welcome dogs for $30/night.

For inexpensive digs, check in to the **Poland Spring Resort** (Rte. 26, Poland Spring, 207/998-4351, www.polandspringresort.com). The 500-acre resort comprises three inns, 10 cottages, three restaurants, an 18-hole golf course designed by Arthur Fenn, Donald Ross, and Walter Travis, a miniature golf course, an outdoor pool, three grass tennis courts, and various lawn games; nightly entertainment is offered. Accommodations are Spartan and dated (think 1970s time warp) but clean. A three-night weekend package including buffet-style, all-you-can-eat breakfast and dinner, lodging, and other activities goes for about $130-190/night, depending upon accommodations, for the whole shebang; add unlimited golf with a cart for $150 pp. Nightly rates begin at $99/room with breakfast. It's not for everyone, but it's a reliable cheap sleep if you're not fussy, and the meals are hearty comfort food. Some rooms are pet friendly ($20/night).

On the shore of Lower Range Pond, 40-acre **Poland Spring Campground** (Rte. 26, Poland Spring, 207/998-2151, www.polandspringcamp.com) has 130 wooded sites ($35-55 for two adults, three children, and one dog). Facilities include an outdoor pool, coin-op showers, a general store, laundry, play areas, and rental canoes, kayaks, and rowboats. There's plenty of organized fun; be prepared for campfires, ice cream parties, hay rides, barbecues, and other activities, although noise rules are enforced. The campground is about 10 miles west of Auburn.

INFORMATION

Pick up a copy of the brochure or visit online for more information about the **Gems of Route 26** (www.gemsof26.com).

GETTING THERE AND AROUND

Poland is about 14 miles or 22 minutes from South Paris via Route 26 and roughly 23 miles from Bridgton via Routes 302 and 11. It's about 11 miles or 30 minutes to Lewiston via Route 11.

Lewiston and Auburn

A river runs through the heart of **Lewiston** (pop. 1,795) and **Auburn** (pop. 1,842)—the Androscoggin River, whose headwaters are in the Rangeley Lakes, courses southeastward until it joins the Kennebec River in Merrymeeting Bay near Brunswick. Surging over Great Falls, the mighty Androscoggin spurred 19th-century industrial development of the twin cities, where giant textile mills drew their power from the river and their hardworking employees from the local community of Yankees, then Irish, French Canadian, and other immigrants. The Québécois and Acadian French, who flocked to mills in Lewiston, Biddeford, Sanford, Augusta, and Brunswick, today constitute Maine's largest ethnic minority. In Lewiston and Auburn, the French-accented voting registers reveal long lists of Plourdes and Pomerleaus, Carons and Cloutiers, and the spires of Catholic churches still dominate the skyline.

Lewiston and Auburn also have quite a sporting heritage in boxing and skiing. World-class boxer Joey Gamache emerged from the local clubs, and the controversial world title fight between Sonny Liston and Muhammad Ali took place here in 1965. Olympic skiers Karl Anderson and Julie, Anna, and Rob Parisien are also local products.

Auburn's Mount Apatite has produced record-setting tourmalines, Maine's state gemstone, as well as quartz and feldspar. Now owned by the city, the mountain is open to the prospecting public.

Lewiston and Auburn, known locally as "the other LA," are still not typical vacation destinations, but they deserve more than a drive-through glance. Lewiston is the state's second-largest city and home to Bates College, a highly selective private liberal arts school and a magnet for visiting performers, artists, and lecturers. Another plus is the easy access to Portland (35 miles away) and Freeport (28 miles), the western mountains, and Augusta (30 miles).

SIGHTS

Bates College

Founded in 1855 on foresighted egalitarian principles, **Bates College** (2 Andrews Rd., Lewiston, 207/786-6255, www.bates.edu) occupies a lovely, wooded campus in the heart of Lewiston. The oldest campus building is red-brick **Hathorn Hall,** built in 1856 and listed in the National Register of Historic Places; one of the newest buildings, the Olin Arts Center, built in 1986, is an award-winning complex overlooking artificial Lake Andrews.

Within the **Olin Arts Center** (Russell St. and Bardwell St., 207/786-6135) are the **Bates College Museum of Art** (75 Russell St., 207/786-6259) and the 300-seat **Olin Concert Hall.** Most college-sponsored exhibits, lectures, and concerts at the arts center are free and open to the public (other organizations also use the concert hall). At 6pm on some Thursdays mid-July to mid-August, free **concerts on the quad** are presented; bring a picnic and seating. The **Bates College Museum of Art** (10am-5pm Tues.-Sat., free), with rotating exhibits, is open all year. A significant stop on the Maine Art Museum Trail, it emphasizes works on paper, especially by Maine artists, including Lewiston-born modernist Marsden Hartley.

The college has won national and international acclaim for the summertime (mid-July-mid-Aug.) **Bates Dance Festival** (207/786-6161, www.batesdancefestival.org), featuring modern-dance workshops, lectures, and performances. Student and faculty programs, most presented in 300-seat Schaeffer Theater, are open to the public and often sell out.

Bates is the repository of the **Edmund S. Muskie Archives** (70 Campus Ave., 207/786-6354, 8:30am-noon and 1pm-5pm Mon.-Fri.),

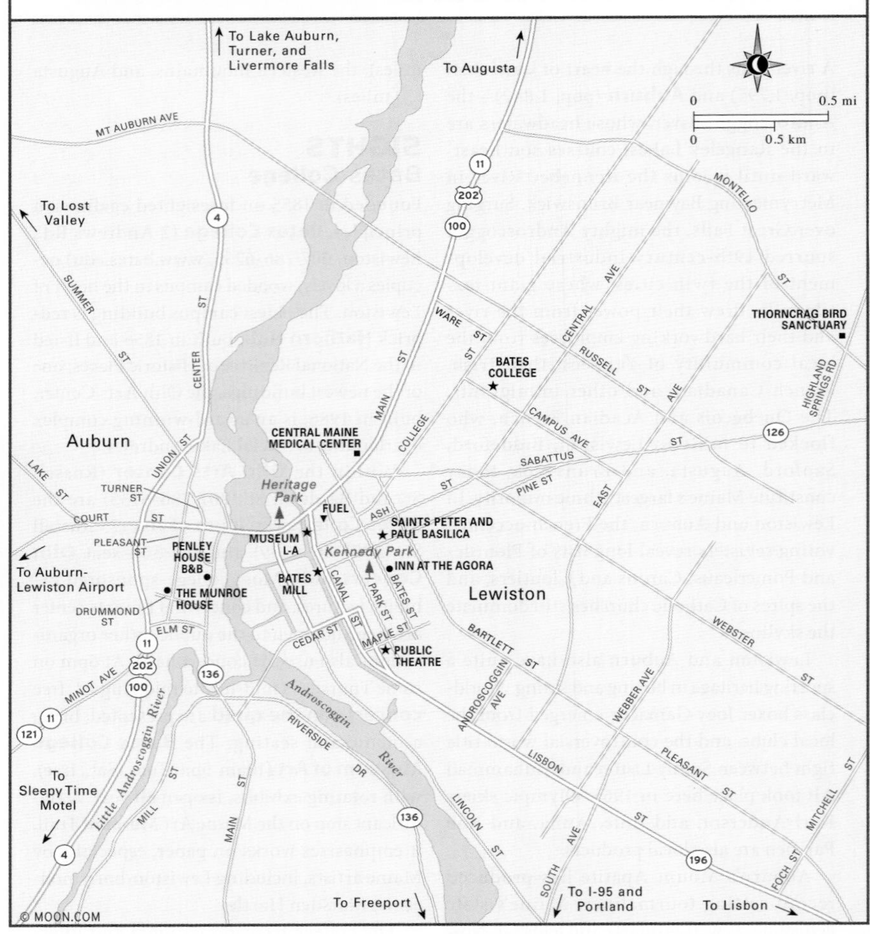

containing the papers of the 1936 Bates graduate and former Maine governor, U.S. senator, and U.S. secretary of state who died in 1996.

At the western edge of the campus, at the corner of Mountain Avenue and College Street, walk up **Mount David** (actually a grandly named hill) for a surprisingly good view of the Lewiston-Auburn skyline.

Bates Mill

Thanks to a progressive public-private partnership, the 19th-century Bates Mill complex, on Canal Street in downtown Lewiston, is being revitalized for a variety of new uses. Occupying 1.2 million square feet in 12 buildings spread over six acres, the mill once produced nearly a third of the nation's textiles. Since 1992, much of the hulking brick complex has been undergoing a long-term makeover—offices, studios, shops, restaurants, and even a museum have trickled in, helping the mill to reinvent itself.

MUSEUM L-A

If you want to understand Lewiston and Auburn, visit **Museum L-A** (35 Canal St., Lewiston, 207/333-3881, http://museumla.org, 10am-4pm Tues.-Fri., 10am-3pm Sat., $5 adults, $4 seniors and students). Appropriately situated inside the Bates Mill Complex, a visit immerses you into the region's industrial heyday; it's almost as if you can hear the machines and chatter as you tour the mill space. Exhibits tell the stories of LA's immigrant communities and document the region's textile-, brick-, and shoe-manufacturing industries. Free tours are available. The museum also partnered to create the online **Franco Trail L-A** (https://franco-trail.herokuapp.com), which maps Lewiston-Auburn's French heritage, making it easy to create a self-guided tour.

Saints Peter and Paul Basilica

The Gothic Revival Roman Catholic **Saints Peter and Paul Basilica** (122 Ash St., Lewiston, 207/777-1200, http://princeofpeace.me), listed in the National Register of Historic Places, is noteworthy for its rose window, a replica of one in the Chartres Cathedral. The second-largest church in New England is capable of seating more than 2,000 for its separate services in English and French. Dedicated in 1938, it was designated a basilica in 2006. Noonday and evening concerts, many featuring the magnificent Casavant organ, are scheduled during the summer.

ENTERTAINMENT

Throughout the year, **Bates College** (207/786-6255 weekdays, www.bates.edu) presents concerts, lectures, exhibits, sporting events, and other activities. Among the summer highlights is the five-week **Bates Dance Festival** (www.batesdancefestival.org) featuring world-class dance companies.

The former St. Mary's Church, considered one of the finest examples of Renaissance architecture in the country, has found new life as the **Gendron FrancoCenter** (46 Cedar St., Lewiston, 207/783-1585, box office 207/689-2000, www.francocenter.org), a performing arts center.

L/A Arts (207/782-7228, www.laarts.org) sponsors **Art Walk LA** (5pm-8pm on the final Friday of the month, May-Oct.).

Lewiston-Auburn's professional theater company, the **Public Theatre** (31 Maple St., Lewiston, box office 207/782-3200, www.thepublictheatre.org), presents musicals and dramas with Equity professionals.

The **Maine Music Society** (207/782-1403, 207/782-7228 box office, www.mainemusicsociety.org) presents classical concerts featuring the Maine Music Society Chorale at the Franco Center and Basilica.

Auburn's riverside Festival Plaza is the venue for the extremely popular **Auburn Community Band Concerts** at 7pm Wednesdays July-August.

Festivals and Events

The **Moxie Festival** (www.moxiefestival.com), a certifiably eccentric annual celebration of the obscure soft drink Moxie, invented in 1884 and still not consigned to the dustbin of history, occurs in downtown Lisbon in mid-July.

August brings the **Great Falls Balloon Festival**, with food, entertainment, a carnival, fireworks, and, of course, balloon launches.

The **Dempsey Challenge** run, walk, and cycle fundraiser in October provides an opportunity to see Dr. McDreamy (actor Patrick Dempsey, who grew up in these parts).

RECREATION

Parks and Preserves

The **Androscoggin Land Trust** (www.androscogginlandtrust.org) protects the area's natural resources. Check the website for places to hike, bike, paddle, and fish; maps; and opportunities such as guided walks or paddles.

Thorncrag Bird Sanctuary

You can bird-watch, hike, cross-country ski, and snowshoe on 372 acres within the city limits of Lewiston in one of New England's largest

1
2

bird sanctuaries. At the 450-acre **Thorncrag Bird Sanctuary** (Montello St., Lewiston, 207/782-5238, www.stantonbirdclub.org, dawn-dusk daily year-round, free), pick up a trail map at the gate and head out on the three miles of well-maintained, color-coded, easy-to-moderate trails—past ponds, an old cellar hole, stone memorials, and benches and through stands of beeches, hemlocks, white pines, and mixed hardwoods; bring a picnic. Throughout the year the **Stanton Bird Club** offers free, open-to-the-public bird walks; call or see its website for the schedule. From downtown Lewiston, take Sabattus Street (Rte. 126) east about three miles to Highland Springs Road. Turn left (north) and continue to the end at Montello Street. You'll be facing the entrance to the sanctuary. No dogs or bicycles are permitted.

Rockhounding

For sheer fun, spend a few hours searching for apatite, tourmaline, and quartz at **Mount Apatite Park** (Hatch Rd., off Rte. 11/121, Auburn, dawn-dusk), a 325-acre park that's been popular with rock hounds for more than 150 years.

FOOD

Quick Bites

Named for the river running through town, ★ **Nezinscot Farm Store** (284 Turner Center Rd./Rte. 117, Turner, 207/225-3231, www.nezinscotfarm.com, 7am-5pm Thurs.-Sun., café to 3pm), Maine's first organic farm, is worth the detour. Besides organically grown produce, the farm makes its own organic baked goods, cheeses, charcuterie, cream products, and herbal products and sells plenty of other local goods. The café makes breakfast and lunch to order ($6-15) and offers themed, outdoor farm dinners on Fridays in July and August ($25-35 pp). The shop sells all-natural wool yarns from the farm's sheep, llamas, alpacas, and goats. Nezinscot also offers **tenting sites** here and on its North Farm pasture ($35). The farm is five miles east and north of the junction of Routes 4 and 117 (about 16 miles north of downtown Auburn). Call ahead to confirm hours if you're making a special trip.

The **Italian Bakery Products Co.** (225 Bartlett St., Lewiston, 207/782-8312, http://theitalianbakery.biz, 6am-5:30pm Tues.-Fri., 6am-3pm Sat., 6am-noon Sun., $4-10) is a great little place to pick up baked goods such as cannoli or bismarck doughnuts; sandwiches, soups, and pizzas for lunch; and daily specials such as Saturday beans. There is no seating.

Forage Market (180 Lisbon St., Lewiston, 207/333-6840, www.foragemarket.com, 7am-3pm Mon.-Sat., 8am-3pm Sun., $3-10) is a grab-and-go market (with seating) selling soups, sandwiches, wood-fired pizzas, and Montreal-style bagels that earned recognition from *Saveur*, along with daily specials.

Family Favorites

In the retrofitted Bates Mill, **DaVinci's Eatery** (150 Mill St., Lewiston, 207/782-2088, www.davinciseatery.com, 11am-9pm Sun.-Thurs., 11am-10pm Fri.-Sat.) specializes in pasta and brick-oven pizza but has a variety of other regional American and Italian entrées in the $14-25 range. A lunchtime pizza buffet is served on weekdays.

Hipsters take note: **She Doesn't Like Guthries** (115 Middle St., Lewiston, 207/376-3344, www.guthriesplace.com, 10am-8pm Mon.-Thurs., 10am-10pm Fri., $8-12), a Maine-certified Green Restaurant, has you covered. Begin with eclectic music, then add local art, live entertainment on Friday nights, and an ecofriendly mission; top it off with inexpensive, well-prepared healthful fare that includes veggie, vegan, and wheat-free choices and even a kids' menu. Expect burritos, quesadillas, soups made from scratch, salads, and similar fare. And don't worry, even if you're not hip, you'll like this place.

1: Saints Peter and Paul Basilica **2:** Munroe Inn

Casual Dining

Fish Bones Grill (70 Lincoln St., Lewiston, 207/333-3663, www.fishbonesag.com, 11:30am-9:30pm Mon.-Fri., 4pm-9:30pm Sat., $12-31), in a renovated mill with handsome brick-accented decor, serves regionally focused American fare both inside and on a terrace. It also offers a two- ($16) or three-course menu ($21) 11am-5pm Mon.-Fri. and occasional wine dinners.

ACCOMMODATIONS

The **Munroe Inn** (123 Pleasant St., Auburn, 207/376-3266, www.themunroeinn.com, $180-200), an elegant restored National Historic Register-listed Queen Anne manse, is rich in exquisite woodwork and stained glass. Five spacious guest rooms and first-floor public rooms are furnished with period antiques. Children and dogs are welcome.

The Queen Anne-style **Penley House Bed & Breakfast** (233 Main St., Auburn, 207/786-4800, www.penleyhouse.com, $125-140) is in Auburn's historic district, an easy walk from downtown attractions. Each of the four air-conditioned guest rooms has a private bath, but three are detached.

Built in the mid-19th-century, the Italianate-style **Inn at the Agora** (1 Walnut St., Lewiston, 855/552-4672, www.innattheagora.com, $230-270) served as St. Patrick's rectory from 1886 to 2009, when the church closed. In 2014, after major renovations designed to keep its architectural features while adding modern necessities, it reopened as a five-suite inn. Breakfast isn't included, but a discount coupon is offered for nearby restaurants. Pets are a possibility ($25).

Charmingly retro and immaculately clean, the six-room **Sleepy Time Motel** (46 Danville Corner Rd., Auburn, 207/783-1435, www.sleepytimemotel.com, $109) offers a lot of bang for the buck. The five-acre property abuts 100 woodsy acres that are laced with three miles of trails for hiking and snowshoeing.

INFORMATION

The **Lewiston Auburn Metropolitan Chamber of Commerce** (207/783-2249, https://lametrochamber.com) serves as the tourism information center for the entire county.

GETTING THERE AND AROUND

Lewiston is roughly 11 miles or 30 minutes from Poland via Route 11. It's 20 miles or 40 minutes to Brunswick via Route 196 and 38 miles or 45 minutes to Portland via I-95.

Background

The Landscape

Maine is an outdoor classroom, a living lesson in what the glaciers did and how they did it. Geologically, Maine is something of a youngster; the oldest rocks, found in the Chain of Ponds area in the western part of the state, are only 1.6 billion years old—more than 2 billion years younger than the world's oldest rocks.

Most significant is the great ice sheet that began to spread over Maine about 25,000 years ago, during the late Wisconsin Ice Age. As it moved southward from Canada, this continental glacier scraped, gouged, pulverized, and depressed the bedrock in its path. Onward

it continued, charging up the north faces of mountains, clipping off their tops and moving southward, leaving behind jagged cliffs on the mountains' southern faces and odd deposits of stone and clay. By about 21,000 years ago, glacial ice extended well over the Gulf of Maine, perhaps as far as the Georges Bank fishing grounds.

But all that began to change with meltdown, beginning about 18,000 years ago. As the glacier melted and receded, ocean water moved in, covering much of the coastal plain and working its way inland up the rivers. By 11,000 years ago, glaciation had pulled back from all but a few minor corners at the top of Maine, revealing the south coast's beaches and the unusual geologic traits—eskers and erratics, kettleholes and moraines, even a fjord—that make the rest of the state such a fascinating natural laboratory.

TODAY'S LANDSCAPE

Along the **Southern Coast,** from Kittery to Portland, are fine-sand beaches, marshlands, and only the occasional rocky headland. The **Mid-Coast** and **Penobscot Bay,** from Portland to the Penobscot River, feature one finger of rocky land after another, all jutting into the Gulf of Maine and all incredibly scenic. **Acadia** and the **Down East Coast,** from the Penobscot River to Eastport and including fantastic Acadia National Park, has many similarities to the Mid-Coast (gorgeous rocky peninsulas, offshore islands, granite everywhere), but, except on Mount Desert Island, takes on a different look and feel by virtue of its slower pace, higher tides, and quieter villages.

Turn inland toward the **Maine Highlands,** and the landscape changes again. The Down East mountains, roughly straddling "the Airline" (Route 9 from Bangor to Calais), are marked by open blueberry fields, serious woodlands, and mountains that seem to appear out of nowhere. The central upland—essentially a huge S-shape extending from the Portland area up to the **Kennebec River Valley,** through Augusta, Waterville, and Skowhegan, then on up into **Aroostook County** at the top of the state—is characterized by lakes, ponds, rolling fields, and occasional woodlands interspersed with river valleys. Aroostook County is the state's agricultural jackpot. The northern region—essentially the valleys of the north-flowing St. John and Allagash Rivers—was the last part of Maine to lose the glacier and is today dense forest crisscrossed with logging roads (you can count the settlements on two hands). The mountain upland, taking in all the state's major elevations and extending from inland York County to Baxter State Park and west through the **Western Lakes and Mountains** is rugged, beautiful, and the premier region for skiing, hiking, camping, and white-water rafting. Here, too, are seemingly endless lakes for swimming, boating, and birding.

GEOGRAPHY

Bounded by the Gulf of Maine (Atlantic Ocean), the St. Croix River, New Brunswick Province, the St. John River, Québec Province, and the state of New Hampshire, Maine is the largest of the six New England states, roughly equivalent in size to the five others combined—offering plenty of space to hike, bike, camp, sail, swim, or just hang out. The state—and the coastline—extends from 43° 05' to 47° 28' north latitude and 66° 56' to 80° 50' west longitude. (Technically, Maine dips even farther southeast to take in five islands in the offshore Isles of Shoals archipelago.)

Maine's more than 5,000 rivers and streams provide nearly half of the watershed for the Gulf of Maine. The major rivers are the Penobscot (350 miles), the St. John (211 miles), the Androscoggin (175 miles), the Kennebec (150 miles), the Saco (104 miles), and the St. Croix (75 miles). The St. John and

---

Previous: Height of Land along the Rangeley Lakes Scenic Byway.

its tributaries flow northeast; all the others flow more or less south or southeast.

The Pine Tree State has more than 17 million acres of forest covering 89 percent of the state, 5,900 lakes and ponds, 4,617 saltwater islands, 10 mountains over 4,000 feet, and nearly 100 mountains higher than 3,000 feet. The highest peak in the state is Katahdin, at 5,267 feet. (Katahdin is a Penobscot Indian word meaning "greatest mountain," making "Mount Katahdin" redundant.)

Maine's largest lake is Moosehead, in Greenville, 32 miles long and 20 miles across at its widest point, with a maximum depth of 246 feet.

CLIMATE

The National Weather Service assigns Maine's coastline a climatological category distinct from climatic types found in the interior. The coastal category, which includes Portland, runs from Kittery northeast to Eastport and about 20 miles inland. Here, the ocean moderates the climate, making coastal winters warmer and summers cooler than in the interior (relatively speaking, of course). From early June through August, the Portland area—fairly typical of coastal weather—may have 3-8 days of temperatures over 90°F, 25-40 days over 80°F, 14-24 days of fog, and 5-10 inches of rain. Normal annual precipitation for the Portland area is 44 inches of rain and 71 inches of snow (the snow total is misleading, though, since intermittent thaws clear away much of the base).

The **southern interior** division, covering the bottom third of the state, sees the warmest weather in summer, the most clear days each year, and an average snowfall of 60-90 inches. The **northern interior** part of the state, with the highest mountains, covers the upper two-thirds of Maine and boasts a mixed bag of snowy winters, warm summers, and the state's lowest rainfall.

The Seasons

Maine has four distinct seasons: summer, fall, winter, and mud. Lovers of spring need to look elsewhere in March, the lowest month on the popularity scale with its mud-caked vehicles, soggy everything, irritable temperaments, tank-trap roads, and often the worst snowstorm of the year.

Summer can be idyllic—with moderate temperatures, clear air, and wispy breezes—but it can also close in with fog, rain, and chills. Prevailing winds are from the southwest. Officially, summer runs from June 20 or 21 to September 20 or 21, but June, July, and August is more like it, with temperatures in the Portland area averaging in the 70s°F during the day and in the 50s at night.

A poll of Mainers might well show **autumn** as the favorite season—days are still warmish, nights are cool, winds are optimum for sailors, and the foliage is brilliant.

Winter, officially December 20 or 21 to March 20 or 21, means deep snow and cold inland and an unpredictable potpourri along the coastline.

Spring, officially March 20 or 21 to June 20 or 21, is the frequent butt of jokes. It's an ill-defined season that arrives much too late and departs all too quickly

Northeasters and Hurricanes

A northeaster is a counterclockwise, swirling storm that brings wild winds out of—you guessed it—the northeast. These storms can occur any time of year, whenever the conditions brew them up. Depending on the season, the winds are accompanied by rain, sleet, snow, or all of them together. Hurricane season officially runs June-November but is most prevalent late August-September.

Sea Smoke and Fog

Sea smoke and fog, two atmospheric phenomena resulting from opposing conditions, are only distantly related, but both can radically affect visibility and therefore be hazardous. In winter, when the ocean is at least 40°F warmer than the air, billowy sea smoke rises from the water, creating great photo ops for camera buffs but especially dangerous conditions for mariners.

In any season, when the ocean (or lake or land) is colder than the air, fog sets in, creating perilous conditions for drivers, mariners, and pilots. Romantics, however, see it otherwise, reveling in the womblike ambience and the muffled moans of foghorns. Between April and October, Portland averages about 31 days with heavy fog, when visibility may be a quarter mile or less.

Storm Warnings

The National Weather Service's official daytime signal system for wind velocity consists of a series of flags representing specific wind speeds and sea conditions. Beachgoers and anyone planning to venture out in a kayak, canoe, sailboat, or powerboat should heed these signals. The flags are posted on all public beaches, and warnings are announced on TV and radio weather broadcasts, as well as on cable TV's Weather Channel and the NOAA broadcast network.

Plants and Animals

Note: This section was written by William P. Hancock, former director of the Environmental Centers Department at the Maine Audubon Society and former editor of *Habitat Magazine.*

Maine is proportionately the most forested state in the nation. It also is clearly one of the best watered. Receiving an average of more than 40 inches of precipitation a year, Maine is abundantly endowed with swamps, bogs, ponds, lakes, streams, and rivers. These in turn drain from a coast deeply indented by coves, estuaries, and bays.

In this state of trees and water, nature dominates more than most—Maine is the least densely populated state east of the Mississippi River. Here, where boreal and temperate ecosystems meet and mix, lives a rich diversity of plants and animals.

THE ALPINE TUNDRA

Three continental storm tracks converge on Maine, and the state's western mountains bear the brunt of the weather they bring. Stretching from Katahdin in the north along most of Maine's border with Québec and New Hampshire, these mountains have a far colder climate than their temperate latitude might suggest.

Timberline here occurs at only about 4,000 feet, and where the mountaintops reach above that, the environment is truly arctic—an alpine-tundra habitat where only the hardiest species can live. Beautiful pale-green "map" lichens cover many of the exposed rocks, and sedges and rushes take root in the patches of thin topsoil. As many as 30 alpine plant species, typically found hundreds of miles to the north, grow in crevices or hollows in the lee of the blasting winds. Small and low-growing to conserve energy in this harsh climate, such plants as **bearberry willow, Lapland rosebay, alpine azalea, *Diapensia,* mountain cranberry,** and **black crowberry** reward the observant hiker with white, yellow, pink, and magenta flowers in late June-July.

Areas above the tree line are generally inhospitable to most animals other than secretive **voles, mice,** and **lemmings.** Even so, summer or winter, a hiker is likely to be aware of at least one other species: the **northern raven.** More than any of the 300 or so other bird species that regularly occur in Maine, the raven is the bird of the state's wild places—its mountain ridges, rocky coasts, and remote forests.

At the tree line and below, where conditions are moderate enough to allow black spruce and balsam fir to take hold, fauna becomes far more diverse. Among the wind- and ice-stunted trees, called *krummholz* (crooked wood), **dark-eyed juncos** and **white-throated sparrows** forage. The latter's plaintive whistle (often mnemonically rendered as "Old Sam Peabody, Peabody, Peabody") is one of the most evocative sounds of the Maine woods.

THE BOREAL OR NORTHERN FOREST

Mention the Maine woods and the image that is likely to come to mind is the boreal forests of spruce and fir. Well-adapted to a short growing season, low temperatures, and rocky, nutrient-poor soils, spruce and fir do dominate the woods on mountainsides, in low-lying areas beside watercourses, and along the coast. By not having to produce new foliage every year, these evergreens conserve scarce nutrients and retain their needles, which capture sunlight for photosynthesis during all but the coldest months. The needles also wick moisture from the low clouds and fog that frequently bathe their preferred habitat, bringing annual precipitation to more than 80 inches a year in some areas.

In the lush boreal forest environment grows a diverse ground cover of herbaceous plants, including **bearberry, bunchberry, clintonia, starflower,** and **wood sorrel.** In older spruce-fir stands, mosses and lichens often carpet much of the forest floor in a soft tapestry of greens and gray-blues. Maine is extraordinarily rich in **lichens**, with more than 700 species identified so far—20 percent of the total found in North America. **Usnea** is a familiar one; its common name, old man's beard, comes from its wispy strands that drip from the branches of spruce trees. The **northern parula,** a small blue, green, and yellow bird of the wood warbler family, weaves its ball-shaped pendulum nest from usnea.

The spruce-fir forest is prime habitat for many other species that are among the most sought-after by birders: **black-backed** and **three-toed woodpeckers,** the audaciously bold **gray jay** (or camp robber), **boreal chickadees, yellow-throated flycatchers, white-winged crossbills, Swainson's thrushes,** and a half dozen other gem-like wood warblers.

Among the more unusual birds of this forest type is the spruce grouse. Sometimes hard to spot because it does not flush, a **spruce grouse** is so tame that a careful person can actually touch one. Not surprisingly, the spruce grouse earned the nickname "fool hen" early in the 19th century, and no doubt it would have become extinct long ago but for its menu preference of spruce and fir needles, which render its meat bitter and inedible.

Few of Maine's 56 mammal species are restricted to the boreal forest, but several are very characteristic of it. Most obvious from its trilling, far-carrying chatter is the **red squirrel.** Piles of cone remnants on the forest floor mark a red squirrel's recent banquet. The red squirrel itself is the favored prey of another coniferous forest inhabitant, the **pine marten.** An arboreal member of the mustelid family—which in Maine also includes **skunks, weasels, fishers,** and **otters**—the pine marten is a sleek, low-slung predator with blond to brown fur, an orange throat patch, and a long bushy tail. Its beautiful pelt nearly led to the animal's obliteration from Maine through overtrapping, but with protection, the marten population has rebounded.

Nearly half a century of protection also allowed the population recovery of Maine's most prominent mammal, the **moose.** Standing 6-7 feet tall at the shoulder and weighing as much as 1,200 pounds, the moose is the largest member of the Cervidae, or deer, family. A bull's massive antlers, which it sheds and regrows each year, may span five or more feet and weigh 75 pounds. The animal's long legs and bulbous nose give it an ungainly appearance, but the moose is ideally adapted to a life spent wading through deep snow, dense thickets, and swamps.

THE TRANSITION ZONE: NORTHERN HARDWOOD FOREST

Although hardwoods have replaced spruce and fir in many areas, mixed woods of sugar

Falling for Foliage

Autumn is a time of spectacular beauty in Maine's northern hardwood forest. With the shortening days and cooler temperatures of September, the dominant green chlorophyll molecules in deciduous leaves start breaking down. As they do, the yellow, orange, and red pigments (which are always present in the leaves and serve to capture light in parts of the spectrum not captured by the chlorophyll) are revealed. Sugar maples put on the most dazzling display, but beeches, birches, red maples, and poplars add their colors to make up an autumn landscape famous the world over.

The colorful display begins slowly, reaches a peak, and then fades—starting in the north in early-mid-September and working down to the southwest corner by mid-October. Peak foliage in far-north Aroostook County usually occurs in late September, about three weeks after the colors have begun to appear. Along the South Coast and Mid-Coast, the peak can occur as late as the middle of October, with the last bits of color hanging on even beyond that.

Trees put on their most magnificent show after a summer of moderate heat and rainfall; a summer of excessive heat and scant rainfall means colors will be less brilliant and disappear more quickly. Throw a September or October northeaster or hurricane into the mix, and estimates are up for grabs.

Predictions are imprecise, and you'll need to allow some schedule flexibility to take advantage of the changes in different parts of the state. Mid-September-mid-October, check the state's **Department of Conservation website** (www.mainefoliage.com) for frequently updated maps, panoramic photographs, and reports on the foliage status (this is gauged by the percentage of dropped leaves in every region of the state). Or call the **Foliage Hotline** (888/624-6345). Another resource for info on driving tours during foliage season is the website of the **Maine Office of Tourism** (www.visitmaine.com).

maple, American beech, yellow birch, red oak, red spruce, eastern hemlock, and white pine have always been a major part of Maine's natural and social histories. This northern hardwood forest, as it is termed by ecologists, is a transitional zone between northern and southern ecosystems and is rich in species diversity.

Dominated by deciduous trees, this forest community is highly seasonal. Spring snowmelt brings a pulse of life to the newly exposed forest floor as herbaceous plants race to develop and flower before the trees overhead leaf out and limit the available sunlight. (Blink and you can practically miss a Maine spring.) **Trout lily, goldthread, trillium, violets, gaywing,** and **pink lady's slipper** are among the many woodland wildflowers whose blooms make a walk in the forest so rewarding at this time of year. Deciduous trees, shrubs, and a dozen species of ferns also must make the most of their short four-month growing season. In the Maine woods, the buds of mid-May unfurl into a full canopy of leaves by the first week of June.

Late spring and early summer in the northern hardwood forest is also a time of intense animal activity. Runoff from the melting snowpack has filled countless low-lying depressions throughout the woods. These ephemeral swamps and vernal pools are a haven for an enormous variety of aquatic invertebrates, insects, amphibians, and reptiles. Choruses of **spring peepers,** Maine's smallest but seemingly loudest frog, alert everyone with their high-pitched calls that the ice is going out and breeding season is at hand. Measuring only about an inch in length, these tiny frogs with X-shaped patterns on their backs can be surprisingly difficult to see without some determined effort. Look on the branches of shrubs overhanging the water; males often use them as perches from which to call prospective mates. But then why stop with peepers? There are eight other frog and toad species in Maine to search for too.

Spring is also the best time to look for **salamanders.** Driving a country road on a rainy night in mid-April provides an opportunity to witness one of nature's great mass migrations as salamanders and frogs of several species emerge from their wintering sites and make their way across roads to breeding pools and streams. Once breeding is completed, most salamanders return to the terrestrial environment, where they burrow into crevices or the moist litter of the forest floor. The movement of amphibians from wetlands to uplands has an important ecological function, providing a mechanism for the return of nutrients that runoff washes into low-lying areas. This may seem hard to believe until one considers the numbers of individuals involved in this movement. To illustrate, the total biomass of Maine's **redback salamander** population—just one of the eight salamander species found here—is heavier than the combined weight of all the state's moose.

The many bird species characteristic of the northern hardwood forest are also most in evidence during the late spring and early summer, when the males are engaged in holding breeding territory and attracting mates. For most passerines—perching birds—this means singing. Especially during the early-morning and evening hours, the woods are alive with choruses of song from such birds as the **purple finch, white-throated sparrow, solitary vireo, black-throated blue warbler, Canada warbler, mourning warbler, northern waterthrush,** and the most beautiful singer of them all, the **hermit thrush.**

Providing abundant browse as well as tubers, berries, and nuts, the northern hardwood forest supports many of Maine's mammal species. The **red-backed vole, snowshoe hare, porcupine,** and **white-tailed deer** are relatively abundant and in turn are prey for **foxes, bobcats, fishers,** and **eastern coyotes.** Now well established since its expansion into Maine in the 1950s and 1960s, the eastern coyote has filled the niche at the top of the food chain once held by wolves and mountain lions before their extermination in the state in the late 19th century. **Black bears,** of which Maine has an estimated 25,000, are technically classified as carnivores and will take a moose calf or deer on occasion, but most of their diet consists of vegetation, insects, and fish. In the fall, bears feast on beechnuts and acorns, putting on extra fat for the coming winter, which they spend sleeping (not hibernating, as is often presumed) in a sheltered spot dug out beneath a rock or log.

Ecologically, one of the most significant mammals in the Maine woods is the **beaver.** After being trapped almost to extinction in the 1800s, this large swimming rodent has recolonized streams, rivers, and ponds throughout the state. Well known for its ability as a dam builder, the beaver can change low-lying woodland into a complex aquatic ecosystem. The impounded water behind the dam often kills the trees it inundates, but these provide ideal nest cavities for **mergansers, wood ducks, owls, woodpeckers,** and **swallows.** The still water is also a nursery for a rich diversity of invertebrates, fish, amphibians, and Maine's seven aquatic turtle species, most common of which is the beautiful but very shy **eastern painted turtle.**

THE AQUATIC ENVIRONMENT

Small woodland pools and streams are, of course, only a part of Maine's aquatic environment. The state's nearly 6,000 lakes and ponds provide open-water and deepwater habitats for many additional species. A favorite among them is the **common loon,** a symbol of north country lakes across the continent. Loons impart a sense of wildness and mystery with their haunting calls and yodels resonating off the surrounding pines on still summer nights. Adding to their popular appeal is their striking black-and-white plumage, accented with red eyes, and their ability to vanish below the surface and then reappear in another part of the lake moments later. The annual census of Maine's common loons since the 1970s indicates a relatively stable population of about 4,000 adults and 250 new chicks each summer.

Below the surface of Maine's lakes, ponds, rivers, and streams, 69 freshwater fish species live, of which 17 were introduced. Among these exotic transplants are some of the most sought-after game fish, including **smallmouth** and **largemouth bass, rainbow trout,** and **northern pike**. These introductions may have benefited anglers, but they have displaced native species in many watersheds.

Several of Maine's native fish have interesting histories in that they became landlocked during the retreat of the glacier. At that time, Maine was climatically much like northern Canada is today, and **arctic char** ran up its rivers to spawn at the edges of the ice. As the ice continued to recede, some of these fish became trapped but nevertheless managed to survive and establish themselves in their new landlocked environments. Two remnant subspecies now exist: the **blue-back char,** which lives in the cold, deep water of 10 northern Maine lakes, and the **Sunapee char,** now found only in three lakes in Maine and two in Idaho. A similar history belongs to the **landlocked salmon,** a form of Atlantic salmon that many regard as the state's premier game fish; it is now widely stocked throughout the state and around the country.

Atlantic salmon still run up some Maine rivers every year to spawn, but dams and heavy commercial fishing at sea have depleted their numbers and distribution to a fraction of what they once were. Unlike salmon species on the Pacific coast, adult Atlantic salmon survive the fall spawning period and make their way back out to sea again. The young, or parr, hatch the following spring and live in streams and rivers for the next 2-3 years before migrating to the waters off Greenland. Active efforts are now under way to restore

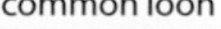
common loon

this species, including capturing and trucking the fish around dams. Salmon is just one of the species whose life cycle starts in freshwater and requires migrations to and from the sea. Called anadromous fish, others include **striped bass, sturgeon, shad, alewives, smelt,** and **eels.** All were once far more numerous in Maine, but fortunately pollution control and management efforts in the past three decades have helped their populations rebound slightly from their historic low numbers.

ESTUARIES AND MUDFLATS

Maine's estuaries, where freshwater and saltwater meet, are ecosystems of outstanding biological importance. South of Cape Elizabeth, where the Maine coast is low and sandy, estuaries harbor large salt marshes of **spartina** grasses that can tolerate the frequent variations in salinity as runoff and tides fluctuate. Producing an estimated four times more plant material than an equivalent area of wheat, these spartina marshes provide abundant nutrients and shelter for a host of marine organisms that ultimately account for as much as 60 percent of the value of the state's commercial fisheries.

The tidal range along the Maine coast varies 9-28 vertical feet, southwest to northeast. Where the tide inundates sheltered estuaries for more than a few hours at a time, spartina grasses cannot take hold, and mudflats dominate. Although it may look like a barren wasteland at low tide, a mudflat is also a highly productive environment and home to abundant marine life. Several species of tiny primitive worms called **nematodes** can inhabit the mud in densities of 2,000 or more per square inch. Larger worm species are also very common. One, the **bloodworm,** grows up to a foot in length and is harvested in quantity for use as sportfishing bait.

More highly savored among the mudflat residents is the **soft-shelled clam,** famous for its outstanding flavor and an essential ingredient of an authentic Maine lobster bake. But because clams are suspension feeders, filtering phytoplankton through their long siphon, or "neck," they can accumulate pollutants that cause illness, including hepatitis. Many Maine mudflats are closed to clam harvesting because of leaking septic systems, so it's best to check with the state's Department of Marine Resources or the local municipal office before digging a mess of clams yourself.

For birds and birders, salt marshes and mudflats are an unparalleled attraction. Long-legged wading birds such as the **glossy ibis, snowy egret, little blue heron, great blue heron, tricolored heron, green heron,** and **black-crowned night heron** frequent the marshes in great numbers throughout the summer months, hunting the shallow waters for mummichogs and other small salt-marsh fish, crustaceans, and invertebrates. Mid-May-early June and then again mid-July-mid-September, migrating shorebirds pass through Maine to and from their subarctic breeding grounds. On a good day, a discerning birder can find 17 or more species of shorebirds probing the mudflats and marshes with pointed bills in search of their preferred foods. In turn, the large flocks of shorebirds don't escape the notice of their own predators: **merlins** and **peregrine falcons** dash in to catch a meal.

THE ROCKY SHORELINE AND THE MARINE ENVIRONMENT

On the more exposed rocky shores—the dominant shoreline from Cape Elizabeth all the way Down East to Lubec—where currents and waves keep mud and sand from accumulating, the plant and animal communities are entirely different from those in the inland aquatic areas. The most important requirement for life in this impenetrable rockbound environment is probably the ability to hang on tight. **Barnacles,** the calcium-armored crustaceans that attach themselves to the rocks immediately below the high-tide line, have developed a fascinating battery of adaptations to survive not only pounding waves but also prolonged exposure to air, solar heat, and extreme winter cold. Glued in place, however, they cannot escape being eaten by **dog whelks,** the predatory snails that also inhabit this intertidal zone. Whelks are larger and more elongate than the more numerous and ubiquitous **periwinkle,** accidentally transplanted from Europe in the mid-19th century.

Also hanging on to these rocks but at a lower level are the brown algae seaweeds. Like a marine forest, the four species of **rockweed** provide shelter for a wide variety of life beneath their fronds. A world of discovery awaits those who make the effort to go out onto the rocks at low tide and look under the clumps of seaweed and into the tidal pools they shelter. Venture into these chilly waters with a mask, fins, and a wetsuit and still another world opens for natural-history exploration. Beds of **blue mussels, sea urchins, sea stars,** and **sea cucumbers** dot the bottom close to shore. In crevices between and beneath the rocks lurk **rock crabs** and **lobsters.** Now a symbol of the Maine coast and the delicious seafood it provides, the lobster was once considered "poor man's food"—so plentiful that it was spread on fields as fertilizer. Although lobsters are far less common than they once were, they are one of Maine's most closely monitored species, and their population continues to support a large and thriving commercial fishing industry.

Sadly, the same cannot be said for most of Maine's other commercially harvested marine fish. When Europeans first came to these shores four centuries ago, **cod, haddock, halibut, hake, flounder, herring,** and **tuna** were abundant, but no longer: Overharvested, their seabed habitat torn up by relentless dragging, these groundfish have all but disappeared. It will be decades before these species can recover, and then only if effective regulations can be put in place soon.

The familiar doglike face of the **harbor seal,** often seen peering alertly from the surface just offshore, provides a reminder that wildlife populations are resilient if given a chance. A century ago, there was a bounty on harbor seals because it was thought they ate too many lobsters and fish. Needless to say, neither fish nor lobsters increased when the seals all but disappeared. With the bounty's repeal and the advent of legal protection, Maine's harbor seal population has bounced back. Scores of them can regularly be seen basking on offshore ledges, drying their tan, brown, black, silver, or reddish coats in the sun. Though it's tempting to approach for a closer look, avoid bringing a boat too near these haul-out ledges, as it causes the seals to flush into the water and imposes an unnecessary stress on the pups, which already face a first-year mortality rate of 30 percent.

Positive changes in our relationships with wildlife are even more apparent with the return of birds to the Maine coast. Watching the numerous **herring gulls** and **great black-backed gulls** soaring on a fresh ocean breeze today, it's hard to imagine that a century ago, egg collecting had so reduced their numbers that they were a rare sight. In 1903, there were just three pairs of **common eiders** left in Maine; today, 25,000 pairs nest along the coast. With creative help from dedicated researchers using sound recordings, decoys, and prepared burrows, **Atlantic puffins** are recolonizing historic offshore nesting islands. **Ospreys** and **bald eagles,** almost free of the lingering vestiges of damage from DDT and other pesticides, now range the length of the coast and up Maine's major rivers.

History

As the great continental glacier receded northwestward out of Maine about 11,000 years ago, some prehistoric grapevine must have alerted small bands of hunter-gatherers—fur-clad Paleoindians—to the scrub sprouting in the tundra, burgeoning mammal populations, and the ocean's bountiful food supply. Because come they did—at first seasonally, and then year-round. Anyone who thinks tourism is a recent Maine phenomenon needs only to explore the shoreline in Damariscotta, Boothbay Harbor, and Bar Harbor, where heaps of cast-off oyster shells and clamshells document the migration of early Native Americans from woodlands to waterfront.

Not until the late 15th century, the onset of the great Age of Discovery, did credible reports of the New World (including what's now Maine) filter back to Europe's courts and universities. Confirmed explorers who visited Maine include Giovanni da Verrazano, Esteban Gomez, and John Rut. By the early 17th century, when Europeans began arriving in more than twos and threes and getting serious about colonization, Native American agriculture was already under way at the mouths of the Saco and Kennebec Rivers, the cod fishery was thriving on offshore islands, Indians far to the north were hot to trade furs for European goodies, and the birchbark canoe was the transport of choice on inland waterways.

In mid-May 1602, Bartholomew Gosnold, en route to a settlement off Cape Cod aboard the *Concord,* landed along Maine's southern coast. The following year, merchant trader Martin Pring returned to England with tales that inflamed curiosity and enough sassafras to satisfy royal appetites. Pring produced a detailed survey of the Maine coast from Kittery to Bucksport, including offshore islands.

On May 18, 1605, George Waymouth reached Monhegan Island, and moored for the night in its harbor. The next day, Waymouth crossed the bay and scouted the mainland. He took five Indians hostage and sailed up the St. George River, near present-day Thomaston. Maritime historian Roger Duncan put it this way: "The Plimoth Pilgrims were little boys in short pants when George Waymouth was exploring this coastline."

Waymouth returned to England and awarded his hostages to officials Sir John Popham and Sir Ferdinando Gorges, who, their curiosity piqued, quickly agreed to subsidize the colonization effort. In 1607, the *Gift of God* and the *Mary and John* sailed for the New World carrying two of Waymouth's captives. After returning them to their native Pemaquid area, Captains George Popham and Raleigh Gilbert continued westward, establishing a colony (St. George or Fort George) at the tip of the Phippsburg Peninsula in mid-August 1607 and exploring the shoreline between Portland and Pemaquid. Frigid weather, untimely deaths (including Popham's), and a storehouse fire doomed what's called the Popham Colony, but not before the 100 or so settlers built the 30-ton pinnace ***Virginia,*** the New World's first such vessel.

In 1614, swashbuckling Captain John Smith, exploring from the Penobscot River westward to Cape Cod, reached Monhegan Island nine years after Waymouth's visit. Smith's meticulous map of the region was the first to use the "New England" appellation, and the 1616 publication of his *Description of New-England* became the catalyst for permanent settlements.

THE FRENCH AND THE ENGLISH SQUARE OFF

English dominance of exploration west of the Penobscot River in the early 17th century coincided roughly with French activity east of the river.

In 1604, French nobleman Pierre du Gua, Sieur de Monts, set out with cartographer

Samuel de Champlain to map the coastline, first reaching Nova Scotia's Bay of Fundy and then sailing up the St. Croix River, establishing a settlement on today's St. Croix Island. During explorations, the duo reached the island Champlain named l'Isle des Monts Deserts (Mount Desert Island) and present-day Bangor before returning to face the winter with their ill-fated compatriots. Scurvy, lack of fuel and water, and a ferocious winter wiped out nearly half of the 79 men. In spring, the survivors abandoned the island and resettled in Nova Scotia's Port Royal (now Annapolis Royal).

Eight years later, French Jesuit missionaries en route to the Kennebec River ended up on Mount Desert Island and, with a band of French laymen, set about establishing the St. Sauveur settlement. But English marauder Samuel Argall reclaimed the territory. By the 1620s, more than four dozen English fishing vessels were combing New England waters in search of cod, and year-round fishing depots had sprung up along the coast between Pemaquid and Portland. At the same time, English trappers and dealers began usurping the Indians' fur trade—a valuable income source.

The Massachusetts Bay Colony, established in 1630, and England's Council of New England, headed by Sir Ferdinando Gorges, began making vast land grants throughout Maine, giving rise to permanent coastal settlements. Among the earliest communities were Kittery, York, Wells, Saco, Scarborough, Falmouth, and Pemaquid.

By the late 17th century, as these communities expanded, so did their requirements and responsibilities. Roads and bridges were built, preachers and teachers were hired, and militias were organized to deal with internecine and Indian skirmishes.

Even though England yearned to control the entire Maine coastline, her turf, realistically, was primarily south and west of the Penobscot River. The French had expanded from their Canadian colony of Acadia, for the most part north and east of the Penobscot. Unlike the absentee bosses who controlled the English territory, French merchants actually showed up, forming good relationships with the Indians and cornering the market in fishing, lumbering, and fur trading. And French Jesuit priests converted many a Native American to Catholicism. Intermittently, overlapping Anglo-French land claims sparked locally messy conflicts.

In the mid-17th century, the strategic heart of French administration and activity in Maine was Fort Pentagöet, a sturdy stone outpost built in 1635 in what is now Castine. From here, the French controlled coastal trade between the St. George River and Mount Desert Island and well up the Penobscot River. In 1654, England captured and occupied the fort and much of French Acadia, but, thanks to the 1667 Treaty of Breda, title returned to the French in 1670, and Pentagöet briefly became Acadia's capital.

A short but nasty Dutch foray against Acadia in 1674 resulted in Pentagöet's destruction ("levell'd with ye ground," by one account) and the raising of a third national flag over Castine.

THE INDIAN WARS (1675-1760)

Caught in the middle of 17th- and 18th-century Anglo-French disputes throughout Maine were the Wabanaki (People of the Dawn), the collective name for the state's major Native American tribal groups, all of whom spoke Algonquian languages. Modern ethnographers label these groups the Micmacs, Maliseets, Passamaquoddies, and Penobscots.

In the early 17th century, exposure to European diseases took its toll, wiping out three-quarters of the Wabanaki. Opportunistic English and French traders quickly moved into the breach, and the Indians struggled to survive and regroup.

But regroup they did. Less than three generations later, a series of six Indian wars began, lasting nearly a century and pitting the Wabanaki most often against the English but occasionally against other Wabanaki. The conflicts, largely provoked by Anglo-French tensions in Europe, were King Philip's War (1675-1678), King William's War (1688-1699), Queen Anne's War (1703-1713), Dummer's War (1721-1726), King George's War (1744-1748), and the French and Indian War (1754-1760). Not until a get-together in 1762 at Fort Pownall (now Stockton Springs) did peace effectively return to the region—just in time for the heating up of the revolutionary movement.

COMES THE REVOLUTION

Near the end of the last Indian War, just beyond Maine's eastern border, a watershed event led to more than a century of cultural and political fallout. During the so-called Acadian Dispersal, in 1755, the English expelled from Nova Scotia 10,000 French-speaking Acadians who refused to pledge allegiance to the British Crown. Scattered as far south as Louisiana and west toward New Brunswick and Québec, the Acadians lost farms, homes, and possessions in this *grand dérangement*. Not until 1785 was land allocated for resettlement of Acadians along both sides of the Upper St. John River, where thousands of their descendants remain today. Henry Wadsworth Longfellow's epic poem *Evangeline* dramatically relates the sorry Acadian saga.

In the District of Maine, on the other hand, with relative peace following a century of intermittent warfare, settlement again exploded, particularly in the southernmost counties. In 1770, 27 Maine towns became eligible, based on population, to send representatives to the Massachusetts General Court, the colony's legislative body. But only six coastal towns could actually afford to send anyone, sowing seeds of resentment among settlers who were thus saddled with taxes without representation. Sporadic mob action accompanied unrest in southern Maine, but the flashpoint occurred in the Boston area in 1775.

Most of the Revolution's action occurred south of Maine, but not all of it. In June, the Down East outpost of Machias was the site of the war's first naval engagement. The well-armed but unsuspecting British vessel HMS *Margaretta* sailed into the bay and was besieged by residents angry about a Machias merchant's sweetheart deal with the British. Before celebrating their David-and-Goliath victory, the rebels captured the *Margaretta,* killed her captain, and then captured two more British ships sent to the rescue.

In the fall of 1775, Colonel Benedict Arnold—better known to history as a notorious turncoat—assembled 1,100 sturdy men for a flawed and futile "March on Québec" to dislodge the English. From Newburyport, Massachusetts, they sailed to the mouth of the Kennebec River, near Bath, and then headed inland with the tide. In Pittston, six miles south of Augusta and close to the head of navigation, they transferred to a fleet of 220 locally made bateaux and laid over three nights at Fort Western in Augusta. Then they set off, poling, paddling, and portaging their way upriver. Skowhegan, Norridgewock, and Chain of Ponds were among the landmarks along the grueling route. The men endured cold, hunger, swamps, disease, dense underbrush, and the loss of nearly 600 of their comrades before reaching Québec in late 1775. In the Kennebec River Valley, Arnold Trail historical signposts today mark highlights (or, more aptly, lowlights) of the expedition.

Four years later, another futile attempt to dislodge the British, this time in the District of Maine, resulted in America's worst naval defeat until World War II—a little-publicized debacle called the Penobscot Expedition. On August 14, 1779, as more than 40 American warships and transports carrying more than 2,000 Massachusetts men blockaded Castine to flush out a relatively small enclave of leftover Brits, a seven-vessel Royal Navy fleet appeared. Despite their own greater numbers, about 30 of the American ships turned tail up the Penobscot River. The captains torched their vessels, exploding the ammunition and leaving the survivors to walk in disgrace to Augusta or even Boston. Each side took close to 100 casualties, three commanders—including Paul Revere—were court-martialed.

The American Revolution officially ended on September 3, 1783, with the signing of the Treaty of Paris between the United States and Great Britain. The U.S.-Canada border was set at the St. Croix River, but, in a massive oversight, boundary lines were left unresolved for thousands of square miles in the northern District of Maine.

TRADE TROUBLES AND THE WAR OF 1812

In 1807, President Thomas Jefferson imposed the Embargo Act, banning trade with foreign entities—specifically, France and Britain. With thousands of miles of coastline and harbor villages dependent on trade for revenue and basic necessities, Maine reeled. By the time the act was repealed in 1809, the bottom had dropped out of New England's economy. An active smuggling operation based in Eastport kept Mainers from utter despair, but the economy continued its downslide.

In 1812, the fledgling United States declared war on Great Britain, again disrupting coastal trade. In the fall of 1814, the situation reached its nadir when the British invaded the Maine coast and occupied all the shoreline between the St. Croix and Penobscot Rivers. Later that same year, the Treaty of Ghent finally halted the squabble, forced the British to withdraw from Maine, and allowed the locals to get on with economic recovery.

STATEHOOD

In October 1819, Mainers held a constitutional convention at the First Parish Church on Congress Street in Portland. The convention crafted a constitution modeled on that of Massachusetts, with two notable differences: Maine would have no official church (Massachusetts had the Puritans' Congregational Church), and Maine would place no religious requirements or restrictions on its gubernatorial candidates. When votes came in from 241 Maine towns, only nine voted against ratification.

For Maine, March 15, 1820, was one of those good news/bad news days: After 35 years of separatist agitation, the District of Maine broke from Massachusetts and became the 23rd state in the union. However, the Missouri Compromise, enacted by Congress only 12 days earlier to balance admission of slave and free states, mandated that the slave state of Missouri be admitted on the same day. Maine had abolished slavery in 1788, and there was deep resentment over the linkage.

Portland became the new state's capital (albeit only briefly; it switched to Augusta in 1832), and William King, one of statehood's most outspoken advocates, became the first governor.

TROUBLE IN THE NORTH COUNTRY

Without an official boundary established on Maine's far northern frontier, turf battles were always simmering just under the surface. Timber was the sticking point—everyone wanted the vast wooded acreage. Finally, in early 1839, militia reinforcements descended on the disputed area, heating up what has come to be known as the Aroostook War, a border confrontation with no battles and no casualties (except a farmer who was shot by friendly militia). It's a blip in the historical time line, but remnants of fortifications in Houlton, Fort Fairfield, and Fort Kent keep the story alive today. By March 1839, a truce was negotiated, and the 1842 Webster-Ashburton Treaty established the border once and for all.

MAINE IN THE CIVIL WAR

In the 1860s, with the state's population slightly more than 600,000, more than 70,000 Mainers suited up and went off to fight in the Civil War—the greatest per-capita show of force of any northern state. About 18,000 of them died in the conflict. Thirty-one Mainers were Union Army generals, the best known being Joshua L. Chamberlain, a Bowdoin College professor, who commanded the Twentieth Maine regiment and later became president of the college and governor of Maine.

During the war, young battlefield artist Winslow Homer, who later settled in Prouts Neck, south of Portland, created wartime sketches regularly for such publications as *Harper's Weekly*. In Washington, Maine senator Hannibal Hamlin was elected vice president under Abraham Lincoln in 1860.

Government and Economy

After the Civil War, Maine's influence in Republican-dominated Washington far outweighed the size of its population. In the late 1880s, Mainers held the federal offices of acting vice president, Speaker of the House, secretary of state, Senate majority leader, Supreme Court justice, and several important committee chairmanships. Best known of the notables were James G. Blaine (journalist, presidential aspirant, and secretary of state) and Portland native Thomas Brackett Reed, presidential aspirant and Speaker of the House.

In Maine itself, traditional industries fell into decline after the Civil War, dealing the economy a body blow. Steel ships began replacing Maine's wooden clippers, refrigeration techniques made the block-ice industry obsolete, concrete threatened the granite-quarrying trade, and the output from Southern textile mills began to supplant that from Maine's mills.

Despite Maine's economic difficulties, however, wealthy urbanites began turning their sights toward the state, accumulating land (including islands) and building enormous summer "cottages" for their families, servants, and hangers-on. Bar Harbor was a prime example of the elegant summer colonies that sprang up, but others include Grindstone Neck (Winter Harbor), Prouts Neck (Scarborough), and Dark Harbor (on Islesboro in Penobscot Bay). Vacationers who preferred fancy hotel-type digs reserved rooms for the summer at such sprawling complexes as Kineo House (on Moosehead Lake), Poland Spring House (west of Portland), or the Samoset Hotel (in Rockland). Built of wood and catering to long-term visitors, these and many others all eventually succumbed to altered vacation patterns and the ravages of fire.

As the 19th century spilled into the 20th, the state broadened its appeal beyond the well-to-do who had snared prime turf in the Victorian era. It launched an active promotion of Maine as "The Nation's Playground," successfully spurring an influx of visitors from all economic levels. By steamboat, train, and soon by car, people came to enjoy the ocean beaches, the woods, the mountains, the lakes, and the quaintness of it all. The only major hiatus in the tourism explosion in the century's first two decades was 1914-1918, when 35,062 Mainers joined many thousands of other Americans in going off to the European front to fight in World War I. Two years after the war ended, in 1920 (the centennial of its statehood), Maine women were the first in the nation to troop to the polls after ratification of the 19th Amendment granted universal suffrage.

Maine was slow to feel the repercussions of the Great Depression, but eventually they came, with bank failures all over the state. The federally subsidized programs of the New Deal, such as the Civilian Conservation Corps (CCC) and the Works Progress Administration (WPA), left lasting legacies in Maine.

MAINE TODAY

Maine's voters and politicians have a national reputation for being independent-minded—electing Democrats, Republicans, or independents more for their character than their political persuasions. Maine has two senators and two congressional representatives. In 2018, it became the first state to permit ranked choice voting for these offices. The governor serves a term of four years, limited to two terms. The state's Supreme Judicial Court has a chief justice and six associate justices.

Maine is governed by a bicameral, biennial citizen legislature comprising 151 members in the house of representatives and 35 members in the state senate. Greater Portland and southern Maine are more liberal, while inland and northern Maine lean more conservative.

Whereas nearly two dozen Maine cities are ruled by city councils, about 450 smaller towns and plantations retain the traditional form of rule: annual town meetings. Town meetings generally are held in March, when newspaper pages bulge with reports containing classic quotes from citizens exercising their rights to vote and vent. A few examples: "I believe in the pursuit of happiness until that pursuit infringes on the happiness of others"; "I don't know of anyone's dog running loose except my own, and I've arrested her several times"; and "Don't listen to him; he's from New Jersey."

When the subject of the economy comes up, you'll often hear reference to the "two Maines," as if an east-west line bisected the state in half. There's much truth to the image. Southern Maine is prosperous, with good jobs (although never enough), lots of small businesses, and a highly competitive real-estate market. Northern Maine struggles along, suffering from its immensity and lack of infrastructure as much as from its low population density.

The coast follows that same pattern. The Southern Coast reaps the benefit of its proximity to Boston. Not only is it a favorite weekend getaway for Boston-area residents, but also it's increasingly becoming part of Boston's suburbs as more and more people move there and commute to the city. Tourism thrives here seasonally. Retail is strong, thanks to Kittery. And traditional maritime-related businesses continue, although real-estate pressures have contributed to their weakening, as fishermen struggle to hold on to wharves and to live near where they work.

According to state economists, Maine faces three challenges. First, slow job growth: Over the past two decades, Maine's has been about half of the national average. Second, changing employment patterns: Once famed for producing textiles and shoes and for its woods-based industries, now health care and tourism provide the most jobs. Third, an aging population: Economic forecasters predict that more than one in five residents will be older than 65 by 2020.

People and Culture

THE PEOPLE

Maine's population didn't top the one million mark until 1970. Forty years later, according to the 2010 census, the state had 1,318,301 residents. Along the coast, Cumberland County, comprising the Greater Portland area, has the highest head count.

Despite the longstanding presence of several substantial ethnic groups, plus four Native American tribes (about 1 percent of the population), diversity is a relatively recent phenomenon in Maine, and the population is about 95 percent Caucasian. A steady influx of refugees, beginning after the Vietnam War, has forced the state to address diversity issues, and it continues to do so today.

Natives and "People from Away"

People who weren't born in Maine aren't natives. Even people who *were* born here may experience close scrutiny of their credentials. In Maine, there are natives and *natives*. Every day, the obituary pages describe Mainers who have barely left the houses in which they were born—even in which their grandparents were born. We're talking roots!

Along with this kind of heritage comes a whole vocabulary all its own—lingo distinctive to Maine, or at least New England. (For help in translation, see the Glossary.)

Part of the "native" picture is the matter of "native" produce. Hand-lettered signs sprout everywhere during the summer advertising native corn, native peas, even—believe it or not—native ice. In Maine, homegrown is well grown.

"People from away," on the other hand, are those whose families haven't lived here year-round for a generation or more. But people from away (also called flatlanders) exist all over Maine, and they have come to stay, putting down roots of their own.

In the 19th century, arriving flatlanders were mostly "rusticators" or "summer complaints"—summer residents who lived well, often in enclaves, and never set foot in the state off-season. They did, however, pay property taxes, contribute to causes, and provide employment for local residents. Another 19th-century wave of people from away came from the bottom of the economic ladder: Irish escaping the potato famine and French Canadians fleeing poverty in Québec. Both groups experienced subtle and overt anti-Catholicism but rather quickly assimilated into the mainstream, taking jobs in mills and factories and becoming staunch American patriots.

The late 1960s and early 1970s brought bunches of "back-to-the-landers," who scorned plumbing and electricity and adopted retro ways of life. Although a few pockets of diehards still exist, most have changed with the times and adopted contemporary mores (and conveniences).

Native Americans

In Maine, the *real* natives are the Wabanaki (People of the Dawn)—the Micmac, Maliseet, Penobscot, and Passamaquoddy tribes of the eastern woodlands. Many live in or near three reservations, near the headquarters for their tribal governors. The Passamaquoddies are at Pleasant Point, in Perry, near Eastport, and at Indian Township, in Princeton, near Calais. The Penobscots are based on Indian Island, in Old Town, near Bangor. Other Native American population clusters—known as "off-reservation Indians"—are the Aroostook Band of Micmacs, based in Presque Isle, and the Houlton Band of Maliseets, in Littleton, near Houlton.

In 1965, Maine became the first state to establish a Department of Indian Affairs, but just five years later the Passamaquoddy and Penobscot tribes initiated a 10-year-long land-claims case involving 12.5 million Maine acres (about two-thirds of the state) weaseled from the Indians by Massachusetts in 1794. In late 1980, a landmark agreement, signed by President Jimmy Carter, awarded the tribes $80.6 million in reparations.

Acadians and Franco-Americans

Within about three decades of their 1755 expulsion from Nova Scotia in *le grand dérangement,* Acadians had established new communities and new lives in northern Maine's St. John Valley. Gradually, they explored farther into central and southern coastal Maine and west into New Hampshire. The Acadian diaspora has profoundly influenced Maine and its culture, and it continues to do so today. Along the coast, French is spoken on the streets of Biddeford, where there's an annual Franco-American festival and an extensive Franco-American research collection.

African Americans

Although Maine's African American population is small, the state has had an African American community since the 17th century; by the 1764 census, there were 322 slaves and free blacks in the District of Maine.

Segregation remained the rule, however, so in the 19th century, black people established their own parish, the Abyssinian Church in Portland. Efforts are under way to restore the long-closed church as an African American cultural center and gathering place for Greater Portland's black community. Maine's African Americans have earned places in history books that far exceed their small population. In 1826, Bowdoin's John Brown Russworm became America's first black college graduate; in 1844, Macon B. Allen became the first African American to gain admission to a state bar; and in 1875, James A. Heay became America's first African American Roman Catholic bishop, when he was ordained for the Diocese of Portland. For researchers delving into "Maine's black experience," the University of Southern Maine in Portland houses the African-American Archive of Maine, a significant collection of historic books, letters, and artifacts donated by Gerald Talbot, the first African American to serve in the Maine legislature. Refugee resettlement programs have created active Somali communities in Portland and Lewiston.

Finns, Swedes, Lebanese, and Amish

Finns came to Maine in several 19th-century waves, primarily to work the granite quarries on the coast and on offshore islands and the slate quarries in Monson, near Greenville.

In 1870, an idealistic American diplomat named William Widgery Thomas established a model agricultural community with 50 brave Swedes in the heart of Aroostook County. Their enclave, New Sweden, remains today, as does the town of Stockholm, and descendants of the pioneers have spread throughout Maine.

At the turn of the 20th century, Lebanese (and some Syrians) began descending on Waterville, where they found work in the textile mills and eventually established St. Joseph's Maronite Church in 1927.

Amish families are increasingly taking refuge in Maine. What began with one colony in Aroostook County has grown to more than a half dozen, including one in Unity.

Russians, Ukrainians, and Byelorussians

Arriving after World War II, Slavic immigrants established a unique community in Richmond, just inland from Bath. In the 1950s, the town was home to the largest rural Russian-speaking population in the country. Only a tiny nucleus remains today, along with an onion-domed church, but a stroll through the local cemetery hints at the extent of the original colony.

The Newest Arrivals: Refugees from War

War has been the impetus for the more recent arrival of Asians, Africans, Central Americans, and Eastern Europeans. Most have settled in the Portland area, making that city the state's center of diversity. Vietnamese and Cambodians began settling in Maine in the mid-1970s. A handful of Afghanis who fled the Soviet-Afghan conflict also ended up in Portland. Somalis, Ethiopians, and Sudanese fled their war-torn countries in the early to mid-1990s, and Bosnians and Kosovars arrived in the last half of the 1990s. With every new conflict comes a new stream of immigrants—world citizens are becoming Mainers, and Mainers are becoming world citizens.

CULTURE

Mainers are an independent lot, many exhibiting the classic Yankee characteristics of dry humor, thrift, and ingenuity. Those who can trace their roots back at least a generation or two in the state and have lived here through the duration can call themselves natives; everyone else, no matter how long they've lived here, is "from away."

Mainers react to outsiders depending upon how those outsiders treat them. Treat a Mainer with a condescending attitude, and you'll receive a cold shoulder at best. Treat a Mainer with respect, and you'll be welcome, perhaps even invited in to share a mug of coffee. Mainers are wary of outsiders, and often with good reason. Many outsiders move to Maine because they fall in love with its independence and rural simplicity, and then they demand that the farmer stop spreading that stinky manure on his farmlands, or they insist that the town initiate garbage pickup, or they build a glass-and-timber McMansion in the midst of white clapboard historical homes.

In most of Maine, money doesn't impress folks. The truth is, that lobsterman in the old truck and the well-worn work clothes might be sitting on a small fortune. Or living on it. Perhaps nothing has caused more troubles between natives and newcomers than the rapidly increasing value of land and the taxes that go with that. For many visitors, Maine real estate is a bargain they can't resist.

THE ARTS

Fine Art

In 1850, in a watershed moment for Maine landscape painting, Frederic Edwin Church (1826-1900), Hudson River School artist par excellence, vacationed on Mount Desert Island. Influenced by the luminist tradition of such contemporaries as Fitz Hugh Lane (1804-1865), who summered in nearby Castine, Church accurately but romantically depicted the dramatic tableaux of Maine's coast and woodlands that continues to attract slews of admirers today.

By the 1880s, impressionist Charles Herbert Woodbury (1864-1940) made Ogunquit the best-known summer art school in New England. After Hamilton Easter Field established another art school in town, modernism soon asserted itself. Among the artists who took up summertime Ogunquit residence was Walt Kuhn (1877-1949), a key organizer of New York's 1913 landmark Armory Show of modern art.

Meanwhile, a bit farther south, impressionist Childe Hassam (1859-1935), part of writer Celia Thaxter's circle, produced several hundred works on Maine's remote Appledore Island, in the Isles of Shoals off Kittery, and illustrated Thaxter's *An Island Garden*.

Another artistic summer colony found its niche in 1903, when Robert Henri (born Robert Henry Cozad, 1865-1929), charismatic leader of the Ashcan School of realist/modernists, visited Monhegan Island, about 11 miles offshore. Artists who followed him there included Rockwell Kent (1882-1971), Edward Hopper (1882-1967), George Bellows (1882-1925), and Randall Davey (1887-1964). Among the many other artists associated with Monhegan images are William Kienbusch (1914-1980), Reuben Tam (1916-1991), and printmakers Leo Meissner (1895-1977) and Stow Wengenroth (1906-1978).

But colonies were of scant interest to other notables, who chose to derive their inspiration from Maine's stark natural beauty and work mostly in their own orbits. Among these are genre painter Eastman Johnson (1824-1906); romantic realist Winslow Homer (1836-1910), who lived in Maine for 27 years and whose studio in Prouts Neck (Scarborough) still overlooks the surf-tossed scenery he so often depicted; pointillist watercolorist Maurice Prendergast (1858-1924); John Marin (1870-1953), a cubist who painted Down East subjects, mostly around Deer Isle and Addison (Cape Split); Lewiston native Marsden Hartley (1877-1943), who first showed his abstractionist work in New York in 1909 and later worked in Berlin; Fairfield Porter (1907-1975), whose family summered on Great Spruce Head Island, in East Penobscot Bay; and Andrew Wyeth (1917-2009), whose reputation as a romantic realist in the late 20th century surpassed that of his illustrator father, N. C. Wyeth (1882-1945).

On a parallel track was sculptor Louise Nevelson (1899-1988), raised in a poor Russian-immigrant family in Rockland and far better known outside her home state for her monumental wood sculptures slathered in black or gold. Two other noted sculptors with Maine connections were William Zorach (1887-1966) and Gaston Lachaise (1882-1935), both of whom lived in Georgetown, near Bath.

Maine Food Specialties

Everyone knows Maine is *the* place for lobster, but there are quite a few other foods that you should sample before you leave.

For a few weeks in May, right around Mother's Day (the second Sunday in May), a wonderful delicacy starts sprouting along Maine's woodland streams: **fiddleheads,** the still-furled tops of the ostrich fern *(Matteuccia struthiopteris)*. Tasting vaguely like asparagus, fiddleheads have been on May menus ever since Native Americans taught the colonists to forage for the tasty vegetable. Don't go fiddleheading unless you're with a pro, though; the lookalikes are best left to the woods critters. If you find them on a restaurant menu, indulge.

As with fiddleheads, we owe thanks to Native Americans for introducing us to **maple syrup,** one of Maine's major agricultural exports. The annual crop averages 110,000 gallons. The syrup comes in four different colors/flavors (from light amber to extra-dark amber), and inspectors strictly monitor syrup quality. The best syrup comes from the sugar or rock maple, *Acer saccharum*. On Maine Maple Sunday (usually the fourth Sunday in March), several dozen syrup producers open their rustic sugarhouses to the public for "sugaring-off" parties—to celebrate the sap harvest and share the final phase in the production process. Wood smoke billows from the sugarhouse chimney while everyone inside gathers around huge kettles used to boil down the watery sap. (A single gallon of syrup starts with 30-40 gallons of sap.) Finally, it's time to sample the syrup every which way—on pancakes and waffles, in tea, on ice cream, in puddings, in muffins, even just drizzled over snow. Most producers also have containers of syrup for sale.

The best place for Maine maple syrup is atop pancakes made with Maine **wild blueberries.** Packed with antioxidants and all kinds of good-for-you stuff, these flavorful berries are prized by bakers because they retain their form and flavor when cooked. Much smaller than the cultivated

Contemporary year-round or seasonal Maine residents with national (and international) reputations include Vinalhaven's Robert Indiana (1928-2018), Lincolnville's Alex Katz, North Haven's Eric Hopkins, Deer Isle's Karl Schrag, Tenants Harbor's Jamie Wyeth (third generation of the famous family), and Cushing's Lois Dodd and Alan Magee.

Crafts

Any survey of Maine art, however brief, must include the significant role of crafts in the state's artistic tradition. As with painters, sculptors, and writers, craftspeople have gravitated to Maine—most notably since the establishment in 1950 of the Haystack Mountain School of Crafts. Craft studios are abundant in Maine, and many festivals include craft displays.

Down East Literature

Maine's best-known author lives not on the coast but just inland, in Bangor: horror master Stephen King (born 1947). Other best-selling contemporary authors writing in or about Maine include Carolyn Chute (born 1948), resident of Parsonsfield and author of the raw novels *The Beans of Egypt, Maine* and *Letourneau's Used Auto Parts*; Cathie Pelletier (born 1953), raised in tiny Allagash and author of such humor-filled novels as *The Funeral Makers* and *The Bubble Reputation*; and coastal-Maine resident Richard Russo (born 1949), author of *Empire Falls*, winner of the 2002 Pulitzer Prize in Fiction and named the year's best novel by *Time* magazine.

CHRONICLERS OF THE GREAT OUTDOORS

The 20th century saw the arrival in Maine of crusader Rachel Carson (1907-1964), whose 1962 wake-up call, *Silent Spring*, was based partly on Maine observations and research.

The tiny town of Nobleboro, near Damariscotta, drew nature writer Henry Beston (1888-1968); his *Northern Farm* lyrically chronicles a year in Maine. Beston's

versions, wild blueberries are also raked, not picked. Although most of the Down East barren barons harvest their crops for the lucrative wholesale market, a few growers let you pick your own blueberries in mid-August. Contact the Wild Blueberry Commission (207/581-1475, www.wildblueberries.maine.edu) or the state Department of Agriculture (207/287-3491, www.getrealmaine.com) for locations, recipes, and other wild-blueberry information, or log on to the website of the Wild Blueberry Association of North America (207/570-3535, www.wildblueberries.com).

Another don't-miss while in Maine is Maine-made **ice cream.** Skip the overpriced Ben and Jerry's outlets. Locally made ice cream and gelato are fresher and better and often come in an astounding range of flavors. The big name in the state is Gifford's, with regional companies being Shain's and Round Top. All beat the out-of-state competition by a long shot. Even better are some of the one-of-a-kind dairy bars and farm stands. Good bets are John's, in Liberty; Pugnuts, in Surry; Morton's Moo, in Ellsworth; and Mount Desert Island Ice Cream, in Bar Harbor and Portland.

Other must-try Maine favorites are **Moxie,** a carbonated beverage; **whoopie pies,** the state's official snack; and, especially in Down East Maine, **periwinkles,** a sea snail familiarly called wrinkles, and **smelts,** a small fish.

Finally, whenever you get a chance, shop at a **farmers market.** Their biggest asset is serendipity—you never know what you'll find. Everything is locally grown and often organic. Herbs, unusual vegetables, seedlings, baked goods, meat, free-range chicken, goat cheese, herb vinegars, berries, exotic condiments, smoked salmon, maple syrup, honey, and jams are just a few of the possibilities. The Maine Department of Agriculture (207/287-3491, www.getrealmaine.com) provides info on markets.

wife, Elizabeth Coatsworth (1893-1986), wrote more than 90 books—including *Chimney Farm,* about their life in Nobleboro.

Fannie Hardy Eckstorm (1865-1946), born in Brewer to Maine's most prosperous fur trader, graduated from Smith College and became a noted expert on Maine (and specifically Native American) folklore. Among her extensive writings, *Indian Place-Names of the Penobscot Valley and the Maine Coast,* published in 1941, remains a sine qua non for researchers.

The out-of-doors and inner spirits shaped Cape Rosier adoptees Helen and Scott Nearing, whose 1954 *Living the Good Life* became the bible of Maine's back-to-the-landers.

CLASSIC WRITINGS ON THE STATE

Historical novels, such as *Arundel,* were the specialty of Kennebunk native Kenneth Roberts (1885-1957), but Roberts also wrote *Trending into Maine,* a potpourri of Maine observations and experiences (the original edition was illustrated by N. C. Wyeth). Kennebunkport's Booth Tarkington (1869-1946), author of the *Penrod* novels and *The Magnificent Ambersons,* described 1920s Kennebunkport in *Mary's Neck,* published in 1932.

A subgenre of sociological literary classics comprises astute observations, mostly by women, of daily life in various parts of the state. Some are fiction, some nonfiction, some barely disguised romans à clef. Probably the best-known chronicler of such observations is Sarah Orne Jewett (1849-1909), author of *The Country of the Pointed Firs,* a fictional 1896 account of "Dunnet's Landing" (actually Tenants Harbor); her ties, however, were in the South Berwick area, where she spent most of her life. Also in South Berwick, Gladys Hasty Carroll (1904-1999) scrutinized everyday life in her hamlet, Dunnybrook, in *As the Earth Turns* (a title later "borrowed" and tweaked by a soap-opera producer). Lura Beam (1887-1978) focused on her childhood in the Washington County village of

Marshfield in *A Maine Hamlet*, published in 1957, and Louise Dickinson Rich (1903-1972) entertainingly described her coastal Corea experiences in *The Peninsula*, after first having chronicled her rugged wilderness existence in *We Took to the Woods*. Ruth Moore (1903-1989), born on Gott's Island, near Acadia National Park, published her first book at the age of 40. Her tales, recently brought back into print, have earned her a whole new appreciative audience. Elisabeth Ogilvie (1917-2006) came to Maine in 1944 and lived for many years on remote Ragged Island, transformed into "Bennett's Island" in her fascinating "tide trilogy": *High Tide at Noon*, *Storm Tide*, and *The Ebbing Tide*. Ben Ames Williams (1887-1953), the token male in this roundup of perceptive observers, in 1940 produced *Come Spring*, an epic tale of hardy pioneers founding the town of Union, just inland from Rockland.

In the mid-19th century antislavery crusader Harriet Beecher Stowe (1811-1896), seldom recognized for her Maine connection, lived in Brunswick, where she wrote *The Pearl of Orr's Island*, a folkloric novel about a tiny nearby fishing community.

Mary Ellen Chase (1887-1973), born in Blue Hill, became an English professor at Smith College in 1926 and wrote about 30 books.

PINE TREE POETS

Portland-born Henry Wadsworth Longfellow (1807-1882) is Maine's most famous poet; his marine themes clearly stem from his seashore childhood (in "My Lost Youth," he wistfully rhapsodized, "Often I think of the beautiful town/That is seated by the sea...").

Poet Celia Thaxter (1835-1894) held court on Appledore Island in the Isles of Shoals, welcoming artists, authors, and musicians to her summer salon. Today, she's best known for *An Island Garden*, published in 1894.

Edna St. Vincent Millay (1892-1950) had connections to Camden, Rockland, and Union and described a stunning Camden panorama in "Renascence."

Whitehead Island, near Rockland, was the birthplace of Wilbert Snow (1883-1977), who went on to become president of Connecticut's Wesleyan University. His 1968 memoir, *Codline's Child*, makes fascinating reading.

A longtime resident of York, May Sarton (1912-1995) approached cult status as a guru of feminist poetry and prose—and as an articulate analyst of death and dying during her terminal illness.

Among respected Maine poets today are William Carpenter (born 1940), of Stockton Springs; Appleton's Kate Barnes (1932-1913), named Maine's Poet Laureate from 1996 to 1999; and current Maine Poet Laureate Stuart Kestenbaum.

MAINE LIT FOR LITTLE ONES

Children's authors of note include E. B. White, who wrote *Stuart Little*, *Charlotte's Web*, and *The Trumpet of the Swan*; Maine island summer resident Robert McCloskey (1914-2003), notably *Time of Wonder*, *One Morning in Maine*, and *Blueberries for Sal*; and Walpole illustrator-writer Barbara Cooney (1917-1999), whose award-winning titles included *Miss Rumphius*, *Island Boy*, and *Hattie and the Wild Waves*.

C. A. (Charles Asbury) Stephens (1844-1931) for 60 years wrote for the magazine *Youth's Companion*. In 1995, a collection of his vivid children's stories was reissued as *Stories from the Old Squire's Farm*.

Kate Douglas Wiggin (1856-1923), author of the eternally popular *Rebecca of Sunnybrook Farm*, spent summers at Quillcote in Hollis, west of Portland.

Essentials

Transportation

GETTING THERE

Maine has two major airports, two major bus networks, a toll highway, limited Amtrak service, and some ad hoc local transportation systems that fill in the gaps.

Air

Maine's primary airline gateway is **Portland International Jetport** (PWM, 207/774-7301, www.portlandjetport.org), although visitors headed farther north sometimes prefer **Bangor International**

Airport (BGR, 207/947-0384, www.flybangor.com). The "international" in their names is a bit misleading. Military and charter flights from Europe often stop at Bangor for refueling and customs clearance, and Portland has a few flights connecting to Canada, but Boston's Logan Airport is the nearest airport with direct flights from worldwide destinations.

PORTLAND JETPORT FACILITIES

Portland's airport is small and easy to navigate. Food options are few, but you won't starve. Visitor information is dispensed from a desk (not always staffed, unfortunately) between the gates and the baggage-claim area.

Ground Transportation: The Greater Portland Transportation District's **Metro** (207/774-0351, www.gpmetrobus.com) bus route 5 connects the airport with downtown Portland Monday through Saturday. **Taxis** are available outside baggage claim.

Mid-Coast Limo (207/236-2424 or 800/937-2424, www.midcoastlimo.com) provides car service, by reservation, between Portland and the Mid-Coast and Penobscot Bay regions. **Mermaid Transportation Co.** (207/885-5630, www.gomermaid.com) services southern Maine.

Car rentals at the airport include **Alamo** (207/775-0855 or 877/222-9075, www.alamo.com), **Avis** (207/874-7501 or 800/230-4898, www.avis.com), **Budget** (207/874-7501 or 800/527-0700, www.drivebudget.com), **Enterprise** (207/615-0030, www.enterprise.com), **Hertz** (207/774-4544 or 800/654-3131, www.hertz.com), and **National** (207/773-0036 or 877/222-9058, www.nationalcar.com).

BANGOR AIRPORT FACILITIES

Bangor's airport has scaled-down versions of Portland's facilities but all the necessary amenities. **Ground Transportation: Community Connector** (207/992-4670, www.bangormaine.gov) buses connect the airport to downtown Bangor. Buses run Monday-Saturday. **West's Coastal Connection** (207/546-2823 or 800/596-2823, www.westbusservice.com) has scheduled service along Route 1 to Calais, with stops en route. **Taxis** are available outside baggage claim.

Bar Harbor-Bangor Shuttle (207/479-5911, www.barharborbangorshuttle.com) operates between the airport, the Greyhound and Concord Coachlines bus terminals, the Bangor Mall, Hollywood Casino, and Bar Harbor.

Car rentals at the airport include **Alamo** (207/947-0158 or 800/462-5266, www.alamo.com), **Avis** (207/947-8383 or 800/831-2847, www.avis.com), **Budget** (207/945-9429 or 800/527-0700, www.drivebudget.com), **Hertz** (207/942-5519 or 800/654-3131, www.hertz.com), and **National** (207/947-0158 or 800/227-7368, www.nationalcar.com).

REGIONAL AIRPORTS

JetBlue partner **Cape Air** (866/227-3247, www.flycapeair.com) flies year-round between Boston and **Hancock County Airport** (BHB, 207/667-7329, www.bhbairport.com) near Bar Harbor, **Knox County Regional Airport** (RKD, 207/594-4131, www.knoxcountymaine.gov) at Owls Head, near Rockland and Camden, and **Augusta State Airport** (AUG, 207/626-2306, www.augustaairport.org). **United** (800/864-8331, www.united.com) provides year-round service between Newark Liberty International Airport (EWR) and **Northern Maine Regional Airport** (PQI, 207/764-2550, www.flypresqueisle.com), in Presque Isle. Through partner **Silver Airways** (801/401-9100, http://www.silverairways.com), United provides daily service, late May-early September, between Boston and Hancock County Airport. Hancock County Airport has rental-car offices for Avis, Hertz, and Enterprise and is also serviced by the Island Explorer bus late June-Columbus Day. Knox County has car

Previous: Bar Harbor's waterfront.

rentals from Avis, Budget, and Enterprise. Augusta has Hertz rentals. Northern Maine has Avis and Budget.

BOSTON LOGAN AIRPORT

If you fly into Boston (BOS), you easily can get to Maine via rental car (all major rental companies are at the airport, but it's not pleasant to navigate Logan in a rental car) or Concord Coachlines bus (easiest and least expensive option). You'll need to connect to North Station to take Amtrak's *Downeaster* train.

Car

The major highway access to Maine from the south is **I-95,** which roughly parallels the coast until Bangor before shooting up to Houlton. Other busy access points are **Route 1,** also from New Hampshire, departing the coast in Calais at the New Brunswick province border, and terminating in Fort Kent at the Quebec border; **Route 302,** from North Conway, New Hampshire, entering Maine at Fryeburg; **Route 2,** from Gorham, New Hampshire, to Bethel; **Route 201,** entering from Québec province, just north of Jackman; and a handful of crossing points from New Brunswick into Aroostook and Washington Counties in northeastern Maine.

Bus

Concord Coachlines (800/639-3317, www.concordcoachlines.com) departs downtown Boston (South Station Transportation Center) and Logan Airport for Portland almost hourly from the wee hours of the morning until late at night, making pickups at all Logan airline terminals (lower level). Most of the buses continue directly to Bangor; three daily non-express buses continue along the coast, stopping in Brunswick, Bath, Wiscasset, Damariscotta, Waldoboro, Rockland, Camden, Belfast, and Searsport, before turning inland to Bangor. The Portland bus terminal is the Portland Transportation Center, on Thompson Point Road just west of I-295. Buses are clean, movies are shown, and there's free Wi-Fi on most.

Concord also provides twice-daily direct service between Portland's Transportation Center and New York City, stopping at 373 East 42nd Street in Midtown.

Concord connects with Cyr Bus Line in Bangor.

Cyr Bus Line (800/244-2335, https://johntcyrandsons.com) offers daily service between Bangor and Caribou, Maine, with stops in Old Town, Howland, Medway, Sherman, Oakfield, Houlton, Monticello, Bridgewater, Mars Hill, and Presque Isle.

Also servicing Maine but with far less frequent service is **Greyhound** (800/231-2222, www.greyhound.com).

C&J (800/258-7111, www.ridecj.com) provides seasonal bus service, late May-early September, between New York City and Ogunquit. It also provides year-round daily service between Boston's South Station and Portsmouth, New Hampshire (connected by bridge to Kittery).

Once-a-day buses to and from Calais coordinate with the Bangor bus schedules. The Calais line, stopping in Ellsworth, Gouldsboro, Machias, and Perry (near Eastport), is operated by **West's Coastal Connection** (207/546-2823 or 800/596-2823, www.westbusservice.com). Flag stops along the route are permitted.

Portland, South Portland, and Bangor have **city bus service,** with some wheelchair-accessible vehicles. A number of smaller communities have established **local shuttle vans** or **trolley-buses,** but most of the latter are seasonal. Trolley-buses operate (for a fee) in Ogunquit, Wells, the Kennebunks, Biddeford, Saco, Old Orchard Beach, Portland, Bath, and Boothbay. Mount Desert Island and the Schoodic Peninsula have the **Island Explorer,** an excellent free bus service operating late June-early October.

Rail

Amtrak's *Downeaster* (800/872-7245, www.thedowneaster.com) makes daily round-trip runs between Boston's North Station and Brunswick, with stops in Wells, Saco, Old

Orchard Beach (May 1-Oct. 31), Portland, and Freeport. In Portland, it connects with the Portland Metro bus. Amtrak trains from Washington via New York arrive in Boston at South Station, not North Station, and there's no direct link between the two. While you can connect via the T (Boston's subway), it's a real hassle with baggage. Instead, splurge on a taxi or take the bus north from South Station.

Ferry

The **Cat** (877/762-7245, https://www.ferries.ca/thecat), a high-speed catamaran car-ferry operates between Bar Harbor and Yarmouth, Nova Scotia, from mid-May to mid-October.

GETTING AROUND

Getting to Maine is easy; getting around isn't. Once here, unless you're visiting a destination with bus service, such as Portland, Bangor, or Bar Harbor, or are content with the trolley system serving the Southern Coast and Acadia's bus service, you'll want a **car.**

The Maine Department of Transportation (800/877-9171) operates the Explore Maine site (www.exploremaine.org), which has information on all forms of transportation in Maine.

Car

No matter how much time and resourcefulness you summon, you'll never really be able to appreciate Maine without a car. Down every little peninsula jutting into the Atlantic lies a picturesque village or park or ocean view.

Two lanes wide from Kittery in the south to Fort Kent at the top, U.S. Route 1 is the state's most congested road, particularly in July and August. Mileage distances can be extremely deceptive, since it will take you much longer than anticipated to get from point A to point B. If you ask anyone about distances, chances are good that you'll receive an answer in hours rather than miles. If you're trying to make time, it's best to take the Maine Turnpike or I-95; if you want to see coastal Maine, take U.S. 1 and lots of little offshoots. That said, bear in mind that even I-95 becomes congested on summer weekends, and especially summer *holiday* weekends.

The interstate can be confusing. Between York and Augusta, I-95 is the same as the Maine Turnpike, a toll highway regulated by the Maine Turnpike Authority (877/682-9433 or 800/675-7453 travel conditions, www.maineturnpike.com). All exit numbers along I-95 reflect distance in miles from the New Hampshire border. I-295 splits from I-95 in Portland and follows the coast to Brunswick before veering inland and rejoining I-95 in Gardiner. Exits on I-295 reflect distance from where it splits from I-95 just south of Portland at Exit 44.

For real-time information on road conditions, weather, construction, and major delays, visit http://newengland511.org.

DRIVING REGULATIONS

Seat belts are mandatory in Maine. Unless posted otherwise, Maine allows right turns at red lights after you stop and check for oncoming traffic. *Never* pass a stopped school bus in either direction. Maine law also requires drivers to turn on their car's headlights any time the windshield wipers are operating and to keep three feet away from bicyclists. Cell phones must be hands-free.

Say It Like a Local

Countless names for Maine cities, towns, villages, rivers, lakes, and streams have Native American origins; some are variations on French; and a few have German derivations. Below are some pronunciations to give you a leg up when requesting directions along the Maine coast.

- **Arundel**—Uh-RUN-d'l
- **Bangor**—BANG-gore
- **Bremen**—BREE-m'n
- **Calais**—CAL-us
- **Castine**—Kass-TEEN
- **Damariscotta**—dam-uh-riss-COTT-uh
- **Harraseeket**—Hare-uh-SEEK-it
- **Isle au Haut**—i'll-a-HO, I'LL-a-ho (subject to plenty of dispute, depending on whether or not you live in the vicinity)
- **Katahdin**—Kuh-TA-din
- **Lubec**—Loo-BECK
- **Machias**—Muh-CHIGH-us
- **Matinicus**—Muh-TIN-i-cuss
- **Medomak**—Muh-DOM-ick
- **Megunticook**—Muh-GUN-tuh-cook
- **Monhegan**—Mun-HE-gun
- **Mount Desert**—Mount Duh-ZERT
- **Narraguagus**—Nare-uh-GWAY-gus
- **Naskeag**—NASS-keg
- **Passagassawakeag**—Puh-sag-gus-uh-WAH-keg
- **Passamaquoddy**—Pass-uh-muh-QUAD-dee
- **Pemaquid**—PEM-a-kwid
- **Saco**—SOCK-oh
- **Schoodic**—SKOO-dick
- **Steuben**—Stew-BEN
- **Topsham**—TOPS-'m
- **Wiscasset**—Wiss-CASS-it
- **Woolwich**—WOOL-itch

Travel Tips

FOREIGN TRAVELERS

Visiting from another country, you must have a valid passport and a visa to enter the United States. The U.S. government's Visa Waiver Program allows tourists from many countries to visit without a visa for up to 90 days. To check if your country is on the list go to http://travel.state.gov. To qualify, you must apply online with the **Electronic System for Travel Authorization** (www.cbp.gov) and hold a return plane or cruise ticket to your country of origin dated less than 90 days from your date of entry. Even with a waiver, you still need to bring your passport and present it at the port of entry. It's wise to make two sets of copies of all paperwork, one to carry separately on your trip and another to leave with a trusted friend or relative at home.

For information on what can be brought into the United States, check the website of the Customs and Border Protection division of the Department of Homeland Security (www.cbp.gov).

SMOKING

Maine does not allow smoking in restaurants, bars, and lounges as well as enclosed public places, such as shopping malls. Few accommodations permit smoking, and if they do, it's only in limited areas or rooms. Many have instituted high fines for smoking in a nonsmoking room.

ACCOMMODATIONS

For all accommodations listings, rates are quoted for peak season, which is usually July-August but may extend through foliage season in mid-October. Rates drop, often dramatically, in the shoulder seasons and off-season at many accommodations that remain open. Especially during peak season, many accommodations require a 2-3-night minimum.

For the best rates, be sure to check Internet specials and ask about packages. Many accommodations also provide discounts for members of travel clubs such as AAA and to seniors, members of the military, and other such groups.

Unless otherwise noted, accommodations listed have private baths.

Maine Inn

Budget Tips

- **Avoid the big-name towns** and seek out accommodations in smaller, nearby ones instead. For example, instead of Damariscotta, consider Waldoboro; instead of Camden, try Belfast or Searsport; in place of Bar Harbor, check Trenton or Southwest Harbor. Or simply explore the Down East Coast, where rates are generally far lower than in other coastal regions.
- **Book a cabin or cottage for a week,** rather than a room by the night. Not only can you find reasonable weekly rentals—especially if you plan well in advance—but you'll also have cooking facilities, allowing you to avoid eating all meals out. Otherwise, small, family-owned motels tend to have the lowest rates.
- **Buy or bring a small cooler** so you can stock up at supermarkets and farmers markets for picnic meals. Most Hannaford and Shaw's supermarkets have large selections of prepared foods and big salad bars and bakeries, and many local groceries have pizza and sandwich counters.
- **Check local papers and bulletin boards for public supper notices.** Most are very inexpensive and provide an opportunity to meet locals and glean a few insider tips.
- **Consider going out for lunch instead of dinner,** or take advantage of early-bird specials or of the Friday-night all-you-can-eat fish fries offered at quite a few home-cooking restaurants.
- **Explore Maine's vast outdoors;** many opportunities are free. Even Acadia, with its miles of trails and carriage roads, is a bargain: buy a park pass and it's all yours to use and explore.
- **Take advantage of free events** like concerts, lectures, farmers markets, art shows and openings, and family events. Most are usually listed in local papers.
- **Use local transportation services** to avoid parking hassles and fees and save gas. There's the trolley network on the Southern Coast and the Island Explorer bus system on Mount Desert Island.
- **Look for special Internet rates or ask about discounts** that might apply to you: AAA, senior, military, government, family rate, and so forth.

FOOD

Days and hours of operation listed for places serving food are for peak season. These do change often, sometimes even within a season, and it's not uncommon for a restaurant to close early on a quiet night. To avoid disappointment, call before making a special trip.

ALCOHOL

As in the rest of the country, Maine's minimum drinking age is 21 years—and bar owners, bartenders, and serving staff can be held legally accountable for serving underage imbibers. If your blood alcohol level is 0.08 percent or higher, you are legally intoxicated.

TIME ZONE

All of Maine is in the eastern time zone—the same as New York, Washington DC, Philadelphia, and Orlando. Eastern Standard Time (EST) runs from the first Sunday in November to the second Sunday in March; Eastern Daylight Time (EDT), one hour later, prevails otherwise. Surprising to many first-time visitors, especially when visiting coastal areas, is how early the sun rises in the morning and how early it sets at night.

If your itinerary also includes Canada, remember that the provinces of New Brunswick and Nova Scotia are on Atlantic time—one hour later than eastern time—so if it's noon in Maine, it's 1pm in these provinces.

Health and Safety

There's too much to do in Maine, and too much to see, to spend even a few hours laid low by illness or mishap. Be sensible—be sure to get enough sleep, wear sunscreen and appropriate clothing, know your limits and don't take foolhardy risks, heed weather and warning signs, carry water and snacks while hiking, don't overindulge in food or alcohol, always tell someone where you're going, and watch your step. If you're traveling with children, you should quadruple your caution.

MEDICAL CARE

In an emergency, dial 911. For non-life-threatening issues, call the closest hospital and ask for the nearest walk-in services.

Southern Coast

York Hospital (3 Loving Kindness Way, York, emergency 207/363-4321); **York Hospital in Wells** (112/114 Sanford Rd., Wells, 207/646-5211); **Southern Maine Medical Center** (1 Medical Center Dr., off Rte. 111, Biddeford, 207/283-7000, emergency 207/294-5000).

Greater Portland

Maine Medical Center (22 Bramhall St., Portland, 207/662-0111, emergency 207/662-2381); **Northern Light Mercy Hospital** (144 State St., Portland, 207/879-3000, emergency 207/879-3265).

Mid-Coast

Mid Coast Hospital (123 Medical Center Dr., Brunswick, 207/729-0181); **LincolnHealth St. Andrews Hospital and Healthcare Center** (3 St. Andrews Ln., Boothbay Harbor, 207/633-1940); **LincolnHealth Miles Memorial Hospital** (35 Miles St., Damariscotta, 207/563-1234).

Penobscot Bay

Penobscot Bay Medical Center (6 Glen Cove Dr., Rockport, 207/596-8000, emergency 207/596-8315); **Waldo County General Hospital** (118 Northport Ave., Belfast, 207/338-2500).

Blue Hill and Deer Isle

Northern Light Blue Hill Memorial Hospital (57 Water St., Blue Hill, 207/374-3400, emergency 207/374-2836).

Acadia

Northern Light Maine Coast Hospital (50 Union St., Ellsworth, 207/667-5311, emergency 207/664-5340); **Mount Desert Island Hospital** (10 Wayman Lane, Bar Harbor, 207/288-5081).

Down East

Down East Community Hospital (11 Hospital Dr., Machias, 207/255-3356); **Calais Regional Hospital** (24 Hospital Ln., Calais, 207/454-7521).

Aroostook

Houlton Regional Hospital (20 Hartford St., Houlton, 207/532-2900); **Northern Light A. R. Gould Hospital** (140 Academy St./Rte. 10, Presque Isle, 207/768-4000); **Cary Medical Center** (163 Van Buren Rd., Caribou, 207/498-3111); **Northern Maine Medical Center** (194 E. Main St./Rte. 1, Fort Kent, 207/834-3155).

Maine Highlands

Millinocket Regional Hospital (200 Somerset St., Millinocket, 207/723-5161); **Northern Light Charles A. Dean Memorial Hospital** (364 Pritham Ave., Greenville, 207/695-5200); **Mayo Regional Hospital** (897 W. Main St., Dover-Foxcroft, 207/564-8401); **Northern Light Eastern Maine Medical Center** (489 State St.,

Bangor, 207/973-7000); **St. Joseph Hospital** (360 Broadway, Bangor, 207/262-1000).

Kennebec River Valley

Maine General Alfond Center for Health Care (35 Medical Center Pkwy, Augusta, 207/626-1000); **Redington-Fairview General Hospital** (46 Fairview Ave./Rte. 104, Skowhegan, 207/474-5121).

Western Lakes and Mountains

Franklin Memorial Hospital (111 Franklin Health Commons, Farmington, 207/778-6031); **Rumford Hospital** (420 Franklin St., Rumford, 207/369-1000); **Stephens Memorial Hospital** (181 Main St., Norway, 207/743-5933); **Bridgton Hospital** (10 Hospital Dr., Bridgton, 207/647-6000); **Central Maine Medical Center** (300 Main St., Lewiston, 207/795-0111); **St. Mary's Regional Medical Center** (93 Campus Ave., Lewiston, 207/777-8100).

AFFLICTIONS

Insect Bites and Tick-Borne Diseases

If you plan to spend any time outdoors in Maine April-November, take precautions, especially when hiking, to avoid annoying insect bites, and especially the diseases carried by tiny deer ticks (not the larger dog ticks; they don't carry these): **Lyme disease, anaplasmosis,** and **babesiosis. Powassan,** carried by the woodchuck tick, is so far extremely rare. As of 2019, mosquito-borne **eastern equine encephalitis** has been diagnosed twice in Maine residents, once in 2014 and once in 2015. The mosquito carrying the Zika virus is not found in Maine.

Wear a long-sleeved shirt and long pants, and tuck pant legs into your socks. Light-colored clothing makes ticks easier to spot. Buy insect repellent with 20-40 percent DEET and use it liberally; pretreat clothing with permethrin. The Maine-based company Dog Not Gone (www.dognotgone.com) produces made-in-the-USA tick-repelling clothing for humans and animals. Not much daunts the blackflies of spring and early summer, but you can lower your appeal by not using perfume, aftershave lotion, or scented shampoo and by wearing light-colored clothing.

For more information, consult the Maine Medical Center's Vector-Borne Disease Laboratory's **Ticks in Maine: What Do I Need to Know** (www.ticksinmaine.com) or contact the **Maine Center for Disease Control** (800/821-5821, www.mainepublichealth.gov).

Rabies

If you're bitten by any animal, especially one acting suspiciously, head for the nearest hospital emergency room. For statewide information about rabies, contact the Maine Center for Disease Control (800/821-5821, www.mainepublichealth.gov).

Allergies

If your medical history includes extreme allergies to shellfish or bee stings, you know the risks of eating a lobster or wandering around a wildflower meadow. However, if you come from a landlocked area and are new to crustaceans, you might not be aware of the potential hazard. Statistics indicate that less than 2 percent of adults have a severe shellfish allergy, but for those victims, the reaction can set in quickly. Immediate treatment is needed to keep the airways open. If you have a history of severe allergic reactions to *anything*, be prepared when you come to the Maine coast dreaming of lobster feasts. Ask your doctor about a prescription for EpiPen (epinephrine), a preloaded, single-use syringe containing 0.3 mg of the drug—enough to tide you over until you can get to a hospital.

Seasickness

If planning to do any boating in Maine—particularly sailing—you'll want to be prepared. (Being prepared may in fact keep you from succumbing, since fear of seasickness just about guarantees you'll get it.) Talk to a pharmacist or doctor about your options. Alternative precautions that may be effective include acupressure wrist bands and ginger.

Hypothermia and Frostbite

Wind and weather can shift dramatically in Maine, especially at higher elevations, creating prime conditions for contracting hypothermia and frostbite. At risk are hikers, swimmers, canoeists, kayakers, sailors, skiers, even cyclists.

To prevent hypothermia and frostbite, dress in layers and remove or add them as needed. Wool, waterproof fabrics (such as Gore-Tex), and synthetic fleece (such as Polartec) are the best fabrics for repelling dampness. Polyester fleece lining wicks excess moisture away from your body. Especially in winter, always cover your head, since body heat escapes quickly through the head; a ski mask will protect ears and nose. Wear wool- or fleece-lined gloves and wool socks.

SPECIAL CONSIDERATIONS DURING HUNTING SEASON

During Maine's fall hunting season (October-Thanksgiving weekend)—and especially during the November deer season—walk or hike only in wooded areas marked No Hunting. And even if an area *is* closed to hunters, don't decide to explore the woods during deer or moose season without wearing a hunter-orange (read: eye-poppingly fluorescent) jacket or vest. If you take your dog along, be sure it, too, wears an orange vest. Hunting is illegal on Sunday.

Information and Services

MONEY

If you need to exchange foreign currency—other than Canadian dollars—do it at or near border crossings or in Portland. In small communities, such transactions are more complicated; you may end up spending more time and money than necessary.

Typical banking hours are 9am-3pm weekdays, occasionally with later hours on Friday. Drive-up windows at many banks tend to open as much as an hour earlier and stay open an hour or so after lobbies close. Some banks also maintain Saturday morning hours. Automated teller machines (ATMs) are abundant along coastal Maine.

Credit Cards and Travelers Checks

Bank credit cards have become so preferred and so prevalent that it's nearly impossible to rent a car or check into a hotel without one. MasterCard and Visa are most widely accepted in Maine, and Discover and American Express are next most popular; Carte Blanche, Diners Club, and EnRoute (Canadian) lag far behind. Be aware, however, that small restaurants (including lobster pounds), shops, and bed-and-breakfasts off the beaten track might not accept credit cards or nonlocal personal checks; you may need to settle your account with cash or travelers check.

Taxes

Maine charges a 5.5 percent sales tax on general purchases and services; 8 percent on prepared foods and candy; 9 percent on lodging/camping; and 10 percent on auto rentals.

Tipping

Tip 15-20 percent of the pre-tax bill in restaurants. Note that the tip is often added to the bill for groups of six or more. Taxi drivers expect a 15 percent tip; airport porters expect at least $1 per bag, depending on the difficulty of the job. The usual tip for housekeeping services in accommodations is $2-5 per person, per night. Some accommodations add resort or service fees; ask before booking and scrutinize bills before adding a tip.

TOURISM INFORMATION AND MAPS

The **Maine Office of Tourism** has an excellent website: www.visitmaine.com. You'll find chamber of commerce addresses, articles, photos, information on lodgings, and access to a variety of Maine tourism businesses. The state's toll-free information hotline is 888/MAINE-45 (888/624-6345). The state also operates **information centers** in Calais, Fryeburg, Hampden, Houlton, Kittery, and Yarmouth. These are excellent places to stock up on brochures, pick up a map, ask for advice, and use restrooms. All offer free Wi-Fi.

The **Maine Tourism Association** (207/623-0363, www.mainetourism.com) also has information and publishes *Maine Invites You* and a free state map.

Peek in any Mainer's car, and you're likely to see a copy of **The Maine Atlas and Gazetteer,** published by DeLorme Mapping Company/Garmin in Yarmouth. Despite an oversize format inconvenient for hiking and kayaking, this 96-page paperbound book just about guarantees that you won't get lost (and if you're good at map reading, it can get you out of a lot of traffic jams). Scaled at one-half inch to the mile, it's meticulously compiled from aerial photographs, satellite images, U.S. Geological Survey maps, GPS readings, and timber-company maps, and it is revised annually. It details back roads and dirt roads and shows elevation, boat ramps, public lands, campgrounds and picnic areas, and trailheads. DeLorme products are available nationwide in book and map stores, but you can also order direct (800/452-5931, www.delorme.com). The atlas is $19.95 and shipping is $4 (Maine residents need to add 5.5 percent sales tax).

PHONE AND INTERNET

Maine still has only one telephone area code, 207. For directory assistance, dial 411.

Cell phone towers are sprinkled throughout Maine; only a few pockets—mostly down peninsulas, in wilderness areas, and in remote valleys and hollows—have no signal. Reception varies by carrier. Internet access is widely available at libraries and coffeehouses. Most accommodations offer Internet access.

Resources

Glossary

To help you translate some of the lingo used off the beaten track at places like country stores and county fairs, farm stands and flea markets, here's a sampling of local terms and expressions:

alewives: herring

ayuh: yes

barrens: as in "blueberry barrens"; fields where wild blueberries grow

beamy: wide (as in a boat or a person)

beans: shorthand for the traditional Saturday night meal, which always includes baked beans

blowdown: a forest area leveled by wind

blowing a gale: very windy

camp: a vacation house (small or large), usually on freshwater and in the woods

chance: serendipity or luck, as in "open by appointment or by chance"

chicken dressing: chicken manure

chowder (pronounced "chowdah"): soup made with lobster, clams, or fish, or a combination thereof; lobster version is sometimes called lobster stew

chowderhead: mischief- or troublemakers, usually interchangeable with idiot

coneheads: tourists (because of their presumed penchant for ice cream)

cottage: a vacation house (anything from a bungalow to a mansion), usually on saltwater

culch (also cultch): stuff; the contents of attics, basements, and some flea markets

cull: a discount lobster, usually minus a claw

cunnin': cute, usually describing a baby or small child

dinner (pronounced "dinnah"): the noon meal

dinner pail: lunch box

dite: a very small amount

dooryard: the yard near a house's main entrance

downcellar: in the basement

Down East: with the prevailing wind; the old coastal sailing route from Boston to Nova Scotia

dry-ki: driftwood, usually remnants from the logging industry

ell: a residential structural section that links a house and a barn; formerly a popular location for the "summer kitchen," to spare the house from woodstove heat

exercised: upset; angry

fiddleheads: unopened ostrich-fern fronds, a spring delicacy

finest kind: top quality; good news; an expression of general approval; also a term of appreciation

flatlander: a person not from Maine, often but not exclusively someone from the Midwest

floatplane: a small plane equipped with pontoons for landing on water; the same aircraft often becomes a ski-plane in winter

flowage: a body of water created by damming, usually beaver handiwork (also called "beaver flowage")

FR: Fire Road, used in mailing addresses

frappé: a thick drink containing milk, ice cream, and flavored syrup, as opposed to a milk shake, which does not include ice cream (but beware: a frappé offered in other parts of the United States is an ice cream sundae topped with whipped cream)

from away: not native to Maine

galamander: a wheeled contraption formerly used to transport quarry granite to building sites or to boats for onward shipment

gore: a sliver of land left over from inaccurate boundary surveys. Maine has several gores; Hibberts Gore, for instance, has a population of one.

got done: quit a job; was let go

harbormaster: local official who monitors water traffic and assigns moorings; often a very political job

hardshell: lobster that hasn't molted yet (scarcer, thus more pricey in summer)

HC: Home Carrier, used in mailing addresses

hod: wooden "basket" used for carrying clams

ice-out: the departure of winter ice from ponds, lakes, rivers, and streams; many communities have ice-out contests, awarding prizes for guessing the exact time of ice-out, in April or May

Italian: long, soft bread roll sliced on top and filled with peppers, onions, tomatoes, sliced meat, black olives, and sprinkled with olive oil, salt, and pepper; veggie versions available

jimmies: chocolate sprinkles, like those on an ice cream cone

lobster car: a large floating crate for storing lobsters

Maine Guide: a member of the Maine Professional Guides Association, trained and tested for outdoor and survival skills; also called Registered Maine Guide

market price: restaurant menu term for "the going rate," usually referring to the price of lobster or clams

molt: what a lobster does when it sheds its shell for a larger one; the act of molting is called ecdysis (as a stripper is an ecdysiast)

money tree: a collection device for a monetary gift

mud season: mid-March-mid-April, when back roads and unpaved driveways become virtual tank traps

nasty neat: extremely meticulous

near: stingy

notional: stubborn, determined

off island: the mainland, to an islander

place: another word for a house (as in "Herb Pendleton's place")

ployes: Acadian buckwheat pancakes

pot: trap, as in "lobster pot"

public landing: see "town landing"

rake: hand tool used for harvesting blueberries

RFD: Rural Free Delivery, used in mailing addresses

roller-skiing: cross-country skiing on wheels; popular among cross-country skiers, triathletes, and others as a training technique

rusticator: a summer visitor, particularly in bygone days

scooch (or scootch): to squat; to move sideways

sea smoke: heavy mist rising off the water when the air temperature suddenly becomes much colder than the ocean temperature

select: a lobster with claws intact

Selectmen: the elected men and women who handle local affairs in small communities; the First Selectman chairs meetings. In some towns, "people from away" have tried to propose substituting a gender-neutral term, but in most cases the effort has failed.

shedder: a lobster with a new (soft) shell; generally occurs in July-August (more common then, thus less expensive than hardshells)

shire town: county seat

shore dinner: the works: chowder, clams, lobster, and sometimes corn on the cob too; usually the most expensive item on a menu

short: a small, illegal-size lobster

slumgullion: tasteless food; a mess

slut: a poor housekeeper

slut's wool: dust balls found under beds, couches, and so on

snapper: an undersize, illegal lobster

soda: cola, root beer, and so on (referred to as "pop" in some other parts of the country)

softshell: see "shedder"

some: very (as in "some hot")

spleeny: overly sensitive

steamers: clams, before or after they are steamed

sternman: a lobsterman's helper (male or female)
summer complaint: a tourist
supper (pronounced "suppah"): evening meal, eaten by Mainers around 5pm or 6pm (as opposed to flatlanders and summer people, who eat dinner 7pm-9pm)
tad: slightly; a little bit
thick-o'-fog: zero-visibility fog
to home: at home
tomalley: a lobster's green insides; considered a delicacy by some
town landing: shore access; often a park or a parking lot, next to a wharf or boat-launch ramp
upattic: in the attic
whoopie pie: the trademarked name for a high-fat, calorie-laden, cakelike snack that only kids and dentists could love
wicked cold: frigid
wicked good: excellent
williwaws: uncomfortable feeling

Suggested Reading

ART, LITERATURE, AND PHOTOGRAPHY

Curtis, J., W. Curtis, and F. Lieberman. *Monhegan: The Artists' Island.* Camden, ME: Down East Books, 1995. Fascinating island history interspersed with landscape and seascape paintings and drawings by more than 150 artists, including Bellows, Henri, Hopper, Kent, Porter, Tam, and Wyeth.

Maine Speaks: An Anthology of Maine Literature. Brunswick, ME: Maine Writers and Publishers Alliance, 1989.

McNair, W., ed. *The Maine Poets: An Anthology of Verse.* Camden, ME: Down East Books, 2003. McNair's selection of the best works by Maine's finest poets.

Spectre, P. H. *Passage in Time.* New York: W. W. Norton, 1991. A noted marine writer cruises the coast aboard traditional windjammers; gorgeous photos complement the colorful text.

Van Riper, F. *Down East Maine: A World Apart.* Camden, ME: Down East Books, 1998. Maine's Washington County, captured with incredible insight and compassion by a master photographer and insightful wordsmith.

HISTORY

Acadian Culture in Maine. Washington, DC: National Park Service, North Atlantic Region, 1994. A project report on Acadians and their traditions in the Upper St. John Valley.

Clark, Stephen. *Following Their Footsteps: A Travel Guide and History of the 1775 Secret Expedition to Capture Quebec.* Shapleigh, ME: Clark Books, 2003.

Duncan, R. F., E. G. Barlow, K. Bray, and C. Hanks. *Coastal Maine: A Maritime History.* Woodstock, VT: Countryman Press, 2002. Updated version of the classic work.

Isaacson, D., ed. *Maine: A Guide "Down East,"* 2nd ed. Maine League of Historical Societies and Museums, 1970. Revised version of the Depression-era Works Progress Administration guidebook, still interesting for background reading.

Jaster, R. S. *Russian Voices on the Kennebec: The Story of Maine's Unlikely Colony.* Orono: University of Maine Press, 1999. A riveting account of the founding of a Russian-speaking colony in Richmond, Maine, in the 1950s. Superb historical photographs.

Judd, R. W., E. A. Churchill, and J. W. Eastman, eds. *Maine: The Pine Tree State from Prehistory to the Present.* Orono: University of Maine Press, 1995. The best available Maine history, with excellent historical maps.

Paine, L. P. *Down East: A Maritime History of Maine.* Gardiner, ME: Tilbury House, 2000. A noted maritime historian provides an enlightening introduction to the state's seafaring tradition.

Woodward, C. *The Lobster Coast: Rebels, Rusticators, and the Struggle for a Forgotten Frontier.* New York: Viking, 2004. A veteran journalist's take on the history of the Maine coast.

LOBSTERS AND LIGHTHOUSES

Bachelder, Peter Dow, and P. M. Mason. *Maine Lighthouse Map and Guide.* Glendale, CO: Bella Terra Publishing, 2009. An illustrated map and guide providing directions on how to find all Maine beacons as well as brief histories.

Caldwell, W. *Lighthouses of Maine.* Camden, ME: Down East Books, 2002 (reprint of 1986 book). A historical tour of Maine's lighthouses, with an emphasis on history, legends, and lore.

Corson, T. *The Secret Life of Lobsters.* New York: HarperCollins, 2004. Everything you wanted—or perhaps didn't want—to know about lobster.

D'Entremont, J. *The Lighthouse Handbook New England.* 3rd ed. Kennebunkport, ME: Cider Mill Press, 2016. Invaluable reference by the historian for the American Lighthouse Foundation.

Woodward, C. *The Lobster Coast: Rebels, Rusticators, and the Struggle for a Forgotten Frontier.* New York: Viking, 2004. A veteran journalist's take on the history of the Maine coast.

MAPS

The Maine Atlas and Gazetteer. Yarmouth, ME: DeLorme, a Garmin company, updated annually. You'll be hard put to get lost if you're carrying this essential volume; it has 70 full-page, oversize-format topographical maps with GPS grids.

MEMOIRS

Dawson, L. B. *Saltwater Farm.* Westford, ME: Impatiens Press, 1993. Witty, charming stories of growing up on the Cushing Peninsula.

Greenlaw, L. *The Lobster Chronicles: Life on a Very Small Island.* New York: Hyperion, 2002. Swordfishing boat captain Linda Greenlaw's account of returning to life on Isle au Haut after weathering *The Perfect Storm.*

Hamlin, H. *Nine Mile Bridge: Three Years in the Maine Woods.* Yarmouth and Frenchboro, ME: Islandport Press, 2006 [orig. pub. 1945]. Hamlin's experiences as a teacher at a remote lumber camp near the headwaters of the Allagash River, where her husband was a game warden.

Lunt, D. L. *Hauling by Hand: The Life and Times of a Maine Island,* 2nd ed. Frenchboro, ME: Islandport Press, 2007. A sensitive history of Frenchboro (a.k.a. Long Island), eight miles offshore, written by an eighth-generation islander and journalist.

Szelog, T. M. *Our Point of View: Fourteen Years at a Maine Lighthouse.* Camden, ME: Down East Books, 2007. A professional photographer documents in words and photos 14 years at Marshall Point Lighthouse.

NATURAL HISTORY

Bennett, D. *Maine's Natural Heritage: Rare Species and Unique Natural Features.*

Camden, ME: Down East Books, 1988. A dated book that examines both the special ecology of the state and how it's threatened.

Conkling, P. W. *Islands in Time: A Natural and Cultural History of the Islands of Maine,* 3rd ed. Rockland, ME: Island Institute, 2011. A comprehensive overview by the president of Maine's Island Institute.

Dwelley, M. J. *Spring Wildflowers of New England,* 2nd ed. Camden, ME: Down East Books, 2000. Back in print after several years, this beautifully illustrated gem is an essential guide for exploring spring woodlands.

Dwelley, M. J. *Summer and Fall Wildflowers of New England,* 2nd ed. Camden, ME: Down East Books, 2004. Flowers are grouped by color; more than 700 lovely colored-pencil drawings simplify identification.

Kendall, D. L. *Glaciers and Granite: A Guide to Maine's Landscape and Geology.* Unity, ME: North Country Press, 1993. Explains why Maine looks the way it does.

Maine's Ice Age Trail Down East Map and Guide. Orono: University of Maine Press, 2007. Information on 46 glacial sites, also available online (www.iceagetrail.umaine.edu).

RECREATION

Acadia National Park and Mount Desert Island

Monkman, J., and M. Monkman. *Discover Acadia National Park: A Guide to the Best Hiking, Biking, and Paddling,* 2nd ed. Boston: Appalachian Mountain Club Books, 2005. A comprehensive guide to well-chosen hikes, bike trips, and paddling routes, accompanied by an excellent pullout map.

Nangle, H. *Moon Acadia National Park,* 6th ed. Berkeley, CA: Avalon Travel, 2018. A Mainer since childhood and veteran travel writer is the ideal escort for exploring this region in depth.

Roberts, A. R. *Mr. Rockefeller's Roads,* 2nd ed. Camden, ME: Down East Books, 2012. The story behind Acadia's scenic carriage roads, written by the granddaughter of John D. Rockefeller, who created them.

St. Germain Jr., T. A. *A Walk in the Park: Acadia's Hiking Guide,* 10th ed. Bar Harbor, ME: Parkman Publications, 2015. The book includes plenty of historical tidbits about the trails, the park, and the island. Part of the proceeds go to the Acadia Trails Forever campaign to maintain and rehabilitate the park's trails. The book is updated regularly; ask for the most recent edition.

Bicycling

Stone, H. *25 Bicycle Tours in Maine: Coastal and Inland Rides from Kittery to Caribou,* 3rd ed. Woodstock, VT: Countryman Press/Backcountry Guides, 1998.

Birding

Duchesne, B. *Maine Birding Trail: The Official Guide to More than 260 Accessible Sites.* Camden, ME: Down East Books, 2009. Authorized guide to the Maine Birding Trail.

Pierson, E. C., J. E. Pierson, and P. D. Vickery. *A Birder's Guide to Maine.* Camden, ME: Down East Books, 1996. An expanded version of *A Birder's Guide to the Coast of Maine.* No ornithologist, novice or expert, should explore Maine without this valuable guide.

Boating

AMC River Guide: Maine, 4th ed. Boston: Appalachian Mountain Club Books, 2008. Detailed guide to canoeing or kayaking Maine's large and small rivers.

Maine Coastal Public Access Guides. Augusta, ME: Maine Coastal Program, Maine Department of Agriculture, Conservation, and Forestry, 2013. Comprises three books: *Southern Region: South Berwick to Freeport, Midcoast Region: Brunswick to Hampden,* and *Downeast Region: Bangor to Calais.* Series covers more than 700 public access points along the coast.

The Maine Island Trail: Stewardship Handbook and Guidebook. Rockland, ME: Maine Island Trail Association, updated annually. Available only with MITA membership (annual dues $45), this book provides access to dozens of islands along the watery trail.

The Northern Forest Canoe Trail: Enjoy 740 Miles of Canoe and Kayak Destinations in New York, Vermont, Quebec, New Hampshire, and Maine. Seattle: Mountaineers Books, 2010. Details and maps the waterway, including highlights en route.

Miller, D. S. *Kayaking the Maine Coast.* 2nd ed. Woodstock, VT: Countryman Press/Backcountry Guides, 2006. Thoroughly researched guide by a veteran kayaker; good maps and particularly helpful information.

Taft, H., J. Taft, and C. Rindlaub. *A Cruising Guide to the Maine Coast,* 5th ed. Peaks Island, ME: Diamond Pass Publishing, 2008. Don't even consider cruising the coast without this volume.

Wilson, A., and J. Hayes. *Quiet Water Canoe Guide, Maine: Best Paddling Lakes and Ponds for All Ages,* 2nd ed. Boston: Appalachian Mountain Club Books, 2005. Comprehensive handbook, with helpful maps, for inland paddling.

Family

Hazard, J. *The Maine Play Book: A Four-Season Guide to Family Fun and Adventure.* Yarmouth, ME: Islandport Press, 2018. Parent-tested ways to keep the kiddos happy and engaged.

Hiking and Walking

Clark, Stephen. *Katahdin: A Guide to Baxter State Park and Katahdin,* 8th ed. Baxter State Authority, 2017. The most comprehensive guide to Katahdin and Baxter State Park.

Collins, J., and J. E. McCarthy. *Cobscook Trails: A Guide to Walking Opportunities Around Cobscook Bay and the Bold Coast,* 2nd ed. Whiting, ME: Quoddy Regional Land Trust, 2000. Essential handbook for exploring this part of the Down East Coast, with excellent maps.

Gibson, J. *50 Hikes in Coastal and Southern Maine,* 4th ed. Woodstock, VT: Countryman Press/Backcountry Guides, 2008. Well-researched, detailed resource by a veteran hiker.

Kish, C. *Maine Mountain Guide: AMC's Comprehensive Guide to Hiking Trails of Maine, Featuring Baxter State Park and Acadia National Park.* 11th ed. Boston: Appalachian Mountain Club Books, 2018. The definitive statewide resource for going vertical, in a handy format. Author lives on Mount Desert Island.

Kish, C. M., AMC's Best Day Hikes along the Maine Coast: Four-season Guide to 50 of the Best Trails from the Maine Beaches to Downeast. Boston: Appalachian Mountain Club Books, 2015. Well-researched, detailed resource by a veteran hiker.

Roberts, P. *On the Trail in Lincoln County.* Newcastle and Damariscotta, ME: Lincoln County Publishing, 2003. A great guide to more than 60 walks in preserves from Wiscasset through Waldoboro, with detailed directions to trailheads.

Internet Resources

GENERAL INFORMATION

State of Maine
www.maine.gov
Everything you wanted to know about Maine and then some, with links to all government departments and Maine-related sites. Buy a fishing license online, reserve a state park campsite, or check the fall foliage conditions via the site's Leaf Cam. (You can also access foliage info at www.mainefoliage.com, where you can sign up for weekly email foliage reports in September and early October.) Also listed is information on accessible arts and recreation.

Maine Office of Tourism
www.visitmaine.com
The biggest and most useful of all Maine-related tourism sites, with sections and search capabilities for where to visit, where to stay, things to do, trip planning, and packages, as well as lodging specials and a comprehensive calendar of events.

Maine Tourism Association
www.mainetourism.com
Find lodging, camping, restaurants, attractions, services, and more as well as links for weather, foliage, transportation planning, and chambers of commerce.

Maine Campground Owners Association
www.campmaine.com
Find private campgrounds statewide.

Maine Dept. of Transportation
www.maine.gov/mdot/
An invaluable site for trip planning, with information about exploring Maine by all modes of transportation; links to real-time information about major delays, accidents, road construction, and weather conditions; and other resources.

Maine Travel Maven
www.mainetravelmaven.com
Moon Maine author Hilary Nangle's site for keeping readers updated on what's happening throughout the state.

PARKS AND RECREATION

Acadia National Park
www.nps.gov/acad
Information on all sections of Acadia National Park. Make ANP campground reservations online.

Baxter State Park
www.baxterstateparkauthority.com
Everything you need for planning a trip to Baxter.

Bicycle Coalition of Maine
www.bikemaine.org
Tons of information for bicyclists, including routes, shops, events, organized rides, and much more.

Department of Conservation, Maine Bureau of Parks and Lands
www.parksandlands.com
Information on state parks, public reserved lands, and state historic sites as well as details on facilities such as campsites, picnic areas, and boat launches. Make state campground reservations online.

Maine Audubon
www.maineaudubon.org
Information about Maine Audubon's eco-sensitive headquarters in Falmouth and all of the organization's environmental centers statewide. Activity and program schedules are included.

Maine Birding
www.mainebirdingtrail.com

A must-visit site for anyone interested in learning more about bird-watching in Maine, including news, checklists, events, forums, trips, and more.

Maine Department of Inland Fisheries and Wildlife
www.state.me.us/ifw
Info on wildlife, hunting, fishing, snowmobiling, and boating.

Maine Island Trail Association
www.mita.org
Membership organization with resources for planning a coastal trip by private boat or sea kayak.

Maine Land Trust Network
www.mltn.org
Maine has dozens of land trusts statewide, managing lands that provide opportunities for hiking, walking, canoeing, kayaking, and other such activities.

Maine Trail Finder
www.mainetrailfinder.com
Find trails to walk, hike, ski, snowshoe, or mountain bike statewide.

Maine Professional Guides Association
www.maineguides.org
Find Registered Maine Guides for sporting adventures, including sea kayaking, hunting, fishing, and recreation (such as canoeing trips and wildlife safaris).

Maine Windjammer Association
www.sailmainecoast.com
Windjammer schooners homeported in Rockland, Camden, and Rockport belong to this umbrella organization; there are links to the websites of member vessels for online and phone information and reservations.

North Maine Woods
www.northmainewoods.org
Essential information for venturing into the privately owned North Woods.

Northern Forest Canoe Trail
www.northernforestcanoetrail.org
Info on more than 350 miles of connected waterways in Maine.

Ski Maine
www.skimaine.com
The go-to source for information on alpine skiing in Maine.

The Nature Conservancy
www.nature.org/wherewework/northamerica/states/maine
Information about Maine preserves, field trips, and events.

ARTS, ANTIQUES, AND MUSEUMS

Maine Antiques Dealers Association
www.maineantiques.org
Statewide dealers are listed by location and specialty, along with information on upcoming antiques events.

Maine Archives and Museums
www.mainemuseums.org
Information on and links to museums, archives, historical societies, and historic sites in Maine.

Maine Art Museum Trail
www.maineartmuseums.org
Information on nine art museums with significant collections statewide.

FOOD AND DRINK

Maine Department of Agriculture
www.getrealmaine.com
Information on all things agricultural, including fairs, farmers markets, farm vacations, places to buy Maine foods, berry- and apple-picking sites, and more.

Maine Lobster Promotion Council
www.lobsterfrommaine.com

All lobster, all the time, with links for lobster boat tours, lobster events, lobster bakes, and ordering Maine lobster, plus recipes for preparing lobster in more ways than you ever thought possible.

Portland Food Map
www.portlandfoodmap.com
A must for culinary travel in Maine's largest city. Information on anything and everything food- and drink-related, including openings, closings, and links to reviews.

Wild Blueberry Association of North America
www.wildblueberries.com
Information on blueberries as well as numerous recipes

Index

A

B

C

D

E

F

G

I

J

K

L

M

N

O

QR

S

T

UV

WXYZ

List of Maps

Acknowledgments

This book is dedicated to all the underappreciated tourism workers in Maine, the volunteers and lowly staffers, the waiters, waitresses, toll collectors, gatekeepers, park rangers, traffic cops, ferry attendants, housekeepers, hostesses and front desk workers, tour guides, and everyone else who has contact with visitors. You make Maine sing. We do appreciate you. You're the real face of Maine. Thank you.

I've lived on the Maine coast since childhood (yes, I will always be a "from away"), and have traveled extensively throughout the state for both work and pleasure, but every time I revisit a place, I find something new or changed, sometimes subtly, other times dramatically. Restaurants open and close. Outfitters change offerings. Inns are sold. Motels open. New trails are cut. Museums expand. Hotels renovate. And on it goes. Which all goes to say, I couldn't have done this without the help of many people, who served as additional eyes and ears.

I'll start with the folks at Avalon Travel who shepherded me through the process: publisher Bill Newlin, publisher and acquisitions director Grace Fujimoto, editorial director Kevin McLain, publishing assistant Ravina Schneider, digital marketing coordinator Crystal Turnau, publicity and marketing associate Erika Lara, acquisitions manager Nikki Loakimedes, contracts assistant Jillian Mannarino, Jane Musser, marketing and publicity associate Erika Lara, graphics coordinator Suzanne Albertson, map editor Albert Anjulo, and especially my editor, Leah Gordon.

More heartfelt thank-yous are due to those who sat down with me and shared insider info, sheltered me along the way, fed me, helped with arrangements, verified information, called me with updates, or simply encouraged me: Nancy Marshall, Charlene Williams, Abbe Levin, Wende Gray, Bob Smith, Connie Russell, Carla Tracy, Devin Finigan, Kristen Levesque, Marti Mayne, Jean Ginn-Marvin, Jed Porta, Chip Gray, Gayle Conran, Rauni Kew, Dale Northrup, Anne and Peter Beerits, Sally Littlefield, Julie Van de Graaf and Jack Burke, Bill Haefele, Susi Homer, Rosemary and Gary Levin, Carol Mahany, Richard Reith, J.J. Roy, Sheila Grant, Phil Savignano, Darcy Lambert, Karen Castaldo, Ruth and Dan McLaughlin, Rachel Crater, Bill Clark, Rick and Debbie LeVasseur, Denise and Wayne Smith, Chris Torrey, Lindsay Downing, Joan Fetsko, Sarah Wills-Viega, and Leah Hobson.

I save my biggest thanks for my husband Tom and my faithful road-trip sidekick Martha Kalina (and her patient left-home husband Rick Skoglund). Between them, they drove me everywhere and didn't complain (too much) when I made them backtrack two or three times along the same stretch of road while seeking an elusive address; waited patiently while I visited practically every restaurant, inn, and bed-and-breakfast from Kittery to Fort Kent, Fryeburg to Calais; and supported me in every way possible throughout the entire process.

And you, dear reader, thank you for using this book to plan your visit to Maine's magical coast. Please, do me a favor, will you? Provide feedback to help make the next edition even better. Visit www.MaineTravelMaven.com or follow on social media to know what's new, changed, or happening in Maine and please, drop a line to share your thoughts and finds.

In these books:

- Full coverage of gateway cities and towns
- Itineraries from one day to multiple weeks
- Advice on where to stay (or camp) in and around the parks

States & Regions

MOON.COM
@MOONGUIDES

Photo Credits

MOON MAINE
Avalon Travel
Hachette Book Group
1700 Fourth Street
Berkeley, CA 94710, USA
www.moon.com

Editors: Leah Gordon, Diana Smith
Series Manager: Kathryn Ettinger
Copy Editor: Callie Stoker-Graham
Production Designers: Suzanne Albertson, Ravina Schneider
Cover Design: Faceout Studios, Charles Brock
Interior Design: Domini Dragoone
Moon Logo: Tim McGrath
Map Editor: Albert Angulo
Cartographer: Andrew Dolan
Indexer: Rachel Kuhn

ISBN-13: 978-1-64049-876-1

Printing History
1st Edition — 1998
8th Edition — June 2020
5 4 3 2

Front cover photo: Autumn in Acadia NP. © Nikhil Nagane | Getty Images
Back cover photo: Colorful kayakers paddle in Boothbay Harbor. © Cheryl Fleishman | Dreamstime.com

Printed in China by RR Donnelley

All recommendations, including those for sights, activities, hotels, restaurants, and shops, are based on each author's individual judgment. We do not accept payment for inclusion in our travel guides, and our authors don't accept free goods or services in exchange for positive coverage.

MAP SYMBOLS

Expressway
Primary Road
Secondary Road
Unpaved Road
Trail
Ferry
Railroad
Pedestrian Walkway
Stairs

City/Town
State Capital
National Capital
Highlight
Point of Interest
Accommodation
Restaurant/Bar
Other Location
Campground

Airport
Airfield
Mountain
Unique Natural Feature
Waterfall
Park
Trailhead
Skiing Area

Golf Course
Parking Area
Archaeological Site
Church
Gas Station
Glacier
Mangrove
Reef
Swamp

CONVERSION TABLES

°C = (°F - 32) / 1.8
°F = (°C x 1.8) + 32
1 inch = 2.54 centimeters (cm)
1 foot = 0.304 meters (m)
1 yard = 0.914 meters
1 mile = 1.6093 kilometers (km)
1 km = 0.6214 miles
1 fathom = 1.8288 m
1 chain = 20.1168 m
1 furlong = 201.168 m
1 acre = 0.4047 hectares
1 sq km = 100 hectares
1 sq mile = 2.59 square km
1 ounce = 28.35 grams
1 pound = 0.4536 kilograms
1 short ton = 0.90718 metric ton
1 short ton = 2,000 pounds
1 long ton = 1.016 metric tons
1 long ton = 2,240 pounds
1 metric ton = 1,000 kilograms
1 quart = 0.94635 liters
1 US gallon = 3.7854 liters
1 Imperial gallon = 4.5459 liters
1 nautical mile = 1.852 km

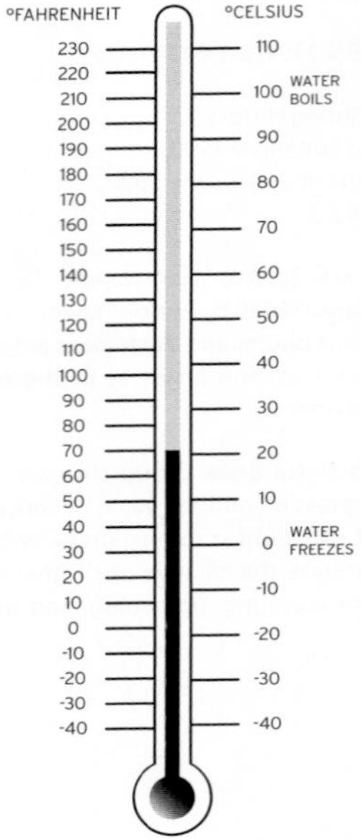

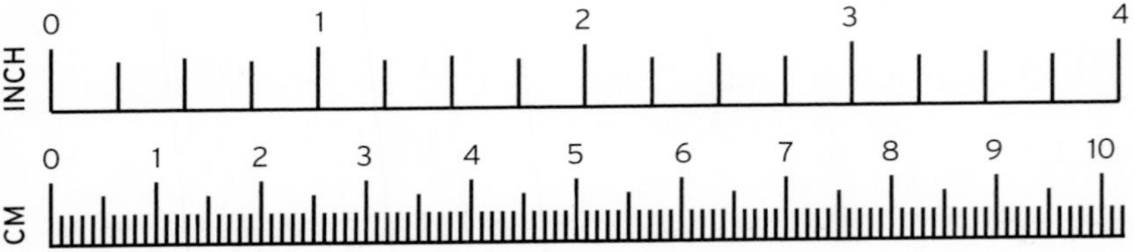